Differential Diagnosis and Treatment in Social Work

Differential Diagnosis and Treatment in Social Work

Second Edition

EDITED BY *Francis J. Turner*

WITH A FOREWORD BY *Florence Hollis*

 THE FREE PRESS
A Division of Macmillan Publishing Co., Inc.
New York

Collier Macmillan Publishers
London

The Free Press
A Division of Macmillan Publishing Co., Inc.
866 Third Avenue, New York, N.Y. 10022

Collier Macmillan Canada, Ltd.

Library of Congress Catalog Card Number: 75–26054

Printed in the United States of America

printing number
       7 8 9 10

Library of Congress Cataloging in Publication Data

Turner, Francis Joseph
   Differential diagnosis and treatment in social work.

   Includes bibliographical references and index.
   1. Social case work. I. Title. [DNLM: 1. Diagnosis, Differential. 2. Social service, Psychiatric.
3. Social service. WM58 D569]
HV43.T8 1976   361.3   75-26054
ISBN 0-02-932731-8

To Bert, brother and colleague

Contents

Death

Part II Psychosocial Pathology 167

Addictions—Alcohol

Addictions—Narcotics

Character Disorders

Sexual Deviations

The Brain-Injured Child

Burn Patients

Cancer

Cardiac Disorders

Cerebral Palsy

Deafness

Diabetes

Factitious Illness

Hemophilia

Suicide

Foreword

How strange it is that not until a half century after the publication of *Social Diagnosis* does a book appear in the social work field addressing itself specifically to the relationship between differential diagnosis and treatment! Over fifty years ago—in 1917—Mary Richmond wrote *Social Diagnosis*, a book dedicated to the then new idea that the social worker, like the physician, must think diagnostically, endeavouring to understand the nature of the disorder with which he is dealing in order to know how to alleviate it. This book so impressed practitioners that for many years it was a text, as if the subject of diagnosis were now understood and social casework could move on to concentrate on problems of treatment methodology. Even in the thirties, when psychoanalytic knowledge was permeating social casework, attention was directed not to diagnostic groupings, but rather to general principles of treatment on the one hand and the specifics of individualization of treatment on the other. It was not until the mid-forties that attention again turned to diagnosis, and the work started by Miss Richmond moved forward with concentration on the psychological component of diagnosis, often designated the "clinical diagnosis." Diagnosis had not been lost sight of during these intervening years, but the principles of social study and diagnosis presented by Miss Richmond seemed to provide sufficient guidelines for the type of diagnostic thinking upon which treatment was based until the mid-forties. This was a highly individualized approach with emphasis on idiosyncratic life happenings that could account for the problem under treatment.

With the emergence of the clinical diagnosis, attention began to turn to elements in personality which characterize some people to a greater extent than others, thus distinguishing a group of individuals who might respond in common ways to certain forms of treatment. It began to be recognized that knowledge of such groupings—of types of disorders, that is—could increase the ability of workers to fashion treatment more appropriately to the differentiated need of the individual. Furthermore, once such commonness was seen, knowledge could become cumulative and what was learned from the treatment of one individual could be put to the service of another suffering from a similar disability.

Dr. Turner's compilation is the first book to bring the results of this development to general attention and to provide the social worker a key to the diagnostically oriented articles of the past ten years. Not only is his selection of articles excellent, but the fact that he read virtually everything available in our English literature before making his selection means that this collection provides a reliable guide to the state of our current knowledge of work with differing diagnostic entities. Inevitably any other author would have made a somewhat different selection. I will leave it to the reviewers to comment on the merits of this or that inclusion or exclusion; Dr. Turner's choices seem excellent to me. His organization of the selections into the stages of human development, psychosocial pathology, physical handicaps, and sociocultural factors is logical and should enable the reader to locate easily material that will throw light on the difficulty about which he is seeking information. If no article is included which deals with the specific subject of concern, much may be learned from an article covering treatment of a related disorder.

In addition to Dr. Turner's contribution in making this material available, his Preface and the introductions to all of the major sections add greatly to the value of the book. I am strongly tempted to underscore some of his excellent points about diagnosis and about the education of the profession, but will content myself with urging you to read the Preface and the Part introductions with care. They contain many astute observations.

In the Part introductions Dr. Turner orients the reader to the writings in the area under consideration, briefly brings out important commonalities, and points to uncovered, or scantily covered, diagnostic areas. In the main, however, he allows the selections to speak for themselves. The coverage of the book is not meant to be exhaustive. The bibliographies within the individual selections will lead the reader to further references.

It is an important sign of the times that this book is addressed to group workers as well as to caseworkers and that in many categories material on group treatment is available. The extent to which these two social work methods supplement each other in treatment and the growing tendency for many workers to want to acquire some competence in both methods is one of the very interesting developments of the sixties. This book should contribute to the common knowledge of the two specialties.

A final contribution of the book upon which I should like to comment is its usefulness as a guide to further compilation of knowledge and to publication. As Dr. Turner notes, there is valuable information dealing with many diagnostic categories in agency records and reports which could be brought to light and published. This book can serve as a guide to prospective writers and to editors as to the gaps in our diagnostic literature. It can also provide points of comparison against which the practitioner reader's experiences can be studied. Articles based on either similar or different experiences should be written. While controlled experimentation and replication is the ultimate task of knowledge building, practical replication occurs constantly in our day-by-day work. Small groups of similar cases can be studied and reported upon, thus providing cumulative information about different diagnostic groupings.

It is altogether appropriate that *Differential Diagnosis and Treatment in Social Work* should appear so soon after the fiftieth anniversary year of *Social Diagnosis*. Dr. Turner is indeed making a substantial contribution to the teaching and practice of social work.

SCHOOL OF SOCIAL WORK   *Florence Hollis*
COLUMBIA UNIVERSITY, NEW YORK

Preface to the Second Edition

It is an interesting experience to write a preface for a new edition of a book, almost ten years after the work on the first edition was carried out. The task appears to divide itself into two components: first, there is the need to explain why the book is being republished, that is, why it is still seen as being a useful contribution to the profession at this time; second, if the book is viewed as still being useful there is the need to explain why it has been altered in the new edition. In the original edition of the book there were 62 articles and in this new one 71, of which 41 are new.

Why the re-edition? I am just as convinced today as before that this type of book provides a necessary aid to the clinical social worker committed to providing efficient and responsible services to clients. Because of the structure of our present delivery system most social workers carry a highly diverse caseload. We have not as yet committed ourselves to a highly structured specialty system. At the same time our periodical literature in clinical practice remains a principal source of new practice ideas and trends. But the periodical literature contained in the better known journals is not easily available to many of our colleagues. Further, with the emergence of several new journals in North America and Europe within the last decade, the question of accessibility becomes even more difficult. Hence the necessity to extract from the literature a series of articles around a common theme. Clearly the question of the utility of collections of articles as compared to independent authorship cannot be ignored. In several of the reviews of the first edition, this question was raised and the emergence of still another collection was decried. In my own view this is not an either/or situation. The present state of practice requires both kinds of books; the collection can present a broad spectrum of current practice issues from a variety of viewpoints, while the single-authorship book presents a longer range, more focused presentation. Both are needed in today's practice.

As before, the underlying unifying concept for the book is the diagnostic component of practice. I am no less convinced of its importance in today's practice even though my perception of its form and content has altered slightly.

Between the time the first edition appeared and the present, we have passed through a period where the whole existence of clinical practice was under attack. As a part of this storm of criticism questions of labeling, classification, and treatment based on diagnosis were severely criticized. Now that this phenomenon appears to be waning, once again we can turn to further efforts at making our work more precise and effective.

I mentioned that my perception of the form and content of the diagnostic component of practice has altered. Let me comment on this. I appreciate more than before that the concept of diagnosis is a much more complex process and activity than has been acknowledged by our field. Although we have often said diagnosis should never, and was never intended to be unidimensional, I think we have nevertheless projected a view that it was a more easily manageable phenomenon with rather clear boundaries than in fact it is.

I began to appreciate this misperception about five years ago. At that time, I observed that a common theme was emerging from students I met in many schools and at many levels. In talking with them it was clear that, although professional schools had done a good job in developing the concept of diagnosis and helping them identify with it, what we had not done was to teach them precisely what to do with the concept, that is, the content of a particular diagnosis. It was then that I became less sure that we are as comfortable about the "how" of diagnosis as our literature implied. Thus, I have become convinced there is still much more conceptualizing and experimentation to be done before we can begin to reach some common ground on the operational components of diagnosis in social work intervention.

In no way does this imply that I am less convinced of the need for greater specificity and precision in our practice. As long as we are committed to the value that what we do for, with, and to clients is somehow related to our knowledge about them, we must continue to connect our perceptions of persons and our professional actions with them.

Clearly, the expanding number of thought systems that are influencing current practice and the thrust to a multi-method form of practice have made our search for more precise diagnostic efforts more difficult. When these two developments are taken into account, in conjunction with the already wide array of significant factors in a client's inner and outer life affecting his functioning, the diversity of services we have to offer, and the wide range of clients' requests and expectations, the search for more precise diagnoses appears almost futile.

There is one other way in which I have modified my perception of diagnosis; this concerns its ever changing nature. I think we have always been aware that diagnosis is a fluid concept but nevertheless have somehow conveyed through the literature and to each other that there was a fixed quality to the fact of diagnosis. That is, we have always said we had to alter it as the case developed, but usually I think we meant that any such alterations would be minimal. I am increasingly persuaded by the spiral concept of diagnosis as portrayed by Gordon Hearn in his writings on social systems.*

* *Social Work Treatment,* Ed. F. J. Turner (New York: Free Press, 1974), p. 350.

Nevertheless, difficult as it is, humbly we must continue the search for unifying concepts that will help to bring order to the complexity. But, at the same time, in our search for unifying concepts we must not overlook the knowledge to be gained by focusing on the specifics of our clients and their situations. Thus, for example, there is still much to be learned about how to deal with the suicidal component of some clients. We can all benefit by improving our techniques in dealing with the psychotic aspects of other clients with whom we work even if our overall focus with them is not related to their symptoms. We know we can be more sensitive and responsive to an addicted client when we have the accumulated knowledge, experience and perceptions of our colleagues with similar situations and behaviors.

Thus, in this second edition, as before, I have sought out, from the literature of the last ten years, articles that combined a focus on the under-standing of a particular facet of human behavior, healthy or ill, and in-cluded related practice-based suggestions aimed at bringing about changes in the identified symptom or problem. Many have found this kind of in-formation helpful in their practice.

As before, I utilized the periodical journals as the principal source of material. In so doing I am aware that there is much unpublished material that exists, although access to it is limited. Again, I found selection difficult. Certainly there was much more material from which to choose. My overall opinion is that the quality of solid clinical articles is improving. One of the new problems in selecting articles this time was the fact that some of our articles are becoming too precise for the goal of this kind of book. Thus, one article might deal with the interconnection between two concepts interrelated in a particular kind of case. Such articles were judged to be beyond the objectives I have for this book and thus, for the most part, were not used.

Once again, I observed that our writings have been uneven with some topics receiving much attention and others very little. I will comment more on this in the introduction to each section. As before, I had hoped to include more articles written from a group focus. A lack of such articles had been one of the criticisms of the first edition. Unfortunately, with the addition of more topics and a new section, I was not able to use all the excellent articles which I located. Some articles written from a one-to-one treatment focus were chosen because the diagnostic component was judged to be stronger, not because of a preference for this modality over groups. Several times, throughout the literature search, I wondered if it might be better to begin to prepare a companion volume that dealt only with group inter-vention with the same categories of client phenomena, rather than try and mix the two types of treatment.

Family treatment articles presented a different problem. A vast amount of family therapy literature exists, as we all know. Interestingly, much of it dealt with particular aspects of family treatment or very precise components of family functioning too specific for the kinds of general diagnostic clusters I had selected. Thus, there are few specific family therapy articles included.

As before, I retained the same fourfold division of articles with the addition of a fifth section entitled "Presenting Problems". I had resisted including such a section in the first edition, but have since decided it gives a fuller profile of the significant components of diagnosis. Thus in practice, in addition to considering the stage and maturation of the person, his psychological makeup and functioning, his physical health, and his sociocultural milieu, we are also interested in the kind of situation he or she presents to us. Again, this could not include full coverage but, rather, an overview of some of the prevalent presenting situations we meet in our current practice.

One of the difficulties in deciding about including new articles was the concomitant one of deciding which ones to exclude from the original group. This was difficult. I did not want to assume that more recent articles were better than older ones. Yet it was apparent that in some categories more recent articles did give a richer perspective of interventions and expanded diagnostic thinking. This was not always the case and at times the original older article was retained, even with the availability of many more recent ones.

There was much less difficulty about authorship. In the first edition I apologized for using social work authorship as a criterion of selection. This was not necessary this time; almost invariably the social-work-written articles were the preferred ones from the viewpoint of quality and the book's objectives. Not only has the content of social work clinical writing improved, but so has the format of the articles. For the most part, the new articles have richer footnotes and bibliographies than the earlier articles. These should provide an additional resource to the reader.

Inevitably, our professional writing goes through repeating series of fads and, hence, some topics are very well covered in the literature while others are scarcely mentioned. At times the decision was which article was to be selected from ten or more and in other situations it was difficult to find a single article.

One of the criticisms of the first edition was the extent to which it reflected an ego psychology orientation. Although this did reflect my own primary orientation this is only a partial explanation. This is where the literature was in 1966. But this too has changed. I was pleased to note that the specific diagnostic articles that make up this book are to an increasing extent trying to reflect a multitheory base. This, of course, is good for the profession, but difficult for planning a book such as this, as it introduces a new variable and a new challenge for choice.

As before, my hope is that we are still actively committed to a search for making the diagnostic component of practice more rigorous, our diagnostic categories more precise, the therapeutic implications from them more interdependent, and outcomes more effective and predictable.

WILFRID LAURIER UNIVERSITY,   *Francis J. Turner*
FACULTY OF SOCIAL WORK

Preface to the First Edition

The primary goal of this book is to help social work practitioners provide more effective treatment to their clients. Obviously such a goal cannot be attained in a total manner; it requires that one segment of the therapeutic process be selected as a substructure. I have chosen to utilize the diagnostic process as a focal point. This segment was chosen because, on the one hand, it is so crucial to effective treatment and, on the other, it has been a weak point in our practice. The method I have chosen is to bring together in four parts a series of articles from the professional literature, each of which deals with a specific diagnostic variable and the resultant treatment implications.

To say that we are living in an age where quantities of available knowledge are rapidly expanding is already a cliché. Such knowledge expansion, with the accompanying proliferation of writings, creates serious problems for practitioners in all disciplines. Social workers in agencies are well aware that much has been written and is being written of import to their day-to-day practice activities. They are also most aware of the difficulty in maintaining anything more than a fleeting contact or haphazard sampling of what is available. Such sampling is often more anxiety provoking than satisfying, as the little reading and formal studying that is possible clearly alerts them to the quantities of material which perforce are left untouched. Concomitant with the awareness of quantity is the realization that all that is written is not necessarily gold; much valuable time can be wasted in locating and reading material which in fact is not as useful as some other might have been.

Someday in the not too distant future, an agency social worker wishing to know quickly and succinctly what has been written about the treatment of a particular kind of client will turn to the agency data-retrieval unit. This in turn will be electronically connected with a national centralized programed library. In a few minutes he will receive a "print-out" of the requested data. As yet such resources, while theoretically possible, are beyond the scope, structure, and resources of our agencies. For the present, agency practitioners wishing to obtain such data must turn to the literature. This is not an easy task. Rarely is there time available to undertake the required search, presuming there are library resources upon which to call. In the meantime books such as this are required.

Most social work practitioners are well acquainted with the major textbooks in individual and group treatment. These have tended to be treatises on treatment in general rather than the specific. Discussions of treatment of specific kinds of problems or diagnostic entities have largely been carried out in individual articles scattered through some 20 to 25 journals and going back 30 to 35 years. Thus, at best, a practitioner can only have a superficial knowledge of the precise type of practice-oriented literature available to him. Because of this, the tendency has been to teach and practice from general rather than specific knowledge and understanding about people and how to treat them. This has been effective, and I believe the majority of our clients have been helped to achieve improved psychosocial functioning as a result of the treatment they have received. When practitioners tend to operate from an intuitive and an *ad hoc* framework, it is clear that diagnosis in anything more than a diffuse manner is unnecessary. Effective as is such a general treatment style, a higher level of competence can be achieved when treatment is consciously and selectively based on a detailed diagnosis of the client. It is my conviction that many social workers would greatly improve the quality of their treatment if experience-based observations and discussions of the treatment implications of diagnostic entities found in the literature of the last few years were readily available to them.

The danger of bringing together articles dealing with specific diagnostic entities or variables is that this collection could be misused. There is the possibility of its being seen as a shortcut, as a "How to do it" book. The prospect of having a resource which will lay out a formula of therapy or a prescription of technique for each diagnostic entity is an attractive one. Unfortunately this is not such a book; anyone who tried to use it in this way would only be disappointed. What it does aspire to achieve is to give therapists some anchoring concepts, some experience-based bench marks, some specific analyses of points of theory which will give direction and basic structure to the treatment of clients. The test of the therapist's skill is a dual one: first, to understand how much his client is like other clients of the same type and thus utilize what the profession has said about them; second, to understand how he is different from all other clients thus necessitating a peculiar combination of therapeutic skills most appropriate to him in his individuality. To follow slavishly a prescribed formulation of treatment because the literature suggests it makes the therapist a technician (and a poor one at that) rather than a professional. Whether this latter is a more serious detriment to treatment than working from no diagnosis is a moot point.

The book is designed to serve as a resource to be used in combination with the "practice wisdom" of the practitioner. It is primarily seen as important for the person in the multifunctioned agency who is called upon to serve a wide range of presenting problems and client types; the practitioner in the small agency and the private practitioner, who does not have a well-endowed agency library and readily available colleague consultation; the student and the teacher. It perhaps won't be as useful to persons in more specialized settings. It is presumed that in such settings there would be a concentration of literature appropriate to the field, for example, the treatment of marital problems. The articles chosen for the book on this former topic or on any topic can only be seen as an overview or a viewpoint rather than an exhaustive treatment or the final word. To aid in a broader coverage than one or two articles could give, bibliographies, wherever present, have been included. Thus a person interested in searching for additional information on a particular syndrome or diagnostic variable is given some leads for further reading.

This book contains a predominance of articles on individual treatment. Originally I had hoped to locate an article dealing with the individual treatment of each topic and another dealing with group treatment. This was not always possible. In the literature there have been more individual treatment-based articles than group-based articles. It is hoped that in the future, there will be more written accounts of appropriate group treatment with other client-types. In seeking group articles for each topic there is a presumed implication that every diagnostic variable lends itself to some form of group treatment. This may be incorrect.

Throughout the articles there can be seen a recurring theme. The social work practitioner of today must be a multiskilled person, comfortable in individual, joint, and group treatment, as well as a person skilled in educative and collaborative activities. This does not imply a generic method in the profession, but the necessity of multiskills, and these at a high degree of competence. Truly, this is a formidable challenge.

One of the unfortunate results of the gap between the professional literature and the mainstream of practice has been a tendency to devalue traditional knowledge. It seems fashionable in some segments of current thinking to suggest that much of our traditional theoretical orientation be scrapped and replaced by newer concepts and practice approaches. It is said that our psychodynamic approaches have failed and are unnecessary in understanding clients. Such presumptive thinking is only as valid as the evidence upon which it is based, and laudatory tributes to new approaches do not establish their validity. If the newer approaches to therapy are more effective than those presently used, then we must adopt them. Responsible professional behavior demands this. To make this comparison requires a full understanding and utilization of the old and the new. I raise this point because of a conviction that much of the disappointment in the results of treatment stems not from a fault in our theory and its applications but from a failure to utilize fully the rich amounts of data, knowledge, and skill accumulated over the years. One of the causes of this failure to tap effectively the rich resources of accumulated professional expertise in our profession has been our reliance on oral tradition and the reluctance to set out in an organized useful way what we know, what we do not know, what has been effective, and what has not.

A further purpose in planning this collection was to highlight the necessity of improved diagnostic habits among practitioners. Is not urging the importance of diagnosis to practitioners but a further example of preaching to the converted? In school and agency recent generations of social workers have been assailed with the triad of study, diagnosis, and treatment. Now every student learns early in his professional training that the unity of the therapeutic process is made up of these three elements. Why then emphasize diagnosis? It is because of a growing awareness of the divergence between our value commitment to the importance of diagnosis and the reality of our practice. Time and time again, records of social workers are examined without being able to locate within them a place where a diagnosis was formulated and set out, which the social worker then used to formulate treatment objectives and goals. That some form of diagnosis is made is indisputable; otherwise there could be no way to account for the large numbers of clients whose psychosocial functioning is markedly improved as the result of the therapist's activities and skills. The process of diagnosis evidently is operating, but the fact of diagnosis is lacking. Why should this be of concern? It is because without the availability of a concrete diagnosis there is no way to assess the effectiveness of our treatment except in a globular way. There is no way of correlating the various forms of social work intervention in relation to particular presenting diagnostic variables and assessing their outcome. There is no way of planfully and carefully improving our effectiveness with our clients. Until we can be more precise in declaring how we assess people and what therefore we choose to do with them and for them, our practice efficiency will remain static.

Why this divergence between fact and process? The answers to this are elusive and uncertain. It is easy to utilize the accustomed mutual recriminatory reflex and attribute this omission to a lack of desired professional behavior. This is too simple and obviously incorrect.

Part of the reason seems to be tied up in our strong commitment to the necessity of individualizing the client and maintaining nonjudgmental attitudes towards him. The process of working towards and from a precise, although flexible and evolving, diagnosis seems to evoke in some an emotional response that in some way the client is depersonalized through categorization and judged through opinion. There is also a fear that diagnosis somehow excludes the client. The thinking is as follows: Treatment in social work requires full involvement of the client; diagnosis is a professional assessment made by us not the client; therefore if we emphasize diagnosis we overlook the client. Obviously this is a misunderstanding of the process.

A lack of experience or perhaps of training also seems to be involved in this underemphasis of diagnosis. If there is a value-based reluctance to diagnosis among practitioners, then it is to be expected that this is a skill which will not be given first-order priority. It is clear that if this skill is not acquired early in a professional career, it is increasingly difficult later to reorient oneself to it. I want to avoid overgeneralizing here; evidently many practitioners are highly skilled diagnosticians. The selections presented here demonstrate this.

Perhaps the most important explanation of this apparent gap in social work practice stems from the complex conceptual base from which we operate. The number of variables requiring assessment and the multitude of frameworks in which these can be assessed presents a formidable and, at times, seemingly overwhelming task for the practitioner.

Because there is not a single theory of psychosocial behavior which can serve as a unifying principle of practice, it is clear that the process of diagnosis must of necessity be a multifaceted one. Since in the diagnostic phase of treatment the therapist is bringing his professional judgment to bear on the information he has about the client, it is presumed that he has a framework in which he can order the data he has about the client and norms against which he can compare his client. In the complexity of our efforts to study our client in a biopsychosocial context, the process of synthesizing, interrelating, and then formulating a professional judgment about the client is indeed a monumental one. This should not deter us from attempting to do so even though we will never reach a point of complete satisfaction with our assessment of the situations with which we are confronted.

It has been implied at times that there is a danger in forming detailed diagnoses and then operating from them. Such a process, it is said, serves to make treatment too rigid by forming a "mind-set" towards the client. It is therefore better to keep our diagnosis flexible and open and permit the utilization of new understanding and perception of clients. It is true that a diagnosis must not become "locked in" so that we operate from it in an inflexible manner. To do this, of course, is a misuse of the diagnostic concept. Obviously, we are going to shift and clarify and make more precise and enrich our understanding of clients; this in turn will affect the goals and methods of treatment we set for and with them. In no way should this deter us from constantly striving to set out clearly our assessments of them. More treatment efforts are ineffective and more client and therapist time is used uneconomically when a diagnosis is not made than there are gains resulting from nondiagnosing in order to remain "flexible and open."

No doubt part of the reluctance to diagnose has resulted from misuse to which nominal diagnoses have been put. I am referring especially to the unidimensional type in which a one-word or a one-expression classification is used. Such terms are used to explain the entire client and by implication dictate the format of treatment. For example, Miss R is a defective, Mr. J is schizophrenic, the B's are a multiproblem family.

On the one hand, if a diagnosis consists of only such labels it deserves to be discredited; on the other, these labels or classifications have their place in spite of the current tendency to disparage them. It is one of the principal assumptions of this collection of articles that we have not used them sufficiently, nor appreciated the extent to which they could help us consciously and deliberately to plan our treatment of clients. That they must be used in consort with many other classifications or labels is also a prior assumption. For effective treatment it is essential to understand the significance of the individual variables designated by the "labels" as well as the peculiar and unique combination of them as presented in the life and person of each client.

Classification in any professional activity must not become an end in itself. Whatever other purposes are served, the process should and must be a pragmatic conceptual tool to assist us in applying the rich and extensive body of knowledge accumulated over the years. Viewing classificatory thinking about clients as a useful tool rather than an absolute helps us achieve some perspective about the classification systems presently available to us. It is clear that we do not have the last word in typologies of clients and the significant variables which must be assessed for effective treatment. Similarly, systems we presently use are far from perfect and complete. It is inevitable that most of them will be replaced as better understanding is achieved and as we become more skilled in integrating the multiple bodies of knowledge from which we draw our understanding of clients.

Our profession does not have a closed body of knowledge. Hence the concepts from which we operate are in constant flux. Theory is formulated in order to be replaced by better theory, better in the sense of helping us more effectively to achieve the treatment goals deemed desirable by the values of the profession. True as this is, we are not thereby excused from utilizing today what we already know.

A further reason for preparing this collection stemmed from a research interest. I was curious to explore the actual situation of the literature. I was aware that articles existed on some categories of clients; for example, we know that there has been a wealth of data on the character-disordered clients in recent years. I did not know how extensive the coverage might be. Have we clearly addressed in our literature the entire range of diagnostic variables customarily considered as being essential to effective treatment? Thus, beyond the wish to produce a book useful to practitioners, I was also interested in locating possible gaps in the literature, to point out strategic areas in which well-thought-out and carefully written articles are required. Some of the gaps which were located will be discussed in the introduction to each Part.

It was further hoped that by bringing together writings which set out our practice, concepts, and thinking in an easily accessible way, practitioners would be given an opportunity to test their "practice wisdom" against the opinions of their colleagues. In this way, we can assess what of our present thinking is still valid, what needs to be replaced with new insights, what can be refined by imaginative experimentation, and lastly, how our traditional understanding of clients can be enriched with new combinations of skills.

There was a further reason underlying this project. From time to time serious concerns have been exhibited as to the extent and diversity of our knowledge. It is hoped that the breadth of areas addressed in the literature and contained here will help to give a better appreciation of the richness of our practice knowledge. On the basis of this idea, I tended to select articles written by social workers over those written by our colleagues in other disciplines. This was not done exclusively, of course, but presuming the articles were judged to be comparable and relevant to the design of the book, authorship by a social worker was used as a criterion of selection. I realize that this can contribute to professional insularity of which we have suffered more than enough. My own conviction is that we are growing to even greater interprofessional collaboration at all levels. To do this effectively and responsibly necessitates that we know our own field well. It is to aid in this latter task that I have kept the book more social work oriented. I do hope, though, that the collection of readings will be of interest and use to members of other disciplines. Of course, some articles written by members of other disciplines were included. Such articles were selected in which the treatment methods discussed were clearly appropriate for social workers. Thus, for example, an article dealing with the pharmacological treatment of depression would not be considered here, although one discussing some form of treatment utilizing relationship therapy would be. In the same way, it is also hoped that some increased appreciation will be gained as to the complexity of client functioning and responsible therapy. Recent conferences and writings have devoted some attention to the possibility of a generic method of practice to be taught to all aspirants to the profession. Much has been said about the necessity for others without comparable training to be able to do some of the direct work with clients presently assigned to social workers. Obviously there is some merit in examining these ideas. It is known that some understanding of treatment principles can be learned by others. It is also obvious to those directly in contact with clients that *more* rather than *less* specialized knowledge and skill is required to understand, involve, and treat many of the persons who come or are referred to us for treatment. There is a growing need for practitioners of a very high level of competence, who have clear and demonstrated diagnostic and treatment skills.

In searching for articles and in selecting them an effort was made to cover all the professional journals which include articles of import to social work practitioners, as well as standard social work journals. I am aware that a considerable amount of data was missed. For example, frequently papers are given at conferences, speeches given to meetings, and reports made to agencies which do not find their way into the mainstream of professional reading. Many of these are of high calibre and should be more widely available. It is hoped that this book will serve to draw out some of these and to encourage people to make their views more broadly known.

Selecting a framework useful for organizing the wide range of topics located in the literature was difficult. The goal was to utilize articles dealing with a specific diagnostic variable or entity rather than a type of service or problem. Thus adoption, unmarried mothers, deserted wives, separated couples, or other problem or service classifications were not employed. It is not always easy to distinguish between a diagnostic variable with specific treatment implications and a problem classification with a multitude of causes so that little or nothing can be said about generic treatment implications. There are some types of situations which are both a problem for treatment and a variable in diagnosis affecting the method of treatment selected. For example, although treatment of unmarried mothers was not included I did include delinquent youth.

I was particularly interested in finding articles which discussed the therapeutic considerations which result from a precise part of our total assessment of the client. It is assumed that all treatment must be geared to the whole person and not to particular parts of that person. It is also understood that there are dangers in categorizing a segment of a client's total psychosocial functioning and selecting our treatment approach specific to that segment. The danger is the well-known one of stereotyping. It is the extent to which the individual person can be partialized and yet treated as a whole that determines the effectiveness of our treatment methods. It is clear that selective treatment skills are necessary with schizophrenic clients, yet there are no schizophrenic clients as such. There are young, recently married, working class, rural-oriented, dull normal, Irish Catholic schizophrenic clients. Our treatment will be most effective when we can begin to understand the significance of each of these variables and whatever others are important and the peculiar combination of treatment methods most appropriate for different constellations of variables.

The variables which were finally chosen were divided into the traditional biopsychosocial traid based on a framework of human growth and development stages. Obviously it would be much easier for all if a unitary theory of psychosocial functioning could be devised so that clients would only have to be assessed along one dimension. Unfortunately, we are a long way from this and for a long time to come we have to live with the problems arising from the fact that societal man is a most complex creature. To try to understand and explain him in a manner that will permit us to aid him effectively to achieve improved psychosocial functioning will demand a complex conceptual framework. Complex as is our present conceptual basis of human behavior, undoubtedly there are other dimensions whose significance we probably do not realize, such as some genetic, cosmotic or time-space factors.

No apologies are made for utilizing traditional psychodynamic headings. It is true that there has been recent serious questioning of the utility of classical dynamic interpretations of behavior. No one denies these present difficulties. They require constant critical re-examination in the light of current practice. This doesn't mean that they are to be ignored; for they have supplied and will continue to supply a framework in which people can be understood and, even more importantly, effectively treated. When they are replaced, as is the lot of all theory, it must be done by validated reliable concepts.

In selecting the headings under which topics were gathered there was an additional difficulty that must always be considered in diagnosis. This is the different levels of precision which exist between and among the various diagnostic variables. The presence or the lack of precision affects the degree of exactness with which we can discuss the treatment implications of each variable. For example, our division of clients by socioeconomic classes is a much less precise variable than the distinction between the types of neuroses or between character-disordered and border-line clients.

As our knowledge about these variables grows and more specificity is developed, our precision in formulating treatment goals and methods will grow also. It is hoped that much of what has been written in these pages will be replaced with further experiences, new concepts, and generalizations. It is hoped that the ideas presented in the various articles will be subjected to the keen scrutiny of our colleagues who are secure in their practice and rich in experience. It is hoped that imaginative, responsible experimentation will provide us with new insights and suggest new therapeutic approaches for consideration. In such instances the most useful form of replacement would be by means of scholarly articles building on the past and adding the new. I would hope most seriously that this book would have to be re-edited in a few years, on the basis of new insights, further writing, and an increased acceptance of our responsibility to translate our knowledge into a form readily accessible to our colleagues.

Much remains to be done in improving our diagnostic categories, in clarifying their definitions and descriptions, in specifying commonly accepted indicators, and in developing optimum treatment approaches. In the meantime the practitioner must use the knowledge presently available to him, fully aware of its inherent limitations. It is the purpose of this book to make one segment of this knowledge more accessible to him.

GRADUATE SCHOOL OF SOCIAL WORK   *Francis J. Turner*
WATERLOO LUTHERAN UNIVERSITY
WATERLOO, ONTARIO, CANADA

Acknowledgments

One of the most pleasant phases of preparing a book is that point just prior to submitting the manuscript; the most difficult work is completed and the time has come to respectfully acknowledge those persons who have been of assistance.

Few professional projects in today's world can be carried out without the assistance of many persons, some of whom contribute to the task without being aware of their involvement. Certainly this is true for this book. In particular, I think of the many colleagues who found the first edition useful and have thus provided me with the necessary stimulus to prepare a second edition.

I am also grateful to my university, Wilfrid Laurier, which granted me leave to spend several months at Oxford where I was able to do the preliminary work for it. In the actual task of scanning the literature and preparing the material, two graduate social work students of WLU, Gay Zimmerman and Cathie Patterson, were of great assistance.

I am thankful also to the staff of The Free Press who have been most helpful and encouraging in developing the format of this second edition.

As before, my most essential assistant was Joanne who views my knowledge of syntax and style with suspicion and thus edited the various drafts of the sections. Francis, Sarah and Anne-Marie have, also as before, been very much a part of the project. On this occasion their major role seems to have been related to using as much paper, scotch tape, and paper clips from my desk as was possible; this no doubt limited the final size of the volume. I am thankful for their involvement.

To all, my appreciation.

F.J.T.

Contributors

The contributors are identified by the professional positions they held at the time the articles were first published.

Margaret G. Frank is Program Coordinator, Advanced Social Work Training Program in Teaching and Consultation on Child Treatment, Judge Baker Guidance Center, Boston, Massachusetts.

Annette Jacobsohn is Senior Caseworker, Westchester Jewish Community Services, White Plains, New York.

Selma Fraiberg is Associate Professor of Social Work, Tulane University, New Orleans, Louisiana.

Ralph J. Kolodny, M.S.S.S., is Research Supervisor, Group Work Department, Boston Children's Service Association, Boston, Massachusetts.

Elizabeth Kerns is Caseworker, Youth Service, Cleveland, Ohio.

Barbara K. Varley, D.S.W., is Professor, School of Social Work, Fresno State College, Fresno, California.

Alice H. Collins, M.S., is Deputy Director, Massachusetts Division of Youth Service, Boston, Massachusetts.

James R. Mackay, M.S.S., is Social Worker, Alcoholism Clinic, Peter Bent Brigham Hospital, Boston, Massachusetts.

Gisela Konopka, D.S.W., is Professor of Social Work and Director, Center for Youth Development and Research, University of Minnesota, Minneapolis, Minnesota.

Miriam Jolesch is Caseworker, Jewish Family and Community Service, Chicago, Illinois.

Joanne Geist is Caseworker in Family Service of Cincinnati and Hamilton County, Cincinnati, Ohio.

Norman M. Gerber is Caseworker in Family Service of Cincinnati and Hamilton County, Cincinnati, Ohio.

Geraldine E. McKinney is Assistant Professor, The National Catholic School of Social Service, The Catholic University of America, Washington, D.C.

Sheldon D. Rose, Ph.D., is Associate Professor, School of Social Work, University of Michigan, Ann Arbor, Michigan.

Barbara Stevens, M.S.W., is Psychiatric Social Worker, in private practice, Berkeley, California.

Sidney Wasserman is from University of Bradford, School of Applied Social Studies, Bradford, Yorkshire, England.

David Soyer is Director, Services to the Aged, Jewish Family Service, New York, New York.

Eda G. Goldstein is Senior Psychiatric Social Worker, New York State Psychiatric Institute, New York, New York.

John Weinberg, Ph.D., is Director of Education and Training, Hennepin County Alcoholism and Inebriety Program, Minneapolis, Minnesota.

C. Andre St. Pierre, M.S.W., is Senior Drug Addiction Counselor, Drug Addiction Treatment Unit, Boston Department of Health and Hospitals, Boston, Massachusetts.

Merl M. Jackel, M.D., is Clinical Assistant Professor of Psychiatry, Division of Psychoanalytic Education, Downstate Medical Center, State University of New York, New York City, and Psychiatric Consultant, Community Service Society of New York, New York City.

Otto Pollack is from Department of Sociology, University of Pennsylvania, Philadelphia, Pennsylvania.

Rosemary Reynolds is District Director for Professional Personnel, Community Service Society of New York, New York, New York.

Else Siegle is Assistant for Professional Personnel, Community Service Society of New York, New York, New York.

Gloria G. Harris is from University of Washington, Center for Psychological Services, Seattle, Washington.

Nathaniel N. Wagner is from University of Washington, Center for Psychological Services, Seattle, Washington.

Beatrice Simcox Reiner is Marriage Counselor, Juvenile Welfare Board, Pinellas County, St. Petersburg, Florida.

Valdemar Hartman, L.L.B., M.S.W., is from Forensic Unit, Toronto Psychiatric Hospital, Toronto, Ontario, Canada.

Sidney Wasserman is Caseworker at Bellefaire, regional child care center and service affiliated with the Jewish Children's Bureau of Cleveland, Cleveland, Ohio.

Lucille N. Austin is Professor of Social Work, Columbia University, School of Social Work, New York, New York.

James F. Suess, M.D., is Professor of Psychiatry, University of Mississippi School of Medicine, Jackson, Mississippi.

Eva Y. Deykin is Co-Director of Research, B.A. Training Program, Simmons School of Social Work and Psychiatric Research Social Worker, Collaborative Depression Study, Boston State Hospital.

Myrna M. Weissman is Chief Social Worker, Yale Clinical Psychopharmacology Unit, and Research Associates, Yale Department of Psychiatry, New Haven, Connecticut.

Gerald L. Klerman is Professor of Psychiatry, Harvard Medical School, Massachusetts General Hospital, Boston, Massachusetts.

Hank Walzer is Psychiatric Caseworker, Children's Division, Department of Psychiatry, and Colorado Psychopathic Hospital, both part of the Medical Center, of University of Colorado, Denver, Colorado.

Richard Stuart, M.S., is Assistant Professor, School of Social Work, Rutgers, The State University, New Brunswick, New Jersey.

Esther S. Marcus is Supervisor, Jewish Family Service, New York, and Faculty, William Alanson White Institute of Psychiatry, Psychoanalysis and Psychology, New York, New York.

Laura Farber is Psychiatric Social Worker, Hillsdale Hospital, Glen Oaks, New York.

Joan Morse is Social Worker, Clinical Treatment Center for Juvenile Rheumatoid Arthritis, Robert B. Brigham Hospital, Boston, Massachusetts.

Doreen M. Winkler, M.S.W., is Social Worker, Lakeshore Psychiatric Hospital, Toronto, Ontario, Canada.

George R. Krupp, M.D., is Psychiatric Consultant, Family Service Association of the Five Towns, Woodmere, New York.

Bernard Schwartzberg is Administrative Director, West Nassau Mental Health Center, New Hyde Park, New York.

Gene A. Brodland is Senior Outpatient Social Worker, Department of Psychiatry, University of Iowa College of Medicine, Iowa City, Iowa.

N. J. C. Andreasen, M.D. and Ph.D., is Assistant Professor, Department of Psychiatry, University of Iowa, College of Medicine, Iowa City, Iowa.

Rosalind Jablon, M.S.W., is Social Caseworker, Tumor Clinic, Bronx Municipal Hospital Center, New York, New York.

Herbert Volk, M.D., is Assistant Professor of Surgery, Albert Einstein College of Medicine, and Cancer Coordinator, Bronx Municipal Hospital Center, New York, New York.

Elliot C. Brown, Jr., is Supervisor, Baker Social Service Unit, Massachusetts General Hospital, Boston, Massachusetts.

Arnold S. Carson, Ph.D., is Clinical Psychologist, Des Moines Child Guidance Center, Des Moines, Iowa.

Steven K. Chough, M.S.W., is Counsellor, Child Guidance Department, Texas School for the Deaf, Austin, Texas.

Mary W. Englemann is Social Worker, Royal Alexandra Hospital, Edmonton, Alberta, Canada.

Kenneth R. Wedel, M.S.W., is Clinical Social Worker, Clinical Center, National Institutes of Health, Bethesda, Maryland.

Alfred H. Katz, D.S.W., is Head, Division of Social Welfare in Medicine, and Associate Professor, Social Welfare in Medicine, Department of Preventive Medicine and Public Health, University of California Medical Center, School of Medicine, Los Angeles, California.

Kathleen M. Hickey is Social Worker, Dialysis and Transplant Unit, Social Service Department, University of Minnesota Hospitals, Minneapolis, Minnesota.

Gladys Lambert is Social Worker, University of Rochester Medical Center, Rochester, New York.

Ann Murphy is Chief Social Worker, Development Evaluation Clinic, Children's Hospital Medical Center, Boston, Massachusetts.

Siegfried M. Pusechel, M.D., is Associate in Mental Retardation, Children's Hospital Medical Center, and Instructor in Pediatrics, Harvard Medical School, Cambridge, Massachusetts.

Jane Schneider is Caseworker, Children's Hospital Medical Center, Boston, Massachusetts.

Sylvia Schild, M.S.W., is Casework Specialist, Child Development Clinic, Children's Hospital of Loss Angeles, and Instructor of Social Work, Department of Pediatrics, University of Southern California Medical School, Los Angeles, California.

Bok-Lim C. Kim is Assistant Professor, Jane Addams Graduate School of Social Work, University of Illinois, Urbana, Illinois.

Jimm G. Good Tracks, M.S.W., is Guidance Counselor, Toyei Indian Boarding School, Ganado, Arizona.

Inez M. Tyler is Medical Social Consultant, U.S. Public Health Service, Division of Indian Health, Window Rock, Arizona.

Sophie D. Thompson is Clinical Social Worker, U.S. Public Health Service, Indian Hospital, Tuba City, Arizona.

Ignacio Aguilar, M.S.W., is Executive Director, El Calvario Community Center, El Monte, California, and Director of Spanish Language Psychiatric Services, Metropolitan State Hospital, Norwalk, California.

Andrew E. Curry is Senior Psychiatric Social Worker, Langley Porter Neuropsychiatric Institute, California Department of Hygiene, San Francisco, California.

Alex Gitterman is Lecturer, Columbia University School of Social Work, New York, New York.

Alice Schaeffer is Social Worker, Jewish Child Care Association, New York, New York.

Esther Fibush is Caseworker, Family Service Bureau, Oakland, California.

BeAlva Turnquest is Caseworker, Family Service Bureau, Oakland, California.

Florence Hollis, Ph.D., is Professor of Social Work, Columbia University School of Social Work, New York, New York.

Berta Fantl, M.S., is Unit Supervisor, Child Guidance Services, San Francisco, Board of Education, San Francisco, California.

Ben A. Orcutt, D.S.W., is Associate Professor, School of Social Work, Columbia University, New York, New York.

Carol H. Meyer, D.S.W., is Associate Professor of Social Work, Columbia University School of Social Work, New York, New York.

Shirley C. Hellenbrand is Lecturer, New York School of Social Work, Columbia University, New York, New York.

Francis J. Turner, D.S.W., is Dean, Faculty of Social Work, Wilfrid Laurier University, Waterloo, Ontario, Canada.

Alice Ullmann is Social Work Supervisor, New York Hospital and Assistant Professor of Social Work, Cornell University Medical College, New York, New York.

Sally Holmes is Caseworker, Family Service of Detroit and Wayne County, Detroit, Michigan.

Carol Barnhart is Caseworker, Family Service of Detroit and Wayne County, Detroit, Michigan.

Lucile Cantoni is Director of Family Life Education, Family Service of Detroit and Wayne County, Detroit, Michigan.

Eva Reymer is Caseworker, Family Service of Detroit and Wayne County, Detroit, Michigan.

Roger Morgan is Post-graduate Research Scholar, School of Social Work, University of Leicester, Leicestershire, England.

Gordon Young, M.D., B.Sc., D.P.H., is Deputy Medical Officer of Health for London Borough of Barnet, London, England.

Elisabeth Lassers, M.D., is Assistant Professor of Psychiatry and Pediatrics, Abraham Lincoln School of Medicine, University of Illinois, Chicago, Illinois.

Robert Nordan, Ph.D., is Assistant Professor of Psychology, Abraham Lincoln School of Medicine, University of Illinois, Chicago, Illinois.

Sheila Bladholm, M.S.W., is Assistant Professor of Medical Social Work, Abraham Lincoln School of Medicine, University of Illinois, Chicago, Illinois.

Jack Adler, Ed. D., is Coordinator of Social Work Training, Jewish Child Care Association, New York, New York.

Irene Fast, Ph.D., is from University of Michigan, Ann Arbor, Michigan.

Albert C. Cain, Ph.D., is from University of Michigan, Ann Arbor, Michigan.

Leona Grossman, M.P.H., M.S.W., is Director Social Work Department, Michael Reese Hospital and Medical Center, Chicago, Illinois.

Ann Wolbert Burgess, D.N.Sc., is Associate Professor of Nursing, Boston College, Chestnut Hill, Massachusetts.

Lynda Lytle Holmstrom, Ph.D., is Associate Professor of Sociology, Boston College, Chestnut Hill, Massachusetts.

Sarah F. Hafemann is Family Court Marriage Counsellor, Milwaukee County Department of Family Conciliation, Milwaukee, Winconsin.

Catherine S. Chilman, Ph.D., is Professor and Research Consultant, School of Social Welfare, University of Wisconsin, Milwaukee, Wisconsin.

Herbert S. Strean, D.S.W., is Associate Professor, Graduate School of Social Work, Rutgers, The State University, New Brunswick, New Jersey.

Donald F. Krill, M.S.W., is Assistant Professor, Graduate School of Social Work, University of Denver, Denver, Colorado.

David J. Klugman, M.S.W., is Co-Chief Social Worker, Suicide Prevention Center, Los Angeles, California.

Robert E. Litman, M.D., is Chief Psychiatrist, Suicide Prevention Center, Los Angeles, California.

Carl I. Wold, Ph.D., is Chief Psychologist, Suidice Prevention Center, Los Angeles, California.

Part 1

Stages of Human Development

The articles in this section were selected to give an overview of the literature dealing with the diagnostic and treatment implications of various stages of human development. This variable is a basic dimension in understanding clients in that it gives an underlying orientation to the method and direction of treatment.

This dimension of diagnosis has always been important for social workers. Considerable attention has been given to it. For example, for many years services and specialties in practice have been formulated around divisions of developmental stages such as services to children, school social work, youth services, marital counseling, and services to the aged. To a great extent the framework of our agencies' structures still tends to divide practice, and thus clients, by some dimensions of age or status. This appears to be changing. There are clear indications that today's practitioners and agencies are called upon to demonstrate competence with a wide range of clients and client problems.

Nevertheless, this differentiating concept is still viewed as critical. Because of the importance of this approach to understanding clients it was anticipated that the literature would provide an abundance of material considering various facets of this continuum. This in fact was the case. During the period since the first edition we have continued to emphasize this component of persons and their psychosocial environment as an essential base to our diagnosis and treatment. That is, the perception we have of clients and the resulting profile of interventive methods, procedures, and techniques are significantly and predictably altered by the stage of development achieved and the roles played therein.

We still continue to write frequently and perceptively about our work with children. The group of four articles selected covers a variety of approaches.

These include direct work with the child; work with the mother; work with the father; work with groups of children; and a new article that gives an overall conceptual framework for working with children. Articles in the literature deal principally with children living in their own homes. Because many social workers work directly with institutionalized children, Fraiberg's article is important.

In general, the literature up to the present has tended to imply that work with children is by definition long term. This recent review shows that we are beginning now to give more thought to the possibility of briefer intervention with this type of client.

In addition, the literature on work with children reflects a heavier emphasis on work with older children. This is interesting. Obviously treatment for the very young child would be directed principally to parents or parent substitutes. With increased collaboration between social workers and pediatricians, it is to be hoped that further articles will be forthcoming that deal with very young children.

Among the children-focused articles, of which about 30 were selected for the final choices, a much wider range of topics and viewpoints was observed than in the earlier review. Thus articles dealing with specific behavioral techniques, focused use of play therapy, educative techniques, therapeutic programs, use of institutional care, and specialized programs for children were located. In addition, we have now began to address the therapeutic implications of dealing with differential components of child functioning, both normal and problematic. A final group of articles to be noted was sociological-developmental in nature: articles that discuss widened perceptions of normal child development as well as sociological observations of children in contemporary society.

The developmental phase of adolescence continues to be well covered in the literature. It is evident that we are making much less of our earlier stress on delinquency as a separate stage of adolescence. Continued stress is put on the necessity of the therapist's own awareness of his or her ideas and attitudes about this period of maturation. Reference is made to the importance of understanding the period of adolescence in our culture both in sociological and in psychological terms to avoid developing an overly pathological viewpoint.

As is to be expected in the literature, we have focused on our changing perceptions of youth in society. Konopka's article was selected because of its twofold thrust on a historical overview and a contemporary understanding of current problems and services, especially institutional services for troubled adolescents.

In our efforts to bring increased specificity to our intervention, more attempts are being made to consider the differential use of newer thought systems and therapeutic strategies in working with adolescents. The Varley article on role theory and the Kerns article on short-term treatment are good examples of this component of the literature.

In the overall literature related to adolescents several new trends were identified. It is interesting that instead of stressing delinquency as we did in the fifties and early sixties we are now looking at other components and roles of the adolescent period. Although space did not permit their inclusion, there is an interesting cluster of articles that focus on such topics as "the adolescent as student," "the adolescent and the changing sexual mores," and "the overall value conflicts of the adolescent." The predominating theme of much of the current literature is a stress on the need for a reconsideration and a reunderstanding of the Eriksonian concept of the search for identity and autonomy of the adolescent.

Many excellent articles are to be found in the literature which deal with various aspects of the marital relationship. In the first two articles in this section there is common emphasis on the prevalence of transference and countertransference phenomena in this type of case and on the necessity of understanding and dealing with these related phenomena.

These articles also reflect a frequent theme of the necessity of using both individual and joint interviews, not as an either/or approach, but in a concurrent manner. The article by Geist and Gerber examines the use of joint interviewing and discusses both the indicators and the specific dimensions of the technique. This is a particularly useful article for persons who have been more accustomed to individual interviews and who are interested in developing this treatment modality as one of their skills.

Wasserman's article looks at a phase of marriage not hitherto given much attention in the literature, the middle years. This article reflects a theme now more evident in the literature. The idea being stressed is that marriage, like the family, has a developmental life of its own and that diagnostically it is important to understand the maturational stage of a marriage to intervene successfully.

In addition to the above theme we are also beginning to give more attention to diagnostic and therapeutic implications of the marriage that is at the point of breaking up. Hitherto it appears that we have tended to see the ending of marriage as a therapeutic failure and have not realized and made use of the need for help and the potential for growth that can exist at this time.

As our writing becomes more sophisticated and precise in the area of human development, we are bringing into focus other aspects of the maturational history of individuals. Thus, along with our rich literature on marriage and family, we have begun to focus on the specific function of parenting as a distinct role with its own problems and interventive implications. As in other client categories increased interest in and consideration of the implications of different thought systems such as behavioral theory, crisis theory, and role theory are found.

The literature is also beginning to reflect the awareness that all adults are not married and that there are other life styles related to the adult stage of maturation. This is an important development in the literature of the last decade. Undoubtedly, in view of current interest, there is more focus on the adult woman than the adult man with such articles taking both therapeutic and sociological perspectives.

In the literature we continue to emphasize our interest and experience with the aged client. In recent years a rich array of articles dealing with both specific and generalized features of this stage of human development has appeared. Our colleagues who write in this area continue to emphasize the extent to which our own feelings and attitudes are an essential part of successful practice with the aged. Soyer's article with its existential orientation reminds us of this fact and adds the further idea that indeed we continue our own maturation through contact with our aged clients.

In the final article in this section, dying, the ultimate stage in human earthly existence is addressed. It is quite remarkable how much this topic, once so denied professionally, has become an acceptable one in the literature. There were some 15 to 20 articles in the final selection from which to choose. Throughout, the authors stress the necessity of seeing the situation, emotionally laden as it is for all, as a professional responsibility, to be met and dealt with in the same manner as any other and not to be avoided out of our own discomfort, or because we misconceive either the client's inability or unwillingness to deal with it.

In conclusion, the stages of human development as a diagnostic variable requiring specific therapeutic consideration serve as an important but not exclusive part of the assessment process. It is clear that extended practice experience has demonstrated there are commonalities in behavior and problems requiring specific and predictable treatment approaches in the various stages and roles of human life. It is also clear, and each author reminds us, that as knowledge of our client expands and as our interventive plan emerges and is modified, a variety of other variables must be considered. In recent years we have greatly enriched our specific understanding of many aspects of the stages of human development. As our knowledge has become enriched so has our awareness that there are many other aspects of this dimension that we have just begun to understand and address as clinicians.

Casework with Children: The Experience of Treatment

Margaret G. Frank

Lenny was a thin, gaunt-looking boy, small for his seven years, with an expression in his eyes that reflected the years of misery he had lived. His stance was stiff, on-guard and watchful. Characteristically he "attacked first," kicking, screaming and trying to bite his caseworker. This was his first visit to a placement agency. He knew he was going to be taken from his home.

What he did not know was that by the time he was to leave home he would agree to go and the residence would no longer loom as a house of horrors. Nor had he any idea that four years later he would emerge from the school nervous about leaving, sad to say "good-bye" to Mrs. Lieb, whose legs he had not bruised for some years. He could not envisage that there would ever be a day when he would proudly sport a report card with B's and two A's, or that he would be able to enter a group of age-mates without fear of rejection. Nor could he imagine that there would be a time in his life when hearing the shrill voices of anger didn't send him into a frenzy.

Barbara, an obese, pimple-faced girl of thirteen, defied her caseworker in their first meeting to "do something about me." Little did this young woman know, who was so hell-bent on evoking disgust and anger, busy negating everything her well-to-do, educated family stood for, that during four years she would move steadily toward the bright, able and charming person that she could be. She had no idea that she could ever be trim and pretty, that she could enjoy, albeit anxiously, her first steps into the dating-game, that working well at school would no longer arouse the dilemmas it had, and could carry satisfactions.

The gratifying development seen in these two children is not unique. Progressive achievement is seen in many children who come to the attention of workers in the children's field. While not unique, neither are such positive outcomes typical. Not all of our work with children is effective. Thus,

Reprinted from *Smith College Studies in Social Work,* Vol. 39 (February, 1969), pp. 127–137, by permission of the journal.

instances of success, while gratifying, are also disquieting in that they identify unrealized possibilities for effective service by marking off and highlighting our failures.

Mental health practitioners and researchers continually question what happens in treatment, what are the elements that enable or induce a child, stunted and thwarted in ego development, to re-enter the main stream and even to experience pleasure in his new-found ego capacities. This search is crucial to the development of the mental health practice and it has particular relevance to those who would teach others. I say this because, if, as practitioners, we are honest with ourselves we would admit that we are not always planful and aware of what we are doing in treatment and why we do it. We are accountable mainly to ourselves and perhaps to a supervisor or consultant. But those who choose to teach others are faced (happily, I might add) with the constant questioning of "the novice": "How did you know to do or say that?" "What made you choose to be silent?" "How should I handle this?" "What should my attitude be?" "Why?"

From my own experience as a practitioner and teacher I have found it useful to view treatment as comprised of two major elements, cognitive and experiential. While the two are, in fact, highly interrelated and inseparable, we should, for the purposes of study, permit them to be artificially separated.

The purpose of this paper is to examine the experiential elements of treatment. While of great importance, the cognitive element will be defined but not elaborated. I have made this choice because, in my opinion, our training lacks the appropriate study of, and emphasis on, the experiential aspects of treatment.

Cognitive Elements in Treatment

Cognitive work in treatment refers to all those steps taken by the therapist to enable the client to understand aspects of himself, why he feels the way he does, why he behaves as he does, what events have influenced his present being.

Such conscious self-knowledge has proven of great value when the client can use his insight to change or modify his behavior. However, too often it appears that measures are taken to clarify the client's behavior more out of the therapist's needs than the client's. Faced, for example, with the rawness of a child patient's need to be emotionally fed, a therapist may state the meaning of his behavior and the reasons for it prematurely. The need to make the behavior understood stems from the threat felt by the therapist possibly of being "swallowed up" by the hungry child. The same clarifications might well be made and be of use to the child later, after a "feeding experience."

There is no question, then, of the importance of conscious understanding as a stepping-stone to growth, and yet we know that such understanding is not enough.

Experiential Element of Treatment

In examining the experiential element I am referring to those aspects of treatment which carry a variety of labels: "corrective experience," "treatment relationship," "friendship." I am concerned with therapeutic procedures involving "the use of self, the use of transference, provision of self as an object for identification." Our interest is in all those actions taken in treatment that provide the client with an emotional experience conducive to growth. As noted before I have, only for purposes of study, separated them from those procedures used to bring about conscious comprehension.

Casework with Children

Before we go into the main topic in depth, I want to digress for a moment. You may have noted that no reference has been made thus far to the discipline of casework or to the process called "casework with children." I feel this needs explanation. I confess that I do not differentiate the work done by caseworkers with children from the psychotherapeutic endeavors of the other mental health disciplines. Following from this, I do not see that the knowledge base of caseworkers should be allowed to be less than that of the other mental health disciplines. But I am all too aware of the reality that little specific training in therapeutic work with children is available for our profession. Less than a handful of schools of social work in the United States offer courses in treatment of children. In the few schools whose doors are open to this need, it's still only a crack—one semester, often without concomitant practical field work. Post-graduate training programs are few and far between. In the face of this paucity of training we find that, in fact, caseworkers throughout our nation are seeing and working with a large number of children whose emotional development has been severely crippled. Perhaps the saddest reality of all is that members of the social work profession have allowed their work with children to go on under such labels as "friendly visitor," "companion," "guardian," yes, even "casework with children," all connoting interventions of lesser importance, necessitating less training and knowledge. It seems that we carry the burden of work but do not fight for the knowledge that is vital to that work.

The historical whys of these realities are not germane to this paper, but noting the existence of these realities is crucial. I said earlier that I do not differentiate between the necessary knowledge base and work done by caseworkers with children from the other mental health professions. But I *do* observe a difference in the child client group generally seen in social agencies from those seen in private practice or even many of the child guidance clinics. These are the children who have not only suffered from *early* emotional deprivations that cause stunted ego development, but they usually have also to contend with *continuous*, on-going tumult and disruption in their environments: The "Lennys" seen in child welfare settings, and the

"Barbaras" seen in homes for unmarried mothers are the children who need many years of therapeutic work to clear away the blocks in their development. These are the children who can use understanding only after they have experienced something in treatment that develops their capacity to use their comprehension. These are the children whose emotional-environmental conditions need the most knowledgeable and artful interventions. Yet, sadly, it is with these very children that many members of the social work profession deny the importance of their actions by calling their endeavors "friendly visiting" or "supportive casework." What follows from this denial is a contentment to proceed spontaneously, intuitively with little of the rigorous planning, knowledge and thought that is deemed part of the practitioner's responsibility when attempting to bring about change in another human being's life. It is my hope that this paper will stimulate members of the casework profession to seek and utilize the knowledge that is available.

As the dynamics of a child's problems unfold it is not difficult to locate the areas in which we wish him to gain understanding of himself and his circumstances. Neurotic distortions in reasoning are obvious and the goal of clarifying these distortions is clear. It is normal for children, at an early age, to see themselves as the center of their universe. It follows, then, that as "good and evil" befall them, they will perceive all happenings as their own doings. A healthy child will mature cognitively and come to understand that there are forces beyond him that cause events. The daughter of a friend demonstrated this beautifully recently when she asked her mother who was yelling at her, "Are you mad at me, Mommy, or at something else?" We can easily understand that Lenny originally saw the disruption of his home, his parents' divorce, his own placement as punishment for his own badness. It was clear that he had to be helped to understand events differently.

Earlier we said, however, that understanding is not enough to free a child to develop.

It is far less easy for a therapist, as the dynamics of a child's problems unfold, to think out planfully what he wants the child to experience with him and from him which will be therapeutic—conducive to his growth.

Corrective Experience

"Corrective" is the label often given to the experiential part of treatment. By this it is meant that the therapist creates an opportunity for the child to re-experience, to rework, to correct earlier phases of his development, phases that are deemed through diagnostic assessment crucial to his problems. Re-experiencing implies setting up conditions which will encourage the child to "slip back," regress to the troubled phase. If the therapist has deep meaning to the child, his handling, responses, attitudes toward the child's behavior become the corrective forces.

Often I have observed a too literal and overly simplified definition of the corrective experience. It is as if the therapist were saying to himself, "I will correct the wrongs done by the parents. I will offer love, acceptance,

warmth, and permissiveness to counter restrictiveness, rivalry, inability to love, et cetera." As important as love, warmth and acceptance are to living and treatment, we have ample proof that they are not enough to bring about growth either in every-day living or in treatment.

One could present another paper on why so many practitioners fill their offices with toys and candies and set about mainly to love and accept their child clients. I want to offer only two thoughts, and briefly, about this kind of practice. One thought has to do with the fact that many people in the mental health profession have not developed a professional self-image which contains the notion that they may be an instrument of pain, even if it is understood intellectually that pain is often a necessary and unavoidable experience in growing. I can recall working with a young girl who had made steady progress. While her mother was gaining in adequacy through her own treatment, I had achieved a strong maternal quality in the transference which had brought about much of her growth. However, the day was coming when she would have to be helped to break her ties to me. The opportunity arose one day when we were observing some animals which were up for adoption. All of her words and actions pointed symbolically to her desire to be taken home by me. Pointing out to her that this was not possible was one of the hardest things I had ever done with a child. First there was the obvious pain of her feelings of being rejected, and then, the uncomfortable for me, ensuing anger, and finally I was also depriving myself of some very pleasurable communications from an appealing child. I remember returning to the clinic later and talking with some colleagues, remarking with only thin humor that no one told me treatment was going to be as painful to do as this. I had never envisaged before that I would do something purposefully which would cause a client to be angry and pained.

The other thought that I want to offer for brief consideration with regard to a "too loving" style of practice is that many of the people who work with the emotionally disturbed do not understand or use their knowledge of normal growth and development. One can find in normal growth and development an important model for the corrective experience. An example of this can be seen in the following situation. Last year I was supervising a caseworker in her work with a young child who was developing rigid compulsive defenses. The history was dramatically clear in showing the sources of these behaviors, for the mother's discomfort with messing was great indeed. The worker had set about to create a "corrective experience." Permission was being given for the child to mess and little by little the child was accepting the permission. I came on the scene at a point when the worker felt that little progress was being made, despite the corrective atmosphere she was providing.

In our discussions we began to concentrate on how "healthy" children learn to deal with their impulses to mess and the demand that they become trained. We came upon the fact that the healthy mother approaches her child with an expectation that he will master his impulses. She offers love and her pleasure as a reward at the same time that she provides him with a

variety of what might be called sublimatory activities. How many children can be observed playing with mud, "washing dishes," slopping in the soapy water at the very period of their lives when they are learning with firmness from their mothers that they must use the toilet. This pursuit became an important guide to the worker. I could not tell her the specific actions she should take with this child, but they were not hard to locate once she had a guide for her direction. Her sessions with the young client began to shift from pure permission to acceptance of the impulse, but with provision of other ways to express it. The boy moved from slopping the office with finger paints to working in more confined areas, to painting with a brush, to working with models where inadvertently his hands always got "messy" from the glue.

Thus far I have discussed the provision of a corrective experience in rather global terms. I have pointed out that it must not be viewed as a simple opposition of parental handling. The practitioner must be comfortable with taking actions which may be experienced as painful by the child (and by himself). I have pointed up the importance of knowledge of the ingredients that go into healthy development to serve as model for corrective experience.

Knowledge and Use of Transference

Somewhat earlier I said that the therapist's responses to the child's behavior have corrective powers *when* the therapist is a meaningful person to the child. Again, we cannot go into the historical reasons behind the fact, but caseworkers have been slow to learn about, understand and utilize the transference phenomena in the treatment relationship. Yet they are there. Sometimes one is lucky, and without awareness treatment can progress because the treatment relationship has room in it for the expression of both love and anger. But all too often practitioners are alert to only the negative. If we know who we are as people, then material from a child of a strongly negative nature: "You're mean. You are not going to approve of this. You are always ready to find fault with me," stands out as obviously stemming from another relationship, and the worker will take steps to diminish the negative qualities. It is not so easy to detect a too positive transference in work with a child. The reason, one can suppose, is that we all find an important positive confirmation of ourselves in the love of a child. If I return to my own experiences with the girl who offered herself up for my adoption, I cannot deny the personal satisfaction that her sentiments brought. There is nothing wrong with experiencing personal satisfaction in work with children, as long as it is also therapeutic for the child. Thus, we must be consciously watchful for the perceptions of us as "the greatest," "the most giving," "the most understanding," no matter how satisfying such expressions may be. What is crucial is that we create room and permission for the expression of both positive and negative feelings.

Our view of transference can be developed further. Time doesn't permit us to go into the history of Lenny's situation, but we can look at an overview

of Mrs. Lieb's work. She rode through many months of his need to attack first. She accepted his anger, gave voice to his reasons for having it, acknowledged the legitimacy of it, at the same time that she stopped his biting and kicking with consistent firmness. She continued to see him at regular intervals until he knew firmly inside himself what she had said in words in their first meeting: "Your anger will not drive me away." Eventually he allowed her to feed him with food, attention, interest and some toys. She had taken on the role of the giving mother. Hard won, she turned this role into the giving mother who expected growth and was pleased by it. By this time Lenny treasured her pleasure in him, even though he had not yet developed pleasure in himself. When the time seemed right she began to relate to him less as the little boy who needed affection and encouragement and more as a developing masculine being.

What should be evident in this brief survey of a course of treatment is that there are phases; transference roles shift sometimes in response to the child's development and sometimes to stimulate changes in the child. I recall an early experience I had in working with a borderline girl. She fantasied herself to be a dog; blonde, pretty, petite, she crawled into my office weekly on hands and knees "arfing" away at me. In the months that followed I learned to communicate with her through some dog dolls and we unfolded the story of her disguise through our play. Months later in conference I was stunned when my consultant asked me when we were going to grow up. Perhaps truthful and a bit unkind, his point was that I had to lead the way in shifting our means of communication. I could not wait for her for she would be content to stay where she was. Years later I received a letter from her in which she wrote, "Remember when we used to talk dog talk?"

Shifts in the transference role are not only determined by stages in the child's treatment, but also by his developmental stages. To exemplify this, we can turn to Barbara who was a most thoughtful and self-aware client in her late latency years. I was clearly her mother. As she moved toward adolescence, however, the nature of our relationship changed and I had to change with it. The doors to self-contemplation closed and there was a frenzied entrance into concerns with men, dating, hair styles, et cetera. This was also a time when the doors were closed to mothers, real and transference. To stay in the picture I became a peer or, perhaps better, an older sister, listening, sharing, consulting and occasionally advising on hair-do, dress, manners, et cetera. Through this she was getting permission to know about and learn to be a woman but not from her mother but rather as so often happens in life, from the older girl, the counselor at camp, the girl on the corner who is a few years older.

Object for Identification

The final theme that I want to bring up as part of the experiential element of treatment with children has to do with the therapist's consciously lending himself as an object of identification. One must assume in such a discussion the child's developmental readiness to use the therapist for purposes of identification. Quite often we will observe that a female client fashions her hair style and dress after her worker. Or we can see a young man walking down a corridor with a gait unmistakably similar to his therapist's. These are the baby steps of identification, the early copying the mimicking that is a part of trying something on for size. The process can become more active and fruitful if we are aware of it and encourage it. I refer now to a period in which a child may begin to ask questions about his worker's life, points of view, behavior, et cetera.

Here I must call to our attention the fact that social workers receive a large portion of "do's" and "don'ts" in their training. "Don't talk about yourself; it is inappropriate," is a tenet that concerns me here, for it can interfere with the opportunities to lend oneself to the child as an object for identification. This does not mean that it is always appropriate for a worker to talk about himself. What it does mean is that there must be constant attention to the material with understanding of its meaning. At one phase, it may be clear that the child is simply trying to deflect the attention to the worker as part of a resistance. But the same concerns and questions at another point in treatment may be part of a deep and meaningful search to "be like you." Barbara, in the latter part of her treatment, was highly active in questioning her worker about the worker's schooling, the necessary preparation for becoming a social worker. It would not have been un-common to see a worker cut off these questions either by saying, "We are here to talk about you, not me," or "I wonder if this is your way of not talking about yourself." Instead she replied simply and directly and these answers followed Barbara's real concerns, her conflict about being feminine and knowledgeable at the same time. Part of her problem was that the two were incompatible.

I am prompted to say that I have become extremely distrustful of any of the "rules" that have been handed down through the years to caseworkers. It makes much greater sense to operate out of a constant quest to understand what the child is dealing with, the meaning of his behavior. Such under-standing leads to a flexibility in responding which is far more likely to be therapeutic.

Summary

I have chosen in this paper to divide treatment, albeit artificially, into two parts: procedures designed to bring about conscious self-awareness, and procedures designed to induce growth through the emotionally corrective experience in treatment. I have concentrated on the latter for several reasons: I have observed as a teacher and practitioner that the children seen by caseworkers are in deep need of a corrective experience. Caseworkers often overlook, or do not understand, the importance of the experiential part of treatment. Too often insight and the techniques that produce it have a glamour which overshadows providing a corrective experience where needed. I have observed in much of casework practice with children a laziness, where the search for the meaning of the client's behavior and the purposefulness of the worker's actions seem to be lacking. Too often the work is merely intuitive and spontaneous but not necessarily progressing.

In discussing some of the elements in the corrective experience I have tried to select the procedures which I see as most therapeutic for the kinds of children caseworkers see in the run of their practice. I have aired some of the misconceptions and misunderstandings that I observe in current practice and have tried to call our attention to the importance not only of knowledge of the child and his problems but also knowledge of the worker. I have noted that the corrective experience must not only offer warmth and acceptance but there must be a readiness to take actions which might be experienced by the child as painful. I have noted that treatment has phases, and that the phases are sometimes determined by the child's own development and growth, but that also the worker must be ready to move both himself and the child in order to stimulate growth. I have suggested that knowledge of the ingredients of normal growth and development is vital as it can serve as a model for the corrective experience.

In short, the therapeutic intervention into the life of a child (or a person of any age) is a serious matter and must be accompanied with a deep sense of responsibility and a wide and deep range of knowledge.

The Treatment of a Type of Chronically Rejected Child

Annette Jacobsohn

Families Requiring Long-Term Treatment

The interest in writing this paper arose in the course of a study in our agency concerning the nature of our long-term cases, i.e., cases that have been or are anticipated to be active for more than two years. The paper does not, however, intend to survey all of these cases but rather to focus on a particular type of long-term case, the treatment of which has been found to be alternatingly frustrating and rewarding.

The type of case I wish to discuss is the one where the child with whom the family and the agency are concerned suffers from chronic maternal rejection, a rejection which is actively aggressive and punitive.

In general, the element of maternal rejection is to a considerable extent accountable for the long-term nature of the treatment required. However, this element is often not discovered or fully taken into account, and, therefore, tends to bedevil the treatment process. This bedevilment takes two forms: apparent improvement takes place after a period of treatment, only to collapse again; secondly, when the contact is then resumed and continued with little further movement one begins to question the usefulness of continued treatment and grows anxious about what seems to be a waste of time.

It is, of course, true that in all cases treatment should be based on a thorough understanding of the intrapsychic and interpersonal dynamics. However, I think that the element of rejection is often overlooked because other factors are also observable, seemingly accessible to treatment and appear to be sufficient cause for the presenting problem. (The presenting problems may actually be of any variety—behavior disorders, neurotic traits, borderline functioning, and so on.)

A brief word about literature on the problem: We have of course become quite familiar with the concept of rejection in the guise of overprotection. Dr. David Levy's book on *Maternal Overprotection* published in 1943 and papers written by him and others dating back to about 1929,

Reprinted with permission of the author and the *Journal of Jewish Communal Service;* from Vol. 39 (Spring, 1963), pp. 293–299.

have defined and elucidated this concept. We have also a number of papers on the individual treatment of rejected children. At the same time we find frequent comments on the difficulty of treating rejected children because their mothers will sabotage treatment.

About the latter type, some comments should be made regarding the concept of rejection. The one word actually covers a rather intricate process and may in a sense be a misnomer except where applied to a situation where the mother has lost all interest in the child. We do use the term *rejection* when we mean the opposite of acceptance. When the mother feels "I can't stand this child; I'd like to get rid of him; he feels like a stranger," we call it rejection. The interesting point is, of course, that she never does what she wishes to do; the rejection never becomes a *fait accompli*. Psychically, the mother needs to have things just as they are, wishing to rid herself of the child and keeping him. From the point of view of the child's psyche this experience of being unloved yet kept also becomes of central importance.

There are a variety of needs in the mother which lead to the wish to reject the child. The particular mother type I am planning to deal with here is the one who unconsciously is using the child as a whipping boy for wrongs she feels have been perpetrated upon her. She might be called the punitive mother, and in the course of being punitive she may also become neglectful, let alone depriving.

I mean to discuss here the treatment only of those cases where a specific child is rejected and other siblings are essentially accepted although they may have various emotional difficulties too. I am excluding the mother who is borderline and whose general ego fragility requires a special kind of treatment approach.

Further, I am referring to rejection which began in early infancy, where we have a history of the mother never being able to feel that she could adequately meet her child's needs. However, in telling us about this the mother will typically speak of the child being "difficult from the start," not that she herself was having difficulties.

It is this very blaming of the child for the difficulties that makes the treatment task so complicated. Sophisticated mothers of our day may of course say that "it must be my fault," but essentially the mothers I have in mind genuinely feel that it is the child who is difficult and provokes their wrath. They will admit their reactive rejection of the child, but not the basic rejection. Their guilt also will be both conscious and unconscious—their conscious guilt brings them for treatment, makes them superficially co-operative often to the point of achieving superficial improvement. Unconsciously, however, their rejection of the child continues and both this and their ensuing unconscious guilt prevents their being related to the child's needs. The child, on his part, is of course truly deprived and truly afraid. In addition, however, his behavior becomes geared toward maintaining himself by being especially controlling and toward revenging himself on the rejecting mother. The fact that he is constantly confronted with his mother's greater acceptance of his siblings adds to the fire. The vicious cycle is thus firmly established.

When we try to understand the punitive mother's need to reject the child we find that this is in response to a sense of herself having been deserted, deep down by her own mother, although consciously she may speak of desertion by mother substitutes which may include sisters, mothers-in-law, even husbands. The resulting rage is expressed toward the child because its actual source cannot be faced. What is referred to here is, of course, the re-awakening of old unresolved dependency problems, not the transitory sense of heightened dependency experienced appropriately by the pregnant woman, or the mother of a newborn infant. If she is left in the lurch during this period for reality reasons she may develop intrapsychic problems, but these are more accessible to consciousness and more easily resolved; she is better able to "forgive and forget" and allow herself the joys of motherhood.

Interestingly enough we find that where rejection of a child takes place there are usually not the overt troubles with families of origin that we find in other situations. It is as if the dependence-independence struggle, the struggle over control and submission, had been suppressed only to re-emerge between mother and child with redoubled force. We find further that there are often no overt marital difficulties but more often that the parents superficially form an alliance against the rejected child. Thus, in a sense treatment of these cases can mean that in order to help the child a lot more people have to become upset than were so originally. The difficulty is, however, that we are often dealing with people whose overall adjustment and functioning in other areas are only "fair" and their ego strengths are not such that one can sanguinely trust that they will survive satisfactorily a challenging of their present adjustment.

Mother's Treatment Needs

In considering treatment approaches in these cases I think we must be really prepared to meet the clients where they are—the reasons why they come and what they expect from us runs mostly counter to why we see them and what we expect to do for them. There is usually a request for the child to be "corrected, straightened out, made to realize . . . ," the mother, herself seeks "guidance and advice . . ." which, if given she subverts and if withheld she will seek elsewhere. All attempts at confrontation or even at being related to her feelings will be strongly resisted with denial, cancellations, excuses, etc. It is therefore quite difficult to establish a "therapeutic alliance." I think that actually the first year needs to be devoted to establishing a relationship of some sort which permits a therapeutic focus to be found. The mother will often continue contact purely in order to assuage her guilt and rather than fight with this, we are best advised to use this time to assess her personality and her needs from stray remarks, behavior, and all available forces, and from a diagnosis more or less "in spite of her," as her direct statements will usually all be geared to how impossible the child is and everything else will be denied. I have found in a particular case that I have been treating, that this groundwork was laid while mother and child had separate workers and that during this time they each felt cared for. The case was then assigned to me for work with both mother and child and interestingly enough I felt that both now benefitted from my knowing the other and my being able to appreciate what they were talking about when they complained. I have also found, with some surprise that my interest in her child and my observations have cheered the mother. It is as if this had given her some hope of yet climbing out of the abyss of guilt and despair. We must remember that the need actually to bring the child for treatment is a shock to the mother because it means that the dangerous game she has been playing has actually had bad results.

It is only when the child has made some progress and the presenting problem is somewhat ameliorated;. when the mother herself has felt fed by our interest in the problem she brings—I am putting it this way rather than our interest in her because she cannot usually stand too direct a relatedness to her feelings—that we can begin to ask the question "Suppose your problem with your child were quite resolved, how would you feel?" The particular mother I have in mind replied jokingly "Oh, I guess I'd have to find someone else to beat up." Never had she admitted directly that she beats the child out of her own need. Then she added with seriousness "I do so wish, though, that I would not do it to a living thing." It was relatively soon after this that she casually began to ask for help with her being generally so aggressive with all her children and for the first time we began to talk directly about her feelings. However I carefully avoid questioning her behavior with her children but I rather use opportunities to express concern about how hard she is on herself. I similarly avoid reference to any negative feelings she might have towards her own mother but note silently that there are more frequent references to the spirit in which her mother raised her.

As this type of mother is in a treatment situation only because of her child and is easily frightened off by anything that suggests her own need for treatment, I use opportunities to comment on her feelings towards her child which are so painful to her. Surprisingly enough when I ask her "What do you think your child really needs?" she replies "If he were treated with kindness and patience he would prosper." What now becomes revealed is that essentially it is masochism that prevents her from allowing herself to be a good mother. She, the punitive mother, is essentially self-punishing. She deprives herself of the enjoyment of meeting her child's needs, she burdens herself with guilt. She punishes herself for her resentment of her own mother.

If at this point we bring her mother in by asking "What would be your mother's attitude on this or that question?" we begin to get a feeling response: "Oh my mother . . . with her there was no such thing as 'I don't want to,' " and so on.

Treatment Needs of the Child

Children who suffer from maternal rejection, I often think, are comparable to children who have been severely physically malnourished or undernourished. Their presenting problems are not necessarily directly attributable to maternal mistreatment or deprivation. However, just as in the case of physical illness the patient will recover more or less successfully in accordance with the relative strength and sturdiness of his body, so the child with a specific psychological disorder will respond more or less successfully in accordance with the relative sturdiness of his ego.

The child who is subjected to maternal rejection, as well as suffering from specific problems in functioning or adjustment, needs to be fed as well as helped to correct his ideas. As in the case of physical undernourishment this process is complicated. The digestive system having adjusted itself to a starvation diet can only absorb small quantities of nourishment and if tempted to take in too much will respond with upset. In psychological terms this is equivalent to the psychic system being threatened by the offer of too much love. In fantasy the affection starved child will long for the good mother, similarly as the person suffering from hunger will dream of the banquet. The disturbed child will have fantasies of being adopted by the worker, fantasies which will occur in response to anyone who is related to the child in an interested, unambivalent manner as long as the child is still capable of affect hunger. These fantasies are accompanied by guilt towards the parents in defense against their jealous retribution. Awareness of this on the part of the worker is of the greatest importance. The child must be given to in order to be strengthened and yet care must be taken that not more tension is created than is bearable. Around this issue runs the debate pro and con over actual physical feeding and giving. Essentially one wants to create an atmosphere and offer a relationship that is conducive to growth and the correction of misconceptions. This, in itself, is the true gift to the child (or any client or patient). Essentially whatever therapist and child client do together must be justifiable in these terms, the relationship must remain a distinct and special one, not play into the fantasies of the child but be conducive to their revelation. This is, of course, in a sense a professional platitude and true of all therapeutic relationships. I am, however, stressing it here because the emotionally rejected child presents a special appeal to the sympathetic adult. As mentioned initially several papers have been written describing in detail the treatment of individual children suffering from rejection and it is not my plan to do this here but rather to point out how some of the difficulties can be coped with. For the sake of accuracy, however, I want to qualify the above by saying that in actuality the rejected child, of course, often presents himself in a manipulative, controlling and often suspicious and highly guarded manner distrusting the very offer of a good relationship.

Theoretically the child could be helped by being transferred to a different, loving environment. In reality we still think that the trauma is too great and recommend placement only in those cases where the active pathogenic factors in the home environment outweigh the trauma of forced separation. The cases which we are discussing here are those where there is enough parental interest in the child that can be positively mobilized.

Why does the treatment of these children take so long? As described above, the child has to take in the therapeutic experience little by little if he is not to get into unbearable conflict with himself and his environment. The contact may therefore continue over several years with the frequency of interviews adjusted to current needs. On the whole, interviews held once a week are more advisable than more intensive contact, in order to avoid over-stimulation.

What the therapist provides apart from a different emotional experience is a means of strengthening the child's evaluation of reality. In a sense the development of seemingly unhealthy defenses were necessary for the child. Protected by guardedness, suspiciousness, manipulativeness, control, he can lead his own life, restricted, deprived but with relative equanimity. Therapy is an interference with these defenses, a demand is made on the child to exercise his critical faculties and keep alive his desires to gain gratification from his environment. This, however, must be done with such caution as to prevent depression or inappropriate acting-out.

Another reason for the long term treatment needs of these children is the fact that the more the child is biologically dependent on the parent the more will he be oriented towards the parent. He can, therefore, only tackle certain problems in his relationship with them as he gains relative independence. From this one might plan to provide contact according to the needs of the developmental period: periods where work with parents is more intensive than with the child and periods where one would encourage the provision of other resources (group work centers, camps, big sisters or brothers) in order to provide special nurture. Then there can be times when only the child is seen weekly and contact with the parents is less frequent.

Treatment Approach with Fathers

In discussing the treatment needs of the fathers of maternally rejected children, I am limiting myself to highlighting what I think are some of the characteristics of their position. We distinguish them here from those fathers who themselves reject their child in primary fashion because the child is experienced as a rival for the fulfillment of their own dependency needs. As in the case of the mothers, I am excluding here too, borderline individuals who need a special treatment approach.

In the cases under discussion our assessment of the family as a whole suggests that the essential treatment considerations need to be given to mother and child. However, we find that the father often has potentially many positives to offer and in involving him it is our intent to help him find areas where he can use himself constructively in furthering the growth of the child without threatening the mother.

Initially, however, he is likely to be in a state of anger, guilt and helplessness. No rational behavior on his part appears to be of any use vis-à-vis the unconsciously determined attitude of his wife. Of course being himself subject to unconscious needs, he will identify with either the aggressor or the victim or punish them both by withdrawing emotionally.

As mentioned initially, we frequently find such a father in superficial alliance with his wife. Having often been somewhat removed from the situation during the child's infancy, having relied either on his wife's apparent "strength" in managing or on the help she received from others, he does not become involved in the problem between mother and child until it has clearly developed to the point where the child has become "the problem" and he feels called upon to exercise his authority to enforce respect for the mother.

As also mentioned above, marital problems are frequently denied in these cases, although their existence is evident from indirect remarks. Just as the child is not enjoyed and is experienced as a burden, so the marriage is not enjoyed actively, there are trivial complaints and the absence of open friction is mistaken for happiness. I think that frequently the husband and wife have met with some defeats in the course of their marriage which have re-aroused old feelings of inadequacy. They feel guilty and in the ensuing mild depression they withdraw from each other and retreat to a somewhat more immature level than they are potentially capable of.

We frequently find that when we first suggest to such a father that he become involved in the treatment process he is quite unproductive. He comes because his wife wants him to, feels that it would be sufficient to work with her as she and he are in agreement one with the other, or that the problem lies between mother and child and he has nothing to do with it. He often disengages himself after a brief contact in the beginning but his interest in what is happening can become aroused at a later point.

When we discover at a later stage that these fathers are capable of making a contribution to the resolution of the problem, we frequently chide ourselves for not succeeding in involving them earlier. However, I think, it may well be true that mother and child have first had to feel the need for treatment and have derived some benefit from it before the father is willing to contribute.

The father will of course have his own personality problems which we would want to understand; however, as long as we are clear that the problem is chiefly between mother and child we may have to let father be out of it until he himself is ready to come. In the particular case I have in mind, the father has been reinvolved through monthly joint interviews with his wife (in the meantime he has regularly brought his daughter for her interviews). I involve him in this way when his wife reported some casually expressed interest by him in the child's treatment and at the same time some wish for his wife to withdraw from treatment herself as she became more acutely upset with herself.

The Integration Process

I should now like to discuss briefly the possibilities of helping the parents and the child to accept each other. This, I think, essentially depends on the degree of movement that the mother can make and in the case I have alluded to above I think this might be possible. As with the mother, with the child, too, we find considerable masochism. She is enjoying the relationship with the worker, has gotten a good deal of negative feelings towards her mother off her chest, but she refuses to talk in response to direct questions, she maintains that "you cannot make me talk" and that she will keep her "secrets." This opportunity for opposition to the worker is welcome as she can live it out safely. Gradually of course the secret begins to emerge—it is her power of being able to make her mother punish her by being very bad and then making her forgive her by being very good. Why should she give up these powerful secret weapons unless she can really be sure that her mother would love her voluntarily? Both mother and daughter can now be shown how they interact and they begin to have a sense of choice about it. The father has been helped to find a place for himself which is neither "away from it all" nor "right in the middle" so that now he is available to do some rescue work when mother and child have gotten themselves into an impasse, and at this point of treatment they will permit him to do this. I think with this we should be able to envisage the maintenance of improvement. Depending then on the age of the child and his growing strength to face up to his own problems some further more individually geared and insightful therapy might be considered.

A Therapeutic Approach to Reactive Ego Disturbances in Children in Placement

Selma Fraiberg

Among the gravest consequences of placement is the child's inability to form new object relationships following loss. A very large number of children in institutions and foster home care are permanently damaged and may never recover the capacity for making meaningful human ties. Frequently the casework treatment of such children is blocked by the characteristic defenses against affect which these children display and by their inability to make an attachment to the caseworker—the indispensable condition for treatment.

This paper describes and illustrates a casework approach that was developed in the course of working with a small group of latency-age boys in institutional placement. The treatment employed a specialized adaptation of an analytic technique that should be entirely within the competence of a caseworker and within the defined limits of casework treatment. It consisted mainly of working through the defenses against affects and of reviving the affects around the initial trauma of placement. Concurrent group treatment was employed for continuing diagnosis, to test the movement in object relationships, and to provide a milieu in which readiness for new ties might be gratified.

This work was part of a program jointly sponsored by the Tulane School of Social Work, the Children's Bureau of New Orleans, and the Protestant Children's Home. In this report I shall confine myself to the casework treatment and illustrate with selected cases.[1] I wish to mention, however, that our experience in the use of concurrent group treatment demonstrated not only the value of the group as an adjunct to casework treatment but opened up the possibility in our minds that for selected cases, group treatment might operate independently to bring about favorable therapeutic results.

The setting in which this work was carried out is in many ways typical of institutions that provide care for the dependent and neglected child in our country. The Protestant Children's Home was built nearly 100 years ago as an orphanage. There is a high iron fence surrounding the grounds and the children are still housed in dormitories according to age groups. The house-parents are mainly middle-aged men and women with limited education

Reprinted from the *American Journal of Orthopsychiatry*, Vol. 32 (January, 1962), pp. 18–31. Copyright, the American Orthopsychiatric Association, Inc. Reproduced by permission of the author and the Association.

[1] All cases reported here were seen in casework treatment on a once-a-week basis.

and, of course, they have no special educational preparation for work with children. Many of the children are severely disturbed and have been placed in the institution because of earlier failures in foster homes. There are no clinically trained staff members. At the time of our study casework services were provided for the children and their families by the Children's Bureau and other agencies in the community.

We chose the Junior Boys Division for our study. The ten boys in this group ranged in age from eight to eleven. The housemother, Mrs. Lindstrom, was a woman in her middle sixties, who somehow managed the difficult job of caring for a group of gravely disturbed children who would have taxed the best gifts of a clinically trained worker. She was strict in her discipline, and some of her demands for good behavior were undoubtedly excessive. But she also had sympathy and affection for her children, and as we worked together she learned to become more lenient and more tolerant in certain important areas.

II

I will begin this report with a description of the treatment of George. George was 11 years old when we began treatment. He was the oldest of five children, all of whom had been placed by the parents two years earlier. At the time of placement the parents were considering divorce. The mother planned to return to work, and the children had become such an emotional and financial burden to her that she appeared dangerously close to a severe depression. The plan was for temporary placement, but as two years passed by it became clear that the mother might never bring herself to reunite her family. The father had disappeared after the divorce.

In preplacement interviews the mother described George as the chief problem among her children. He was described as very stubborn and aggressive and subject to stormy outbursts of temper. In the early months of placement at the institution George presented the full battery of his behavior problems. Both the institution and the school reported belligerence and bullying of other children, much fighting, and provocative behavior. But gradually, the record shows, George gave up his fighting and his bullying and became a rather passive and tractable child. The complaints now were of another order. He had become whiny and fearful of bigger boys in the institution. He brought constant complaints of being beaten up by the bigger boys and of having his toys destroyed by them. About the second complaint the boys in his group seemed genuinely baffled and claimed that George himself had been seen destroying toys that his mother had sent him and would then accuse other children of having broken them.

Along with this shift from active to passive came two new developments. George had begun to gain weight rapidly, and at the end of the first year in placement he had gained 30 pounds. During the second year he continued to eat voraciously and to gain weight. He was about 40 pounds overweight when I first met him. He had wet the bed occasionally prior to placement. By the time internalization of his conflicts had been completed, at the end of the first year, George had become a constant bed-wetter. Often he wet two and three times a night.

When I first saw George he was an obese, sluggish youngster with a round pink face. He never smiled. His nails were bitten to the quick. His speech was mushy, indistinct—devoid of affect.

In the early interviews with George I was impressed by certain characteristics of his relationship with me. He was affable, superficially friendly, garrulous, and yet he was completely uninterested in the new caseworker. One had the impression that caseworkers were interchangeable, that one would do as well as another. He was sorry that he had to give up his previous worker. He had even expressed some regret to her when he learned of the transfer, but none of this feeling could be recovered when I invited him to talk about his feelings about the transfer. I began to understand that his relationship to me, to previous workers, and to members of the institutional staff derived from his feeling of helplessness. We were protectors against the danger of hunger, abandonment, and a variety of physical dangers. And because these relationships were important only for providing need satisfaction and protection, any one member of the staff could substitute for another. During the first months of treatment he almost never mentioned his housemother, Mrs. Lindstrom, unless I initiated discussion through questions. This, I learned, was not to be taken as a deficiency in the capacities of the housemother; it was a result of George's absence of interest in or involvement with the adults who cared for him. During the same period he never showed any interest in me or curiosity about me.

Like most children in placement George clung to a fantasy about his parents and the reasons for his placement. His mother, in the fantasy, wanted all of her children at home but she didn't have enough money to keep them. When she saved enough money she would bring the children back home. There was no criticism of his mother and there were no reproaches. On many occasions the mother neglected to visit the children when she had promised. George, if he discussed these occasions at all, reported them factually and without affect.

Our earliest work, then, began to deal with the defenses against affects. I used every good opportunity to give George permission to feel and to show him omissions of justifiable feelings of anger or disappointment and displacements of affect. Very early in treatment we began to understand why the defenses against aggression were so strong. On one occasion when George got into a fight with one of the boys in his school (and it was indeed nothing more than a mild fight in which they pushed each other around), George spent the better part of his hour alternating between restrained fury at his enemy and fear that he would be sent away to a correctional institution for delinquent boys.

There were two components in this exaggerated fear of consequences for aggression. One, of course, was the expectation that any aggression, no matter how mild, would result in his being sent away. The other clearly was that the exaggerated punishment was equal to the strength of the undischarged aggression; he was afraid of the destructive power of his rage. Through a number of examples of such exaggerated fear of punishment I began to help George see that he was really afraid of his own feelings, that the anger inside was so strong at times that he feared that if it came out he might really hurt someone. I helped him to understand that the more he talked about his feelings in the interview the less need he would have to fear these feelings.

Gradually we began to understand various forms of displacement of anger. George's fear of attack by other boys, his constant complaints of being picked on, began to diminish when he understood how these fears were to a certain measure tied up with his fear of his own anger. Sometimes I could draw his attention to his savage nail-biting as he talked about anger, and he was impressed to see how feelings could be connected with such a symptom. We went further and began to establish some links between bed-wetting and the feelings of anger and fear that he kept inside him.

Yet he was only able to experience anger and resentment toward other children. He could in no way acknowledge feelings of anger toward the adults in the institution, toward teachers, or toward me. Once when I felt he was struggling with hostile feelings toward me I asked him what he thought would happen if he should feel angry toward me and tell me. And he said, without a moment's hesitation, "Why you would go away!" He said this with such conviction that I could tell him now that I thought that this fear was connected with a real happening in his life, that this must have been the way he felt when mother placed him in the home. I said that all children are afraid that if they are naughty or have any angry thoughts mother or daddy might go away and leave them, and I said that when children are placed away from home they can't help but feel deep inside that maybe it was because of something they had done or because they had been naughty.

From this point on in the interview George seemed to be struggling with all kinds of feelings. Several times he was in tears or close to tears. I encouraged him to talk more about mother and father and his feelings about placement. When he began attacking his nails again I tried to get him to tell me what he was feeling. Was it possible, I asked, that even when a child loved his parents he might feel some anger toward them, too, for disappointing him? With this George turned away so that I might not see his tears, and in a voice full of fury he said, "Sometimes I think I'm gonna be in this place for four more years and that I'm never going to go back to my own home."

As more and more feeling welled up within him he began to talk for the first time about the beginning period of placement. He remembered when his mother first told the children they were going to a Home. He didn't know what it would be like and he even thought it would be fun to live in a place with many other kids and have swings and slides. "And then I remember the first night and everything was so strange and I woke up in the middle of the night and it was dark and I didn't know where I was and my bed was all wet. . . . And then the next day when I woke up I looked out of the window and I saw all the bars around the place and the gates were locked." (The "bars" were the high iron fences around the 100-year-old institution.) I said, "I think it must have made you feel as if you were in jail. It must have made you feel that being here was like a punishment." He nodded in silence.

In this session we established the first connections between George's fear of his aggressive impulses and his feeling that placement was a punishment for being bad. This hour initiated many new developments. George, who had been the scapegoat of his group and who exhausted the adults of the Home with his whining and constant complaints of persecution, now began to fight back. George was as astonished as his former tormentors were. There was tremendous relief in him when he found that he could fight back and hold his own even with the older and more powerful boys. For a while it was difficult to keep the fighting under control. I got him to exercise some judgment in the fighting and to get a good measure of his rage and hostility back into the therapeutic hours where it might do some good. At the same time I was in close communication with George's housemother and with the director of the institution. Their understanding of the meaning of this behavior enabled them to handle a number of difficult situations with a firm and non-punitive approach. After a few weeks the aggressive behavior subsided to something close to normal for a boy of this age. Now we saw that George was no longer afraid of his own aggression or afraid of monstrous punishments for having aggressive feelings.

From this we could understand that one of the decisive factors in the transformation of aggression had been the experience of separation. To be aggressive was to invite abandonment, and when our work established the connection between these two factors and the separation experience George could experience anger once again. With even this much work there was some symptomatic relief. George's nails, which had been bitten to the quick, were now beginning to grow. The bed-wetting improved temporarily. Also there was now considerable improvement in schoolwork, with George boasting that he was getting a better report card than he had ever had in his life.

Yet the whole area of his ambivalence toward his parents remained barely touched at this point. Now, however, there was a new theme in George's communications. He worried about people dying. He worried about his father. He didn't know where he was. He could be dead for all anyone knew. He missed his Dad. Sometimes he worried that his mother might die. From his fantasies it was very clear to me that his fears were closely connected with destructive wishes toward his parents. I now understood, too, another reason why it was so difficult for George to express even mild hostility toward his parents. For the child who is separated from his own parents the hostile and destructive wishes are necessarily more dangerous than for the child who still has his parents. For all children the physical presence of the parents is a reassurance against the danger that the loved persons may be harmed or destroyed by the child's own bad wishes. In the absence of his parents George could not tolerate his own dangerous fantasies, for he could not have reassurance against the omnipotence of his thoughts.

"Is it really true," George wanted to know, "that you could put a curse on someone and make them die?" He didn't think so but he had seen a story on television once. In one session he brought forth a number of such stories having to do with fictional events in which evil wishes brought about the illness or death of "someone." When I began to relate these fears to his own fears that bad wishes might harm someone he quickly denied that he ever had such thoughts. Then, very tentatively, he began to explore this dangerous territory with me through offering stories about a fictional boy who did have such thoughts. In the course of this hour we talked about his fears that bad wishes could come true and I again linked these fears with the experience of placement and the feelings that angry thoughts could cause someone to go away. At the end of this session George, for the first time since I had met him, looked relaxed and happy.

In the play-group meeting the following week George did something unprecedented. He got angry toward his group leader for allowing someone to use his materials and he announced that he was quitting the group. But when he told me about this experience in his next session he assured me that he didn't really intend to quit the club. He liked his group leader a lot; he just got good and mad at her that day. Sally, he reported marveling, had not been mad at him; she was "real nice about it." He seemed tremendously uplifted by this experience. It was one of the first occasions offered us in which George could allow himself to show hostility toward an adult whom he liked and to do so without fear that he would lose the love of that person.

During the same week George's housemother reported a most interesting set of observations. For several days George had been playing baby, in a clowning act in the dormitory. The big 150-pound baby crawled from one end of the room to the other, under beds and under furniture, emerging to be petted like an infant by Mrs. Lindstrom, who went along with the game with some amusement. At the same time Mrs. Lindstrom reported that George had become very affectionate toward her, telling her how swell she was and how he loved her. He even made a written declaration of love in the form of a mock certificate of honor with her name on it.

These events marked another turning point in George's treatment. Now we began to see the beginnings of a strong positive attachment to Mrs. Lindstrom and qualitatively richer relationships with both the director of the institution and his play-group leader. And at just this point we were suddenly confronted with some new behavior that baffled all of us. With all the gains on the side of relationships with adults and with all the new satisfactions that he seemed to be receiving, George was now involved in conflict in another sphere. Both the group leader and the housemother reported that George was in constant battle with Jimmy, one of the scapegoats in his group. George had appointed himself chief tormentor of Jimmy and constantly provoked fights with him. From various pieces of material in treatment I was certain that George's hatred of Jimmy was based upon an identification with him but I could not clearly establish the basis of this identification.

Then in one interview when George had spent most of his hour reciting a litany of hate against Jimmy I asked him what he thought was the trouble with Jimmy, what made Jimmy behave this way. "I'll tell you!" George said promptly. "He's full of hate. That's what his trouble is. Just full of hate. That's why he steals, too. Just full of hate." I replied, "Well, you may be right. But why do you think he is full of hate?" The answer was, "I don't know and I don't care." I said, "I think he is full of hate because he feels that nobody loves him." And then to my surprise George said, "Then I guess me and him is in the same boat, 'cause I ain't got nobody to love me either." He began to cry. "I'm just as bad off as he is. I ain't got no Daddy and my Mama, I don't think she's ever gonna take us home and I think the only way I'm gonna get out of this place is when I'm big enough to work."

Now I asked if this made George wonder if his mother loved him, too? He nodded, choked up. I asked if this made George "full of hate" at times, too, because he could not understand why his mother had done this? He hesitated, then said painfully, "Sometimes." Now for the first time George could express his bitterness toward his mother and his longing for her. In this interview he talked about how fat he had grown; he remembered that he had not been overweight before coming to the Home. I helped him see how miserable and lonely he must have been and how eating was a way of easing the hurt then and now.

From this point on in treatment George's ambivalence toward mother became accessible to us with the full strength of the powerful feelings involved. He no longer consoled himself with the fantasy that his mother was going to take the children back, and he made the heartbreaking observation that mother herself no longer talked about making a home for the children again.

On one occasion when two of the boys in his group were preparing to return home, several of the other boys circulated stories that they, too, were going home—stories that were really painful fictions. George was overwhelmed with jealousy and spent hours in bitter tirades against his mother. During this time he became involved in open conflict with his mother and there was one episode in which the strong feelings of George and his mother initiated a Sunday afternoon drama. The mother had taken the children home for a Sunday visit. George was apparently short-tempered and volatile for most of the day, quarreling with his mother and each of his siblings in turn. At one point when George and his brother Martin were bickering, the mother lost her temper and sent both children out of the house and locked the door. The two boys pounded on the door and screamed to come in but the mother would not open the door. George was in a fury as he told me this story.

When we sorted out all the complicated feelings in this episode I was able to show George two aspects of his reactions. On the one hand were the real and justifiable reactions to being locked out of the house. In another way, I suggested, the whole episode hurt him so deeply because it made him feel that mother didn't want him in her home, that she was "sending him away" and that being closed out of his house was just exactly the way he felt living away from home. With this George's rage began to subside and he began to struggle with tears.

As we worked through the ambivalent feelings toward mother during these months George showed considerable growth in all areas of his life. That summer after the first eight months of treatment we all observed that George had actually become a happy child. His relationships to his housemother and the director of the home were warm and spontaneous and he could even afford now to express negative feelings toward them at times. At one period during the summer, when George's mother began to speak about the possibility of bringing her children back home, George's reactions were very interesting. He was genuinely happy at the prospect but, he told me soberly, he would miss Mrs. Lindstrom and the director very much. He said that if he went back to his mother he would ask the director if he could come back to the Home to visit "maybe three times a week." However, his mother changed her mind again, and even this George was able to manage, with understandably strong feelings but without regression.

In summarizing the casework achievements in the fall after ten months, we saw that George had demonstrated his capacity to make new love attachments and that his relationship to his own mother had grown freer. There was less overt conflict with mother now, and with increased satisfactions in other areas of his life he seemed able to accept the pain of separation and mother's own limitations. He was able to handle his relationships with other boys within the institution with confidence and without undue aggressiveness. But he could fight when he needed to. There was now real pleasure in school and in learning—an unexpected and welcome bonus for treatment. Arithmetic was still a rough spot, mainly because of academic deficiencies brought about by three years of daydreaming in class, but George was energetically applying himself to mastery of tables and other fundamentals neglected since the third grade and his teachers reported favorably on his progress. There was some modification of the symptom picture that came about very clearly through the therapeutic work on the defenses against affects. Nailbiting, for example, disappeared completely. The voracious eating was curbed. There were no further weight gains and even some slight weight reduction. (I made no effort to deal with eating as a symptom except to occasionally connect eating with longing and aggression.)

But the enuresis remained. Clearly the casework treatment that had centered on affects and their transformations would not bring about symptomatic relief in this area. I knew that the enuresis was intimately connected with fears concerning masturbation and sex play, and until this material could be worked through there was no possibility of cure. In the second year of treatment it was necessary to modify the therapeutic approach in order to deal successfully with the sexual conflicts associated with the enuresis. This part of the treatment does not concern us here, of course, since we are primarily concerned with the method employed in the first year for bringing about the restoration of object ties.

In summary, those conflict areas and transformations of affect that were clearly reactive to the separation from parents were accessible to the casework treatment approach I have described, and the morbid process proved to be reversible.

It was undoubtedly an advantage to the therapy that George was already in latency at the time that separation from his parents took place. And yet we were most interested to see that in another of our cases, ten-year-old Brian, who was placed in the institution at the age of four, we had a therapeutic achievement that surpassed our expectations. I shall only briefly mention this case for illustrative purposes. . . .

Brian, when I first saw him, was one of the most severely depressed children I had ever seen. He was completely passive and withdrawn, a sad little gnome who sat on his bed looking into space, and who had no connections to any other human being. No one within the institution could say at this point that he had a relationship to Brian. I realized from reading his record that periods of severe depression had recurred throughout his stay at the institution dating from age four. There were other periods when he seemed less depressed, but characteristically he was withdrawn, and the picture of a grave, unsmiling, silent little boy remained little changed during the six years of placement. Brian's mother was described as mentally ill (diagnosis not available) and four of the six children were placed after mother demonstrated her inability to give even physical care to the children. Brian, the youngest, was mother's favorite. Throughout placement she has maintained contact with him through visits. The ties to father and his common-law wife were also maintained on an irregular basis.

My private estimate of the possibilities of reaching Brian through casework treatment was a pessimistic one. Brian had no conscious memory of a time before placement and the remaining ties to the parents were very thin. His capacity for object ties could not be judged. Ego functioning had broken down in vital areas. He had failed his last grade in school in spite of good intelligence.

Almost as soon as the caseworker began to touch upon "feelings" with Brian she found herself the object of transference reactions that were so dense and complex that at first we had great difficulty in understanding the events of treatment. At the beginning there was no evidence of a strong positive transference in the treatment sessions and yet the passive and lethargic little boy began to come alive and began to communicate with adults and other children at the Home. There was no question that the tie to the caseworker had meaning and value to him, yet many hours were spent in almost complete silence. Previous caseworkers had also reported such silent hours with Brian.

As the caseworker repeatedly encouraged expressions of feeling, and gave permission to feel, Brian became visibly afraid. And when feeling first emerged in these sessions it came through in the form of terrible inarticulate grief and rage. He would kick savagely at the chair while he sat mute and helpless. He would cry hopelessly and inarticulately. It was as if the grief and rage were so elemental that there were no words that could express them. As more and more affect emerged the caseworker found herself in the center of a strange, wordless drama, the object of passionate hate and longing yet walled off from understanding by the child's silence.

There were no words, we thought, because there were no conscious memories to which these feelings could attach themselves.

But as the pressure of these painful affects grew stronger we began to see elements of the past revived in the present. During a period when the caseworker saw many reactions in Brian that showed that he was jealous of other boys who came to see her, Brian characteristically closed her out. Then on one occasion at the close of the interview Brian refused to leave and finally buried his head in his arms and burst into tears. He could not speak of his grief, but the next hour he entered in a hostile mood and for the first time put his rage into words. He didn't want to see the caseworker, he said. He wished she weren't his caseworker. He wanted to be left alone. Then, in a passionate outburst he accused the caseworker of liking other boys who were her clients better than she liked him, and he burst into tears. When the caseworker attempted to talk with him he ran out of the room. In the next sessions he renewed his fury with the caseworker, and finally in one climactic hour he screamed, "I hate you! I hate you!" and then, sobbing, said, "Go see Roger. Go see Jimmy. Not me." At one point he jumped on a chair to reach a storage cupboard and pleaded with the caseworker to give him everything that he saw, crayons, glue, and color books. Finally he desperately demanded that she give him a model airplane that belonged to another child. When the caseworker explained that these things must remain in the office he began to cry and shouted, "You won't give me *anything!*" He ran out of the room sobbing.

Only after Brian could express grief and rage and longing in transference to the caseworker was he able to express his positive feelings for her and enter into a relationship that showed affection and trust. It is important to note that during this whole stormy period in transference, there was very little affect outside of treatment; all these strong feelings centered on the caseworker. In every other area—in the institution, in the play group, and in school—all of our reports showed Brian reaching out to people and finding pleasure in play and in schoolwork. He had become spontaneously affectionate toward his housemother; he had a strong attachment to his play-group leader, and as we followed his development in the play group we discovered skills and qualities of leadership that surprised all of us. Group treatment made a substantial contribution to the therapy by providing opportunities for growth and a favorable milieu for Brian's growing capacity for object relationships. It is also important to note that Brian, who had been failing in school the year before treatment, completed this academic year with an excellent report card.

In Brian's case, then, the affects associated with loss of the love object in the preoedipal phase were revived in transference, and the casework treatment permitted a reliving in the transference of grief and rage, with recovery of the capacity for object ties and excellent gains in ego functioning.

The therapeutic results in Brian's case surpassed our expectations. From an analytic point of view there is much in this case that I wish we understood better. The specific connections between events in transference and events in the past could not be established through a casework treatment; these could only be known through employing an analytic method. And we do not understand how a depression of such severity should have responded so favorably to a casework treatment. We cannot be certain, of course, that in a child with such severe depressive tendencies the tendency will not reassert itself. But this recovery through casework treatment is still a substantial gain, and the child in latency who can make attachments once again and who can feel again may be less vulnerable in adolescence and later life.

III

In such cases as these, a child who has once experienced ties to the original object—however ambivalent these may have been—can recover the possibility of making new attachments through a therapy directed toward reviving affects and working through the experience of loss. As we should expect, the method will not have any usefulness in those cases where a child's inability to attach himself derives from failure to establish meaningful human ties in the earlier stages of ego development. In one of our cases, for example, our earliest superficial observations led us to expect a favorable outcome in treatment. Pete seemed less damaged than any other child in our group. While his relationships were qualitatively poor there were no signs of serious withdrawal and no symptoms. But as we worked with Pete in casework and in the group we discovered that we had erred gravely in our original assessment. After eight months we found that none of us felt he really knew this child. Pete was charming, ingratiating, and somehow unconnected with any other person in his environment. We began to see that here there was real impoverishment in the ego, a deficiency and an incapacity in forming human ties that was not reactive to object loss but that derived from failures in human connections in the earliest phases of personality development.

In those cases where the child's inability to form new object ties is a reaction to loss with consequent transformations of affects we have, I believe, a generally favorable condition for recovery through therapy. One of the strongest therapeutic assets we have in working with such children in placement is the readiness to form a transference neurosis. As Anna Freud pointed out many years ago in her remarks on transference in child analysis, when a child is separated from his original love objects and moved to a new environment he may be expected to transfer to the new environment libidinal and aggressive impulses that originated in the relationships to the original objects. The condition of placement, of separation from the original objects, makes possible the development of a true transference neurosis.

If we observe closely during the early weeks and months of placement we can often find a variety of behaviors directed toward foster parents, cottage mothers, and caseworkers that are clearly repetitions of earlier experiences with the original objects. In a treatment home or institution with clinically trained personnel we can actually make use of these transference reactions in therapy and help the child achieve insight into his behavior. Or it may happen that reliving the past in the present with the corrective afforded by a benevolent institution and its personnel may, in itself, bring about the resolution of old conflicts. The transference neurosis and its handling should provide the key to the therapeutic effects of milieu therapy.

Now in the institution in which our work was carried out and most other institutions that provide custodial care for neglected and dependent children we have no clinical facilities and the houseparents ordinarily have little training to equip them to understand the complexities of child behavior following placement. The child's grief or withdrawal in the initial stages of placement is experienced by the cottage parents as a reproach or a criticism, as if they had failed to make the child happy. Mourning, then, is seen as something that must be gotten over quickly, and the cottage parent may exert himself in making the child happy and making him forget.

After an initial period of emotional neutrality toward the substitute parents we can usually expect some transference reactions to manifest themselves; old conflicts are revived in the new setting. Many children struggling with the crushing burden of their ambivalence toward the parents who deserted or surrendered them will transfer the hostile and negative feelings toward the new objects and preserve an unambivalent love for the absent parents. In the absence of clinical training, the cottage parent can hardly be blamed for reacting with injury and perhaps with anger to the child's repudiation of him and to the negative and provocative behavior that the child produces. The behavior from the cottage parents' point of view is bad behavior, "sassiness," impudence, and ingratitude—an indication to the cottage parents that this child needs to learn who is boss. There may be a period of conflict for a while and then we may learn that the child is much improved, that he is settling down in the institution and making a better adjustment. It sometimes happens, as in the case of George, that these achievements, which make the child far easier to live with, were made at the expense of symptoms, ego restrictions, and loss of the capacity to form new ties. The whole process is invisible to the cottage parents and no blame should be attached to their failure to understand this most complex sequence of behavior.

This brings us to examine the prophylactic measures that grow out of such studies of children in placement. The morbid process that eventually brings about a transformation of affects will only be visible to clinically trained eyes. This means that the caseworker of the child in placement must regard the first months following placement as the critical period, the time when the morbid process can be halted and reversed because the affects associated with separation are still available. Direct work with the child during this period and educational work with the cottage parents and other institutional personnel could make this a period of working through the reactions to placement. When grief and longing and reproaches to the parents are regarded as permissible feelings by the cottage parents and such feelings can be communicated to the caseworker by the child, the child may not have to resort to pathological defense. When hostility is transferred to the new objects and to the caseworker himself, cottage parents may be helped to understand the irrational feelings of the child, to see these feelings as displacements, and to deal with them without defensiveness and counter-aggression.

The caseworker, himself, is often the object of the child's hostile feelings —realistically as the person who took the child away from his parents, in fantasy as the kidnapper of helpless children, and as a convenient transference object for hostile feelings toward the parents. If the caseworker makes use of the feelings that have attached themselves to his person and his role and if he makes use of transference reactions to cottage parents and institutional personnel, he can help the child to examine these feelings and to see them also as part of the ambivalence toward the original parents. It should then be possible to work through the ambivalent feelings toward the parents and to help the child find new solutions in his new environment. Only then is the child free to make new attachments in the institution.

Acknowledgments

The writer wishes to express appreciation to these colleagues who collaborated in the program: Miss Ethel van Dyck of the New Orleans Children's Bureau carried major responsibility for the casework treatment in consultation with the writer. Miss Rita Comarda of Tulane University School of Social Work was supervisor of group treatment. Miss Sally Matlock, at that time a student in the Tulane School of Social Work, was leader of the treatment group. Miss Miriam Gaertner, director of the New Orleans Children's Bureau, Miss Adele Eisler, assistant director of the Children's Bureau, and Mrs. Carol Hamrick, director of the Protestant Children's Home, gave generously of their time and counsel throughout our study.

The writer served as coordinator and consultant for the project and carried one child in casework treatment.

Discussion

CATHARINE D. BERWALD: It is a pleasure to hear and discuss a paper which is so interesting and so lucid. The subject is one of tremendous importance for all persons concerned in any way with children who must be placed away from their own homes, whether in institutions or foster homes. The damaging effect of the separation on the child, if the separation is not worked through, is all too familiar. But so often the agencies and workers responsible for these children do not know what to do, and they compound the damage by putting the child through placement after placement without recognizing what the difficulty is. Lack of staff, inadequate facilities, etc., are often given as excuses. The work described in this paper was done, not in a treatment institution or a psychiatric clinic, but in a custodial institution with no clinically trained staff. This excellent work was done under the direction of one consultant who had the knowledge and experience necessary to define the treatment aims and teach the various people involved what they needed to know to accomplish the aims.

A positive aspect of this work was the deliberate limitation of the therapeutic goal, namely, the working through of the trauma of separation to free the child for new relationships. The case material presented makes clear exactly how the procedures used brought about their results, and those results ought to encourage other agencies to try to do likewise. However, the work described emphasizes the ability of the therapist to know what to say, how and when to say it, and above all, what not to say. This ability is the hallmark of the experienced therapist. It indicates a high degree of training, or an excellence of supervision which is often not available in agencies. There can be a danger in expecting performance beyond the real ability of caseworkers; this is a danger of which Mrs. Fraiberg is well aware, and she has dealt with it in her excellent paper on professional responsibility. Perhaps the answer would be for child placement agencies and institutions to make sure that there is on the staff someone with the necessary training and experience to give the kind of leadership described in this paper.

I was especially happy that Mrs. Fraiberg included a description of the work with the cottage parents and emphasized the importance of teaching them to understand the child and his behavior so that they could support the child's therapy. Her emphasis on the importance of their understanding transference manifestations was of interest. In my own experience such training of cottage parents has been of the greatest importance in enabling them to support individual treatment as well as to handle the children in a way consistent with the therapeutic goals. This kind of training of cottage parents has implications for work with foster parents as well. This is exactly the kind of help foster parents so often need.

The particular use of the group work sessions in conjunction with the individual treatment was intriguing. Our institution has used them in a similar way and I was curious to know more of the details of the coordination of the two in this situation. I would like to know the nature of the contacts with the parents of the children, the handling of visits, and the differences encountered in working through the trauma of separation with children whose parents were no longer in the picture. Of course, this is not at all fair. Mrs. Fraiberg gave us exactly what she said she would, an effective measure to deal with a problem which is so important, and so often neglected. I hope she will write more about this project, but, in the meantime, this paper can be an important influence in the whole field of child welfare because it proves what really can be done to correct the damaging experience of separation in children and to prepare them for the new relationships they so badly need.

A Group Work Approach to the Isolated Child

Ralph L. Kolodny

Physical illnesses or injuries have an emotional impact, whatever their genesis and time of onset. It may be said that, irrespective of a child's emotional adjustment prior to the advent of an incapacitating illness or accident, it is virtually inevitable that emotional difficulties will follow in its wake.

Social group workers must be particularly concerned with the child's problems of social adaptation, which frequently reflect these difficulties and often compound them. Aside from his own hypersensitivity regarding his physical disability, it is more than likely that the physically handicapped child will be confronted in his neighborhood with a group of normal children who at best show but limited tolerance for his inability to participate adequately in play. This may deprive the handicapped child of those intimate associations with peers through which youngsters normally dilute the intensity of their attachment to parents and work out a more realistic and effective relationship with the world outside the home. It also places a heavy burden upon the child's family, who must provide the major resources for his recreational life.

One way to meet the problems inherent in this situation is to provide services for groups of handicapped children who meet in centrally located agencies under various auspices. Here the handicapped child may be able to reach out safely to others his own age, learn to feel more at ease with his condition, and find opportunities as he matures to take action with other handicapped people on matters of common concern. Groups of this kind perform a vital function and their growth has been heartening. They cannot, however, readily be used for homebound children, nor do they directly affect the handicapped child's relationships with his normal peers, the majority group among whom he must make his life. In fact, such groups may serve unwittingly to "ghetto-ize" the handicapped child and inhibit his entry into other relationships and experiences from which he could derive stimulation and gratification, given the proper opportunities and support.

Recognition of these facts has stimulated some organizations and agencies to involve handicapped children in substantial social contacts beyond those they have with their handicapped fellows, and to bring

Reprinted with permission of the author and the National Association of Social Workers, from *Social Work*, Vol. 6, No. 3 (July, 1961), pp. 76–85.

handicapped and normal children together in various types of groups.[1] The Department of Neighborhood Clubs of the Boston Children's Service Association has been extremely active in this effort for the past twenty years. Hopefully, our experiences will offer guidelines to others interested in this particular group of children and this important segment of group work practice.

Throughout its existence the department has primarily concerned itself with the socially isolated child.[2] Because of this it has been called upon to provide service to boys and girls with a wide variety of physical handicaps, including a number who are homebound. These children are referred by hospital social service departments, specialized agencies for the handicapped, and—occasionally—parents. In most instances the department does not place these children in groups made up of others who are similarly handicapped. Its usual procedure is, instead, to form a club around each of the referred children in his own neighborhood, the other members of the club being drawn from among his physically normal peers. This provides the handicapped child with an opportunity to participate in the kind of group experience that would ordinarily be inaccessible to him because of his physical limitations, the reluctance of his peers to reach out to him, or his own reticence.

There are many questions to be considered in any undertaking of this kind. The issues range from those of a medical, psychodynamic, or group dynamic nature to those which relate to staff development, interagency relationships, and costs.[3] Of central importance are questions pertaining to intake, group formation, and programing. The following material focuses on these three aspects of the department's work and illustrates the procedures and problems involved in each. It also suggests the type of contribution this approach can make to the over-all rehabilitation of the handicapped child.

Intake Policies and Group Formation

The department has consciously avoided formulating a detailed and fixed set of policies regarding the kinds of children whom we will accept for service. Our feeling is that with our present knowledge it would be premature for group work agencies to establish neatly defined criteria in this regard. It

[1] Among such agencies have been the Community Council of Greater New York, through its demonstration project on group work with the handicapped; the Girl Scouts and Boy Scouts of America, and the New York Herald Tribune Fresh Air Fund.

[2] For a general description of the department's service see Ralph Kolodny, "Research Planning and Group Work Practice," *Mental Hygiene*, Vol. 42, No. 1 (January 1958).

[3] Some of these issues have been discussed in other presentations or articles. See Marjory Warren, "Meeting the Specialized Needs of Handicapped Children Through Group Work," *Proceedings of the Tenth Governors' Conference on Exceptional Children* (Chicago: State of Illinois, Commission for Handicapped Children, 1953); and Ralph Kolodny, "Therapeutic Group Work with Handicapped Children," *Children*, Vol. 4, No. 3 (May-June 1957).

is important that considerable latitude be permitted a department such as this if it is to explore the boundaries of group work with the handicapped and is not to exclude children whose situations appear on the surface to be untreatable, but who might actually be reached by this service. We do have criteria upon which the disposition of referrals is based, but these are broadly conceived rather than sharply defined.

In order to be accepted for service the child must be socially isolated or likely to become so after hospitalization. He cannot be so intellectually retarded that he will have obvious and continuous difficulty in understanding children his own age. He may be emotionally disturbed, but not to the extent that he will be unlikely to tolerate relationships with others in a group or have any interest in program activities.[4] The child need not be ambulatory, but if he is not, he must be able to engage in a substantial range of sedentary activities. If these requirements are not met and a case cannot be accepted, the department helps the referring agency to find other resources for helping the child.

The department's acceptance of a referral does not, of course, bind the child referred and his parents to accept the service. Preliminary interpretation of the service is made to them by the referring medical social worker, but it remains for the group worker, through one or more home interviews, to make the final interpretation. If during these interviews the child and his parents decide they wish the service (in a substantial majority they do), the worker then begins the process of forming a group.[5]

Suggestions for potential group members are usually first obtained from the youngster and his mother. If they are not in a position to suggest members, the worker, with their permission, then uses neighborhood schools or agencies as resources for this purpose. As he discusses suggested members with parents or with school or agency personnel, he keeps the following requirements in mind in assessing their suitability for the group: (1) the member should be about the same age as the referred child; (2) he should be able to accept a limited and sometimes sedentary type of program; (3) he must be able to control impulses to act out physically; (4) he should not be so competitive that he will be unable to tolerate the demands for attention which the referred child may make upon the leader; (5) he should not have displayed excessive fear of the referred child's condition if he has had previous contacts with him; and (6) there should be some likelihood of his being enthusiastic about the idea of a club as something he himself might enjoy.

Following these discussions the worker makes home visits to suggested

----

[4] The existence of an emotional disorder in a case referred for service becomes one more factor to be assessed. Evaluation of its implications for group work can be made by the worker, who has the benefit of the suggestions of the child's therapist, if there is such, and the advice of the department's psychiatric consultant. It is not considered by itself a sufficient reason for nonacceptance of a referral.

[5] In 1956, for example, in 9 of the 12 cases referred the parents and the child decided that they wanted the service.

members and their parents in order to interpret and enlist their interest in the group. Unless he is patently unsuited for the group, if a suggested member indicates a desire to join, he is allowed to do so. While this policy sometimes leads to difficulties, a rigid screening system for membership would be most difficult to operate. The use of diagnostic testing in order to evaluate suitability for membership, for example, would give rise to many complications. Even were parents to permit such testing, which is unlikely, the procedure would lead to serious problems arising from the exclusion of some of the children tested. Moreover, the selection of members according to narrowly specific criteria is often made unfeasible by the limitations of the peer population in the neighborhood.

The groups the department forms are kept purposely small—usually from five to eight members. Most begin by meeting in the handicapped child's home. As soon as it is feasible, however, meeting places are rotated so that the homes of other members are used as well. If a youth-serving agency exists in the neighborhood, meetings may be held there, occasionally at first and later regularly. The choice of meeting place and the process of movement to other meeting places depend upon a combination of factors: medical restrictions on the handicapped child's movement, his emotional readiness to leave his own home for meetings, the physical suitability of the home for meetings, the availability of neighborhood resources, and the age of group members.

Problems During Referral and Formation Periods

The problems that develop during the referral and formation period are equal in importance to those that arise once the group is under way and must be given equally close attention. We have found it necessary to disabuse ourselves of the notion that parents, in their gratitude for an opportunity to move the handicapped child out of isolation, will welcome this service without reservation. Most parents, of course, want their children to lead less constricted lives. At the same time, it is only natural for them, because of the various pressures to which they have been subjected in the course of their children's illnesses, to display some ambivalence when presented with the offer of this service. Isolation of the child may be bad, but exposure also has its drawbacks and parents have strong feelings about it. Under these circumstances close contact between the referring agency and the department becomes particularly necessary during the referral and formation period. Both the referring caseworker and the group worker must be prepared to be quite active at this time. Through accepting parental anxieties and hostilities, searching with parents for contributions they can make to the group, and showing an interest in parents as individuals, they can support them to a point where they will be able with some security to share the child with a new outsider.

Parental ambivalence is not always severe or immediately obvious, but its existence is inevitable. The group worker, therefore, must be alert to its presence and, when it is extreme, willing to understand and move with the parent as he or she hesitates, vacillates, and behaves in what may appear to be an immature way. Mrs. L, mother of a 7-year-old girl with nephritis, offers a case in point. She displayed some interest in a club for her daughter when the caseworker at the hospital spoke to her about it. The department worker who telephoned her later discovered, however, that she had some reservations. The worker suggested that she could visit Mrs. L at home to discuss them, but Mrs. L thought she would rather come to the office. An appointment was made for the next week. On the morning for which it was scheduled Mrs. L called to ask for a new time. This was set. Shortly afterward the department worker called the caseworker at the hospital and was surprised to learn the following:

> Mrs. L had come to the hospital social service office that morning and it was from here that she had called to cancel the appointment. She had made no appointment with Miss N (the caseworker) but had "just dropped in." Mrs. L had expressed much concern about the club to Miss N. She was afraid Alice (her daughter) wouldn't know how to play with other children. Miss N explained that this would be the purpose of the group, to help Alice learn to play with children her own age. Mrs. L wanted to know specifically what the group would do and Miss N mentioned that the group worker would help the members to carry out their own ideas. When Mrs. L expressed some concern that Alice wouldn't have any ideas, Miss N reassured her that the group worker would also have ideas and suggestions. Miss N reported that by the time she left Mrs. L seemed interested in the group again. Miss N believed that Mrs. L is feeling guilty about having someone else come in and do what she thinks should be her job. It became apparent, she said, that actually Alice doesn't have any friends. When Mrs. L wondered where the group members would come from, Miss N was able to reassure her by pointing out that they could come from the immediate neighborhood or nearby school.

The department worker sent a letter or reminder to Mrs. L about the next appointment, but she again canceled. She did, however, respond favorably to the renewed offer of a home visit. She and her daughter were at home when the worker came and a thorough exploration of their questions took place. The group began to meet a month later. Shortly afterward Mrs. L had another interview with the caseworker, who called the department worker and advised her that Mrs. L "seemed much more relieved about the group and was very pleased."

It is necessary also to recognize what this new experience means to the handicapped child himself and to realize that, along with the promised pleasure, it poses a threat of sorts. The group worker needs to try to reduce the child's anxiety over participation in a club by seeing him several times before the group begins to meet and building a relationship through which the child can begin to perceive him as a source of support. During these contacts he can also help the child by relating this experience to other experiences with which the child is familiar and to skills and interests he has already developed.

Objectives

Once a group begins to meet, the leader's basic objective in his work with the handicapped child is to help him to function within the limits imposed by his handicap, but also to learn through experience the range of activities and relationships available to him despite his physical condition. Care is exercised not to deny the child's incapacities or force him to compensate for a lack of ability by becoming hyperactive. The aim is to help him discover, through testing in a protected situation, alternatives to social withdrawal or overcompensation.

Within the context of this objective various goals are developed, not only on the basis of the child's physical handicap, but also in relation to his feelings toward himself and his conception of the attitudes of others toward him. For example, in cases where the handicapped child is a homebound boy, one of the department's objectives is to provide reinforcement, through a male leader and peer group, for the child's sense of his own masculine identity. His exclusive association with his mother for long periods makes this important.

Helping the child to develop and begin to follow through on realistic vocational goals is an important objective in work with the severely handicapped youngster, who may keep this matter on the level of fantasy unless the worker, through programing and marginal interviews, enables him to take concrete steps in this direction. This attention to vocational goals, expressing the worker's confidence in the child's adequacy, can also increase the child's faith in his own capabilities.

Although the worker does not focus directly on helping the child to gain insight into, and resolve, the basic feelings associated with his handicap through the group experience, he is concerned with helping him to face and handle more adequately the problems in social relationships that accompany it. He is therefore interested in reducing whatever need the child may have to deny the reality of his handicap. At the same time, especially with the homebound child, one of the worker's objectives is frankly, through activities, sometimes to divert the child from preoccupation with his condition. Excitement and change in the life of such a child are too often confined to negative experiences such as a reinjury or recurrence of symptoms. The club gives him an opportunity to anticipate a potentially pleasurable event each week and to develop relationships with others which may afford him emotional gratification between meetings. This can help to relieve some of the depression associated with his condition.

In speaking of goals it should also be made clear at this point that, although by design this paper is focused exclusively on the handicapped child himself, this is not the case in the leader's actual work with the group. On the contrary, he is concerned with and attentive to the feelings and interests of all the members. Department workers pay close attention to the developmental needs of each group member and are also prepared to help with crises in the lives of members both within and outside the club whenever these occur. Adolescent members of a department club, for example, use this type of group as they would any other, for ventilation, information, and support around heterosexual matters, educational and vocational aspirations, and the problems of growing independence from the family. They are encouraged to do so by the worker, who uses his understanding of individual and group dynamics and his program skills to provide guidance and outlets in these areas to all the members. In addition, department workers from the very outset make themselves available as social workers to the families of all members of their groups and are frequently called upon to counsel parents or help them to use appropriate social, psychological, or medical resources. The department does not regard the normal children as figures to be exploited for the benefit of the handicapped child. While the latter may have a markedly greater need for relationships than other members, our aim is to make his association with them *mutually* advantageous.

There are five major aspects of the approach used by the worker in helping the handicapped child to move toward the goals described. These are:

1.   Accepting the handicapped child's maladaptive behavior, such as overdependence, denial, and overcompensation or withdrawal.

2.   As trust develops, helping him to become more aware of the effects of this behavior on his relationships with others, and of alternatives to it.

3.   Enabling other members to react without undue deference or serious antagonism to his demands on the worker by giving them consistent individual attention, which includes the provision of opportunities for the ventilating of feeling about this experience.

4.   Beginning with program activities well within his ability and even sometimes giving him special preparation for them.

5.   Later, challenging his tendency to cling to the familiar through exposing him to carefully planned activities which are not beyond him, but which do clearly call upon him to extend himself.

In implementing these steps the worker must give careful attention to the conditions governing group interaction which are created by the presence of a youngster who is in some ways severely limited in his physical movement and whose feelings are profoundly affected by this limitation. The kinds of considerations to which the worker must pay heed might best be illustrated by a discussion of some of the issues involved in the use of program activities in a group of this type.

Programing

In groups composed of physically normal children, shoving, pulling, hugging, and wrestling are often prominent features of social interaction. The handicapped child and the members of his group, however, must exercise considerable restraint in regard to the direct expression of feeling through physical activity. The handicapped child may be fearful of his own aggressive impulses—active physical contact with another youngster may be actually dangerous for him. The other members must in some cases curb their tendency to grab or push, even in a mild way, and the usual opportunities for aggressive play of a direct sort may be denied them in this setting. Under these conditions it is important that the group's program include activities through which the generalized aggression that members may feel can be expressed and sublimated. In groups in which the handicapped child has very limited ambulation and there can be only minimal physical activity, the worker can still provide experiences through which aggressive impulses may be expressed in a controlled and enjoyable manner. The effect of the activities the worker introduces in order to provide those experiences depends, in large part, upon his relationship with the members. If he is unable to accept even verbal expressions of hostility among members or toward himself, no activity he uses is likely to provide appropriate channels for aggression. If, however, the worker feels some hostility to be inevitable, is prepared to accept it, and believes that aggression can be utilized for constructive ends, he can create a climate in which sublimation can take place.

In devising activities for this purpose he may rely on a variety of media. Wide use can be made of materials that can be struck and pounded. Clay modeling and woodworking are, of course, quite useful in this connection. Balloons may be substituted for balls in games which require throwing and hitting. Other media are also available. In round-robin story-telling, for example, in which one member begins and the others continue a story, an opportunity is afforded members to ventilate hostility if they wish and to exercise their creative urge at the same time. Some sedentary games provide youngsters with a chance to "attack" without hurting or being hurt and to "fight" without destroying. The game of "battleship" is of this type. In this game through plotting ship locations on a sheet of graphed paper, youngsters can figuratively sink each other's vessels until one team's fleet is "destroyed." Anticipation and excitement are built into this kind of game, and for the handicapped child especially, but for other members as well, there is an opportunity to release aggression that is potentially beneficial to all concerned. For, under these circumstances, youngsters may be helped to understand that, although giving vent to aggressive impulses through physical movement against another person cannot be countenanced in this type of club, the expression of aggression in some forms is natural, permissible, and constructive.

Although a well-structured and stimulating program is essential to the development of this type of group, it is important not to overemphasize this aspect of club life. Since the range of physical activity of members is limited by the presence of the handicapped child, a worker may feel under some compulsion continually to encourage the use of program activities which will create a "lively" atmosphere in the group. Implicit in this is the assumption that the handicapped child and his fellow members can only be happy when they are intensely involved in specific projects that engage all their attention. Unless he is careful, the worker may reinforce the handicapped child's tendency to rely excessively on organized projects and games as a basis for relating to others. Often such a child feels uncomfortable or even threatened if he has to relate without such props; though they bring him in contact with others, they enable him at the same time to maintain his psychological distance. While in the initial stages of the group these external supports may be essential, as the group develops the worker should encourage the attempts of members to discover spontaneous ways of relating to one another. It should also be recognized that the handicapped child in particular needs opportunities to disengage himself from activities without feeling disapproval by the worker or the other members of the group. It is important that he be given latitude to *be* with others without continually having to *do* something.

One of the persistent themes that runs through the program of a group is that of "movement." The worker is interested in helping the handicapped child to mobilize whatever capacities he has to move physically and to move out to others emotionally. It is expected that the personal investment of the worker in the child's emotional growth will be great. It should also be recognized, however, that he may likewise come to have a substantial stake in the expansion of the child's physical movement. This may stem from his concern that the child improve in every respect, but it may also be related to his own inability to face the child's realistic physical limitations. Consequently, there is always the possibility that a worker will overestimate a youngster's physical capabilities and program accordingly. This may not cause irreparable damage, but it does create unnecessary difficulties and reinforces whatever inability the child has to function within the bounds of his handicap.

To be sure, a worker will want actively to help a child make maximum use of his physical abilities. When increased physical activity can be of benefit to the child, a worker does well to devote substantial efforts to seeking out and using outside resources as well as the club program itself for promoting this.

Even as he looks for opportunities to help the child in this way, however, the worker has to avoid an exaggerated emphasis on increasing his physical activity, and to be wary lest—rationalizing his approach by saying he does not want to repeat in the group the inhibiting overprotection a youngster is receiving at home—he subtly pressure him to move beyond his physical limits. Naturally the worker wishes to avoid being overprotective. Perhaps the most direct way to accomplish this, however, is to make sure that any activity which clearly has an element of danger in it for the handicapped child is kept out of the program of the group; in this way the leader will not be forced to be unnecessarily protective.

Effects of the Service

Questions of formation and programing are interesting, of course, but what of results? Have we seen improvement in the attitudes or behavior of handicapped children in our groups? We have seen constructive changes. We are fully aware of the complexity of this matter and the need for caution in making judgments. We have had our share of difficulties and failures. Our experiences do lead us to believe, however, that a service such as that offered by the department can be of substantial psychological benefit to many physically handicapped children.

In the case of Steve, a 12-year-old double amputee, one sees this in the contrast between the youngster's frightened response to his club's first cook-out and his reaction to this same activity a year later. The first time, despite his expression of interest and intensive preparation by the worker, Steve could not bring himself to go. He did not come to the assembly point, and when the worker stopped by his house he found Steve had suffered an anxiety attack and had been left exhausted by a severe siege of vomiting. Steve and his mother were distraught at this point and expected rejection by the worker, who had to go to considerable lengths to reassure them before going off with the group.

Some months later, however, after intensive work with Steve in the group and with his mother and Steve outside it, the youngster was able to consider going on another cook-out when this was proposed at a club meeting. This time he was ready at the appointed hour, and although at first fearful that he would be in some way overwhelmed, he soon entered into the activity with great spirit, helping to set the fire, volunteering for clean-up, and even participating in a baseball game after arrangements were made so that he could play. Throughout the afternoon he kept telling the worker what a pleasant surprise everything was.

For Linda, an 11-year-old-girl with *spina bifida*, the benefits of the service became apparent after many months when she was able finally to relate, first to the worker and then to her fellow members, without anxiously concealing some of the more unpleasant aspects of her physical condition. Having come to trust in her acceptance by others, she could treat such things as her use of a catheter quite openly rather than as a dark secret. This, in turn, made it possible for her to share happily in important new areas of activity with the other members. These developments were recorded by the worker, who first began to notice a change in the youngster on one occasion when she met her at school before a trip. Linda's catheter had become caught in the upper part of her brace, causing her some discomfort. When the worker offered to help, Linda reacted with embarrassment. Their ensuing conversation is described by the worker as follows:

I asked her if she felt funny talking to me about things like the catheter. Linda said she didn't like to think about it. I said that it was certainly easy to understand that she might be sensitive about being different from most people in this respect, adding, "But you know, Linda, I can still like you and want you to like me." Linda grinned broadly and commented that she thought I was the best club leader she had ever had.

Several weeks later when some of the members suggested an "overnight" at camp the worker was struck by Linda's ready assent and her subsequent eagerness to go. All Linda asked was that she have "some privacy." When the group planned for the trip at a later meeting Linda spoke quite openly of the medical supplies and apparatus she would have to take along. On the "overnight" itself her growing assurance and comfort with the physical aspects of her handicap became clearly apparent. At bedtime Linda permitted the worker to accompany her to the bathroom while she emptied her catheter bag, and then indicated that she wouldn't mind if the girls stayed in the room while she changed her clothing, as long as they kept looking at the fire and toasting marshmallows. The worker describes her behavior as follows:

> Linda spoke throughout in a normal tone of voice about these more personal things and the other girls could hear very easily what was being said. She apparently feels very much at home with them. They, in turn, evinced little interest in what she was doing, whatever their underlying curiosity. After everyone had changed into her pajamas, they went to bed and, after talking a bit, fell asleep. When we visited town the next day Linda declined offers of being pushed, and wheeled herself around the shops. She was showing a noticeable amount of independence by this time and I was not asked to push the chair or lift and carry as much as before.

In some instances there occurs a substantial alteration in the handicapped youngster's capacity to respond positively to the demands of approaching adulthood. This is seen in the following abstract from a summary report of Tim, who was referred to the department by a medical social worker when he was 13.

> Tim suffered from a rare congenital disease of the skeleton characterized by brittle bones, and had sustained 25 fractures during the first 13 years of his life. He was referred to the department because he was profoundly isolated from his peers. An extremely intelligent youngster, Tim had many scientific interests. He rarely followed through on these interests, however, but confined himself to fantasies about becoming a scientist. We attempted to help him give concrete expression to his vocational aspirations and learn ways of fulfilling them realistically. During the three years his group was in existence Tim and his fellow members were introduced through various program activities to a variety of scientific projects and procedures. He developed hobbies around electronics and radio. The department worked closely with Tim's home teacher in encouraging these hobbies. At the age of 16, having had no fractures for three years, Tim began to attend high school. He did extremely well there, displaying a genuine talent in technical subjects and a striking ability to make friends with his classmates. Tim is now a college sophomore and on the way to a scientific career.

There are, of course, many problems and questions connected with our approach which will continue to concern us and which demand intensive study. We need, for example, to extend and deepen our knowledge of the impact of this type of group experience on the normal as well as the handicapped children who participate in it. We need better understanding of how to handle the tensions that sometimes arise between the handicapped child and his parents as a result of the increased independence the child has acquired through the group experience. As we help the child to relate to his normal peers we also have to learn more about how to help him, at the same time, to feel comfortable with and a part of his own minority group, the physically handicapped. Finally, we not only need to increase our understanding of the meaning of the behavior of group members but must also constantly examine our own feelings as workers in this kind of situation.

The investigation of problems such as these presents all group workers with a continuous and arduous task. If, however, we are persistent in carrying it out, we can with greater assurance help handicapped children in increasing numbers to participate in and draw emotional nourishment from group experiences with their peers.

Planned Short-Term Treatment, a New Service to Adolescents

Elizabeth Kerns

Despite the well-documented need for changes in agency delivery of services, little has been published on how these changes can be effected. For example, how does the staff of a traditional casework agency shift its emphasis from long-term therapy to short-term treatment? (It is assumed that such a change is relevant to some of the needs of the agency's clientele and to the community's comprehensive plan for welfare services.) For a staff to evolve a planned short-term treatment (PSTT) approach encompasses much more than consideration of the time element; it makes new emotional and technical demands on the workers. Emotionally, each worker must feel secure and must be sufficiently flexible to examine his current practice and then be prepared to deal with problems which may arise from this examination. Technically, the worker is required to reconsider the philosophy of casework, develop more refined skills in the formulation of diagnostic assessments and treatment plans, reorganize the range of treatment procedures, and terminate at the time mutually agreed upon in initial contacts with clients. Within the framework of these factors, this article describes the experience of the staff of Youth Service of Cleveland in learning to deliver services to adolescents through planned short-term treatment.

Youth Service, a voluntary casework agency for over fifty years, offers counseling to young people, between the ages of twelve and twenty-one years, and their parents living in the metropolitan Cleveland area. It has a small staff of seventeen experienced professional social workers who have specialized skills in treating adolescents. During 1968, 1,315 teenagers were served in individual and group counseling. With the community's growing social awareness—in part a reflection of new federal programs—came an increasing demand for services and a volume of applications which traditional treatment methods could not meet in the foreseeable future. This gap between available services and adolescents' needs for services prompted the

Reprinted from *Social Casework*, Vol. 51 (June, 1970), pp. 340–346, by permission of the author and the Family Service Association of America.

agency to hold a one-day meeting to review in depth, specific areas of work; to appraise the community resources, the needs of adolescents, and the role of Youth Service within this existing structure; and to decide on the options and priorities for innovation and change. First priority was given to learning short-term treatment as a method of choice to provide more service without sacrificing the quality of treatment.

The formal learning process began with a series of weekly staff development seminars under the leadership of Harry Rubinstein, who was casework director until February 1969. These sessions were used initially for discussion of readings from a selected bibliography and of seminars with Lydia Rapaport on crisis intervention. Because few of the referrals to Youth Service met the criteria of a crisis as defined in the literature, planned short-term treatment was eventually chosen because it seemed applicable to a broader range of case situations. (Although the techniques for planned short-term treatment and crisis intervention are not mutually exclusive, there are differences in the theoretical concepts.)

Planned Short-term Treatment

The name *planned short-term treatment* (PSTT) is borrowed from Howard and Libbie Parad.[1] PSTT makes the structured use of time an important treatment variable. In PSTT, the client and worker must reach a mutual agreement to work together toward a specific goal within a given number of sessions. (This agreement constitutes a contract.) During the last sessions, the participants in the contract must evaluate what has been accomplished in relation to the goal. They then decide to terminate or to continue for an additional number of sessions with the same goal or a new goal. (This decision is referred to as renegotiation of the contract.) The terms *contract* and *renegotiation* may or may not be used directly with the clients, but the process and expectations of PSTT must be considered carefully because the client's full understanding and participation are essential.

The seminars on PSTT raised many philosophical and technical questions of which few can be answered fully after only a year of practice. These early questions included the following: (1) How long is short-term treatment? (2) Is it applicable to adolescents? (3) What does time mean to teenagers and adults? (4) Is the time limit perceived as another deprivation? (5) Does the time limit serve as a protection for the adolescent in his struggle for independence, or is it used as a defense maneuver against coming to grips with the problem? (6) What kinds of case situations are appropriate to PSTT? (7) What happens when confrontations are made early in the contact? (8) Is it necessary first to establish a "good working relationship"? (9) How does the worker enable teenagers—especially the younger, inarticulate ones— to focus on a specific problem? (10) Can good service be given

[1] Howard J. Parad and Libbie G. Parad, A Study of Crisis-Oriented Planned Short-Term Treatment: Parts I and II, *Social Casework*, 49:346–55 (June 1968) and 49:418–26 (July 1968).

when the goal is so limited and many other problems still exist? (11) Does termination present a problem for the worker in letting go and in not being certain that the treatment will be effective?

Reading, discussing, and theorizing can go only so far; sooner or later action must follow, and this action can be very difficult when it involves major changes. Nevertheless, the staff was encouraged to begin trying the PSTT approach. The cases were fully recorded and, in subsequent seminars, reviewed session by session as the treatment was taking place. One of the difficulties was to refrain from simply referring to the content of the case but instead to focus on the differences inherent in the PSTT process. The following condensed case situations and corresponding discussions demonstrate the action of PSTT.

An Adolescent Boy's Problems

Mrs. B, a sixty-two-year-old black mother of eight, referred her youngest child, sixteen-year-old David, for help. According to the mother, David had displayed no serious problems until the age of fifteen. The father had died when David was five, and later David suffered a prolonged grief reaction, becoming socially withdrawn, although he was quiet and conforming at home. At the age of fifteen, he grew rapidly, began to break the close tie to his mother, and became a rebellious adolescent. Since then he had become increasingly aggressive and rebellious at home. He had been in a series of fights at school and his performance deteriorated alarmingly. The mother had gone to juvenile court for help and was referred to Youth Service. David refused to come, but several months later asked that his mother contact the agency.

In the first appointment, the worker was struck by David's high degree of anxiety as manifested by marked head and shoulder tics. David denied any problems; he had come because his mother nagged him. The worker tried to help him understand the differences between Youth Service and Juvenile court and between a psychiatrist and a social worker. David relaxed enough to tell that when he had entered high school, he had been taunted by other boys and fights had resulted. Art was his major interest, and he had been removed from class because of his fighting. Could the worker help him get into art class? Also, he needed a job and wanted to get into weight lifting. He went on to tell of living in a bad neighborhood and having to cope with "things you [white worker] never experienced." David thought that one more interview should take care of his problems, but he was willing to take part in five sessions with the major goal of getting into an art class.

In spite of David's obvious, deep-seated problems, the worker chose PSTT, with admission to art class as the major goal because it was a goal David could accept. This frightened boy felt overwhelmed by his environment and was struggling to gain some control over his situation. The activities he desired were attempts at constructive sublimation; the worker saw this as ego strength. The five sessions would allow an opportunity to give specific help regarding the art class and, it was hoped, an experience in mastery and self-respect. There were actually seven interviews over a three-month period. In the first five appointments there were two major themes, the first of which was being admitted into an art program. David saw himself quite powerless in this process and expected the worker to do it all for him. The worker used this attitude to express understanding of David's feelings about himself and to encourage him to do more for himself. This led to discussion of the establishment, black-white relationships, and power.

The second theme was life in the inner city—the immense danger and the possibility of getting killed at any time. This discussion was motivated partly by bravado and partly by an effort to impress the worker with his knowledge of life, but primarily David conveyed how overwhelmed he felt by the impossibility of doing well and surviving in his environment. The worker recognized the realities but pointed out David's improved and better behavior as an indication that he could manage and succeed. (No effort was made to relate his pessimism to the death of his father.) There was marked decrease in the anxiety symptoms during interviews.

Through the joint efforts of David and the worker, he did enter an art program at a settlement house. With difficulty, arrangements were made with a black school counselor for David to get back into the art program at school. This action necessitated the worker's active intervention; otherwise David would have been lost in the negativism of the inner-city school.

A sixth appointment was agreed upon, pending the school's making final arrangements for David's reentering art class. David arrived for the appointment extremely distraught and angry. The school counselor had "flaked" him off. Despite earlier planning, the counselor said it was not his responsibility, and David should see the art teacher himself. The counselor had acted as if he did not recognize David or had ever heard of him. David was extremely angry; however, he left the office and managed to get through the whole day without getting into trouble in spite of his anger and hurt. The worker gave David a great deal of support for his managing his anger but raised the question about his giving up on himself and not seeing the teacher. The boy insisted that he "didn't have a chance." The worker was aware of the reality factors in this perception and agreed to see the art teacher. A school visit revealed the confusion and lack of concern in the school. Insistence upon a complete check of David's current progress showed marked improvement, and the art teacher was then willing to readmit him.

David was quite relaxed in his last appointment and told of plans to run for the student council. He stated that he was the most articulate boy in his class and that "some things needed to be changed" at school. Almost incidentally, David expressed his satisfaction with art class. He minimized the worker's role, saying he probably could have done it himself but he was "lazy." In his disparagement of the worker, David seemed to be struggling for the worker's recognition of and respect for him as an equal. The worker indicated that in part David needed the help of an adult, but that he had done most of it himself, as his better grades and better control had gained him readmission to art class. David started a discussion of black nationalists, black pride, and so forth. He hoped that someday no one would feel superior to anyone else on the basis of race. He himself was feeling equal to others. David seemed to be feeling much better about himself. He and the worker discussed future contacts. David felt he could go on his own; if he needed the worker, he could always call. The worker fully supported this attitude.

Treatment Techniques

This case shows that the whole treatment in PSTT can take place in the time span approximating the study period of a more traditional, long-term approach. The worker cannot use the beginning sessions primarily for the purpose of evaluation and development of a relationship. The nature of the client-worker relationship differs in PSTT from long-term treatment in that the aim is *not* to build a therapeutically dependent relationship with the resulting transference reactions becoming a focal point of treatment. In PSTT the dependency is not heightened, but rather the relationship takes advantage of the client's potential for independent problem solving. (It is recognized however that in any relationship, transference and counter-transference reactions do occur.) The worker in the David B case used the PSTT relationship to provide a corrective experience—namely, that some adults can be trusted to help in gaining self-mastery. At this time in his development, David could not have tolerated the dependent kind of relationship required for long-term therapy involving personality restructuring; but PSTT did provide an experience in constructive problem solving that he could apply to other areas, such as the student council.

In the very first appointment, the worker must be clear about and accept the problem for which the client is both concretely and preconsciously seeking his help. Starting at the concrete level follows the social work maxim of "starting where the client is"; with David, it was getting into an art class. At a preconscious level, David seemed to be asking for help with conflicts of dependency, which were handled by the worker within the context of the concrete request. At the same time, the worker must assess the problem in relation to the client's personality, current social situation, and past life experiences. The client and worker mutually must agree on a stated goal to be worked upon within a specific time; the more clearly the goal is delineated, the easier it becomes to evaluate goal-directed behavior. The worker, as the helping person, must then formulate a plan by which the goal may be accomplished and that enables the client to complete the tasks that will solve the problem. In order to remain oriented toward a goal, the worker must closely observe the course of treatment session by session.

The treatment techniques in PSTT are not really new, but they must be used differently from the way they are used in long-term treatment. The all-important sense of timing is crucial to meeting the goal. A major difference lies in the fact that the worker confronts the client early in the contact with behavior patterns that interfere with his problem solving. In long-term treatment, the worker is much less active and attempts to develop the client's self-awareness so that he can make these connections for himself. Consequently, in PSTT, the worker places more emphasis on what Florence Hollis referred to as "procedures of direct influence" and "reflective discussion of the person-situation configuration" and less emphasis on sustaining and encouraging "ventilation" procedures that promote the more dependent relationship necessary for accomplishing the personality-restructuring goals of long-term therapy.[2] Collateral contacts in PSTT must be made quickly so that they can be incorporated into the treatment plan. In the David B case, the worker facilitated planning through contacts at school and at a settlement house.

Termination of the treatment process is in a sense begun in the first interview when the contract is made for a specific number of sessions. The important element of short-term treatment is not so much the length of time but the planned nature of the process. There is no magical set number of sessions, although sometimes it is helpful to connect termination with some significant event, such as the end of a grading period for a school problem. Many adolescents can present their own plans for the number of sessions; in other cases, the worker must suggest a plan. In the David B case, the time limit was a compromise decision between the client and worker.

After termination, the agency administration must support PSTT with a "revolving door policy" that allows for flexible intake and prompt service as they are needed by clients returning for help with another problem. There are two positions on casework follow-up: some workers think such a contact promotes positive transference to the agency on the part of the clients, lessens their feelings of rejection, and facilitates their returning if further service is needed; others say that the follow-up is an indication of the worker's lack of confidence in his own work and in the client's ability to judge when he needs to return. Both ways have been tried, and the use of follow-up is left to the discretion of the worker.

A Teen-aged Girl's Difficulties at School

A second case illustrates PSTT with a younger adolescent—a girl whose presenting problem is more vague and whose motivation for help is limited. The case of Martha demonstrates the PSTT process of diagnosis, treatment, and termination. A contract for eight appointments was established with the goal of helping Martha to do better at school and to try to control her laughing, talking, and losing her temper. Follow-up contact with the school indicated that there was considerable improvement, and the goal was reached.

Martha Ellen, a fourteen-year-old girl, lived in the inner city with three

[2] Florence Hollis, The Sustaining Process, Direct Influence, and Ventilation, *Casework: A Psychosocial Therapy* (New York: Random House, 1964), pp. 83–116.

siblings and her mother. They were supported by public assistance and social security payments. Martha was referred to Youth Service by the assistant principal at a junior high school where Martha had begun the seventh grade a few months earlier. In school, she was disruptive and unable to control talking and giggling; she refused to accept discipline from teachers. She had average ability and performed well academically. Martha and her mother initially agreed to the referral because of fears that juvenile court and placement might otherwise be involved.

PSTT was chosen for this case because neither the girl nor her mother seemed to feel there was a problem they could not talk about easily, and they showed little interest in counseling. At the worker's suggestion, a contract was made for eight appointments, with the goal of helping Martha to do better at school and to try to control her behavior in school. In the course of treatment, Martha was late for two appointments and missed one; the mother was seen three times.

Martha did not begin to concentrate on the problem until the fifth session, at which time she talked of her inability to control laughter when the boys made comments about the teachers. In the next session, she demonstrated the problem in the interview situation: she came with a friend, Jean, and they were laughing and out of control in the waiting room. In a discussion between the worker and Martha about what made Jean giggle, the elements of sexual excitement and embarrassment became more evident. Martha then wanted to invite Jean to the last two sessions to see if she could help in clarifying the problem.

For the seventh appointment, Martha and Jean came about fifteen minutes late and were laughing as they arrived. At first it was difficult for them to overcome their giggling. The worker welcomed Jean and explained that she and Martha were working on the problem of giggling in school. Jean acknowledged that she was familiar with this problem, had some difficulties herself, but that she could usually stop herself, especially after a teacher called her mother. When the worker questioned them about the laughing, both girls readily said that the boys made them laugh by using words that had obvious sexual connotations. The worker tried to elicit the meaning of the words and the girls' feelings about them. Martha claimed she knew but could not explain what they meant because they were too nasty. Eventually Martha was able to say that the words meant "when a man and woman get together."

After several attempts to make the girls talk more freely, the worker was convinced of their inadequate sex information. The worker explained that "getting together" was called intercourse or sex relations, and she suggested that perhaps they knew other names for it. There was an almost breathless silence as the worker described the sex act and pointed out that intercourse was the way to have children, but it was also the way for a man and woman to show their love and appreciation for each other. At first there was absolute silence, but a look of relief on both girls' faces. They were very quiet now, and Martha finally asked, "Is that all?" The worker could not learn more about her thoughts. Both girls then started talking about the movies at school on sex education which had hinted that somehow the man and woman got together. Mothers always gave a lot of prohibitions. Martha's mother said to "keep your dress down and don't act all trampy." Jean's mother warned her not to make the mistake of having different children by different men. This raised questions about pregnancies out of wedlock and whether one could have sex relations without being in love. At the end of this session, Martha asked Jean to come back for the next week.

By helping them understand some of the facts, the worker relieved some of the anxiety and enabled Martha to better control the giggling. In the last session, despite Martha's earlier intention to leave at the end of eight sessions, she was ambivalent about termination. However, there was nothing specific she wanted to work on further. By identifying her ambivalence, Martha was then free to terminate with the understanding that she could come back if other problems arose. The focus with the mother was to help her understand Martha's sexual curiosity and preoccupation with growing up and to help the mother give needed social and sex education information appropriate for a fourteen-year-old.

"Growing Pains" of Staff and Agency in PSTT

This kind of pioneering presented exciting challenges, but the staff and agency experienced "growing pains" in the actual carrying out of PSTT. Some workers were able to assimilate the PSTT approach into their practice more easily than were others. The ease of assimilation seemed related especially to the following factors: the worker's casework philosophy, his willingness to assume a directive role, his view of the meaning of time, his ability to work well under pressure, and his general adaptability.

Although there are reports of studies that show encouraging results with short-term treatment, the staff and agency experienced some anxiety about whether "experimenting" with adolescent clients and their families was justified. Another big question concerned the values of and attitudes toward the psychoanalytic model of long-term treatment, which is often seen as the foremost type in the "hierarchy of therapies." Was PSTT a second-best sort of treatment or was it really the casework treatment of choice for many clients? It was often difficult for the worker to accept for the focus of treatment the limits of what the client considered to be his problem. Much self-discipline was required to remain focused on the problem as circumscribed by the goal. This difficulty, coupled with the workers' concerns that improvement through PSTT was a "flight into health" rather than a real working through of the problem, made them reluctant to terminate. Thus workers frequently neglected to evaluate the treatment process with clients prior to the final session. Some workers whose practice had always been very goal oriented found it difficult to subject their mode of treatment to a time limit. The support of the total staff and agency administration was of prime importance in helping the individual worker with his own difficulties in learning PSTT.

After several months of experience with PSTT, the full recording had produced material too voluminous for study purposes. A mimeographed form, to be filled in by the worker after each session, was devised to take the place of the usual agency record. This new record form began with a fact sheet that included information about the intake, the PSTT design and rationale, the renegotiations, and the termination. Under the heading of *Presenting Problems* was the problem for which the adolescent and his parents requested help as well as the worker's evaluation of the problem in relation to the client's personality structure, current social situation, and past life experiences. After this, the mutually set goal for the PSTT contract and any changes in the goals at renegotiation points were stated. Then the worker outlined his plan for accomplishing the goal. A description of the course of treatment was included next and the content of each treatment session was related to four questions: (1) What use of the time factor was made in this session? (2) What clarification did the worker make in this session of problem, goal, or dynamics; confrontations; or connections? (3) What was the client's reaction to the worker's clarification? (4) What evidence of goal-directed behavior did the client show in this session? Finally, the termination process was reviewed by answering the following questions: What goals were reached? How, in the opinion of the adolescent, the parents, and the worker, was the treatment plan effective or ineffective? The client's and worker's reactions to termination were also recorded. Most of the staff thought that this form of recording helped make the learning of PSTT a more conscious process.

Conclusion

During the first year of learning PSTT, approximately 10 percent of the case situations at Youth Service were handled by this method. The staff planned to continue the intensive study of PSTT with the goal of using it for at least half of the cases, so that in the future the long-term case might be the exception.

Although many questions still remain unanswered, some of the early fears about PSTT proved to be unfounded. The PSTT approach is helpful with adolescents, who, while they are forming their own identity, are already overly concerned about whether they are normal. Referral to an agency often confirms their worst fears about themselves; the PSTT approach mitigates some of these fears by setting a time limit. This seems to tell the teenager that he is not so badly off, and frees him to work on his problem. The planned time limit forces workers to use their diagnostic acumen in assessing clients and their problems and to formulate appropriate plans for treatment, all within the first session. Workers must make full use of every contact and deal directly and immediately with the material presented by clients. This kind of intensive approach is taxing for workers, but it also defines more realistically what help the agency and worker can offer.

Actual practice has revealed that the appropriateness of a case situation for PSTT and the degree of success in meeting the goal are not determined by the problem or psychiatric diagnosis but rather by (1) the kind of goal for which the client and worker are willing to strive; (2) the positive, intrapsychic, and external factors in the adolescent's and family's life situation which can be utilized in problem solving; and (3) the skill and confidence of the worker. In summary, this was the Youth Service staff's initial learning experience with planned short-term treatment—a practice problem concerning other agencies too—in an attempt to find a new way of delivering services.

The Use of Role Theory in the Treatment of Disturbed Adolescents

Barbara K. Varley

Because of the special nature of the developmental tasks of adolescence, in which the fragility of the ego presents a major problem, the application of social role theory is particularly appropriate in the treatment of disturbed adolescents as a structural basis both for diagnosis and for treatment. Therapeutic principles derived from ego psychology should be utilized, but the simultaneous application of the concepts of social role theory enables the therapist to view the psychodynamics of the disturbed adolescent within a social interactional context and to approach his treatment from this vantage point.

Specifically, the following three major concepts from role theory warrant attention: role, multiple roles, and role conflicts. *Role* can be defined as a pattern of actions either intentionally taught or accidentally learned that are performed by a person in an interactional situation.[1] Implicit in the concept of role are expectations in regard to rights and expectations in regard to obligations, which may be analyzed in both objective and subjective terms. The way in which one enacts a role depends, therefore, on one's perception of the role in relation to others, and faulty role performance can arise from failure to perceive either oneself or others clearly. The enactment of a role becomes further complicated by the fact that each individual has *multiple roles,* the complex of roles associated with the various statuses he occupies.[2] Thus a male adolescent may have, concurrently, the status of son, student, group member, scout, and so forth and be called upon to enact, concurrently, the corresponding roles. Different rights and obligations are associated with the enactment of each specific role, and each role is differentially cathected. Such a complex of multiple roles has, therefore, the potential for *role conflict.*[3] Whereas only one role can be active at any given

---

[1] Theodore R. Sarbin, "Role Theory," in *Handbook of Social Psychology*, Gardner Lindzey (ed.), Addison-Wesley Publishing Co., Reading, Massachusetts, 1959, pp. 225–26.

[2] Robert K. Merton, *Social Theory and Social Structure* (rev. ed.), The Free Press, Glencoe, Illinois, 1957, pp. 369–70.

[3] Charles W. McCann, "Social Role Theory," in *Canada's Mental Health Supplement #25,* January 1962, Mental Health Division, Department of Mental Health and Welfare, Ottawa, Canada, pp. 5–6.

Reprinted from *Social Casework,* Vol. 49 (June, 1968), pp. 362–366, by permission of the author and the Family Service Association of America.

time at the behavioral level, the obligations associated with two or more roles may come into play simultaneously, forcing an individual to make a decision about which role has priority. In addition, "the opportunities for role conflicts are increased . . . due to the increasing specialization of the family, the fragmentation of relationships through multiple institutions and the resulting increase of different roles carried by each person."[4] A teenager may, for example, frequently experience a role conflict in regard to his felt obligations to his peer group, on the one hand, and his parents, on the other, which necessitates a behavioral choice based on a decision about priority.

Identification of the various roles of the patient should enable the therapist to assess the patient's perception of his roles in terms of rights and obligations; to identify conflicts between the patient's perceptions of his roles and the perceptions of those with whom he interacts; and to determine, when the patient has perceived a role correctly, whether or not he is able to execute it appropriately. An assessment of the patient's performance in his various roles should allow the therapist to identify treatment goals and objectives clearly and to establish priorities among them. The therapist and patient can concentrate their efforts on the role in which the patient is demonstrating a breakdown in performance, or they can focus on the roles that are producing the greatest conflict. Improved performance in an important role or resolution of role conflicts should result in a better adjustment in other areas.

Concepts from role theory appear to have particularly valid application in the treatment of adolescents, both because a fragility of ego is characteristic of adolescent years and because the roles of adolescents in our society are poorly defined. The dynamic problems faced by all adolescents are intensified in the disturbed adolescent—defined in this article as one who has failed in establishing ego identity and manifests this failure in feelings of loneliness and self-diffusion.[5] Behaviorally, the lack of a sense of identity is most frequently reflected in a distrust of adults, a loss of peer-group relationships, and a record of performance in school or on the job that is not commensurate with ability, even though it may be adequate. Disturbed adolescents have a low tolerance for frustration and very few, if any, mechanisms for coping with insecurity, anxiety, and fear.[6] Since their former defenses no longer work, adolescents experiment intensely with multiple defenses; as a result they find themselves in a constant state of fluidity, which seriously complicates therapeutic intervention. As Irene Josselyn has indicated, the very nudity of the conflicts revealed by some adolescents is a warning that the ego is too exhausted to build adequate defenses and thus cannot stand the

[4] *Ibid.*, p. 5.

[5] Eveoleen N. Rexford (reporter), "Child Analysis," a panel report centered around Erik H. Erikson's paper "Adolescence and Identity," presented at the Midwinter Meeting of the American Psychoanalytic Association, 1953, *Journal of the American Psychoanalytic Association*, Vol. II, April 1954, p. 328.

[6] Fritz Redl and David Wineman, *Children Who Hate*, The Free Press, Glencoe, Illinois, 1951.

additional strain of disturbing insight.[7] Under such circumstances it seems highly important that the therapeutic intervention be systematically planned, clearly structured, and oriented to the adolescent's present reality.

Diagnosis

In the diagnostic phase the therapist's analysis of the adequacy of the adolescent's role performance—including his perceptions of rights and responsibilities, his execution of them, and his role conflicts—allows the therapist to perceive the sources of the adolescent's discomfort. Such an approach subordinates consideration of the patient's psychosocial developmental history and emphasizes the here and now, which is the more tolerable focus for the adolescent's overburdened ego. An analysis of his multiple roles and role conflicts, however, obviously incorporates an assessment of the dynamic balance among the ego, id, and superego.

Since the execution of any role consists of patterned actions that are learned, this task is obviously a function of the ego. For the disturbed adolescent, ego dysfunction may have precluded earlier role learning and may prevent current role learning. In such cases the adolescent experiences difficulty in determining his rights and obligations in any given relationship and experiences conflict within himself as he struggles with his perceptions of what others expect of him vis-à-vis his ability to meet expectations at a behavioral level. When the disturbed adolescent distrusts adults—which he so frequently does—he cannot use the process of identification as a means of learning adult roles, for identification demands an emotional investment that his feelings of distrust prevent. In addition, a loss of peer relationships by the disturbed adolescent often precludes peers as a source of role-learning for him. Thus, the adolescent's capacity to take on new roles has frequently been seen as an important diagnostic indicator of ego strength.[8]

Because the disturbed adolescent's self-image is diffuse, he has only limited ability to sort out demands made on him by his various roles—as son and as friend, for example—and to establish priorities among roles—that of student versus that of sports participant, for example. He cannot readily discriminate between himself and others or between roles, and he has difficulty in sorting and weighing the rights and obligations associated with his various roles. The degree to which he can make such differentiations and evaluations is an indicator of the level of his ego functioning.

It seems axiomatic that an adolescent who is suffering pronounced intrapsychic conflict will have difficulty in making choices among the obligations associated with his roles, that he will experience role conflict. In turn, his inability to establish priorities intensifies his intrapsychic conflict.

---

[7] Irene Josselyn, "The Ego in Adolescence," *American Journal of Orthopsychiatry,* Vol. XXIV, April 1954, pp. 233–34.

[8] Herbert S. Strean, "Role Theory, Role Models, and Casework: Review of the Literature and Practice Applications," *Social Work,* Vol. XII, April 1967, p. 79.

Thus, the greater the role conflict manifested by the disturbed adolescent, the greater the fragmentation of his ego. The reverse need not necessarily be so, however: that is, a lesser degree of conflict may reflect a faulty perception of roles rather than stronger ego functioning and a greater ability to make choices.

Basically, the roles that require diagnostic evaluation are located on two planes of interaction: primary and secondary. The primary plane of interaction involves, for the adolescent, family and peer-group relationships, whereas the secondary plane involves reference groups—ethnic, cultural, religious, occupational, and so forth. The sources of the adolescent's discomfort are most likely to be located in the primary plane and to be, specifically, either conflicts between peer-group and family roles or dysfunctioning within a given role arising from a faulty perception of rights and responsibilities, as in the role of a son, or an inability to execute appropriate behavior despite clear perception of the role, as in the role of student.

As is apparent, diagnosis is not a delimited operation, but an ongoing process. The diagnostic picture is subject to revision and change based on the adequacy of the adolescent's current perception and performance of his roles.

The Therapeutic Endeavor

Although the therapeutic endeavor with each adolescent is unique and requires individualized management, there are some generic principles for planning and structure. First, the therapist should state explicitly how he views his own role and how he and the adolescent can work together. Second, he should discuss with the adolescent what is expected of him during treatment—the adolescent's role. In addition, the therapist should clarify the structure of the interviews—time, place, duration, and the like. He should discuss his availability for interviews at other times—especially in emergencies, because there are many crises in the life of an adolescent—and his availability by telephone. Some therapists have found that allowing an adolescent to telephone them at home in the evenings or on week ends enhances the development of a working relationship,[9] and, by and large, their experiences have indicated that adolescents generally do not abuse the privilege, though they usually find it necessary to do some initial testing of the new-found warmth and acceptance it implies. When the disturbed adolescent is hospitalized, his response is also more appropriate if the expectations of him within the structured, but tolerant, milieu of the hospital are definite and explicit.

Crucial for the therapeutic aspects of the diagnostic phase is the adolescent's involvement in the evaluation process, including mutuality in the consideration of his role performance. A lack of agreement between therapist and adolescent only adds further discomfort and confusion to that already

[9] Barbara West and Frank T. Rafferty, "Initiating Therapy with Adolescents," *American Journal of Orthopsychiatry*, Vol. XXVIII, July 1958, pp. 627–39.

caused by the adolescent's ego diffusion, whereas agreement provides the adolescent with a beginning sense of direction. On the basis of a shared evaluation, the therapist and patient can, together, identify short-term treatment goals and objectives and establish priorities.

Besides providing a focus for the therapeutic endeavor, the use of role theory in the treatment phase serves a number of different purposes. A disturbed adolescent struggles violently with feelings of insecurity, anxiety, and fear: a permissive treatment orientation has the potential for intensifying such feelings, whereas a mutually agreed-upon treatment focus provides a structural limitation for the adolescent's vacillations. A disturbed adolescent has, at best, a low tolerance for frustration: the application of role theory as a structural base for treatment reduces his feelings of frustration—as he copes, with limited psychological resources, with the unknowns and fears inherent in the problem-solving process. By focusing on the role difficulties of the present, the therapist can protect the adolescent from the strain of achieving insight that may be further disturbing. Thus, treatment intervention based on role theory concepts has the potential for enabling the adolescent to mobilize his ego strengths for the resolution of interactional conflicts. And successful resolution of faulty role perceptions or faulty role enactment leads to a beginning sense of ego identity.

Case Illustration

John, eighteen years of age, was hospitalized for several months while experiencing an acute psychotic episode. Initial exploratory interviews with him indicated that prior to hospitalization he had been experiencing an inability to *perform* in his major roles as son to father, son to mother, member of his peer group, and student in freshman classes. He had been performing more successfully in his roles as brother to sisters and brother to brothers. His capacity to *perceive* the rights and responsibilities associated with his roles was limited and inconsistent, with the result that he experienced confusion, anxiety, and failure. He was least able to perceive his role as son to father. He was best able to perceive his role as student, but his performance was not commensurate with his ability.

Together, the caseworker and John decided to focus primarily on his relationship with his father. Both believed that if he could resolve the conflict he felt in that relationship and achieve a more stable, continuous interaction with his father, difficulties in other roles would diminish. Therefore, many interviews were directed to examining the father's expectations of John and John's expectations of the father and establishing and facilitating communication between them. Thus treatment was focused on their current interaction, John's perception of that interaction, and John's behavioral response in the relationship. As John came to function more adequately in his role as son to father, his performance as student began to improve and his conflicted responses in other roles lessened. Later other roles were identified for closer examination, and John furthered his perception of the expectations involved in them and, thereby, his capacity to fulfill them.

Conclusion

The major advantage of the use of role theory in the treatment of disturbed adolescents is that it provides a system by which priorities in treatment can be established. And establishing treatment priorities with adolescents is especially necessary, for they are already experiencing scatter and vacillation. Moreover, the disturbed adolescent who cannot easily tolerate probing into his developmental history can become positively involved in a therapeutic process that is focused on current realities. At the same time, the clear definition of the roles of the adolescent and the therapist diminishes the threat to the adolescent in their inevitably intense interaction. For the disturbed adolescent, this highly charged interaction has potentially destructive elements, for his ego is not strong enough to tolerate the threat; old defense mechanisms are no longer working and new ones are not yet established. Moreover, if the roles of the adolescent and the therapist are well defined and discussed, the probability that the patient will be able to handle the transference constructively is increased. Such structuring prevents further ego diffusion, which can occur if the adolescent's perception of the therapist and himself is not consistent with reality. The therapist cannot permit himself to be viewed either as a surrogate parent or as friend. He must be and remain what he is, a person who is interested in the adolescent and trained to help him resolve his difficulties. The adolescent must realize that the therapist's concern for him is based on professional regard for him, not personal interest in him.

In summary, role theory can be constructively utilized in the treatment of disturbed adolescents, first, in the diagnostic phase, as a basis for a systematic approach to understanding the adolescent's social milieu, his perception of his interactional complex, and his ability to perform his roles; second, in the treatment phase, as a basis for setting goals and objectives and establishing priorities; and, last, in the interactional process between the therapist and the adolescent, as a structure for controlling transference and countertransference elements.

The need of the disturbed adolescent for role clarification is critical. Inherent in the treatment process there are both the potential for meeting this need specifically and the potential for adding to the adolescent's role confusion and ego diffusion. By maintaining clarity of roles and functions, the therapist can encourage and enable the adolescent to achieve ego identity, to build on his ego strengths, and to discover his own unique self.

Casework Treatment of Delinquents Who Use the Primary Defense of Denial

Alice H. Collins and James R. Mackay

It is accepted today that casework is an essential tool in the treatment of clients in the correctional field and increasingly, caseworkers are finding that practice in this field is rewarding and challenging, calling on the skills they bring from a broad background of training and experience. Conversely, caseworkers with experience in corrections find their understanding of the client who is labeled "delinquent" illuminates their practice in regard to the client who has not been legally delinquent, but whose personality patterns are similar to those seen in the field of corrections.

This paper is based on casework experience with several hundred boys seen at intake, reviewed during their stay at four facilities and seen again at parole and on return for violation of parole. Emerging from this came the belief that there was a group of boys which could be identified, at least in part, by their unwillingness to admit the need for help. Many techniques were tried in an effort to reach these seriously delinquent boys who did not appear to be able to benefit from the program that met the needs of other boys. They were seen as belonging to the group who used the defense of denial in so massive a manner that it appeared to control their entire personality structure.

Forms of Denial

In general, such children are felt to be brazen liars when they are interrogated by the police or appear in court, and are so seen by the general public when their remarks are publicized. The denial of guilt may range from a flat "I wasn't there. . . . I wasn't driving, I was at home when it happened. . . . I didn't do nothing. . . ." to a denial of responsibility, an admission that the act might have occurred but that he was not a willing participant and therefore, not guilty. "He made me do it. . . . I just seem to pick the wrong kids to hang around with. . . . He said it was his car. . . . How should I know it was stolen? I was drunk. . . ."

Such statements may be what the public believes them to be—lies to

Reprinted with permission of the authors and the National Association of Social Workers, from *Social Work*, Vol. 4, No. 1 (January, 1959), pp. 34–43.

avoid punishment—yet to the professional eye and ear there is a difference between them, although it is not an easy difference to delineate. It rests, perhaps, in the voice and expression of the child making the statement in that he does not show the avoidance of glance, change in color, involuntary physical movements of the person suppressing or distorting the truth. He is wide-eyed and inappropriately calm and open in manner. He shows a different picture from the child who is lying because, actually, he is not lying—he is telling the truth as it appears to his conscious mind.

In his thinking, it follows logically that if he did not commit any offense, he needs no help now toward avoiding trouble in the future. Sometimes he makes it clear that he will not accept help because he should not be under the care of the agency in the first place, and, in fact, has no problems but the false ones of which he is accused. The more the offense is discussed in an attempt to establish a base for the need for help, the firmer becomes his denial of such need.

The child may use more subtle means to ward off help by agreeing that the offense was serious, that he should not have been involved but that he does not need to discuss it further because the whole experience "has been a lesson to him" and he will never again be guilty. He may use phrases gleaned from previous contacts with social workers and relatives to point out that he recognizes that no one can help him—he must help himself and he intends to do so. There is nothing really wrong with him now, he made a mistake in the past. He knows that and he will make no more in the future. Sometimes he may go on to describe his new-found conscience, his clear understanding of right and wrong, and his appreciation of the offer for help which he has demonstrated he does not need. It is not unusual for such conversations to take place even as the authorities are investigating a repetition of the first offense.

Even if the offense is not discussed by the caseworker and help is offered without reference to the authoritative setting which brings the child to the attention of the worker, the same tactics are met, though perhaps differently used. In the face of the most rejecting and demoralizing home situations that the child knows are known to the caseworker, he may assert that he does not need help from an "outsider" because his parents have been so good to him "they gave me everything" and conditions will be entirely satisfactory to him once he is free of the present restraints. Some of this applies to school where he did well, and to his relationship with his friends, who all liked him. Why, then, should he need the help the caseworker offers?

One other form that denial takes is seen more recently among the older children who are intelligent and who have been seen earlier in childhood by mental health agencies or have had access to books or television and movies concerning mental illness. Such children may acknowledge the act they have committed as being wrong and ask for a "psychiatrist," pointing out that since they are clearly mentally ill, they are not responsible. If treatment is then attempted in response to the request for help, it rapidly develops that the child wants to be cured from "outside," by a kind of psychological magic while his defense against his real feelings remains intact.

As has been reported by other investigators,[1] these are children who have known early experiences with rejecting, variable parents who have been unable to give them the consistent gratification that would have served to relieve their primary anxiety; at the same time their external environment has been threatening through the actual deprivation of essential physical care. The majority of such children have experienced loss of even such poor parental figures as they had—either through desertion, death or social action—and have experienced such loss more than once.[2]

The unrelieved anxiety so generated would overwhelm the weak ego if it permitted itself to feel it fully so that the ego has resorted to denial in order to defend itself and survive. Such denial may take one of two forms—fantasy and word and act.[3]

Most children give up this defense as the ego grows more able to cope with the anxiety aroused by internal and external stimuli, but children for whom the rewards of parental love are withheld and for whom the demands of reality are too harsh may cling to this defense or regress to it. The children under discussion here, because of the nature of the internal and external climate in which they grew up, were not able to develop to as high a level of ego functioning as is normal. They have continued to use denial as a defense so that it has become increasingly impregnable as the anxieties of their reality increased with the years.

Method of Treatment

While often the defense has served so well that there appear to be no signs of it, it must be constantly borne in mind that the anxiety is still there. Thus, in treatment, when anxiety is aroused, it is to be expected that the defense of denial will be mobilized, since this is the chief way which the ego has perfected for protecting itself. For casework success, an approach must be made to the problem of lowering anxiety if the defense is to be modified or abandoned for one which does not restrict the personality to a primitive level of development. Such an approach is made when the caseworker, as a result of the diagnostic appraisal, attempts to meet the child in the

[1] Beatrice R. Simcox and Irving Kaufman, M.D., "Treatment of Character Disorders in Parents of Delinquents," *Social Casework*, Vol. 37, No. 8 (October 1956), pp. 388–395.

——, "Handling of Early Contacts with Parents of Delinquents," *Social Casework*, Vol. 37, No. 9 (November 1956), pp. 443–450.

Also see Fritz Redl and David Wineman, *The Aggressive Child* (New York: The Free Press, 1957); August Aichorn, *Wayward Youth* (New York: Meridian Books, 1953).

[2] Irving Kaufman, "Three Basic Sources for Predelinquent Character," *The Nervous Child*, Vol. 11, No. 1 (October 1955), pp. 12–15.

[3] Anna Freud, *The Ego and the Mechanisms of Defense* (New York: International Universities Press, 1946), p. 89.

area that is of the greatest concern to him—in the difficulties he is having in maintaining his homeostasis. If this appears to overemphasize the importance of the defense, it is because this is precisely what the child himself is doing.

The method of treatment described below as having some measure of success with such children consists in the modification of the external reality and the restoration of loss to the point where anxiety is reduced. This is accomplished through the relationship of the child and the caseworker who presents himself as a kind, accepting, and consistently controlling parent figure. The relationship is dependent on the quality of the reality experience the child is having at the same time. The caseworker must see to it that, simultaneously with the development of the relationship, the reality is manipulated to contribute to the conditions of gratification which are necessary to these children. The duration of the treatment varies with the degree of ego damage but it is rarely accomplished in a short time.

As in every casework situation, a dynamic diagnosis is essential to successful treatment. If interviewing and testing reveal denial to be a major defense, the caseworker must consider in what ways it is used and how far it has restricted the ego, so that he may estimate the anxiety and depression that he knows are present and gauge the likelihood of the modification of such behavior. It must be borne in mind that if the defense of denial in fantasy persists too long, serious mental illness may result.

Whether the caseworker arrives at the diagnosis alone or with the help of other professional disciplines, he must now make a treatment plan that will take into account how best to help the child who refuses to admit his need. Nor is it sufficient to make plans for casework treatment alone. It is also necessary that the reality conditions of his life be made to contribute to his treatment. It is important for the caseworker who sees him in the institutional setting to make sure that the daily program of the child is interesting to him and offers some immediate rewards for good behavior, limitations upon loss of control, and an opportunity to succeed.

As casework proceeds, the worker needs to maintain a warm, accepting attitude but avoids agreeing with the denial. He accepts it as real to the client and may also, without contradiction or being punitive or insistent, state the attitude of society as personified by the judge, the police, and the probation officer. He does not try to "prove anything" but makes his position on the side of adult authority plain.[4] This is most difficult in the frequent cases where the caseworker recognizes that because of family background, cultural prejudices, and other handicaps, the child "never had a chance." His empathy for the child may lead him into resentment against the authority figures involved and the expression of this.[5]

[4] Martin Falsberg, "Setting Limits with the Juvenile Delinquent," *Social Casework*, Vol. 38, No. 3 (March 1957), pp. 138–142.

[5] Elliot Studt, "The Contribution of Correctional Practice to Social Work Theory and Education," *Social Casework*, Vol. 37, No. 6 (June 1956), pp. 263–269.

Three Cases

Jack was an illegitimate child, his mother having been committed to a school for the feebleminded immediately following his birth and not released until he was 12 years old. He lived in a succession of foster homes, none for more than two years, up to the time of his commitment to a training school at 13. Although he was found to have average intelligence, he had been in special classes most of his school life.

At 13, he came to the attention of the court, shortly after his return to his mother on her release. He was committed on the second offense and had spent some time in two training schools with brief paroles home. Repetition of the offense and one long and one short runaway during which he was involved in homosexual offenses with an older man led to his commitment to a closed training school. He was seen weekly by a caseworker over a period of fifteen months, at which time he was paroled.

Jack maintained that he was "sent away for nothing" for most of the first interviews. He minimized every offense, characterizing the pocket-book snatch from an old woman and the destruction of property as boyish pranks done with his friends. When the caseworker continued to point out the reality of his appearances in court, especially as a partner in frequent homosexual acts with the same man, he indignantly exclaimed, "Somebody committed an unnatural act on me . . . I didn't commit an unnatural act on him!"

During these early weeks, Jack was unable to conform to the rules of the training school. He wandered about where he knew he would be caught. While his infractions of the rules were punished, an effort was also made to find something in the program to interest him. This was difficult since he expressed no preferences and would participate in any placement only as far as he had to. He finally showed some interest in music and was accepted by the music teacher as a drum student, a placement he enjoyed and worked at.

Bob was committed when he was 12 for participating in a series of breaks into stores and gas stations. He was 15 when he was seen and on his second stay at the training school, having been returned for a second series of breaks, the last one involving $1,200. He was the only child of his mother's second marriage; he had an older brother who was married and in another city, and an older sister in a state mental hospital. His parents were divorced when he was 9 years old because of his father's drinking and extramarital affairs, the same reason for which his mother had divorced her first husband. His mother was a waitress in a nightclub and was said to drink to excess and to have a boyfriend of poor reputation.

In the early interviews, Bob did not minimize his guilt; in fact, he added details not known to the police. He pointed out repeatedly that while on his first parole he had been "mixed up," now he was all straightened out and there was no reason why he should not go home and "keep out of trouble." He maintained that the only problem he had was "how soon I can get out of here and go home"; he knew he could get and keep a job where his mother worked, everything would be all right, and there was nothing he wanted or needed to discuss with the caseworker.

In the institution he was involved in two violent fights with another boy and then he virtually isolated himself for some time, not talking or playing with other boys, volunteering for extra work with the avowed intention of "keeping out of trouble and getting home."

Tony was committed at 16 for an assault on a woman, for staying away from home nights and for being a "stubborn child," having been unknown to the courts until he was 14. His mother died when he was 3 years old and after some time in the homes of relatives, his father remarried and took him to live with him, the stepmother, an older brother, and younger stepbrother. At the time of Tony's commitment, the brother had married and left the home. Tony's father was interested in him but could not withstand the force of the stepmother's dislike of the boy and her insistence that he or she must leave the home. Tony had above-average intelligence, did quite well in school, and had musical talents. He impressed people as a most attractive boy.

He admitted his offenses and his trouble with his stepmother without apparent affect, but insisted that in the future he could and would return home and avoid difficulty. "If somebody starts getting on my neck or something, now I just walk away." He professed to like all the staff of the training school, and indicated that he understood himself very well and needed no casework help.

In the institution he was pleasant, compliant, and was given privileged placements as well as a leading part in the school play.

As in every casework relationship, as the interviews continue the worker accepts the material the client now begins to bring in and evaluates it in terms of its use to the client. It is likely now that the client will test out the caseworker in small, unobtrusive ways concerning the keeping of appointments, his attitude toward other members of the staff and other boys, the confidentiality of the interview (which the client will test out over and over again), and his willingness to be too acquiescent about the client's negative expressions toward others. The extreme ambivalence of the boy toward authority and the concomitant elements of control in the authority relationship are clearly seen at this time. It might be said that in a sense the child is trying to prove to himself that it would be foolish and unsafe to lower his defenses, to trust this person, and that he can only continue to survive as long as he denies his own ability to grow up and relate to reality as more than a very young child. Thus, the client presents himself on the one hand as a dependent child, passively wishing help, and then as an independent, aggressive individual not in need of help and questioning the motivation of the social worker who wants to help him.

In effect, the client at this time is in a very painful situation. He desperately fears to discover that this relationship, like all others he has known, will lead to loss, pain, and the renewal of the feelings of helplessness and loss against which he initially defended. At the same time, his testing behavior on the surface implies the converse—that he does not wish help and has little interest whether treatment continues or stops. However, within the relationship, he has found what he has wanted in a parent figure. If he lowers his defenses and lets himself become really involved with this person, he is vulnerable again to the pain of loss and the depression it engendered.

It is at this point in the treatment process that little progress is apparent. There is repetition of earlier material and the client appears to be unwilling or unable to move into new areas. The interviews are marked by a bored attitude on the part of the client, who makes it clear that he is there only under duress. There is a constant fencing on the part of the client, or at best, admissions and insights which prove on examination to be superficial— merely new angles of a well-tried defensive system.

In the face of this apparent impasse, the social worker may feel that nothing of importance has been accomplished except, perhaps, the perfection of the defensive system of the client. If the case is terminated at this point, there is almost the assurance that the delinquency, or a similar one, will be repeated. The child will appear to be the type of offender whom one sees categorized as bad, unteachable, not willing or able to profit from treatment, and consequently only to be reached through punishment. In actuality, it may be said that the child is fearful of moving deeper into a relationship that would expose him to a repetition of an earlier experience against which he is highly defended. The child must be allowed to continue to test the relationship, with the caseworker helping by remaining a constant figure and pointing out the reality of the relationship to the client.

Same Defense but Subtle Change

The caseworker will soon note that a subtle change has come into the client's behavior. While he uses the same defenses as heretofore, there is a new quality in this phase of the treatment process that is difficult to define or describe. For a period of time, there has been defiance in the denial—anger, rigidity in voice and manner. What is now apparent is perhaps analogous to that moment in the blind, raging temper tantrum of the young child when the alert parent senses that the fear and anger have blown themselves out and the continuing uproar means "Help me to stop!"

This same indescribable change seems to come into the relationship between the worker and the child. While the child maintains the same outward attitude of rejecting help, he comes to the interview with more enthusiasm, he smiles more often, he may "kid" with the worker, get angry or "fresh" with him, use more obscenity, and be more truly communicative. It is as though he were trying out the new relationship, but he is quick to retreat to the earlier position behind his defenses if any pressure is applied.

Excerpts from an interview with Jack, after thirteen months of weekly meetings, are given here. His progress in the institution had been very stormy although the administration had tried to recognize even small gains.

CASEWORKER: What have you been doing this week?
JACK: Nothing.
CW: What?
JACK: You heard me. Nothing. . . .
CW: Were there some things you didn't want to talk about?
JACK: Not necessarily.
CW: *Are* there some things?
JACK: You asked the same question twice and you'll get the same answer twice—not necessarily!
CW: I was hoping the second time I'd get a different answer! (*Both laugh.*)
JACK: I wouldn't say there were some things I don't want to talk about . . . it doesn't bother me. . . . I just don't care. . . . (*yawns*). . . . I didn't sleep much

last night. (*Here follows an involved story about listening to a friend's borrowed radio.*) I wish I could get one from somewhere of my own. I ain't writing to my cousin no more.

cw: Why not?

JACK: Huh

cw: Why not?

JACK: Ah, she's full of s——, always feeding me that stuff . . . what do I care? . . . don't make no difference to me.

cw: What does she say?

JACK: She's always telling me "You can't go home." What is she telling me that for? I don't care. . . .

cw: Why?

JACK: I don't know. She says my mother's still sick over the last time. (*weak laugh*) . . .

cw: Did you ask her if you could go there?

JACK: (*softly, yawning*) Yeah. About a thousand times. I'm sick of it. When I get out . . . I'm not going to live there. I wouldn't live there.

For several interviews, Bob began by saying everything was "peaches and cream," but when the caseworker pointed out to him that he was spending most of his energy *not* thinking about the things that troubled him, he was able to talk about his early memories of his father whose early life, he had heard, was "just like me," shifting quickly again to statements about his boredom with the interviews. In the institutional program, his behavior was well under control and he was given some cottage responsibilities and played on a cottage basketball team.

Tony came to the interviews pleasantly and on time. He discussed what he professed to have heard his cottage master say—that "They are getting rid of this school soon," and that if he wished, he could ask the court to transfer him to an adult prison which he thought would be a much better place to "serve his time." He was still convinced that he would get into no more difficulties when he returned home because now his stepmother understood him better and wanted him. He mentioned talking all this over with his cottage master who agreed that he had "learned his lesson." He continued to have excellent behavior reports although he made no special friends among the boys.

Relaxation of Defenses

The caseworker is now at a crucial point in the treatment process and one most difficult for him. As the client gradually feels able to move deeper into the relationship in the direction in which he has been slowly moving over the past several months, there is a relaxation of the defenses. Within the safety of the treatment situation, the client is able to recognize that there is a pattern in his previous behavior and that this defensive structure has meaning for him. As the child is now faced with material that previously was inaccessible, he becomes highly anxious and the depressive feelings that have been buried are now felt directly. This is a stormy time in the relationship— the client often refuses to talk to the caseworker, accuses him of all kinds of deceptions, sets traps to demonstrate his unreliability, or refuses to come to interviews at all. He appears to be using every possible way of provoking the caseworker to reject him and terminate this painful period of beginning growth. He is almost in the position of a man, very painfully hurt in an accident, who begs his rescuers not to touch him because he cannot face the pain of healing.

At this interview Jack had flagrantly violated rules and had to be restricted to his room. He expressed disgust at seeing the caseworker and maintained that there was nothing to talk about, nothing was bothering him. When the caseworker refused to accept this, Jack countered by telling him of some of his homosexual activity in the training school which was not known to the administration, talking about it in a tone calculated to show how little he cared to conform to the standards he knew were acceptable and clearly provoking the caseworker to anger and rejection. The caseworker expressed his displeasure with such behavior, said he hoped it was thing of the past now and left, reminding Jack that he would see him next week.

For six interviews Bob's responses were monosyllabic—he had no problems, he found the interviews boring. In answer to any question he said, "I don't know." He said he saw no sense in coming to the interviews and wondered if "somebody" was working to prevent his parole, going on to accuse the caseworker directly of telling his cottage master about some drinking Bob had confided in the caseworker. To a question about what he wanted to talk about at one of these interviews, the reply was "Nothing."

At this time, he was refused parole home because of his mother's drinking, and when the caseworker tried to talk to him about that, he replied, "If she drinks, she drinks. It's got nothing to do with me."

He was having many arguments with the cottage personnel.

Tony continued to talk of his wish to go home and said, "My father says it'd be different if I come home now." The caseworker asked, "What does he mean?" Tony replied: "He said he was going to talk to her" (*stepmother*). Tony had a weekend at home and reported it as "perfect." While he insisted that he had no worries other than whether and when he would be permitted to return home, he was always polite and changed the subject frequently rather than refusing to answer the caseworker's questions.

The caseworker told Tony that he was going to be away on army training for two weeks. Tony appeared hardly to hear this but a moment later exploded into a long diatribe about the people at the training school who "leave you alone and don't talk to you," ostensibly centering on the administration's withholding final information about his return home. That night he made an unprovoked attack on a boy so hard that the boy had to be hospitalized. Since this was completely out of keeping with his usual behavior, the administration was inclined to believe his story that it was accidental and he was not punished.

Beginning of Emotional Growth

If the worker is strong enough to weather the final period of testing out described above and perseveres through it, he encounters the depression that the lowered defenses now allow to break through, flooding the ego with the threat of potential loss, of helplessness and pain. The client blames the caseworker for his unhappiness and at the same time clings to him in an acute dependent relationship. It is often difficult for the caseworker to deal with his own feelings of guilt at this point since he may feel that he has brought about too much suffering. He may also be concerned that the client may be permanently fixed in his dependence on him.

If, however, he can accept the client's feelings as a sign of positive growth, he will find that this stage does rapidly move over into that of growth in a more emotionally mature fashion. It is, indeed, rewarding after months of sparring and constant gains and losses, to see the client begin at last to show insight, to make appropriate sexual identifications, and to demonstrate the beginning of a useful superego development.

It is vital at this time in treatment that the external reality also prove rewarding to the client, since it is against the reality that the defense was erected in the first place. In the institution, it is important that progress be rewarded with tangible evidences of the pleasure of the staff in the boy's increasing maturity. Exception to institutional routines should, if possible, be made for the boy at this time and should be explained as resulting from a recognition of him as a more responsible individual. If possible, the reality of the community to which he will return should be made attractive to him, and if this is not possible, he should be helped to find resources there which are ready to help him as he needs them. Tangible rewards, letters, and visits will be more meaningful than words or a passive willingness to accept his application for help.

In the final interviews, Jack talked of his feelings when he had been confined to his room.
JACK: I don't like to be in my room.
CW: You'd rather be in the program?
JACK: I don't like to be in my room, period. . . .
CW: What happens when you are?
JACK: Nothing happens—I just get restless and bored. . . . When I got at this point anywhere else, I ran away.
He discussed the fact that he was trying to keep himself free of homosexual involvements and the manner in which he had found the staff, formerly seen as implacable enemies, as able to help him.
CW: You mean you are afraid you will get involved with him? (*a homosexual boy whom Jack has described as "a jerk" whom he hates*)
JACK: That's right, you hit it on the nose. . . . I just pay no attention. . . .
CW: Because if you did, you're afraid—
JACK: I'm not afraid to get into trouble. I just don't want to have anything to do with him, period. If I get into trouble or not . . . He's got a lot of kids into trouble.
CW: The masters know?
JACK: They know, don't worry. They ain't stupid either. . . . One day he was in his room and I was trading funny books with him and I had a whole stack of funny books and Mr. C came over and he said, "Jack, I know you was having nothing to do with him—just trading books—I know," he says, "just pay no attention to him and you won't get into trouble!" I says, "I was just getting books" and he says, "I know!" He wasn't telling me like—you know—me and Mr. C get along good.
CW: So you're trying to keep away from D?
JACK: That's what I'm trying to do *most*.

Bob started the interview by saying that he wouldn't mind going to live with his brother if his mother would come too, because in his home town there was "nobody to hang around with but kids that have been in trouble, just hang around with a couple of them and before you know it, you're in trouble again." From this, he went into an angry account of the cottage relief matron he could not adjust to, and the caseworker accepted his angry feelings. At the next interview, he talked of his decision to go to his brother's house although his mother would not join them now, and went on to talk about his mother's drinking, saying that she always drank some, "like everybody else" except when he got in trouble and then it got worse. And he went on to say that she told him his father had taught her to drink—repeating his belief that he was just like his father. In the last interview, before he left for his brother's home, he discussed realistic plans for work and school, expressed some fears about the trip, and about making new, nondelinquent friends, and accepted reassurance in a mature manner. He followed out his plans and continued to do well.

When the caseworker came back from his trip, Tony hastened to tell him about the assault "accident" although he mentioned he had not told his father. He admitted to some worries about how things were going to go when he reached home and said he thought he would like to have "someone to talk to" when he left.

Because of his excellent institutional record, he was permitted to go to a work placement where he did so well he was "rewarded" by being allowed to go home at his urgent request and without consultation with the caseworker. Two months later he was returned for violation of parole because of two "unarmed assaults."

As with other such personality disorders, it is inevitable that regressions will occur when the conditions which caused the original difficulty are reactivated, as they often are in the difficult reality situations in which most of these clients must live. Loss of a friendly employer, a change in caseworker, the removal of a friend, all may bring a recurrence of the depression and a remobilization of the early defense against it. For this reason, such clients should be continued in some contact with their caseworkers for as long a time as possible after active treatment is terminated. If this is done, or if the worker to whom the case is assigned in a new agency understands the long road the client has traveled before, such regression can frequently be used for additional insights as the client comes to realize that he has not really "lost everything." No claims are made that such clients will be able to function as freely and with as great a degree of maturity as those whose early lives were not so severely traumatized. But they can function adequately, with a degree of happiness to themselves and safety to the community.

Summary

Clients who use the primitive defense of denial are frequently seen on correctional caseloads where they are placed by authoritative agencies.

To work successfully with such clients, the caseworker needs to recognize that this defense is held against the pervading depression felt by the client who has known early loss and rejection and who controls the resulting anxiety created by his reality situation by denying it and resisting any relationship which may cause a repetition of the early experience. Because the client is reacting against reality, it is essential that during treatment the environment be made as consistent and rewarding as possible.

The cases studied were institutionalized boys in training schools for delinquents. In treatment, the caseworker presented himself as a warm, accepting, consistent adult, identified with authority but not involved with institutional management. Treatment was carried on this basis for a long period of testing out on the part of the client who appeared to need to fend off the relationship he actually longed for, for fear of the loss which relationship had brought him in his earlier experiences. When treatment was continued in spite of his denial of need, and the environment was used positively, a period of depression followed the lowering of the defense and the beginning of emotional growth. Such growth was rapid and with the development of a more mature defensive system, the depression was greatly alleviated so that the client was enabled to live comfortably and safely in the community.

Our Outcast Youth

Gisela Konopka

In 1966 there were 51,000 young people in public institutions for delinquents, a 16 percent increase over 1964. It is not only the number of institutionalized youngsters that is alarming; it is their complete state of dependency and the stripping away of their self-respect during their confinement.

> "When I was placed in a detention center, I was told to strip and take a shower. I had to do it in the presence of the matron and two male attendants," explained a girl.
>
> "Ha!" laughed a counselor in an institution for older adolescent boys. "We fixed him when we caught him after he ran away. He lost his pants."
>
> "I just won't keep quiet," spit out an angry and fiery 14-year-old girl. "Even if they put me in isolation again for ten days like last time."

In the late fall of 1968 a 13-year-old Indian boy hung himself in a jail where he had been kept in solitary confinement for six weeks. His crime had been to run away from home and become involved in a car theft. Excuses for his long isolation were made on legal grounds: the law requires that a youngster be segregated from adult prisoners and be held until both parents can meet together with the officials—but the boy's parents were separated. There was and is no recourse for these children.

Solitary confinement and degrading practices have gone on for a long time. Books have been written about them. Standards have been set. Once in a while certain treatment techniques appear and are hailed as panaceas— "guided group interaction," "milieu therapy," "behavioral conditioning," and so on. Yet the total situation does not really change.

We frequently do not build on past experiences. For far too long a constant seesaw between "permissiveness" and "treating them rough" has been permitted. It is necessary once and for all to clarify our goals on the grounds of our knowledge and experiences and translate these goals into tangible practice.

Present Practice and Historical Precedents

There is a great deal of talk about institutions as treatment facilities. Let us look first at the present state of these institutions and how the general public and many professionals view them.

Reprinted with permission of the author and the National Association of Social Workers, from *Social Work,* Vol. 15, No. 4 (October, 1970), pp. 76–86.

Most institutions for delinquents are located in rural areas removed from the centers of professional services that are considered necessary for these young people. Sentence to an institution is usually expressed in terms of removal from the community. When the youth is released from the institution, he is said to be "returned to the community."

What does all this mean? It means the intentional casting out of a human being. The only parallel of similar treatment is in leper colonies and mental institutions. Hospitals that treat physical illness are within the community, and in recent years a real attempt has been made to attach units for mental patients to them. This is not the case with institutions for delinquents except for a few private centers that are usually classified as institutions for the emotionally disturbed.

The casting-out concept is based on the long and disastrous history of corrections and institutions for delinquents. It is also related to the common historical concept of delinquency as a willful act committed by a "bad" person.

In ancient times treatment of the adult or juvenile delinquent was based on the accepted concept of retaliation. There were no correctional institutions. Retaliation meant physical punishment that supposedly was related to the deed (usually mutilation in some form). At times retaliation meant compensation of the victim or his relatives by the offender. A third form was banishment, sometimes as slave labor. Almost until modern times some European countries transported criminals to colonies for penal service or placed them on penal islands such as France's Devil's Island or Australia when it was colonized by the English. Imprisonment was actually used in those periods only for detention.

In the Middle Ages the concept of correctional institutions was related to the philosophy of the Church in relation to man. The Church did not necessarily ask for punishment, but it did ask for penance. Early prisons resembled monasteries, with cells, bare cots, and occasional flagellation. (Is it not strange and tragic that we are still using these same forms in the twentieth century?)

Protestantism stressed hard work as necessary for redemption and so the concept of work, especially hard labor, entered these institutions. Many of the practices still found in both adult and juvenile institutions had their origin in the way religious groups saw the road to redemption. The system of silence (especially at meals), which is still observed in some institutions for juvenile delinquents, and the continued use of solitary confinement (to "give them time to think") stem from the view of the gentle Quakers, who saw silence as essential to salvation.

Removal from the community was therefore only partially based on a wish to punish the individual. In earlier times it was seen as the only way to protect society from dangerous elements and to redeem the individual for an eternal life.

The Industrial Revolution brought other changes. Correctional institutions were a source of cheap labor and high profits for manufacturers who used inmates to help keep down the rising labor movement with its demand for higher wages. At the same time the expanding economy demanded that such institutions become self-supporting. This meant that in a rural country such as the United States was then, institutions had to have farms and produce their own food. There are still adult and juvenile institutions that have adjoining farms, although for several decades it has been known that such work does nothing to rehabilitate city youngsters.

Another strong influence on institutions was the form of military discipline perfected by the Prussians in the late eighteenth century. The Prussian court developed a highly disciplined army from a conglomeration of people, mainly in two ways: (1) a total obliteration of individuality by the utmost uniformity in clothing, barracks living, and drill and (2) the maximum use of fear as a motivating force—severe beatings, incarceration, and isolation. Total obedience to absolute authority was demanded.

Change in the treatment of delinquents came with the establishment of the juvenile court, the first of which was established in Chicago in 1899 and was concerned primarily with neglected children. Many of the children in correctional institutions were not delinquent in the modern sense, but children who had been neglected and were institutionalized for their own protection. In that period foster homes and other forms of treatment like parole and probation were born. Yet in general, the institutions themselves continued to retain many of the physical characteristics of the penal institutions of earlier times as well as absolute obedience to authority. The young people stayed in institutions until they became adults and could be placed for employment, usually totally broken or consumed with deep hatred and bitterness.

Twentieth-Century Changes

The twentieth century, often called the "Century of the Child," brought new insights that had some influence on institutions for juvenile delinquents. In some instances more child- or youth-centered activities were introduced, as was the concept of education of the delinquent. It was thought that by teaching the child good habits and specific school and work skills, he could be rehabilitated. Training workshops were added. The designation "training school" is a result of this approach. It was based on the theory that the human being is a cognitive person and a creature of habit. There was some understanding of the impact of the milieu, but this was predominantly viewed as the physical environment.

Muckrakers in America and reformers in Europe attacked the slums— the crowded, ugly urban living situation—as the breeding ground of delinquency. To provide healthier surroundings, new institutions continued to segregate the delinquent, but were built on spacious grounds and cottage-type living quarters replaced mass dormitories.

This period was followed closely by a revolution in the understanding of the human being. Freud and his followers stressed the significance of instincts, human behavior partially based on unconscious motivations, and the immense importance of learning to handle instincts in a positive way rather than in neurotic or acting-out behavior. The major educational or treatment tools were seen as being intensive individual contact with the person in need of help or change and active participation of the patient in understanding the dynamics of his own behavior. It was Freud's deep concern for the inviolate dignity of the individual that insisted on this kind of participation rather than on acceptance of authoritarian edicts or omniscient manipulation by an outsider. Some of Freud's pupils, especially Adler, added to this basic theory an understanding of the significance of the peer in addition to the person in authority. Adler therefore stressed the group as an important treatment tool.

In his writing the sociologist Georg Simmel foreshadowed the theory of modern social group work. He too stressed the importance of participation in decision-making. Experiments in self-government were made in some institutions for delinquents, such as the George Junior Republic, founded in Freeville, New York, in 1895.

Unfortunately World War I interrupted the beginning of this enlightened era, making international communication among reformers impossible. The militaristic mood supported forces that wanted conformity, obedience, and discipline in institutions. After the war toppled the monarchies that had brought it about, strong forces supported by political power began reforms in government, education, and correctional institutions, especially those for youths.

The Reform Movement

Before 1918 German institutions, as well as the country's total educational system, had been based on the model of the Prussian army and a caste and class system. Reaction to this was strong. Almost every program that is today considered progressive or innovative was instituted during this period. Unfortunately no evaluative surveys were made because research techniques were limited at that time. Yet simple indexes such as the number of runaways in a specific institution show clearly that the methods of the reform movement had a positive impact.

The reformers' concept of the institution was as an educational and therapeutic community. They tried to combine the individual influence of an adult who respected young people with a total, stimulating, warm environment in which the students (as they were called rather than inmates) were encouraged to help each other. Art, music, and drama were deemed as important as therapeutic discussions. The reformers especially rejected the concept of the outcast. Parents, boyfriends, and girlfriends were invited into the institution so that the youngster never felt totally separated from his environment. The aim was not retaliation, redemption, protection, or strict obedience.

Karl Wilker, director of the Lindenhof (formerly one of the most notorious institutions for delinquents in Berlin) and one of the great reformers of that period, expressed the institution's aim and its rationale in a few short paragraphs:

> The Lindenhof was a beginning for the realization of human brotherhood, was a seedling toward a community of human beings, was a cell of a reborn human organism. . . . There was a strong belief that something different was possible, that one could move in a new direction in delinquency treatment which is not punishment or retribution, not a poor substitution for school or a poor substitution for the parents. . . . That it could be: a true school for life, and education that provides an opportunity for development of human potential. . . .
>
> One cannot base this direction as previously on the concepts of "waywardness" or "dangerous youth." And one cannot base it on the concepts of "inborn goodness" or "evil." The base can only be the young person himself and, today, usually the deprived child because this is the child we meet. . . .[1]

One of the major aspects of this program was that staff and students were seen as equals, as friends who had to develop mutual trust. Compare this with still-prevailing practices. The following is taken from a recent letter from a young man who has gone through the delinquency institutions and prisons:

> Perhaps I am guilty of overgeneralization, but out of the context of my current environment, it is my observation and guarded conclusion that, for the most part at any rate, a "Holier Than Thou" philosophy seems to be characteristic of the general correctional atmosphere. Needless to say, this enforced "caste system" between inmates and professional staff is not especially conducive to harmonious relationships. Nor does it breed the trust, confidence and respect that is necessary if any real, worthwhile rehabilitative processes are to be accomplished. Of course, it would be redundant for me to say that this dilemma is strictly confined to the institutional environment. We know that it isn't. I do think, however, that the very nature of confinement tends to intensify rebellious attitudes towards authority and, to a large degree, the reinforcement and exaggeration of pre-existing attitudes are made just that much more chronic. What I'm trying to say is that you don't train a dog by placing him in a cage and poking sticks at him. I honestly do think that the greatest obstacle to be overcome in the area of corrections is the problem of communication between inmates and staff. I am unable to suggest how this might best be accomplished or what alternatives may be available. What I am able to predict with a certain degree of certainty is that little progress is likely to be made in the area of inmate-staff relationships until it is recognized that inmates are human beings rather than statistics. Enough said!

The reformers of the 1920s definitely understood that to achieve any change the total human being has to become involved. That means one cannot direct oneself only to the brain or to the emotions or simply to automatic imitation of certain behavior. One must address oneself to the total human being in his interaction with others. Wilker and his associates addressed themselves in treatment to the present situation of the young person, helping him to gain hope through tangible possibilities in the future and to gain insight by some view of the past.

[1] Karl Wilker, "*Fursorgeerziehung als Lebensschulung, Ein Aufruf zur Tat,*" *Die Lebensschule* (Berlin), Heft 3 (1921).

In Germany itself these amazing reform movements were totally destroyed by the advent of the Nazis, who brought a return to the concept of inherent badness and therefore to the system of the outcast and conformity through strict obedience. In some European countries such as in Scandinavia and in a few isolated places in England, the reform movement approach continued.

Institutions Today

In the United States no such political upheaval as the 1917 and 1918 revolutions occurred. Institutional treatment of juvenile delinquents represented through all these years a conglomerate of all the historical concepts, with occasional spurts of "innovations" that in reality were not new.

Delinquency institutions today—with few exceptions—manifest practices based on the concepts of retaliation, redemption through work or silence, strict obedience enforced through military-type discipline, protection through custodial care, education through provision of mostly vocational and often outdated training, sometimes individual or group therapy unrelated to the rest of the milieu, and especially an overall separation from the community. Here is a quote from a newspaper report:

> Mary was scheduled to go home last Friday. But she wasn't told and she ran away from the school the previous weekend.
>
> Two days later, school authorities found her at a friend's house. Now she may not be released for six more months.
>
> Mary is 12, quite pretty but nervous. . . .
>
> "Let me tell you a secret. I'm not going to be here tomorrow. I'm spending Christmas at home, even if I have to spend another year here."
>
> Mary said her father had just gotten home from three years in Stillwater Prison and, "I want to see him."[2]

Both the school (institutional) authorities and the girl base their actions on the premises of retaliation and removal from the community.

The same day that the newspaper article appeared—December 25, 1968—the newspapers were headlining the extraordinary feat of man's circling the moon. What made this possible?

1. The capacity and willingness of scientists to discard old concepts when proved ineffective or based on incorrect premises.

2. The constant, patient building on knowledge derived from many different sources and many different people.

3. Teamwork of thousands of individuals and organizations.

4. No fads begun by throwing out catchy phrases.

[2] *Minneapolis Star*, December 25, 1968, p. 1C.

5. Experimentation with sharp and honest evaluation.

6. Enough money to make such a complex venture possible.

Delving into the secrets of human behavior and human relations is as exciting and adventuresome as spaceflight. Yet in this area this country is the most backward, for the following reasons:

1. We are not willing to discard old, ineffective concepts proven to be useless.

2. We do not build on knowledge derived from past experiences and many people.

3. We do not use widely spread teamwork.

4. We follow some catchy fads.

5. We do not use sharp evaluation, even when possible—we either just continue what has traditionally been done or excuse our poor practices by blaming someone else (the legislature, the public, and the like).

6. Society as a whole does not spend money with needed generosity in any area concerned with human beings.

We are especially at fault in the treatment of adult or juvenile offenders. It has often been said that the reason for this is our punitive attitude toward the offender, the ancient instinct of revenge. This is surely part of it. Yet another major reason is that the method of casting out, of removing the undesirable one, has proved comfortable. They are not in our midst; they are invisible; they cannot be heard. The institutions "taking care" of them are neither bothersome nor enjoyable because they are so far removed. They make headlines when someone escapes, only to further strengthen the belief that the people in them must be kept away from the "good" population.

The model of institutions for juvenile delinquents must be built on what we know or think we know of human motivation, of developmental stages of the growing person in a given culture. Surely knowledge changes and theories are not perfect in any field, but especially not in a field that deals with the complexity of human beings. A model for the institutional treatment of delinquents and its theoretical rationale follow.

Community-centered Treatment

Any treatment of juvenile delinquents must be community centered. The reason for this is our present understanding of the nature of the human being as a

social being. The central drive of every human being, besides the biological
life instinct, is to have meaning, to be someone. This central drive can even
overcome the life instinct, as can be seen in the cases of martyrs and people
dedicated to causes. Paton wrote beautifully about this when he said:

> To mean something in the world is the deepest hunger of the human soul,
> deeper than any bodily hunger or thirst, and when a man has lost it he is no
> longer a man.[3]

This, then, means the basic life-giving force of self-respect, of dignity.
Self-respect and dignity are not self-made. They grow out of human relationships—the relationship between child and parent, encounters between
young and adult in any other social contact, and between peers and colleagues. If self-worth is not nourished by these relationships, the human
being loses it and reacts in some highly predictable ways:

1. He may withdraw totally into a mental illness, thus turning away from
other human beings.

2. He may submit to any demand placed on him from the outside, but
without any inner consent, simply following the powerful pressure on him.

3. He may strike out against others, their property or their person.
Whatever forms he "chooses," he hates himself and others; he suffers.

Delinquency has been explained in the past by poor parent-child
relationships, the impact of slums, poor habit-training, or bad group associations. All these can be brought down to a common denominator, namely,
the disastrous impact of a human and physical environment that makes a
person lose self-respect.

It is obvious, then, that treatment must provide in concentrated form
the vital missing ingredient that should have been available in normal life.
Most present-day correctional institutions do exactly the opposite. Separation from the community—the casting out that immediately carries with it
the label of badness—intensifies the lack of self-respect and therefore increases the hate.

It is therefore logical that the first principle of treatment has to be to
maintain the young person in the community, to give acceptance, to let
him become part of the community. This means completely different
alternatives to mass institutions, even if the young person needs to leave his
own family. The alternatives are these:

1. Group homes of approximately five to six youngsters inside the cities
and towns. These must not be false imitations of a family but small, active
youth communities. In such homes the young person gains self-respect,
mostly through relationships with a small group of peers, with the help of

---

[3] Alan Paton, *The Long View* (New York: Praeger, 1968), p. 19.

accepting and capable adults who use every opportunity offered by the total living situation to enhance the youngster's self-respect. The neighborhood will have to be involved in the creation of good group homes because it too, including the schools, must become part of this pattern of concentrated acceptance.

Recently, for example, a group home was established for delinquent girls. The girls developed well when they felt part of the existing friendship patterns, school activities, and the like. But then some neighbors began agitating against "such influences" in their area "on principle," not because the girls had done anything to harm them. It was then that the girls reverted to their patterns of hate and became destructive.

All communities will have to learn that one cannot isolate oneself into neat little corners away from the "bad" people. In fact those in neat corners become the bad people, because they harm the total fabric of human society, which is dependent on mutual help.

2. For young people who are not yet able to relate to an everyday community situation, to specific stresses and strains of the normal school or work situation, and whose distrust is deep, small institutions with some self-contained, built-in learning and treatment services would be appropriate. Those too must be within or close to the centers of population so there is no sense of isolation and individual flexibility in the use of existing community facilities is possible. Such institutions may house approximately twenty-five young people—subdivided into much smaller living groups—with a strong emphasis on building a strong and coherent community within the larger community.

The mass institution as it exists today definitely must be *out*. There are usually two objections to this statement: (1) smaller facilities are too expensive and (2) removal of delinquents from the community is necessary to protect society from their violence.

The answer to the first argument is that the use of community facilities, the opportunity to share costs with others, the avoidance of costly building programs, and less recidivism will make community-based homes less expensive than the existing institutions. The saving of human lives—of offender as well as of victim—surely demands the full use of existing knowledge rather than the timid adding of a small piece of something good onto existing ineffective institutions.

To the second objection it can be said that the number of violent, seemingly untreatable, youngsters is quite small. A limited number of closed institutions will be needed, but those should have outstanding staff and give intensive care.

involvement of the Offender

Any treatment of delinquents must constantly involve the young person in his own fate. This means that one does not do *to him*, plan *for him*, diagnose *about him*.

Trust is essential for positive human relations. It grows out of having experienced honesty, of knowing where one stands with another person. Most delinquents have been exposed to an unpredictable and therefore untrustworthy adult world. To counteract this, every contact with the delinquent must be carried on with openness. Staff must offer an opportunity for the young people to be just as honest, even if it is at times painful to experience their form of honesty. This is different from what is found in the everyday world. There obviously exists a great deal of dishonesty, often called "politeness," "politics," or "tactics." Yet although treatment means preparation for the real world, it cannot exactly duplicate real life because more trust and dignity must be given to the delinquent to make up for early deficits and to give him a base to enable him to resist the painful disappointments of life and handle them with courage. People can live through the disappointment of misplaced trust if they have learned to trust at all. Only then can they act in a way in which others can trust them.

Openness has generally been missing in the treatment of delinquents, not only by ignorant or vicious staff members, but often by knowledgeable, even well-meaning ones. Their manipulative treatment of offenders is rationalized by various theories:

1. Psychoanalytic theory—poorly comprehended—gives excuses for a certain omnipotent attitude: "One has to diagnose," "The clinician knows best," or "It is too early to share insights with the youngster in trouble."

2. Operant conditioning frequently uses punishment and reward without teaching the young person why a certain behavior is unacceptable or acceptable. Speaking about race relations, Pettigrew described the fallacy of this approach:

This vicious circle is analogous to what psychologists describe as "avoidance learning." Suppose in an experimental setting, a subject's forefinger is repeatedly shocked electrically immediately after the flashing of a light. Very quickly he learns to avoid the painful shock by lifting his finger as soon as he sees the light flash on; in other words, the subject is conditioned in the classic Pavlovian paradigm. But consider what happens when the electric shock is no longer applied. How can the subject acquire knowledge of the change? As long as he withdraws his finger at the light, he can never discover that the light is no longer associated with a shock. This is the critical feature of avoidance learning.[4]

Enhancement of Self-respect and Self-confidence

Any treatment of delinquents must provide experience that enhances self-respect and self-confidence. Insight and self-understanding are hard for any human being to gain and demand a rather high degree of sophistication. When a delinquent, for instance, is quoted as saying, "I will not run away from this

[4] Thomas F. Pettigrew, *A Profile of the Negro American* (Princeton, N.J.: D. Van Nostrand Co., 1964), pp. 162–163.

institution because it only means running away from my problems and I know I will always take my problems with me," this may represent insight, but it may simply be parroting something he has been told over and over again. He knows the "reward" for such expression is release from the undesirable institution.

Yet even if one assumes that the statement represents true self-insight, the necessary ingredient that creates change—the seed of true self-confidence —comes only from having *experienced* the capacity to do something well. Experience is more than talk. It means, for instance, working on projects that give a feeling of accomplishment. For most young people it means some accomplishment in school. Most delinquents hate school because they feel so woefully inadequate in their schoolwork. They say that school means nothing to them, that they are smart enough. Yet they do not feel that way. They simply are afraid of renewed failure. A gifted young woman, a mathematician, volunteered her services to an institution for delinquents. The youngsters made it clear that they thought algebra was boring, stupid, and totally unnecessary in the real world. She neither contradicted them nor forced them into the usual routine of learning. She merely asked them to look into the newspapers for one week and cut out any item they thought had some relationship to mathematics. She then helped them make a poster from those items. The youngsters became excited about showing visitors which items each had cut out. They were proud of their own discoveries. This small accomplishment led to an interest in algebra.

For institutional treatment programs this concept means that a high degree of individualization is necessary to discover the youngsters' specific capacities. One must begin with simple enough tasks to permit the youngster to have an initially successful experience and then move to more demanding projects. The development of skills therefore has to be both present and future oriented.

Hope for the Future

Any treatment of delinquents must constantly provide hope for the future. Human beings make an effort on their own behalf or on behalf of others only when they think there is some hope of success. It is a societal phenomenon that unrest and drive toward change usually do not occur when repression is the strongest, but when there is a beginning of the possibility of change. This has often puzzled history students. They wonder why revolutions break out just when things are getting better. Our present knowledge of psychology explains this. Only hope of success starts action. If we want young people in trouble to become motivated toward change, we must provide tangible opportunities for them to gain hope.

A famous boxer once told how he had belonged to a delinquent gang because he saw no hope of ever getting out of his bleak surroundings. He said: "The change in me occurred when I first believed that I could make money legitimately." Hope for young people who have been deprived for a long time does not consist of telling them of rewards that have to be post-poned for a long time. What is the use of being told "You will be released if you behave for eight months?" The time period is long, "behaving" means pleasing the powers one hates, and release means only the absence of some-thing bad, not something positive. It is reminiscent of Socrates' words when his chains were removed: "It is wonderful to know how it feels to be with-out chains."

Hope must grow out of the constant experience of fulfilling certain needs: finding warm approval instead of constant nagging or indifference, earning money for something on which one has worked hard, taking a trip to fulfill some of the deep yearning for adventure usually denied to most delinquent youngsters. The more young people experience some fulfillment of hope, the more they will be able to prepare for goals a little more removed. Here is where John Dewey's theory of learning by doing and experiencing, the social group work theory with its stress on tangible group action, and Glasser's recent reiteration of the significance of the consideration of present and future in treatment flow together.[5]

Provision of Positive Human Relationships

Any treatment of delinquents must provide for significant and positive human relationships. In their daily encounters staff and peers become the most significant therapeutic agents. It is true that many youngsters will need special services by psychiatrists, social workers, and special teachers, but the most important relationships are with those with whom they have daily contact, especially counselors. Everybody on the staff must not only know a great deal about adolescents, but be capable of producing the kind of atmosphere conducive to self-respect and trust. Wilker wrote in 1921:

> Most significant to us, to my collaborators and myself was the human being. The mutual relationship from man to man is one of the incredible miracles in the cosmos.[6]

This kind of attitude must be shared by each staff member. In fact, the present separation of cottage life, individual and group therapy, school, and community involvement has become obsolete. Everything in such a treatment community must include learning, experiencing, relearning, and developing trust, hope, and self-respect. Staff and young people must become one community. This does not mean that the roles of adults and youths are the same, but they certainly must not carry the aspect of inferior and superior that are a hangover from the concept of the military institution. Staff members may and must have various competences and skills and yet the disastrous hierarchy among them must disappear. It has led and still leads to frustration, especially for those who are on the low rung of the

[5] William Glasser, *Reality Therapy* (New York: Harper & Row, 1965).
[6] Karl Wilker, *Der Lindenhof* (Heilbronn a. Neckar, 1921), p. 40.

ladder. Because of this situation youngsters become the targets of their own anger.

For many years we have talked about counselors or houseparents as the hub of the wheel in the institution, but we have only given lip service to this idea. They are not considered professionals equal to the other staff members and they are not required to have special training, with the exception of some token in-service training. Professional education in its best sense is needed for people who carry this task and they must be given the privileges and compensations as well as the heavy responsibilities of a true professional.

With a well-selected and well-trained staff one would not have to worry about creative programming. The staff will not be afraid of offering experiences that entail some risk. They will allow young people to learn something about participation in community action, either on their own behalf or on behalf of others in a world that will no longer tolerate passive submission. They will not be afraid of letting boys and girls meet together in a world that more and more asks for responsible decision-making in every area of personal conduct. To learn this, young people must be exposed to the experience of enjoyable and dignified relationships between the sexes. They will then make these decisions on grounds of mutual respect instead of exploiting each other.

Such staff members will understand the young people as youngsters— as adolescents, not as criminals. They will know that they must provide outlets for the strong drives of that age group instead of putting them into a stultifying straitjacket. And finally such staff will not be afraid to let the community know what they are doing as most are today. Most institutions have become insulated kingdoms in which administrators are free to act as autocrats, benevolent or malevolent. The public is allowed "in" on special days. The institutions actually believe the propaganda they disseminate on visiting day. Yet, in the writer's own memory, some pictures stand out:

> Approximately forty years ago, as a young student, I visited one of the most progressive institutions at that time. After a walk through it, with its walls in the most modern, beautiful colors, and after hearing the glowing report of the superintendent, we left happy in the knowledge that here was a truly excellent place. I found I had forgotten something and returned half an hour later only to see the superintendent and four strong women overpowering a pale 17-year-old who cried that she did not want to stay there. They were not only restraining her, they were beating her. I also remember the furious and tight-lipped face of the superintendent when she saw me.

And only recently when community volunteers actually began to work in one of the "better" institutions, they heard orders coming over the loudspeaker and saw youngsters placed in isolation without any human contact for as long as ten consecutive days. None of this can happen if staff become responsible and if the treatment of the delinquent becomes community based.

Summary

The models for treatment of delinquents are group homes and somewhat larger group living units within the community with approaches based on present-day psychosocial knowledge. The touchstones of this understanding of the human being are self-respect, human interrelatedness, capacity to change, and hope as a motivating force.

We can start today with the establishment of such community units. Since the larger institutions still exist, we must at least introduce into them all the forms of dignified treatment necessary while beginning to phase them out.

To return to the writer's thoughts when the astronauts circled the moon on a cold winter night and our horizons widened: Human problems are far more difficult to solve than those of space, yet we can learn something from this achievement. We can learn to build patiently on knowledge derived from many different sources. We can learn to work with others to achieve. Our knowledge regarding delinquents is not as imprecise and vague as we sometimes think. The concept of the dignity of the human being is really not as subjective or even as controversial as it is often presented. If we can only start one or two communities on the ideal model, then on a jubilant day like that night in December we can stand together with capable young people and say: "It worked."

Casework Treatment of Young Married Couples

Miriam Jolesch

During the early years of marriage, a young couple is likely to be exposed to a number of sources of potential conflict. Each partner must effect an emotional separation from his own family; each must achieve a sense of personal identity; each must learn to accept the role of husband or wife. Together the partners must gain a sense of identity as a family unit, over and above their identity as separate individuals. Accomplishing these developmental tasks may be so difficult for one, or both, of the partners that the marriage becomes threatened. Often, however, young couples having such difficulty can master the conflicts and crises typical of early married life if they are given casework treatment. This article is based on the author's experience in working with twelve young couples; in every instance, both marital partners were engaged in treatment.

In each of the twelve cases the request for help was based on the problem of unsatisfactory marital interaction. In eleven cases the wife was more concerned about the couple's failure to achieve gratifying interdependence in the marriage than was the husband. Most of the marital partners were in their mid-twenties; all of them were high school graduates, and some had had further education. The majority of the couples had been married from three to six years. They were economically secure, and the men had made a satisfactory vocational adjustment.

The Initial Period

The chief complaint verbalized by each of these young wives had to do with her feeling that her husband wanted to maintain his separateness from her and her distress at the emotional distance between them. In some instances the wife was troubled because her husband seemed to have so little time to spend with her and their children, although he managed to do many things outside the home. In other instances the complaint was not about outside interests but about the time and attention the husband

Reprinted from *Social Casework,* Vol. 43 (May, 1962), pp. 245–251, by permission of the author and the Family Service Association of America.

devoted to his possessions, either at home or at work. Invariably the wife was lonely and felt disappointed and hurt by her husband's lack of attention. She saw the basic problem as one of the husband's failure to show interest in her in return for her efforts to build a give-and-take relationship with him. She was insistent that her husband as well as she would have to have help if the marriage were to be maintained.

The young husbands, however, were relatively unaware of the interaction problems that so disturbed their wives. They did not believe that there was a serious problem in the marriage, and they resisted applying for marital counseling. Most of them came to the agency in anger, often under the wife's threat of getting a divorce or after the couple had been separated for a short period. The reciprocal processes operating in their marriages were obviously provocative and depreciating to both partners, and neither partner was receiving the gratification he needed.

In ten of the twelve cases studied, the worker noted during the intake process that the wife had greater perceptiveness and sensitivity than the husband, and that she had also achieved a more advanced state of emotional maturity. She was miserably unhappy and freely expressed her anxiety. She seemed to be struggling to re-create the gratifying aspects of the family life she had experienced in the past, but her husband, who was well defended against anxiety, was unprepared to help her. Typically, the husband was threatened by the wife's desire for closeness, while the wife was threatened by the husband's need to isolate himself and put distance between them. Often the wife behaved in such a way that the interpersonal tension derived from the husband's avoidance of closeness was increased. For example, one young wife always managed to be talking on the telephone when her weary, uncommunicative husband returned from work. She never had the dinner ready; the children's clothing was always strewn around the room where her possession-centered husband would stumble over it and have to pick it up.

The central therapeutic problem with these couples was to engage and sustain the husband's motivation to use casework treatment, since he was the partner who evinced little concern about those aspects of the marital relationship that created so much anxiety and dissatisfaction in the wife. The same worker treated both partners in the twelve cases; treatment was considered successful in ten of the cases. In large measure the favorable outcome can be attributed to three factors: (1) use of a combination of joint and individual interviews for the purpose of identifying individual reactive patterns basic to the conflict in marital interaction; (2) timing of the joint interviews so that they were held only after each partner had made a positive transference to the caseworker and had become engaged in an examination of his own role performance; and (3) focusing of treatment efforts on the interactional conflict. A couple was considered to have been treated successfully when the partners discovered that they could handle their problems to their own satisfaction and when it was clear to the worker that they had achieved a degree of interdependence that was gratifying to both of them.

The Intake Phase

The M case illustrates the typical interpersonal problems experienced by these young couples and the casework techniques used during the intake, exploratory, and treatment phases of the cases.

Mr. and Mrs. M—26 years of age and the parents of two boys, age $3\frac{1}{2}$ years and 1 year—reminded the worker of a plump, ruffled robin redbreast and a dismal little wren as Mr. M plowed into the office ahead of his wife for their intake appointment. Mrs. M repeatedly accused her husband of resenting marriage and of being power- and success-hungry. She threatened to divorce him unless he would agree to having marital counseling. Mr. M, sitting at some distance from his wife, did not deign to glance at her; he was flushed, angry, and impatient with her complaints. He kept glancing at his watch as he stressed his fear that he would be late for an important business engagement. Speaking rapidly, he insisted that they did not have a marital problem: Their only trouble was lack of time to be together. When they did talk, his wife said silly things or asked silly questions that he had no time to answer—as she was doing now. He was convinced that the answer to her unhappiness was for her to join organizations, as his mother had done. He wanted the worker to know that he did not believe in marital counseling or any kind of therapy. He had come to the agency this time just to please his wife; he was too busy to stay for any lengthy discussion, and he did not expect to return.

When an applicant requests help in solving a marital problem, the intake interview is a joint one unless a serious objection is expressed by one of the marital partners. This type of interview affords the worker an excellent opportunity for perceiving both the verbal and nonverbal aspects of the marital interaction. In the case under discussion nothing that either Mr. or Mrs. M might have said in individual interviews could have conveyed so vividly Mr. M's feelings of puzzlement and anger, and Mrs. M's feelings of utter defeat, disappointment, and disparagement as did their unverbalized responses to each other. The very fact that Mr. M had come for an interview, and the puzzled quality of his negative reactions, gave the worker the impression that Mr. M, as well as his wife, did have some investment in the marriage. Emotional factors were blocking these people from functioning appropriately in their marital roles to such an extent that they seemed to be obtaining little real gratification from their marriage. Mr. M was getting satisfaction from his work and studies, and from indulging in an adolescent type of recreational activity with other young men. Mrs. M was extremely unhappy and maintained a passively hostile, hopeless attitude. She felt completely frustrated in her efforts to create a new and more congenial pattern of living.

As did many of the husbands in the cases studied, Mr. M tried in the joint intake interview to prove that his wife was wrong and that there was no marital problem. He insisted that he worked hard, provided well for his family, loved his children, and respected his wife, and that a man could not be expected to do more. He was angry. At first he insisted that he would be wasting his time if he kept appointments in the future because he was sure he could put his wife "on cloud nine" if only he had the time. However, as the interview progressed Mr. M began to recognize his wife's feeling of loneliness, hopelessness, and disappointment as a wife. He then agreed that he could manage to find the time to come in for a few more interviews. The worker did not mention his feelings of anger, but stressed the importance of finding time in which to attain the couple's mutual goals.

Mrs. M brought out little material other than her reiterated charge that her husband was eager for power and success, and that he was thoughtless, selfish, and disinterested in her and the children. It was the worker's impression that old conflicts had been revived in this marriage, as so frequently happens in early married life. The key problem was one of engaging the resistant partner, Mr. M, in order to determine whether treatment could be effective in helping the couple make new or better adaptations so that they could sustain the marriage.

It quickly became apparent to the worker that cases such as the ones considered here might easily be lost at the point of intake. Although most of these couples did not reveal markedly serious pathology, they seemed to be in danger of divorce unless both partners became engaged in improving their ways of interacting. The relative emotional health of the wife was the primary factor that operated to bring the husband to the agency. It also proved to be an important factor in the wife's decision to get a divorce in the two situations in which the husband could not be engaged in the treatment process. Casework experience has shown that it is often the deeply self-punishing wife who chooses to remain in an ungratifying marriage.

The joint intake interview is an important medium for engaging the resistant partner because in this interview the presenting problem can be observed and focused by the caseworker in terms of its interacting effects on the marital relationship. At intake, the worker must focus on the form rather than on the content of the interview. The content is made up of the complaints—the charges and the countercharges one partner makes against the other—and the resultant emotions expressed. The form is constituted from the interplay of roles and the patterning of interaction resulting from this interplay. As the discussion in the joint intake interview is focused by the caseworker on the form of interaction—what is said, what is shown, what happens, and what all of this means in the marital situation—the two partners usually begin to be engaged in viewing their marital conflicts. As they do so, one partner's denial of marital conflict is weakened, as is the attacking posture of the other. This joint intake interview also enables the partners to confront their own feelings in a more unified manner. Each partner derives some measures of awareness that each must assume a degree of responsibility for attaining their mutual goal of sustaining the marriage.

The Exploratory Phase

In the intake process the worker should clarify the next steps to be taken and should design at least a tentative therapeutic plan in which both clients will have the motivation to participate. The important point to decide in the M case was whether joint or individual interviews would be better during the exploratory phase. The worker chose individual interviews on the basis of her initial diagnostic impression that Mr. M was reluctant to develop the close interdependent, or give-and-take, relationship his wife sought, and therefore was not ready for further joint interviews. Individual interviews were selected as the best means for obtaining a clearer grasp of the origin and severity of this problem for Mr. M, as well as for testing his capacity to mature within a therapeutic relationship. The worker's clinical impression of Mrs. M, who demonstrated anxiety combined with both a sensitivity in relation to her husband's needs and a real desire to give as well as to be given to, was that of a person with neurotic character traits and certain self-defeating tendencies.[1] The worker believed that in individual interviews with Mrs. M it would be possible to elicit quickly personal data needed as background for determining whether clarification of certain areas of her neurotic conflict which contributed to the marital problem would strengthen the marriage.

The young couples studied repeatedly transferred to their marital situations the fantasies and expectations they had had in relation to their parents. In working with the couples, the worker always found it important to explore the key relationships of each partner with his own parents. During the exploratory phase, individual interviews were chiefly used *1]* to obtain more quickly and economically personal and historical data needed to clarify certain aspects of individual behavior that seemed to be contributing to the interactional disturbance; *2]* to meet the need for an individual relationship with the worker, especially for the purpose of quickening individual maturation; *3]* to give the client an opportunity to talk to the worker in private, without his having to expose his feelings and attitudes to the partner and thereby build up resistance to treatment; and *4]* to relieve excessive anxiety.

The worker's tentative diagnostic impression in the M case was that Mr. and Mrs. M had not been able to achieve a satisfying degree of interdependence even after five years of marriage and the birth of two children, both of whom were planned. Mr. M, whose anxieties about his capacity to be a husband were well defended, was hectically pursuing his own goals. He perceived his wife as an object of gratification, just as he had perceived his father's relationship to his mother in that light. Direct interaction between the M's was minimal. Mrs. M was intensely frustrated, and she

---

[1] For a discussion of character neurosis, see Otto Pollak, Hazel M. Young, and Helen Leach, "Differential Diagnosis and Treatment of Character Disturbances," *Social Casework*, Vol. XLI, No. 10 (1960), pp. 512–17.

had a very poor self-image. Mr. M worked long hours in his father's business, in which he had a small part interest. Three nights a week he rushed home for a quick bite of supper before hurrying away to teach business classes in an extension course. His wife served him his meal. Then, while he ate and listened to news reports on the radio, she went next door for a cup of tea with her mother. Mr. M was very proud to have been asked to teach; he could not understand why his wife seemed so disinterested in his teaching. Usually he was so keyed up after his classes that he felt the need to unwind by going with some of his men students to listen to progressive jazz. Thus he stayed out until one or two in the morning three nights a week. Another two nights were devoted to studying at home. On one of these two evenings Mrs. M went out to play mah-jongg with some of her women friends. Sunday was the only day the family was together as a unit. Mrs. M, however, could not enjoy being with her husband this one day in the week because she could not recover sufficiently from her feelings of being deprived and depreciated—feelings that had become intensified because of her isolation from her husband during the other days of the week. They had established few gratifying patterns of marital interaction. Each partner wanted the other to sense his feelings intuitively and to meet his needs without being asked to do so.

Mr. and Mrs. M indicated clearly that they were both struggling to achieve maturity but were still clinging to the fantasy of the all-wise or omnipotent parent. Each one was following the identical pattern of his own parents. Each—but Mr. M in particular—was incompletely identified with his own sex role. Mrs. M had moved haltingly and uncertainly into the role of wife. She had exercised some of her mature, feminine impulses to give and to share, but her husband was unable to meet her countervailing need to be given to and nurtured. The worker decide to offer Mrs. M individual treatment as a means of restoring her self-confidence. The aim of individual treatment for Mr. M was to help him examine his role performance as a husband and father and to test his capacity to mature emotionally. It was considered important for them to be treated by the same caseworker so that, in both individual and joint interviews, the focus could be kept on their shared, long-term goal of finding their new identity as marriage partners. Although each of them seemed to have the desire to love and to be loved, they were not certain how they could achieve this goal together.

The Treatment Phase

The M's were treated over a period of five months. There were twelve individual interviews with Mr. M, nine individual interviews with Mrs. M, and seven joint interviews. Following the exploratory phase, treatment was based on the fact that the M's had enjoyed a brief period of mutual satisfaction prior to the birth of their second child. The first child had been conceived during the first year of marriage. Subsequently, the M's were separated for a year while Mr. M was in the Army. The second child was conceived soon after his return. Fathering this boy may have reactivated an unresolved childhood conflict against which Mr. M defended himself through his overdetermined, aggressive drive for success. His keeping himself emotionally distant from his wife was a defense against his deep feelings of inadequacy, or perhaps his oedipal guilt. His functioning as a husband was impaired. He was not particularly uncomfortable in the relationship except for his resentment of what seemed to him to be the unrealistic and undeserved nagging of his wife. He felt that she should be understanding and supportive of his goals. Always a few minutes early for his interviews, he came armed with books on accounting and business psychology, which he studied assiduously in the waiting room. In the first four interviews he talked at length about his interests, his studies, his accomplishments, and his pursuit of ambitious but reasonable goals for himself and his family. He felt that it was unrealistic for him to use precious time in keeping appointments with the worker when he had no problems. He was startled when the worker asked why he came early, but he quickly explained his need to keep ahead of schedule if he were to get through all of his daily activities.

Since Mr. M's narcissistic defenses seemed well integrated into his personality structure, the worker questioned whether Mr. M could accept a self-image that was less than strong, powerful, and successful in every way. Did he really need a wife's love and companionship? Repeatedly he emphasized that he saw no value for himself in having interviews with the worker. Eventually he admitted reluctantly that he liked to come: He enjoyed talking to the caseworker; he felt understood and respected; he wished he had more time. Later, when Mr. M began to think about his own sense of always being pressed for time, the worker believed that he was becoming involved in trying to work out new goals in his marriage. In his individual interviews he then began to examine his self-image, particularly the aggressive posture that he had developed in order to please his father. As he dealt with key areas of experience in his childhood, he began to reveal his feelings in relation to certain aspects of his behavior.

During this period Mrs. M was also having individual appointments. She was quickly able to face her own self-defeating patterns. After spending some time in discussing her interaction with her husband, she began to talk about her fear of asserting herself or of expressing anger. She made a connection between these fears and her childhood feelings as the older of two sisters. She had felt that her sister, who had developed a chronic cardiac condition at the age of six years, had pushed her away from the love and protection of her parents. Mrs. M began to understand her earlier pattern of suppressing anger toward her sister, whom she envied, and of passively waiting and hoping for attention and consideration. She learned to see that she had transferred this pattern into the marriage, and that she was behaving in a similar fashion toward Mr. M.

The Joint Interviews

The worker began to use joint interviews, in addition to individual interviews, at the mid-point in treatment, when each partner was showing some capacity for examining his own self-image and role performance. Joint interviews can be used productively when each partner has become able to attach the appropriate feeling to his own attitudes or behavior. Such interviews should bring into focus whatever is occurring in the present experiential or interactional situation. When the defensive behavior of each partner has diminished, the couple can begin to examine their interactional patterns. Joint interviews with the M's were held in the same week as the individual interviews to facilitate a more mature type of communication. Each of them grew not only in capacity to examine his own and the other's negative attitudes and patterns but also in ability to discover positive reactions he had previously denied. Reality distortions were corrected as the joint interviews progressed. Each partner became increasingly aware of his own unrealistic expectations of the other.

When an impasse was occasionally reached in a joint interview, or when their old reactions flared up, each partner was motivated to explore his immature pattern in the individual interview. This use of both individual and joint interviews tended to discourage regression. It was through the joint interviewing process that Mr. and Mrs. M first realized the faith they had in each other. After the long period of mutual frustration, each had become doubtful that this was so. The irrational fears each one had had were now removed. The process had begun in individual therapy, when Mr. and Mrs. M each had resolved some of their difficulty in expressing aggression. Their discussions in joint interviews hastened the process of neutralizing their fear of loving and hating the same person.

Treatment was terminated by mutual consent when both Mr. and Mrs. M felt that they no longer were withdrawing from each other. Both found that they were now having more gratification in their married life than they had believed possible. Mr. M had given up staying out late after his evening classes. Mrs. M noticed that her husband had been able to stand up to his father on a few occasions. She had stopped asking foolish questions. Mr. M proudly stated that his wife was even able to suppress her dislike of "blood and thunder" stories and was permitting him to tell her about a few of his experiences in the Army. Mr. M summed up his concept of what had been the major gain from their marital counseling experience in the simple statement, "I have matured."

In the 12 cases studied, it was found that joint interviews were used most effectively at the point where each partner is beginning the process of self-examination in the individual interviews. One caseworker shared by the marital partners seemed to represent to each of them a parent who was interested but neutral. Through the corrective emotional experience provided by the worker, the sense of personal worth of each partner was enhanced, and he became more tolerant toward the other. Usually the more highly motivated and relatively more mature partner had become less anxious by the time the joint interviews were instituted. As his anxiety lessened, his capacity to be more tolerant and to express himself verbally increased. This improvement in the healthier partner helped to sustain the motivation of the less motivated partner. In joint treatment interviews the caseworker must repeatedly communicate to the couple the way in which each partner's actions and reactions cause or exacerbate their mutual problems. As the worker repeatedly points out the various manifestations of the partners' behavior, the partners can begin to tolerate each other's individual ways of reacting. Each can begin to identify with the other as they face, and work together on, their contradictory feelings. Essential to this process is the caseworker who, they have both come to believe, knows, understands, and supports their mutual aim of finding security and gratification in the marriage. In this transference situation the caseworker represents a parent figure who supports their mature aims and who strengthens them in their separation from their parents. Changes in their perceptions occur. The adolescent fantasies they have carried into marriage fade away and are replaced by genuine object relationships.

Conclusion

These young married people had a deep wish to make a success of their marriages, but they were uncertain about how their aims could be achieved. In a majority of these cases the period following the birth of the second child was one of particular stress and crisis. After they were engaged in treatment, these partners wanted the family caseworker to help them achieve a new identity as marriage partners. In most instances delayed maturation was the fundamental cause of the marital problem. The wives, on the whole, seemed more ready to fulfill a marital role than did the husbands. The average time required to treat the younger couples in this group was from five to seven months. Similar methods were used successfully in two cases in which the partners were in their mid-thirties, but the time required was one year in one case, and twenty-two months in the other. The findings in the cases studied support the conclusions of Howard Parad and Gerald Caplan that stress reactivates earlier conflict and that help given at a time of stress can promote growth and maturation.[2]

---

[2] Howard J. Parad and Gerald Caplan, "A Framework for Studying Families in Crisis," *Social Work*, Vol. 5, No. 3 (1960), pp. 3–15.

Joint Interviewing: A Treatment Technique with Marital Partners

Joanne Geist and Norman M. Gerber

Joint interviewing is a valuable technique in the treatment of certain marital partners, especially when they have a mutual interest in a particular problem or problems within the marriage. For the purposes of this paper, joint interviewing is defined as one or a number of planned casework interviews of an hour's duration of husband and wife together by one caseworker.[1]

In the Family Service of Cincinnati and Hamilton County, married clients are usually interviewed separately at intake by a worker in a centralized intake department. An attempt is made to have the same intake worker interview both marital partners, but usually at different times. Usually, the partners are then assigned to the same caseworker for ongoing treatment. This worker may decide to see both partners in separate interviews, to have one partner treated by another worker, or to refer one partner to another social agency or to a psychiatric treatment resource. He may decide to work with only one partner or, in certain cases, he may see the partners in joint interviews. Whatever decision he makes is based on a treatment plan that is indicated by the psychosocial diagnosis.

The intake worker attempts to gain as much understanding of marital interaction as possible. The knowledge gained may lead the continuing worker to select joint interviewing as a primary technique to be used in the

---

Reprinted from *Social Casework*, Vol. 41 (February, 1960), pp. 76–83, by permission of the author and the Family Service Association of America.

[1] For discussion of joint interviewing, see particularly: Sanford N. Sherman, "Joint Interviews in Casework Practice," *Social Work*, Vol. IV, No. 2 (1959); Max Siporin, "Family-Centered Casework in a Psychiatric Setting," *Social Casework*, Vol. XXXVII, No. 4 (1956), p. 167; M. Robert Gomberg, "Family Diagnosis—Trends in Theory and Practice," *Social Casework*, Vol. XXXIX, Nos. 2–3 (1958); Victor W. Eisenstein, M.D., *Neurotic Interaction in Marriage*, Basic Books, Inc., New York, 1956; M. Robert Gomberg, "Family Oriented Treatment of Marital Problems," *Social Casework*, Vol. XXXVII, No. 1 (1956); David Hallowitz, Robert A. Clement, and Albert V. Cutter, M.D., "The Treatment Process with Both Patients Together," *American Journal of Orthopsychiatry*, Vol. XXVII, No. 3 (1957); Rex A. Skidmore, "The Joint Interview in Marriage Counseling," *Marriage and Family Living*, Vol. XVII, No. 4 (1955), p. 349.

treatment process. He may also arrange joint interviews at other points in treatment if it appears that joint interviews would be of greater benefit than individual interviews to the marital partners involved. As the St. Paul study indicates, "Our choice of interviewing plan must depend upon what we see is needed and upon our skills in the process of planning and conducting interviews."[2]

"Marital diagnosis," the term used in this paper, refers to a clear understanding of the individual diagnosis of each partner and additional understanding of the marital interaction between them. The twelve cases used as the basis of this discussion included nine couples that continued in treatment, and three that did not continue. All the clients involved had character disorders; some of them were quite disturbed while others were relatively healthy.

In considering the use of joint interviews, the caseworker sees the following factors as diagnostically important: marital interaction, the degree of involvement of each partner, and the degree of concern of each partner. Of greatest single importance is the ability of each partner to maintain an interest in and to use his concern about mutual interests. It has been found that a concern about mutual interests, expressed by both marital partners, becomes the basis for establishing the focus of treatment and for maintaining a treatment relationship. "In treatment, joint interviewing has merit only if the participants can feel some togetherness in their desire to focus upon a common problem. Lacking this, individual interviews become necessary until this condition can be met."[3] One cannot stress too strongly the fact that the partners must have an interest that is mutually shared and to which they both relate in coming to the agency. Also it is diagnostically important to discover the factors that have led to upsetting the marital balance, since this knowledge will clarify the quality of the interaction and will lead to a further understanding of the dynamics of the marital relationship. When joint interviews are used, understanding the marital interaction takes on even greater meaning in relation to the worker's helping these persons find more satisfactions from each other in the marriage, as well as in restoring the equilibrium in the marriage and thereby benefiting the children.

Diagnostic Indications for Joint Interviewing

In casework with marital problems, certain situations occur that seem to indicate the desirability of planning joint interviews. The caseworker's use of these situations as diagnostic clues to the need for interviewing marital partners together has grown out of an increased understanding of marital interaction and a growing awareness that a variety of techniques is needed in helping to restore marital balance.

[2] *Casework Notebook*, Family Centered Project, Greater St. Paul Community Chest and Council, Inc., St. Paul, Minn., 1957. See Chapter 13 on family interviewing.

[3] *Casework Notebook, loc. cit.*

1. *When there is a breakdown in verbal communication between marital partners.* At intake each partner may speak of not being able to discuss his concerns with his spouse. Restoration of communication between them sometimes is extremely difficult when individual interviews are continued. Each partner is expressing the same worries and concerns as the spouse but neither can share them with the other in a way that leads to a solution of the difficulty. The joint interview can help to create an atmosphere in which the partners attempt to re-establish communication with the help of the caseworker.

> Prior to joint interviews, Mr. and Mrs. A each expressed the feeling of being "left out" by the other. In individual interviews they made some of the following remarks: "My husband doesn't take me anywhere. He only wants to work or stick his nose in a book. He married me to have a housekeeper. I want to feel close to him but he won't let me." "My wife never gets up to fix my breakfast. She wants a handyman around but not a husband. She gets all upset about meeting people. I'd like my friends to meet her but she doesn't want to." Despite the worker's encouraging them to discuss these complaints with each other, they did not do so. In joint interviews each of the clients did discuss these complaints and the caseworker was able to help them explore their feelings and increase their ability to talk with each other without constant distortion.

2. *When there is distrust of the other partner's actions.* Marital partners may misinterpret feelings and facial expressions, as well as words. Because of this distrust, the nonjudgmental role of the caseworker, in separate interviews, can be misinterpreted as taking the partner's side, particularly when the caseworker raises questions about the behavior of the partner who is being interviewed. In a joint interview each has a chance to see that the caseworker raises questions about the other in order to help them as a couple to find their own solutions. Thus they are able to see the caseworker and themselves more realistically.

> Individual interviews with Mr. and Mrs. B led to the following situation. When Mr. B was seen alone he frequently voiced his suspiciousness about his wife's sexual role with the male worker. Alone, Mrs. B consistently provoked situations that would add to her husband's suspiciousness and then condemned his lack of faith in her ability to be a loyal wife. When the worker tried to help each of them by raising questions about the other, his effort was misinterpreted to mean that he disbelieved the statements made. When the worker was able to bring them together in a joint interview and then raised questions about their suspicions, they were able to handle the matter and to solve part of the conflict.

3. *When the degree of security of one or both marital partners is too slight for them to work individually with the same worker.* Some clients seem unable to permit the spouse to see the worker individually; but when they are seen as a couple they are able to work productively on their problem. This kind of competition for the caseworker's attention can be put to constructive use. Unresolved sibling rivalry may be the reason for a client's inability to feel secure in separate interviews. If so, separate interviews may arouse the feeling

that he needs to compete for a parent's love and attention and that he is inadequate. These feelings can sometimes be dispelled by participating in joint interviews and being reassured that the worker is as interested in him as in his partner.

> After joint interviews were begun in the C case, it became apparent that Mrs. C was suspicious of her husband's relationship with his female caseworker and that he derived pleasure from fostering the suspiciousness. Mrs. C had not been able to reveal this in individual interviews, but could bring it up in joint interviews when she could observe that her fantasies were without a basis in reality. Mr. C could express his anger toward the caseworker for not favoring him and could recognize that his provocativeness was delaying the restoration of marital balance which he actually desired as strongly as his wife did.

4. *When there is a lack of focus in individual interviews.* Sometimes the material presented and discussed in individual interviews, although apparently meaningful, results in little or no change in the marital situation. The case-worker needs to be aware of the client's current living situation and his expressed desire for some change. Often individual interviews are used to drain off complaints about the partner, and the area of mutual concern is not given enough attention.

5. *When the client himself asks for joint interviews and the caseworker senses the client's intuitive knowledge that this is the best method of solving a particular problem.* The caseworker should examine the client's motivations when he requests joint interviews. Often the worker will interpret this request as the client's effort to control the situation when this may not be the meaning of the behavior.

> The C's mentioned above asked for joint interviews after a long period of individual interviews. The caseworker, although dubious about the wisdom of this procedure, was willing to try it because treatment progress had come to a standstill. In retrospect it appeared that the clients had sensed the best method of help for them. Marital balance was fairly quickly restored. Although the case has now been closed a year, the caseworker has been in touch with the couple and they have continued to feel able to solve their problems together without disruption of the marital balance.

6. *When the caseworker senses intuitively that the use of joint interviews would be the treatment method of choice.* The caseworker may be unable to give explicit diagnostic reasons for his method because less is currently known about this method of interviewing than about individual interviews, and, hence, he is less familiar with it.

> Mr. and Mrs. D had been known to the agency since 1954. In their first contact with the agency they were both seen by the worker in individual interviews. They failed to return after one contact. When they returned to the agency in 1956, each partner was assigned to a different worker. Again, after one interview each, they discontinued. In 1958 they again applied to the agency for service. The worker felt that joint interviews ought to be tried

because no other treatment method had worked. When the marital partners were seen in joint interviews they were able to express their mutual concern about their 5-year-old child who was quite destructive in his acting-out behavior toward his peers. In joint interviews the worker was able to help Mrs. D with her fears about losing control over her child and at the same time was able to relate to Mr. D and help to reduce his sense of exclusion from his wife's concern.

Treatment Techniques

We have found certain treatment techniques to be particularly successful in joint interviewing. Before initiating joint interviews with a couple, the worker should clarify with each marital partner the fact that they will be talking together to work toward a solution of their problems because of their mutual concerns.

1. *Limit setting.* It is extremely important for the worker to set limits as a means of enabling the marital partners to tolerate their anxiety in a more comfortable manner. Setting limits is an aid in focusing the interviews as well as in helping the marital partners channel their energies toward constructive and appropriate handling of their mutual concerns. The caseworker sets limits by not allowing one marital partner to be overcontrolling in the verbal communication during the joint interview. By suggesting to the more passive, nonverbal partner that his opinion is needed, or that it is important for him to raise questions about what the marital partner is saying, the worker enables both partners to reach some balance in solving the problem through communication.

It is important to stress that doing this does not mean permitting the couple to have a free-for-all in the office. Instead, it provides an opportunity for carrying on the interview within a structured atmosphere in which the caseworker is the leader. When both partners become too vociferous in their comments, the worker attempts to maintain control by diluting the emotional charge that is taking place between them. He tries to retrace the first steps of the argument by seeking the facts, thus enabling the marital partners to develop ideas about how their own behavior and distortions have led to the argument. At the same time the marital partners are able to gain some control of their impulses for more profitable use in the future. The worker's presence offers a protective atmosphere which enables the clients to accept the limits he has placed on them. Thus he can provide a healthy ego ideal to which they can relate themselves as treatment progresses.

In the beginning of treatment Mrs. B monopolized the joint interviews. She clearly indicated that she was a hysterical, masochistic personality. Mr. B, a suspicious, hostile personality, only evoked tears from Mrs. B when he talked to her. Consequently, he tried to avoid saying anything. However, Mrs. B would manipulate him into a position where he would lose control and yell loudly at his wife. Mrs. B, becoming hysterical, would depreciate her efforts as a wife and mother. The worker commented that they had not come to the office to yell and fight with each other, since this would not solve the problems they faced as parents. The worker added that, since they were paying a fee, he thought they should try to use the hour to their best advantage. Although this helped to calm them down somewhat, Mrs. B continued to bait Mr. B. The worker suggested directly that she get hold of herself and try to tell him what had happened, step by step, that had led to this argument. Mr. B just sat in the chair, daring the worker to ask him his side of the argument, which by plan he wasn't going to give. When the worker asked for his opinion about what his wife was saying and he refused to give any, the worker suggested to Mr. B that he, the worker, would not allow any outbursts by the wife while Mr. B was speaking, since Mr. B had not interrupted when she had spoken. Only then were they able together to discuss the situation with the worker.

2. *Clarifying the distortions and lack of trust in each marital partner.* It is our opinion that either partner's distortions are essentially a defense, masking his own uncertainties in handling his feelings, and that they result in perpetuating an unhealthy marital interaction. When these distortions are clarified, a balance in the three-way therapeutic relationship can be maintained.

In one joint interview Mr. B stated that he wished they could save money; he'd like to invest in stocks. Mrs. B turned to the caseworker and said, "You see he doesn't want me to have a new vacuum cleaner." She then told her husband that they would save more if he'd help her to go over the budget. He then told the caseworker, "My wife never wants me to have anything. I want a new electric drill but I just have to give all my money to her." Their distortions, so obvious to the caseworker, had to be painstakingly pointed out to each client. An entire interview was focused on the above remarks and it took genuine effort on the part of each client to think through these angry reactions and try to understand how they had come to feel this way.

3. *Universalizing and educational techniques.* We have found that using the technique of universalization helps marital partners such as these through giving them an idea of what other people do and why they do it. The use of educational techniques also can serve as a demonstration, in a general way, of how certain situations can be handled. Thus, the worker can help the marital partners by relieving some of their anxieties and by presenting to them a healthy ego ideal to which they can relate. Quite frequently, marital partners try to place the caseworker in the position of a referee on a specific point which, on the surface, is so isolated from the main problem that its discussion does not help in reaching a solution. Thus, through the caseworker's helping the marital partners to focus on the general rather than the specific by referring to what other people do and think, facts are elicited that enable both marital partners to move toward a specific solution of their problem. Moreover, the caseworker avoids being put in a position of being a referee and can place the responsibility for solving the problem with the marital partners.

Mr. and Mrs. D were upset about the acting-out behavior of their 5-year-old child. What was clearly indicated in the material they presented was the need for psychiatric evaluation of the child. Both Mr. and Mrs. D spoke about a specific incident when the child had thrown bricks at another child. Everything about him except this incident seemed to have been blotted out. The worker suggested that they talk more about the child's behavior and tried to relate this discussion to a more generalized concept of what is normal or abnormal behavior. When the parents were able to focus on a more educational approach, which in itself did not have as much pain for them since focus was taken away from their own child, they were able to comprehend that some of his behavior was serious and to accept the plan necessary to help the boy.

4. *Transference and countertransference.* In a joint interview, the worker has to be keenly aware of the multiple transferences that take place. One must remember that when two people are interviewed together, they naturally present two differing sets of evidence. Hence, the worker has an opportunity of observing the interaction between the marital partners. We have found that, if the caseworker is not aware of his own involvement and his own reactions, he is more susceptible to manipulation by the marital partners than would be true in a one-to-one relationship. If the worker takes sides or succumbs to the more controlling marital partner, the treatment process is adversely affected. Since it is quite easy for the worker to leave the nonverbal partner completely out of the discussion, he should be mindful that he may have to divide his time between the marital partners so that each receives equal attention from him. If he is aware of his own feelings and reactions to the clients, he is able to understand more fully the types of logical resistance that occur in the treatment process, since these are not blurred by the illogical resistances that occur because of his countertransference reactions. As the clients progress in treatment, the worker continues to re-evaluate the transference and countertransference reactions.

> Mrs. E was a controlling, depreciating woman who seemed to antagonize everyone. The worker's initial reaction to her was a feeling of being overwhelmed. He appeared to be controlled by her just as her husband felt he was. When the worker realized how he was reacting to Mrs. E, he was able to handle her attempts at control in a non-rejecting way, thus affording Mr. E the opportunity of presenting his ideas and opinions in the joint interview. The worker tried to bring Mr. E into the discussion by asking him, "Do you have something to add to this?" or by suggesting, "I'm sure this is of concern to you, too."

Terminating Treatment
with the Use of Joint Interviews

In terminating treatment, the joint interview can be used not only with clients who have previously been interviewed together, but also with marital partners who by design have been seen in individual interviews. It is our opinion that if the focus of treatment has been on marital and family relationship problems rather than on individual personality problems, the joint interview may be validly used at the point of termination regardless of whether the treatment design has involved joint or individual interviews by the same worker.

A joint interview at termination gives focus to the problems the marital partners have worked on; it also permits the worker to summarize for both of them together their efforts in reaching a solution. It affords an opportunity for the worker to verbalize the gains and the successful use the marital partners have made of casework treatment. Too frequently, caseworkers think that terminating a case should end their contact with the clients they have helped. It is our feeling that joint terminal interviews should be related to the positive interaction in the marriage. If, in the future, the partners should need help they can both be assured that the agency considers each of them equally important to the health and welfare of the family. Their knowledge that the agency feels that they used help well will enable them to return, should the need arise.

> At a point where Mr. and Mrs. F were feeling much more comfortable together and positive about their marriage, it seemed appropriate to terminate treatment. Two joint interviews were held after two years of regular individual contacts with Mr. and Mrs. F by the same worker. Mr. and Mrs. F told the worker separately, and then together in the last interview, that their marriage was much improved but was still no bed of roses. Each felt that he understood the other person better, as well as himself. They could talk together about their problems with some tolerance and without a need to become angry. We all felt that this was an appropriate time to discontinue treatment.

Contraindications for Joint Interviews

There seems to be a variety of factors involved in the failure of joint interviews. It has been our experience that these factors seem to fall into three main categories: the accuracy of the caseworker's diagnostic understanding of the two clients involved, the caseworker's own comfort in using joint interviews, and the quality of interaction between the two clients.

In consideration of joint interviews as a treatment method to be used over a period of time, the diagnosis of each client involved needs to be carefully considered. Joint interviews should not be used, for example, when one client is extremely narcissistic or has an oral aggressive character structure. The need of such a person to be given attention as an individual is so great that he cannot use a joint interview for solving a problem that is of concern to another person as well.

> Mr. and Mrs. G were being seen by the same worker individually about a marriage problem involving Mrs. G's inability to trust her husband to pay the bills and Mr. G's refusal to share his financial worries with her. Each expressed a desire to continue the marriage and felt that their problems stemmed from financial difficulties. Each felt that if they could come to some agreement about how to spend their money their marriage would be happier. The caseworker attempted joint interviews because of their expressed mutual concern. In the joint interviews each accused the other of untruthfulness and they drew farther apart. Each began to phone the caseworker in attempts to build himself up and to tear the other down. Mrs. G was diagnosed as having a hysterical character disorder. She viewed herself as depreciated and long

suffering. Mr. G had an oral aggressive character structure with some anal features. His financial manipulations were somewhat dishonest, he had extensive debts, and he withheld from his wife, as long as possible, all information about money.

Although the G's expressed a mutual concern, they could not make use of joint interviews at the particular time these were introduced. Mr. G's pattern of keeping information from his wife was his method of punishing her for her inability to gratify him or to satisfy his dependency needs. His need for a one-to-one relationship made it impossible for him to tolerate sharing the caseworker. Mrs. G's need to depreciate both herself and her husband was too strong for her to put the joint interview to use.

The caseworker must always be aware of his own feelings of competition, his degree of anxiety about expressed hostility, and his countertransference feelings toward both clients in joint interviews. Most workers are uneasy about joint interviewing, since this is not only a seldom used technique but is one that involves a different use of oneself. They are sometimes tempted to plunge into joint interviewing without full evaluation of all the factors involved (as in the G case above) because the couple seems so clearly to have a sustained mutual concern.

The quality of interaction between two clients needs to be evaluated carefully before the worker attempts joint interviews. The difference between success and failure in the use of this technique seems to lie in the degree of competitiveness between marital partners. Hence, sound diagnostic understanding is extremely important. All-pervasive competitiveness disrupts the interaction and prevents success in joint interviews. Such competitiveness can represent a demand for the caseworker's attention in terms of attempting to gain gratification or to depreciate the partner in the caseworker's eyes. If the caseworker is to succeed in keeping the interview focused on the area of mutual concern, the clients must be able to tolerate having their competitiveness put to constructive use. If the greatest need of one or both partners is to ally himself with the caseworker against the other, joint interviews will fail.

Mr. and Mrs. H came to the agency because Johnny, age 7, was failing in school. Mr. H rejected him completely since he was Mrs. H's illegitimate child, while he lavished affection on his own three younger children. Although Mr. and Mrs. H both expressed concern about Johnny they quickly focused on their stormy marriage. Joint interviews were attempted. However, the high degree of competitiveness outweighed their mutual concern and each partner battled for the caseworker's attention. Each picked at the other in a depreciating fashion, in a seeming attempt to destroy the other person in the eyes of the caseworker for the purpose of gaining all the caseworker's love and attention for himself. After a trial period contacts were discontinued.

Evaluating Progress in Treatment

There are several clues that one can use in evaluating the progress made in joint interviews. One is the manner in which the marital partners start to ignore the caseworker in the conversation. As they begin to relate more and more to each other, are able to contain their anxiety rather than to act it out, and can focus on the problem about which they are mutually concerned, there is not only less distortion in the way they relate to each other but also less and less argument. Moreover, they are able to talk about improvements in their situation and to look directly at each other as they talk. Sometimes they even turn their chairs to form a circle with the worker so that each is more obviously included in the conversation. The more passive, quiet, nonverbal partner becomes a little more vocal, and expresses his feelings and attitudes without provoking the wrath of the more vocal, controlling partner.

> Initially Mr. and Mrs. B literally sat with their backs to each other talking to the caseworker as if the other marital partner were invisible. As treatment progressed they started to face each other, then to talk to each other, and finally they left the caseworker out of their conversation entirely.

Summary

Because the family service agency is concerned with marital interaction and its effect on children and the total family unit, it should consider using joint interviewing as one treatment technique. This technique may help to restore the marital balance so that marital partners can mobilize all their strength to handle crisis situations. In the final analysis, it may assist in restoring family balance.

We have found that the ability of each marital partner to maintain an interest in, and put to use his concern about, the couple's mutual interests is the greatest single factor in the success of joint interviewing. The diagnostic clues and treatment techniques offered here have been developed on the basis of our experience in using joint interviews with clients who have diagnosed character disorders. We are not sure that the same would hold for the treatment of clients with neurotic problems. We realize that our formulations require further study and practice. We feel, however, that we have been able to demonstrate the effectiveness of joint interviewing in a small number of cases and trust that our findings will be useful to others.

Adapting Family Therapy to Multideficit Families

Geraldine E. McKinney

Much has been written about family therapy as an effective approach in the resolution of family problems, but little has been said about how it can be adapted for use with multideficit families to increase the family's motivation and capacity and the opportunities available to its members. Family group casework is not a substitute for the necessities of life that society should provide but is treatment for family dysfunction, such as faulty or inadequate parenting, problems of children, or basic emotional needs that have not been met adequately.

Worker activity is guided by the premise that the family as a group can develop more strength to cope with maturation and family roles and tasks by an emphasis on transactional processes within the family rather than by casework with individual family members. Traditional family group casework techniques must be modified to successfully engage the participation of families whose members have little reason to hope for success in dealing satisfactorily with people directly involved in their lives. Such families generally are not willing to risk involvement that could lead to further rejection or failure. Although sharing many of the distinguishing features commonly associated with "multi-problem," "hard-to-reach," or "hard core," the term "multideficit" more accurately characterizes such families. Here the emphasis is on what is missed or not attained rather than on problems or lack of motivation to change. In her article, "Can CaseworkWork?," Helen Harris Perlman defines what we really mean when we discuss these lacks. Discussing concepts developed by Abraham H. Maslow, she states: ". . . . human beings are driven by two major kinds of needs: one, to fill in 'deficit needs,' that is, to gratify basic biological and psychosocial wants; and, second, to fulfill 'developmental needs,' that is, to gratify strivings

Reprinted from *Social Casework,* Vol. 51 (June, 1970), pp. 327–333, by permission of the author and the Family Service Association of America.

for growth, competence, self-actualization."[1] These basic needs include hunger and sex, love and affection, a dependable economic "floor," and the feeling that one belongs to and is a part of society.[2]

In "The Broken Family," Otto Pollak analyzes the important distinction between the broken family and the uncompleted family—"[the former] is characterized by loss, [the latter] by luck of attainment."[3] Both Perlman and Pollak emphasize the important difference between what has been gained and then lost and what has never been acquired. This paper will discuss the latter circumstance.

Effects of Unmet Multideficit Needs

To offer effective service, set realistic goals, and know what to focus on to meet the needs of the families we are discussing, caseworkers must understand what happens when these tangible and intangible needs are not met. (We have been accused of being too general and ambiguous in our efforts to help individuals and families resolve problems or prevent them from occurring or escalating. Because our goals have not necessarily been those of our clients, our efforts have often not been fruitful.) What happens when many of the family's basic needs have not been met and there is little hope of attaining them? If parents continually experience inadequate housing, food, and clothing, as well as inadequate fulfillment of affectional needs, tensions and anxieties mount to the point where the energies needed for being an adequate parent are channelled into a struggle for basic needs, often in an indifferent and hostile environment and at a terrific cost in self-esteem and role performance. Often added to these hurdles are ill health, mental or physical disabilities, discrimination, lack of useful job opportunities, and inadequate schooling.[4] These various combinations of personal and environmental stresses and deficits make adequate social and parental functioning impossible.

Having been deprived themselves in so many areas of their lives, parents can contribute little to the growth and development of their children. In their struggle to have their own needs met, they have not had the opportunity or energy to learn appropriate adult role functions or child-rearing practices, because consistent, stable, growth-producing figures often were absent from their lives.

If we give up in discouragement and decide that massive societal change is the only answer (it certainly is a major one), we do multideficit families a terrible disservice. Those who have worked successfully with such families and can view them more clearly recognize that for the most part they share

---

[1] Helen Harris Perlman, "Can Casework Work?", *Social Service Review*, 42:443 (December 1968).
[2] Ibid.
[3] Otto Pollak, The Broken Family, in *Social Work and Social Problems*, ed. Nathan E. Cohen (New York: National Association of Social Workers, 1964), p. 321.
[4] Perlman, "Can Casework Work?"

with better-situated families the same values—education for their children, significant job opportunities, the wish to be more adequate parents, and to have their own "place in the sun." Success in helping the multideficit family depends on the extent of the deprivation, including a clear distinction between what must be supplied by the larger society and what social workers can do in working directly with and in behalf of these families.

What Can Family Group Casework Offer?

An important tenet of family therapy is that the family is an open system with a life of its own, and when one member is having some difficulty the other members in the household are affected.[5] Therapy deals with the communication processes unique to this family system. The use of the term family group casework in this article has been influenced by *Family Group Casework*, a monograph by Donald R. Bardill and Francis J. Ryan. Their concepts utilize those already known to social caseworkers and in the author's view can be readily adapted to work with multideficit families.[6]

What does family group casework have to offer that can be more effective than casework with individuals or parents? How do we engage the family in this effort?

Family group casework, with its emphasis on transactions and communication within the family and with significant others, focuses immediate attention on the family as a unit. This point needs stressing because often the multideficit family is seen as an amorphous collection of individuals vying with each other for attention or for the immediate meeting of their own needs, often at the expense of the others. This attention to the family as a constant allows the worker to be flexible in giving importance, when indicated, to family members as individuals within the context of the family, to parental functions, and to parent-child and sibling relationships.

Family interviewing aids in stimulating motivation (or in protective service situations stirs up some discomfort if serious problems, such as delinquency or neglect of children, are affecting family members) by allowing the family members to talk about how they would like the situation within the family to be different. It then enlists their help in examining together possible realistic solutions. This appeal to collective as well as self-interest is very important to people who think and act in concrete, self-defeating, and stereotyped ways and whose survival and affectional needs predominate. Not to be minimized is that family group casework provides a safe arena in which to risk sharing feelings and thoughts, leading to the

---

[5] A broader definition of family may need to be considered. A useful and realistic one is two or more people, adults and children, not always related, who share common concerns and are economic, cultural, or emotional resources for each other.

[6] Donald R. Bardill and Francis J. Ryan, *Family Group Casework: A Casework Approach to Family Therapy*, rev. and enl. ed. (Washington, D.C.: Catholic University of America Press, 1969).

growing recognition and acceptance that it is natural and expected to experience opposing emotions about important people and events in one's life.

It has been demonstrated over and over that initial work with an individual concerning family problems often leads him to drop out because tentative decisions arrived at between the worker and the client are often sabotaged by other family members' apathy, suspicions, projections, and distortions. Such pressures, overt or subtle, on the person not yet committed to working on the problems affecting his or her family lead to vacillation and withdrawal from agency contact.[7] Reaching-out techniques, with the family as the unit of attention, can be reassuring and less anxiety provoking.

An Illustration of Initial Resistance and Subsequent Engagement

Miss T, age twenty-eight, and her three illegitimate daughters, ages eight, ten, and thirteen, had been known to various health, welfare, and juvenile agencies for years. The T family, living in an urban inner-city area, received Aid to Families with Dependent Children (AFDC). Miss T, who had had a hysterectomy two years earlier, had never fully recovered and seldom followed the doctor's advice to lose wieght and have periodic medical checkups. The youngest daughter was mildly retarded. The girls were frequently truant from school because Miss T did not insist on regular attendance and had them care for her and the apartment when she was not well. When the girls did go to school, their clothing was usually shabby, ill fitting, and dirty.

Miss T herself did not take care of her personal appearance and gave the impression of being mentally dull. She had been apathetic and uninterested when approached by workers concerned about the children's truancy, shabby appearance, and misconduct in school. Repeated attempts to get Miss T to talk with the teachers about the girls' fighting and poor attendance led to sporadic school visits ending in outbursts of anger at the teachers.

The family lived in an apartment building also housing Miss T's mother and grandmother, both of whom had always told her what to do and how to rear the children. Although she ignored their suggestions, she used them to keep an eye on the girls when she left for the evening with a man. She never allowed a man to spend the night in her home, saying it would not be right for the girls to know of her activity, and besides a worker had once told her that if she did, she would be reported for neglect. The mother handled the girl's increasing interest in boys by saying, "Don't let those boys mess with you or you'll have a baby."

Any attempts to discuss her parental responsibilities or poor household

---

[7] Helen Harris Perlman, Intake and Some Role Considerations, *Persona: Social Role and Personality* (Chicago: University of Chicago Press, 1968), pp. 162–76.

management was met by hostility, apathy, or projection. Her relationship with the girls was more that of a sibling than of a parent. Although she gave lip service to her parental functions, there was never any transition to action. The girls were aware of this and seldom paid any attention to her feeble efforts to get them to behave. The apartment was chaotic, with no place to hang or put clothing and no place for the girls to study.

A worker with a family group casework orientation was assigned to work with the family. Miss T and the girls, used to caseworkers' visits, were apathetic and suspicious. Although aware of more basic problems in need of attention, the worker engaged the mother and girls in a discussion of what realistic and concrete things they would like to see changed to make life less troublesome for them.

The girls, after some prodding, talked generally about the hatefulness of the teachers, their dislike of school, and how they were laughed at by the other children because of their appearance. Miss T and the girls complained about the lack of drawer space in their apartment and how there never was enough money to use the laundromat to keep their clothing clean. All agreed that the lack of adequate and clean clothing was the problem that bothered them the most. In discussing what could be done about it, the worker learned that the girls did their own shopping at the thrift shop because Miss T did not like to be seen in public in her own shabby clothing.

When the girls were younger, the grandmother took responsibility for seeing that Miss T and the girls had clothes to wear. When asked about getting some clothing for herself, Miss T said her mother and the workers told her that her children should always come first. Asked what they thought of this, the older girls stated they wanted their mother to look nice. The girls decided that Miss T needed a coat and dress, and then she could help them buy their clothes. The worker affirmed the girls' desire for Miss T to have some decent clothes but noted Miss T's reluctance, although she had smiled her approval, actually to plan the shopping trip, even after they worked out plans to shop at a store where time payments could be made. The worker, aware of the grandmother's earlier role in buying for Miss T and the girls, asked if she herself could accompany them on this venture. The suggestion was met first with surprise and then with relief. Plans continued for the shopping trip, with every detail discussed and decided on by all in advance to prevent any possible mishap from occurring.

Subsequent interviews with the family over a period of many months centered around laundry problems, devising ways of fixing the apartment so clothing and household goods could be more neatly arranged, and working out a way of making the AFDC checks meet their basic financial needs. Choice of colors for painting the apartment became a collective enterprise; Miss T's longtime boyfried provided the paint.

From the very beginning, whenever appropriate, the worker reinforced Miss T's position as the girls' mother while allowing for some dependence and recognizing the complexities of living and rearing children in the "inner city." Broken appointments became less frequent and testing of the worker's interest and concern diminished. Finally, as the relationship became more firm, Miss T told the worker she guessed she'd better go to the school to see what "all the fuss was about." This decision came after some family talks with the worker about the pros and cons of education.

Miss T told the girls and the worker about her own feelings of inferiority and stupidity while in school, which led her to drop out in the eighth grade. She wished her mother had made her stay in school so she wouldn't "be so dumb now." The worker rehearsed with Miss T what she might anticipate at school and how she might react. At first, Miss T wanted the worker to accompany her, but as the date grew closer she felt she could handle it alone.

As small successes and confidence in the worker increased, Miss T discussed her fear of the older girls' getting pregnant. Further interviews with Miss T and the girls led to realistic discussions about sex and what the girls wanted for themselves when they grew up. Distortions were cleared up for both Miss T and the girls. Separate interviews were held between Miss T and the worker about the place of the boyfriend in Miss T's life. The girls and Miss T were gradually able to see themselves as separate individuals with their own needs as well as in their roles as members of a family. As motivation to work on current life situations increased, so did capacity, because the worker provided opportunities within their reach. Goals were short range and realistic. When they were appropriate, they were decided on by all concerned; thus the integrity of the family was enhanced.

Worker Activity

In the foregoing illustration, much of the worker's activity consisted of getting the family to help her understand the way things were and to discuss ways of figuring things out. It is also evident that family interviewing can help all members examine bothersome situations together, get experience in partializing, and devise steps leading to resolution of a family problem. The worker will often meet a barrage of angry feelings, particularly in the early stages and before the family members are actively engaged. It is essential that such feelings be credited but not allowed to continue. They should be discussed openly and freely and, if destructive, the consequences examined.

The worker emphasizes the desirability of clear communication by insisting on feedback so that decisions and actions are understood by all. This feedback is particularly important when family members give lip service to what is under discussion to please the worker or to curtail further discussion. By serving as a model of clear communication, by looking at all steps and facets of a decision with the family, the worker helps the family members begin to take more responsibility for their words and actions. For persons used to acting without much conscious thought or putting such thoughts into words, small early successes gained from carefully planned decision making can be very reassuring as well as pattern setting. Trust and hope are built as the family and worker puzzle out and work together on the problem at hand. The worker's words and actions emphasize the family as a unit, give status to the roles of each person within the unit, and respect both. Gradually, family members begin to realize, emotionally and intellectually, that what affects one member will have an effect on all. Also, they begin to see for themselves how their own actions have results that are beneficial to the family.

The relationship is based on how the worker can help the family accomplish its goals. All worker responses are ego enhancing and related to observable facts, including facts about feelings. The worker must develop and make a real part of his practice an awareness of the various modes of verbal and nonverbal communication. Any improvement in functioning, no matter how small, should be noted and commented on so that change can be seen as desirable and rewarding. No daily or life task is too insignificant to discuss if it has impeded successful role functioning within the family. This means the worker must be acutely sensitive to using every opportunity to clarify and reinforce appropriate role performance. The worker must be aware that selectivity and timing are also important in order not to overwhelm family members or move beyond their current capabilities.

Areas of Family Group Casework

Family group casework encompasses the same areas as work with individual members of multideficit families, for example, education to help the family operate more effectively in the community and live a more satisfactory life, establishment of sounder child-rearing practices, and encouragement of open communication. The latter must emphasize helping family members realize that what is said should reflect what is meant, thereby eliminating double messages and putting others in impossible double binds. For example, the worker can immediately observe and comment in a nonthreatening way when a mother tells her daughter Susie to see that the children behave but under no circumstances should she hit them. Unless the children and Susie know what is allowable and what alternatives can be used, Susie is put in a double bind and the children know it, and all are confused and act accordingly. [8]

Another example of how family group casework can be helpful in clarifying role functions is work with teenagers, where the problem is helping a teenage boy stay out of further trouble. Family interviewing can be most effective in getting the members to recognize and talk about the many areas that could be contributing to the difficulty, such as unclear expectations, lack of understanding of children's developmental stages— including wants and desires and how these might affect the situation—and situational or environmental pressures not clearly understood or appreciated, such as lack of money, peer and gang relationships, influence of mother's male companion. The teenage unmarried mother living at home, with or

[8] Charles H. King, "Family Therapy with the Deprived Family," *Social Casework*, 48:206–7 (April 1967).

without her baby, is often expected to assume the role of an adult for which she has had no preparation, either physically or emotionally. Family members as well as society have expectations for role performance that do not take into consideration all that goes into the preparation needed for assuming new roles. In the family interview, role expectations are discussed practically with attention to their emotional components. Here, feelings can be discussed that can lead to clearer understanding and more realistic expectations.

Worker as Advocate

Because many multideficit families are the victims of societal lags and intentional or unintentional indifference by institutions important to their survival and well-being, the worker may have to serve as an advocate when he and the family have identified a stumbling block to resolution of a problem and there are reasonable expectations for success. For example, a mother and her school-age children discussed the latter's refusal to eat the free school lunches because they, as well as other poor children, were embarrassed and humiliated by school personnel administering the program who insisted that "the welfare children" and those unable to pay be the last in line to receive their lunches. This announcement was made to the assembled children at the beginning of each lunch period. The justification was that it made it easier to count the number of free lunches distributed. Individually, mothers has asked the school to change this practice, to no avail. With agency backing, the worker, his client, and other interested mothers collectively approached the school principal and succeeded in having the practice changed.

Of utmost importance in working with multideficit families is that tasks to be performed and problems to be solved be talked about, made specific, and be within the family or member's capability, minimizing the possibility of failure. Therefore, individual and collective strengths and limitations within the family must be periodically evaluated. Family group casework is a decided asset here because problems can be thrashed out, shelved, partialized, or acted on, depending on the readiness of the family or person. The worker is a model with whom adults can identify, acting as flexibly as necessary in allowing for parental dependence while teaching and reinforcing change and self-mastery. Children begin to see positives in their parents as they grow in their ability to assume more appropriate or adequate roles. While allowing for individual differences and even encouraging them, the worker is active and direct in engaging family members to discuss their views of appropriate behavior as well as his own. The worker constantly seeks to get feedback and to correct obvious distortions. Because of the worker's direct involvement in many facets of the family's life, to have every member present all the time may not be necessary. The worker and the persons directly involved would decide.

Goals of Family Group Casework

Family group casework seeks to bring together, whenever possible, cognitive ability and feelings; through this union real improvement and maturation can take place in family functioning. However, with multideficit families this process is often a slow one and the worker needs patience. He must be content with modest goals. In dysfunctional families, roles are often distorted in the growth process and family members need opportunities to grow and take charge of themselves. We grow when we are able to put pieces together. Family group casework is a method for helping multideficit families acquire this growth.

Active involvement in the community and enlisting the aid of other workers, agencies, or significant others is an important part of the worker's repertoire. However, these involvements should always include, at least through discussion and through participation if possible, those family members most affected. Discussions can be held within the family group on the best way of working with the schools or the housing authority and what will be involved in visits to the food stamp office or clinic. If part of the casework plan, the imaginative use of paraprofessionals in certain instances could be added. Parents' needs are considered as well as those of the children. The importance of parental decisions is upheld but family members' participation in looking at the probable outcomes reinforces the family as a unit and the members as individuals with their own thoughts and feelings. The parents' gradual assumption of more adequate role functioning increases and solidifies the whole family's autonomy to function to its capacity.

It is important to mention the role of the worker in meeting affectional needs of parents who have been deprived before they in turn can give more valuably to their children and reach out in more adult ways to others.[9] If the worker emphasizes the family as a unit and every person's growth potential, he can give affection in acceptable ways and still maintain the integrity of the family and its members. Besides being a person who is comfortable with giving, the worker must recognize that he neither can nor should completely become the person sought for, consciously or otherwise. However, we do know that is it possible to help parents achieve more satisfying relations with others once their own feelings of self-worth are enhanced.

Summary

This paper has shown that family group casework concepts—outreach, advocacy, attention to initial engagement, limited goals, emphasis on growth

[9] Irving Kaufman, "Helping People Who Cannot Manage Their Lives," *Children*, 13:97 (May–June 1966).

potential, and flexibility in worker response—can be more effective with multideficit families than work with individual family members when the worker regards the family as a dynamic unit and increases its motivation, capacity, and opportunities to more adequately perform social roles and tasks. Agencies interested in expanding their services to utilize this approach must be willing to restructure caseloads, take a position on advocacy, and institute more flexible hours because of the necessity for home visits, accompaniment, and community work. The use of paraprofessionals should be carefully considered, not as a substitute for but as a part of effective services to multideficit families. For those interested workers engaged with multideficit families, who have little familiarity with family group casework concepts, a workshop, seminar, or course should be available to help them adapt their skills. Workers wishing to practice in this area should be able to tolerate frustration, be satisfied with small gains, have a real respect for differentness, and be comfortable with dependence while helping others grow toward interdependence.

The Parent

A Behavioral Approach to the Group Treatment of Parents

Sheldon D. Rose

Group work, like casework, has been defined as a method of treatment whose purpose is the improved social functioning of clients.[1] Although the social work literature abounds in descriptive typologies and case studies aimed at facilitating the practitioner's diagnostic skills, few articles have pointed to a specific set of procedures of intervention available to the social worker for the amelioration of the client's problems. In the absence of a theoretical foundation that would aid in specifying the worker's actions, little progress in this direction could be made. With the introduction of learning theory into social work, however, conceptual tools became available for describing in detail a large number of procedures of intervention, many of which have been systematically evaluated and effectively demonstrated in a variety of contexts.[2]

In contrast to the recent introduction of learning theory in social work, the small group has long been used by social workers. Social-psychological studies have demonstrated the power of the group to modify its members' behavior and attitudes.[3] Many operational hypotheses concerning the group's specific attributes are available to the social worker.

In developing a behavioral approach to the group treatment of parents,

[1] For a detailed description of this specific orientation to social group work, *see* Robert D. Vinter, "Social Group Work," in Harry L. Lurie, ed., *Encyclopedia of Social Work* (New York: National Association of Social Workers, 1965), pp. 715–724.

[2] *See* Edwin J. Thomas, ed., *The Socio-Behavioral Approach and Applications to Social Work* (New York: Council on Social Work Education, 1967). *See* especially Leonard Krasner and Leonard P. Ullmann, eds., *Research in Behavior Modification* (New York: Holt, Rinehart & Winston, 1965).

[3] For a review of findings pertaining to the implication of power for the behavior of group members, *see* especially Barry E. Collins and Harold Guetzkow, *A Social Psychology of Group Processes for Decision-Making* (New York: John Wiley & Sons, 1964), pp. 152–165.

Reprinted with permission of the National Association of Social Workers, from *Social Work*, Vol. 14, No. 3 (July, 1969), pp. 21–30.

the author has taken advantage of the empirical findings derived both from learning theory and from small group theory.[4] Since social workers are more familiar with small group theory, this paper will emphasize the procedures and principles derived from learning theory. Examples will be given that have been drawn from the experiences of five second-year students at the University of Michigan School of Social Work who worked with groups of parents and utilized some or all of the procedures reported here. The students worked primarily with parents from the lower socioeconomic strata in a settlement house, child guidance clinic, family service agency, public welfare agency, and school service agency. The groups ranged in size from three to eight members and met once a week for as few as five to as many as sixteen weeks.

Assessment

One of the major difficulties of parents who come to an agency is the inadequacy or inappropriateness of their child management procedures—the skills necessary to cope with their children's behavior. The purpose of behavioral group treatment is to increase their repertoire of procedures and to teach them the appropriate conditions under which these techniques should be applied.

Before the parent can be taught these skills, it is necessary to determine the child's presenting behavioral problem.[5] The parent learns to state the problem in terms of observable behaviors that occur or fail to occur in specific situations. He is also shown ways of estimating (or counting) how often they take place, since it is the frequency that is most often changed.

[4] A behavioral approach refers to a treatment approach that focuses on behavioral change and is based, at least in part, on learning theory. The author is by no means the first to describe a behavioral approach to the treatment of parents. Within the same theoretical framework, the following authors suggest a variety of procedures for parental training, many of which are not included in this article: Leopold O. Walder, Shlomo I. Cohen, Dennis E. Breiter, Paul G. Daston, Irwin S. Hirsch, and J. Michael Leibowitz," Teaching Behavioral Principles to Parents of Disturbed Children," unpublished manuscript, University of Maryland, College Park, Maryland; B. R. Patterson, Shirley McNeal, Nancy Hawkins, and Richard Phelps, "Re-programming the Social Environment," *Journal of Child Psychology and Psychiatry*, Vol. 8, No. 3-4 (December 1967), pp. 181–196; Salem A. Shah, "Training and Utilizing a Mother as the Therapist for Her Child" (mimeographed); Salvatore Russo, "Adaptations in Behavioral Therapy with Children," *Behaviour Research and Therapy*, Vol. 2, No. 1 (February 1964), pp. 43–47; L. O. Walder *et al.*, "Mothers as Behavior Therapists for Their Own Children," *Behavior Research and Therapy*, Vol. 3, No. 1 (February 1965), pp. 113–124.

[5] In this paper the author has tried to avoid the technical terminology that assumes the reader has a background in learning theory. An excellent introduction to this material as it applies to behavior is Arthur W. Staats and Carolyn R. Staats, *Complex Human Behavior* (New York: Holt, Rinehart & Winston, 1963). These authors review some of the more important research findings on the application to human subjects of behavior modification procedures derived from learning theory. *See also* the quarterly journal *Behavior Research and Therapy*, from 1963 to 1967, for case examples and recent research findings in this area.

Because most parents are not accustomed to speaking in specific terms about behavior and many lack observational skills that are a prerequisite to any description or counting, in most groups considerable time is given to training them to do so.

This training involves observing social situations, counting specific behaviors, charting these behaviors, and reporting the results to the group. In order to increase the probability of success, the parents first observe and count behaviors with which they are not especially concerned, e.g., the number of times the child leaves and enters the room, the context and number of situations in which he smiles or laughs. As they gain skill in observation, they note the frequency of the behaviors with which they are concerned, e.g., complaining, temper tantrums, soiling, teasing a sibling, being a truant. At this point a baseline—an estimate of the frequency of the behavioral problem prior to any endeavor at change—is established.

The baseline makes it possible to evaluate the degree of the child's behavioral changes as treatment progresses. However, in the experiences described in this paper, several difficulties arose that frequently made it necessary to rely on indefinite estimates or to forgo a baseline completely. Some of these problems were the parents' different levels of comprehension, their inadequate training, "forgetting," and a lack of co-operation by one of the spouses.

There is considerable evidence to support the contention that the events that follow a given behavior or the immediate consequences of that behavior have a strong influence on subsequent performances of it.[6] This is one of the basic precepts of learning theory and it forms the foundation for many forms of intervention. For this reason, parents are taught to observe and describe the immediate results of all their child's behaviors with which they are concerned. One set of consequences over which the parents have the most control are their own reactions—emotional, verbal, and motor. Once the parents are able to describe their responses, a major part of the treatment involves assessing them and training the parents in new or more appropriate ones.

In order to determine which behaviors should be modified, the worker also reviews the long-range consequences of each behavioral problem with the parents. In this process, many parents discover that the ultimate effects of one set of behaviors are relatively unimportant or, because of the consequences of previously unconsidered behaviors, they warrant immediate attention.

The following example is an excerpt from a group meeting in which some of the aspects of assessment are demonstrated:

> Mrs. M complained that her 11-year-old daughter had frequent temper tantrums. The members inquired about the conditions that led to them. Mrs. M, after reflecting a moment, indicated that her daughter responded this way

[6] *See* Krasner and Ullmann, *op. cit.*, esp. chaps. 5–12; and Staats and Staats, *op. cit.*, pp. 35–115.

whenever the mother said "no" or she became frustrated in any way. When asked what happened when she had these tantrums, Mrs. M said she usually gave her daughter exactly what she wanted in order to quiet her down. Mrs. W asked what might eventually happen if this habit were to persist. Throwing up her hands, Mrs. M replied that it would drive the whole family out of their minds and probably her teacher and friends, too.

The members then suggested to Mrs. M that she was maintaining the behavior she wanted to eliminate by rewarding her daughter after the temper tantrum. This implied the change procedures to be used: Mrs. M would have to find some alternative response to the temper tantrum, such as ignoring her, walking away, using calm verbal expression, and/or isolating her until the tantrum wore off.

Goal-Setting

After assessing the problem, each set of parents is helped by other parents to establish a goal of the desired frequency or intensity of behavior they would like to see their children achieve. The goals are formulated along the same dimension as those in relation to the presenting behavior or the conditions under which a behavior is appropriate. As is true of initial behavioral problems, the criteria of specificity and the description of the impinging conditions are essential in the statement of goals. The kind of goals dealt with include increasing the frequency of studying to one hour an evening, eliminating temper tantrums, reducing the frequency of fighting with a sibling to twice a week, learning new ways of responding to external stress or limitations, discriminating between situations in which loud, raucous play is appropriate or inappropriate, and increasing the frequency of coming home on time to every evening.

The worker also evolves with each parent or set of parents the goal each parent expects to achieve for himself by the end of treatment. Many parents are initially hesitant to look at ways in which they themselves must change in order to establish the desired changes in their children and, as a result, prefer to focus solely on the changes in the child. The worker may postpone encouraging the parent to make explicit the goal of his own behavioral change in the first phase of treatment. However, the need for parental change usually becomes obvious as soon as the children's behaviors are evaluated.

Examples of goals for parental change include ignoring temper tantrums and providing attention for more desirable behaviors, establishing rules and routines and ways of maintaining them, giving rewards in a consistent rather than haphazard manner, and learning and practicing the forms of manifesting interest in the child's school and recreational activities.

The processes of assessment and goal-setting begin in an intake interview and are continued in the group. Dealing with these tasks in the group provides each parent with an opportunity to help others specify their problems and impinging conditions and to observe on repeated occasions the relation of these conditions to the problem. The group members gradually take over from the worker the responsibility of determining whether the problem and goal are sufficiently specific and the conditions adequately described. By analyzing and dealing with problems other than their own, they increase their problem-solving skills in general and are better able to cope with new problems that may arise after the group terminates.[7]

Modifying Children's Behavior

After each set of parents decides which behavior they will seek to modify first, they begin to learn procedures for altering it. These procedures usually involve modifying antecedent and consequent conditions to improve the performance of desirable behaviors and decrease the performance of less desirable ones.[8]

Some examples of modifying antecedent conditions are the use of routines (when none existed previously), the introduction of models who have acceptable characteristics that are likely to be imitated, the elimination of seductive parental behaviors that previously triggered off undesirable behavior, and the use of cues to help the children remember the desired behavior. Examples of modifying consequent conditions are systematically applying limits, rewarding on a frequent and consistent basis, time-out procedures, and withholding attention or other rewards when they seem to be maintaining the undesirable behavior.

Extensive case examples of these techniques are to be found in the literature.[9] For this reason, in the remaining part of this paper the author will largely concentrate on the procedures used by the worker in teaching parents to become behavior modifiers.

Modifying Parents' Behavior

In order to teach the parents the techniques to be used, the following behavioral teaching procedures are utilized by the worker: programmed instruction, model presentation, behavioral rehearsal, and behavioral assignments. These should be included as a total group plan in such a way that each client may achieve his stated goals. Each of these procedures also

---

[7] *See* Arnold P. Goldstein, Kenneth Heller, and Lee B. Sechrest, *Psychotherapy and the Psychology of Behavior Change* (New York: John Wiley & Sons, 1966), pp. 212–259.

[8] The reader could rightfully raise the question of what is desirable and who determines the desirability of behavior. For purposes of this paper, the author has avoided such a discussion. The behavior modifiers more frequently allude to adaptive and maladaptive behaviors. *See* Leonard P. Ullmann and Leonard Krasner, *Case Studies in Behavior Modification* (New York: Holt, Rinehart & Winston, 1965), p. 20, for a definition of maladaptive behavior from the learning theorist's point of view.

[9] A large selection of such case examples is to be found in *ibid.* and recent issues of *Behaviour Research and Therapy*.

involves the other group members in some way in helping work toward the goals of treatment.

Since most parents are not able to learn to do everything at once, simple techniques are taught first, which are followed gradually by more complex procedures and combinations of different procedures. Usually parents try out each step between sessions. Although these techniques are usually integrated into a sequential plan, for purposes of analysis each will first be discussed separately.

Programmed Instruction

When treatment is viewed as a learning process, one can use the same techniques to teach new behavior that have proved effective in teaching academic subjects. One such technique is programmed instruction.[10] In the project, extensive use was made of a programmed instruction book on child management in which the writers train the parents to use a number of basic concepts and principles for working with their children.[11] Some of the principles on which the book focuses are increased consistency in parental behavior, the use of rules to provide increased consistency, and guidelines for selecting and enforcing rules. The book is especially effective for disorganized parents or those who have difficulty in limiting their children. It seems to be less effective for excessively orderly parents and strict disciplinarians. The following example from the book is a discussion followed by an exercise:

A. Selecting a Rule

1. What Is a Rule?

Any demand made on a child by a parent is a rule. Any task he must perform is a rule. Any decision regarding what he may have or may not have, what he may do or may not do—any such decision is a rule. Many parents dislike establishing rules. Usually they feel guilty when they require the child to do something which is unpleasant. They are not aware that consistent enforcement of a rule makes the world safer and more comfortable for the child.

Parents sometimes disguise rules to ease their guilt. They say, "Wouldn't you like to do the dishes?" or "Do you want to take a nap?" If the only

---

[10] *See* Staats and Staats, *op. cit.*, pp. 415–424. In this section, the writers discuss the principle of and values underlying programmed instruction as it applies to academic subjects. For a complete bibliography of programs applicable to social work practice, *see* Edwin J. Thomas and Roger Lind, "Programmed Instruction as Potentially Useful in Social Work Education: An Annotated Bibliography," *Social Work Education Reporter*, Vol. 15, No. 1 (March 1967), pp. 22–27, 33.

[11] *See* Judith M. Smith and Donald E. P. Smith, *Child Management: A Program for Parents* (Ann Arbor, Mich.: Ann Arbor Publishers, 1966).

acceptable answer to the question is "yes," it is a rule—regardless of the way it is stated. It would be much less confusing to the child if Mother said, "Do the dishes now," or "It's naptime."

Some rules are "long term." They must be enforced again and again over a long period of time. These rules usually govern the performance of a chore or a family routine. In each item below, choose the long-term rule.

· · · · ·

23. (a) Mark must cut the grass every Saturday afternoon.
    (b) Mark can earn 50c by weeding the garden.

24. (a) Mother provides Joan with an alarm clock.
    (b) Joan must dress herself without help before she leaves for school.

25. (a) Jeanine has to do the dishes on Monday and Friday.
    (b) Jeanine's brother asks her to substitute for him on Wednesday.

26. (a) Everyone must wash his hands and face before eating dinner.
    (b) It is often necessary to turn on the light in the dining room if the sun has set.[12]

There are several ways in which the program can be used. The first is to assign a number of principles and exercises each week to be completed at home. In the group meeting, the responses are discussed and applications to the parents' specific situations are suggested. Since the Smith and Smith program requires approximately a seventh-grade level of reading, some variation was required for several of the groups with whom the project members worked. In one group, the worker would prepare simplified excerpts from the program that were then discussed in the group. He asked the parents to complete the exercises during the meeting and helped them with concepts or words they did not understand. In most groups the entire book was not used. In some groups additional exercises were designed that taught other principles. Programmed instruction was the major basis of treatment in one group. In another group the parents thought the program was for parents with younger children and preferred discussing their own examples. In the remaining groups, programmed instruction was used to supplement the many other procedures used.

Model Presentation

When situations are presented in which some of the parents think the principle is difficult or impossible to enforce, the worker may suggest

[12] *Ibid.*, pp. 19–20.

appropriate parental responses and/or may encourage the other members to make suggestions. But such advice, although helpful, is seldom sufficient to add new behaviors to the parent's repertoire or to eliminate ineffective ones.[13]

To demonstrate appropriate behavior, the worker or a parent who has solved a similar problem plays the role of the parent. The other group members play the significant others in the situation. The parent whose problem is being enacted is the director. In this capacity he instructs the other members in performing their roles and defines the conditions that have led to the problem.[14]

In training the members, the worker may initially play all the roles.[15] When the parents begin role-playing, the situation is highly structured, i.e., the roles are predetermined in discussion. If notes describing each of the roles are distributed to the participants, anxiety about role-playing is usually reduced. The worker points out that dramatic ability is not essential and that as soon as the point has been made, the action will be terminated. Another way to reduce initial anxiety is to announce in advance that no situation should be played longer than five minutes. After some discussion the role-playing may be continued.

The role-play situation may be repeated several times until the parent feels comfortable enough to try it himself. The cast may be modified or various aspects of the situation may be adapted to simulate more nearly the varied conditions of real life.

In evaluating the role play, the entire group is encouraged to discuss the appropriateness of the parent's actions. The worker first discusses with the group what the probable consequences of these actions would be. Then the group discusses alternate actions and examines their probable effects. The members may also discuss the problems of applying any of these actions to their own situations.

There are several additional techniques for model presentation that do not involve role-playing and may be used instead of or, preferably, in addition to it. One is to invite parents from previous groups to tell their techniques for handling similar problems. Another is to present the case histories of such parents. Popular films or television programs in which characters have coped with similar problems may also be used.

---

13 For empirical evidence of this statement, *see* Arnold A. Lazarus, "Behaviour Rehearsal vs. Non-Directive Therapy vs. Advice in Effecting Behaviour Change," *Behaviour Research and Therapy*, Vol. 4, No. 2 (August 1966), pp. 209–212.

14 For an excellent summary of the principles and implications of model presentation for behavioral change, *see* Albert Bandura, "Behavioral Modifications Through Modeling Procedures," in Krasner and Ullmann, *op. cit.*, pp. 310–340.

15 For an extensive discussion of the possibilities and limitations of role-playing for treatment, *see* Raymond Corsini, with the assistance of Samuel Cardone, *Role-playing in Psychotherapy: A Manual* (Chicago: Aldine Publishing Co., 1966).

Behavioral Rehearsal

Behavioral rehearsal refers to the client's performance of behavior in the treatment situation that he would like to perform in the real-life situation. Lazarus, in a controlled experiment, has demonstrated the greater effectiveness of behavioral rehearsal in comparison to "advice-giving" or a "reflective-interpretive approach" in the treatment of persons who are unassertive.[16] Experience suggests that the approach can be used in the treatment of a wider range of behavioral problems than those used by Lazarus. It has been used by the parents to practice such behaviors as setting limits, establishing new reward procedures, ignoring situations that previously they could not ignore, and even using behavioral rehearsals with their children. Practice in the simulated situation seems to facilitate performance in the real situation by reducing the anxiety associated with it.[17]

Behavioral rehearsal usually follows some form of model presentation. Prior to a person's performance of his own role in a family situation, the worker and the group members review exactly what new behaviors the parent is to perform. After the first rehearsal, the other members evaluate the performance and make additional suggestions for alterations. The situation is repeated at least once. Then the parent is given a behavioral assignment to perform some of the behaviors rehearsed with the group in the real-life situation. It is seldom possible in one session for each person to rehearse his situation. In the course of several meetings, however, it is helpful if everyone who is willing has the opportunity to perform at least once. It is preferable to begin with situations that have implications for several, if not most, of the group members.

Behavioral Assignments

One of the major problems of group and individual treatment is a lack of concern about generalizing change to situations outside the treatment situation. Although role-playing focuses on extra-group situations, it is performed within the group context. Moreover, it demonstrates and provides practice but does not assure performance in the real-life situation. For these reasons, at each meeting behavioral assignments are given to group members so that they may try out newly learned behaviors outside the group prior to the next meeting. The following are four requisites for the successful performance of a behavioral assignment:

1. The assignments should be highly specific. The client should know exactly what he must do and the conditions under which the given responses

---

[16] *See* Lazarus, *op. cit.*, pp. 205–212.

[17] The empirical evidence for this assumption has been discussed by Goldstein, Heller, and Sechrest, *op. cit.*, pp. 97–109.

should be performed. Furthermore, if certain unexpected conditions arise (e.g., illness), or if the appropriate conditions do not occur, alternate behaviors, such as telephoning the worker, should be developed.

2. The client should be able to handle the assignment, i.e., there should be a high probability of success. If the client succeeds early in treatment, it is more likely that he will continue to try behavioral assignments.[18]

3. The client should commit himself, at least verbally, in front of his fellow group members to attempt the performance of his assignment. If the client states exactly what he is going to do, it will be more difficult for him to hedge or explain away his failure.

4. The client should report the details of his attempt to carry out the assignment to the group. Without such monitoring procedures, it seems that assignments are soon neglected. Monitoring by the other group members serves both as a reward for trying the task and a source of information about how it can be done more effectively the next time.

Initially, the assignment may be suggested by the worker on the basis of the previously mentioned criteria. The client, together with the other group members, works out the details. The worker then asks the client if he understands and thinks he can perform the assignment within the allotted time. If not, the assignment is adjusted accordingly. Once he has had some experience in applying the criteria, each client develops his own assignment with assistance from the others.

Each assignment must be viewed as being part of a sequence. As one assignment is completed, a slightly more difficult one should be given. The sequence should ultimately lead to the attainment of the treatment goal. The completion of each assignment is, in a sense, the achievement of a subgoal.

Two examples that point up the interrelationship and sequence of the aforementioned techniques are the following:

Mrs. L, Mrs. A, and Mrs. B complained that their children never did chores in the house. After the Smith and Smith program on enforcing rules had been discussed, Mrs. M demonstrated in a role-playing incident (model presentation) how she set and enforced rules. She was followed by Mrs. L who rehearsed behaviors in which she enforced a daily bed-making rule (model presentation). Then Mrs. A played her own role in a situation in which her daughters refused

---

[18] Success in task performance has been shown by D. G. Marquis, Harold Guetzkow, and R. W. Heyns, "A Social Psychological Study of the Decision-Making Conference," in Guetzkow, ed., *Groups, Leadership and Men: Research in Human Relations* (New York: Russell Sage Foundation, 1963), pp. 55–67, to be related to several indications of satisfaction. Success is probably experienced as an intrinsic reward and, therefore, according to learning theory, should function to increase the probability that the behaviors that preceded it would occur with greater frequency or intensity.

to do the dishes (behavioral rehearsal). Mrs. M prompted Mrs A. about what she should say. Finally, the group gave Mrs. L, Mrs. A, and Mrs. B the assignment of developing and enforcing a rule with one of their children (behavioral assignment) and reporting to the group at the next weekly meeting.

Mr. and Mrs. N had difficulty limiting the acting-out behavior of their son, aged 11. The group members discussed the antecedent conditions of the child's behavior and the previous ways in which Mr. and Mrs. N responded to it, which included showering him with attention, arguing with each other, and pleading with the child to stop.

The worker suggested several alternative responses, such as immediately removing the child from the scene of the acting out without discussion. Mrs. McA, who had used this procedure effectively, demonstrated how it should be done. The worker played the role of the son (model presentation).

Mr. and Mrs. N were hesitant about role-playing but were willing to describe exactly what they would do (behavioral rehearsal). They agreed to try it out during the week (behavioral assignment). The worker pointed out that they could expect an increase in the undesired behavior before the situation got better, and Mrs. McA affirmed this from her experience.

Other group members thought it would be helpful if, after this first attempt, Mr. and Mrs. N would call Mr. and Mrs. McA to tell them what had happened so they would not have to wait until the next meeting (monitoring the behavioral assignment).

Relationship

Since relationship is a core concept in the present-day practice of social work, a description of its place in the behavioral approach seems necessary. Although the worker does not focus on relationship-building as a means of intervention, the low rate of discontinuance and the frequent verbal expressions of satisfaction suggest that quite rapidly he becomes a highly attractive individual.

The factors that contribute to relationship-building appear to be the following: (1) The worker provides a highly structured situation in which answers are given to the clients' specific problems. (2) The worker readily recognizes and rewards achievement. (3) Accomplishments are clearly defined in such small steps that everyone achieves something between and during every meeting, which affords the worker ample opportunity to be rewarding. The feeling of success even in small things may be in itself an important internal reward for many parents. (4) Since goals, procedures, and assumptions of treatment are made explicit, the situation is not ambiguous. This reduces anxiety and, in turn, increases the worker's attractiveness.[19]

The social worker does not set aside his natural warmth, understanding, or acceptance of the clients with whom he works. He adds to his skills in relationship the more specific techniques espoused in this paper. The parent, too, is taught that the techniques are to be applied in a warm and understanding social climate. Since the parents cannot be taught warmth, it is

---

[19] For a discussion of the relation between ambiguity, message threat, and the therapist's attractiveness, *see* Goldstein, Heller, and Sechrest, *op. cit.*, pp. 171–177.

sometimes helpful to teach them the physical manifestations of it. In doing so, there is some support for the assumption that the appropriate feelings will eventually follow the behavioral manifestation.[20]

Value of the Group

There are many therapeutically facilitating aspects of the group, most of which are common to all group treatment approaches. In a group there is an abundance of models for the client to imitate. Although clients are treated for the absence of behaviors necessary to deal adequately with their children, almost all parents have within their repertoire adaptive behaviors they can demonstrate or teach to other parents in the group. The worker encourages and structures imitation of those behaviors appropriate to each client in terms of his individual treatment goals. The group also provides a large variety of role-players for model presentation and behavioral rehearsal.

When the cohesiveness of the group is high, approval and disapproval of the group members function as effective controls.[21] Encouraged by the worker, members tend to create a norm of accurate accounting of extra-group activities. Thus the group may be an especially efficient means of monitoring behavioral change outside it. With the worker's help, the group members also develop norms for working on their problems, being specific as opposed to global, and participating in discussion and role-playing. Thus the parent, in observing and participating in the treatment of others, develops a range of solutions for a range of problems.

Conclusion

In the groups in which the behavioral approach was used, most parents claimed at termination that they were better able to handle their problems and many felt they would be better able to cope with any new problems their children might have. The workers, too, stated that it was helpful to have prescriptions for what they could do to help the parents. They also indicated that it was easier to prepare for meetings and evaluate outcomes than in previous treatment situations.

Although the outcomes reported in this paper are the results of a

---

[20] *See* Gerry Brosky, "The Relation Between Verbal and Non-Verbal Change," *Behaviour Research and Therapy*, Vol. 5, No. 3 (August 1967), pp. 183–192. Brodsky demonstrates how verbal behavior follows nonverbal learning. If it is assumed that verbal behavior is an indication of the feelings of the individual, this supports the present author's contention that feelings can best be changed by first changing behaviors associated with them (the author's limited experience also supports this contention).

[21] Compare B. M. Bass, *Leadership, Psychology and Organization Behavior* (New York: Harper & Bros., 1960), p. 60. On the basis of extensive research experience, Bass points out that the more attractive the group, the greater the rewards that may be earned by its members.

demonstration project and are anecdotal in nature, they are sufficiently promising to encourage an expansion of this approach and an exploration of the use of additional behavioral procedures to facilitate still further the treatment of parents in groups.

The Psychotherapist and Women's Liberation

Barbara Stevens

In all forms of therapy, regardless of the therapist's theoretical stance, the female patient tends to model herself on the therapist.[1] Therapies that are considered successful end with the patient's personality and value system more congruent with the therapist's than they were at the outset.[2] Existing research indicates that this is unavoidable and that rather than protest against it, therapists should recognize and use it.

An important result of this recognition necessarily involves the therapist's extensive self-examination of his own value system. This article presents an analysis of the role of women in our society, identifies the values underlying that analysis, and discusses the implications of women's liberation for the practicing therapist.

If one attempts to define a woman's role, it immediately becomes clear that despite marked progress in opening up professions and trades to women and despite the fact that one-third of the work force in this country is female, a woman's primary roles are still those of wife and mother. When a woman deviates from these roles—when she earns "real" money—she is thought of as filling a man's role.

Role Inadequacies

Homemaking has been touted as the ultimate in self-fulfillment, as the mystical realization of a woman's total self. It would certainly be bizarre to maintain that all men can find fulfillment by becoming lawyers; we

---

[1] *See*, for example, Gerald Albert, "Identification Therapy," *Psychotherapy: Research and Practice*, Vol. 5, No. 2 (Summer 1968), pp. 104–107; and Richard G. Farmer, "Values and Personal Style in Psychotherapy," *Psychotherapy: Theory, Research and Practice*, Vol. 6, No. 2 (Summer 1969), pp. 131–136.

[2] David Rosenthal, "Changes in Some Moral Values Following Psychotherapy," *Journal of Consulting Psychology*, Vol. 19, No. 6 (December 1955), pp. 431–436.

Reprinted with permission of the author and the National Association of Social Workers, from *Social Work*, Vol. 16, No. 3 (July, 1971), pp. 12–18.

know that different men have different needs, talents, and drives. There is no evidence to indicate that women are less varied in this respect. Yet when a female infant is born, her parents can predict what her primary occupation will be in twenty-five years: she will be a wife and mother, first, if not exclusively. No such prediction can even be attempted for a male baby.

Homemaking is essentially a stultifying, self-negating role. If a women works as a domestic, cleaning homes and caring for other people's children, it is clear to everyone that she is filling the most menial and boring job. Yet the same job, unsalaried in one's own home, is considered exciting, rewarding, and creative. This is indeed an amazing leap in logic.

Today most people recognize that only the most acrobatic rationalization can make cleaning floors a creative experience. But the myth persists that caring for small children means combining the roles of teacher, minister, doctor, psychologist, and inventor. This is undoubtedly true for a short time each day. The remaining time is spent in endless drudgery and nerve-wracking boredom. Insofar as a woman can find the inner discipline and the time to pursue something of substantial value to herself, she is subjected to continual interruption from children who really do need an adult's attention and supervision. Motherhood—basically a joyous and wonderful experience —becomes a prison that warps the souls and minds of women when it is imposed as a twenty-four-hour-a-day job.

Just as men need to grapple with the whole world, women need to make a place for themselves in the larger society outside their neighborhood. Volunteer work can be meaningful, but in a culture that measures worth in terms of money, "not paid" usually implies "not valued." Most people need to be paid for emotional as well as economic reasons. The pace of our society today and the demands of jobs and professions are such that no one can successfully take ten years off to raise children. Ten years off means no seniority, atrophied skills, forgotten knowledge.

Despite the fact that the needs for meaningful work is probably as strong in women as it is in men, the mystique persists that it is unfeminine to succeed, to be capable, to achieve. Only a castrating woman could surpass a man. Along with Freud and Deutsch, our society and the social work profession label women intrinsically passive. The fact that most social workers are women has not helped the profession to exert leadership in challenging this myth. Rather it seems to have reinforced the profession's subservience to psychiatry—the male profession.

Being primarily a wife and mother means being primarily a nonbeing. Although it has become trite to mention it, the assumption of her husband's name and consequent loss of her own on being married have tremendous emotional significance for a woman. Her status and social class follow her husband's—regardless of what other roles she plays. Professional women are invariably asked in social and business situations: "And what does your husband do?" This question is a basic part of evaluating a woman.

The roles of wife and mother deprive a woman of her identity in a still more basic way. These roles are intrinsically passive. They require the subjugation of oneself to the needs of others—a husband and children. But the concept of identity requires the assertion of that identity. No self can survive for long if it never stands up, if it never occupies space. And the mere act of occupying space necessarily invites conflict with others who want that space or want to move through it. The myth of woman as a passive-dependent creature who cannot and should not stand up and assert herself has restricted humanity to the male sex.

Women as well as men need some clear area in which they can express and develop their unique individuality. This is not to deny the many intrinsic joys of caring for others. The emotional satisfactions of motherhood are indeed extensive. But they do not substitute for an identity; they enrich one. To develop the multitudinous facets of oneself, to establish a clear identity, a human being must first define him- or herself in some direct relationship to the larger society. The absence of such a self-definition leads to feelings of insignificance and impotence.

Oppression of Both Sexes

The division of sex roles in this society oppresses men as well as women. Men are saddled with the entire financial burden, not only of their children, but also of their doll-wives. This is indeed a burden in our inflationary and materialistic society. And manhood has been equated with financial success, which makes the threat of failure even more potent. Men are even denied meaningful contact with their children, to the detriment of both. Just as women are not permitted to express their assertive needs, men are not permitted to express their dependent needs. Whole people, however, have both sets of needs.

Thus women's liberation cannot mean that women will fill men's roles. In its deepest sense it means the liberation of both sexes from the sterility of imposed, pre-fabricated roles. It means the freeing of all human beings to develop themselves fully. Both sexes would be able to display the entire gamut of personality types without fearing that they would lose their sexuality in so doing. Society as a whole would assume some of the financial and physical burdens of caring for children—perhaps as the Israeli kibbutzim do or in other ways—and all adults would have greatly expanded opportunities for exploring and expressing themselves.

Freedom and the absence of imposed modes of behavior are threatening ideas. It is far easier to be a Babbitt than an Arrowsmith, far simpler to be Mrs. John Smith than Lucy Stone. Hopefully, we can someday create a more secure, less anxiety-ridden society, in which increasing numbers of human beings can be people instead of stereotyped shadows. Until that time the specific task of the psychotherapist is to help people move toward the goal of self-development by assisting them in self-exploration, self-acceptance, and self-realization.

Implications for Psychotherapy

Obviously, women's liberation has profound implications for the practicing therapist.[3] The therapist's underlying attitude toward his female patient is communicated in subtle and uncontrollable ways. If he sees her as a passive and dependent being whose true happiness is to be found in moderate submission to her husband, adoration of her children, and personal immersion in the joys of housekeeping, he will communicate this attitude to her, no matter how hard he attempts to be neutral. This attitude will permeate his whole stance—the areas in which he seems most interested and on which he chooses to focus, his demeanor, tone of voice, posture and most minute facial expressions.[4] Therapists like to pride themselves on the speed with which they "psych patients out." But patients psych out therapists too—and fairly rapidly.[5] How therapists feel about themselves, how they relate to others, what kind of behavior makes them uncomfortable or they approve of are readily seen by patients. Moreover, they provide extensive clues for deciphering the therapist's values and beliefs about women. Thus unless a therapist can truly empathize with a woman's need to assert herself and develop herself socially and intellectually—as well as physically and emotionally—he cannot help her to develop her human potential.

Insofar as a therapist accepts society's role prescription for women, he is implicitly accepting the value judgment that underlies it: that women are basically inferior to men.[6] Thus even when no specific role conflicts are at issue in therapy—when "women's issues" are never mentioned—the therapist's unconscious attitude toward his patient is to some extent antitherapeutic. Because his contempt for her is usually ego syntonic for her, it may do no more than perpetuate her own self-contempt; it certainly will not help her overcome that self-contempt.

With the exception of those patients whose object relations are so impaired that they are virtually nonexistent, a woman's situation brings her into constant contact with people who define her in destructive and con-

---

[3] For purposes of simplicity, the male pronoun will be used throughout to refer to the therapist. This is not meant to imply that female therapists are necessarily less accepting of oppressive societal standards for other females than are male therapists.

[4] Theodore Reik, *Listening with the Third Ear* (New York: Grove Press, 1948), chap. 14.

[5] Fred E. Fielder and Kate Senior, "Exploratory Study of Unconscious Feeling Reactions in 15 Patient-Therapist Pairs," *Journal of Abnormal and Social Psychology*, Vol. 47, No. 2, Supplement (April 1952), pp. 446–453.

[6] There seems to be no other possible explanation for assigning an entire sex to a role that, although nearly impossible to perform well, is so under-valued by our society that totally inadequate persons with no preparation for the role are not only permitted but encouraged to perform it. Hence the often-heard statement: "No need to worry about her future—she can always get married and have a family."

stricting ways. By the time she starts therapy, she has introjected many if not all of these destructive stereotypes. Unless the therapist can truly understand tnis and take the side of her self against these introjections, no matter how buried and repressed that self is, their work together cannot succeed. This means that the therapist must frequently watch for hints of intellectual and societal strivings that have long been repressed and denied.[7]

All therapists need and use some theoretical model to help them diagnose and treat their patients, and no theorctical model accepts the patient's definition of her problems as ultimately correct. Over and over again patients ask therapists to help them never to be angry, to be satisfied in self-restricting jobs, and to end their headaches and depression without disturbing their repressed anger. In fact, the patient's initial description of her problem is rarely even related to her definition of her problem after six months of therapy. This is not because the therapist has imposed his values on her, but because he has helped her to explore her inner feelings and needs without imposing his moralistic judgments and because his theoretical formulations have guided him in understanding her and therefore redefining her problems.

Theory Versus Values

It is important to differentiate between theory and values. Theory is an attempt to describe reality on the basis of those facts at one's disposal, without morally judging the objective reality. Values are moral judgments one makes about this reality. Because few established facts exist about human psychology, values are inevitably present in the choice of a theory.

The vast bulk of this discussion of sexual roles in our society is theory, comparable to the theoretical idea which all therapists impose on their patients that all human beings are subject to anger. Thus the statement that if a woman develops her potential and allows her inner self to find expression, she will not continue to be exclusively a wife and mother is theoretical, not a value judgment. Clinicians must evaluate this statement and, if they believe it to be true, must use it to help them understand and treat their female patients.

The value judgment underlying this theory is that women have as much potential and inner worth as do men. This author wants to impose that value judgment on her patients, since one of her major goals is to enhance the patient's self-image. Because therapy inevitably involves substantial modeling of the therapist by the patient and significant reshaping of patient's values toward those of the therapist, it is incumbent on therapists to examine and acknowledge their values instead of to pretend a nonexistent neutrality.

[7] Many therapists believe that the therapist must not impose values on his patients. If a patient is happy being exclusively a wife and mother, the therapist must not challenge her because he feels that a woman cannot be fulfilled in these roles. Thus watching for hints of frustration is interpreted as imposing values on a patient. This author believes that concern about imposing values is a diversion from the real issues involved.

In addition, it is important to distinguish between manipulating a patient regarding her actions and maintaining one's analysis of a patient's psyche, even if she disagrees with that analysis. Occasionally a therapist will attempt to influence the course of a patient's life; he may intervene by forbidding a woman to have a child or attempt to persuade a patient to move out of her parents' home. These are both attempts to impose one's analysis on a patient and are acceptable and common in therapy, although such actions are controversial, especially if clumsily done.[8] Therapists have considerable insight into people's motivations and needs, which should be used in working with them. For example, although therapists should not necessarily try to push housewives into the labor market, it is incumbent on them to explore the constricting and oppressive aspects of the housewife role with their patients. Thus they must develop some understanding of the actual ways in which women are oppressed in our society in order truly to understand women.

Societal Explanations

There are societal explanations for feminine masochism, self-hate, and penis envy, problems that many, if not all, women experience on some level in our society. Women are kept down in our society. They are not promoted to administrative positions, even in women's professions like teaching and social work. They are shunted from classes that would prepare them for demanding careers, hired last and fired first in industry, paid consistently less than men for the same jobs, and generally ignored in intellectually demanding situations. In such an environment, the intrapsychic orientation in psychotherapy is not sufficient. It is essential that this orientation be supplemented by an understanding of the social causes of emotional problems.

As long as one maintains that penis envy is essentially an inherent characteristic of women—that little girls, on noting the difference between their anatomy and that of little boys, universally and necessarily are jealous—the psychotherapeutic focus must be toward accepting and modifying women's feelings of anger and inferiority. In fact, the orthodox view is that women's feelings of inferiority are accurate. As Freud says:

> A woman often frightens us by her psychical rigidity and unchangeability. . . . There are no paths open to further development . . . as though, indeed, the difficult development to femininity had exhausted the possibilities of the person concerned. As therapists we lament this state of things.[9]

When one recognizes the sociopolitical basis of these feelings of self-

---

[8] *See* F. A. Coyle, Jr., and Phillip Erdberg, "A Liberalizing Approach to Maladaptive Fundamentalist Hyperreligiosity," *Psychotherapy: Theory, Research and Practice*, Vol. 6, No. 2 (Summer 1969), pp. 140–142; and Charles B. Truax et al., "Effects of Therapist Persuasive Potency in Individual Psychotherapy," *Journal of Clinical Psychology*, Vol. 24, No. 3 (July 1968), pp. 359–362.

[9] Sigmund Freud, *New Introductory Lectures on Psychoanalysis*, James Strachey, trans. (New York: W. W. Norton & Co., 1965), pp. 134–135.

contempt—when one admits that they are realistic because we live in a male-dominated society—one need no longer postulate an inborn genital and characterological deficiency to explain them. Just as investigation of the familial causes of schizophrenia has freed us from the medieval belief in demons as the cause of madness, recognition of the social causes of a female's feelings of inferiority should free us from belief in inborn causes. This understanding of the true roots of feminine self-hate also leads to a recognition that a woman's conscious attempts to change her social situation —through political action or personal confrontation with her life situation— are constructive and necessary moves towards overcoming these problems.[10]

Case Illustration

The following case illustrates many of the points made in this article:

> Mrs. M had recently separated from her alcoholic husband (at his initiative) and was extremely depressed and lonely. She was anxious about her ability to live alone and to raise her sons and was excessively dependent on her husband for such day-to-day matters as rides to medical appointments. Despite her re- latively unambivalent feeling that she would be better off divorced and the fact that a previous therapist had supported the decision to separate, Mrs. M was so terrified of the prospect of being independent that she found it impossible to end her relationship with her husband.
>
> Mrs. M was a depressed young woman who covered her depression with anger, which was the only emotion readily available to her. She was constricted and moralistic, with a rigid, punitive super-ego that left her paralyzed with guilt for every minor sin. Also, she saw herself as valueless and despicable.
>
> In the first four months of therapy she worked out many of her feelings of hurt and anger vis-à-vis her husband and was able to view him with increased calm and rationality. She became more able to identify the real feelings beneath her quick anger and to accept anxiety, depression, hurt, and loneliness as admis- sible, if painful, parts of herself.
>
> After several months of therapy, realistic financial considerations made it im- portant for her to find a job. Mrs. M had never worked, but the therapist's support and Mrs. M's increased stability and self-knowledge enabled her to find a job as an aide in a hospital. The emotional impact of this job was amazing. In one week her affect changed from depression to self-satisfaction—she felt valuable and needed. It seemed as though the self-confidence she had been building in therapy had been proved through this one experience of being paid for rendering service. This change in affect was essentially maintained for the remaining three months of therapy.
>
> A short time later Mrs. M discovered that she was pregnant (by her husband). By this time she had filed for divorce. Just how much the pregnancy represented a repressed wish to resume the marriage was unclear. Certainly, she was still ambivalent about divorce. Her feelings about another child, though, were rela- tively unambivalent: she saw another baby as an intolerable burden. It would prevent her from continuing work, which she now saw as a major source of satis- faction as well as an economic necessity. She felt that she was not an especially good mother, her children were not gratifying to her, and she certainly did not want to raise another child alone.

[10] Zira DeFries and Lilo Grothe, "Les jours de mai, 1968—Barnard College," *Adolescence*, Vol. 4, No. 14 (Summer 1969), pp. 139–162.

The therapist raised the possibility of an abortion. Mrs. M's Catholicism and her rigid, moralistic attitude made this decision exceptionally difficult, but she did get a therapeutic abortion. She was able to discuss her anger at having been "pressured" into the abortion and to recognize that the abortion had been something that she truly wanted beneath her super-ego prohibitions. Furthermore, she was able to resolve her shame and guilt sufficiently to tell her friends and family about the abortion.

Mrs. M emerged from this traumatic experience with a strengthened belief in her ability to cope with crises. She began dating a man who, whatever his problems, did not drink and treated her with respect. She made the difficult and realistic decision to move to the town where her mother and sisters lived so that she would be away from her ex-husband. She felt much less fearful about her ability to support herself and cope with her life.

This case clearly shows how a woman can improve her self-image and reduce her irrational dependency and masochistic tendencies by actively opposing society's stereotype of her. Mrs. M's angry stance was false: beneath her anger was a fear that she was totally unable to deal with the world alone. This terror of being alone was one major factor in keeping her chained to her husband. The fact that she had never worked built and reenforced her negative self-image and dependency. The combination of economic pressure and therapeutic support enabled her to get a job, but it was the job itself that triggered remarkable emotional progress. Her self-image was greatly enhanced by her discovery that she could support herself and her children, that she could function as a full adult. Also, her desire to form an emotionally satisfying relationship with a man helped her to leave her husband emotionally and begin dating other men.

Masochism was one of the most important drives in Mrs. M's personality. Her marriage to an alcoholic and her overwhelmingly punitive super-ego were two major expressions of her masochistic tendencies, as were the guilt and shame she experienced about the abortion. Although her religion did in fact oppose abortion, a less masochistic woman would have had no trouble in rationalizing her decision not to have a baby. Mrs. M's decision to abort the baby was a testament to the progress she had made in combating her masochism. By demonstrating to herself that she was not the slave of her body, she took a step toward overcoming that self-enforced slavery and enhanced her belief in her ability to control her destiny.

Conclusion

It is beyond the scope of this paper to explore the individual etiology of Mrs. M's problems. The various patterns of relationships in her family that built her dependency to its irrational proportions, determined her feelings of inadequacy and self-hate, and developed her fear and envy of men have not been examined. It is certainly not enough to note that Mrs. M's problems were similar to those of many women in our society. Merely recognizing the ways in which society supports and maintains women in their self-hate and passivity is certainly not adequate for an understanding of any patient. The specific roots of these feelings must be explored for each individual patient.

Many influences converged to produce Mrs. M's masochism, feelings of inadequacy, excessive dependency, and depression. What is important is the dramatic way in which Mrs. M's confrontation of and behavioral opposition to the female stereotype resulted in her emotional progress. Although Mrs. M had little awareness of herself as a liberated or oppressed woman, she took some important steps to liberate herself, economically by finding a job and biologically by getting an abortion.

In most women the societal aspects of neurosis are less striking and dramatic, and no such confrontation occurs with the female role. However, on some level every female in our society—certainly every disturbed female— has conflicts between her needs and society's expectations, and a therapist must be sensitive to this fact if he is to be successful with women. The more he helps his patients to honor and express their inner selves, the more likely it is that they will strike out in new role directions. When patients do attempt to develop new roles for themselves, the therapist must be prepared to support them.

The Middle-Age Separation Crisis and Ego-Supportive Casework Treatment

Sidney Wasserman

It has become increasingly apparent in mental health research that the years forty to sixty-five—middle-age—when human beings are at their most responsible, fullest, busiest phase—are the most neglected by theorists and researchers. It is that time of life described as "the crisis point of growth or regression" yet we still know so little as to what determines how individuals caught up in the middle-age crisis grow or regress.

Erik Erikson has conceptualized the normal ego crisis as "generativity versus stagnation," whereby the middle-aged person is primarily interested in establishing and guiding the next generation. On the opposite end of the spectrum, the ego threat is being "unable to generate and guide," to become stagnant and unfulfilled (Erikson, 1959). Many clients who are referred to social agencies are caught in the latter spiral, hopelessly *de*-generating, continuously frustrated and impotent in their ability to guide the next generation—their own adolescent and emerging young adult children. By the time the couple and/or family comes to the attention of a social agency, the marriage and mental health of all members concerned are at serious risk. The adolescent emancipation crisis has ascended in the faces of the 'descending' parents.

This built-in generational paradox gets superimposed on a myriad of conflicts and problems. Middle-aged fathers are often interacting with adolescent sons at a time when the fathers themselves are most vulnerable regarding loss of role, failure in job promotion and prestige, and the threat of younger men eagerly waiting to take their place. Middle-aged mothers are commonly plagued with psychological anxieties around menopause, fearing loss of sexuality along with the physical reality of loss of fertility. All of this happens while their adolescent daughters are rapidly approaching their prime sexual years.

Reprinted from *Clinical Social Work Journal*, Vol. 1 (Spring, 1973), pp. 38–47, by permission of the author and publisher, Behavioral Publications, 72 Fifth Avenue, New York, New York 10011. Copyright 1973.

In our eagerness to rescue the adolescent, social caseworkers frequently convey a sense of helplessness and hopelessness in reaching out to the middle-aged couple who are so unresolved at this time of their life cycle. Aside from the individual dynamics of the mothers (who are often struggling with unrelenting needs to consume and absorb in relationships within their immediate environment) and the fathers (who concomitantly reverse and turn inward overwhelming feelings of aggression), we need also to perceive such clients within a larger context. Frequently, there is a broader theme operating and, as practitioners, we perhaps tend to overlook the obvious. Just why are our caseloads so overloaded with children absorbed by such "grasping" mothers and "self-involved, indifferent" fathers? Why do we so often find that when the adolescent is emerging toward young adulthood and possible independence that the crisis looms so much larger? Exactly what does this mutually opposing time of life mean to the individuals caught in this psychological-social bind? Can this be theoretically explained only along social-economic determinants, or are there psychological components which need to be highlighted and clarified for ourselves?

In studying the past histories of clients, it is not unusual to find that there has been a marked tendency, on the part of the wives and mothers particularly, to be overinvolved with the children—often a son. However, during the adolescence of the child, an increased sense of desperateness is often within the parents. This appears to be primarily related to the fact that the youngster's crisis of adolescence not only sets off the parents' unresolved adolescence but overlaps the parents' crisis of middle age. As Dr. Stanley Cath has said: "As one becomes aware of sexual decline in the self, one's children may be emerging as vibrantly alive and extremely sexual." Thus, he goes on to say: "the parents become most upset when either sons or daughters turn outward and away" (Cath, 1965).

There is growing recognition that the less commitment to the marriage itself, the greater is the stress and difficulty in letting go and separating from the children. Not uncommonly social caseworkers inject into their diagnostic workups the phrase: "poor marital matrimonial relationship" and then appear to proceed as though this assessment had never been made. Inversely, the parental pattern of getting overinvolved with the youngster gets repeated by the social caseworker. In so doing, we lose sight of what the marriage is all about, its ingredients, etc. Perhaps this oversight has a purpose. It enables us to avoid facing up to a pretty depressing fact; that is, that there are millions of marriages which are anything but ideal, and this can be threatening to us as caseworkers. Loveless marriages were frequently contracted from the start while countless others "fell out of love" many years ago. Such marriages all too commonly have sought to gain from the children what the marriage partner has been unable to provide and, most likely, what earlier parental relationships never provided. What we find is an oft-repeated pattern of a mother-son and or father-daughter 'hang-up.' And we find these components reflected across the socio-economic class spectrum.

Middle Age: A Time of Assessment

Though it is vitally important to assess the individual dynamics of each partner, as well as the marital interaction, we need to gain a clearer assessment of the marriage itself: its past, its present, its potential for further growth, and how the middle-age separation crisis is being dealt with.

The best of marriages encounter heightened tensions at this time. The individual partners have to adapt to disillusionment and statistics show that the highest divorce rate is in the thirties-to-early-forties age group. According to Dr. H. V. Dicks of Tavistock Clinic, the disillusionment is "an awakening to the difference between youthful expectation and sober reality" (Dicks, 1968). After thirty-five, we come to know that we will not conquer new worlds, or achieve all that we had hoped to. Most of all, we are confronted, and yes, affronted, by the reality that we really are mortal. For many, a sense of imprisonment sets in and a feeling of restlessness. The "old wars" surface again but this time the marital partner becomes the displaced scapegoat. When this happens, each partner harbors increased disillusioning thoughts regarding going through middle and old age with such a companion. Each tends to relish phantasies of earlier relationships and affairs, feeling that John Smith or Mary Brown would have been the 'right' person. The marriage is on trial and each partner is thinking about what it holds for the future, if anything. The climacteric years, with their physical concomitants, only heighten the realization that "time is running out."

The weaker the basis of the marriage, the looser the ties, the greater the ambivalence and the more difficult it is for the partners to cope with this time of life. In such circumstances, the marriage partner attempts to ward off this painful assessment process and instead clings desperately to the emerging adult-child, refusing to give permission for the young person's further development. In surveying a cross section of case recordings in various settings, clients repetitively tell workers: "He (the child) is all I have. I love him (her) so much. My life wouldn't be worth living if he (she) wasn't around." Neither partner feels supported by the other and many have reached the point of saying: "What's the use of trying?" The wife will complain that the husband has little affection for the child—"he's jealous"; the husband complains that the wife is "babying" the son. Each are busy sending out all kinds of overt and covert messages to the children about "letting parents down" and leaving them to face old age alone. Guilt-arousal is used consciously, but more often unconsciously, as a mechanism of control. If the children succeed at least in some form of physical emancipation, a number of unrewarding marriages then collapse. Significantly, the youngster going off to a university, or into the armed services, or getting married, or moving into his (or her) own living quarters (particularly, the last child leaving home) often brings the crisis to a head. For some partners the "emptiness" of the marital relationship is too much to bear. The purpose of having "lived together" seems to have disappeared. Such clients have been heard to say: "It was all for the children. As far as I am concerned, I only put up with him (her) because of them." Is it any wonder that so many of the young people caught in such a bind are so ambivalent themselves about leaving their parents to cope with future years of "nothingness"? Some adolescents will actually verbalize the fear that the parents will now divorce, or "do something terrible" to each other. At the same time, the adolescent is usually quite unaware of his own needs to manipulate the situation (e.g., to play one parent against the other) and of his deep-seated desire to remain tied to one or both of the parents. Consciously, he protests for independence and freedom. Unconsciously, he longs to be nurtured and protected from the unknowns of the outside world.

All this does not mean to imply that social, economic, and cultural stresses do not impinge on the stability of the marriage. Of course they do, and we know that the most solid of marriages can undergo acute crisis states—even crumble—under overwhelming external stimuli. However, we also know that the firmer the commitment to the marriage, each partner to the other, the greater is the ability to withstand and cushion various external stresses. When the bonds are weak, the tendency to distort reality increases, sometimes to monstrous proportions. Thus, for example, economic, religious, and racial-cultural differences are often realistic stresses which occasionally get overinvested with all kinds of irrational meanings. The "weak" partner interprets these differences in accordance with his own personal dynamics. As stress increases, so does the need to overproject one's own inadequacies and anxieties onto the partner.

Diagnosis and Prognosis

Perhaps the most disconcerting of efforts is the gaining of recognition and insight into the balance of strengths and weaknesses in the marital interaction at this time in the life cycle. A basic question seems to be: To what extent is the present marital upheaval precipitated by the "normal" crisis of middle-age, reassessment of the marital relationship, and the letting go of the children? Or, to what extent is it a representation of what has smouldered just below the surface (preconscious) for many years, whereby the problems of middle-age, etc., only exacerbate the essentially weak marriage commitment? It is possible to err in either direction in the over-all diagnosis. At times, the worker may tend to underestimate strengths and to assess the present crisis as symbolic of a poor marriage, without clarifying to what degree the marriage is struggling with some reasonably "normal" maturational upheaval. When this happens the worker can easily lose sight of what has been positive in the marriage and where there has been good indication of mutuality.

Mr. and Mrs. K. had been married thirty-seven years and each were insisting that there was no possible way to save the marriage. The last of three sons was now leaving home to get married and the other two sons had taken over the small family business. Mr. K. had been "pensioned out" by his sons. Each partner, in individual and joint interviews, markedly projected onto the other why the marriage was failing. Mr. K. repeatedly insisted that Mrs. K. no longer cared to provide him with decent, warm meals, as well as other needs of his (physical and sexual). Mrs. K. maintained that Mr. K. only sat around the house complaining, whining, and getting in her way. After a prolonged testing-out period with the caseworker, both Mr. and Mrs. K. cautiously began to talk about their feelings of being let down by their children, of coping with late middle-age and approaching old age. Each spoke of their roles being taken away and each nurtured their own hurts. After several sessions of such verbalization there was a noticeable lessening of projection. Each could begin to bring forth remembrances of the 'good years' in raising the children together.

As in all crisis assessments, it is oft times confusing as to where the marital ego strengths lie. From the above situation, one can prognosticate rather hopefully that the partners, encouraged and supported by the case-worker, can now begin to turn to each other for increased gratifications. But what about the innumerable marriages where there has been a pronounced lack of mutuality—at best a pseudo-mutuality? What about those marriages where the sadomasochistic interplay has provided such a weighted amount of negative gratifications?

Mr. and Mrs. R. spoke of having fallen out of love within the first five years of their marriage. As far as they were concerned they were filling out a "life sentence," living under the same roof and upholding some pretences for "the sake of the children" and community. Earlier years of turbulence and verbal assaults were replaced by months of mutual silence. Any exchange was passed through the children; e.g., "Tell your father (mother), etc." Recently, in honor of their seventeenth wedding anniversary they took a three-hour auto drive to a large metropolitan city. Within the over-all six-hour trip not a word was was exchanged between them. Mrs. R. concentrated on smoking one cigarette after another. Mr. R. focused his eyes on the road and drove the car. Both agreed (in response to the caseworker's question) "We have nothing to say to each other; it's been this way for years."

With such situations, or in marriages where the theme is one of violence, drunkenness, extra-marital relations, child-beating, etc., the temptation to mark off or dismiss the couple is very great. Certainly, the prognosis is usually a very guarded one. However, in many of these marriages there are, in spite of gross negative elements, many interactions which possess latent strengths and underlying degrees of discomfort with the status quo. Each partner is harboring deep-seated feelings of failure and low self-esteem. The challenge of case-work, or any form of therapeutic help, is how to tap into, capitalize on and exploit the discomfort and desire for change. In other words, the question is how to make the demoralizing behavior toward each other as ego-alien as possible. It can be anticipated that those marriages which have been characterized by varying degrees of neurotic interplay will be more likely, with support, to come to grips with the "normal" crisis of middle-age and of separation from children. However, where the acting out within the interaction is of gross proportions, and the behavior is ego-syntonic, the ability to deal with the present crisis is lessened. It is the purpose of this paper to underscore the importance of the middle-age separation crisis and to deal with it in treatment as a means of strengthening the marital partners' egos, individually and collectively. With earlier and clearer recognition of this crisis, the worker increases the possibility of freeing latent strengths which have been disguised or hidden; these may exist even in the most destructive of interactions. Granted, the more destructive the relationship the greater is the likelihood of the need for negative gratification. However, within differential diagnostic thinking, it is important to also assess the individual partner's accessibility to professional intervention, his (her) potential for discomfort with the interaction, and the covert seeking of help.

Treatment

As indicated earlier, it is frequently observed that during the early phase of treatment the marital partner's need to focus on the children, or project onto the partner the present difficulties, is pronounced. It is important, in reaching out, to recognize that this projection is defensive and needs to be respected. Though we have often diagnosed a "poor marital relationship," we have also erred by moving too quickly into the area of the marriage itself, and threatened the desperate defenses of the partners. Many practitioners are somewhat uneasy in "going along" with the defense. However, the anxious, "consuming" mother needs to hear the worker emphasize and verbalize how difficult it is to cope with an adolescent who seems to be wanting things his own way and showing less and less gratitude. Or, that the worker can appreciate the difficulty of feeling unsupported by one's partner. The "up-tight" father needs to hear concern and support as to his distress regarding his needs: i.e., lack of attention, job frustrations, etc. All this must be balanced with what has been identified in the diagnostic workup as the positives in the situation. Not infrequently such mothers put much stress on their immaculate housekeeping standards, their thrifty management of limited economic housekeeping resources, and their rendering of excellent physical care to the children. These need to be supported and held up as indicators of good parenting. So too, the fathers are often reasonably good workers nad have established loyal and conscientious work records. Others have had sporadic work records but the desire to have stuck with it has always been there. The reality, as well as the wish, needs to be supported.

It has been stated that destructive interaction needs to be made ego-alien as early as possible. As the partners send out clues related to their interactions: e.g., "all we ever do is fight," or, "we never talk to each other," etc., the worker needs to respond somewhat incredulously. The response should always be based on concern for the individual partner, as well as themselves as a couple. Such remarks as "I know you really do not want to be like this," or, "it concerns me that you do this to yourself, as well as to each other," or, "how upsetting it must be to keep on at each other this way—what do you want to do about it?" are indicated in that they serve as reminders to the individual partners that they are again lowering their own self-esteem.

By attempting to make the destructive interaction ego-alien, we simultaneously move toward formulating the interactional problem for the partners. The worker needs to exaggerate the conflict in order to demonstrate what they are doing to themselves, as well as to each other. By so doing, the worker supports the healthy part of the ego which seeks to gain greater maturity and self-control.

The worker can usually measure the effectiveness of the approach by the degree of response on two levels: (1) the diminishing of the acting out within the marital situation, and (2) the beginning establishment of trust within the therapeutic relationship. As basic trust begins to crystallize, along with the lessening of destructiveness, the worker can gently begin to inject such realities as to the difficulty in raising children for so many years and then having to cope with their beginning to move off on their own. Also, it is important to universalize the fact that all parents have this struggle at this time of life and that this is not an easy time for any of them.

> Mr. A. began to respond to the individual support and attention he was being given by the worker, in that he gradually talked about his fear of having been overlooked in his marriage. He spoke of his feeling that the marriage was never important to his wife; that she wanted it only for the sake of having children. Mr. A. moved on to say that he always felt unimportant to his wife, that she only tolerated him. As far as he was concerned she was giving to the children what rightfully belonged to him. This is why he was feeling a kind of resentment toward the children, especially his son.

> Mrs. A. slowly injected remarks about the marriage. She stated that they started raising a family shortly after they were married. She feels that she and her husband "never really got to know each other" and before they knew it, they were "bogged down with the kids." In time, she talked of how she always felt unsure of herself and that her husband wanted too much from her. In fact, she felt let down in that she was wanting him to give her the confidence and affection which she felt she always lacked. Instead, she felt like she had to raise him, along with the children, and she resented having to do so. She was determined that their son was not going to be like the father, but somehow, it had all gone wrong. If anything, she feels her children now resent her.

To reach the above stage in the treatment process takes much patience, time, and perseverance on the part of the worker. It is not meant to imply that there are pat phrases and magical words to get the necessary responses from our clients. However, what is implied is the importance of testing out ways to free clients in order to bring forth some of the above doubts and apprehensions. Doing so reflects a full appreciation for the middle-age separation crisis. Such clients need permission to face up to such feelings. With catharsis, the partners are frequently relieved to hear that each has a right to be *first* in the eyes of the other; that the marriage should have precedence over the children; that it is all right to 'mother' one's husband to varying degrees; and that it is permissible to risk and demonstrate some affection for the other.

With the beginning of this new-found freedom, clients have been heard to express some positives about being middle-aged. Feeling more supported by the other, they talk of "enjoying life at fifty." The wives appear more resigned to the implications of menopause, recognizing the end of their fertility but not necessarily of sexuality; some come to regard it as a time of welcome release from childbearing. In fact, some wives have been somewhat taken back in that "mothering" their husbands a bit more brings a warm response and that motherly affection is what "he has been wanting all along." Having themselves been nurtured and encouraged in the relationship with the worker, each partner feels freer to risk and to test new methods of interacting with the other. Also, having faced up to the fear of being unloved and unlovable appears to make the dreaded reality less threatening, somewhow easier to cope with and easier to bear.

It must readily be admitted that there are marital interactions where the characteristic pattern of mutual destruction is so ingrained as to provide minimal opportunity for therapeutic intervention. Knowledge and skill in such instances is, as yet, underdeveloped and undefined as to how to ignite the necessary discomfort and desire for change. Nonetheless, practitioners have not always utilized to the fullest the knowledge and skill available in testing out potential for further growth and development. Not infrequently, practitioners opt for the quickest or easiest avenue (e.g., referrals to other agencies; remaining concentrated on the child; or outright hostility to the parents). Consequently, it is found that the short-cut all too often proves to be ineffective, expensive, and ultimately to perpetuate both acute and chronic crises.

The Practitioner's Dilemma

Earlier it was indicated that the attitude of the worker in identifying and categorizing various "poor marital relationships" is significant. The possibility of one's own inner family struggles being rearoused now requires some elaboration. Helping clients through the middle-age separation crisis means being confronted with: (1) disenchantment regarding the marriage ideal myth and (2) that realistically no one comes from a home where the marriage was "perfect" or "made in heaven." As practitioners, all of us have had earlier life experiences where we felt caught between parental loyalties. Therefore, overidentification with the adolescent can noticeably obstruct one's ability to reach out to the parents.

On the other hand, many workers are today in the "prime" years, with adolescents of their own. A number may understandably be struggling with "letting go," reassessment of their own marriages, and the internal strains of various ambivalent pulls. Dealing with the middle-age couple in crisis means opening up one's own internal conflicts and binds. And so, how much easier it is to keep middle-aged parents at a distance! At least one is protected from any of one's own discomforts.

However, as in all effective means of help, the greater the self-awareness that can be brought to the interaction with clients, the greater is the ability to inject objectivity and thereby increase the opportunity for client growth. We do not come to our clients purified and absolved of all conflicts. Rather, self-knowledge hopefully leads to enhanced tolerance and patience which so often soothes and heals the hurt of others. Most of all, by helping individuals and couples over the middle-age separation hurdle, we provide an opportunity for the persons involved to rediscover each other. For many, it is a chance to discover each other for the *first* time.

References

1 CATH, S. H. "Some Dynamics of the Middle and Later Years." In H. J. Parad, (Ed.), *Crisis Intervention*. N.Y.: F.S.A.A., 1965.

2 DICKS, H. V. "The Seven Ages of Man." In *A New Society Pub.*, Special Edition: (Prime of Life: 30 to 42), London: 1968.

3 ERIKSON, E. "Identity and the Life Cycle." In *Psychological Issues*, Vol. 1, No. 1, N.Y.: International University Press, 1959.

Reverie on Working with the Aged

David Soyer

This is a personal piece. I tried it several times with footnotes, jargon, and case histories, but it didn't go. It didn't say what I felt. It must be personal, for it touches not on professional knowledge and techniques but rather on some lines of thought and feeling set off in one social worker by the experience of working in a service to the aged.

The Jewish Family Service has a special unit, Services to the Aged, to serve clients sixty years of age and over.[1] The range of people served is great—from the physically, mentally, and ego intact client who has generally lived life fully but for a number of reasons (retirement, widowhood) is now struggling with problems of relationship and self-image, to the other extreme of the seriously deteriorated recluse, lying in offal, without family, frightening and alienating neighbors by stinking, breeding roaches, opening gas jets, and letting the plumbing overflow. The intensity of service varies just as widely—from a telephone contact with adult children, giving them information that may help to unsnarl the unbelievable red tape facing people in today's cities, through varying combinations of concrete services, to intensive individual, family, or group counseling over a long period of time. Although the ranges persist, our staff feels we are facing an ever increasing percentage of crises involving some form of dissolution of the individual or family. It imposes great pressure on caseworkers.

If one works with the aged and yet has friends who are swingers, seeking kicks, trying to make it in our youth culture (perhaps to fight the specter of their own middle age), one sometimes has to wonder, What am I doing here? To one degree or another, the worker with the aged is bucking the beat of today's world. His values and his clients are laughed at, scorned, or dreaded. He may be torn between what he believes in and his desire to be "in" with the world around him. Work with kids? Great, man, I love kids.

---

[1] The unit has been transferred to a new multiple-function agency, The Jewish Association for Services for the Aged.

Reprinted from *Social Casework,* Vol. 50 (May, 1969), pp. 291–294, by permission of the author and the Family Services Association of America.

Work with the aged? Isn't that depressing? One doesn't have to document each ad for youthful skin or sing each song about young love to know what is hip and what is square.

Yet through just such an assault upon one's beliefs and sensitivities can grow affirmation of them. The question What am I doing here? can turn into What can I gain as a social worker and person through working in this setting? One might also ask, Does this specialty have something to give to social workers in other fields? I know that I shall take these feelings and thoughts with me wherever I go.

Each of us becomes absorbed in different aspects of the profession at different points in his career-life. Each agency, each client group, each set of colleagues adds to this never finished making of the social worker. For me, more and more, it is the core values that have drawn me. It sometimes seems that as we careen ahead, becoming more scientific, adding theory, exploding theory, developing treatment techniques, abandoning them, rediscovering them in different language, we make something simple into something very complicated. Perhaps it is a search for simplicity that turns me to thinking of values. Yet without them all our theories and techniques become sophistry or manipulation rather than social work.

Long before I thought of social work as a career, there was a family I loved in whose home I often was and whose mode of life still inspires me. The Father, whom I shall call My Friend, was an alcoholic who rarely worked. When controlling his drinking, he would spend his days, pug-nosed and square-jawed, sitting in his undershirt next to a cold-north-lighted window in that old, top floor New York apartment. On an antique cherry-wood table he slowly, methodically shuffled a deck of cards and laid out and played countless games of solitaire. Morning until night, day after day. The cards grew soft and pliant, then limp (though somehow never frayed or dog-eared), and the numbers and spots were worn off them. The games were interrupted only by trips to the kitchen for cups of scalding, pitch black coffee. How many days? How many games?

Then suddenly but still deliberately, My Friend would set aside the cards, take a pad of yellow, lined paper, and start to write (writing was his life-myth, his entrée into the Bohemia of the day). Page after page of yellow paper was covered. He never talked about what he wrote; never showed it around; never, to my knowledge, sent it anywhere. Though always curious, it was a long time before I sneaked a look. One day My Friend went down to buy cigarettes and I read in the manuscript. It was all repetition with seemingly one basic idea: Man has two types of value— instrumental value, which consists of what he possesses, what he produces, what he is "worth," and intrinsic value, which is his value as a human being—just for being a human being. It was the intrinsic value that meant the most. It was My Friend's way of saying, I am worth something after all, for I am human.

It is not surprising that a quarter of a century later while working with aged clients my thoughts go back to My Late Friend. There is a certain purity about working with the aged, especially those who are beyond the production years. One does not justify this work on the basis of crime prevention or helping to develop untapped, potentially productive forces or freeing the oppressed so as to ward off summer insurrection or any other instrumental value. One justifies it only on the basis that each human being has value—intrinsic value, the meaning and dignity of being human. So many of our clients we serve for this reason alone. That is why social work is concerned about those in whom our society loses interest.

I believe that working with the aged is one of those fields in social work that, by setting forth the issue so clearly, gives the worker a chance to test, temper, and affirm this core value of our profession.

But far deeper than one's sense of values—more soul-pervasive than any professional commitments—is the confrontation with one's own mortality; for working with the aged brings the worker face to face with the decline and end of the individual life. For him who is ready for it, this confrontation can open the experience so well described by Pascal, as quoted by Rollo May: "When I consider the brief span of my life, swallowed up in the eternity before and behind it, the small space that I fill or even see, engulfed in the infinite immensity of spaces which I know not and which know not me, I am afraid, and wonder to see myself here rather than there, now rather than then. . . ."[2]

We have seen untimely death in our time, wars and riots, and the special impact of the King and Kennedy assassinations, but the effect is different. The death of the younger person may be far more tragic; yet it is less inevitable. It does not underscore man's mortality, for its very tragedy is in the fact that the younger person *might have* lived. The decline and death of the older person reminds us that this must eventually happen to all.

We deny and avoid the issues of aging and death. One therapy group of men and women in their sixties and seventies gave clue after clue that these subjects were on their minds, and yet the therapist never responded or helped them bring out their preoccupation and fears. In staff meetings on the aged I have found myself dwelling on great achievements of older people, of artists in their eighties, actively producing good work, being discovered and rediscovered, sometimes for the third or fourth time; of an aged pope opening new directions to a far-flung and ancient church; of statesmen and national leaders still effective in their later years. Haven't we all tried to find some comfort in such examples—comfort that decline and death can at least be put off? Yet, at the end of a meeting I had to catch myself; recognize why I was bringing up these examples; and realize that, at least in the corporal sense, even these great and long-lived figures are mortal.

Each receives the impact of this confrontation in his own and private way (and we have not really opened this to each other enough in our staff

[2] Rollo May, The Origin and Significance of the Existential Movement in Psychology, in Rollo May, Ernest Angel, and Henri F. Ellenberger, eds., *Existence: A New Dimension in Psychiatry and Psychology* (Basic Books, New York, 1958), 18.

discussions). Some young case aides seem almost unable to really comprehend aging and death: it is so far in the future for them, and time has not yet started to rush by. Some older workers (and some clients) seem to have come to peace with it, through life experience early or late. I wonder sometimes if it is the person in the middle, the one just emerging from the sense of omnipotence and physical indestructibility of youth who is most open to the impact. But perhaps factors other than one's stage of life are more important in one's receptivity to the awareness of man's mortality. Recently a young case aide told me she had been having such thoughts since she was eight years old.

The ways of coping with this awareness are also varied. There is the usual gamut of defensive reactions—denial, avoidance, reaction formation. For some with deep religious faith there seems a drawing upon this faith. And for others there is a slow groping for comfort, for meaning—a groping that may well find an existential course: "Death in any of its aspects is the fact which makes of the present hour something of absolute value. . . . 'I know only two things—one, that I will be dead some day, two, that I am not dead now. The only question is what shall I do between those two points.' "[3]

This confrontation with man's mortality and a successful coping with it can be a most precious professional and personal experience. Of course one can have it without working with the aged; and just as certainly many who work with the aged are not open to it. Yet if one is open, then working with the aged can surely stir deep feelings on life, decline, and death and on one's relationship to them.

This next thought has developed through work in several agencies but has become clearer to me through the perspective of working with the aged.

It has been "the thing" recently for social workers to beat themselves about the biases—usually class and race bias—and the problems in understanding and communication they cause in working with clients from other backgrounds. There is another bias that many of us bring, and that is a bias in favor of some image of normalcy or health. Consciously or unconsciously, the teachings of cultural anthropology notwithstanding, despite our "nonjudgmental attitude," most of us want our clients to move toward "health," and for most of us this includes marriage, children, job success, keeping out of trouble (although the new "advocates" among us would not necessarily go for this), and freedom from symptoms.[4]

When one works with younger people and the world is open and one is looking ahead, there can be a terrible striving to make one's client normal within whatever definition the worker has of that concept. In work with the aged the perspective is different. There is a look backward. No longer is there the dream of what life may become, but there is a stark look at what

[3] Rollo May, Contributions of Existential Psychotherapy, in May, Angel, and Ellenberger, eds., *Existence* . . . , 90.

[4] See Henry Miller, Value Dilemmas in Social Casework, *Social Work*, 13:27–33 (January 1968).

it was. There is a search for the things that gave life meaning. Sometimes they have been big: the coming to America, the founding of a labor union or of a family. Sometimes they are smaller: memories of old baseball stars, of neighborhoods or countrysides as they were long ago, bitter-sweet thoughts of old business ventures with high hopes and small returns. A friend once told me a story of his ghetto childhood. There was an old homosexual who lived in a furnished room on the block. One day a group of kids decided to rough him up. They broke into his room and found it lined with delicate constructs of paper and cardboard, prissily arranged. In their cruelty they not only beat him up but also tore the place apart. My Friend remembers the man pleading, not for an end to the beating, but for them to stop tearing apart the order of his one-room world.

I believe that working with older people can sensitize a social worker to the little treasures, the moments, the paper shreds that give meaning to a life.[5]

The longer I work in settings where the potential of the client group is severely limited, the smaller grows my bias for normalcy. When an eighty-year-old man shows a tenderness toward a canary (provided by his creative social worker) that he could never feel for any of his three wives, I can accept that tenderness as precious. As against isolation I will cherish homosexual or hippie bonds. The crotchety contentiousness of a bedridden old woman is welcome versus apathy.

But perhaps this is to state it too negatively. There is a larger point to be made. It is that the spectrum of human experience and potential is unbelievably broad. It ranges from the lonely furnished-room dweller working on his paper scraps to the world shaking scientist, artist, or statesman. We social workers must expand our views of life to appreciate as much of that range as we possibly can. In a previous article I argued that social workers often chisel down the aspirations of clients (with handicapped clients used as example) in the name of being "reality oriented."[6] The argument here is that because of his own aspirations for the client the social worker may fail to see, the worth of small, perhaps eccentric, but personal experiences. Is it that our sense of normalcy has a leveling, centering effect upon our work, blocking off for us the outer ranges of the life scale—the great, if unrealistic, aspiration on the one hand and the tiny, closed in, yet individual life style on the other?

One more image comes to mind, a composite of Cardinal Cushing's recital at President Kennedy's funeral and the words blending into a song by the folk singer Pete Seeger: "To every *thing there is* a season, and a time to every purpose under the heaven."[7] (I am told that this passage can be interpreted rigidly, that it can be taken to mean that there is only one proper time when each purpose can come to pass. But that's not how it

[5] See Fred Berl, Growing Up to Old Age, *Social Work*, 8:85–91 (January 1963). See especially the section on Economizing One's Resources, 88–89.
[6] David Soyer, The Right to Fail, *Social Work*, 8:72–78 (July 1963).
[7] Eccles. 3:1.

affected me. Followed by its chain of opposites, it seems to sing an acceptance of the breadth of man's purposes.)

This has been a comment on what working in a special setting for the aged can mean in the professional and personal development of a social worker. (1) It can be a testing and affirmation of certain of the basic values of our profession, especially of the intrinsic value of the human being, a value much in need of affirmation in today's violent and dehumanized world. (2) It can confront the social worker with man's mortality and open him to a deep struggle with this most basic existential dilemma. Some resolution (religious? existential?) of this struggle can have great personal and professional meaning. (3) The perspective gained in working with the aged—the looking backward upon a life—can broaden one's sensitivity to the full range of human experience. One's view of normalcy is shaken, and one can be readier to accept and affirm the small and eccentric satisfactions in life, as well as the great ones.

Social Casework and the Dying Person

Eda G. Goldstein

The idea of writing this article germinated from the experience of sharing the last nine months of life with a young woman dying of cancer. It is ironic that a casework process narrowly defined as psychotherapy to a dying patient should be an experience so revealing of how social casework can be alive. It also seems ironic that new perspectives on the unit of help, the object of help, the role of the helper, and the helping process[1] should stem from a nine-month, in-depth experience with one client, even though that experience involved many systems that helped, hindered, or had needs in their own right. It is stranger still that what intuitively seemed right in casework with a dying woman may have implications for a reconceptualization of casework practice.

Ecological Perspective on Death

This article discusses death in the framework of an ecological perspective or life model. As described by Carel B. Germain, this view is committed to "individualizing social work services," with an emphasis on the transacting forces in a person's total life space. It highlights the creative capacities of man and the processes of growth and adaptation as the organism and environment find their "mutual fit." It affirms the therapeutic potential of natural life processes rather than "contrived clinical processes as treatment media in an artificially created setting."[2]

A discussion of death in a proposed life model can draw on Erik H. Erikson's notion of the life cycle, with its stages composed of developmental

[1] Morris S. Schwartz, Charlotte G. Schwartz, and Mark G. Field, *Social Approaches to Mental Patient Care* (New York: Columbia University Press, 1964), p. 85.

[2] Carel B. Germain, Social Casework, in *Goals for Social Welfare 1973–1993: An Overview of the Next Two Decades*, ed. Harleigh B. Trecker (New York: Association Press, 1973).

Reprinted from *Social Casework,* Vol. 54 (December, 1973), pp. 601–608, by permission of the author and the Journal.

tasks, the successful resolution of which strengthens adaptation and a sense of identity. Here, death is seen as the final stage, a biopsychosocial one, also having certain adaptive tasks for the individual and the environment. Crisis theory also highlights task mutuality. In addition to its emphasis on ego adaptation, it enables the conceptualization of the normal and mutual processes which those affected by a crisis—in this instance death—go through.

As soon as one speaks of an interpersonal context, concepts about transactions between or among people or other systems become salient. The lens shifts from the intrapsychic or the family system to the relationships among various aspects of a particular situation. As our lens shifts, so must our way of describing what we see and how we deal with its change. William E. Gordon infused the person-in-situation complementarity with new life when he described the central concern of a social work technology as "the matching of people's coping patterns with the qualities of impinging environment for the purpose of producing growth-inducing and environment ameliorating transactions."[3] By putting social work at the interface between the person and environment, Gordon draws attention to the need to address the transaction between the two, since a change in the environment can have positive repercussions for the individual. The life model is committed to the idea that there are "qualities of impinging environment" which can be therapeutic, if correctly "matched" to the person's "coping patterns." These ideas provide the unifying framework for the following discussion which, while dealing with the problem area of death, is aimed at understanding how to apply an ecological perspective.

Reversing the traditional order of starting with the person, it seems important here to understand certain qualities of impinging environment. A crucial aspect is the contribution of our culture in determining personal, professional, and societal responses to the dying person. That there are many societies in which death and dying are not avoided should prompt us to ask what it is that determines American attitudes toward death. John P. Spiegel[4] in work on cultural values describes people along five value orientations. He concludes that the American middle-class person is future-oriented, highly individualistic, concerned with doing, expectant of triumph over nature, and convinced that man is neutral regarding good and evil. In a culture that puts so much stress on the future, on activity, and on mastering nature, death represents a prospect too dismal to face. It is the end.

These value orientations are reflected in our advanced medical technology which is dedicated to saving lives and wastes no time, service, or

[3] William E. Gordon, Basic Constructs for an Integrative and Generative Conception of Social Work, in *The General Systems Approach: Contributions Toward a Holistic Conception of Social Work*, ed. Gordon Hearn (New York: Council on Social Work Education, 1969), p. 7.

[4] John P. Spiegel, Cultural Variations in Attitudes toward Death and Disease, in *The Threat of Impending Disaster*, ed. George H. Grosser, Henry Wechsler, and Milton Greenblatt (Cambridge: Massachusetts Institute of Technology, 1964), pp. 283–99.

resources on comforting the dying patient and his family. We use our technology to minimize the impact of death rather than to humanize its occurrence. This process can be seen in the bureaucratization of death; hospitals develop expeditious methods of classifying and routing dead patients, and funeral arrangements are formalized, conveniently sparing family and friends the responsibility of and participation in caring for the dead.

Events prior to a death are equally mechanical and depersonalized. Severely ill people rarely die in familiar environments. Increasingly, people die in hospitals, often after being whisked away from their families. Patients and families are often not told the truth about the illness. Children are not allowed to visit. The sick individual and his family are treated as if they have no right to an opinion. They are left in a state of helpless despondency.

Of this grim state of affairs, Elisabeth Kubler-Ross writes that it is not our culturally determined attitude toward death which is crucial but our allowing scientific advancements to be used to help us defend against our universal fear of death. She writes that "we displace all our knowledge onto machines, since they are less close to us than the suffering face of another human being which would remind us once more of our lack of omnipotence."[5]

The writer's personal and professional response to death reflected this avoidance phenomenon until her client developed terminal cancer and casework that was originally aimed at helping the client to live a fuller life changed to helping her to die.[6]

Case Illustration

Without warning, Mrs. P, a thirty-six-year-old housewife and mother of a six-year-old son, was rushed to a city hospital dealing mainly with malignant diseases after a weekend of abdominal pain and rectal bleeding. Within two weeks, a malignant tumor of the colon was removed. During the operation, metastasis to the liver was observed and it was estimated that she had six months to a year to live. The medical staff told Mrs. P about the malignancy but not about the metastasis nor her prognosis. She was told the operation had been successful. Her husband and her mother, a physician, were told the truth. During this time the writer, a social worker at a nearby psychiatric teaching hospital, decided to continue working with Mrs. P who had been her client for over a year and a half.

The client, her family, and the social worker were thrust into a system which, in addition to its understaffing and overcrowding, conspired to keep patients from learning the names and natures of their diseases. The staff had a ritualized defense pattern to keep secrets. Thus, if Mrs P mentioned death, the nurses changed the subject. When the doctors saw Mrs. P, they either smiled and re-

---

[5] Elisabeth Kubler-Ross, *On Death and Dying* (New York: Macmillan Co., 1969), pp. 4–8.

[6] Adapted from Eda G. Goldstein and Sidney Malitz, Psychotherapy and Pharmacotherapy as Enablers in the Anticipatory Grief of a Dying Patient: A Case Study, in *Anticipatory Grief*, ed. Arthur Carr, Ivan K. Goldberg, Austin H. Kutscher, David Peretz, and Bernard Schoenberg (New York: Columbia University Press, in press).

assured her, chiding her for her fears, or else went briskly about their business. The staff did not use names of illnesses, even with one another. One would have to go to the carefully guarded chart to understand the nature of an illness. The patients basically reacted to their own illnesses the way the staff culture defined them. Patients learned what was expected and did not ask questions. At the same time, the patients, including Mrs. P, were left alone to question the inconsistencies they perceived. For example, Mrs. P knew she was in a cancer hospital rather than in the affiliated voluntary hospital from which she had been transferred after the initial examination. She saw others around her leave, only to return and die even though they, too, had been told their operations were successful. She witnessed the lower echelon of personnel covertly administering extra pain medication to some patients whose suffering was intense. She watched her mother take doctors aside for whispered conversations. She knew she was receiving chemotherapy but she could not reconcile this with her favorable prognosis. Like the families of most of the patients, Mrs. P's family knew the truth; they were given the responsibility of whether to share this information, but they were never encouraged to do so. The patient was completely excluded from the decision-making process.

Because of understaffing, the social service staff of the hospital were deployed to handle financial matters or to take referrals for concrete services, but these services were rarely obtained for patients who were terminal. The director of social work openly resented the attention Mrs. P received; "she is going to die anyway." The director objected that it disrupted the other patients to see one patient getting professional social work attention and that it reflected poorly on her own staff.

This situation is not unusual. There are endless variations. One can question whether organizational efficiency or a collective avoidance of the needs of the dying patient and his family accounts for these patterns. It is a cliché but one with the earmark of truth to cite the needs of the health professions to defend against death.

This avoidance became real in Mrs. P's situation, not only among the staff of the city hospital but also among the writer's colleagues at the teaching hospital, the psychiatrist supervisor, the psychologists, and the nursing staff who knew Mrs. P well because of their earlier research interest in her depressive episodes. Of a large staff, only one person ever visited Mrs. P in the hospital and when Mrs. P came to the social worker's office, those who previously had joked with her were suddenly much busier, often with their usually open doors shut.

In this light, it is understandable though tragic that in 1965 when Kubler-Ross wanted to begin her research on the dying patient she could not get physicians to give her permission to interview a terminally ill patient.[7] She recounts the relief and gratitude of most of the terminal patients on being able to talk about their fears, once she finally gained access. Similarly, two researchers learned in interviews with patients, families, nurses, and physicians the patterns of the staff thinking that the patient was an expert at denying, while the patient clearly made frequent obvious references to his plight. Different people visiting the same person would come away with opposite points of view. Each would hear what he wanted to hear.[8] The crucial point is that the feelings exist, whether or not we choose to hear them.

[7] Kubler-Ross, *On Death and Dying*, p. 20.
[8] Thomas P. Hackett and Avery D. Weisman, Reactions to the Iminence of Death, in *The Threat of Impending Disaster*, p. 301.

This point was illustrated in session after session with Mrs. P who, while maintaining a surface denial of her plight, would plunge from a euphoric mood to crying about the constant pain that frightened her. On one occasion, she came to her session in despair because she thought her husband no longer found her attractive. She poured out feelings she thought he had about the ugliness of her body and then realized that she felt this way about herself. She knew she would never be the same and she cried for what she had lost of herself. In a home visit, the social worker found Mrs. P in good spirits with a new hairdo and a bright new dress with matching shoes. Although the patient modeled her outfit for the social worker, insisted on serving tea, and entertained her by playing the piano, she sang nostalgically of the countries in which she grew up, about time passing, people parting, and flowers dying.

What is it that the dying person experiences that creates so much fear in those around him? How does the patient cope with death in the face of these societal and organizational obstacles? In asking these questions one takes the first step in reconceptualizing the problem.

What emerges in account after account of interviews with dying patients and their families is the agonizing loneliness, the feeling of being apart from the lives of others, experienced by the dying patient.[9] For the family, the universality of their feelings of helplessness and grief is the dominant theme.

Some of these feelings are poignantly described in Tolstoy's *The Death of Ivan Ilych*:

Ivan Ilych saw that he was dying and he was in continual despair. Why deceive myself? Isn't it obvious to everyone but me that I'm dying, and it's only a question of weeks, days . . . And none of them knows or wishes to know it, and they have no pity for me . . . The deception, the lie, which for some reason they all accepted. . . . This deception tortured him—their not wishing to admit what they all knew and what he knew, but wanting to lie to him concerning his terrible condition, and wishing and forcing him to participate in that lie. . . . He wept on account of his helplessness, his terrible loneliness . . . a loneliness in the midst of a populous town and surrounded by numerous acquaintances and relatives but that yet could not have been more complete anywhere—either at the bottom of the sea or under the earth—during that terrible loneliness Ivan Ilych had lived only in the memories of the past. . . . It was true, as the doctor said that [his] physical sufferings were terrible, but worst were his mental sufferings which were his chief torture.[10]

It is this all-too-often grim situation that an ecological perspective would attempt to correct. Early descriptions of dying patients focused on their need to withdraw libidinal cathexis from the body and from loved ones. The writing on death is replete with references to the death instinct, object loss, and the premorbid personality characteristics of the individual that

---

[9] For example, see Ruth D. Abrams, Social Casework with Cancer Patients, SOCIAL CASEWORK, 32:425–31 (December 1951); Audrey T. McCollum and A. Herbert Schwartz, Social Work and the Mourning Parent, *Social Work*, 17:25–36 (January 1972); Harriet MacLauren, In the Hour of Their Going Forth, SOCIAL CASEWORK, 40: 136–40 (March 1959); and Janet N. Norton, Treatment of a Dying Patient, *Psychoanalytic Study of the Child*, 18: 541–61 (1963).

[10] Leo Tolstoy, *The Death of Ivan Ilych and Other Stories* (New York: American Library of World Literature, 1960), pp. 131–50.

might determine his response to death. Social work literature in this area in the 1950s reveals a strong conviction that the dying patient should not be avoided and admonishes social work as a profession not to turn its back on the human spirit. There is an awareness of a unique position for the social worker in being a member of a team involved with setting up a suitable medical-social plan. There is recognition of the effects of, and on, the family group. However, one has the sense that there was no theory to highlight how the social worker's key position in the milieu could be utilized to promote active positive involvement by hospital, family, and patient in the dying process with the view that such involvement would be beneficial to all.

Even with the increased attention to the ego's adaptive capacities and the way the reacting environment can play a positive role, dying was still viewed as a state to be coped with, not one which one could experience with a greater sense of mastery. Before a new framework could be applied, perhaps some new pieces had to be added.

Crisis Theory Used in Life Model

Crisis theory opened an avenue of exploration leading to the identification of phases that people normally experience after traumatic occurrences or crises. A mental health goal would be to allow or enable the natural processes to occur. One can only make sense of the development of crisis theory if one takes cognizance of the developments in ego psychology. Is the crisis-theory ego, with its novel resolution of old conflict abilities, a stronger and more autonomous ego than the one that defends against death only by decathexis? This is a view of the ego that sees its development in terms of crisis resolution regardless of whether the crisis is a catastrophic event, a change that calls forth such new coping mechanisms as marriage or the birth of a child, or another developmental stage of the life cycle.

Crisis resolution is seen not merely as curative or preventive but as ego-enhancing. Every crisis has identifiable tasks and every successful crisis resolution calls forth and strengthens the ego's adaptive capacity. All crises, throughout the life cycle, allow for ego mastery. The view of man is not of someone bound by the past, static in the present. The paradigm that Erikson's eight stages of man encompass can be any point in the individual or family life cycle, and the person or family is not necessarily bound by previous life-styles or ways of coping.

One principle of intervention emphasizes assessing and utilizing all resources that exist in the client's total life space in order to bring about crisis resolution. The term *life space*[11] is used here to highlight the need for understanding the ongoing life experiences of a client and for utilizing

---

[11] For example, see Fritz Redl, The Life-Space Interview, *American Journal of Orthopsychiatry*, 29:1–19 (January 1959); Joel Vernick, The Use of the Life Space Interview on a Medical Ward, SOCIAL CASEWORK, 44:465–69 (October 1963); and David Wineman, The Life-Space Interview, *Social Work*, 4:3–17 (January 1959).

various aspects of it for therapeutic purposes. The therapist can be anyone in the environment. These ideas are extensively elaborated in establishing milieu therapy, where an attempt is made to actually structure the environment to be nurturing to ego adaptation and mastery.

What do crisis theory, ego development—particularly as viewed by Erikson—concepts of life space, and milieu treatment contribute to help a terminally ill woman with little more than six months to live? What does crisis theory tell us about the efficacy and humaneness of a value system based on avoidance of death? How can it combat the loneliness and despair she will experience and the helplessness and grief of the family? How can it enable the adaptive functioning of the ego until death? Is there a message for social casework practice in dealing with this human and systems dilemma?

A Positive Approach

First, a redefinition of the meaning of death seems in order. Is there any reason why the dying patient and those around him can not be allowed to have their crisis, calling forth coping mechanisms that allow for successful crisis resolution? Rather than viewing death as necessitating an emotional decathexis from life, it can be seen as a developmental phase involving active preparation by the ego of the individual and positive involvement by the family. Preparation can be related to practical matters or anticipatory grief. Concrete planning for the future of the survivors of the deceased has usually been taken out of the decision-making process of the dying person, as if he or she should be spared the pain, but actually because professionals and family either kept the knowledge of impending death from the individual, could not tolerate the pain of open discussion themselves, or did not realize or know that this could be a beneficial process.

Preparation also exists in relation to grief work for the dying patient and those close to him. For the dying patient, this mourning must be done in advance of death. It involves coming to terms with multiple losses and with how one has lived one's life. Erikson's eighth stage, ego integrity versus despair, can be precipitously thrust on someone whose life is being cut short. Because of the way society, professionals, and families handle the reality of death, this grief work is done in isolation without the mutual support of all those involved.

The crisis for Mrs. P and her family was immediately apparent. Mrs. P was shocked and terrified to learn of her malignancy following surgery. She cried and expressed anger at "the double curse" of having both a psychiatric and physical illness. "I want to live. I don't know how I ever wanted to kill myself." Mrs. P's mother, who had openly attempted to break up Mrs. P's marriage, in addition to blaming Mr. P for his wife's condition berated the social worker. She exclaimed, "Why didn't you stop them from telling her she had cancer? Why didn't you keep this from happening?" Mr. P was stricken by his wife's prognosis but proceeded to deny the inevitability of her death, refusing to discuss the situation, plan for his son, or prepare the child for the future.

As Mrs. P regained her equilibrium, the word *cancer* loomed large in her thoughts. Uppermost in her thoughts was her desire to help her son reach manhood, and she "bargained" for enough years to accomplish this. Her mother and her husband disagreed on the best way to help.

We can outline the mutual needs and tasks involved in this crisis. Mrs. P and her family needed to mourn each other—to share angers, hopes, pains, nostalgia, and intimacy. Yet, paradoxically, as is generally the case, those closest to the situation were least able to tolerate the demands of this task. They needed to plan for Mrs. P's son, yet Mrs. P. was kept in the dark about her prognosis and the chronic battle between mother and husband prevented their coopera- tion. The relationship between father and son was strained because of Mr. P's need to deny the situation. Mrs. P had many months ahead of her. How was she going to live them?

Our new definition sharpens the focus on death in life and raises the question of how professionals, and social workers specifically, can influence, deliver, or coordinate services to enable ego mastery, social functioning, crisis resolution, and environmental amelioration in relation to this avoided, or neglected, aspect of life. More specifically, if the goal is the enablement of the dying patient and his family to deal with this crisis with optimal mastery, what must be valued, what must be known, and what must be done, given the perspective in which this discussion of death has been placed? What is the unit of attention or the object of help? Who should be the helper, and what goes into that process?

The process with Mrs. P was defined narrowly. Mrs. P left the hospital ex- pecting to regain her strength, but, in spite of her hope and brave struggle to function normally, she recognized that her weakening condition meant she was dying. It would have been better if her family could have rallied to help her or if the social worker could have been able to mobilize the progressive forces within the family, thus enabling them to perform a therapeutic function. In this particular situation, it was felt to be futile to try to mobilize the family to help Mrs. P in a way they had never been able to do before because of their chronic disharmony. Mrs. P had a lonely road to travel and she remained the focus of treatment.

The treatment process was geared to helping Mrs. P achieve the tasks she identified for herself and those that were intrinsic to her illness. For example, her courage seemed important to her. She strove for a bravery and independence she felt she had missed, and she asked the social worker to help her to be more independent in assuming the responsibilities of wife and mother. She outlined a plan for self-improvement, better family relations, and more pleasures.

The more difficult task was the gradual and painful process of enabling Mrs. P to share her fears of death so that she would find an internal peace. It was moving to watch this woman, who was so physically weakened, function so well for the four months between hospitalizations. Her energy, the look of alertness in her eyes, and her mood were remarkable. She spent a great deal of time with her son, visiting his teacher and going to PTA meetings. She revived some friend- ships and joined a choir composed of mothers of school children. She got some of her rights back at home in relation to financial allowance and budgeting. She showed a sensitivity to her son's needs which had previously been absent; often she seemed to be compelled to make up for lost time with him. At the same time she cried through session after session about her feelings of isolation and abandonment, about her physical pain and appearance, about the mistakes of her past, her despair about the future, her fears about being forgotten by her son and replaced as a wife and mother, and her deep sorrow at not seeing her son become an adult. She was able to forgive herself for being what she considered a bad mother and decided her son would turn out all right. In the last hours of her life she felt reassured by his get-well card that she would never be forgotten and that he would be cared for.

There are many old elements in the handling of this case. It was an individual casework process, although the social worker did help the family, worked with staff in the hospital system, and maneuvered to get better medical treatment for Mrs. P. What is also common is the use of a professional social worker in the process. What is new was the awareness of the transacting elements in the total situation and the view that Mrs. P had adaptive capacities which could be mobilized even as she died. What was also new was the assessment of the needs of the hospital staffs, the family, and the patient and the awareness of alternatives to the way the case was handled. The process was not the only way nor necessarily the best way. The family, the hospital system, or our cultural attitudes themselves could have been the locus of intervention. The ecological perspective has a wide umbrella. It is a facilitative process. One intervenes to set certain ameliorative or growth-enhancing processes in action. What could have been new might be the use of anyone in Mrs. P's environment to embody the therapeutic function.

The questions of who or what should be the unit of attention, what should be the process, and who should do it have complex ramifications. Collective professional experiences reveal that the answers are largely determined by where one happens to be located. Thus, it is not unusual that a psychiatrist[12] saw intrapsychic conflict and individual change as her unit of attention, that a social worker[13] involved with parents of dying children should work with the family, that a social work administrator[14] saw her staff as the link between the hospital, the family, and the patient, and that a group worker[15] utilized her role on a medical ward of terminally ill patients to influence the total milieu's management of fatal illness.

Educators who are physicians, nurses, social workers, and others in the health professions have conceptualized the problem of dying as an educational one. The ministry is becoming aware of its strategic position, and even architects have begun to see the interface of that portion of life which is known as death to be an area for architectural design.[16]

These approaches are catalogued to illustrate that each way of conceptualizing the problem leads to giving help to someone in particular. The helping person may or may not play a traditional helping role. Similarly, the helping processes need to be broadly defined. The aim is not to deal

12 Norton, Treatment of a Dying Patient.
13 McCollum and Schwartz, Social Work and the Mourning Parent.
14 Elizabeth R. Prichard, Planning for the Terminally Ill Patient: The Social Worker's Responsibility, in *Anticipatory Grief*.
15 Zelda P. Leader Foster, How Social Work Can Influence Hospital Management of Fatal Illness, *Social Work*, 10:30–35 (October 1965).
16 Henry J. Wald, A Hospital for Terminally Ill Patients, in *Anticipatory Grief*.

with either the person or the milieu, but to address their mutuality. In the case of a dying person, the patient can derive comfort in closing his life in accordance with his own ideas about proper dying, and the family and hospital can benefit.

Very specifically, families can be helpful with terminal care. This assistance may be especially useful in understaffed, overcrowded facilities. It can also keep family members productively involved with tasks to accomplish. Mrs. P's mother felt better when she, a physician herself, gave injections to her daughter. Having the relative become a worker in the situation may be mutually beneficial. While initially resenting Mrs. P's mother, the nurses came to rely on her for the physical care of her daughter. Rather than viewing the relative as an outsider, the hospital can benefit from the help, and the relative feels useful. The family also needs and has a right to prepare for death in terms of anticipatory grief.

The staff in an instutional environment can derive satisfaction from actively helping someone face death. This feeling reduces the need to defend against feelings of closeness and helplessness. Other patients, as well, can take comfort from the caring way death occurs rather than be silently terrified of its dehumanization. One day Mrs. P remarked about the nurse who had been transferred from the ward, "She was probably too soft." Mrs. P had previously spoken of the tender way in which the nurse took care of her dying roommate.

While it is the writer's view that Mrs. P was helped, those in her environment were not helped, nor were they able to help her. They could not find useful roles for themselves that would ease the burden or allow transcending it, and they were not encouraged to find such roles. It was not because the family was unique. Families are not prepared for, or supported in, viewing themselves as effective helpers in the dying process in most situations. They are robbed of what can be a growth experience.

The social worker has a unique location. He is generally "at the crossroads of life . . . at the location on the scene of the natural life event [that makes] help available and more possible."[17] The social worker in his various roles in agencies where the dying person may be found is not only at the transition point between life and death but truly at the interface between person and environment. We do not have enough professionals to treat all the individuals or families in crisis, nor can all of us converge on the medical establishment and influence its policies and practices. However, in these so very human situations that we encounter, can we not find creative ways of using ourselves and the resources available to us and to our clients to enhance "growth-inducing and environment ameliorating transactions"?

An ecological perspective involves viewing the total situation and intervening at the place that will set in motion adaptive natural processes. It is a model that values the individual but does not necessarily rely on an

[17] Carol H. Meyer, *Social Work Practice: A Response to the Urban Crisis* (New York: The Free Press, 1970), pp. 158–61.

individual casework process by a professional worker. It is an approach that allows the situation to determine the nature of the assessment and intervention rather than being based on dehumanizing, inaccurate, and narrowly conceived labels of persons. It is a perspective that calls forth the best in people rather than expects the worst, thus creating a self-fulfilling prophecy.

Part 2

Psychosocial Pathology

In recent years the provision of individual, family and group treatment by social workers for persons with problems in psychosocial functioning has taken its place in the psychotherapies. Thus the psychodynamics of clients have received considerable attention in the professional journals. Recent trends in the literature have shifted to a heavier emphasis on the social aspects of man's behavior. This does not imply, as at times is suggested, that the psychological dimension should in any way be minimized, or that the two dimensions of psyche and social should be considered mutually exclusive spheres. Neither does an emphasis on the social aspects of the client presume that we have exhausted all there is to know about the treatment of the dynamic aspect of man's human makeup. On the contrary, although the professional literautre has put heavy emphasis on the psychodynamic components of man, the coverage has been far from exhaustive. Some areas have been given special attention; others have been overlooked.

Selecting the framework by which to order the articles in this section was difficult. This is not surprising because of the wide variation in terminology that still exists as well as the varying approaches to categories of personality dysfunctioning still used. Although most systems have much in common there are variations. For example, frequent references are made in the literature to the treatment of the alcoholic. As well as being considered a separate category of problem, such persons are also at times categorized in terms of character disorder or as persons with borderline functioning. Similar problems exist in the classification and location of the spectrum of behaviors described as sexual deviations. The reordering of the material in this section is an effort to relate the contents to current usage.

From the numerous articles about the treatment of the alcoholic client, one has been chosen. This article emphasizes both the magnitude of the problem in our society and the need for specialized knowledge and skill in the therapeutic intervention with this type of client. The need for careful diagnosis of each client, a carefully defined multifaceted treatment strategy and a continuing awareness of one's own attitudes and reactions are stressed. In other articles located in the literature about the alcoholic similar themes were observed, including the need for a differential understanding of causality and a multiservice approach to management and control.

Problems of drug addiction have received considerable professional and popular attention. The article selected for this edition presents a less pessimistic view of the effects of the therapy than is commonly observed. St. Pierre stresses the importance of understanding the lack of motivation to change in the addict and suggests a series of strategies where heavy emphasis is put on confrontation and the development of intellectual understanding of addiction. In addition, there is focus on the client achieving some beginning awareness of the place of feelings in his life and behavior. In other articles, as with the alcoholic, emphasis is put on societal and professional values as an important component of effective help.

One of the marked changes in the literature reviewed for this edition was the increased interest in and identified competence of social workers dealing with problems in the sphere of sexual functioning. Clearly this is partially related to the societal attitudinal shifts about human sexuality. It also reflects the availability of new knowledge and techniques of change. In particular, there is increased acceptance, through clinical experience, that modification and control in many areas of sexual deviation or problem functioning do not require the uncovering and resolution of unconscious origins. Significant gains can be made from the viewpoint of improved control, changed attitudes, and enhanced growth. There are, as well, the beneficial effects on functioning resulting from the reduction of anxiety, fear, and guilt that accompany these problems. Current practice experience indicates that clients frequently bring such problems to agencies. While there is a continuing suggestion in the literature that many social workers may not as yet be comfortable with this kind of difficulty in their cases, yet the marked increase in literature available does indicate a changing attitude and comfort in this area. Hartman's discussion of the importance of group methods with some forms of sexual problems was repeated in several other articles related to this topic.

The treatment of neurotic clients was the original basis from which Freudian theory was developed and which in turn greatly affected the development of social work theory and practice. Clients with various neurotic problems are frequently found in the caseloads of social workers. Articles dealing with this type of client problem have increased in the professional literature. Of specific note is Austin's article, a classic in the field. This reminds us that our interest lies not only in the developmental dynamic problem itself but in the problems in psychosocial functioning stemming from it; this holds true for the client himself as well as significant persons in his life.

Depression is a topic in which there has been a marked increase in available material for social workers. It is gratifying to find a rich number of articles from which to select for this topic. A few years ago there were scarcely any. We have many clients who are exhibiting depressions of various kinds and it is essential that we be more knowledgeable about this frequently misunderstood and overlooked cluster of symptoms.

Borderline clients are another group whom we are meeting more frequently in practice. Hopefully, we are learning to recognize and deal with them more effectively. Again, the literature on this topic is expanding.

The final group of articles in this section deals with the treatment and management of psychotic behavior. Within our literature there has been a considerable amount written about the treatment of schizophrenia even though many social workers would consider this group of clients beyond their competence. Esther Marcus suggests in the first article on this topic that such clients make up a "large proportion of caseloads in community agencies and clinics." This paper then reviews and examines the current thinking on this problem, pointing out the wide dimensions of the concept. The articles dealing with direct treatment of the schizophrenic, included in the collection, all emphasize the theme of reality-oriented relationship therapy. In addition to our direct work with the schizophrenic client the literature reminds us of the need to consider the "significant others" in the client's life, especially the family, in our assessment and treatment. Also, there is an increasing interest in the use of groups with these persons.

Apart from the treatment of the schizophrenic client there is a remarkable absence of consideration of other forms of psychotic behavior in the literature. For example, the manic-depressive client and the paranoid client are rarely mentioned. Although the true paranoid is not frequently met, persons with paranoid tendencies and mild to moderate forms of paranoid schizophrenia are frequently found in the clientele of our agency. There appears to be as much oral tradition of how not to deal with such persons as there is an absence of articles and formal discussion of their management. Some references dealing with paranoid ideas are included in the articles on schizophrenia, but these are only incidental to the main theme. I suggest there is no group of clients which arouses more discomfort and uncertainty than these. Many of them continue to function at a level which keeps them out of institutions, but their constant difficulties in social adjustment still bring them and their families to agencies.

Conclusion

To aid clients effectively to achieve improved psychosocial behavior it is essential to address their psychodynamic functioning. Although the professional literature indicates that a high degree of attention has been focused on this area, it is clear that coverage has been far from thorough; thus, it requires constant updating and examination for gaps and omissions as well as for discussions of new experiments in treatment using different theoretical viewpoints and modalities.

Addictions—Alcohol

Counseling Recovering Alcoholics

Jon Weinberg

The magnitude of the problem of alcoholism—which afflicts about 5 percent of the population over 15 years of age—is gradually coming to the attention of the public. In general, those in the helping professions have contributed relatively little toward effective intervention in the problem, primarily because their training has not provided a basic understanding of alcoholism.

This article focuses on treating recovering alocholics—those who recognize their illness, have stopped drinking because they realized the central role it was playing in their difficulties, are currently sober, and intend to maintain sobriety. The term "recovering" is used instead of the more typical "recovered" to stress the chronic nature of the disorder and the patient's eternal susceptibility to relapse.

Many sober alcoholics do not seek counseling because, when their illness is arrested, they return to their premorbid level of adjustment, in which they were reasonably healthy. Others do not seek it because they are successfully following a program of recovery such as Alcoholics Anonymous (AA), which has a strong mental health component. Some who need counseling avoid it. They believe—often with considerable justification—that their potential counselor might not be knowledgeable about alcoholism and might even do them more harm than good.

However, a considerable number of alcoholics do seek counseling after attaining sobriety, and some stop drinking during treatment. The suggestions for counseling given in this article are designed to make professional social workers more aware of the special problems of the recovering alcoholic, to help them avoid common pitfalls (such as identifying alcoholism as secondary or symptomatic, rather than the primary disorder), and to point out techniques and attitudes that have proved effective.

Reprinted with permission from the author and the National Association of Social Workers, from *Social Work*, Vol. 18, No. 4 (July, 1973), pp. 84–93.

Family Involvement

Alcoholism has usually been described as a family illness. This does not imply, as many believe, that the spouse is in some way responsible for the alcoholism. Rather, it means that other family members, especially the wife or husband, are caught up in the pathological processes of the alcoholic's illness in such a way as to develop parallel emotional and/or behavioral problems. Successful treatment for the recovering alcoholic often hinges on involving the spouse effectively in the counseling process.[1]

It is obviously preferable to involve the spouse directly—through joint counseling interviews, for example—but this is not always possible. When it is not, the counselor, with the client's knowledge, is strongly advised to maintain at least occasional telephone contact with the spouse. Self-delusion, or at least marked rationalization, which develops along with the more visible aspects of the illness, is a cardinal feature of alcoholism. Thus it is virtually imperative for the counselor to have an independent source of information about the client's behavior outside the interview situation. The client may be reporting sobriety when he has been drinking; or he may indicate that everything is rosy at home when he has actually been moody and irritable, perhaps getting close to a slip. Without independent information, the counselor may be falsely lulled into a feeling of optimism, which would be followed by resentment ("I was conned") if ultimately disastrous events occurred as a complete surprise. Counselors whose values make them rankle at such "prying" into the client's life beyond the interview may be more successful with nonalcoholics.

One problem frequently encountered in the early phases of recovery is the disappointment or resentment stemming from unrealistic expectations. The alcoholic often expects the family to greet his sobriety with the utmost enthusiasm and gratitude. Unfortunately, the family has been previously conditioned by a thousand broken promises, and may be skeptical or distrustful rather than thrilled. The alcoholic in turn feels let down or angry. Similarly, the family may expect the sober alcoholic to begin functioning at full capacity, to "make up for lost time"; the reality often is a gradual recovery from the physical and psychological ravages of the illness. The alcoholic is taught in recovery programs such as AA to put sobriety ahead of everything, including his family. This may necessitate frequent attendance at AA meetings, avoidance of overwork, and other therapeutic measures. The family may not believe that these activities are vital to recovery. The counselor's role is to help the alcoholic and his family understand and accept the feelings each has, and educate them regarding appropriate expectations, always emphasizing the patience both sides must have to deal with a serious illness that was years in the making.

A special caveat is in order with respect to women alcoholics who are

---

[1] *See* John F. Mueller, "Casework with the Family of the Alcoholic," *Social Work,* 17 (September 1972), pp. 79–84.

married. Many husbands of recovering alcoholics deal with the problem of alcoholism largely by denial, unlike most wives of alcoholics, who more typically try sincerely to be cooperative and understanding. Although the husbands may acknowledge the improved behavioral functioning in their wives, they often resist the use of the alcoholic label or only pay lip service to it. A man may consider his wife's alcoholism a blow to his pride, and if he is a heavy drinker, her abstinence may be a threat. The increasing self-confidence and independence that is likely to accompany her lengthening sobriety often poses an additional threat.

The counselor should attend closely to such factors, working directly with the husband when possible. Since the husband of an alcoholic seldom makes himself available to the counselor, the wife should be helped, as far as possible, to avoid feeling discouraged or sabotaged by the lack of understanding and support. She is more likely to have to depend on herself and other sober alcoholics for the reinforcement needed to maintain recovery.

The Fallacy of Reasons

Both the genesis of alcoholism and its optimal solution are extremely controversial issues. Most people in the helping professions (and the public at large) have a strong bias toward the view that alcoholism is psychogenic and that its solution primarily involves unraveling the presumed psychological roots of the disease.

The author's position, by contrast, is that intrapsychic factors alone do not account for alcoholism and that the search for its psychological origins cannot provide an appropriate or effective solution. Further, he believes that, with some exceptions, alcoholics have a genuine illness with biological and cultural as well as psychological factors in the etiology. An enormous amount of evidence has accumulated from research, which unequivocally contradicts the notion of an "alcoholic personality," but many mental health professionals cling tenaciously to this myth.[2]

The view that alcoholism is a complex, chronic disorder without an established etiology has several implications. The counselor should remember that a great many disorders are successfully treated even though the etiology is obscure. What does successful treatment involve? What are the priorities? Sobriety—not simply healthy psychological functioning—must be given primary consideration because it seems that an abnormal reaction to alcohol is a life time proposition for the vast majority of alcoholics. The evidence at present suggests that no matter how well psychologically alcoholics may become, few can ever return to social drinking.[3]

---

[2] *See,* for example, Edwin H. Sutherland et al., "Personality Traits and the Alcoholic: A Critique of Existing Studies," *Quarterly Journal of Studies on Alcohol,* 11 (1950), pp. 547–561; and L. Syme, "Personality Characteristics and the Alcoholic: A Critique of Present Studies," *Quarterly Journal of Studies on Alcohol,* 18 (1957), pp. 288–302.

[3] *See,* for example, R. E. Reinert and W. T. Bowen, "Social Drinking Following Treatment for Alcoholism," *Menninger Clinic Bulletin,* 32 (1968), pp. 280–290.

Although the causes of alcoholism have not been established, the counselor can profitably examine the reasons for drinking, about which more is known. The reasons for drinking are not equivalent to the reasons for alcoholism; they do not explain alcoholism, nor are they necessarily abnormal in any way. In fact, virtually all the reasons why alcoholics drink are the same as the reasons why many nonalcoholics drink at times.

The counselor should become familiar with these reasons so that he can help the recovering alcoholic be on guard for the stimulus cues that are likely to precipitate a response of alcohol or other drug use. In other words, the counselor can forewarn the recovering alcoholic of what he can anticipate and can point out alternative responses and guide him toward them, thus offering constructive help in avoiding relapses. For example, both alcoholics and nonalcoholics may drink to become more relaxed and voluble at a large social function. In recovery, the counselor can help the alcoholic by teaching him how to be socially comfortable at a party without using chemical aids. Similarly, having a few drinks to relieve tension after a hard day at work is a habit the culture generally condones, but alcoholics in recovery must learn other strategies for unwinding.

It is important to note that, as the examples demonstrate, the recovering alcoholic must strive for superior, not average, emotional adjustment because in our society the average person at times uses alcohol and other drugs instead of internal coping mechanisms. This is a luxury the sober alcoholic cannot afford.

Alibis and Antabuse

A cardinal feature of alcoholism is the alibi system that the alcoholic must develop to maintain the addiction. That is, a person must become delusional in the sense of denying reality and blaming factors outside himself for the terrible problems actually produced by the drinking; otherwise, he would be forced to give up the chemical—hardly the solution an alcoholic prefers. However, the alibi system does not automatically fade away with sobriety. Since most alcoholics stop drinking under great pressure by their families, their employers, or the courts, or under the duress of some situation that has precipitated a crisis, they may still fail to perceive reality and instead blame their problem on their "rotten spouse," their "bigoted boss," or the unfair judicial system.

A person with such delusions, although reluctantly sober, is not yet a recovering alcoholic because he has not recognized his illness as the source of his difficulties. The counselor should treat such a person essentially the same as he treats a practicing alcoholic—that is, teach him about the illness and help him to see reality in terms of the harmful consequences of his drinking.

The alibi problem also occurs with those who are in recovery and even with those who have long been sober. This is called "stinking thinking" in AA terms, and counselors should be aware of some of the many forms it may take. These include:

1. Minimizing retrospectively the harmful consequences of drinking: "I was never that bad."

2. Attributing alcoholism to factors no longer present, thus implying that the illness may have waned: "That job I had would make anybody an alcoholic."

3. Suggesting that a beverage with a lower alcoholic content will be safe: "A little wine with dinner won't hurt me, and besides my husband will be happier if I join him."

4. Showing self-pity: "Nobody understands how rough it is for me."

5. Clinging to resentments or blaming others: "Those kids of mine had just better straighten out, and my wife too."

6. Disparaging or avoiding his AA group: "Those people at AA are really hypocrites. Anyhow, I can't go Monday nights during football season."

These examples of the resurgence of the alibi system are a signal that relapse may be lurking around the corner. It is critically important that the counselor not only avoid reinforcing these often seductively plausible rationalizations, but also make a direct, persistent attempt to bring the person's thinking back to reality. This may require a combination of forceful confrontation and diplomatic delicacy that will tax the counselor's ingenuity. The counselor must remind the client of the nature of his illness and show him that his thinking in alibis is preparing him for drinking again. At the same time, the counselor has to maintain an atmosphere of acceptance that will encourage the client to continue the counseling process.

A special word is in order about clients who are on Antabuse (disulfiram), an inexpensive deterrent drug taken daily that causes an extremely unpleasant physical effect when any alcohol is ingested. In general, the counselor should consider highly suspect any decision that the client makes on his own to discontinue this medication. The client may give an extremely plausible reason—such as "I am doing so well now, I just don't need it"—but in most cases he is planning to drink even though he is not aware of it.

The counselor should try to persuade the client to delay his action for an arbitrary period, perhaps two or three months, and then the decision can be jointly reconsidered. If he insists on discontinuing the drug, the counselor can explain the dangers of the unconscious alibi system, but should not be surprised if the client relapses before the next counseling session.

Routine and Rest

The collective experiences of alcoholics—and of those who work with them regularly—have yielded a number of commonsense conclusions that few professional counselors are aware of.[4] These may sound trivial, but they often spell the difference between maintaining sobriety and relapsing, especially in the first year or two of recovery, and for many even far beyond that.

A primary point is related to changes of routine. It is best for the recovering alcoholic to develop a stabilized life routine, and most do so. A drinking problem arises when something unusual or different occurs. Two important examples are business trips out of town and any type of vacation, from a weekend at a nearby resort to two or more weeks far away.

Frequently environmental changes seem to awaken a desire for drinking, and the counselor should discuss the risks in advance with the client. Similarly, the client should be prepared for an inclination to drink whenever a change in job, a move to a different neighborhood or town, or some other important shift in scenery or routine is impending. The counselor should make certain that clients who are in AA are informed about meetings in places they will be visiting while away from home, and attendance should be strongly encouraged.

Another important caution involves rest. It is fairly typical for the recovering alcoholic to be an unusually hard worker. In some instances, in his zeal to make up for lost time, he tackles more than he is physically capable of, with resultant fatigue and a greatly increased risk of relapse. The counselor should generally advise a client to forget trying to do two taxing jobs even if he is debt ridden. He can instead pay off the creditors more slowly. Or the housewife and mother of five might well be counseled to leave the kitchen floor for another day instead of laboring until midnight. Naturally, the rest of the family should be helped to understand the necessity for putting the alcoholic's sobriety first.

Flare-ups and Flashbacks

The early phases of recovery from alcoholism involve a complex physiological readjustment of the organism to an unaccustomed state— a state of complete freedom from ethyl alcohol. A variety of medically significant laboratory findings are typically noted immediately after withdrawal, but within several weeks such conditions generally return to normal. Clinical observation suggests that a physiological rather than an environmental hypothesis better accounts for sporadic abnormalities in psychological state that some alcoholics experience during recovery.[5] These abnormal states, which may be called flare-ups, typically include general irritability, tension, and/or depression. Their cardinal characteristic is a complete lack of any reasonable psychological explanation. On the contrary,

---

[4] *See*, for example, Elizabeth D. Whitney, *Living with Alcoholism* (Boston: Beacon Press, 1968).

[5] *See*, for example, J. Milam, *The Emergent Comprehensive Concept of Alcoholism* (Seattle, Wash.: Alcoholism Center Associates Press, 1972).

they occur with fairly sudden onset in spite of the most favorable environmental circumstances.

A further diagnostic clue—which favors a physiological etiology—is the tendency for such states to occur for most people at specific time spans during recovery. Flare-ups most frequently occur from the fifth to the seventh week, from the fifth to the seventh month, and from the eleventh to the thirteenth month of the recovery period, but there are wide individual variations. They usually pass within a few days.

The counselor should be aware of this phenomenon in order to warn clients and reassure them by stressing the transitory nature of flare-ups. Clients will otherwise feel bewildered and discouraged, since their efforts to recover seem to be sabotaged, and relapse is a threat. The wise counselor will not only avoid compounding the problem by insisting on a search for psychogenic explanations, but will explain the flare-ups before they arise.

Recovering alcoholics often have anxiety dreams in which they are drinking. Or, despite not drinking, they may wake up with a hangover feeling, especially after a party. Or they may experience in other episodes the kinds of feelings formerly elicited by drinking. All these phenomena may be conveniently labeled flashbacks. Again, the counselor needs to reassure the client about the normality of the occurrence, carefully avoiding psychodynamic speculations.

Humility

A pervasive goal in most psychological counseling is enhancing the client's self-esteem, which is nearly always low—and alcoholics are certainly no exception. Counseling the recovering alcoholic-dependent person does, however, introduce an apparent paradox with regard to ego-building. For successful recovery, both self-confidence and humility must be sought. A comprehensive understanding of alcoholism is needed to appreciate fully the critical importance of humility, but a brief rationale may be helpful.

In his illness the addicted person becomes completely self-centered and even grandiose. He believes he can manage his life if others do not interfere. Usually recovery can begin only after his life has begun to crumble in one or more ways and he has finally abandoned the delusion that he can manage everything. Once in recovery, he must continue to acknowledge that a host of people, events, and conditions influence what happens in his life.

Failure to attain and retain this humble perspective of his power to control his own life usually leads to a return to what AA calls "the big I," or the grandiose idea that one has total control. This is quickly generalized to the use of alcohol or other drugs—which of course "I" can manage—and the result is relapse. Although some alcoholics, by single-minded involvement with AA, do seem to combine grandiosity and sobriety successfully, this is unlikely to occur among clients who seek counseling.

In practice, the counselor should have little difficulty in directing the alcoholic client toward both self-esteem and humility. He works to build self-esteem by helping the client to accept himself as a worthwhile person, recognize his assets, set reasonable goals.

The counselor works to develop humility by emphasizing recognition of reality. He may point out examples illustrating that people do not fully control outcomes in their lives:

1. An executive intends to be on time for an appointment but a traffic snarl makes him an hour late.

2. A father means to take his family on a picnic but thunderstorms upset the plan.

3. A student studies hard for a test but an attack of flu impairs her performance.

Above all, the alcoholic cannot control the outcome of his drinking. His illness renders him as powerless over the effects of alcohol as the diabetic is over the effects of excess sugar.

Morality

Counselors are usually well aware that their own values and attitudes influence the way they interact with their clients. Experiences derived from counseling alcoholics suggest that moral values are especially significant to this population. The great majority of sober alcoholics seem to have traditional, often somewhat rigid, moral values, even though the active stages of the illness have brought about the temporary deterioration of such values.

The most effective counseling strategy for alcoholics is to reinforce behavior consistent with their conventional values, unless these are demonstrably self-defeating and therefore desirable to modify. The counselor should recommend that they avoid behavior contrary to their values because it is highly probable that even relatively low levels of guilt may precipitate a relapse into drinking. While other types of clients may be quite willing to suffer mild or moderate degrees of guilt in order to reap the benefits of "immoral" behavior—and may occasionally drink to relieve guilt without getting into serious trouble—the recovering alcoholic should be encouraged to live up to his own values scrupulously.

The two most common problem areas are honesty and sex. Dishonesty or cheating, whether in job applications, income taxes, interpersonal behavior, or other aspects of life, poses a real hazard to recovery. Even when signs of guilt are not immediately evident, guilt feelings, often unrecognized, tend to grow and eventually erupt in the form of relapse. With regard to sex, the counselor should adopt a highly conservative stance. Any nonmarital sex relations contrary to the values of recovering alcoholics carry an enormous risk. If both partners in a relationship that is counter to their values are chemically dependent, a joint relapse is a near certainty.

In addition to the guilt component, many alcoholics (especially women and homosexuals) have developed a strong association between "illicit" sex and a state of intoxication. Engaging in the former will be likely to awaken a craving for the latter, with disastrous results. Although he may have a long-range counseling goal of helping the client adopt new values or of breaking up old behavioral associations, the counselor must focus primarily on steering the alcoholic toward keeping sober. This means the client has to move with the utmost caution in the area of morality.

Relapses

Because alcoholism is a chronic disease, its victims are subject to relapse throughout their lives. Some counselors may believe that a cure is possible, but the majority accept the fact that sobriety for any length of time is no insurance against a return to the destructive consequences of drinking. Most alcoholics do in fact experience one or more relapses during the recovery process, especially in the first two years. Disastrous slips after twenty years or more of sobriety are by no means unknown.

The attitudes and actions of the counselor may be critically important when his alcoholic client has a relapse. A major hazard is that the counselor may reject the client, overtly or covertly. Since most social workers intellectually accept the chronic nature of the disorder, rejection probably originates in latent moralistic attitudes toward alcoholism. Or a counselor's rejection of an alcoholic may be derived, at least in part, from a sense of inadequacy because of the client's apparent failure to benefit from counseling.

To ascertain his real feelings about alcoholics, the social worker might ask himself the following questions:

● How do I react when clients with other types of chronic problems take a turn for the worse?

● Do I get angry, for example, at a chronic schizophrenic who stops his medication and must be rehospitalized?

● Do I condemn the obese client who departs from his prescribed diet?

● Do I denounce the borderline student who fails to adhere to the agreed-upon study schedule?

If the answer to these questions is yes, then the counselor should look at his own self-concept in relation to his professional role. If, however, he does not feel angry and rejecting toward some types of clients, but does toward the relapsing alcoholic, he has yielded to the entrenched cultural attitude of judging his client as morally inferior and thus unworthy or unmotivated.

It is worth remembering that our society generally stacks the deck in favor of relapse. Although the alcoholic's sobriety initially delights the family and most other people important in his life, they tend after a time to assume that the problem has ended, that the person is cured. Sooner or later well-intentioned but uninformed friends and relatives will encourage or even pressure recovering alcoholics to try drinking "like gentlemen or ladies" now that they have "reformed." The power of social conformity may jeopardize recovery as much or more than the internal psychological stresses on which most counselors focus.

The counselor's role when relapse occurs is to help interrupt the drinking if he has an opportunity to do so. He may assist by advising the family to take forcible action, since the client is not likely to be available to him. He should also avoid condemnatory judgments when the client returns and help the client examine the probable causes of the relapse with an eye toward future prevention.

Alcoholic Anonymous

Professionals typically have mixed feelings about AA. On the one hand, nearly everyone acknowledges the superior effectiveness of AA in comparison with professional mental health treatment for alcoholics.[6] On the other hand, for varying reasons, counselors tend to have negative feelings or at least serious reservations about the AA approach. Some feel it is too religious. Some suggest that it involves too much dependence or rigidity. Others object to the zealous or smug attitudes of some AA members.

The author believes that AA offers an outstanding program, both for recovery from alcoholism and for general emotional adjustment which those counseling the alcoholic should strongly endorse. Careful study of the Twelve Steps of AA reveals the following major components, telescoped and grouped for the sake of brevity.[7] In the first three steps, the alcoholic acknowledges the crux of his problem and commits himself to the necessary solution. In the next four steps, he takes an honest look at himself, shares this information with a special person, and works to modify his behavioral deficiencies. Through the succeeding four steps, he continues to scrutinize himself honestly and humbly, trying to follow a virtuous path—that is, behaving sensibly toward his fellow man. Finally, in the last step, he assists others by teaching them what he has learned.

Individuals rigorously applying these principles may reap rich benefits, not only in sobriety, but in a highly satisfying emotional life and rewarding relationships with others. Al-Anon and Neurotics Anonymous are self-help

---

[6] *See*, for example, James C. Coleman, *Abnormal Psychology and Modern Life* (Glenview, Ill.: Scott Foresman & Co., 1972), p. 421.

[7] For a fuller explanation of the AA program and the common objections to it, *see* Jon R. Weinberg, "Alcoholics Anonymous: An Interpretation for the Professional." (Mimeographed by the author, 1972.)

organizations for those who are not chemically dependent on alcohol. They utilize the identical program because of its established effectiveness.

In addition to the twelve-step program, AA provides for the alcoholic a fellowship that offers immediate and complete empathic acceptance to individuals who have been widely rejected and who have come to despise themselves. This is of critical importance to many in the initial phases of recovery. Furthermore, AA groups represent virtually the only social subculture that assures permanent positive reinforcement of lifetime abstinence, and they are immediately available to replace the former "drinking buddies."

As for the common objection that AA is too religious, it should be noted that the program is spiritual but not religious in the sense of being tied to organized religion or the tenets of any particular faith. Agnostics and atheists are free to interpret the program in ways acceptable to their values.

Then there is the criticism that AA is too restrictive and rigid. AA has no eligibility requirement except a sincere desire to be sober. However, those trying to follow the program should adhere to it closely for the same reason a diabetic should scrupulously follow his diet-insulin regime. If that is rigidity, the author endorses it.

Smugness? Some individual AA members may be smug, just as some ex-smokers are. And some are zealous, just as some Democrats, abortion advocates, and ecology enthusiasts are. People tend to take notice of the vocal minority—in AA as in any group—and forget that most of the half million AA members are living as productively and unobtrusively as anyone else.

The author believes the principal points about AA that the counselor should consider are the following:

1. The AA program should routinely be recommended even if the counselor does not fully understand it, simply because of its effectiveness. The client frequently resists, offers alibis, or otherwise tries to avoid becoming involved. As a rule, counselors should patiently persist in the advocacy rather than accept the alibis. Of course, it would not be necessary to advocate AA for someone who had never been in it, but had long been sober.

2. A referral to AA should be personal rather than general. Ideally the counselor should contact AA and arrange for the initial visit, rather than simply telling the client "Go to AA."

3. Clients should be asked to refrain from making a judgment about the program until after they have attended regularly for at least three months. Objections to a specific AA group may be valid and one change of group is often legitimate. After that, the counselor can assume that the client is resisting the program, and his alibi should not be supported.

4. If the client is already established in AA, the counselor should be wary

of declining attendance and any other sign that the alcoholic is avoiding AA, since such avoidance is often a forerunner of relapse.

Other Psychoactive Drugs

The use of psychoactive medication for recovering alcoholics is an extremely controversial issue. The author's position is definitely a conservative one, based on the disastrous experiences of a great many recovering alcoholics. No doubt, some alcoholics have been able to use such drugs without harm. However, since what will happen in the individual case cannot be predicted, one must be thoroughly persuaded that the potential benefits outweigh the known risks.

Prescribing such drugs is obviously a medical decision, but counselors may need to take responsibility for advising alcoholic clients in regard to seeking or using certain kinds of drugs, because most physicians have had no relevant training in drug dependence and may have been misled by pharmaceutical houses about the risks of most of these medications.

The drugs of greatest risk are those chemically related to alcohol in that they act primarily as a depressant of the central nervous system. These drugs, which produce both physical and psychological cross-dependence, include all hypnotics and sedatives and nearly all minor tranquilizers.

Thus any sleeping pill and all the popular minor tranquilizers—regardless of the alleged safety from dependence promised by the manufacturer—pose a twofold hazard to the recovering alcoholic. Besides the obvious risk of substituting one chemical for another in a harmful fashion, a danger that is probably greater is often observed. Because the prescribed drug creates in the brain a state sufficiently similar to the state created by alcohol, it strongly awakens a desire for the drug of first choice, alcohol. Many alcoholics with years of sobriety have been innocently sentenced to instant relapse by a simple prescription.

In addition to the drugs chemically related to alcohol, all narcotic analgesics—including allegedly safe synthetic narcotics—should be avoided unless medically imperative. Over-the-counter medications intended to sedate or tranquilize are also risky, as are antihistamines and other cold medicines. For example, one of the most familiar nighttime cold medicines is 25 percent alcohol. Even trips to the dentist have been known to cause a relapse for alcoholics who were given a form of pain killer that resulted in a "high" feeling. The general rule of thumb to keep in mind is that drugs arousing strong pleasurable feelings or those paralleling the effect of alcohol should be taboo. It is irrelevant that the manufacturer or the prescribing physician may have given the client assurance that the drug is not hazardous; they do not fully understand chemical dependence.

Psychoactive medications that do not ordinarily generate problems for an alcoholic include all major tranquilizers and the antidepressants (excluding amphetamines and other pure stimulants). In some cases when counseling alone does not dispel marked symptomatic anxiety, it may be advisable to suggest that the client request small doeses of a major tranquilizer rather than the ubiquitous minor tranquilizers. If alcoholic clients who are using any of the foregoing drugs described as hazardous report no problems with them, the counselor should accept this as accurate only when counseling is manifesting satisfactory progress and when a knowledgeable person can certify the client's statement about his drug use and general progress.

Role of the Social Worker

The most important potential contribution that social workers might make in the treatment of alcoholism would be to move from intellectual recognition that alcoholism is a prevalent problem to direct application of appropriate helping strategies in clinical practice. First and foremost, social workers should systematically screen all adult clients, prior to launching into treatment of the presenting problem, to see whether they can rule out a diagnosis of alcoholism. The alcoholic will derive little or no benefit and much time will be wasted if his treatment focuses on secondary or interdependent individual, family, or marital problems.

When alcoholism is identified, the next task is to deal directly with it. This includes educating the client and his family about the illness, working toward an acceptance of the problem, and obtaining a commitment to helpful action.

The third task is to guide the client toward whatever action seems most appropriate. This may involve referral to a specialized treatment agency or self-help group, but generally counseling with the social worker should continue.

Unhappily, social workers, like other professionals, are seldom trained to perform effectively the three tasks described. This deficiency can best be remedied by seeking competent remedial training from professionals and/or paraprofessionals who have the specialized knowledge required.

The author has conducted many such training sessions and has found that, in general, social workers are highly receptive to learning more about strategies for identifying and dealing with alcoholics. Gaining such practical knowledge should help break the vicious cycle that the professional untrained in this specialized field may experience: first, he feels inadequate to deal with alcoholism and is unreasonably pessimistic about it; then, he avoids or minimizes the problem when counseling the alcoholic; subsequently, he verifies his initial feelings (a self-fulfilling prophecy) as the treatment fails to help.

This paper has dealt mainly with the social worker's fourth task in treating the alcoholic: to understand the complexities of the recovery process in such a way as to enhance the effectiveness of psychotherapy for the sober alcoholic. As the social work profession begins to carry out the first three tasks more effectively, vastly increased opportunities will be presented for dealing with the fourth task. Ultimately, social workers may be pleasantly surprised to learn that treatment of the alcoholic, rather than being the one massive disappointment that many have supposed or found it to be, is actually one of the more gratifying social work experiences.

Motivating the Drug Addict in Treatment

C. Andre St. Pierre

If one were to tour the existing drug treatment facilities, the complaint heard most regularly would be about the drug addict's impoverished motivation. Furthermore, it would be seen that many treatment settings have established standards of motivation as the ruling criterion in their admission policy. As a result, the more pathologically progressed addicts, unable to show adequate motivation, are most likely to fail the intake evaluation. If they do manage to be admitted, their ability to remain in the treatment facility is questionable. Thus when they return to the streets, their situation is unaltered.

These addicts, unfortunately, represent the portion of the addict population with the largest habit; they are involved in the more extreme antisocial behaviors and are the greatest source of contagion. Although these addicts are doing the most damage to themselves and the community, they are the most untouched by therapeutic contact. It is of utmost concern that there has been a significant increase in the number of unmotivated addicts. Somehow these persons will have to be included in some type of treatment program. The contagion factor alone makes this an urgent problem. Thus one can see the pressing need for developing effective methods to foster motivation. It is to this end that this paper directs itself.

The methods used to foster motivation derive from the author's continuing experience as senior drug addiction counselor for the Drug Addiction Treatment Unit of the Boston City Hospital. Since opening in August 1966, the unit has functioned as a voluntary walk-in outpatient clinic. It is directly supervised by the hospital's department of psychiatry and is part of the city's Department of Health and Hospitals.

During the initial years of operation, various casework counseling techniques were experimented with on a small scale, with the intent of selecting the most successful for incorporation in future treatment programs. The resistant drug addict was treated with supportive techniques such as educational counseling, persuasion, ventilation, environmental manipula-

Reprinted with permission of the National Association of Social Workers, from *Social Work*, Vol. 16, No. 1 (January, 1971), pp. 80–88.

tion, and work rehabilitation. Also used were such psychotherapeutic techniques as clarification, interpretation, and limited insight therapy. The end result was that some patients were rehabilitated and helped to live relatively drug-free lives. A review of these successful cases showed that in moving from an unmotivated to a motivated state, patients experienced a series of four major successive developmental phases or processes.

Intake experience with a significant number of addicts provided further evidence of the patient's need for a developmental process of motivation. On intake several patients were confronted with the fact that they loved the feeling heroin gave them and were not prepared to give it up. (At the time—prior to January 1969—the treatment unit had no methadone withdrawal program, nor did these specific patients seek inpatient care, so these two incentives for coming to the clinic could be ruled out.) These patients were therefore challenged about why they had come to the clinic at all. They stated their intention of continuing drug use, but said further: "Tell me why I'm using drugs. Convince me not to take drugs." One wonders, in retrospect, if these patients were not unwittingly giving counselors a formula that could be used to motivate them. Similar pleas have been heard since, some patients even asking to be hypnotized to deliver them from their plight.

Evidently it is not a question of willpower alone that prevents an addict from rejecting drugs. In reaching for drugs the addict uses the ego defense mechanism of blocking, whereby for the crucial moments of temptation he shuts out all good judgement, the disastrous consequences, and often actually what he may have learned in therapy. He thereby becomes emotionally free to take the drug, so to speak. Blocking is used by almost everyone almost every day of his life, in particular to cope with fear and anxiety about death. It would be extremely difficult to function were one unable to shut off painful feelings. The addict, on the other hand, uses blocking to his disadvantage, not allowing himself to experience negative feelings about drug use, since this could mean a denial of the needs the drug will meet immediately or the satisfaction it can so quickly provide.

Awareness of the developmental phases the addict passes through on his way to a drug-free life and of the patient's need for motivation to discontinue drug use led to formulation of a scheme of motivational progression that is currently being used to potentiate motivation in the patient. The four goals are as follows:

1. Confrontation of the patient with his addiction.

2. Development in the patient of an intellectual understanding of why he uses drugs.

3. Development in the patient of an intellectual conviction that drugs are harmful to him.

4. Development of an awareness in the patient of the role his feelings play in his addiction.

The obvious dynamic of this process is that each step involves strengthening the patient's ego so he can move on to master the succeeding, more difficult step. The validity of the process may be found in the observation that this was how successful patients chose and were enabled to progress toward motivation to discontinue drug use. As a basis for a better understanding of this means of motivating the unmotivated drug addict, the current addiction problem as seen clinically will first be discussed and the addict's lack of motivation will be explained.

The Addict Population

Heroin has again become the drug of choice for at least 95 percent of the patients now being treated. This upswing in the use of heroin has occurred at an alarming rate over the past year. Two or three years ago the clinic population of young drug addicts were abusing a smorgasbord of drugs indiscriminately: LSD, amphetamines, barbiturates, codein-containing cough syrup. A second change in the type of person being treated is that whereas the typical heroin addict of a few years ago was in the mid- and late 20s, the addicts now being treated are in their late teens and early 20s. These young heroin-users are supporting $30–$100-a-day habits by living outside the law.

As has been the pattern for the last four years, drug addiction continues to spread to all classes of society. Also, as drug addiction makes inroads in the general population, any attempt to delineate a typology of personalities with a disposition to drug addiction has less and less validity.

Many of the youngsters now becoming addicted are bright and capable. They have the usual transitory emotional upheavals of their age such as having to make school, work, and sexual adjustments and to adopt some philosophy of life. It is likely that, had drugs not been available to them, many would eventually have resolved their difficulties and taken a place in society. This is why it is so important that law enforcement agencies are supported in their efforts to curtail the availability of addictive drugs.

The Drug Experience

The question is often asked: Why do teenagers start using drugs? To begin with, the adolescent takes drugs out of such varying motives as curiosity, thrill-seeking, rebellion, and the need to belong to and be accepted by another individual or a peer group. Drugs, especially narcotic drugs, introduce the experience-seeker to a new realm of feeling. He experiences them as a "wonderful world of feeling"—a satiating euphoria, the "high." One young addict reported that after experiencing his first heroin high he had exclaimed to himself: "Why didn't they tell me such wonderful feelings existed?" The addict can conceive of nothing in the real world that could produce a comparable feeling in him. A significant number of heroin addicts made the statement that unless the world could provide them with a feeling to compensate for the loss of the high, they would never be able to give up heroin. For this reason an addict usually scoffs when it is suggested that he search for substitute satisfactions.

Addicts have stated that the closest feeling to the high is the sexual orgasm, but even this falls far short of the satisfactions of the former. They explain that orgasm lasts for a matter of minutes, whereas the glow from heroin often is felt for an hour and, through repeated injections, as long as a day and a half. Patients reported their sexual lives to be greatly diminished while on drugs. Some spouses complained about the resulting long periods of sexual abstinence forced on them by their mates' addiction. Drugs are seen to suppress the addict's sexual drive almost totally, there being a definite shift of libido from sexual goals to a paramount pursuit of the drug experience.

Another facet of the craving for drugs is the immediate and often complete relief drugs will give from psychic tension. One can see how the experience-seeker can become the oblivion seeker. Drugs zero in quickly on anxiety. In contrast, therapy is slow and tedious and often cannot compete with the immediate relief afforded by drugs. This naturally places the counselor at a significant disadvantage.

The presence or absence of satisfactions in the patient's life does appear to have a definite correlation with the tenacity with which he holds onto the drug once having experienced it—the typical clinic patient became addicted after his first few drug experiences. Exploration of patients' lives—interpersonal relationships, marriage, sex, and work—shows that a significant majority had never experienced a sustained feeling of well-being. The anxiety-free drugged state therefore became for them a novel and cherished experience. One explained: "The only time I feel normal is when I'm on drugs; I didn't realize how tense and depressed I was until I started using drugs." Another patient, struggling through his fifty-third straight day of barbiturate abstinence, telephoned his counselor to pour out the anguish and torment he felt in having to cope with his employer, his mother-in-law, and his wife. "I can't stand it," he complained. "I didn't realize what these pills meant to me. I'm holding the pills in my hand now and I feel I could kiss them." The addict is caught in a mammoth struggle. For the majority, escape from painful feelings was the most frequent motivating factor in drug dependency.

However, for many youngsters it was a total lack of satisfaction in life from which they fled. Many gave the following as a reason for taking drugs: "I was bored; there was nothing else to do." They appeared to be giving life an ultimatum: each moment, day, or week must provide satisfaction—or else drugs would be taken. Realistically, the everyday world holds no such promise. Just as we must learn to live with and tolerate our day-to-day depressions, a tolerance must be acquired for periods without satisfactions.

Nevertheless, a way is usually open for one to do something about depression or to work at achieving some satisfactions. This is where the addict is trapped: He will not work at anything; he makes little attempt to solve his problems—he must meet with instant success. Often he feels doomed to fail. Many addicts are almost completely lacking in aggressiveness in this regard.

Resolution of inner conflicts and environmental difficulties does not necessarily free the patient from the captivating power of the drug experience. After two years of intensive treatment several barbiturate addicts achieved considerable insight, were freed from somatic symptoms such as headaches, has settled into good jobs, and reported their sexual lives as satisfactory and that stress from intrafamilial relationships was at a minimum. Yet despite these tremendous gains and newfound satisfactions they relapsed—and relapsed badly. There was at first a weak attempt to rationalize their relapses by exaggerating the slightest personal or familial stress. With repeated confrontation by the counselor they admitted their replases were indefensible. No motive came to their immediate awareness and they resigned themselves to having to cope with the raw compulsion to take drugs. Further exploration revealed the compulsion to be repetition of the drug experience, to achieve the especially appealing feeling of well-being it gave—a feeling apparently not capable of achievement by these patients in any other way.

Motivation

The question arises of how it can be said that an addict who comes voluntarily to a clinic for help with his problem is not motivated at least to a slight extent. This question might best be answered by describing the addict's typical approach to treatment. Usually, the first explanation the addict offers—especially if he is a heroin-user—is: "I'm sick of the hassle." He then explains as convincingly as he can that the hardships he endures in obtaining drugs prohibit his continuing to use them. The appropriate affect expected of someone serious about treatment may or may not be present. Many times the addict recites in rote fashion the catastrophes he has experienced as a result of his addiction and says that he is determined to avoid them in the future. Sensing the counselor's desire to help, the addict may "put the bite on him for methadone." What initially is a subtle request for this relief-giving withdrawal medication explodes into a demand for an unalienable right if the request is not granted. Obviously, life without drugs is foreign to the addict at this period in his life.

It is necessary here to define what is meant by movitation. Motivation, as intended in this paper, is the condition that exists when a patient displays appreciable incentive to struggle against the drug compulsion. Motivation has also to be considered from its conscious and unconscious aspects.

At best patients were seen to have mixed feelings about abstention from drugs. Invariably they appeared to have a mental reservation that they would use drugs if they felt the need, but with "proper management." An illustration is the case of a patient rated as having a favorable potential for rehabilitation. His clinic attendance was above average and he was intent on problem-solving. He had been in treatment about one year when one day his wife reported that he had ripped off the bathroom molding and torn away some of the kitchen planking. On confrontation the patient admitted he had felt a strong craving for pills and had forgotten in what crack he had hidden his supply. It came out later in therapy that he had been taking the pills all along, being careful to hide such activity from his counselor. Such deception on the part of a patient is not unusual. The pull of the drug can be astonishingly strong.

Regarding the unconscious factors, it was clinically evident that patients were not fully aware of their great lack of incentive. They overworked the ego defense mechanisms of denial and projection, which obviously interfered with this awareness. Denial was used in two ways. The addict rejected the reality of his physical and personal deterioration and indulged himself in the wish-fulfilling fantasy of the "beautiful feeling of heroin," thereby shutting out the "madness of it all." Projection was found to be especially useful in avoiding the uncomfortable reality of responsibility for continuing the addiction. For example, when methadone was denied, addicts often said: "You're forcing me to go back on the street and use drugs." To this the counselor was tempted to say: "Why is this a crisis? What have you been doing for the past two years?" Another projection frequently heard was the addict's blaming his relapse on another person: "A friend stopped by and gave me some."

A minority come to the clinic because they see it as a refuge. They are tired and physically ailing. The mad hustle to scrape money together to meet the day's drug need has become too much. Their arms are badly scarred—at times badly swollen from infections—and their veins have collapsed from injection abuse. This group searches for a haven in which to recuperate, even if it is a hospital.

In January 1969 the unit began prescribing methadone on a more liberal basis. By June 1969 the number of addicts coming to the treatment unit increased 500 percent. Thus one can readily see the importance of withdrawal medication to the addict and conversely the weakness of his motivation without this incentive. So although the counselor sees the patient sitting before him in his office, the patient, so to speak, is still outside. He is not a participant. There is as yet no appreciable struggle against the drug compulsion. Clinicians will agree that a sincere desire to abstain totally from drugs is rare. Even the patient himself is usually openly pessimistic about his ability to live without drugs.

The importance of motivation as the essential ingredient of treatment is, of course, self-evident. Without it treatment would never get off the ground. The drug addict, as evidenced in the preceding pages, more often than not is thoroughly unmotivated. The crucial task therefore becomes one of motivating the unmotivated.

The technique used in the program under discussion consists of the counselor's helping a patient to attain the four developmental goals listed previously. These will now be discussed in detail, with a descriptive evaluation of application of the technique to patients who have benefited from it.

Confrontation with Addiction

This process consists of effecting a tolerable degree of confrontation of the patient with the following issues:

1. He is in a crisis situation. The cause-and-effect relationhsip between the situation and the drug abuse is explored in detail.

2. He likes the way drugs make him feel.

3. The counselor is aware of his lack of motivation. The counselor presents as an illustration of this the fact that if the patient could maneuver out of his present crisis situation he would most certainly be on the street that very moment hustling for his next fix. He is told that he has manipulated his environment and relationships to the utmost to be able to take drugs and coexist in a society that condemns such abuse. Now his back is up against the wall—he is sick or someone has exposed him and he is threatened with jail of a similar catastrophe.

4. He is pursuing drugs at a primitive instinctual level, disregarding possible harm to others. Consequently society, out of self-preservation, might decide to jail him.

5. In denying his addiction or projecting culpability for it he is using primitive defense mechanisms that must be given up.

Confrontation as a technique in motivating the addict is not a new concept. It was pioneered by the self-help group of ex-addicts in Synanon with favorable results.[1] Synanon's use of the technique involves a vigorous attack on the addict's attempts at rationalization, denial, and projection so as to strip him of these defenses. In the initial encounter the patient's statement that he wants to quit taking drugs might be met with such retorts as: "How can you say you want to give up drugs? You like them—they're good to you," and "You're a phoney." Benefiting from Synanon's experience, other treatment settings such as Daytop Lodge on Staten Island, New York, and the Boston State Hospital Drug Addiction Treatment Unit have since adapted the confrontation concept to their programs.[2]

Understanding Why Drugs Are Used

With rare exceptions the addict has little insight into his use of drugs other than that he likes the way they make him feel. Actually patients never

[1] Louis Yablonsky, *The Tunnel Back: Synanon* (New York: Macmillan Co., 1965).
[2] Joseph A. Shelby and Alexander Bassin, "Daytop Lodge: Halfway Home for Drug Addicts," *Federal Probation*, Vol. 28 (December 1964), pp. 46–54; and David Myerson and Joseph Mayer, "Treatment of Drug Addiction," unpublished paper, Boston State Hospital Drug Addiction Treatment Unit, 1969, p. 13.

gave the matter much thought before it was brought up in therapy. They really had to be helped to see that they were taking drugs to meet certain needs, emotional as well as physical. Simply asking the patient: "What do drugs do for you?" often established what drugs really meant to him. It is most important that the patient verbalize these needs in order to return the crucial focus to his own words.

Invariably all patients brought out directly and indirectly two major reasons for drug use: (1) they thoroughly enjoyed the satiating euphoria of the high and (2) the drug brought considerable relief from psychic pain, tension, and anxiety. Patients verbalized quite easily that drugs relaxed them. Surprisingly, however, patients soft-pedal the importance of the high to them. Only later as therapy progresses does the overwhelming importance of the high and its primacy in the patient's relapse emerge.

The clinical observation is that the standard psychodynamic formulations for explaining relapse become secondary to new drives generated in the personality after the patient has tasted the effect of drugs. The pleasure principle now appears to take hold. What is now being dealt with is a hungry man who has a new appetite, an appetite for the feeling he knows drugs will give him. The chief motive for relapse was observed repeatedly to be the attempt to recapture the first high—such is the impact it has made on the addict's mind and feelings. Bringing this to his awareness eventually elicits a concession by the patient that this is the case. This proved to be extremely important in giving the patient an understanding of why he was using drugs.

The self-destructive impulse appeared for most patients to be a component part of addiction. Additional guilt brought on by addiction compounded the situation. In this regard patients reported taking larger and larger dosages in order to achieve the desired oblivion. Also, the need to expiate showed itself as the addict flirted dangerously with death by overdose. The clinical picture viewed here is that of the addict standing motionless, arms hanging limp, observing himself plunging headlong downhill to self-destruction and doing nothing about it. He apparently splits himself off from his feelings, using the ego defense mechanism of isolation, and thereby does not see himself as a participant in this tragedy. When challenged by the counselor with: "You see what's happening; why don't you do something about it?" the addict usually replies with a naïve rationalization: "I don't know how." Were the patient able to be more honest his reply would be: "I won't struggle," which is the crux of the motivation problem.

Knowing Drugs are Harmful

On intake the unmotivated patient was seen to have rationalized a philosophy to sustain himself against society's condemnation and his own guilt feelings. Quite often he was eager to match wits with the counselor, at times investing much effort in trying to convert the counselor to his own point of view. The patient would emphasize the good feeling drugs gave him and how they enabled him to function in stressful situations with which he felt he could not otherwise cope. He had not permitted himself to think about the harmful consequences of drug abuse.

It was here that the counselor presented a strongly convincing case against drug abuse. The following four characteristics of drug addiction were impressed on the patient:

1. There is an overpowering desire, need, or compulsion to continue taking drugs and to obtain them by any means.

2. There is a tendency to increase the dosage steadily.

3. There is a psychic and generally a physical dependence on the effects of the drug.

4. There is an effect detrimental to the individual and society.

Actually the counselor agreed with the patient that the heroin high, for example, was a satiating, exceedingly pleasurable sensation. Were it not for the accompanying harmful consequences of heroin addiction, its popularity would be assured and, as one patient put it: "We would have a real cool world." For clarification purposes, the counselor used the analogy of poison-coated candy.

Another technique used was repeatedly to dig up the dirt and hurt associated with addiction, throwing them up to the patient at appropriate times—again a device used successfully by self-help groups such as Synanon. The patient was further informed that in extended drug abuse there is drastic personality deterioration and eventual immobilization. The evidence of this was too fresh in the patient's life for him to deny. Often at this point the patient was seen to be really listening for the first time. There was some depression and a beginning identification with treatment goals.

An outstanding delusion was that the patient could control his use of drugs. "Chipping," the addict calls it: using drugs only at convenient intervals such as on weekends. The problem, of course, is sticking to this system. In group discussions patients assumed two opposing views on "chipping." The younger addicts who had been into drugs only for a year or so aggressively defended their ability to control the habit; the older, seasoned addicts shook their heads, cautioning that they had once felt the same way but had been unable to do so.

The reality of the situation appeared to be that in heroin addiction, as with all other forms of addiction, one is unable to stick to a system. The addict finds himself psychologically helpless to set any limits on his use of drugs. He becomes "greedy," as some patients put it. Furthermore, changes are going on in his body; a tolerance develops. The body demands more and more of the drug to achieve the desired feeling, and eventually high dosages are needed simply to prevent withdrawal sickness. There is no status quo—and this fact has to be reinforced continually.

Awareness of the Role Feelings Play

In this phase the patient has to be helped to develop an appreciation of the power feelings have over his behavior. Typically (which is likely the condition of the majority of the general population), the addict is unaware of the world of feelings. He goes through life without understanding why he feels the way he does. With regard to his addiction, rational thinking and behavior are submerged under waves of impulses. He has to learn the distinction that exists between knowing and feeling. He may know that drugs are destructive; however, his feelings may not respond according to his best interests. His impulses might continue to demand gratification despite the injurious consequences. The patient is told that his *knowing* could be considered an expression of the intellectual portion of his personality, whereas his *feelings* are the expression of the instinctual forces.

A psychiatric technique found considerably effective at this stage in treatment is splitting of the ego judgmental executive force of the personality into the observing self and the experiencing self. This involves having the patient become aware of his adult, mature, rational self as opposed to his childish narcissistic demanding self with its associated uncontrolled impulses. The counselor supports mature, addiction-free behavior and discourages infantile narcissistic pursuits. Thus the patient's observing self enters into an alliance with the counselor and begins to struggle with the personality force that does not understand the word "no."

When the patient has mastered the stages of knowing why he uses drugs, developing an intellectual conviction that this is self-destructive, and achieving some insight into his feelings, his ego is seen to be in a much stronger position to contain and attempt mastery of his craving for drugs. What was observed clinically was an excruciating turmoil in and struggle on the part of the patient. Some patients compared it to taming a wild animal in themselves, a predicament that can readily be appreciated.

Conclusion

When the patient begins to move from his passivity and shows a willingness to struggle against the drug compulsion, then it can be said that he is motivated. Of course this motivation will have to be revitalized repeatedly and at best is achieved by a slow process—six months to two years in treatment is not unusual.

The writer's analysis of the motivational technique described is that it succeeds largely by virtue of two means, namely, fragmentation of the problem and elucidation:

1. *Fragmentation* because there is a splitting up of the seemingly overwhelming task of mastery into workable sectors. Patients were observed to

manifest changes in attitude during the four phases almost despite themselves. Hostility toward the counselor accompanied some of the changes, real evidence that he was breaking through their resistance. The patient was now more exposed to his own painful thoughts and feelings and saw the counselor as being responsible for this.

2.   *Elucidation* because a geniune enlightenment develops in the patient as he is exposed to new perspectives on himself and his addiction problem. He is also exposed to a learning process. His ego is strengthened as a result of this activity and moves toward an identification with treatment goals. By persuasion, by using the inductive process of reasoning, and by introducing real conviction, the technique succeeds in helping the patient reach the conclusion that he must act—he must struggle against the drug compulsion.

The bulk of the patient's work is done in ongoing therapy. This will necessarily involve the patient's feelings—some how attaining an understanding that the sufferings attached to drug addiction outweigh the satisfactions. As a consequence the patient will make the ultimate decision that "It just isn't worth the hassle," as some put it. Next the patient must learn to live with the deprivation of the pleasurable feeling the drug gives. This will require practice on the part of the patient—in struggling, in self-denial, and in coping with the ultimate goal: mastery of his craving.

Clients with Character Disorders

Merl M. Jackel

In the present state of psychoanalytic knowledge, the classification "character disorder" is subject to a great deal of confusion. One can readily understand why this is so if one remembers that at the turn of the century psychiatry as a whole did not even accept the concept of a psychogenic cause, as opposed to organic causes, for mental illness. Except for psychopaths, whose condition was generally thought to be constitutional and hereditary, persons with what we now diagnose as character disorders were not considered to be in need of treatment by a psychiatrist. Thus the psychiatric classification "character disorder" has actually been a result of the scientific investigation done by psychoanalysts. The concept that a person responds in accordance with certain repetitive patterns that push him into characteristic difficulties has been developed only in the past thirty years. Also relatively new is the idea that these patterned responses have a marked bearing on an individual's choice of career, choice of mate, marital unhappiness, and antisocial conduct. Because these conceptualizations are new, our knowledge is still scattered and our classifications unsatisfactory.

Before discussing the difficulties of identifying and understanding character disorders, I should like first to define *character* and then to make some observations about character traits. One dictionary definition of character is as follows: "those peculiar qualities impressed by nature or habit on a person which distinguish him from others." This is a broad, descriptive definition that I think is useful. Perhaps it could be made more explicit as follows: Character consists of those characteristics or qualities impressed by nature or habit on a person which individually or in their relationship to each other both distinguish him from others and make him resemble others.

Most analysts define character on the basis of ego functioning. Fenichel says: "Thus the ego's habitual modes of adjustment to the external world, the id, and the superego, and the characteristic types of combining these modes with one another, constitute character."[1] Nunberg defines character

[1] Otto Fenichel, *The Psychoanalytic Theory of Neurosis*, W. W. Norton & Co., New York, 1945, p. 467.

Reprinted from *Social Casework*, Vol. 44 (June, 1963), pp. 315–322, by permission of the author and the Family Services Association of America.

as "a synthesis of many traits, habits and attitudes of the ego."[2] For myself, I am inclined to agree with those who question the soundness of defining character solely in terms of ego functioning. English and Finch use a broader definition, including under character "the sum total of an individual's behavior which is peculiar to him."[3]

I consider character to be a composite of many traits, which are usually established in childhood and which remain more or less unmodified throughout life. These character traits are highly heterogeneous, and a delineation of them will vary in accordance with the frame of reference in which they are viewed.

Factors Influencing Character Formation

Although it is impossible, in a brief presentation, to list all the many factors that influence the formation of character, I shall enumerate a few of them to show that character cannot be regarded merely as a collection of defense mechanisms.

Heredity

Certainly heredity is an important determinant of character formation. First, it is an important determinant of the individual's intelligence and physical characteristics. How important this is to character formation can be seen in the effect on a person of being unusually tall or short, unusually good-looking or ugly, unusually intelligent or dull. Probably, also, heredity plays a role in the potentiality for ego development, the strength of instinctual drives, and the strength and choice of ego defenses.

Constitution

Mothers report, and scientific observation has confirmed, that siblings often reveal marked differences even immediately after birth. For instance, infants may differ in their response to loud noises as early as the second day of life. Some children are more irritable, others more passive. There are undoubtedly constitutional variations that help or hinder the individual in dealing with all the problems in the development of the id, the ego, and the superego. Such variations may determine the extent to which a particular child is traumatized by the demands of his mother or of his environment.

Rate of Physical and Physiological Maturation

Children develop physically and neurologically at different rates. As a result, a certain demand may be readily accepted by one two-year-old, for example, and be obviously traumatic for another. Again, the child who is

---

[2] Herman Nunberg, *Principles of Psychoanalysis: Their Application to the Neuroses,* Madlyn Kahr and Sidney Kahr (trans.), International Universities Press, New York, 1955, p. 303.

[3] O. Spurgeon English and Stuart M. Finch, *Introduction to Psychiatry,* W. W. Norton & Co., New York, 1954, p. 232.

able to talk at an early age does not require as much action as a child who is late in talking. The former child may attempt to deal with frustration by thinking and talking; the latter is forced to act in order to get what he wants, and acting rather than using words may become an entrenched pattern. Similar examples can be cited in relation to early or late muscular coordination, bowel control, and so on.

Congenital Defect or Early Illness

The effect of congenital deafness or blindness on character formation need not be emphasized. Congenital deformity, even if corrected, can be traumatic. For instance, an infant's being in a cast throughout the first year of his life or an eighteen-month-old child's experience of prolonged physical pain may produce a profound effect.

Identification

Identification plays an important role in the formation of character structure. The ability to imitate and identify develops early in a child's life. In the course of maturation a series of identifications takes place, most significantly with one or the other of his parents. These identifications are largely unconscious and are somewhat indiscriminate. They are modeled on the child's own understanding of the person with whom he is identifying and not necessarily on what the person is really like. His identifications determine much of what becomes his conscience and his ideals in life. When he is older, his conscious ego may reject or struggle against identification. For instance, a boy may struggle against his identification with his mother. Similarly, my adult woman patients often express the following idea: "The one thing I don't want is to be like my mother, but every day I find I am becoming more and more so." Sometimes the struggle goes on unconsciously and the person behaves compulsively in a way opposite to that of the person with whom he has an unconscious identification.

Psychosexual Development

One of the basic contributions of psychoanalysis is the concept of the influence of psychosexual development on the formation of character. Many factors affect psychosexual maturation, and hence character formation, but I should like to stress particularly the fact that it culminates when the oedipal conflict is resolved (or when the person fails to resolve it). It is at this time that significant regressions occur, identifications are established, and modes of defense become crystallized.

Defense Mechanisms

The term *defense mechanisms* is at present not clearly defined. Anna Freud, who introduced the term, limited its scope to defenses developed by the ego to protect itself from dangers arising out of the instinctual drives. Since the ego is capable of using concurrently a wide variety of mechanisms to defend itself, agreement on which are defense mechanisms and which are not is difficult to obtain. It is probably simplest to include only the ten that Anna Freud specifically mentioned.

In the process of erecting defenses—an entirely unconscious process—the ego always undergoes changes that are either modifying or inhibiting in nature. It should be emphasized that defense mechanisms are not pathological per se; on the contrary, they are important determinants of normal character formation and serve the purposes of adaptation and maturation.

Character Traits

Character traits, in general, are habitual modes of reaction. They differ widely, however, in accordance with the clinical diagnosis of the individual. Thus the character traits in character disorders have certain qualities that distinguish them both from psychoneurotic symptoms and from "normal" character traits.

Normal Character Traits vs. Psychoneurotic Symptoms

Normal character traits can be said to have existed all of the person's adult life, and their dynamics can be traced back to childhood. By contrast, psychoneurotic symptoms usually have a more limited history, and a patient can often state more or less accurately when they began.

Character traits involve broader, more complex reactions than psychoneurotic symptoms do. Compare, for instance, the compulsive neatness, orderliness, and cleanliness of the housewife with a limited symptom such as a hand-washing compulsion. Character traits also have the quality of predictability. It is this quality to which we are referring when we say that a person is or is not acting "in character." It may also be present in pathological character formation—for example, in the girl who repeatedly falls in love with the wrong man or in the man who marries three or four times, each time a woman who turns out to be frigid.

Finally, *character traits are ego-syntonic whereas neurotic symptoms are ego-alien.* This differentiation is of special importance in making a diagnosis.

Normal Character Traits vs. Character Traits in Character Disorders

There is a rigidity in the reactions or behavior of a person suffering with a character disorder that is not present in the character traits of the normal person. For example, the normal person may respond with anger in a work situation where he feels he has been injured. At the same time, he can co-operate with authority figures without feeling he is being submissive. The person with a passive-aggressive character disorder cannot respond in this manner. He is rigid or "fixed" in two ways. In the first place he sees everyone around him as trying to dominate him; he is unable to discriminate between his boss, his wife, and a Hitler. This makes him angry, either consciously or unconsciously. Neither can he distinguish accurately between situations in which anger is justified and those in which it is not. Furthermore, his reaction to his own anger is also fixed; he may, for example, react passively to any situation that might elicit his anger. This rigidity or inflexibility, this inability to discriminate among various kinds of stimuli and react to them appropriately, distinguishes the pathological character traits from the normal.

Rigidity of response can take any of several forms. There may be a fixed emotional response to a variety of situations, to a specific emotion, to any situation that would precipitate a specific emotion, or to a specific situation. An example of the first kind of response is found in the person who reacts in all situations as if he were being humiliated. I recall a woman of this type. If she was accosted by a man, she felt humiliated. If she was not, she felt humiliated. If she was told what to do, it was humiliating. If she was not told what to do, she was being ignored, and this too was humiliating. If she was not able to do something, it was humiliating; if she was, it was humiliating that she had to perform such undemanding tasks. Regardless of the situation there was only one emotional response available to her.

A fixed reaction to a specific emotion is exemplified by a woman I knew who never recognized or exhibited feelings of jealousy. In situations that might stimulate such feelings, she would react with feelings of pity. She was never jealous of other women but pitied many of them.

My last example is of a fixed response to a specific situation. The patient, a twenty-six-year-old single woman, described going to a moderate-sized business firm to apply for a job. In the office she saw a young man to whom she felt attracted. As soon as she was told he was the boss, her feelings changed to anger, and in her mind she became critical of him—her "characteristic" attitude toward bosses.

Problems of Definition and Classification

I should like now to suggest a definition of character disorders and to discuss some of the reasons for the widespread confusion that clouds our understanding of this category of emotional or behavioral dysfunctioning. *Character disorders form a large and heterogeneous group of emotional or developmental disturbances that are usually ego-syntonic and that evidence themselves primarily by abnormalities in the person's habitual pattern of behavior.*

One of the reasons why the term *character disorders* is often confusing is that, as has been suggested, it is used to cover such a very wide range of emotional and behavioral difficulties. In discussing one particular type of character disorder, a speaker or writer sometimes gives the impression that his remarks apply to all character disorders. Obviously, if he has in mind the "actor-outer," his remarks will not make sense to a person who has in mind a compulsive personality. It is important to be as specific as possible about the kind of character disorder one is discussing. Any attempt to deal with character disorders as if they were a homogeneous group of disabilities leads to insurmountable difficulties.

Another source of confusion is that a variety of terms—*personality disorder, neurotic character, character neurosis, behavior disorder, actor-outer*—are used synonymously with *character disorder*. It should be noted, too, that the American Psychiatric Association, in its official classification of mental and emotional diseases aimed at promoting the use of common terminology among psychiatrists, uses the term *personality disorder;* it does not recognize the term *character disorder*. None of the terms used is completely satisfactory, but a social worker should be familiar with all of them. It is particularly important that he know the exact kind of character disorder an author of a professional article is discussing.

One further source of confusion in attempting to classify the character disorders should be mentioned—the fact that several different frames of reference can be used. One, for example, is the level at which libidinal fixation has occurred. The classic example of this is, of course, Freud's description of the anal character: the character traits of orderliness, obstinacy, and parsimony were found to be preponderant in persons whose instinctual life is fixated at the anal level. Similarly, one can speak of oral and phallic characters. But there are other frames of reference—defense mechanisms, social standards, or descriptive similarities.

It is of great importance in understanding nomenclature to appreciate the difference between a primarily descriptive approach and a dynamic approach. A *descriptive* approach has to do with a mode of behavior or the characteristics of a symptom or group of symptoms as they are seen clinically by an observer. A *dynamic* approach has to do with the motivation of these symptoms or of a particular piece of behavior, conscious or unconscious. The same behavior may have several different kinds of motivation, just as a particular motivation may be manifested by various types of behavior. In the official nomenclature of the American Psychiatric Association a third frame of reference is used—one based on society's reaction to the behavior of the person. This classification, the "sociopathic personality disturbances," includes such entities as antisocial reaction, dyssocial reaction, the sexual deviations, and the addictions. Thus, variations in the frame of reference lead to a lack of homogeneity in diagnostic classifications.

Fenichel attempts to classify character disorders according to the reaction of the individual (ego) to internal needs.[4] One group is classified on the basis of how the individual reacts to his conscience (or superego); others are defined by how the individual reacts to his sexual and aggressive drives. These groups are then subdivided. Such an approach makes for a cumbersome number of individual character disorders and at the same time fails to cover the field.

Such confusion emphasizes the fact that psychoanalysis is still a developing scientific endeavor and that analysts are not as yet clear enough about character disorders to be able to establish a satisfactory classification. We might settle for the idea that we are studying various aspects of human personality and that in different character disorders certain factors are more significant than others. It follows that in studying a particular aspect one

[4] Fenichel, *op. cit.*, pp. 463–540.

frame of reference may be more rewarding than others. It seems to me, too, that the frame of reference should also be determined by the purpose for which the classification is being used. For some purposes a purely descriptive approach will be satisfactory, whereas others will require a dynamic approach.

Acting Out

One of the terms frequently associated with character disorders, *acting out*, originated in psychoanalysis. Analysts noted that some patients, instead of remembering and verbalizing the traumatic situations of their childhood, would unconsciously "act out" these early situations outside the analytic hour. As might be expected, many of these patients were people who in their daily lives tended to use action as a means of dealing with tension. As a result, common usage soon broadened the term to include all such people. The major characteristics of the person who acts out are one or more of the following:

1.   An inability to tolerate tension is general, accompanied by a need to discharge tension by action. Frustration tolerance is minimal, and postponement of gratification is impossible.

2.   An intolerance for *any* unpleasant affect. When threatened by such a feeling, he must immediately do something to get rid of it.

3.   A pervasive misunderstanding of the present in terms of the past. People in present life are not perceived or responded to as they actually are but are used as stand-ins for the re-enactment of childhood conflicts and defenses.

4.   A tendency to repeat again and again the same experiences or behavior patterns.

The third of these characteristics is apt to lead the caseworker to misinterpret the client's reaction as either a transference reaction in the analytic sense or an attempt at manipulation. Superficially, the reaction of the person who acts out may resemble the typical transference reaction of the neurotic. On closer examination, however, it is found to be much more indiscriminate. Often it takes place with people the client scarcely knows. The relationship lacks depth, is based on the role or function of the other person rather than on the person per se, and is readily exchanged for other relationships. This distinguishes it from typical transference. In a sense, the client does try to manipulate the worker, but the manipulation is not usually conscious and is not simply a struggle for power. Rather, it results from his misunderstanding of the present in terms of the past. Unconscious dynamics always underlie the client's manipulative attempts.

The fourth characteristic—repetition—represents the person's attempts to somehow master traumatic events that he failed to master in childhood. An excellent example of how complicated the process may become and how the original drives and defenses may be transformed is a case reported by Alexander in 1930.[5] I should like to cite it to illustrate the four broad types of pathological reaction that are possible for an individual confronted by a traumatic situation.

As a boy, the patient had persisted in taking his milk from a nursing bottle up to the age of at least five. His siblings teased him for it. As a compensation for this teasing he developed the ability to ride his bicycle in the street alone—a feat somewhat beyond his age. He still took his milk from the bottle. In the patient's adult life, these traits persisted as follows: He expected his wife to guess his every need and satisfy his desires without being asked (the bottle); in business, however, he was capable, daring, and successful (the bicycle). This equilibrium was satisfactorily maintained until a new boss was appointed, who dominated and used the patient. In essence, this removed the patient's defense (bicycle). He then "seduced and had as his mistress" the wife of a superior. This, then, was the new defense, the re-establishment of masculinity (the bicycle). At home, he continued the usual demands on his wife (the bottle).

At the point where the new boss was introduced, this patient could have reacted in one of four ways:

1. Developed a *psychoneurosis*. For example, he could have developed a street phobia that kept him at home and thus have avoided being exposed to the new boss.

2. Become *psychotic*. For example, he might have become paranoid about his boss.

3. Developed a *psychosomatic* symptom. For example, he could have developed colitis or a stomach ulcer, which would have allowed him to avoid his boss on days of particular distress.

4. Solved his conflict by a complicated piece of behavior, in which he used people to re-establish a defense. By reacting in this way, the patient revealed that he had a *character disorder*.

Borderline State

I think it important to make a few comments about the "borderline state." This term, which is essentially descriptive rather than dynamic, has come into common use as psychiatrists and caseworkers have been seeing

[5] Franz Alexander, "The Neurotic Character," *International Journal of Psycho-Analysis*, Vol. XI, 1930, pp. 300–302.

more and more people who are seriously ill but not clearly psychotic. Three points of view on the borderline state should be noted:

1.   Some psychiatrists maintain that the term *borderline state* expresses the therapist's ignorance of the correct diagnosis when he has not made an adequate examination of the patient. They assert that, at best, it is only a temporary diagnosis—one that can serve until a definitive diagnosis can be made. Knight, who has written extensively on the subject, points out that difficulty in making a diagnosis is based in part on the fallacious assumption that a patient must be either psychotic or neurotic.[6] Actually, schizophrenic patients frequently complain about symptoms that are clearly psycho-neurotic—for example, compulsive rituals or extensive phobias. If the psychiatrist looks beyond the patient's presenting symptom, the schizophrenic process becomes obvious. I have always maintained that a full psychiatric diagnosis includes the patient's character structure—for example, a phobic reaction in a passive-aggressive personality, or schizophrenia with phobic symptomatology.

Knight further points out that it is entirely possible for some ego functions to be severely damaged while others remain relatively intact. In most borderline patients the ego functions that are impaired are integration, concept formation, judgment, and realistic planning. Their defenses against the eruption of id impulses into consciousness are also weak. On the other hand, their more general intellectual functions, their conventional adaptation to the environment, and their ability to sustain superficial object relationships may be well maintained. These people can be highly successful in their vocations, but usually their accomplishments are not in line with their abilities.

2.   The second point of view is that certain persons are overtly psychotic at certain times and latently psychotic at others. In other words, such a person has sufficient ego to be in contact with reality, adjust to it, and use good judgment at certain times. However, the ego adjustment is so tenuous that a seemingly minor upset can result in a psychotic break. At a time when such a person's condition is severe, he may be diagnosed as having ambulatory schizophrenia or latent schizophrenia; when it is not as severe, the pre-psychotic state may be regarded as either a character disorder (less disturbed) or a borderline state (more disturbed).

3.   The third point of view is that mental health and psychosis represent the two extremes on a continuum; there is an area in between, in which a person is not psychotic, not neurotic, and not healthy—he is "borderline." The differentiation is based on the extent to which psychotic thinking has invaded the ego. Hence, the difference between character disorder and borderline state is one of degree.

[6] Robert P. Knight, "Borderline States," in *Psychoanalytic Psychiatry and Psychology: Clinical and Theoretical Papers*, Robert P. Knight and Cyrus R. Friedman (eds.), International Universities Press, New York, 1954.

Treatment Considerations

Treating the client with a character disorder is a difficult task. One of the primary reasons is that a character trait is acceptable to the ego; in other words, it is ego-syntonic. Usually the client has no urge to do anything about his pathological character traits because he is not conscious of their making him suffer. A client may, for example, ask for help with a marital problem, feeling that he has chosen the wrong mate and that if he had a different mate he would have no problem. He has no idea that he himself is emotionally disturbed. Another client, like a person I knew who wanted the therapist to help him get rid of feelings of guilt when he cheated or stole, may want to rid himself of a normal reaction and retain a pathological character trait. In brief, one can say that treatment of the client with a character disorder should have as an initial aim making the ego-syntonic trait ego-alien or ego-dystonic.

It is sometimes said that clients with character disorders lack motivation. This is certainly not true. Clients are *always* motivated, but the caseworker may not assess the motivation correctly. For example, a client may come for casework treatment with the conscious goal of working out a marital problem but with the unexpressed need to prove that she was in the right in her conflict with her husband—in order to counteract unconscious feelings of guilt. She may then interpret the worker's efforts to improve the marital relationship as efforts to show that she was in the wrong. Thus, she may react in the treatment situation with indifference or resentment. If the caseworker fails to recognize the basic motivation, which has been frustrated, he is likely to interpret the client's reaction as a lack of motivation.

One of the caseworker's first tasks in treatment is to establish a relationship with the client. To do so, he must have an understanding of the client's conscious and unconscious motivations for coming to the agency. Having established a relationship and accurately appraised the client and his situation, the worker can then use the relationship and his understanding to convert ego-syntonic behavior gradually into an ego-dystonic symptom. If before this happens the client succeeds in changing his environment or by other means getting rid of his presenting discomfort, he is apt to lose interest in treatment. Until the client is helped, through treatment, to become aware of having a problem that requires him to make a change in himself, little can be accomplished.

Occasionally it is important for the caseworker to determine early in contact with the client whether a particular piece of behavior is a psychoneurotic symptom or a character trait. One example is the client who is late for his first few appointments. Is his arriving late a character trait, or is it a transitory symptom related to his anxiety about coming to see the worker? If lateness has been a problem all his life or if he is late for any appointment even when he is looking forward to it, the worker can assume that his behavior in this respect is a character trait. As such, it has a complicated set of dynamics, is apt to be overdetermined, and serves an important function in his psyche. Interpreting to him that he comes late because he is angry at the worker or because he fears what will emerge in the interview can have no meaning to him, even though the interpretation may have elements of truth in it. Interpretations of this kind often lead to fruitless arguments that use up all the interview time, and the client leaves the session frustrated and resentful. He is likely to miss his next appointment or to discontinue treatment entirely.

This kind of client is extremely difficult to work with. The worker must, however, accept the client's lateness as a part of his character; any attempt to "attack" it or modify it by direct interpretation is doomed to fail. There is no one solution to the problem of dealing with it, but the worker must be flexible in his approach. Sometimes the interview hour may be prolonged so that the client can feel he has got something out of it. Or the worker may explore how the client has dealt with the problem in the past and reinforce the solution the client has worked out. Knowing what techniques to use and choosing the most appropriate depend on the worker's psychodynamic understanding of the client.

Another problem for the caseworker is to avoid being misled by what the client presents as reality. Since his character traits serve many different functions in preserving him from anxiety, the client tries desperately to arrange his outer life so as not to disturb them and his inner life so as to justify them. For example, a man may report that his marriage to a frigid woman is creating a sexual problem for him. It may be true that his wife is frigid; but it may not be true, as he is implying, that he would have no sexual problem if he were married to a more responsive woman. Because a client with a character disorder is inclined to use rationalizations, the worker must be careful not to assume that the reason he gives for doing something is his real reason.

I should like to add one final caution in relation to treatment. Once the client progresses to the point that his behavior is no longer ego-syntonic, he is likely to become depressed or anxious and may develop neurotic or psychosomatic symptoms. If the worker fails to recognize that the appearance of these symptoms does represent *progress*, he may become frustrated and angry at the client at the very time when the client is beginning to improve. After evaluating the ego-dystonic symptoms and the client's reactions to them, the worker can help him by letting him know that his new discomfort represents progress. As appropriate, the caseworker can then help the client use the discomfort to become motivated to improve his social functioning or to reach a decision to get psychiatric treatment.

Conclusion

One of the complications in understanding character disorders is that often the therapist sees only the end product of a series of vicissitudes in the development of a character trait. For instance, a character trait may start as a source of gratification; but as the child develops, it takes on several additional values, a series of defenses, and perhaps secondary gains, which make an understanding of the total personality an impossibility without a thorough analysis. By way of reassurance, I should like to stress that a caseworker is not an analyst; he cannot know all the analyst knows about dynamics and, at the same time, know something about social work. Part of the caseworker's confusion about character disorders is due to five important facts: (1) the study of character disorders is a developing scientific endeavor; (2) such knowledge as has been formulated is scattered, lacks integration, and is not clear even to those who specialize in the field; (3) the classifications that have been developed are designed for more or less severe character disorders and not for the more normal character development to which they are sometimes inaccurately applied; (4) caseworkers are apt to develop anxiety about not knowing, even in cases where it is not possible to know; (5) caseworkers often set their treatment goals too high. Recognition of these facts may help the worker avoid unwarranted frustration.

There is just so much a caseworker can know about the dynamics of character disorders, since even the specialists have not yet been able to organize their formulations into a sound theory. However, the caseworker should recognize that no one can attempt to formulate dynamics until he has an accurate and detailed description of the person's behavior in a variety of situations. He can get this most satisfactorily by studying the client's *present* rather than his past. Too often workers are inclined to substitute extensive dynamic formulations of childhood, which must be largely speculative, for a clear description of the client as he *is*, of how he came, and of why he wants treatment.

Treatment of Character Disorders: A Dilemma in Casework Culture

Otto Pollak

In the treatment of character disorders, social caseworkers deal with three groups of difficulties. The first concerns the nature of the condition itself. The main difficulty in work with persons with character disorders is that, because of the primitive ego structure of the persons afflicted, the therapist and the client must engage not only in a process of unlearning faulty reaction patterns but also in a process of diversification and creation in social development. Clients require a type of therapy which emphasizes

Reprinted from *Social Service Review,* Vol. 35 (June, 1961), pp. 127–134, by permission of the author and The University of Chicago Press. Copyright, 1961 by the University of Chicago.

psychological nurture more than gains in understanding, identification with the ego of the therapist, and therefore acceptance of limitations rather than liberation from maladaptive restrictions. Sometimes the course of therapy shows movement even through the development of a neurosis as a step toward health.[1]

Second, the nature of our civilization not only seems to elicit the development of character disorders in an increasing number of people but it also lends support to the persistence of such disorders. From individualism to egotism there is only one step. From romantic love to unrealistic expectations regarding gratifications that can be demanded from the marriage partner there is equally only one. And from such unrealistic expectations to the limitation of one's own giving and the resultant violation of reciprocity in marital interaction the distance is not long either. In a materialistic society id gratifications are prominently offered in overt and hidden form, while the waning power of a generally accepted morality leaves superego forces unsupported. That under such conditions all compromise between id and superego should be weighted on the id side need not be surprising. Most of all, however, a society that mistrusts authority and extols rebellion is likely to furnish many rationalizations to a person whose psychic structures leads to acting out rather than to internalization of conflict.[2] In this cultural framework, psychoanalysis, with its liberating impact upon conventional restrictions in the expressions of sexuality and hostility, has become overextended in the popular mind. Our current civilization, therefore, continually feeds new strength into the resistiveness to treatment of clients who are afflicted with character disorders.

The third complex of difficulties which caseworkers encounter in their therapeutic efforts with this group of clients stems from their own professional culture. These difficulties will be presented here in hypothetical form as a basis for scrutiny and discussion by practitioners. The central thesis presented is that caseworkers have made their greatest professional advances in an orientation of theory and practice concerned with the treatment of the classic symptom neuroses and with character disturbances accompanied by guilt, while they are now faced with clients who exhibit character disturbances which are relatively guilt-free and which lead to conflict in interaction with other people rather than to intrapersonal conflict in the client. Caseworkers find themselves, therefore, sometimes entrapped by the principles of a method of casework which does not appear appropriate for the new group of clients who seem to dominate the case loads of family welfare

---

[1] Rosemary Reynolds and Else Siegle, "A Study of Casework with Sado-masochistic Marriage Partners," *Social Casework*, XL (December, 1959), 545–51; Effie Warren, "Treatment of Marriage Partners with Character Disorders," *Social Casework*, XXXVIII (March, 1957), 118–26; and Otto Pollak, Hazel M. Young, and Helen Leach, "Differential Diagnosis and Treatment of Character Disturbances," *Social Casework*, XLI (December, 1960), 512–17.

[2] Otto Pollak, "Social Factors Contributing to Character Disorders," *Child Welfare*, XXXVII (April, 1958), 8–12.

agencies today. Apparently every success in fighting discomforts in the social sphere is followed by new discomforts which could not have been foreseen. Success in the fight against infant mortality necessitated increased concern with the management of sensory disorders which survived perinatal injuries. The gain in survival of the middle-aged has brought into focus the problems of degenerative diseases. And apparently our successful fight against the symptom neuroses has increased our difficulties in finding means of effective treatment of character disorders.

In order to clarify the nature of these difficulties, it may be helpful to describe the syndrome from which clients with character disorders seem to suffer. The constellation commonly described as a character disorder, as distinguished from a character neurosis, seems to present a constellation of massive projection, ego-syntonic behavior, insistence on self-justification and the need for change in others, insensitivity to the needs of others, hopelessness, and inefficient exploitation of others.[3] Mere inspection of this constellation of characteristics will suggest that casework help oriented to guilt and discomfort in self-perception will find itself without points of easy contact with clients so afflicted. It may serve, however, the task of reorientation which diagnostically oriented casework requires if the difficulties in this respect are elaborated and analyzed. That "therapeutic techniques that are effective with neurotic clients are not appropriate with character disorders"[4] has been clearly recognized and frequently stated in the literature. What has to be elaborated and presented to the profession is the fact that the principles of casework appropriate for the treatment of neurotic clients have by and large been generalized in the subculture of the profession so that principles appropriate for the treatment of character disorders present problems in the professional culture as it has developed. These difficulties will be presented under the headings of relationship difficulties, difficulties in setting goals, and difficulties in treatment methods.

Relationship Difficulties

The outstanding difficulty in establishing a positive relationship with clients afflicted with character disorders stems from the fact that professional training and experience of social caseworkers produce a personality which is the opposite of the personality encountered in such clients. A high degree of self-awareness, sensitivity to the nature of his interactions with others, and ability to give of himself for the benefit of others are the attributes which we find and welcome in successful caseworkers. The client suffering from the impact of a character disorder upon his relationships with others is a person who uses projection, is insensitive to the need of others, and is unable to give

[3] Pollak, Young, and Leach, *op. cit.*, p. 513.
[4] Beatrice R. Simcox and Irving Kaufman, M.D., "Treatment of Character Disorders in Parents of Delinquents," *Social Casework*, XXXVII (October, 1956), 388.

in interaction with others. Since the essential quality of a positive relationship is a feeling of "at-oneness"[5] with somebody else, it can easily be recognized that there will be difficulties in the initial interaction between the caseworker and such clients. Opposites have little chance to establish rapport from the start. It is therefore understandable that Effie Warren has found it necessary to publish a warning to caseworkers against the temptation to expect such clients to volunteer facts about their own part in the marital relationships and to cut short such persons in the first interview by bringing them back to a consideration of their own behavior.[6] This, however, is only a consideration of the problem as far as the caseworker is concerned.

It is probable that the client also becomes consciously or unconsciously aware of the contradiction between his own personality and that of the caseworker. On the conscious level, at least, the very personality of the caseworker may present a reproach to the client with a character disorder. Very few of us are able to perceive a person as being helpful if he is very different or if he is actually the opposite of what we are. The client would much rather sense in a therapist a fellow sufferer than a person who is a stranger to his condition. On the other hand, the therapist probably finds it easier to treat a person whose condition he has experienced than one whose experience he has never known. Since self-selection, screening in admission interviews, and professional success in social casework probably have resulted in selection of personnel more inclined to neurosis than to character disorder, the sympathy created by similarity between therapist and client is unlikely to exist between the caseworker and the client with character disorder. The only at-oneness which may come quickly is the id stimulation which the caseworker receives from the client, i.e., the acting out stimulation, the vicarious gratification of receiving without giving, of expressing hostility and hoping to get away with it. Against this type of at-oneness the professional caseworker will be on guard, of course, but even being on guard presents a special strain and for that reason may be the cause of still another difficulty in establishing a positive relationship with this type of client.

Always exploiters of human relationships, clients with character disorders will be tempted to exploit the caseworker by using his skills for their own pathological needs. Such clients have probably come to the agency because they have found their exploitative efforts in human relations ineffective. What they want is first of all an increase in the accessibility to exploitation in their marriage partners or children. Unconsciously, at least, they want to become better exploiters rather than more giving persons. Even though they accept the need for self-change, they want most of all to free themselves only of those aspects of their behavior which interfere with their raid on the personal resources of others. The caseworker will not be able to accept either of these goals and thus by professional conviction about health in human relationships will become in fact an opponent of the client.

[5] Helen Harris Perlman, *Social Casework: A Problem-solving Process* (Chicago: University of Chicago Press, 1957), p. 66.

[6] Warren, *op. cit.*, p. 120.

Casework culture extols reciprocity in human relationships; character disorder defies it.

This basic difference expresses itself also in an incongruity between the perceptions of the client and the perceptions of the caseworker. As a result of the fruitful contact which social casework has had with dynamically oriented psychiatry, the professional perception of caseworkers is geared to individual diagnosis. The caseworker wants to understand the client who presents himself to him as a person in a situation; the client with a character disorder perceives only his situation as unsatisfactory and is entirely concerned with the part that others play in his interpersonal relationships. The client sees what he does not get; the caseworker sees—largely—what the client does not give.

Within recent years the perception of caseworkers has shown signs of reorientation toward the diagnosis of interpersonal relationships and family groups. Yet all these understandings and diagnostic formulations are based on individual diagnoses of the persons involved. In consequence, it is extremely difficult for a caseworker to establish a common frame of reference with such clients from the start. Even, for instance, if the caseworker manages to keep in diagnostic focus two marriage partners with character disorders, the two will be concerned only with what they do not get while the caseworker will be concerned with what both of them do not give. This contest makes it difficult for the caseworker to establish a common goal with the client early in the contact, even though establishing such a common goal is elementary.[7]

The caseworker must learn to be patient with this client group and to be satisfied with agreement with the client on the desirability of certain subgoals which from the point of view of casework cannot be accepted as the sum total of desirability. In the last analysis, of course, the caseworker must see the goal in such cases in the capacity of the client to meet the needs of others. The suggestion made by Rosemary Reynolds and Else Siegle[8]—to connect with the client's narcissism in a logical discussion of behavior changes which will make things easier for him—presents for the caseworker the difficulty of trying to use a condition in the client which represents immaturity and pathology. In this respect some reorientation will probably be necessary to make the suggestion by Reynolds and Siegle an easily workable procedure. The solution may lie in the proposition that maturity and immaturity are designations of conditions which in their purity are unlikely to be found in clients. People are more or less geared to reciprocity, more or less self-concerned, and the caseworker must learn to use the client's potential in these respects without the mental reservation that he is actually fostering the undesirable or is arresting the client's development.

Perhaps most significant, however, is the fact that clients with character disorders are prone to attacks of depression and hopelessness which make

[7] Lenore Rivesman, "Casework Treatment of Severely Disturbed Marriage Partners," *Social Casework*, XXXVIII (May, 1957), 244.

[8] Reynolds and Siegle, *op. cit.*, p. 549.

them need persistent encouragement and support from the caseworker. In this respect the culture of casework makes the helping task difficult. Caseworkers notoriously underestimate their effectiveness and are therefore cautious in predicting or promising significant improvement to the clients. It might be worth investigating how many cases are lost after one or two contacts simply because caseworkers hesitate to hold out definite hope to depressive clients. While it may be impossible, due to the nature of the condition, to establish with the client a framework of common understanding and common goals, it may be possible to establish with him a framework of common expectations regarding his improvement and to renew such a framework when the client has a relapse into depressive moods.

Goals

There is no aspect of the helping process in which the culture conflict between a caseworker and the client with character disorder expresses itself more clearly than in treatment goals. If it is correct, as is often assumed, that most therapists have a neurotic personality basis, then it is within their own professional and, perhaps, therapeutic experience that the treatment process is liberating rather than binding. Guilt and anxiety are decreased, spontaneity is increased, self-blame and self-restriction are eased. The client with a character disorder, however, brings to the casework process a personality structure which requires binding instead of liberation, the creation of a measure of guilt and anxiety rather than emotional release from such conditions, restriction of behavior in place of maladaptive spontaneity. To the caseworker who considers these treatment goals it must look therefore as if he were about to take from the client something which he, the worker, has achieved at the price of great effort and emotional investment. People who have become liberated find themselves in a position in which they are to set up limitations for the client and in which they have to help the client toward an internalization of limitations.

In the treatment of character disorders, there is a surface implication of taking away rather than of giving which is in direct contradiction not only with the culture of casework but with our culture in general. Having grown out of material giving, casework still wants to "give" to the client in emotional and psychological respects. Actually, treatment methods appropriate in character disorders demand more such giving than any other type of diagnostically oriented casework, but this giving is method, not goal. The goal is one of taking away from the client his spontaneity in acting out his needs for gratification and expression, his freedom from guilt, his unconcern with others. What the worker does take away from the client in goal-setting is something which we all somewhat regret that we have lost in our upbringing and development—freedom for the id.

Furthermore, social caseworkers sometimes are still under the impact of the goal definition in the *Report on Scope and Methods* of the Family Service Association of America which was formulated with an orientation to people suffering from an excess of guilt and the resulting disabling conditions. It will be remembered that the report identified two treatment aims of social casework: (1) to support and maintain the client's current strengths by helping him mobilize capacity and resources to meet his current life-situation, and (2) to modify the client's attitudes and patterns of behavior by increasing his understanding of himself, of his problems, and of his part in creating them.[9] Neither of these two aims seems to meet the needs of the client with a character disorder. Support and maintenance of his strength are not appropriate because the client does not have enough strength. In modifying attitudes through increased understanding, the emphasis is on cognition; the client is to be helped to become the scholar of his misery. In the character disorder, on the other hand, treatment aims at more than either of these goals suggests. It aims at growth of motivation. To achieve this requires a much greater investment by the caseworker than helping the client to maintain strength or to increase understanding. The report is an invitation to do either too much too soon or not enough. What the client with a character disorder needs is, to borrow a term from computer language, "input" which will enable him in the long run to produce emotional and interpersonal "output." He must be invested in to become able to pay interpersonal dividends. Before such an investment is fully made, understanding will not be accessible to him, and what glimpses of understanding he may gain will probably be abused as the rationalization of further acting-out. In terms of goals, then, understanding will never be enough to help these clients; before they can become able to gain understanding they must be motivated to interact with others in a giving rather than in an exploiting way.

Treatment Methods

As far as treatment methods are concerned, the life-history approach, particularly the dwelling upon childhood experiences, is likely to prove of doubtful therapeutic value. Eliciting of childhood experiences and the feelings which accompanied them is necessary for liberation from morbid anxieties, but is not indicated for the creation of a readiness in the client to accept limitations and restrictions. In the person with a character disorder there is nothing to be gotten rid of because there is not enough there. Delving into the past can bring the client into stronger contact with his id impulses. What is appropriate in order to undo the impact of an overstrict superego is contraindicated in the absence of an adequately developed one. In a way both client and caseworker are deprived of the intellectual gratification resulting from a genetic diagnosis. Since this gratification, however, would furnish for the client only justification for his non-giving and exploitative behavior, the caseworker in turn must learn to get along without it.

[9] *The Scope and Methods of the Family Service Agency: Report of the Committee on Methods and Scope* (New York: Family Service Association of America, 1953), p. 7.

If caseworkers are concerned about a relatively low degree of success in work with character disorders, they must remind themselves that they start with many handicaps created by past learning. Perhaps one of the outstanding therapeutic reaction patterns which caseworkers have had to learn is permissiveness. In a world in which everybody has evaluated the client and has shown him various degrees of dissatisfaction with his performance, the at least overtly non-critical attitude of the caseworker has made it easy for the client to distinguish between therapist on the one hand and spouse, parent, employer, and members of the peer group on the other. In the treatment of character disorders this clear-cut differentiation is likely to be lost. Since a strong element of nurture and personality rearing has to be incorporated into the therapeutic effort, the setting of norms and limits, at least indirectly and later on directly, has to enter the complex of therapeutic interaction with the client.

"Rearing" demands more giving—and more denying—than conventional therapy, be it supportive therapy, clarification, or insight therapy. Along with permissiveness, the caseworker must abandon inactivity. Clients with character disorders require praise for even very minor achievement, for sporadic even if abortive effort. When they break appointments, they require more reaching-out from the caseworker than a simple letter or a telephone call. They require sensitivity and response to their hopelessness; they require advice and guidance.[10]

On the other hand, there are certain conventional patterns of casework influence which seem inappropriate. Feelings are not to be elicited because the client already suffers from too great a flow of feeling into action. He is "acting out" and suffers the consequences. To release his feelings further and thus to increase his acting out might bring him into conflict with the authorities, might lead to the breakup of his marriage, or might induce panic.

Setting limits, on the other hand, may furnish an easy cover for the countertransference of the caseworker. Since these are clients who are likely to tax the potential of the caseworker for empathy, countertransference is perhaps a greater danger here than in the treatment of other types of pathology. To be forced into a limit-setting relationship by the nature of the disorder is likely to make it more difficult for the caseworker to become aware of the emergence of non-therapeutic reactions on his part to the client.

There is also the trying demand for prolonged—and renewed—therapy which the elements of nurture and rearing in this type of treatment present. Our general culture has come to value speed as a sign of efficiency. Casework, as well as psychiatric treatment, has not remained unaffected by this tendency. Treatment of clients with character disorders, however, does last longer and moves less perceptibly than even long-term treatment which caseworkers, who do not yield easily to cultural pressure, have defined as standard.

[10] Warren, *op. cit.*, p. 123; Reynolds and Siegle, *op. cit.*, p. 549.

Professional Maturity and Social Change

The caseworker who has read this paper may well be left with the following impressions: (1) that he has heard all these treatment suggestions before, and (2) that there is no peace in the development of treatment techniques and of theoretical clarifications. Both impressions are correct, but the implications of fatigue and impatience which they carry may be based on an erroneous assumption. It has always been part of our culture to believe that one final effort might free us from burdensome aspects of human existence. We accept war only as a means to end all wars. We buy blue chips in order to be able to forget all about them. We court a person who might make a desirable mate and after marriage abandon efforts to further his affection and positive responses. In reality there is no peace and there are no final solutions. Every effort creates new problems, and every solution of these problems creates new ones in turn. Caseworkers appear frequently to be exhorted to return to methods of treatment and to approaches which one or two decades ago they were called upon to abandon. Such exhortations are not recantations, they are not the abandonment of fads, they are not the expressions of artificial obsolescence. The ability of the helping professions to remain aware of the swings of the social pendulum and to be able to respond to them seems to be the sign of a high degree of professional maturity.

A Study of Casework with Sado-masochistic Marriage Partners

Rosemary Reynolds and Else Siegle

Can a couple whose married life is a continuous physical or verbal battle, or at best an armed truce, be helped by casework treatment? If so, in what ways? Which casework methods and techniques seem to be most effective? In an effort to find the answers to these questions, a study of a group of cases in which a marked sado-masochistic pattern characterized the relationship between the marriage partners was undertaken in the Community Service Society of New York. The term sado-masochism is used here to describe the simultaneous existence of submissive and aggressive traits in each spouse which lead to a high degree of destructiveness in the marital

Reprinted from *Social Casework,* Vol. 40 (December, 1959), pp. 545–551, by permission of the authors and the Family Services Association of America.

relationship. In other words, the partners tend to suffer and to inflict suffering on each other.

After perusal of seventy-five cases in which certain sado-masochistic characteristics had been noted, the following criteria were used to select a group of comparable cases for more detailed study: (1) marked sado-masochistic aspects in the personality structure of each partner, which interact in the marriage relationship, had been confirmed by the same psychiatric consultant; (2) extreme verbal or physical hostility, or both, has been employed by the partners throughout the marriage; (3) at the time of application to the agency, the marriage had existed at least a year and there had been no prolonged separations; (4) both husband and wife had had casework treatment in the agency. Nine cases that met these criteria were used as the basis of this study. Extensive information was available in the case records. Selected study findings on the following topics will be presented: (1) significant social and psychological characteristics of the couples and their families; (2) the casework goals set and the degree to which these goals were achieved; (3) the treatment method and techniques used in these cases.

Social Characteristics

The social characteristics of these nine couples were markedly similar. All were attractive men and women in their late twenties or early thirties. The average length of marriage was five years, and eight of the nine couples had either one or two children, only one of whom was over ten years of age. These adults were intelligent and had had more than the usual amount of education, since seven of the eighteen clients were college graduates and only three had not completed high school. All nine couples were self-supporting, and two-thirds of the husbands earned more than one hundred dollars a week. Eight men were employed in professional, white-collar, or skilled artisan work and their steady employment records and regular raises indicated at least average job functioning. All but one family lived in a comfortable four- or five-room apartment. Two wives were working outside the home at the time of application to the agency.

What had led these intelligent young couples, with incomes adequate to provide security and comfort for themselves and their children, to apply to a social agency? Five of the nine couples came because of marital troubles, the other four because of difficulties with their older child. No couple applied immediately following a fight in which one or the other partner had suffered physical injury. Each applicant and referral source agreed that the situation had remained essentially the same over a period of time. The intake interviews with these clients were characterized by each person's concentrating on his or her own needs and voicing repeated complaints about the spouse's failure to understand or to be helpful. These complaints were the dominant theme even when the central presenting problem was a child's difficulties.

In fact, fighting and quarreling between husband and wife remained the central theme throughout the casework contact. The marital relationships in these nine families appeared never to be truly calm and relaxed although there were brief lulls between storms. Any subject—children, relatives, sex, money, food, or laundry—could precipitate an argument. The relationships between these husbands and wives seemed to be dominated by their continuing struggle to gain control over each other. The husbands complained bitterly that their wives belittled, nagged, bossed, and criticized them; and the wives objected strenuously to their husbands' leaving them alone, not helping them at home, and not telling them everything. Verbal and physical quarrels were the result. The caseworker observed that it was during the period of relative calm between "big fights" that one partner would choose to do something known to provoke the mate—the husband would stay out until midnight when his wife expected him to come home for dinner, or the wife would neglect to have a suit pressed for her husband when he had an important business engagement. However, although each spouse complained of the other's unreasonable behavior and temper, and frequently threatened to leave the partner, only four of the nine couples had ever separated, and the longest separation had lasted only two weeks.

The tenacity with which these men and women clung to each other appears even more noteworthy when one considers that, on the surface at least, all aspects of each marriage seemed rife with irritation. In no case was there joint planning and handling of the family income; consequently, arguments about money matters were frequent. Most of the wives actively disliked being homemakers and left the responsibility for doing the housework, in large measure, to the husbands. The couples had no mutual interests or close, comfortable relationships with relatives or friends. Their sexual interest and response were far below the average for couples in their twenties and thirties; the majority of the women were frigid and most of the men had potency difficulties. In each instance, contraception posed a problem because neither partner was willing to accept responsibility. The coming of children had been unplanned in most instances and their arrival had increased the tension between the partners. The children's development and adjustment were seriously hampered by the strife between the parents. Particularly the older child, when there were two in the family, showed marked disturbances such as learning problems, stammering, thumb-sucking, excessive masturbation, inability to make friends, and so forth. In addition, there was clear evidence that more than half of these older children had become enmeshed to some degree in the parents' sado-masochistic behavior. Provocative behavior between parent and child, similar to that which led to parental fights, occurred consistently and, in turn, ended with the child's being severely punished and scolded.

To these nine couples, strife within the home was not a new experience. Each of these clients had come from a home torn by dissension, quarreling, and bitterness between his parents during his childhood. Affection had rarely been shown and punishments had been frequent. Each had left home at an early age to become a wage-earner because either the parental home was broken up or space was needed for a younger family member. Nevertheless these men and women had not entered marriage after only a brief acquaintance; the shortest courtship period had been nine months. In fact, seventeen of the eighteen clients had had grave doubts about marrying the present spouse, because they had known during the courtship that they did not share the same expectations of married life. Each had gone ahead with the marriage because he had expected the partner to change. Instead the partner had not changed and, as could have been anticipated, the home life of these nine couples and their children had been fraught with dissatisfaction, irritation and quarreling.

Psychological Characteristics

The psychological characteristics of these eighteen men and women were as markedly similar as were their social characteristics. The clinical diagnoses all lie within the range of severe character disorder, borderline schizophrenia, or schizophrenia. Examination of the ego functioning of these clients revealed that, aside from having better than average intelligence, other important aspects of ego functioning were seriously impaired. All of them showed distorted judgment, unsound reality testing, and extremely low tolerance for frustration. Since they were highly narcissistic, they had only a limited capacity to form mature object relationships. Their over-use of the defense mechanisms of projection and rationalization tended to create situations in which each felt isolated and misunderstood; their superego functioning appeared to be childlike and sometimes defective. Since their behavior was often determined by the fear of being caught, they tended to engage in questionable behavior when external controls were lacking. The absence of a mature ego or superego in these parents adversely affected their children's character development.

As a group, these were extremely impulsive, dependent men and women who lacked the ability to perceive the effects of their behavior on others. Sixteen of the eighteen frequently experienced great anxiety, but the areas in which anxiety was manifest were quite diverse. Varying types and degrees of depression and many types of psychosomatic difficulty were the most common symptom formations.

Sado-masochism was present in a high degree in all these eighteen clients. Each of these individuals revealed both sadistic and masochistic aspects, but the balance of sadism and masochism varied with each couple. In fully half of the families the husband was the more masochistic, but his sadistic side was also in evidence. The extent to which each spouse openly provoked the other was striking. A wife who knew that her husband liked a well-run house would allow dirty dishes to accumulate for several days and would forget to do the marketing. A husband who knew that his wife was possessive, insecure, and jealous would leave poems written to another woman where his wife would find them, and would stay out late without explanation. Often these individuals could describe specifically what had aroused the angry and cruel behavior in the other partner, and yet repeatedly would do that very thing. It appeared that each person had a strong underlying need to maintain this sado-masochistic relationship.

Achievement of Treatment Goals

When faced with such self-centered, impulsive clients who act out their hostility in such an extreme fashion, caseworkers often despair of effecting any beneficial changes in the family situation. Yet the findings[1] of this study revealed that substantial improvement had taken place in seven of the nine families. It should be noted that no basic personality change was attempted or brought about through casework methods, but it was possible to modify the destructive pattern of functioning of these men and women. The length of the casework contact with these families averaged twenty-two months; the longest period was four years.

The following are the four treatment goals most frequently selected for casework activity with these couples. (1) *Improvement of the marital balance through modification of the sado-masochistic relationship.* This was a goal in seven cases in which the couples expressed concern about their marriage. In all seven families the provocative behavior between husband and wife lessened, and in six cases the degree of change was marked. Physical abuse stopped almost entirely in four of the five families where this had been a serious problem. (2) *Improvement in the children's situation, particularly that of the older child, by reducing the parents' sadistic attitudes and behavior toward the children.* This was a goal in eight of the families. In five of them better parental handling of the children resulted. The gains made by these older children were confirmed by reports from school teachers, doctors, and group leaders. (3) *Improvement in sexual adjustment, when the wife's limiting the amount of sexual activity had been extremely upsetting to the husband.* In two of the three cases in which this was a goal, both husband and wife confirmed that noticeable improvement in this area has taken place. (4) *Increase in the ability of these couples to manage their current reality situation.* This was a goal in all nine cases; in six, better care and management of the home, finances, and health were clearly evident.

Importance of a Positive Relationship

The fact that it was possible for casework treatment to influence favorably the functioning of most of these couples warrants closer examination of the factors operating and the methods employed to bring about these

---

[1] The evaluation of the results of casework treatment was based on the expressed statements of the clients, the opinions of the caseworker and supervisor, and the conclusions of the study team. As had been found in other studies of the effectiveness of casework service, clients gave a higher rating to the value of the help received than did caseworkers.

changes. The material in these records clearly shows that a positive relationship between client and worker must exist if the desired shifts in behavior and attitudes are to take place. It is recognized that in every treatment relationship more effective results can be brought about if the client-worker relationship is essentially positive. With these sado-masochistic couples, however, a positive relationship appears to be one of the major determinants of the degree of success that can be obtained through casework. The experience of having a person—the caseworker—continue to be interested in and solicitous of their well-being in spite of their ill-advised behavior, seems to have made it possible for change gradually to take place in these highly narcissistic, dependent individuals who had always felt unwanted and unappreciated. When such an essentially positive relationship between worker and client was absent, the sado-masochistic acting out appeared to have become accentuated. Yet, the very traits that characterize these sado-masochistic clients frequently tend to arouse either negative reactions or negative countertransference in a caseworker. Unless a caseworker is continuously alert to his own reactions, and plans early and frequent supervisory conferences and psychiatric consultations in cases of this type, he is apt to find himself responding negatively in three areas: (1) against the partner who is more obviously abusive and cruel, because of his own identification with the more mistreated spouse, not fully recognizing the latter's less obvious provocative behavior; (2) against the parent's open abuse of a child, because of his own identification with the child; and (3) against the great rigidity, self-righteousness and projection of the markedly compulsive and ambivalent clients.

In view of the importance of sustaining an essentially positive client-worker relationship in spite of provocative behavior, the question has been raised as to whether it is preferable to use one or two workers in treating sado-masochistic couples. The findings of this study are not decisive on this point since both plans were used in these nine cases with varying degrees of success.

It is also extremely important for the caseworker to ascertain each client's true situation and manner of functioning in this type of case. Owing to the characteristic way in which such clients project and distort, the caseworker needs to employ a variety of means to ensure that his own thinking is based on as correct an appraisal of facts as possible. Only under these circumstances is the caseworker in a position to help the client learn to evaluate reality factors more accurately.

Factual Data

This study highlighted the importance of having simultaneous casework contact with both husband and wife in order to obtain necessary factual information and even to approximate the reality of the situation. The frequency with which either partner is seen may vary periodically. Simultaneous contact also enables the worker or workers to understand better the family balance and to base casework treatment on it. At least one home visit is indicated since this, too, provides the worker with an opportunity to see for himself the actual interaction between various family members in the home setting. For instance, one worker had tended to discount a compulsive husband's complaints about his wife's poor housekeeping, until she visited by appointment in the afternoon and found soiled diapers on the living room floor, the room bare of curtains and pictures and the table loaded with unwashed dishes from several meals.

Collateral contacts are also essential. Through visits to schools, doctors, and others, the worker is able to correct for himself the client's inaccurate perception of the situation and can open the way for the client to make more fruitful use of such outside resources. Recognizing that sado-masochistic persons frequently tend either to deny or to exaggerate facts, the worker needs to use every available opportunity to correct his own impressions and thinking.

Four Supportive Techniques

Supportive treatment was the method selected by the caseworkers for dealing with all eighteen clients in this study. In the light of the clinical diagnoses of these men and women—from severe character disorder to schizophrenia—one would anticipate the use of this method. Although many techniques are used in the supportive method, only four proved to be the cornerstones upon which successful treatment of these clients was based. The four techniques[2] employed most frequently and with best results were logical discussion, advice and guidance, the setting of realistic limits, and reassurance. These techniques are particularly appropriate for use with sado-masochistic clients who, as has been stressed earlier, show seriously impaired ego functioning and childlike superego development. Through the consistent use of these techniques by a worker for whom the client feels trust and respect, it was possible to help these persons learn to assess their current life situation in a more realistic manner and, to some extent, to curb their self-damaging acting out.

Logical discussion was the technique most frequently used and most effective with all these clients. Since these were intelligent men and women, they themselves at times raised questions about their impulsive behavior. They responded well when the worker helped them again and again to appraise the true situation and anticipate the consequences of their behavior. For example, after one husband had given numerous illustrations of quarrels with his wife, the caseworker suggested to him that if he wanted peace at home, as he had said so many times, he would do well to stop making teasing and sarcastic remarks to his wife which he knew always upset her. Although

---

[2] A more complete presentation of various techniques employed in the supportive method of casework treatment will be found in *Method and Process in Social Casework*, Report of a Staff Committee of the Community Service Society of New York, Family Service Association of America, New York, 1958.

this man had not been able to reach this conclusion by himself, he gradually accepted the idea and quarrels at home became less frequent. Certain clients seemed able to make use of logical discussion in some areas and not in others. One wife made good use of points discussed in relation to her health and use of money, but anything discussed in relation to her older son had no apparent effect on her behavior. Since these were highly narcissistic persons, the use of logical discussion was most effective when the consequences to themselves were highlighted by the caseworker. It was thus possible to bring about considerable modification in their tendency to project blame on others and, also, to lessen the extent of their provocative behavior.

The technique of offering advice and guidance was also particularly well suited to the needs of these individuals. In order for the client to make use of direct suggestion, however, the worker had to proceed slowly and patiently and only after an atmosphere of trust and confidence had been established. Advice and guidance were found to be especially useful in working with these women in areas such as budgeting, household management, and care of the children. Here, too, when the worker's suggestions were made from the point of view of the woman's self-interest, they were more readily accepted. The emphasis had to be placed on "this will be easier for you" not on "this will be better for Jimmy."

The setting of realistic limits by the worker was demonstrated to be an important part of the treatment process in certain instances where a client showed markedly uncontrolled behavior and poor judgment. For example, after hearing from one woman the details of how she would hit, scratch, and bite her husband when angry, and after the husband had come to the office with a black eye and nail-raked face, the caseworker told her that such behavior could not continue. She pointed out to this woman that she was no longer a small child, and that a grown woman does not behave in such a manner. The worker also reminded her of her husband's frequent threats to leave her and added that some day he might do this. After this interview the client did curb this form of acting out, and the husband commented with relief that he was gratified that his wife had stopped attacking him. Improvement in the couple's situation can be furthered by such direct intervention on the part of a worker but, obviously, this technique should be employed sparingly and with discrimination. It should also be noted that when a worker who has an underlying critical attitude toward a client attempts to set such limits, further destructive acting out may be anticipated, since the worker is viewed by the client as a critical parental figure.

Similarly, the technique of giving reassurance, when used realistically and with restraint, proved beneficial. In the treatment of these dependent, self-doubting individuals, well-timed reassurance, when offered by a person whose opinion was respected, frequently lessened anxiety. For example, when the caseworker reminded one mother that a recent physical examination had showed her son to be in good health, the mother's worry about his poor appetite decreased. Although giving reassurance did not touch the client's fundamental problem, it still brought some relief to these men and women who had only a minimal ability to judge facts and feelings accurately for themselves.

In summary, these four techniques proved to be particularly suitable in the treatment of these clients, since they are designed to assist a person to perceive and appraise reality more accurately, to anticipate consequences, to make wiser decisions, to restrain dangerous impulses, and to develop the capacity for behaving in a more rational manner. The intent of casework treatment with these persons was to improve defective ego and superego functioning to whatever degree was possible.

Another technique, ventilation, was used to some degree with all these clients. Many times it was appropriate to encourage these men and women to speak freely of things in their home life with which they were so preoccupied. In certain cases, however, ventilation was encouraged to a greater extent than was advisable, considering the treatment objectives. This occurred under the following circumstances: when too much sado-masochistic gratification was engendered through the detailed description of events; when such telling encouraged the client's tendency toward projection; when there was danger of stimulating borderline schizophrenics to bring out repressed material. Material in this study indicates that the technique of ventilation should be used cautiously with sado-masochistic clients whose diagnoses range from severe character disorder to schizophrenia, since the encouraging of too much emotional release may lead to further breakdown in the client's already precarious functioning.

It was observed in a few instances that when the worker had attempted to secure and use early childhood material in an effort to give the client more understanding of causative factors in his situation, the client's current functioning deteriorated. It is understandable that such a person, whose sense of reality was poor and whose defense structure was fragile, could profit from obtaining some dynamic understanding of his current reactions but could not make use of a genetic approach. When treatment was focused on the present, observable improvement took place.

Conclusion

From the study of these nine cases, it was possible to indentify certain common characteristics of the sado-masochistic marriage pattern. The study also throws light on what treatment goals may be achieved, the effectiveness of certain treatment techniques, and the dangers to be guarded against when working with this type of marital relationship. Treating couples whose marital relationship is predominantly of a sado-masochistic type requires a large investment of time, skill in casework, and great self-awareness and self-discipline on the part of the caseworker. This study indicates that, although no fundamental change in the underlying sado-masochistic pattern can be brought about through casework methods, the pattern of functioning can often be modified. This finding becomes even more significant when it is recalled that the study shows that the sado-masochistic pattern of the parents frequently becomes the characteristic pattern of the children, particularly of the older child. Unless the sado-masochistic responses and behavior of the parents are reduced in extent and degree, the children are likely to relate to other people in this same destructive manner. Consequently it is extremely important that appropriate casework treatment be made available to such persons, not only for their own benefit but in order partially to interrupt this pernicious chain reaction from generation to generation.

Sexual Deviations

Treatment of Sexual Dysfunction and Casework Techniques

Gloria G. Harris and Nathaniel N. Wagner

"Social casework incorporates within its processes both scientific knowledge and social values in order to achieve its ends" (Hamilton, 1959). With this statement, Gordon Hamilton's classic text introduces the basic assumptions and methods of social casework. More than a philosophical stance, this statement may be viewed as constituting a professional mandate. Ethical responsibility requires that new knowledge which may contribute to the alleviation of human emotional suffering be incorporated into professional practice. The potential utility of employing the techniques developed by Masters and Johnson for the treatment of sexual dysfunctions within the on-going casework relationship is, consequently, both suggested and explored in this paper.

The authors of this paper are of the opinion that sexual counseling may be effectively employed in an out-patient or social agency setting, independent of medical supervision. Evidence for this opinion lies in the successful utilization of Masters and Johnson's techniques with an increasing number of couples who have received the benefits of sexual counseling at the University of Washington Psychology Clinic. The Psychology Clinic is a training facility which is presently gaining a reputation in the Seattle community as a resource for the treatment of sexual problems.

Success of Treatment Approach

Masters and Johnson estimate "conservatively" that half the marriages in this country are either presently sexually dysfunctional or imminently so in the future (Masters and Johnson, 1970). As a result of their findings, the average troubled couple stands a 75–80 percent chance of having their dysfunction corrected. Obviously these marriages cross-cut racial, socio-economic, and social class boundaries.

Reprinted from *Clinical Social Work Journal*, Vol. 1 (Winter, 1973), pp. 244–250, by permission of the authors and publishers, Behavioral Publications, 72 Fifth Avenue, New York, New York. 10011. Copyright 1973.

Without detracting in any way from the magnitude or quality of the monumental work by Masters and Johnson, their approach clearly has roots in techniques of behavior modification. Treatment of female dysfunction has been reported by Brady (1966), Haslam (1965), Lazarus (1963), Kraft and Al-Issa (1967), and Madsen and Ullmann (1967). Impotence and premature ejaculation has been described by Cooper (1963, 1968), Lazarus (1965), Kraft and Al-Issa (1968), and Semans (1956). These studies received little attention prior to the national recognition, both professional and public, that the work of the St. Louis group received. It is interesting to note that despite the fact that the greatest percentage of professional activity of the St. Louis group is in the area of sexual counseling, they continue to be known as "The Reproductive Biology Research Foundation."

Although Masters and Johnson's first book, *Human Sexual Response* (1966), was primarily intended for a scientific audience, their more recent book, *Human Sexual Inadequacy* (1970), may be more easily understood and employed as the source of information in sexual counseling by sophisticated nonmedical professionals such as clinical social workers. In addition, an officially authorized and endorsed explanation of the original publication entitled *Understanding Human Sexual Inadequacy* (1970) which is intended to be read by lay persons, is available in an inexpensive soft-cover edition.

Masters and Johnson's approach is both biological and psychological in its orientation. Despite a recognition of biological factors, sex is not mechanized. On the contrary, the contribution of interpersonal relationship variables to sexuality is fully appreciated; it is to some extent this aspect of their approach which brings it appropriately within the province of those who deal with marital difficulties of broad scope. Masters and Johnson's dual emphasis views sexual functioning as an interaction between the biological and psychosocial spheres. Strong negative signals from either system may result in dysfunction for an individual of either sex. The psychosocial system includes the existence of positive values and attitudes toward sex. The biophysical system includes the presence of a healthy body and anatomically functional sex organs. These two systems are seen as capable of reinforcing and complementing each other.

Masters and Johnson's scientific data reports failure in only 20 percent of 790 cases of male and female dysfunction which were treated for two weeks and later followed up for five years. Their most stunning success has been in the treatment of premature ejaculation, for which they report that only 5 of the 186 men with this problem were not cured. By use of a "squeeze technique" in which the female grasps the penis when the man indicates his readiness to climax, a 98 percent success rate has been achieved. This technique is used in conjunction with supportive, educational, communication, and reflective techniques.

Success of Out-Patient Approach

The success rate at the University of Washington Psychology Clinic, where couples remain in their own homes and are seen two or three times a week rather than taking up residence in St. Louis for two weeks, is equally striking. The average length of treatment in our adapted program is from three to ten weeks. As in Masters and Johnson's work, our accomplishments with the problem of orgasmic dysfunction are less astounding, but at the same time, results are much better than those commonly reported with conventional therapeutic techniques, and they are obtained in a considerably shortened period of time. Ejaculatory incompetence and secondary impotence have also been successfully treated in our out-patient setting.

As in Masters and Johnson's original program, a couple who applies to our clinic is first required to have undergone a recent physical examination in order to rule out biological or anatomical deficiencies which may be contributing to the dysfunction. Because we do not include a medical person on the treatment team, a competent medical examination is an absolute prerequisite. The couple is initially interviewed by a male-female cotherapist team. Dual sexual counseling teams give each member of the marital unit a "friend in court," a person who is sympathetic to and identified with the unique feelings and attitudes of the same-sexed client. This conjoint interview is not unlike the typical initial casework interview. Attempts are made to elicit the clients' feelings, both past and present, and tenative diagnostic impressions regarding the nature of the presenting problems are formed. The importance of forming a meaningful relationship with the clients and the difficulties in seeking professional help for private, often embarrassing problems are recognized.

Following the intake interview(s), a decision whether or not to accept a couple for treatment is made. Several factors are taken into consideration in arriving at this decision; they include client motivation and the likelihood of treatment success for a particular sexual problem. For example, our experience has indicated that nonorgasmic women who are able to achieve climax with manual manipulation are less likely to attain orgasm during intercourse using Masters and Johnson's sexual counseling approach than women who have never experienced orgasm.

The St. Louis program has provided surrogate partners for single clients whereas the University of Washington Psychology Clinic is not in a position to do the same (it is our understanding that the St. Louis surrogate partner approach is presently in abeyance pending the outcome of litigation). Each sexually dysfunctioning client must bring his or her own partner although it is not required that the couple be legally married. Established liaisons are equally acceptable to our program as long as both partners share a willingness to participate and to cooperate in the sexual counseling regime.

There are other ways in which our program differs from that in St. Louis. Masters and Johnson's treatment costs $2500 and is thus available largely to affluent clients, although a sliding scale is used for a large number of cases. Our program employs a sliding scale which enables many lower socio-economic clients to receive help and denies no one treatment because of lack of funds.

Once a decision has been made to accept the couple for treatment, a highly detailed psycho-social-sexual history is gathered. A copy of the form used by Masters and Johnson in their program is included in their 1970 book. Appropriate male and female roles in marriage, conceptions of effective sexual functioning, life-cycle influences and events, self-perceptions, and awareness of and response to sensory stimuli are among the areas explored in this phase of the program. Issues of embarrassment, misunderstanding, discomfort, and conflict as well as of pleasure and of enjoyment are carefully delineated. Often this phase makes the client aware of aspects of his own functioning which were previously unrecognized. In addition, an atmosphere in which feelings and attitudes may be freely and unashamedly discussed is established.

Once the history-gathering phase has been completed, the standard "round-table discussion" in which communication between the partners is encouraged and misconceptions are corrected is conducted. The cotherapy team presents to the clients a probable explanation of the causes of their problem. Misinformation, unrealistic expectations, communication failures, and destructive behavior patterns are elucidated. The therapists emphasize to the couple that neither of them is considered solely dysfunctional but rather, the relationship between the partners is the client. The round-table discussion is set up as a four-way dialogue. Special relationships between an individual client and therapist are avoided. Often for the first time in their marriage, the clients begin here to express to each other their worries and their fears about sexual performance.

The next phase of the program has been called by Masters and Johnson the "sensate focus." These exercises are based upon the recognition that touch is a vital part of human communication. In order to achieve the fullness of sexual expression, the partners must touch each other in a communicative way. This form of communication is viewed as the single most important source of sexual stimulation. For many people, these exercises provide the first opportunity to both think and feel sensuously without pressure to proceed to intercourse. Genital areas are excluded in this non-demanding period in an attempt to reestablish and to relearn new habits which in turn may lead to successful sexual functioning. Successful sexual functioning is an extremely important component of a successful marital relationship. Our experience suggests that it may in fact be an essential component.

Following positive reactions and progress in the sensate activity, participation becomes more active. The specific direction of the activity is determined by the particular sexual dysfunction for which help is being sought. The case illustration which follows is intended to further illuminate the use of sexual counseling techniques in an outpatient setting.

Case Illustration: Premature Ejaculation

Mr. and Mrs. E, aged 27 and 25, were married 10 years when they were referred to the Psychology Clinic for treatment of Mr. E's chronic premature ejaculation. A family agency caseworker who had formed a close working relationship with the couple in the course of several months of marital counseling made the referral. The E family, like many other couples with sexual problems of long standing, recently learned of the possibility of cure with Masters and Johnson's techniques, but their caseworker felt unable to assist them in this sensitive area.

The E's economic and educational level is representative of many clients seen in casework practice. Mr. E, a high school graduate, is employed as a carpenter. His wife has an 11th grade education, has never worked, and is relatively unconflicted regarding her role as a housewife.

Mr. E is a slim, pleasant looking man who speaks with an occasional slight stutter which appears unpredictably. Mrs. E is a stockily built woman with attractive, girlish features. In the initial conjoint interview with the co-therapist team, Mrs. E explained that she has grown increasingly angry that her husband leaves her unsatisfied and only obtains relief for himself. She married as a 16-year-old virgin and had not expected sexual pleasure for herself. Her mother had avoided sexual discussion, and from Mrs. E's limited conversations on this topic with friends, she had formed an impression that others, like herself, performed the sexual act in marriage as if it were a duty.

Despite disappointment and disinterest in her early marital experiences, for many years she had pretended involvement and had not shared her real feelings with her spouse. Recently, however, Mrs. E learned that a cure for her husband's problem might be obtained and that she should appropriately expect sexual fulfillment for herself.

Mr. E reported that when his wife began to complain about his selfishness, he became quite hopeless and discouraged. All of his varied efforts at ejaculatory control had been unsuccessful in the past. Around this time, the E's started to "bicker" a great deal which led them to seek casework assistance.

Mr. E further described other areas of his life in which poor control had been problematic. Specifically, he had been an army sergeant stationed in Vietnam several years ago and had impulsively killed a 17-year-old draftee who called him "quick draw E," referring to an incident in which Mr. E had illegally drawn his gun. Mr. E stated that he had felt no particular previous animosity toward his victim; he simply lost control of his temper. As a result of this incident, Mr. E received a "secondary manslaughter" sentence of which he served only six months. The sentence was commuted with the aid of powerful political intervention.

In the intensive history taking phase of the program, it was further established that Mr. E had "almost lost control" several times since the fatal incident. The last time had been with an elderly neighbor who accused Mr. E's son of stealing. Mr. E had pushed the man around and "if he hadn't backed off, he might have been wiped out." Mr. E expressed some concern about and awareness of his poor impulse control and spontaneously connected his deficit with early childhood experiences which included a punitive, authoritarian father and seductive, infantile mother. He preferred, however, to focus his discussion on the sexual symptom for which he was seeking professional assistance.

Mrs. E told her interviewer that she finds it difficult to share her feelings with her husband and that she has always been embarrassed to talk in front of men about sexual matters. Despite her limited sexual experience prior to marriage, Mrs. E confided that she had a brief affair while Mr. E was in Vietnam. She had, through that experience, been astonished to discover that lovemaking could be satisfying. It took her several years, however, to discuss this subject with her husband. When she finally did, she couched the discussion in terms of what she had learned from "talking with the girls."

The Psychology Clinic's affirmative decision to accept this case for sexual counseling was based primarily on the assumption that the probability of Mr. E's performing another impulsive, violent act would be greatly reduced if he could become more sexually competent. Mastering control in the sexual area might enable the client to generalize this experience to other areas of his life. Since the likelihood of successful treatment of Mr. E's sexual problem was extremely high, based on both Masters and Johnson's results as well as our own, our decision was further bolstered.

During the sensate focus phase, the E's exhibited rather atypical resistance. They did, however, ultimately cooperate. The quality of their interpersonal communication remained limited since neither partner desired increased closeness, and the cotherapy team respected the goals which they had elected for themselves. In spite of the several limitations and rather severe pathology exhibited in this case, Mr. E overcame his chronic premature ejaculation problem in only a month and a half of twice weekly sexual counseling sessions.

Analysis

The effectiveness of the sexual counseling approach described in this paper may be attributed to several factors. First, there appears to be evidence that dual-sex teams of therapists are more successful than individual therapists. Understanding the sexual responsivity of the opposite sex appears to be enhanced by the presence of a professional interpreter. The importance of this factor is also suggested by Masters and Johnson's finding that it is extremely difficult to elicit reliable material when the sexually dysfunctional male patient is interviewed by a female therapist.

Second, if the therapy team functions well, it plays a catalytic role in marital communication. Verbal exchange is deliberately encouraged between patients, and thus the marital partners increasingly learn to share and to understand each other's needs. The ultimate level in marital unit communication is sexual intercourse. Without question, sexual functioning is not the total of any marital relationship, but few marriages which lack a positive sexual component can exist as effective, complete, and ongoing entities.

Finally, the premise that attitudes and ignorance rather than psychopathology or physical illness are responsible for most sexual problems is basic to Masters and Johnson's sexual counseling approach. These attitudes and their accompanying behaviors have been learned and can be unlearned. Misconceptions can be corrected, attitudes can be modified, and dysfunctional symptoms can be replaced with appropriate responses without any evidence of symptom substitution. Through the use of a building block technique in which new behaviors are attempted step-by-step, the marital unit is gradually deconditioned and reconditioned. Successful treatment enables a couple to relinquish irrational performance fears and goal-oriented behaviors and to share a revitalized, life-enhancing sexual relationship.

References

1 BELLIVEAU, F., and RICHTER, L. *Understanding Human Sexual Inadequacy.* New York: Bantam Books, 1970.

2 BRADY, J. P. "Brevital Relaxation Treatment of Frigidity." *Behavior Research and Therapy,* 1966, *4,* 71–77.

3 COOPER, A. J. "A Case of Fetishism and Impotence Treated by Behavior Therapy." *British Journal of Psychiatry,* 1963, *109,* 649–652.

4 COOPER, A. J. "A Factual Study of Male Potency Disorders." *British Journal of Psychiatry,* 1968, *114,* 719–731.

5 HAMILTON, G. *Theory and Practice of Social Case Work.* New York: Columbia University Press, 1959.

6 HASLAM, M. T. "The Treatment of Psychogenic Dyspareunia by Reciprocal Inhibition." *British Journal of Psychiatry,* 1965, *111,* 280–282.

7 KRAFT, T., and AL-ISSA, I. "Behavior Therapy and the Treatment of Frigidity." *American Journal of Psychotherapy,* 1967, *21,* 116–120.

8 KRAFT, T., and AL-ISSA, I. "The Use of Methahexitone Sodium in the Systematic Desensitization of Premature Ejaculation." *British Journal of Psychiatry,* 1968, *114,* 351–352.

9 LAZARUS, A. A. "The Treatment of Chronic Frigidity by Systematic Desensitization." *Journal of Nervous and Mental Disease,* 1963, *135,* 272–278.

10 LAZARUS, A. A. "The Treatment of a Sexually Inadequate Man." In Ullmann and Krasner (Eds.) *Case Studies in Behavior Modification.* New York: Holt, 1965.

11 MADSEN, C. H., and ULLMANN, L. P. "Innovations in the Desensitization of Fridigity." *Behavior Research and Therapy,* 1967, *5,* 67–68.

12 MASTERS, W. H., and JOHNSON, V. E. *Human Sexual Response.* Boston: Little, Brown and Company, 1966.

13 MASTERS, W. H., and JOHNSON, V. E. *Human Sexual Inadequacy.* Boston: Little, Brown and Company, 1970.

14 SEMANS, J. G. "Premature Ejaculation: A New Approach." *Southern Medical Journal,* 1956, *49,* 353–357.

Casework Treatment of Sexual Confusion in Character Disorders

Beatrice Simcox Reiner

In a large proportion of cases of marital conflict, uncertainty about his psychosexual identity is a problem presented by one or both partners. According to its severity and the ways it is expressed, this problem is referred to as sexual confusion, sexual distortion, failure to fulfill the sexual role, or sexual role reversal. Caseworkers often approach such cases with natural uneasiness because of the seemingly random expression of psychosexual maladjustment and the fact that they have been exposed to a variety of generalizations on the subject. One of these generalizations is that sexual disorders cannot be treated by caseworkers. Another is that lack of psychosexual identity is caused by a combination of cultural influences and individual factors[1]—an explanation that, without more clarification, may convey a discouraging sense of inevitability. Perhaps it would be worth while to examine the effect on casework practice of various generalizations about psychosexual identity, and to see if some of its expressions may be viewed in a more meaningful way.

An Unscientific Approach to Sexuality

No other generation of caseworkers has been so subject to the temptation of succumbing to easy generalizations as is the present one. Evidence may be found in Morton Teicher's article "The Culture of Concepts" and in the letters to the editor it stimulated.[2] In spite of the heat engendered, however, the correspondents seemed to agree that it is imperative that concepts be

Reprinted from *Social Casework,* Vol. 43 (December, 1962), pp. 538–545, by permission of the author and the Family Service Association of America.

[1] Sue Vesper, "Casework Aimed at Supporting Marital Role Reversal," *Social Casework*, Vol. XLIII, June 1962, pp. 303–304.

[2] Morton I. Teicher, "The Culture of Concepts." *Social Casework*, Vol. XLII, December 1961, pp. 491–93. "Readers' Comments." *Social Casework*, Vol. XLIII, February 1962, pp. 86–88.

formulated and that the most important issue is the way the caseworker uses them. A similar conclusion was reached by Victoria Olds in her clarifying article about role theory.[3] Caseworkers are influenced, however, not only by concepts drawn from psychology and sociology that are finding their way into casework thinking but also by some much less specific sociological generalizations that have gained currency in the mass media. These latter generalizations represent oversimplifications that can become clichés or catchalls preventing the caseworker from engaging in further questioning. In the end, too-ready acceptance of theories that have no scientific foundation may lead the worker to adopt an attitude of hopelessness about the possibility that individual clients can change.

Caseworkers should be suspicious of "popular" sociological theory that offers too pat an explanation of human phenomena. One of the best ways of achieving understanding about the relationship between cultural change and individual psychosexual development is the traditional method of case exploration. Within any conceptual framework we employ, it is only through careful case-by-case study that we can understand the similarities and differences that occur and the backgrounds of the characterological phenomena we see. We tend to forget that, as caseworkers, we have access to more dynamic case material on these issues than any other professional group, since our clients represent a cross section of American life and since our interview material has a high degree of validity because clients give it in the context of a meaningful relationship.[4] In this period of extensive generalization we must retain our curiosity, value our observations, and re-evaluate our own attitudes. We should not forget that significant new knowledge usually gives rise to more questions than answers.

At a recent meeting attended by family caseworkers,[5] Otto Pollak speculated that caseworkers are operating on the basis of Victorian or pre-Victorian concepts of masculinity and femininity, and tend to be disturbed by unfeminine women or unmasculine men. As a result, they may be working against the cultural stream and be unreceptive to the possibility that new cultural modes of expression of the relationship between the sexes are emerging. Perhaps Pollak's analysis is correct. Are caseworkers suffering from a separation between thought and feeling that permits them to believe that personality is a mixture of male and female components while their emotional reactions are still influenced by an outdated "norm" of sexual behavior?

Moreover, caseworkers should give up the naïve belief that somewhere in the world there are large numbers of "normal" families, unknown to them because they come in contact only with pathological families. Irving Harris

[3] Victoria Olds, "Role Theory and Casework: A Review of the Literature." *Social Casework*, Vol. XLIII, January 1962, pp. 3–8.

[4] Beatrice Simcox Reiner, "Some Meanings of Identity for Casework." *Smith College Studies in Social Work*, Vol. XXXII, October 1961, pp. 1–19.

[5] Middle Atlantic Regional Institute of the Family Service Association of America, Bryn Mawr, Pennsylvania, June 1961.

has done his best to explode this myth.[6] In recent mental health surveys of mid-Manhattan and of a semi-rural county in the Maritime Provinces of Canada, it was estimated that the mentally "healthy" in these areas represented 18.5 per cent and 17 per cent of the population, respectively.[7]

Another possibility for confusion lies in the fact that Western culture not only blurs the differences between what men do and what women do but simultaneously makes us acutely aware of the male or female "image" created by certain external signs. The power of advertising is such that the average client has become adept at reproducing the proper image and the average caseworker is unconsciously influenced by it. Assessing the male or female identity of a client is not a simple task; the most feminine-appearing woman may be the least motherly or sexually adequate, and the most virile-appearing man may be able to love no one but himself.

Sexual Identity and the Character Disorders

Psychoanalytic theory holds that true male or female identity is achieved only when the oedipus conflict has been resolved; therefore, most persons with neuroses or character disorders are confused about their sexual identity and role. Caseworkers are familiar with some of the sexual aberrations associated with the neuroses, but they are less knowledgeable about the sexual confusions manifested by persons with character disorders. I should like, therefore, to review briefly the problems of sexual identity associated with various types of character disorder. I shall place special emphasis on the anal-erotic and the phallic-urethral types, since many of the obvious and marked problems of sexual identity are to be found in persons fixated at these levels of psychosexual development.[8]

In the oral-erotic character disorders, sexuality represents the gratification of thinly disguised oral needs, including the need for closeness and for kinesthetic pleasure. Sexual promiscuity in a person with this disorder may indicate that these needs are insatiable and that he is engaged in an endless search for the all-gratifying lost mother.

The person who has an oral-sadistic character disorder also expresses his oral needs through sexual behavior, but his affect is somewhat different. In contrast with the oral-erotic person, his early experience of severe oral deprivation has made him pessimistic, angry, and convinced of his un-

[6] Irving D. Harris, *Normal Children and Mothers*. Free Press of Glencoe, New York, 1959.

[7] Reported in *Mental Hygiene News*, New York State Department of Mental Hygiene, May 1962; based on a paper by Dorothea C. Leighton, John S. Harding, and Charles C. Hughes, of Cornell University, presented by Dr. Leighton at the annual meeting of the American Psychiatric Association, Toronto, Canada, May 7–11, 1962.

[8] Beatrice Simcox Reiner and Irving Kaufman, *Character Disorders in Parents of Delinquents*. Family Service Association of America, New York, 1959, pp. 37–65.

worthiness. Through a form of identification with the aggressor, he has come to believe that he does not deserve much. As a result, his love relationships often have a masochistic quality, as if he has no right to expect anything better, or he gets vicarious satisfaction from a relationship with someone even more needy than himself. Within this group of severely deprived persons are to be found the addict and the potential addict.[9] The sexual role is relatively unimportant to the person with an oral character disorder, since all his relationships are basically those of mother and child. Only with resumption of the growth process can we expect any change in his psychosexual behavior.

The person with a character disorder of the anal-erotic type, which represents fixation at the earliest stage of toilet training, is engaged in rebellion against controls. To such a person, masculinity and femininity are synonymous with strength and weakness, independence and dependence. He shows signs of being bisexual and is unwilling to give up either aspect of sexuality. A parent with this disorder often wants to fulfill both the maternal and the paternal roles in relation to his children. Furthermore, he has a somewhat confused identification both with the parent who controls and with the child who rebels. Rebellion against control may be revealed in rebellion against all accepted standards, as is the case with the "beatnik." It may also be expressed in difficulties with employers or, more constructively, in unusual or creative approaches to artistic or practical problems. The lack of a clear sexual orientation frequently results in a broken marriage or in competition with the spouse over which should assume the male role and which the female. The client with this type of character disorder resists discussing his sexual confusion as such, since he knows it is socially unacceptable; at the same time, he does not find it entirely ego-alien.

Casework treatment of the client with an anal-erotic character disorder consists in helping him form a relationship with the caseworker that can permit a resumption of emotional growth through new identifications. Resumption of emotional development is a slow process, but it can activated if a treatment relationship can be established and maintained. Treatment consists, in part, in helping the client form new concepts of masculinity and femininity that do not include the old stereotypes of strength and weakness, exploiter and exploited.

A person with an anal-sadistic character disorder, for whom sexuality has a strong sado-masochistic component, usually holds rigid ideas about the proper sexual role for a man and for a woman. When he has some doubt about his own masculinity or femininity, he adheres to these rules of behavior even more strictly. If his marital partner has an anal-erotic or a phallic-urethral character disorder and is inclined to make his own rules, the marital conflict is intensified.

[9] "Report of a Three Day Conference on Narcotic Addiction and the Teenager: Prevention, Control, Treatment." In-Service Training Department, New York City Youth Board, New York, October 1959.

The Phallic-Urethral Character Disorder

Problems of sexual identity often emerge with particular clarity in the treatment of the client with a character disorder of the phallic-urethral type. Since he is fixated at the pregenital level of development dominated by the penis, he is acutely conscious of sex differences and inclined to be preoccupied with them. Characteristic traits of this type of client include exhibitionism, competition, motility, and facility in manipulation. He wants to have the best or the most of everything, and he wants to be admired.

Although the phallic period of development encompasses the oedipal phase, the person with a phallic-urethral character disorder has predominantly pre-oedipal characteristics. For the most part he does not reveal the neurotic symptoms, the hysterical behavior, and the preoccupation with triangular relationships that characterize the person struggling with unresolved oedipal conflicts. Occasionally he may have transitory hysterical symptoms, especially if he presents a "mixed" type of pathology. For the most part, however, he resembles the child who either has not yet reached the oedipal phase or has retreated from it.

Why does a person become fixated at the phallic-urethral stage of psychosexual development? As is true of earlier pregenital fixations, one or more of three important factors are likely to have affected his development: loss of a parental figure, marked inconsistency of early handling, or family troubles affecting the parents that coincided with a crisis point in his psychosexual development. One frequently finds that he has suffered from particular kinds of loss or inconsistency: absence of the father or of a father-substitute during the phallic period; identification with the mother through close and intimate contact with her; reversal of roles by father and mother; insufficient maternal tenderness coupled with brutal rejection on the part of the father; a tendency for the parents to bribe the child by giving him "things" instead of affection; or the parents' need to equate the child with a phallus and stimulate his showing off, combined with failure to meet his needs on his own level. Such a child experiences no true latency, but continues to indulge in sexualized aggressive behavior throughout childhood and into adult life. As an adult, he is primarily narcissistic and has poor capacity for establishing relationships, although he may be charming and seductive.

Since the person with a phallic-urethral character disorder has an infantile superego structure, consisting of partial and inconsistent identifications with the parents, he suffers from objective anxiety rather than guilt. In other words, the sources of his anxiety are external rather than internal. Like persons with other types of character disorder, he allows himself to feel very little anxiety; he avoids it by seeking gratifications (chiefly some form of personal aggrandizement), by experiencing speed or motion, or by manipulating others. Power and possessions are important to him. Caseworkers may be misled by certain similarities between this client and the anal-sadistic client, but the differences between them must be accurately assessed if treatment of either one is to be successful. The person with a phallic-urethral character disorder seeks *power* to promote his own ends; the person with an anal-sadistic character disorder seeks *control* to defend himself from his own forbidden impulses (and those of others) and from his projected aggression, thereby assuring his own safety. Similarly, the phallic-urethral person's use of possessions for conspicuous consumption is different from the anal-sadistic person's investment in owning things as a protection against need or as a self-reward.

The person with a phallic-urethral character disorder is well attuned to our culture. He is aware of what others think of him. He is prone to use effectively the advertised trappings of sex (perfume, cosmetics, jewelry, clothes, and cars) in order to create the impression he regards as male or female. This behavior is part of his search for identity. To the woman of this type, holding a job may be an assertion of her femininity rather than a sign of masculinity. She wishes to be admired as a woman, and a job may put her in contact with men who treat her as a sexual object, who "kid" with her, or who are fatherly to her. In certain jobs she may also get vicarious feminine pleasure—for example, by making other women beautiful. Before the caseworker decides whether the woman client's wish to work has primarily a male or a female connotation, he needs to know what the job means to her, possibly on several levels.

Case Illustration

In the case of the J's, discussed below, the caseworker's failure to understand the meaning of Mrs. J's problems of sexual identity resulted in slowing up the casework process.

> The J family came to the attention of a family service agency when Mr. J complained that his wife was spending more and more time in a dress shop owned by her parents. After several interviews the caseworker was inclined to attribute Mrs. J's behavior to childish dependence on her mother and to a rejection of femininity. It was some time before the worker secured sufficient additional material to clarify the real meaning of Mrs. J's behavior. In her relationship with her mother, Mrs. J actually revealed few of the characteristics of a small, dependent child. Rather, what became evident was her fixation on her mother as the primary love object (inverse oedipus) and as her major source of identification. Moreover, this line of work reassured Mrs. J about her own femininity through her identification with her mother, who worked to make other women beautiful, and through her modeling in fashion shows.
>
> Mrs. J's lack of interest in housework was not based on rejection of the feminine role. In her childhood, the household chores had been done by a neat, unglamorous aunt who was restrictive with Mrs. J and against whom she had rebelled passively. Therefore, in Mrs. J's mind, doing housework was not associated with being feminine. Her mother's only interest in the house had been in buying furniture. One of the chief battlegrounds between Mr. and Mrs. J was what Mr. J regarded as his wife's extravagance in furnishing the house.
>
> Mrs. J's father had been the more maternal parent. It was from him that she had developed a certain potential for parenthood, but it had been obscured by her struggle to be loved by her mother. Like her mother, she had returned to work as soon as possible after the birth of her baby, leaving his care to paid

housekeepers. During his infancy, she had often lingered at work to avoid his feeding time because she felt that his poor appetite was a sign that he rejected her.

Mrs. J had always been embarrassed when her husband demanded a show of affection from her in front of her parents. Her reaction was not the inhibited response of the girl with an oedipal conflict who fears her mother's disapproval of her affection for any man who represents the father. Rather, it was caused by her perception of the competition between her mother and her husband as the primary love object. (The inverted oedipus represents the early passive oedipal attachment to the mother that, in the case of the girl, precedes the active oedipal wish for the father. The combination of a seductively dominant mother and a disappointingly passive father can contribute to the girl's failure to develop further. When treatment of such a girl is successful, oedipal wishes begin to emerge.) Mrs. J's intense jealousy of her younger sister, toward whom her mother had developed a seductive attitude after Mrs. J had stopped working, provided some confirmation of her attitude toward her mother. Mrs. J was also depressed, since she was cut off from all her main sources of narcissistic supplies.

Mrs. J had married a man who was passive like her father and who appeared easy to manage. However, he also represented some aspects of her mother, especially the disapproving, punitive ones. The fighting between Mr. and Mrs. J was described by the caseworker as a battle for "control." Actually it was more than that—it was a fight for "power," a fight to establish who was the boss. The words "control" and "power" may seem to be synonymous, but clinically they hold different connotations for treatment. The fight for power is typically phallic-urethral in its competitiveness, whereas the fight for control suggests anal-sadistic anxiety about control of the impulses.

Some Aspects of Treatment

Once the problem of sexual identity was opened up in the casework interviews, Mrs. J showed her eagerness to work on it—a reaction character-istic of many female clients with phallic-urethral character disorders. Some of them are avid readers of "confession" magazines or other forms of popular literature that offer them some comparisons with their own lives. Such a client is likely to say, "I could write a book myself." Many of them have had a history of lifelong oral deprivation combined with disappointment in the father who was lost or who submitted to the mother's domination. (There is some indication that having a father who was "lost" leads the woman to act out more extensively the ambivalent wish for a father.)

The woman who has a phallic-urethral character disorder suffers from low self-esteem, which must constantly be bolstered through her interaction with others. She has an intense longing to be understood, which is often the key to establishing a casework contact with her or losing her as a client at the very beginning. She is sensitive to conventional platitudes that miss the essence of her feelings. There is wide variation among such clients in the depth of their sensitivity and, therefore, in the length of time before they can trust the caseworker. The client whose character disorder has a strong anal-erotic component may quickly reach the point where the caseworker can, with a light touch, hazard a guess as to what is going on, in the knowledge that the client, whose basic wish is to do everything herself, will toss the suggestion aside good-naturedly if it is incorrect. Another client, however, for whom being understood is a primary aim, will feel that a wrong explanation by the worker creates a barrier in the relationship and is evidence that the worker is just like her mother. In spite of this strong wish to be understood, the woman with a phallic-urethral character disorder often has a fear of closeness that is related to losses she suffered in childhood. This fear should alert the caseworker to the importance of being always available to the client but not letting the relationship become an intense one.

The strength of the phallic-urethral fixation and the extent and kind of acting out are always related, however, to the severity of the client's early losses and the patterns she evolved in adolescence for dealing with them. The chief hazard in treatment lies in her tendency to become depressed, which may, in turn, lead to increased acting out, if not to attempted suicide. In many instances, the acting out itself is motivated by strong self-destructive impulses.

The male client who has a phallic-urethral character disorder is frequently more difficult to engage in treatment than his female counterpart, because his search for psychosexual identity so often takes a more symbolic form, such as preoccupation with making money or with "hot rods." He tends to be less articulate, since in our culture talking about oneself and philosophizing are regarded as feminine. The threatened break-up of his marriage sometimes keeps him in treatment, and it is then possible to form a relationship with him that will permit discussion of his defensive behavior. For example, in the J case discussed above, Mr. J was able to see how his attempts to "prove" himself by undertaking "impossible projects" were related to his lack of identification with his father and had been intensified by an incapacitating illness at a critical time in his childhood.

Other Manifestations of Phallic-Urethral Disorder

The phallic-urethral character disorder has a wide variety of manifestations. For example, Mr. or Mrs. J, both of whom are "uneasy," resemble the early adolescent who is attempting to establish himself as a person. Another manifestation is to be found in the blatantly exhibitionistic "pyschopath," who exploits any situation for his own ends and seems devoid of conscience, guilt, or conflict. Included in this diagnostic category are many "call girls"[10] and Don Juans. The proverbial "psychopath" is someone who appears "larger than life" because of his mobility, his unconflicted aggression, and his ability to charm. His lack of genuine sexual identity and his inability to establish relationships are betrayed by the trail of broken marriages and liaisons he leaves behind him. Only rarely does a person with this severe type of phallic-urethral character disorder come for help to a social worker or

[10] Harold Greenwald, *The Call Girl.* Ballantine Books, New York, 1958.

sustain the contact if he does come. The problems for the caseworker who has such a client are finding a casework goal that will seem worth while to him and controlling his tendency to manipulate the worker. An excellent example of this process is to be found in Nathan Ackerman's description of his treatment of Jim.[11]

Another type of phallic-urethral character disorder is characterized by ego restriction. To the person with a restricted ego, sexual expression and open aggression are taboo. He denies the desire to compete with others and emphasizes the virtues of getting along with people. In contrast to the exhibitionism and the fondness for conspicuous consumption displayed by the "psychopath," his tastes are subdued and he underplays the importance of possessions. The person of this type has a fear of whatever is different from himself and shows a tendency to marry someone with whom he can identify. This behavior resembles a characteristic, transient stage of early adolescence—the stage of denying sexuality and of loving only a person who is like oneself. A married couple who share this disorder maintain a kind of "collusion"[12] to deny sexual differences; thereby, envy, anxiety, or aggressive feelings are avoided. Sexual relations either are severely restricted or merely give the partners a sense of becoming one. In such a marriage, the crisis comes when one partner begins to have feelings, possessions, or activities of his own—in other words, when he resumes the interrupted growth process. Children are often regarded as alien intruders into the marital relationship.

Erik Erikson has ascribed ego restriction, in part, to the abdication of parental roles; the male ideal is exemplified by the maternal grandfather rather than by the father, who is more like a big brother. Sexual rivalry with the father is thereby excluded from consciousness.[13] Margaret Galdston Grunebaum has made a further contribution to the understanding of ego restriction in her discussion of the frequency with which such clients have "secrets." These may be the client's own or their parents' extramarital affairs, the physical or mental illness of relatives, or business difficulties that involve legally questionable practices.[14] Such secrets are undoubtedly a factor in a surprising number of cases, if one can judge from the difficulty encountered in getting more than scraps of history from many of these clients. In some cases, childhood sexual experiences—incestuous or other—may comprise the secret.

Anna Freud has suggested that restriction is one of the methods adopted by the ego for the avoidance of pain, especially by that of the older child,

---

[11] Nathan W. Ackerman, *The Psychodynamics of Family Life*. Basic Books, New York, 1958, pp. 240–246.

[12] *The Marital Relationship as a Focus for Casework*. Family Discussion Bureau, Tavistock Institute of Human Relations, Codicote Press, London, 1962.

[13] Erik H. Erikson, *Childhood and Society*. W. W. Norton & Co., New York, 1950, pp. 267 ff.

[14] Margaret Galdston Grunebaum, "A Study of Learning Problems of Children: Casework Implications." *Social Casework*, Vol. XLII, November 1961, pp. 461–68.

whose greater freedom of physical movement and increased powers of psychic activity enable his ego to avoid such stimuli without performing so complicated a psychic operation as denial. Her examples include children who refuse to compete because of the hopeless rivalry of the oedipus phase and those who want to avoid the disagreeable realization of the differences between the sexes.[15]

Fulfilling the Parental Role

A marriage based on ego restriction in both partners may appear to be a mutually satisfactory one, and the pathology may be revealed only through the children. The parental failures in such a marriage are illustrated by an episode in a case served by a family service agency.

> Mr. and Mrs. D were referred to the agency by their family physician, to whom they had complained about the behavior of their seven-year-old daughter, Helen. They were ashamed of her boastfulness about possessions and of her fantasy of the military heroism of an uncle. Her behavior was the exact opposite of their own refusal to be ostentatious, competitive, or aggressive. They were also worried by her lack of friends and her tendency to stay in the house and read. In the third interview Mrs. D described Helen's behavior with the new puppy they had just given her in the hope that it would force her to go outdoors. In the middle of the night Helen had heard the puppy crying. She had taken her pillow downstairs, lain down beside the puppy's pen, and talked to it, but had made no attempt to pick it up. The caseworker asked Mrs. D, "Do you know what she said to the puppy?" A startled expression came over Mrs. D's face as she replied: "Yes. She was telling it what it should do and what it shouldn't do." Mrs. D was an intuitive woman who had not succeeded in restricting all her feelings; she did not need to be told that Helen's concept of parental tenderness was one of "telling what to do and what not to do." She did, however, need help in translating her intuition into action that would enable her to share the child's feelings and relax some of her own restrictions.

The inability of the parent with a severe phallic-urethral character disorder to understand his child's feelings points to the basic fact that his own have never been valued. It is frequently found that in his childhood he was rewarded handsomely with possessions or privileges for disregarding his own feelings and allowing himself to be manipulated in accordance with his parents' desires. His relationships are therefore shallow and he tries to allay his loneliness with glamour, speed, money, and power. As Hans Morgenthau says, "The lust for power is, as it were, the twin of despairing love. Power becomes a substitute for love. What man cannot achieve for any length of time through love he tries to achieve through power: to fulfill himself, to make himself whole by overcoming his loneliness, his isolation."[16]

[15] Anna Freud, *The Ego and the Mechanisms of Defense.* International Universities Press, New York, 1946, pp. 100–113.

[16] Hans J. Morgenthau, "Love and Power." *Commentary*, Vol. XXXIII, March 1962, p. 249.

Treating Sexual Confusion

Although the individual variations seem endless, clients who suffer from sexual confusion do present recognizable patterns that have meaning to caseworkers. The sexual confusion of a person with a character disorder, like his other ways of behaving, thinking, and feeling, is likely to bear some relation to his fixation at a pregenital stage of development. In this respect his sexual behavior differs from that of the neurotic. The neurotic's behavior is dominated by defensive activities of the ego that are designed to reconcile the demands of the superego and of the id. The most familiar neurotic manifestations are, perhaps, the symptoms and behavior of the hysteric and the perversions and undoing rituals of the obsessive-compulsive. The traditional prohibition against the caseworker's dealing with sexual problems can readily be understood, since the neurotic manifestations, involving deep unconscious mechanisms, were recognized and understood by psychiatrists much earlier than the character disorders were. The treatment of the sexual confusions of the person with a character disorder depends, however, not on analyzing ego defenses and increasing the client's tolerance in handling the demands of the id but on helping him resume the growth process through a relationship with the worker.

When he has made a sound diagnosis, the caseworker can help marital partners who have phallic-urethral character disorders to establish improved male-female relationships, in which the husband and the wife supplement each other rather than compete for the male and female roles. A valid diagnosis depends on both a sound conceptual framework and the caseworker's development of an intuitive diagnostic sense based on his perception of qualitative differences in client attitudes. Through the study of individual cases, caseworkers may also make a significant contribution to an understanding of the sexual problems common to our culture and of the process by which cultural change takes place.

Some Observations of Group Psychotherapy with Paedophiles

Valdemar Hartman

Since the early days of mankind, children have been playing an important part in the lives of adults. According to time and culture, attention has been shown to them by individuals as well as by social institutions. It may be generalized that children are almost totally dependent upon the social environment and that adults are the ones who shape the environment, *eo ipso*, the onus for providing a suitable environment for their development rests upon the significant adults in the child's life. Opinions about "a suitable environment" may vary according to time and culture. Thus, in ancient Greece with its emphasis on the free, uninhibited expression of sexual instincts, a paedophile may have been regarded as "a man with refined tastes." In our culture the paedophile's choice of a child as an object of sexual interest is not condoned. It is viewed as a threat to the child's physical and emotional development—and also violates our Judeo-Christian ethical principles.

One of the cornerstones of our legal system is the protection provided for those unable to protect themselves according to the doctrine of *parents patriae*. Thus the paedophile may face not only society's strong disgust but also prosecution and severe penalty under the criminal code.

Historically, methods of dealing with paedophilic behavior vary. In medieval times such severe punishment as burning alive was meted out. More recently, we find incarceration and asexualization. However, the aim has remained the same: to curtail paedophilic behavior in the interests of protecting our children and preserving our ethical norms.

The new insights into human behavior and motivation brought about a search for more effective methods of controlling paedophilic behavior. It brought, also, emphasis on the doer's personality as the basis factor in motivating this behavior. The rehabilitative idea, having as its focus changes in the offender's attitudes, was seen as a compromise between the emphasis on individuality on the one hand, and our need to maintain social conformity on the other. This rehabilitation idea is becoming a part of a basic philosophy in dealing with our fellow citizens whose behavior grossly deviates from our accepted norms and is perceived as threatening and therefore evoking repercussions from society.

Reprinted from the *Canadian Journal of Corrections*, (October, 1961), pp. 492–499, by permission of the author and the publisher.

One of the relatively recent developments in the search for such effective methods of dealing with paedophilics is the application of group psychotherapeutic techniques for the investigation and treatment of paedophilia. Such research-oriented group psychotherapeutic sessions have been established at the Forensic Clinic of the Toronto Psychiatric Hospital.

The following remarks are gleaned from my experience as the therapist of this group, which has been in existence for the past fourteen months. The limits of this paper make necessary highly selective reporting, and an occasional oversimplification is unavoidable. The report is based upon direct observation in leading the group and also upon discussions of the transcripts and the tape recordings which take place at the regularly held group psychotherapy seminars at the Forensic Clinic. Attempts will be made to recapitulate some significant material pertaining to individual dynamics and group interaction as well as to present some tentative conclusions.

In reviewing the literature, there appears to be agreement about the definition of Paedophilia ("love of children" in translation). It denotes sexual interest in children; the emphasis being on the immaturity of the sexual object. Regarding the etiology there is a wide divergence in emphasis. The inferred dynamics often appear to be contradictory. No studies pertaining to group psychotherapy of paedophiles appear to have been published. Generally there is a paucity of writings referring to this form of sexual deviation.

It is understandable that in establishing this group, our objectives were to learn more about paedophilia and group interaction while at the same time helping the patients to effect better controls over their paedophilic urges.

In order to facilitate the optimal therapeutic group interaction, the proper selection of group members is of extreme importance. In selecting members for this group, the main criteria were patient homogenity in psychopathology and roughly equal intelligence levels. Soon, it became necessary to limit the group to heterosexually-oriented paedophiles only. As for homosexually-oriented, the discussions were too anxiety-provoking and intolerable. Also, to avoid a too-great age discrepancy, the age limits were arbitrarily set from 20–35 years. A variety of occupations were represented. The I.Q. of the group were bright normal or in the superior range, one was a university graduate. The majority were married with small children of their own.

All were previously assessed by a clinical team consisting of a psychiatric social worker, a psychologist and a psychiatrist as having capacity for psychotherapy. There were doubts expressed regarding their motivation for treatment, however. While all of them had acted out their paedophilic urges for a number of years, one over a period of fifteen years, none had previously thought of seeking help. Their present attendance at the clinic was made compulsory by a court order or a threat that charges would be laid unless treatment was initiated. All of them were currently experiencing paedophilic urges. The majority of them experienced quite compulsive urges and most were acting them out. The relative absence of guilt was observed as common to all the members of the group. In general, the patients were anxious, mildly depressed and dissatisfied with life.

In deciding upon the treatment approach, the integration of the presently available knowledge of individual dynamics regarding paedophilia, together with concepts derived from analytic group therapy, was regarded as an ideal to be strived for. Thus, while the group itself was seen as the therapeutic tool, no group goals were externally imposed. Treatment was individually oriented with reliance on unrestricted verbalization in the group. Evidently, since this was a research oriented group, the sessions were not limited to alleviation of the symptoms but were aimed at uncovering of the underlying causes, clarification and insights.

In determining the role of the therapist in the group, it was evident that the traditional permissive catalyst is essential to ensure uninhibited discussion. But we faced a group where for the majority of the members their deviating sexual urges had already become to a great extent ego syntonic despite the reality factor that even an attempt to act out these urges would bring serious social consequences. The decision was made to show firmly on which side the therapist stood as a reality tester. Evidently there also was a need for an equally firm show that the disapproval of their paedophilic urges did not imply that the therapist was chastising or condemning them as human beings. While it may be said that this stand appears not to have interfered with the sessions, it should be indicated that an everpresent danger existed in the form of possible identification as a forbidding authority figure, with the threat of a possible loss of the therapeutic effect.

Essentially the group sessions could be looked upon as a continued process of investigation and clarification. The main reliance was on interaction, unconscious and conscious, verbal and non-verbal, between group members present at the sessions, and on reactions to the purposeful activities of the therapist as a catalyst and reality tester.

In the development of the group several phases could be observed. Of these phases, the beginning or integrative phase is arbitrarily selected for a more elaborate description. Before discussing this phase, it should be remembered that none of the group members had been a self-referral. All had been subjected to compulsory attendance at the sessions. Thus it is not surprising that their initial attitudes in the group ranged from overt resentment regarding the enforced attendance, to benevolent noncommittal attitudes with regard to the help that was offered. This resistance and resentment at being involved was later aptly described by a probation officer to whom a group member on his reporting day had confided that "you can make me attend but you cannot make me talk."

This may partly explain why the integration of the group as a meaningful therapeutic instrument took some four or five months of weekly one and a half hour sessions. During this period, absences and late coming, as well as demonstrative nonparticipation in the sessions and testing of the therapist, were common features. The most frequently used defence mechanism was that of primitive denial. For example, that there was no sexual element in their urges and does not everyone love children? This was followed by rather generalized projections of guilt. Later, very slowly and cautiously, dissatisfaction with life in general started to develop as group themes. Yet avoidance of any sexual theme was a common feature. Around the third month, their dissatisfactions became more concrete assuming the form of highly emotional criticism of their wives as well as deep resentment, bringing out their own lack of a normal degree of aggressiveness. The use of projection in blaming the sexual attitudes of the wives for the gradually acknowledged urges toward children as sexual objects was instrumental in undoing the denial. Around the fourth month, the group was intensively engaged in exploring the reasons for their sexual attraction to small children. There was full attendance at nearly every session, and the group became well-motivated, learning why they are not able to control their paedophilic urges.

It is reasonable to question what had happened and why such a startling change had taken place in a relatively short period of time. The answers are to be looked for in the already available knowledge about group dynamics. In a simplified way, it may be said that the experience of the new relationships provided by the group with the supportive and anxiety-reducing influences implicit in this treatment approach made possible the reduction of the individually employed defences to the point where introspection became possible with developing self-awareness and the wish for a change. This wish for a change had been an important development since in treatment where benefits are to be achieved by psychological means, adequate motivation for change appears to be the condition *sine qua non*. Evidently, the significance of the supportive aspects of the group cannot be over estimated.

A more detailed observation of this phenomenon was possible some ten months later when a totally unmotivated paedophile under court order to attend, was added to the group. It was most striking to see how the group members' attitudes, most of them on an unconscious level, dealt with the new member's resistances and finally absorbed him into the group, in a surprisingly short period of time. That the achieved motivation has been a lasting one could be evidenced by the fact that of the original group, all members continued their attendance well beyond the legally imposed obligation to attend the clinic (in most of the cases this had been for a period of six months). One member left the group after an attendance of eleven months while the others are still attending.

In describing the individual roles in the group constellation, it could be said that the members had a great tendency to relate to each other and to the therapist as they presumably had related socially in childhood experiences of the past. Thus the significant features were sibling rivalries and distorted attitudes about meaningful figures of an early period of development. While this was utilized for information-getting as well as effecting better reality testing, the emphasis was on "here and now." As already mentioned, the therapist was not a neutralist from the very beginning of the sessions. It was made clear that he does not approve the paedophilic acts even if he tries to understand them. At the beginning stage it was also assumed that a direct prohibition might have to be applied after the neurotic material had been verbalized in the group and some understanding achieved. Such prohibition, in fact, never had to be imposed by the therapist since it came from the group itself and in much stricter form than the therapist could have possibly applied successfully.

In discussing the content of the sessions, certain dominant group themes could be well distinguished by their frequency and intensity. The changes and developments individually and groupwise could be clearly noticed by the changed emphasis and content of the themes. Thus, after reduction of the basic defences, the group's attentions were focused on their sexual difficulties. The slowly emerging insight that sexual difficulties are only a part of their interpersonal difficulties, focused the group associations on the total personalities of the members with the realizations of their own personality inadequacies. No doubt, this was provoking major anxiety and again support of the group as well as the part-identification with the therapist should be stressed as a factor in making the tensions tolerable and in not provoking withdrawal from sessions.

More specifically, the prominent group themes were: dissatisfaction with wives (all but one member were married); concern about paedophilic urges; dissatisfaction with self for not being sufficiently aggressive; apprehensions about adult women and the need to master them; curiosity about the female genitalia, and apprehensions about impaired masculinity.

In the therapist's evaluation, the central theme of the discussion was the perception of adult women as an unspecified danger (the castrating element appeared to be only one aspect) and the rationalization that the group members could not face an adult woman because of the certainty of refusal and ridicule on her part. The resulting anxiety appeared to be discharged by what to them was a total mastery of a paedophilic object via some form of sexual contact with the female child—not necessarily intercourse, however.

While the focal conflict no doubt remained paedophilia, the elements of other sexual deviations, such as exhibitionism, fetishism, voyeurism as well as some confusion about sexual identity, by no means always remained peripheral in the discussions.

It may be of interest to note that in the discussions of the group I currently have in therapy, a new theme is emerging, namely, the search for a connecting causative link between paedophilic urges and the satisfactions they provide in terms of feelings of mastery and masculinity.

In comparing the individual assessments with the findings in the group, in every case the assessment by the clinical team could be confirmed. The disturbance in normal childhood development had been a prominent feature. All the members of the group had experienced either a physical or psychological absence of the father. The mother had taken the dominant role in the family. In every case, this had resulted in an actual or perceived trauma and the real or perceived attitudes of the mother appeared to haunt each patient's life in an exaggerated form.

In placing emphasis on the possible influence of mother's attitudes in the individual dynamics, this should not be regarded as a monocause for paedophilia or evidence that mother had been a monster. No evidence could be found that the group verbalizations indicating disturbances in mothering could be the result of mother's own psychopathology or were created by father or by a neurotic interaction in the marriage unless a thorough psychosocial assessment of the parental family as a unit had been made. Of a more immediate therapeutic concern was the impression gained from the session, that the group members' present family situation actually could be regarded as a continuum of childhood experiences. The description of their attitudes, the persistent slips in mixing up the mother and the wife and the occasional flare-up of a power struggle in the marriage, even with due allocation for the possible distortions in perception, gave some indication of the intensity of the remnants of the childhood experiences.

At the Forensic Clinic, we offer the wife of the patient a continuing professional contact. In the cases where the wife attended, little progress was made with her due to extreme defensiveness on her part. In some cases we noticed that she attempted to make it difficult for the husband to attend the sessions. For example, she might choose the day when group meetings were to take place for entertaining guests or shopping. Evidently this is an area for deeper exploration.

In returning to the stated objectives in the establishment of this group at the Forensic Clinic, namely, to learn more about paedophilia and group dynamics and to provide immediate treatment for patients, the experimental nature of this undertaking is stressed, and that evaluation of this experiment is based on clinical impression (social functioning being the only external measurable criteria). It is felt that the group sessions are an excellent research media, at the same time providing a possibility for effecting changes in patients' attitudes towards their paedophilic urges. While clearly we cannot talk about "a cure" of paedophilia we can talk about reduced paedophilic urges and ability to control these urges, and over-all improvement in functioning in the community.

In a simplified way, it can be said that there were different degrees of improvement. All group members appeared to have lost the compulsive nature of their paedophilic urges and to be more or less capable of restraint.

Considering further these limited gains, we had the experience of two patients acting out after imposing adequate self-restraint for over half a year. This was precipitated by stress related to personality dynamics regarding which the patient had gained little insight. The group, with the member present on each occasion, were able to explain the acting-out behavior with reference to significant events in the patient's early life together with activating factors in the development of the group.

In concluding, it is emphasized that the purpose of this paper is not to uncover new insights about paedophilia or group techniques or to depict group psychotherapy as a panacea for curing individual and social ills. It is intended to stimulate some thinking about the possible pragmatic value of this technique, as well as to indicate the need for further extension of the concept that treatment may be a substitute for incarceration, by showing that group treatment of paedophilics is feasible. Does this bring us closer to the idea that legal responsibility should not necessarily be associated with punishment by imprisonment?

Bibliography

ABRAHAMSEN, D. *Who are the Guilty?* New York: Grove Press Inc. 1952.

———. *Report on Study of 102 Sex Offenders at Sing Sing Prison.* Utica: State Hospital Press, 1950.

BAK, R. C. "Aggression and Perversion" in Lorand, S. and Balint, M. edit. *Perversions: Psychodynamics and Therapy.* New York: Random House, 1956.

FOULKES, S. H. and ANTONY, E. J. *Group Psychotherapy.* Toronto: Penguin Books, 1957.

FRIED, E. *The Ego in Love and Sexuality.* New York: Grune & Stratton, 1960.

KARPMAN, B. "A Case of Paedophilia", *Psychoanalyt. Review,* 37:325, 1950.

———. *The Sexual Offender and His Offenses.* New York: 1954.

SLAVSON, S. R. *Analytic Group Psychotherapy.* New York: Columbia University Press, 1950.

Casework Treatment of a Homosexual Acting-Out Adolescent in a Treatment Center

Sidney Wasserman

In this paper I should like to focus on an adolescent whose primary symptom was homosexual acting-out behavior. The main attempt will be toward demonstrating that casework techniques can be applied in such cases, with encouraging results. In addition, the treatment of this adolescent is within the milieu and controlled setting of a residential treatment center.

Because of the severity and deep-rootedness of the problem, the treatment should be done only under close casework supervision and psychiatric consultation. Conferences between the caseworker, casework supervisor and psychiatrist were held to determine the applicability of casework to this boy.

Because of our limited knowledge in the treatment of sexual deviations such as overt homosexual behavior, we caseworkers approach individuals of this symptomatology with understandable reluctance and hesitancy. Certainly the significance and handling of such a symptom in an adult may differ considerably from that of an adolescent. This is specifically so because such behavior in adolescents is frequently part of the normal adolescent conflict.

We know that with the onset of puberty the adolescent is torn asunder. At this stage of life there is an upsurge of libidinal energy which breaks down the rapport that had temporarily resulted between the ego and id (during latency). Impulses (aggressive and sexual), which during latency were brought under balance, at adolescence create an onslaught which overwhelms the ego and superego. The adolescent suddenly indulges in activities which heretofore had been considered taboo and he (or she) begins to resist and rebel against all forms of authority.[1]

The adolescent whose behavior is manifested by the symptom of homosexual acting-out presents a unique problem. It is at this period of life that the

[1] Anna Freud, *The Ego and Mechanisms of Defense*, 158–70.

Reprinted from *Mental Hygiene*, Vol. 44 (January, 1960), pp. 18–29, by permission of the author and the Journal.

adolescent is seeking identifications. Frequently the young person forms an attachment to another of his or her own sex and age which takes on the form of passionate friendship and love. Because of the pressing conflict of instincts, the attachment may be expressed by overt homosexual behavior. It is therefore difficult to determine at what point the adolescent is forming a homosexual, pathological adjustment which may become a fixed pattern and perhaps be irreversible, and what is merely the "temporary" acting-out which will gradually be replaced by stronger inner controls and defenses.

In working with this particular adolescent boy, it became extremely important that the psychiatric recommendations and suggestions be such that they could be implemented by casework technique and the environment. Because the homosexual problem in this case had become a conscious matter to the youngster, the casework treatment needed to be geared to reality and ego support. The amount of ego needed to be determined as well as the degree of reality assessment and inner anxiety. Sublimating outlets for the aggressive and sexual impulses and activities that would be supportive and stimulating to the ego had to be provided by the environment.

This is the case of A, a tall, sandy-haired green-eyed, sharp-featured, bright, handsome young man of 19 with a well-built body of almost classic proportions. He was placed at the treatment center when he had just turned 14 years old. At the time, he appeared older than his age owing to his almost mature-looking build, his outward poise and politeness and his well-dressed appearance.

He is the eldest of three boys and one girl, his brothers being four and a half and six years younger, his sister seven years younger. He comes from a mixed marriage; his father is Jewish, his mother Gentile.

Since the age of five (according to the parents) A presented problems. He lied and stole, and was uncooperative in any routines such as eating, washing, family rules, etc. For periods of time he was enuretic. In general, he was very immature, even infantile, and tended to isolate himself from both peers and adults. Occasionally he was extremely provocative to younger boys and sought out opportunities to beat them up. In spite of superior intelligence, he did poorly in school, failing in several subjects and receiving gratuitous D's in others.

A severe and hostile atmosphere existed between A and his mother, who was controlling, aggressive, ambitious and competitive with him. She had a strong need to mold him into a submissive, polite boy. The marital situation was a poor one in that the husband was most passive and reluctant to assume a more assertive role as husband and father. He worked in a factory and was consistently reminded by his wife of his inadequacy as a successful breadwinner. In all, the role of disciplining the children was left to the mother, which was undoubtedly overwhelming and frustrating for her. A had particular difficulty with his next younger brother C, whom he described as always being favored by his parents, particularly his mother. A seemed almost indifferent to his other siblings.

As his behavior progressively deteriorated, it became of extreme necessity to remove him from the rejecting, tense environment of the home. On his arrival at the treatment center he made a most promising, appealing, initial impression, but underneath the clean-cut, wholesome look was a deeply angry, damaged, frightened, sensitive, unloved child who had, in a large sense, given up on himself.

In brief form this, then, is the history of A and some of the presenting problems. It did not take long to observe that the pleasant, seeming outgoingness of this boy was superficial—and he didn't allow relationships to develop beyond the superficial. During the first six months of casework interviews, A handled all reality discussion by flights into fantasy. He insisted on talking about jet guns, model rockets and "super bathyspheres." He denied any reason for being at the treatment center except difficulty in school and escaped all discussions as to feelings around placement and separation from home.

During this period, it was decided through supervision, psychiatric consultation and a staff planning conference that the caseworker should hold up reality whenever possible. It was felt important that in order to reach this boy the caseworker should talk at some length with him about rockets, jet guns, etc., and of his plans to construct such projects. The psychiatric thinking, at the time, was that such inventions might be a projection of himself and the telling of these inventions to his caseworker might be his way of wanting the worker to be his friend. Talking to A about rockets and guns was seen as a means of establishing a relationship with A and of breaking through his defense of being totally self-reliant, independent and self-sustaining. By so doing, we hoped that A's feelings would then come to the fore and the desire for a relationship would take hold.

At the end of the first six months there was the first discovered incident of A's engaging in homosexual play with one of the younger boys of another cottage. This was then followed by A's first admission that he "hated" the center. His homosexual acting-out with younger boys increased. When confronted with this by cottage personnel and the caseworker, he was vigorous and hostile in his denial. With the emergence of this acting-out came increased overt hostility along with frequent withdrawal and isolation. However, there was a decrease of fantasying, especially with the adults in the cottage, and as he gave up the fantasying, the overt homosexual behavior continued. Throughout the first year of casework contacts, A's defenses seemed to be primarily projection and denial manifested by flights into fantasy. He was also suspicious, and frequently accused others of spying on him.

Throughout that fall he developed a strong, homosexual attachment to a 12-year-old boy. A freely admitted that he "loved" the boy very much, "more than he ever loved" his parents or brother. At this time it became necessary to set up extra controls and supervision for A to protect him as well as the other boys. He was not allowed in the younger boys' cottages (unless accompanied by an adult) and he could not invite them up to his room.

The group contagion of the problem, because of the normal existence near the surface of such feelings in adolescents, can present considerable difficulties in maintaining outer controls and limiting the acting-out whenever possible.

The previous summer, I had worked as a counselor with A in his cottage. By the end of the summer he had told me of his homosexual feeling toward the 12-year-old boy to whom he had such a strong attachment. In the fall when I returned to the center as a caseworker (A's worker was leaving) A was assigned to me.

In his first interviews with me he referred back to the previous summer when he admitted his homosexual problem to me. I accepted what he said but did little or no exploring except to underline that this was a problem and that he seemed worried. Over a series of interviews he admitted his concern more and more and began to bring out that he feared he could not control his acting-out. This admission came after I took a definite stand to the effect that having and talking out these feelings was all right but that acting them out was unacceptable. This became the theme of our contacts for about six months.

During this period, on the basis of the presenting material the psychiatrist pointed out that A could be treated only if he felt more anxiety. This caution was based on the fact that A was acting-out and showing little concern about his behavior. The acting-out interfered with treatment and it would have to be brought under control before he could be reached. The lack of anxiety, it was stressed, made treatment of such overt behavior unpromising. However, it was decided that I continue to try to stir up his anxiety by pointing up his behavior as unacceptable and by telling him that he was expected to learn to control it. The need to hold up reality to him and to support his weak ego whenever possible was stressed by the psychiatrist.

With the implementation of these suggestions and direction, A became noticeably anxious. He began to hide his face, when talking to me, shielding his eyes with his fingers and looking down at his feet. He spoke of how "ashamed" he was and said he would "rather be dead" than talk of his homosexual feelings. I had to assure him that talking was right. When he spoke of his fear that he would not be able to control his feelings, I was reassuring but firm. I let him know these feelings were rough on him but said he was expected to learn to control them; this was what society and the center expected of him. Furthermore, I told him he didn't help himself by acting-out as he involved another person, and this was serious. I underscored my concern for him. His behavior could only bring trouble and hurt and unhappiness. He had been hurt and unhappy enough.

With this kind of empathizing, A slowly started to bring out his negative feelings toward his parents, particularly his mother. He felt his parents did things wrong and said he couldn't stand it when his mother yelled and screamed at him. He recalled the constant arguments in the home and said he was always fighting with his mother, sometimes with his father, and practically all the time with his brother. He brought out that his parents had often sent him away. He recalled that when his brother C was born he was sent to an institution for six weeks. He was mistreated there and, according to him, his parents didn't seem concerned. He felt he had been tricked into coming to our center. He had thought he was coming to a "glamorous" setup and had not been told that this was an institution for emotionally disturbed children. He hated his parents for sending him here. It seemed to him that the only children who came here were those who were "useless and whom nobody wanted." He wondered if "this is really life?"

By that winter A began being extremely hostile to me. One day after I had watched a basketball game at the center's gym, in which A participated, he came for his appointment and blasted me. I was "spying" on him. He didn't want me ever to come to the gym again. When he calmed down he was able to admit that seeing me outside the office was upsetting to him. In the next moment he exploded and insisted that I was "not curing" him. The only reason he was coming for his interviews was to let me know how much he hated me.

Concurrent with these expressions of intense hostility toward me, there were rather dramatic changes in the cottage. A became an active participant in group activities and was thoroughly enjoying the participation. He began to stay with the group and to take on a leadership role. The boys showed a real respect for what he had to say and offer, and his ideas started to be "picked up." He appeared to be more genuine and friendly. Most of all, there were fewer and fewer incidents of overt homosexual behavior. Though his sexual behavior was better controlled, he was most stimulated in the evenings when the boys took showers. He would wait until all showers were taken and then he would sneak into the bathroom. If sexually aroused when accidentally seeing a boy in the nude, he would start to yell, have a temper tantrum, and then bring himself under control.

In his casework interviews, his hostility, after about six months, began to lessen. He spoke of feeling better and talked about being in a "neutral zone," of not feeling sexually attracted to either boys or girls. For the first time he recognized that he was being helped, and the tone of his conversations began to change from "I can't be helped" to "I have been helped." At one point he said: "When I came here, I knew right from wrong but it made no difference to me, for I had no past and I didn't feel I had a future. Now I can look at my past a little bit and I feel I have a future. I was like a little boy in a big world and I felt very lost."

After two and a half years of failures and marginal work in school, A completed junior high school with D's and some C's. His greatest difficulties were in concentrating, in his short attention span and in continually daydreaming. However, the first signs of a freer, spontaneous manner appeared and there were the beginnings of achievement.

Late the following summer A was seen by the psychiatrist (in order to verify casework impressions). It was felt that he was showing better control of his sexual problems. He refused to discuss his sexual problems with the psychiatrist, which was indicative of having built up some defenses around this. He related on reality subjects, which suggested increased ego strength. The psychiatrist felt I should allow A to talk about his homosexual problem as much as he wanted.

Around that period, A was also re-tested by the psychologist. Two and a half years before his tests revealed a picture of a boy functioning intellectually in the bright normal range (full scale IQ 114). Now his intellectual level was in the superior range (full scale IQ 121). Two and a half years before he resisted any forms of self-expression by maintaining a rigid guard and refusing to expose himself. Now he was still somewhat restricted but he showed a remarkable change in the freedom and spontaneity of expression within the bounds he had set up. He showed a neurotic type of adjustment but more social awareness.

For the next six months, however, A seldom spoke of his homosexual feelings except to say that from time to time he got aroused and anxious. But he was able to keep these feelings under control. With the internalization of his anxieties and the controlling of his acting-out, he showed more concern about his physical health. Through most of his interviews, he kept telling me that his heart was beating too fast and that he feared it would stop or that "a bubble or something like it" was trying to pass through his heart.

As he spoke of his life, he said: "What can I do? I can't live with my parents. I have no future, my life is ruined, there is no one to love and if I can't love my parents, there's no one." I acknowledged his concern around this and also pointed out how far he had come, particularly in showing better control of his behavior.

With the lessening of verbalization of his homosexual feelings, and the revealing of increased inner controls, the diagnostic picture changed. It had been about a year and a half since the psychiatrist had indicated that A could be treated only if his anxiety became apparent and that this could occur if his acting-out could be brought under control. Now homosexuality was seen as a neurotic symptom; the boy would require intensive treatment. The psychiatrist suggested that I point out to A that he could talk to me about his sexual problems but that he might someday need more intensive help from a psychiatrist. He felt it important that I point out to A those goals and areas in which I could be of help to him. A's signs of increasing ego strengths, according to the psychiatrist, made the prognosis more favorable.

At the same time, in supervisory conferences, it was felt important that I help A to see his parents more realistically, to see that they were confused and unhappy. I might point out that as a child he couldn't help reacting the way he did—with anger. It was important, however, that he realize he had his own life, that though he couldn't change the past he had a responsibility to himself about the future. We needed to help him develop a concept of self and to recognize himself as separate from his parents. The symbiotic and seductive relationship with his mother could be countered by helping him to see his separateness and to see that what he wanted and did with his life rested with him.

In the months that followed I began to initiate and implement the plan that evolved in the shared thinking of the psychiatrist, supervisor, staff conferences and myself. By the following winter A was letting me know that I wasn't "giving him enough." He kept expressing the wish that I were a psychiatrist, and spent much of his appointment time wanting to know why I didn't become a psychiatrist. He informed me that he was still occasionally bothered with his feelings toward boys but said he could control them, adding that sometimes he didn't even have to think about controlling them— "it just comes natural."

Around that time he showed a strong interest in hypnotism and insisted he was going to hypnotize other boys on campus. I was definite in stating that hypnotizing other boys was very serious and was prohibited. A exploded, demanding that I allow him to hypnotize others. He insisted that I never allowed him to do anything. A few days later I was visiting in the cottage when A called down from his room and asked me to come up. When I arrived I found him in the process of hypnotizing one of the boys. I asked the boy to leave. After the boy left A raged at me. When he calmed down I pointed out that he was not a physician, that he had done something illegal and dangerous, and that I did not want any harm or hurt to come to him.

In a pathetic, grateful manner, he answered: "When I lived at home my parents never allowed me to grow up or do anything for myself. Sometimes I did things behind their backs and then I felt bad inside. Because you mean so much to me and I don't want to feel bad I won't hypnotize others."

Somehow I felt this incident may have paralleled in A's mind the time his mother walked in on him and his brother C when they were involved in homosexual play. A couple of weeks earlier A had recalled this episode in an interview with me. He remembered how hysterical his mother had become and how she had screamed at him about his "naughtiness and filth." Furthermore, she had protected A's brother and had blamed A entirely for luring his brother into it. This was devastating to A.

Early the following spring A began talking to me of his feelings toward girls. He said he was no longer so shy, and found it easier to talk to girls. He began to hang around the girls' cottage and started to learn to dance. Several girls showed a pronounced willingness to get closer to A, but their eagerness frequently made him withdraw from them. He talked then of being more interested "in photography than in girls."

His hostility toward his parents lessened. He was seeing that although his parents were no different, he could get along better with them during his periodic visits home. One day he said: "Before I came here I just existed, but now I am a person." He asked me if I knew the "turning point" in his life and then added: "When you became my caseworker." After telling me this, he became demanding and angry, and maintained that I never did anything for him. He wanted a car. Why wasn't I a psychiatrist? At one point he asserted that I was a "nice guy" but as a caseworker, "you stink." At another point he yelled at me: "Don't you realize that what you say affects my life? You make me sick. Every time we talk I go back to the cottage with an upset stomach and a headache."

That fall, four years after coming to the center, A began speaking of leaving and going home to live, "where school is easier." He started hypnotizing boys from my caseload. In psychiatric consultation I stressed the feeling that A seemed distressed about his feelings toward me and that aside from anger he somehow wanted to run from me. The psychiatrist pointed out that A was expressing homosexuality through hypnotism and was having a homosexual relationship with me by hypnotizing boys of my caseload. He needed to deny my importance to him and I needed to bring it out. It was felt that I should point out to him the defense and denial of his feelings. By so doing I would be supporting his ego and at the same time pointing out that it was one thing to have these feelings and another to act them out.

As I did this with A, he insisted that he was upset because I was a "lousy caseworker" and not important to him. I brought out that it was all right for him to have feelings toward me. If I weren't important to him I couldn't help him. Slowly he mellowed and said: "When I was a homosexual I used to believe I could not be cured. You told me you thought it was too early to tell and you thought I could have feelings toward girls. At first I didn't want to have feelings for girls, but now I have and maybe you can help others the way you helped me."

During that winter A continued to address himself to his leaving the center and to his future. He showed considerable concern about his inability to function on a higher academic school level. He was less sure that he could learn in school "if he wanted to." He became most angry at me whenever I pointed out that he had big ideas about his future but did nothing about them. For example, he spoke of going to college but didn't study. I questioned his desire to go to college. He insisted that he did and pointed to his parents' desires and expectations. When I wondered what his desires and expectations were for himself, he showed confusion and anger. I had, consistently, to separate him from his parents and to emphasize the importance of formulating his own goals according to his own needs and desires.

What was most noticeable in his interviews from about the fourth year of treatment to his discharge after five and a half years of treatment was that his homosexual problem no longer became the focus of our discussions. I slowly moved from defining what was permissible (talking) and what was not (acting-out) toward emphasizing that the past could not be changed but that if he wanted to do something about his present and future, he could.

Significantly, during the spring before discharge, when he was particularly anxious about his feelings of separation from me, he said: "I'm afraid that you see me by my past and as I was." He justified the changes that had come about in him by saying: "Each person has a pattern. If one is raised in a pigsty, he lives like a pig. I grew attached to my mother and I had problems. I didn't know another way of life. Then I came here, and I wanted to change. It wasn't easy. I had to fit into a different pattern, the right one. Lots of times I didn't think I could change, but I did, and now I've learned to do things that give me satisfactions. I don't have to slip back."

The summer before his discharge, A was active in the campus council. He also had but one more semester to go before completing high school. During the summer he went to his home community to be with his parents as his father had been paralyzed. A's mother brought considerable pressure on him to stay home and assume the "father-husband" role. In conflict, A returned to the center and began his final semester of school. He needed assurance that it was all right for him to plan for himself. I recognized that, as unfortunate as his father's illness was, taking on the responsibilities of the household was too much to ask of the boy. A took a part-time sales job in one of the local department stores; he felt he had to help his parents financially.

As he became calmer about the home situation, he once again focused on himself. He spoke of being able to enjoy "little things like people and everyday occurrences." He went on to say that he accepted the fact that he would "never be a very happy person." He spoke of graduation, and of going home to live and then on to college at the start of the fall semester. At one point he said: "Don't worry. I'm not going to stay home indefinitely. I'll go to college and then the service. You see, I am really thinking of myself."

A few months before discharge A addressed himself to the changes that had occurred during his five years of treatment. Interestingly, he summarized: "I knew reality but I didn't want to change. I did it for you, but I think the environment may have been just as important as you. It's like one big experiment all mixed together, and it came out well. One thing I can say for myself: I think I like life, and that feels good."

At the time of his graduation, during one of his last talks with me, he summed up his treatment: "There are three things that happen to a kid in treatment. First, he needs to be removed from the environment that was making him unhappy. Second, he comes to the center where he is shown new ideas and a better world. And third, he has to want to change. But once he is shown that he has problems, he usually wants to change." He ended by telling me that what he wants most in life is "knowledge" and that only by "learning" does he truly think he'll ever be "happy."

It would be deception to conclude that A is now "cured." His problems around aggression, sexuality and inadequacy continue to plague him, but his ego has developed sufficiently that he can cope with these conflicts and use his abilities more adequately. It is very likely that at some later time in life he may very well need additional help and treatment.

At the point of discharge he had become quite the "lady's man" and enjoyed a more comfortable social relationship with girls. As he became involved with a particular girl, however, he frequently or eventually dropped her, feeling he couldn't trust her.

His fear of rejection by girls and women often provoked him to reject them as a means of defense. He sensed the capacity for love and the potential to give within women but feared the possibility of their withholding or withdrawing love. Whether he could work this out sufficiently to make an adequate adjustment remained to be seen.

A came to the treatment center consumed with hate and guilt. At the time, his homosexual acting-out was an attack against all the deprivations and injustices that had been inflicted upon him against his will. Each aggressive sexual act only increased his guilt and created further anxiety, necessitating further acts and additional guilt. Such a socially unacceptable and threatening symptom brought on considerable environmental hostility for him. He was in desperate need of love, acceptance and understanding, and the symptom of homosexuality was, in a way, a defiant act and manner of gaining love at any level, as well as a symbol of his tremendous castration anxiety and the fear of taking on a more masculine role. It is interesting that his homosexual partners were invariably younger boys (about his brother C's age). Because C as well as his brother J and sister B were so favored in A's mother's eyes, is it any wonder that A sought what made the younger ones, particularly C, so loved, adored and acceptable? At the same time, he could hostilely bring his brother and all "younger brothers" down to his level (which, according to A's self-image, was of the lowest form).

Perhaps the greatest all-encompassing quality which prevailed within A was his engulfing feelings of unending loneliness. He was in frantic need of a relationship, one that could accept him and maintain social standards which gave him the control that he lacked and longed for. The giving up of the symptom was more than he bargained for but it became possible because of his desire to please a loved adult. In attempting to control his acting-out, he became noticeably more anxious and conflicted. His ability to suppress and later repress these impulses began to increase, however, and his inner controls became effective in coping with outer stimuli. With the ability to control came stronger feelings of enhanced self-worth and confidence. Having an opportunity to express his anxiety, fears and self-hate not only alleviated the pressures and served cathartic purposes but enabled him to rebuild his defenses and redirect libidinal energy into culturally acceptable modes of behavior.

It is interesting to note that the facing of the homosexual symptom and the conflict concerning it led to discussion of A's basic feelings of hate and retaliation, which he harbored and repressed against his parents (particularly his mother). What emerged was an overwhelmed, damaged child who had identified, to a great degree, with the aggressor (his mother) in order to avoid complete annihilation. He had endowed her with magnitudes of power and even admired this all-powerful force which had become almost a monster in his life.

On the other side of the coin was his anger at his father. He looked to the male of the family for the protection he sought from his mother, but he found an uninvolved, passive, frightened man who allowed the mother to rage and lash out without stopping her. To A, this could only mean further rejection and abandonment.

In treatment, the caseworker played a constant and consistent ego supportive role. At times he became the target which absorbed the anger projected and transferred on to him by the boy, whose hate needed to be released and accepted without retaliation. As A began to see to whom his hostility was directed, he began to bring his parents, especially his mother, down to human-sized proportions. Slowly he learned that women were not necessarily female Cossacks who flung sabres about on helpless boys. This became most evident when he began to relate on a closer level to his female resident cottage counselor, a kindly, intelligent, non-threatening, maternal woman. This was not done without months and even years of testing intermingled with all sorts of accusations and verbal attacks. This was A's pattern in every attempt at relating. He needed to provoke and reject others because he himself feared attack and rejection. Even today he sometimes resorts to this method of relating, when he is limited by someone in authority or when he senses his need for acceptance by a person in authority.

After years of testing the counselor, one day he told her: "Do you know that you and my caseworker are the two most important people in my life?" At that point he endowed the counselor and caseworker with all the qualities that he felt lacking and that he wished for in his own parents.

A crucial point in A's treatment was when he re-enacted through his worker the homosexual acting-out with his brother C, in the presence of his mother, by hypnotizing another boy when it had been defined (by the worker) that this practice was unacceptable. A was needing to re-live and undo this traumatic experience and was attempting to master it by repeating it. According to Thompson:[2] "In the transference, the patient repeats his childhood experiences, both good and bad. It is further observed that not only do people tend to repeat earlier life situations in the transference, but there is a general tendency to repeat life patterns over and over again. Human behavior is dominated even more powerfully by the tendency to repeat former patterns of life than by the pleasure principle." With the re-enactment A was finally able to see that the adult was interested in protecting him and wanted no harm to come to him. The worker did not condemn and reject; instead, he limited A's action because of his concern for A's well-being, which to the boy was an indication of love and acceptance. What followed was a recognition on A's part that he had done things behind his parents' back that made him feel "bad." He now felt that he no longer needed to resort to this pattern of behavior. He was now freer and able to use his resources much more adequately.

At no time in treatment did the caseworker interpret to A the boy's fears of castration, homosexual-masturbatory or incestuous fantasies. Such an interpretation would generally be avoided in casework. (The caseworker may

---

[2] Thompson, Clara, *Psychoanalysis: Evolution and Development.*

not be able to select his clients but he can be selective in how he deals with them. A variety of casework approaches can be applied.) Instead, in this case the worker chose to provide casework that was ego-supportive, on the theory that this had much to offer an adolescent whose primary symptom was homosexual acting-out. It was an educational process in which the worker held up reality to the adolescent and thus supported his weak ego. He pointed out the unacceptable behavior (homosexual acting-out) conveyed the feeling that the adolescent could control this, and supported him when he did show control.

For example, to bring the homosexual acting-out of A under control and to bring his anxiety to the surface, the worker had to take a definite, firm, non-punitive stand based on his concern and his desire to protect. To have been indefinite and non-committal would have been permissive and would almost have encouraged further acting-out. Such an approach might unconsciously have meant to the adolescent that the worker lacked standards, and eventually the acting-out might have become a delinquent interplay with the worker. By being firm and insistent, the worker practically coerced the adolescent into facing his anger, hate and anxiety. A was given confidence through the relationship and as a stronger ego developed, he saw that he could function successfully in many areas (as a campus council participant, athlete, cottage leader, student, salesman, etc.).

Empathy and acceptance were also important. A needed to know and understand that the worker was aware of the existence of his feelings and of how difficult they were to live with. As treatment progressed, the worker focused on the concept of self and supported the healthy part of the boy's personality. He helped him to see his separateness, to evaluate his parents more realistically, and to see, first through the worker's interest and then through other relationships, that he could be liked.

Today A manages to live with his parents and is about to enter his freshman year at a state university. There is every indication that he will be able to make an adequate adjustment to life. However, if his problems again overwhelm him, he has strengthened himself enough to know that help is available to him and he will seek it.

In such a case, psychiatric consultation helps the caseworker to understand the diagnosis, to delineate the problem and the dynamics involved, and to set realistic goals within the framework of casework methods. The casework supervisor guides the worker toward helping the adolescent learn to accept his parents, to emancipate himself from them, to develop a concept of self and to use his potentials. This combination of effort—psychiatric consultation, casework supervision and casework—brought this case to a successful conclusion.

Bibliography

BYCHOWSKI, GUSTAV, "The Ego and the Introjects," *Psycho-Analytic Quarterly*, 24 (1955), 516–26.

————. "The Structure of Homosexual Acting Out," *Psycho-Analytic Quarterly*, 23 (1954), 48–61.

FREUD, ANNA, *The Ego and Mechanisms of Defense*. New York, International Universities Press, 1946.

FREUD, SIGMUND, *Basic Writings of Sigmund Freud*. New York, Random House, 1938.

GRAUER, DAVID, "Homosexuality and the Paranoid Psychoses as Related to the Concept of Narcissism," *Psycho-Analytic Quarterly*, 24 (1955), 516–26.

JOHNSON, ADELAIDE M. and S. A. SZUREK, "The Genesis of Antisocial Acting Out in Children and Adults," *Psycho-Analytic Quarterly*, 21 (1952), 323–43.

KOLB, L. C. and ADELAIDE M. JOHNSON, "Etiology and Therapy of Overt Homosexuality," *Psycho-Analytic Quarterly*, 24 (1955), 506–15.

LEWINSKY, HILDE, "Features from a Case of Homosexuality," *Psycho-Analytic Quarterly*, 21 (1952), 344–54.

LITIN, E. M., M. E. GRIFFIN and ADELAIDE M. JOHNSON, "Parental Influences in Unusual Sexual Behavior in Children," *Psycho-Analytic Quarterly*, 25 (1956), 37–55.

SPERLING, OTTO, "Psychodynamics of Group Perversions," *Psycho-Analytic Quarterly*, 25 (1956), 56–65.

THOMPSON, CLARA M., *Psychoanalysis: Evolution and Development*. New York, Hermitage House, 1950.

Dynamics and Treatment of the Client with Anxiety Hysteria

Lucille N. Austin

The first attempts to utilize psychoanalytic psychology in casework were associated with the neurotic client and his punishing superego. Guilt-relieving techniques, together with permissive and nonjudgmental attitudes on the part of the caseworker, came to be accepted casework procedures. Over the years, there has been a tendency to use these procedures in an all-inclusive way, rather than selectively. It is now clear that treatment techniques must be based on a clear understanding of the relationships between the various parts of the personality structure and of the underlying unconscious conflict, and that these dynamics differ in different clinical entities. In the various neuroses, as well as in psychoses and the character disorders, there are wide variations in ego strength, the severity of the superego, defenses, symptoms, and characteristic modes of behavior.

A re-examination at this time of treatment formulations about casework with the neurotic client, and particularly those with anxiety hysteria, may be useful. Although there are indications that the caseloads of social agencies and clinics are made up increasingly of clients with character disorders and "borderline" problems, it seems likely that a large number of clients are still in the neurotic category. In many instances, these cases are incorrectly diagnosed as character disorders. I believe, too, that anxiety hysteria is sometimes confused with compulsive neurosis, to the disadvantage of persons in the former category.

In this paper, I shall highlight the clinical features of anxiety hysteria and then discuss (1) the nature of the problems that clients in this category present in initial contacts; (2) the typical features of the life history as a diagnostic aid; and (3) some treatment considerations.

Reprinted from *Ego Psychology and Dynamic Casework*, edited by Howard J. Parad and published by the Family Service Association of America, New York, 1958. (Originally published in *Smith College Studies in Social Work*, Vol. 27 [June, 1957], pp. 167–187). Permission granted by the author and the Association.

The Clinical Picture and Dynamics of Anxiety Hysteria

In Freudian terms, the central conflict of all the neuroses is the oedipal conflict.[1] Capacity to love is established but remains partial under the influence of the oedipal ties to the parents and the incomplete resolution of the problem of bisexual identification; the neurotic does not accept masculinity or femininity. His ego is relatively well organized and developed, but it is weakened by the conflict between the demands of the id and the prohibitions of the superego.

Whereas the compulsive neurotic reacts to the oedipal disappointment by regression to the anal level of operation and manifests problems of anger, the anxiety hysteric reacts by regression to the phallic period, that is, the conflict remains focused in the psychosexual sphere. In the phallic stage of development, heterosexual desires are strong but they are blocked by castration anxiety, fear of punishment, and oedipal guilt. Furthermore, the genital organ of the heterosexual love object is refused full recognition, as if recognition of the difference would be an admission of inferiority. The hysteric handles these conflicts by maintaining bisexual identifications, repression of sexual strivings, and the development of symptoms that are, in themselves, abnormal sexual expressions. Sexual feelings are also displaced on nonsexual relationships and situations, so that a kind of pseudo-sexuality pervades all activities and contacts.

The problems of aggression in the hysteric are predominantly those of erotic aggression, rather than the hostile aggression of the pre-oedipal stage. In the child the aggressive and sexual feelings are intertwined when he perceives his parents as a couple; his resulting anger is in response to the oedipal situation and not to frustration because of unmet dependency needs. Some of the aggressive feelings are conscious or preconscious but they may be somatized or turned against the self.

The characteristic defenses in anxiety hysteria are repression, displacement, and projection. The characteristic symptoms are pervasive anxiety; anxiety as a neurotic symptom attached to a special situation that represents the neurotic conflict; conversion symptoms; fear of abandonment, death, and mutilation; phobias; and sexual inhibitions ranging from shyness with the opposite sex to impotence and frigidity.

Hysterical "acting out" is a marked feature. It is a turning from reality to fantasy and is an attempt to induce others to indulge in daydreaming in order to obtain some relief from anxiety and guilt or to evoke punishment. It is sometimes confused with the "acting out" of the character disorders; in anxiety hysterics, the behavior is neurotically determined by the oedipal wishes.

[1] Otto Fenichel, M.D., *The Psychoanalytic Theory of the Neuroses*, W. W. Norton & Co., New York, 1945, Ch. XI; Helene Deutsch, M.D., *Psychoanalysis of the Neuroses*, Hogarth Press, London, 1932, Parts I and II; Sigmund Freud, *Collected Papers*, Vols. I and II, Anglobooks, New York, 1952, *The Problem of Anxiety*, W. W. Norton & Co., New York, 1936.

In character structure the anxiety hysterics are in many respects most nearly "normal." They show vivid dramatic qualities associated with the excitement and exhibitionistic features of the neurosis. They have lovable qualities, based partly on their fear of losing love which makes them eager to please others. They are more capable of love than the ambivalent compulsive, who provokes rejection as a justification for his own hatreds. Hysterics have considerable charm, imagination, feeling, and sensitivity. They may indulge in chaotic behavior but it has a romantic and colorful flavor. The extensive fantasy life, which they develop as a refuge and as a substitute for unpleasant reality, gives color to their conversations and actions. Their child-like qualities, such as seeking protection, are often acceptable and appealing, particularly in women. Their many real strengths and abilities, combined with a defensive capacity to simulate more adequacy than they feel, enables them, more often than not, to conceal their illness.[2]

The degree of character disturbance ranges from the relatively outgoing person to seriously repressed, restricted, disorganized, helpless, and anxiety-ridden individuals whose neurosis is not held in bounds. In some cases, pregenital factors are in the foreground; in others, compulsive features are mixed with hysterical features, making for a more complicated illness and character structure.

Etiologically, anxiety hysteria may be based in part on a constitutional predisposition but is chiefly rooted in sexually stimulating events—in infancy and in the period between three and seven years—which make for sexual precociousness. Childhood sexual seductions, which are reported in the life history as conditioning factors, are kept secret by the hysterical child because of guilt about his complicity and his wish for sexual excitement and pleasure.[3] His attitude is different from that of other children who speak more freely of sexual matters because they were not responsive to seduction. Karl Abraham says, "The tendency to experience sexual traumas repeatedly is a peculiarity which we can often observe in adult hysterics. . . . Hysterics are those interesting people to whom something is always happening. Female hysterics in particular are constantly meeting with adventures. They are molested in the public street, outrageous sexual assaults are made on them, and so forth. It is part of their nature that they must expose themselves to external traumatic influences. . . . People of this kind have a similar tendency in childhood."[4]

In all neurosis there is suffering; the suffering, combined with the

---

[2] Karl Abraham, *Selected Papers on Psychoanalysis*, Hogarth Press, London, 1949, Ch. XXV.

[3] Freud's original formulation concerning sexual trauma and childhood sexual seduction (*Collected Papers*, "The Etiology of Hysteria," Vol. 1, p. 183) was later altered (*Collected Papers*, "Sexuality in the Neuroses, " Vol. 1, pp. 276–277) to take cognizance of "the deceptive memories of hysterics concerning their childhood" and the fact that often a fantasy of seduction was a defense against the memory of sexual activities practiced by the child himself, for example, masturbation.

[4] *Op. cit.*, p. 57.

transference capacity of the hysteric, provides the leverage for both case-work and analytic treatment. It is possible to work with the ego if the ego feels pain and the person senses the irrationality of his feelings, symptoms, and behavior.

The case records of these clients show certain clinical features and the influence of the neurosis on their social functioning. I shall now present some material on the nature of the expressed problem and conflict in the initial contact, and the typical features of the life history.

The Nature of the Expressed Problem and Conflict

In the initial contact, these clients show marked anxiety, ranging from an acute anxiety state to diffuse and pervasive anxiety feelings. The anxiety is accompanied by feelings of inadequacy and inferiority, of not being loved and appreciated. In general, the anxiety hysteric, at the point of the intake interview, gives an appearance of being sicker than he is, while the intact paranoid schizophrenic or the person with a character disorder may appear healthier than he is.

The presenting problems may take the form of difficulties in family relationships, in the job situation, or in personal adjustments. They have a special meaning, however, for the anxiety hysteric. The external event which touches off the anxiety can be seen to be overdetermined by the neurosis. To the anxiety hysteric, certain problems with a child, a marital partner, an employer, or the circumstances of a physical illness, loss of work, and so on, signify a psychosexual danger. He anticipates the loss of love and the veri-fication of his unfitness and inadequacy as a whole man or woman, as well as punishment for trying to exercise sexual rights and privileges. The com-pulsive neurotic, in contrast, tends to interpret similar events as attacks or as attempts to weaken his controls and to expose his anger and retaliative wishes. Because the hysteric has not regressed to the same level, his psycho-sexual conflicts are partially conscious or, when repressed, are thinly dis-guised. In the treatment of these cases, the caseworker must endeavor to bring the conscious sexual conflicts into focus, since the client will continue to suppress, project, and displace them until he is given permission to talk openly about them.

The hysteric frequently presents his marital problem in terms of differ-ences and incompatibilities in all areas other than the sexual. He usually states that the other partner is the one at fault.

In a typical case, a wife reported that she had decided to separate from her husband because they could not agree on ways of raising their children and quarreled over money. She said she had lost interest in sex because her husband had hit her several years before. Only later could she talk about her sexual problem and the fact that she had grown up without a father in the home. She had heard only negative talk about men from her mother and she did not know how to relate to them. She said she had not learned to give herself in the sexual relationship and achieved an orgasm only occasionally.

Many times these clients will make a beginning contact and then become frightened. They minimize the problem they came with or make a "flight into health" as a resistance to going on with treatment.

> In one case, after a few interviews the woman said that "it is best to forget it all" and that she was doing all right and did not want to continue. With encouragement from the caseworker, she was able to tell about an early sex experience in which "a man took advantage of her when she was intoxicated." Then she was able to tell that she was the aggressor in current sexual relationships with her husband, and that he was often impotent, which was disturbing to both of them. Later she arranged for him to come to the clinic for help.

Sometimes the conflict is expressed in terms of not being able to choose between a home and a career.

> One woman at the beginning of contact was in an acute anxiety state. She said she had a wonderful home, husband, and baby but that she "felt cooped up and as though there were no escape." She had become pregnant immediately after marriage and had had to give up an art career. In later interviews, she described her childhood and told about her father's violent temper. Her mother had been an unhappy woman who felt tainted by sex and she had conveyed these ideas to her daughter who had always been afraid and inhibited sexually. Going to work, obviously, was safer than being a wife.

Some women express their problems initially in terms of feeling pulled between husband and children or between the husband and mother; others have conflict about managing money and difficulties in homemaking.

A man's problem may be expressed in the work situation. The conflict is often centered on employers who, he thinks, belittle him; or he may have anxiety about not doing his job well or feelings of dissatisfaction because he has not found himself vocationally. This group of cases, because of the clear displacement of the oedipal rivalry with the father onto the employer and the sexualization of the work situation, might well be classified as "work difficulty—oedipal type."

In child guidance cases, where the mother's predominant concern is about the child's sexual interests—whether he is four years old or adolescent —the problem is unmistakably a displacement. If the child is young, the mother is fearful of injury to him and is overanxious about his illness. If he is an adolescent, she fears he will get into sexual difficulties and therefore frowns on heterosexual friendships. These mothers often take pride in being frank about giving sexual information to their children but reveal that they are either inhibited in answering questions or seductive in their overemphasis on sex and in their discussion of inappropriate sexual material. The compulsive mother, on the other hand, usually focuses the problem on her fear of losing control over the child and her fear of his aggression and destructiveness.

In the medical social work setting, hysterical clients tend to be difficult and fractious. They shop from clinic to clinic when the doctors find nothing wrong organically, or when they cannot accept a diagnosis and relax under competent medical care. Illness produces undue anxiety because it is associated with castration fears. Sexual fantasies are clearly evident in their exaggerated fears of body injury. Illness is also viewed as punishment for sexual pleasure.

In the initial interviews, the client is not likely to mention symptoms other than his anxiety. He does not think of phobias, conversions, or obsessive thoughts as symptoms but as idiosyncrasies. He may not mention situations he completely avoids, but in talking about less dangerous situations he may reveal the presence of organized symptoms. Phobias particularly are obscured by the avoidance measures which he uses to keep them quiescent. Incidentally, I think the caseworker's failure to recognize symptoms and to inquire about their presence frequently results in inadequate data for use in psychiatric consultations. The absence of data may be a contributing factor to the idea that symptom neuroses are not frequently found in agency caseloads.

The client in early contacts often succeeds in leading the caseworker away from the path of building a sound treatment relationship into a morass of transference gratifications. His neurotic need for love and his phobic need for protection form the basis for an initial positive transference. The hysteric often shows marked improvement even after the first interview. His appearance improves and he is vocal in his gratitude for the help he has received. He does this to create a bond between himself and the caseworker as well as to ward off further work on his problem. He usually has extensive fantasy about the worker. Through permissible flattery and conventional interest, he tries to satisfy his curiosity about the worker as a person. As he weaves his fantasies, he is able to blot out any facts that he wishes to ignore. A transference goal—to be loved for himself—supersedes the goal of securing help with his family relationships and other problems of adult adjustment.

The narcissism and the defense of wish-fulfilling daydreams lead the hysteric to an avoidance of hearing anything he might construe as negative criticism; the compulsive, in contrast, provokes criticism and rejection. The hysteric has a tendency to volunteer only a few factual details and has difficulty in giving a consistent, coherent account of what is actually going on at home or at work. He skips from topic to topic. He talks in such a vivid, interesting way that the caseworker may fail to note that he is giving an exaggerated dramatic version of what happened. He demonstrates that he is a talented person, worthy of love and recognition. He produces feelings, not facts. This way of communicating differs from that of the compulsive neurotic. The latter chooses words carefully. He underplays rather than overstates, and gives detailed facts without apparent feeling because the feeling has been isolated.

In many respects, at the points of early contact as well as later, the hysteric seems to be repeating much of his early behavior with his parents. In childhood he had to pretend innocence in order to keep the parent from knowing how much he knew about sexual matters and how intense was his sexual life. An element of scorn for adult stupidity is also reflected as a transference response, especially when he senses naivete and repression in the caseworker.

The client tends to hide his negative transference reactions because he cannot take the chance of losing a source of gratification and protection. When he does venture a negative response, it is often in the form of a childish attempt to let the caseworker know he is displeased. These responses take the form of play in order to disguise the extent and reality of the negative feelings.

As a last comment about problems in the initial contact, I should like to note that it is not always easy to recognize panic anxiety or acute anxiety states. Certain common errors are made in diagnosis. The caseworker may think the client who cries and expresses despair is deeply depressed. The degree of depressed affect, however, cannot be measured by the amount of anxiety expressed. The hysteric's tendency to exaggerate—to believe that all is lost and the worst has happened—must be taken into account; often self-pity, rather than depression, may be the prevailing affect. The phobic client who is seeking protection may give the impression of being a deeply dependent person. Immobilized by his anxiety, he seems uncertain, childlike, and helpless, and, at first, gives no evidence of his real ego strength. In some instances, the caseworker may suspect that the hysteric is psychotic; he may talk wildly and excitedly, show signs of disorganization, and express fears of insanity. A premature referral of such cases to psychiatrists will only add to their fears.

In the early interviews with hysterics, the caseworker should remain calm and supportive, in order to test out the client's ability to regain his ego strengths and to get treatment started with a correct diagnostic appraisal.

The Typical Features of the Life History

The life history is an invaluable tool in the formulation of both the clinical and the psychosocial diagnosis of persons suffering with anxiety hysteria. I therefore will present some typical features of their histories.

Childhood

The life history of these clients usually reveals the presence of the neurosis in childhood. They were fearful, anxious children. They were afraid to go to school, afraid to be away from mother, afraid of the dark, and afraid of new experiences. The women frequently speak of themselves as "good little girls, too afraid to be anything else." They were frequently depressed and moody and took things hard. Toys and pets were overinvested with libidinal significance. The men were often enuretic into latency. They were onlookers rather than participants in sports and frail in physical build, at least in their own comparison to their fathers. They were mothers' boys, not just in the passive, effeminate sense, but "mother's little man" with good manners and consideration for the mother's friends.

Most of these clients remember some of their sexual curiosity, fear, and preoccupation. They express anger because their parents did not give them sexual information. Most of them remember being discovered masturbating and being caught in sexual experimentations with siblings or playmates. These memories are still sources of guilt in adult life because of the parents' excitement, threats of punishment, and predictions of dire consequences. They were sometimes taken to a doctor for examination and were often the object of family concern. The client's memory of such events sometimes goes back only as far as his adolescence, but it seems likely this is a screen memory covering earlier sexual traumas and experiences. These memories, because they are fraught with guilt, are usually brought up only when treatment has advanced and the relationship to the worker is well established.

> One man, who later became mentally ill, had an overdeveloped sense of responsibility for his young sister; he was obsessed with a feeling of responsibility for not having told his family about a man who molested his sister when she was 11 and he an adolescent. He had come downstairs at dusk and saw a man attempting to rape his sister. The man ran and he chased him. He knew him but he did not report the episode to his parents or to the police. Sex was a tabooed subject in his family.

The women often report being molested by men in the neighborhood or by relatives.

> A woman client reported that she remembered being taken to a doctor at the age of 6 or 7. The doctor gave her an internal examination and she felt a sharp pain in the genital region; she had always believed that he pierced her hymen. He had become hostile because her neck was dirty. Her mother had come in at this point and, instead of siding with her, had sided with the doctor. She had always wanted to express her anger at her mother for not protecting her. She thought her husband had always suspected that she had had sex experience previous to marriage. She was not able to tell her mother that she was pregnant with her first child until after three months. She showed shame and anguish in telling these incidents.

Adolescence

The life histories of both men and women in this group show a difficult adolescence. Menstruation for women and pubescence for men were fearful experiences.

> One woman, who began menstruation at 14, had no difficulty at first; she said it proved her womanhood and she used it to get out of housework. Then she began to have little fainting spells, but was not clear about the details. In adulthood she still felt depressed and irritable during menstruation.
> One man reported that he was completely unprepared for changes that took place in his body when he approached puberty. He said that he had grown up in complete ignorance about sex. When nocturnal emission occurred for the first time, he did not know what it was. He had earlier been enuretic and thought the emission was a form of the same thing. As it continued he became worried about his health and at last mentioned it to his father who merely shrugged and said, "Well, now you're a man." A kindly family doctor later explained the matter to him.

In adolescence both sexes were shy, had marked feelings of inferiority, and had problems in dating. The girls had crushes on teachers and older women which were more intense than is usual for girls of their age. They had more girl friends than boy friends, and in several cases the girl dated only the man whom she subsequently married; frequently he was an older man. The husbands are described as gentle and understanding, "not sexual like a lot of men." The woman usually seemed grateful to the man for marrying her, feeling that it was unlikely that anyone could have loved her.

The men also had been slow in dating and showed a tendency to separate sexual and tender feelings in their discussions of premarital sexual relationships. They often married women who were sexually inhibited. Neither the men nor the women were promiscuous before marriage and generally did not have extramarital relationships. Rather they would form strong nonsexual attachments which aroused guilt because of their oedipal nature.

These clients have many fears about the effects of adolescent and childhood masturbation, including the fear of insanity which often continues into adult life. The women clients usually do not talk easily about masturbation, but they give evidence of their guilt.

> One woman, early in contact, mentioned her fear of becoming psychotic. She had marked feelings of inadequacy and had always felt second to her brother, who had graduated from college. When she finished high school, she felt unable to decide anything for herself and had been unable to make her wishes about employment or possible further education known to her parents; she felt hurt because of their lack of interest. Through an aunt she obtained a job as an attendant in a state mental hospital, remaining there for a year and a half. She frequently felt panicky and spent many sleepless nights wondering whether she would become psychotic. She pictured herself as socially awkward and dumb.

Relationship to Family Members in Childhood

From early childhood the relationship of the hysteric to the parent of the same sex is characterized by hostile competition, with an accompanying overdevotion to the parent of the opposite sex. Both sets of feelings are guarded through defenses of rationalization and projection. The woman frequently says, "No one liked my mother," and "Everyone loved my father." Overdevotion to the parent of the same sex is a defense against the underlying hostility. The oedipal feelings toward both parents are usually so apparent that caseworkers have difficulty in believing that the clients themselves are not conscious of them.

It is not uncommon for a woman to recall incidents of being embarrassed in adolescence because her father was mistaken for a boy friend. In some women, the negative feeling toward the father may be high, particularly if he had deserted the mother and the daughter; if he remarried, the daughter feels it as a double insult. In one case, the woman said that her father had beaten her with a strap and connected her fear of being a woman with her father's treatment of her. Yet she vaguely sensed that she loved him.

In general, the complaints of the hysteric against his parents are in terms of their unwillingness for him to get ahead, rather than in terms of neglect, which is the chief complaint of borderline and psychotic clients. The hysterics believe that the parents stood in their way. The women feel that their mothers did not train them in housework, did not prepare them for marriage, and did not give sex information. Basically they feel that the mothers did not want them to marry or to have babies.

In many cases, these clients are still in touch with their parents; after marriage many live near them and often live with them for a period. They usually are psychologically overinvolved with them; they are concerned about the affairs of family members and dependent on them for advice in making decisions. The women clients often resent the closeness to their mothers and what seems like their interference, but are unable to tell them so. They sometimes neglect their own families to help their parents.

Sibling relationships are also marked by extreme rivalry, since a particular brother or sister often plays a role in the oedipal conflict. The hostility toward the sibling may carry over to their relationships with their own children, particularly if one child becomes identified with the hated sibling. In the case of women, we find the birth of a brother often had increased penis envy and made feminine adjustment more difficult. Both men and women show strong reactions to having had a crippled or retarded sibling, since the actual presence of handicap heightened their castration fears.

Health Histories

In all age periods of the hysteric, health problems are prevalent. These clients have a tendency toward illness and they overemphasize ordinary illnesses when they occur; after illness, they usually require a long convalescence. Childbirth is fraught with changes for the women and surgery is frightening for both men and women. They have fear of cancer, tuberculosis, and various infections. They worry about nourishment and their weight; obesity is a frequent problem. Some are afraid to go to doctors and others go at the first sign of any sickness.

School Histories

Learning difficulties are frequent in latency and adolescence as a result of sibling rivalry and of preoccupation with daydreams. Also, learning itself is sexualized since it is connected with childhood sexual curiosity.

Work Histories

The choice of a career is complicated by rivalries with parents and fear of competition. Work that involves exhibitionistic qualities, or that calls attention to the person, is often given up in favor of a more anonymous role; if it is not given up, it is carried with anxiety. Work activities are sexualized for both men and women, with resulting anxiety. When the person does succeed in school or work, he feels that something is wrong. He believes that he does not merit the success, or that he got it by cheating, or that his superiors did not evaluate him correctly. The women are torn between homemaking and having a career, often alternating between them and unable to combine them comfortably.

In the women, the motivation to work is in part a masculine identification, but in part a defense against the fear of the feminine role. Their frequent use of their mothers to care for their children while they work is again related to the oedipal conflict; they feel they must turn the children over to their mothers. At work the women are competitive with men but not in as revengeful a way as the compulsive women.

Friendships

The woman hysteric often maintains a friendship with an older woman, or with a series of them in turn. Such friendship is motivated by an over-compensated hostility to the mother. Others find women friends dull and prefer the company of men; with them they may be provocative and flirtatious or they may establish platonic friendships. The men maintain relationships with other men through clubs or informal groups which have in them a strong, unconscious sexual element. The marital partner in both instances senses a threat to the marriage and is likely to quarrel about the other's friends.

In summary, the life histories of persons with anxiety hysteria have similarities to histories of persons with other disturbances. On the whole, however, persons in this group have a stronger tendency to grow and develop than many other clients. They make achievements in spite of problems, largely because there is less ego impairment. Oedipal problems, rather than pre-oedipal problems, are predominant in childhood, in adolescence, and in adult life. Fear of sex and preoccupation with sexual matters and the separation of sexual and tender feelings are their chief problems.

Treatment Considerations and Techniques

The treatment of this group of clients, in general, should be designed to help them to develop some self-awareness as a means of strengthening the ego. Not all, of course, have the ego strength, the motivation, or the supporting favorable conditions to make such treatment possible; these persons, however, can benefit markedly from supportive treatment because of their transference capacity. The choice of treatment should be determined by the evolution of the content and the extent of the neurotic conflict and of the transference and countertransference factors.

I should like to discuss first the countertransference problems that enter into the treatment of these clients.

Caseworkers often have difficulty in engaging clients in a discussion of sexual problems. In a way, caseworkers have acted as if all of sex is unconscious. Since caseworkers do not work with the unconscious, they have tended to rule out sexual matters. Hostility seems to be an easier topic for them to discuss, perhaps because the values of helping clients express anger have been more adequately formulated. The caseworker is able to elicit anger with a feeling of safety and with assurance about the correctness of his technique. Also, the extensive experience in working with the compulsive neurotic has added to the sense of safety; the compulsive's many defenses against complying with the caseworker's suggestion that he vent his anger serve as a protection. The caseworker in these cases may "chip away" at the hostility, but it comes forward so slowly that nothing very frightening happens.

In any event, the hysterical client, with his emotionality and sexuality, appears to frighten the caseworker. The current generation of caseworkers, as well as clients, have been brought up by parents who retained the repressed attitudes of the puritanical previous generation, even though many give lip service to new sexual freedoms. Thus client and worker alike are likely to be wary of talking about sex. In working with the hysteric, whose central neurotic concern is sexuality, the worker should focus on sexual matters relatively early in treatment. If this is not done, the client is likely to terminate contact, using whatever help has been given to relieve his guilt and raise his morale. Such help may be useful but it does not have the value of sustained treatment of the core problem.

When we read case records, we see that the hysteric is seldom able to take the initiative in talking about sex. He hints at it or reveals it through projection or displacement. For example, a client talking about his work frustrations may also be expressing feelings about his sexual inadequacy. The caseworker, therefore, must feel free to ask about possible sexual problems, thereby giving the client permission to talk about them. In order to do this, the caseworker must overcome any feeling he may have that sex is a fearsome topic or that talking about sex is a form of seduction. If the caseworker fails to give the client an opportunity to explore his disturbing sexual problems, he will represent the disapproving or repressive parent who made the child feel guilty, or sent him elsewhere for help, or forced him to hide his sexual concerns.

Handling the anger of the oedipal conflict is doubtless more frightening to the caseworker than handling the hostile aggression related to the pre-oedipal period. Since there is considerable justification for the anger of the client who was deprived in his earliest years, the caseworker can agree with his feelings and offer sympathy. The "unjustified" anger of the neurotic presents more complex problems, for both client and caseworker. The caseworker's own anger, fear, and guilt associated with the oedipal situation may block his ability to help clients with their feelings. He must be able to tolerate his own anxiety and guilt if he is to help them reduce the power of their punishing superego.

In the treatment of the hysteric, the transference relationship is of particular significance. Freud identified the hysterical neuroses as transference neuroses and therefore amenable to standard psychoanalytic procedures. In casework treatment, the positive transference response of the hysteric places the caseworker in a position of primary influence. Certain standard casework techniques, therefore, may have a deeper influence with this group of clients than with others. I shall discuss briefly four techniques: (1) manipulation, (2) emotional release, (3) clarification, and (4) selected interpretations.

1. Manipulation

By manipulation, I refer to the technique delineated by Dr. Grete Bibring.[5] The main elements are the construction of a corrective relationship and intervention in the client's environment.

The anxious or phobic client needs a calm and consistent relationship because his own anxiety and his tendency to misconstrue or distort relationships keep him stirred up. He needs to be sure he is appreciated and respected, since he feels inferior and unworthy of love. He wants love so badly that frequently in his life he has paid too high a price for it; he often sacrifices his own individuality and his reality wishes. He will tend to repeat this pattern in his relationship with the caseworker. He needs a relationship in which sacrifice is not demanded of him; instead, he needs attention and an opportunity to voice his hopes and aspirations as well as his despairs. The caseworker should construct a relationship that will contain the elements both of a corrective parent and of a kindly person who operates on an objective reality level. A link with the ego, with the person's strivings to improve his functioning, should be established early. The client's problems in functioning must be defined and the goal of working on them must be established and kept in the foreground in order to give a boundary to the treatment and to help in controlling the transference.

The sex of the worker may be an important consideration in casework with these clients, but this question needs further study. In some cases, there has seemed to be a readier response when the female client has been assigned to a male worker.

> In one case, after an initial embarrassed beginning, a woman client clearly responded positively to a nonseductive man worker, who showed respect for her as a wife and mother and who encouraged her to improve her relationships with her husband and son. She believed that her father had belittled her and as a result she had felt unattractive and unable to compete as a woman.

In another case, it is probable that improvement was accelerated when a man client was assigned a fatherly caseworker.

> The client's current work difficulty was tied up with his rivalry with his father. He had repressed his negative feelings about his mother, who died when he was 17, and spoke of her in idealized terms. The worker played the role of an encouraging father who wanted the client to succeed; he made active job suggestions that were in line with the client's capacities. Later he also had contact with the wife so that she could continue to give her husband the support she had given him during the courtship and early days of the marriage. A woman worker might have reactivated a complicated attachment to the mother.

[5] Grete L. Bibring, M.D., "Psychiatric Principles in Casework," *Journal of Social Casework*, Vol. XXX, No. 6 (1949), pp. 230–235.

If a woman worker works with the woman client, careful steps must be taken to prevent the client from regressing into an overdependent attachment. Such an attachment can best be avoided by dealing with her as a grown-up woman and a mother. She should be supported in her maternal role and be helped to work out conflicts that interfere with her assumption of it. Problems of child rearing can be profitably discussed with the expressed aim of helping her be a better mother. If the problem is a marital one, the caseworker should make it clear that the aim is to help her get more out of her marriage. If both partners are involved in a treatment relationship, separate workers may be desirable to avoid recreating the oedipal triangle.

The caseworker's intervention in the management of family life can serve a useful function in both marital and child guidance cases.

> In one case where the mother was reacting to her son's growing independence and attempts to free himself from her seductive love, the worker encouraged the father to become more active in doing things with the boy. The father's participation in the boy's life not only supported his attempts to develop normally, but it also brought relief to the mother by reducing the temptation to cling to her son.

Giving advice about such matters as moving away from irritating parents, changing jobs, and the use of social resources can be psychologically helpful. Changes in their reality situation can give clients protection from phobic stimuli and can reduce the opportunity for neurotic gratifications. When this kind of advice is offered in a reasonable way, these clients do not react with the same degree of negativism that compulsive neurotics do. Often they feel relieved when the caseworker gives advice that is at least partially in line with what they want; usually they can carry out the advice with the sanction and support of the worker. The worker must, of course, guard against becoming an omnipotent figure; the best safeguard is to base his activity on the conflicts and discomforts described by the client.

2. Emotional Release

The skilful use of guilt-relieving techniques usually bring about a cessation of acute anxiety in these clients. Symptoms subside or become less disturbing. Since the neurotic has introjected the ambivalently held love object, the conflict continues in the superego. The conflict can be modified through identification in the course of a meaningful relationship with a parental surrogate. The new introjection can reinforce the positive side of the ambivalence and effectively overpower the negative. A continuing warm relationship gives added strength to the positive identification.

In some cases, the power of the superego may be further reduced by the development of new ego defense mechanisms. Interpretations can be made that result in depersonalization of anger and in new displacements and rationalizations. The client can also gain substantial relief from anxiety if he is permitted to discuss his current sexual inhibitions and fears, as well as his memories of adolescent sexual conflicts that are conscious or near conscious. Being given permission to talk about these problems, in itself, reduces their danger. Guilt can also be reduced if the caseworker universalizes the problem; many of these clients have never discussed sexual matters with their own age group, either as children or adults. The superego of the hysteric is harsh, but it is not as implacable as the superego of the compulsive neurotic.

3. Clarification

Clarification techniques, ranging from simple educational discussions to the more elaborate process of separating reality and fantasy, should be utilized. Specifically, these clients need to be helped to make a new appraisal of their reality situations, which are usually relatively good, and to find new opportunities for enjoyment. Even when reality difficulties are present, they are usually not as serious as the hysteric fears them to be. The caseworker must recognize that these clients have been trying to escape internal danger by attaching the danger to reality situations. In many instances, the caseworker is drawn into handling the reality problems only to find that the client produces a new set. Sometimes, of course, help can be given only with each adverse reality problem as it appears. However, in situations where the ego is relatively strong and the neurosis not too pervasive, the client can develop some degree of awareness as he is helped to see his repetitious behavior patterns and to make connections between childhood feelings and current adaptations.

4. Selected Interpretations

Certain interpretations of the meaning of the client's behavior can be made in the later stages of treatment. These interpretations should be of the kind that will help the client realize the undue influence of his parental ties and his childhood feelings on his current functioning. The connection between his typical ways of reacting to situations and his need to work against his own best interests can be pointed out. Further discussion of his sexual problems and the way they interfere with his personal relationships may also be helpful. Some modification of sexual conflicts often takes place under the influence of the transference. Also, hysterical clients can be helped to gain useful insights through discussion of conscious and preconscious feelings and experiences; the deeper oedipal material, of course, is not touched. By working with the social components of the instinctual conflicts, the caseworker can help the client achieve considerable emotional relief. For example, a man's fear of sexual intercourse is frequently lessened after he has discussed his fear of being dominated by his wife. A discussion of the client's feeling of personal and social inadequacy can carry deeper meanings, thereby relieving the underlying feeling of sexual inadequacy.

> In the case of the mother and son mentioned previously, the mother became angry because the boy's caseworker gave him a present. She expressed her anger to her caseworker after the latter had talked with the father and advised him to associate himself more actively with his son. The worker raised the question of jealousy and the mother, in this interview, admitted her jealous

feelings and then talked freely about her close relationship with the boy during his first four years while her husband was in service. She was able to see that she had subtly kept him from developing a good relationship with his father during the subsequent years. She brought out feelings of anger against her husband for leaving her alone during these years, although realistically she knew he had been drafted and had no choice. She also reported that she never had a satisfactory sexual relationship with her husband. The caseworker suggested that she might be withholding in the sexual relationship to punish her husband for leaving her and that she accused him of being unloving, whereas this might be her problem. The woman in subsequent interviews was able to make connections between her anger at her husband and her childhood feelings of being insufficiently loved by her father, who preferred her brother. Her relationship with her husband improved during contact and she gained considerable self-confidence.

In another situation, a married woman, who had been in treatment for some time, started an interview by saying that she should never have married. Her mother had told her that men cannot be trusted. Her mother, even now, would like to take care of her and her children, and put Mr. R, her husband, out of the house. She made these statements in a half joking way. When the caseworker asked whether the mother knew that things had been going a little better, Mrs. R looked startled and said she had not discussed her affairs with her mother recently. She then asked whether she would be disloyal to her mother if she allowed herself to be more fond of her husband. The caseworker commented on the incongruity of the question, and soon after Mrs. R began to report about the good times she was having with her husband. Later she started to look for a new apartment, stating that they needed a pleasant place to entertain friends. She also said that she knew it is important for a father and children to be close to each other. In one interview she said that, if her husband would be patient with her, she believed their sexual problems could be straightened out.

In general, clients with anxiety hysteria are relatively well on their way to adult adjustment. Their capacity for a certain degree of love for the marital partner and for the children, and their ability to be partially satisfied and successful in work, can be considered positive indications for treatment. The strong urge to equal their parents, even on a neurotic basis, is an active conflict which can be used to motivate treatment. Usually the material about their parental relationships comes early in the contact and is accompanied by deep feeling. Their overinvolvement with their parents and the influence of the parents in their current reality situation make the central problem readily available for discussion. Also, their current relationship problems with the marital partner and the children provide many opportunities for fruitful discussion.

Conclusion

It is important to conclude this discussion of treatment with the note that sometimes casework treatment should be viewed as preliminary to psychoanalytic treatment. Although casework treatment may be the method of choice in some cases, in others such treatment can only bring partial or temporary relief. Psychoanalysis is a specific treatment for this neurosis and offers possibility of resolution of the basic conflict. Analysis should be considered, if possible, for young persons, particularly young adults, who have such pervasive anxiety and symptoms as to prevent marriage, disturb a marriage, or interfere with their successful functioning in parental and work roles. It should also be considered for young women who are fearful of childbirth or have been traumatized by the birth of their first child. It should be considered also for all clients who are symptom ridden to the point where the only avenue to treatment is to work with the unconscious content of the problem.

The adults who suffer from anxiety hysteria are handicapped in the performance of their social and sexual roles. Since this neurosis is rooted in an unresolved oedipal conflict, its resolution often requires analytic treatment. Casework treatment, however, can serve to reduce the client's anxiety and to restrict the influence of the neurosis on the client's functioning. If the caseworker identifies the neurosis and understands it dynamically, he can help many of these persons live satisfying and productive lives.

Short-Term Psychotherapy with the Compulsive Personality and the Obsessive-Compulsive Neurotic

James F. Suess

With the increasing incidence of neurotic personality disorders in the psychiatrist's case load and the general pressure of a shift toward short-term dynamic psychotherapy, the present-day psychotherapist is moved to consider possible techniques to satisfy both of these conditions. This paper offers psychotherapeutic interventions found to be useful with patients manifesting compulsive ego patterns. Even within the limits of short-term therapy many of these people can be moved toward growth and change. To understand the problems that will confront the venturesome therapist, one should first survey some of the ego patterns and personality features that characterize this group of patients.

General Qualitative Ego and Personality Features

These patients have been described as ambivalent, rigid, cold, and retentive and with such little affectual transmission that they have difficulty becoming emotionally involved in a significant interpersonal relationship (1). The compulsive person keeps firm control over his feelings and impulses by maintaining only detached, impersonal relationships. His attitude is that this is the only way to relate to others without arousing in himself feelings of surrender, submission, or exploitation. These fears of becoming emotionally involved and then hurt accompany attitudes of being eventually thwarted or rejected. It is also common for these people to secretly hate themselves and others for what they see through the magnifying lens of their hypertrophied superego. For these reasons the pathologically compulsive person may be very resistant to any form of insightful psychotherapy unless the relationship helps him to establish a feeling tone of openness and trust with his therapist.

This type of patient considers himself to be "logically minded," when actually his thinking is tightly compartmentalized, with much intellectualization but with very little affect. He has been described as follows: "He may

Reprinted from *American Journal of Psychiatry*, Vol. 129 (1972), pp. 270–275. Copyright 1972, the American Psychiatric Association.

know the words, but he doesn't hear the music." The patient accepts the intellectual part of his ego as being desirable, logical, and strong but avoids the affective component of his ego as being illogical and at times frightening. This is clearly seen in the defense of compulsive working or obsessive thinking to avoid recognition of affect and impulses in daily life. Compulsive verbosity also serves the patient a similar defensive purpose in the psychotherapeutic session.

Because of this compartmentalization the patient has extreme difficulty in relating insight from psychotherapy into his daily life, either from one interview to another or even from moment to moment in the same interview. This resistive process greatly impedes movement in treatment. In a similar isolating fashion the patient's solely factual intellectual awareness of his present or past will rarely produce relief from his emotional symptoms. With such a life-style of ambivalence, doubting, isolation, self-control, and rigidity, the patient's ego (conscious or otherwise) will not allow him to wholeheartedly take part in the therapeutic endeavor. Also, his characteristically firm control over his feelings and behavior may bind his spontaneous efforts toward health, in or outside of the therapeutic setting, to the point of helplessness. He becomes immobilized when faced with decisions and resistively uses rationalization and explanation. Nevertheless, in an aggressive manner, the patient may expect quick results from psychotherapy or demand detailed directions from the therapist in a one-two-three fashion.

Mobilizing and Recognizing Feelings

One of the goals of dynamically oriented psychotherapy is to make the unconscious conscious by loosening repression and suppression (2). This applies not only to impulses and information but, more importantly, to their related feelings. It is best brought about at first by helping the patient to become aware of his feelings in the current interview situation. This is of critical importance since it is the current attitudes and reactions to his present life that perpetuate the patient's symptoms and discomfort. In the interview the patient must be helped to recognize his compulsive, defensive behavior, to relax his doubts and control, and to begin to respond adaptively, with realistic feelings and behavior, to the therapist. The goal of the interviewer is to free the patient's feelings, to help him realize himself now.

Characteristically, compulsive patients have frozen their feelings for much of their lives. Because of the rigidity of their compulsive structure it is difficult for them to give up their defenses and change; even though they really long for expression their fear, doubt, and guilt prevent them from trying. Consequently, the interviewer should consistently push for the patient's feelings and not his words, particularly in relation to his current life and especially in the interview situation.

The compulsive patient will experience great difficulty in recognizing any of his feelings, so the therapist must initially help in the identification of feelings from the patient's verbalizations, voice tone, facial expression, body movement, and other nonverbal cues. The kinesics and linguistics, as well as the purely lexical meaning of the patient's communication, should be used in this process. Only by identifying feelings and then experiencing them as not noxious (for whatever reason they might have been thought to be) can the patient be encouraged to begin to respond to them appropriately. Feelings can then become ego syntonic and accepted, instead of ego dystonic and denied.

Assistance to the patient is best offered when the therapist picks up the feeling tone from the patient's verbal and nonverbal behavior and, by feedback, allows the patient to concurrently recognize what his emotions are: "You sound angry." "You look disgusted." "You appear uncomfortable inside." With his sensitive understanding the therapist can often close gaps in the patient's awareness by an empathic recognition of emotions, in the manner well characterized by Theodor Reik (3).

The interviewer should encourage the patient's attention to the present affective meaning of his pathological behavior rather than to its genetic or historical origin. Otherwise, the patient may get lost in historical facts and rumination, which can be used as resistance to the basic goal of releasing feelings and using adaptive responses. For this reason one should avoid theoretical, philosophical, or intellectual discussion of material that the patient will use as a defense.

The patient may prefer to deal with incidental areas of his life so as to avoid inspection and expression of the personal feelings and attitudes that are at the core of his difficulty. This can also be evidenced by the patient who focuses attention on tangential people in his life—neighbors, fellow workers, and friends—in analogy to himself. Frequently the patient will correctly detect the behavior and defenses of others but be blind to the application of this material to himself. Again, by intellectualizing about someone or something else, he avoids the necessity of becoming aware of his own feelings and pathological defenses.

The assumption is often made that the compulsive person's blocked emotions comprise only anger, hostility, or helplessness. This is far from true. Tender, warm, affectionate, and sexual feelings also become constricted in his attempt to ward off other emotions. The important idea, again, is how these affective states are expressed, and if they are not expressed, why not. Only by recognizing and adaptively responding to his feelings can the patient grow and mature emotionally through his experience with the interviewer and later be encouraged to generalize into his daily life by working through the same process with other people (4). The patient can then make a realistic judgment of the nature, intensity, and direction of his feelings and what actually happens when he responds to them.

To appreciate the extent of the emotional constriction in these patients, one need only hear their accounts of being angry once a year, of seldom allowing themselves feelings of self-satisfaction and self-esteem, and of rarely or never responding with tears or tender emotion, which they find embarrassing. The patient should be helped to explore his feelings in such areas as sex, money, control, selfishness, family, authority, and self-esteem. He may defend himself by stating, "Everything there is fine." The therapist, however, should not be too easily dissuaded from further inquiry. After all, the patient is there for relief of a problem, and the intensity of his denial may bear a highly positive correlation to a conflict area.

From the awareness of himself and the world that he gains in the therapeutic interviews, the compulsive patient is surprised when he finds that other people feel happiness or anger, fear or anxiety, and at times disgust or even hate for themselves. Slowly he will learn that others can recognize and accept the appropriate use of their emotions without danger of self-doubt or vulnerability. The patient must then begin to realize that he can also do this, for it is the fear of the omnipotence of his thoughts and the overpowering strength of his feelings that makes the compulsive person cautious. His thinking and feeling control him; they are his master, rather than being used in his service. This is why the patient may at first be detached about his feelings and refer to them as a foreign body or "that thing in me."

The process of helping the compulsive patient become aware of his emotions is quite difficult; it is seldom accomplished by one confrontation with a situation or transference experience. Thus the interviewer must continually help the patient determine what feelings and attitudes he is defending himself against and help him experience them and respond adaptively. Because of the rigidity of his compulsive personality, it is extremely difficult for the patient to give up his defenses and change. Accordingly, confrontation and working through are a tedious process (4).

The Process of the Interviews

It is difficult to establish a trusting relationship with the compulsive patient. However, this must be done before meaningful therapy can begin. Also, the patient's problem of isolation of feeling and action must be recognized and appreciated. This problem is often evidenced by the patient's inability to report feelings and events from past or present experiences. He gives the initial picture of composed order and rigid control in which it is difficult for him to say or express anything, and he may then confront the interviewer with silence. "I don't know anything to talk about." "You'll have to get me started today." "You'll have to pull out of me what you think I need to know."

Rather than be eager to move in, the therapist should wait for the patient to act on his own behalf. This will heighten the emotional level of the interview session and may help the patient to become more aware of his feelings and projected demands. In addition, the more the therapist talks, the less the patient will talk and discover about himself. With a decrease in the quantity of the patient's verbalizations, the therapist may at times be tempted to turn the interview into a question-and-answer period in the belief that this will keep the session moving. However, the amount of actual therapeutic progress thus produced is questionable. Instead, the therapist should put such silent episodes to use by interpreting their defensive nature.

If he does not deem it economically desirable to wait out the patient to the point of self-action, the therapist may feel impelled to become more active and directive. Such a therapist might say, "Do something, even if it doesn't work out; then we will talk about it." One apocryphal therapist, in a more vulgar (but appropriately anal) manner, said, "Shit or get off the pot." In these maneuvers, however, the therapist must recognize that he may be preventing his patient from exercising uncritical and reasonably free choice in his life. After all, this is what the patient needs in order to experience self-realization without self-doubt. He needs to feel self-generated activity and feeling without becoming guilt-ridden or overwhelmed with feelings of duty and obligation.

The therapist can often facilitate the therapeutic process by reducing the patient's abnormal guilt from an overpowering superego. This can be done by suggesting to the patient the possibility of less critical self-interpretations, by comparing the patient's attitudes in a given situation with those one might reasonably expect of a person with a more tolerant superego, or by not responding in ways that the patient is willing to project into the therapist's (presumably healthy) superego (5). This technique, which has been called "Letting the patient borrow the therapist's superego," establishes in the patient a self-criticizing identity more compatible with pathologically guilt-free living.

In another way of exercising control the patient may come to the interview prepared, having decided beforehand what to talk about. He may bring a list of topics and questions or articles from magazines, newspapers, or books. Thus compliance with the so-called basic rule (6) of freely reporting current thoughts and feelings is extremely difficult, and the patient uses these maneuvers as a defense against it.

Some patients may be superficial and exhibit a compulsive verbal chaos. The content of such interviews is at times repetitive, tangential, and unfocused, and there is an emphasis on trivia, which may be presented endlessly. The patient should not be encouraged to use the interviews for intellectual discussion or prolonged accounts of obsessive and compulsive symptoms with their isolating potential. The therapist should be prepared to interpret the defensive characteristics of such activity and then focus on the emotion, rather than on the content of what has been isolated. He can do this by encouraging the patient to look into the immediate life situation that provoked feelings of anger, doubt, fear, and so forth, which the patient repressed and defended against with his obsessive or compulsive mechanisms. As in the treatment of patients with other neurotic personality disorders, allowing the obsessive-compulsive patient to talk at length about his symptoms *per se* will interfere with the progress of therapy.

The patient's recognition and acceptance of his feelings do not come about quickly; weeks may pass before he can usefully recognize the presence of a specific feeling or the affective meaning of a particular interpretation. Even then it will not be of maturing value unless he makes it a part of his active life experience. Until this happens the patient may handle such insight by telling the therapist, "I understand all of that, but what difference does it make?"

Intellectualization is often used by the patient as a defense against the emotional understanding of his pathological behavior. For example, the patient may incorporate psychiatric clichés into his speech as if they had emotional significance. At times the patient may engage in self-analysis as an intellectual exercise. "I know I missed my father's friendship and comfort as a boy, and I'm always looking for a pat on the back now." This recognition is usually devoid of any emotional awareness of the actual content and is seldom followed by an active change in the patient's attitude or behavior. The patient uses such pseudo-insight of the past to avoid the deeper recognition and resolution of related feelings in his present life.

Patients will sometimes observe the therapist's office library and ask for journals or books to help in their "self-understanding." The alert therapist will recognize this as another type of defensive maneuver for further intellectual isolation. Should the therapist comply he will find to his dismay that the patient will barrage him with countless details from such readings and therapy will bog down. The therapist should avoid this pitfall regardless of how well-intentioned the patients may sound.

At times the patient may become superficially aware of his subsurface hostility and dependency fears but still respond to this knowledge in a negativistic fashion similar to the mechanism of undoing. That is, the patient in his daily life may consciously do the opposite of what he is aware may be to his advantage, as learned from interpretation or verbalized insight in therapy. This may go on for weeks or months before the patient reports it. Such subtle hostility and passive-aggressiveness can come into focus when the patient shows no manifest clinical improvement and then blames the therapist. Upon exploration it may then become apparent that the patient is not carrying his intellectual and emotional insights into his life situation, where the genuine benefits are experienced.

Some patients search for "the key," "the missing pieces of the jigsaw puzzle," or "something awful in the past" as an easy solution but at the same time as a resistance against examining the present. In others there is an obsessive doubt about making up one's mind as to reality and the appropriate decisions that should follow. The patient alleges that he can see both sides of an issue but can make no choice, or he can see the choices as involving only the extremes of the possibilities available. Some have explained this by saying, "With me it's either black or white; there's no gray." For them only the finite, the discrete, and the obvious offer security and the least chance for error, whereas a responsible, inexact choice or judgment signals the anxiety of doubt or guilty uncertainty.

For this reason compulsive patients are very literal in the meaning and interpretation of verbal communication from the therapist. Therefore, subtleties, nuances, or cleverly worded interpretations should not be used early in the treatment process. For a considerable time these patients can respond only to the rigid distinction and security of black and white. After they are able to discover "gray," the area of flexible judgment, they can affectively see the more subtle manifestation of feeling, behavior, and defense.

As another method of evasion of meaningful material during the interview, the compulsive patient will abruptly change the subject of his discussion. The therapist should first try to determine the possible significance of such a shift, since the temporal relationship in the sequence of the patient's verbalizations often replaces the causal relationship. If this is not readily apparent the interviewer can inquire, "How did we get on this?" "How is this really connected to what you were talking about?"

The interviewer should not introduce situations that can encourage ambivalent or intellectual responses. For example, one should avoid asking such multiple-choice questions as "Whom did you like better, your father or mother?" This can entangle the patient in futile intellectual indecision.

Often the patient will ask the therapist's advice and if the therapist should offer any, he will find that the patient will either pay no attention or will find fault with it. Eric Berne succinctly described this as the game of "Why don't you—yes, but . . ." (7). The therapist must also be cautious about the ever-present risk of fostering dependency. Such dependency encourages the patient to continue his self-doubt and denies him the possibility of the self-satisfaction that comes with active resolution of one's problems.

It is extremely important that the therapist not become caught in such a power struggle or battle of words, meanings, and intellectual opinions with the compulsive patient. This struggle may be manifested by the patient's making issues out of the appointment schedule, fees, office furniture, personnel, and so forth. He may also attempt to extend the length of a session, bring up meaningful material at the end of sessions, and find fault with the meaning of an interpretation or make false generalizations from it. These situations should be recognized for what they are and should be handled carefully; otherwise, they will offer the patient further areas for resistance and provoke him to battle. The therapist is cautioned not to respond to, but rather to interpret, the resistance and repetitious nature of such traps (8).

Therapy is often slowed because the patient expects that the therapist can read his mind or understand something that he has never verbalized. For this reason the interviewer should hear the patient's account of an event in order to avoid any confusion between what the therapist knows factually and what the patient may expect him magically to know. The therapist should not allow the patient to avoid presenting material in the session by referring the therapist to "my records with Dr. A., to whom I've told all this" or to "my chart at B. Hospital." The compulsive patient may also omit some relevant details that he has thought about, assuming that the therapist magically knows about his current or past thoughts. The patient is surprised to learn that the therapist has no such awareness and really cannot perceive the patient's thoughts.

The interviewer is well advised not to jump too quickly to conclusions from minimal data, since this may reinforce the patient's concept of the interviewer's mind-reading ability. The patient tends to expect supernatural things anyway. It is this type of magical belief in the omnipotence of thoughts that allows the patient to equate the feeling or thought of activity with the actual performance of deeds or to feel that the use of words has the same effect as the actual expression of the behavior. The therapist should clarify this magical distortion and encourage the mobilization and activity of related feelings and thoughts in an adaptive way without the dire effects and results that the patient fearfully expects (9).

Conclusions

Since the patient will constantly use the defenses of intellectualization, isolation, ambivalence, and undoing, it is the therapist's task to help him recognize them for what they are and set them aside (10). Only then can the patient perceive the nature of his emotional life and direct his feelings and abilities in a mature fashion toward realistic goals. These changes will not occur quickly with the compulsive patient, who feels more comfortable with rigid structure and order. He resists change since change to him implies dangerous loss of control and frightening uncertainty. The compulsive person would more willingly cling to what he knows and experiences, no matter how unpleasant, than change to something that may be better but is yet unknown and unexperienced.

The therapist best serves the patient by encouraging him to deal with the conscious and unconscious controls and doubts that inhibit his feelings and behavior, as well as to recognize his irrational guilt and unfelt hostility. The therapist should encourage the patient to lay aside his uncertainty and doubt in the recognition of his feelings and behavior toward the therapist and then with other people in his current life. The patient's recognition, acceptance, and use of affect is still one of the guiding principles of effective dynamic psychotherapy.

References

1 FENICHEL O: *The Psychoanalytic Theory of Neurosis.* New York, W. W. Norton & Co, 1945.
2 ALEXANDER F: *Fundamentals of Psychoanalysis.* New York, W. W. Norton & Co, 1948.
3 REIK T: *Listening with the Third Ear.* New York, Farrar, Straus, and Co, 1949.
4 FROMM-REICHMANN F: *Principles of Intensive Psychotherapy.* Chicago, University of Chicago Press, 1950.
5 SYMONDS P M: *Dynamics of Psychotherapy,* vol 2. New York, Grune & Stratton, 1957.
6 FREUD S: "Recommendations for Physicians on the Psycho-analytic Method of Treatment (1912)," in *Collected Papers,* vol 2. Edited by Jones E. New York, Basic Books, 1959, pp 323–333.
7 BERNE E: *Games People Play.* New York, Grove Press, 1964.
8 SULLIVAN H S: *Clinical Studies in Psychiatry.* New York, W. W. Norton & Co, 1956.
9 SALZMAN L: *The Obsessive Personality.* New York, Science House, 1968.
10 REICH W: *Character Analysis.* New York, Noonday Press, 1949.

Treatment of Depressed Women

Eva Y. Deykin, Myrna M. Weissman and Gerald L. Klerman

Introduction

Depressions are among the most common forms of mental illnesses.[2] The exact incidence is difficult to determine as the availability of tranquilizers and effective anti-depressant drugs often facilitates the remission of depressive symptomatology without psychiatric intervention. Although a large proportion of depressed patients are treated by their family physicians, a great many others apply for psychiatric help. Psychiatrists in private practice have estimated that between 60 percent and 75 percent of their private patients are suffering from some degree of depression.[1, 11]

While the term depression has been used to describe reactions as varied as mild emotional malaise to the severe forms of psychotic melancholia, in this paper depression refers to the clinical syndrome consisting of a number of symptoms sometimes appearing singly and sometimes concomitantly in the same patient.[5] These symptoms include painful subjective feelings of hopelessness, despair, helplessness, worthlessness, guilt, and emptiness; somatic symptomatology such as headaches, gastro-intestinal discomfort, chest tightness, difficulty in breathing and urinary problems. Insomnia, fatigue, appetite loss, weepiness, retarded speech, and anxiety are also features of the depressed state.

The onset of depression can be either rapid or gradual. While it is not always possible to delineate the exact time of onset or a precipitating event, the patient and family generally agree that the patient's current state marks a radical departure from his normal mood and behavior. Families of depressed patients will often describe the patients as particularly strong individuals to whom others could turn in times of crisis. In this respect, depressed patients differ from other mental patients, especially schizophrenic patients, who even in periods of remission often lead marginal lives requiring significant societal supports.

Reprinted from *British Journal of Social Work*, Vol. 1 (Fall, 1971), pp. 277–291, by permission of the authors and the Association.

In recent years, there has been an increase in the number of depressed patients seeking psychiatric help. It is not clear whether this rise represents greater incidence, a growing sophistication in the medical and lay population about mental illness, or an increase in the availability of local community mental health centers. Psychiatric facilities are seeing more depressed patients, and frequently at an earlier stage of illness. While there probably always will be patients who postpone psychiatric treatment until their symptomatology becomes intolerable, an increasing proportion of depressed patients now seek help while only mildly or moderately ill and can be treated as outpatients.

This paper discusses casework techniques useful in treating depressed patients whether in the hospital or in outpatient clinics. Our experience is derived mainly from adult females who were generally married. The focus of casework has been on the patient and her immediate family. In spite of the homogeneity of this group, it is suggested that the casework techniques discussed here have relevance to other groups of depressed patients, including males and unmarried females.

Since caseworkers perform different roles depending on the institutional setting, this paper integrates experience of caseworkers in hospitals and outpatient clinics. In the hospital setting, the caseworker's role was a collaborative one with the physician. The primary focus of work was with the patient's family and occasionally participating with the psychiatrist in conjoint family-patient therapy. Conversely, in the outpatient clinic, the caseworker's major function was direct work with patients. In this instance, the caseworker was an important liaison between the patient and psychiatrist who saw the patient only briefly to regulate anti-depressant medication.

Given these differences, the paper addresses itself to the various issues arising from the casework treatment of hospitalized and outpatient depressed women; the role casework plays in their drug treatment; and the influence of casework on their recovery phase and aftercare. The hospitalized patient is permitted to assume the sick role;[13, 7] legal responsibility for the patient is assumed by the hospital and clearly understood by its staff, the patient and her family; and the hospital constitutes a structured environment where life influences on the patient are somewhat controlled and observable. In contrast, the outpatient is not usually viewed as sick but rather as a person with a problem. This perception frequently causes the patient's family to have a lower tolerance for a diminution of the patient's usual social functioning.[16] Since outpatient treatment occupies only one or two hours a week, the patient's major involvement is still with her family thus reducing institutional dependency, and maximizing early re-establishment of normal functioning.

The Hospitalized Depressed Patient

Hospitalization almost always produces major stresses for both the patient and family. The separation of the patient from her family generates difficult role readjustments. Hospital admission initiates a definite change in a depressed person's status and added responsibilities for the family. For the depressed patient, a change in status may be difficult to accept, often it is interpreted as a loss and tends to intensify and confirm a patient's feelings of worthlessness. Many patients relate their self-esteem to performance of their role; thus a patient may wonder whether she is still a good wife and mother when she is unable to perform the usual wifely and motherly functions.

The newly hospitalized depressed patient may experience feelings of abject dejection. Occasionally, these feelings are so intense that the patient may be unable to convey her psychic discomfort and can only make statements like 'you don't know how badly I feel' or 'no one who feels like I do can ever feel well again'. In the face of this overwhelming pessimism it is useful for the caseworker to maintain a stance of strong hope and qualified reassurance. This is justified because most depressive episodes are time limited, and even without treatment the majority of severely depressed patients will improve if they can be prevented from committing suicide during the acute illness.

Working with such pessimistic patients can be extremely trying. The patient's unremitting expressions of hopelessness to the exclusion of any other sentiments appears to provide no basis for a therapeutic alliance. It is not unusual for the caseworker to begin to feel angry and impotent. During the initial phase, support and reassurance should be maintained, but the words carefully measured so as not to challenge the patient into becoming sicker. It is often therapeutic for the caseworker to agree that he cannot fully feel the patient's pain but that he has seen patients who have expressed similar despair and who, in time, have recovered. It is essential for the caseworker to be aware of the possiblity of a negative counter-transference, and to acknowledge to himself his own feelings of anger and frustration. The awareness and control of such feelings is important since anger, frustration, or veiled impatience are frequently perceived by the patient as rejection or loss of control on the part of the caseworker. This situation may be particularly threatening to patients with strong dependency needs and whose own control of impulsivity is shaky.

The Impact of Depression and Hospitalization on the Patient's Family

Even before hospitalization, many families have to deal with the discrepancy between the patient's former functioning and her depressed state. Some relatives are unprepared to cope with role reversals and may themselves become discouraged when their emotional needs are unfulfilled. While this reaction can be seen in any relatives, it is most evident in the patient's spouse. Many husbands develop symptoms similar to those of the patients, especially somatization. In such marriages, it appeared that both the patient and spouse were vying for the position of the 'sick' person. Therefore, in initiating casework with such a family, the caseworker should anticipate this pathologic competition.

A spouse who has had to assume many household responsibilities may feel overwhelmed and resentful. Concentrated attention to the patient without any exploration or acknowledgement of the husband's position tends to entrench the spouse's feelings of burden and to diminish his ability to cope with these responsibilities. A simple acknowledgement of the spouse's difficulties may suffice to support him over this trying period. Occasionally, the caseworker has to initiate intensive work which may include helping the spouse to modify his existing living patterns.

The interruption of the characteristic interpersonal family balance, whether it be between spouse and patient or between the patient and other relatives, may have repercussions on all other family relationships. The nature of the relationship between the patient and her significant relatives, such as children, parents, or siblings, is sometimes expressed in the content of her symptoms. For example, some patients present symptoms which have a decidedly sado-masochistic flavor, and the intensity of these symptoms has been noted to vary according to who is with the patient at any given time. Patients with somatic symptoms frequently suffer an exacerbation of symptoms when they are visited by certain relatives, but verbalize considerably less somatic discomfort when alone with the therapist. Chasin and Semrad[4] have commented on this phenomenon, and make the point that hypochondriacal symptoms serve both to arouse guilt in family members and as safeguards or defenses for the patient against the open expression of hostility. Careful observation of the content of the patient's symptomatology and the method of expressing it may serve as a useful tool in determining where the patient's interpersonal impasses lie.

Casework with the Patient and Family

The patient's difficulty in communicating is a major source of her interpersonal difficulty. The depressed patient may have lost the capacity for the traditional and accepted forms of direct expression, and compensates for this by disguised communication through symptoms or other primitive symbolic and non-verbal communications. As one recovered patient eloquently described it, 'I felt as if I were at the bottom of a well calling for someone to help me, but all that came up were muffled sounds'. Like others who have worked with depressed patients,[17] we have noted that as the patient's capacity for appropriate verbal communication increased, somatic and depressive symptoms diminished.

The caseworker can be of significant help in reinstituting meaningful communication between the patient and family. One possible technique for re-establishing communication is a family conference in which the patient and family members are given the opportunity to express their perceptions of illness, their expectations of treatment and hopes for the future. A family interview held either at admission or shortly thereafter can serve as an important diagnostic aid allowing the caseworker to observe existing interactions and provides a psychologically protected setting in which difficult or painful subjects can be discussed.

It is not surprising to find that communication between patient and family is frequently inadequate and distorted when one considers that hospitalization represents a last resort to a problem for which no solution has been found. A careful history of the events leading to hospitalization will usually reveal unsuccessful adaptive measures undertaken by both patient and family to avoid or postpone hospitalization. Frequently the unsuccessful measures involved the change or modification of role performances among family members.[15] The failure of such role modification usually provokes anger, and a growing impatience with the patient's limited functioning. Maladaptive communication can be viewed as the by-product of the frustration, guilt and anger felt on all sides.

The patient's relatives may indicate their anger covertly, through messages with ambiguous or contradictory meanings. For example, some families try to 'cheer up' the newly admitted patient by pointing to the misfortunes of others. The hidden message is 'maybe you are not trying hard enough'. The caseworker may be able to modify this interaction by pointing out the correct message thereby appealing to the family's conscious wishes for the patient's recovery. It is at times advisable to point out the latent hostility in such a message. Once the family is able to recognize its hostility, it can usually express it in more appropriate ways, thereby lessening the ambiguity of communication.

A more serious form of distorted communication is seen in the families who wish to exclude the patient from information they share with the caseworker. These families characteristically contribute little during a joint interview or will totally agree with the patient, but will then indicate to the caseworker that there are other facts which they will disclose later. Allowing oneself to become a party to this type of secret sharing is not only harmful to the patient but damaging to the success of any casework subsequently undertaken with the relatives.

A variant of this pattern occurs in families who wish to withhold any 'bad news' from the patient on grounds that it would aggravate the patient's condition. The caseworker should encourage families to share all significant happenings—good and bad—pointing out that should the patient react badly, the family and the treatment staff would be available for help. On the other hand, exclusion of the patient from knowledge shared by other family members would deny the patient her adult status and thus increase feelings of alienation and worthlessness. Families who find it particularly difficult to discuss what they feel to be traumatic news can be helped to do so in the setting of a joint family-patient interview. Many families have been surprised to find that the patient was able to tolerate and deal with the news in a mature way.

There is a number of families whose interaction with the patient is so poor, that lying and conscious distortion of reality constitute the dominant form of communication. While this group is not a large group, it does present a serious challenge for casework treatment in that these families' wishes for the patient's recovery are markedly ambivalent. While it is possible to help these families work through their ambivalence towards the patient, occasionally it is necessary to intervene in order to protect the patient by limiting direct visits.

Sometimes the poor communication between family and patient is due not so much to their inability to verbalize but rather to a fear that their shared meaningful interaction would lead to a discussion of intolerable or taboo topics. Foremost among intolerable topics is suicide. A depressed patient who is sick enough to be hospitalized is often also potentially suicidal. For this reason, it is important to establish whether the patient is suicidal and if so, to what degree. A forthright discussion of suicide potential between patient, family and clinician accomplishes several goals. First of all, if a patient has suicidal thoughts it is essential that the hopsital staff responsible for the patient know it, and it is equally important that the family know it, especially when the patient makes weekend visits home. Secondly, in asking about suicide, the clinician conveys to the patient that her distress is taken seriously. This often helps establish a basis for a working relationship. Lastly, the honest exploration of what many people consider a 'taboo' subject opens the way for the discussion of other forbidden topics especially those which have to do with unacceptable hostility and aggression. A striking example of this was one newly admitted patient who when asked about suicidal thoughts, blurted out with obvious relief, 'I've never thought of killing myself, but I have had thoughts of killing my mother'. Contrary to the belief of some families, an exploration of suicidal potential does not 'put ideas into the patient's head'. Patients are usually quite frank in their talk of suicide if given the opportunity, and are grateful for the chance. It is particularly important, for patients who are worried about their impulses, to verbalize suicidal fantasies with someone who takes them seriously. This lessens a burden which otherwise the patient would have to bear alone.

Initiating Casework with the Acutely Depressed Outpatient

In contrast to hospitalization, the patient maintains her status within the family in outpatient treatment. The important consequences of this difference need be stressed. While certain aspects of the patient's roles may have to be performed temporarily by others in the family, the basic family role structure is not as radically altered as in hospitalization. This facilitates the gradual resumption of usual duties as the patient recovers. Patients who can be treated in outpatient settings are either those who have significant familial supports or those who have less florid symptomatology than their hospitalized counterparts.

In the acute phase of illness the performance of ordinary tasks requires considerable effort for the depressed patient. The patient frequently expresses a strong desire to rest and be nurtured. In this situation, casework therapy has three tasks: (1) the reduction of symptoms, (2) the restoration of the patient's social functioning, and (3) the initial exploration of the patient's maladaptive patterns of behavior. Before the caseworker begins to explore the patient's maladaptive patterns of interaction, it is important that at least a small degree of her usual social functioning be restored. Premature exploration can add to the patient's feelings of despair.

Casework during this early phase is predominantly supportive in nature. Specific techniques include advice, encouragement, reassurance, reduction of guilt, ventilation, and direct help to modify the environment.[9] Since many patients deny deeper problems when they are recovered, the casework relationship established during this early phase may provide a more enduring bond for deeper treatment.

Unlike the hospital setting where the patient has twenty-four hour attention, outpatient therapy occupies only a few hours a week. Family demands on the patient continue the rest of the week. Although considered a patient by the treating staff, she is still 'Ma' to a family who is both disturbed and perplexed by her decreased performance and lessened capacity of affection. The family's anger and confusion are reinforced when mother, who used to bake her own bread and noodles, can't make the morning coffee.

Casework undertaken during the acute phase of depression must deal with the patient's conflict and ambivalence over her wish for regression. A supportive relationship should allow the patient to feel accepted despite her symptoms, but not because of them. Although symptoms are acknowledged, focus is not maintained on them and the patient is encouraged to discuss herself and her feelings. A useful technique is to explore the daily demands made on the patient and to reassure her that inability to meet these demands is part of the illness and will improve. This serves to decrease any unrealistic expectation the patient has for herself. At the same time, the few non-expendable household tasks are identified, allowing the patient a degree of mastery.

Many patients treated on an outpatient basis spend long, unstructured days at home alone doing very little. Some of these patients are ashamed to discuss their daily routine as they tend to view inactivity as a personal failing rather than as a symptom of illness. One formerly active and conscientious mother of six, persistently avoided discussing her household routine with the caseworker while remaining preoccupied with her somatic symptoms. Weepiness and constipation, she finally admitted, were less of a disgrace than her inability to take care of her house and children. These discussions were useful in decreasing the patient's feeling of guilt and isolation and served to relieve the immediate distress.

Because of the disorganized nature of many depressed patients' lives, it is both useful and therapeutic for the caseworker to provide a measure of structure. Appointments at regular and specified times once or twice a week help to accomplish this. The importance of keeping these appointments should be emphasized. Appointments on an irregular schedule are not recommended during the early phase. A regular, externally imposed appointment schedule makes it easier for a patient to work out her plans and, conversely, this structure has a beneficial effect on symptoms. Other patients who have an enormous need to please the social worker may attempt to cancel appointments when they cannot report improvement in their clinical condition. The caseworker should interpret setbacks as part of the normal and temporary course of the illness and not necessarily related to a lack of progress.[12] The value of seeing a patient at her best as well as at her worst should be stressed. Missed appointments can be followed up by a telephone call, and at times, a home visit.

Family Involvement in Outpatient Treatment

Despite the obvious need for involvement, the family of an outpatient can more easily exclude itself from treatment. In a hospital setting, the patient's family is almost always involved at intake when it provides historical information and later on when it visits the patient. An outpatient, on the other hand, is frequently self-referred and provides her own history.[14] Often she seeks treatment without her family's knowledge. Unlike the hospitalized patient who may blame the family for placing her in the hospital, the outpatient is more likely to express guilt for her diminished performance within the family unit.

The frequent intricate balance between the depressed patient's clinical symptoms and family relationships has been well documented.[6, 10, 15] Often the successful treatment of a depressed outpatient is dependent upon the quality of the family's involvement. The outpatient living at home is constantly subject to familial pressures and irritants. Unless the patient has made a dramatic suicide gesture or exhibits psychotic symptomatology, the family may not perceive her condition as an illness. Furthermore, as outpatient therapy does not initially produce immediate impact on the patient's life, the family often has difficulty in perceiving the patient as sick. The family's reactions to the patient's decreased activity may range from direct accusations—'Why don't you get off your behind and do something', to more subtle messages such as, 'You ought to get a new job, take a course, get a hobby'. In either case, the family's frustration and misinterpretation of the illness is conveyed. To some families, the hours spent at the clinic may loom as a mystery, an intrusion of privacy and a source of anxiety. One husband suspiciously asked his wife, 'When you go there, do you blame everything on me?'

Although families of outpatients are tolerant, to a degree, of the patient's decrease in performance, diminished communication and hopeless affect, this tolerance is not endless and comes with a price. Daily confrontation with the patient's gloomy affect as well as the necessity for the family to assume some of the caretaking may foment additional conflicts. For example, the daughter of one patient became withdrawn during her mother's depression. It was gradually learned that this child feared that any misbehavior on her part would result in her mother's suicide.

In contrast to families of hospitalized patients who have little or no difficulty in perceiving the patient's symptoms as part of an illness, the families of outpatients frequently are amazed to learn that the clinic staff considers the patient a sick person in need of professional help and medication. This difference in perception has implications for the family's willingness and ability to involve itself therapeutically. Family conferences, as with inpatients, geared to eliciting the family's perception of the illness are generally non-threatening to families who deny problems. In addition, these conferences serve to define the patient's illness as well as to give recognition to the added burden the family bears, thereby laying the groundwork for the family's more intensive involvement.

Casework and Drug Therapy

Pharmacotherapy is widely used in the treatment of depressed patients. While the physician is ultimately responsible for the prescription and regulation of drug therapy, the social worker is often instrumental in the interpretation of this therapy to both patient and family and in dealing with the hopes and anxieties arising out of drug treatment. Here, the caseworker has a dual function: to help the patient and family accept drug therapy and to relate to the physician possible problems which the patient reports in the taking of the medication. It is necessary for the caseworker to have a working knowledge of the action of the drugs used, their effectiveness, common side effects, toxicity, and the time needed before drug effects can be expected.

The function of the caseworker in relation to medication is diminished in the hospital where drugs are dispensed by nurses who remain with the patient until the medication is swallowed. In the hospital, therefore, the caseworker's primary function is to interpret drug treatment to the family, and to allay their anxiety if they do not see immediate improvement. The most common questions and anxieties families express regarding medication refer to the possible addictive qualities of the drugs used, and to whether the patient will have to take the medication for the rest of her life. At times, the hospital social worker may have to stress to the family the patient's need to continue taking medication while on home visits and after hospital discharge, even when improvement is clearly evident. In cases of potentially suicidal patients who go home on visits, the social worker should call the family's attention to the fact that the patient has medication with her and if necessary, ask a responsible relative to dispense the drug. Occasionally, a patient may be taking an anti-depressant drug which can prove toxic if taken in combination with a variety of common foods. If this is the case, the social worker should instruct the family as to the patient's diet while on home visit, and explain the need for the elimination of certain foods.

In an outpatient clinic, the role of the caseworker in pharmacotherapy becomes much more important since medication cannot be as well controlled as in the hospital. In outpatient settings, it is crucial for the caseworker to gain the patient's and family's confidence and co-operation. It is not unusual for the patient and her family to become discouraged by the lack of immediate improvement which is often interpreted by the patient as further proof that she is 'hopeless'. Conversely, when the improvement does occur, the patient and family may assume that the depression has been cured and may have considerable conflict about continuing medication fearing a possible dependency on it.[18] In either case, the social worker is in a strategic position to interpret the expected sequence of events, to reassure the family and patient about the delayed effects of the drug and to encourage them to continue.

Equally important is the social worker's communication with the physician who is prescribing and regulating anti-depressant medication. In treating the outpatient, the social worker is usually the first, and sometimes the only person, to hear of unusual or persistent side effects. In addition, the social worker should mention to the physician any indication of increased alcohol intake, impulsivity, or suicidal ideation in the patient, as a month's supply of medication in the hands of an impulsive, suicidal patient can be disastrous.

The caseworker's professional relationship with the doctor is an important accompaniment of combined drug and casework treatment. The ideal patient says, 'drugs help, but not with everything'. The caseworker helps with the other issues, predominantly in the realm of interpersonal relationships. The area of therapeutic responsibility and eventual credit for patient improvement are well mapped out. More often, one or all of the following problems arise. The patient uses the medication and doctor to reject the caseworker and make him feel unneeded. The patient attributes magical powers to the pill, and may reject looking for antecedents to the depression. As one patient told the caseworker, 'if anyone knew what caused my depression, they'd get the Nobel prize. At least, the pills make me feel better.'

If casework is initiated after the patient has improved symptomatically as a result of medication, the caseworker may feel like 'Johnny-come-lately'. Fantasies of rescuing the patient are thwarted and can lead to a negative counter-transference. In addition, the patient may be angry about being treated by a 'lesser' person, and may wonder if she is less interesting now that she is less symptomatic. Casework becomes interspersed with the patient's memories of 'the good doctor'. The patient, after many months of combined drug and casework therapy, ends by attributing improvement to her medication. Even the most disciplined caseworker will have some negative reactions.

Casework with the Recovering Patient

Most depressed patients, whether they were treated in a hospital or as outpatients, begin to show significant improvement within a few weeks of starting on anti-depressant medication. Feelings of helplessness, hopelessness, insomnia and diminished appetite are relieved although some residual sadness may continue. At this point, the hospitalized patient begins to show more interest in the outside world. She wants to know what her family is doing, how they have coped during her absence and may even begin to resume part of her usual role by giving advice to her family and participating in decision making. At the same point of recovery, the outpatient, on the other hand, may be far more advanced in her social functioning, since she was never removed from her family.

It has been suggested that with symptomatic improvement the patient is more able to focus her energies on understanding the causes of the depression. This is only partially true; two groups of recovering patients can be identified: those who feel so well that they find looking to psychological antecedents runs counter to the positive effects of medication and those who do, in fact, have renewed energy and willingness to explore their intrapsychic and interpersonal difficulties.

The first group tends to lose interest in casework as the depression lifts. When they do attend, they are not interested in engaging in reflective consideration of their problems or in historical material. They continue to dwell on routine daily activities, in order to show how well they are doing. In one study, the common characteristic of this group was found to be their good marital relationships and stable social situations. Family conflicts which existed were covert, and the illness served to gain additional attention from family and friends. Their usual daily functioning, when well, was good, and they had no critical social problems.[15] Often they had some concurrent medical problem, which they believed brought on the depression—e.g. hormone shots or an operation. They tended to over-evaluate the drug effects and the doctor who treated them. They denied the extent of their illness as soon as they recovered. It was difficult for the caseworker not to partake of this denial as the patients seemed to be bubbling over with good health and activities. Casework·with this group was similar to that described for the depressed 'latent conflict patients' of Deykin et al.[6] Such casework was geared to the reestablishment of interest in activities, work, and friends rather than to a confrontation of underlying conflicts. Insight development was minimized, and the reinforcement of successful adaptation, prior to illness, stressed.

The following case is an example of the patient who was uninterested in ongoing casework when recovering:

Mrs. S. was a fifty-year-old married housewife with one previous depression. Her current illness was attributed by her to hormone shots for menopausal symptoms. A number of family stresses in addition to the patient's menopause could have contributed to the precipitants of the depression. Her only son, to whom she was devoted, married. She and her husband had purchased a smaller home and were unsuccessful in the sale of their first home, increasing their financial burdens. The maintenance of two houses stressed the patient's excessively high standards of cleanliness. Her husband had taken a second job to ease their finances, which left her alone at night. Therefore, she had lost the company of her husband and son at the same time. After a six-week course of antidepressants, the patient's acute symptoms subsided. During the acute phase of her illness, her husband gave up his second job and the family rallied around, giving her much help and attention. While the patient was recovering, she quickly resumed her pattern of 'over-doing'. Casework interviews consisted of detailed reports of her activities to show how well she was doing. These included new recipes, square dancing with her husband, etc. She hardly could recall that she had been ill. Casework supported and encouraged her new interests, and the patient, after a few months, could see no need for continuing interviews as she was doing so well. Her obsessive compulsive adjustment remained intact and eight months after her illness she reported feeling better than she ever had.

A second group of patients consists of those who were quite interested in continuing casework once they recovered from the acute illness. They saw casework as an opportunity to understand antecedents and often said, 'Now that I feel better I can really look at what was bothering me'. These patients did not separate the depressive illness from social and personal problems, and feared that failure to relieve these problems could result in relapse. They saw the depression as an inability to cope with accumulating stress. The most common stress was overt marital conflict. The illness served to further alienate the spouse rather than win his sympathy. The frustrated need for object relations and interpersonal gratification because of the poor marriage served to motivate these patients into a therapy situation which would meet some of these basic needs. They were usually eager to engage in long-term casework, and came at least once and often twice per week for interviews. Continued family conferences, in which expectations and conflicts between the patient and other family members could be explored, were found extremely useful. Like the depressed 'overt conflict' patients described by Deykin et al., therapy was geared to helping the patient view family conflict in a more appropriate way and to seek constructive means of dealing with reality.[6] The patient in individual sessions was helped to identify precipitants to depression.

This woman is an example of a patient motivated for continued case-work while recovering from a depressive illness:

Mrs. E. was a forty-year-old housewife with four children and no history of depressive illness. Although her marriage had always been stormy, the family stayed together. About one year prior to her depression, a number of changes resulted in increased family disintegration. Mr. E. lost his job and moved the family over 1,500 miles away. Mr. E. could not find employment, and his wife took a job to support the family. Their two teenagers left school and went to live with relatives. Mrs. E. had an extra-marital affair and contemplated divorce, which was against her religious belief and caused her tremendous guilt. She became acutely depressed when she and the family finally did return home. She felt she had lost self-respect, and withdrew from her family, spending days on end without speaking to them. They in turn, angered by her withdrawal, re-taliated by doing whatever they felt would displease her.

Summary

This paper has focused on some issues in the casework therapy of hos-pitalized and outpatient depressed women. While the clinical symptomatology presented by both groups of patients may be very similar with the exception that outpatients, in general, have less bizarre or florid symptoms, the difference between the twenty-four-hour hospital and the outpatient clinic produces separate kinds of problems and necessitates specific casework techniques.

The hospitalization of a depressed patient causes a certain degree of alienation of the patient from her family. Treatment should address itself to the restoration of appropriate communication and interaction between the patient and family. The cloistered nature of the hospital is useful in that it allows for the direct observation of the methods which families and patients employ to communicate with one another and thus provides the caseworker with valuable information into the nature of interpersonal conflicts as well as to possible ways of resolving them. Joint family-patient interviews, at least in the initial phase of casework, have proved to be valuable both as a diagnostic aid and as a means of fostering open and free communication between patient and family.

In treating an outpatient, on the other hand, one is faced with the problem of preventing the alienation of the patient by the family; of encouraging both the patient and family to allow the patient to maintain her status in the family unit while at the same time relieving her of some of her usual duties. In working with the depressed outpatient one should be cognizant of the patient's need for rest and recovery and at the same time, the family's demand for her continued role performance within the home.

The initial goal of casework should be the restoration of the outpatient's personal and environmental mastery rather than the exploration of maladaptive patterns. Early family involvement in the patient's treatment is particularly important because the family has to assume the burden of caring for a depressed patient at home.

In addition, the caseworker treating outpatients has a special responsibility regarding the patient's drug treatment. This often calls for the early detection and reporting of negative side effects and for dealing with the family's and patient's ambivalent feelings towards the continuation of medication. Potential professional rivalries between caseworker and physician have been identified.

During the recovery phase, the outpatient's motivation for intensive casework is related to the degree of her ongoing social and marital stresses. Those patients with few overt social problems may not be interested in casework as a means of insight into the underlying causes of their depression, but rather choose to use the relationship with the caseworker as a means of support, while they are re-establishing their relationships and activities disrupted by the illness.

Acknowledgments

The authors are indebted to, and would like to express their appreciation to, Ruth Bullock, Effie Geanakoplos and Shirley Jacobson, Clinical Caseworkers, for their discussion of their cases in hospital and outpatient settings.

References

1 AVNET, HELEN H., 1962. *Psychiatric Insurance.* New York: Group Health Insurance.

2 AYD, FRANK J., 1969. *Recognizing the Depressed Patient.* Grune & Stratton (New York).

3 BURKE, LEE, DEYKIN, EVA, JACOBSON, SHIRLEY, and HALEY, SARAH, May 1967. "The Depressed Woman Returns." *Archives of General Psychiatry,* 16.

4 CHASIN, R. M. and SEMRAD, E. V., October 1966. "Interviewing the Depressed Patient." *Hospital and Community Psychiatry,* 17:283–6.

5 COMMER, LEONARD, 1969. *Up from Depression.* Simon & Schuster (New York).

6 DEYKIN, EVA, JACOBSON, SHIRLEY, KLERMAN, GERALD, and SOLOMON, MAIDA, June 1966. "The Empty Nest: Psychosocial Aspects of Conflict Between Depressed Women and Their Grown Children." *American Journal of Psychiatry,* 122, No. 12.

7 FREEMAN, H., LEVINE, S., and REEDER, L. G., 1963. *The Handbook of Medical Sociology.* Prentice-Hall (Englewood Cliffs, New Jersey), pp. 111–19.

8 HANKOFF, L. D., and GALVIN, JOHN W., July 1968. "Psychopharmacological Treatment and Its Implication for Social Work." *Social Work,* 13, No. 3.

9 HOLLIS, FLORENCE, 1966. *Casework: A Psychosocial Therapy.* Columbia University School of Social Work (Random House, New York).

10 JACOBSON, SHIRLEY, and KLERMAN, GERALD L., February 1966. "Interpersonal Dynamical of Hospitalized Depressed Patients' Home Visits." *Journal of Marriage and the Family.*

11 KLINE, N. S., 1964. "The Practical Management of Depression." *Journal of the American Medical Association,* 190: 732–40.

12 LEVIN, SIDNEY, January 1965. "Some Suggestions for Treating the Depressed Patient." *Psychoanalytic Quarterly,* 34:48.

13 PARSONS, T., 1951. *The Social System.* The Free Press of Glencoe, Inc. (New York).

14 PAYKEL, EUGENE S., KLERMAN, GERALD L., and PRUSOFF, BRIGITTE A., 1970. "Treatment Setting and Clinical Depression." *Archives of General Psychiatry,* 22.

15 SPIEGEL, JOHN P., 1957. "The Resolution of Role Conflict Within the Family." *Psychiatry,* 20.

16 SPIEGEL, J., and BELL, N. W., 1959. "The Family of the Psychiatric Patient." in *American Handbook of Psychiatry,* edited by S. Arieti, Vol. 1, pp. 114–49. Basic Books (New York).

17 STUART, RICHARD, April 1967. "Casework Treatment of Depression Viewed as an Interpersonal Disturbance." *Social Work,* 12: No. 2.

18 UHLENHUTH, E. H., LIPMAN, R., and COVI, L., 1969. "Combined Pharmacotherapy and Psychotherapy." *Journal of Nervous and Mental Disease,* 148, No. 1.

19 WALZER, HANK, December 1961. "Casework Treatment of the Depressed Parent." *Social Casework,* 42, No. 10.

Casework Treatment of the Depressed Parent

Hank Walzer

A parent's depression may have a devastating influence on his child's development. The psychiatric literature has amply described the pathological effect on a young child of physical separation from the mother-person.[1] Emotional or psychological separation may produce equally tragic consequences. Such separation may take place when a parent is depressed and his feelings and thoughts are turned inward, away from his child. Casework treatment of the depressed parent should therefore be of particular concern to those working in the interests of children.

In keeping with the current trend toward family-centered treatment, the Children's Division of the Department of Psychiatry at the University of Colorado Medical Center has stressed the need for including both parents in the treatment. The Division's approach to treatment of the child tends to be holistic, that is, to recognize the interdependence between the child's treatment and the treatment of the family as a unit. In this article the focus is on techniques that are useful in modifying parent-child relationships when the parent has the particular problem of depression. Many parents who seek treatment for a child come to the clinic in a helpless, depressed mood that has resulted from the stress created by the child's problems. This is a common condition. The parents considered here, however, are those whose depressive symptoms cause disturbances in the parent-child relationship, although the parents are not so severely incapacitated that they need psychiatric treatment.

---

[1] John Bowlby, *Maternal Care and Mental Health*, World Health Organization Monograph, Geneva, 1951; Anna Freud and Dorothy T. Burlingham, *War and Children*, International Universities Press, Inc., New York, 1943; René A. Spitz, "Hospitalism: An Inquiry into the Genesis of Psychiatric Conditions in Early Childhood," *The Psychoanalytic Study of the Child*, Vol. 1. International Universities Press, Inc., New York, 1945, pp. 53–74.

Reprinted from *Social Casework*, Vol. 42 (December, 1961), pp. 505–512, by permission of the author and the Family Service Association of America.

Definition and Symptoms of Depression

The depressed person suffers from an undue sadness or dejection that impairs his ability to sustain vital relationships with others and severely restricts or inhibits important life activities. A depression may be characterized by feelings of discouragement and downheartedness, or it may be a hopeless despair. Bowlby states that not all depressions are pathological. For example, a bereaved person's grief may be a perfectly natural reaction to a realistic loss. Bowlby defines pathological depression as "depressive illness," or "melancholia."[2] In melancholia, as contrasted with normal grieving or sadness, the real source of the emotion is largely unknown; the person reveals a strong attitude of self-depreciation. When an individual is in this state, his lowered spirits may bear little relation to his external circumstances.

There are several common symptoms of depression. The depressed person makes vague complaints of fatigue that impedes normal functioning regardless of the amount of sleep or rest he obtains. He seems to be saying, "I'm tired of all the demands people make on me; I have nothing left over to give them." He may experience insomnia at night and may awaken early in the morning, or, conversely, he may sleep excessively as a means of escaping from the troubles that beset him. His appetite may diminish, with the result that he loses weight. Shifting somatic complaints may plague him, and changes in behavior such as withdrawal, indifference, or boredom often occur.

Dynamics

The person who is depressed suffered in infancy some disappointment, loss, or abandonment at the hands of the cherished love object or mother-person upon whom he was totally dependent. His resultant rage was repressed for fear of further rejection or retaliation by the mother-person. Abraham has called attention to the reactivation of the early infantile pattern of deprivation brought on by a correspondingly serious loss in the current life of the adult.[3] Freud discovered that the depressed person's self-reproaches are chiefly directed against the image of the lost love object.

> [The self-accusations] fit someone else, some person whom the patient loves, has loved or ought to love. . . . So we get the key to the clinical picture—by perceiving that the self-reproaches are reproaches against a loved object which have been shifted on to the patient's own ego.[4]

---

[2] John Bowlby, "Grief and Mourning in Infancy and Early Childhood," *The Psychoanalytic Study of the Child*, Vol. XVI. International Universities Press, Inc., New York, 1960, pp. 9–53.

[3] Karl Abraham, "The Infantile Prototype of Melancholic Depression," *Selected Papers on Psychoanalysis*, Basic Books, Inc., New York, 1953, pp. 464–70.

[4] Sigmund Freud, "Mourning and Melancholia," *Collected Papers*, Vol. IV, Ernest Jones (ed.), Basic Books, Inc., New York, 1959, p. 158.

The love object has been introjected, and the anger has been turned inward upon the self; depression is the result.

To the depressed parent, the child may unconsciously represent a significant figure from the past. The parent may then attempt to use the child to meet his own unfulfilled need to be mothered. The child who is tied to the parent in this way (partially because of the parent's needs and partially because of his own ambivalence) may actually mother the parent. On the other hand, the parent may also gratify his own need for nurturance by infantilizing the child. Since the child cannot possibly gratify the parent's needs, the parent feels frustrated, and the child becomes to him an ungiving person.

In some instances, the depressed parent perceives in his child the bad part of himself (the introjected figure), and he repeats the mistakes of his own childhood in the current parent-child relationship. One father said, "I see John hating himself for things I hate myself for—not having friends, being easily hurt, and so on. So maybe I hate John when I see him act that way because I hate those things in myself."

Bibring has theorized that the structure of depression is complicated by the ego's awareness of its helplessness. He has likened the ego's feeling of helplessness to the helplessness of the small infant who is totally dependent on the mother-figure for gratification. Therefore, any experience that intensifies feelings of helplessness and loss of self-esteem may create a pre-disposition toward depression.[5] The dynamics of each case vary, however, in accordance with the individual's life experiences. Bibring has cautioned that not all depressions are the result of loss of dependency gratifications in childhood. However, " 'the orally dependent type' . . . represents perhaps the most frequent type of predisposition to depression. . . ."[6]

Bowlby, too, has pointed out that not all depressions have the same dynamics. He has emphasized the importance of separation or loss of close contact with the mother as a major factor in depression. Yet, he has questioned the "assumption that the syndrome . . . can be explained only on the supposition that an essential in its dynamics is aggression directed against the self. Could it not be due simply and solely to the rupture of a key relationship and the consequent intense pain of yearning occurring in a young child?"[7] The problems of the depressed individual cannot be attributed solely to unresolved childhood conflicts, either. The current family situation of the parent may also be a significant factor in the intensification or reduction of depression. The family of a depressed person is often unable to tolerate or cope with the person's failings and inadequacies, and the members may react with bewilderment and anger as their own needs are not met.

---

[5] Edward Bibring, "The Mechanism of Depression," *Affective Disorders*, Phyllis Greenacre (ed.), International Universities Press, Inc., New York, 1953, pp. 13–48.

[6] Bibring, *op. cit.*, p. 36.

[7] John Bowlby, "Grief and Mourning in Infancy and Early Childhood," *The Psychoanalytic Study of the Child*, Vol. XVI, International Universities Press, Inc., New York, 1960. p. 35.

These reactions, in turn, further damage the depressed person's self-esteem. As Gomberg has stated, ". . . the diagnosis of the individual [should] . . . not be in a vacuum but rather within the context of the social and emotional environment in which he lives, adjusts, suffers, fails, or succeeds."[8]

The Child Guidance Problem

When the depressed parent comes to our Child Guidance Clinic, he is usually at the stage where he feels overwhelmed and immobilized by the demands his child is making on him. He often speaks in a helpless, self-condemnatory manner about his inability to cope with the child. An excerpt from an initial interview typifies this kind of problem: "I don't know what to do with him (the patient) anymore. Anything I say is wrong, and nothing I do works. I don't know what to do. Maybe I'm too lenient. I don't know anything anymore. He thinks he's a hot-shot; he's too bossy."

The depressed parent often fears that the child will criticize him or stop loving him unless he meets certain demands. His underlying fear of rejection and his fear of his own hostility provoke the child into attempts to manipulate and control him. Frequently, the child tries to manipulate the parent by confronting him with his own ambivalence. The child will say, "You hate me" or "You don't really love me." The guilt-ridden parent will then continue to appease or mollify the angry, unsatisfied child while suppressing his own growing resentment. The unrelenting guilt, nourished by smoldering resentment, perpetuates the vicious cycle of inconsistent, ambivalent handling of the unfortunate child who then acts in such a manner that his parent's guilt is increased.

Supportive Treatment

Depression may interfere with normal functioning to such a degree that the parent has difficulty in meeting the requirements of his parental role. Even everyday tasks may become a burden. The caseworker, therefore, should give the parent a good deal of support in the form of encouragement, reassurance, and praise. The basic ingredient of supportive treatment is the worker's communication of warm concern, understanding, and acceptance of the parent's problems.

Guidance and Environmental Manipulation

One means of enhancing the parent's self-esteem and decreasing his feeling of helplessness is the worker's judicious use of advice and educative techniques. For example, a guilt-ridden, highly intellectual mother who

---

[8] M. Robert Gomberg, "Trends in Theory and Practice," Part 2 of "Family Diagnosis," *Social Casework*, Volume XXXIX, Nos. 2–3 (1958), pp. 73–74.

suffered from fatigue "could not get things done" because she constantly had to interrupt her housework to be with her preschool child. The worker suggested to the mother that she give the daughter play materials and invite her to play in the same room in which the mother was working. On another occasion, this mother complained about having to put the daughter to sleep in the parents' bed because the child was so frightened. The worker explained why this was not good for the child and proposed that the mother, who was an avid reader, try reading in the daughter's bedroom until the child fell asleep.

The depressed parent often feels burdened by his child's demands. Utilization of various community resources, such as nursery school, summer camp, or youth group, can relieve the parent of certain pressures. At the same time, the child can form constructive relationships with his peers and with adults other than his parents. However, the worker should wait until there has been some lessening of the parent's guilt before he broaches the matter of using community resources. Otherwise, the parent may feel too guilty to permit the child to be separated from him.

The Handling of Anger and Guilt

The technique of universalization, in which the worker generalizes about emotional reactions, is an important method of reducing guilt and lessening the demands of a severe superego. The depressed parent can benefit from the worker's universalization of the emotion of anger. At times the worker's therapeutic questioning of the parent's need to be self-condemnatory can alleviate some of his guilt. The worker must be careful, however, not to create more guilt by offering too much sympathy. One chronically depressed mother remarked helplessly that whenever her son became angry she felt she was an utter failure. She castigated herself because she believed that if she had handled the situation properly he would not have had a temper outburst. The worker questioned whether the child's anger necessarily implied that the mother was a failure, and said that all children become angry at times. The mother then told of an instance in which she had handled the child well, and the worker was able to offer his support. The caseworker must be aware that the depressed person wishes to be punished and expects to be rejected, especially when he receives dependency gratifications. The worker's support of the parent may release a good deal of guilt, which the worker must then deal with. One mother, temporarily adopting the role of the worker, asked anxiously, "How are things going?" When the worker pointed out the mother's concern, she expressed guilt about not having been able to give sympathy to a sick friend. As a result, she felt bad about receiving support from the worker. The mother wondered whether the worker planned to continue seeing her and spoke about past rejections. She wept as she voiced her fear that the worker, too, would let her down.

The Recognition and Ventilation of Hostile Feelings

When a positive relationship with the parent has been established, the worker may be able to help him externalize the hostility that he has turned in upon himself. The worker must be careful not to liberate too much hostility in the beginning phases of treatment because the depressed person has had to employ tortuous defenses against expressions of anger and resentment. The worker should avoid using such terms as "mad" or "angry," and should instead use words like "disappointed," "let down," or "annoyed." Sometimes, through the use of an incident unrelated to the parent's family life and its emotion-laden relationships, the worker can help the parent recognize that he does have angry feelings. For example, Mrs. H, who was active in scouting, felt deeply criticized when she was "bawled out" by a scout leader for "being eight minutes late" to a meeting. Mrs. H remarked that it "was a hell of a thing," and she laughed with relief when the worker jokingly pointed out to her that perhaps she wished the leader to "go to hell."

I have found that the ventilation of anger can be made more acceptable to some depressed parents when I use mildly aggressive words such as "heck," "hell," and "damn," which are used commonly in everyday conversation. Through identification with me, the parent can use these words as vehicles for his own anger. It is important for a caseworker to be able to sense correctly the client's readiness for the use of this technique. Moderate and appropriately timed use of the vernacular can become an integral part of supportive casework treatment when intermingled with encouragement, reassurance, and suggestion.

The afore-mentioned Mrs. H complained of her inability to cope with her nine-year-old daughter, Virginia. Whenever Mrs. H attempted to control the child's behavior, Virginia would say, "Mother, you're angry with me," and would have a temper tantrum immediately. Mrs. H would then experience a typical depressive reaction. She would turn her resentment against herself and helplessly back down in her demands on Virginia, or she would go to bed because of her deep feelings of failure and guilt. At times she infantilized her daughter by combing her hair, brushing her teeth, and bathing her. She felt that Virginia was "so sweet" at these times, and caring for the child gratified her own dependency needs. Virginia, in turn, would wait upon her mother when she was ill and would bring her medicine, tuck in the blankets, caress her forehead, and verbally console her. Mrs. H received very little emotional support from Mr. H, who also suffered from periodic depressions and an undiagnosed gastrointestinal disorder. He often berated his wife for "letting the kids run her," but he undercut her shaky authority by telling their two daughters to "take care of your mother" when he went off on business trips.

During the four years immediately preceding her casework treatment,

Mrs. H had been seen monthly by a neuropsychiatrist for supportive treatment and drug therapy because her feelings of depression had been intensified by a hysterectomy. Deprivation in her early life was a major factor in her continued predisposition to depression. She described her mother as a narcissistic, critical, selfish person who "did not care for us," and her father as a shadowy figure who was chronically ill and who had died when she was 16 years of age. A sister three years her senior had cared for her and had assumed almost full responsibility for her. In order to communicate with her mother, Mrs. H had had to go through a chain of command: her older siblings had acted as intermediaries between her and her mother.

As Mrs. H experienced the acceptability of her feelings within the casework relationship, she was gradually able to bring out her anger toward Virginia. Some of the supportive techniques discussed earlier are illustrated in the following series of excerpts from interviews with Mrs. H:

> Mrs. H proudly related how she has learned to be more consistently firm about the limits she sets for Virginia. She laughingly told of one incident when Virginia accused her of being angry with her. Mrs. H said she had retorted, "You're right, I'm damned angry." During this hour Mrs. H reported that she no longer found it necessary to bathe and dress Virginia, and that the child was doing this herself.
>
> In an interview a few weeks later Mrs. H reported that Virginia had had a temper tantrum over Mrs. H's refusal to write a Thanksgiving story for her as a part of a homework assignment. Mrs. H had handled Virginia's underlying fear about her inability to write the story by exclaiming, "Hell, you can do it if you try." When Mrs. H remained firm, Virginia was able to write her own story. Mrs. H then read it and complimented Virginia on what a fine job she had done. The child responded by saying, "You're the best mother." Mrs. H had some lingering guilt feelings that she had been too "forceful" with Virginia about the story. The worker pointed out how Mrs. H had brought out the best in Virginia, and discussed the meaning of the child's accomplishment in terms of a growth experience.
>
> In the next interview Mrs. H reported humorously that after using a cuss word with Virginia, the child had remarked with surprise in her voice, "Mother, I wouldn't talk that way, but I like it when you're so hardhearted." The worker helped Mrs. H to see how important it was for Virginia to sense her mother's firmness and strength, and how, in turn, this contributed to the child's security.

Experiential or Relationship Therapy

In a subsequent interview, Mrs. H recalled the time when she had been pregnant with Virginia. She revealed a good deal of guilt-laden material concerning her shock and anger at discovering her unwanted pregnancy. Her reliving of this experience during the interview, and her use of the casework relationship to become more constructively assertive with her daughter, indicated that she had moved into a more intensive treatment relationship. This shift in relationship at a certain point during supportive treatment takes place in many instances of casework with depressed parents.

Alexander and French,[9] Austin,[10] Kaplan,[11] Levine,[12] and others have labeled this intensification of the relationship and its therapeutic implications "experiential," "relationship," or "intermediary" therapy. According to these writers the relationship provides a "corrective emotional experience." The client finds that the caseworker does not respond in the manner the client anticipates as a result of his earlier relationships and experiences with parental figures. This new kind of relationship provides a model for healthier identifications. As one parent commented, "Now when things aren't going well, something you have said flashes through my mind." The goal of experiential therapy is the modification of the client's personality pattern, or some change in his behavior which will decrease his vulnerability to external pressures. Restrictive ties to parental figures are loosened by the reliving of certain feelings and attitudes that have caused problems in the past. In some instances "casework carried out with an understanding use of the transference relationship, plus attempts at clarification and at giving the client intellectual awareness of the way the past interferes with present functioning, can result in the development of degrees of insight which will lead to better integrative behavior."[13] In many cases, however, the therapeutic relationship can lead to change even when the client does not have intellectual awareness.

Use of the Casework Relationship

I have found that it is frequently necessary to undertake experiential therapy as part of the casework treatment of the depressed parent if important changes in the parent-child relationship are to occur. Perhaps this is because deprivation in the parent's earliest relationships is a major factor in his depression. Mrs. T, the submissive, depressed mother of Mary, a preschool child, illustrates this point. During Mary's infancy Mrs. T's depression had contributed to the child's affect deprivation, which had caused a serious disturbance in the child's ability to develop meaningful relationships with her parents, teachers, and peers. Mr. T was a coldly intellectual man who was almost completely involved in his own career and who had been unable to give his wife the support she needed when she had been overwhelmed with the care of the child.

> During her interviews, Mrs. T commented on how tiring it was for her to be alone all day with Mary because of her own need for companionship and understanding. Her forced smiles quickly dissolved into tears, and she

[9] Franz Alexander and Thomas Morton French, *Psychoanalytic Therapy*, Ronald Press Co., New York, 1946.

[10] Lucille N. Austin, "Trends in Differential Treatment in Social Casework," *Journal of Social Casework*, Volume XXIX, No. 6 (1948), pp. 203–11.

[11] Alex H. Kaplan, "Psychiatric Syndromes and the Practice of Social Work," *Social Casework*, Volume XXXVII, No. 3 (1956), pp. 107–12.

[12] Maurice Levine, "Principles of Psychiatric Treatment," *Dynamic Psychiatry*, Franz Alexander and Helen Ross (eds.), University of Chicago Press, Chicago, 1952, pp. 307–66.

[13] Kaplan, *op. cit.*, p. 111.

cried frequently. She would do housework all day and then go to bed exhausted. There was a striking parallel in her relationship to her own mother, who also was described as having done housework all day and having been "too busy" to play with Mrs. T when she was a child. Mrs. T cried softly as she spoke of her deep need for "someone who would be a companion to me, who would laugh and talk with me"—someone who would be different from her cold, over-controlling mother who was "so much older."

Following the ventilation of these feelings, Mrs. T reported that she and her daughter had played store together, using a makeshift cardboard box. Mrs. T had saved empty food containers for the "store." Mary would delightedly buy and sell food, and Mrs. T would take on the roles of customer and grocer as her daughter wished. Mrs. T improvised play money to add an extra touch to the game. She also had tea parties, using Mary's toy cups and saucers, but real tea and cookies.

Thus, as Mrs. T relived some of her feelings about past deprivations, she was able gradually to become more spontaneous and giving toward her child. She did not make any insightful statements about how the repetition of past problems had affected the mother-daughter relationship of the present. She did, however, experience this insight emotionally as she became more able to find new ways of relating to her child.

A parent can use the casework relationship to test new ways of behaving in an assertive manner, ways that can then be used in other life situations. For example, in a later interview Mrs. T reported that she felt tense whenever she decided to use her own judgment rather than follow the worker's advice in a particular situation. The worker stressed that it was all right for her to disagree and to make her own decisions. Mrs. T commented, "I'm learning that," and in a subsequent interview reported that she had taken the initiative in organizing a Great Decisions group.

The Recognition of Dependency Needs

The parent may be helped to gain a measure of insight into how his own wishes to be mothered are satisfied through the child. In pointing out to the depressed person that he has passive-dependent wishes, the worker must be tactful and must offer reassurance that these wishes are acceptable. The parent may then become aware of his ambivalence toward significant figures who have in some way frustrated or exploited his dependency needs. For example, in one interview Mrs. H, who was discussed earlier, brought out painful memories of her own mother. This subject had been touched off by a visit from her mother, who was making the rounds of various relatives' homes. Her mother suffered from a heart condition and required Mrs. H's constant attention when she visited her.

Mrs. H related sadly that she had always had the feeling that "when mother is around you should be quiet and keep away." She felt that her mother was more like a grandmother to her because of a wide age difference, but that there had always been a distance between them. Mrs. H wanted to "make it up to Virginia because of the attention I lacked." The worker explained that mothers often give their children the love they themselves have missed and in this way also "make it up to themselves." The worker reminded Mrs. H of the sensation of warmth and closeness she felt when caring for Virginia, and gave examples of her infantilization of the child. Mrs. H reflected on this and realized she had "always looked for a mother." She described how utterly dependent she had become on a close friend, to the extent that the friend had often taken Virginia (as an infant) to the doctor and had even arranged the appointments. On one occasion the doctor had angrily asked both adults, "Who is the mother here?" Later the friend had died of a heart attack. Mrs. H commented significantly that "I was almost relieved after her death because I felt freer." Later in the hour Mrs. H was able to acknowledge her anger toward her mother, who also made many demands on her and yet was unable to assume a maternal role toward her.

Insight into the Sources of Anger and Guilt

Once a parent is encouraged to feel that the emotion of anger can be appropriate or justifiable, the worker may be able to move into the area of feelings of anger and guilt that are inappropriate in the present because they are related to childhood experiences. Kaplan indicates that "a degree of insight" can be achieved with clients who have fairly good ego strength. He succinctly states the following general rule as a guide: "The weaker the ego strength, the more supportive the casework; and conversely, the stronger the ego strength, the more intensive the casework."[14] Therefore, when a depressed parent exhibits relatively good ego strength, it may be possible to uncover the source of his anger in a childhood situation and relate it to current relationships with his child and other family members. In this way, restrictive ties to the past are loosened so that the parent is able to obtain some degree of insight into his relationships with others. The effort to decrease the severity of the superego, however, must go hand in hand with the client's increasing awareness of his anger.

> Mr. R constantly berated himself, thought himself worthless, and felt helpless in dealing with the significant people in his life. His relationship to his mother had been marked by a seductive dependency and overcloseness. He reported that when his mother died he went into a reactive depression lasting a year. Since then, despite his predisposition to depression, he has been able to hold a responsible position as a district manager of a large wholesale store. His wife contributed to Mr. R's need to berate himself. She had a belittling, provocative manner of relating to him, in contrast to a seductive way of relating to an adolescent son. The family seemed to be paired off; Mr. R. had a "special bond" with nine-year-old Teddy (the patient) and an almost maternal overconcern for the child's welfare. Whenever Mr. R returned home from work feeling blue, he would sit up late and watch television with his son on his lap.
>
> In casework treatment Mr. R needed to paint with heavy black-and-white strokes the picture he gave his parents. He described his father as the angry and punitive villain, while his mother was depicted as saintly and all-giving. When the case was taken for psychiatric consultation, it was decided that Mr. R needed to explore his ambivalent feelings toward his mother. Gradually Mr. R was helped to recognize that his feelings of helplessness and his wish

[14] Kaplan, *op. cit.*, p. 112.

to "stay under the covers" were related to his mother's overprotection of him. He recognized that his mother "had taken something away from him" by her over-solicitous behavior. His mother's role in keeping him apart from his father, as well as his guilt in having his mother all to himself, became evident. He brought out his fear that his adolescent son might displace him in his wife's affections much as he had displaced his own father in his mother's affections. Mr. R began to have a clearer picture of his father as a weak person who was, analogously, dependent on Mr. R's mother and a rival of Mr. R for her attentions. Mr. R was helped to clarify his fear of losing his mother: "Mother was my entire world, and I couldn't go against her." His need to feel close and safe made it necessary for him to suppress his anger lest he be rejected or suffer retaliation. The theme of his introjected guilt concerning his mother was, "How could I be angry with you? Look at all you have done for me." In an earlier interview Mr. R had said, "When I married my wife, I was very mean to her and cross all the time." Now he saw that the reason for this behavior was that he had been unconsciously asking himself, "Why is this woman keeping me from Mother?" He recognized his ambivalent tie to his mother, who would say, "Come live with me; you're sick, you need my help." Mr. R summed up his feelings by saying, "That's why I always had to feel I was bad." He then related this material to his fear of making the same mistake with his son, and was able to recognize that he must permit the boy to grow up.

Conclusion

Supportive techniques of encouragement, reassurance, guidance, and utilization of community resources can be helpful in fostering attitudes of self-respect and adequacy in the depressed parent. As the casework relationship is intensified, the "corrective emotional experience" can free the client from certain feelings and attitudes that have caused disturbances in the parent-child relationship. The parent is then enabled to try out newer and healthier modes of relating to the child.

Although casework treatment will vary according to the client's motivation for change and the degree of his ego strength, the worker should not make an "either/or" choice between supportive treatment and insight therapy. Both types of treatment, and the techniques appropriate to each, can be utilized profitably in casework treatment of the depressed parent.

Borderline States

Supportive Casework with Borderline Patients

Richard Stuart

Patients diagnosed as borderline are appearing in increasing numbers in all types of social agencies, yet at the same time "classic" neurotics are showing up in fewer numbers. Is this because our skills at diagnosis have improved? Is this because there is more serious illness? In either case, it is clear that a large number of patients diagnosed as borderline account for a vast proportion of treatment time in family agencies, mental hygiene clinics, public assistance centers, and the like. Therefore, to make the best use of available resources and to insure the highest quality of service, it is essential that the meaning of the diagnosis and the treatment considerations be formulated carefully.

The goal of this paper is to suggest a casework approach to help the patient adapt more successfully to his environment. First we shall describe the behavior and personality characteristics of the borderline patient. Then we shall attempt to describe how specific aspects of the therapeutic situation lend themselves to the use of certain techniques. This will include a description of general treatment considerations and various sources of potential change. Last, we shall suggest a cluster of techniques designed to aid the patient in strengthening his hold upon reality.

The borderline state is a stepchild of diagnostic thinking. There are some who regard it as a point on the classic continuum between neurosis and psychosis while others regard it as a separate entity.[1] In the first view, the borderline state ranges from severe, complex, and somewhat disabling neuroses to relatively benign psychoses. The condition is regarded as somewhat flexible with the patient moving back and forth between neurosis and psychosis in response to inner and outer pressures.

In the second view, the borderline state is seen as a stable, precise

[1] Jerome Weinberger, "Basic Concepts in Diagnosis and Treatment of Borderline States," in Howard J. Parad, ed., *Ego Psychology and Dynamic Casework* (New York: Family Service Association of America, 1958), p. 112.

Reprinted with permission of the author and the National Association of Social Workers, from *Social Work*, Vol. 9, No. 1 (January, 1964), pp. 38–44.

diagnostic entity which, while it resembles both neurosis and psychosis, has features that clearly differentiate it from both. While there may be shifts in the severity of his symptoms, the borderline patient has difficulty in perceiving his environment accurately, but he does not display the kind of thought disorder characteristic of the psychotic. In the literature dealing with the treatment of the borderline state, this second point of view prevails, as it does in this article.[2]

"Borderline state" refers to a group of symptom patterns whose common denominator is a predominance of narcissistic control with a resultant weakness of secondary ego processes.[3] These patients have a sense of inferiority that leads to a deep dependency upon others who appear omnipotent in contrast to their own sense of powerlessness. They have a tendency to retreat from object relationships,[4] although this withdrawal may be temporary and partial.[5]

Because of the chronic tension of aggression and anxiety, these patients have had too much pressure to be able to consolidate ego gains. As stated by Knight:

> Some ego functions have been severely impaired—especially, in most cases, integration, concept formation, judgment, realistic planning and the defending against the eruption into conscious thinking of impulses and their fantasy elaboration. Other ego functions, such as conventional (but superficial) adaptation to the environment and superficial maintenance of object relationships may exhibit varying degrees of in-tactness. And still others, such as memory, calculation, and certain habitual performances may seem unimpaired.[6]

Despite the defects in secondary ego processes, there are no clear breaks with reality in the form of hallucinations, delusions, or ideas of reference. The clinical picture is often dominated by the presence of either strong neurotic symptoms such as hysteria or obsessive-compulsivity, somatic complaints, and/or severe and frequent manic-depressive shifts. These patients thus have a proneness to narcissistic injury with impulsive attempts to re-establish equilibrium characteristic of the infantile personality, showing an unevenness of development and an inadequate self-image.

[2] Adolph Stern, "Psychoanalytic Investigation of and Therapy in the Borderline Group of Neuroses," *Psychoanalytic Quarterly*, Vol. 7, No. 4 (1938); Leo Stone, "The Widening Scope of Indications for Psychoanalysis," *Journal of the American Psychoanalytic Association*, Vol. 2 (1954), p. 582: Robert Knight, "Management and Psychotherapy of the Borderline Schizophrenic Patient," in Robert Knight and Cyrus Friedman, eds., *Psychoanalytic Psychiatry and Psychology*, Vol. 1 (New York: International Universities Press, 1954); Melita Schmideberg, "The Borderline Patient," in Silvano Arietti, ed., *American Handbook of Psychiatry*, Vol. 1 (New York: Basic Books, 1959).

[3] Robert Knight, "Borderline States," in Knight and Friedman, *op. cit.*, p. 102.

[4] Edith Jacobson, "Transference Problems in the Psychoanalytic Treatment of Severely Depressed Patients," *Journal of the American Psychoanalytic Association*, Vol. 2 (1954), p. 597.

[5] Otto Fenichel, *Psychoanalytic Theory of Neurosis* (New York: W. W. Norton & Co., 1945), p. 444.

[6] Robert Knight, "Borderline States," in Knight and Friedman, *op. cit.*, p. 102.

Behavior and Personality Characteristics

Despite the severity of their pathology, borderline patients may present themselves as relatively intact persons because of their use of obsessional defenses, denial, omission, projection, and so forth, or they may fashion eccentric environments which provide at least partial gratification for their extreme needs. The illness may be diagnosed through the use of such "soft signs" as frequent blocking, peculiarities of word usage, obliviousness to implication, or oversuspiciousness. An inappropriateness in feeling tone is also found. Expressions of feeling are sudden in onset and cyclic in patterning. Frequently they are out of proportion to their stated causes with the effect often being "undone" by an inappropriate gesture such as a smile or a peculiar concern with detail. In presenting their initial problems, borderline patients may move off from a specific statement in an associative manner without returning to their starting point. Logical errors are common, particularly in deductive processes, and some self-effacing conclusion is almost inevitable. They often refuse to accept responsibility for their own actions and see themselves as the mere pawns of events. This has the effect of reducing their responsibility for the past and serves as vindication for dependency in the present. There is an ahistoric quality to their view of themselves, with an inability to accept the role of the past in their present lives and a constant hope for, and fear of, the future.[7]

Because of the combined impact of depression and anxiety, borderline patients often feel that they cannot mobilize themselves to meet any new challenge. They receive little reinforcement from others in their personal lives because of their proclivity for surrounding themselves with persons whose resources are as limited as their own, and because their demands are unreasonable or insatiable. Owing to their dissatisfaction, they often withdraw and their frequent complaint is one of loneliness or isolation in a world which is angry partly by projection and partly as a response to their provocation. The view of a hostile, uncaring world leads to counteraggression, which causes conflict because it also coincides with dependence upon others. In the writer's observation such conflicts partly explain the frequently bizarre speech mannerisms and the tic-like patterns which represent the intrusion of strong impulses into object relationships. Consistent with the apparent paradoxes they display, these patients usually have some degree of insight into the nature of their conflicts and can clearly express it, although they lack the appropriate affective understanding which would make their insights useful.

General Treatment Considerations

The treatment of choice with borderline patients is an ego- and reality-oriented supportive method. It is generally agreed that psychoanalytic procedures are contra-indicated. This is because the patient has difficulty in controlling the

[7] Jacobson, *op. cit.*, p. 600.

temporarily induced autism and regression, because the semidelusional form of thinking undermines secondary ego processes, and because the somewhat detached attitude of the analyst (which serves as a catalyst for transference) can reinforce the irrationality in the interpersonal relationships of borderline patients.[8] This point of view prevails even though it has been argued that nonanalytic procedures are directed to the less mature aspects of the patient's personality[9] and that the only means of achieving true personality change is through genetic understanding.[10]

However, it must be pointed out that the ability to use interpretation leading to insight presupposes the ability to make cause-and-effect connections and to use symbolism in thought which serves as a delay function. Borderline patients are notably weak in these areas. They cannot take sufficient distance from interpretations to convert them into useful insight, and tend to react to the interpretation as thought it were censure leading to a narcissistic wound. This reaction may provoke more acting out.

Relationship is a central factor in any supportive treatment, and with borderline patients it is particularly important. Conditioned by life experience to think of themselves as inferior to others in their world who are viewed as having great power, these patients tend to establish an illusory and magical transference which leads to great dependency and is based on fear and aggression.[11] The borderline patient's hypersensitivity and negative expectations lead to a suspiciousness and a tendency to overreact to imagined rejection which makes his assessment of the caseworker's countertransference as crucial an issue as is the transference phenomena in the treatment of neurotics.[12] Indeed one of the chief problems is the worker's ability to handle his own feelings of defensiveness and emotional strain which prolonged exposure to the patient's provocation must produce.[13] The factors that can negatively influence the relationship are the excessive demands of the patient and the reaction of the worker if his approach tends to be inflexible. The most effective rapport is one which reveals the caseworker as a flexible, alive, and reasonable person with definite views when problems of human values are concerned, and with reliable reactions to stress situations. It is only then that the patient can experience the worker directly, with a minimum of fantasy elaboration. The patient can use the worker's sense of calm and assurance to reinforce his own more reasoned approaches. Through

[8] To the author's knowledge only Gregory Zilboorg, "Ambulatory Schizophrenias," *Psychiatry*, Vol. 4, No. 2 (May 1941), advocates the use of unmodified psychoanalysis with borderline patients. Because of the lack of clarity in diagnostic thinking, however, comparison of treatment approaches is hazardous.

[9] Stone, *op. cit.*, p. 588.

[10] Frieda Fromm-Reichman, *Principles of Intensive Psychotherapy* (Chicago: University of Chicago Press, 1950), p. x.

[11] Jacobson, *op. cit.*, p. 599.

[12] Silvano Arietti, "Aspects of Psychoanalytically Oriented Treatment of Schizophrenia," in Samuel C. Scher and Howard R. Davis, eds., *The Outpatient Treatment of Schizophrenia* (New York: Grune and Stratton, 1960), p. 115.

[13] Stone, *op. cit.*, p. 597.

an effective relationship it is possible to begin to overcome the patient's sense of helplessness and confusion and to minimize his defensiveness and hostility. The patient then is able to use the worker as a source of active help in organizing energy to overcome pressing problems and he will be willing to experience the anxiety of some degree of self-examination perhaps for the first time.

Three Sources of Change

The focus of treatment of the borderline patient is to provide experience which will reinforce secondary ego processes in order to help the patient develop more effective means of meeting his own needs in a socially acceptable manner. This requires simultaneous work with both implicit and explicit therapeutic processes.

First of all there is the *formal* aspect of the relationship. The process of establishing a therapeutic relationship has change value in and of itself. Borderline patients almost invariably enter treatment with a subservient attitude which is abruptly changed into an aggressive defensiveness when any pressure is brought to bear on making a closer examination of his life situation. This reaction can be minimized when the worker succeeds in helping his patient to see that the process is exploration and not condemnation. If the relationship can survive this period of testing, the patient is likely to have a fairly strong, positive feeling for the worker because of the all-or-nothing nature of his functioning. This positive relationship is associated "with the repression of overwhelming patterns of experience."[14] Implicit in the treatment situation is a new set of operations which requires that the patient come regularly for interviews in which he sits and talks about his problems, rather than act them out impulsively. He must forego the wish for immediate gratification of instinctual desires in favor of discussing means of obtaining more permanent future rewards. He must set aside his wished-for immediate gratification from the social worker. In so doing, he implicitly accepts some responsibility for his unhappy state and also some responsibility for initiating changes. In addition, he accepts an implicit accountability for his actions as they are to be discussed with the worker. Thus the establishment of a treatment relationship calls into play such ego forces as communication, reasoning, delay of discharge, realistic perception, and control of hostile and sexual impulse both in and outside the casework situation.

In addition to this implicit, formal aspect of the relationship which helps the patient control himself there is a second element of change, namely, implicit *informal* acceptance, which is an important therapeutic factor. Freud suggests that there are three sources of self-regard: the residue of childish narcissism, the residue of experience which serves as a fulfillment of the ego ideal, and gratification of the object libido. The borderline patient intermixes the last two sources superimposed over faulty early development,

---

[14] Sigmund Freud, "On Narcissism," in *Collected Papers*, Vol. 4 (London: Hogarth Press, 1957), pp. 58–59.

and thereby induces a self-fulfilling prophecy of failure. Acceptance of the healthy, adaptive enterprise of the patient contributes to what has been termed a "developmental relationship," at the same time that it helps him contain the aggressive and sexual elements which have complicated his interpersonal relationships in the past.[15] In discussing the therapeutic implication of his observation, Freud remarks that patients will become attached to "whoever possesses an excellence which the ego lacks for the attainment of the ideal," and will seek the "cure by love which he generally prefers to the cure by analysis."[16] This points up a central casework problem: the need to balance acceptance with provocation to change. The worker must avoid the pitfall of unqualified acceptance of the maladaptive behavior of the patient for this can reinforce the patient's feeling of hopelessness. To do this, one must build into the interviews a spirit of examination which emphasizes the areas of potential change.

The third source of change is found in the consequences of the *supportive procedures*. Support is implied when the caseworker probes for new information or offers some form of advice. Furthermore, focusing the patient's concern upon a particular problem not only demonstrates the caseworker's interest, but it also reinforces perception of the problem, which forms the basis for developing a new defense. At the same time it creates a channel for directing activity. This idea is embodied in Freud's comment on various nonanalytic procedures which are "not concerned with the origin, strength and meaning of the morbid symptoms, but instead emphasize something—a suggestion—and expect this to be strong enough to restrain the pathogenic idea from coming to expression."[17] Edward Glover developed this idea further, viewing the process as "neglect combined with counterstimulation."[18] The patient must do or think something new (such as obsessional ceremonial or fixed idea) or take up some counterattraction (anticathexis, cancellation, undoing, expiation). This process is backed by "strong transference authority, which means that . . . by borrowing strength from the suggestionist's superego, a new substitution product is accepted by the patient's ego. The new 'therapeutic symptom construction' has become, for the time, ego-syntonic."[19]

These new defenses are adopted provisionally at first and can only become truly established after considerable time. If treatment is cut short or interrupted, they are likely to evaporate, and this is their chief limitation. When the positive transference is of sufficient duration and intensity, a process of incorporation occurs, consistent with the narcissistic orientation of this group of patients, with the patient taking over the caseworker's suggestions.

[15] Weinberger, *op. cit.* p. 116.

[16] Freud, *op. cit.*, pp. 58–59.

[17] Sigmund Freud, "On Psychotherapy," *Collected Papers*, Vol. 1 (London: Hogarth Press, 1957), p. 254.

[18] Edward Glover, *The Technique of Psychoanalysis* (New York: International Universities Press, 1955), p. 360.

[19] *Ibid.*, p. 361.

The goal of this supportive treatment is the formation of new defenses which will enhance adaptation and improve the means of satisfying narcissistic needs. *No attempt is made to modify the patients' basic personality patterns*, although if changes in adaptation can be maintained long enough, some alterations are likely to occur.[20]

Improving Secondary Ego Processes

The efforts to improve rational control are founded upon techniques that will both control anxiety and reinforce secondary ego processes. Among the techniques are logical discussion, labeling, focusing on the present, anticipatory transference clarification, and reassurance. While borderline patients are not amenable to so-called "insight treatment," this does not preclude their gaining some measure of new self-understanding. The patients are quite capable of understanding the *processes* of their functioning, while at the same time they may be unable to gain insight into the dynamic *structure* of their personalities. The structure includes the underlying infantile conflicts, the process includes the manner in which these conflicts are expressed in daily life. The borderline patient may consistently misrepresent the world around him, may rush immediately into action without delay, may fall to pieces readily or repeat self-destructive rituals: these are process considerations. In work with personality structure the social worker is concerned with *why* certain objects are chosen over others, in work with process with *how* the individual behaves with respect to the objects which he chooses.

A crucial aspect of a psychological process is the cognitive component. George Kelly suggests that "a person's processes are channelized by the ways in which he anticipates events."[21] By this it is meant that all men have a reasoned conception of how the world behaves and how they can best integrate themselves into that world. This conception is partly within awareness and partly not so. It is psychological in nature, and therefore not necessarily logical—with key dimensions ignored or distorted consistent with momentary need. The pattern of its reasoning tends to be somewhat stable and can therefore be studied so that consistent patterns may be brought to light. A knowledge of these patterns can then be used by the individual to guide his own behavior.

Once the casework relationship is established, it is possible to explore with the patient the inner consistencies of his behavior and to elucidate the patterns of recurrent dysfunction. Merely establishing connections between previously isolated instances of behavior "makes the ego relatively stronger

[20] Florence Hollis, "Analysis of Casework Treatment Methods and Their Relation to Personality Change," *Smith College Studies in Social Work*, Vol. 32, No. 2 (February, 1962).

[21] George Kelly, *The Psychology of Personal Constructs*, Vol. 1 (New York: W. W. Norton & Co., 1955), p. 46.

in its relationship to the deeper forces within [the] personality."[22] Establishing these connections in the treatment situation helps to limit the self-punishment which is generally associated with the introspection of borderline patients and establishes a pattern for self-study. Once the patterns have been identified, they may be labeled, and once labeled they become more easily recognized and useful in future planning.[23] The label also helps to distinguish what is and is not included in a pattern. For borderline patients this has the effect of further reducing self-deprecation and it is then possible to see the relatively healthy areas of functioning more clearly.

Labeling is a simple matter once the consistencies are known. When a patient has a tendency to see all authority figures as hostile or to foresee personal failure as an inevitability, labels such as "childish fearfulness" or "dismal-Dan approach" may be applied. The labeling process implies a value judgment that certain behavior does not work, or, in the patients' terms, is "bad." It is thus made ego-alien or encapsulated.[24] This moves it away from what the patient identifies as his core identity, his "me." This is reinforced by the worker's selective support of the healthy aspects of the patient's ego, and by the patient's identification with the worker who is analyzing the patient's thought and behavior.

In this approach, attention is focused on the present all the time, with discussion of the background minimized as much as possible. An understanding of the present is far more useful to borderline patients than a rehashing of the past, which often leads to a recurrence of guilt and despair. Furthermore, the caseworker has no "authority" in matters of the past so this limits him to an ex post facto, verbal process. The most emotionally meaningful level of existence for the borderline patient, whose approach is ahistorical, is the present success or failure of his attempts to obtain narcissistic satisfactions. Therefore, the worker can establish a meaningful contact with his patient by limiting it to the focus on the present. Furthermore, it is necessary to keep in mind the totality of current functioning of borderline patients, since they are more sensitive to changes in equilibrium than most patients. Thus, before attempting to modify any bit of behavior, the worker must evaluate its adaptive significance in addition to its immediacy and salience. In an active approach such as this, when the patient's self-dosing is slightly curtailed, there is a danger of unleashing more acting out because of poor timing or indiscriminate activity.

Since the general focus of concern is the patient's interpersonal relationships, both the worker-client relationship and the various extra-therapeutic transferences may be examined during treatment. An important mechanism for keeping treatment going is "anticipatory transference clarification"

[22] Otto Fenichel, *op. cit.*, p. 555. These connections have also been termed "integrative interpretations" by Lee Stone, "Psychoanalysis and Brief Psychotherapy," *Psychoanalytic Quarterly*, Vol. 20 (1951), pp. 215–237.

[23] John Dollard and Neal Miller, *Personality and Psychotherapy* (New York: McGraw-Hill Book Co., 1950), Chap. 18.

[24] Paul Federn, "The Analysis of Psychotics: On Techniques," *International Journal of Psychoanalysis*, Vol. 15 (1934), pp. 209–215.

which helps to offset the acting out of narcissistic wounds.[25] Because the casework relationship is an aspect of the patient's current reality, it may be the subject of discussion, but not in terms of its analog to the patient's formative experiences. Rather it must be regarded as an arena for the operation of patterns that have been labeled and which dominate the patient's general adaptation.

A great deal of reassurance may be required at the start of treatment and at key periods of anxiety. As with all patients, reassurance must be realistic and must also be directed toward healthy parts of the personality. An attempt should be made to shift the focus of reassurance from the patient himself to his accomplishments in adjustment as these accrue. The self-assurance that results from perception of successful, mature experience will be far more durable than the self-assurance that depends on the transference relationship.

Conclusion

Borderline pathology has been defined as (1) a variety of generally impulsive symptom patterns (2) whose common denominator is a predominance of narcissistic control (3) with a resulting weakness in secondary ego processes. These three factors influence the treatment method which is quasi-educational in nature and based upon engaging the healthier parts of the personality in an attempt to improve the level of adaptation. An initial attempt to reduce harmful tension and to reduce the impact of depression is designed to provide sufficient motivation for the patient to move into a limited amount of self-scrutiny under the worker's guidance. Then an attempt is made to introduce rational delay mechanisms as a means of coping with stress. These mechanisms take the form of anticipatory labels of either impulsive activity patterns or their cognitive representations: they become ego-alien and can be reckoned with by the patient in tempering his own reactions.

While this procedure draws upon intellectualization and isolation as defenses, it derives emotional meaning from three sources. First, it is the existence of a strong casework relationship the formal aspect of which makes the treatment possible and which lends considerable emotional significance. Second, as the relationship begins to be effective, the patient starts to derive reinforcement from his improved control, which allows a more self-fulfilling redirection of energy. Third, some energy is gained from his habitual faith in, and reliance upon, magical measures. The introduction of new defenses makes positive use of this tendency. The treatment is limited by the fact that considerable time is needed to integrate the new growth experiences and by the fact that it is dependent upon a continuous relationship with the worker and may deteriorate upon separation. If dependency is skillfully controlled during treatment, however, and some provision is made for sustaining contacts, the latter problem can be minimized.

[25] Stone, *op. cit.*, p. 231.

Ego Breakdown in Schizophrenia: Some Implications for Casework Treatment

Esther S. Marcus

The last decade has seen considerable increase in systematic attempts to understand the dynamics of schizophrenia and to apply this understanding to the treatment of schizophrenic patients. As the over-all knowledge about schizophrenia has grown, there has been increasing recognition of the numbers of people—people without florid symptomatology—to whom this diagnosis applies. We now know that the schizophrenic personality structure has many manifestations and that the degree of social functioning can vary enormously. In some individuals, the diagnosis is fairly obvious; in others, only careful clinical evaluation and perhaps the use of projective tests can detect the thought disorder pathognomonic of schizophrenia. Some individuals can live a lifetime with the ego defect covered over. In others, increasing dysfunction may be stimulated by any number of inner and outer stresses. Frequently, it is the manifestation of the problem in social and interpersonal areas which causes these people to seek help—and to seek it at a social agency. Under the diagnostic labels of ambulatory, incipient, latent, or borderline schizophrenics, they make up a large proportion of the caseloads in community agencies and clinics. In addition, caseworkers frequently have contact with acutely disturbed schizophrenics, either by assisting in hospitalization or by later collaborative treatment in the mental hospital. The posthospitalized schizophrenic may also be receiving casework help. The worker's role and the goal of treatment naturally vary from case to case and are influenced by the setting. It is hoped, however, that increased understanding of some of the dynamics of schizophrenia and of the principles of treatment will make more effective the help given all these clients.

The subject of schizophrenia is vast, and the areas of new and helpful knowledge are many. However, I shall limit myself in this paper primarily to a discussion of the structural changes that occur in the schizophrenic personality in the process of breakdown and their significance for understanding the communications and treatment needs of the schizophrenic. I shall also consider some implications for casework treatment.

Reprinted from the *American Journal of Orthopsychiatry,* Vol. 31 (April, 1961), pp. 368–387. Copyright, the American Orthopsychiatric Association, Inc. Reproduced by permission of the author and the Association.

Dynamics

The pioneers in the psychological treatment of schizophrenia started with their ability to sense intuitively what the patient was attempting to communicate. Once there was recognition that schizophrenic productions have meaning and can be understood, there was increasing effort to find a key to an over-all understanding of schizophrenic manifestations. This particular aspect of the study of schizophrenia (and its application in treatment) was given considerable impetus by Paul Federn, whose work was published in comprehensive form in 1952 (3)*. Federn saw the loss of cathexis of the ego boundary, with its attendant loss of a sense of personal identity, as the central feature of schizophrenia. He saw the ego boundary as having the function of a sensory organ that separates the individual from the outside world. A person with a well-functioning ego boundary senses clearly what is inside—whether thought, memory, or fantasy—and what is outside, i.e., a real object or event in the external world.

Freeman, Cameron, and McGhie (4) applied Federn's concepts to their study of a number of chronic schizophrenic patients. They found that regardless of the etiology of the disorder, this "disturbance of the development and maintenance of adequate ego boundaries [is] . . . the central feature of the schizophrenic disease process" (p. 49). With the disruption of the ego boundaries, the schizophrenic experiences uncertainty as to his own existence. He loses a sense of himself as a distinct entity, separate from the external world. He can confuse himself, and parts of his body, with others or with objects in the immediate environment. There may be a vague unclarity as to whether an experience pertained to him or to someone else.

This loss of a sense of personal identity affects not only current experience, but also the patient's capacity to experience himself in a continuum. Although the memory of events may continue, the sense of order and duration is often lost. Intervals in time and place lose their meaning. Events of the distant past may be felt as having just taken place. For example, an apparently coherent, although scattered, woman complained bitterly in an intake interview about the difficulty of having her 90-year-old mother to care for. The interview was well advanced before the worker became aware that the mother had actually been placed in a nursing home four years before.

In the breakdown of ego boundaries and the dissolution of an integral ego, the secondary processes and functions of the ego become impaired. Such functions as perception, memory, and ability to synthesize, to integrate, to comprehend, to organize are affected to varying degrees. What emerges is primary process thinking. Logical thought processes give way to archaic, infantile ways of dealing with the world. Rules of logic, of time and space, of cause and effect cease to exist. The world is perceived in terms of magic and wish fulfillment. Instead of orderly, reality-oriented thought

---

*References will be found at the end of the chapter.

processes, there is the use of the primary process mechanisms of displacement, condensation, symbolic thought, and concrete thinking. The impairment of the capacity for abstract thinking is a major feature of the thought disorder. It is seen, for example, in the literal interpretations of proverbs frequently given by schizophrenic individuals.

> One fairly intact, well-functioning woman, when asked the meaning of the proverb "People who live in glass houses shouldn't throw stones," replied that the glass might break.
>
> It is illustrated in the behavior of a young man with an extremely high IQ who was, however, failing in college. He was amazed and uncomprehending when he failed a one-credit "snap" course because of overcutting. It was finally possible to discover that he had not kept track of his absences in this course because in the first session the instructor had told the students that the course was so easy they could "pass it without coming to class"! This same young man could not understand why he received a zero on an essay question in which he was asked to discuss the effectiveness of the inflationary measures utilized during the depression. His answer that "they were fairly effective"—showing both concrete thinking and condensation—seemed to him a satisfactory response.

The loss of a sense of personal identity, the fusion of the inner and outer world, with little ability to localize and organize stimuli arising from either source, and the replacement of secondary thought processes by primary process thought mechanisms help explain much of the bizarre behavior of the psychotic schizophrenic. I shall examine only a few of the grosser manifestations, keeping in mind the fact that to a lesser degree the same process operates in the less acutely disturbed schizophrenic. There is the "schizophrenic's susceptibility to environmental stimuli, which he is [however] unable to perceive in their proper order and context" (4, pp. 61–62).

> An example of this was a client who was engaged in an apparently jumbled and incoherent conversation. As she was listened to, it became apparent that the talk was in part a response to inner stimuli; i.e., as a thought came into her mind she might express it or she might counter it as if responding to someone else's voice. This talk was interspersed with responses to external stimuli not immediately obvious to the interviewer. For example, there were responses to snatches heard from other people's conversations. There was an apparent response to the blowing of a car horn, which must have implied to her that someone was double parked, because she then admonished the imagined culprit, etc.

Freeman et al. (4, p. 62) found that "this incorporation of random stimuli into the patient's stream of talk was very common and explained much of the apparent bizarreness and lack of purpose in the speech content."

The phenomenon of hallucinations can be understood when viewed in terms of the breakdown of the outer and inner ego boundaries. Freeman et al. point out that the breakdown of the ego boundary and the "reduced awareness of the mental and bodily ego, leads to an experience of the thought processes as divorced from the control of the individual, and therefore as alien and externally located. . . . Thus the patient's own thoughts, lacking ego feeling and therefore a sense of inner 'belongingness' are perceived by him as externally located auditory and visual experiences" (4, pp. 64 and 65).

The breakdown of the secondary process mechanisms also helps explain the formation of delusions. The *purpose* of the delusion, as pointed out by a number of authors (1, 2, 3), is to cope with the havoc caused by the breakdown of the ego boundary, when the world becomes strange, chaotic, fragmented, and incomprehensible. There is an attempt to explain the confusion caused by the perceptual disturbances and to make some order out of chaos. This is done, however, in terms of a false reality, i.e., a reality in which rules of logic, cause and effect, etc., do not exist. For example, if the schizophrenic feels that people know his thoughts, he might explain this by the existence of a machine that reads the mind—or, on a somewhat higher level—by the fact that his wife must be telling his secrets.

> One client, a butcher, complained that there was a conspiracy to drive him out of work (otherwise, how explain that he lost one job after another?), that he was being given conflicting information about prices, that his fellow employees frequently pushed his arm so that he cut the meat incorrectly, and that he was being distracted from his work by whisperings regarding his personal life. It was quite obvious that these delusional ideas were his attempts to explain increasing periods of lack of contact during which he became oblivious to his surroundings and to the passing of time, engulfed in his own unintegrated past. His confusion made it impossible for him to remember which prices were in operation at the moment, and he might cut the meat in response to an order given three days before.

Important for our purpose is some consideration of the course that the illness takes. Eissler says that "the schizophrenic process may take its full course or may come to a standstill at any point of its development" (2, p. 164). Federn indicates: "The personality disintegrates slowly, reality perception still controls the more important falsifications, and a rather good adjustment may last for many years with a very slow change to the better or the worse. Therefore psychotherapy has a good chance to protect an individual against recrudescence of the disease" (3, p. 170). He makes a distinction between latent schizophrenia, i.e., a personality in which the underlying structure is a schizophrenic one, but overt psychosis is kept in check, and early or incipient schizophrenia. He says that "the therapeutic aim is to prevent a latent schizophrenia from becoming a manifest one. For this reason the diagnosis of latent schizophrenia should be made early. Even though it may be impossible to prevent the outbreak, the attempt is worth our while since the outcome of schizophrenia is unpredictable in any case" (pp. 169–70).

Eissler says that preceding the acute outbreak of the illness there is frequently a period of withdrawal. "It seems as if the ego has fought a long time to keep up its interest in the world, then a sudden collapse sets in. . . . More often the period of withdrawal is clinically mute, long lasting and not noticed by the patient's environment, often not even by the patient himself" (2, p. 160). In the second phase, that of collapse, the patient feels confused, dreamlike, disorganized, unable to comprehend what is going on around him; the ego is fragmented; everything is unreal and chaotic. In the state of restitution, when the ego again pushes toward reality, one finds the delusional system setting in—the attempt to explain the psychotic perception of the world. These three stages are separated thus primarily for purposes of discussion. In actuality, it is not always possible to tell whether the delusions are part of the initial phase or the postacute phase. Eissler has pointed out that a patient may be in all three phases at the same time. In addition, he has found that some patients do not go through the second stage, but form delusions in what he calls a "short-cut" manner (p. 160).

In evaluating the seriousness of a patient's illness, Eissler says that he is "convinced that a prognosis . . . cannot be made in terms of whether the patient is smearing feces or is orally fixated. The decisive point is the extent of regression in the ego and possible destruction of higher ego functions" (2, pp. 160–161). In considering the effect of the illness—i.e., whether the higher ego functions have been preserved, temporarily impaired, or permanently damaged—it is necessary to know the extent to which these functions had been developed prior to breakdown. There is considerable variation. For example, in some individuals executive ego functions may be highly developed; in others, very little. Even after acute breakdown, some schizophrenics may show considerable residual capacity for synthetic thinking—even when this thinking is coupled with a defective sense of reality as manifested in delusional ideas.

Although these dynamics have been described in terms of the acutely disturbed, their understanding is important in working with the less disturbed schizophrenic; the variations we find are of degree rather than kind.

Treatment

Many writers agree that the earlier in the course of the illness the patient receives treatment, the more favorable the prognosis. However, establishing and maintaining contact with these individuals present special problems. Some of the problems in initial contact have been discussed elsewhere (7). We know that frequently these clients do not ask for help in the usual sense. They present themselves, and their communication needs to be understood. More than with the neurotic client, the decision about appropriate activity rests with the worker. The schizophrenic client has little ability to synthesize an entire situation, to know what is wrong, and to present some formulated solution—no matter how potentially unhelpful—with which he requests help.

> For example, in one rather extreme case, the client began, in the intake interview, by talking aimlessly, could not say what was wrong or why she had come, and finally said that she did not know what to prepare for dinner. The worker, realizing the degree and nature of disturbance that this behavior portended, began to clarify, in a simple and active way, what the woman's

living situation was. What emerged from this and subsequent contacts was that this schizophrenic woman and her two children had been cared for by her mother, who had recently had a stroke. The client stated that she had no one other than her mother. While not factually true, her statement was psychologically true. Her siblings had at first provided a housekeeper, but when the mother improved slightly, withdrew her on the assumption that the client could take over the tasks. In a state of helplessness and abandonment as acute as that of a young child, and just as incapable of visualizing a solution, she presented the immediate and crucial problem confronting her—without her mother, she and her children were in danger of starvation. The worker gave simple instructions regarding food, provided assurance that the agency would stand by and work out some plan to help, and kept in telephone contact over the weekend, in order to hold the situation together pending exploration of other plans.

Sometimes these clients are able to ask for help with a specific problem. Less frequent, however, is the request for help with personality difficulties. There is little sense of "This is me, this is how I function in relation to situations and people, these are the people I cannot get along with, these are the situations I cannot cope with." In addition, any suggestion of a personal problem (i.e., of there being something wrong with the individual) generally is devastating, and too intolerable to face. As they continue, withdrawn clients generally have little ability to state what they are getting from contact or why they want to go on. In several cases in which clients had shown evidence of considerably improved functioning and a decrease in withdrawal, and in which the relationship with the worker was extremely important, there was no concomitant ability to verbalize this. While in their own indirect way they all indicated a need for continued contact, their comments were typified by the vague "I think you helped me with my thinking." Some could point only to concrete reasons. For example, one client was not ready to stop seeing the worker because he still had a problem—his parents had not yet moved out of their junk-filled apartment! However, even his ability to state definitely that he needed to continue represented considerable progress.

Much of the treatment activity is determined by the extent to which the schizophrenic's communication is understood. The difficulty in grasping the communication varies, depending on the extent of destruction of higher ego functions, and the extent to which the communication is in primary process language. With some clients the communication is fairly direct; with others less so.

For example, one client, the butcher earlier mentioned, in an acute psychotic state and in need of immediate hospitalization, telephoned while his wife was being seen and told the worker that he was thinking of buying a cemetery plot for himself, his wife, and their children. He said that until now what had kept him from killing his wife was the thought that his children would be left alone. He had decided that perhaps it would be better if they all went together, and he was going ahead with the arrangements. But he was not going to let anyone put him in a hospital. The worker assumed that he was letting her know that the flimsy controls over his impulses were breaking down. His spontaneous comment about hospitalization indicated that somewhere there was some awareness that he was ill and in need of it; and his comment was in response to this inner awareness. The worker then went on the assumption that he would be relieved by hospitalization. She was positive in suggesting it to the wife, who arranged for an ambulance. When the police and the ambulance arrived, the wife was quite surprised by her husband's meekness, but even more so by his lucid statement that if she was really arranging to take him to the hospital, then he was glad to go because he wanted treatment. This was a startlingly lucid comment in the midst of days of acute paranoid disturbance.

In another situation a posthospitalized young woman with a well-developed delusional system revolving around her religious beliefs complained to the worker that a demon in the form of a bird had been recently alighting on her shoulder and singing popular songs—something which was against her strong religious convictions. The worker surmised that this was an expression of emerging conflict over her rigid morality. She therefore worked with the client on the idea that some very religious people saw God as not frowning on lighter things like popular music and that it would be understandable if she as a young person was interested in it. The "bird" shortly thereafter disappeared.

Two major aspects of work with schizophrenics are the need to establish affective contact with the individual and the need to strengthen his enfeebled ego. The two are separable primarily for purposes of discussion, because generally the establishment of affective contact is the framework for all other treatment principles. The patient must in some way begin to experience an emotional connection with the therapist. This in itself is an important part of treatment, is ego strengthening, and is essential if further work is to be done. Eissler, in discussing the break with reality, has pointed out that in the course of it "a real person [the therapist] can be cathected by the patient with narcissistic libido and at that point the breakdown of the ego boundary, the fusion between ego and world, can be at least temporarily stopped" (2, p. 145).

Much has been written in psychiatric literature about the qualities in the therapist that bring about this situation. Sechehaye (8), Fromm-Reichmann (5), Hill (6), and others have emphasized various aspects. Whatever method one uses, the wish to penetrate the isolation of the individual and to establish a connection with him is important. The therapist's need to be there for the person, to become part of his life and his world, and to feel that he, the therapist, will stop the internal destruction that is taking place, is vital. Eissler points out that the doctor "should believe in his own omnipotence; the patient's recovery must be of high emotional importance to him" (2, p. 164). Whatever the therapist's underlying motivation, the need to "rescue" the other individual must be strong.

Care must be taken to avoid activity or behavior that is likely to arouse negative feelings toward the worker. The capacity for object relationships is poor, and the relationship with the worker can easily be disrupted by a negative reaction. The effect of this disruption is greater and more far-reaching than it is with the neurotic client.

For example, after an extended contact with one well-functioning, borderline schizophrenic woman, the worker pointed out that the client had difficulty in seeing something new if it came from the worker, and that this apparently interfered with the gratification that the client was getting out of her newly found and growing ability to see and understand her own behavior. Although the client was able to see this intellectually, her emotional reaction was that the worker was trying to take something away from her—this new-found area of gratification—and therefore the worker temporarily became the "evil mother." In spite of a very positive relationship, the client went through a period of increased disorganization, re-experiencing some feelings of estrangement and of increased helplessness, none of which had been in evidence for some time previously. With a neurotic client, although the reaction of annoyance at the worker might be similar, one would not expect the same kind of total effect on the client's functioning.

The same care should be applied in dealing with any significant object relationship. Negative reaction to parental figures should not be elicited precipitously. In spite of the destructiveness that may exist in the parental relationship, or may have existed in the past, the tie, however tenuous, to the object, i.e., the parent, may be crucial in maintaining a connection with reality. In addition, unconscious identification with parental figures may make premature emphasis on their negative qualities narcissistically destructive.

Much of the treatment activity aimed at ego strengthening is determined by the schizophrenic's lack of awareness of subjective feelings, difficulty in separating the internal from the external, and general impairment of the sense of personal identity. These clients need help in knowing what they are feeling, what they are reacting to, what others are feeling. The most obvious surface feelings such as sadness, hurt, annoyance are frequently not perceived and not expressed directly. Suggesting, for example, that the fidgety client is feeling restless, and may want to leave, may appear simple but can be meaningful to a person who has little tangible sense of himself. They need help in identifying symptoms of the illness in order to counteract secondary threats to the ego. Where there has been impairment or destruction of the secondary functions of the ego, such as ability to concentrate, to organize, to work—the client may see this as laziness, incompetence, or stupidity. Recognizing these changes as symptoms can help counteract the guilt, self-criticism and feelings of inadequacy. Identifying the various symptoms that make up anxiety or depression can also be of considerable relief to an individual who sees them in a fragmented form and experiences the reactions as mysterious and frightening. In relation to any symptom, the hope can be held out that with treatment it could be modified.

The executive and synthesizing functions of the ego having been disrupted in the process of breakdown and as a result of it, anything that encourages a feeling of mastery and of ability to cope with internal and external pressures is vital. Activity aimed at helping cope with internal pressures is frequently related to reducing guilt and anxiety, counteracting feelings of helplessness and helping the person deal with the conflicts which are overwhelming him. What these are is frequently conveyed through the fantasy, delusion, or hallucination, which is a communication in primary process language. Once the process of breakdown has begun it is accelerated by the emergence of unacceptable and previously repressed impulses and fantasies, or as Federn holds, improperly decathected previous ego states. Freeman et al. point out that "the hallucination or delusion is invariably stimulated by the patient's present experiences . . . such activity is closely related to the patient's earlier experiences, but fully understood only when its relevance to the present events is appreciated" (4, pp. 70 and 71). This means that "listening sympathetically" to this kind of material and at the same time looking for the first opportunity to shift to "reality" matters is not necessarily the most helpful way of dealing with the situation and overlooks opportunities for understanding, and helping the client understand what is going on for him.

This does not mean that the emergence of fantasies should be encouraged and that efforts should be made to obtain details for their own sake. If, however, the material that is presented is examined for its specific connection with the individual's immediate life situation, this scrutiny will of necessity determine the detail that needs to be elicited.

> For example, in one interview a posthospitalized client spoke in an agitated fashion, reliving the horror of her pregnancy and delivery ten years before. The worker focused first not on what had been so disturbing about that pregnancy, but on what was stimulating this material at this particular time. She was able to obtain sufficient facts to conclude that it was probably connected with the woman's having had intercourse without contraceptives the night before. Although, in response to the worker's comment, the client claimed that she was sure she was "safe," actually the thought had occurred that she might conceive. Once the fantasy was there she responded to it emotionally as if it were fact, and all the old unintegrated terror was evoked. The worker pointed out that she was reacting as if she were pregnant, and reinforced the realistic appraisal that it was very unlikely, and that even if she were to conceive, a pregnancy now need not be the same as the previous one. When her agitation diminished, it was possible to help her examine somewhat more dispassionately what had gone on during her pregnancy ten years before that had made it such a nightmare for her.

Even in the acute period of the disturbance, when "the patient's ego feels itself at one with the schizophrenic symptomatology" (2, p. 131), some vestige of reasonable ego remains. The fact that the client does not spontaneously share regressed or bizarre fantasy or activity may be part of the attempt by the remaining intact portions of the ego to continue to keep it in check. If, however, the material is agitating to the client and arouses anxiety about "insanity" or some other self-critical reaction, ignoring its existence is not helpful, for these reactions themselves serve as an undermining force. If the client provides any indication that such a force is operating, the worker needs to get enough of an idea of what is going on to counteract the secondary reaction. This does not mean that the behavior or preoccupation should be sanctioned by the worker or the client. The recognition that there is something wrong with the ideas or behavior can be tacitly affirmed, while the self-flagellation is converted to an interest in understanding the purpose—frequently defensive—that the ideas serve.

> For example, a woman whose husband was dying felt guilty about her fantasies revolving around her contemplated life after his death, and frightened and disturbed by the fact that she had recurrent fantasies about his corpse. Without eliciting details about the corpse fantasies, and thus inadvertently encouraging the preoccupation, the worker brought out the mere fact that she had them. The client was considerably relieved to have the realistic horror in her husband's impending death affirmed, and her fantasies explained as one part of her attempt to make the unknown future less frightening.

Frequently, behavior that the client is distressed about and that the worker himself may question can be dealt with as an effort on the client's part to cope with his life, thus avoiding trouble with either the client's or the worker's superego and the undermining of healthy—as against archaic— superego reactions.

> For example, a client who had been married chaotically to several deteriorated men was able, with help, to free herself from the last. She went to work for the first time in her life and, in addition, established a much quieter and less destructive relationship with a man who helped support her. She began to berate herself for allowing this relationship to continue and yet was obviously unable to give it up. The client's self-criticism, focused on its lack of permanent satisfaction and the damage to her growing child, was not disputed. However, the worker highlighted both its improvement over previous relationships and its representation of a growing ability, in the face of a difficult situation, to do something about it. Instead of returning to her psychotic mother, as she had done in the past, she had been able this time to find someone to help take care of her while she needed this help. The various other ways open to people in her situation, which she might eventually be able to use, were discussed. The worker in this way bolstered the ego ideal by pointing up the client's own implied more mature standards, and by retaining them as a goal. The client can be told that as he feels better, less frightened, and stronger, he will more and more act in accordance with a realistic ideal.

A vital part of treatment is to diminish feelings of helplessness. Frequently these are heightened by the client's feeling that a decision has been taken out of his hands or that he is at the mercy of others. The recognition of this in itself can offer some relief, and where possible, helping him see his contribution to the specific situation can counteract the feeling of helplessness. This effect can be achieved, for example, by pointing out when there is enough specific evidence that the client had something to do with another's negative response to him, or with the termination of a relationship. Helping the person cope with frustration and tolerate intense feelings is ego strengthening. The fact that a need, for example, is great can be recognized. However, the extent of the need can sometimes be explained as being the result of the degree of deprivation suffered as a child. This can help diminish somewhat the overwhelming reaction when the need is not met. In general, recognizing painful feelings but conveying the conviction that these can gradually be examined, understood, and coped with, can afford relief. All this allies the client with the worker and mobilizes the ego to work on the reaction instead of merely continuing to be overwhelmed by it. At the same time, it offers a sense of the worker's support.

> For example, in an interview with a woman who was expressing extreme feelings of unworthiness and a sudden inability to deal with the smallest routines, the focus was first on clarifying the onset of the current reaction. It appeared to have been stimulated by a rejection she had experienced the previous week from her husband. Pointing out that her feeling about herself hinged almost totally on others' reactions to her—in this case, her husband's—and that she experienced no sense of self-worth apart from others' approval, directed her interest to this reaction as a mechanism, as something that had its roots in her past and did not need to remain that way. This was pointed out as part of her problem, one which could with time be worked through, so that she could then cope with other people's reactions to her without being overwhelmed.

The worker needs to align himself with the healthy part of the ego, to help the client combat such manifestations of the illness as paranoid reactions. Federn says:

> In treatment, those parts of the ego which still function with adequate distinction of thoughts and reality must be employed as allies. Only with their help can the repair of the deficient part be accomplished (2, p. 167). The latent schizophrenic who begins to become psychotic learns . . . to resist his inclination suddenly to attribute the character of certainty to previous ideas of reference. He himself undergoes the experience that his conscious, critically directed attention is able to correct the beginning falsifications (p. 193).

The focus in the foregoing discussion has been on the intraphysic aspects of treatment aimed at ego strengthening. Space does not permit a discussion of the very important topic of the role of family interaction in either disturbing equilibrium and accelerating the process of breakdown, or in supporting improved functioning. The separation between "internal" and "external" has been made for purposes of discussion, and with complete recognition that it is an artificial one, since the personality is always dually oriented to internal processes and the social environment. Intraphysic and interpersonal processes can generally be defined only in relation to each other—as the last example demonstrates. Nor is it possible to discuss here the wide range of environmental and social measures, and the dynamics of family-oriented treatment. I would like to touch briefly, however, on one aspect relating to external pressures, and relevant to our present topic—considerations in the worker's decision regarding direct involvement in the environment.

One factor in this decision is the client's awareness of his external situation and whether he can keep the worker informed of what is going on.

> For example, the young man who thought he could pass the course without coming to class had no awareness of whether or not he was functioning effectively. He rarely grasped what was expected of him. In the midst of failure, he had the impression that he had done all his assignments or that he had done well on an examination. When he began to express some interest in wanting to do better, the worker established regular contact with the teachers

and kept informed of his actual performance. It was possible in this way to interpret reality to him, help him cope with its demands, and prevent the accumulation of additional avoidable failures.

In general, when there is any indication of difficulty in functioning and when the client is a poor informant, the worker's being "in on" the client's life is important.

For example, the client who "had been helped with his thinking" had a good possibility of obtaining a very suitable job. He presented no anxiety about the coming job interview. It was only the worker's very specific interest in how he was planning to handle it that revealed that he was probably going to talk himself out of the job, because of some involved reasoning about not wishing to show how desperately he wanted it. By being in on this situation, the worker was able to help him approach the interview much more effectively.

Direct intervention is usually indicated when the client cannot deal effectively with the situation, when it is of importance in his life, and when the worker's intervention will not be experienced as destructive. In one case, intervention might have saved a job for a client, but he felt too threatened by the exposure involved to justify intervention.

The worker's attitude about the environment is important. To be effective he cannot be immobilized by feelings similar to those of the client. He must not feel that the environment is immovable but, on the contrary, must have the conviction and zeal of the mature parent: he nurtures all evidence of growth and maturation; he helps the individual cope with the demands that are made on him; he helps him avoid or postpone situations that he is not ready to cope with and that will be ego weakening; he can sense what disappointments are tolerable and which are intolerable, trying to help avoid the latter and cushioning those he cannot prevent. And when a situation becomes too much, he takes over—if the client permits.

In ego strengthening, the use, emphasis, and timing of any of the treatment principles described vary with the needs of each client and the specific nature of the ego problem. For example, helping the client become more aware of *what* he is feeling seems to be important in early contact with withdrawn clients—the ones who are losing contact without anyone's being aware of what is taking place. The more agitated client who is involved in a more active internal struggle and who shows more evidence of such secondary symptoms as delusions and hallucinations usually requires a more complex approach, involving the counteracting of feelings of helplessness and the diminution of the intensity of some of the conflicts. The case of Mrs. A exemplifies one set of needs and the treatment derived from the principles discussed above.

Mrs. A came to the agency after not following through on two earlier applications. A woman in her early twenties, she had been married twice. The intake worker saw no evidence of serious illness. Mrs. A described a severe marital problem, but placed the blame for all the difficulty on her husband. She was annoyed when the intake worker alluded to Mrs. A's own feelings, and she insisted that it was only Mr. A who needed help.

She subsequently telephoned to refuse the appointment offered by the continued service worker, stating that her husband had changed his mind about using the agency's service. She sounded somewhat incoherent. The worker made an effort to help her come in at least once, but Mrs. A refused.

When Mrs. A called back two months later, she did not ask for an appointment but went into a tirade against her husband. When the worker finally suggested that it might be a good idea for her to come in to see her, she hesitatingly agreed, with interpolated comments that she did not see what for, etc.

In the first interview, her disjointed, rapid-fire monologue bordered on incoherence. She seemed hostile, out of contact, and talked as if the worker were attacking her. She alternated between tirades against her husband and angry defense of herself. She gave information and then had no recollection of having shared it, wanting to know suspiciously how the worker knew these things about her. She did not respond directly to clarifying questions asked by the worker, but would lapse instead into what appeared on the surface to be an unrelated tirade. It was apparent, however, that she had heard what the worker said but that the questions evidently evoked unbearable feelings with which she attempted to cope through her outbursts. For example, the worker's asking whether she and her husband were still together or apart was apparently intolerable, because Mr. A had left her. She could not state this fact because it was too painful, and she responded instead with an outburst about what a disturbed person he was.

It was apparent that Mrs. A's ego boundary was poorly cathected. She felt internal accusations as coming from the outside. She was confused about the meaning of others' behavior, responded to isolated statements, and was unable to grasp anything but the literal meaning. She had apparently been behaving in a panicked, impulsive, aggressive fashion. She was suspicious and somewhat fragmented.

The worker's focus then shifted to an attempt to reach Mrs. A, diminish the agitation, and establish a connection with her. The internal attacks had to be diminished, and she had to be strengthened so that she could cope with what currently felt like an intolerable situation, arousing intolerable feelings. In some way, she needed to be helped to perceive the worker as a supportive figure—one who would help her in her struggle against the encroaching illness.

The worker gave up any attempt to obtain the simplest facts. Instead she responded to the underlying panic—indicating awareness of how frightened, alone, and deserted Mrs. A must have felt and must still be feeling, and how little way out she saw. She was told that such feelings would account for some of the things she had apparently done in the marriage. (Without being specific to Mrs. A, the worker guessed from the latter's defense that she apparently, among other things, had locked her husband out, gone home to her mother, and refused sexual relations.) There was recognition of her inability to comprehend her husband's behavior, and simple explanations were offered as to what he probably meant. There was an attempt to diminish the self-critical reactions which were intolerable and experienced as coming from the outside. She was offered the possibility that with help from the worker she could learn to understand why she did things, could exercise more control over what happened in her life, improve her judgment, and eventually lead the kind of life she wanted for herself. The idea was that initially the control and improved judgment would be a result of the worker's "being in on" her life with her.

During the initial interview—and a number of the early interviews—Mrs. A's shifting and fluid "ego feeling" was graphically in evidence. As she felt relief and some sense of mastery, she quieted down, was aware of the worker, and gave information directly. When this became too painful, she reverted to a defensive tirade and appeared to be out of contact. Her struggle to cope with her feelings of abandonment was evident as she grasped eagerly at the worker's suggestion that she might again at some time in the future be in a position to *choose* a man.

At the end of the first interview the suggestion of further appointments was made on the basis of the worker's desire to help with the many problems and decisions facing Mrs. A, and without allusion to any personality difficulties contributing to her problems in her marriages. Mrs. A, who was temporarily relaxed and in contact at the end of the first interview, agreed to return on the basis that she thought the worker understood her. If the worker thought that she could help her and she should return, she would.

As the contact progressed, a clearer picture of Mrs. A's personality emerged. Evidence of the thought disorder and of the poorly cathected and fragmented ego boundaries pointed to a diagnosis of schizophrenia, but there were indications that the process was not far advanced. Her ability to integrate experiences was quite faulty. Her behavior was random and impulsive: she had no ability to evaluate her behavior or to connect it with subjectively experienced emotions. Feelings were unintegrated, and behavior was determined by whichever feelings erupted. Judgment of other people was extremely poor. Her sense of self as separate from other people—as a distinct entity both in the past and present—was also poor. For example, there was constant fighting among all her relatives; between her mother and her father, who had separated when Mrs. A was two, but were not divorced; and between her mother and the latter's married lover. When Mrs. A was involved by the others in these arguments, she responded as if she was one of the other family members. Mrs. A's excellent grooming represented a positive carry-over from a time when she took pride in her appearance. Currently, however, it was apparently being done automatically and she was surprised when others commented on it, since generally she felt dirty and unattractive. She frequently spoke of herself in the third person. She would talk to herself as one would to a child. As the contact with the worker progressed, she would imagine what the worker might say to her in a specific situation and she would talk to herself in that way.

Mrs. A had paranoid ideas, with shifting insight into them. When contact was advanced she told the worker that she was afraid she had ideas of persecution, with awareness that her reaction was not rational. At other times, particularly at points of severe distress, she had minimal insight into her delusions, which, however, were never florid and did not get out of hand. For example, she thought that someone, "a man", came to the house during the day as evidenced by an unflushed toilet and by a disappearing skirt; and that there were mysterious phone calls which were really from her husband, who was calling both to upset her and to communicate with her. She went as far as considering going to the district attorney's office, but decided to discuss it with the worker first.

She felt little connection with people. As contact progressed, she put into words the dreadful sense of isolation—of being all alone in her own barren world—that she frequently struggled with. She felt confused by much of what went on around her. After two or three months of contact, she had no recollection that her worker was not the same person who had seen her in intake. However, by the time she left treatment, she recalled her much more specific response to the intake worker: that the latter talked in a way which Mrs. A was unable to understand, doing so deliberately to confuse her, because she was against her—"as I felt everyone else to be at that time." Here we see the paranoid reaction to explain her inability to comprehend.

Mrs. A's terror of helplessness—of being under someone else's control—was often in evidence. She had had a paranoid reaction when she had entered a hospital for minor surgery. An extremely traumatic event in her life had been her temporary placement in a shelter at the age of three, during which she had screamed constantly.

The executive functions of Mrs. A's ego were least impaired, and this had probably been important in counterbalancing the disintegrative process. At points of stress, when a situation felt unbearable to her, she *did* something. The behavior might not be thought through, or it might not be the best way of coping with a situation, but she at least acted to relieve the pressure temporarily. She had left home at 17 when the situation there had become too much for her. She became a band singer, going through all the steps involved in interviews, auditions, etc. She opposed her parents in her decision to marry her first husband shortly thereafter; then divorced him. When she felt herself on the verge of a breakdown during the chaotic and tumultuous breakup of her second marriage, she decided that she had to be able to support herself outside show business, and so forced herself—to the extent of muffling her phone—to study stenography until she was able to obtain "respectable" work as a stenographer. However, in many of these situations as she recalled them, she had no awareness of what had motivated her behavior, and, even more, she had the feeling at times that someone else was doing these things, not she.

When she came to the agency, she had nowhere else to flee. She was staying with her mother, who sounded like a rather unrelated, helpless person, somewhat afraid of her daughter, and tending to be controlled by her. She felt herself degraded by two broken marriages, so that fleeing from her mother into the arms of another man when her tension mounted at home was no longer a solution. At the time, she was actually more clinically disturbed than she had ever been.

Mrs. A did not need help in dealing with her external situation in the way schizophrenic clients often do. She was quite capable of getting a job, for example, or of getting any legal information she needed. When she finally decided to move with her mother to another community, she made all the arrangements for housing and employment transfer. What she did need help with, however, was in acquiring a sense of herself as a person, beginning to tolerate, experience and be aware of feelings, and integrating these both currently and in relation to her past relationships. Goals were to help her develop better judgment and to diminish the tendency toward impulsive behavior with its destructive results.

In working with her there was, initially, a cautious attempt to arouse her interest in understanding the reasons for her behavior. For example, when it was obvious that she had no idea why she had left home at 17, the fact that something must have been going on to bring about this move was presented for her consideration. Her curiosity was stimulated by the very fact that she had no idea as to what this could have been. Since she did tend to take on as her own other people's reactions to her, emphasis was put on expressing the worker's goals for her. For example, she did not have to rush into meeting other men. She was young and needed to choose carefully; the worker wanted her to gain sufficient understanding of her life, so that she could avoid other mistakes, etc.

Mrs. A did have a capacity for awareness. Whenever the worker pointed out that she was reacting as if the worker were accusing her and asked where these accusations came from, Mrs. A would, with amazement, agree and puzzle about herself. This tendency to puzzle, to try to understand herself, was encouraged. Mrs. A experienced considerable pleasure when she began to *feel* reactions, look at them, and understand them, rather than strike out impulsively. For example, she described a visit with her sister, with whom she generally became embroiled in upsetting and incomprehensible quarrels. She was aware of her usual feeling of anger but then realized that it was aroused by her mother's playing favorites rather than by anything her sister had done. The anger dissipated, and she did not follow her usual pattern of lashing out at the sister without knowing why. Mrs. A stated that even if this one realization were the only change she experienced as a result of her interviews, it would have been worth the entire contact. The importance to her and to any individual of this sense of mastery, of knowing what is going on inside himself and what he is reacting to, and the sense that reactions are then under control rather than mysterious and uncontrollable, cannot be overemphasized.

Mrs. A gradually moved from the feeling that she had initially expressed —that she found herself saying things in the interview that she did not want to think—to the attitude that she incorporated from the worker: she wanted to understand herself and some of her unhappy feelings so that she would not have to continue her life in so impulsive a fashion.

Her delusional reactions were generally handled by touching on the conflict behind them. By the time she brought these in it was possible to suggest, for example, in relation to the mysterious phone calls, that perhaps, in spite of her anger at her husband and her disappointment with him, she missed him and at times wanted him back. It was interesting (and showed Mrs. A's attitude toward feelings) that the first time she became aware of positive feelings toward her husband, she brought this to the worker as something that she thought she could tell the worker, but that no one else would understand; she thought her mother would be angry with her if she knew that Mrs. A felt this way. There was constant interpretation to Mrs. A of emotional reality and explanation of her own and others' reactions; i.e., what she felt, what a relationship was like, how people reacted. Her recognition that the odd behavior of her family was psychologically rather than genetically determined was important in counteracting her conviction that she came from bad stock.

During the course of the contact, as her annulment was becoming final, she experienced increasing tension that she would now be under her mother's "jurisdiction." Concurrently, the mother was hospitalized after a minor accident. The latter's increased self-absorption and demands on Mrs. A stimulated an increase in Mrs. A's feelings of both being abandoned and unappreciated by her mother. The old impulse to run away from home came to the fore. This time, however, it was possible to get to all the feelings of rejection, of abandonment, of anger at the mother, of being consumed by family quarrels. She was able to recollect for the first time the similar feelings that she had actually had prior to previous flights from home. She was aware that she would have fallen into the arms of any man who offered to take her out of the chaos and confusion that she associated with life with her family. Yet this time she recognized that this was no solution and that it only led to further difficulty. She also began to separate the confusion outside and the confusion inside. She began to recognize the sense of help-lessness at not really understanding the adult world. She began to grasp that others' reactions to *her* were frequently a response to her behavior and feeling toward *them*. During the contact, she quite on her own did some volunteer work at a foundling home. Discussing in detail with the worker the reactions of the children was a reliving, and an attempt to integrate, the feelings that she had experienced when she had been placed.

She terminated contact after about a year by moving with her mother to another city. Aside from her own desire to go to a new community, Mrs. A, who had planned this move over a period of months, felt that it would finally enable her mother to obtain a divorce. She planned to contact a local agency, should she feel the need for further help. At the time she left, psychiatric evaluation, which had been utilized twice in the early months of treatment, indicated that the disintegrative process had been arrested and reversed, with expansion in healthy ego taking place. She was not at all out of contact. She looked back both on the past year and on her life with much greater awareness and understanding. There was less impulsive behavior and she controlled this tendency when it arose. She had begun to learn to deal with the psychotic portion of the ego. There were no current delusions. Although there were transient paranoid reactions, she usually identified them and could frequently see what went into them, so that she could move from the reaction to the underlying feelings. She could tolerate and look for mixed feelings. She was aware of her difficulty in sensing what people were like. Although the thought disorder was still there, she had been helped to weather a difficult situation, without acting out as she had before. Hopefully, the gains she had made would help her cope with her ongoing life somewhat more effectively.

Mrs. A's leaving was hard on the worker, who was left with a feeling that the job was not completed and with the wish that—like a parent—she could have guided her charge into greater development. In addition there was a retrospective doubt as to whether the decision not to try to see the mother—which had seemed so valid—had really been sound. But the worker needed to be satisfied with the growth that had taken place and the hope that, should there be signs of increased difficulty in the future, this young woman, having had a positive experience with the worker, would again turn to a professional person for help.

Conclusion

The subject of schizophrenia is vast; the patients are many; the symptoms are varied; their needs are different. Schizophrenia has been described as psychiatry's number one riddle. The theories of etiology range from organic illness of an as yet unknown cause to a disturbance brought on by early traumatization in the child's relationship with his parents leading to subsequent behavioral maladjustment. The theories of treatment vary. At one end are those who see only organic therapy, the prognosis remaining poor. At the other end are those who see no essential difference between the schizophrenic and the neurotic patient. The theory of the latter group has to some extent been a reaction against the hopeless attitude toward schizophrenic patients that was frequent in the past.

Casework practice has to some extent reflected the attitudes prevalent in psychiatry. Some agencies have in the not so distant past still held that they would not take on schizophrenics for treatment—on the assumption that little could be done for them or that they belonged with psychiatrists. Others have assumed that there was no essential difference between the schizophrenic client and other clients. The treatment approach in these latter instances frequently did not take into consideration the special problems and so often came to grief.

The intent of this paper has been to highlight some of the recent theoretical explanations of schizophrenic manifestations. Schizophrenics are neither hopeless nor are they like everyone else. An understanding of the nature of the ego structure of schizophrenic clients is important for case-workers because it makes clear that caseworkers can be of help, but that the help must be based on a clinical grounding that considers the client's special treatment needs.

The factors to be considered in deciding which clients appropriately belong with the caseworker and which need to be treated by a psychiatrist are complex and have not been discussed here. Once the schizophrenic client is in our office, however, it is important to establish contact with him, irrespective of what his long-range treatment needs may be. There is a wide variety of help that clients can get from any treatment. For some, lasting integration and change takes place, with increased capacity for coping with their lives. Others may not experience permanent personality change. Treatment may have helped them weather a difficult period and may have been a preventive of possible deterioration. The help given any schizophrenic individual is important, for it may affect the ultimate course that the illness takes. At times, this help needs to be offered without active verbal participation on the part of some of these clients, because, in spite of their desperate need, some can never acknowledge verbally either their need for help or their need for another person. But for any caseworker, in whom the need to "rescue" is strong, the knowledge of the help he has given can carry emotional meaning for a long time. A relationship implies the involvement of two people, and, as the worker remains a part of the client, so the client remains a part of the worker.

References

1 ARIETI, SILVANO. *Interpretation of Schizophrenia*. New York: Brunner, 1955.
2 EISSLER, K. R. "Remarks on the Psychoanalysis of Schizophrenia," in Eugene B. Brody and Fredrick C. Redlich (eds.), *Psychotherapy with Schizophrenics: A Symposium*. New York: Internat. Univ. Press, 1952.
3 FEDERN, PAUL. *Ego Psychology and the Psychoses*. New York: Basic Books, 1952.
4 FREEMAN, THOMAS, JOHN L. CAMERON and ANDREW McGHIE, *Chronic Schizophrenia*. London: Tavistock Publications, 1958.
5 FROMM-REICHMANN, FRIEDA. *Principles of Intensive Psychotherapy*. Chicago: Univ. of Chicago Press, 1950.
6 HILL, LOUIS B. *Psychotherapeutic Intervention in Schizophrenia*. Chicago: Univ. of Chicago Press, 1955.
7 MARCUS, ESTHER S. "Initial Contacts with Incipient Schizophrenic Clients." *Soc. Casewk.*, 39: 551-559, 1958.
8 SECHEHAYE, M. A. *Symbolic Realization*. New York: Internat. Univ. Press, 1951.

Casework Treatment of Ambulatory Schizophrenics

Laura Farber

This paper deals with some theoretical aspects of casework with ambulatory schizophrenics, and with a number of specific treatment techniques that are particularly applicable to work with these persons, although they are also used with other diagnostic groupings. The discussion is focused on one aspect of casework with the schizophrenic person—direct treatment in which the objective is improvement in his social functioning. The techniques described are based on the understanding of ego functioning. Since this presentation is drawn from the writer's experiences as a caseworker in both the in-patient and out-patient services of Hillside Hospital, the word "patient" will be used throughout.

Because the number of schizophrenics living in the community seems to be increasing, their treatment is a problem that confronts not only caseworkers in psychiatric clinics, but also caseworkers in many other settings. Clients with similar, if not identical, problems come to the attention of all community social agencies. If caseworkers are to be effective in their work with schizophrenics and are to be dealing with more and more of them, it is imperative that they have adequate clinical knowledge of the nature of the personality disturbance called "schizophrenia." Such knowledge will influence the way in which cases are handled since it will enable the caseworker to know in advance the problems he is most likely to encounter.

The term "schizophrenia" has not been clearly defined. It holds different meanings for different people; there are wide areas of disagreement about it and no single treatment approach can be proposed. Although there are characteristic modes of schizophrenic functioning, and schizophrenic patients resemble one another to some degree, they can actually be distinguished from one another in respect to the degree of their affective thinking, and behavioral disturbances.

We are primarily concerned with what is generally called ambulatory schizophrenia. The term as used in this paper includes individuals whose ego functions are not so markedly impaired that they cannot maintain themselves with some measure of effectiveness in the community. A large number of patients known to the Out-Patient Clinic of Hillside Hospital fall within this group. For the most part they show none of the dramatic symptoms, such

Reprinted from *Social Casework*, Vol. 39 (January, 1958), pp. 9–17, by permission of the author and the Family Service Association of America.

as hallucinations, delusions, and bizarre behavior, which commonly are diagnostic indicators of schizophrenia. However impressive, these are but accessory symptoms, characteristic only of the more advanced stages of illness, and they may be altogether lacking in the ambulatory patient.

Characteristic Symptoms

The characteristic symptoms of the ambulatory schizophrenic patient are those that are fundamental to schizophrenia, in that they are always present but in varying degrees. As outlined by Bleuler, these symptoms are: disturbances of association, disturbances of affectivity, the predilection for fantasy as against reality, and the inclination to divorce onself from reality.[1] These disturbances constitute failures in acquired ego functions. In the later stages of schizophrenia these symptoms may be readily discernible, but their manifestations are more subtle in the ambulatory patient and often not immediately recognizable. For example, after several interviews, it becomes apparent that many of the patient's verbal communications, regardless of specific content, consistently lack a certain vital clarity. Or, while listening to a patient, one may suddenly realize that a sentence or two, flowing smoothly along with everything else that he has said, is inappropriate to the context.

It is important to note the extent of impairment in the ego functions of the ambulatory schizophrenic; specifically, impairment in the areas of judgment, perception, organization, self-preservation, synthesizing of experience, and reality testing. Not all these functions may be uniformly affected in any one patient. Since a failing ego has but limited "coping" energy, defenses are created in order that some degree of cohesiveness may be maintained and disintegration avoided.

A schizophrenic may thus be viewed in part as a person who is to some degree regressed and who, like the infant whose boundaries between himself and others are vague, has intense needs, lacks controls, and is sensitive to slight indications of psychic danger. In reality, however, he is not the infant who is moving ahead on the road and who has not yet learned to differentiate himself from the environment. He is, instead, the adult on the path back, having undergone life experiences, many of which have created anxiety so painful that he has had to withdraw into himself from the world about him. His disorder is thus an ego-defensive function.

The ambulatory schizophrenic's tolerance for pressure may be decreasing as he struggles with unconscious impulses threatening expression. Because his feelings are so easily stimulated, getting close to external objects is a risky business, and the patient maneuvers to maintain distance. Such patients often complain, during initial interviews, that the world seems cold,

[1] Eugen Bleuler, *Dementia Praecox; or, The Group of Schizophrenias*, translated by Joseph Zinkin, International Universities Press, New York, 1950.

empty, strange, and alien. Other parts of the schizophrenic's personality may be intact, however, and in a number of respects he is like others rather than different from them. The caseworker should relate to and thus strengthen these stable parts of the patient's personality. At the same time the caseworker should be respectful and accepting, although not encouraging, of the existing impairments since these are also part of the patient's unique differences and individuality. It may be necessary first to meet the patient's infantile needs to some degree in order later to strengthen his more mature drives.

Preserving Ego Defenses

The casework process is primarily one of reorienting the patient to his present social reality, rather than one of attempting to help him resolve internal psychological conflicts. Although casework treatment with schizophrenics may frequently be geared toward the maintenance of present levels of functioning, in order to prevent further deterioration, it need not exclude the possibility that some degree of modification in adaptive behavior may be achieved. Treatment goals as well as treatment techniques should be flexible. The basic casework approach to schizophrenic patients rests, however, upon attempts to nurture carefully and to preserve their ego boundaries and defenses. The worker's efforts are directed toward massive support of ego defenses and reinstatement of ego functions with particular emphasis on reality testing if this is failing. The degree to which these efforts are successful depends upon the establishment of the worker-patient relationship. Casework with schizophrenics is based upon the traditional broad techniques of support and clarification, and within these wide categories a variety of specific approaches may be used. Caseworkers achieve good treatment results with these patients even though the techniques employed may vary from worker to worker. Choice of specific techniques frequently grows out of the uniquely personal manner in which a particular caseworker relates to an individual patient, and it was from individual experience that the writer arrived at some of the following formulations.

The formerly warranted prudence of many caseworkers in attempting to work with schizophrenics—a prudence that resulted from the potential dangers and unpredictable nature of casework treatment of them—has blossomed into anxious caution which may be limiting and incapacitating. Although schizophrenics make challenging patients, they also inspire pessimism, precisely because they are difficult to treat. A pessimistic attitude in itself may handicap a caseworker in attempting to achieve results that are realistically possible. If the casework goals set are flexible and considerate of the patient's limitations, the worker can afford to be optimistic. Because the treatment course with the schizophrenic is often stormy and, by our usual standards, the gains are relatively small, caseworkers are often ready to call the patient "untreatable" or "unreachable." Although this may be true at times, it is preferable in the beginning for the caseworker to be as flexible as possible in relation both to treatment processes and to goals, rather than for him to begin with the assumption that the patient is beyond help.

Reality-Oriented Treatment Approach

Some caseworkers treat many patients, including ambulatory schizophrenics, by means of what may be called the laboratory method. They are advocates of "objectivity" and "neutrality," who seem to regard their function as that of providing a screen for the patient on which he may safely project a wide range of thoughts and emotions, which the caseworker then "interprets." The development of this method may in part be attributed to the early development of casework in analytically oriented settings where caseworkers were brought into close contact with the ideas of classical analysis, some of which were then modified for casework purposes. Although this approach is desirable and effective with some patients, it may be not only useless but even harmful with schizophrenics, since it may foster an impersonal and passive attitude on the part of the caseworker.

A passive casework approach may encourage both regressive withdrawal and anxiety. The atmosphere of remoteness which it creates serves perfectly as a setting for the silent patient, or for the patient who is introspective. The schizophrenic patient, on the other hand, needs actual direction in turning his attention toward externalities. The simple fact of the caseworker's "being there" is of particular benefit to the schizophrenic, but it may not be sufficient in itself. The necessary atmosphere of mutuality resulting from the interaction of two human beings will not be achieved if the caseworker's contribution and participation are limited to his merely being present or occasionally punctuating silent listening with a few words. The caseworker cannot establish the effective relationship through which all treatment gains are achieved if he sits in remoteness from the human struggles confronting the schizophrenic patient.

In working with the schizophrenic patient, the caseworker should utilize an active, reaching-out, reality-oriented approach in which he establishes what can be called a "controlled" involvement—controlled, that is, by the realistic limits of the worker-patient relationship of which he never loses sight. An active casework approach will furnish the schizophrenic—a person whose perception of the external world is blurred as a result of his anxiety and whose ego boundaries are ill defined—with what he needs, the opportunity of relating himself to a real person from whom he can gain a clear and dependable image. The nature of the schizophrenic's problems demands that the caseworker represent a segment of reality, and thus the worker must allow his own feelings to be acknowledged in order to enter into his relationship with this patient.

The caseworker's genuine emotional responsiveness to the feelings of the schizophrenic may evoke in the patient a variety of personal feelings toward the worker from which he may build a fantasied relationship which transcends professional limits. Problems may arise if these feelings exceed the level of moderate strength. It is usually desirable for the patient, although he is characteristically ambivalent, to have predominantly positive feelings for the caseworker, since there is less danger of serious difficulties resulting from overpositive than overnegative feelings. If a patient reveals strong feelings of affection for the caseworker as a person, it is extremely important that such expressions be graciously and respectfully accepted. To the schizophrenic patient these may be represented by a cautious offering of a precious gift. Interpreting them as "transference" feelings, truly meant for another person, as might be done with non-schizophrenics, can be devastating to this vulnerable person and may be experienced by him as harsh rejection.

It is often difficult, yet necessary, to discover ways in which it is possible to reject the feelings but not the patient. It is possible to accept expressions of positive feeling and then to translate them into broader terms. For example, a man in his twenties expressed affectionate feelings for a female caseworker and made references to being sexually attracted to her. The caseworker accepted his feelings as meant for her, and since she knew him to be a shy person with strong feelings of isolation, commented that he seemed to be really telling her that he was beginning to feel some closeness toward other people, which was a healthy gain. She added that she was pleased to hear this and that, although he seemed to feel attracted to her as a woman, she felt that he needed her most, and that she could help him best, as his caseworker. In doing this, the caseworker refused the role of girl-friend, yet she did not reject the patient since she made clear to him her desire to continue to relate to him in her professional role.

On the other hand, strong negative feelings toward the caseworker can create serious problems as they can disrupt the treatment relationship. In his active role the caseworker is bound to display some of his own individual personality characteristics, some of which the patient may dislike and respond to with anger. These negative feelings must first be listened to and accepted; but it then is helpful for the caseworker to intiate discussion of the circumstances relevant to their being expressed—why the patient is preoccupied with his dislike for the worker at this particular time. His preoccupation may be a reaction to something the worker has unwittingly said or it may simply be a means by which the patient can avoid talking about himself. Generally speaking, in order to assist the patient in identifying the reason for his feelings, and in order to reduce the possibility of distortion, the caseworker has to be free enough to disclose his own feelings and the meaning of his actions so that they may be objectively examined. The frequently used casework technique of responding to questions with questions —for example, asking "why" when the patient asks a somewhat personal question—must frequently be discarded with the schizophrenic, particularly if negative feelings are to be kept within reasonable limits.

The Patient-Worker Relationship

It is important that the beginning phases of treatment be concerned primarily with the establishment of the vital patient-worker relationship, particularly since the schizophrenic is often unusually resourceful in defending himself against interpersonal involvements. The manner in which the early interviews are handled may either greatly facilitate the development of the relationship or make it practically unattainable. It may be added that the schizophrenic patient who has established any degree of relationship will repeatedly test the caseworker's ability to remain constant, the extent of his interest, and his capacities to tolerate the patient. The relationship, once established, is, in any event, but precariously maintained. During the early stages of contact, the ways in which the patient tests may often be subtle. His attitude may be one of quiet scrutiny. If, so to speak, the caseworker passes the first tests and the relationship moves forward, the testing becomes more direct and piercing, and may produce in the caseworker anger, helplessness, or anxiety, none of which are comfortable feelings. Although it is distressing to witness the schizophrenic's need to confirm the caseworker's reliability over and over again, it is also painful at times for the caseworker to be in the position of test target.

Where the work setting offers a time-limited period of treatment, it is even more necessary for the caseworker to provide the stimulus and assume the initial responsibility for establishing the relationship, as this cannot be left to chance nor delayed until the patient makes a move. Each caseworker must make continuous efforts in his own individual manner to emerge as a solid object on which the patient can focus and to which he can also cling at times if necessary. Fundamental attitudes such as empathy, warmth, and respect are often insufficient, particularly with those patients who are constricted or detached. These attitudes must be accompanied by energetic efforts to induce the patient to direct his attention away from himself and toward the external world in the person of the caseworker. In addition to the highly important non-verbal communications such as glance, gesture, and posture, these efforts include verbal communication in which it is not only what the caseworker says that matters, but, equally important, how it is said.

The effectiveness of speech very much depends upon the tone of voice and the feeling qualities that accompany the words. The caseworker, on certain occasions, should have a suggestion of conviction, firmness, or insistence in his voice. Language is a potent means of communication and may be used freely, although not as the sole means. Not only should the caseworker be actively inquiring by continuing to ask questions despite sparse answers, but also he must be active in responding by commenting frequently upon the patient's remarks so that the patient at least knows that he is being heard. Although schizophrenics are persons for whom non-verbal communication assumes special significance, they frequently need to have the worker's support, interest, and attention demonstrated in words.

Exploring the Patient's Problems

Casework usually starts with an exploratory phase during which the nature and scope of the problems confronting the patient are determined. Casework with the ambulatory schizophrenic places emphasis on the problems the patient is encountering in his handling of current reality situations; thus the initial focus should be on the facts and feelings surrounding the circumstances of the patient's coming for help. Although these facts and feelings may seem obvious, the obvious can often be obscure. The caseworker cannot assume that these are at all clear to the schizophrenic patient, but rather should assume that they need to be both established and clarified. Thus, it is often valuable for the caseworker to put what appears to be the obvious into words. Many schizophrenics are unable to verbalize concretely their need for help, and the caseworker must often do this for them. The caseworker takes his cues in doing this from what the patient has thus far said and from his non-verbal attitude, and thereby attempts to convey some understanding of the patient's feelings.

It is possible to anticipate the patient's probable attitudes toward seeking to help because his fears, doubts, confusions, and expectations are not basically different from those of other patients although they certainly may be more intense. Many of these patients cannot be expected to focus on, or even to identify, their problems. The caseworker may have to identify the patient's unexpressed concerns and, at times, emphatically state them. During this process the caseworker does not depend solely upon verbal explanations; he acts out his function, thereby demonstrating to the patient how casework operates. He conveys something of what his help involves, and what he and the patient may attempt to do together, so that the patient's expectations of him will not get so far out of touch with what is actually possible of achievement in the situation that the patient becomes angrier and more frustrated.

As a result of the caseworker's verbalizing for the patient and bringing some of his feelings into the open, the patient may visibly experience relief of tension. It seems to be enormously encouraging to the schizophrenic to feel that another person has managed to understand at least a part of what he is feeling and has shown respect for him by communicating this to him. The fact that he can be understood implies further to him that his feelings are not unusual nor are they beyond the pale of human understanding. In addition, the schizophrenic is very concerned about whether the caseworker is a competent person. For example, during an initial interview a patient, in a challenging manner, said to the caseworker: "If I tell you my problems, what more can you do for me besides giving me empathy?" This attitude of infantile defiance is not uncommon, and it may be wiser for the caseworker to answer such questions directly as they arise than to postpone or avoid answering them.

Encouraging Verbalization

One technique that may be used to encourage the schizophrenic patient to verbalize involves the caseworker's giving him something specific to which to relate. For example, a patient reported that he attended a family social function which he did not enjoy. He could not on his own say why it was so unpleasant, nor could he answer the caseworker's questions. The caseworker then made use of his knowledge of this man's characteristic difficulties and suggested a possible reason why he had failed to have a good time. The worker suggested that the patient did not feel comfortable because he felt obliged, as he usually did when his mother was present, to limit his freedom of action for fear of evoking criticism from her. As a result of the caseworker's stating this one possibility, the patient had a specific factor on which to focus and to which he could respond. He then said that he had actually been made uncomfortable by something else—the presence of a fellow employee whom he had not expected to be present. This comment was pursued and led into a discussion of the patient's interpersonal relationships on his job—an important area of functioning which it had not previously been possible to discuss.

Something may be gained, also, from the worker's venturing an opinion regardless of whether it eventually proves correct. A need on the part of the worker to be correct most of the time hinders vital spontaneity and defeats the objective of bringing the patient's thoughts, feelings, and attitudes into the open where they may be realistically appraised. A possible error or what may actually be a difference of opinion helps the schizophrenic to separate his attitude from his total self as he considers the different ways in which a situation can be viewed and described. If the caseworker can acknowledge being wrong without being defensive, the patient is provided with the opportunity of seeing the worker more accurately and realistically as another fallible human being. As a result he may not need to regard his own mistakes as unique or devastating, and may be freed from some feelings of inadequacy. For example, a patient in her early thirties was involved in a chaotic marital relationship and vehemently denied that she in any way contributed to the violent battles that took place regularly. She projected the entire responsibility for these scenes onto her husband, thereby stabilizing her own rage toward him. For many months, while viciously criticizing neighbors whom she felt were pitying her, she nevertheless presented herself to everyone as the victim of her husband's abusiveness.

At the beginning of the contact there were but few attempts made to discuss these projections with her since the casework relationship was tenuous. As the relationship developed, so did an identification with the worker, and the patient gradually revealed more specific information as to how these arguments arose. During one particular interview, the caseworker managed to elicit details that indirectly revealed that the disagreement under discussion had resulted from her insisting to her husband that she had been right in her evaluation of a particular situation when she had actually not been. She was able to examine realistically the circumstances under which this argument had arisen when she was reminded of some of the mistakes the caseworker had made during the contact and was then asked why she found it so hard to admit the possibility of human mistake in herself.

Holding the Patient to Reality

Since certain schizophrenics are vague and confused in their thinking, it is important for the caseworker to consider ways in which the patient may be held to discussion of important realities so that the interviews do not become "much ado about nothing." These patients readily escape into irrelevancies and generalities, avoiding topics of significance by all sorts of circuitous means, and some become more anxious as they become more confused. The caseworker must listen intently to the patient who rambles, or the one who talks compulsively, in order to understand what he is trying to convey and in the hope of picking up at least one significant statement which then may be pursued. If a patient dwells on a circumstantial narrative about a situation that is irrelevant to his difficulties, it is the caseworker's responsibility to direct his interest elsewhere. This may be accomplished by referring back to an area discussed previously, bringing it to the patient's awareness in a general way so that the topic does not appear to be abruptly changed. Once it is in front of the patient it may be followed by a question that requires a more specific answer. Sometimes a patient resents the worker's firm attitudes in interrupting his verbal wanderings, and he feels thwarted and angry. Since such feelings may hinder further communications, the caseworker should help the patient realize that his anger is related to the worker's activity and that this reaction is understandable.

Dealing with Anger

Most schizophrenics suffer from pervasive or chronic feelings of rage to which the term "unassuageable anger" has been applied.[2] In his struggles with rage, the schizophrenic will feel more secure from his own impulses if the caseworker's strength or control serves to reinforce his own impaired ego. Although the caseworker may feel more comfortable in being permissive, he must often be firm and even demanding since the patient needs external controls. The caseworker must set limits, but not arbitrarily, and these limits may be more acceptable to the patient if he is given reasons as to why they are necessary. A 20-year-old patient, whose grandiose schemes

[2] Karl Menninger, M.D., "The Diagnosis and Treatment of Schizophrenia," *Bulletin of the Menninger Clinic*, Vol. XII, No. 3 (1948), pp. 96–106.

revealed poor reality testing, frequently expressed anger toward the case-worker. One day, during a period when she was particularly distressed, she became furious with the caseworker when the latter refused to comply with a request to write a letter to the patient's sister in her behalf since the worker felt that the patient was capable of handling this on her own. Feeling helplessly angry, the patient grabbed a small ash-tray from the caseworker's desk. The caseworker did not wait for the minute to pass during which the patient might have returned it to its place, but instead ordered her to put it down and gave as the reason the fact that she would not allow the patient to hurt either one of them. When the patient did not respond even after the caseworker repeated this, the caseworker reached over and removed the object from the patient's hand. The patient was shown that the case-worker possessed the control the patient lacked.

The schizophrenic is caught up in a circle of anger; the original anger, after being expressed, brings guilt, which in turn creates additional anger. Whether the verbal expression of hostility is subtle or blatant, it is wise to clarify it at once since otherwise the patient may be left with discomforting guilt. This unmitigated anger of the schizophrenic may be a further problem in treatment since he may project a good deal of it onto the caseworker and thus may readily feel that the worker is attacking or rejecting him. In addi-tion, by verbally attacking the caseworker and attempting to disparage him or to prove him worthless, the schizophrenic attempts to prove that he in no way needs the worker, and thus he increases his provocative testing as the relationship assumes importance and his anxiety mounts.

Dealing with Paranoid Ideas

A large number of schizophrenics, particularly when under stress, develop paranoid ideas which serve to ward off anxiety but in many instances create social difficulties. Since new experiences are frequently terrifying to the schizophrenic, he may develop suspicions regarding the intentions of others. Whether the expression of the paranoid idea is directed toward the caseworker or toward another person in the patient's environment, immedi-ate handling is nevertheless called for lest the distortion become more involved. The caseworker neither agrees nor disagrees with such ideas, but accepts them as what the patient is experiencing. If the caseworker disagrees with a distortion, the patient may become more cautious or may be forced to elaborate.

One way in which the caseworker may deal with paranoid distortions is illustrated by the following brief case excerpt. A 20-year-old man was being seen regularly with particular focus on his problems in employment and residence. A few weeks after beginning a new job that was potentially promising, he told the caseworker about his idea that co-workers were laughing at him as he passed their desks; hearing the murmur of their voices as he reached the other end of the office led him to believe that they were also talking about him. The caseworker first approached the patient's reactions to what he perceived, which were feelings of fear, anger, and rejection. With persistence she then attempted to elicit factual material about the circumstances under which his ideas had arisen. She asked questions about the office situation in general, about particular people of whom the patient was suspicious, and inquired as to whether the patient had ever felt this way before in any other situation. At the same time she attempted to create some doubts in the patient's mind and to have him consider alternative meanings, through questions such as, "What other explanations might there possibly be for their laughing?" She did not deny the validity of the patient's feelings, but indicated that she was dubious about the validity of his perception.

In order to strengthen the patient's reality-testing ability, the case-worker should elicit details of the reported situation. With these details the caseworker can then review the relevant circumstances step by step, trying to pull them together into some sort of objective sequence of events, so that the patient can become aware of the relationship between the actual situation and his feelings abouts it. In this case, the patient was helped to relate his own feelings of humiliation resulting from a public criticism by his supervisor, to his later feeling of being laughed at by others. Since effective reality testing depends to some degree on the identifications supporting it, it may be advisable for the caseworker to assume a position of critically examining the patient's attitudes toward the worker himself so that the patient may then assume a similarly critical attitude in relation to his own actions and those of others. The caseworker should be explicit, frank, and detailed in his discussions with the suspicious patient in order to prevent some, although certainly not all, of his potential misinterpretations. There should be no tacit understandings with these patients, and absence of comment regarding a distortion may mean to the patient that the worker is tacitly giving consent.

Conclusion

The casework approach outlined in this paper can best be called "directive." Some of the difficulties that frequently arise during casework treatment of the schizophrenic patient have been described, and techniques for handling them have been suggested. It is recognized that this is a complex area of treatment in which further exploration and experimentation are needed. Although one cannot suggest final answers to many of the questions posed, caseworkers should be willing to be flexible in experimenting with various, and possibly new, treatment techniques.

Part **3**

Physical Handicaps

The physical condition of a client and his health is one of the important areas of the total situation which the social worker must consider in diagnosing and planning treatment. This is not to suggest that a medical assessment of the client is the social worker's responsibility. Rather, his task is to assess the extent to which the life patterns, problems and potential for psychosocial functioning as presented by the clients are affected by his physical condition.

This responsibility rests both in the assessment phase and in the selection of treatment goals and methods. It presumes, therefore, some knowledge of physical functioning and of the client's attitude towards his health. Certainly in every case the implication to individualize must be kept in mind; the therapist would seriously err if he considered that all clients with particular handicaps or disease entities were to be treated the same. However, the necessity to individualize does not imply that we cannot acquire some understanding of clients by considering the common factors of their physical condition. For example, only when we understand how much a particular blind client is like other blind clients can we individualize him, and thus understand how he is unique and different.

There is a further reason for considering the client's physical state. Frequently, our work with people will involve helping them understand, accept, and cope with various physical problems of other family members. As well as assisting in this recognition and the working through of feelings, we will also aim at helping them to cooperate with, and at times participate in, the treatment of the afflicted family member. As suggested in the articles presented on the retarded and other forms of brain damage, there may be considerable resistance and denial on the part of the family, loath to accept such a diagnosis. This in turn frequently limits the potential of the client to mature and progress.

The appropriate involvement of other significant persons in treatment requires the social worker to understand the nature of the physical condition its manifestations and effects on patients and others. Also we must have the same understanding of various medical procedures related to a condition. There are several difficulties which can arise from a failure to understand the client's physical condition. Some of these are to support the patient's denial of a diagnosis, to overlook manifestations of illness, to miss seeing changes in a situation or to avoid supporting and encouraging cooperation in medical treatment.

Although it is not our primary task, we do have a responsibility to recognize obvious physical problems. Certainly I am not implying that we should be diagnosing medical conditions. Nevertheless, we do need to be aware of some of the possible physical conditions and their manifestations which clients tend to deny or not recognize. Again, we can use the example of a mildly brain-damaged child. It would be tragic if, due to lack of awareness of easily recognized patterns, such a child were treated as a reactive type of problem to a family situation instead of as a child with a physical handicap. In the Krupp-Schwartzberg article it is suggested that some of these children can go unrecognized for some time because of unawareness of the therapist and of the patients' families. In multiprofessional settings the cooperation and amalgam of several disciplines assist in this regard and social workers are more attuned to these areas. It is much more difficult and yet much more crucial for social workers in nonmedical settings to be equally aware has of physical symptomatology.

With the growing importance of social workers in health fields, as well as an increased psychosocial orientation in psychiatry and medicine, it is evident that social workers are going to be involved much more with persons suffering from, or recovering from, various physical illnesses. The increase of shorter hospital stays, home care for patients, widespread rehabilitation programs, retraining programs, and publicly supported insurance programs will all demand that social workers be even more physically oriented than has been our custom in recent years.

The selection of articles presented in this section is not all inclusive. It does represent a sampling of the range and focus of articles relevant to this area as found in recent literature. It is evident and understandable that the topics addressed in the literature reflect trends in medical interests. Thus illnesses such as tuberculosis, where social work was once heavily involved, are no longer given much attention in the literature. On the other hand, kidney diseases, cardiac conditions and cancer all are frequently discussed.

Many of the articles located for consideration in this section were of a "one-of-a-kind" category, that is, they were not selected from a large group of several articles dealing with the same topic. I mention this point to emphasize the irregular and almost haphazard pattern of writing in this area of our literature. A beginning search was made into the principal medical journals to locate articles of direct relevance to social work. Two things were quickly observed: first, the overwhelming amount of medical data covering the vast variety of topics both macroscopic and microscopic; second, the paucity of social work contributions to such medical journals although other disciplines such as sociology and psychology have contributed. In addition to the areas mentioned above there are two other areas which have received a particular emphasis in social work literature. These are the fields of retardation and blindness, especially blindness in children. Again, the reason for this is not clear. It may be that these conditions are generally untreatable and to a great extent unchanging for the person afflicted. Thus, the principal difficulty is in the area of necessary psychosocial adjustments for both the clients and the families. Of these two areas, mental retardation has by far the greatest number of articles. Besides those used in this section there are many others which could have been utilized.

Several articles included in this section of the book deal with various forms of cerebral dysfunctioning. A common trend can be observed throughout them: (1) the necessity for understanding the nature of the handicap; (2) its effect on the psychosocial development of the person; and (3) its effect on the significant others in the client's life. The authors all emphasize the relationship capabilities in these types of clients and the frequency with which we underestimate their potential for improved functioning.

As mentioned above, social work treatment of retarded clients and their families has been given heavy emphasis in the literature. Separate approaches to the many problems presented by these clients and their families are discussed in the articles included here. Emphasis is put on the necessity of knowing the family's attitude towards retardation and its possible interference with therapy. The theme of individualizing and building our treatment on diagnosed strengths rather than presumed limitations is highlighted.

One interesting trend noted in this most recent review of the literature is that we have now begun to give almost equal emphasis to clients of all ages and stages of development, unlike earlier days when we directed much of our attention to child patients.

The articles in this section are listed in alphabetical order rather than grouped by related conditions since the social work literature has been uneven with regard to specific physical and medical problems. The format of the articles in this division is varied: some contain a detailed analysis of the particular symptom and a consideration of the treatment implications; others discuss the analysis of a particular approach to treatment; others outline a program of service; still others offer the analysis of one of a few cases. As a totality they do represent a rich overview in a general way of social work treatment of physically handicapped persons.

Although the focus of most of the articles in this section is specific, it is clear that there are diagnostic and treatment concepts with import for other forms of illness and handicap. Thus the concept of adjustment to the crisis of blindness and the analysis of the adjustment process can be applied to similar crisis situations resulting from the onset of illness or disease. The themes of denial of the illness and damage to the concept of body image and adequacy are important ones that appear in several articles.

Even though much of the material has been written from an isolated viewpoint, I think sufficient experience and sufficient material now exists to begin to develop a general theory of working with physically ill or handicapped people. There are some indications that this is happening. A group of articles was located with just such a generalized focus as, for example, those that discussed work with the chronically ill patient or handicapped patient or fatally ill patient. It is hoped that such further synthesizing and generalizing work will continue.

Katz's article on hemophilia emphasizes our dual responsibility. That is the necessity to incorporate into our practice with physically ill or handicapped patients generalized knowledge and skills, but then to apply them individually adjusted to the need of each client or group of clients.

Although each topic discussed in these articles points out the necessity for specific knowledge, only one underlines the need for specific skill. In Chough's article on deafness the need for different forms of communication skills is discussed. The author emphasizes the desirability of some social workers developing knowledge and skill in communicating directly with the deaf. The frequently used method of utilizing interpreters and translators is discussed and the familiar problems, frustrations and limitations associated with this method are highlighted. It would be hoped that our increased knowledge and awareness of communications would encourage us to expand our repertoire of communication skills.

Conclusion

This group of articles is interesting, important and useful. Yet it is thought that a wealth of additional knowledge and skills, both generic and specific, has been accumulated through the professional cadre concerning the treatment of the psychosocial ramifications of physical handicaps. This material should be made available to the general stream of the professional literature for two reasons. The first is to help all practitioners to expand their knowledge of persons from the viewpoint of their physical potential. The second reason is perhaps more important, that is, to use the practice wisdom of our colleagues in the health fields to develop more generally based practice theory that has wider applicability than to a particular area of practice.

Arthritis

Making Hospitalization a Growth Experience for Arthritic Children

Joan Morse

Since John Bowlby focused attention on the traumatic effects of separating sick children from their parents for an extended period, clinicians have hesitated to recommend prolonged hospitalization for children.[1] Treatment procedures in a hospital setting seem especially frightening and painful to children, for their fears and fantasies magnify the real discomforts of the medical milieu.[2] Well-meaning efforts of staff and families to compensate young patients for the discomfort they are experiencing by giving them presents and special privileges may afford them so much secondary gain that they find more immediate gratification in remaining ill than in becoming emotionally committed to the long, often difficult, struggle to regain their health.

The treatment of juvenile rheumatoid arthritis sometimes requires a prolonged hospital stay to achieve remission of the illness or to prevent or correct deformities resulting from the disease. Experience at the Robert B. Brigham Hospital in Boston has shown that, without prolonged hospital care, some children who have juvenile arthritis will inevitably be crippled.

Specialized treatment of rheumatic disease in adults and children has been provided at the Robert B. Brigham Hospital for most of its fifty-year history. Recently, in 1963, with the impetus provided by an initial grant from The National Foundation, a multidisciplinary group was organized for the study and treatment of juvenile arthritis, and members of the Social

---

[1] John Bowlby, *Child Care and the Growth of Love*, Penguin Books, London, 1955, based on the report *Maternal Care and Mental Health*, World Health Organization, Geneva, 1951, pp. 139–49.

[2] Veronica B. Tisza and Kristine Angoff, "A Play Program for Hospitalized Children: The Role of the Playroom Teacher," *Pediatrics*, Vol. XXVIII, November, 1961, p. 841; Edward A. Mason, "The Hospitalized Child—His Emotional Needs," *New England Journal of Medicine*, Vol. CCLXXII, February 25, 1965, p. 408.

Reprinted from *Social Casework*. Vol. 46 (November, 1965), pp. 550–556, by permission of the author and the Family Service Association of America.

Service Department became particularly interested in examining the psychosocial changes that occur in children requiring prolonged hospitalization.

During the first year of the program five girls required long-term hospital care, extending from seven to twenty-four weeks. By coincidence, each child represented a different age group, ranging from infancy to adolescence. The ages of the girls were as follows: Susan M, one and a half; Rosella J, three and a half; Mary L, six; Barbara T, eight; and Christine F, thirteen and a half. Each child showed marked psychosocial and physical improvement between the date of admission to the hospital and the date of discharge. Thus far, the results of the study demonstrate that long-term hospital care can not only correct swollen joints and flexed limbs but also improve the child's total functioning within the family unit. These dual gains can be achieved, however, only if attention is paid to the whole range of social, emotional, and environmental problems associated with juvenile arthritis.

To accomplish this task, the social worker in such a setting as the Robert B. Brigham Hospital must have broad professional competence, including ability to work intensively with parents, and must have an active interest in modifying detrimental environmental factors and sufficient flexibility to function as a member of the hospital team. The skills needed have been described by Harriett Bartlett as those of "the experienced worker in action not as a caseworker or consultant but as a professional social worker, assessing situations and moving from one appropriate method to another, with full awareness of the nature of the decisions involved and the professional components of each activity."[3]

The Illness and the Patients

Juvenile rheumatoid arthritis is a generalized disease of unknown etiology that runs a variable, often intermittent course. The onset of symptoms, which may be acute or insidious, begins before puberty. These symptoms may include fever, pain, stiffness, and the swelling of one or more joints. Twice as many girls as boys develop juvenile arthritis.[4]

Studies by The National Foundation have estimated there are 50,000 patients in this country with the juvenile form of rheumatoid arthritis. J. Sydney Stillman, M.D., chief of the medical service of the Robert B. Brigham Hospital, suggests, however, that with better diagnostic criteria and more widespread recognition of this disease, a more accurate figure, including children and adult patients in whom the disease developed before they reached adolescence, would approximate 250,000.

The medical regimen prescribed varies with each patient because the

[3] Harriett M. Bartlett, "The Widening Scope of Hospital Social Work," *Social Casework*, Vol. XLIV, January, 1963, pp. 8–9.
[4] Henry K. Silver, C. Henry Kempe, and Henry B. Bruyn, *Handbook of Pediatrics*, Lange Medical Publications, Los Altos, California, 1955, p. 527.

natural history of the disease is unpredictable.[5] Treating patients with severe symptoms requires close co-operation between medical and orthopedic specialists, the patient's intensive use of physical and occupational therapy, and a high standard of nursing care. Although observers have long believed that emotional, social, and environmental factors influence the course of juvenile rheumatoid arthritis, research is needed to validate this assumption.

At the Robert B. Brigham Hospital, a special weekly clinic known as the Clinical Treatment Center for Juvenile Rheumatoid Arthritis was started in December 1963. A social worker interviews the parents, and often the children as well. The Social Service Department assumes responsibility for providing casework services, particularly for the families in which the child requires hospitalization.

During the first nine months, seventy-five patients with a definite or probable diagnosis of juvenile arthritis were examined at the clinic. Most of the children received out-patient care, supplemented by one week of intensive examinations in the hospital; only the five children to be discussed in this article required prolonged hospital care. In addition to having certain general symptoms, they all had difficulty in walking or were unable to walk at all at the time of admission, and they had all failed to respond to previous treatment.

These children came from middle-class and lower-middle-class families. In each case both parents were alive and the father was employed at the time of the patient's admission; none of the families had ever received public assistance. All the parents had been born in the United States; they ranged in age from twenty-four to forty-two. There were two, three, or four children in each family.

The children were provided with ward accommodation. Their pattern of care was somewhat similar although their treatment was individually prescribed. The regular staff provided them with similar nursing service. The children received physical and occupational therapy daily. They were examined by orthopedic consultants, who prescribed casts, traction, splints, braces, and crutches during the course of treatment. All the children were able to walk by the time they were discharged.

The staff members of the juvenile arthritis center met weekly. They were responsible for making treatment recommendations for the hospitalized children and for the out-patients. Two internists specializing in rheumatology, the child psychiatrists, the pediatricians, the physical therapist, the occupational therapist, and the social worker assigned to the center attended the conferences. An orthopedist was on call as needed. These sessions, which were marked by free communication and exchange of ideas, resulted in the formation of united decisions by the staff regarding patient care.

The child psychiatrist who served as a consultant for the inpatients

[5] Regina Fiesch, "Counselling Parents of Chronically Ill Children," *Pediatric Clinics of North America*, Vol. X, August, 1963, p. 766.

made suggestions about the ward milieu and the management of the patients, and he was available regularly as a consultant to the staff providing direct service to the patients and their families. Formal psychotherapy, however, was not available to the children during their hospital stay.

Economic Stress

Serious financial burdens are a frequent and disturbing problem for families with arthritic children.[6] A lack of funds for the direct and indirect cost of medical care can threaten the social well-being of the entire family. The following case illustration shows the worker's effort to help one family cope with these burdens.

> Susan M's family lived in a rural area of a state where employment opportunities were limited. Her father's earnings were sufficient only for the family's fundamental living expenses. The parents had already borrowed money, using their car, insurance, and furniture as security, to pay for Susan's two-week stay in another hospital. During those two weeks, slender Mrs. M had lost ten pounds "from worry."
>
> Before Susan's admission, when she was eighteen months old, the referring physician told the social worker of the family's limited financial position, and the worker was able to obtain funds for a sixteen-week out-of-state hospital stay from the agency that serves crippled children.
>
> The worker found Mr. and Mrs. M to be thoughtful and considerate of each other's needs and Mrs. M to be warm and loving with Susan. It was not surprising, therefore, that the first person in the hospital to whom Susan responded positively was an exceptionally warm and motherly nurse. As Susan improved, the occupational and physical therapists assumed a major role in her care, using play techniques in teaching her to exercise. Helping Susan to learn new words became a favorite project for the entire staff. She also learned to feed herself.
>
> Since the relationships within the family were good, the social worker focused her efforts on preventing any further distress as a result of the economic and emotional strain of having a child hospitalized far from home for a prolonged period. Money for travel expense was obtained so that Susan's parents and her brother and sister could visit her weekly. Between visits the family was informed by letter of Susan's progress during critical periods of her illness. Before Susan was discharged, funds were made available to allow Mrs. M to live near the hospital for two days while she learned how to help Susan exercise.
>
> Mrs. M was able to accept help without becoming overly dependent on the worker. She was emotionally strong enough to entrust Susan to the hospital in spite of her deep concern for her, and, later, when her daughter was discharged, she was able to resume caring for her with obvious joy.
>
> When Susan returned to the clinic for follow-up care, it was hard to believe that this adorable blonde child who ran about, calling hospital staff members by name, had been described by her doctor as a "pale, unresponsive lump" when she was admitted to the hospital.

[6] Robert H. Manheimer, Katrine R. C. Greene, and Frances Kroll, "Juvenile Rheumatoid Arthritis in New York City, 161 Cases," *Archives of Pediatrics*, Vol. LXXVI, May 1959, p. 181.

Separation Anxiety

Separation from his mother is a particularly difficult problem for the rheumatoid child.[7] Nevertheless, the child's physical separation from the parents during the hospital stay may be viewed as a crisis that can be used to help both parents and child gradually begin to develop a psychological separation from each other.

Rosella J, three and a half years of age, was referred to the child psychiatrist two days after admission because she cried and refused to eat and was vomiting. When Mrs. J. visited the hospital, she would only peep at her youngster through the ward door. Meanwhile, the staff characterized Rosella as "totally unmanageable." In addition to having temper tantrums, she was rebellious, manipulative, combative and resistive.

The psychiatrist thought many of Rosella's symptoms stemmed from anxiety and fright as a result of the way her mother had handled her admission to the hospital. The child had been told she was entering the hospital for a "vacation," and she had come to fear she was abandoned. In consequence of these circumstances, the social worker initiated a long-term relationship with the mother to help her learn more effective ways of assisting her daughter.

Mrs. J had to be helped to accept the need for casts, exercises, braces, and crutches so that Rosella herself would co-operate with the doctors and physical therapists in using these aids. It was also necessary for the worker to win Mrs. J's confidence in him and the rest of the staff so that the mother could visit Rosella without interfering with treatment procedures, criticizing the hospital, or bringing sweets before a meal. Even learning to terminate a visit by assuring Rosella that she would return the next day was difficult for this mother.

In the process of establishing a relationship with Mrs. J, the worker learned the reasons for the disturbed behavior that had provoked Rosella. Rosella, who was the youngest child, was conceived when her mother was expecting menopausal symptoms rather than another pregnancy—and Mrs. J's mother also had given birth to a menopausal child, who suffered from epilepsy and was a patient in a state institution. Mrs. J's father had died shortly before Rosella began to show symptoms of arthritis. Mrs. J had been overwhelmed by her recent loss and by her special fear that Rosella, like her sister, would suffer from a chronic illness.

The mother seemed too volatile and too suspicious of authority to be able to modify her own behavior by self-understanding. The social worker hoped, however, that a corrective relationship would help Mrs. J control her constant interference with Rosella's treatment.

After several informal meetings on the ward, sometimes preceded by the social worker's taking Mrs. J by the arm to help her break away from her clinging daughter, Mrs. J felt comfortable enough to come to the worker's office for weekly appointments. Gradually, she came to enjoy discussing each aspect of Rosella's progress. Her criticism of hospital routines diminished as she began devising ways in which she could use her own energies to work creatively with her daughter and other young patients; for example, Mrs. J helped them make decorations for the Thanksgiving and Christmas holidays.

---

[7] Gaston E. Blom and Babette Whipple, "A Method of Studying Emotional Factors in Children with Rheumatoid Arthritis," in *Dynamic Psychopathology in Childhood*, Lucie Jessner and Eleanor Pavenstedt (eds.), Grune & Stratton, New York, 1959, p. 127.

The next step was to help the mother gain confidence in her own ability to handle Rosella, before she was discharged. Appointments were scheduled for practice sessions with the physical therapist, but Mrs. J failed to appear until the social worker helped her understand that she would not be judged by her daughter's performance. Finally, six months after her admission, Rosella was transferred to a day hospital program until she was ready to enter nursery school two weeks later. During this period the staff was able to follow Rosella's progress, and the worker continued to reinforce Mrs. J's decision to allow her daughter to enter school.

When Rosella was interviewed by the nursery school director, he made this statement: "She proved quite delightful, less shy than I anticipated. She shows good signs of responding to our program."

Emotional Constriction Related to Maternal Deprivation

A marked inability to express feelings was observed among the twenty-eight children with rheumatoid arthritis who were studied intensively at the Massachusetts General Hospital from 1948 to 1954;[8] this trait was typically observed in children with a history of maternal deprivation. Such an association of emotional constriction and maternal deprivation was particularly obvious in Mary L, an exceptionally "good" six-year-old child from a small town in Vermont.

Mary rarely complained, although no one visited her. She formed superficially rewarding relationships with everyone she met at the hospital and was soon a "ward pet," surfeited with presents she hardly seemed to notice. Indeed, Mary's ingratiating behavior suggested she was severely deprived to the point of "almost failing to distinguish between one adult and another."[9]

When the social worker first began to see Mary regularly, she talked blandly about nonexistent brothers and sisters. Later, she felt comfortable enough to discuss family pets, her two real younger sisters, and, finally, her parents. Although Mary gave no indication of any family strains, the staff was concerned about her tendency to fantasy and her mother's failure to visit. The social worker telephoned Mrs. L and arranged for her to travel to the hospital for an overnight visit.

Mrs. L, aged twenty-four, looked tired but youthful. She had separated from her twenty-eight-year-old husband after a difficult and troubled winter. The family had lacked adequate heat, clothing, and food because Mr. L had been spending most of his wages from the local lumber mill on liquor. Contemplating divorce, Mrs. L had taken the children to her sister's home in another small Vermont town. There Mary's arthritis, which had been symptomatic for a year, had grown worse. The local pediatrician had referred Mary to the center, and Mrs. L had remained in Vermont with her other children.

Mrs. L had dropped out of high school because of her pregnancy and had been married shortly before Mary's birth. After two subsequent pregnancies, a hysterectomy had been performed when she was twenty-three years old. Mr. L's sister had moved next door, and she had often left her own children with Mrs. L while she and her brother went out drinking with friends.

---

[8] Gaston E. Blom and Grace Nichols, "Emotional Factors in Children with Rheumatoid Arthritis," *American Journal of Orthopsychiatry*, Vol. XXIV, July, 1954, p. 595.

[9] Eleanor Pavenstedt, "Environments That Fail To Support Certain Areas of Early Ego Development," in *Ego Development and Differentiation*, Vol. II, Forest Hospital, Des Plaines, Illinois, 1964, p. 11.

When Mrs. L mentioned her idea of seeking divorce, the social worker talked to her about making arrangements for the children, especially about her eligibility to receive an AFDC grant. As the mother began to feel less trapped by her hostility toward her husband, it became apparent that she still cared for him. She also began to realize that his presence in the home would mean much to Mary.

By the end of her one day's visit to the hospital, Mrs. L felt she understood her own feelings well enough to make some decisions. She planned to rent an inexpensive apartment in her sister's town, close to a school Mary could attend and close to her husband's work. She planned to encourage him to join them.

By the time Mrs. L had made these plans, Mary had begun to feel comfortable in the hospital; in fact, she was sufficiently secure to be naughty at times. She delighted in "buzzing" into the men's ward in her wheel chair, and she became careless about picking up toys. Mild discipline was established to prepare her for her return home and her experiences in school.

Mary completed the first grade one year after she was discharged. Her social adjustment seemed excellent. She was happy and relaxed as she talked about her sisters and schoolmates, sledding, and birthday parties. Both parents accompanied her to the clinic when she returned for visits during the year. Her boyish, backwoods father was as pleased with her progress as her hardworking mother. At the time of Mary's last visit, the pediatrician noted she was doing well "with just the right amount of co-operation and resistance."

Psychological Illness

Psychosocial factors influence the clinical course of juvenile rheumatoid arthritis in many patients treated at the center. It has been necessary, however, to hospitalize only one patient during the first year of the project because her psychological illness made improvement at home impossible.

Eight-year-old Barbara T could not walk, although the swelling in her ankle joint had subsided as a result of bed rest at home. Frightened, depressed, and apprehensive, she continued to remain in bed, or in a wheel chair, with her leg prominently displayed. Because her doctor feared her leg muscles would atrophy, he recommended hospitalization. In part, he also wanted to determine the effect that separation from her parents would have on her symptom. The information the social worker obtained in interviewing the parents helped the staff plan an effective program of treatment.

Mr. T was a tall, handsome, athletic man. He disliked being employed on the early morning shift at a shoe factory. In the afternoon and evening he cared for Barbara and her brother while his wife went out to work. Because of Barbara's illness, he had had to stop coaching the Little League baseball team on which his twelve-year-old son played.

Vivacious, energetic Mrs. T was a strikingly attractive brunette. After she organized her home in the morning, she left to work from 4 P.M. until midnight at a modern electronics plant. Mrs. T loved her work, at which she excelled, and enjoyed spending the extra money she earned, a good part of which she spent on new clothes and coiffures.

Barbara's health had been good until the spring preceding her hospital admission, when she had begun to feel pain in her ankle. Shortly thereafter, a hysterectomy had been performed on Mrs. T. When the mother had returned to work in September, Barbara had once again spent the rest of the day after she returned from school with her father and brother. Later that fall, the rheumatologist had observed the hot, swollen ankle symptomatic of her arthritis.

A week after Barbara entered the hospital, her spirits improved. In fact, she soon became quite coy. With a disarming smile, she discussed her then normal-looking leg with the psychiatrist.

After considering her psychosocial history and her clinical symptoms, the staff concluded it was dealing with a combination of juvenile arthritis and conversion hysteria. Barbara, perhaps feeling threatened by spending so much time with her father and brother, had wanted her mother to stop working. According to the psychiatrist's speculations, she felt guilty when her mother underwent surgery and temporarily made her wish come true; her inability to walk, even after the swelling of her ankle subsided, might have resulted from Barbara's need to feel punished for wanting her mother to become sick again so that she would have to stay at home.

The therapeutic problem was to establish an emotional climate in the hospital that was sufficiently different from the one at home to permit Barbara to give up her difficulty in walking. The secondary gain Barbara derived from being immobile was decreased by limiting the attention and presents she received from her family. The staff gradually helped her to participate in an active program. The occupational therapist was instrumental in helping her to learn to cook; she had never shared this activity with her mother because her father had prepared the evening meal. In contrast to her father, who showed much anxiety about her illness, her male physician purposely assumed an attitude bordering on indifference.

For seven weeks, until she herself wanted to walk, Barbara resisted all attempts of the staff to help her. For a few days she worked hard with crutches, and then she went home for a trial weekend visit, which was successful. One week later she was discharged. In three weeks, she was playing with her friends and riding her bicycle and had resumed a full schedule of activity at home.

During Barbara's hospital stay the social worker interviewed Mrs. T weekly to help her understand the psychological and physical components of her daughter's illness. Accepting the existence of a psychological component was painful for Mrs. T, since, as a consequence, she gradually had to recognize that the role reversal she fostered at home might be influencing her daughter's symptoms. Yet, by the time Barbara left the hospital, Mrs. T had arranged a leave of absence from her job and was awaiting an appointment at the local child guidance clinic where Barbara might be helped by psychotherapy.

Parental Denial

Denial is perhaps the most common psychological defense mechanism resorted to by orthopedically handicapped children and their parents.[10] When the medication prescribed alleviates the disease, families tend to minimize its intensity and thus delay seeking the best treatment.

Thirteen-year-old Christine F was literally waddling when she was admitted to the hospital. Symptoms of juvenile arthritis had been evident in her ankles, wrists, fingers, elbows, and shoulders for four years. The cortisone medication prescribed by a local doctor had helped this adolescent maintain a level of

[10] "Emotional Reactions of Orthopedically Handicapped Children," in *Feelings and Their Medical Significance* (published by Ross Laboratories, Valley Stream, N.Y.), Vol. VII, January, 1965, p. 1.

activity that satisfied her father; Mr. F was pleased Christine had missed only two weeks of school throughout her four-year illness. A self-made man, he proudly described his daughter as "independent and self-negotiating."

Unfortunately, cortisone is a drug that has powerful side effects. Obesity and osteoporosis were two of the more serious side effects that resulted from Christine's use of it. Her osteoporotic bones lacked calcium and strength, and some of the spinal vertebrae had been compressed. Not until the compressed vertebrae caused this usually stoic girl to experience acute agony did the family decide to seek specialized medical care.

Eleven weeks after her hospital discharge Christine was no longer dependent upon cortisone to "keep going." She became less restrained emotionally and cried sometimes, first in an interview with the psychiatric consultant, and later as she talked with the social worker and struggled to gain a more mature understanding of her illness. She continued her excellent study habits and was supervised by a teacher at the hospital and a tutor at home. Christine completed her eighth-grade work on schedule, and she was walking well enough when high school opened to take her place there along with her classmates. She lost weight, adopted an attractive new hair style, and in manner and appearance became a more outgoing teen-ager.

Her parents freely expressed their feelings to the social worker, discussing their previous attempts to obtain medical care for Christine, their disagreement about what should have been done, and their feeling of responsibility for her present handicaps. After improving their comprehension of her illness, the parents were able to arrange a more realistic school program for her, so that all her classes were located on one floor, and allowance was made in her home schedule for adequate rest and appropriate exercise.

Conclusion

Upon admission to the hospital all five children discussed in this article presented evidence of psychosocial difficulties in addition to active rheumatoid arthritis. By the time they were discharged from the hospital seven to twenty-four weeks later, both their social and physical functioning had improved.

Just as more than one factor may have precipitated the onset or exacerbation of juvenile arthritis, more than one factor may be cited to account for the improvement in the total functioning of these children after a period of hospital care. Undoubtedly, the patients did feel better physically. Their parents had had an opportunity to gain from the doctors and the social worker a better understanding of the disease itself and how their attitudes might influence its course. The parents increased their competence by attending teaching sessions on physical therapy and by observing appropriate activity for such children in the Occupational Therapy Department.

Although the family of each child experienced special strain when she was hospitalized, the parents were relieved of the physical burden of providing for her care. Having the hospital assume this responsibility can lessen the guilt of parents who blame themselves when their child's condition deteriorates at home.

Although other factors operated simultaneously, these patients showed the benefit of having participated in an appropriate social work program designed to modify the family response to illness and to preserve family strengths. The parents in this program received both environmental and psychological assistance. Depending on the situation, the social worker offered the parents a supportive or a corrective experience, or she helped the parents clarify the meaning of the child's illness and of the parental role in treatment. In staff conferences the social worker exchanged ideas with other staff members and interpreted the changing needs of patients and their families.

Nevertheless, prolonged hospitalization remains a potential psychosocial hazard to the family and child. Invalidism can be increased, and progress toward maturity can be thwarted by emotionally unhealthy hospital practices. Long-term hospital care is also expensive to both the family and the community. Yet, with some types of chronic illness, such as juvenile rheumatoid arthritis, there are times when there is no alternative if the crippling process is to be arrested or minimized. In cases in which potentially harmful parent-child relationships exist, the crisis of hospitalization may provide an opportunity for therapeutic social work intervention. Appropriate attention to the patient-family constellation can transform the child's stay in a hospital from a possibly damaging experience into one that promotes his social and emotional well-being as well as his physical health.

The Blind: Psychological and Emotional Needs

Doreen M. Winkler

Since formalized work with the blind began in North America about 1828, a good deal has been thought, written and said about their physical needs and how best to meet them. Much less attention has been paid to the psychological and emotional needs of blind individuals and their families. Perhaps this is because much less is known about these needs. Or, there may be a reluctance on the part of both blind and sighted people to become involved in discussions of them. The psychological needs created by blindness are important not only to blind people themselves but to all those who attempt to assist them.

This paper explores some of the psychological needs blind people and their families have: what they are, why they exist, and why they are often unmet. There are three major needs.

First, a person who is congenitally or adventitiously blind needs to know as honestly and objectively as possible the facts about his condition. The individual must be given accurate data and emotional help to accept and adjust. Second, a blind person needs to be rehabilitated according to the individual requirements of his personality and circumstances. He cannot be reconstructed according to a mold his rehabilitators have made for him. Third, in so far as possible, a blind person needs to have some control and power to shape his own destiny.

To achieve this third goal, he needs skilled intervention of an objective, knowledgeable worker to help him consider possible alternatives, to make realistic decisions for himself, and to attempt goals that are within his capabilities.

In part, all people have these needs. But with the advent of blindness, such psychological needs become intensified, urgent, and all-encompassing.

My observations and impressions have come from my personal experiences as a congenitally, totally blind person; and from my professional

Reprinted from *Social Worker,* Vol. 40, No. 4 (December, 1972), pp. 262–269, by permission of the publisher.

experiences as a social worker variously employed in a family service centre, a child guidance clinic, a medical clinic of a general hospital, a treatment ward in a psychiatric hospital, and, briefly, in the Social Service Department of the Canadian National Institute for the Blind in Toronto.

The Need to Know

Dr. Louis Cholden, in his writings, argues that blind people need to know as quickly and as realistically as possible the unvarnished truth about their condition, and to adjust and accept that as a prerequisite to rehabilitation.[1] Secrecy is harmful to all concerned because it leads to distortions of reality.[2] Some sightless people begin and even successfully complete their education and training without accurate knowledge about their condition and without help in dealing with it emotionally. They do this, however, at great uncounted cost to themselves and, in some instances, to their families as well.

Parents of blind children are in need of special help. Their burden of anxiety and remorse is usually clearly evident. Because feelings are often irrational, most parents will inevitably blame themselves for what has happened to their child. If the marriage is not a strong one they will invariably blame one another for the occurrence. Such parents need a skilled counsellor to give factual information about their child's condition, and emotional support to sustain them in the crisis. Some form of marital or family therapy should always be made available to these parents for short periods of time.

Certain psychological factors account for information being witheld from the sightless and their families. Dr. Cholden suggests it may be partly due to society's concerted efforts to prevent such persons from accepting their blindness as a fact.[3] Such efforts may begin specifically with the attitude of the ophthalmologist. This physician has devoted his life to the conservation and preservation of sight.[4] Its loss in one of his patients may cause him to react emotionally rather than clinically.

Blindness in one of his patients may mean loss of self-esteem, loss of prestige among his colleagues, or injury to his reputation. His patient may no longer believe in his ability to treat him or he may hold him responsible for his blindness.[5]

Out of his own discomfort with blindness, or out of his need to spare the patient the pain he himself feels, he may distort or minimize information.[6] In fact, he may choose an even less desirable alternative and avoid the

---

[1] Louis S. Cholden, M.D., *A Psychiatrist Works With Blindness*, American Foundation For The Blind, New York, 1958, p. 23.

[2] *Ibid.*, p. 16.

[3] *Ibid.*, pp. 76–77.

[4] *Ibid.*, p. 22.

[5] *Ibid.*, p. 23.

[6] *Ibid.*, p. 23.

patient and his family altogether, assigning the task of information-giving to someone less qualified. If he does discuss the patient's condition at all the doctor's attitude will be conveyed by what he says, and the manner in which he says it.[7]

If the doctor holds out hope that his patient may live a full and productive life as a blind person that patient may be able to begin to think of his condition in a rather more positive light. If, on the other hand, he views blindness as a tragedy or as something akin to death, his patient will tend to reflect that attitude. If the experience of being informed is a negative one, the blind person may direct all the hostility he feels to the ophthalmologist and refuse further treatment which he may urgently need.[8] By being misinformed or misguided about his blindness, his family may have their worst fears confirmed and either blame themselves for what they do not know, or embark on an endless and painful search for miraculous cures.

If false hopes are repeatedly offered to the patient he may be prevented from coming to terms with his blindness and this will invariably hinder his adjustment to it.

Reluctance to Disclose Condition

Some ophthalmologists may be reluctant to disclose information to a blind person because of what happens when he is told of his condition. Dr. Cholden described his initial emotional shock as a state of being "frozen," immobilized, unable to think or feel.[9] This is disturbing to the observer. Yet it is Dr. Cholden's belief that such a reaction on the part of a blind person is natural and essential, and must neither be prevented nor blocked. Time is needed by the blind person to recognize his inner strength to deal with the next phase of his adjustment. When his emotions return the first thing he feels is loss, the loss of his sight. Dr. Cholden describes the experience of a blind person that follows his initial shock as one of normal, reactive depression. His symptoms are those common to all reactive depressions: self-recrimination, feelings of hopelessness, self-pity, lack of confidence, suicidal thoughts, and psychomotor retardation. For a few days he may not want to get out of bed and he may have trouble eating and sleeping. In parents of blind children who experience this depression some genocidal fantasies may be present.

When this "expression of grief over the lost sense"[10] has run its natural course and the blind person begins to do some minor activities on his own he will be able, with skilled assistance from a counsellor or therapist, to start working on adjusting to his handicap.

At some time in his life the congenitally blind person must experience a process of mourning for his *lack* rather than his *loss* of sight.

[7] *Ibid.*, p. 25.
[8] *Ibid.*, p. 22.
[9] *Ibid.*, pp. 25, 73–75.
[10] *Ibid.*, p. 20.

In the initial stages of blindness a person will find contact with other sightless people very helpful to him. Dr. Cholden conducted group therapy with newly-blinded residents at the Kansas Rehabilitation Centre for the Adult Blind. He was impressed by the recurring themes around which discussions revolved. He found, for example, that many blind people felt their fears, anxieties, and emotional problems, were peculiar to themselves. He observed that "It is amazing to a blind person sometimes to know another feels uncomfortable in a silence, or that his blind friend is fearful when he is lost."

A blind counsellor who has made a good adjustment to his own handicap is often better qualified emotionally and has greater depth of intellectual understanding of his newly or congenitally blind client than do his sighted colleagues. An early visit by a well-qualified blind worker to parents of a blind child is likely to give them more hope for their child's future than any number of visits by a sighted worker.

Dr. Cholden suggests that, in most cases, the blind person should be isolated from his family during his initial stage of depression as well-meaning members will tend to interfere with or try to prevent the mourning process.[12] The author is inclined, however, to share the opinion of Dr. Robert Scott that "a family crisis precipitated by the onset of blindness in one of its members is a family problem and not generic to blindness".[13] Experience in working with many families in crisis has been that whenever one member is suffering pain or loss all members feel that pain or loss in some way. The mourning process so necessary to a blind person's acceptance of his handicap is equally necessary to his family's acceptance of it.

Forces Blocking Acceptance of Blindness

Even though adequate information has been given to blind persons and their families and they have received help in working through the first stages of shock and grief, many of them continue to have difficulty accepting and adjusting to blindness. Many external and internal forces thwart their efforts to do so.[14]

1. There is resistance to change in the human personality that makes it hard for everyone to accept a new self-concept. The sightless individual may feel that he will never be fully accepted by society. And he may see little need to reorganize himself in another, perhaps more painful way.

2. This observation underscores Dr. Cholden who writes that, according to his personality make-up, every individual will have his own individual reaction to blindness. Some reactions though are common to many. For

[11] *Ibid.*, p. 37.
[12] *Ibid.*, p. 27.
[13] Robert A. Scott, *The Making Of Blind Men*, Russell Sage Foundation, New York, 1969, p. 76.
[14] Cholden, pp. 76–77.

instance, people who have always depended on others will react in an even more dependent way to being blind. Blindness may be used by them to rationalize the gratification of those needs. They may try to prolong the period of regression that often accompanies the onset of blindness because they enjoy the attention and extra affection their family and friends have shown them because of it.[15]

Another person may see his blindness as a new way to controlling family members, or as a means of absolving him from family responsibilities. Some may use their blindness to punish themselves or their families in some way, or force sacrifices to be made on their behalf because of it. Still others may use their blindness to justify their recriminations against the world.

Sometimes a blind person who is enjoying his dependent role is encouraged in it by members of his family.[16] Many families sabotage a blind member's efforts to make a satisfactory adjustment.[17]

3.   A blind person's adjustment may be hampered by the stereotypes he and others around him may believe concerning "the blind".[18] Some of the more common stereotypes are: (a) that of the blind beggar, completely dependent, constantly demanding charity in an inferior role;[19] (b) that of the blind genius, able to overcome all odds at great cost to himself, and magically able to do things no one else can;[20] (c) the notion that the blind have extra perceptions by which they can be guided, which the sighted do not have;[21] (d) the idea that the blind live in a "world apart", with spiritual qualities, aesthetic preoccupations and inner thoughts others cannot have;[22] (e) the assumption that blind people live in a "world of darkness" and that most of them are docile, melancholy, helpless and dependent.[23]

4.   Closely linked with stereotype beliefs are what Dr. Cholden refers to as "the irrational feelings concerning blindness and its sexual meanings and historical connotation as punishment for sin."[24] Psychoanalysts' investigations have furnished proof of the close, unconscious connection between the eyes, vision, and sexual activity.[25] Child psychiatrists have often observed children in play therapy to expect punishment by blindness for masturbation or sexual curiosity. These unconscious connections often cause exaggerated, irrational responses by the sighted, and greatly affect the blind person's image of himself.

[15] *Ibid.*, p. 19.
[16] *Ibid.*
[17] *Ibid.*, pp. 68–69.
[18] *Ibid.*, p. 21.
[19] *Ibid.*
[20] *Ibid.*
[21] *Ibid.*
[22] Scott, pp. 21–22.
[23] Cholden, p. 77.
[24] *Ibid.*, p. 20.
[25] Scott, pp. 18, 24.

Out of these fears and irrational feelings the notion may arise that blindness is a stigmatized condition which causes the sighted to regard the sightless as their physical, moral and emotional inferiors, or, as somehow contaminating with the power to inflict physical or psychic damage.[26] Dr. Scott emphasizes that few blind people can ignore the stereotype beliefs of the sighted. Some actually come to believe in them themselves and so internalize them. Others try to insulate themselves against them or reject them as false. In either case, Scott's argument maintains that "these beliefs are a fact of life for the people who are blind". They must be reckoned with in some way.[27]

5.   A blind person may be psychologically blocked in his adjustment by his knowledge that his blindness makes him part of a minority group which may represent to him a lowered social status and reduced self-worth.[28] It certainly means that he is different, and his encounters with the sighted are likely to confirm his feeling.[29]

More could be said about the obstacles to adjustment blind people encounter. The author's experience supports Gloria Sewell's conclusion, drawn from the findings of her study, that "every sightless person could benefit from professional help to build a sufficiently strong self-image to cope with community attitudes and his own feelings of difference" and to assist him in his integration into the sighted world.[30]

Rehabilitation Is Not Always Successful

However, as Dr. Cholden suggests, a person who has been independent and mature, and accepts and adjusts to blindness, is not always successfully rehabilitated.[31] I share the view of Dr. Cholden that all blind persons are motivated to adjust to blindness, and to be rehabilitated, but there are many blocks that hinder the utilization of their motivation. As was indicated at the beginning of this paper, much is known about the physical needs of the blind. Much is known about their physical rehabilitation—how to teach braille and mobility skills, and so on. But, as Dr. Cholden has pointed out, much less is known about "making a frightened handicapped person courageous or a dependent client desirous of independence."[32]

Dr. Scott's sociological study vividly documented in his book, *The Making of Blind Men*, dramatically reveals that many sighted persons and

[26] *Ibid.*, p. 117.

[27] *Ibid.*, p. 77.

[28] *Ibid.*, p. 30.

[29] *Ibid.*

[30] Gloria Sewell, *The Adventitiously And Congenitally Blind*, School of Social Work, University of Toronto, unpublished master's thesis, Toronto, 1964, p. 98.

[31] Cholden, pp. 20, 67.

[32] *Ibid.*, p. 64.

workers in organizations for the blind clearly do not want to know the answers.

The thesis advanced by Scott is "that blindness is a learned social role. People whose vision fails will learn the attitudes and behavior patterns that the blind are supposed to have in their relationships with those with normal vision and in the organizations that exist to serve and to help blind people."[33] Further, "the needs of the blind are not determined from scientific studies of the impact of blindness on the functioning of the human organism. They are invented to justify the creation of programs and institutional arrangements required to palliate community reactions and fears about blindness."[34] Since the blind person must rely on the sighted for assistance in the most ordinary situations he finds himself automatically placed in the sighted person's debt and he may be restricted in his ability to reciprocate.[35] Therefore, as Scott emphasizes: "The blind person, by virtue of his dependency, is the subordinate in a power relationship."[36]

Within organizations for the blind there are also factors which prevent many blind people from receiving much-needed assistance. The findings of Scott's study indicate that, although there are many blindness agencies in the United States, only about one-quarter of the blind population is helped by them.[37] They are mainly blind children who can be educated and blind adults who can be employed. For the most part, the elderly, unemployable, uneducable, and multiple-handicapped blind are excluded or minimally served.

Traditionally, blindness has meant or at least implied total absence of vision so that most of the programs of blindness agencies have been geared to the needs of the totally blind.[38] For example, in many agencies braille is taught to some who, with the aid of special lenses, can read enlarged or ordinary inkprint. People with partial vision are frequently trained to do jobs devised for totally blind people when, with a few minor adjustments, they might be able to continue in the jobs they held before their vision began to fail.

Scott's study also shows that when a person is legally "blind," he ceases to be "a sighted person with visual difficulty" and becomes "a blind person with residual vision".[39] His problems are seen not so much as medical ones but more as sociological ones pertaining to his adjustments to his disability, whether or not this is the case. Once accepted by the blindness agency, Scott's theory maintains, the person who has difficulty seeing is taught how to behave like a blind person.[40]

[33] Scott, p. 71.
[34] *Ibid.*, p. 91.
[35] *Ibid.*, p. 36.
[36] *Ibid.*, pp. 118–19.
[37] *Ibid.*, p. 73.
[38] *Ibid.*
[39] *Ibid.*, p. 74.
[40] *Ibid.*, pp. 76–80.

Two Approaches to Rehabilitation

Dr. Scott outlines two approaches adopted by blindness workers in rehabilitation agencies for the blind. The premise of the first is that blind people can be restored to a high level of independence enabling them to lead a reasonably normal life but this is only possible after they have come to fully accept the fact that they are blind, with the implication that this is a permanent role they must assume.[41] The second approach acknowledges that the first is noble but impractical for most blind people. It holds that blindness creates enormous obstacles to independence which can be overcome only by a few, highly-talented blind people through great personal effort. A more realistic objective is to provide an environment to which blind people can accomodate easily.[42] This "accommodative" approach assumes that most blind people are incapable of true independence, that most blind people prefer their own company, and that most blind people need to perform special kinds of work because of their disability.[43]

Scott's investigation shows that, as recently as 1968, although most agencies in America theoretically accept the "restorative" approach, most practise the "accommodative".[44] There are economic, political and sociological pressures which make this necessary.

When a sightless person comes for help with his blindness he has some definite ideas about his needs or about what problems he has that must be dealt with before he can cope with his situation. The place to which the blind person comes for help, and the means by which he is sent there, has significance in relation to his knowledge about it as well as how he is received. If his need for self-determination in planning his program of rehabilitation is ignored, he will react in a number of ways. His anxiety may cause him to present himself inappropriately as resistant or acquiescent. His views about his blindness are essential to an understanding of how best to help him with it. If, as so often happens, he is listened to very nicely and later finds his opinions have been discredited or dismissed as inaccurate or superficial, he may react with so much anger that he will leave the agency feeling more confused, frightened and frustrated than when he came to it. Thus he may fail to avail himself of the agency's services he needs, wants, must have, and indeed, to which he is entitled.

In the rehabilitation process, Scott discovered, "the blind person is rewarded for adopting a view of himself that is consistent with that of his rehabilitator's view of him, and punished for clinging to other self-conceptions. He is told that he is insightful when he comes to describe his feelings and personality as his rehabilitators view them and he is said to be blocking or resistant when he does not."[45]

[41] *Ibid.*, pp. 80–84.
[42] *Ibid.*, 84–89.
[43] *Ibid.*, p. 93.
[44] *Ibid.*, p. 90.
[45] *Ibid.*, p. 119.

Many clever blind people learn to behave as they are expected to and demonstrate "insightfulness" in order to receive tangible services or proceed through the agency's course of rehabilitation to make use of its programs. Such a person learns to play the rehabilitation game in much the same fashion as the prisoner learns to walk the straight line in order to be paroled, or the psychiatric patient learns to recite all the right responses in his therapeutic sessions in order to procure his discharge from hospital.

Summary

This paper has identified three basic psychological needs I believe to be common to all unsighted or partially-sighted persons. The need to be informed as quickly and honestly as possible the facts of his condition and to receive professional help in accepting and adjusting to it. The need to be given rehabilitation assistance as an individual and not sociological reconstruction as a blind person having thoughts, feelings and abilities that sighted and many blindness workers believe he must have because he is blind. The need to be a partner with his rehabilitators in planning for a future as a sightless person and to be allowed some psychological autonomy in shaping his own destiny according to his personal preferences and desires.

Obstacles that hinder many blind people in their adjustment have been explored. The difficulties many blind people and their families encounter in meeting psychological needs have been examined primarily in the light of observations and research of Doctors Cholden and Scott.

Workers in rehabilitation agencies and educational institutions for the blind must employ great flexibility and imagination in their work with blind people. They use techniques and skills based on scientific knowledge of human behavior rather than on subjective experience with blindness and the unsighted. They must listen well to what each individual has to say about his problems with blindness as well as his feelings about being blind. The simple fact is that those who have difficulty seeing or who cannot see at all are, after all, individual persons who happen also to be blind persons. From this very simple fact comes the conviction that if a person's needs as an individual are not accounted for or met satisfactorily, his needs as a blind person will never be understood and total life adjustment will never be complete and happy.

The Brain-Injured Child

The Brain-Injured Child: A Challenge to Social Workers

George R. Krupp and Bernard Schwartzberg

The brain-injured child has been given little attention as a treatment entity by social workers in the fields of child welfare, family casework, foster care and adoption, and psychiatric casework. In recent years, however, several agencies have discovered that an increasing percentage of children under care or referred for service seem to fall within this category.[1]

The social worker can be of considerable assistance in the recognition of this disability, and in getting the parents to accept the diagnosis. In the agency, the parents can obtain the counseling they need, and also can be directed away from inappropriate casework therapy for the child. When a total therapeutic regime for the child is required, it can be planned and followed through within the casework setting.

In considering the caseworker's role with the parents of a mentally retarded child, Kelman notes, "A particularly crucial function . . . is that of guidance or treatment of parents. . . . they have a right and a responsbility to participate closely in planning for [the child's] care. . . . Some parents have experienced profound difficulties in caring for their . . . child, owing to the nature of the child's condition, to their own subjective difficulties, or, as is usually the case, to a combination of the two."[2] He adds that they should be encouraged to participate in planning, not only for humanitarian reasons but also to ensure that the treatment program instituted may be carried on appropriately in the home. These proposals also are sound in regard to the parents of the brain-injured child.

The social worker's role in helping the brain-injured child is: (1) to provide counseling and guidance for the parents, and (2) when desirable, to provide the child with direct help, including the necessary therapy when the agency is equipped to give it, or appropriate referral when the agency

---

[1] The source material for this paper was drawn from the experiences of the authors when they were associated with the Family Service Association of the Five Towns, Woodmere, N.Y.

[2] Howard R. Kelman, "The Function of a Clinic for Mentally Retarded Children," *Social Casework*, Vol. XXXVII, No. 5 (1956), p. 239.

Reprinted from *Social Casework*, Vol. 41 (February, 1960), pp. 63–69, by permission of the authors and the Family Service Association of America.

is unable to provide direct service. The family service agency, whose case-work treatment is family oriented and which can provide a range of services, lends itself well to such a program.

The parents' feeling of bewilderment and confusion concerning the child's behavior is a crucial problem. Special attention should be given to the fact that many of these parents have not been able to accept the diagnosis of brain injury, despite their having been advised of it—sometimes years before—by various doctors, clinics, and special educational resources. Because of their anxiety and lack of knowledge, the parents frequently fight against the acceptance of this diagnosis. They often mention the child's highest level of performance as proof that the child is not retarded or damaged, and ignore other areas in which the child functions poorly. This tendency is not surprising, since the brain-injured child's behavior is almost always erratic or spotty. Hence, the parent rationalizes and cites scores of examples to disprove the previous diagnosis and recommended course of action. Invariably, in the first contact with the caseworker, the parent will deny the child's condition, and complain that the case has been mishandled in the past.

The brain-injured child is frequently brought to the attention of the social worker either by the parents because of his poor school adjustment, or by the school itself because of his poor educational achievements. Sometimes the referring school or parent is also concerned about the child's high degree of volatility as well as by his lack of any real social adjustment.

It has been estimated by various authorities that the incidence of children suffering from this condition is much larger than the public realizes. For example, Weir and Anderson note that a large proportion of the 5 per cent of failing children in the school system in Rockford, Illinois, was suffering from the results of brain injury.[3] That such a comparatively large proportion can go generally unrecognized may be due, in part, to the fact that the parents see the children primarily in the protected environment of the home. When the child goes to school, he is then observed in relation to his learning ability and in new social situations that create anxiety. His atypical behavior leads to a recognition of his condition. Frequently the school and the family are in conflict because the parents do not accept the school's observations and recommendations. The social worker should not be involved in this struggle, but must maintain his focus on the meaning of the child's behavior.

Behavior Characteristics

The particular behavior defect that the brain-injured child manifests depends upon the area of the central nervous system that is damaged. If the intracranial centers that initiate and co-ordinate muscular activity are the

[3] Homer F. Weir, M.D., and Robert L. Anderson, M.D., "Organic and Organizational Aspects of School Adjustment Problems," *Journal of the American Medical Association*, Vol. CLXVI, No. 14 (1958), pp. 1708–1710.

areas involved, the consequence may be cerebral palsy. If the areas of the brain that are concerned with intelligence are affected, one consequence may be mental deficiency. The injury of the particular areas that control speech and sight may result in distorted sensory perception. Disorders of other areas may produce epilepsy. If the damage occurred early in life and the involvement is diffuse, the result may show itself in altered behavior in relation to many functions. It is the child who falls within this last category who is of primary concern in this discussion—the child who usually has no gross motor or sensory disturbance and whose intelligence is average or even above average. It is this child whose disability often goes unrecognized. Frequently, such a child is diagnosed as having a severe behavior disorder, as being mentally defective, or as suffering from schizophrenia. Once the clinician is familiar with the clinical picture, brain injury is not difficult to recognize, but proving the diagnosis is often difficult.

No behavioral act is the result of a single preceding or predisposing event; and every act has both conscious and unconscious components. A particular symptom may have both physiologic and psychodynamic determinants. Although the organic factor is one of several factors that influence the child's total adjustment and personality, the behavior patterns of brain-injured children reveal a distinctive similarity. The parents, too, reveal a distinctive similarity in that they are almost always anxious and worried and usually give a confused and contradictory description of the child's history and present functioning.

The common behavior characteristics of the brain-injured child have been described by numerous authors.[4] He is different from others of similar age and development. He tends to be outside, or on the periphery of, the group and presents a strikingly erratic performance. This erratic and inconsistent performance is what causes the parents (and frequently the social worker and the school teacher) to be perplexed. This erratic quality has resulted in their describing the child's behavior as poorly integrated, variable, unco-ordinated, inconsistent, strange, queer, and lacking in stability. The child tends to be hyperactive or hyperkinetic. He is often described as overactive, hypermotile, or driveless. His behavior is often characterized by sudden rages, irritability, lability, and uncontrolled impulsivity. The lability in the intellectual sphere is evidenced by his poor concentration, distractibility, and short attention span. Frequently such children have difficulties with number concepts and with arithmetic owing to their difficulty in conceptualization. Instead of grasping number concepts as a

[4] See particularly: Harry Bakwin, M.D., "Cerebral Damage and Behavior Disorders in Children," *Journal of Pediatrics*, Vol. XXXIV, No. 3 (1949), pp. 371–382; Alfred A. Strauss and Laura E. Lehtinen, *Psychopathology and Education of the Brain Injured Child*, Vol. I, Grune and Stratton, New York, 1947; Lauretta Bender, *Psychopathology of Children with Organic Brain Disorders*, Charles C. Thomas, Springfield, Ill., 1955; Edgar A. Doll, "Mental Deficiency vs. Neurophrenia," *American Journal of Mental Deficiency*, Vol. LVII, No. 3 (1953), pp. 477–480; and Charles Bradley, "Organic Factors in the Psychopathology of Childhood," *Psychopathology of Childhood*, Paul H. Hoch and Joseph Zubin (eds.), Grune and Stratton, New York, 1955, pp. 80–104.

whole they will count out the number. An example is a five-and-a-half-year-old who, when asked how many coins (4) were shown to him, had to count each coin separately to the total of four; he could not perceive the four as a whole.

Another characteristic usually noted is perseveration or the tendency to repeat behavior whether or not it is appropriate. This tendency is frequently assumed to be a form of negativism, particularly when the child refuses to give up or shift his activity.[5] Because the child's attention may be distractible but also highly perseverative the behavior picture is confused. Another trait frequently found is low tolerance for stress and frustration. The child may be attentive when it pleases him to be so, yet hopelessly inattentive when efforts are made to control him. For example, a ten-year-old child was able to sit and listen to records at home for long stretches of time but was unable to sit still at school for more than five minutes. Moreover, the brain-injured child is almost invariably ostracized by other children. Often, he has poor muscular co-ordination and finds it difficult to ride a bicycle, tie his shoelaces, or engage in sports.

If the clinician specifically asks about the types of behavior described above, it is astonishing how frequently the child's behavior will then be described in these terms. One of the bewildering aspects of his behavior is its sudden and frequent change. The child will have periods during one day or for days when everything goes well and he appears to be relatively bright; then there will be periods when everything goes wrong and he appears and acts quite stupid. His anxiety readily becomes intensified and disrupts his performance; his conduct is unpredictable and alternates between infantile and more mature behavior. His ability to establish rapport alternates with inaccessibility, and his affectionate acceptance of others alternates with negativistic withdrawal.[6]

Authorities have advanced various hypotheses to explain these behavorial phenomena[7] in terms of the basic brain injury. In summary, they all seem to agree that these children have the following defects which the uninjured do not have: (1) Faulty powers of inhibition and control, motor and emotional; the child is forced into actions that are not intended. (2) Disturbances of perception. Perception is more than receiving stimuli; it is an act or a process in which meanings are attributed to the sensed stimuli. (3) Predisposition to anxiety due to impaired organization, confused interpretation of the environment, and early postural reflex disturbance. The child has impaired visual-motor performance, with a corresponding inability to distinguish foreground figures and background details. There is a sort of confusing-the-forest-for-the-trees response. Distortions of body image are also present. (4) Secondary psychological defense mechanisms related to the repeated frustrations (anxiety) encountered by the brain-

[5] Charles Bradley, *op. cit.*

[6] Edgar A. Doll, *op. cit.*

[7] See especially Alfred A. Strauss and Laura E. Lehtinen; Lauretta Bender; Edgar A. Doll; Charles Bradley, *op. cit.*

injured child and his parents. These may be character reactions such as meticulousness, clinging or withdrawal; psychoneurotic reactions such as phobias, obsessions, and compulsions; psychotic reactions such as schizophrenic thinking disturbances and specific disabilities.

Diagnosis

Despite the ease of making a diagnosis in typical cases of brain injury, clinicians frequently fail to make it. One of the reasons for this failure may be the erroneous assumption that this diagnosis implies a hopeless future. The fact is that such a child tends to improve as he grows older and develops greater ego control. An accurate diagnosis can be made if the clinician bears in mind the six following considerations. These are given in what seems to be their order of value to the clinician.

1. The composite picture described above and the developmental history. These distinctive patterns must be present. They constitute the soundest basis for making a diagnosis of brain injury.

2. The child's performance on judiciously selected psychological tests. These must be administered by a psychologist *sensitive to the special problems of the brain-injured child.* In our opinion the psychological test is almost always more significant for the diagnosis than the neurological examination. Without positive findings on the psychological tests a definite diagnosis is difficult to make.

3. Past medical history. Prenatal factors, such as toxemia, abnormal vaginal bleeding, maternal infection. Prenatal factors, including trauma, anoxia, prematurity, Rh incompatibility. Postnatal factors, including trauma, meningitis, encephalitis, convulsions, cerebral hemorrhage.

4. Neurological investigation. The presence of neurological disabilities strongly supports the diagnosis. Pediatric neurological examination should emphasize postural reflexes, eye convergence, motility, and the manner in which the child relates to other individuals. Such evidence may not be present if organic factors are in operation. Thus, Silver notes, "Fully 20 per cent of all children seen in the Bellevue Hospital Mental Hygiene Clinic suffer from organic defects incurred during prenatal, paranatal or neonatal life. . . . In them . . . classic neurological examination . . . gives essentially normal results."[8]

5. Consideration of the family background and of other members of the family. If the child is extremely disturbed, but the family is well adjusted

[8] Archie A. Silver, M.D., "Behavioral Syndrome Associated with Brain Damage in Children," *Pediatric Clinics of North America*, Vol. V, No. 3, W. B. Saunders Company, Philadelphia, 1958, p. 688.

and the mother in particular is not schizophrenic, rejecting, or controlling, the clinician should consider the possibility of an organic defect.

6.   Electroencephalogram. This is of limited value, since it can be positive when organic findings are absent and negative when they are present. Much too much emphasis has been placed on this diagnostic procedure.

The child who has suffered a severe brain injury in early life, and the child who presents typical schizophrenic symptoms (autism, bizarre thinking, merging with the environment, withdrawal from people) following a period of normal development are not too difficult to distinguish diagnostically. There are, however, many children for whom a differential diagnosis is not easy to make. Some children seem to have both conditions. Many workers in the field feel that the same cerebral defects or dysfunctions associated with mental retardations or brain injury may and do induce certain patterns of disorganized thinking which are termed schizophrenic.[9] The authors agree with this but use the term "schizophrenic" only when no organic factors are revealed in the clinical picture, the psychological tests, and the history.

The Role of the Social Worker

In working with the brain-injured child and his parents, the social worker should have three main objectives: (1) recognition of the brain-injured child; (2) formulation of a treatment plan for him and his family; (3) offering assistance in carrying out the treatment plan.

Recognition

The social worker needs to acquire a basic understanding of the clinical entity known as the brain-injured child, and the meanings of each aspect of the child's behavior. He should recognize not only the individual elements of the syndrome, but also the combination of factors which characterize this diagnosis. He needs to know both the emotional and the physical reasons for the child's behavior and for the lack of impulse control. Above all, he needs to understand the relationship of the organic brain damage to the child's educational and social adjustment. This knowledge enables him to help the parents to understand the child better, and to work out a treatment plan with the school and other community resources.

Paramount in the worker's mind must be the fact that the brain-injured child has specific disabilities in the area of perception, and that his ability to conceptualize is impaired. This child finds it difficult to master two and

---

[9] See Max Pollak, "Brain Damage, Mental Retardation, and Childhood Schizophrenia," *American Journal of Psychiatry*, Vol. CVX, No. 5 (1958), pp. 422–428; and Joseph Wortis, "Schizophrenic Symptomatology in Mentally Retarded Children," *American Journal of Psychiatry*, Vol. CXV, No. 5 (1958), pp. 429–431.

three dimensions, he responds more to details than to the whole, his motor and emotional controls are poor, and he needs to repeat experiences. When the social worker recognizes that the child's perception is defective and that his learning ability is thus impaired, he will be able to understand better why the parents are so confused in their assessment of the child's intellectual capacities. Many of these children have average and above average I.Q.'s, yet fail miserably in school and in new learning situations. For example, the parents of one child who had been examined by several clinicians could not accept the diagnosis. By making tape recordings of the child's responses to their questions, the parents attempted to prove to the examiners that the child was not so slow and retarded as all the examiners had indicated. When one listened to the tape recording it was quickly apparent that the child had good ability in rote matters and that they had given him indirect clues to the correct answers. Hence, they were overoptimistic in assessing the results. It should be emphasized that in order to understand the child's behavior and his poor learning ability one must recognize his difficulty in abstract thinking and in conceptualization. For example, one child could take measurements of two halves of a table but could not add them together to get the whole.

A social worker alert to this diagnosis will notice the child's gait, posture, and facial expression. He will observe the particular speech characteristics—immaturity, slowness, and an echoing quality. A history of erratic behavior, hyperactivity, impulsivity, and social unacceptability, significant information derived from the genetic history, and the above observations should immediately suggest to the worker the need for psychologic and psychiatric consultation to confirm the diagnosis of brain disorder.

The psychiatrist is in the best position to help the social worker understand the medical and neurological implications of brain injury. He may make his contribution as a member of the staff of the psychiatric clinic, as a consultant in a family or children's agency, or as a teacher of a seminar in which all the members of the casework staff of the agency participate. He may also be used as a diagnostician who sees the child for a diagnostic interview to ensure the validity of the diagnosis made.

Formulation of a Treatment Plan

The worker in a social agency needs to take into consideration the assets and liabilities of the parents, as well as the nature and extent of the injury to the child, and the limitations of the child's functioning because of the damage. In general, however, an appropriate treatment plan includes counseling and guidance for the parents, referral to a medical resource for medical or drug therapy needed by the child, some sort of relationship therapy when indicated, and suggestions for modification of the average educational plan, such as placement in a special class or securing a teacher of the homebound, if this is possible. When the school does not permit any modification of the usual curriculum, or when the parents are unwilling or unable to benefit from a counseling or guidance relationship, it may be necessary to work out plans for the child away from his home—foster care, placement in a treatment institution or in a specially structured educational setting. The psychiatrist usually participates in formulating the plan.

The brain-injured child has a weak ego and a history of repeated failure in handling his own needs and his environmental pressures. Special educational techniques are required to help him develop ego mastery. These are divided into two main groups by Kaliski[10] and include "experiences in everyday living, awareness and interpretation of each other's needs, feelings, forming relationships (adults and peers), getting acquainted with the community, its structure, its resources, its needs, civic responsibilities," and "learning the skills and acquiring the tools necessary to function independently in our culture." An atmosphere in which the child is relaxed and in close contact with the teacher is a most important tool for his educational retraining.

It should never be taken for granted that the child will understand and follow ordinary verbal directions, especially when time and space relationships are involved. The brain-injured child has difficulties in perceiving the relationships and similarities between things in the world around him, which is the basis for abstract thinking. He often perceives things quite differently from the normal person and his attention is distracted by any insignificant or meaningless detail. Therefore, it is important to avoid any unnecessary or distracting stimuli.

At the same time, each task the child is asked to perform must be concretized for him. It must be broken down into its component parts, and each one must be made concrete. For example, the child may be unable to tie his own shoelaces. The special educator, educational therapist or psychologist who is helping him learn to perform this task can do so only by over-concretizing the material. Each step is broken down into its simplest elements. The child learns each step in minute detail, and gradually learns to put the steps together. Or again, the child may know his multiplication tables and spelling by rote. He may know that two times three is six, but he does not know why it is six. The educator may use diagrams and teach him by adding two threes. What he already knows by rote can be used in developing conceptualization in this way; thus, multiplication and division are spelled out.

The child's attention has to be directed through the use of special techniques, because one of his major limitations is his inability to concentrate on ordinary visual or auditory stimuli. This can be done through specially designed visual stimuli such as lights, color, or forms, or through special auditory stimuli. In addition, certain kinesthetic approaches may be used to increase conceptualization. For example, the special educator may hold the pencil with the child, and go over the letter that is being taught, or the letter may be made out of clay, pinned out flat, and then traced with a stick

[10] Lotte Kaliski, "The Brain Injured Child—Learning by Living in a Structured Setting," *American Journal of Mental Deficiency*, Vol. LXIII, No. 4 (1959), pp. 688–695.

or the finger. These and other kinesthetic approaches increase the child's comprehension by moving from the concrete to the abstract. Although special techniques have been developed, educators of the brain-injured child by no means have the final answer for educating him. As Strauss and Lehtinen state, "what we present today is only a vague, preliminary 'scouting' in the field of defect and disease and as yet we do not even know to what extent our efforts toward alleviating disease and defect are efforts in the right direction."[11]

Assistance in Carrying out the Treatment Plan

In establishing a treatment program for the brain-injured child, the social worker must be aware that any plan will involve three groups of people: the school authorities, including the psychologist, principal, and classroom teacher; the family physician or pediatrician; and the parents themselves. Even the child with superior intelligence usually has had a history of failure in school, and the referral to the agency often comes at a point of desperation. Thus, it is vital to secure the co-operation of school personnel in working out a special program, or in securing greater understanding of the child in the regular curriculum if this is possible. Hence, the school psychologist should be included in the plan as early as possible in order to make sure that the other school authorities, including the classroom teacher, understand the child and his problem and work to help him within the school setting.

Second, especially when drug therapy is part of the child's treatment (other than in a psychiatric clinic) the co-operation of the family physican must be secured, since it will be he who administers the drug treatment in conjunction with the consultant psychiatrist of the agency, and relates this treatment to the total physical functioning of the child. His co-operation in the planning should be secured as early as possible.

Finally, the major task of the social worker, that of giving guidance or casework counseling to the parents or parent substitutes, is carried on simultaneously with the other aspects of the treatment plan. The parents or foster parents are thus enabled to accept the diagnosis and plan on a continuing basis and to handle their own personal feelings which may interfere with their seeing the child as in need of special help.

Conclusion

The brain-injured child must be understood in terms of his biological damage, his psychological defense mechanisms, and the environmental forces acting on him. The social worker also needs to be aware that the child tends to improve as he grows older.

The social worker, therefore, needs to be alert to the overt signs which point to the existence of this type of damage in order to carry out his function

---

[11] Alfred A. Strauss and Laura E. Lehtinen, *op. cit.*

of providing service to the brain-injured child and his parents. He must see his role as one of helping the parents to secure additional direct help for the child when it is needed while providing concurrent counseling. Consultation with or participation by both psychiatrist and psychologist is essential to any social agency considering a program of this nature.

The social worker cannot be expected to assume the responsibility for making the clinical diagnosis of the brain-injured child. He should, however, be able to spot the chief behavioral characteristics and typical history of this type of child, and to understand some of the dynamic implications of the child's psychopathology. Unless he is able to do so, time will be spent needlessly in exploring the possibility of other diagnoses, in interviewing the family members, and often in attempting inappropriate casework treatment of the child. This is not only an inappropriate use of the caseworker's time, but also does the family and child a disservice.

When the social agency clearly sees its responsibility in helping a brain-injured child, and does the job in a professional and competent manner, it can be of considerable assistance to both the child and his parents. In this way, the social worker helps the child, the family, the school, and the community in which the child lives. All benefit from the social worker's efforts, and the child is able to lead a more fruitful and productive life.

Adjustment Problems of the Family of the Burn Patient

Gene A. Brodland and N. J. C. Andreasen

Patients who have been severely burned experience an intense and varied trauma involving catastrophic injury, severe pain, possible cosmetic or functional deformities, and a threat to their sense of identity and worth. Hospitalization is usually prolonged. During this time, the family of the burn patient often remains with him to comfort and console him. Because most of the attention of the medical staff is focused on the suffering patient, the family members remain in the background and few people are aware of their suffering and emotional needs. Yet, just as the patient himself must adjust to his injury, so the family must go through a complicated process of understanding, accepting, and adjusting to the illness and distress of the loved one.

The adjustment problems of the adult burn patient have been the subject of only a few studies, and the problems of his family have drawn still less attention.[1] Studies done in England have examined the grief reactions of parents of fatally burned children and pathology in the parents which may have contributed to behavioral problems in surviving children.[2] One follow-up study of ten children and their parents, an average of four

Reprinted from *Social Casework*, Vol. 55 (January, 1974), pp. 13–18, by permission of the authors and the Family Service Association of America.

[1] N. J. C. Andreasen, Russell Noyes, C. E. Hartford, Gene A. Brodland, and Shirlee Proctor, Management of Emotional Problems in Seriously Burned Adults, *New England Journal of Medicine*, 286: 65–69 (January 13, 1972); David A. Hamburg, Curtis P. Artz, Eric Reiss, William H. Amspacher, and Rawley E. Chambers, Clinical Importance of Emotional Problems in the Care of Patients with Burns, *New England Journal of Medicine*, 248: 355–59 (February 26, 1953); and David A. Hamburg, Beatrix Hamburg, and Sydney DeGoze, Adaptive Problems and Mechanisms in Severely Burned Patients, *Psychiatry*, 16: 1–20 (February 1953).

[2] Helen L. Martin, J. H. Lawrie, and A. W. Wilkinson, The Family of the Fatally Burned Child, *Lancet*, 295: 628–29 (September 14, 1968); Helen L. Martin, Antecedents of Burns and Scalds in Children, *British Journal of Medical Psychology* 43: 39–47 (March 1970); and Helen L. Martin, Parents' and Children's Reactions to Burns and Scalds in Children, *British Journal of Medical Psychology*, 43: 183–91 (June 1970).

and a half years after injury, discovered recognizable psychological disturbance (usually depression) in eight of the mothers and none of the children.[3] This morbidity is high, and it suggests that further examination of the reactions of families is needed.

The observations presented in this article are based on a study done over a period of approximately one year on the burn unit at the University Hospitals in Iowa City. A total of thirty-two adults and their families were evaluated psychiatrically on admission and were interviewed daily thereafter until the time of discharge. Initial evaluation was based on complete psychiatric and social histories and mental status examinations. The patients ranged in age from twenty to fifty-nine with a mean of thirty-six, in total body surface burn from 8 percent to 60 percent with a mean of 29 percent, and in duration of hospitalization from two and one-half weeks to three months with a mean of one month. Patients outside the age range of eighteen through sixty or with severe mental retardation were excluded.

The relatives of the burn patient appeared to go through an adjustment process, similar to that of the patients, involving two stages. The first stage was one of acute shock and grief analogous to the acute physical and emotional trauma experienced by the patient himself. In the second or convalescent stage, the relatives had overcome shock and disbelief; they rationalized and accepted the fact of the injury and its accompaniments and began to assist the patient in the process of recovery.

Initial Reactions of Relatives

The family's first reaction on arriving at the hospital is usually relief that the patient has not died or been burned more severely. Rationalizations that "it could have been worse" provide an affirmative basis from which to begin coping with the stress that they face. In this first stage, the relatives express little concern about the potential scarring that might take place. Their primary concern is for the recovery of the patient, no matter what his appearance on recovery. The following case history illustrates the initial reaction of many families in the first stage of hospitalization.

> Mr. S, aged twenty-three, was severely burned in a car-truck accident. Having been pinned in the truck cab which caught fire, he sustained third-degree burns over 45 percent of his body. He was transferred to the burn unit two and one-half weeks after being burned and remained hospitalized for two and one-half months. His wife, who visited him daily, expressed her feeling that the scarring which might result was not important. She said she "would be happy if he could get well no matter what his condition is, so the kids will have a father." She demonstrated a considerable amount of quiet desperation; tears were often evident when she expressed her feelings.

Despite expressions of relief that the patient has not died, the fear that the injury might ultimately prove fatal lingers with many relatives. Some-

---

[3] Aldo Vigliano, L. Wayne Hart, and Frances Singer, Psychiatric Sequelae of Old Burns in Children and Their Parents, *American Journal of Orthopsychiatry*, 34: 753–61 (July 1964).

times this fear is expressed overtly. Interwoven with these feelings is a well-repressed wish by some relatives that the patient would die and thereby avoid the pain and frustration that lie ahead of him. Relatives of patients who die as a result of burns support this idea; when informed that a loved one has died, they often comment, "It is probably a blessing for he won't have to suffer any more now." Such feelings are usually suppressed because of the guilt they could arouse. The case of Mrs. K illustrates this reaction.

> Mrs. K, aged twenty-four, was burned in a natural gas explosion in her home. Her husband suffered more severe burns and subsequently died. Her comments following his death indicate a degree of relief. She said, "I will miss him and it will be hard without him. He won't have to suffer for months and months. I'm glad God took him soon. I know he wouldn't want to live being terribly burned as he was. His death was a blessing." Mrs. K probably would not have said this before his death but as she rationalized in an attempt to face reality, these feelings were allowed to come to the surface.

During this early period, the relatives and the patients form feelings of trust or mistrust toward the medical staff. When a patient suffers from pain and fear, he and his relatives have to decide whether everything is being done medically to insure his comfort and recovery. Occasionally, patients and relatives question the competence of the staff and feel that the patient is the object of experimentation. The extended waiting period prior to skin grafting is often seen as abandonment and may lead to feelings of mistrust. Such feelings were expressed to the psychiatric social worker more often than to the medical staff. Relatives were concerned that by expressing angry feelings toward the staff they might jeopardize the patient's relationship with the staff.

> Mr. L sustained a steam burn while working on a construction job. After skin grafting failed to take, the patient became suspicious and remarked that the resident doctor was practicing on him as if he were a "guinea pig." He requested that the social worker arrange for a transfer to a private doctor or to another hospital. He did not want to talk to the nurses or the staff doctor about this change, because it might cause hard feelings. It was determined later that his problem centered on the lack of communication between the resident and the patient. The problem was resolved when the resident made conscientious efforts to explain the treatment procedures more fully to the patient.

Soon after admission, a number of extensively burned patients experience confusion and disorientation as a result of an acute brain syndrome that often accompanies burn trauma. Many relatives found this reaction stressful. Sometimes a patient was verbally abusive or assaultive, and relatives had a difficult time in deciding whether this behavior represented his true feelings or whether it was the result of delirium. Relatives were frightened by this sudden "mental illness" and needed reassurance that delirium is a common occurrence in burn patients and that once the burn begins to heal, the delirium passes.

> Mr. R, a twenty-eight-year-old farm hand, was burned over 60 percent of his body in a natural gas explosion. About a week and a half after admission to the burn unit, he became delirious. During his periods of confusion, he thought of a

period during his second year of marriage when his wife had had an extra-marital affair. Mr. R angrily expressed the belief that this affair was still going on. His bewildered wife thought that this problem had been resolved eight years before. Mrs. R needed reassurance that his accusations were a result of his delirium. After Mr. R recovered, he denied any feelings of suspicion toward his wife.

Another source of difficulty for relatives is the psychological regression that is often observed among the burn patients. Patients who have been quite self-sufficient in the conduct of their daily lives before being hospitalized often become complaining, demanding, and dependent during hospitalization. The family, unaccustomed to this behavior, becomes alternately confused and angry. They want to respond to the patient's needs but are confused by demands that seem so out of character. Relatives become angry when the patients do not give them credit for their efforts and continue with their childlike behavior.

Reactions after Initial Crisis

During the second phase of adjustment, the family is assured that the patient will survive and begins to consider the process of getting well. The family members begin to recognize that they and the patient still have many weeks in the hospital ahead of them. The patient and his relatives usually have no prior knowledge of the treatment and procedures required for recovery; now they begin to ask questions of physicians and nurses about the process of healing, dressing changes, grafting procedures, and so on. Often relatives of other patients on the ward are important sources of information, just as they are sources of reassurance. The family of the patient must prepare themselves psychologically for an extended stay in the hospital. From a practical standpoint, family members must make arrangements for their own physical well-being during this period and establish "a home away from home." This often involves spending days at the hospital and nights in a nearby motel.

The pain the patient suffers is a primary problem at this time, and it often results in a sense of helpless frustration in the relatives. The patient seems to become increasingly cognizant of his pain once the threat of death has passed. He then begins to verbalize the pain, at times in tones of desperation. The helplessness which relatives feel in handling this pain produces conflict. On the one hand, they try to do everything within their power to aid the patient by making him physically comfortable and providing emotional support. On the other hand, relatives sometimes feel the staff could relieve pain more adequately by the administration of analgesic medication. The relative often is in a precarious position, trying to maintain a good relationship both with the patient and with the medical staff. Few persons understand fully the principles followed in the use of pain medication. The following example illustrates the development in one relative of mistrust of the staff.

Mrs. B was burned when she and her family were trapped upstairs in their burning home. She broke her arm when she jumped from a second-story window to escape the flames. Because of the burns, the staff were unable to put her arm in the correct cast. The arm was very painful. Because of her complaints of pain and her mother's frustration in attempting to alleviate the pain, the mother confronted the nurse with the accusation that the staff was neglecting her daughter by not giving her enough pain medication. Once the problems inherent in using potent analgesics for long periods of time were explained in detail, the patient's mother was much relieved and could again be supportive to the patient.

Another source of pain occurring during this period is the process of autografting. The donor site, from which the skin for grafting is taken, often is more painful than the burn site itself, causing great distress to the patient. Further, the patient must lie quietly after the grafts have been placed, increasing the sense of helplessness felt by both patient and relatives. The fear of doing something that might disturb the graft is a significant cause of anxiety.

The frequent trips to the operating room for skin grafting are yet another source of anxiety. The fear of anesthesia must be faced each time the operative procedure approaches; the patient is anxious about being put to sleep and having to relinquish control. This anxiety is often sensed by the relatives.

Reactions during Recovery

Still later in the recovery period, the problem of pain is supplanted by one of itching, which creates a problem for the relatives who try to help the patient to tolerate each new stress. It often seems that total recovery will never arrive and that one discomfort is simply succeeded by another.

Another major problem faced during the recovery phase is fear of deformity. Most families initially expect grafting to restore fairly normal appearance. What medical personnel consider an excellent job of skin reconstruction is often viewed by the lay person as almost grotesque. Thus, patient and family tend to be disappointed by the results of grafting and to find a gap between their expectations and those of medical personnel. During this stage of recovery, the patient begins to prepare himself for facing the outside world by realizing that scarring and deformity may have made him unattractive and unacceptable to others with whom he has previously associated. He becomes hypersensitive to initial reactions and wonders what reactions he will find himself meeting the rest of his life. Relatives have similar fears.

The relatives' reactions are the first ones that the patient observes, and his distress is increased when he sees revulsion. A fairly typical case of family reaction was noted in a follow-up study of burn patients.[4] A young mother

[4] N. J. C. Andreasen, A. S. Norris, and C. E. Hartford, Incidence of Long-Term Psychiatric Complications in Severely Burned Adults, *Annals of Surgery*, 174: 785–93 (November 1971).

who had been hospitalized for three months eagerly anticipated seeing her children. She was greeted by her five-year-old with "Yuk, Mommie, you look awful." Adult family members, on the other hand, tend to recognize intuitively that they need to be supportive and to help the patient establish a denial system. Yet, providing a reassurance that they do not always sincerely feel is often quite stressful for them. Only with time and thoughtful support on the part of doctors, nurses, and relatives can the patient resolve his feelings about disfigurement and come to realize that angry red scars eventually fade and that his appearance will gradually improve.

Sometimes relatives carry an additional burden because of their feeling that they have contributed to or caused the accident in which the patient was injured. Even when the relatives have had nothing to do with the injury, some feel guilty; they explain this feeling on the basis of not having foreseen the possibility of the accident and not having taken steps to prevent it. Eventually, the relative resolves his guilt feelings and achieves a rationalization that relieves him of full responsibility for the accident—for example, that the accident happened because it was God's will, because it would draw the family together, or because of the carelessness of others.

Notable throughout the recovery period is the difficulty that relatives have in dealing with the patient's need to express his feelings. They find it difficult to strike a balance between letting the patient describe his feelings about being burned and possibly handicapped and providing adequate emotional support. Sometimes relatives attempt to discourage the patient from expressing feelings of grief or fear and try to be constantly supportive and optimistic. In preserving their own comfort, they sometimes unwittingly deprive the patient of a necessary safety valve.

There are also relatives who become overwhelmed by the emotional stress of sitting at the bedside of a loved one and sharing his suffering. Many are reluctant to leave the bedside in the early stages of recovery, fearing that something might happen while they are gone. Occasionally, relatives become too depressed or anxious and must be asked to leave the ward temporarily to regain their emotional equilibrium. Remaining at the bedside of a burned patient is an unusually draining experience for his relatives. Much like a young child, the burn patient tends to focus only on himself and provides little support in return, leaving little opportunity for relatives to converse or receive support from others.

Recommendations from This Study

A burn injury is a traumatic experience for the uninjured relatives, as well as the patient himself. The families of the burn patients face multiple stresses and adjustment problems. They go through essentially the same phases of adaptation as the patients, for they must cope with anxiety about death, communication difficulties with the medical staff, fear of deformity, and the boredom of a prolonged hospital stay, as well as enduring the trauma of watching a loved one suffer. In some respects, their suffering may be greater than that of the patient. Although they do not suffer pain directly, they must stand by in helpless frustration, their guilt over the fact that the injury occurred at all further enhanced by their guilt about the anger which they must inevitably feel sometimes. Although they do not fear death or deformity for themselves directly, they must face these threats more immediately than the patient. Few patients are informed of their prognosis soon after admission and, if they were, their minds would be too clouded by trauma to comprehend it fully; however, relatives can not be shielded from this information, and they receive it when their minds are usually in a state of heightened sensitivity and alertness.

Relatives may provide valuable assistance on wards by helping to feed the patient, by providing companionship for him, and often by encouraging and assisting him with exercise and physical therapy. Nevertheless, nurses and physicians provide primary care, and the role of relatives must inevitably be simply a supportive one. This role is a difficult one to fulfill in such an emotionally draining situation unless the person providing the support receives support from others for himself. On the burn unit, this need was often met by the relatives of other patients. Although there was no formal effort by the staff to enhance such relationships, relatives often pooled their information about treatment methods, compared notes on the condition of the patients, and consoled one another when things were going badly.

Hospital burn units could learn a lesson from this phenomenon and formalize it in several ways. Relatives could be helped greatly if hospitals prepared a simple pamphlet to be given to them on arrival, explaining simple facts about injuries from burns and the operation of the unit. It should state the visiting hours established and describe the daily routine, the purpose of unfamiliar treatment methods such as the use of silver nitrate and sulfamylon, the rationale behind the use of milder and preferably oral analgesics, the usual course of recovery from a burn injury, the nature of the grafting procedures usually done, and so forth. A glossary of unfamiliar terms—*autograft, zenograft, debridement*, for example—should be included. Because of the complex nature of this type of injury, burn treatment units are often run quite differently from other hospital facilities, and relatives can not carry over any prior hospital experience. For example, they find it difficult to understand the infrequent use of potent analgesics, although this practice usually becomes acceptable when they realize that the long-term use required in a burn injury might lead to dependence or addiction. On the affirmative side, on some burn units, rules about visiting hours are flexible and most relatives are permitted to remain with the patient as long as they wish.

A second way of providing communication and understanding among relatives would be the establishment of group support meetings. A group composed of family members or close friends of patients currently on the burn unit could meet at a regularly scheduled time once or twice weekly. The group would remain in existence, although the membership changed as the patient population changed. Ideally, this group would be conducted by a pair of group leaders—a psychiatric social worker and a nurse or physician who are members of the burn unit treatment team. A physical therapist, a dietitian active on the burn unit, and a psychiatrist familiar with the problems of adjustment to chronic illness would be other potential members or guest visitors.

The establishment of such a group would serve several purposes. It would demonstrate to the beleaguered relatives the interest and concern of the hospital staff, sometimes prone to leave relatives out of the picture because of their concern for primary patient care; regular group meetings would make efficient use of the professionals' time and experience. The meetings would also serve to educate relatives about problems of burn trauma, particularly when discharge draws near. Family members often take on primary responsibility for the patient at discharge and they greatly need adequate information about wound care, the need for continuing physical therapy, and the problems of emotional and social adjustment. The group discussions would provide relatives with an open forum for raising questions and for airing complaints. They would provide emotional support by strengthening the bonds formed between family members and alleviate some feelings of fear, frustration, futility, and boredom. Such a group would not be designed as therapy, but as a means of sharing strength and information. Limited experience with such group meetings on burn units indicates, however, that often staff members also receive information and support from them.

A final way for social work staff to be effective on a burn unit is perhaps the most obvious. Families of patients often suffer significant financial expenses, and even after the patient is discharged the period of rehabilitation is prolonged. Family members and patients need to receive information about funds available to assist in the high cost of hospitalization, funds for care of dependents, and opportunities for vocational rehabilitation. An experienced and sensitive social worker can often provide subtle emotional support by demonstrating his concerned involvement as he offers his resources of information and interest to the family.

Revealing Diagnosis and Prognosis to Cancer Patients

Rosalind Jablon and Herbert Volk

The social and psychological concomitants of cancer are profound and extensive, and a treating physician inevitably needs to grapple with these allied issues. Present medical thinking also holds that it is inadequate to treat a "disease." The doctor-patient relationship must encompass concern and activity to help a patient with the anxieties evoked by the illness and the treatment process. Though this philosophy is widely supported, medical practice frequently falls short of the espoused goal. Typically the physician's explanation for restricting his activity to the treatment of disease is that he does not have the time for more than this. It is tacitly assumed thereby that a doctor would have the skillfulness generally to help patients in the broader sense. The authors question this premise and propose that it is rather the other way around. The difficulty in implementing comprehensive medical care arises out of the failure of medicine to understand the problems and skills involved in attaining this quality of service, and as the medical profession achieves greater appreciation of the complexities of treating a "human being," it will find both the time and means to do so. Toward this goal, the ensuing discussion offers some deeper understanding of a critical problem in managing the breast cancer patient. This is the issue of revealing diagnosis and prognosis to the patient.

The thinking expressed in this paper is mainly based upon experiences with breast cancer patients attending the tumor clinics of the Bronx Municipal Hospital Center, a New York City general hospital. The authors believe these patients to be representative of the general breast cancer patient population, but this is an inference based upon observation rather than statistical demonstration. Breast cancer patients include women with operable disease as well as patients with advanced inoperable or recurrent postoperative malignancy. Generally the patient with early operative mammary cancer is a younger woman than the patient with advanced metastatic cancer. However, within our population there is no predictable correlation between stage of illness and age of the patient. In this study

Reprinted with permission of the authors and the National Association of Social Workers, from *Social Work*, Vol. 5, No. 2 (April, 1960), pp. 51–57.

patients are differentiated according to broad age groupings, since it is believed that this criterion is both meaningful and functional; more concretely, it offers the medical practitioner the clearest and most usable guide for dealing with the problem under discussion.

In determining the appropriate type of medical treatment for the breast cancer patient, the stage of the disease is clearly the critical differentiating factor. However, in studying the sociopsychological trauma incident to the illness and the kind of social casework service needed by the patient, the most significant (and readily observable) differential factor is typically the age of the patient. Since our paper is concerned with the latter area, we are classifying our patients into two broad age groups—the first, women in the age range from 35 to 50 years; the second, women 70 years and over.[1] The significance of this specific chronological classification is the differentiation between persons functioning at sharply different phases of the life cycle, and therefore typically carrying very different social roles in living. The age group 35 to 50 is generally made up of women who are actively connected with others in the roles of mother, wife, friend, and working person. These patients are usually aware and mentally alert. The life experience and self-image of this woman is oriented toward being socially and physically adequate and self-reliant. In contrast, the patient 70 years and over has few active relationships, her social role is minimal; frequently she is dependent on other adults (married children) or she is alone in the community. She is a less aware person; her total life pattern, psychically, biologically, and socially, is largely adjusted to passivity and dependence. Women whose age is between these two ranges, 50 to 70 years, constitute the most heterogeneous group, but our studied population showed no significantly different characteristics among these patients as compared with the patients of the preceding two groups. This leads us to include the 50- to 70-year-old patient in either one of the aforementioned patient groups; the appropriate choice will depend upon the grouping with which her particular living patterns are most comparable.

Illness, as any life event, is an experience which occurs within the broader life picture; and the meaning and dimensions of any experience are synthesized out of its significance within the broader whole. The full life picture for the women of 35 to 50 years is radically different from that of the woman of 70, and therefore the social and psychological meaning of disease at these different stages of life will necessarily also be sharply different. In line with this, the treatment role which social casework offers these patients will need to vary, derived from the difference in meaning and impact of the illness in the total life configuration of the patient.

The nature of a social casework service to any person is bounded and

---

[1] Age alone does not automatically define and categorize the vital qualities of a particular personality and her life involvements. In discussing large groupings of patients, however, age is the most applicable single criterion for classifying patients into homogeneous subgroups based on sociopsychological factors. The writers accept that more extensive study may yield finer or changed age groupings as more precisely significant.

determined by that person's awareness of his situation. The most vital life fact for the cancer patient is his illness; and a casework service will need to be geared closely to the patient's understanding of his medical condition. This pertains both to concrete services which can be offered, as well as to what can be an appropriate focus of counseling help. In illustration, one can only handle irrational fears about cancer with the patient who has been medically informed of his diagnosis.

Should the Patient Be Told?

There have been sharply differing attitudes in the medical profession about whether to reveal diagnosis to a cancer patient. General agreement exists only about the need for sharing diagnosis with a responsible relative. The philosophy opposing sharing diagnosis is the more entrenched and long-standing one, whereas those who argue for greater candidness with patients represent more recent thinking. Advocates of each opinion have written effectively for their beliefs. Each side points for justification to a particular sequence of traumatic eventualities that may ensue when the patient either is made aware of his illness or is "protected" from his diagnosis. It is unfortunate that each school of thought largely ignores the logic and experiences of the other. However, review of the literature, observation of professional practice in the Bronx Municipal Hospital Center, and discussion with medical personnel of other New York City cancer centers reveal that these two opposing philosophies exist more in terms of theoretical speculation than in daily medical practice.

Practicing physicians exposed to both views reject a dogmatic use of any one theory of patient management. They express the need to individualize in giving medical information, recognizing that any piece of knowledge may be helpful to one patient but destructive to another. Medical practice, however, is at a still different point, lagging far behind intellectual conviction—in fact, few patients are told a cancer diagnosis. In view of this dichotomy between conviction and practice, it is important to examine the opinions traditionally offered on the issue, "Should the patient be told?"

Those who believe that it is generally more helpful to conceal a malignant diagnosis from the patient present the following reasons:

1. The awareness that the illness is cancer precipitates too great an emotional burden. The usual patient would respond with panic or depression, thus destroying his capacity for productive living during his remaining span of life.

2. Most cancer patients do not want to know the truth about their illness. Though generally not stated explicitly, the sequence to this is assumed to be: this patient knows what is best for himself, and the doctor will be most helpful by respecting the patient's wishes.

Those who argue for informing a patient of his diagnosis and prognosis point to the following observations:

1.   It is virtually impossible to deceive a cancer patient effectively about his illness. His own awareness, the infinite subtle communications brought him in his relationships with others (family and medical personnel), will transmit clues to the truth.

2.   Inasmuch as most cancer patients suspect their diagnosis and become aware at some point of their medical course, attempts to conceal it with unduly optimistic statements breed distrust, resentment, and emotional isolation in the patient. The patient needs to feel trust in his doctor, the support and closeness of friends and relatives in bearing his illness; he is deprived of these when fed unrealistic and unconvincing promises.

3.   There are patients who have known their diagnosis and who have had the strength to continue productive living. They have demonstrated that there can be greater values and ease in being aware of one's real condition.

4.   Most laymen are to some degree emotionally and knowledgeably irrational about illness. A patient suspecting cancer but advised otherwise is also frequently left alone to harbor many irrational fears. To the degree that there is doctor-patient trust and the illness can be discussed openly, a doctor can learn the patient's fears and help him understand his illness more rationally and to take measures in his own behalf.

Each of these points of view expresses a partial truth of human psychic life and human relationships. Still unanswered, however, are two key problems: first, perceiving the unique way in which each patient integrates these strands within himself; and second, judging therefrom the most helpful course of medical management for the specific patient. In essence, we see both views as having contributed theoretical insight; but the task still untouched concerns the skillful management of a therapeutic relationship with an individual patient as this relates to the sociopsychological trauma inherent in malignancy. And in considering the latter, the specific questions now needing re-evaluation are the following:

1.   Medicine accepts the validity of comprehensive care and differential management in dealing with the cancer patient. Yet practice continues to conceal diagnosis, and differential management is sparsely evidenced. What factors can explain this? Is existent practice meeting patients' needs?

2.   How can one differentiate what should be told to whom? Can we begin to formulate significant criteria to help judge whether a particular patient should be informed of his diagnosis and/or prognosis—or the reverse?

3. In malignant illness where the social and psychological meaning of the affliction is most profound, is it the best practice to place sole responsibility upon the physician for determining the psychologically best course of patient management? Is the medical doctor generally adequately equipped to help the patient with the emotional trauma?

In the Bronx Municipal Hospital Center Breast Clinic, patients are not usually told their diagnosis. Our experience is that many patients, certainly women below age 50, suspect their true illness and carry this terror-laden knowledge only lightly veiled.[2] Most patients are ambivalent about corroborating their suspicions. They demonstrate strong need to avoid exploring their fears; yet, equally tenaciously, they distrust medical and familial reassurances about their illness. Overtly these patients frequently appear to come to the resolution of keeping the truth barred behind a thin veneer of desperate hope. Yet many of these same patients do have the strength on occasion to ask directly, "Do I have cancer?" This situation constitutes the basis upon which it is argued that the cancer patient usually does not want to know the nature of her illness, and that the doctor will be most helpful by following her wishes. However, this thinking needs critical evaluation.

A Psychosocial Approach

The human being cannot bear isolation, and man's psychic structure inevitably strives against this. On conscious and unconscious levels, we devise ways to re-establish threatened interpersonal connections, tenuous as these ways may be. A sense of isolation breeds guilt, inadequacy, and fear, and we search to avoid experiencing ourselves as isolated from others. Death is isolating—not only for the dying, but also for the living. Further, the values of our culture also tend to emasculate man's capacity to deal with the inevitable facts of infirmity and death. Dependence and inadequacy, inherent in any illness, are defined culturally and experienced individually as bad and to be feared. Doctor, patient, and family members are all subject to these emotional forces; and consciously and unconsciously, we will all try to shield ourselves from meeting human mortality and weakness. Thus, the cancer patient who chooses overtly to deny the threat of malignant illness comes to this solution within a milieu which encourages evasion. In infinite direct and subtle ways, we who are well discourage this patient from facing us with his frightening, alienating truth. Should he want to know a malignant diagnosis, he may first need to "help" the living to bear his tragedy before he can be given his own right to do so. Ilse S. Wolff reports just such a situation most movingly. A young nurse recorded her experience with a patient in the late stages of bacterial endocarditis:

[2] This observation is widely confirmed in other studies dealing with the cancer patient's awareness of his illness. A bibliography is available from the authors.

. . . Every day when she entered his room, she felt a strong upsurge of feelings of guilt. She was going to live, while he, of her own age, was about to die. "I know he wanted to talk to me; but I always turned it into something light, a little joke, or into some evasive reassurance which had to fail. The patient knew and I knew. But, as he saw my desperate attempts to escape and felt my anxiety, he took pity on me and kept to himself what he wanted to share with another human being. And so he died and did not bother me."[3]

Need we not ask to what extent our continuing "humane" denial of medical reality with a cancer patient may be protective of our own defenses against the impact of death, inadequacy, and pain? Also, to what degree does our practice reflect intertia? We continue to do what is more familiar, thereby following the path of least resistance—intellectually, psychologically, and socially—for both doctor and patient. Inasmuch as medicine still cannot cure cancer, can this diagnosis cause some sense of guilt and defeat for the doctor, making it difficult for a sensitive physician to reveal a malignant diagnosis? There has as yet been no serious, scientific exploration of the question of what is therapeutically best for the patient himself.[4]

Medical opinion generally agrees that it is necessary to individualize the doctor-patient relationship, but that it is difficult to judge what is best in dealing with an individual patient's anxieties and questions. Truly this is so. Today there exists a large body of knowledge concerning skilled, therapeutic intervention in the social and psychic life of man by means of a trained relationship. Psychiatry, social work, and psychology are all disciplines involved in this content. The general medical practitioner or surgeon can only rarely be skillfully aware of all the many facets of his patient's social and emotional life, yet this doctor is asked to judge and to act with helpfulness in relation to a patient coping with the trauma of malignancy. It is also he who must carry final responsibility for what is told a patient regarding his medical condition, since the physician must be responsible ultimately for the patient's care. It is this situation which necessitates that those trained in dealing with human behaviour and interpersonal relationships contribute to medical understanding of these perplexing problems in patient management.

Professional staff will be better able to evaluate the social and psychological facets of a patient's life when they have some clear and specific criteria by which to guide them. Such objective criteria need to be understood as guides to facilitate arriving at an individualized approach to patients, through highlighting some of the important, common differentials among patients. Guiding criteria must be applied together with careful individualized judgment, never in a dogmatic, mechanical manner. It is within this

---

[3] Ilse S. Wolff, "The Magnificence of Understanding," in Samuel Standard and Helmuth Nathan, eds., *Should the Patient Know the Truth?* (New York: Springer Publishing Company, Inc., 1955), p. 32.

[4] All the studies seen by the writers deal with this major question only in a tangential or philosophic manner. Nevertheless, the data available do tend to challenge the continued widespread practice of withholding diagnosis from the cancer patient.

framework that we have drawn up the following tentative recommendations which have been useful to the authors in evaluating the question of whether a breast cancer patient should be informed of her diagnosis and/or prognosis. Though the specific recommendations which are presented apply only to the breast cancer patient, it is our opinion that this report has wider pertinence in pointing out a useful direction of thinking in relation to all cancer patients.

Recommendations for Interpreting Diagnosis

Unless there are major contraindications, the patient with breast cancer up to 50 years of age for whom there is probability of medical control of the disease for a substantial period of life should be advised of her diagnosis. However, along with this, it is vital that the patient's concepts of the disease are essentially accurate. The patient must be told clearly first, that she is not doomed, and second, the few cautions she will need to observe. The patient between 35 and 50 years is typically a woman actively participating in many relationships; often others are dependent on her. She is an aware, thinking person, whose self-image is geared to being adequate. Such patients almost invariably suspect their true diagnosis; reassurances to the contrary are rarely effective. This person's many active involvements in community and family groups hold the constant threat of temporarily allayed suspicions being restimulated, the truth becoming known, under circumstances in which realistic medical knowledge and assurance are least available.

Such a woman is more probably a person with strong motivations for life, inherent in her biological and social status. The motivation toward life carries with it both the need to feel herself in control and the strength to face trauma. It is these forces that impel the younger woman to express a persistent, though conflicted, desire to know her diagnosis in contrast to the older patient who will usually deny the illness far more effectively. The same drives in the younger patient can, however, also be channelized into other directions if the patient is permitted an alternative. They can be available to the patient in facing her true diagnosis and still reaching out for continued satisfactions in living. It is our experience that the anxiety of the younger patient is frequently interwoven with fears about the welfare of others, primarily her children. Realistically, knowing her illness (when there is still a hopeful prognosis) may release a parent from corroding uncertainty and conflict and free her energies for planning constructively for her child and herself. It is also important to realize that honest, realistic reassurance will generally be more effective and sustained than false over-optimistic hopes. Similarly, our own capacity to deal with the patient's anxieties will be more secure when we are not burdened with gross untruths.

The woman under 50 years whose illness is at an advanced stage presents different problems. Her social roles and emotional and intellectual attitudes have been described. However, the patient's more critical medical status produces grave differences in her emotional resources and needs, as compared with the patient of the same age whose disease is controlled. The advanced cancer patient will be experiencing more or less prolonged debilitation and physical pain, relieved usually only for brief periods. There can be no hopeful prognosis of sustained freedom from disease. Death is advancing inexorably. The patient's accelerating symptoms of pain and disability will intensify anxiety and hopelessness. On an overt level the patient may evidence an intense, desperate desire to live, but one can safely assume that this is far from the entire emotional matrix. At our present point of understanding, it is wiser with most of these patients to conceal diagnosis, but this decision must always be determined discriminatingly in relation to the particular patient—not mechanically out of inertia.

It is pertinent to be aware of two vital considerations with the advanced cancer patient. First, does the patient herself convey strong need to know her diagnosis? Obviously, if she does not want this knowledge, it will not be of therapeutic use to her, but will only increase her anxiety and despair. Second, there are some persons for whom uncertainty and not knowing are intensely upsetting and emotionally draining, since for them unsureness is emotionally synonymous with total loss of control. This patient will press to know the diagnosis in an effort to subdue the feeling of loss of control. This is a most difficult patient to manage, since the same unbearable psychological threat of loss of control is also inherent in the patient's medical status. To tell such a person her diagnosis contains the danger of intensifying the very anxiety which drives the patient to demand the diagnosis. The most helpful management may be to share as much real understanding about the illness and prognosis as is asked by the patient, and which can be given without revealing diagnosis or the inevitable fatal prognosis. The disease can be explained, to the extent of the particular patient's understanding, in terms of the organic processes involved (sufficiently broadly as to conceal the diagnosis); as a chronic, inflammatory condition responsive to palliative measures for varying periods of time. With this kind of understanding, the person may be helped to feel a sense of greater control of her life, since understanding is a force which can yield a greater sense of adequacy and active participation.

For the woman over 70 suffering from either operable or advanced cancer, there is generally no therapeutic value in knowing the nature of her disease, and in our experience, this patient rarely requests this. Her biological and social life level is such that she is essentially adjusted to passive, dependent living. She is aware of and accepts the fact that illness and incapacity are virtually inherent in her stage of life. She has both diminished need and strength to cope with life's traumas in an active participating way. To give the patient the knowledge of her diagnosis and prognosis would generally precipitate added anxieties and would serve no useful purpose for the patient's remaining life.

Interpreting Prognosis

What should be told a breast cancer patient requires differentiation between sharing diagnosis and dealing with questions of prognosis. To be aware that one is living with an incurable illness, or that one faces a danger of possible reactivation of disease, does not involve the same degree of psychic threat as is contained in the knowledge or suspicion of inevitable fatality. To the degree that a patient is able to face the realities of her life, her capacity to make constructive adjustments is enhanced. Many who could not bear knowing a diagnosis of cancer can sustain the knowledge that their illness is chronic, or holds the danger of reactivation. In many instances it would be far more helpful to give the cancer patient this kind of realistic, prognostic picture, rather than to permit false or overly optimistic concepts of cure. A case in point would be the young breast cancer patient who becomes pregnant without knowing the risks of reactivating the disease, because of the factors involved in hormone levels during pregnancy.

In our experience we found it advisable to inform the advanced cancer patient that her disease is chronic, though amenable to palliative measures, rather than to permit or encourage her to build hopes of cure. New therapeutic agents which can bring temporary regression of disease may be interpreted by the patient as a cure, regardless of whether the doctor corroborates this. However, the potential dangers in this unrealistic understanding are too great to be justified by the transient value for the patient of believing or hoping that a cure is possible. The patient who anticipates cure is implicitly directed to live unrealistically; she is unprepared for what does occur and misunderstanding interferes in feasible planning for her life. Moreover, when there is protracted illness with periods of clinical relief and then further progression of disease, the patient who has been awaiting cure will become confused, resentful, and distrustful of the medical relationship. She will feel deceived and increasingly isolated from family and doctor as her unreal hopes are slowly shattered by the stark truth of her experiences.

Conclusion

In proposing these beginning guides to differentiated medical management of the breast cancer patient, we emphasize that the criteria used—age and stage of disease—cannot be applied mechanically, without evaluation of their substantive appropriateness to the particular patient. They are to be understood as guides, not substitutes, for differential diagnostic judgment with each patient. The significant individual characteristics of each patient must always be considered.

Cardiac Disorders

Casework with Patients Undergoing Cardiac Surgery

Elliot C. Brown, Jr.

Recent developments in cardiac surgery, including the cardio-pulmonary by-pass machine, synthetic material prostheses for valve replacement, and surgical approaches to the relief of coronary artery disease, are presenting new opportunities and challenges to patients with heart disease. Those for whom there was no recourse twenty years ago may now have surgery that will at least enable them to survive. Others, for whom the prospect was one of stable existence, but with severe limitation, may achieve or regain a full, active life. Surgeons are addressing themselves to the amelioration of a broadening range of heart ailments. Vastly increasing numbers of patients are undergoing the various procedures. In 1970 at Massachusetts General Hospital, 530 cardiac surgery procedures were carried out. This number represented an increase of ninety-seven cases over the preceding year, and in each of the several years before that, there were somewhat smaller increases in the total number of procedures. In the first year's experience with a new surgical treatment for certain kinds of coronary artery disease, approximately twenty-five patients received the operation; in the second year of its use, approximately one hundred and fifteen patients underwent surgery.

The risks, expressed statistically in percentages and mortality rates, continue to decline. The challenge to each individual patient remains the same: to dare to undergo what is ironically at the same time a life-threatening, life-saving, and usually elective operation and to agree to incur almost inconceivable amounts of acute anxiety and physical and chemical assault on the organism.

The challenge to caseworkers in this exciting field also remains the same, but the number of patients involved has trebled and quadrupled. We are challenged to develop greater skill in assessing the psychosocial history and functioning of people coming to surgery, especially in appraising ego strength and capacities for coping with anxiety. There are seemingly

Reprinted from *Social Casework*, Vol. 52 (December, 1971), pp. 611–616, by permission of the author and the Family Service Association of America.

infinite demands to be placed on clearly finite and often overextended manpower resources. We must further the application of sound generic concepts to the special setting of the cardiac surgical service.

We are challenged to develop the skill to enable patients with a wide variety of personality structures and from various social environments to cope with the acute stresses of the surgery period itself, so that they can take full advantage of the objective improvement surgery gives them. Casework in this field draws on the main body of personality theory and on the special insights of crisis theory. It requires skill at initiating a supportive relationship where the concerns, perhaps because they are so extensive, are often either vaguely formulated or displaced to the most distant, concrete issues. The caseworker must also learn to be comfortable with all the paraphernalia of a modern hospital's surgical service, offering a relationship that transcends the particular awe-inspiring, intimidating instruments of modern medical technology.

The Literature

The plight of the patient facing heart surgery has received increasing attention in recent years. Drawing on the earlier works of Erich Lindemann, Helene Deutsch, William Bainbridge, and others, investigators have focused on the cataclysmic, life-threatening, or traumatic aspects of the surgical experience.[1] They describe the psychologic stress and delineate common coping mechanisms. The studies of the newly developed coronary care units (CCU's) by Thomas Hackett, Julia Ezra, and others have infused an awareness of the peculiar stresses of that setting.[2] Donald Kornfeld and others have suggested that the environment of the recovery room, with its exotic equipment, eerie science-fiction atmosphere, hypnotically monotonous and repetitive sounds, and disruption of usual sleep-wake patterns, explains why 38 percent of the patients in their sample had episodes of acute delirium.[3] Another sizable group of investigators believes that the disruption and alterations of normal biochemical variables account for the changes in ego functioning that many patients experience.[4]

[1] Erich Lindemann, Observations on Psychiatric Sequelae to Surgical Operations in Women, *American Journal of Psychiatry*, 98:132–39 (July 1941); Helene Deutsch, Some Psychoanalytic Observations in Surgery, *Psychosomatic Medicine*, 4:105–15 (1942); and William Seaman Bainbridge, Consideration of Psychic Factors in Surgical Diagnosis and Procedure, *Psychiatric Quarterly*, 4:414–24 (1930).

[2] Thomas P. Hackett, N. H. Cassem, and Howard A. Wishnie, The Coronary-Care Unit: An Appraisal of its Psychologic Hazards, *New England Journal of Medicine*, 279:1365–70 (December 19, 1968); and Julia Ezra, Casework in a Coronary Care Unit, *Social Casework*, 50:276–81 (May 1969).

[3] Donald S. Kornfeld, Sheldon Zimberg, and James R. Malm, Psychiatric Complications of Open-Heart Surgery, *New England Journal of Medicine*, 273: 287–92 (August 5, 1965).

[4] S. J. Hazan, Psychiatric Complications Following Cardiac Surgery: Part I, A review article, *The Journal of Thoracic and Cardiovascular Surgery*, 51:307–19 (March 1966).

Much of the psychiatric literature, especially the recent literature, is focused on the etiology of postcardiotomy delirium. That phenomenon is interesting, but it is, after all, apparently a self-limiting condition, whatever its etiology, and it may be occurring less frequently than in the earlier days of open-heart surgery.[5] This material is of limited usefulness to social workers primarily concerned with the long-range readjustment of patients following surgery.

Many investigators report undertaking successful therapeutic interventions to limit disorientation and hasten successful ego adaptation to the stresses of the surgery.[6] The time perspective in which most of these studies have been carried out is limited to the "perioperative" period itself, a few days on either side of the surgery. Thus, any appraisal of the patient's psychological makeup is handicapped by the pressures of time, the anxieties of the present crisis, and the limitation of an often hasty, frequently a historic, retrospective evalutaion.

Casework Evaluation

For the social worker to help patients endure and recover from the experience of cardiac surgery, it is necessary to carry out a thorough psychosocial evaluation of patients coming into cardiac surgery. If it is done well in advance of the surgery itself, such an evaluation can be the basis for deciding the nature of the casework help offered each patient and the kind of consultative help the caseworker can provide to nursing and other personnel caring for the patient during the actual admission. It is this approach that is used at Massachusetts General Hospital and that will now be described in greater detail.

The psychosocial evaluation seems the best procedure for gathering important information about the patient. Properly done, it provides a historical perspective to the description of the patient in his current predicament, and it inventories those personal and social supports available to the patient through this crisis period. This assessment is the key to determining what sort of casework supportive relationship to offer and to providing accurate information useful to the many people who will work with the patient. The systematic appraisal goes far beyond merely affording each patient the opportunity to ventilate his fears about the surgery itself. Indeed, in some instances, this material should not be uncovered.

We try to determine the general level of functioning of each patient. How well has he or she done in the role of husband or wife, breadwinner or housekeeper, parent, employee? Further, we try to gain a full understanding

---

[5] Stanley S. Heller, et al., Psychiatric Complications of Open-Heart Surgery: A Re-examination, *New England Journal of Medicine*, 283: 1015–20 (November 5, 1970).

[6] Janet A. Kennedy and Hyman Bakst, The Influence of Emotions on the Outcome of Cardiac Surgery: A Predictive Study, *Bulletin of the New York Academy of Medicine*, 42: 811–49 (October 1966).

of what the heart disease means to the patient and of the effects the manifestations of the illness have had on the patient's life. Has the patient found ways to cope with these successfully, or has he yielded and retreated to a more limited life than seems medically necessary? Have there been important secondary gains to the patient, extra attention from an otherwise not-too-attentive spouse, for example? Or has the illness been used to avoid certain stressful roles and situations, to gain exemption from important obligations? If so, does it seem that modifications in the patient's psychic economy can take place which will enable him to give up the prop of his illness? This aspect can often be gauged by learning what the patient's expectations are for after surgery. Those patients who may not be able to relinquish the illness often have exceedingly modest hopes for improvement and seem unable even to have the fantasy of being really well.

To what extent is coming to surgery an unexpected crisis? Patients with rheumatic heart disease have, in a very real sense, been chronically ill for some period of time previous to surgery. If the proposal of surgery is received as an unexpected blow, denial must certainly have been a principal coping mechanism.

What are the patient's usual methods of coping with anxiety? Are there any analogous situations to the present one that might provide clues?

What is the history of recent and remote losses? The threat of death or of the loss of some important function during the impending surgery usually evokes a reexperiencing of such losses. Many patients appear to work over previous losses, and the urgency of these feelings often puzzles and frightens them.

Finally, what is the social setting in which the patient will come to surgery? Can he count on the support of important family members, or will quiescent tensions be aroused that will prevent others in the family from communicating emotional support to the patient?

Treatment Plan

From the evaluation, a casework treatment plan is formulated. This plan provides for a series of judgments and decisions based on the worker's understanding of the patient and his situation. These decisions determine the nature and intensity of the relationship, the frequency of visits, and the kind of transference the worker hopes to encourage.

Some patients require frequent visits for reassurance. Under these circumstances, the worker may be cast in something of a parental role. He likely will have to be active and giving in a parental way, finding things out, giving information, and paving the way for the patient. He should convey his readiness to step in and help sort things out if the stress becomes too much for the patient.

Other patients would interpret such activity as a sign that the caseworker considered them not strong enough to endure the tensions of the situation. To communicate such an idea would clearly be nonsupportive, and for these patients something quite different is indicated. One would hope to nurture a peerlike relationship—casual, measured, and carefully respectful of the patient's independent competence. If the worker is too active, he may undermine the patient's confidence in his own ability to negotiate a difficult road. Patients in this group may need to mask their need for support with specific requests and concrete concerns. The worker should answer the specific request, hoping to discover other acceptable ways to respond to the unstated wish for help.

Some patients ask for help in dealing with the mysteries and intricacies of the surgical experience itself. They want information about what will happen to them, what the machines are, who the various technicians are, and what the tests are for. These are usually people who use intellectual techniques to gain a feeling of mastery over their situations. Providing full and complete information helps because it gives them the tools they use best to cope with frightening situations.

Other patients ask, in one way or another, to be spared the details of what awaits them. Directly or indirectly, these patients usually seek a general reassurance that the hospital staff is concerned about their well-being and stands ready to lend a comforting presence to the proceedings. Although other patients may be primarily concerned with the technical competence of their physicians and surgeons, patients in this group seem most responsive to the charisma of their physicians.

From the foregoing descriptions, it is clear that there are wide variations in how patients respond to the crisis of the cardiac surgery experience.[7] Fortunately, caseworkers have a wide variety of tools and skills available to help each individual patient.

Our expertise at focusing on ego strengths and undergirding defenses helps patients cope with the acute anxieties of the surgical period. Our skill at using concrete services—finding funds to pay for surgery, making blood bank arrangements, helping families cope with financial crises during the surgical period, and making discharge and follow-up plans—meets real needs. It also opens the way to helping patients with their emotional responses to their illness without labeling them "needy" or "dependent." Finally, the caseworker is the member of the team best equipped to develop and disseminate a clear awareness of the interpersonal setting in which illness and recovery take place.

Illustrations

Mr. B was an example of someone who used a request for concrete help as a way of asking for assistance in mastering his fears concerning the illness and surgery. The family sought social service help just after Mr. B was admitted for aortic valve replacement. They wanted aid in preparing and pursuing an application

---

[7] For an excellent typology, see Chase Patterson Kimball, Psychological Responses to the Experience of Open Heart Surgery: I, *American Journal of Psychiatry*, 126: 348–59 (September 1969).

for public assistance for the period of time Mr. B would be out of work because of the surgery. They appeared worried about a weekly income, although Mr. B still had extensive sick-time benefits. They seemed immobilized by anxiety and had made almost no preparations during the two months they had known about the impending surgery. Seen together at Mr. B's bedside for the initial interview, they were smiling and jovial, but there were undercurrents of inarticulated, massively denied fears relative to Mr. B's situation. The financial concerns were the only specific focus for these fears.

At an interview alone shortly thereafter, Mr. B was more open about his fears. He cried several times while the worker was taking a fuller history and as the special meaning of the illness and the need for surgery became clear.

There had been major deprivations in Mr. B's early years. Mr. B's father had spent nearly all of those years in a mental hospital suffering an organic, deteriorating brain disease. Mr. B had been reared by his mother and there had been no adequately functioning men to serve as models for him.

The three years leading up to Mr. B's admission had been ones in which the B family, and Mr. B in particular, had suffered several reverses or disappointments. At great expenditure of energy and entirely on his own, Mr. B had put himself through school, but shortly after moving into his third professional position, he had been "furloughed," when a recession in the industry led to major economy moves by the company. Mr. B sought the security of a clerk's job in a government agency—a safe job, but one considerably below his potential.

Shortly thereafter, the older child, an eighteen-year-old girl, announced that she was pregnant and subsequently married the father of the child. In addition to his feelings about his daughter's pregnancy, Mr. B also had to adjust to the fact that his new son-in-law was of a different ethnic and religious background. Mr. B said he wished his daughter had "given him time" to get his affairs in order so that he could give her away properly, but it seemed clear that he felt he had failed as a father and somehow forced his daughter into her course of action.

In this context, and from remarks in the interview, it seemed clear that Mr. B considered the surgery one more reverse, another thing to contend with, a crisis that he had somehow brought on himself or a cruel fate had visited upon him, and from which it was unlikely he would emerge unscathed. His confidence in his own competence had been severely sapped by his other losses and reverses. His guilt and disappointment led him to expect the worst.

The caseworker's tasks were clear. The financial situation was quickly clarified and the B family was reassured. Then, in the few days between the referral and the surgery, the caseworker helped Mr. B to see the illness and surgery as a medical event being competently handled, diluting as much as possible Mr. B's association of it to other reverses. By generalizing Mr. B's feelings and pointing out his good judgment and good functioning, the caseworker sought to decrease Mr. B's guilt over various past events, strengthening his picture of himself as a competent person deserving another chance at good health, important to his family, and potentially to his profession.

Mr. B's surgery went smoothly, and after a suitable convalescence he returned to the security of his clerk's job. Six months later, he was able to return to employment in his chosen field. Mr. B had been restored to the good level of functioning he had shown prior to the reversals.

Patients who have major problems with dependency present special difficulties to the caseworker and to all those caring for them. It is usually hard to assess the extent of their need for support. They often adopt a counter-dependent, cold, or aggressive way of relating that alienates the staff and heightens the chances that the patient will undergo surgery without sufficient preparation.

> Miss C worked as an occupational therapy aide at a regional center for crippled children, but she sheepishly said she really "couldn't stand" sick children. Being a patient was very difficult for her. She disliked the "implied dependency"; she wanted to be left alone when she felt sick rather than be comforted, and she kept most of her feelings to herself. She said that occasionally when she was alone, she might "break down" in response to anxiety, but it was important to her to be in perfect control when she was with people. It was difficult to know for certain where this feeling originated, except that all five girls in her family had apparently been forced to become self-reliant prematurely, when the patient's father deserted the family and her mother became more withdrawn. Even during Miss C's admission, the mother seemed preoccupied with her own health and only secondarily concerned about Miss C. The mother regarded the surgery as something her daughter was being given, and thus something she, the mother, was being deprived of. It seemed unlikely that the mother would be much support, but Miss C had erected barriers against acknowledging that she wanted or needed such encouragement.
>
> Through the preoperative period, Miss C maintained the most abrasive facade regarding anxieties about the surgery. Although she appeared tense and concerned about what it was going to be like, she made a point of not giving in and admitting how upset she really was. When the caseworker tried gently to speculate about how Miss C must be feeling and the kinds of questions she must have, she berated him for not being able to read the clues in her rather immobile face. After all, he was the social worker!
>
> A social service note in the medical record suggested that preoperative teaching and preparation of this patient should be casual and matter of fact, and that it should be carried out even if there were no indication from the patient that it helped. It was necessary in working with Miss C to avoid the connotation that such preparation was to make the experience comfortable, to relieve anxiety, or in any other sense to coddle the patient.

Concerns about death and dying are often denied, displaced, or projected. When such concerns are expressed more directly, the patient will usually have discovered some way of partially neutralizing his feelings. Frequently, this fact is clear from what the patient says.

> Mr. R was a thirty-six-year-old man, the father of seven children. He had rheumatic heart disease with severe aortic stenosis. Of special significance was the fact that Mr. R's mother had died in the operating room having open-heart surgery six years prior to Mr. R's admission.
>
> Preoperatively, Mr. R was able to talk about his misgivings about the surgery, relating it directly to the loss of his mother. Fortunately, he saw the hospital as having made a valiant attempt to save her. He saw himself as in quite a different position: younger, without other major diseases (his mother was diabetic), and benefiting from medical advances in the intervening years.

When the concerns are expressed directly and no adequate way to defuse them has been found, the patients present a striking picture. They seem globally anxious, distraught, panic stricken, with agitation and tears never far away. They grasp at straws of reassurance from whatever source, but nothing comforts them for long. Ironically, they often hide their distress from the physician, usually out of a wish not to seem childish or weak. These patients present management problems post-operatively if they are not helped to develop better ways of coping.

Mrs. F was such a patient. Lying there, frightened before her surgery, searching every visitor's face for some clue as to how they thought she would do, clinging, weeping and wordless, to each of her children in turn, she seemed strikingly different from the competent, controlled person the caseworker had interviewed several months before. During the intervening time, Mrs. F had suffered a stroke which was probably caused by her heart lesion. She had recovered fully, but that emergency evidently heightened her awareness of the risk of death from the surgery. She had apparently no way to come to terms with this threat.

The caseworker knew her early history in detail from the initial interview. Mrs. F's life was a chronicle of ultimately successful struggles against great odds: a poor, unassimilated, old-world Italian family, a difficult marriage to an immature man, and chronic economic problems which interfered with her attempts to educate her several bright children. In ruminating about her life, Mrs. F seemed certain she had never made a correct decision, although evidence of her good judgment was all around her.

The caseworker began the discussion by observing that Mrs. F held on to her children "as if she thought she'd never see them again." Mrs. F seemed relieved to be able to share her fears about dying. She confided that what particularly distressed her was her fear that more would be demanded of her, in relation to courage, stamina, and emotional fortitude, than she could muster.

Once these issues were clarified, the caseworker was able to help Mrs. F come to terms with her situation and make peace with the people she might not see again. More important, she was helped to apply her "when the going gets tough, the tough get going" philosophy. As Mrs. F began to tell the caseworker of other difficult situations and how she had been able to handle them, she became much less distraught and much more actively involved in her own preoperative preparation.

After the surgery, she had to spend more than twice the average time in the surgical intensive care unit, perhaps because she had been so ill preoperatively. Yet, despite a day or so of being disoriented about place and time, she emerged intact and has begun what promises to be a complete recovery.

Summary

A method of providing ego supportive casework treatment to patients undergoing cardiac surgery has been described. The treatment begins with the recognition of the particular stresses of this kind of illness and of the setting in which surgery and initial recovery take place. The content of a casework evaluation for these patients is suggested, as well as the development of a casework treatment plan based on diagnostic understanding. The case illustrations show something of the range of responses to the cardiac surgery situation which patients demonstrate and the casework activity involved.

Technical Alterations in the Psychotherapy with an Adolescent Cerebral Palsy Patient

Arnold S. Carson

Within the last decade the practice of psychotherapy has broadened in spectrum and has become sufficiently eclectic to be useful with mentally retarded children, character disorders, sex offenders, stutterers and a variety of other classifications (5)*. With broader application, specialized techniques have been developed.

The purpose of this paper is to add to the continuing effort to develop clinical skills for working with people who are typically considered "poor psychotherapeutic risks." Specifically, the short-term psychotherapy of a 14-year-old cerebral palsy patient will be described with particular emphasis upon obstacles to treatment and the technical alterations which were developed to overcome these obstacles.

Theoretical Considerations

Much has been written about the effects of physical handicap upon the ego and the subsequent adjustment of the handicapped youngster (1, 2, 4, 6, 7, 11, 12, 13). There is little doubt expressed in the literature that the severe physical handicap of a child carries with it, as one of the side effects, some degree of ego impairment. Psychoanalytic theory places special importance on the physical self, both in differentiating the self from others and in the development of the ego.

> In the development of reality, the conception of one's own body plays a very special role. At first there is only the perception of tension: that is, of an "inside something." Later, with the awareness that an object exists to quiet this tension, we have an "outside something." One's own body is both at the same time. Due to the simultaneous occurrence of both outer tactile and inner sensory data, one's own body becomes something apart from the rest of the

*References will be found at the end of the chapter.

Reprinted from *Mental Hygiene*, Vol. 48 (April, 1964), pp. 249–256, by permission of the author and the Journal.

world and thus discerning of self from nonself is made possible. The sum of the mental representations of the body and its organs, the so-called body image, constitutes the idea of *I* and is of basic importance for further formation of the ego (8, pp. 35 and 36).

Other noted psychologists have commented on the importance of physical self for personality development from different theoretical frames of reference (9, 10, 14). However, Wright cautions theoreticians against presupposing a straight-line correlation between physical handicap and emotional disturbance during adolescence. "Although physique carries a particularly heavy emotional loading during adolescence, it is not correct to conclude that any single physical deviation will invariably or even probably produce distress." (14, p. 181.)

Ausubel adds: "The psychological consequences of deviation will depend on 'social and individual attitudes toward nonconformity,' the strength of intrinsic attitudes of self-acceptance and the possession of compensatory assets" (3, p. 102).

In addition to the structural aspects of personality development in physically handicapped children, the writer has noted a number of consistent psychodynamic factors which have had particular applicability in the understanding of adolescent cerebral palsy patients with medium to severe crippling.

The physical and social development of the child with cerebral palsy is slowed down. His motility is impaired. Often he is incontinent until the age of 7 or 8 and sometimes dependent upon urinary bags throughout his life. In addition to toilet training, personal responsibility for cleansing, dressing, eating and speaking often need be postponed. Many of these youngsters are carried over the shoulder of their parents to the period of preadolescence.

Undoubtedly these atypical patterns of development predispose them to severe dependency problems as they get older. Consequently, the adolescent cerebral palsy patient in psychotherapy will often fight off a dependency relationship with the therapist or succumb to it so readily that there is little potential initiative manifested.

In their psychosexual development a post-oedipal development is an exception. Most of these youngsters remain partially to totally fixated in the oral and anal phases of development. So much attention and energy has had to be given to the functions of eating and eliminating that they often remain the chief avenues of sexual gratification even in adulthood. Genital sexuality is often hampered until these adolescents can work through their feelings regarding extended handling of their sexual organs by their parents during ages where there should be a quiescence in parent-child intimacy. It is worth noting that the prolonged physical dependency of the crippled child upon his parents sometimes makes it necessary for these parents to ignore some of the taboos essential in the normal child-parent relationship.

A number of obstacles to psychotherapeutic treatment with the cerebral palsied youngster follow from the research, theory and clinical observations:

1.   Strong dependency needs continue to be buffered by the ever-present palsy.

2.   Affliction at birth precludes the opportunity to develop a more favorable self-image.

3.   Self-sufficiency with inadequate personal equipment is a feeble alternative to the gratification derived from being cared for in the bathroom, at the dinner table and in the bedroom.

4.   The "why should I be the one who is afflicted?" question is one that tends to set off a severe depressive reaction, while the answer is sought.

5.   The avenues for sexual growth and exploration are limited by the lack of motor co-ordination, the rejection by peers of the opposite sex, and the conveyed fears of adults concerning their development in this area.

Case History

Bob T was born in 1947. Mrs. T was anemic during the pregnancy. He was delivered after $7\frac{1}{2}$ months of carriage; labor was forced for $2\frac{1}{4}$ hours; toes were bruised; and legs remained in a triangular position for three weeks. The baby breathed spontaneously at birth and weighed 7 pounds 2 ounces. Bob was a healthy baby and was circumcised a few days after birth. He had the usual immunizations at 6 and at 9 months. He was able to finger-feed at one year and spoon feed at two. Head control was established at three months, and he could roll over about the same time. He began to crawl at three years and could stand without support at four years.

At the age of $8\frac{1}{2}$ months Bob was diagnosed as a "congenital spastic." He was placed on a Prostigmine Regime until the age of two. Loss of eyelid droop and muscle tone improvement was noted. At two the standing diagnosis of cerebral palsy with general loss of muscle control in the abdominal and gluteal muscles was established. Bob was fitted for an abdominal corset in 1952 and long leg braces in 1953. He continues to wear these physical aids. Physical therapy case notes have the following repetitive pattern: slight gains, broken appointments, case temporarily inactive, reopened, slight gains, broken appointments, etc.

Bob's father is a self-made man from an Italian-English, Roman Catholic cultural background. He has attended college over the past 10 years and has gained inservice training in the field of metallurgy. Mrs. T is from an English-German, Roman Catholic background. She has been trained as a commercial artist but is employed full-time in the home caring for her 4 children, of whom Bob is the oldest. Bob, age 14, is followed by a brother, age 13; a sister, age 8; and a brother, age 3.

At the age of 7 Bob was tested with the Stanford-Binet, Form L, and earned a score within the bright normal range of intelligence. He received homebound teaching until the age of 9 when he was placed in a school for handicapped children. At the age of 10 he was transferred to a different school and reacted to the transfer with an episode of soiling his pants two to four times a month. Bob's pediatrician prescribed 10 mg. of Aterax per day to tranquilize the anxiety assumed to be underlying the soiling. Throughout the period of school attendance, Bob was described as being resistant to learning and to the school's physical therapy program.

Bob was referred for psychotherapy because of his underachievement in school and physical therapy, his constant regressions into unrealistic fantasies and general immaturity.

Administration of Treatment

Bob was seen once a week in an outpatient orthopedic clinic. His physical therapy, occupational therapy and social service were enlisted at times as aids to treatment. The therapist was a post-doctoral fellow in the counseling service of Merrill-Palmer supervisors. There were 29 treatment hours with Bob, an equivalent number of supervisory hours, and a total of 5 interviews with Mr. and Mrs. T.

Treatment

The therapist was cautious about working with Mr. and Mrs. T because of their dissatisfaction with previous psychological contacts. They consented to treatment for Bob but were weary of having people telling them how to rear their children. The goals of therapy were to help Bob understand his passive resistance, "smart aleckiness," and find ways of handling his impulses which would not elicit rejection from others.

A second goal of treatment was to put Bob's fantasies to the test of reality. The initial stages of therapy were devoted to establishing a positive working relationship with the patient.

The therapist initially defined the modes of operation with the patient in too-rigid a manner. He expected a boy of 14 with better than average intelligence to be able to utilize verbal therapy on a time-limited basis. It became apparent that Bob (who emotionally was more like an 8 or 9 year old) could not utilize classical methods of treatment.

The first six interviews were a period of no movement. Bob was not willing to trust or reveal himself to someone who was not going to allow him to function in his typical manner. He was only comfortable when he knew the person he was with and could control the other person with this knowledge. He continually asked the therapist personal questions and would test the boundaries of the therapist's discipline. (The patient would open the therapist's drawers and want to read case notes.)

With the advent of no therapeutic movement, the therapist, with the help of his supervisor, made a number of changes in the mode of operation. Play materials such as clay, crayons and games were offered. At times the entire verbal therapy was carried out during a game of checkers or darts. The time limits of treatment were made more flexible so that the patient could determine if he wished to continue treatment or not.

The therapist would help the patient to help himself through a variety of experiences. One that was particularly meaningful to the patient was grasping his hands, fisherman style, and walking down the stairway with him. This activity elicited some anxiety from the therapist and the patient since both were aware that if either slipped they would tumble down the stairs entangled in 60 pounds of braces.

The therapist made a constant effort to help Bob become more aware of his strengths. Bob has a definite asset which he undervalued. Although crippled, he has definite artistic ability. The therapist began talking with him about how he could use his talented hands. Movement became rapid with the newer modes of operation.

Bob brought in his concerns about having his sexually matured body handled, dressed and cleansed by his mother and young female attendants at school. Fortunately, Mr. and Mrs. T had observed Bob's increased motivation in school and loss of belligerent attitude and now were willing to accept help from the therapist in rearing him. The therapist helped the father to accept more responsibility in caring for Bob at the toilet, shower, and other places where physical contact and exposure were necessary.

Bob began to identify with the therapist strongly and would carry the therapist's program of helping him to help himself into the home. Around the middle phases of therapy the patient began expressing many angry feelings toward his father and mother.

Bob's wish to murder anyone who would put him a wheelchair (Mr. T threatened Bob with a wheelchair if he did not carry out his physical exercises) was considered seriously by the therapist. The therapist considered with the patient the possibilities of committing murder within the context of the patient's handicapped motility and lack of finances. Realization of the extent of his handicap elicited the patient's basic feelings of inadequacy. Bob made a plea to sail off to some primitive island where he could live alone.

The therapist considered this plea for alienation again in terms of its possibility. This brought a new surge of hostility from the patient, directed and expressed toward the therapist. Bob believed that as he grew older he would be able to walk without crutches, drive a low-slung sportscar, marry easily, have a family and earn lots of money as a metallurgical engineer. No one had ever delineated for him fact from fantasy and possibility from probability. The therapist worked closely at this point with the orthopedic surgeon, and it was determined that Bob might be able to drive in an especially-equipped car and, from a physical point of view, marriage and sexual relations might be possible. Walking without crutches was pretty much out of the question.

All fantasies that the patient brought in were entertained in terms of their reality value. The patient became very indignant when the therapist called the U.S. Navy recruitment office with him present in order to establish that he could not join the Navy, as he had fantasied.

His unwillingness to accept his crippling was brought to a head during an interview in which Bob and his parents were seen together. The purpose of this interview was to discuss vocational possibilities for Bob. For the first time, during this interview, Mr. T approached Bob with the fact that he could not perform the work of a metallurgical engineer with his handicap. The therapist confronted Bob with the impossibility of his driving a low-slung sportscar. With Bob's anger welling up inside of him, Mrs. T commented sympathetically, "This is a hard pill for Bob to swallow." It was for her, too.

An alternate modality in which treatment was carried out was psycho-sexuality. Purposeful sex education assured Bob that he could discuss his concerns in this area during the interview. Gingerly, at first, he revealed strong voyeuristic tendencies and an anal conception of birth. At first he depersonalized his drawings pertaining to sex.

The therapist, utilizing knowledge from early experiences with Bob, extended himself by drawing on paper some of his own conceptions of sexuality. Two essential needs emerged from the psychosexual modality of treatment. The patient tried to use the therapist as a procurer of porno-graphic material and experiences. In some of his more daring hours Bob demanded that the therapist bring his secretary into the office, make her undress and leave him alone with her. The second need, the desire to be nurtured, was brought into the interview in an interesting manner. Bob became very secretive, demanded confidentiality, then confessed that the reason girls shun him is because he cannot use his hands adequately to cleanse himself after defecation. His rationale for being shunned by girls was understood by the therapist as a powerful defense against rejection, buffered by taking on the characteristics of a buffoon in appearance and behavior to ward off inner sadness and to explain the rejection. This in-terpretation was confirmed when Bob, attending a camp for crippled children, became interested in a girl and soiled his pants seven times in 48 hours in order to explain a seemingly inexplicable rejection from her.

In spite of his reaction to rejection from girls, gains were noted in a number of areas. Bob now looks and behaves more like a 13-year-old than a 9- or 10-year-old. He has lost his "smart alecky" attitude. He is responding well in school and physical therapy. There have been some basic revisions in Bob's self-concept. He realizes much more his physical handicap and his vocational assets.

Generally, his fantasy life is filled with more potentially productive ideas. Specific familial conflicts have been resolved because Bob no longer sits back and instigates fights between other family members. He is more able to express both positive and negative feelings toward his father. The remaining problems in the area of Bob's ability to cope with rejection from peers are still handled by soiling.

Discussion

Bob admitted to no dependency needs, although he depends upon another individual in almost every aspect of his life. After reactive, arrogant independence was given up by the patient, the therapist chose to ward off a severe dependency relationship and afford the client with help in helping himself. This alteration served as a buffer against a too-speedy regression and, at the same time, helped to increase the patient's skills in handling day-to-day situations.

The self-image of a palsied child is based upon his accomplishments during childhood. Unfortunately, the child with palsy is handicapped in those skills which are attributed with primary importance during childhood; i.e., walking, talking, bowel and bladder control, feeding, etc. The inadequate self-image can be countered through "foresight therapy." In addition to having the child recall his past experience, the therapist directs the child into fantasies about himself 5, 10 or 15 years henceforth. Some of these fantasies have proved to be as bizarre as early childhood nightmares.

The fact that "something is wrong with me" is sometimes given to bizarre speculation about how the patient can be "righted" or punished. "Foresight therapy" affords the therapist with the opportunity to correct anxiety-ridden images about the future and to educate the patient on his potential vocational assets.

The difficult problem of how to help the patient part with infantile sexual gratification was encountered in the case illustrated. Although adolescents sense the inappropriateness of having adults of the opposite sex care for them at the toilet and shower when they are sexually mature, the repressed sensual gratification obtained from such care is a powerful deterrent against giving up such experiences. The promise of adult heterosexual relationships is vague for the palsied adolescent. In the case illustrated the therapist did not dwell on the patient's infantile gratifications but instead enlisted the aid of the parents in changing the patient's outlets for sexual gratification. The patient only began to grope for more mature ways of meeting his sexual impulses when father replaced mother as his attendant at the toilet and shower.

The palsied adolescent's question of why should he be the one who is afflicted precludes an intelligible intrapsychic answer since the affliction is not something that the patient wrought. The analogy which might help clarify this answer is that of the brain-damaged adolescent asking the question of why should he be so confused. In both cases their burden is not something they purposely wrought; yet as adults they will be expected to accept responsibility for what they are.

In the case illustrated, the patient was comforted by the therapist pointing out that everybody has burdens to bear to a greater or lesser degree. Dark skin, lack of money, limited intelligence, cowardliness or marital problems are some of the many burdens people bear. He conveyed to the patient that as he matured he would continue to be judged by some fearful people for his palsy, but the primary criteria for his own worth would be his manner of coping with his palsy.

Summary

The purpose of this paper was to describe psychotherapy with a 14-year-old cerebral palsy patient. Particular emphasis was placed on the obstacles to psychotherapy brought about by the physical affliction and the technical alterations which were used to overcome them.

Theories, research and clinical observations in the field of somato-psychology all point to some degree of ego deficiency in medium to severe crippling from birth. Problems specific to cerebral palsy which have previously precluded psychotherapeutic intervention were (1) the affliction buffering dependency needs, (2) lack of opportunity for development of positive self-image, (3) gratification of pre-oedipal sexual strivings by significant adults, and (4) the seemingly inexplicable rejection of those afflicted.

Technical alterations in psychotherapy were discussed, utilizing a case study to illustrate implementation of technique. The therapist warded off a severe dependency relationship by helping the patient to help himself. Opportunity for developing a positive self-image was afforded by "foresight therapy," a process of exploring and analyzing progressive fantasies in addition to regressive fantasies.

Pre-oedipal sexual strivings were frustrated through manipulation of the familial environment and exposing the patient to a purposeful program of sex education. Actual rejection and feelings of rejection were handled by helping the patient to use his personal assets effectively and to ward off implied or felt worthlessness.

Acknowledgment

The author wishes to express his appreciation to Carolyn Pratt, Ph.D., who so ably supervised the case presented here.

References

1 ADLER, A., *Study of Organ Inferiority and its Psychical Compensations* (New York: Nervous and Mental Disease Publishing Co., 1917).

2 ALLEN, F. H. and G. H. J. PEARSON, "The Emotional Problems of the Physically Handicapped Child," *British Journal of Medical Psychology*, 8(1928), 212–36.

3 AUSUBEL, D. P., *Ego Development and the Personality Disorder* (New York: Grune & Stratton, Inc., 1952).

4 BARKER, R. G., "The Social Psychology of Physical Disability," *Journal of Social Issues*, 4(1948), 28–38.

5 BYCHOWSKI, G. and J. L. DESPERT, *Specialized Techniques in Psychotherapy* (New York: Grove Press, Inc., 1952).

6 CRUICKSHANK, W. M., "The Impact of Physical Disability on Social Adjustment," *Journal of Social Issues*, 4(1948), 78–83.

7 CUTSFORTH, T. D., "Personality Crippling Through Physical Dis-

ability," *Journal of Social Issues*, 4(1948), 62–67.

8 FENICHEL, O., *The Psychoanalytic Theory of Neurosis* (New York: W. W. Norton & Co., Inc., 1945), 35, 36.

9 FITZGERALD, D. C., "Success-Failure and T.A.T. Reactions of Orthopedically Handicapped and Physically Normal Adolescents," *Journal of Personality*, 1(1950), 67–83.

10 HENTIG, H. VON, "Physical Disability, Mental Conflict and Social Crisis," *Journal of Social Issues*, 4(1948), 21–27.

11 McANDREW, H., "Rigidity and Isolation: A Study of the Deaf and the Blind," *Journal of Abnormal Social Psychology*, 43(1948), 476–94.

12 SHELDON, W. H., in collaboration with S. S. STEVENS and W. B. TUCKER, *The Varieties of Human Physique: An Introduction to Constitutional Psychology* (New York: Harper & Row Publishers, Inc., 1940).

13 WRIGHT, B. A., ed., *Psychology and Rehabilitation* (Washington, D.C.: American Psychological Association, 1959).

14 Wright, B. A., *Physical Disability: A Psychological Approach* (New York: Harper & Row Publishers, Inc., 1960), 13–85, 162–78.

Casework with the Deaf: A Problem in Communication

Steven K. Chough

The caseworker dealing with the deaf client faces a frustrating problem regardless of the agency with which he is affiliated. The difficulty in communication is a paramount problem in any social work service for the deaf. In practice, the caseworker as well as the psychiatrist, psychologist, physician, rehabilitation counselor, or other professional is faced with the problem of communication and its distortion at every step in his work with the deaf client. The natural result is difficulty in understanding the client as a person, his problems, his feelings, and his potential strengths. The importance of communication cannot be overemphasized. Without communication the client-worker relationship cannot be established and help cannot be given.

It is difficult to discuss or describe the "typical" deaf person, because people who are termed deaf may vary widely in the degree of hearing loss, methods of communication used, their attitudes toward their deafness, and many other factors. They experience and interpret culturally engendered frustrations or gratifications according to their own personality and developmental history. It is, therefore, not advisable to assume that all deaf persons face the same kind of problems or respond to these problems in the same way. Perhaps emphasis should be placed on the principle that deaf persons are just people and, as such, are subject to the same problems as the unhandicapped.

Keeping this variability in mind, one can note certain general characteristics in terms of "deafness." There is, perhaps, a communicative difference among those who are deaf at birth or become deaf in early childhood, those who become progressively deaf because of gradual loss of hearing in later life, and those who become deaf suddenly in adulthood. The distinction among the communicative ability in these three categories of the deaf is too complex to discuss here. For the purposes of this paper the term "deaf persons" is used to describe both those totally deaf from birth or early childhood and those partially deaf or hard-of-hearing who are unable to understand normal conversation.

Reprinted with permission of the author and the National Association of Social Workers, from *Social Work*, Vol. 9, No. 4 (October, 1964), pp. 76–82.

It is estimated that today there are approximately 250,000 deaf children and adults in this country. "In a representative crowd of 700 Americans, we find no more than one who is deaf."[1] The deaf pass unnoticed and are pretty much lost in the general mass of people. "They have no *visible* characteristics that set them apart. They generally become known only as communication demands reveal their severe disability."[2]

In social work literature, authors discussing work with the deaf usually have focused on persons with partial hearing loss and on communication through the use of a hearing aid; the communication problem in work with severely deaf clients and the need for skills in communicating with them have received little attention. There is a possibility that much is missed with the deaf client in any social agency or health facility when communication is limited. It is hoped that this article, dealing with the effect of communication obstacles, various methods of communication used by the deaf, and the need for skills in communication, will be of some help to social workers in recognizing and dealing with the communication problem in order that the casework method may be utilized with the deaf. When a caseworker is mentioned in this paper, reference is being made to one who himself is a hearing person.

Effect of Communication Obstacles

One of the most basic needs of human beings is to communicate with others.[3] Each of us is aware of the fact that communication is not only the key to intellectual comprehension but also a medium for the expression of feelings and emotions. Dr. Rose Spiegel states:

> Communication is a dynamic process—an experience in itself and also the gateway to other experience. Communication not only is a psychobiologic means, it is also an end—a process whose fulfillment brings its own gratification.[4]

She continues by saying that communication is a process that has, in a sense, some of the quality of growth and maturation, because a person has been shaped as a personality by his specific life experience in communication with others. Of significance, too, is the statement of Dr. Jurgen Ruesch, an outstanding authority on communication in psychiatry, to the effect that

> since man needs a certain amount of gratifying communication in his life in order to learn, to grow, and to function in a group, all events that significantly curtail communication eventually will produce serious disturbance.[5]

[1] Boyce R. Williams and Elizabeth A. Chase, "Deafness: New Approaches," *Rehabilitation Record* (November–December, 1960), p. 17.

[2] *Ibid.*

[3] Robert L. Sharoff, M.D., "Enforced Restriction of Communication: Its Implications for the Emotional and Intellectual Development of the Deaf Child," *American Journal of Psychiatry*, Vol. 116 (November, 1959), p. 445.

[4] "Specific Problems of Communication in Psychiatric Conditions," in Silvano Arietti, ed., *American Handbook of Psychiatry*, Vol. 1 (New York: Basic Books, 1960).

[5] "General Theory of Communication in Psychiatry," in Silvano Arietti, ed., *op. cit.*

Helmer R. Myklebust, a psychologist specializing in work with the deaf at Northwestern University, explains that

> man is highly dependent on his senses. Through his senses come the sensations which contribute to his experience. Upon the information he receives from his senses he builds his world, his world of perception and conception; of memory, imagination, thought, and reason.[6]

The ordinary infant does not first learn how to read but learns to comprehend and use the spoken word; he acquires auditory language. Dr. Edna S. Levine, an authority on psychology of the deaf with rich experience in working with deaf children and their parents, mentions Sigmund Freud as having acknowledged the importance of hearing in the metaphor "ego wears an auditory lobe."[7] Language, depending to a large extent on hearing, is the form that conveys ideas or messages, especially in interpersonal relations. "The existence of speech and language for all human beings seems to be bound to the human propensity for symbol-making."[8] Many scholars have long declared that without language human nature almost ceases to exist. Language is, it is seen clearly, the symbolic reservoir of the feelings, emotions, ideas, attitudes, and motives that are involved in the expression and perception of human experience and behavior.

The emotional development of the deaf, then, can scarcely remain unaffected by the barrier to comprehension. When a deaf child attempts to learn all aspects of language, an auditory sense deprivation limits to a large extent the world of experience. Since learning language, including reading, is initially a matter of hearing, the deaf child in school must work much harder than the hearing child to remember and memorize. Because of the language deficiency created by this sense of deprivation, the deaf child is faced with difficulty in understanding what is put before him and has trouble expressing himself. His vocabulary is built slowly and may be limited. It can be concluded that the lack of language is a great obstacle to thinking itself and to psychosocial maturation. It is, however, a serious mistake to assume that the imperfect language used by a deaf person means defective mental ability.

> An inability to communicate creates barriers to the satisfaction of basic needs. Since the individual's well-being depends in large part on his ability to satisfy his own need harmoniously with the needs of others, the deafened person may experience considerable frustration both from inner, emotional sources and from outer, social situations.[9]

The majority of deaf persons have learned from experience that they cannot avoid meeting further frustration in communication. Because of difficulty in, or in some instances lack of, means of communication there

---

[6] *The Psychology of Deafness* (New York: Grune & Stratton, 1960), p. 1.
[7] *The Psychology of Deafness* (New York: Columbia University Press, 1960), p. 25.
[8] Spiegel, *op. cit.*, p. 917.
[9] Esther W. Fibush, "The Problem of Hearing Loss," *Social Casework*, Vol. 36, No. 3 (March, 1955), p. 125.

can be nothing for some but a life of deprivation, loneliness, and dissatisfaction. It is difficult for the deaf to communicate their problems, their frustrations, their needs, and their hopes.

> In addition, they are apt to be sensitively aware of their own shortcomings, and even more so of the indifference and misconceptions of the hearing world about the need and problem of the deaf.[10]

Sharoff warns parents of deaf children not to restrict them from expressing themselves through natural communication, because such restriction can affect their ability to grow to emotional and social maturity.[11]

When deaf persons' communication with hearing persons becomes extremely frustrating, they are apt to seek ways of defending themselves by withdrawing or aggressively controlling the exchange of conversation. However, for them the real problem is not deafness in itself but the fact of living in a hearing world. Actually they live in mental isolation and suffer the lack of healthy socialization. Most of them are uninformed and misinformed about many things pertaining to the hearing world and even to the deaf world.

Methods of Communication

The communication methods used widely by the deaf in this country are speech, lip-reading, writing, finger-spelling, and sign language. Speech and lip-reading are referred to as "oral communication," sign language and finger-spelling as "manual communication."

Finger-spelling or the manual alphabet is defined as "the regular letters of the alphabet formed by standard positions of the fingers of one hand, and words and sentences are thus spelled out in straight language."[12] Sign language refers to "an ideographic method of expression in which words and ideas are graphically formulated through codified gestures of the arms, hands, and body aided by facial expression."[13] While the characteristics of the sign language are more colorful, lively, and dramatic than other means of communication, it has some disadvantages, especially those of grammatical disorder, illogical systems, difficult expression of abstract ideas, and linguistic confusion.

The combination of oral and manual communication is referred to as "the simultaneous method" or "multiple communication." This is characterized by the use of the sign language and finger-spelling, with the individuals at the same time speaking. By "speaking" is meant either vocalization or movement of the lips without actual speech. In practice, when a hearing person, while using manual communication, speaks, the deaf person to whom he is talking can read his lip movements while watching his hands

---

[10] Levine, *op. cit.*, p. 40.
[11] Sharoff, *op. cit.*, pp. 443–446.
[12] Levine, *op. cit.*, p. 321.
[13] Levine, *loc. cit.*

as well. When the latter speaks aloud while using manual communication, the hearing person can listen to him. If the deaf person speaks inaccurately or unclearly, the hearing person can move his eyes quickly to the other's hands, picking up his meaning from the sign language and finger-spelling. Understanding the deaf individual's speech depends upon both his ability to speak and the hearing person's familiarity with the speech of the deaf; it is probably best for the later to watch the manual communication as well.

Finger-spelling has some advantages over sign language, especially in that it permits use of the names of people and places, technical or abstract words, and certain words that cannot be expressed by sign language. Its major values are accuracy and exactness. To many deaf persons, however, telling a story or listening to it through the manual alphabet only is slow, dull, colorless, and emotionless. They prefer a combination of sign language and finger-spelling to any one of the other methods. A number of the deaf, as well as the hard-of-hearing, can read lips and speech with amazing skill. The oral method is a desirable medium for those who can understand normal conversation. Unfortunately, though, the majority of the deaf are poor in speech and lip-reading. Just as many people do not have a natural ability in music, many deaf persons do not have a natural talent in the art of lip-reading.

Casework services with the deaf through written communication can be successful but are available to a limited number of highly intelligent deaf persons. Many deaf people confess a difficulty in comprehension when this method is used, admitting that they usually guess at meanings on the basis of familiar words. Just as hearing people prefer oral or spoken communication to written communication, so do almost all deaf people prefer manual communication. The written method seldom can express the emotional tones the worker needs to grasp, and the slowness of this method may affect the flow of ideas and feelings. The less formal education the deaf client has received, the more difficulty the worker may have in communicating with him through the written method alone.

The author agrees with Levine's statement:

> Manual conversation eases the strain of lip-reading and talking in prolonged interviews and enables the subject to relax somewhat while still continuing to converse. This is a particularly important consideration in cases of emotional disturbance, in which the writer has noted a preference for manual communication even on the part of habitual oralists.[14]

In the simultaneous method, if a deaf person misses a word or a statement on the lips, he always has the manual method to fall back on, because manual communication is perceived more adequately than lip movements.

> Even the most expert lip-reader is grateful for the larger visual area presented by the hands when used along with speech. . . . The average deaf person finds himself watching the lips, with his peripheral vision getting assurance from the

---

[14] Levine, *op. cit.*, p. 166.

hands that he is not missing anything. In this manner we have a communication procedure that is exact and free from guesswork.[15]

In addition, multiple communication can be of great value in developing speech and improving skills in lip-reading.

Need for Communication Skills

Few social workers are trained in the skills necessary for social service to the deaf; still fewer know how to cope with the communication problem in actual practice. Also, hearing workers frequently encounter a feeling of uselessness and hopelessness when assigned to help deaf clients with whom they feel they cannot communicate. Because of the unusual communication skills necessary, the social worker with the deaf has been limited in utilizing his usual knowledge and skill. He cannot talk with the client.

Because of lack of adequate communication, few deaf clients and patients are able to describe themselves or their needs adequately. How can the caseworker encourage the essential dignity and self-worth of these deaf clients? How can they be helped to develop and utilize their strengths? How can they be helped to feel like useful and adequate citizens in the community? How may they be assured of a worker who has both an understanding of and appreciation for the problems of the deaf? If communication is recognized as a prime factor in the caseworker-client relationship, how, then, can the simultaneous method be used by a worker to help the deaf improve their social functioning?

The following is an example of how deaf clients suffer because of communication obstacles and of how they can be helped through use of multiple communication with the caseworker.

> Mrs. A was a congenitally deaf woman with two children. Because the father had been out of the home for some time she had received Aid to Families with Dependent Children for six years. An earlier caseworker, unable to communicate with her even through writing because of her limited education, had obtained the sparse social information in her case record from her children and other relatives. Little or nothing was known about Mrs. A's feelings or her perception of her situation. She had been severely isolated much of her life, and limited social and educational experience had followed a traumatic childhood.
>
> Early work with Mrs. A was educational, not traditional casework. She was helped to understand the standardized sign language, improve her knowledge of English and of basic mathematics, and learn to tell time with the aid of a special type of clock. She was encouraged to go out of the house, to use public transportation, and to risk herself in socialization with other deaf people. Eventually she was able to move into a rehabilitation program, learn a trade, and accept employment in competitive industry. Communication with this client was not easy, but the use of the sign language combined with fingerspelling permitted the exchange of thoughts and ideas necessary in the educative and casework process.

[15] Mervin D. Garretson, "The Need for Multiple Communication Skills in the Educative Process of the Deaf," *The Banner*, published by the North Dakota School for the Deaf, Vol. 72 (March, 1963), p. 3.

Some of the general psychosocial factors prevailing among the deaf should be considered. After graduating from a school for the deaf, a great number of deaf persons tend to maintain association with other deaf people through various organizations of the deaf. Their tendency to seek social satisfaction from other deaf persons rather than from hearing people has given rise to a complicated social system. Many deaf persons, although desiring to seek out other deaf people, may for various reasons be unable to do so, leaving them no choice but to withdraw and live in a world of loneliness.

Some clients seems to feel ashamed or uncomfortable in asking help from social agencies, especially the public welfare agency, because they regard their need for public assistance and casework help as an indication of failure. Since deaf people constitute a small group in any given city, they may know almost every other deaf individual, and are likely to feel uncomfortable in the presence of other deaf people if they are known as recipients of public assistance. Capable deaf people have great pride in their own achievements and abilities. More specifically, as a class they are proud of their economic independence. Consequently, many of them are highly critical of deaf recipients of public assistance or have little respect for them. Such facts discourage economically deprived deaf clients from seeking out other deaf people socially. The social worker needs to be sharply aware of this psychology of the deaf in relation to their stereotyped concepts of social work.

Suggestions for Caseworkers

In work with hearing-impaired clients, as well as all hearing clients, the caseworker endeavors to help them lead a useful and satisfying life. The worker should remind himself that he is not treating a deaf client as a disabled person but as a human being whose disability is an integral part of his personality.

The caseworker should accept the deaf client as he is and help him maintain his self-respect and personal dignity. He needs to be able to "give and take" freely with all types of deaf clients in order to establish rapport. He then will be able to enable them to bring out the important feelings, their hopes, and the significant aspects of their lives that they may have had difficulty sharing with others.

Caseworkers can help hearing-impaired clients a great deal through arranging for medical examinations, the purchase of hearing aids, and planning for auditory and speech training. However, it is an erroneous conclusion that a hearing aid and remedial training will soon put everything to rights. Those who are hard of hearing or have a speech defect may need much more help than a hearing aid can give them. What is important in considering any casework service are:

1. Assessing the factors in the deaf client's personal and social development.

2. Assisting him on the basis of this assessment, in coming to grips with the reality of his problem and in helping him work toward personally acceptable and realistic goals.

3. Helping him in locating and using various resources in the community.

4. Assisting, when necessary, in coordinating the various services available to him in his rehabilitation program.

When the hearing caseworker begins working with the deaf, he is apt to seek a third person who is capable of interpreting for the deaf client. It is not easy, however, for the worker to gain rapport with the client with a third person present. When the interpreter is a parent or other relative, it may be especially difficult for the worker, because the person may perform the role of collaborator by talking *about* rather than *for* the deaf client. In such interviews there is always the danger of the interview becoming a conversation between the worker and the interpreter. It should be kept in mind that the caseworker is responsible for maintaining the focus on the deaf client, not on the interpreter. When the hearing-impaired client gains confidence in the worker though skilled communication, he will often prove to be a highly co-operative interviewee.

The manual alphabet is the unified, standardized method all over this country, but in the sign language there are many "dialects" in different areas, just as in oral communication used by hearing people. In addition to mastering the sign language together with finger-spelling, the worker may need to master dialects as much as possible. When he is faced with unfamiliar gestures used by the deaf interviewee, he may ask him what is meant. The deaf client will usually be glad to explain, for he can thereby feel useful. Too much help requested of the client by the worker may, however, affect the role expectations of each and alter the relationship.

When the caseworker needs to obtain information about a deaf client from other persons, the deaf client must know why the worker wishes to see others, and what purpose will be served. The client should participate to the extent that he gives the worker permission to obtain the information and the worker discusses with him how important other people can be in relation to a better understanding of his situation.

In the case of a joint or family interview while the deaf interviewee is present, the caseworker should continuously let him know precisely what is being discussed. If the client wants to say something, the interviewer should break off his discussions with the other persons and listen to him or explain as well as he can exactly what they are discussing. It should be realized that the deaf client has learned in the most heartbreaking way how to wait. Keeping him involved in the caseworker's thinking and planning will help greatly in breaking down his isolation and impassiveness and enable him to develop more desire to participate in the casework plan.

Summary

The most significant need in the successful practice application of social work with the deaf is the recognition that the great barrier in communication is the first problem encountered by hearing caseworkers new to work with the deaf. In the usual interview situation, the client has a chance to tell his own story in his own way and the worker has an opportunity to hear his problems, needs, and feelings as the client expresses them. On the other hand, there seems to be an inability or natural reluctance on the part of a hearing caseworker unfamiliar with the deaf to overcome the communication obstacles that exist. There is apparently an equal inability on the part of deaf clients to tell their story to the uneasy and awkward interviewer.

As the casework relationship with the deaf client is developed, the worker learns how he feels about his hearing loss and his unsolved problems and finds the range of his motivations, capacities, and opportunities in the process of the social diagnosis and treatment. Deaf people usually place their confidence in a hearing worker who is skillful in multiple communication and who has acquired an understanding and appreciation of the general problems of the deaf. The caseworker, therefore, is urged to learn these communication skills so that he can talk with the deaf in the most relaxing way. As Ruesch has stated:

> If we attempt to explore the secrets of psychotherapy, we invariably fall back upon its first and most important requirement—that, in addition to the patient, there must be another person present who is accessible and visible, who can be talked to, and who is ready to understand and to respond. Once interpersonal feedback is established, the exchange elicits in the patient the sensation of pleasure. To be acknowledged is pleasant; to be understood is gratifying; to be understanding and to agree is exciting. This gratification becomes the driving force which induces the patient to seek further improvement.[16]

Caseworkers who work directly with deaf clients or patients are much in need of preliminary preparation, as are any professionals who specialize in new fields. It is suggested that there should be at least one caseworker trained to communicate with the deaf in a large agency or hospital in which deaf recipients are helped or are designed to be helped. Where can he learn the sign language and finger-spelling? There are many available sign language facilities provided by schools for the deaf and by city clubs, state associations, religious organizations, and fraternal orders for the deaf. The period of learning manual communication depends to a great extent upon the individual's ability and motives, ranging from several months to several years. It must be realized that learning manual communication is an art, just as is learning any foreign language.

It is hoped that the hearing social worker who is confronted with the problem of communicating with deaf clients will use his skills and make a

---

[16] Ruesch, *op. cit.*, p. 904.

real effort to help the clients achieve mutually acceptable and realistic goals. While skill in communication is but one phase of the casework process, it is an extremely important one, basic to the application of other aspects of the casework method. If the significance of adequate communication with the deaf is realized by social workers, more deaf clients may accomplish the reality and gratification of full citizenship.

The Diabetic Client

Mary W. Engelmann

Diabetes Mellitus is a common disease in North America. In Canada alone there are approximately 200,000 known diabetics. This figure will undoubtedly increase as detection methods improve, and as greater medical knowledge enables diabetics to enjoy longer and healthier lives. Social workers in both medical settings and community agencies can expect to see more individuals with this chronic condition in the future.

At first glance it would not seem that this handicap is particularly serious. Diabetes does not have a marked effect on the victim's appearance and no stigma is attached to it. The well-regulated diabetic can, with few exceptions, participate in most activities and he meets with relatively little discrimination in job-seeking.[1] Is it necessary then for the social worker— whether in a medical setting or not—to be concerned about the implications of this handicap? The answer can be found by examining the illness more closely.

In diabetes, more than in any other chronic illness, there is a delicate interplay between the victim's emotional life and satisfactions and his ability to live with and control his condition. The requirements for adequate diabetic control can affect the person's attitude to himself and his inter-personal relationships. Much depends on the previously existing personality patterns of the individual and the interaction of his family life. Those persons who have made reasonably satisfactory adjustments find it easier to cope with diabetes, though even in the best of circumstances, there are periods of stress, anxiety and anger. For the person with problems, whether emotional or environmental, diabetes can be particularly upsetting and difficult.

[1] A. H. Kantrow, M.D., "Employment Experiences of Juvenile Diabetics", *Diabetes*, Vol. 10 (1961), pp. 476–481. This article is a report on a survey of the employment experiences of the alumni of the camp for diabetic children in New York.

Reprinted from *The Social Worker*, Vol. 35 (February, 1967), pp. 6–10, by permission of the author and publisher.

Emotional Health and Control

An understanding of the interaction between emotional health and diabetic control, along with an understanding of some of the specific anxieties and problems encountered by the diabetic, should enable the social worker to assist him more skillfully.

There are varying degres of diabetic severity. The older individual who develops diabetes generally has a milder form of the illness and his diabetes can be controlled through diet alone, or through diet and oral medication. In a person under forty years of age, diabetes is generally more severe, requires insulin therapy, and is often much more difficult to control.

Diabetes and Emotional Stress

While diabetes is generally considered to be an inherited condition, due to a metabolic defect, there is some indication that it can be precipitated by emotional stress. Some studies suggest that the onset of diabetes may have been preceded by a period of deprivation, particularly loss of emotional support, unconscious conflict and depression.[2] Obviously, in such situations, the individual is weakened in his ability to cope with the meaning of the diagnosis. The new diabetic may be shocked, frightened, and even have moments of panic. He may feel a sense of despair because he faces a lifelong incurable condition. The amount of technical information he must absorb about diet and insulin therapy can seem overwhelming, and he may have doubts about his ability to care for himself. Along with this great increase in anxiety can come feelings of inadequacy and insecurity as he is faced with the awareness of physical limitation, dependency on insulin and continuous medical supervision.

Parents of a diabetic child have many of the same reactions as the adult diabetic, and often have a great sense of guilt. Irrational feelings of having neglected their child, or of having passed on a hereditary defect are present in almost every instance. The parents of a diabetic child are often overwhelmed by the technical information given them. Parents, at such a time, need the opportunity to discuss their anxiety and receive supportive help in developing their strengths and capabilities.

Diabetes is controlled through a therapeutic regime consisting of a restricted diet, insulin injections, and regular exercise. Adequate rest and regularity in meals are important. As it is a condition which must be regulated on a day-to-day basis, diabetes must be controlled by the patient

---

[2] P. F. Slawson, M.D., W. K. Flynn, M.D., E. J. Kollar, M.D., "Psychological Factors Associated with the Onset of Diabetes Mellitus," *JAMA—Journal of the American Medical Association*, Vol. 185, No. 3 (1963), pp. 96–100. E. Weiss and O. W. English, *Psychosomatic Medicine, A Clinical Study of Psychophysiologic Reactions*, 3rd Edition 1957, pp. 334–335.

himself or, in the case of a young child, by his parents. The doctor can determine the initial regulation, can advise, and can help in illness or emergency situations, but the diabetic himself is responsible for the actual treatment.

Emotional upsets, in addition to illness, will have a definite physiological effect, actually raising the blood sugar level, thereby adding to an already complicated job.[3] Diabetic coma and insulin reactions are two serious and immediate complications which can develop. In the former, the blood sugar level becomes too high, and the person loses consciousness after a period of time. In the latter, which can come on suddenly, the blood sugar level drops too low, and causes aberrant behaviour and, in the latter stages, results in unconsciousness. Both if untreated, can lead to death.

Control Can Create Resentment

What meaning does this have for the diabetic individual and his family? The diabetic cannot "adjust" to his diabetes and forget about it. In order to control it effectively, he and his family must be constantly aware of and concerned about it. This situation can create resentment and irritation. The other members of the family find that, at times, their lives and social activities are limited by the diabetic's need to adhere to his regime. For children and adolescents this regime will add to already incipient feelings of being different. Diabetic women may have added concerns about their adequacy as it is difficult for them to carry pregnancies to completion. It is obvious that, even in the best of circumstances, there are going to be periods of rebellion, frustration and resentment.

In a disturbed situation diabetes can add to an already charged atmosphere and be used by both the diabetic and his family in an attempt to solve neurotic conflicts. The diabetic regime can become the focus for arguments which usually reflect existing and more deep-rooted personality conflicts. The anger and frustration that all diabetics and their families feel will be exacerbated, added to more basic hostility, and reflected in destructive ways towards self and others. This can result in the diabetic's denial of the illness and in a lack of adequate concern, manifested in deliberate overeating or neglect of insulin requirements. In this way the diabetic can control, and indirectly hurt, his family. As he becomes ill, he gains attention and sympathy but, at the same time, adds to his guilt feelings of being a burden. All of this can create a vicious cycle of anger, illness, guilt and depression. The immature, dependent diabetic may use his poorly controlled diabetes and resulting illness as a way of meeting his emotional needs.

[3] D. G. Prugh, "Psychophysiological Aspects of Inborn Errors of Metabolism," in H. I., V. F., and N. R. Lief (eds.), *The Psychological Basis of Medical Practice*, New York, Harper & Row, 1963, p. 421.

Personality Patterns in Diabetes

Some observers say that dependent, passive behaviour is a frequent personality pattern in diabetes. Their views are summarized by Dr. David Hawkins:

> While a wide variety of individual personality patterns are seen in diabetes, clinicians have over and over commented on the frequency of marked passivity, masochism, extreme oral dependency, and frequent retreats into illness in these patients. Rosen and Lidz noted that the refractory diabetic patient "reacted to sibling rivalry by regressively seeking maternal attention by becoming helpless and demanding or negativistic rather than through more active measures". It is easy to see that this illness with its emphasis on diet would facilitate regression to whatever oral dependent behaviour was potentially present in the patient, and there is considerable evidence that in many individuals a passive dependent character structure antedated the onset of the clinical disease. Mirsky postulates that there is an inborn, metabolic problem from birth, even though signs and symptoms of the disease do not become manifest until later, and that this interferes with the development of a confident and mature outlook.[4]

Other observers emphasize that these diabetic personality patterns are the result of and not the cause of the disease. Doctors Philip Isenberg and Donald Barnett, in writing about the personality of the juvenile diabetic, say the following:

> What we have outlined above suggests that there are bound to be certain similarities in the group of diabetic children because of the traumatic effect of the onset of the disease on most families. The persistent vulnerabilities and character trends which have been studied and reported on are probably the consequence of the disease and not its cause. What has been reported is a certain suppression of emotions, a feeling of being oppressed by a frustrating outer world which forces the patients to subordinate themselves to its demands. As a group they feel somewhat restricted and have been shown to be less spontaneous and free in the expression of their emotions and fantasies. Since therapy aims to control the disease by imposing restrictions on diet and requiring certain routines to be fulfilled many claim this tends to increase the feelings of being oppressed and frustrated.[5]

Insulin injections can carry implications of self-punishment or self-multilation to the diabetic. If injections must be given by a member of the family, similar fears with consequent guilt can result for the nondiabetic. The strict regime may carry the implication of punishment and authority and may reactivate in the diabetic earlier unresolved conflicts.[6] Diet restriction may be linked in the individual's mind to a restriction of love

---

[4] D. Hawkins, M.D., "Emotions and Metabolic and Endocrine Disease," Lief, *op. cit.*, pp. 274–275.

[5] P. Isenberg, M.D., and D. M. Barnett, M.D., "Psychological Problems in Diabetes Mellitus", *The Medical Clinics of North America*, Vol. 49, No. 2 (1965), pp. 1127–1128.

[6] F. Upham, *A Dynamic Approach to Illness*, New York, Family Service Association of America, 1949, pp. 91–92.

or affection, with the result that he may, denying the seriousness of this for his illness, have periods of over-eating, even gorging himself.[7]

The marital partner, fearing that the diabetic may become totally dependent on him, and perhaps resenting the inevitable partial dependency, may become over-solicitous and concerned, thus accentuating the diabetic's sense of being handicapped. Insulin reactions can come on suddenly, even in the best-regulated diabetic. They can be embarrassing as well as dangerous and can result in the diabetic being at times dependent for life or death on his marital partner, family or occasional associates.

Reaction Manipulation

Reactions can be used by both the diabetic and the non-diabetic for control and manipulation. A beginning insulin reaction has some resemblance to an anxiety attack. There have been instances when a diabetic thought he was suffering from fairly frequent reactions but was actually suffering from anxiety (blood sugar levels were found to be normal or above normal).[8]

A case history reported in *Diabetes,* the journal of the American Diabetic Association, illustrates some of the interaction between neurotic disturbance and the control of diabetes.[9] A young woman diabetic was ensnared in a conflict between her parents and her husband. She was unable to decide whether to be the dependent child of her parents or develop a mature relationship with her husband. In spite of the fact that there were frequent arguments and scenes between all members of the family, the presence of tension was denied.

This young woman was admitted to the hospital five times in one year in diabetic coma, always following a family argument. There was ample evidence that there was no neglect of insulin treatment or diet, and that the comas were her attempt to escape from her problem. She could retreat into the relative safety and neutrality of the hospital and at the same time receive attention and sympathy. Psychiatric help enabled both her and her family to develop some insight and alleviate the tension-producing situations. As a result her diabetes came under much better control.

Much has been written about the particular problems that are encountered in the family with a diabetic child and about the importance of seeing that the child's emotional growth is not blocked by the condition. There are some particular problems that may be encountered when diabetes develops in a family where there is already a disturbed parent-child or marital relationship. All parents have some resentment about the extra care and responsibility required by the diabetic child. However, in some instances, the child himself may be resented and rejected. Parents may show

[7] Lief, *op. cit.*, p. 420.

[8] E. Weiss and O. S. English, *op. cit.*, p. 342.

[9] G. L. Schless, M.D., and R. von Laveran-Stiebar, M.D., "Recurrent Episodes of Diabetic Acidosis Precipitated by Emotional Stress," *Diabetes,* Vol. 13, No. 4 (July–August, 1964), pp. 419–420.

this by using the diabetic regime in a punitive way under the guise of achieving good control. Over-protection and over-anxiety can accentuate the child's sense of handicap and may be an expression of hostility. Parents may, by using the rationalization that the child must become independent, give the child too much responsibility for his diabetic control and then blame him when things go wrong. A history from the records of the Social Service Department of the Royal Alexandra Hospital, Edmonton, illustrates this latter point.

A diabetic child, aged eight years, was the third of four children. There was much conflict between the parents. The mother, a nervous tense woman, suffered from asthma. The father, quiet and passive, was somewhat aloof from the family situation. Neither parent understood diabetes adequately and neither was able to enforce the necessary discipline concerning diet and rest. The child was given a great deal of responsibility for his own diabetic care. When difficulties developed and he had to be hospitalized, he was blamed by his parents for this.

It would appear essential that the social worker be aware of the ramifications of diabetes in working with afflicted clients. Recognizing this the New York City Diabetic Association has set up a special counseling service for diabetics. This service not only works directly with diabetics, but also provides specialized information on diabetes to community agencies.[10]

While many diabetics appear to be able to cope successfully with their condition, there are always a number who fail to do so and stumble through life with an increasing complex of physical and emotional problems. It is these people who are most likely to come to the attention of social agencies, and it is in working with them that a knowledge of the particular problems of diabetes is necessary.

[10] A. H. Kantrow, M.D., "A Vocational and Counselling Service for Diabetics," *Diabetes*, Vol. 12, No. 5 (1963), pp. 454–457.

Factitious Illness

A Therapeutic Confrontation Approach to Treating Patients with Factitious Illness

Kenneth R. Wedel

Factitious illness has received attention in the medical literature for a number of years. Broadly defined, this diagnosis includes patients who, for a variety of little-understood reasons, simulate real patterns of illness and/or symptomatology suggesting real illness. The illness ranges in severity from the so-called "Munchausen's syndrome," a term applied to patients who chronically wander from hospital to hospital seeking admission by distorting their medical histories, to self-induced simulated disease or common malingering.

Petersdorf and Bennett have described the most commonly used methods of creating factitious fevers.[1] Patients may hold the thermometer next to a hot water bottle, steam pipe, light bulb, flame, and the like; shake it; or produce a higher reading by rubbing the teeth, gums, or anal sphincter. Another method is to substitute the thermometer offered by the nurse with one from a cache of thermometers that the patient has set at various readings. Patients have also been known to inject themselves with vaccines, toxoids, and pyrogenic substances to produce a real fever.

A comprehensive review of the literature on factitious illness has been made by Spiro, who found the psychiatric literature contained only three reports of factitious illness.[2] The medical literature, however, described thirty-eight cases with various presenting symptomatology. The behavior of these patients in the hospital was characterized by uncooperativeness and hostility. Following diagnosis of factitious illness, their most common reaction was to sign out of the hospital against advice. Only sixteen of the

Reprinted with permission of the National Association of Social Workers, from *Social Work,* Vol. 16, No. 2 (April 1971), pp. 69–73.

[1] Robert G. Petersdorf and Ivan L. Bennett, "Factitious Fever," *Annals of Internal Medicine,* Vol. 46, No. 6 (June 1957), pp. 1039–1062.

[2] Herzl R. Spiro, "Chronic Factitious Illness," *Archives of General Psychiatry,* Vol. 18, No. 5 (May 1968), pp. 569–579.

thirty-eight patients were seen by a psychiatrist, and generally the motivating factors for the illness were not discussed.

A central theme in the literature is the hostility of hospital staff toward the patient that is common when factitious illness is diagnosed, with immediate hospital discharge prompted by either the patient or the physician as the result. One approach to the control of serious factitious illness is the "black book"—a list of names kept in hospital emergency rooms to identify patients who chronically wander from hospital to hospital. English physicians have sometimes initiated legal action when all other methods have failed.[3] In general, the literature emphasizes both the waste of valuable medical resources and the human and economic loss to such patients and their families.[4]

The Study

Ten patients took part in the clinical study of fever of unknown origin conducted at the Clinical Center, National Institute of Allergy and Infectious Diseases, National Institutes of Health.[5] Seven of the patients were female and ranged in age from 16 to 41 years. The three male patients were much younger: two were 11 years old and the other was 13. Five of the patients worked in medically oriented occupations: three were registered nurses, one was a pharmacist, and one was a medical laboratory technician. Psychiatric diagnoses and social histories did not reveal any common characteristics among the patients, but five of them had recently experienced a death, tragic accident, or severe illness in the family. Follow-up data were available for five patients; of that group, four made a satisfactory readjustment, as measured by completion of recommended psychotherapy and freedom from factitious illness, and one patient refused to be seen by the consulting psychiatrist and left the hospital against medical advice when her factitious illness was verified. She later died under circumstances that suggested suicide.

At the Clinical Center it has been found that a multidisciplinary approach involving medicine, nursing, social work, and psychiatry is most successful in working with patients exhibiting factitious illness. Central to the approach is the recognition that factitious illness represents the patient's attempt to cope with emotional problems. Although the patient may not acknowledge or recognize that his problems are emotional, he has managed to convey his desperate need for help by placing himself in the hands of physicians and other hospital staff. An understanding response by the staff

---

[3] P. Blackwell, "Munchausen at Guy's," *Guy's Hospital Report,* Vol. 114, No. 3 (1965), pp. 257–277.

[4] Joseph J. Bunim et al., "Factitious Diseases: Clinical Staff Conference at the National Institutes of Health," *Annals of Internal Medicine,* Vol. 48, No. 6 (June 1958), pp. 1328–1341; and Spiro, op. cit.

[5] The study began in 1960, and of the 175 patients seen to date, ten were found to have factitious illness.

makes it possible for this disguised request to become more direct and opens the door to treatment planning.

Confrontation Process

The first step in the confrontation process is the search for organic disease. As organic causes for fever are ruled out, suspicion grows that the illness may be factitious. Clues that signal the possibility of factitious fever to the ward physician are the absence of laboratory data to substantiate fever and an unusual fever pattern. To determine whether the patient may be switching thermometers or manipulating them in order to produce a high reading, the nurse remains with the patient while his temperature is being taken. The serial numbers of thermometers also may be checked. A room search by the ward physician and head nurse has revealed substitute thermometers, unauthorized drugs and chemicals, and needles and syringes in some cases.

Following the verification of factitious illness, the ward physician requests a psychiatric evaluation. The psychiatrist is asked for (1) an analysis of the patient's personality dynamics together with a diagnostic impression, and (2) advice and assistance when the patient is confronted with his factitious illness. Particular attention is paid to any contraindications to confrontation, such as the risk of suicidal or psychotic behavior.

After the psychiatric evaluation is completed, a meeting of the patient, senior staff physician, ward physician, head nurse, social worker, and psychiatrist is held so that the senior staff physician (who has primary responsibility for the patient) can confront the patient with the factitious nature of his illness. The patient is given an opportunity to react after the confrontation. Frequently his reaction will be one of defensive anger, which is usually directed at the confronter, i.e., the senior staff physician, who serves as a lightning rod for the patient's emotions. Because the patient's intense initial need to storm and protest is accepted, he usually will not need to vent his angry feelings later on staff members who must give him day-to-day care. As a result, they are able to offer support to the patient as he goes through the difficult period of readjustment. At the conclusion of the meeting, the patient is reassured that he will have time to come to terms with the experience and plan for his return home.

During the confrontation a redefinition of the illness takes place for both patient and staff. Prior to this, the major goal was to diagnose an organic cause for the fever. Following confrontation, the goal of medical care is to interrupt effectively the patient's maladaptive behavior pattern. To be successful in this, the confrontation process must be firm, but gentle and nonpunitive. The patient must be helped to remain in the hospital long enough to work through the worst of his feelings of rage and shame, to begin reconstructing his shattered self-image, and to experience the staff's continued acceptance of him as a person who is worthy of concern and has not wholly forfeited the staff's trust.

Social Work Practice

Social work services are provided for all patients admitted to the study. Contacts early in the patient's hospitalization are valuable because (1) the broad diagnostic category "fever of unknown origin" may encompass a number of serious illnesses or it may mask emotional problems, (2) a final diagnosis of factitious illness is a possibility, and (3) the exhaustive medical workup may in itself be a source of anxiety and stress. The casework relationship is an important tool in cases of fever of unknown origin, but the worker recognizes that most of these patients are unable to form mature and trusting interpersonal relationships and they will relate in different ways—some will be guarded and defensive, while others will reach out for understanding and sympathy. The worker also avoids probing to uncover the patient's underlying feelings in order to minimize disruption of emotional defenses essential to the patient's functioning. Attacking these defenses would only increase the patient's resistance and blunt the relationship. Thus the initial treatment goal is to support the patient through the medical diagnostic workup, to convey the worker's commitment to him as a person, and to develop a contact with enough meaning to the patient so that the worker can help him when his defenses are breached by the confrontation procedure.

If the social worker has succeeded in developing a firm supportive relationship with the patient, it is helpful for him to be present at the actual confrontation. His presence can be regarded as a commitment to be with the patient during a difficult time. The worker has heretofore been accepting of the patient's emotional defenses and is not an active participant in the confrontation, but his presence symbolizes his alliance with the goal of medical treatment—the interruption of maladaptive behavior patterns. As a witness, he is better able to handle the patient's subsequent need to distort the intent of the confrontation.

Once the confrontation has taken place, the social worker shares with the rest of the staff a number of therapeutic tasks, all of them carried out in a spirit of acceptance and continuing concern. The patient feels stripped and may be tearful, anxious, or storming. He may cloak his sense of shame and helplessness in attacking or defensive behavior, or he may withdraw; however, his feelings of being worthless and untrustworthy nevertheless come through. The social worker and other staff members can help the patient handle his sharp and conflicting feelings about the confrontation. He will need a "winding down" period for self-reassessment and for consideration of the treatment recommendations, and his heightened anxiety often can be used constructively to help him accept psychotherapy—a concrete step in relinquishing old patterns. Arrangements for psychotherapy after discharge are usually made by the patient and the local referring physician. In some cases the social worker may assist with these referral arrangements, but his most important function is to be a source of support and encouragement to the patient. He may also be called on to help the patient's family understand the patient's illness in terms of his emotional needs and problems.

Illustrative Case

The case of Mrs. A, a 39-year-old registered nurse admitted for fever of unknown origin, illustrates the confrontation approach to treatment. Her medical history revealed numerous hospitalizations in the past for excision of a benign cyst of the breast, hysterectomy, suture granuloma of the colon, hiatal hernia, cystitis, gastritis, and fever of unknown origin. During the year prior to her most recent admission, the patient suffered from fever with associated aches and pains and had been unable to work.

Social work contacts with Mrs. A began at the time of admission. In early interviews she was friendly but guarded when talking about her life situation. As the casework relationship developed, she expressed concern that even the experts would not find the source of her illness. She also disclosed that she had not advanced professionally to her satisfaction because she was unable to get along with superiors. However, she was quick to deny that her medical or employment history indicated any adjustment problems. Despite the system of denial and superficiality maintained by the patient, she seemed to regard the social worker as a safe person with whom she could share negative feelings about the unpleasant aspects of hospitalization.

Shortly after admission, the nursing staff discovered that Mrs. A was substituting thermometers each time her temperature was taken. In order to confirm this, the serial numbers of thermometers given to the patient were compared with those on the thermometers handed back. This documented information was kept in the patient's medical record.

The diagnostic medical evaluation revealed no organic basis for the patient's fever. The psychiatric evaluation described her as a fairly rigid individual with many dependency needs and a strong defense of denial concerning her psychosomatic illness. No evidence of psychotic or pre-psychotic behavior was found.

In a meeting with the senior staff physician, ward physician, head nurse, and social worker, the patient was confronted with the fact that she had been switching thermometers. A nonaccusatorial, understanding, straightforward approach was used by the senior staff physician to describe the staff's concern about her. The patient was told that there were no physiological findings to explain her illness and her behavior indicated she needed therapy for her emotional problems. Furthermore, she would be given ample time to consider the recommendation for therapy and to make plans for her return home.

During the confrontation the patient maintained her composure and insisted that she did not understand the matter of differing serial numbers because she had not switched thermometers. She was not questioned further about this and was allowed to save face when the senior staff physician indicated that several laboratory tests would be repeated to confirm past findings.

Following the confrontation, Mrs. A became markedly anxious, began weeping, and remained in her room. After she had regained her composure somewhat, she verbalized to the social worker her anger toward the senior staff physician for saying that she had switched thermometers. She continued to deny that she had switched them and wondered how anyone could now believe her. How could she face the nurses who would soon arrive for the evening shift? Several hours after the confrontation, however, she confided individually to the head nurse, senior staff physician, and social worker that she actually had switched thermometers because she believed she must have a fever if her physical ailments were to be given sincere consideration.

Following the confrontation, hospital care was continued for several days so that Mrs. A could prepare for her return home and make preliminary plans for the future. She was able to make constructive use of the casework relationship by discussing her fears and misconceptions concerning psychotherapy, which helped to reduce her ambivalence about accepting the recommended treatment. She was doubtful that her former supervisors would approve of her undertaking psychiatric treatment and felt her future employability would be jeopardized if she did so. With encouragement, however, she contacted her own physician, who assured her he would not divulge the factitious nature of her illness to her former employer and would arrange for her to obtain therapy in her own community.

Conclusion

Factitious illness is an expression of a complex network of psychosocial and physiological factors that are not clearly understood. It is clear, however, that this illness is not merely a malicious hoax perpetrated by the patient; it is the desperate plea for help of a person who has been unable to devise a better solution for his emotional problems.

A hospital team that understands the message of the patient's behavior and has a treatment plan geared to his emotional needs will not react with hostility toward the patient or punish him through premature discharge. The primary social work contribution to treatment is to develop a relationship with the patient that will help carry him through the difficult period of confrontation with the factitious nature of his illness. Following confrontation, this sympathetic but reality-based support sustains the patient as he struggles to abandon modes of behavior that have been so damaging to him.

Some Psychosocial Problems in Hemophilia

Alfred H. Katz

Hemophilia is a congenital, chronic illness, about which relatively little is known although it affects some 40,000 persons in the United States.[1] The medical problems it presents are far better understood than are its psychosocial aspects. The latter have received little attention in this country except for an early paper by Cohen and Herrman and a fragmentary outline for psychiatric research by Poinsard.[2] This discussion is an attempt, based on some years of association with the problems of hemophiliacs, to sketch some of these psychosocial factors, since social workers may encounter persons with this illness in the course of their work.

Hemophilia is a hereditary ailment characterized by excessive bleeding. It is not yet subject to cure, but in the past two decades various therapeutic advances have been made in the direction of stopping or controlling hemorrhaging and in the management of some resultant problems. Genetically, hemophilia is the product of a sex-linked recessive gene which is transmitted by females, but which primarily affects males. It also occurs, but quite rarely, as a result of genetic mutation. In recent years a number of related "bleeding disorders" have been found, which are milder in symptomatology than classical hemophilia, and which can be differentially diagnosed by refined laboratory procedures.

The severity of hemophilia varies from individual to individual although, generally speaking, severity remains comparatively stable among afflicted members of the same family. Some physicians (and patients) believe that there is a cyclical or seasonal variation in the onset and severity of bleeding

---

[1] Although the figures regarding the incidence and prevalence of hemophilia vary and are not definitive, this figure, given by Dr. Armand J. Quick of Marquette University, is the most commonly accepted estimate.

[2] Ethel Cohen and R. L. Herrman, "Social Adjustment of Six Patients with Hemophilia," *Pediatrics*, Vol. III (1949), pp. 588–596. Paul Poinsard, M.D., "Psychiatric Aspects of Hemophilia," in *Hemophilia and Hemophiloid Diseases*, Brinkhous, ed., University of North Carolina Press, Chapel Hill, 1957.

Reprinted from *Social Casework*, Vol. 40 (June, 1959), pp. 321–326, by permission of the author and the Family Service Association of America.

episodes. Others believe that there is no such seasonal change, but that with maturation the affected individual learns to take better care of himself and is therefore less prone to situations where bleeding may be touched off.

With the introduction in the past twenty years of methods of banking blood, and particularly with the development of methods of processing human plasma through freezing or lyophilization, the treatment of hemorrhages has been greatly facilitated and the mortality rate among hemophiliacs has declined sharply. Owing to the volatility of the coagulative factor, the hemophiliac requires transfusions of blood or blood derivatives that have been freshly prepared, if the bleeding is to be stopped.

Although hemophilia is comparatively rare, it poses such severe problems of medical management and of psychosocial stress to the patient and his family that it must be considered a serious health problem for those affected and for the community. Not only does the moderately-to-severely affected individual have frequent, and at times almost uncontrollable, bleeding from external abrasions and sites, but even more serious forms of internal bleeding can occur from no apparent cause. Such bleeding episodes may be extremely painful, and often result in orthopedic problems. Hemophilic arthropathy, as it is termed, arises from such repeated bleedings into joint spaces. Orthopedic abnormalities and permanent damage to muscles and joints can occur from this type of bleeding. The approach of orthopedists and psychiatrists to appropriate measures of therapy and correction for such problems still varies considerably, and much of the therapeutic work that is being done is on an experimental basis.

Social Problems in Hemophilia

From this brief review of medical problems it can be understood that, both for patients and for their families, hemophilia reproduces many or most of the psychosocial problems of other forms of congenital chronic illness, but with some added special features. Prominent among the latter are the extreme feelings of distress, guilt, and self-reproach experienced by the parents of newly diagnosed sufferers, especially by the approximately 50 per cent who are unable to trace a history of hemophilia in their families, but who are suddenly confronted with a child bearing this "hereditary taint," who forever after needs special care.

The protective care of the hemophilic infant and young child has to be extremely thorough to prevent the trauma that can result from normal childish exploration of the environment—crawling, body contact with furniture and floor, sharp-edged toys, and so forth. From a tender age the hemophilic infant must be protected from the more strenuous forms of physical contact with playmates and play objects; at the same time normal curiosity, growth, and socialization have to be fostered through stimulation by other means. *Thus the most general and pervasive psychosocial problem for these parents is to give their child physical protection and, at the same time, avoid making him overdependent and eventually a psychological invalid.* This all-pervading problem imposes tremendous burdens on the self-restraint and psychological maturity of the parents, siblings, and others in the hemophiliac's immediate environment. When he reaches school age, these problems are aggravated. The necessity of reaching a viable balance, of treading the narrow line between physical protection and psychological overprotection now involves teachers, playmates, and others in the child's environment.

The possibility of danger to the child is aggravated by the fact that frequently the young hemophiliac offers no external physical signs of his condition and thus appears to other children to be completely normal. Perhaps because of the difficulty of limiting the child's physical activity at this time, the school years are often the period of most frequent occurrence of hemorrhagic episodes. It is common for hemophiliacs to miss many weeks of the school term as a result of requiring rest and immobilization after, or between, periods of hemorrhage. Repeated bleeding can also lead to weakness and anaemia, with their effects on vitality and energy levels. The loss of time in school involves not only possible academic retardation and its important emotional concomitants, but the equally important loss of contacts with other children, of the socializing effects of play, and of the maturational benefits of social activity within a peer group.

It is also clear that if a hemophilic child is born into a family in which other male children are not affected by the disease, he tends to pre-empt major attention in the family, and there is a consequent withdrawal of attention from siblings.

Among the urgent and continuous pressures confronting the parents of a hemophilic child are the threat of being called upon at any moment to secure emergency medical attention for a hemorrhage; the consequent necessity of staying close to sources of such care; and the cost of such attention, not only in relation to the services of a physician, but particularly in relation to the replacement of blood or blood derivatives that may be used in transfusions. On the latter score, in some parts of the United States the American Red Cross does supply blood or blood products for hemophiliacs without requiring replacement by the individual user. In other localities the voluntary organization of hemophiliacs—The Hemophilia Foundation— may assume the responsibility and sometimes can cover the emergent needs of a particular family. Since, however, a hemophiliac may require as many as fifteen to twenty pints of whole blood to meet the exigencies of a single episode —and in the course of a year may require as many as one or two hundred pints of blood—this voluntary organization is usually overwhelmed and cannot meet all the requests. Thus, the drain on the finances and the energies of afflicted families is enormous. In those localities where blood or blood derivatives have to be purchased, the minimum cost to the family is $10 or $12 per unit, exclusive of administration fees. Therefore, the financial drains are constant, chronic, and severe; and these drains have important psychosocial consequences in increasing intra-familial tensions and in promoting shame, withdrawal, and social isolation tendencies.

Other medical costs result from the frequent hospitalizations that are necessary for hemophiliacs. Although many of these families have hospital insurance, it is not at all uncommon that a hemophiliac will require repeated hospitalizations every few weeks and thus exhaust within a short time the coverage by hospital insurance for the whole year. In some states, Crippled Children's programs may carry a portion of the cost of hospitalization, but eligibility for such aid is frequently defined by the state only in relation to the performance of corrective orthopedic procedures and is not available for the simpler procedure of treating a bleeding episode and its sequelae.

Such other emergent costs as those for transportation, ambulances, appliances and braces for those orthopedically afflicted, and special fees of medical consultants are all constant accompaniments of this condition.

As indicated above, the area of schooling and vocational preparation is a critical one for the hemophilic child. In this regard, parents require much help, counseling, and support in order to understand the importance of maintaining the child's independence, autonomy, and self-reliance insofar as possible, and to handle the child appropriately.

Problems of Adults

One of the striking observations regarding the hemophiliacs with whom I had contact was of the number of young adults in the group who lacked a stable occupation. When referrals of young men who were mild or even moderate sufferers were accepted by the State Division of Vocational Rehabilitation, the possibilities of their becoming self-maintaining were found to be excellent. However, this resource was little known and not widely utilized by the families of sufferers. It was my experience that social service assistance is rarely sought by or extended to adult patients in hospitals or attending clinics. The hospital social services for hemophiliacs tend to concentrate efforts on the problems of young children, their eligibility for assistance under Crippled Children's programs, and other such tangible services as camp arrangements, which are helpful and which carry a good deal of meaning for parents.

What has been found lacking, however, has been an approach to the hemophiliac through a program of counseling and advisement that would start at an early age, and that would tend to forestall the development of some of the special problems the hemophilic adolescents and young men encounter. The following case example illustrates some of these problems:

> Harry B, aged 26, a sufferer from classical hemophilia of moderate severity, had lived in a small suburban community of New York all his life. He was a handsome young man, with no orthopedic involvements; yet he had been in and out of hospitals for years for treatment of hemorrhages and resultant internal complications. Harry was the only hemophiliac in a family of four sons. His father was a retired ship-building worker who received a pension. The three brothers—one younger and two older—worked at manual trades.
>
> Of apparently normal intellectual capacity, Harry had finished two years of high school after an elementary schooling that was irregular owing to his frequent illnesses. He was 19 when he decided that he felt awkward with the

younger high school students and simply dropped out. He had had no jobs, but amused himself at home by watching television and playing records. He did not go out socially, but had one close friend, a young man who had taken an interest in him and had attempted to arrange blood donations for him.

Harry played the piano and spoke of wanting to become a musician. He wanted to study at a school where he could learn to make transcriptions for jazz orchestras. He could not, however, afford to attend such a school, and did not know whether, after taking such training, he would be able to get a job in this field.

Harry verbalized his interest in such vocational planning, but had not followed through on suggestions that were made to him of discussing the plan with the State Vocational Rehabilitation Division. This failure to follow through seemed to be a characteristically apathetic approach to his own situation.

It is clear that casework help to Harry and his parents would have had to begin when Harry was much younger if realistic vocational counseling and referral were to take place. In extending casework help to his parents, the caseworker would have had to take into account the special medical and psychological problems experienced by the hemophiliac during various phases of his development. To be helpful, the caseworker would have had to be aware of the very special frustrations and anxieties that both Harry and his parents had encountered. As this case reveals, the caseworker must be particularly aware of the problems associated with the hemophiliac's adolescence. In addition to the maturational stresses of normal adolescence, the hemophiliac experiences growing awareness that he is afflicted with a chronic disease, one that has multiple implications for marriage and parenthood roles and for the highly valued role of worker in our culture.

The adolescent hemophiliac thus may call into question his own adequacy in relation to most of the important adjustment indices in the adult world. Unless he is helped to explore and understand the ramifications of these feelings and reactions by means of a professional relationship, he can easily lose his way, and, like Harry B, retreat into a chronic passive dependency which is not realistically related to his actual medical condition. I found particularly noteworthy the number of such apparently "lost," passively dependent, apathetic, and depressed personalities encountered among young adult hemophiliacs. That I also encountered a relatively small number of comparatively active and outgoing individuals, who had made what seemed to be a good adjustment to their illness and disability, should also be stated. In perhaps a majority of cases there were problems of overdependency and passivity. It should be possible for many hemophiliacs, through skilled casework help, to achieve a better adjustment that will involve coming to terms with limitations in relation to their image of themselves, their possibilities of becoming vocationally active, and their problems of social life.

A readily acceptable focus for such casework help to adolescents and young men would seem to be the area of vocational planning. The possible range of occupations that can be followed by the hemophiliac is limited by several factors: (1) the innate capacities of the individual; (2) the severity and frequency of occurrence of disabling episodes; (3) the presence and degree of correction of orthopedic defect; and (4) the attitudes of potential employers. Within a framework of such limitations, hemophiliacs have been able to function in the professions, in education, small businesses, and clerical occupations. Generally speaking, severe physical exertion is not advised, although one encounters hemophiliacs who are laborers, bus and truck drivers, machinists, and workers in other active trades. Awareness of the many vocational possibilities open to him and of available community resources for helping him secure employment in one of them can be decidedly therapeutic for the young hemophiliac, even without exploration of deeper, underlying feelings.

The problems of social life are also acute for the young adult who suffers from his constant awareness of the implications of his condition for marriage and parenthood. Awareness of such problems frequently imposes a pattern of withdrawal from group or individual relationships, which in turn intensifies his feelings of loneliness, isolation, and depression. Through simple encouragement, some young men have been helped to try, and have found considerable support from, planned participation in social and recreational activities with other handicapped or non-handicapped persons.

Problems of Female Relatives

One of the most serious areas of conflict is that experienced by the female members of a hemophilic family. Their conflict arises from the fact that they may be carriers of the defective gene, although they are not personally affected by the illness. Genetic data indicate that there is a fifty per cent chance that the daughter of a male hemophiliac will be a carrier of the defective gene. There is a fifty per cent chance that a male child born to a carrier will be a hemophiliac. *All* the daughters of a female carrier of the gene are themselves carriers. Thus, in the well-known instance of Queen Victoria, who was a hemophilic carrier, all her daughters were carriers; they married into the royal houses of Spain, Germany, and Russia, where, among their male children, several hemophiliacs were subsequently found.

There is at present no reliable test which indicates whether or not the daughter of a hemophilic male is herself a carrier of the defective gene. Researchers are continuing to try to develop such a test but so far without success. In view of this, the psychological situation of the potential carrier is understandable. Attitudes range from shame, and the impulse to conceal the possible hereditary defect, to withdrawal from social contacts and extreme depression. It has been found that the daughters can be helped through professional or lay sources to face realistically the alternatives that confront them. Some daughters of hemophiliacs, for example, have been ready to take a chance on marriage and motherhood; they may rationalize their actions by the belief that, first of all, they have a "fifty-fifty" chance of having a healthy son; or that the care of a hemophilic child is not such a tremendous burden and is to be preferred to childlessness; or they may be convinced that the improvements in therapy developed over recent years, and the prospects of current research, give promise of more effective control or even a cure. Some women have sought to adopt children rather than to risk a perpetuation of the defective gene. Adoption has been arranged, to the writer's knowledge, in several instances, both within and outside the structure of social agency services. It is of interest to note that among hemophilic families known to me, there are several with two or more affected sons, and that such multiple-sufferer families are found in religious groups that do not have prohibitions against birth control practices.

Therapeutic Aspects of Help to Hemophiliacs

Like other groups of the specially disadvantaged and handicapped, hemophiliacs and their families can draw great strength from group associations. In those communities where the voluntary agency concerned with their problems exists, these families have been able to work out generally superior arrangements for blood procurement, medical services, and special schooling. The less tangible advantages of participation in such "self-help" groups are also worth stating. Among these are: (1) overcoming the sense of isolation and overwhelming distress, frequently experienced by parents as a first reaction to the diagnosis of hemophilia; (2) provision of accurate information regarding problems of medical management, child care, blood procurement, and so forth; (3) socialization through contacts and exchange of experience with other families who can contribute to knowledge about developmental phases and problems that can be anticipated; (4) provision of organized or informal opportunities to discuss the parents' fears, frustrations, and satisfactions arising from the particular difficulties of caring for a hemophilic child; (5) opportunity to discuss broader and longer-range problems that can be anticipated on behalf of the child so that planning can be done; (6) possibility of securing through group action better facilities of a therapeutic and educational nature for their children; (7) cathartic effects of such personal participation, which helps to relieve anxieties by channeling them into constructive outlets.

As stressed in the foregoing, it seems to me that casework services are extremely important for both parents and patients, to help forestall and minimize some of the problems that have been described in this article. Such assistance can help to define and resolve for the parents some of the major feelings that may inhibit their handling their child in a way that combines necessary physical protectiveness with maximum psychological self-reliance. Early establishment of a relationship with a caseworker enables the hemophilic youngster to express his own perceptions, fears, anxieties, and wishes about himself, that for one reason or another cannot find adequate expression in his family group. Vocational planning can and should be instituted early in order to assist the hemophiliac to "capitalize his losses" by turning to academic or quiet hobbies, to make up for the fact that he cannot be an active participant in body contact athletics and rough games. Early counseling is particularly imperative for the individual who does not have the intellectual endowment suitable for pursuing academic courses of study, in order to steer him to an appropriate and consistently pursued course of preparation leading toward ultimate employment.

The older adolescent and the young adult need constant encouragement and opportunity to discuss their personal problems and reactions in other than the emotion-fraught home situation. One way social workers can also help in this area by arranging special opportunities for group participation in existing social agencies, community centers, and informal clubs. Posing these problems and needs, however, does not answer the question of who in the community, that is to say, what professional group, will take responsibility on behalf of such patients. From my experience with hemophiliacs, I should estimate that not more than twenty per cent of the afflicted families in a large city have had contacts with social agencies. Although individual situations must be dealt with individually, it is apparent that once the definite diagnosis of hemophilia is made, the resultant psychosocial, educational, vocational, and other social problems of a patient and his family are numerous, diverse, long-continuing, and almost uniformly present. It would seem of great benefit, then, to have centers established for information, referral to appropriate resources, and, if possible, direct casework and related services—such as group counseling—that would utilize specific knowledge of the condition and its effects. The hemophilia associations are not yet strong enough nor do they have financial resources sufficient to provide such services, although they recognize the necessity for them. It would thus seem that in this, as in other fields of chronic illness, the community is in need of a new type of casework service, one that offers comprehensive information and knowledge of resources appropriate to meeting the needs of the chronically ill, along with some direct services of both a casework and a group character. The challenge of meeting the needs of the hemophilic patient and his family is a persistent and urgent one for social workers in all settings.

Impact of Kidney Disease on Patient, Family, and Society

Kathleen M. Hickey

The National Kidney Foundation estimates that over seven million Americans now suffer disease of the kidney. More than 125,000 people in the United States die from kidney disease each year. If transplantable kidneys were available, seven thousand of these persons could be saved.

The long periods of chronic illness, repeated hospitalizations, and the overwhelming amount of stress placed on patients and families have implications for social work. It is the purpose of this article to provide information about kidney disease and methods of treatment and to point out some of the social problems in order that social workers might be better prepared to assist clients with kidney disease. The material in this article is drawn from experience at the Kidney Transplant Service of the University of Minnesota Hospitals, a teaching facility of 826 beds, with 125,000 outpatient visits each year. The Kidney Unit has 25 hospital beds and 220 patients attending the Transplant Out-Patient Clinic.

The person who is faced with the loss of kidney function manifests a state of crisis. Permanent kidney failure formerly resulted in death; choices today are limited to implantation of another person's kidney, kidney dialysis, or death. Two methods of treatment offer a chance for life—hemodialysis (use of artificial kidney machine) and kidney transplantation.

Hemodialysis has shown itself to be a feasible means of prolonging the lives of people with permanent kidney failure. The treatment procedure involves implantation of tubes (cannulas) into the arm or leg of a patient. The cannulas are inserted into the artery and vein and are connected by a shunt that lets the blood flow from one cannula to the other between treatments. When a patient comes in for treatments, the cannulas are connected to tubes leading to the artificial kidney machine that removes the impurities from the blood. The patient must spend several hours lying in bed attached to the machine, as a dialysis may take from four to twelve hours and is required two or three times a week.

Reprinted from *Social Casework,* Vol. 53 (July, 1972), pp. 391–398, by permission of the author and the Family Service Association of America.

Kidney transplantation, which involves grafting of an organ from one individual to another of the same species (homograft), has now advanced to the stage in which it is the treatment of choice for persons with permanent renal failure. Successful transplantation removes the patient from the "sick role"; dialysis does not. He feels better, sources of stress are lessened, and he is able to assume a functioning role. The aim of transplantation is to restore the individual to a normal functioning life.

Physicians have intensified research and study on kidney transplantation as a method of treatment for several reasons. (1) Deaths were numerous among young people; (2) kidney transplantation is technically the easiest method to perform; and (3) the kidney is the only vital paired organ of which a human being can lose one and still survive well. Also, if the body does reject the new kidney, the patient can be maintained on the artificial kidney machine. It is anticipated that improved immuno-suppressive drug therapy, organ preservation, and more accurate tissue typing will, within the next few years, greatly reduce rejection reactions and increase the chances of longer life.

The University of Minnesota Hospitals has a liberal admission policy. Although a patient must meet certain medical criteria, social and economic factors do not play roles in a patient's acceptance. Patients also do not have to be state residents. Those rejected by other centers and those with disease or complications, such as diabetes, are accepted. Because of these factors, social problems are perhaps more prevalent and severe.

In 1971, eighty patients received kidney transplants; of this number, sixty-three were adults, and seventeen were children under sixteen years of age. Of the group, thirty-four received cadaver (deceased, nonrelated donor) transplants. All the children and twenty-nine of the sixty-three adults received kidneys from blood-related donors. When a patient receives a kidney of a related donor, his chances for survival with a functioning kidney are much greater.

Surgical illness is a "human experience" and produces new adaptations that may or may not be pathological. The dramatic character of transplantation surgery diverts attention from social problems inherent in the medical procedures, such as failure of the operation to meet expectations of the patient and family, disruption of family equilibrium, and investment of public funds to meet these costs. Renal failure and transplantation precipitate a crisis that may be defined differently by the patient and family. The crisis situation may mobilize or it may incapacitate them.

The discussion that follows will be based on the experiences of the social worker assigned to the Kidney Transplant Unit. The social worker assists the staff by obtaining detailed information in the form of social histories concerned with the impact of the disease on the patient and his family. The major functions of the social worker are to help the patient face his current environment and work through his feelings, fears, and attitudes and to help him strive toward a realistic adjustment and plan for his future life after discharge. The social worker explores the interaction and dynamics of members of a family—their attitudes, ways of communicating, and patterns of coping. Adherence to the patterns of a past life is not always indicative of the future but may identify specific problem areas. The focus is on helping families retain their integrity and functions.

The social work role varies with each patient. It consists of (1) helping the individual to understand the extensive treatment plan, (2) counseling with the patient and family in working out acceptance of the medical problem and methods of modifying some of its aspects by exploring ways for more satisfying relationships, (3) assessing readiness for acceptance of help from community and similar resources, (4) acting as a resource person and liaison with community agencies, (5) providing casework services to assist the patient and family, and (6) offering public education.

In order to coordinate information to assist the physician so that the patient can receive maximum benefit of treatment at University Hospitals, the "Hospital Team Conference" was initiated and is concerned with a comprehensive program for total care. The team attempts to alleviate forces that interfere with the patient's ability to receive and accept medical care. There is also considerable interaction and intense involvement among patients and between patients and staff. Social systems that characterize hierarchy among the patients are evident. Codes and rules are established, and patients redefine these roles and set up new expectations and responsibilities of which the staff must be aware in order to meet the needs. A therapeutic environment is encouraged by the staff through team conferences, physical therapy, occupational therapy, and diversional activities.

The Chronically Ill Patient and Hemodialysis

Hemodialysis prolongs the life of patients by the use of the "artificial kidney." Patients unable to receive a kidney transplant, those awaiting a cadaver donor, and patients who have had rejected transplants are maintained on dialysis. The treatment procedure can return a patient to a reasonably normal existence but presents some physical side effects and psychological complications. Although hemodialysis alleviates the uremic syndrome and the patient generally feels better, there are diet restrictions, problems with blood pressure, feelings of weakness, impotence, periodic hospitalizations, and shunt complications (clotting), any of which may prevent participation in living activities. Most patients experience some degree of apprehension before dialysis and tend to become most anxious at the beginning and end of the treatment when the shunt is disengaged or when technical difficulties arise. Attention span is often short, and it has been noted that some patients defend themselves against their anxiety by intellectualization or through sleep. Dialysis can be a frightening experience as a patient is able to observe his blood leaving and returning to his body. He may experience various degrees of fantasies and distorted body imagery, and he may view himself as not wholly human. The dialysis technician and nurse, who are particularly close to the patient, must deal realistically with the patient's anxieties concerning the machine. After dialysis, temporary weakness and nausea from salt and water loss is present; this weakness is often accompanied by lethargy.

Thus, hemodialysis does not completely alleviate difficulties of renal failure, and patients may be faced with a future of chronic illness. Patients, however, may function adequately in the "sick role." The passive dependent person probably will make an adjustment to dialysis but may have difficulties in long-term adjustment after a successful transplant. Patients on dialysis are also placed in a dependent situation and may never accept the shunt as an integral part of themselves. The cannula is a constant reminder of their condition and dependence on the dialyzer. A state of mental depression is not uncommon and follows the general grieving sequence of stages. At first patients tend to use denial; then they go through a period of grief and mourning, followed by anger and frustration, which may give way to depression or regression. Then constructive attempts are made to adjust to the illness and treatment plans. (A temporary depressive phase is also noted immediately following transplant.)

It is not uncommon for the patient on dialysis to violate a dietary or fluid restriction. Patients are carefully taught about permitted and forbidden food and its significance in relation to their illness and life. Nevertheless, patients frequently refuse to eat designated foods, request foods they know they are not allowed, or eat in the hospital canteen. Food can assume great importance for the patient under stress. The traditional methods for relieving anxiety and tension, other than food, are often not permitted for the dialysis patient. He may be advised to stop smoking or restrict alcoholic and fluid intake. He may not be allowed lengthy trips or participation in rigorous activity. These prohibitions may result in hostile feelings, and the patient may attempt to use his diet to control his situation, seek gratification, and release his stress. Another form of behavior that might be interpreted as an act of resentment, denial of illness, or desire for self-harm is the patient's neglecting to take care of his shunt.

Long-term dialysis requires sacrifices on the part of the patient and his family because of the special requirements and frequent trips to the hospital for dialysis. The patient and family members may resent this intrusion on family life and display open hostility and guilt, often directed at the staff. The patient's self-image and role can change greatly during this period.

The time of dialysis (day or night) and the distance to the center are important factors in the patient's total rehabilitation and his ability to be gainfully employed or perform household duties. Thus, chronic hemodialysis has a profound psychological impact on the patient and his family.

The Transplant Patient and His Family

The transplant patient must plan to remain under medical supervision for an indefinite length of time. The prospect of transplantation presents freedom from pain and provides an opportunity to engage in meaningful activity. Conflict may arise between the patient and family. The patient may feel more threatened by new independency in assuming the "healthy role" than by facing death. The choice of a kidney donor requires family decisions that can produce a high degree of stress. This decision-making crisis in kidney transplantation is unique; all the members of the family know that one could be saved by the sacrifice of another. The act of donation may be inconsistent with other life patterns and may not follow a rational decision-making process. Man is used to identifying with a model, and the lack of norms and customs to use as guidelines would appear to cause a great amount of tension and stress. The patient knows that if he receives a kidney from a family member, his chances for survival are twice as good as they would be from a cadaver kidney. Reactions to receiving a cadaver kidney have not been studied extensively; however, from observation, attitudes vary from curiosity about the person who donated and how his death occurred to indifference and relief that the patient does not have to be concerned about family responsibilities or obligations to the donor. Some relatives reveal a sense of grief about the inability of the family members to contribute toward saving the patient's life. The attitude regarding the donated cadaver organ seems to differ between recipient families and donor families, the latter probably viewing donation as a gift and sacrifice.

The length of the interval between the first knowledge that a transplant is needed and the time of the surgery influences psychological attitudes. The patient exhibits various degrees of psychological decompensation pertaining to the donated kidney, based on intrafamilial relationships and personality makeup. Particularly if the recipient is an adult, he will look beyond his immediate family for a potential donor. Role obligations for family members (siblings, aunts, or other close relatives) are unclear in our culture with the possible exception of parents' donation to children. Parents who donate seem to feel that their donation is not so spectacular or extraordinary but something natural to do for their child. Siblings appear unclear about this obligation to donate a kidney. Realistically, the donation of a kidney would cause the donor discomfort, loss of work time, and a small risk of kidney loss for himself later in life. Some families are subjected to many pressures, and the decision to donate a kidney may be a very stressful process. Many of the patients do not approach the entire family but request another member to do so, and this member may play a key role in the recruiting of donors. The patient usually has a good idea if a family member will not volunteer because of ambivalent family relationships; he accepts this fact and is satisfied to wait for a cadaver donor. However, in less close relationships, decision-making can be very difficult. Studies are currently being conducted by Dr. Roberta Simmons of the Sociology Department at the University of Minnesota on the nature of this crisis, focusing on the extended family and on the relative who does not donate a kidney. It has been observed that some relative donors, however, may question their responsibility for the recipient's life; likewise, the recipient may feel threatened in taking the kidney. There is also some indication of feelings of greatness versus hypochondrism on the part of the recipient and donor. In general, donors postoperatively display pride and increased self-esteem and handle their emotions and physical discomfort well.

Patients, both adult and child, become quite sophisticated and knowledgeable about their medical conditions. The patient takes an active part in his treatment program and is able to understand and speak the medical terminology. He learns about the detailed functions of the kidney and about the complex medications and their purposes. "Dialysis and transplantation" are explained thoroughly to him. The kidney disease patient understands his medical diagnosis and prognosis and the reasons for his renal failure in more detail than do most chronically ill patients. The medications given after transplant are essential for the life of the new kidney and the patient's life. The patient knows this and must accept the medications, which may produce observable side effects and impose psychological implications. The first year post-transplant is probably most crucial; problems such as rejection of the organ will most likely occur during this time period. Thus, even after discharge from the hospital, patients often must be readmitted for rejection episodes. This threat, which continues to cause work and home disruptions, adds to the patient's fears.

The high level of emotional involvement in regard to the donation and possible rejection of the new kidney may arouse great anxiety, grief, and disruption of family equilibrium. Rejection of a transplanted kidney produces changes in relationships and a breakdown in defenses. Changes in roles and in the patient's total life situation may be consequences of chronic illness or kidney rejection. Successful transplantation, however, also may produce new life situations and adaptations that do not automatically insure total social and psychological rehabilitation.

The changes in total life situation and attitudes of the transplant recipient may, for example, influence women to change their attitudes in regard to childbearing as against adoption of a child. Marital and sexual relations that have been altered drastically because of the patient's uremic condition during dialysis treatment may make the post-transplant adjustments difficult. Employment retraining may be indicated. Conflicts or problems existing prior to transplantation, on the other hand, may be resolved following a successful transplant.

Teen-agers who receive a transplant have special problems. Absences from school, loss of friends, and conflicts in regard to sex and dating appear to be common. The adolescent is apt to find his body image and identity more of a problem than he can handle.

The social problems a child with kidney disease faces differ from those of the adult. His lack of knowledge and immaturity make the medical treatment plan less well understood and more frightening. Often the child's personality is formed during lengthy and recurrent hospitalizations. The parents' fears and concerns and the limitations of the illness influence the child's development.

Children frequently identify very strongly with a kidney that has been received from a parent donor. For example, a thirteen-year-old boy who received a kidney from his father stated, "I have the only kidney for a boy my age that flew forty missions over Germany."

The parents of a child who has a successful kidney transplant must learn a whole set of new adjustments. Their general concerns and over-protection must be modified to enhance the child's normal development. Siblings who have had competitive feelings and resentment because of special favors and privileges accorded the ill child may add to the difficult readjustment of parents and patient. At times, even the marriage itself must be rebuilt and the entire family relationships recast, requiring assessment, time, and work. Most families need the services of a caseworker during this process.

The social workers in hospitals need to be sensitive to the reactions of patients and relatives so that they can provide guidance and support when needed. During the patient's hospital course, he usually seeks out other patients and compares progress. Strong friendships may form, offering each other a great deal of support. On the other hand, inaccurate information is often exchanged. Relatives, too, may misinterpret another patient's medical status and assume that the same fate is in store for their relative. When a patient becomes acutely ill or dies, the other patients generally become agitated, withdrawn, and depressed; feeling tones are easily picked up and transferred one to another and should be discussed. Because of the critical nature of the illness, the social worker must be able to understand and recognize his own feelings about death and have substantial medical knowledge so that he can empathize with and relate to all patients' families.

Financial Costs and Community Responsibility

The cost of medical care for kidney transplant patients ranges from $10,000 to $80,000. The average cost at the University Hospitals is approximately $16,000 for total inpatient care exclusive of professional fees. Chronic dialysis treatment may amount to between $5,000 to $15,000 on a yearly basis, whereas it is hoped that transplantation is a one-time expense. Eventually, these costs will decrease because of shorter hospital stays and medical advances. The principal sources of financial help at the present time are private insurance, federal research grants, and public welfare programs. Thus, the financial costs entailed by chronic hemodialysis and transplantation impose a problem for the patient, his family, and society. Loss of economic, social, or personal status can become a serious problem and can greatly affect the patient's adjustments and capacity to function. Economic variables directly influence family attitudes as do those of culture, religion, sex, age, and length of illness.

The middle-class patient, who may have insurance coverage and a fairly adequate and stable salary prior to hospitalization, may be required, when his insurance coverage is less than his expenses, to apply for welfare assistance—a plan difficult for many to accept. Furthermore, because they own ' property and have financial assets, many are ineligible for public assistance until legal income requirements are met. The tragedy is compounded for farm patients who are faced with the necessity of selling their land and sacrificing their livelihood and financial independence. For patients residing outside the metropolitan area, there is the additional financial strain of transportation and maintenance costs. Most welfare departments and communities are not able to authorize funds to meet these expenses.

Major financing for the medical expenses of these patients comes from public funds under Title XIX of the Social Security Act. The provisions of the act make it possible to provide complete care for these patients. However, state plans, the interpretation of the act, and procedures by local community agencies impose limitations that create difficulties. The large amount of money required to provide medical care for patients who have severe renal disease, moreover, may be more than a community considers justifiable for one individual. The alternatives are for those in medical practice to refine technical methods to reduce costs and for the federal government to grant financial assistance to institutions involved in development of new methods of medical care. Kidney disease is a major community health problem and thus has serious implications for every community whose social agencies cannot offer constructive services to help these patients.

Among men and women under twenty-five, kidney diseases are the second highest cause of work loss in the United States today. From age twenty-five on, these kidney-related diseases are the fourth highest cause of work loss. The Kidney Foundation, the only major voluntary agency relating itself to the total problem, states that one of every twenty-five persons in any community suffers from some form of kidney disease. Thus, in order for the patient to receive maximum benefit from medical care, his financial, social, and psychological needs must also be met by the community and society.

Employment

Generally, when the patient who has had a successful kidney transplant is ready for discharge from the hospital, he has no vocational restrictions imposed upon him. Ideally, the patient can return to his former job. Realistically, however, his former job may not be available. The prolonged treatment and hospitalization, the financial costs, complexity of medications, periodic checkups at the hospital, and drastic changes in the patient's life situation may have interfered with work performance and resulted in loss of his job. Overprotection is often manifested by family members; it impedes the patient's return to work and independency and interferes with his rehabilitation. Patients, too, fear that harm may come to the new kidney if they engage in strenuous work or extracurricular school activities. Because the majority of patients receive Social Security Disability or county assistance, it is difficult for them to relinquish this aid until they are secure in a new job. Employers hesitate to hire persons who receive Social Security Disability. Many employers do not understand the nature of kidney transplants and do not wish to risk employing someone who might be readmitted to a hospital at any time. Thus, patients may be rejected because they have received an organ transplant. The primary reason generally given is the restrictions imposed by insurance and union policies of large companies.

Physical side effects produced by medication, such as cushioned face, may also prevent patients from seeking the type of employment they want or from resuming past activities. Family relationships and support are important in determining the patient's successful rehabilitation and his return to a level of activity that is equal to, or surpasses, the level prior to the onset of kidney disease.

Vocational rehabilitation and counseling services should be enlisted prior to the patient's discharge from the hospital. Studies focused on defining "rehabilitation" and "adjustment" pretransplant and posttransplant would be useful with the recognition that definitions vary. The mere fact that a person has returned to work following transplantation does not automatically conclude that he is "rehabilitated." The quality of the individual's functioning must be explored. When the gainful employment he has returned to is satisfying to him and to his needs, employment can be used as an indicative factor of rehabilitation.

Moral and Ethical Aspects of Transplantation

Transplantation of human organs is a new era in medical history. The availability of new surgical techniques that prolong and save the lives of thousands of individuals makes it necessary to examine current beliefs concerning the use of organs from the bodies of other people. There are fears within the population regarding the donation of organs, as evidenced by the customs and the mass media. The value of the body, fear of mutilation, sickness, and future health are all considerations and should be correlated with religious beliefs, socioeconomic status, sex, age, race, and culture.

The development of living organ banks is an attempt to institutionalize societal fears. The signing of a donor card may represent a wholesome impersonal aspect, although it is questionable whether people view this action realistically or view it as socially desirable. In the past it has been thought that people who sign cards donating vital organs to a medical center to be used for others are from the better educated, higher socioeconomic groups and view this act as humanitarian. Recent studies, however, indicate that people in the lower socioeconomic groups also wish to make a donation of parts of their body—possibly as a contribution to society or from religious motivation.

The use of organs from the body of a healthy, functioning individual raises moral questions. The extent to which one individual may impose on another is an ethical consideration. The rights of people to safeguard their own bodies can never be denied. In some of these instances the moral and family pressures on donors impose obligations that deny this right.

Another ethical aspect of the procurement of organs involves the purchase of organs for transplants when immunological techniques are perfected. More organs would then be available on a cash-negotiation basis. Because American culture is based on paying for what one receives, this action might not be disturbing to the population. If purchase of organs were authorized, the use of family and cadaver donors would be less of a necessity. However, purchase of organs raises the difficulty of determining price. A high price for organs would certainly discriminate against the poor. The selling of organs might also be interpreted as a partially suicidal gesture. Through laws, it is likely that attitudes and customs regarding transplantation and donation may change, and donation may come to be viewed as a social obligation rather than as a gift or sacrifice.

At the University of Minnesota Hospitals the criteria used for selection of people to receive a renal transplant or to be maintained by hemodialysis are based primarily on medical decisions. As yet, the quality of life the patient will be able to lead or the contributions he can make cannot be determined or defined without enlisting value judgments. Transplantation provides a "potential" life with a new organ. The moral issue is, "Are we doing what we are supposed to do?" Focusing on the quality of life and on transplantation and developing ways of improving present situations are needed.

Other questions raised pertaining to the moral and ethical aspects of transplantation might include the high costs of maintaining dialysis and transplant units of equipment and of training of specialized personnel. People undoubtedly will question the future of transplantation and the possible creation of genetic pools. There are also ambiguities concerning whether to view transplantation as research or treatment, thereby affecting the cost-benefit ratio.

Technical problems of transplantation are now being surmounted and the risk of death reduced. Perhaps we should also look at what technology has not accomplished. Technology may change or eliminate some of the forementioned problems. For example, selection criteria may never have to be defined if the use of mechanical or animal organs replaces the use of human organs in transplantation.

Kidney transplants are successful and are becoming a socially approved procedure. Society lags behind the technological aspects of transplantation, and we must prepare ourselves to meet the psychological and social needs imposed by transplantation in order for these members of society to return to a functional life. The social worker, who has direct contact with the patients, staff, and community agencies, has a professional obligation to transmit accurate information to the public and inform agencies of the needs of certain groups of people in an attempt to establish new resources or change existing attitudes and conceptions.

Conclusions

Social factors are being recognized as important components of kidney disease. Extreme importance is attached to the period following acute illness when the patient regains his health. The patient's attitudes toward kidney disease range from acceptance, resentment, and feelings of inadequacy to withdrawal and exclusiveness. Attitudes of the family members can result in increased dependency, overprotection, and unwanted sympathy. The patient who returns to the community sometimes needs complete economic and social rehabilitation, or he may undergo only relatively minor adjustments. The psychological manifestations are manifold, especially in patients and families when transplantation has failed. The threat or fear of rejection and the high degree of emotional involvement can prevent the patient from resuming his normal life.

In describing some instances of family conflict, decision making, stress, and the impact of kidney disease on the patient, on his family, and on our society, is not intended to imply that the information presented is valid for all potential transplant candidates. In many instances, dialysis, donation, and transplantation run a fairly smooth course and only minimal amounts of rehabilitation are required in order for the patient to resume a fully functioning life.

A program of early social evaluation in the course of the illness should be designed to detect patients whose defenses and coping patterns seem ineffective. The degree of personality disintegration that may accompany organ transplantation has made it evident to medical personnel that a more comprehensive program must be developed to meet the total needs of these patients.

This is a new era in medical history, which offers an opportunity for health to thousands of people with kidney disease. The social worker has an essential contribution to make to the total treatment plan. The new developments present a challenge to social workers to use their skill and knowledge to assist patients to obtain the greatest benefits from medical care and to participate in the healthful living that new treatments promise.

Patients with Progressive Neurological Diseases

Gladys Lambert

Unlike the patient with an acute but transient illness, the patient with a progressive neurological disease is faced with an incurable, debilitating illness that may eventually lead to total physical dependency and a shortened life span. The long, slow, course of the disease causes overpowering anxiety in both the patient and his family, especially in those instances where other family members have had the same disease or where the patient knows other persons with the same diagnosis whose condition is more advanced than his. The dread of, and then the horror of, being unable to walk, feed oneself, get out of bed, and take care of one's toilet needs has been graphically described by articulate patients.[1] As the patient becomes increasingly helpless and disabled, he and his family are called upon to make new and difficult emotional adjustments that frequently require social work intervention.

Progressive neurological diseases, which affect the brain and spinal cord, are primarily of unknown etiology. They vary in onset from early childhood and middle age to the later years of life. Multiple sclerosis, Parkinson's disease, and Huntington's chorea, a hereditary disease, are common in this group. Although symptoms vary with each disease, some fairly typical ones include involuntary irregular movements of the face, head, and hands; transient paralysis and weakness of extremities; instability of gait; and numbness and loss of sensation in various parts of the body.

Basic Considerations

The patient with a progressive neurological disease is confronted not only with the normal stresses of living but with the additional problems and limitations inherent in his illness. The adjustment he makes depends to a large extent on his previous level of social functioning, the nature of the

Reprinted from *Social Casework,* Vol. 55 (March, 1974), pp. 154–159, by permission of the author and the Family Service Association of America.

[1] Georgia Travis, *Chronic Disease and Disability* (Berkeley, Calif.: University of California Press, 1966), pp. 111–12.

illness and its meaning to him, the existence of significant others who rally around him and are available to help, and his access to concrete resources. These factors, when applied to the patient, can provide the social worker with psychosocial diagnostic clues to the patient's coping potential and can serve as the basis for formulation of a treatment goal and plan.

The patient with a satisfactory life adjustment prior to illness is more likely to cope adequately than a person whose previous adjustment has been poor or at best marginal. In evaluating the pre-illness level of social functioning, consideration should be given to the nature of the patient's previous family and social relationships and the extent to which these have been sustained and positive. His performance in such roles as spouse, parent, and worker provides clues about previous adjustment.

The physical limitations of a progressive neurological disease invariably interfere with the patient's performance of his previous role responsibilities. In our culture the husband carries primary responsibility for providing the family income. When he is the patient, the family is threatened with a loss or reduction of income and frequently a lower standard of living. For many men, the role of provider is a source of both status and deep personal satisfaction. Having to relinquish this role can result in a loss of self-esteem, a feeling of inadequacy, and an accompanying depression. Such reactions are culturally reinforced by the value our society places on productivity, self-reliance, and physical strength, particularly for men.

The patient who is a wife and mother may find it increasingly difficult to handle responsibilities attached to these roles. If she is the mother of an infant or young child, she may be unable to lift him or otherwise minister to his physical needs. Housework may become increasingly difficult. However, the reaction of each patient to these limitations will depend on the meaning they hold for him. Jeanette R. Oppenheimer points out that some individuals and families gain new satisfactions in the patient role because it serves to meet long-existing but previously unfulfilled needs. For many patients, however, the reverse is true. In his role as a patient, the individual may expect to be considered helpless and deserving of sympathy and tender care; he may anticipate that others in the family will take on protective functions and attitudes. These actions and attitudes, however, do not always come spontaneously from family members, who are charged with his care while simultaneously being affected by his abdication of his customary role. They may resent the onerous duties placed on them and the patient's release from his own duties.[2]

The patient's ability to cope can be greatly influenced by the support and encouragement of friends and family. If the patient is married and has relatives who can share some of the responsibilities of the overburdened spouse, the adverse repercussions of the illness on the marital relationship are often less excessive. However, the too-ready response by the family to the patient in his new role may create further problems for him as he experiences the loss of a role that had deep meaning; he may feel no longer

[2] Jeanette R. Oppenheimer, Use of Crisis Intervention in Casework with Cancer Patient and His Family, *Social Work*, 12: 48 (April 1967).

needed or valued.[3] When there are no family or friends, or the relationship is extremely poor, the patient may rely heavily on the social worker for help in coping with the problems confronting him.

The availability of resources in the community can alleviate some of the more concrete problems facing the patient and his family and allow time for long-range planning. These resources may include various programs—frequently financed through medical insurance and local welfare departments—that provide for physical care of the patient at home and care of young children in the family. Although such programs exist in many communities throughout the country and render valuable help, they do not adequately meet the needs of the patient with a progressive disease because the help offered tends to be time-limited whereas the patient's needs often are not. Commercial programs which do not have this built-in limitation are usually prohibitive in cost for most middle-income families. In addition to the need for long-term home care services, community respite programs would be invaluable in offering temporary physical and emotional relief for families from care-taking responsibilities. Unfortunately, many communities have not yet addressed themselves to the long-term needs of this patient group.

Sometimes the problem faced by the patient and his family is not a lack of access to concrete resources but rather a reluctance to accept what is available. Applying for social security disability benefits and other forms of assistance may symbolically represent an admission of disability and dependency which neither the patient nor his family is yet ready to face.

Treatment Implications

The social worker in a medical setting is in a particularly good vantage point to intervene and help the patient and his family begin to cope with emotional and social aspects of a progressive neurological disease and prevent family dysfunction. Because the patient frequently visits a clinic or hospital for treatment of his illness, he is accessible to the worker. For some persons it may be less threatening to accept help with psychosocial problems in a setting which has medical treatment as its primary function.

If the patient and his family are to be helped to cope with a progressive neurological disease, it is important that the social worker not be overwhelmed by the disease process itself and that he keep the medical diagnosis in its proper perspective. The diagnosis should be viewed as a source of clues to the possible areas in which the patient and his family may need help.

In treating the patient, it is essential that the social worker provide opportunity for him to express and clarify feelings about his illness. Those in his immediate environment, his family and friends, often feel threatened by such expression and may overtly and covertly prevent him from doing so. The expression of feelings can liberate emotional energy needed to cope with the changes and limitations in his life and lessen his need to displace anger and frustration onto family and the medical team. Irving N. Berlin notes that he has known a number of seriously handicapped neurological patients

---

[3] Ibid

for whom the continued opportunity to express their feelings about their handicap, without an attendant show of anxiety, helplessness, and hopelessness from the therapist, has helped them to focus their attention on the realities imposed by their handicaps and to proceed to do what they could to earn their own livings, to be productive, and thus to be more satisfied with themselves and happier despite severe and incapacitating handicaps.[4]

Since the patient's feelings are never completely resolved and often need to be dealt with during various stages in the progression of the illness, it is extremely important for the worker to be aware of his own feelings about the illness and to bring these under conscious control. Unless he is able to do so, he will be less prepared to help the patient with his feelings.

The patient's use of denial in coping with his illness, particularly when it is first diagnosed and during its early stage of progression, is fairly common and has been much discussed in the literature.[5] Denial can serve a useful purpose and should not be questioned unless it interferes with the patient's treatment and makes it impossible for him to handle reality problems precipitated by his medical condition. The use of denial is a signal that the patient is not yet emotionally able to face his illness and all of its implications for him and his family. Each patient has his own timetable for acceptance.

Case Illustrations

The following case summary illustrates early intervention of the social worker, initiated to help a patient with multiple sclerosis express and clarify feelings about his disability and begin to cope with his situation.

Multiple sclerosis generally afflicts the patient during the most productive years of his life, between the ages of twenty and forty. The fatty substance called myelin, which acts as a protective covering for the nerve fibers of the spinal cord and brain, disintegrates, thereby blocking and distorting nerve impulses which control speech, vision, movement, and balance. Although early symptoms may disappear, over the years they reappear in more severe forms, resulting in paralysis and often urinary and bowel incontinence.

> Mr. B, aged thirty-four, married and father of five children aged seven years to twenty-one months, was referred to the hospital social worker by his physician because of Mr. B's concern about his family's income during his hospitalization. He was hospitalized following the onset of blurred vision and paralysis of limbs. The tentative diagnosis of multiple sclerosis was confirmed. Nine years earlier, he had experienced transient visual difficulty and at that time there was conflicting medical opinion as to whether he had multiple sclerosis. Mrs. B, a full-time housewife and former registered nurse, was expecting their sixth child. Two years earlier, when Mr. B accepted a research position with a pharmaceutical company, they had moved into a new community, leaving behind relatives and friends.

[4] Irving N. Berlin, A Review of Some Elements of Neurology: Part II, *Journal of Social Casework*, 37: 493–500 (December 1956).
[5] Harry S. Abram, Psychological Responses to Illness and Hospitalization, *Psychosomatics*, 10: 218–23 (July–August 1969).

Mr. B was an intelligent, capable young man who took pride in his role as husband and provider for his family. Mrs. B derived gratification from her role of wife and mother. In the marital relationship, she appeared maternal and more dominant, with no desire to work outside the home.

The worker saw Mr. and Mrs. B during and after hospitalization to help them adjust to his illness and its repercussions on their life. There was periodic consultation with Mr. B's physician and the nursing staff regarding his medical condition, prognosis, extent of impairment, and capabilities. This information was essential to the worker in helping the B family plan realistically for the future. Mr. and Mrs. B were given the opportunity to express their feelings about Mr. B's illness. Mr. B reacted to his diagnosis with depression and a verbalized fear of becoming dependent on "public charity." He expressed disapproval of disabled people he had known who lacked initiative and expected others to take care of their needs. Such feelings reflected his own conflict and anxiety about dependency.

After leaving the hospital, Mr. B returned to work for approximately eight weeks. However, a subsequent exacerbation of his condition, resulting in further weakness of limbs and unsteady gait, made it impossible for him to continue working. Although eligible for veteran's and social security benefits, he initially denounced each as charity and was only able to accept these sources of income when a representative of the Veterans' Administration pointed out that he should consider the needs of his family. The social worker recognizing Mr. B's need to deny his dependency needs, supported his rationalization that he had decided to accept help only because of his concern about the needs of his family. The family was able to manage on a reduced income chiefly as a result of their ability to economize.

Mrs. B, faced with her husband's illness as well as her pregnancy, avoided discussion of her own dependency needs. Because of her nursing background and experience, she understood a great deal about Mr. B's illness. Although she generally used strong intellectual defenses, she expressed a sense of loss and anger toward Mr. B for permanently depriving her of some aspects of companionship which he had not fully gratified previously. She recalled her own fondness for dancing and her attempts to prod him into dancing with her. Now, because of his condition, there was little possibility that he would ever be able to dance.

Looking ahead to the future, Mrs. B expressed the philosophy of enjoying to the fullest each day spent with her family. She used casework help to handle reality problems resulting from Mr. B's illness. The worker responded at the level Mrs. B sought and gave her advice and guidance about procedures and requirements for social security benefits and temporary public assistance. Mrs. B expressed a sense of shame in having to accept the latter and needed an opportunity to discuss her feelings and receive support from the worker before proceeding with the application.

In anticipation of Mrs. B's confinement, the worker helped her to consider various alternatives for the care of the children, and she was able to ask a relative to help. Following Mr. B's discharge from the hospital, both partners experienced some difficulty adjusting to his presence at home all day. The noise of the children distressed him and he expressed his feeling that his wife was not strict enough with the children. She complained that he was underfoot frequently and began to explore possible outside activities which would take Mr. B out of the home for a portion of the day, since he was ambulatory with the aid of a cane. Mrs. B, who had a retarded brother, suggested Mr. B volunteer his services at a local center offering day care activities for retarded children. Mr. B became enthusiastic about the volunteer experience, and the worker encouraged him to discuss his role at the center, supported his involvement, and gave recognition for his contribution to the children at the center who needed his interest and help. When Mr. B again saw himself as a productive person and when his self-esteem increased, the couple's relationship also improved.

As this case illustrates, a progressive neurological disease has emotional implications, not only for the patient but for his family as well. Sometimes it is not until the patient develops residual impairments that the full implications of the illness become an emotional reality. Since all relationships contain some ambivalence, the negative, resentful feelings of the patient's spouse and other family members are bound to increase as the patient becomes increasingly helpless and dependent on their care. Because they recognize that the patient is not responsible for his condition, they often feel guilty about these feelings; they then may become rejecting or depressed and over-protective of the patient. By helping family members express their ambivalent feelings without responding in a judgmental way, the social worker can help them cope with their responsibilities in a way which is constructive for family and patient.

The patient's increasing helplessness may upset the previously established balance in the marital relationship. A frequent area of difficulty is the change in the patient's ability to meet the needs of his spouse. Highly vulnerable are those marriages in which the ill spouse had played a protective nurturing role toward a highly dependent spouse. The increasingly disabled spouse may also be unable to meet the sexual needs of his partner or to fulfill his own. The nature of the couple's companionship frequently undergoes a change. Some previously shared social and recreational activities may need to be modified or curtailed and other substitutes found.

The following case illustrates the role of the social worker in sustaining a couple during the acute and terminal stages of the wife's progressive illness and prolonged hospitalization.

Mrs. R, a thirty-one-year-old married woman, mother of six children ranging in age from twelve years to seventeen months, was hospitalized because of a severe exacerbation of multiple sclerosis. She was unable to walk or sit upright in a wheelchair. She could not feed, bathe, or dress herself and was incontinent. Mrs. R's condition had been originally diagnosed shortly after the birth of her youngest child. Since then she had been hospitalized for brief periods but had been able to resume her normal activities as wife and mother.

She was referred for help to the hospital social worker by a staff nurse because of the concern Mrs. R expressed regarding care and supervision of her children. Mr. R, a construction worker, had been at home recovering from a back injury but was now ready to return to work.

This was the second marriage for both Mr. and Mrs. R, whose first marriages had ended in divorce. The present marriage had been plagued by long-standing differences over disciplining the children, especially the three older ones who were born during Mrs. R's first marriage. She was extremely protective of them and saw Mr. R as too strict and rigid. The two children of Mr. R's first marriage lived with his ex-wife in another state. Despite this area of tension in their relationship, they had positive feelings for each other. They shared common goals, had middle-class aspirations, and were buying their own home.

The social worker explored with them various alternatives for the care and supervision of the children and helped obtain a homemaker from the county department of social services. Later, the three children of Mrs. R's first marriage went to stay with their paternal grandmother who lived nearby. When the homemaker was placed in the family, Mr. R returned to work. The worker maintained periodic contact with the county department of social services throughout the seven months of Mrs. R's hospitalization. There was a sharing of information regarding her condition and the family's adjustment to the homemaker.

Mr. R, a rather passive, dependent man, had relied on his wife to make decisions regarding the family, and he continued to do so, with her acquiescence. To the worker, he showed considerable sorrow over her illness and he expressed his dependency on his wife by complaining about the lack of comfort and care when the house was run by the homemaker. The worker recognized his longing to have Mrs. R recover and return home to him.

Mrs. R, an intelligent, determined woman, displaced her anxiety about her illness onto continuing anxiety about the children. Under the increasing stress of her condition, complicated by a pulmonary embolism, she became quite paranoid for several weeks. She suspected her husband of poisoning her, transmitting a venereal disease to her, and seducing her ten-year-old daughter. There was no evidence to substantiate these suspicions, which subsided once her condition improved.

There was a change in social workers when, after three months of hospitalization in the neurology division, Mrs. R was transferred to the rehabilitation unit. Although Mrs. R's illness resumed a downhill course with a poor prognosis, she was able to spend some weekends at home with her family. Before the weekend visits began, the worker visited the home to evaluate its adequacy and determine the kind of equipment Mrs. R would need.

Both partners continued to use denial and to express hope in coping with Mrs. R's poor prognosis. They formulated plans for their future together in anticipation of her recovery and return home. Mrs. R continued to focus on the needs of her children. She was concerned about the academic performance of the eight-year-old daughter of her first marriage who was in a classroom for emotionally disturbed children. The worker conferred with the school personnel and shared pertinent information about Mrs. R's condition, interpreting the needs of the family.

The worker consulted frequently with members of the rehabilitation team regarding the changes in Mrs. R's physical condition. Because there was no improvement in her ability to function, the worker began to help Mr. R to consider the chronic care needs of his wife. Because of his dependency on Mrs. R and because he saw placement as essentially an unloving act, he was insistent on taking her home when discharged. However, as her condition further deteriorated, the focus shifted to helping him face the imminent loss of his wife.

After Mrs. R's death, Mr. R came to see the worker and talked about his wife's death and the plans he had made for the care of the children, following consultation with the county department of social services. The children of Mrs. R's first marriage were to remain with their paternal grandmother. Two children of his marriage to Mrs. R were to live with his mother in another state and the remaining son, a first-grade pupil, would continue to live with him. He had arranged to have his cousin supervise the child while he worked.

Summary

Because of the difficulties which patients with progressive neurological diseases and their families must face, they often need the help of a caseworker periodically during the course of the disease. The worker can help the family to cope with the members' ambivalent feelings about the patient while helping the patient to clarify his feelings and maintain a sense of self-worth and dignity. This task is exceedingly challenging in a society that places a high premium on self-reliance and productivity.

Group Work with Parents of Children with Down's Syndrome

Ann Murphy, Siegfried M. Pueschel, and Jane Schneider

Social workers are increasingly stressing their role in prevention of social maladjustment. Frequently, however, they lack access to groups of people sharing a common crisis. Children with birth defects do not ordinarily come to the attention of social workers unless the family manifests some adjustment problem or there is need for specific social planning. Even then, contact is apt to be limited to resolution of a particular issue with selected families. Patterns of coping which are maladaptive have been identified. Retrospectively, they would indicate that if help had been available to the family when attitudes were being formed, the current problems might not have developed.

For one and one-half years, the authors had an opportunity to meet families coping with the impact of discovering that their newborn child had Down's syndrome. This is a chromosomal aberration resulting in a characteristic physical appearance and mental retardation. It is more commonly and incorrectly known as mongolism. Following closely nearly seventy families of infants with Down's syndrome in a group experience provided insights into the dimensions of such a crisis, the range of responses, and the kinds of support professional people and the community can offer. The group also served as a therapeutic resource for the participating families in working through the trauma of giving birth to a defective child.

Background of Study

In September 1970, the developmental evaluation clinic of the Children's Hospital Medical Center in Boston received a grant to evaluate the effect of a drug (L-5-hydroxy-tryptophan-pyridoxin) upon the motor, language,

Reprinted from *Social Casework*, Vol. 54 (February, 1972), pp. 114–119, by permission of the authors and the Family Service Association of America.

and intellectual development of young children with Down's syndrome.[1] A multidiscipline team of anthropologist, neurologist, nurse, pediatrician, physical therapist, psychologist, speech therapist, and social worker was organized to document the progress of new-born children on all major parameters of development. One-half the children received the medication and the other half a placebo, but the identity of the members of each sample was unknown both to the parents and to the professional staff involved in the evaluation. The parents of all the children were instructed in motor and sensory stimulation. They were cautioned that all of these efforts would, at most, facilitate the development of the child and were not expected to be curative. Appointments were initially scheduled at three- to four-week intervals, and as the child's health and family were stabilized, the frequency decreased. Comprehensive evaluations were to take place every six months during the first three years. Children were recruited for the program by informing all pediatricians and maternity hospitals within a 150-mile radius of Boston of the existence of the project and by encouraging referrals of newborn infants. The babies ranged in age from one week to three months at the time of the first appointment, but typically they were about two weeks old. The clinic program was unusual because of the high proportion of fathers who attended, in contrast to other clinics in the hospital.

The social worker's original plan was to interview all families at the first appointment, when the baby was six months old, and again at one, two, and three years of age, to assess their responses as the different dimensions of the handicap became apparent. The objective would be to study factors which influence a family's adaptation to a child with this type of birth defect.

Common Initial Concerns of Parents

The birth of a child with Down's syndrome places a great stress on the parents. What has been anticipated as a joyful occasion is characterized by a sense of loss, grief, and mourning.[2] The medical staff handle their own disappointment by suggesting institutionalization, by avoiding the parents, or by exhorting them to love the child, thereby betraying their underlying negative feelings. Specific facts on what the diagnosis entails or how the child may develop are frequently lacking, and there is little opportunity for the parents to check their fantasy that they have given birth to a monster against a more objective reality. Many are afraid to look for what they might see; a common expectation, for example, is that the infant will have a very large head. It is not surprising that a number of parents misinterpret the term *mongoloid* to mean mongrel. When they do look it is difficult for them

---

[1] This work of the clinic was supported by National Institute of Child Health and Human Development (Bethesda, Maryland) Grant HD-05341–01 and Maternal and Child Health Service Project No. 928, U.S. Department of Health, Education, and Welfare.

[2] Simon Olshansky, Chronic Sorrow: A Response to Having a Mentally Defective Child, *Social Casework*, 43: 191 (March 1962).

to reconcile what they have heard with the rather normal appearance of the baby.

A typical assumption is that the child will be an object which they will feed, while he in turn will do nothing but lie there. Some parents resist touching the child because they fear becoming involved by claiming the child as their own. Friends and hospital personnel contribute to the unreality by not sending greeting cards, not photographing the baby, or failing to list the birth in the community newspaper. Some parents illustrate their feelings of low self-esteem by expressing surprise that friends would want to come and see them. Often they do not know anyone else with such a child, and their grief and mourning is compounded by a sense of isolation. Up-to-date reading material is not readily available in the maternity hospital or even in the local library, and what exists is often based on experiences with institutionalized children with this defect.

All the families studied expressed positive feelings about the opportunity to participate in a program in which their child would receive some help and they themselves would receive some support and would participate in activities which might be remedial in nature. In only three of the families was there sufficient indication of disorganization or acute emotional disorder to indicate need for intensive casework treatment. However, all were struggling with feelings of sadness, depression, concern as to cause, and a need for information; these feelings rather than focused conflicts are part of the process of living with a child with a defect. What seemed indicated was a continuing experience which would allow for discharge of feelings, examination of fantasies and fears, and development of constructive adaptive patterns. Since all appointments for the program had been scheduled on the same day of the week for the convenience of the staff, there were at least five or six families present in the waiting room at any given time. It seemed appropriate to consider whether a group experience might offer the additional support such parents appeared to need.

Formation of the Group

All families were informed at the time of their first visit to the clinic of the opportunity to meet with other parents. Parents who were still questioning the accuracy and finality of the diagnosis usually deferred participation until their second visit. Although they placed a varying value on group attendance, all but two families elected to participate. The meetings were held in a small conference room within the clinic area. The atmosphere was informal and coffee was served. Parents usually preferred to bring their babies into the group, although facilities were available for child care. The group composition varied but there was usually a nucleus of people who had been enrolled in the program for some time and who knew each other from previous group meetings. The pediatrician joined the group for the last half hour to answer questions on Down's syndrome, expected development, medical complications, and genetics. The group meetings usually lasted one and one-half hours, although sometimes parents remained in the room to talk after the meeting was over.

The function of the social worker was to facilitate introductions, assist the group in identifying topics for discussion, and encourage participation by the more reserved members while limiting the more aggressive ones. When individuals denied negative feelings or worries which might have been appropriate, the worker verbalized these for the group, allowing others to bring such topics into the discussion. She also assisted the group in exploring fears and questions at a somewhat deeper level than they might have done spontaneously and in functioning as a resource person in terms of information about the diagnosis and clinic and community programs. Typically, the parents related quickly to one another, volunteered data about themselves, and directed personal questions to others. They usually felt free to disagree or to correct one another's misconceptions. Members were particularly supportive and protective of new group attendees; a number of parents formed friendships outside the group. They frequently referred to the fact that the availability of the group and the clinic program diminished their feeling of isolation.

> I look forward to coming; it must be like psychotherapy. I don't feel so alone. It recharges me so I feel strong enough to continue . . . . If I couldn't come here, I would get depressed and then it might affect my baby's development and I would not be able to give to him in the way that I should.

Working Through the Diagnosis

The group experience served as a vehicle to work through feelings regarding the diagnosis. Each new member was usually asked how he was told about the diagnosis; this query gave him an opportunity to describe the experience and to express his feelings of shock, anger, disappointment, and fear. "I was so elated after the birth, then it was as though I had nothing at all. It took me a while to realize I still had a baby, a husband, and a home." At this point the longer-term members reviewed their own experiences, usually with diminishing intensity of feeling as time passes. They discussed freely what they had feared their child would be like, for example, a monster who would be able to do nothing, out-of-control, or dangerous. They then described their relief at the child's actual responsiveness and development as a person. All parents used the group to assist them in comprehending what the diagnosis meant in their child and to reconcile the word and its stereotypes with his presence, a process which usually requires four to five months.

> Sometimes he looks it, sometimes he doesn't. When he's awake his tongue sticks out and then you really notice it.

> I don't know whether to pick him up or not when he cries. He stops crying if I do. He has caught on already and they say he is retarded.

> I feel so much better when I am with the baby. When we are apart my imagination takes over.

For some parents, discussing feelings about the diagnosis in the group was a preparation for talking about the diagnosis with relatives and friends. On each occasion when they had to speak of it to another acquaintance the original sadness and anxiety were reawakened. The group was utilized to clarify their thinking about how and whom to inform about the diagnosis and what terms to use that would be understandable while avoiding the stereotypes that would be conjured up by the word *mongoloid*. "People are curious. They seem to think you have a monster or a freak. When you hear *mentally retarded* you imagine it will be different from normal." Before moving to a new neighborhood, one parent asked the group whether she should introduce herself by saying that she had a child with Down's syndrome, as though this were her most important characteristic. The group members discussed the mourning reaction of their friends who were unsure of how to approach them and the parents' need to take the initiative to help friends relate comfortably to them and to the baby. Advice was solicited and given on how to discuss the child's handicap with their other children and how to anticipate their questions.

The behavior of the professional staff in maternity hospitals was discussed in detail during the group meetings. All members agreed that any person who broke such news to a family was likely to become the target of angry feelings. A few parents described sensitive and supportive experiences with hospital staff. "They let the baby stay with me longer and let my husband hold him." A majority complained about lack of information, avoidance by hospital personnel, and hindrance of their contact with their child.

> My baby suffered the first social rejection at the hands of his obstetrician.

> The nurse in the hospital told us we should put our baby's name on a waiting list for an institution in case she should turn out to be severely retarded. When I asked her what this meant, she said, "Well, if she becomes dangerous to others."

The group allowed the parents to gain some perspective on what kind of people have children with Down's syndrome. Group members varied in age from seventeen to the mid-forties and were from various socio-economic and educational levels and ethnic backgrounds. For some parents the involved baby was their first child; some had as many as nine other children. Sometimes they speculated on what they all had in common that caused them to create such children. There was much interest in research to identify causal factors and in physical characteristics or attitudinal factors as possible precipitants.

Obtaining Perspective on Child Development

The group allowed the parents to compare the development of their baby with that of his peers.

> I wouldn't want to compare him with a normal child. It only discourages the parent.

I can't live in a void, I need to talk with other mothers. That's why it's good to get together because you can compare with other kids like him.

They held one another's children and discussed how the characteristics of Down's syndrome were manifested differently in each child.

There was much mutual questioning regarding growth and development, feeding and sleep patterns, temperament, and level of responsiveness. They offered one another advice on specific methods of effective management. This information was particularly supportive to those group members who were parents for the first time and who would ordinarily have used friends, relatives, and literature as guides to develop competence in child care. Those who had other children were sympathetic to parents whose first child was the involved child; the new parents suggested that perhaps it was easier for them because they had no point of comparison. All the group members shared their excitement and joy at each accomplishment of the child. A few parents avoided their peers with normal children of the same age because they resented those children's normal development. Sometimes friends avoided them out of guilt because their own child was normal. Those group members whose children had cardiac lesions compared notes on diagnosis and prognosis, and those whose children had had diagnostic procedures prepared the parents whose children were about to undergo them. A vital aspect of the clinic's program was that the parents felt that the clinic was a place where their child was valued as a person; in general, the experience seemed to enhance their self-esteem, sense of adequacy, and normalcy.

A frequent topic was what the future will bring in terms of the child's development and the parents' ability to cope with his special needs.

Will I still love him the way a parent should when his handicap shows more?

It's fine now, for me it's later, people staring. I don't know whether I will be able to cope with a child who won't be toilet trained or walk until late. . . . I also fear the future, but I shut my mind.

I worry who will take care of him after I am gone. Will other children be cruel to him and tease him?

Some parents were more oriented to the future than others, but after a few months most parents concentrated on the present and anticipated only the next phase of the child's development. Anxieties about the future were handled in the group by discussions of the hope that social attitudes would change and resources become more available.

Another major concern of the younger couples was in planning future pregnancies. The attitudes varied from plans for another child very soon to compensate for bearing a defective child to refusal to accept such a risk although adoption might be considered. One couple whose child was critically ill with heart disease conceived another "in case he died." A pregnant woman could not imagine herself bearing a normal child.

The Value of the Group Experience

The literature on crisis theory emphasizes the vulnerability or accessibility of the individual under stress to the influence of significant others in his environment. Lydia Rapoport describes stress as associated with a rise in tension, some personality disorganization, reactivation of old unresolved conflicts, a general feeling of helplessness, and some cognitive confusion. She identifies three aspects of a healthy resolution of a crisis: correct cognitive perception of the situation, management of affect through awareness of feelings and appropriate verbalizations leading toward discharge of tension, and development of patterns of seeking and using help.[3] What forces come into play during the crisis period may be more influential than previously existing personality characteristics of the individual in determining his ultimate adaptation to stress.

Parents of a newborn child with Down's syndrome described themselves as being in a state of shock, lacking in self-esteem, and beset by fantasies and fears. They were actively looking to those around them for emotional support and information in order to reorient themselves. "One of the most frightening things is the process of finding direction." They wanted facts about what such babies are like, what they can do, and whether they will be able to function like other children in such activities as walking, communicating, and caring for themselves.

Reading material which contains these facts, preferably supplemented by pictures of such children in natural settings, is a basic need. A notable example is *David*, a book that describes the experience of a couple who have a child with Down's syndrome, their initial ambivalence, and subsequent resolution of their concerns during the early years of their child's life.[4] Many of the parents in the group saw themselves as potential leaders in making such resources available to others.

Meeting other people undergoing the same stress can provide an invaluable opportunity to test reality. The immediacy and intimacy stimulated by the common experience is of a different quality from that characteristic of contact with a professional person. The closeness of the bond to the group mitigates feelings of isolation and depression. Members could see how the other children appeared and acted. The discovery that other parents had similar feelings and fears reassured them of their own adequacy and sanity. Some parents served as role models to illustrate that it is possible to survive such an event. The group provided them with an opportunity to test themselves in a protected environment preparatory to dealing with the stresses of the larger community. The parent of an older child with Down's syndrome commented, on meeting the group of parents, that she was im-

[3] Lydia Rapoport, The State of Crisis: Some Theoretical Considerations, in *Crisis Intervention: Selected Readings*, ed. Howard J. Parad (New York: Family Service Association of America, 1965), pp. 22–31.

[4] Nancy Roberts, *David* (Richmond, Virginia: John Knox Press, 1968).

pressed with their openness and degree of comfortableness in discussing the problems of their children in contrast to her own experience at that stage.

The development of any child poses certain stresses for his parents, and typically these are more intense for the parents of handicapped children. Each new crisis reactivates unresolved issues of the past. As the child approaches the age of school entrance or of adolescence, patterns of coping may become increasingly maladaptive. The opportunity to work through the grief of bearing a defective child at the time of diagnosis and to receive support in building a positive relationship with the child can provide a more secure foundation for dealing with the future conflicts which will inevitably arise.

The opportunity for social workers to meet with groups of families having a common stress focuses attention on those common needs which are not being met by professional people. Although the staff of maternity hospitals have nearly abandoned advising institutionalization for children with Down's syndrome, they apparently have not substituted adequate supportive services to families. This fact stimulated the staff of the developmental evaluation clinic to enlist the help of these families and others in designing a more constructive approach to discussing the diagnosis of Down's syndrome with a family as a basis for an educational program for professional people. Siblings also are in need of information and supportive services. With the assistance of these parents, such a program has been implemented for them.

Although the experience described in this article concerned families of children with Down's syndrome, some of the conclusions may apply also to families of children with other birth defects which have a disruptive effect on the evolution of the parent-child relationship. Some of the clinic experience paralleled the descriptions of David M. Kaplan and Edward A. Mason as well as Lydia Rapoport in their studies of families of premature infants.[5] Other life-threatening neonatal problems—those requiring prolonged initial hospitalization or those where the infant's appearance or functioning is predictably deviant—undoubtedly interfere with the parents' ability to accept the child as their own and threaten their self-esteem or sense of adequacy. More thought should be given to the therapeutic potential of a group experience for such parents in the setting which supplies treatment to the child.

Such a group experience can be instructive to the professional because it focuses attention on major themes and the needs of a group of people rather than on the unique stress and adaptation of individuals. Two developments which emerged from this group work were an educational program for professionals on the needs of parents who had given birth to a child with Down's syndrome and a program of information and support for the siblings of such children.

[5] David M. Kaplan and Edward A. Mason, Maternal Reactions to Premature Birth Viewed as an Acute Emotional Disorder, *Crisis Intervention*, pp. 118–28; and Lydia Rapoport, Working with Families in Crisis: An Exploration in Preventive Intervention, *Crisis Intervention*, pp. 129–39.

Counseling with Parents of Retarded Children Living at Home

Sylvia Schild

In the light of the emergent philosophy and prevailing practice of encouraging home care of mentally retarded children, a re-examination of the casework counseling technique with parents is indicated. Until recent years, social workers in the field of mental retardation were primarily located in institutions and the focus of casework with families was usually geared around the problems of placement planning. With the advent of special clinics for early diagnosis and evaluation of retarded children, attention shifted to parental feelings and reactions and to ways of counseling parents more satisfactorily. The need for a sympathetic, supportive approach to the parents has been well established with the recognition that the impact of the retarded child is deeply disturbing to the ego-functioning of the parent.[1] The importance of having as complete a knowledge and evaluation of the child's problem as possible has been accepted as a necessary counterpart to being able to provide a meaningful explanation to the parents of the child's difficulty and to give consideration to the parental questions and emotional involvements related to having a retarded child.[2]

Social workers in specialized clinics and social agencies are now dealing not only with the areas of diagnosis and placement, but with the complex task of helping the family and child live together more comfortably in the home. The purpose of providing maximum benefit to the child needs to be interlocked with minimal stress to total parental needs and family functioning. Both the child and the family are faced with making adequate adjustments to and in the community in which they live. Unless these ends are achieved, maintenance of the child in the home serves little purpose.

Professional workers, in supporting a philosophy of home care for retarded children, must be keenly aware of the responsibility to know how to help families achieve this goal with maximum ease. This paper proposes to examine some aspects of counseling with parents of retarded children

Reprinted with permission of the author and the National Association of Social Workers, from *Social Work*, Vol. 9, No. 1 (January, 1964), pp. 86–91.

[1] *See* Helen Beck, "Counseling Parents of Retarded Children," *Children*, Vol. 6, No. 6 (November–December, 1959), pp. 225–230; and Alexander Hersh, "Casework with Parents of Retarded Children," *Social Work*, Vol. 6, No. 2 (April, 1961), pp. 61–66.

[2] A. Wheeler Mandelbaum, M.D., "The Meaning of the Defective Child to Parents," *Social Casework*, Vol. 41, No. 7 (July, 1960), pp. 360–367.

living at home that are characteristic of the problem and that may lead to a better understanding of how to work with these families. These observations are drawn from experience in counseling with families receiving services in the Child Development Clinic at the Children's Hospital of Los Angeles. The clinic is a diagnostic and counseling center primarily for retarded children less than age 6. The observations thus are related to the early adjustment of the preschool child and his family, although they may be generic to the problems of the older retardate as well.

Ambivalence of Parents' Feelings

Enormous ambivalence of feeling is evoked in a parent when he learns that his child is retarded. Feelings of rejection, dejection, and disappointment collide with anxious hopefulness, doubt, anger, and self-pity. Strong emotions of guilt mix with protective parental reactions; resentment, confusion, and insecurity become pervasive. It is this ambivalence that characterizes initial work with families of retarded children. These conflicting emotions are never completely resolved, as the long-term aspect of the problem and the repeated crises that stem directly from the fact of the child's handicap stir up the ambivalence from time to time. To help the parent, it is necessary to ferret out the positive aspects of the ambivalence and help him to build on these so as to find some answers to the problem immediately at hand. Thus, ambivalence is dealt with in relation to the immediate crisis situation on a reality basis and by focusing on the areas that are conducive to meeting the needs of the family. The following case illustrates this point:

> A young couple had just heard the diagnosis of retardation for the first time. In the hostile tirade the mother loosed on the social worker, she vehemently denied that this catastrophe could be true, attacked the doctors, blamed herself. Toward the end of the outburst, she cried out, "Nothing I ever do is perfect. How will I ever be able to raise this child?" In this plea for help the social worker recognized the mother's immediate fear and denial of the diagnosis as resulting from her shaken confidence in being able to successfully handle her mothering role with the defective child. The positive aspect of the ambivalence, underlying the fear of inadequacy, was her intense desire to be a good mother. This was an area that could be worked with realistically in counseling, since she was indeed performing successfully in her mothering role with her two older children. The husband's support to his wife was encouraged. With help and attitudinal change, this mother was enabled to depend again on her own inner strengths and resources in coping with the child; this in turn paved the way toward better understanding of the child's limitations and freed her to work on other aspects of the problem.

A factor accounting for sustained ambivalence toward a retarded child is that the parents are deprived of the opportunity to project any blame for the problem onto the child himself. It is too difficult in any rational way to blame the child for his own defect. This differs from situations in which, when social pathology exists and becomes reflected in disturbed parent-child relationships (for example, in emotional disturbance and delinquency), the parent realistically is able to hold the child partially responsible for a share of the problem. This serves to alleviate some parental guilt and lowers resistance to accepting help. In the area of mental retardation the self-accusatory parent, who feels that he alone is in some way accountable for his child's limitations, is very well known.

It is an accepted fact that part of the resistance of the person seeking help stems from his feeling of responsibility for the problem. When guilt is intensified, the resistance to help will be proportionately increased. Because of this, those endeavoring to help parents of retarded children must be aware that heightened resistance is usually due to the inwardly projected guilt of the parent. In counseling, this guilt needs to be alleviated and an emphatic understanding of the problem area imparted to lower the parent's resistance, freeing him to benefit from the offered help. Most parents hope to hear an authoritative and sympathetic endorsement of themselves, of their human and parental competence, and of their right to blame themselves for what has happened.[3]

One way of ameliorating the guilt of parents is to counsel them together in joint interviews. This helps to focus on the mutuality of feelings and responsibility shared by each parent and aids to shift away from individual parents the assumption of self-blame for the problem. The joint interview technique often may help to restore the marital balance around the mutual concern for the child so that the parents are better able to mobilize all their strengths to handle crisis situations.[4] Although mothers are generally entrusted with the major care of the child, management is a joint responsibility of both parents. Too often the father's role and share of responsibility are overlooked, especially when it is the mother who assumes the task of taking the child for his medical care and transmitting the medical information and advice to her husband. Joint interviewing frequently serves as a device to engage the father actively and to give due consideration to his concerns and attitudes, as well as to those of his wife. Counseling parents together is supportive and enables them to concentrate their energies, not as much on the fruitless searching for why this has happened to them, but more productively on how they can better perform in their parental roles in order to benefit their child.

Changes Required of Parents

The hard reality that needs to be faced is that with the presence of a retarded child the family is no longer the same and it cannot be reconstructed as it was before the arrival and impact of the defective child. Perhaps the area of greatest difficulty that needs to be resolved in the counseling process is the changes required on the part of the parents to meet the special needs

[3] L. Kanner, M.D., "Parents' Feelings about Retarded Children," *American Journal of Mental Deficiency*, Vol. 57 (1953), pp. 375–379.

[4] J. Geist and N. M. Gerber, "Joint Interviewing: A Treatment Technique with Marital Partners," *Social Casework*, Vol. 41, No. 2 (February, 1960), pp. 76–83.

of the retarded child. These often conflict with parental functioning that heretofore was considered satisfactory.

Often the management of the retarded child is perceived by the parents as being no different from their performance with their normal offspring. Counseling needs to be directed toward helping parents to see that their attitudes and feelings relative to mental retardation per se have indeed shifted their own parental behavior.

> One mother complained constantly of her child's temper tantrums. The disturbance the child was creating was upsetting to the entire household and the mother felt at her wit's end. The parents were beginning to feel that to keep the child in the home was almost impossible. The mother stated she was handling the problem behavior exactly as she had in the past coped with similar behavior in an older child.

> Closer examination revealed that in reality the mother, caught up in her disappointment and her attitude that a mentally retarded child was totally worthless, considered the child not worth bothering to discipline. Also, the father was unsupportive, leaving all discipline to his wife. Hence, the mother responded to the tantrums with anger and helplessness, and was permitting herself to be manipulated by the child. The youngster, having no external controls put on his behavior, became increasingly infantile and difficult. This gave validation to the low value placed on him by his mother.

> When the mother gained some insight and understanding that she was reacting differently to this child than to her normal offspring, she began to cope with the problem. Her self-esteem increased with her more effective management of the child. In addition, the father was helped to participate more meaningfully in the child's discipline, thereby giving his wife emotional support. As the child's behavior improved, the parents acquired a new appreciation of him. This in turn helped them to evaluate better the considerable potential latent in their mildly retarded son and to enjoy a more favorable relationship with him in the home situation.

The resistance and ambivalence of the parents in counseling are amplified also by the nature of the new stresses encountered merely by virtue of being the parent of a retarded child. The problem of keeping the retarded child at home is determined by a number of factors, such as sibling relationships, social status, family attitudes, the degree of deficiency in the child, and so on. These are all potential problem areas and the ability with which problems that might arise in these areas are handled and solved vary from family to family, situation to situation.

The new stresses arising from the presence in the family of a retarded child are not pathological as such, but should be viewed as a normal complement of problems for the situation that may affect the parent-child relationship and to which adjustments need to be made. When a pathological situation (i.e., divorce) is imposed on a family and is disruptive to family functioning, the focus in counseling must be directed toward the realistic problems that occur as a result of the pathology.[5] It has been pointed out that the presence of a retarded child in the home is often a precipitating

---

[5] H. Pannor and Sylvia Schild, "Impact of Divorce on Children," *Child Welfare*, Vol. 39, No. 2 (February, 1960), pp. 6–10.

factor in individual or family maladjustment or breakdown.[6] The family that is able to adjust satisfactorily to the impact on it of a retarded child has also to deal adequately with the many normal problems that occur in relation to the situation. Their attitudes, feelings, care and management of the child, and the like must all be taken into account.

These normal problems attending the presence of a retarded child in the home must be dealt with on a reality basis to permit the best possible solutions to be effected. Some of these problems are met often in other handicapping conditions of childhood: the increased dependence of the child on the parent, confusion and lack of finiteness in medical diagnosis, crumbling of parental aspirations for the child, rehabilitation and training problems, and the like. However, there are some conditions that occur uniquely in the case of the mentally retarded child and his parents.

One solution, which is culturally sanctioned, is often freely available to parents of the severely and moderately retarded. This is the opportunity to relinquish responsibility for care of the child to an institution if, considering the degree of his intellectual impairment, the child is eligible. Granted that placement holds the parents to a modicum of responsibility and is indeed an appropriate solution in many situations, there still is a need for recognition that this alternative presents conflict for the parents and may impair efforts to effect a successful adjustment in the home. From the time that parents are told that their child is eligible for institutionalization the ambivalence about the child and the problem increases. Again, this ambivalence needs to be handled in counseling, with the focus geared to the positive aspects inherent in the successful fulfillment of parental roles and responsibilities.

Counseling Should Be Spaced

One difficulty occurring in counseling with parents is that the resistance of the parent is sometimes insidiously supported by the behavior of the child himself. The parents may move well initially in shifting to more positive attitudes and methods of handling the child only to be thwarted by the slow movement of the child in responding to improved parental functioning. Although intellectually the parents can relate the slow pace to the child's mental limitations, they often become frustrated emotionally and can react by feeling that the counseling is unproductive. This can cause reversion to easier, more familiar patterns of behavior. The counselor, too, can become uneasy and impatient by the slow pace of the child's response and may fail to support the parents' efforts adequately or project blame on the parents for failure to utilize the counseling.

The most immediate help, consequently, occurs when the parents are

---

[6] Robert M. Nadal, "A Counseling Program for Parents of Severely Retarded Preschool Children," *Social Casework*, Vol. 42, No. 2 (February, 1961), pp. 78–83.

[7] Charlotte H. Waskowitz, "The Parents of Retarded Children Speak for Themselves," *Pediatrics*, Vol. 54 (1959), p. 319.

having critical emotional distress and help can be directed toward easing their personal difficulty rather than being geared to change in the child himself. Casework for this latter goal, which is focussed around the management and behavior of the child, can perhaps be best provided when spread out over proper and widely spaced intervals to give the child an opportunity to react and develop at his own speed.

A review of the reactions of forty parents to diagnosis and counseling emphasized that the parents needed time to take in the extent of their problem and solutions needed to be worked out step by step. Also, parental questions did not arise in an organized, crystallized fashion but gradually, as the child grew.[7] When the element of time is taken into consideration and work with the family is structured over appropriate intervals, the parents are able to bring into counseling some growth on the part of the child that might not otherwise have been apparent if counseling around the child had been sustained on an intensive basis. In other words, parents need intensive casework help at times of crisis situations but, in addition, they need a continued contact. The latter can be less intensive and made available to them over a longer period of time. Such counseling should be properly spaced and educationally focused, to help the parents with the practical problems of daily living with their retarded child. This help is often crucial in determining if the child can live in his own home and in strengthening and sustaining the mental health of the total family unit.

Counseling related to everyday living experiences with the retarded child helps to sustain the parents' motivation to continue in a program designed to improve the child's behavior and to develop his potential. Parents need to deal with concrete situations—the success they achieve in such common daily experiences tends to ameliorate the problems of living with a retarded child. For this kind of approach the caseworker must have a keen knowledge and awareness of normal growth and development. To help the parents understand their child's behavior, it is important to assist them in relating behavior to normal functioning and expectations of children as well as to comprehend the limitations in their own child and its implications.

Summary

In summary, this paper has discussed some aspects of helping parents who have retarded children living at home. The following points were suggested:

1. Professionals counseling parents to keep their retarded child at home assume an additional responsibility to learn how to help the parents achieve this goal comfortably. This implies not only increased understanding of the problems faced by the parents, but also better awareness and skill in involving and sustaining parents more effectively in the counseling process itself.

2.   The key factor to be dealt with in the counseling process is the ever present ambivalence of the parents about their retarded child. Movement toward satisfactory solution of problems is more easily attainable when the positive aspects of the ambivalence are used constructively to meet feelings and to free parents for changes in attitudes.

3.   Guilt feelings of the parents are enhanced by the fact that they cannot rationally project any responsibility of blame for the problem on the child himself. These guilt feelings heighten the resistance to meaningful participation in counseling. Involvement of both parents in joint counseling is one way of alleviating the inwardly directed guilt and of helping parents to focus on more rewarding functioning in their parental roles with the retarded child.

4.   The presence of a retarded child changes the structure of existing family relationships. One area of great difficulty is that former parental functioning may prove to be inadequate in meeting the needs of a retarded child. Parents need help in seeing that their attitudes and feelings relevant to mental retardation per se affect their parental behavior.

5.   There are many new stresses affecting families of retarded children that should be viewed as normal problems for the situation and that need to be dealt with on a reality level. Some of these, such as the easy access to shifting responsibility of the child through institutionalization and the slow reaction of the retarded child to parental teaching and management, are unique and may hamper counseling efforts.

6.   Parents are best helped at times of crisis, but counseling geared to improvement of the child's behavior and to daily living can be structured over spaced intervals planned to compensate for the slow movement and the maturation of the child and to offer sustained support to the parents.

The importance of more and better knowledge about how to help these families has been best expressed by a parent who has written:

> The greatest single need of parents of mentally retarded children is constructive professional counseling at various stages in the child's life which will enable the parents to find the answers to their own individual problems to a reasonably satisfactory degree. . . . We need guidance from someone who can help us to see that this thing which has happened to us, even though it may be a *life-shaking* experience, does not of necessity have to be a *life-breaking* one.[8]

[8] Mrs. Max A. Murray, "Needs of Parents of Mentally Retarded Children," *American Journal of Mental Deficiency*, Vol. 63, No. 6 (May, 1959), p. 1084.

Part 4

Sociocultural Factors

Interest in the sociocultural aspect of client functioning as a necessary ingredient of the diagnostic process continues to be of import and concern within the social work literature. There has been an abundance of written and verbal enthusiasm about these rich and fertile fields. Important and influential as this emphasis has been on practice attitudes and understanding, the amount of material written by social workers concerning direct practice implications of these data has not been remarkable, at least not if the professional literature is used as an indicator. The need to do more has been frequently stressed; the results have been uneven.

It is clear that progress is being made although the initial enthusiasm and interest following the impact of the Stein and Cloward book *Social Perspectives on Behavior* has waned somewhat. There is still interest in the overall concept of sociocultural factors but the coverage in the literature is uneven. Clearly certain topics are emphasized more than others. This itself is probably a reflection of the socioculutral climate in which we live and practice.

Obviously social work is just beyond the beginning point of translating the importance of these dimensions into generalized therapeutic considerations. It is interesting that all the articles examined for inclusion in this section of the book were written after 1959; they are recent articles reflecting the beginning trend to incorporation.

It is evident that the articles in this section point out more gaps in the literature than in the other areas in this book. Nevertheless, these articles not only reflect a trend toward increased development of this dimension in our practice but clearly point out their rich potential for treatment. An interesting observation is that this is the only section of the book which does not contain any specifically group treatment article. This is surprising.

It would seem that some of the diagnostic dimensions of sociocultural factors would be particularly available to group approaches. If, for example, the Kluckhohn work on value orientations is considered, especially the dimension of "relational value orientation," it could be hypothesized that collaterally oriented persons would be expected to involve themselves more easily and presumably more effectively in group treatment than individually oriented clients. Also one would expect that a client who had a strong value orientation that emphasized the family and the extended family would be particularly well suited for famliy therapy. To date, this has not been discussed in the literature.

Certainly the component of this topic on which we have focused the greatest attention is that of ethnic differences. In the first edition I had wondered whether we needed a great number of articles dealing with various racial or cultural differences, or whether we should move immediately into a search for a more general theory related to ethnic differences.

Whether correctly or not, we have obviously decided upon the type of article focused on specific groups rather than efforts at general theory building. Thus, in the search this time many more articles dealing with additional ethnic groups were found than in the previous search. It is clear from each writer's work that there is more conviction about the nature and impact of differences than on the possibility of general theory. It seems that each author is saying the group about which he is writing is so different from any others that there can be little to learn about other groups. Each new group requires a new assessment of diagnosis and treatment.

Thus we must await further experience with focused emphasis before we can move to some general considerations of ethnicity as a variable in diagnosis and treatment.

As is to be expected from the sociohistorical events of the past decade, there has been considerable emphasis on the black-white situation as a component of treatment. The literature is rich with such articles examining this phenomena from all sides. The earlier Currie article is still an important one for this topic. The one by Getterman-Schaeffer identifies the obstacles and difficulties in working in a mixed racial situation and the new Fibish-Turnquest article examines a further dimension of the interaction between therapists of different races.

In addition to the above topic, it was pleasant to observe that we are beginning to turn more attention to the native Indian client as a component of practice. The Good Tracks article focuses on a specific value orientation, that of noninterference and its potential obstacle to intervention.

The importance and significance of class factors as a diagnostic variable have been given less attention in the literature than ethnic factors. Of the articles addressed to this variable, more attention has been given to lower-class clients than other classes. This is to be expected since this segment of society has long been presumed the special interest of social workers.

All the articles dealing with the lower class emphasize the grossness of this category. Within the term is included a wide range of problems, persons, forms of behavior and differences. There is a tendency in the articles to give most attention to the multiproblem and severely economically deprived families living in submarginal conditions. Implied in this is the erroneous idea that membership in the lower class presumes the need for treatment.

Florence Hollis acknowledges the usefulness of social class as a diagnostic variable and the necessity for modification of treatment emphasis rather than distinct methods in formulating treatment plans. She also stresses the lack of precision of the variable and the danger of letting it become a stereotype. Fantl and Meyer emphasize the necessity to understand the impact of the clients' milieu on their functioning to avoid seeing psycho-pathology rather than reaction to stresses and conflicts in the life situation, and to diagnose and treat individually rather than by generality. Orcutt's article moves the conceptualizing of work with lower-class families forward, as she has schematized the overall strategy with this type of client from a systems theory approach.

Clearly we have focused the bulk of our writings about the class variable on the lower class client. Important as this is, it continues to be essential for the development of practice theory that we examine other segments of the class structure. I sense that we are still not comfortable in declaring our interest in and commitment to clients from other segments of the socioeconomic continuum. I suggest that we have overreacted to some of the criticisms about our failure to meet the needs of the poor and thus not conceptually focused on other non-lower-class clients. This is in contradiction to the fact that we still serve large numbers of them. I suggest that, although not popular, class is still an important variable in both diagnosis and treatment and must be given more attention in the literature.

Obviously, the range of clients receiving social work treatment is widening to include all facets of society. It would be helpful to the whole profession if our colleagues would make more available their experiences with clients from different classes. The private practitioners could make an important contribution here, as they are presumed to treat clients from parts of society not always found in the regular clientele of agencies.

Personal and group values are dimensions that have received particular attention in recent years. To date, work in this area has indicated some interesting leads for practice which must be given further attention. Some correlation between values and interview content has been demonstrated as well as value differences between workers and clients.

Clearly, in our society, there are clients who are in stress as a result of value conflicts, or in value transition and turning to us for help with this stress. We are now more comfortable with the concept that values are an important component of the client-worker situation and that some difficulties in the relationship formerly seen as transference and related resistance phenomena are indeed caused by value differences. There is still much to be done in this area with both more experience and more practice-based research required to help clairfy the therapeutic significance of values.

Status and role are two further areas of the client's sociocultural profile to which further attention in our literature is required. Some work has been done on the impact of the professional status and both the implicit and explicit authority components of it. More is needed. From the viewpoint of role, we know that in contemporary society many clients are involved in some aspect of role change—sometimes recognized and sometimes not. Certainly, at times, such periods of transition can be a growth experience for persons, or can be the source of crisis. To date we undoubtedly have developed some expertise in this area that should be more widely discussed in the clinical periodical literature.

One final concept that has not been significantly evident in the literature is the importance of a client's religious identity as a component of treatment or indeed as a source of stress. This too is a facet of the sociocultural makeup of a person, but one with which we seem to be uncomfortable. We have developed significant components of our service delivery systems along sectarian lines but, interestingly, have not given much attention in our own literature to the way this facet of the client's or worker's psycho-social profile can be an asset to treatment or, indeed, a source of conflict and stress.

Conclusion

It is clear that extensive and interesting gains have been made in the profession regarding the incorporation of social science concepts into practice. It is equally clear that much still remains to be done to translate our interest in and appreciation of these concepts into operational case-directed activities. Obviously, other dimensions of a sociocultural nature have not been fully explored, as mentioned above. The search for similarities, in clients' sociocultural functioning along selected dimensions, that can help us more effectively develop and apply a profile of treatment technique most applicable to the individuality of the client and his situation, can be observed in all the contributions.

Ethnicity

Casework with Japanese and Korean Wives of Americans

Bok-Lim C. Kim

In recent years the social work profession has become sensitive to the injustices of racism and poverty and their dehumanizing effects on society as well as on the immediate victims. Popular responses to these conditions have been pleas for institutional changes, rearrangement of priorities, and development of new resources including legal solutions to deal with human suffering. These efforts are timely but, with the zeal of a missionary, some proponents question and minimize the relevance and effectiveness of social work focused on individuals. Although there are still some professionals describing the needs and values of individualized work, their voices are lost among the cries for larger-scale social change. Despite the claim that individual clients or families are not being forgotten, the tenor and climate of the time is marked by "systems change" through community action programs, social policy, and legislation.

In this climate one becomes uneasy about segments of the population that desperately need individualized services. Among the many such disadvantaged groups, the immigrants of Asian origin are least understood and written about. They are not studied less because they have fewer problems but because there is a common belief that the close-knit family and kinship structures of this group aid their members' welfare.[1] This group's ignorance of available facilities and reticence to seek public help are other factors.

The number of foreign-born wives and children of United States servicemen admitted by this country since the end of World War II under

Reprinted from *Social Casework*, Vol. 53 (May, 1972), pp. 273–279, by permission of the author and the Family Service Association of America.

[1] Pei-Ngor Chen, The Chinese Community in Los Angeles, *Social Casework*, 51: 591–98 (December 1970).

the special immigration acts is staggering.[2] Not all of these people need community-based social services but, based on percentages of the general population which need and use public and voluntary services, the number of families with one Korean or Japanese parent who may need such services is large. However, there is a relative paucity of literature on this subject in the professional journals of behavioral and social sciences. There is even less reference in the social work literature to intermarriage, particularly between Korean or Japanese women and United States servicemen.

Several factors seem to account for this lack of attention. First, the number of Korean and Japanese applicants to social agencies is negligible because of the unfamiliarity with and timidity toward American social services. Moreover, the group is largely concentrated near military installations or in large metropolitan areas where its members become isolated, nearly invisible segments of American society. In addition, if worker-client contacts are established through such groups as the American Red Cross, family service agencies, or the protective services units of public welfare, the barriers of language, culture, and social class hinder meaningful communication. At best, the concrete and immediate needs of clients are met by the social worker who has a nagging and uneasy feeling that all available skills and resources are not being fully utilized.

Literature on Intermarriage

Several studies with inconclusive findings on American-Japanese intermarriage have been published.[3] Depending on the particular group studied and the measuring instruments used, the findings are only fragments of a comprehensive picture of intermarriage. Two of the main deficiencies in these studies seem to be the lack of background information on the couples and an incomplete understanding of the circumstances under which courtship and marriage took place.

Despite common problems of language and assimilation, Asian and European wives are distinctively different; Korean and Japanese wives came from countries which had little cultural interchange with America up to the end of World War II. When a Korean or Japanese wife leaves her

---

[2] Six provisions enacted by the U.S. Congress since 1945 relate to admission of wives, fiancées, and children of citizens of the United States. The first four acts between 1945 and 1952 were enacted to benefit alien wives, fiancées, and children of the U.S. citizens in the Armed Forces. The latter provisions regulate entry of close relatives of the U.S. citizens and permanent resident aliens. There have been 330,975 European and 147,587 Asian wives of U.S. citizens entering this country since 1945. The further breakdown pertinent to this article of Asian wives by nationalities is Japanese, 55,456 and Korean, 13,904. The figures were obtained from the U.S. Justice Department, Immigration and Naturalization Service Annual Reports, 1945–1970.

[3] Gerald J. Schnepp and Agnes Masako Yui, Cultural and Marital Adjustment of Japanese War Brides, *American Journal of Sociology*, 61: 48–50 (July 1955); and Ansem Strause, Strain and Harmony in American–Japanese War-Bride Marriage, *Marriage and Family Living*, 16: 99–106 (May 1954).

family, friends, and way of life to come to America, her husband is the sole guiding and supporting person.

Study Samples

Data from one group (Group A) were obtained from forty-seven Korean women and their American servicemen fiancés from September 1958 to July 1959. They received premarital counseling at the Protestant chaplain's office in Seoul, Korea. The original intention was to provide casework service for Korean wives and their mates in the common adjustment tasks anticipated in the United States. Through the provision of counseling service, the author began to question the couples' capacity to use highly specialized social services in the United States. Doubts were also raised about the American agencies' readiness to provide the types of service that these people needed.

Data from a second group (Group B) were obtained from the International Institute of Los Angeles. Casework service was provided from May 1961 to March 1962 to ten Japanese wives of American servicemen who were stationed in Japan.

Data from a third group (Group C) were derived from eight cases—one Japanese and seven Korean interracial families. This writer gave consultation to social workers, clergymen, and police from 1964 to the present. She provided intensive casework service for two years to one of the eight families. The nature and scope of the problems presented by all three groups of Korean and Japanese families appeared to be highly similar, and it was this factor that prompted this article.

Robert K. Merton defines intermarriage as:

> . . . the marriage of persons deriving from those different in-groups and out-groups other than the family which are culturally conceived as relevant to the choice of a spouse. . . . The standardized rules of intermarriage range from prescription and social approval to proscription, and social disapproval. These polar extremes give rise to two distinguishable types of intermarriage; the first representing conformity to the rules, called exogamy; the second, involving prohibited deviations from the rules, may be called cacogamy.[4]

Intermarriage between Korean or Japanese women and American men (Caucasian, Negro, Mexican, or Indian) is difficult to categorize because this phenomenon is relatively recent, and the attitudes of members of the respective ethnic groups have not been systematically studied. Norms and practices of mate selection are influenced not only by societal customs but by such conditions as size of groups, sex and age compositions, and degree and type of social contact. In the unusual circumstances brought about by the Korean conflict and the defeat of Japan, there was a breakdown in and disregard for traditions and norms in order to accommodate and adapt to

[4] Robert K. Merton, Intermarriage and the Social Structure: Fact and Theory, *Psychiatry*, 4: 362 (August 1941).

the situation. Therefore, incidence of intermarriage between American servicemen and Korean or Japanese women should be considered an outcome of unusual postwar conditions rather than a normal trend.

Background and History of Groups A, B, and C

Data from three groups studied under different geographical, circumstantial, and temporal conditions are discussed in this article. Although the wives were of different nationalities—Korean or Japanese—they experienced a similar cultural orientation concerning mate selection, courtship pattern, role expectation, and moral code for females. These two countries historically shared the religious and cultural heritage of Buddhism and Confucianism.

There are striking similarities in the backgrounds of the women in Groups A and B in relation to childhood experiences and the circumstances under which they met, were courted by, and married their husbands. In addition, they were born and raised during the war years. Although the end of World War II had different meanings for Koreans and Japanese politically, socially, and economically, the most important impact on these women who were in their latency period at the end of the war was the weakening and resultant questioning of authority figures and existing cultural mores. The American way of life as represented by occupational troops and Hollywood movies was indiscriminately imitated by the impressionable young generation as an expression of dissatisfaction with and revolt against the older generation who had caused destruction and suffering and, in the case of Japan, the humiliation of defeat. The conditions during and after the Korean conflict were comparable to the post–World War II conditions in Japan. There was mass destruction, loss of millions of lives, uprooting of the general population, plight of millions of refugees from North Korea, and presence of large numbers of American troops.

Group C women had experienced the Korean conflict during their preschool years; they had hazy memories of these years. Although Group C was less systematically studied than Groups A and B concerning background and circumstances under which courtship and marriage had taken place, some differences were noted. The women in Group C all had at least a ninth grade education; nearly one-half had lived with one or both parents until they began to associate with American servicemen; one-third had worked as waitresses or cashiers at the military establishment. Economically there seemed to be less compelling reasons for this group to associate with servicemen than for Groups A and B to do so.

The women in Groups A and B came from poverty-stricken families who had subsisted on scanty resources for most of their lives. Most women in Groups A and B and about one-half of Group C came from rural families who had experienced seasonally related hunger. In Group A only one-fourth had lived with one or both parents up to the age of ten, and the remainder had had to shift for themselves as burdens on unwilling relatives or as orphans in orphanages. As they matured physically, they turned to prostitution as a source of support. Those women with parents living had to work to supplement the family earnings. The prevalence of early deprivation for the women in Group A is directly attributable to the partition of Korea in 1945 and the Korean conflict of 1950 which produced refugee orphans, widows, and disabled. Compared to Group A, Groups B and C women fared better in relation to familial protection and education.

At the time when they met their husbands, these women were all economically and physically independent of parental authority because of death or enforced separation. This fact is highly significant in these two countries where unmarried girls traditionally can not and will not leave familial supervision and protection until they are married.

The varying degrees of early and chronic economic and emotional deprivation of Groups A and B seemed to have left profound and indelible marks on the developing personalities of these women. The most characteristic and common feature in their attitudes and behaviors is their focus on the immediate present. Its manifestation is conditioned differently by their respective subcultures. The dynamics operative in Group C's difficulties are less easy to determine because of the lack of accurate background information; however, explanation can be suggested in relation to disruption in role complementarity to be described later.

Prostitution in Korea

In Korea there are hierarchies among the women who cater to American servicemen. The first, and lowest, are uneducated and inexperienced women who are tightly controlled by illegal operators of the houses of prostitution. The second group includes more aggressive women who solicit customers on the street or in stores and clubs on a daily basis. The third group consists of fairly intelligent and experienced women who have built up "connections" during their careers so that they are able to maintain relatively stable relationships with one soldier at a time.

The third group usually unites against exploitation by slick native operators, interpreters, black-market middlemen, and proprietors of bars, dance halls, and houses of prostitution as well as against the soldiers who may treat its members unjustly or abusively. This group has leaders who are experienced, resourceful, intelligent, and maternal toward group members.

Women in this study who came for premarital counseling usually came from the third type of prostitute. This is the same group from which children of mixed parentage were offered for intercountry adoption. Within these relatively stable relationships, promises of marriage were often given by soldiers, seemingly out of their own needs for dependent and sustaining relationhsips. Most of the women during their careers of one to ten years were given several promises of marriage without fulfillment.

Seldom were contraceptive means employed. The idea that a soldier would marry more readily if there was a child born to the union was still held, although the results did not substantiate this feeling. When there was no prospect of marriage, however, abortion was generally employed.

This third group enjoyed relative financial security and prestige among other less fortunate members of their trade. The group cohesion was particularly strong in times of crisis, such as illness, disappointments from broken promises of marriages, and desertion. The members would provide financial help and emotional support.

Even higher in status among prostitutes was a small colony of women who had finally attained legal marital status with American servicemen. Legality and permanence of relationship, in addition to the many privileges of this status, placed them in a far superior and coveted position.

Composition of Group A Men

The men in Group A were equally divided between professional soldiers and draftees. The age range was twenty-five to thirty-four, and this marriage was the first for most subjects. The educational level was higher than that of their fiancées; the majority of men had completed at least the seventh grade. However, their own lack of family stability resulting from death, desertion, separation, divorce, and marital conflicts was a prominent feature of this group. Fewer than one-half of these men had lived with their mothers up to the age of ten, and even fewer had lived with their fathers that long. The rest had lived with relatives, in foster homes, or in residential centers.

The unanimous reason given for marriage to their present partners was that "she is the first person who makes me feel important." With one exception, all of the men openly and unhesitatingly described various degrees of dissatisfaction and unhappiness with their childhood experiences and a wish to forget and sever ties with their memories and people from the past. Most of the men had no definite plans for their future occupations and places to settle. This uncertainty seemed to be related to their wish to dwell on the immediately gratifying present, and they were very much like their fiancées.

Relationships Before and After Marriage

Within Groups A and B the length of cohabitation before legal marriage was from six months to three years. Very few women met their husbands through legitimate work; most women met them while working as prostitutes. Although physical attractiveness played a part in the initial phase of the relationships, this and other attributes of the women—such as, personality, education, and social background—seemed to have relatively little bearing on the men's decision for marriage. Instead, it appeared that the decision depended primarily on the men's emotional needs and previous life experiences which conditioned them to be favorably disposed to marrying

Oriental women. They perceived these women as a limited threat to their masculinity compared to American women.

Many of these men discovered that in their relationships to Oriental women their feelings, comfort, and welfare were given precedence. Thus, for the first time they felt accepted by solicitous, unquestioning women who respected them. In turn, the women considered themselves rescued from their insecure socioeconomic position. Their energy and activities revolved around serving and gratifying the needs and wishes of their men.

Handicapped by a language barrier, by an ignorance of American culture, and by limited social experiences, these women failed to view the men in realistic terms; they considered them masculine and potential security giving mates. For these women and others like them, the United States evoked romantic impressions of physical and economic security because it was believed that no one was hungry or cold. Marriage to American soldiers symbolized eternal security and happiness, an insurance against suffering and want.

Under this peculiar combination of misery and hope, needs and their gratification, and threat of war and efforts to preserve peace, couples with diverse cultural and social backgrounds were thrown together. For many men the position and conditions in which they found themselves were totally strange. Thousands of miles from home, housed in army Quonset huts, and surrounded by barren hills and shabbily dressed natives, these men felt that life had an unreal quality. For the women who spoke, ate, and thought as Koreans, the experience of living with Americans who behaved differently made life appear equally unreal. This atmosphere created optimal conditions for misrepresenting one's self and misunderstanding of one's partner. Both men and women were free to distort and exaggerate their past experiences and status, and in doing so they convinced themselves that these wish-fulfilling fantasies were true. It was also easy to deny negative aspects of the present reality or the future because the couples' special circumstances supported these fantasies. A man who had sustaining affectional ties in the United States seldom made this type of relationship more than a convenient arrangement. Those men who lacked and hungered for affectional ties became involved and legitimatized their relationships by marriage.

When the commercial relationship culminated in legally sanctioned marriage, a couple should have made a distinct and conscious change in their respective roles, from a customer and a prostitute to a husband and wife. However, this change very seldom took place while the couple stayed in Korea or Japan. The marriage continued with an autocratic husband who demanded and received obedience and compliance from his wife. His infantile dependency needs and his gratitude were interpreted as expressions of his affection in "American style." The wife's only major concern was the fear of desertion by her husband after reaching the United States; this fear was related to her feelings of inferiority *vis-à-vis* American women.

Although the husband's pay was inadequate by American standards, many army privileges and local market conditions made it possible to live luxuriously while overseas. The interracial couples were considered the social aristocracy of their small subculture, and they experienced feelings of adequacy, acceptance, and superiority.

The reactions of the women's relatives and friends to the marriages were generally favorable because such a marriage was considered the only way to escape the status of a prostitute. Any misgivings the relatives had were related to their permanent separation from the women and their own loss of financial support when the women emigrated to the United States. The reactions of the men's relatives ranged from opposition to indifference.

Adjustment in the United States

A brief description of Group B derived from casework service is significant. Nine wives of the ten were between twenty and thirty-three years old; eight had at least a ninth grade education. Eight couples had three or more children, all under age seven. The husbands included five Caucasians, three Negroes, and two Mexican Americans. Only three wives were living with their husbands; five were either separated or divorced through desertion; and two wives had husbands who were on overseas duty. One-half of the women were in the United States less than three years; the longest stay was six years. Seven women were referred from other social agencies, and three were referred by clients of the agency.

When they came to the agency, all of the women had a combination of family problems, including inadequate income, substandard housing, need for medical care, work adjustment, and problems associated with living without husbands. Singularly absent from these women's environments were supportive relatives or friends.

A couple who had courted and married in the unique circumstances previously described had very limited opportunity to practice the normal roles of husband and wife. A husband who had lived and worked on army installations and had spent his off-duty hours among other interracially married couples using pidgin English and smatterings of Korean or Japanese failed to recognize that his wife had none of the advantages that he had enjoyed and that she needed his help and support in learning to communicate and behave in new ways. It was his responsibility to perceive, interpret, guide, and teach his wife the community values, modes of interpersonal relationships, and proper responses. However, this process was the very task in which husbands in Groups B and C has failed; consequently, they jeopardized the marriage and exposed their wives to the traumatic experience of emotional and physical desertion. Wives in such a situation seemed to fare better when the husbands remained with them and were stationed on a military base where there were other interracially married couples.

Difficulty in communication had once afforded an excuse for avoiding the inadequacies of both wives and husbands. Eventually this inability to communicate became a glaring deficiency and a handicap in mutual understanding and adjustment. Out of his own need for support, the husband expected his wife's speedy acculturation and adjustment. His own insecurity, frustration, and anxiety were projected onto the wife, and bitter complaints about her total dependency accompanied the frequent and violent fights. The previously docile wife tended to counter his accusations with rage and threats of self-destruction.

A wife who was separated from her culture and friends experienced an acute sense of isolation and loss which was further enhanced by the different linguistic, physical, and behavioral responses of her new environment. New ways of living which called for a changed pattern of response threatened and confused her and generated anxiety. Seemingly simple tasks, such as shopping, use of public transportation, telephoning, banking, and visiting with neighbors, became major undertakings. Even a kind neighbor's gesture of friendship became a source of anxiety because the Oriental wife did not know what was offered or expected of her in return. All of these factors confined her and her activities to the radius of her immediate dwelling and accentuated her loneliness and preoccupation with her problems.

A husband who once had valued his wife's submission often became angry when he felt overburdened by her essentially dependent attutides of passivity and her uncritical acceptance by his opinions and commands. The wife's fear of desertion was heightened by his irritability and insensitivity to her needs. Her own fear prevented her from seeing the panic and insecurity that he experienced in his adjustment to civilian life. It was difficult for her to perceive her husband as a frightened person needing her understanding and support rather than as a person who had once appeared omnipotent.

Casework Implication

The needs and problems presented by the wives of these couples require casework intervention strategies developed in recent years for working with families with a range of problems. The problems and tasks associated with the establishment of casework relationships, skillful utilization of various community resources to meet clients' urgent economic, medical, social, and housing needs, and involvement in the educational process of helping the clients to use such resources were common to the three groups.

However, here the similarity seems to end. In relation to capacity the wives in all three groups had surmounted earlier deprivation and succeeded in elevating their status. Strength, ingenuity, and resourcefulness were seen in most women of Groups B and C after their urgent environmental problems and needs were met. Although the wives appeared to be disorganized and apathetic initially, they demonstrated strong determination to work out their problems so that they could raise their children in this country; they felt the children would experience less discrimination here for their racial mixture and would encounter better opportunities for education and employment.

There are several culture-bound characteristics which need special handling by social work practitioners. The submissive attitudes should not be confused with dependency. The reluctance of Oriental women to express their needs, feelings, opinions, and thoughts should not be equated with an absence of such emotions. The most effective casework service in combination with environmental help is provided by role interpretation, modeling, and rehearsal. In this process the client is provided with an opportunity to perceive, interpret, and respond appropriately to her new world. Introduction of an interpreter, perhaps a student or businessman from the client's country, to facilitate worker-client communication should be planned only after evaluating the interpreter's attitude toward these women and explaining the purpose and nature of his role in the context of service.

The casework goal depends on the nature of the client's problems and needs, her capacities and motivation, and the resources of the agency. The writer's experience has indicated six months to two years of intensive casework service of a supportive and educative nature to produce a minimally self-sufficient client.

The meaning and value to these women of service focused on the individual are twofold. First, a client is prevented from resorting to such drastic actions as suicide, mental or physical breakdown, or a return to her country where equally difficult obstacles await her and her children. The ramifications of such actions on the welfare of children are deleterious. Second, with their capacities and resources restored, these women can become warm and nurturing mothers as well as helpful neighbors and friends who can reach out to other women in similar stressful situations.

A study of interracially married couples of Korean and Japanese women with United States servicemen should be undertaken to further illuminate the elements and conditions necessary for successful adjustments of such couples. Social workers could then focus their efforts on providing preventive services through casework, meeting the deficiencies, and creating optimal conditions for successful adjustment in the environment of these couples.

Native American Noninterference

Jimm G. Good Tracks

The standard techniques and theories of social work that bring positive results with many groups, including lower-class Anglo-Americans (Anglos), Negroes, and assimilated Mexicans, are not successful when applied to native Americans.[1] In fact, all the methods usually associated with the

Reprinted with permission of the author and the National Association of Social Workers, from *Social Work*, Vol. 18 No. 6 (November, 1973), pp. 30–34.

[1] The author's experience indicates that the statements made in this article apply to the Navajo and the tribes of the Northern and Southern Plains. Much that is said here might also be true of the Pueblo and other tribes.

term "social work intervention" diminish in effectiveness *just to the extent that the subject has retained his native Indian culture*. The reason is that any kind of intervention is contrary to the Indian's strict adherence to the principle of self-determination. The less assimilated and acculturated the individual, the more important this principle is to him. Some time ago Wax and Thomas described this principle as noninterference.[2]

Many human relations unavoidably involve some influencing, meddling, and even coercion or force. Indians feel, however, that Anglos carry these elements to an extreme while professing an entirely different set of values. Anglos say they price freedom, minding one's own business, and the right of each person to decide for himself, yet they also think it right to be their brother's keeper, to give advice and take action in their brother's best interest—as interpreted by the Anglo, in and by the Anglo social context.

In native Indian society, however, no interference or meddling of any kind is allowed or tolerated, even when it is to keep the other person from doing something foolish or dangerous. When an Anglo is moved to be his brother's keeper and that brother is an Indian, therefore, almost everything he says or does seems rude, ill-mannered, or hostile. Perhaps it is the Anglo's arrogant righteousness that prevents him from grasping the nature of his conduct. But if the Indian told the Anglo that he was being intrusive, the Indian would himself be interfering with the Anglo's freedom to act as he sees fit.

Coercion and Suggestion

Coercion appears to be a fundamental element in the peoples of Western Europe and their colonial descendants. All the governments and institutions of these societies use a variety of coercive methods to insure cooperative action. Traditional Indian societies, on the other hand, were organized on the principle of voluntary cooperation. They refrained from using force to coerce.

In recent times Euro-American societies have tended to rely less heavily on physical violence, but they have only replaced it with verbal forms of coercion and management. Anglo children appear to be taught by their elders, peer groups, and mass media to influence, use, and manipulate others to achieve their personal goals. They begin to try to manipulate others early in life while at play and in their relationships with adults. They continue to improve their manipulative skill throughout their lives as they study psychology and apply it to marriage counseling and psychotherapy. Their newspapers print "Dear Abby" letters from people who want someone else to tell them what to do or how to make others do as they wish. This ability is rightly called a tool essential for living and achieving success in Anglo society. Anglo economic development and exploitation could not

---

[2] Rosalie H. Wax and Robert K. Thomas, "Anglo Intervention vs. Native Noninterference," *Phylon*, 22 (Winter 1961), pp. 53–56.

otherwise exist. But even when verbal manipulation has superseded physical force, it still remains a form of coercion and constitutes interference. This does not disturb Anglos who feel there is a distinction.

Even a nondirective teacher utilizes some coercion when he wants his pupils to acquire a certain skill, express themselves with certain prepared materials, or participate in a group activity. It appears that the compulsion to interfere is so habitual among Anglos that even when they have no particular business to accomplish in a conversation, they will still tend to be coercive. For instance, one person may remark that he wishes to buy a new car. Someone will immediately tell him where he should buy one and perhaps what kind. In the most friendly manner Anglos are always telling each other and everyone else what they should do, buy, see, sell, read, study, or accomplish—all without any consideration of what the individual may want to do.

But whether it is a subtle suggestion or an outright command, it is considered improper behavior and an interference by Indian people. The Indian child is taught that complete noninterference in interaction with all people is the norm, and that he should react with amazement, irritation, mistrust, and anxiety to even the slightest indication of manipulation or coercion.

Respect and Consideration

The following incident illustrates noninterference in the simplest of matters. I was visiting my cousins when one of them put on his coat and said he was going down town. He had no car, so one could assume he was going to walk. I restated his intention and volunteered to drive him. The cousin showed noninterference with my activities by not asking or even suggesting that I drive him, although that is certainly what he wanted. If he had asked directly and I had not cared to drive him, I would have been put on the spot. I would have been forced to refuse unobligingly or agree unwillingly. But by simply putting on his coat and announcing his intentions, he allowed me to accept or reject his desires without causing bad feelings for anyone. I could volunteer to take him or pay no attention to his actions.

A cross-cultural misunderstanding might occur in the following way. A non-Indian guest at my mother's home, having enjoyed a rice dinner, might pay my mother this compliment: "Your rice was so good! I should be happy to have your recipe, if I may. And do you want some of my rice recipes in exchange?" The offer of recipes might strengthen friendship among Anglos, but to an Indian it cancels the compliment. If my mother had wanted other recipes she would have suggested it to her guest. When the guest makes the offer on her own initiative, it implies she did not really care for my mother's rice and knows a better way to prepare it. If the guest had talked only about various ways of preparing rice, she would have given my mother the opportunity to ask about any that interested her.

An Indian will usually withdraw his attention from a person who interferes. If the ill-mannered person does not take the hint, the Indian will leave. In the event he is unable to leave, he will attempt to fade into the background and become unnoticed. In this way, he will avoid provoking the ill-mannered person to further outbursts and at the same time save the person embarrassment by not witnessing his improper behavior. This reaction also reprimands the one who interferes in a socially sanctioned manner. At such times, an Indian can only wonder at the person and wish he could leave. On occasion, however, when pushed beyond endurance, he may lose his self-control and drive the aggressor away with verbal or physical force.

Much delicacy and sensitivity are required for Indian good manners. If one is planning a gathering, for example, a feast to give a child his Indian name, one does not urge people to come. This would be interfering with their right to free choice. If people wish to come, they will come. Under most ordinary circumstances, an Indian does not even speak to another unless there is some indication that the other desires to turn his attention to him. If one wishes to speak with another, whether it is a friend, relative, or spouse, he will place himself in the person's line of vision. If the person's behavior does not indicate an acknowledgment of one's presence, one waits or goes away until later. Should one be talking with a friend and without forethought bring up a subject that may be sensitive or distressing to the listener, the latter will look away and pretend not to hear or suddenly change the subject.

The rules of etiquette are generally followed even by many assimilated Indians. They express a deep respect for the interests, responsibilities, and pursuits of other people. The same respect can be seen even in the behavior of young children. They play in the midst of adults who are having a conversation and yet never interrupt. A child may come and lean for a while against his parent or relative, but without a word or act of interference. Only in an emergency does a child try to attract an adult's attention, and then in a way that will not interrupt the adult's activity. A child who gets hurt playing, for example, might come in crying and then go lie down on a bed. The adult hears the crying and decides if he wishes to attend to the child. A bold child who wants something quietly comes up to his parent, stands there a while, and then whispers the request. It seems that even the youngest Indian children do not bother older people when they are preoccupied.

This behavior is taken for granted by Indian people as the proper way to behave. Learning it probably takes place on an unconscious level. Indian infants and those beginning to walk do not make loud attempts to attract their parents' attention as Anglo babies do. This suggests that demanding attention is actually taught the Anglo infant. Indian adults do not respond to interfering demands, so the child does not learn coercive methods of behavior. This does not imply that Indian children are never aggressive, but only that the culture does not reward aggression when it interferes with the activity of others. Indian children are taught to be considerate through the example of their elders, and the adult treats the child with the same respect and consideration that he expects for himself. It is generally against the child-rearing practices of Indian people to bother or interrupt their children when they are playing or to make them do something against their will, even when it is in their own best interest. Some Anglo educators show their ignorance of this principle by condemning Indian parents for not forcing their children to attend school.

Implications for Practice

This principle explains much of the general failure of social workers to treat the social and psychological problems of Indian clients. There are other factors, of course, such as the Indian's perception of the worker as an authority figure representing a coercive institution and an alien, dominating, and undesirable culture. The physical appearance of the worker is another factor, and so is his ignorance of the manners of Indian people. The relationships that both client and worker have with the agency make for further complications, but an understanding of the principle of non-interference can still have an important effect on the worker's role. It can teach him what to expect in his social work relationships with Indian clients and thus enable him to be more effective in helping Indian people.

From an Indian client's viewpoint, the worker is expected to perform only the superficial and routine administrative functions of his office. Clients may request him to increase their aid grants, to draw upon some of their own funds from the agency Individual Indian Monies (IIM) accounts, to assist with a government form, or to submit a boarding-school application. These tasks involve no real social involvement, as involvement is understood both by Indians and non-Indians. The Indian client does not allow or desire the worker to have any insight into his inner thoughts. That would not be a proper part of work.

This expectation does not, of course, correspond to the professional social worker's own concept of his function. A worker could become quite frustrated just shuffling papers about and doing little actual social work when there might be plenty of social problems evident among his clientele. Nevertheless, the worker must not intervene unless the people request an intervention, and he is likely to wait a long time for such a request. The credentials of his profession, his position, status, knowledge, skills, achievements, and authority, though respected by the agency, are in most cases completely without merit among the Indians. Such things belong to Anglo culture and are not readily translatable into Indian culture. His standing in the Anglo community does not give him a license to practice intervention among Indian people.

The explanation for the social worker's initial uselessness is easily given. His professional function is generally performed from within the Indian culture, and no foreign interference is desired or contemplated. If a man's problems seem to be a result of his having been witched, for example, he will seek out the properly qualified person to help him alleviate the condition. He will have no need of any outside diagnoses or assistance. Should a personal or family problem be of another nature, it is addressed again to the proper individual, an uncle (mother's brother) or a grandfather—not to a foreigner such as the social worker. In every case, the people utilize the established, functional, culturally acceptable remedy within their own native system.

Worker's Approach

Can a worker ever convey his potential for helpfulness to Indian clients without breaking their norms? How can he do this while they adhere to the principle of noninterference?

Patience is the number-one virtue governing Indian relationships. A worker who has little or no patience should not seek placements in Indian settings. Native temporal concepts are strange to the non-Indian. Some non-Indians even believe these concepts are unstructured and dysfunctional, and perhaps they are—in the Anglo conceptual framework. But the social worker's success may well be linked with his ability to learn "Indian time" and adjust his relationships accordingly.

Native temporal concepts have no relation to the movements of a clock. They deal in terms of natural phenomena—morning, days, nights, months (from the native concept of "moon"), and years (from the native concepts of "seasons" or "winters"). Ignorance of these concepts makes it impossible to understand the long time it takes any alien to become established in the Indian community. For although they are seemingly without interest, perhaps even indifferent to the new worker, the people will at length carefully observe the manner in which he presents and carries himself. It would be well for the worker to know how slow this evaluation process is likely to seem, for he must not become impatient. The evaluation will progress in accordance with native temporal concepts. Perhaps in a year or so a majority of the people will have come to some conclusions about the worker's character. Basic acceptance comes only after there has been enough observation to determine with reasonable assurance that the worker will not inflict injury with his activities.

There is little or nothing the worker may do to expedite the process; to push things along would be interfering with the process and the people. In the meantime, as he performs his superficial functions for the people, he may discreetly interject bits and pieces of his potential for further assistance. But discretion is needed to the utmost in order to avoid the slightest coercive suggestion. If the worker inflicts a coercive tone in conversation and thus thwarts an individual's self-determination, it could be a major setback and perhaps mean complete failure with that individual.

Only time can bring the fruition of the worker's occasional hints. One day a person may decide to test the words of the worker with a real problem. It would not be a preconceived act, discussed beforehand in the community, but merely an impulse on the part of one individual to find out the truth of the worker's boasting. Nevertheless, there will be many among the people who are likely to be aware of it.

A great deal may depend upon this trial case, perhaps the entire future relationship between the worker and his clientele. The worker should recognize the importance of this opportunity and be keenly aware of its possible ramifications. A positive solution to the test problem can be the best way to advertise the worker's potential usefulness. A success will travel quickly by word of mouth throughout the close-knit Indian community, and as the good word spreads the worker's worth to the community becomes recognized. Other clients will come forth.

It will never be necessary to perform "social work intervention" and interfere with an individual or the community norms. The people will incorporate the worker into their functional system. He will perform social work in agreement with the native system rather than try to intervene on the basis of a foreign system. Otherwise he would alienate the people.

An alien, it should be noted, is anyone who is not a member of the tribal group. Among Navajos, a Cheyenne would be as alien as an Anglo, though his acceptance may be more readily attainable.

Working within the System

Needless to say, this discussion has excluded numerous complications that are always present in reality, but an effective approach to the non-interference norm is basic to any social work with Indians. If the worker is ever mindful of this norm and how it conditions his role and acceptance, he should be able to deal with the other problems.

A continued adherence to engagement from within the preexisting native framework will assure the confidence and trust of Indian clients. In time they may use the worker to assist with personal problems pertaining to matters outside the native system and even with problems inside the native system that for one reason or another cannot be resolved by the regular native approaches. In the latter case, however, the problem would actually be resolved by a regular approach, inasmuch as the worker would have *become* a native approach by functioning within the native framework.

But even then it should be kept well in mind that the worker is still an alien. His degree of acceptance is based entirely on how well he is able to work within the preexisting native systems and norms. Perfect acceptance comes only with the loss of the worker's alien status, which cannot be achieved except through adoption by Indian people. To become one of the people is, of course, most unlikely, but not impossible.

Cultural Factors in Casework Treatment of a Navajo Mental Patient

Inez M. Tyler and Sophie D. Thompson

Planning aftercare service for a non-English-speaking Navajo Indian who has been a long-term mental patient presents the social worker with two specific kinds of problems. Not only must he deal with the usual problems associated with the discharge of a mentally ill patient, but, in addition, he must deal with problems that are unique to the Indian culture. The case discussed in this article illustrates the importance of the worker's under-standing the Navajo language and culture.

The Navajo woman who returned home had been a mental patient for twenty years in a hospital located at a great distance from her family and homeland. The worker showed unusual skill in utilizing her knowledge of the patient's cultural background to help the patient and her family achieve a realistic view of her return home. In this case it is of special interest to note the process by which certain specific cultural beliefs were incorporated in the patient's symptomatology. Before a discussion of the case is presented, however, information is given about the Navajos and their mode of living in order to provide some understanding of their orientation to problems involving health and medical care, and how this sociocultural orientation may affect casework treatment.

Cultural Background

With an estimated population of 90,000 the Navajo is the largest Indian tribe in the United States, living on 14,450,369 acres of land in the states of Arizona, New Mexico, and Utah. Their complex social and economic problems are compounded by cultural and language barriers that separate them from the dominant society. Their poor roads, their inadequate trans-portation facilities, and their low educational attainment further serve to increase their isolation. During the past ten years, however, there has been

Reprinted from *Social Casework*, Vol. 46 (April, 1965), pp. 215–220, by permission of the authors and the Family Service Association of America.

great progress in making available to the Navajos an opportunity to be educated in local day and boarding schools and in the public schools of "bordertowns" that lie outside the reservation.

Traditionally, the Navajos are a semi-nomadic people whose principal livelihood is gained from herding sheep. They are accustomed to move with the sheep to new grazing land. They live in octagonal hogans, built of logs and mud; the floors are dirt, and a smoke hole is cut in the roof. The one-room hogan may shelter an entire family composed of from two to twelve or more persons. The Navajos do not live in villages, and the family groups are often separated from one another by long distances. In many instances the members of a traditional matrilineal extended family, including grand-parents, parents, and daughters and their husbands are still found living near one another. In general, however, no more than four or five hogans are located in one place. The hogans lack indoor sanitary facilities and electricity. Neither water nor wood is readily available, and each family must haul its water from a distance, perhaps so much as twenty miles. The storage of hauled water has become less a threat to the Navajo's health since the people learned in a sanitation program supported by the Public Health Service to build platforms for the steel water containers.

The traditional Navajo religion is oriented primarily to maintaining health and curing illness. One of the simplest and clearest statements of Navajo religious thought and its relationship to health was made by Mary and John Collier, Jr.:

> The basis of Navajo religious thought is that the universe and all the earth peoples function according to rules. The misfortunes of sickness and premature death are the result of not following the rules. Navajos hold ceremonials to restore order in the individual by performing exact rituals which will require supernatural forces to withdraw their punishment, or the sickness, from the individual. To be well you must obey the ancient rules, and the chants and ceremonies are routines to re-establish the broken routine.[1]

Medical and Psychiatric Facilities

In 1955 the responsibility for the medical care of Indians living on reservations was transferred from the Bureau of Indian Affairs to the Division of Indian Health, a part of the U.S. Public Health Service responsible for all health services to Indians and Alaskan natives. Six hospitals, three field health centers, and a number of health stations provide preventive and curative health care to Navajos living on the reservation.

The staff of the Division of Indian Health is especially concerned about the high rate of illness among mothers and children and the high rate of infant mortality; they are also concerned about the high incidence of accidents and the identification and care of people suffering from emotional

---

[1] Mary and John Collier, Jr., "The Basis of Navajo Religion," in *Societies Around the World*, Vol. I, I. Sanders and others (eds.), Dryden Press, New York, 1953, p. 300.

problems and mental illness. Providing comprehensive health services to patients on the reservation is complicated by problems of communication, shortage of staff, and other factors already mentioned.

The Public Health Service contracts with state and private mental hospitals to provide psychiatric care for the Navajos, since psychiatric services are not available on the reservation. In past years mentally ill Navajos were committed to federal hospitals located hundreds of miles from their homes, where, because of the language barrier, they received only limited care. Some Navajos have remained in such institutions for as long as twenty years, or even longer. Recently emphasis has been placed on using psychiatric facilities that are near the reservation. Efforts have been made, when medically feasible, to arrange for patients previously sent to distant hospitals to return to their reservation. Mrs. Y was one such patient, whom the caseworker helped to return home after a long absence. In this instance, the caseworker was the only trained Navajo caseworker on the reservation.

Case Illustration

In the late 1930's Mrs. Y was living with her children in her mother's extended family kinship group. Following the death of one of her relatives in this camp, she was accused—apparently by an aunt and a sister with whom she had quarreled—of killing the relative. The court records do not contain a clear statement of the circumstances surrounding the death of the relative. Mrs. Y was hurriedly convicted, and her mother was unable to see her before she was taken from the reservation.

Mrs. Y could not converse in the prison because no one there understood the Navajo language. She became depressed and resistive and developed symptoms of emotional disturbance, such as vomiting and refusal to eat. As a result she was transferred, within a few months after her imprisonment, to a mental hospital in the East. At this hospital the patient spoke to no one for many years and lay huddled, in a fetal position, in a blanket on the floor. She continued to be resistive and apprehensive, spoke to no one, and refused to be examined. Attempts to speak to her through an interpreter were unsuccessful, but it was not clear whether the problem stemmed from the inadequacy of the interpreter or the inability of the patient to communicate with him.

Gradually Mrs. Y began to show improvement and became less resistive. She spoke her native language, began to smile, ate well, slept well, and was quiet and pleasant. She showed some interset in others about her, and as she continued to improve, she began to take care of herself and to eat her meals with a group of other patients. By then twenty years had passed since she had been imprisoned, and she was over fifty years of age.

After the hospital staff inquired at the Division of Indian Health regarding plans for discharging Mrs. Y, the caseworker on the reservation contacted her daughter, who was then an adult with a family of her own. She also contacted Mrs. Y's mother and sister in order to include them in the planning for her return to the reservation. The family members were pleased to receive news about the patient, and they were also pleased at the possibility that Mrs. Y might return home after such a long separation. During a visit to the social worker's office they tape recorded a message to Mrs. Y, and the tapes, along with photographs taken that day, were sent to her.

The Caseworker Visits the Patient

It was hoped that Mrs. Y could be either discharged or transferred to an institution closer to her home. The reservation caseworker visited her at the hospital on a number of occasions in an attempt to arrive at an accurate evaluation of her condition. On the first occasion the patient eyed the worker apprehensively. The worker said hello in Navajo and told Mrs. Y she had come from the Navajo country to see her. The patient continued to look at the worker and remained silent. The worker asked the patient if she were a Navajo. She replied yes, and then tested the worker's Navajo origin by asking her to name the clan to which she belonged. Because the worker was able to speak in Navajo and understand the patient's feelings and cultural background, Mrs. Y could express her feelings to her freely.

The worker learned that Mrs. Y strongly resented her removal from her home, and she held her family and relatives responsible. With each succeeding visit to the patient, her feelings about having been "hauled away" seemed to increase. "They destroyed me, trampled me in the dirt, stripped away my clothing, took me apart joint by joint." At this moment she pointed to her knees, shoulders, and elbows. "They brought me to shame, they made me nothing. I crawled begging to go back, I had no pride [self-respect]. I am nothing, only a stranger here, I have no will, no thinking, no right to say yes or no, to decide. . . ."

To questions regarding her wish to return home, she replied, "I'm not in authority; that's not for me to decide." Who was the authority? "I don't know." The doctor asked her if she would return home if *he* said she could do so. Again she said it was not for her to decide. She had no right; she was only there. Then she said, "It costs money. How will I pay?" Assurance that her transportation would be paid did not help her to make her decision.

The doctor asked her if she knew she was in a hospital. She replied, "*Hwo'la* (I don't know)." Was she aware of the nature of her illness? "*Hwo'la.*" The caseworker asked whether she knew that she had been sick in her "thinking process." Again she replied "*Hwo'la.*" The doctor then asked her if she had ever killed anyone. She promptly shook her head and replied "No, no." Would she kill anyone? Again her answer was, "No, no." Whenever her family was mentioned, she began a monologue. She spoke about them in a rapid, breathless way, and her set speech sounded like something she might have memorized, something she was repeating automatically. When the worker asked her which members of the family were responsible for her imprisonment, she replied, "All of them." The only members of her family whom she exempted were her children, whom she thought of as small and helpless. She showed her feelings for them when she said she had "nearly died for them." The worker and the doctor thought that if the patient could change or moderate her attitude, she could be discharged and return home. To help her mother's family understand her illness and attitude, they decided that the worker should visit them.

The Caseworker Visits the Family

On the reservation the caseworker discussed the plan to discharge Mrs. Y with the patient's mother, her daughter and son-in-law, and her two sisters and their husbands. They showed interest in the plan and were anxious to have the patient returned to them. The women in the family were an impressive group, attractive, healthy, and friendly; each of them had an excellent sense of humor. Mrs. Y's mother, old but alert and intelligent, was obviously the matriarch of this extended family group. Her rule was not rigidly authoritarian. Instead, she exercised a guiding influence on each of the independent families in the camp. The worker was impressed by the dignity, pride, and self-assurance displayed by the family; it seemed that they might have been descendants of an influential and ancient lineage of medicine men.

The women were very interested in hearing about the patient and asked many questions about her: How did she look? Was her hair turning grey? Did she look "as old" as her sisters at home? What kind of clothes did she have? Could she still speak Navajo? Did she still remember them or the children? What had she said about coming home? Had she commented on their photographs and the tape recordings of their voices? The worker reported her observations of the patient and the feelings she had expressed about the family. They, in turn, told the worker a little of the history of the patient's departure from home. The mother, as head of the household, then took the proper steps to call together community leaders and councilmen and learn their reactions to her daughter's proposed return and to help them understand her illness.

The Patient's Return to the Reservation

It took several months to arrange for the transfer of the patient to a general hospital on the reservation. Mrs. Y was given appropriate clothes and was accompanied on the flight by an attendant. She recognized the caseworker at the airport. From the beginning she was cheerful and in good contact. On the ride from the airport to the hospital she talked in Navajo about her trip: "A morning cab ride to the airport, boarded an airplane, three stops en route, scared, and near the end of the trip, vomited." This experience seemed to remind her of her abrupt separation from her family when she had been taken to prison. She conversed well and spoke of her family when the worker told her that she was on her way home. Mrs. Y said "I didn't know where we were going, but I just stayed right behind her [the attendant]." She said she had suffered "for nothing" for many years and recalled that her mother had not witnessed her removal from home. An aunt had delivered her to the "wolves" to destroy her mentality. They cast a spell over her and took complete possession of her mind to the extent that she could no longer think or feel. In her own words, "I just gave up to them."

Wolf is a colloquial Navajo term meaning *witch*. Clyde Kluckhohn and Dorothea Leighton emphasize the strength of witchcraft beliefs among Navajos, even today, and the deep-seated fears associated with them: "What counts is that belief in witches is universal and that there are deep fears, much gossip and countless and widely current anecdotes."[2]

Throughout her stay at the hospital on the reservation, Mrs. Y's adjustment was satisfactory. She was assigned to a ward occupied by other Navajo women. At first she sat by her bed most of the day, but soon she began to exchange a few words with the women. Later, in talking to them, she said that she had been away from home a long time. She wondered whether she still owned any sheep and whether she retained authority to make decisions in her own home. She enjoyed a ride with the worker around the reservation to look at flocks of sheep, people riding horseback, an occasional wagon on the road, and of course, the hogans. She said that these sights brought back memories of her people. They stopped at the store, and the worker permitted the patient to make her own purchases so that she could learn whether or not Mrs. Y was capable of making decisions by herself. Mrs. Y purchased cookies and candies and paid the correct amount to the clerk.

The patient became aware of the difference between her short hair and the long hair of the other Navajo women, which was plaited in the traditional Navajo knot. Navajo women feel that long hair adds to their attractiveness, and it enhances their self-image. Several times the patient made reference to her hair, and the worker felt that long hair would help her regain her self-esteem.

Mrs. Y's mother, sister, niece, daughter, and two small grandsons visited her the day after she arrived at the hospital. Mrs. Y had no difficulty in recognizing her mother, but the other members of the family had to introduce themselves to her. She readily accepted her grandchildren, hugged the baby occasionally, and inquired about the identifying characteristics of her son-in-law—his parents, clan, origin, and so forth. She was obviously happy to see her family. She said that until then she had been afraid to believe that she was really home. Her mother gave her information about her brothers and sisters and her other relatives and her neighbors. Although Mrs. Y's ability to express herself in Navajo was somewhat limited, she conversed rationally and coherently with the family. When they attempted to plan for her return home and asked her how she would like her clothes made, she kept saying, "I have no authority; I cannot decide." Her daughter told her that

[2] Clyde Kluckhohn and Dorothea Leighton, *The Navaho*, Harvard University Press, Cambridge, Massachusetts, 1946, p. 172.

her refusal to make decisions was part of the past life that she had left behind her. Now she was home, among her people, and she was again entitled to all her rights and privileges. She was a person again. She could now make decisions, and the family would help her.

Mrs. Y, however, still feared members of "the old regime" who had taken her away from her home. Her mother explained that "the old regime" no longer exercised authority over the Navajos, but Mrs. Y did not quite understand this. The patient continued to refer to the aunt who had sent her away, and her family reassured her by telling her that this aunt had died. Mrs. Y asked the worker to tell the officials of her return in order to learn about their reaction. She also talked about a bracelet taken from her when she had been imprisoned.

Mrs. Y was confused about the reasons for her imprisonment. She believed that she was the victim of the jealous, now deceased, aunt who had sought to bring evil upon her. She spoke again of "Navajo wolves" (human beings in wolf skins) turned loose upon her, crawling upon her hogan, and running riot in her mind. Her daughter, who had been ten years old at the time of her mother's imprisonment, remembered these animals crawling on the hogan at night and scaring the whole family. The worker surmised that these ideas, rather than being manifestations of the patient's illness, were a part of the Navajo culture. Kluckhohn describes the way the Navajos believe these "witches" behave:

> Witches are active primarily at night, roaming about at great speed in skins of wolf, coyote and other animals (bear, owl, desert fox, crow). This is one bit of witchcraft lore with which even the youngest Navajo is familiar. Indeed, ["wolf," in the Navajo language] I have found to be the most common colloquial term for "witch."[3]

Since Mrs. Y was able to adjust to life on the reservation successfully, the worker believed she would be able to adjust to living among her people without great difficulty. She still needed help with the unresolved problems of "the wolves," symbolic in Navajo culture of everything evil and to her of her fear in connection with her traumatic separation from her people. She also needed assurance that she had a secure place with her family and in the community. The family could help her with this problem, but the worker thought it advisable to request support from the community agencies for both the patient and her family.

Two months later the worker made a home visit and found Mrs. Y baby-sitting for her niece. She had just finished feeding four children, aged four, three, two, and one, and washing the dishes. She apologized to the worker for not giving her something to eat, explaining that she was not in her own home. She was cheerful and talked of helping her mother with the cooking and other chores; she also helped to prepare the wool for weaving. Mrs. Y was anxious to weave, but her mother had advised her to wait, because she still suffered from nocturnal episodes of vomiting and diarrhea.

[3] Clyde Kluckhohn, *Navajo Witchcraft*, Beacon Press, Boston, 1962, p. 26.

At night she was afraid of something she could not identify, but during the day she had no problems. These symptoms may well have indicated her persisting fear of witchcraft. Her family had arranged for some ceremonies to be performed that were designed to cure Mrs. Y of her illness, and they were planning for more of them. These ceremonies are the basic Navajo method of curing illness, including illness caused by witchcraft. Kluckhohn and Leighton state:

> The most efficacious reassurance for victims of witchcraft is provided, therefore, by the unusual, complicated, and costly prayer ceremonials, with many relatives and friends in attendance, lending their help and expressing their sympathy.[4]

The particular ceremony recommended by the Navajo diagnostician depends on his identification of the supernatural cause of the illness. The ceremonies vary in length from one to nine days. Many relatives and friends gather to participate in them, bringing together the efforts of the community for the well-being of the patient. In this way they provide a positive emotional support for the member of the community who is ill. The Public Health Service doctors have come to recognize the continuing importance to the Navajos of their ceremonies, and in some cases they encourage the use of native methods of treatment along with those of modern medicine.

In a second home visit the worker learned that Mrs. Y had made marked improvement. She was living in her own home and taking full responsibility for herself. She had woven a number of rugs and was pleased to be back on the reservation. Mrs. Y spoke of the "voices inside her," but she recognized them as a part of the past and they no longer guided her in her actions.

Summary

The case discussed in this article illustrates some of the problems social workers encounter in the rehabilitation of patients who have been hospitalized for long periods. Long-term care of patients in hospitals located at considerable distances from their families and communities often fosters the development of symptoms associated with institutionalization. Although the patient's illness may be in remission, his ability to relate to family and community is thwarted by his isolation from them. Members of minority groups may, of course, be even more isolated than patients who are members of the dominant culture.

Some of the problems the social worker encountered in helping a Navajo Indian return to her home after an absence of twenty years were resolved because the worker understood the patient's cultural beliefs and customs and was able to communicate with her in her native language. The worker helped the family understand Mrs. Y's illness and her attitude toward them, which was essential in securing the family's participation in planning for her return home.

Casework service is especially needed in helping mental patients who

---

[4] Kluckhohn and Leighton, op. cit., p. 175.

have been hospitalized for a long time to bridge the gap between living in the hospital and living in the community. It is especially important to involve the patient's family and community agencies in planning for the discharge of such patients.

Initial Contacts with Mexican-American Families

Ignacio Aguilar

Schools of social work have, for the most part, been oblivious to the need for adapting methods of practice to minority groups. Rather they teach practice derived from a generic method that is dictated primarily by the majority. Yet much social work practice is carried out in the United States with minority groups and, too often, social workers apply it by a blanket method supposedly effective with all people.

Each minority group has its own problems and personality—derived from long-existing cultural and moral values, language, patterns of behavior, socioeconomic conditions, ethnic background, and many other factors. Social work practice in a minority community shows that besides the variations that must be made in the generic method to suit individuals, certain adaptations should be made in applying social work methods to the specific minority group.

During ten years' experience in a California community made up mainly of Mexican-Americans, the author learned from the people in the community how to adapt some of the key concepts and techniques of social work to the needs and the life-style of Mexican-Americans and how to avoid some common obstacles to the development of goodwill.

This article briefly outlines different cultural values and patterns of behavior—and barriers to assimilation in an alien society—which the social worker should consider in making initial contacts with Mexican-American families. How social work method was adapted in this initial contact phase in order to provide effective counseling is illustrated by a case example of work with a family in the author's community.

Initial Contact

There is no doubt that one of the most important and difficult processes in social work is the beginning phase, that is, starting to work with a client. Green and Maloney describe this phase as one in which

> ... emotional interaction takes place. The worker focuses on an emotional engagement with a purpose, explores the possibilities of person(s), agency and

Reprinted with permission of the author and the National Association of Social Workers, from *Social Work*, Vol. 17, No. 3 (May, 1972), pp. 66–70.

worker finding a realistic *common purpose*. On the other hand, the client(s) naturally and rightly questions moving into a relationship with the worker.[1]

Since the first encounter determines the dynamics of the relationship and the kind and quality of the interaction between worker and client, a correct start is vital.

Awareness of differences, an understanding of why the differences exist, and experience in dealing with people of the specific minority group— all these are important to the social worker in establishing feelings of friendliness and confidence from the outset. Without them, a worker can unknowingly arouse antagonism or cause the client to withdraw in fear or confusion.

Patterns of Living

The social worker in a Mexican-American community finds that his ways of work are strongly influenced by the people's patterns of living, which differ in many respects from those of people having a Protestant Anglo-Saxon background. Consideration of concepts, attitudes, and patterns of behavior that are likely to have a marked effect on the beginning stages of social work method can help to assure that vital correct start.

The leisurely opening. When Mexican-Americans meet to negotiate or arrange affairs, the first step is to set the climate or *ambiente*. A preliminary period of warm, informal, personal conversation precedes the discussion of the concerns that brought them together. Jumping into the middle of serious and controversial affairs—as many persons in the United States are inclined to do—seems confusing and even discourteous to most Mexican-Americans.

Language. Language is, of course, one of the main problems in working with non-English-speaking people. How can a social worker help people if he cannot communicate with them? How can a common purpose be established if that purpose cannot be discussed? How can a worker start where his clients are and proceed at a pace comfortable to them when he cannot even start at all? Obviously, for any social worker in a Spanish-speaking community, fluency in the language is a tremendous asset and for those dealing directly with clients it is a necessity—both for communicating and establishing rapport.

Attitude toward the law. Having to deal with the law is considered shameful by the average Mexican-American family, and the family members are disinclined to accept it as a common practice. The social worker needs to reassure his clients that dealing with the law offers them an honorable way of protecting their interests and legal rights. He will also have to explain their relation to such persons as probation officers and the police and tell them about legal services available to them. Knowledge of the basic elements

---

[1] Rose Green and Sara Maloney, "Characteristics of Movement in Phases of the Social Work Relationship." Unpublished paper, University of Southern California, Los Angeles, 1963. (Mimeographed.)

of the Mexican system of law, as well as the system in the United States, will enable him to interpret these subjects more intelligibly to his clients.

Influence of religion. Religion plays an important role in the Mexican-American home and shapes the lives of the entire family. As Heller notes:

> Some observers have reported that the church continues to exercise a strong influence in the Mexican-American community. For example, Broom and Shevky contend that "the church is the principal agency of cultural conservatism for Mexicans in the United States and reinforces the separateness of the group." They specify that they have in mind not only the parish organization of the Catholic Church but also the Protestant Missions "with their functional sectarian attributes." There seems to be little doubt that the "religious factor" (to use Professor Lenski's phrase) plays an important role in the rate of acculturation of Mexican Americans.[2]

Role of the male. The concept of the male in society and in the family is important to the understanding of the person of Mexican ancestry. It is not only a concept of philosophy, it is a way of life, quite different from the "American way of life." Paz describes the *macho* concept as follows:

> The ideal manliness is never to "crack", never to back down.... Our masculine integrity is as much endangered by kindness as it is by hostility. Any opening in our defenses is a lessening of our manliness.... The Mexican macho—the male—is a hermetic being, closed up in himself, capable of guarding both himself and whatever has been confided to him.[3]

The traditional role of the husband and father in the Mexican-American family is explained by Heller, as follows:

> According to the traditional norms the husband is regarded as the authoritarian and patriarchal figure who is both the head and the master of the family, and the mother as the affectional figure in the family.[4]

The extended family. To Mexican-Americans the extended family is of great significance in their pattern of living; they take it for granted that in time of trouble they can always count on the family to help out. Again quoting Heller:

> Not only in size, but also in organization the Mexican-American family displays an unusual persistence of traditional forms. It continues to be an extended type of family with strong ties spread through a number of generations in a large web of kinships. These ties impose obligations of mutual aid, respect and affection.[5]

Barriers to Cooperation

The social worker dealing with Mexican-Americans may well find that there are certain obstacles to be overcome before he can gain his clients'

---

[2] Celia S. Heller, *Mexican American Youth: Forgotten Youth at the Crossroads* (New York: Random House, 1966), p. 19.

[3] Octavio Paz, *The Labyrinth of Solitude*, Lysander Kamp, trans. (New York: Grove Press, 1962), pp. 29–31.

[4] Heller, op. cit., p. 34.

[5] *Ibid.*, p. 34.

confidence and they can work together smoothly and effectively in endeavoring to solve problems. These obstacles may involve attitudes of other people with whom the Mexican-Americans associate or they may be related primarily to the clients' own attitudes.

Prejudice. Unfortunately, in many sections of the United States Mexican-Americans—especially the families of poor and unskilled workers—are likely to encounter prejudice. This can occur within the community at large, can reach out to the children in school, and can even be found among persons in the helping professions.

Unfriendly or antagonistic feelings conveyed by insensitive people in positions of authority hinder the progress of such families in becoming assimilated and assuming responsibility. These families with limited financial resources and limited knowledge of English are likely to become the target of prejudiced individuals reluctant to help those who do not fit readily into the mold of middle-class American society. Too often, help is not offered at all. Or it may be offered in such a way that acceptance requires departure from familiar behavioral patterns. Indeed, prejudice in its purest and ugliest manifestations becomes one of the most common problems the minorities face in their encounters with helping professionals. It can also be one of the social worker's greatest obstacles to building confidence.

The strange system. It is hard for the parents in a Mexican-American family to understand the "system" with which they have to deal as they endeavor to cope with their problems. It becomes in their minds a kind of hydra-headed creature, with authorities cropping up from all sides to make demands upon them and press in on their privacy. Yet these families have to learn how to deal with the system if they are to become active partners in the process of being helped. They have to learn how to exercise their rights and to assert their self-worth and esteem as human beings in a society they do not understand. As Hollis notes:

> This emphasis upon the innate worth of the individual is an extremely important, fundamental characteristic of casework. It is the ingredient that makes it possible to establish the relationship of trust that is so essential to effective treatment. From it grow the two essential characteristics of the caseworker's attitude toward his client: acceptance and belief in self-determination.[6]

For truly effective social work practice with minority groups, the social worker must learn as well as the client. Much more needs to be done in the way of teaching the uniqueness of the cultures of these groups to social workers and others in the helping professions if they are to provide worthwhile assistance to those who need the most help.

The following case illustration presents only the beginning stages in working with a typical family in a Mexican-American community in California. With further involvement, all other orthodox social work methods had to be modified somewhat in order to help the family fully.

[6] Florence Hollis, *Casework: Psychosocial Therapy* (New York: Random House, 1964), p. 12.

Case Illustration

Family X is made up of the parents and three children: a girl 6 years old and two boys, aged 7 and 16. Mr. and Mrs. X were legally married at one time, but because of serious marital problems and pressures from Mrs. X's family were divorced three years ago. However, they managed to resolve their problems and came together again; the church never considered them divorced. The family lives in a small house in the back of a large empty lot that has not been taken care of properly. Weeds have taken over the majority of the land, so that they conceal the house.

The probation department referred Family X to the community center because neither the father nor the mother were able to communicate in English. The probation officer explained that this family needed counseling and also "someone who could speak their language." The parents were unable to control their 16-year-old son, Freddy, who had been placed on probation for running away from home regularly.

Mrs. X had been told to call the center for an appointment. This might have been sufficient to start the helping process for an Anglo-Saxon Protestant family; for a Mexican-American family it was not. Not only was it difficult for the family to overcome the shame of having to deal with the law, but Mr. X—who made all the decisions—had been disregarded by the probation officer. It was decided that establishing contact was up to the center, on the assumption that this would be difficult or impossible for Mrs. X.

Establishing Contact

The director of the community center called Mrs. X, identifying himself in Spanish as a social worker who knew that her son had been in some trouble, and explained that the center was a voluntary not a governmental agency. It was suggested that Mrs. X ask her husband if he could come with her to the center. She agreed to do so and to call back later in the evening when her husband came home from work, adding, "It is good to talk to someone who can speak Spanish." The fact that Mrs. X had been asked to consult her husband about a conference for the two of them put her in a situation in which she did not have to decide on her own. Her husband was now involved in the decision-making.

A few days later Mr. and Mrs. X came to the center for the interview. True to Latin custom, the first hour was leisurely, the talk mainly about familiar things that they could comfortably share with the worker. Conversation centered about Mexico, where they had lived until about two years before. They shared information about their respective families and mentioned how difficult it was for them to get used to the American way of life. Here they had no close relatives nearby to whom they could turn when problems arose. It was disconcerting for them to have to bother people outside the family.

Alien Surroundings

It was no wonder that Mr. and Mrs. X were having a hard time, not only with their son, but with the society surrounding them, which was completely alien to them and highly threatening to their way of life. In their own little house at the end of the big lot, hidden by the growing weeds, they had found an island isolated from the outside world—up to the time that their son had gotten into trouble. But then they had to face the world, and it was difficult to understand and more difficult to be understood.

They were not pressed to talk about their son's situation in detail. They decided to come back the following day to talk about this problem after the probation officer had come to see them.

The purposes in mind for this first interview were accomplished: to meet Mr. and Mrs. X personally and to establish a comfortable relationship that would lead to a partnership once they were able to share their problems with the social worker. The next step would be to share a common purpose, in this case, helping Freddy.

Mr. X was included in the helping process from the beginning. Had he been left out, it would have meant that Mrs. X was assuming an improper role, that Mr. X was being put down by her, and that his role as head of the household plus his *macho* role were being jeopardized.

The following day Mr. and Mrs. X came a little late to the meeting and were reluctant to talk about their conference with the probation officer. Mr. X just kept silent, looking down. Mrs. X, red-eyed, finally said, "I am very ashamed. You should have heard what the probation officer said about us. He blamed us for all the troubles with Freddy and said that if we were not able to speak English we should go back to Mexico. Perhaps worst of all, our daughter heard all of this because she had to translate for us."

It was suggested that they arrange to meet the probation officer the next time at the center; there the social worker could translate for them and make the necessary interpretations. Thus the harmful effect of the probation officer's prejudices against them would be minimized. Mr. and Mrs. X were assured that they had certain legal and moral rights that had to be respected —among them the right to be treated as human beings. Major differences between the systems of law in the United States and Mexico were explained, as were the functions of the probation department and the role of its officers.

Mr. and Mrs. X then seemed somewhat relieved and looked less tense and fearful. Mrs. X thanked the social worker and, looking at her husband, said: "We are not ignorant and dumb. We just did not understand anything about what was happening."

This family is not unusual. Nor are its problems. Many families in minority communities are facing problems like these every day. The situations can be far more critical when compounded by illness and poverty. Preparing the social worker in advance to serve such families effectively— rather than leaving it up to him to learn on the job from the community —offers a challenge to the schools of social work.

The Negro Worker and the White Client: A Commentary on the Treatment Relationship

Andrew E. Curry

When the caseworker and the client are members of different racial groups, the factor of race becomes an important variable in the casework treatment process. In this attempt to examine the subjective reactions and responses of the white client and the Negro worker in the treatment relationship, certain sociological and psychological influences on the relationship will also be considered.

It is a truism that, in casework practice, the worker must understand and exert some control over psychological responses, such as transference and countertransference. It is equally necessary that he take into account the sociological matrix in which the psychological responses occur. The clients' sociological supplies—his values, norms, and reference groups—should be assessed as carefully as his psychological supplies. In spite of the general acceptance of these principles, relatively little systematic attention has been given to their application in treatment of a client of one race by a worker of an other.[1] Casework supervisors, however, frequently have to deal with the profound consequences of this particular kind of client-worker relationship. Consider, for example, the Negro worker with a predominantly white caseload who is overly conscientious about adhering to the fine points of eligibility; or the "socially conscious" young white worker who plans relatively lavish budgets for Negro families only; or the white worker who makes a biased judgement that a Negro mother is refusing to let her mentally

---

[1] Luna Bowdoin Brown, "Race as a Factor in Establishing a Casework Relationship," *Social Casework*, Vol. XXXI, March 1950, pp. 91–97; Inabel Burns Lindsay, "Race as a Factor in the Caseworker's Role," *Journal of Social Casework*, Vol. XXVIII, March, 1947, pp. 101–107; Eric Layne, "Experience of a Negro Psychiatric Social Worker in a Veterans Administration Mental Hygiene Clinic," *Journal of Psychiatric Social Work*, Vol. XIX, Autumn, 1949, pp. 66–69. For the view that a patient is best treated by a member of his own race or religion, see C. P. Oberndorf, "Selectivity and Option for Psychiatry," *American Journal of Psychiatry*, Vol. CX, April, 1954, pp. 754–58.

Reprinted from *Social Casework*, Vol. 45 (March, 1964), pp. 131–136, by permission of the author and the Journal.

ill child enter a psyciatric hospital because her welfare check will be cut while he is there. This short list of examples could easily be extended.

In a pioneering paper, Leonard Simmons discussed a phenomenon called "Crow Jim" and its effects on the practice of a Negro worker. Simmons defined "Crow Jim" as a form of Negro racial prejudice—"animosity, hostility, and bitterness felt by Negroes toward whites and a predisposition of Negroes to descriminate against them."[2] Elsewhere, the transference and countertransference reactions of the members of a treatment group and their Negro therapist were examined in two articles,[3] but aside from these efforts and that of Simmons few guideposts are to be found in the professional literature for caseworkers and supervisors who must deal with the problem.

In this article the relationship between white client and Negro worker is discussed from the standpoints of (1) the casework relationship and the vicissitudes of rapport (or lack of it), (2) relevant aspects of ego psychology, and (3) the nature of the underlying social factors that sustain certain modes of thought, racial tensions, and intergroup conflicts. Each of these has crucial importance for caseworkers and supervisors, educators, agency executives, and others concerned with the refinement of practice skills.

The subject is relatively difficult to examine because of the near-impossibility of gaining sufficient distance from the events of the day to be objective and clear-headed. Everyone seems to be taking part in some way in the current social revolution. For some persons change is occurring too quickly; for others it is not quick enough. Interracial group tensions now permeate every aspect of our contemporary society, and there is no reason to believe that the client-worker relationship is immune to them. The casework relationship, by its very nature, is a product of the mutual perceptions of client and caseworker—perceptions based on what each has been taught to see and what he needs to see.[4] These perceptions cannot be divorced from affects, which are "indices" of the dynamic and economic conditions obtaining in the "psyche."[5] More importantly, however, they cannot be divorced from each individual's attitudes, beliefs, and social norms. Affects and attitudes are embedded in the fabric of each personality and in the ethnic subculture from which each has drawn his values, biases, hopes, and fears. Through careful study of this subject, social workers may obtain "a clearer picture of value orientations based on ethnic backgrounds."[6] They

---

[2] Leonard C. Simmons, " 'Crow Jim': Implications for Social Work," *Social Work*, Vol. VIII, July, 1963. p. 24.

[3] Andrew E. Curry, "Some Comments on Transference when the Group Therapist is Negro," *International Journal of Group Psychotherapy*, Vol. XIII, July, 1963, pp. 363–65, and "Myth, Transference, and the Black Psychotherapist," *Psychoanalytic Review* (scheduled for publication).

[4] See Solomon E. Asch, *Social Psychology*, Prentice-Hall, New York, 1952, Chapter 8, pp. 223–27.

[5] Marjorie Brierley, *Trends in Psycho-Analysis*, Hogarth Press, London, 1951, p. 55.

[6] Herman D. Stein, "The Concept of Social Environment in Social Work Practice," in *Ego-Oriented Casework: Problems and Perspectives*, Family Service Association of America, New York, 1963, p. 74.

may also learn more about the ego's response to the normative structure of the environing community—about how the ego sustains its identity in the flux of social change.

The Client's Image of the Negro Worker

The reaction of a white client to a worker is presented in the following case, in which the worker's sensitive use of the situation enabled him to establish contact with the client despite her initially negative response.

> Miss K was an unmarried thirty-three-year-old white woman who had been diagnosed as suffering from a "schizophrenic reaction: chronic un-differentiated type." She was then on convalescent leave from a psychiatric hospital, having been released as greatly improved. Altogether, she had been hospitalized four times as a mental patient. On meeting the Negro worker in the initial posthospital interview, she explicitly stated that she did not like his race, his looks, or his office. She said she would not return again and that the worker would have to drag her into the few evaluation interviews required by the state. The worker acknowledged his concern and his sympathy for her feelings. He wondered if there might be some subject they could talk about, and he made some general comment about appreciating her frankness and honesty. His efforts failed to engage her at that point, but about three weeks later she telephoned and asked to see him. She said she was "feeling funny again" and was thinking about suicide.
>
> She came to the interview promptly, and immediately said that she had been feeling very bad ever since she had said "those nasty things" to the worker. The worker pointed out that he did not recall her saying anything more than that she did not like Negroes, and he had appreciated her honesty. He reminded her that the function of the agency was to help her and that he had been appointed to see her for that purpose. Miss K, appearing to relax, said that she must have been *thinking* some "funny things"; perhaps she had not *said* them after all; anyway, perhaps she should talk with the Negro worker, since she was always having "dark thoughts." The worker said that he did not know what the "dark thoughts" were but that, if she wanted to help him understand, they could arrange to see each other regularly. Miss K accepted, commenting that maybe she would have something to live for then.

The worker undoubtedly resented Miss K's "attack" on him. Perhaps he was even hurt deeply; however, he never lost sight of her reference to suicidal thoughts. As many workers do, he wondered about the client's social frame of reference as well as about her psychological needs. (One must wonder also about the worker's frame of reference here. Was he more "social worker" than "Negro social worker"? This kind of question, touching on the articulation of professional identity, awaits study.)

In terms of Miss K's response to the Negro worker, what was her "social context of action?"[7] The discussion that follows is concerned not with the broad issues of social psychology and social action but with the

[7] Alex Inkeles, "Personality and Social Structure," in *Sociology Today*, Robert K. Merton, Leonard Broom, and Leonard S. Cottrell, Jr. (eds.), Basic Books, New York, 1959, p. 273.

response of individual clients, since the action of an individual in any situation—particularly a stressful one—reflects personal motivations however much it also reflects the determining influences of the social environment. The forces in the environment, in turn, can be reflected in individual action only to the extent that they are mediated through the personality.[8] The social environment, of course, varies from neighborhood to neighborhood in a community and from state to state in different parts of the country. A client living in Oregon would be expected to respond differently from one living in Virginia because of the differences between those states in the position of the Negro.

The Meaning of "Negro" in a Social Context

Prejudice is often based on a faulty chain of reasoning according to which the world is divided into two groups of people, we and they: " 'they' are different, therefore inferior; if inferior, we are justified in disliking them and in treating them as inferiors. . . ."[9] The treatment "they" receive can be structured and sanctioned by complex and rigid patterns of discrimination. Currently a major effort in the United States is aimed primarily at upsetting the structured patterns of discrimination. Once these are changed, it is thought, then individual beliefs, attitudes, values, and perceptions will also change. This view may be valid, but it should be recognized that many of the attitudes of prejudice are not manifested in institutionalized patterns of discrimination but in the various modes of thought (fantasy and myth, dreams and superstitions) that reference groups nurture. The white Southerner is quick to remind the white Northerner of this subtle point.

In the social context, the designations *Negro* and *white* are emotionally laden signs and symbols that have important sociopsychological stimulus value. Krech and Crutchfield, in considering this stimulus value, stated that there are two different functions that the beliefs and attitudes of racial prejudice can serve: *"1]* There are the beliefs and attitudes of racial prejudice that serve *in defense of the self,* and *2]* there are the beliefs and attitudes of racial prejudice that serve to maintain the individual's *identification with society."*[10] In the definition that each (self and group) makes of its own integrity, the meaning of *Negro* may be symbolic of something that for some unknown reason can be expressed in no other way. That is to say, there is more meaning in the sign/symbol *Negro* than is expressed in group norms and values. We will need, ultimately, to learn how such meanings come into being. To say that attitudes are socially determined is an inexact way of saying several things. We may agree that the formation and change of attitudes can only take place in the setting of

[8] Inkeles, *loc. cit.*
[9] S. Stansfeld Sargent, *Social Psychology*, Ronald Press Co., New York, 1950, p. 449.
[10] David Krech and Richard S. Crutchfield, *Theory and Problems of Social Psychology*, McGraw-Hill Book Co., New York, 1948, p. 456.

significant social and emotional relations. But one is hard put to know, at this stage of our knowledge, what *significant* means—to whom, when, and in what part of the country.

Using Help and the Response to Authority

The white client often has difficulty in recognizing and accepting the Negro worker's authority and his ability to help him solve his problems. In this context the concept of "Crow Jim" attitudes in the Negro worker may be studied profitably. As a professional helper, the Negro worker encounters the same problems as his white counterpart; he must be able to establish a good helping relationship and empathize sufficiently with the problems and needs of his client. But the Negro worker's professional task is more difficult because he must deal not only with the client's expected psychological resistances to using help on the terms prescribed by the agency's function but also with the sociocultural and characterological resistances stimulated by his being a Negro.

These resistances are different for the client in a Vermont family family agency and the client in a Georgia public welfare agency. It may be easier for the Vermonter than for the Georgian to associate the Negro worker with authority. Because of the social traditions in Georgia, however, it may be easier for the client there to percieve the Negro as one who gives service; he will screen out the authority aspects of the worker's role. In both situations, the white client's perceptions need to be observed and studied on two fundamental levels: his perception of *Negro worker* and his perception of *Negro*. When the white client has little difficulty in perceiving that the Negro worker possesses the authority vested in him by the agency, the community, and his profession,[11] it is evidence that the client's ego is able to manage an extremely complex situation. Difficulties arise when the worker's and the client's subtle responses to *Negro* and *white* begin to spill over into the professional contractual relationship between them. Stable interaction is most likely to occur when client and worker share the same norms and expectations and when optimum cathexis exists between them. The social distance between client and professional worker[12] is being carefully studied by social scientists. These may also be an "emotional distance" that needs equally careful study.

Much supervisory time is undoubtedly spent in tackling this complex issue. Typically, both the client and the worker make a great emotional investment in the casework relationship. Their perceptions, biases, likes and dislikes, fears, and fantasies each influence their reality-testing and self-obser-vation, their identity and self-image.[13] When the variable of race is added,

[11] Andrew E. Curry, "The 'On-Call' Contract with the Schizophrenic Leave Patient," *Napa State Hospital Quarterly*, Vol. IV, January, 1963, pp. 18–21.

[12] Charles Kadushin, "Social Distance Between Client and Professional," *American Journal of Sociology*, Vol. LXVII, March, 1962, pp. 517–31.

[13] Roger R. Miller, "Prospects and Problems in the Study of Ego Functions," in *Ego-Oriented Casework, op. cit.*, pp. 108–126.

it seems to function like a Rorschach card capable of stimulating a wide range of reactions that indicate the underlying emotional frame of mind of the helper and the person being helped.

Emotionally Distorted Perceptions

The reciprocal responses of Negro worker and white client should not, however, be conceived of as transference reactions. *Transference* is a psychoanalytic construct used to denote an irrational and infantile attribution of characteristics to another person and a response to him in terms of these attributes. When complex symbolic processes, fantasies, fears, and counterphobic reactions are motivated by characteristics the other person does possess, such as a black skin, such responses are not transference reactions. Rather, they are residuals of fairy tales, folk tales and children's stories that deal with darkness, bogeymen, badness, and evil. Their psychodynamic import is great, and they complicate still further the already complex problem of dissolving racial tensions based on prejudice. For example, if either *white* or *Negro* signifies threat, the ego can deal with this *external* perception by avoidance. The person can pattern his social relations in accordance with the doctrines of segregationists and restrict his social activities with Negroes. The *internal* perceptions, however, give the ego no such possibility of escape.[14] Even if extensive sociological changes occur (desegregation, integrated services, open housing practices, and so forth), subtly distorted perceptions can still persist in the psyche, beyond the reach of conscious control.

The Negro worker must be willing to allow himself to recognize the existence of these emotionally distorted reactions in the client and in himself. He must also be willing to risk discovery that his clinical practice is being affected by his own insidious reactions. He must make this effort because he is professionally responsible for the establishment of a therapeutic casework relationship. He may gain a measure of comfort and security from knowing that his profession and his agency have made clear their belief in such values as the dignity of the individual, equal opportunity, and social justice. But all the social-psychological information in the world will not produce sound, conflict-free casework practice unless the Negro worker has examined his own emotional reactions.

There is no getting around the fact that a great deal of emotion is interwoven in the fabric of interracial relationships. The Negro worker and the white client (and the white worker and the Negro client as well) will find that their interactions are highly charged with emotions that they may not be completely aware of or are not able to handle. The consequences of being a Negro, in relation to the range of responses a white client may make, are not at all equivalent to those of being fat or bald or ugly—the symbol *Negro* has much more affect and stimulus value. It is both incorrect and clinically unsound to argue that the dynamics of the casework process are not affected

[14] Angel Garma, "The Genesis of Reality Testing," *Psychoanalytic Quarterly*, Vol. XV, April, 1946, p. 161.

by the worker's race. Both the worker's and the client's responses to it, whether deeply unconscious or preconscious, can stimulate or impede the establishment of a sound casework relationship.

Transference and Countertransference

The fantasies and fears developed by the white client because his worker is a Negro can have a crucial effect on the eventual manifestation of the transference, as it is related to resistances and the working through of resistances. The white client's reactions are also influenced by the countertransference of the Negro worker, his self-image, and his reactions to the white client. Because of the regressive pull in the accompanying fantasy systems of both client and worker, great anxiety can be stimulated in the worker, especially if he harbors neurotic resistances to identifying himself with his race. If the client becomes aware of the worker's reactions, the resulting interference with communication precludes effective treatment.

Countertransference phenomena are probably present in every treatment relationship. The worker habitually deals with them in various nonverbal ways. Often, however, they are either ignored because the worker does not know what to do with them or repressed because he responds to them by first developing anxiety and then defending himself against the anxiety. On the conscious level, Negro-white relationships are directly related to a person's values, ethics, group norms, and social-political philosophy. Some interesting dimensions of countertransference are revealed, however, by focusing on the unconscious and preconscious power of *black* and *white* as symbols that appear in the fantasies of the Negro worker.

When the Negro worker's reactions to his own race are unresolved and overly complicated and the white client's reactions to him are hostile or unfriendly, the worker's reactions take two distinct, though not unrelated, forms: (1) the countertransference of defensiveness, which is derived from the unconscious conflicts about his color; (2) the countertransference of interaction, which is derived from the white client's negative reaction to the worker. In either case, the Negro worker's reaction is based upon his unconscious need or wish not to be a Negro, not to be what he is. His unwillingness to allow the white client to accept him as he is further interferes with the progress of treatment, since this acceptance is essential in therapy.

The white client's whiteness as an image for fantasy may constitute a difficult situational exigency with which the Negro worker is unable to cope.[15] The Negro worker's counterresistance and counterphobic reactions to his blackness may actually be manifestations of his questioning his own sense of identity. When the white client becomes aware of these reactions, he is called upon to bear too heavy a burden. In one sense, he is called upon to "treat" the feelings of the Negro worker who has failed to work through his feelings about his color. In another sense, the client may find himself being

---

[15] See Gert Heilbrunn, "Comments on a Common Form of Acting Out," *Psychoanalytic Quarterly*, Vol. XXVII, January, 1958, p. 88.

used as an audience before whom the Negro worker plays out his own fantasy, or personal myth, that he is really a "Negro white". Uncomfortable with himself and preoccupied with his own hatreds and fantasies about blackness and inferiority, the Negro worker inevitably arouses tensions and anxieties in the white client. If the worker is able to recognize his effect on the client, he can take advantage of it, as was illustrated in the case of Miss K, to further the process of treatment; in other words, he can use race as an important tool in treatment. He cannot do so, however, if he is not ever mindful of "Crow Jim" attitudes and countertransference contaminations of what could prove to be an advantageous situation. Working through the client's displaced reactions to the therapist or caseworker is the *sine qua non* of all the psychological therapies.

When the worker's race is used by the white client as the point of departure for an attack on him, it constitutes a source of great anxiety for the worker. He may get anxious about the threat to the client's ego identity, which may result in hypercathexis of the client's ego defenses.[16] He may get, anxious about the threat to the client's ego-ideal, superego commands, or reference group norms, which may result in the client's overvaluing these commands and norms. Or he may get anxious about the meaning of *black skin* in the fantasies of the white majority and in their evaluation of minority groups. Such an attack creates resistances in the client and counterresistances in the worker that neither of them may be able to overcome.

It is important to remember that in the history of psychoanalysis, the phenomena of transference and countertransference were understood before there was a comparable understanding of character. As a result, transference phenomena and character were for a long time considered separately. It may well be that with further developments in the study of character and ego psychology, the phenomena of transference and countertransference will become clearer, particularly as they are affected by race.

Summary

Because social workers practice in a wide variety of settings, they are in an ideal position to observe and study the effects of the client's race, ethnic group, and reference group on several important aspects of the treatment relationship—on his perception of the worker and of the agency and on his utilization of service. They are also in an ideal position to observe and study their own attitudes, values, and prejudices, which affect their perceptions of clients. It is hoped that the thoughts presented here will contribute to such study.

[16] See Erik H. Erikson, "Ego Development and Historical Change," in *Identity and the Life Cycle* (*Psychological Issues*, Vol. I, No. 1, Monograph 1), International Universities Press, New York, 1959, pp. 18–49. Erikson points out that "the suppressed, excluded, and exploited unconsciously believe in the evil image which they are made to represent by those who are dominant" (p. 31).

The White Professional and the Black Client

Alex Gitterman and Alice Schaeffer

As we become increasingly conscious of the depth of racism in our society,[1] and as tensions between blacks and whites continue to surface, it is imperative to examine the impact of these racial pressures on the helping professions—especially upon those encounters that find the white professional trying to serve the black client. It is not an uncommon experience, for both black client and white professional, that the supposedly therapeutic contact is a frustrating and unsatisfying one during which service is neither delivered nor received. Each party may tend to "explain" this result by blaming the other, and at present there is a substantial body of literature—professional and popular—attacking the inadequacies of both white professionals and black clients. The stereotypes are familiar: the middle-class white professional is labeled as distant, unfeeling, uncaring if not actually racist, malicious, and punitive;[2] the lower-class black client is stigmatized as unmotivated, resistant, inaccessible, and lacking mature personality development and family organization.[3]

Because of these negative experiences, the question has been raised within the professional and lay community as to whether white professionals can, indeed, provide meaningful service for black clients. This question has stimulated vigorous debate and will continue to do so for years to come. It is not the intention of the writers to attempt to answer this question. Rather they choose to view the present situation as given—one in which because of social service manpower conditions and the needs of this country's population, white professionals *do* work with black clients and will continue to do so. Therefore, the crucial issue becomes, *How* will this work be carried out—what can white professionals *bring to* and *do in* the encounter with black clients to make their services most useful? The writers address themselves to this concern by (1) identifying the obstacles emerging from the black-

Reprinted from *Social Casework*, Vol. 53 (May, 1972), pp. 280–291, by permission of the authors and the Family Service Association of America.

[1] See, for example, National Advisory Commission on Civil Disorders, *Report of the National Advisory Commission on Civil Disorders* (New York: Bantam Books, 1968).

[2] Kenneth Clark, *Dark Ghetto* (New York: Harper & Row, 1965), p. 77.

[3] James Farmer, Stereotypes of the Negro and Their Relationship to His Self-Image, in *Urban Schooling*, ed. H. C. Redman and R. L. Featherstone (New York: Harcourt, Brace & World, 1968), pp. 135–50.

white encounter that impede the development of a helping relationship; (2) offering a professional vision, a frame of reference, that lends itself to a meaningful black-white engagement; and (3) presenting case material to demonstrate one worker's struggle with these obstacles.

Obstacles Inherent in the Black-White Encounter

The problems confronted in the white professional and black client encounter may be perceived as emerging from, and being obstacles to, the joint effort rather than as flaws or faults of one party or the other. Three basic situational factors define the framework and substance of the encounter between middle-class white professional and lower-class black client: institutional racism, social distance, and mutual unknownness. These factors greatly influence what the client and professional bring to the encounter and how they perceive and deal with each other.

The encounter occurs in the context of American society—its culture, norms, and values. This context is essentially a racist one based on a history of black slavery and oppression within a culture of white dominance and supposed superiority.[4] Race is a crucial dimension in American culture and carries with it a host of rigidly institutionalized roles and connotations. Both black client and white worker have experienced this racial dimension in the course of their lives; indeed they have been conditioned to it. They have adapted to it, reacted against it, incorporated it, rejected it, struggled with it—each in his own way—but certainly they have not been able to avoid a self-consciousness about race and its significance in America.

One direct consequence of the institutionalized racial positions of blacks and whites is social distance. This consequence is further accentuated by the differential of available opportunities through which whites are able to attain greater social mobility than blacks.[5] In many ways, the specific helping encounter represents a microcosm of these societal conditions. The white professional is of the middle-class, well-educated, and functioning within and according to the rules of the established system. He has a fair degree of power over his own life as well as power over his client and the service his client needs. The lower-class black client tends to be poor, is less well-educated, and has fewer tools and opportunities to help him negotiate

---

[4] See, for example, Stokely Carmichael and Charles V. Hamilton, *Black Power* (New York: Vintage Books, 1967); Eldridge Cleaver, *Soul On Ice* (New York: McGraw Hill, 1968); Louis L. Knowles and Kenneth Prewitt, *Institutional Racism in America* (Englewood Cliffs, N.J.: Prentice Hall, 1969); August Meier and Elliot Rudwick, *Black Protest in the Sixties* (Chicago: Quadrangle Books, 1970); Malcolm X, *The Autobiography of Malcolm X* (New York: Grove Press, 1964); and Sidney M. Willhelm and Elwin H. Powell, Who Needs the Negro?, *Trans-Action*, 1: 3–6 (September–October 1964).

[5] For statistical description, see Elizabeth M. Eddy, *Walk the White Line* (New York: Vintage Books, 1964), p. 12; Clark, *Dark Ghetto*, pp. 34–55; Michael Harrington, *The Other America* (Baltimore: Penguin Books, 1965), pp. 65–82; and Arnold M. Rose, Characteristics of Socio-Economic Status Amongst White and Non Whites, in *Urban Schooling*, ed. Redman and Featherstone.

the established system on its own terms. As he perceives it, he has little power over his own destiny, including the outcome of his encounter with the white professional. Both parties perceive that the white professional has the upper hand—both in the larger society and in the specific encounter between them.

As a result of these conditions, there emerge two separate and distinct experiences, each somewhat unknown and alien to the other. It is this very quality of mutual strangeness which characterizes the initial black-white encounter. It may be camouflaged, denied, or rationalized. The void may be filled by stereotyped "knowledge" and preconceptions, but the essential unknownness remains. Not only are the two different, but, not having lived or known each other's differences, they can only speculate about them. They see each other and the world, and are in turn viewed and treated by the world, in different ways.

Thus separated by race, money, education, social position, power, and lack of real knowledge of and feeling for the other's life experience, the white professional and black client come together. They face each other and are confronted with the necessity of doing something together. The reactions they may have to each other and to the situation in which they find themselves are the dynamics of the encounter with which they must cope in order to work together. In essence, both professionals and clients are what they are, based upon their past experiences and the society in which they live and interact. They do not know each other; they do not trust each other. Indeed, they most probably have many feelings about each other, themselves, and their respective positions which in reality impede the development of trust and concomitant mutual honesty. First, there is suspiciousness and fear between them. "What is the other really thinking and feeling? What does he really want? What does he really mean? How much does he hate me, blame me, or want to con me? How can he hurt me or take advantage of me?" The phenomenon of fear and suspicion has been discussed and documented in many sources as coming from the black client.[6] It is an equally active dynamic for the the white worker. It is an inevitable consequence of the three basic factors already identified. This phenomenon is in part a reaction to, and in part a precipitator of, the fear and suspiciousness of the black client. It is both a defense and an offense. Regardless of whether the white professional is aware of it, the black client usually is.

There is also anger between them. Once again, much has been written, especially in recent years, of the rage that is felt by black people.[7] The white worker also feels anger of which he may or may not be aware. He may be angry at the black client for being so troubled, or helpless, or dependent, or

[6] Grier and Cobbs identify the fear and suspicion as a defense for survival and refer to it as "cultural paranoia . . . in which every white man is a potential enemy and every social system is set against him unless he personally finds out differently." See William H. Grier and Price M. Cobbs, *Black Rage* (New York: Bantam Books, 1969), p. 149.

[7] Grier and Cobbs, *Black Rage*, pp. 1–17, 152–67; and Charles Silberman, *Crisis in Black and White* (New York: Vintage Books, 1964), pp. 58–67.

hard to reach. He may be angry at himself for his inability to do very much to really help his client; or he may be angry at the client for being angry at him. The anger is there on some level. It is most likely that the client perceives it even if the worker does not.

There is also pain between them. This pain is one of the most complex dynamics because it stems from so many different sources. There is pain and suffering connected with whatever presenting problems caused the client to seek service. There is, of course, the underlying pain of being black in white America. There is also the pain felt by the worker in response to his client's pains and in reaction to them. In addition, there is the pain from the guilt felt by each party—guilt by the client at having problems with which he cannot cope and in being in a subordinate and powerless position—and guilt by the worker at having the feeling that he is somehow responsible for his client's problems or that he cannot really do anything to alleviate them. Most profoundly, there is guilt caused by repressed anger and other negative feelings experienced by both.

Furthermore, there is defensiveness and guardedness between them. Keeping each other at arm's length may decrease the hurt and danger, make them less vulnerable, and somehow ease the struggle. If they blame each other, perhaps they can avoid looking at themselves. If they have ready answers for all accusations, real or imagined, perhaps they need not really listen to each other or touch each other. If they try to relate by masking their feelings, perhaps they will be safer. They may deny, avoid, project, rationalize, internalize, externalize, or just plain lie. The defensiveness and guardedness between worker and client are of the encounter and are not characteristic of either worker or client. Rather, they become a reaction and an obstacle between them, which come out of the situation and must be perceived and dealt with as such. In a real sense, both worker and client are simultaneously victims and perpetuators of these obstacles.[8]

A Professional Vision

Nevertheless, there is hope. Despite the obstacles between them, worker and client do express a need for each other in the very act of coming together. The client requests some kind of help, and the worker and sponsoring agency

[8] For good discussions on the white professional and black client relationship, see Julia Block, The White Worker and the Negro Client in Psychotherapy, *Social Work*, 13: 36–42 (April 1968); Dorcas Bowles, Making Casework Relevant to Black People: Approaches, Techniques, Theoretical Implications, *Child Welfare*, 48: 468–75 (October 1969); Esther Fibush, The White Worker and the Negro Client, *Social Casework*, 46: 271–78 (May 1965); Esther Fibush and BeAlva Turnquest, A Black and White Approach to the Problem of Racism, *Social Casework*, 51: 459–66 (October 1970); Jean Gochros, Recognition and Use of Anger in Negro Clients, *Social Work*, 2: 28–34 (January 1966); Harold Rosen and Jerome Frank, Negroes in Psychotherapy, *American Journal of Psychiatry*, 119: 456–80 (November 1962); and Barbara F. Shannon, Implications of White Racism for Social Work Practice, *Social Casework*, 51: 270–76 (May 1970).

indicate a willingness to try to provide it. This force pulling them toward each other even while myriad counter forces are pulling them apart may be seen as a potential underlying symbiotic attachment between worker and client.[9] William Schwartz has postulated a "symbiotic" relationship between the individual and society:

> ... each needing the other for its own life and growth, and each reaching out to the other with all the strength it can command at a given moment ... [based on] ... the person's urge to belong to society as a full and productive member and the society's ability to provide certain specific means for integrating its people and enriching their social contributions.[10]

This formulation suggests that a fully realized and healthy society can develop only through fully realized and healthy people and that to the extent that any segment of the population is diminished, total society suffers. It is therefore in the interest of the whole society to enable every single member to become fulfilled and productive, and it is in the interest of every individual member to have a healthy society in which he can grow. On the other hand, a counter potential also exists—one in which the relationship can become parasitic and mutually destructive. These potentials represent two extremes on a theoretical continuum, neither of which exists completely in a real society. A part of one potential, however, coexists with a part of the other in any given situation. The question to resolve is: Toward which potential do we want to strive?

In the specific encounter between the white worker and black client, occurring in an admittedly imperfect and sometimes destructive society, there is still potential for a symbiotic relationship. It is found in the fact that the worker is employed by an agency that has been charged with the responsibility of serving people who have difficulty obtaining and utilizing society's resources. Concomitantly, lower-class black people in need of assistance are encouraged to look to these agencies to provide the needed services. Thus, there is a direct societal mandate for workers and clients to attain a goal together. This goal may or may not be realized, and the forces impeding it are tremendous. However, because such a symbiotic potential exists— because the racist, master-slave, parasitic microcosm can be countered by a mutual need, mutual aid microcosm—the potential can begin to be uncovered and realized through a professional orientation.

The orientation envisions the helping process as a mutual endeavor between active participants, each trying to reach and touch each other in the giving and using of help. This emphasis on mutuality is crucial because it counters the superiority-inferiority dynamic within the relationship. It says that it takes *both* participants to do the job—that they are equally important, that they must listen to each other, that they must recognize each other's rights and responsibilities, and that they must respect each other.

---

[9] *Webster's New International Dictionary*, 3d ed., s.v. "symbiotic."

[10] William Schwartz, The Social Worker in the Group, in *New Perspectives on Services to Groups: Theory Organization and Practice* (New York: National Association of Social Workers, 1961), p. 15.

The notion of active participation directed toward reaching and touching each other emphasizes the emotional engagement deemed necessary for the accomplishment of real work. It sets up a demand for involvement, sharing, and feedback between white worker and black client in opposition to passive or secret observation and analysis. This part of the vision attempts to counter the forces of isolation, alienation, and unknownness. It says, "Get in there and do, open up, make mistakes, express what you are feeling and thinking." It also encourages the worker actively to support the client's desire and efforts to combat the social conditions affecting his life by struggling beside him. It says that the worker cannot be an uninvolved outsider who ignores or minimizes those societal factors that contribute to his client's problems. What is envisioned is an endeavor in which client and worker jointly tackle relevant social problems in contrast to the situation depicted in Kenneth Clark's indictment of unhelpful professionals.

> The pervasive need to turn one's back on any clear evidence of man's inhumanity to man exemplified in the cool objective approach is possibly most clearly seen . . . in the detached professionalism of many social workers. . . . Some members of these helping fields too often define as objectivity, what to the client, feels more like insensitivity. Furthermore, in their preoccupation with the problem of the individuals and their insistence upon reducing him to a manageable system of assumptions, the disturbing and dehumanizing social realities behind his personal agonies may be avoided.[11]

The foundation of this professional orientation is the belief that the black client has the right and capacities to determine what he wants to do and the strength to move himself in that direction. With this perspective, the worker does not set himself up as the omniscient expert trying to direct or control his client. Carl Rogers states that "it is the client who knows what hurts, what directions to go, what problems are crucial, what experiences have been deeply buried."[12] The worker reaches for what lies within the black client—his desires, dreams, aspirations, strengths, creativity. It is the client's life; he must live it in his own way. The worker struggles to become a source of help, a resource to be used by the client as he grows. If the worker really believes in the client, he can lend himself in the encounter without having to impose himself. Thus, the potential conflict between different value systems—between different judgments of right and wrong, sickness and health—is mitigated. Such judgments are basically irrelevant. What matters is the client's choices and the development of his ability to recognize his options and take advantage of them.

The worker can give of himself freely, offering his knowledge, opinions, and feelings. He can also offer a vision of how things might be different for the client by affirming the client's right and ability to use what he wants on his own terms. Thus, the vision emphasizes the client as his own person, making his own way. This vision contrasts with a view of the black client

---

[11] Clark, *Dark Ghetto*, p. 77.
[12] Carl Rogers, *On Becoming A Person* (Boston: Houghton Mifflin, 1970), pp. 11–12.

as powerless, submissive, inferior, or someone to be led by the expert. The worker strives to stay with the client as he offers his faith in the client himself.

> Can I meet this other individual as a person who is in process of *becoming*, or will I be bound by his past and by my present? If, in my encounter with him, I am dealing with him as an immature child, an ignorant student, a neurotic personality . . . each of these concepts of mine limits what he can be in the relationship. If I accept the other person as something fixed, already diagnosed and classified, already shaped by his past, then I am doing my part to confirm this limited hypothesis. If I accept him as a process of *becoming* then I am doing what I can to confirm or make real his potentialities.[13]

Finally, the orientation is essentially a *human* one in which white worker and black client struggle to gain the freedom to reveal themselves as real human beings. It is based on the belief that growth occurs primarily through interaction between real people who have weaknesses and strengths, flaws and attributes, and who can benefit by revealing them and coming to grips with them and each other.

> Crisis, shock, confrontation, resistance, struggle, rejection, defeat as well as joy, silence, the excitement of discovery, the peaceful smile, the gesture of affirmation and growth—all these enter into the process of therapy in which real persons rather than ghosts engage in the challenging struggle of wills and the ennobling pursuit of meaning and value in living.[14]

The orientation challenges the unknownness between worker and client by demanding that their feelings—including the rage, fear, and mistrust— be shared and squarely faced. If the pain is avoided, the humanness is avoided; life is deadened; black client and white worker remain apart, relating to each other only through masks. The obstacles between them grow because they are not confronted; they destroy all potential for real help to be given or received. Only when the risks are taken, when the pain is felt and lived through, when there is struggle and confrontation, when black client and white worker open themselves to each other, can they be freed to experience the caring that can be between them.

> The essential ingredient is the capacity of the therapist to love his patient— to say to him that . . . you have a listener and companion who wants you to make it. If you must weep, I'll wipe your tears. If you must hit someone, hit me, I can take it. I will, in fact, do *anything* to help you be what you can be—my love for you is of such an order.[15]

Case Illustration

The following excerpts illustrate the struggles of one white social worker and one black client to begin to establish a helping relationship based on mutual honesty and trust. The focus on the helping relationship does not

---

[13] Ibid., p. 55.
[14] Clark Moustakas, *Existential Child Therapy* (New York: Basic Books, 1966), p. 3.
[15] Grier and Cobbs, *Black Rage*, p. 180.

imply that the development of this relationship was the primary concern of worker and client. Rather, the central focus was, and had to be, the services desired by the client and the joint efforts of worker and client to meet the client's needs. However, aside from specific concrete assistance which could be offered somewhat impersonally, the major part of their work together involved struggling with intimate and painful problems and necessitated a sharing, honesty, and trust between worker and client. Thus, the helping relationship was the vehicle through which service could be offered. The excerpts selected trace the course of the work between client and worker, highlighting both the obstacles within the encounter and the efforts made to deal with these obstacles.

Mrs. R, a thirty-year-old, black mother of seven children, called the neighborhood social service office to request help in finding summer camps for her older children. The worker receiving the call was a twenty-two-year-old, unmarried white woman. After discussing the request briefly on the telephone, the worker offered to gather information on camps and to meet with the client in her home to discuss the matter further.

The Struggle for Mutuality

From the beginning, the worker emphasized the need to develop a mutual definition of what was needed, ways to proceed, and expectations of each other. Her reason was to let Mrs. R know that they would have to be real partners in the endeavor in order to get anywhere and that neither one could impose a point of view upon the other. This beginning was an attempt immediately to challenge the potential obstacles of distance and power differential. These obstacles, although present in every helping relationship, are heightened in the black-white encounter because of institutionalized racial attitudes in America. The worker realized that she would have to demonstrate that she really meant her words of mutuality by listening for subtle cues, drawing out critical responses, and guarding against pushing Mrs. R into actions about which she might be hesitant.

> WORKER: I brought Mrs. R information about camp for the children and talked enthusiastically about their going. She seemed pleased but began anticipating that things might be wrong with the camp. At first, I tried to explain away all her objections; then I realized she might have mixed feelings about sending them to camp or might fear I was trying to railroad her into just any camp. I tried to draw out this feeling by saying that maybe all these questions on her mind made her unsure about wanting to send the children away to camp. She said she did want them to go but only to a good camp. I added, "And one you can see for yourself is good, not just because someone says it." She smiled and said she had to make sure. I said that I was glad she checked me before I started running away with my enthusiasm and that it certainly was up to her to get all the information and make the final decision on which camp was best.

The client responded to the worker's efforts to extend herself—willingness to work in Mrs. R's own home, promptness in gathering camp information, and responsiveness to Mrs. R's wishes—by beginning to share some of her other concerns. These concerns included Mrs. R's despair about her severe obesity and her desire to obtain a homemaker so that she could enter an inpatient weight reduction program, her difficulties with her ten-year-old son who had been expelled from school and was frequently in trouble in the community, her sense of being overwhelmed by the demands of raising seven children without a consistently available husband and father, and her struggle to survive the strain of coping with the institutions impinging on her life—welfare, schools, housing.

The worker made an offer of help with these concerns, trying to present an intensive, flexible service that Mrs. R could make use of in her own way. Although no attempt was made to deal with racial factors explicitly in the early sessions, the worker made every effort to set a tone of partnership, respect, and getting to know each other which would challenge the potential obstacles of the black-white encounter.

> WORKER: After about an hour (at the third interview) I said, "Listen, I want to ask you about an idea I've been thinking about, and I hope you will be able to let me know what you really think about it." I asked her about the possibility of my using my last few months at social service to get her really started in help for herself and her family, by seeing her three times a week and being available to her for a variety of services: just talking, helping in meetings with such other agencies as housing and management, helping her with physical tasks, or figuring out problems about the children. She smiled and said no one ever had done this for her before. I said I wanted to lend a hand to her efforts and maybe things could be worked out better for her. She then began talking about past workers who had tried to help her and how little they had accomplished. I said that I heard a warning, like the one she had made once before, that we should not get our hopes up because nothing could be done.
>
> She sighed and said no one ever really did anything for her. I said I could understand that it often seemed hopeless and maybe it seemed too much even to try again. She said that maybe this time would be different. I agreed, but hearing her express this hope worried me that she might expect the impossible of me or become angry or frustrated if changes took a long time. She laughed and said sometimes she became angry at her worker. I said she had a right to get angry and could at me, but still we could not accomplish miracles and maybe she would be disappointed again. She said, "I know, just one step at a time." I said I thought it was not much, but it was all we had. She said, "That and more nerves than brains." We both laughed.

The specific course of the work was guided by the nature of the problems being tackled by worker and client. If concrete assistance or material goods were needed, the worker lent her efforts to the client's own attempts to obtain them. If outside systems or institutions needed to be dealt with to obtain better services for the client, worker and client strategized together, with the worker accompanying the client, whenever necessary, to lend support, skills, and influence. If the client was struggling with personal and family problems, the worker offered help with these problems.

Always, the emphasis was on the task at hand and developing the best ways for worker and client to work together to deal with the tasks before them. The obstacles and tensions within the black-white encounter were viewed as potential impediments to a successful service and therefore had to be confronted and challenged in order for the work to proceed.

Emphasizing through Honest Sharing

Having decided, however tentatively, that they wanted to try to work together, black client and white worker had to struggle to begin to close the gap of distance and unknownness that separated them. They had to risk revealing themselves, thereby becoming more vulnerable, but also more human and accessible to each other. In defining themselves for what they were and how they felt, worker and client were confronted by their real differences—not only in race, but in class, education, social position, and outlook on life. This was a painful, halting process. There was no right way to do it. In the struggle, a bond began to develop between them.

> WORKER: We talked a while longer and I had to leave. As I stood up she said, "That's a nice dress, you look good today. Are you gonna meet your boyfriend?" I thanked her but must have appeared embarrassed. She said, "Why do you always get embarrassed when I ask about your boyfriend?" I was silent a few seconds, and then said that she was right in sensing that I did get embarrassed. I said I was not sure why, but thought it might be because I did not feel I should share my personal life with her since I was there to help her. She said maybe if she knew I had problems, she wouldn't think about her own so much. I said maybe that was true but it wouldn't help her work on her problems to think about mine. She said, "You have problems? Don't kid me." I asked, "Do you believe I don't have problems as you have?" She agreed. I said that I knew she thought I had a better life than she had and was more fortunate, and in many ways it was true.
>
> I said that sometimes I guess she'd resent me for it because I was in a position to help her, and she might wish that the tables were turned. She smiled a knowing smile and said that such a situation would be nice. Then she asked, "You do have some problems, don't you?" I said that I did and I guessed all people had problems, although they might be of a different nature. She said that she sometimes felt life was bad only for her and that she wished others had their share too. I said it was natural to feel that way, especially when things were going bad for her. I said it was all right even when she wished I would find life a little difficult.
>
> One day she asked me where she could buy inexpensive beds (two of her children needed beds). I suggested a large department store. Mrs. R howled, slapped me on the back, and said, "Girl, you are crazy." Her friend joined in the laughter. Then they informed me about the prices at the store. I admitted I had never shopped for beds and was just guessing. I felt embarrassed by my ignorance and guilty that I had never had to learn to shop with as little money as she had to do. I did not know what to say, yet it seemed all right to say nothing.

Confronting Anger and Suspiciousness

If there was to be real honesty between them, worker and client had to face the painful areas of negative feelings in the relationship. Especially in a black-white encounter in which anger, tensions, and fears are almost built into the situation, an attempt to deny or avoid them would have implied that the relationship could not withstand them and that honesty had to be limited to "nice" feelings. Moreover, when it really came down to the basic issues, they still had to "play the game" with each other. Making this black-white experience different necessitated squarely acknowledging the negative feelings. This acknowledgement was a difficult task, and at times the worker's own apprehension prevented her from tackling it. Nevertheless, the necessary direction remained clear even when it was not successfully followed.

WORKER: Then she began talking about another social worker, an investigator she had known. She said she liked them mean and rough; then she could hate them and know they were enemies and that there was to be a battle. She said the nice ones were sneakier and they double-crossed one with a smile. I asked, "Do you always have the feeling that you can't trust anyone, that behind the smile they don't like you and will double-cross you?" She said the worst thing was that the smile cooled off her anger and took her off guard. I said, "That sounds as if it could mean me, at least sometimes. I know you're still afraid to trust me and I have a good idea of the reason, since you have been let down so often."

I said that I also knew that sometimes when she was angry, I cooled her off by being nice. I cited a recent incident when I had not visited when she expected me and then I telephoned to say I was sorry, so that she didn't feel she could scold me after that. She laughed and said, "You are something else, you even remembered that." I said I thought she did too. I asked if she had been very angry at me then. She laughed and asked, "What do you think?" I replied, "But you couldn't show it or tell me?" She said it didn't seem worth the effort, and then I had called to apologize. We both smiled at this "cooling out" piece. I said that maybe now that we have talked, it will be easier for her to tell me next time I upset her or make her angry or make her feel any kind of way. She nodded and said, "Maybe it will."

During the next half hour, the sarcastic exchanges that seemed to mask deep feelings were very frequent. First she said, "I hear you have a maid—like a rich kid." I said I guess sometimes she thought of me as a rich person. She laughed and said she didn't, but she knew I surely was not poor and couldn't know how hard it was for poor people. I said that was true, and sometimes it would bother her, that maybe life was better for me and that was one reason I could help her. She said that I was a "do-gooder."

At this time I should have picked up her anger, but I did not. I said I just wanted to help her and her children if I could. Then she said, "I bet you'll leave here as soon as you can get something easy." I said that I guessed she thought that I wanted to leave as soon as I could. She said, "Sure you do, you're just here to get experience, like the student teachers. I don't blame you." She went on to say that she would do the same thing in my place and go where it was easier.

I asked if it would make any difference if I said it wasn't true for me, that if I could get a job here, I would stay. What I meant was that my words would not change the feelings she had about me. However, she said, "Sure if it's true, say it; I don't think you are a liar." I said, "What I mean is that some part of you does think I'll pick up and run to a nice rich area in the suburbs as soon as I can get out of here, and just my words won't really affect that." She laughed and said, "Well, you will go back to the suburbs, won't you?" I said I could see how angry she was about the possibility that I might leave her. She said that she wasn't angry but that she just knew how it was. I said that I presumed that all people who helped her eventually left her. She could not respond to this statement, but again asked if I was leaving. I said that I had told her before that I would be leaving in May—not because I wanted to, but because my job here was over. I realized that by making excuses I was cooling her out but I could not tolerate her anger and sadness coupled with my own.

Challenging Racial Obstacles

Although racial position and attitudes were deeply entwined in every experience and feeling between worker and client, it was important in the course of the work to confront the racial dynamic explicitly. Again this area was painful, and the temptation to avoid it and feign "color-blindness" was great. The worker had to demonstrate her own willingness to reveal her racial attitudes before Mrs. R would risk sharing hers. It was crucial that worker and client relate directly to themselves as white and black and not discuss race on a theoretical plane, denying its impact on themselves and their work together. Only by facing their differences and trying to share the meaning of their own black and white experiences could they begin to bridge the gap of racial distance and unknownness.

WORKER: Mrs. R said that the only other person she had ever talked to a long time ago was Miss O, a social worker, and she was different too. I asked if she were black or white. She said she was white, then stopped to think and said, "I'd never have believed I could talk like this to a white person." She said that the way white people treat colored people made her angry. She said it made her angry that she had to call white ladies "Miss" and they called her "girl" or "Frances." She said, "If you're white, you're right, if you're black, stay back."

I said that blacks did have a pretty bad deal in America and I would expect her to be angry and bitter. She said life was difficult for a black person and the whites never let them pick themselves up. She added that mixed marriages made her furious because it was "like the black needed the white to get ahead." She commented that it just infuriated her to see an interracial couple in the street. I asked her why she felt so strongly about it, as if it were a personal insult. Mrs. R replied, "Listen, it is an insult. My mother looked white and I was the black child of the white mother and that was a terrible feeling."

She began talking about herself and how she had never had a break in life. Then she said, "Colored people never get much—no decent jobs, no education, nothing." I said I knew it was very rough to be black in America. She said, "It's rougher than you could know, you just can't imagine." I said, "I guess you're saying I really can't know how it is, how it feels, what it's like to be black because I'm white." She said that was true and that the black people had it worse than any others; they just received a rotten deal from the whites. I said, "I'm one of the whites; does it bother you sometimes that I have more than you, that I can't even begin to know how life is for you?" She said, "No it doesn't bother me, that's life." Then she paused and said, "Yes it does bother me, it bothers me a great deal. The whites can do anything and get away with it, but let a black man or a black child make a slip and they get the works!"

She continued, "And you know the worst part is when the northern whites make like they care, and we know they don't. At least in the South they're honest; they hate us and they say it." I said, "I guess I fit in here too; I am one of the whites who acts as though she cares, and you're not sure whether I do. Maybe you are not even sure if I don't hate you." She shrugged and we were both silent. I said it was hard to get that out and now we felt uncomfortable, but it was good that we had made a start in talking about this subject—her feelings about being black and my being white did matter, and so did my feelings, and we should try to share them.

Challenging the Sense of Worthlessness and Hopelessness

The intensity of pain and hardship suffered by Mrs. R was sometimes enough to overwhelm both worker and client and caused both to experience despair, defeat, hopelessness, worthlessness, self-blame, and guilt—all obstacles to productive work together. While the worker was struggling to deal with these feelings within herself, she also had to show Mrs. R her faith in her and her vision of hope and progress for her. At the same time, she had to guard against making empty declarations of concern or minimizing Mrs. R's tremendous burdens. The worker had to show sincere concern. By letting Mrs. R's pain touch her, by opening herself to the closeness between them, and by staying with Mrs. R through difficult times, the worker showed that she cared, that Mrs. R mattered to her, and that she believed in what Mrs. R could accomplish.

WORKER: I did not try to talk her out of her sadness. When she seemed to have run dry and looked to me, I said, "For a while I guess you'll just feel totally hopeless and not even have the energy to try to do something but after a time this hopelessness will get less and your stronger part will come out, and then I'll ask you what you want to do." She showed a spark of anger and said," *Do*, there's nothing that can be done." I said I didn't believe that and knew that some part of her didn't believe it either and would want at least to try. She challenged me and said, "You tell me what to do, how to make all the problems go away." I said, "Now you are challenging me to do the impossible and I can not. Let us pick one problem and try to work on that." She began discussing her obesity—the embarrassment, physical discomfort, and her resulting isolation. As she gave vent to these feelings, she started to think of ways to deal with the problem—specifically, inpatient weight reduction programs. We began to think through the steps needed to get her into one of these programs.

Mrs. R indicated the way she would like all the arrangements to be made and we began developing strategies for proceeding. At one point I said to her, "Listen, I've never fooled you up to now, and I'll try not to as we work together. We both know it will be very difficult for you to lose weight and begin to make things better for yourself and your children; however, something about you makes me believe in you and your ability to do it and get some of that better life you want." She was silent for a while and then said, "No one ever said that to me before."

As I stood up I must have sighed because she said, "You're gonna go crazy, taking my problems so seriously." I asked if she meant I shouldn't take her problems seriously because they weren't my own. She said social workers never really cared about their clients; they just listened and nodded and then forgot. I was silent for a few seconds and then I said, "I have to care, I know you and I have feelings for you." She was stunned and said, "You know, I think you're really telling the truth." I asked, "Did you think no one could really care about you?" She said she didn't think anyone ever really did. She kept marveling, almost talking to herself. She said, "You really did something; I just told you about that money and expected you'd forget about it and then you go and think about it and even tell your supervisor and then you come up and do something. You really did something for me." She repeated, "I think you really care." I could only nod. As I walked through the door she said, "You know, if you don't change; I mean, if you somehow manage not to get hardened so that you hear so many problems that they don't mean a thing, you're going to be a good social worker."

Contact as Real Human Beings

Through it all, Mrs. R and her worker were just two people—of different race, class, social position, background and fortune—but still just two people struggling, against tremendous obstacles, to do a job together. They accomplished no miracles, overturned no oppressive structures, proved no major point, and left no lasting mark upon the world. Although they had a great impact upon each other, they were not really changed in dramatic or visible ways. They continued to function in their own worlds, in their own ways, separated by so much, and still scarred by the racism of America. However, because of their step-by-step efforts, they began to make a dent on the terrible problems that had previously overwhelmed Mrs. R and on the feelings of helplessness and powerlessness that had made her believe things could never be any different. They made only a beginning. They struggled and suffered and shared and fought and loved and cried. With every moment of profound and intimate sharing, they reaffirmed the potential of two human beings to reach and touch each other.

WORKER: I winced and Mrs. R noticed it. She said, "I guess you think I'm a bad mother." I said, "I know you saw me react when you yelled at Tony and I won't lie to you. I don't think you're a bad mother, but it bothered me to hear the way you talked to him. It bothers me even more because I know that's not really how you are or how you want to be. When you talk to me you come across so differently. I believe you want to be a good mother and want to give them something good. However, when you let all your anger and hurt come out on them, you're hurting them and going against what you really want." She was silent and I said, "Maybe you're thinking, 'Who is she to tell me these things; she doesn't know how miserable it is and what a poor life I've gotten stuck with.' " She replied, "That's true, you don't know, so it's easy for you to talk, but still I don't always want to yell and be mean to the kids. It's just that sometimes I get so angry that things are like this for us that I'm afraid that if I beat them I'll kill them so I try to yell and let the anger out so I won't hit them so much."

I said that I had some idea what it must feel like, although I couldn't feel it as she could—how just seeing the children reminded her of all she wanted for them and couldn't give them, and also how they prevented her from having freedom and the things she needed in her own life. She shook her head slowly and there was pain in her eyes, "That's some of it; there's so much more; I'll try to let you know how it is."

We talked about her needing help to manage all her problems and her large family. I supported her feeling that it was not her fault that she needed help and that her problems were real and very serious. She told me about the group she had been in at the mental health clinic because her social worker there believed it would be good for her to have something to do and people to talk to other than her children. Then she found it was a group for recently released hospital patients many of whom were still psychotic. They talked to themselves and sometimes lost sight of reality for moments. She said she was very frightened by them and also upset that she was placed in a group with them. She said, "Look, I know I'm nuts, but I'm not that nuts. Maybe someday I will be, but let me get there in my own time. When I have a nervous breakdown, I want it to be my very own and not taught to me by members of my therapy group!"

I literally howled at this speech. She was very pleased that I responded in this way, and we both laughed. I said I knew she wasn't really kidding and had a great deal of serious feelings about this problem, especially about being crazy, but she'd said it in such a great way, seeing the comedy of the situation, that I had to laugh. She said, "Sometimes if you don't laugh at ridiculous but painful situations, you just go nuts." I said, "You know I'm glad you let me see this part of you, the part that can laugh and be warm even in the midst of pain." She said, "You know, I'm glad we can laugh together."

Conclusion

The writers have identified those critical societal conditions of institutional racism, social distance, and mutual unknownness that profoundly influence the white professional–black client encounter. In this encounter, as in society, it is the white professional who has the perceived and defined power, status, and control. This predefined, institutionalized role relationship triggers deep feelings of mistrust, anger, fear, pain, and resentment within both worker and client. These feelings represent potential obstacles to the development of a helping relationship through which desired services can be delivered. Certain kinds of social services, such as assisting in budget preparation or making referrals, may be effectively offered without the establishment of a helping relationship. However, when desired services involve more complex needs and deeply felt and intimate struggles, the helping relationship becomes a crucial vehicle. Moreover, this relationship can be effective only to the extent that it is open, trusting, and real. Thus, those obstacles that impede the development of such a helping relationship must be dealt with by worker and client in order for them to work successfully together.

The writers have attempted to define some of the specific obstacles within the white professional–black client encounter and have offered a way of approaching and dealing with them. The writers do not suggest that the basic social problems involved in institutional racism will be mitigated through the described frame of reference or social work skills. To provide an effective and needed service to the black client does not change the society in which he must continue to live. To the extent that some segment of a black client's life can change and become more satisfactory to himself, however, something significant has been accomplished. The primary proposition is that by challenging the obstacles of the white professional–black client encounter and by working in such a manner that worker and client can build a helping relationship based on trust and honesty, the client can begin to demand and receive more of those services he needs and desires.

The specific case illustration demonstrates how a deepening helping relationship—in which both worker and client struggled against the obstacles keeping them apart to make themselves known, real, and available to each other—freed the client to demand and make use of ever more extensive and intensive services. By developing trust in the worker, the client was able to demand a variety of services. She obtained country camp placement for her older children, secured minimum standards from the Department of Social

Services, and developed a more successful working relationship with the Department of Social Services worker. She also improved communication with her housing manager, clarified the fine system and successfully challenged several situations in which fines had been incorrectly levied, gained reinstatement of her son in public school, was admitted into an inpatient weight reduction program, and obtained homemaker service for her children. In addition, she was enabled to open new avenues of understanding and exchange among family members, develop a greater emphasis on dealing with family problems without violence and recriminations, and begin to deal with deep sources of family tension.

In essence, the client's acquisition of entitled services was always the major emphasis, rather than the work on the obstacles in their relationship. However, only to the extent that the worker and client were able to "reach and touch each other as real human beings" was it possible for genuine services to be delivered.

A Black and White Approach to the Problem of Racism

Esther Fibush and BeAlva Turnquest

The basic commitment of casework is a dual one—to both the social and the psychological approaches to human problems. Because of this commitment, "a diagnosis of an individual's unhappiness ... cannot ignore a diagnosis of the sickness of society and what it is doing to the person's life."[1] There can be no doubt that white racism qualifies as major social pathology in the United States. Its significance to the lives of its black victims has been powerfully documented, and there is increasing recognition of its contribution to the problems of other minority groups.[2]

From the environmental standpoint, racism is expressed in political, socioeconomic, and cultural institutions that enable the dominant white group to promote its own material interests at the expense of other groups. From the psychological standpoint, it is expressed in a number of related attitudes whereby white individuals attempt to promote their own psychic security through an assumed superiority to members of other groups. Racism

Reprinted from *Social Casework,* Vol. 51 (October, 1970), pp. 459–466, by permission of the authors and the Family Service Association of America.

[1] Bertha C. Reynolds, The Social Casework of an Uncharted Journey, *Social Work,* 9: 16 (October 1964).

[2] Documentation exists in great variety, dating back to abolition days. A noteable recent addition to the literature is William H. Grier and Price M. Cobbs, *Black Rage* (New York: Basic Books, 1968).

is thus not only a means by which white people maintain a very real environmental advantage but also a mechanism for attempting to maintain a psychological advantage.[3]

Racist attitudes in individuals both arise from and contribute to racist institutions. In the treatment situation, the caseworker sees the ways in which the social pathology is interwoven with individual psychopathology. Although psychological racism takes a variety of forms and serves a variety of purposes, depending on both the social and the individual dynamics involved, it always includes the assertion of an assumed superiority on the basis of race. Identification with one's own racial group does not in itself constitute racism. Racism arises when racial identity is seen and used as a mark of superiority or inferiority inherent in a person by reason of his racial group membership. Racism ranges from overt white supremacist attitudes to various covert attitudes, including unconscious fantasies about imagined racial characteristics.

Institutionalized racism is a flagrant wrong and must be eliminated through social and political action. Casework treatment is in no way a substitute for such change, nor is the caseworker excused from participating in advocacy or activism when these are indicated. In his daily practice, however, the caseworker remains primarily a therapist and a clinician. In this capacity he conducts with the client, white or black, a search for mental health that rejects the concept of superiority or inferiority on the basis of color.

There have been numerous studies of the social and psychological factors associated with prejudice in white people.[4] There has also been some discussion of the impact of racism on the treatment of white patients by black therapists.[5] The scarcity of literature by white caseworkers on the subject of white racist clients suggests that there has been avoidance, denial, or repression of a painful subject. Caseworkers have concentrated a great deal of attention on the black victims of racism. It seems high time that more attention be given its white carriers.

---

[3] The concept of racism used here is formulated from several sources. It rests in a general way on Gordon W. Allport, *The Nature of Prejudice* (Cambridge, Mass.: Addison-Wesley, 1954). It is also influenced by Stokely Carmichael and Charles V. Hamilton, *Black Power: The Politics of Liberation in America* (New York: Vintage Books, 1967); and by Whitney M. Young, Jr., *Beyond Racism* (New York: McGraw-Hill, 1969).

[4] See T. W. Adorno et al., *The Authoritarian Personality* (New York: Harper & Brothers, 1950); George Simpson and J. Milton Yinger, *Racial and Cultural Minorities: An Analysis of Prejudice and Discrimination* (New York: Harper & Brothers, 1958); and Bruno Bettelheim and Morris Janowitz, *Social Change and Prejudice* (New York: Free Press of Glencoe, 1964).

[5] See Leonard C. Simmons, "Crow Jim": Implications for Social Work, *Social Work*, 8: 24–30 (July 1963); and Andrew E. Curry, The Negro Worker and the White Client: A Commentary on the Treatment Relationship, *Social Casework*, 45: 131–36 (March 1964). From the standpoint of psychoanalytic psychotherapy, see interview with Dr. William H. Grier, A Negro Therapist Discusses Treating the White Patient, *Roche Report: Frontiers of Clinical Psychiatry*, 4: 5, 11 (March 15, 1967).

Clinical Study

This article is the outcome of a collaborative exploration into white racism by a black caseworker and a white caseworker. Its purpose was to understand the ways in which racism plays a part in the client's problems or defense against problems, in the interaction between client and caseworker, and in the caseworker's attitude toward the client. It was believed that the black-white relationship is a significant factor in casework treatment and might be used as an important tool in the treatment of white racist clients.[6]

The setting was a family service agency in a west coast urban community that has presently a minority population of 40 percent and a "minority" school population of approximately 70 percent. Although the agency continues to serve a substantial number of white middle-class clients, a survey conducted in February 1969 showed that minority clients constituted 44 percent of all clients seen, and that 22 percent of agency clients had incomes below the $4,000 "poverty" level, with another 32 percent at incomes below $7,000. It is an agency that has no present access to funds for financial assistance or to any other direct means of altering the environmental reality for economically deprived clients. It must, therefore, count heavily on what can be accomplished by casework alone.

Clients who come to a family agency are not representative of the population at large. They are a highly selected group—in large measure a self-selected one. They see themselves in need of a kind of help that their image of the family agency suggests will be offered them. Within this client population there are few white clients who express extreme racist attitudes, just as there are few black clients who express extreme hostility toward whites—this situation is doubtless a factor of the self-selection involved. Of this client population, a number of cases were examined from the standpoint of racism as a treatment consideration; some of them were chosen as case examples.[7]

Attention was given not only to the case material but also to the caseworkers' reaction to it and to their reaction to each other in the course of their discussion. Discussion was deliberately free-flowing, to encourage the expression of personal as well as professional reactions. There was a conscious effort to recognize factors related to racism wherever they were found—in client or caseworker, black or white—and to trace them to their psychological and social sources.

It became clear very quickly that there would be no simplistic application of either sociological or psychological concepts, that each case had its

---

[6] Curry, The Negro Worker and the White Client, p. 135.

[7] For the sake of simplicity, examples presented in this study are all of individual treatment cases. Both workers also carried cases in family group therapy and in joint marital counseling in which racism was a factor. The black worker also was conducting group therapy with two racially mixed groups in which, of course, racist attitudes played some part.

unique configuration of factors from both sources, and that the caseworker's interpretation might in itself be a stereotype of psychoanalytic, sociological, or personal derivation. Discussion between caseworkers provided a check on each other's assumptions, with the black worker speaking from the standpoint of a black life experience and the white worker from that of a white life experience.

As a working hypothesis for this study, racism in the white client was defined as a defense mechanism indicative of the individual's failure to achieve a sense of identity as a human being of dignity and worth. It was seen as being used primarily in defense against anxiety-provoking feelings of inferiority or inadequacy, shame or guilt. It was thought also to exist in a latent state, coming to conscious awareness or overt expression when other, more habitual modes of defense were threatened.

This definition of racism was adopted for purposes of casework treatment and may or may not have wider application. It represents primarily an effort to find a more therapeutic approach to racism in white clients than just to deplore it.

Some Case Examples

There were many white clients with whom the subject of race did not seem to need discussion. Some of these clients were obviously so engrossed in other problems in their lives that it would have been inappropriate to introduce the subject. Others had already begun to come to grips with the problem of racism and were actively combating it in some way, so that discussion would have been superfluous. A few white clients brought up the subject of race with the black worker; there were others, however, with whom the caseworker felt an undercurrent of feeling that suggested that the matter of color be brought into the open.

The purpose in discussing the subject was primarily to free the treatment situation from unnecessary anger and guilt arising from avoidance or denial of the difference in color. It was found that whenever it was possible to discuss the black-white confrontation with a white client (whenever, that is, the subject was not too threatening to the client), the discussion proved to be ego-strengthening. Not only did it free emotional energy for the pursuit of treatment, but it often enabled the client to grapple with other, more realistically threatening situations in his life. The need for such discussion did not arise with the white caseworker, but it was felt that the coincidental advantage of the opportunity to explore and help the client understand the meaning of a special kind of emotional encounter was thereby lost.

The person-to-person encounter between black worker and white client means different things to different clients. For some it is so highly charged emotionally that the worker's blackness becomes a paramount factor in treatment. Such was the case with Miss G.

Miss G was a young white woman who was described by the white intake worker as attractive and articulate, with a problem involving the excessive use of fantasy but with no apparant difficulty entering into a casework relationship. Miss G was assigned to the black worker, who immediately noticed that Miss G was acting out some fantasied role in the casework setting just as she did in her real life situation. During the first treatment hour, the black worker felt that her blackness was interfering in some way, but she did not feel sure enough of this appraisal to bring it up during the session. Miss G canceled her second appointment.

In the next session, Miss G plunged into a discussion of her feelings about black people, her surprise at the worker's being black, and her fear that she might inadvertently say something offensive to the worker. Exploring these remarks, the worker found that some of Miss G's feelings were attributable to her lack of contact with black people and her considerable contact with white people who spoke of black people in a derogatory way. Surprisingly, in this area Miss G had not made use of fantasy, and exploration of the subject of black-white relationships proved to be her first venture into a search for authenticity.

In this instance, the black-white encounter precipitated the client into a "real" relationship in which she had to grapple honestly with authentic feelings, thus bypassing the habitual defense system and laying the groundwork for the development of healthy ego-functioning.

There are some white clients who appear to have such deep feelings of empathy with black people that one would expect to find them actively engaged in combating racism. When in fact they are not so engaged, the black caseworker might well suspect an effort at ingratiation. This is not always the case, however, as exemplified by Mrs. T.

Mrs. T's problem was her inability to take action. She suffered from anxiety about her own aggression and was unable to assert herself or even to express her feelings in most situations. This was especially true in her marriage, and it was the marriage that was the focus of casework treatment. As Mrs. T gained insight into her problem, she was delighted to find herself openly and freely expressing disagreement on racial issues with her covertly and sometimes overtly racist acquaintances.

At the other extreme, there are white clients who show evidence of deep feelings of anger and hatred toward black people, yet can accept psychological help from a black caseworker.

Mr. S came to the agency reluctantly at the urging of a relative. He was entertaining ideas of suicide and had, over a period of several months, almost starved himself to death. His depression had been precipitated when his wife of many years had left him for another man. Mr. S told of the many plans he had in mind to kill this man. There was something about the way Mr. S talked that prompted the worker to ask if the "other man" had been black. Mr. S confirmed this and added that he had to admit that it was this fact that prompted such murderous feelings.

Having been helped to bring this emotionally fraught matter into the open, Mr. S was able to continue the interview in a more spontaneous way. Because the black caseworker had reacted to him with positive subjective feelings, a rapport was established that enabled Mr. S to recognize his need for treatment and made it possible for him to follow through on the worker's referral to a clinic. One might speculate that the black worker's ability to accept Mr. S's racist feelings provided relief from his immobilizing anger and guilt, freeing him from his obsessive murderous fantasies sufficiently to seek the psychiatric treatment he needed.

The white client may initially have a greater feeling of safety with a black caseworker than with a white worker. Ironically, this sense of trust arises in part from the inferior position imposed upon the black person in a white-dominated society. Moreover, because the black worker may seem at so great a social distance from the realities of his own life, the white client may experience an additional feeling of safety. As treatment progresses, however, there may be development of regressive transference with all its hostile negative elements.

Mrs. L was divorced from her husband but continued to cling to him through a variety of manipulative maneuvers that indicated a severe dependency problem. She was assigned to a white worker and responded to supportive treatment by making some progress toward more independent functioning. The basic problem went untouched, however, and when the white worker left the agency, Mrs. L felt she needed to continue. She asked to be assigned to the black worker who had seen her at intake. This worker had initially had a negative reaction to Mrs. L although Mrs. L had not at that time expressed any racist attitudes.

When the black worker shifted from a simple supportive role to a focus on the intense dependency needs, the negative transference came to the fore, and with it all the previously concealed racist attitudes. Exploration of these feelings indicated that Mrs. L had fastened onto those stereotypes of black people that most reflected her own character problem: dependency, efforts to win acceptance by ingratiating behavior, and various other aspects of childlike or impulse-indulging action. The black worker had intuitively reacted at intake to a defense mechanism in Mrs. L that touched directly on the problems and adaptive techniques developed by black people in a racist society and on Mrs. L's unconscious racist feelings. It became clear that Mrs. L was attempting to deal with ego-dystonic traits by means of projection onto a scapegoat.

The black worker must find some way of handling his own feelings about racist material for the therapeutic benefit of the client.

As the negative transference emerged, Mrs. L's derogatory remarks about black people became more and more difficult to tolerate. The fact that Mrs. L tried to resolve her guilt by seeing her black caseworker as the one exception to the stereotypes served only to "add insult to injury." Mrs. L was not ready for an interpretation of the stereotypes as a projection of her own problems, and the worker feared that any attempt at such an interpretation would be an acting out of her own anger at Mrs. L and therefore destructive to the client.

Discussing the countertransference problem with her white colleague, the worker realized that her attempt to suppress her own anger at racist remarks was unrealistic, despite her awareness of the underlying psychological problems that prompted them. She therefore decided to talk with Mrs. L about her anger.

Mrs. L's reaction was surprise. Recognizing that the worker did indeed feel anger and that such anger was a natural response by a black person to racist remarks, Mrs. L could see that she tended to be unaware of other people's feelings in all her relationships. This was a problem she was ready to work on.

Treatment could then proceed on the basis of Mrs. L's insight into her interaction with people in her real-life situations, and the development of further negative transference and countertransference was avoided.

If treatment can accomplish its purpose without special attention to racist attitudes, there is some possibility that the client's racist attitude may simply drop away as he no longer needs it.

Miss J was illegitimately pregnant. Her problems involved conflict with her mother, anger at rejection by her father, and inability to compete successfully with her more demanding siblings for the limited emotional and material supplies in the family. She was from a white, low-income, working-class family that often had to seek help from "the welfare" and that habitually used racist sentiments to deny their own feelings of inferiority and inadequacy. She was able to function well at work but was in danger of losing her job when her pregnancy became known. Miss J quite freely expressed occasional racist opinions.

The white worker ignored these expressions, concentrating on helping Miss J make a plan for leave of absence from work, adoption placement for the baby, and a program for additional education. The crucial factor was to bypass "welfare" in the process, thus effectively separating Miss J from the family pattern of recourse to a kind of help that she felt degrading and humiliating. As Miss J worked her way up the status scale, her self-esteem grew, she no longer needed to feel superior by means of racist attitudes, and she began associating on equal and friendly terms with black colleagues and acquaintances.

Judging from the limited evidence obtained, Miss J's use of racism may have been superficial, primarily a status factor. She had sufficient ego-strength so that when a few doors were opened for her, she could satisfy her need for upward mobility and was then able to adopt a value system appropriate to her more secure environmental situation. One might speculate that because she had not been using racism as a basic personality support, she might have given up her racist attitudes more quickly with a black worker who symbolized the middle-class values toward which she was striving.

There is an occasional instance of a white client for whom racism is not merely a defense mechanism but the very ground on which he stands.

Mr. R came to the agency because he disapproved of his daughter's association with "hippies," a group of white liberal high school students who were tutoring black children in a ghetto area. Mr. R, at fifty-eight, was essentially a defeated person, separated from his wife and alienated from his children, struggling to maintain upper middle-class status among more successful business and professional men within his own reference group. He not only disapproved of his daughter's being in direct contact with black people, whom he saw in every way as inferior, but also of her having close social contact with "gentiles" for fear she might marry outside her faith. Mr. R's sense of personal failure was so great, both emotionally and socioeconomically, that he had retreated into a fantastically narrow concept of his own "in-group" and viewed all outsiders as dangerous threats to what little security he could feel within his self-imposed ghetto.

Mr. R was himself the victim of one variety of racism and the carrier of another. His "identification with the aggressor" had become for him a necessity of life. The white worker decided not to attempt any confrontation with him; whether or not the confrontation implicit in a black caseworker's presence in a counseling capacity might have been more therapeutic for him is questionable. Fortunately, it was clear from Mr. R's report that his daughter had sufficient ego-strength to pursue her own purposes despite her father's objections.

From the standpoint of casework treatment, the matter of racism seemed to be a peripheral factor with Miss J and a central one with Mr. R. In neither instance did the casework relationship itself provide the opportunity for a direct therapeutic encounter. The significant factor from the standpoint of treatment, however, was that the casework relationship could proceed successfully where racist stereotypes were not an essential defense mechanism, as with Miss J, but was entirely blocked where racism constituted a major character defense, as with Mr. R. This finding suggests that the ways in which racists attitudes are used in the defense system may provide an important diagnostic and prognostic clue for treatment.

The treatment possibilities are ordinarily not so easily evaluated, however, because racism is likely to be but one component of a complicated network of defense mechanisms within the personality structure. When it is difficult to assess the significance of racist attitudes to the total treatment picture, the white worker may be confronted with his own conflicts in regard to racism. He may wish to disassociate himself immediately from the client's attitudes, but if he does so, he risks the possibility that the client will feel rejected or attacked and will drop out of treatment. If he disregards the racism, he must be able to handle his own sense of participation in racist guilt so that his own emotional reactions will not block treatment.

Because racist attitudes often provide a defense against awareness of anxiety, such attitudes may contribute to the resistance that arises during the course of treatment and must be dealt with in some way. Dealing with these attitudes will be double difficult when racism is ego-syntonic to the client, not only because it contributes to his psychic comfort but also because it corresponds to his perception of a real-life situation. If the white caseworker attempts to deal with racist stereotypes as an incorrect perception of reality, the client may experience this attempt as an attack on his cognitive functions; the matter could then easily degenerate into an "argument" that encouraged the client in intellectualization and rationalization.

It may be necessary for the caseworker to remind himself that the primary purpose of casework treatment is not to attack the defense mechanisms as such, but to strengthen the client's ego capacity sufficiently so that he no longer has need of destructive or self-destructive defenses. It is the ego that perceives reality and that provides the means for dealing with the life situations so as to maximize the attainment of satisfaction. The ego also, however, erects defenses against the awareness of painful emotions and thus blocks its perception of some very significant inner realities; in the pursuit of physic comfort, the ego often handicaps itself in performing its own basic task. The caseworker must therefore be prepared to enlist the ego in an exploration of inner emotional factors as well as of outer reality circumstances.

Mrs. M came to the agency about her son, age seven, who was soiling. On exploring the social situation, it became apparent that Mrs. M needed supplemental financial assistance and was probably eligible for Aid to Families with Dependent Children (AFDC). She was unwilling to apply, stating that the welfare department favored "Negroes," and indicated her feelings about black people by a facial expression that suggested she was smelling something unpleasant.

The white worker commented on her statement and was able to help Mrs. M decide to make an AFDC application. She did not comment on the facial expression because her own reaction to it was so intensely negative. It was obvious, however, that the facial expression was a nonverbal clue to the meaning of the child's symptom. It later became apparent that Mrs. M's background of economic and emotional deprivation had produced in her a self-hatred that her son was acting out, and that her feelings about black people were actually her feelings about herself.

The worker focused on the reality problem of financial need without also exploring the psychological implications of the nonverbal communication. Having failed to come to grips in the initial encounter with the racist attitude, the worker's guilt mounted, and when Mrs. M again made a racist statement, the caseworker expressed direct disagreement. By that time, regressive transference elements were operating, and Mrs. M ostensibly accepted the disagreement without objection. She then became involved in a sadomasochistic relationship with a man of minority group identification, acting out her problem instead of trying to understand and deal with it in therapy. Ego-oriented casework provided no direct access to the unconscious factors involved, the opportunity for using the racist material to reach a deeper level of emotion was gone, and the case was eventually closed without any real progress having been made.

The case of Mrs. M exemplifies the dilemma for the white caseworker. Had the racist attitude been picked up immediately, the caseworker would have found it extremely difficult to use it in some constructive way. An immediate response would have had the advantage, however, of eliciting a "real" rather than a "transference" reaction from the client, and thus might have prevented the client's acting out later in treatment. By the time this study was undertaken, the damage had already been done, and it was too late to test the proposition that discussion with a black colleague might be the most useful kind of consultation for such a problem.

In handling his own feelings about racism, the white worker is often a novice. The black worker has the painful advantage of having had to cope with his reactions to racist attitudes all his life. The problem of dealing with racist defense mechanisms therapeutically requires all the understanding and creativity that black and white workers together can bring to it. Even so, it is possible that the treatment of choice for certain racist clients would be group therapy in a racially mixed group, in which the client could face the irrationality of his racist attitudes without direct confrontation with a caseworker.

Conclusion

Judging from the clients studied, racist attitudes in clients must be viewed as an important casework consideration, both from the standpoint of diagnosis and of treatment. The evidence suggests that the presence of a black caseworker sometimes represents a therapeutic encounter in itself. There is also some indication that confrontation by a black worker taps a deeper emotional level with some white clients than is available in ego-oriented treatment with a white caseworker, indicating that the racial composition of a staff has direct bearing on the effectiveness of its treatment program. This evidence does not, however, excuse the white caseworker from facing his own problems in working with racist clients—and perhaps, in some instances, disqualifying himself.

It would also seem that while black people necessarily suffer from the white assumption of superiority, white people do not necessarily gain a corresponding advantage in psychic security (despite their very real advantage from the exploitation of racist institutions). Racist defense mechanisms do not promote, at least in white applicants for casework help, a viable sense of self-esteem, and may indeed be a diagnostic clue indicative of failure in some important ego task. There seems to be considerable reason for caseworkers to shift some of their attention at this time from the black victims of racism to its white carriers. The carriers of the disease may in fact be sicker than its victims.

Where there is sickness in society, everyone is in need of healing—the carrer as well as the victim, the caseworker as well as the client. The first and basic task is to make whatever changes are necessary to bring the society from sickness to health. The caseworker who deals with the individual client, family, or small group is obviously not contributing much to this larger task. Nevertheless, in his daily practice, he may be doing something to limit the spread of the disease.

During the course of this study, both caseworkers realized that any conclusions they might hope to reach would be less important than their growing sense of security in talking together about a subject that is as emotionally charged for caseworkers as for clients. What had started primarily as an intellectual enterprise became an emotional experience in which they were able to share openly and honestly their feelings about black-white relationships. Both became convinced that without such emotional communication between black and white staff members, casework practice will take on its own sterile and intellectualized stereotypes, with both black and white clients.

Caseworkers may read all the "right" books, say all the "right" things, and participate in all the "right" causes, but if black and white do not share their feeling as well as their thinking, they will remain handicapped in achieving their goals. In view of the experience of one such venture, it would appear that when black and white caseworkers talk together freely, the black-white relationship becomes a source of strength and security that has a direct carry-over to work with all clients, black and white.

Intellectually speaking, this study represents only a tentative and preliminary effort to understand and deal with the problem of racism in the treatment situation. Emotionally speaking, however, the implications could be as vast as was James Baldwin's vision in *The Fire Next Time*:

If we—and now I mean the relatively conscious whites and the relatively conscious blacks, who must, like lovers, insist on, or create, the consciousness of the others—do not falter in our duty now, we may be able, handful that we are, to end the racial nightmare, and achieve our country, and change the history of the world. . . .[8]

[8] James Baldwin, *The Fire Next Time* (New York: Dial Press, 1963), p. 119.

Socioeconomic Class

Casework and Social Class

Florence Hollis

Students of social-class phenomena have observed that many persons follow a life style that is characteristic of the particular socioeconomic class to which they belong. If this observation is valid, caseworkers should attempt to answer two questions. To what extent are differences in life style of major importance for casework among people of different socioeconomic classes? The second question goes further and can be stated more specifically: To what extent is it true that a person who is impoverished needs a kind of casework that is basically different from the kind needed by a person who has an adequate income? Before presenting some of the data available that may help us to find answers to these questions, I should like to call to mind the concern that social workers—family caseworkers, in particular—have traditionally shown for low income and impoverished families and to emphasize the fact that service to these families continues to be a responsibility of family service agencies.

A Long-Held Commitment

The wave of concern now being felt in this country for those who are not sharing in our general prosperity, who are underfed, shabbily clothed, and poorly housed, is reminiscent of the spirit of the early and middle 1930's, when a cure was sought in social reforms that were primarily economic in nature. Social workers viewed the mass unemployment of those years chiefly as the result of failures in the economy. We constantly fought the opinion so often expressed by comfortably employed and employing citizens that "people are too lazy to work"; and we sought to show that, except for a small minority who were socially disturbed, the physically fit unemployed would gladly return to work as soon as work became available. Moreover, we were insistent that, until work was available, adequate financial assistance had to be provided so that families could live in decency. The validity of our point of view was amply sustained by the events of the late thirties and the war years, when public assistance rolls shrank to a small fraction of their former size and thousands of persons, previously classified as completely unemployable, again became wage-earners.

Reprinted from *Social Casework*, Vol. 46 (October, 1965), pp. 463–471, by permission of the author and the Family Service Association of America.

Today we are again aroused by the problem of poverty, as automation, migration, lack of education, and other factors combine to prevent full employment of our potential labor force. More jobs there must be; but the new jobs will be different from the old ones, and workers must be provided with the skills needed to fill them. The school drop-out is the symbol of the new concern, associated as it is with delinquency and unemployability, rooted as it is in conditions that are derived from the very fact of poverty itself.

Obviously social work is not a complete answer to the problem of unemployment. Overcoming this social ill will require the efforts of many disciplines, but social work does have work to do with the individuals who have been victimized by joblessness. Although personal problems are not a major *cause* of unemployment, they often are the end *result* of the social deprivations and pressures brought about by the poverty created by unemployment. Once these poverty-induced problems have become imbedded in the individual, employment alone can no longer cure them.

Within the social work sphere, casework carries the major responsibility for direct work with individuals and families grappling with the day-by-day realities of life without an adequate income. Dealing as it does with both the individual environment and the individual personality, casework alleviates some of the pressure of poverty, on the one hand; on the other hand, it attempts to undo, or to help the individual overcome, the damage his personality has suffered from years, or even a lifetime, of grinding and humiliating deprivation.

This obligation to the victims of poverty has been recognized by casework ever since its beginnings. But despite the widespread recognition among the casework leaders of the thirties of the need for casework services in public assistance,[1] in most states relatively little emphasis was subsequently placed upon the training of graduate caseworkers for the public assistance field. This was in contrast to the situation in child welfare, where the Children's Bureau had long been able to give leadership to the development of adequately trained personnel. Today the aspirations of the public welfare workers of the early thirties are about to become a reality. The current push for the expansion of income-maintenance programs on an insurance instead of a "needs" basis and for the long-needed simplification of eligibility procedures will increase the opportunities for providing casework service under public auspices and so increase the demand for professional skill in working with low-income families.

Family caseworkers in voluntary agencies are also deeply engaged in serving low-income families. In the past thirty years casework service to middle-income clients has greatly expanded. Its value to persons above the poverty line has been demonstrated, and caseworkers have developed a

---

[1] Elizabeth H. Dexter, "Has Casework a Place in the Administration of Public Relief?" *The Family*, Vol. XVI, July, 1935, pp. 132–37; Rosemary Reynolds, "Do We Still Believe Case Work Is Needed in a Public Relief Agency?" *The Family*, Vol. XIX, October, 1938, pp. 171–77.

methodology particularly relevant to problems of personal and interpersonal adjustment. But the family agency's extension of its service to middle-income clients by no means signifies that it has abandoned casework with low-income families or work with practical problems. Problems of personal and interpersonal adjustment are not a monopoly of middle- and upper-income clients. The poor have psychological problems too! Although family agencies vary in the socioeconomic make-up of their caseloads, a survey made up by the Family Service Association of America showed that, in 1960, 72 per cent of the clients interviewed and 67 per cent of those who had five or more interviews were in the lower or lower-middle class. The lowest socioeconomic class (the group which approximated the population designated as Class V in the August Hollingshead two-factor index of social position) accounted for 43 per cent of all clients interviewed and 37 per cent of those who had five interviews or more.[2] Clearly, the family agency is deeply involved in serving the economically deprived.

Confusions About Class Differences

Turning now to the question concerning social class differences in life style and their significance for casework, I should like to comment on some of the confusions inherent in this subject. The first confusion is the result of lumping together—as if they were all the same—multiproblem families, hard-to-reach families, and impoverished families. Although there is considerable overlapping of these groups, they are by no means identical. Reports of the St. Paul study of multiproblem families indicate that more than 25 per cent were above the public assistance income level and that 53 per cent functioned above the marginal level in economic practices. Furthermore, 64 per cent functioned above the marginal level in their relationship with the worker.[3] Similarly, many low-income families are not multiproblem families, nor are they all hard to reach. Countless low-income families can use casework service, once it is made available to them, with no more difficulty than can financially secure families. Their problems are augmented by their poverty and consequent pressing, practical problems, but they are not *necessarily* hard to reach.

The second confusion about the matter of class differences arises when low-income families are erroneously viewed as a homogeneous cultural group. It is easy to recognize that within this group are found many older persons and families, reduced to poverty by illness or other misfortune, who really belong to the middle class by virtue of their educational level and their

[2] Dorothy Fahs Beck, *Patterns in Use of Family Agency Service*, Family Service Association of America, New York, 1962, p. 26, supplemented by a memorandum, August, 1964.

[3] Ludwig L. Geismar and Beverly Ayres, *Families in Trouble*, Family Centered Project, Greater St. Paul Community Chest and Councils, St. Paul, Minnesota, 1958, p. 48; Ludwig L. Geismar and Beverly Ayres, *Patterns of Change in Problem Families*, Family Centered Project, Greater St. Paul Community Chest and Councils, St. Paul, Minnesota, 1959, p. 39.

previous employment. After these segments are eliminated, however, the term "culture of poverty" is sometimes used to refer to the ways of life of clients whose incomes approximate the level of public assistance or are even less—and many non-public-assistance families fall in this group—who have not finished high school, who are able to do only unskilled work, and who are, often, members of "female-based" families.

It is frequently claimed that persons in this latter type of low-income family tend to lack motivation for self-improvement, to feel that their lives are controlled by fate rather than by their own efforts, to prefer present to future gratification, and, therefore, to be uninterested in long-time planning. They are supposed to be "expressive" in the sense of acting out feelings and emotional needs rather than controlling them, to have a poor time sense, to project the blame for their troubles on external forces, to be unable to express feelings in language or to comprehend abstractions, to have no belief in the value of talking as a way of solving problems or straightening out feelings, and so to be inaccessible to what is called "traditional case-work."

In actual fact, how much homogeneity is there in this low-income, poorly educated, vocationally unskilled group? In it can be found first- and second-generation families from many ethnic backgrounds; old American families—white, Negro, and Puerto Rican—who have recently migrated to the city from rural areas; and families that have lived in the same general area for three or more generations. These families also vary widely in religious affiliation, in family structure, and in education. The educational gap between the illiterate or barely literate individual and the high-school dropout is surely as great as that between the high-school graduate and the holder of a graduate degree.

And to what cultural influences will these different kinds of low-income families be exposed? All will be influenced to some degree by the dominant middle-class culture. They will be influenced by the values and customs of the blue-collar working class of which they are a part. They will be influenced by the values and customs of their parental families if these differ from their own culture and by the values and customs of any subgroup that they themselves may comprise.[4] Robert Merton, Lloyd Ohlin, and Richard Cloward hold very persuasively that a significant portion of juvenile delinquency in low-income families is caused by one aspect of this fact—that is, by the conflict between the high aspirations youngsters have assimilated from middle-class culture and the meager opportunities available to them for realizing these aspirations. There is every reason to believe that many, many low-income, poorly educated individuals do not share a common "culture of poverty." Hylan Lewis and Camille Jeffers stress the diversity

---

[4] For similar points of view, see William L. Yancey, *The Culture of Poverty: Not So Much Parsimony*, a paper based on research sponsored by the National Institute of Mental Health, Grant No. MH-09189 (unpublished); Jerome Cohen, "Social Work and the Culture of Poverty," *Social Work*, Vol. IX, January, 1964, pp. 3–11.

found among lower-class individuals in the Child Rearing Study in Washington, D.C.[5] In the Stirling County study it was found that there was "more diversity than consensus . . . and . . . a tendency . . . toward isolated behavior and unpredictability."[6] Richard Slobodin says of Upton Square, "individuality and idiosyncrasies of character flourished there as they do not at present in conformist middle-class society."[7] In work with low-income families we must steer clear of any tendency to stereotype. Stereotyping can lead to undue discouragement, unwillingness to persevere, the offering of even less service than the client can use, and even abandonment of the willingness to try to help at all.

The Effects of Persistent Poverty

At the same time that we resist the temptation to stereotype, we should be alert to any data that can add to our understanding of either the personalities of low-income persons or the situations by which they are confronted. Material based upon participant observation is particularly valuable when combined with psychological understanding. Caseworkers are beginning to join sociologists in studies of extremely deprived families. Louise Bandler, in her report of the South End Family Program in Boston, describes work done with thirteen extremely deprived Skid Row families.[8] The mothers in these families were virtually children, competing with their own offspring as if they were siblings; their households were completely disorganized; the parents were so inarticulate that they literally did not have words for their emotions, or knowledge of abstraction, or even such fundamental knowledge as why a baby cries.

The workers in this program found that they could visit these clients without an invitation and that if they returned regularly, chatted in a neighborly fashion, and offered help with practical problems when they could, they would be allowed to stay. They might then have the chance to demonstrate that a baby stops crying more quickly if someone feeds him,

[5] Hylan Lewis, "Culture, Class and the Behavior of Low-Income Families," a paper given at the Conference on Lower Class Culture, New York, N.Y., June 27–29, 1963, sponsored by the Health and Welfare Council of the National Capital Area, Washington, D.C. (unpublished); Hylan Lewis, "Child-Rearing Practices Among Low-Income Families," *Casework Papers, 1961*, Family Service Association of America, New York, 1961, pp. 79–92; Camille Jeffers, "Living Poor," a report for restricted circulation, Child Rearing Study, Health and Welfare Council of the National Capital Area, Washington, D.C. (unpublished).

[6] Charles C. Hughes and others, *People of Cove and Woodlot*, "Stirling County Study of Psychiatric Disorder and Sociocultural Environment," Vol. II, Basic Books, New York, 1960, pp. 394–95, cited by Lewis, "Culture, Class and the Behavior of Low-Income Families," *op. cit.*

[7] Richard Slobodin, " 'Upton Square': A Field Report and Commentary," Child Rearing Study, Health and Welfare Council of the National Capital Area, Washington, D.C., 1960, p. 13, cited by Lewis, "Culture, Class and the Behavior of Low-Income Families," *op. cit.*

[8] Louise S. Bandler, "Casework with Multiproblem Families," *Social Work Practice, 1964*, Columbia University Press, New York, 1964, pp. 158–71.

changes his diaper, turns him over, or picks him up than if he is yelled at or hit. Gradually the workers learned that even these little-girl mothers wanted to do better by their children than they themselves had been done by; that the mother yelled at the baby and hit him partly because she actually did not know why he was crying or what else to do and partly because the crying made her feel so bad—so inadequate in the care she was giving her child.

Both experience and study show that long-time poverty results not only in actual deprivation of food, inadequate and shabby clothing, crowded and run-down housing but also in illness or at least depleted energy, a strong sense of inferiority or lack of self-esteem, and often a great sensitivity to criticism, even though this sensitivity may be overlaid by defensive hostility, denial, and projection. The client who is the victim of persistent poverty is often discouraged to the point of being chronically depressed. He almost surely has underlying resentment, anger, and disbelief that the caseworker— a well-dressed, healthy, well-educated member of the middle class—can respect him or be relied upon to help him. Motivation and aspiration are often not absent; but disappointment after disappointment and frustration after frustration may have forced him to bury his hopes for himself—if not for his children—so that he will no longer be vulnerable to so much pain. Jeffers has observed a cycle in the aspiration level of low-income families: the unrealistically high goals of early life are replaced by discouragement, embitterment, and apathy, except for the hope that the children will succeed where the parents have failed.[9]

Oversimplifications Concerning Poverty

Much has been made in recent years of the failure of the middle-class worker to understand the ways of the lower-class family. The implication has been that caseworkers seek to impose their own middle-class values and goals inappropriately on the lower-class client. Perhaps the sheer size of the problem of helping these families and our frustrations at the slow progress we have made have led us to do some scapegoating of our own. Perhaps we have created an easy victim by accusing the middle-class worker of imposing his values on lower-class clients. If this does, in fact, occur, it is indeed an error. But an even greater error is the more subtle one of failing to see the aspirations and motivations—the craving for liking, respect, and help—that may lie beneath the client's hostile, couldn't-care-less, touch-me-not exterior. (We should remember, too, the months of hard work that sometimes are required to overcome the resistance of the economically secure client.)

Guilt, too, can be underestimated or not perceived because we are accustomed to look for certain behavioral signs more common to the middle class. Deborah Shapiro's preliminary study of illegitimacy among girls of different classes and racial backgrounds indicates that both the parents and the children in low-income Negro families share in the general cultural

[9] Jeffers, *op. cit.*

disapproval of bearing children out of wedlock.[10] The sense of alienation, or anomie, so often cited as prevalent in low-income groups may well be due, in part, to the real lack of group-accepted, internalized norms of conduct that make the individual's behavior predictable to himself so that, in a sense, he knows himself as a stable entity. But it may also be a reflection of his lack of self-esteem—a lack induced partly by the attitudes of others and partly by his own dissatisfaction with his inability to achieve the goals he has set for himself.

It must always be kept firmly in mind that a family's life style is influenced not only by the amount of its income but also by its ethnic background and religious affiliation, the educational level of its members, its place of residence (urban or rural), and—perhaps more than any other factor—family structure. The fatherless, or "female-based," family—or, to put it another way, the family in which the father's relationship is tenuous— is found so frequently in the low-income group that our observations of the behavior that appears to be characteristic of this type of family structure often color our conclusions in regard to the total group. (It is estimated that this type of family makes up about 40 per cent of the lowest income group.) Much of the behavior of adolescent boys in these families seems traceable to the effort of the growing boy to escape the domination of his mother by identifying with an exaggeratedly aggressive and tough ideal of masculinity. The significance of this factor of family structure and behavior, as contrasted with economic differences, was highlighted in a recent study of twenty adolescent boys who were making a poor adjustment to school despite their having superior intelligence. Richmond Holder and Edliff Schwaab found that these boys had been cared for in early life by parent substitutes; their mothers were dominant in the home but preoccupied with affairs outside the home; they had too little contact with their fathers; they had a negative feeling toward education, a sense of futility and indifference toward their own future work, a lack of motivation, a desire for success by magical means, a poor self-image, an orientation to pleasure-seeking, and a lack of impulse control.[11] Without doubt these boys would have been school dropouts had they not been the children of *wealthy* parents suffering from an overdose of *affluence*.

The Old and the New

Having answered the first question by citing a number of characteristics commonly found in persons who have been subjected to poverty over a long period of time—but which are by no means absent in other strata of society—

[10] Deborah Shapiro, *Social Distance and Illegitimacy: A Report of a Pilot Study*, Columbia University School of Social Work, New York, 1965.

[11] Richmond Holder and Edliff H. Schwaab, "The Impact of Affluence on the Personality Functioning of Adolescent Boys in Treatment," a paper delivered at the Annual Meeting of the American Orthopsychiatric Association, New York, March, 17–20, 1965 (unpublished).

we can now turn to the second question. To what extent do such differences as do exist point to the need for a different kind of casework for people from different classes? Those who feel strongly that casework with low-income families is different often speak of "traditional casework" and characterize it as a form of psychotherapy designed for verbal, well-motivated, middle-class neurotics. To anyone truly knowledgeable about modern casework, this description has a curiously nostalgic but hollow ring. Where, oh where, has the middle-class neurotic gone! It is true that the middle-class client does not find the office interview by appointment the same kind of obstacle to getting help that the low-income client may find it. But is the ceremony of an office interview the essence of casework? As a matter of fact, it is only in the child guidance clinic, the mental hygiene clinic, and the family service agency that private interviewing rooms are the prevailing mode. Even in these agencies, much that proved so disconcerting about the home interview of a few years ago is no longer so troublesome, as the use of joint and family interviews has increased. As one of my students put it, "Why should it be harder for the caseworker to listen to the turned-on television set of the resisting, home-visited client than to the weekly intellectualizing of the resisting, office-appointment client?" Resistance may take different forms in different classes, but it certainly is not unknown in work with economically secure people.

Earlier in this article reference was made to certain characteristics of casework practice with the low-income family—the use of the home visit, the worker's persistence in visiting even when the family seems to be resistive, the need to overcome the client's initial distrust partly by "doing for him" rather than relying wholly on the verbal handling of the resistance. Practical problems certainly play a larger part in work with disadvantaged families than they do in casework with those who are economically secure. There is a greater need for actual demonstration and for giving information. The importance of the worker's maintaining an accepting, noncritical attitude in order to overcome the client's lack of self-esteem and lessen his inner feelings of guilt and unworthiness cannot be overestimated. The worker must refrain from counterattack when the client's hostility bursts through and must avoid challenging the client's defenses except under special circumstances, for example, with certain types of acting-out delinquents. Over and over again the literature stresses the critical importance of these familiar components of casework practice in work with the low-income family.

A few ingenious new techniques and new combinations of familiar procedures have been devised recently. Rachel Levine has reported the worker's use of games, arts, and crafts during the home visit as a means of observing the family members' behavior patterns and of teaching, by demonstration, less destructive and hostile ways in which they can relate to one another, the use of words instead of acting out to settle differences, and so on.[12] Frank Riessman advocates role-playing and other game-like

[12] Rachel A. Levine, "Treatment in the Home," *Social Work*, Vol. IX, January, 1964, 19–28.

devices and suggests the use of "helper therapy" as is now done by Alcoholics Anonymous and similar organizations.[13] Indigenous homemakers and home teachers have been used as an adjunct to the treatment process at Mobilization for Youth in New York City. This organization has also established neighborhood service centers through which emergency help can be given and from which referrals for more sustained service are sometimes made. Riessman also recommends that service be available in the evenings and during week ends.

Another facet of casework with the low-income client, which is frequently mentioned in the literature, is the importance of accepting him for service at the point of crisis. Waiting lists are particularly inappropriate for this group. Moreover, the likelihood that the client will be reached and held in treatment is thought to be significantly greater when he is assigned directly to the worker who will be responsible for the case. A change of workers after the first interview should be avoided. It is widely recognized that what Riessman has called "anticipatory socialization" will usually be necessary: the client will have to be gradually aided to understand how talking can help, that there is something he can do about his own situation, and that the worker has no magic but that by their talking together ways can be found to make life somewhat better. This process is often equally necessary with the middle-class client!

Much has been made of the difficulty of the worker's finding the right words to use with the low-income client, particularly in the discussion of feelings. There are, of course, some clients with whom this is truly a problem. Most workers report, however, that if they use simple, everyday English, they have no difficulty. Intellectualization and the use of technical language is helpful with neither lower-class nor middle-class families.

How Basic Are the Treatment Modifications?

In the foregoing discussion we have been noting certain techniques and styles of working that seem to be particularly useful in the casework treatment of low-income families. Do these techniques and styles constitute a brand of casework that is entirely different from the "standard brand"? Or are they only relatively minor variations? In discussing this question of methodology, I should like to refer to my own recently developed classification of casework procedures.[14] In this classification distinction is first made between direct work with the client himself and work in the environment on the client's behalf. Direct work with the client is then subdivided into six major sets of procedures, the first four of which also apply to environmental work:

[13] Frank Riessman, *New Models for a Treatment Approach to Low Income Clients*, Mobilization for Youth, New York, March, 1963 (unpublished).

[14] Florence Hollis, *Casework: A Psychosocial Therapy*, Random House, New York, 1964, Chapters IV, V, VI, and VII.

1. Sustaining procedures in which the worker shows interest in the client and acceptance of him, and, by making reassuring comments, tries to increase his self-confidence or decrease his anxiety.

2. Procedures of direct influence in which suggestions, advice, and sometimes admonition are given in an effort to guide the client's behavior.

3. Exploration and ventilation.

The next three types of procedure deal with communications involving three types of reflective consideration:

4. That pertaining to current person-situation interaction

5. That pertaining to the dynamics of response patterns and tendencies, and

6. That pertaining to early life factors of developmental significance to present ways of functioning.

Indirect work—that is, casework with others on the client's behalf—makes use of the first four of these sets of procedures and an additional one, the mobilizing of resources.

Practically everything the worker does in the traditional casework treatment process can be classified under one of these headings. Different client problems and different personality diagnoses call for various blendings of these procedures and various emphases. If this classification is applied to casework with low-income families, what do we find?

First, we certainly find that environmental treatment—indirect work—is of very great importance. Here the worker must exercise resourcefulness, persistence, and ingenuity; he must be skillful in working with other social agencies and knowledgeable about both agency and nonagency resources. He must often work with other persons on the client's behalf; and though the contact may be of short duration, an interview with such a person calls for skill in all the procedures used in direct work with the client, with the exception of dynamic and developmental understanding. Furthermore, legwork as well as telephone work is essential. Over and over again it has been demonstrated that the initial building of the relationship with the client in the economically hard-pressed group is greatly facilitated by skillful environmental work. Be it noted, however, that environmental work is also of great importance with children and older people and with many seriously disturbed clients with or without a good income.

In direct work with the client, it seems quite clear that the client of low income with little education usually needs a large measure of *sustainment*—comparable, in fact, to the amount needed by the depressed or extremely anxious or guilty client in the better educated, economically comfortable group. The need for sustainment has been stressed over and over again in the material produced by workers who have been concentrating on casework with the low-income client. He is often highly distrustful of the caseworker, and if his self-esteem is low and his fear of criticism pronounced, he will need a very large measure of the expression of interest and concern, of respect for him and his abilities, and of the worker's desire to help him.

Much of the literature also emphasizes that this client more often needs *suggestions and advice* than do others. To a degree this may be true, but the worker must carefully assess whether or not a particular client really does need this approach. The low-income client is often quite capable of thinking about himself and his situation if the worker sticks close to the realities of life and to the client's true concerns, and if he uses words that are simple and expressive. If the client does, indeed, need suggestions and advice, the worker must be sure that his standing with the client is on firm enough ground to make his advice acceptable—to say nothing of the fact that it must be advice well attuned to the client's values and circumstances.

Exploration may sometimes proceed at a slower pace than with the more verbal, better-educated client. But once the low-income client's confidence has been established, he is likely to speak freely, particularly of feelings of anger and frustration, sometimes directed against the worker himself. The worker's acceptance and understanding of these feelings, combined with his continued interest in the client and his nonretaliation, will go a long way toward establishing a firm relationship.

As with the middle-class client, when the low-income client is able to think things through for himself, it is preferable that he do so. Simplicity of language and slowness of thought should not be mistaken for incapacity. As with most clients, whatever their income, in reflective discussion the emphasis will often be on understanding practical problems, understanding other members of the family, and foreseeing the outcome or effect of the client's own ways of acting and handling things rather than on intrapsychic understanding. The client's learning to see reality clearly, and thinking of what to do about it, often occupy the major part of his interview time. In this process, the worker may have to take more initiative in giving information, explaining, and demonstrating than would be necessary with the better-educated client.

In the worker's use of demonstration his clarity about what is to be conveyed and his careful judgment about the right time for transmitting it effectively to the client are based on the same knowledge that underlies his use of the verbal procedures through which the client is led to greater understanding in other forms of reflective consideration. Moreover, it should by no means be assumed that the low-income client does not need to, and is unable to, understand his own feelings; the way in which he responds to the environment; and those happenings in his daily life that touch off his feelings. Poor education is not synonymous with low intelligence, and simple ways can be found to express fairly complicated ideas if the worker has enough ingenuity to devise them.

It is probable that the caseworker makes less use of procedures designed to encourage reflective consideration of dynamic factors in the personality and factors of developmental significance when the client has had little education, but these procedures are not entirely ruled out. As a matter of fact, contrary to popular impressions, caseworkers make relatively little use of these procedures, even with the middle-class client. Some of the doubts expressed about the appropriateness of "traditional casework" for low-income families reflect a gross misunderstanding of the nature of present-day casework treatment; it should not be confused with psychoanalytic psychotherapy, which is practiced by psychiatrists. Casework is noted as much for its emphasis on environmental and supportive work as for its techniques of clarification and experiential treatment. In all its various procedures special emphasis is given to the value of a warm, accepting relationship as both a supportive and a corrective experience for the client. The caseworker's attempts to effect personality change are limited to specific modifications of the client's ego or superego that can be brought about through an understanding of conscious and preconscious content, through a corrective relationship, and, under certain circumstances, through environmental changes. Casework does not attempt to effect a basic reorganization of the client's personality through his gaining insight into deeply buried experiences. The emphasis of present-day casework is on helping people to deal with their immediate problems, to understand others better, and, when appropriate, to bring about limited but highly important changes in their ways of functioning and, therefore, in their personalities. For many low-income people these are by no means impossible goals.

Summary

There are, indeed, differences between casework with the average low-income, poorly-educated client and casework with the average middle-income, well-educated client. But these are differences in specific techniques and in emphases rather than in basic casework *method*. Work with impoverished families involves the use of all the procedures valued in work with more advantaged groups. In addition, it requires the use of certain innovations or modifications of traditional techniques—for example, demonstration and role-playing, which have heretofore been used chiefly in work with children and with borderline or recovering schizophrenics.

In trying to understand clients of low income, we must beware of the stereotype. They differ from one another fully as much as do clients in the middle class. At the same time, we must be sensitive to the effects of grinding deprivation, of poor education, of being devalued in a status-minded society, and often of growing up in a fatherless family in a neighborhood where opportunities for crime abound and opportunities for reaching the goals to which their membership in American society leads them to aspire are very, very scarce.

We must also guard against depriving these clients of the opportunity of receiving adequate casework help by our holding stereotyped and erroneous preconceptions about their limitations. The caseworker trying to help impoverished families needs not only all the skill in both diagnosis and treatment that he needs in work with other types of families but also great ingenuity, resourcefulness, flexibility, and patience. Above everything else— as the work of Overton, Henry, Wiltse, Fantl, Cloward, Riessman, Bandler, and many others has amply demonstrated—he needs to have faith in the possibility that the client is capable of change and a deep desire to help him do so.

Acknowledgments

I should like to acknowledge the contributions of three students— Rosalyn Lowenstein, Alice Schmacher, and Mary E. Woods—to the content of this paper. Their term papers were of distinct value for both information and ideas.

Casework in Lower Class Districts

Berta Fantl

This is not more than an attempt to describe our initial impressions, changing attitudes and approaches following our move from a downtown school child guidance center into neighborhoods where poverty, crowded housing, lack of community facilities and delinquency are as high as services of trained social workers are rare. Without benefit of a research team or even a limited caseload our impressions are open to revisions and, hopefully, they eventually will be subjected to systematic investigation.

Ethnic Composition, Social Class, and Family Structure

The majority of our clients are Negroes, many of them from the South. Among other ethnic groups are American Caucasians, a considerable number of Latin American families, a sprinkling of Chinese and Filipinos, European immigrants, re-located American Indians and a few Samoans. Economically, occupationally and socially our clients belong to the lower, lower classes. If there is a recession they are the ones who are hit first and hardest. Many are one-parent families who are receiving Aid to Needy Children. Even if there is a father in the home, his wages as an unskilled laborer may not be sufficient to support a family without supplementation from public aid. The size of families is large; six to nine children are more the rule than the exception, and 11 to 16 children in one family is not uncommon. Whether natives of the United States or foreign-born, many families came from rural—frequently impoverished—backgrounds. They are living in low-rent public housing built during World War II to accommodate the influx of war workers and now gradually being replaced by permanent housing projects.

During this unforseen expansion little attention was paid to such other needs of tenants as neighborhood centers, schools, proper sidewalks or streetlights, adequate bus services. Many of the organized churches are located in adjoining districts. Most of our clients attend church regularly; some walk a far distance, while others belong to informal religious groups

---

Reprinted with permission from *Mental Hygiene*, Vol. 45 (July, 1961), pp. 425–438.

right in the projects. Several of our clients are ministers or assistant ministers. Their positions seem to give them status within their group and provide them and their families with a few socially approved outlets. We are told that people who are upwardly mobile leave the more isolated districts as soon as they are able to do so. This coincides with the wishes expressed by clients.

Perception of Clients by Others and Clients' Low Self-Concept

Members of various service professions who work hard and conscientiously frequently feel isolated. There is little status or challenge[1] to work in our area and many ask for a transfer to a "better" district as soon as they get here. They have trouble understanding and communicating with the various ethnic groups and they feel that their efforts to help people are not appreciated. Some are inclined to consider our clients "lazy," "dumb," "people on relief," "bad" and "indifferent."

This perception of our clients is reflected in the low concept the clients have of themselves, especially in relation to the helping "outsider." Depending on the strength or weakness of their core identification with their own cultural group, clients may feel worthless, hopeless and helpless in dealing with the endless cycle of daily stresses and deprivations. They are highly conflicted and confused about when to call for help from one of the many authority figures—the police, housing authority, school, public welfare, court—or when to reject them. They feel self-conscious about their speech and clothing and uncertain about how to act in initial contacts. They may have nothing to say or they may flood us with material which seems of little relevance to the question of why the school referred Johnny. It is up to the worker to size up the situation sensitively, to put the parents at greater ease and—through listening, questions and restatements—to engage the parents in meaningful discussions. We may have to listen to many other problems pressing on the parent's mind before we get to talk about Johnny, as well as obtain adequate information about Johnny's developmental history and other background information which frequently has little meaning to the client.

Even young children seem keenly aware of their lack in social skills. A nine-year-old, proud of the knowledge he gained in school about the Revolutionary War, asked his worker to show him "which is right and which is left." Another boy, supposedly retarded and in a special class, expressed his liking for his new teacher "because he does not just tell kids to do things; he shows them how they are done."

Early last school year we engaged in some heated discussions on whether some of the things we responded to in clients, or even occasionally

---

[1] Caseworkers are not exempted from this status dilemma. Occasionally "professionalization" of services is equated with an increase of referrals from professional sources, with a decrease of services to unskilled laborers and the appearance of a clientele which is less economically deprived—despite an economic recession—and with scheduled versus unscheduled appointments.

initiated, were "therapeutic" or "educational" and if the latter, were they within our function? As the school year wore on, those doubts must have become dissipated, since whenever we were able to enhance a client's concept of himself as emotionally or socially more adequate, we realized that we had accomplished a step toward helping him to see others differently and to relate to them in new ways.

Lower, Lower Class and Working Class District

Casework in a lower, lower class district poses somewhat different problems from a more regular working class district. In a working class district there is a higher degree of family cohesiveness, more permanent male figures with whom to identify, membership in labor unions and a greater pride in achievements in spite of recurring obstacles, including unemployment. The lower, lower class district has an aura of being caught with no way out, daily drudgeries with few rewards and an almost greater hanging together and understanding for each other in times of trouble than a common purpose and mutual joy in the rare moments of calm.

On the other hand, people in our districts show a great need for contact with the "outside world" and a genuine appreciation for any little thing accomplished or gesture extended to them. A call to a mother who is ill or a card as a reminder of Mother's Day to the members of our Mothers' Group was responded to warmly and elaborately and mentioned for several weeks. Among the 150 referrals made to us from one of the most deprived districts, we do not remember one family whom we were unable "to reach" as long as we met the clients in a way which made sense to them and as we did not expect them to respond in some stereotyped "therapeutic" fashion.

Function of the School Child Guidance Services

The major functions of the School Child Guidance Services are direct services to clients, consultation to school personnel and participation on community committees. Because of the high number of referrals to us and our desire to give quick services to the school, *our direct services to clients* consist mainly of one or two intake interviews or a brief series of interviews accompanied by psychological tests. Such intakes or short-term evaluations are followed up whenever indicated by referrals to appropriate community resources, mostly family agencies and psychiatric clinics. Each worker also carries a small continued treatment load, but the major function of direct service is in the area of intake and evaluations with referrals elsewhere.

Consultation services to school personnel, as a complex and rapidly expanding function of the Child Guidance Services, grew out of the realization that as professional workers we have a commitment to develop— gradually and thoughtfully—techniques to effect the health and welfare of larger groups of people. We also realized that knowledge and skills need to be used cautiously and imaginatively and in more ways than one. The goal of consultation is to enable school personnel to deal more effectively—in their professional roles as administrators, counselors, teachers—with the many disturbing school situations they encounter. Consultation is not focused on the teacher as a person, but on the problem situation and the professional role the teacher is asked to perform. With increased interest in giving equal services to "tough" as well as middle-class districts, *participation of caseworkers in community committees* and neighborhood councils became a small yet integral part of their daily activities.

When we moved into very deprived neighborhoods we were ready for some surprises, but we did not realize how poorly our former way of referring cases elsewhere would work for all but a handful of "non-typical" clients. As our communication with clients increased, just the reverse seemed to happen between us and our usual referral sources, all of which are located downtown.

We found ourselves conversing in different languages. Even when we knew that clients needed and wanted help we could not be sure that the client would keep appointments at a certain hour and day in a district strange to him and far from his home. Even when we were convinced of the client's good intelligence and ego strength in the face of insurmountable difficulties, we found ourselves at a loss to know whether his "ego capacity" to "use treatment" would be exactly what the worker on the other end of the line had in mind. We soon could see that our limited time was better spent with clients or on community committees than by trying to explain the need for flexible services to individual workers who were caught in those structures of the agencies which were geared to another echelon of clients.

Acute Stresses and Ego Defense

Families with "social crises" are referred to us—a suspension of a child from school for stealing, continued misbehaving, using "foul language," "breaking into" a school with a group of other young children.[2]

Acute stress situations, even with *clients with whom we continue to work,* are much more common than internalized conflicts, guilt and self-blame. Anxiety is expressed by blaming others, by apparent indifference, passivity and depression-like behavior. We have much to learn about how clients cope not only with inner conflicts but also with stresses[3] which are largely

---

[2] Our referrals come from elementary and junior high schools. However, because of the size of the families we are aware of the problems of older teen-agers.

[3] In Myers, Jerome K. and Bertram H. Roberts, *Family and Class Dynamics* (New York: John Wiley & Sons, Inc., 1958), 15 and 16, Dr. Myers makes the useful distinction between *external presses* and *internal stresses*. A press is a potential pressure on the individual from the environment; it may be either *stressful* or *supportive*. Emotional stress, on the other hand, may add to the individual's negative presses.

produced by outside circumstances—irregular employment, no food in a society of plenty, repeatedly experienced social barriers and cultural strains. We have become cautious about the terms we are using to diagnose and describe clients' difficulties. Not only norms for behavior or style of impulse expression may be influenced by ethnic group identification and class structure; we also will need to examine carefully what additional factors to consider when we describe the ego's mode of dealing with inner and outer conflicts.

Denial of difficulties, projection-like behavior and the sometimes long-winded "rationalizations" by clients are not necessarily the neurotics' rigid distortions of reality. Often it is an anticipation based on repeated reality experiences during which the client experienced attacks and injuries to his self-image.[4] As soon as the client senses that the worker understands his underlying anxiety of being "attacked," the "denials" and "projections" seem to diminish quickly—although often only temporarily and, first, in relation to the worker. It seems to us that the neurotic client experiences some level of emotional and social enrichment before he resorts to his symptoms as a compromise. We doubt that our clients experienced the same type of emotional and social enrichment since their biological drives and resources were nourished in a different social environment and exposed to a chronicity of stressful situations.

Toward an Understanding of Deviant Group Behavior

Current casework practice cannot, without adaptation of methods and techniques, be applied to large families, who frequently come from rural areas and whose needs and wants for love, affection and security are the same as everyone else's but whose value system as to time, property rights, manner of speech and clothing, expression of feeling and sex behavior are different from the conventional norm. In attempting to emphasize the social side of human behavior, there is perhaps a tendency to overstress the "differences" in human beings or to lose oneself in generalizations. It is well to remember that people differ only in degree and that they are much more alike than they are different. The differences might be small, yet subtle enough to obscure communication between different groups of people, and after all *communication—verbal and nonverbal*—with an *adequate understanding for the subtle aspects of the situation under which communication takes place* is the vehicle for all treatment.

To know the way the client *is likely* to view his problem, the agency and the worker, from his ethnic point of view or class position, are of utmost importance in the design of new services. Therefore it is not merely a matter of "reaching out" or decentralizing offices before services with certain client

---

[4] Although the author takes full responsibility for any opinion expressed in this article, she is indebted to Erika Chance, Ph.D., research associate, Department of Psychiatry at Mount Zion Hospital in San Francisco, for her helpful criticism and discussions.

groups will become more effective. This must not be misunderstood to mean that just because a client is a member of a certain milieu, he will respond a priori in an expected manner. People and milieux are much more complex, and in the last analysis *each client's problem is inevitably unique and personal*; it is the product of the individual's biological equipment and his life experiences. However *certain types of problems* occur more commonly under certain *subcultural pressures* which are operating in the client's life experience.

When working in certain neighborhoods one cannot help being impressed by the high number of deviant behavior patterns. Of course what defines "normal" or "deviant" behavior is relative to each society. Therefore what may seem an "antisocial" act to the school may be normal—if not expected—behavior for clients. This does not necessarily mean that parents or children are without conflict about conventional values and expectations. Our commitment to democracy—with the ideal of an equal success goal for all, supported by our social institutions and mass media—instills a desire for a better life, i.e., a middle-class life style which hardly anyone can escape. Who the ones actually are who achieve these goals, to what stratum of society they are more likely to belong, what price in strain they or society may have to pay for the pursuit of such aspirations is another story.

Deviant behavior as a *group response* can be understood only by a thorough knowledge of environmental pressures. It is a form of adaptation to strain when conformity to societal expectations is positively motivated, yet at the same time frustrated and unacceptable.[5]

To the individual—regardless of society's prescription of what is "normal," "deviant," "good" or "bad"—only those groups to which he has actual and not fictitious access make sense—where he can learn skills necessary for group membership, where he is recognized as "someone" and is able to relate without losing face. The cultural milieu is an intermediary between the larger social norms and the individual chooses certain behavior forms to give greatest tension relief from particular strains and stresses. It is important for social work to pay increased attention to those societal strains induced by inconsistent demands and promises which lead to the formation, changes and disbandments of subcultural groups[6] and which influence the various behavior adaptions of groups[7] to which the individual belongs. Although we are far from having arrived, we gradually are becoming equipped to see the environment take on new and systematic dimensions; until now we were not able to give it—as an uncharted plot—more than

[5] See Cohen, Albert K., *Delinquent Boys* (Glencoe, Ill.: The Free Press, 1955), 179.

[6] As an example of the development of a subcultural ideology see Cloward, Richard A., *New Perspectives for Research on Juvenile Delinquency* (Washington, D.C.: U.S. Department of Health, Education and Welfare, May, 1955), 80–92.

[7] See Dubin, Robert, "Deviant Behavior and Social Structure;" Cloward, Richard A., "Illegitimate Means, Anomie, and Deviant Behavior;" and Merton, Robert K., "Social Conformity, Deviation and Opportunity Structures," *American Sociological Review*, 24 (April, 1959), 149, 164–76, 177–89.

vague recognition. This is not an irresponsible take-off into interdisciplinary skies but a challenge for the social work profession.

A Look into the Future

There is presently a great need among caseworkers to clarify to what degree a "presenting symptom" is due to psychopathology and to what extent is a cultural adaptation to the client's group memberships. Although we can expect the dichotomy of what is "personal" and what is "sociocultural" to disappear eventually, at present it exists perceptually.[8]

With increased knowledge about the client's dynamic environment, we shall be able to differentiate systematically between *various types* of deviant group adaptations, their formation, persistency and operations.[9] This will lead to a differential diagnostic and treatment approach, much-needed to make treatment fit the client. Erikson's concepts of ego identity, social role and perception by others, his repeated emphasis on mastery, pride in workmanship, the need for individualized opportunities offer the most perfect synthesis of biological drives, childhood identifications and added societal expectations presented thus far.[10]

Our present diagnostic and treatment skills, sensitively tuned and refined to deal with situations of intrapsychic conflicts, will need broadening to include those environmental aspects which influence the client's psychodynamics. Our colleagues in group work are developing treatment approaches of which we in clinics and in public and private agencies are taking notice.[11]

In no way minimizing the major importance of intrafamilial experiences on the personality structure, we began to realize that other meaningful individuals and groups may have a profound impact on clients' behavior and on the developing personality. For many lower class children, the peer group provides emotional if not physical security; it is a place to be recognized, an orientation to what is right and wrong, what to say and to whom and under what circumstances.

[8] We might eventually conceive of a continuum with more or less "pure" psychogenic disturbances on one pole. For instance, as a school agency in a lower, lower class district we did not receive a single referral of school phobia in a two-year period. Although there will be exceptions to this, on the whole mothers do not have *this type* of emotional investment in their children, and fathers are shadowy figures. On the other end of the continuum we may place "strictly" sociocultural reasons for deviant behavior like the delinquent gang in a well-integrated criminal adult subculture. Most cases will fall somewhere in between the two poles.

[9] See Cloward, Richard A. and Lloyd E. Ohlin, *New Perspectives on Juvenile Delinquency* (New York: New York School of Social Work, Columbia University, 1959), 169, Mimeographed.

[10] Erikson, Erik H., "Identity and Life Cycle," from *Selected Papers: Psychological Issues* (New York: International University Press, 1959), 171, Vol. 1, No. 1.

[11] Lerman, Paul, "Group Work with Youth in Conflict," *Social Work*, 3 (October, 1958), 71–77; and "Hard to Reach Youth Project" in *Befriending Troubled Youth* (Chicago: National Federation of Settlements and Neighborhood Centers, 1958).

People have many links between their inner selves and their environments and many different perceptions of what roles to take. They see themselves as persons they think they are; they have other concepts of what they want to be or should be; they have a desire as to how they want others to see them, and. they are afraid of how others see them. A person takes one role with respect to some people and another role with respect to others. As the person grows up and as he works, marries and has a family, roles may change with time and in different settings.[12] A certain amount of role experimentation and "sameness" or continuity in self-perception and role-taking are necessary for the development of a wholesome identity. From a group point of view (and every individual belongs to some groups) minority adaptations to majority norms may be complicated by double identities which may result in ambivalent identities or even self-hatred and negative group identity. This means that certain individuals already psychologically prone to develop a negative identity are more likely to develop it under certain subcultural pressures.

Viewing our client from this broader perspective, we may want to learn more about his actual and imaginary group associations, in other words about "significant others" who influence his values and aspiration level. Who are the ones he admires or hates? Whom does he want as his friends? What are their values and goals? To what group does he actually relate and have access? In other words, what are his "social" frustrations, his actual social barriers which are so important to us in our work with clients of various ethnic groups and lower social classes? In what way can we help to strengthen his inner self and widen his social opportunities for a more productive life for himself and others?

Practice Approach

Incomplete as our knowledge about human behavior may be, we felt secure enough to make our services as easily accessible, available and uncomplicated for the clients as we were able to do within our limitations of time, being greatly understaffed and dealing with overwhelming problems. We reconsidered such things as the 50-minute hour and careful selection as to whom we see and whom we do not—which in our district means no services whatsoever. To be sure, our approach is very family-centered; if anything, we are *more family- and community-oriented* than we ever were, but this does not mean that parents have to make a formal application for services or keep their weekly appointment six times in a row before we dare to see a child. We feel that our clients are neither that delicate nor our techniques that precarious.

We do not make home visits without some evaluation of what is best, realistic and most integrative to the total situation of each family. We are

[12] Erikson, Erik H., *op. cit. See also:* Merton, Robert K., *op. cit.*, Chap. VIII, pp. 255–386.

surprised how few home visits we actually make, yet a firm belief has evolved that a "reaching out" visit in the client's home or in his yard or wherever we find him right then—for 30 minutes to two hours—might be more therapeutic than an office visit three weeks hence. Remember, we are dealing with acutely felt stress and "social crisis," i.e., an immediate situation as far as the client is concerned and as chronic as the situation may be from our point of view. Postponement of even concrete gratifications, let alone "therapy" or "talking out a problem," is not the usual neighborhood pattern.

If someone has trouble in our neighborhood, he is more likely to get into a fight right then, to swear, to tell his neighbors how wrong the other guy was. Therefore, we do not expect clients to be "motivated" for help in the way we used to perceive motivation, and we do not expect verbalization of "inner conflict." We listen to "projection-like" behavior and "rationalizations" in the same way we used to listen to "insight" and "self-blame," and we accept withdrawal and passivity as if the client would express an urgent desire "to bring about a change within himself," great as his resistance to such change may have been.

If one deals with these types of ego defense, the immediate interaction between the client and the worker becomes extremely important. The client is apprehensive about the worker, because, up to that point, to come to an agency to "talk out one's problems," had not been the accepted thing to do within his social setting. The worker has to demonstrate through his attitude and behavior that he can be of help; this is more of a personal task, "an achieved status"[13] than when he works in a clinic or agency which is highly esteemed by the client population. The worker is also exposed to the community's pressure to do something about the "antisocial" actions of the clients, and he must know what the clients' behavior means to his own defenses.

The mutual focus on the immediate situation makes it possible for the client to identify with the worker; this is more important than an emphasis on insight, although a certain amount of increased self-understanding frequently will result. The worker is a participant/observer in each interview situation; he has to know when to intervene, when to deal with some distortions, when to be supportive and when to listen questioningly. In order to do that, the worker has to understand the client's situation truly in its social context. He has to evaluate realistically the client's social handicaps, along with his emotional difficulties, to clarify and show him possible avenues out of his dilemma, offer concrete help if necessary or state that such help is not available. Clear, forthright and correct statements are ego-supportive. Mere passive listening on the part of the worker may be felt as hostility and may increase anxiety of "acting out" behavior. However, if the worker intervenes insensitively, the client is likely to withdraw.

[13] Lerman, Paul, "Group Work with Youth in Conflict," *Social Work*, 3 (October, 1958), 76.

In clients who are judged derogatorily by the community, the desire to relate, together with their fearful anticipation needs special consideration.

By successfully helping clients around, "immediate" crisis situation, the following may be accomplished: (1) Some relief is experienced in his ability to control his behavior, and (2) There is a growing feeling of confidence in the worker because he understood the client's feeling of extreme anger, fear of losing control or isolation from others, without becoming frightened, "hopeless" and discouraged about the client or deserting him as other helping professions might have done in the past. We know of examples of complete silences and passivity in the initial interviews, followed by *"reaching out" on the part of the client* when the worker continued to drop in on the client. One of those clients is now among the most active participants in our Mothers' Group; this does not mean that she attends every session or that she is always on time. She has six children under eight years of age; there is a different orientation toward time in her culture, and we do not minimize her resistance against involving herself in a close relationship.

Other Methods of Support

The emphasis in treatment is on the integrative capacity of the clients, on strengthening the healthy part of their defense structure and on an emotional relearning of interpersonal experiences as well as on neurotic conflicts. Since it is easier to project blame onto external circumstances, it is important for the worker not to overidentify with the client's difficulties and to distinguish when discrimination and other cultural material is used defensively to obscure intrapsychic conflict. With clients whose egos are rather impoverished and who have relatively low internalized tension build-up, the need in treatment is less on abreaction than for strengthening their controls and for the enhancement of their self-concept so that they feel less overwhelmed and helpless. For this we have to look not only for anxiety, anger and conflict (of which they have plenty) but also for such positive experiences and opportunities accessible to them as joy and mutual satisfaction.

We found it gratifying to come across an article by Jerome D. Frank,[14] which stresses this, among other important points. Anyone working with "hard to reach" families knows about the endless crises and often clinically defined traumatic experiences which haunt them. In our Mothers' Group, which is composed of clients we never thought we would "reach" let alone see join a group, emotions and content become so heavily loaded with stories of violences, jails and brutalities that one of the coleaders spontaneously responded (to what we are starting to call "flood release") by asking whether there was anything enjoyable in their daily lives. Since cruelty and other abuses could not fill their entire day, how did they get started in the morning, and what was a "typical" day like? This openly

[14] Frank, Jerome D., "The Dynamics of the Psychotherapeutic Relationship," *Psychiatry*, 22 (February, 1959), 17–39.

guided expectation of what can be discussed and looked at in addition to "problems" had amazing repercussions for the following group sessions and resulted in a number of beneficial changes in the family lives of these mothers.

Joint Interviewing

We began to see jointly both parents or whole family groups on a continued basis. Our impressions here are tentative and we are aware of the much more systematic efforts in family interviewing taking place in our field. So far we have found continued joint interviews useful and supporting the *strength* in a family situation (although differences are aired) when, to begin with, there are evidences of some family cohesiveness. In families who are psychologically pulled apart we do not find this to be the case. Our major focus is on the family as a unit—its collective strength, stresses within the unit, problems and strains in relation to the community and possibilities and limitations of growth potentials. We focus on the individual to assess his roles and the possible strains on these roles which lead to his inadequate functioning as a member of his family. We found individual interviews for a severely disturbed family member an important adjunct to the joint sessions. To work gradually toward a more conceptualized frame of "family identity"—as expressed by Kermit Wiltse[15]—with families who are socially and culturally handicapped seems an important task. We are neither so naive nor foolish to think that the road ahead of us is an easy one.

Unimportant and "superficial" as it may sound to those who are more interested in the hidden aspects of behavior, the mere act of pulling up chairs, getting and talking together in the presence of a person who is interested, ready to observe, restate and clarify what is said and observed, and who is not hesitant to make occasional appropriate suggestions, may have great meaning for the internal aspects of the family structure. It also may be the beginning of a more gratifying experience between the family and the community. The worker then becomes truly a specialist in human relations. "Interaction" and "communication" per se have little meaning unless the worker as a participant/observer is sharply tuned to the psychological and environmental forces operating in clients and between himself and his clients. He has to understand his clients' and his own verbal and nonverbal behavior and expression as well as his own attitudes, which are based on his background and experiences; these are likely to color his perception and feeling for the situation which is confronting him.

Our experience in joint interviewing has been short and limited so it is perhaps a little presumptuous to present a brief and partial example of what happened in a family we had known for six months. Only because similar trends were noticed in working with other families do we believe

---

[15] Wiltse, T. Kermit, "The Hopeless Family," *Social Work*, 3 (October, 1958), 20.

that our preliminary report warrants mention here and that it may be of interest to others:

The family is large—16 children ranging in age from a new baby to a twenty-three-year-old. Fourteen are living at home. Without exception, all of the school age children are reported to have had *serious* behavior difficulties in both school and community, although these difficulties are too numerous to list here. The parents are Negroes, born in the South where they began hard work on farms at an early age, with a minimum of educational or other opportunities to prepare them for the more competitive life they would seem to like for themselves and for their children.

This family may be somewhat different from their neighbors—or at least different from those with whom we come in contact—because the father not only has a steady job but one which also ranks high among unskilled laborers, considering his ethnic background and limited early opportunities. Also, the parents stayed together over the years despite severe marital discord. Like other clients, they easily perceive their children as "bad" and "headed for jail," especially when they misbehave in the community. Yet, despite their anger and expressed disappointment, they seem to have real concern and warmth for each other and for the children. There is real babying and enjoyment of the tiny ones, but this turns into harsh treatment, hollering and punishment as soon as the children are no longer babies. There is endless pride in the older children who succeeded in the army, in white-collar jobs or in college.

We contacted the family by phone regarding what was an *immediate* and *major* crisis in school. The parents, feeling haunted by the police, the court and the school, did not want anything to do with us. The mother was sure that we, like everyone else, were against her, after her and sure to drive her children into jail. The worker was primarily a listener throughout the entire 30-minute telephone conversation but she did ask a few relevant questions, admitting that the situation was an awful mess and spelling out, tentatively, some alternatives to think about.

The mother's tirade subsided, and when the worker suggested that it might be a good idea to get together sometimes to meet the father and whichever children were around, the mother asked, "Right now?" For the next few weeks the worker met with this family every week for two hours or more. The parents were always present; of the older children, those participated who wanted to come or those who presently had problems at home or in school.

The little ones stormed in and out of the room, sometimes trying busily to make friends with the worker. It should be noted that most of the joint interviews were conducted in our offices upon mutual agreement between parents and worker; that we went back to home visiting when it became too difficult for the mother to pack up her family because of her advanced pregnancy; and that at no time was a meeting canceled or broken.

We found that in the beginning, as was our experience with other families, complaints were raised against school, police, court and neighbors and then shifted to bitter accusations against each other. The worker listened, restated some of the problems, asked questions and finally picked out *one* area—among the many expounded on lengthily or repeatedly ("flood release") or touched upon briefly—about which something could perhaps be done. After the customary initial "no," substantiated by reasons frequently based on realities, the worker succeeded—by further questions, listening to feelings expressed and by realistic appraisal of the situation in her own mind—in pointing out a number of ways the situation could be handled more satisfactorily.

As we carefully tapped the ego strength of the clients (in our case it is the strength of the family) by empathizing with some of the clients' difficulties for which there are no ready answers[16] and as we realistically attempted to clarify and sift out possibilities within the clients' reach, we found the family became less hopeless and less helpless about the many real and imaginary odds stacked against them. They began to look actively for resources in the family and community which could handle a few things differently. The court, the police, the many injustices and social barriers experienced became less the cause and object of attack for "all problems," although in time of renewed crisis they are likely to respond with their old pattern, not infrequently with some justification.

In the fourth session, one of the adolescents who rarely talked at home, even without a stranger around, grudgingly expressed his anger—if not his rage—that his parents would call on the police to beat him up, take him away for a day[17] when he was "bad" or he would take off from home to get away from the noise and quarrels. Both parents seemed truly surprised that all of this would bother the boy to this extent, and father and son finally talked to each other after months of silence.

Space does not permit us to report on the worker's contacts with the school, the nurse and court, all of which we find to be an equally important part of our work.

After seven joint interviews several shifts had taken place. After eight years of employment the father got up the courage to explain to his white foreman that he was needed at home in the evenings; within days he was working on a different shift. He and his older boys started to talk to each other; the mother began to reconsider whether "all that was wrong" with her daughters was that they were "rotten and spoiled." The father said if it had not been for his wife he would have left a long time ago since she is the one who holds the family together; this remark led his wife to bake him a cake for his birthday.

The following sentiment about the worker was expressed by the mother: "That's the first time anyone talked to us like that; usually I am treated like an animal." The father remarked: "The 'right' kind of people never speak to us; we have to pick our friends where we can find them."

Open House Afternoon

Our original plan was to set aside three hours each week during which two workers would be available to see school-referred clients either in a group or in individual interviews. We called our group "Mothers' Group" because of the small numbers of fathers in our caseload. At this writing we had held 25 sessions and we were as excited as we were "tentative."

As a start we thought of our open house afternoon as a social affair— to acquaint clients with our services and with each other. We reasoned that the group meetings gradually might become more problem-centered and that a core of clients might emerge who could go into a regular group therapy session. We gave a good deal of consideration to whom we would

---

[16] Sometimes a brief statement by the worker—such as "that's surely tough"— may convey to the client that the worker is fully aware of the impact of his experience, and the client may be able to move on to an area of more productive discussion or activity.

[17] The "authorities" are frequently called in to settle personal disputes among our clients which a middle-class family would handle by themselves, or perhaps through a friend or lawyer.

want to select for the more "therapeutic" group, through what methods, and to which clients might be better suited for individual interviews.

We had a slow start, especially with our "Mothers' Group," since unintentionally we became too selective and too slow about inviting mothers to the group. With clients who avoid tension build-up and who respond best to help when internal and external pressures are great, a "waiting list" of even two or three weeks becomes meaningless. Things changed as soon as we made the group the starting contact with a new client, with perhaps a 15 to 30 minute interview preceding the first group session. Our most responsive clients come from very deprived neighborhoods. We never could claim perfect attendance, but from the beginning the meetings seemed meaningful to the mothers. The sessions are not only problem-centered; they are more family- and self-focused with "less projecting out" than are some of our individual interviews. In many ways we expected this, since discussing problems in a group may be less threatening than discussing them in individual interviews. The refreshments and babysitting arrangement we tried to work out are incidental to the meetings. We are surprised about the leadership quality and initiative our mothers show in the group, considering that the neighborhood is said to have no potentials for any kind of leadership. Some of the clients have been coming from the beginning while some others who came once or twice keep in touch with us by phone or by unexpected office visits. At times a father might show up or an older daughter and not infrequently clients arrive a day earlier or at 10:00 A.M., instead of 1:00 P.M., and we talk to them,—pointing out the correct time of the meeting but listening to their problems anyway.

Although the group attendance of mothers might be irregular, we can be sure of a prompt knock on the door from a group of six- and eight-year-olds who started to drop in on us on the afternoons following the mothers' meeting. Some are the sons of clients, and we usually notice them roaming the streets, since they are too disruptive and restless to take part in the organized after-school activities. We recently contacted a neighborhood center in another district and our inquiry about the possibility of obtaining a group worker for these boys met with a favorable response. Unfortunately we have neither staff nor time to respond to the many groups of youngsters who come by, first to look us over, next to return to "sit around the big table and talk" or use the playroom, or report some important news or who just come and say nothing.

Putting Back the "Social"

In our diagnosis and tentative treatment plans we try to deal with the "social" in the client's environment in more than a descriptive way. To say that a client or his family lives in a slum area, that there are 15 siblings, that the family is Negro or Filipino, that the father is an unskilled laborer, presently unemployed and therefore unable to pay for casework services or "not ready to use casework services," is not sufficient for our purpose. The client's exposure in the social structure brings about different stresses and strains which impinge on his "psychological" make-up from without. This is true whether he belongs to the upper, upper classes or to the lower, lower classes, as our clients do. The strain and stress systems differ, depending on where the client and his family is located in the social structure, and to what ethnic, occupational or religious group he belongs. Although greatly pressured with requests for services, we do not feel that our time is ill spent because clients are not "motivated" for help, have little "insight" and do not readily phone for an office appointment. We consider every cultural improvement we are able to bring about to be a psychosocial improvement— in the true sense—for the client.

Johnny or any of his siblings may steal because they are just plain hungry and the swiping of food, money and toys is not such an exceptional misdeed in Johnny's neighborhood. More often than not, he steals continuously because there exists an emotional conflict of one kind or another in addition to all the other social handicaps within his family—disturbed or changing parent figures, older siblings in trouble with the law or unemployment with all its emotional, physical and social implications. Johnny may or may not have experienced emotional and physical traumata at an early age; he is living *presently* in a situation which does not prepare him for a socially useful life. Some of the children may be less "emotionally sick" than we think they are and our chance to treat them and their families with our present psychological techniques remain slim unless we gain a deeper understanding of their environmental stresses.

In addition to Johnny's or his family's psychopathology (*which needs to be treated* whenever it is present) where are the *strengths* in Johnny's situation? What is left of his family unit, including older siblings, grandparents, etc., and what are his positive resources for growth and social integration? Who are his peers; what kind of behavior pattern do they show as a group and what is Johnny's attachment, relation and role to them? Who are the "significant others" outside his family—teachers, nurses, ministers, policemen —whom we could enable to have a more satisfactory relationship with Johnny and his family? Family caseworkers and clinicians will need to expand their horizons—if they are not doing so already—to collaborate more freely, more effectively, less preciously and confidentially with other agencies around so-called "multiple problems families" and to *develop techniques*[18] *to further communication and understanding between various key figures and the clients.* The best planned casework job with a family might falter. as long as the children's teachers and others who come in contact with the family perceive the family as "no good" and "hopeless." We deal not just with child-parent relationships; we also need to *deal with the community perception of the clients.* For example, to enable a teacher, through case-centered conferences, to have Johnny—who is a poor learner in addition to being a disturbing nuisance—accomplish a small task which he was never

---

[18] Caplan, Gerald, *Mental Health and Consultation* (Washington, D.C.: U.S. Department of Health, Education and Welfare, 1959), 269.

able to accomplish before will give both teacher and child a sense of mutual satisfaction. This might not seem much but if repeated, Johnny and children with similar problems might develop friendlier relationships with their teachers.

Johnny might not go to school for another seven years being perceived as lazy and a nuisance, the only consistent self-image he ever was able to form—until he becomes convinced of it, too—that this is his place in society. Many misunderstandings between people and misconceptions about people are caused by cultural differences, distorted expectations and a breakdown in communication. This leads to increased anxiety and stereotyped perceptions of each other. Once we become clear as to what these differences are we may be able—by helping others in the community—to deal more satisfactorily with our clients.

By its mere existence a service like ours—small and incomplete as it is— demonstrates to the neighborhood and to the other key figures (probation officers, police, nurses, etc.) that they are no longer alone to tackle problems which are overwhelming, that someone thinks, spends money and time to work with "those" families that we too fail at times, no matter how hard we try. Let us remember that it is tought to live or work in certain districts. We try to become part of the neighborhood and this seems the easiest part of the job. The schools, the police and the merchants welcome the opportunity to talk to someone about the way they see the problems; we need them just as urgently, for as caseworkers we can no longer work in a professional vacuum. We have to understand the place we occupy in the community along with all the other helping professions; we have to be clear about our professional value system and goals which may be slightly different from the other helping professions; we have to be more accepting and more understanding and less punitive, just as we need to be clear about how the clients are viewed by the community and how they may perceive us.

Putting back the "social" into social work, therefore, does not just mean making more home visits and doing otherwise "exactly what we have done before." Nor does it mean returning to "old-fashioned" social work, although this would be better on many occasions than doing nothing.

It means seeing the environment in a new, dynamic way and becoming cognizant of the social processes which impinge on the individual from without.[19]

Our perception, in the light of new knowledge of what is important, is changing as new formulations of diagnosis and treatment are developed.

[19] Stein, Herman D., "The Concept of the Social Environment in Social Work Practice," *Smith College Studies in Social Work*, (June, 1960), 188–210.

Casework Intervention and the Problems of the Poor

Ben A. Orcutt

Casework will not eliminate poverty, although it has historically addressed itself to the troubles of poor people. The elimination of poverty is an economic and social complexity involving the productive economy of a nation, the social fiber of its people, and transfer of income,[1] and it requires a national commitment, with multidimensional strategies for intervention. In the past decade much emphasis has been laid on poverty amid affluence in this country; politicians, economists, academicians, social workers, and others have spoken out on its insidious effects and offered ideas for its eradication. The mass of literature that has emerged on the profile, incidence, causes, and economic solutions to poverty has contributed to the awakening of Americans to the deplorable plight of a substantial proportion of the citizenry.[2] It has emphasized the fact that poverty was not to be equated with personal defects, but could be the result of social conditions, institutional structures, market fluctuations, technology, and crises beyond individual control.

It is recognized that to deal with poverty, broad economic and social measures are required: economic growth, full employment, a minimum wage, educational and training opportunities, social and health insurance, income maintenance for those outside the labor market, and a guaranteed income floor under the working poor.

The purpose here, however, is to discuss social work intervention aimed directly at maximizing the social functioning and potential of impoverished

Reprinted from *Social Casework*, Vol. 54 (February, 1973), pp. 85–95, by permission of the author and the Family Service Association of America.

[1] Robert J. Lampman, Transfer and Redistribution as Social Process, in *Social Security in International Perspective*, ed. Shirley Jenkins (New York: Columbia University Press, 1969), pp. 29–54.

[2] For example, Mollie Orshansky, Counting the Poor: Another Look at Poverty Profile, *Social Security Bulletin*, 28: 2–29 (January 1965); ibid., The Shape of Poverty in 1966, *Social Security Bulletin*, 31:3 (March 1968); Margaret S. Gordon, ed., *Poverty in America* (San Francisco: Chandler Publishing Co., 1967); Leon H. Keyserling, *Progress or Poverty* (Washington, D.C.: Conference on Economic Problems, December 1964); John Kenneth Galbraith, *The Affluent Society* (Boston: Houghton Mifflin Co., 1958); Michael Harrington, *The Other America: Poverty in the United States* (New York: Macmillan Co., 1962).

individuals and families. One should be especially concerned with those poor people who are most vulnerable to stress and disorganized patterns of family life as a result of psychological and social scarring from lives of impoverishment, inadequate parents, discrimination, and drug abuse and whose social values and life-style are generally regarded as outside the mainstream. Social casework as a mode of help is appropriate to all troubled individuals and families, regardless of their economic and social circumstances, but it is a vital strategy for attack on the incidence and perpetuation of social problems associated with poverty. It is overly simplistic to assume that adequate income alone will eliminate the problems of poverty although it is a major device. For masses of families, this is a tenable assumption, but for many more who are products of long-term, generational poverty, social deviance, and more entrenched psychosocial problems, intervention beyond income is required. Intervention is particularly needed to interrupt the cyclic patterns of inadequate parenthood and prevent children from developmental hazards. The use of social casework services oriented to understanding and treatment of life stresses is a fundamental strategy for intervention and must be built into any current program that seeks prevention, rehabilitation, and the maximizing of the social functioning potential of its citizens. Carol Meyer,[3] in stressing prevention, suggests the availability of the social worker, prior to the onset of problem and breakdown, in such social institutions as Social Security offices and day care centers. In these marketplaces for the citizenry, stress, crisis, and potential problems may be identified with appropriate intervention. Another important point of entry for services is the public family agency, disassociated from the stigma of public welfare, which can host a range of family and children's services responsive to the magnitude of daily problems that occur in conflictual personal and family relationships or in the work and social environment. The public family agency could serve to restore and rehabilitate as well as to prevent dysfunction and would complement, not displace, the valuable services of voluntary family and children's agencies. There is extensive work to be done in both the public and private sector to strengthen and protect families.

The casework focus within the social work practice system is a direct service to individuals, families, and groups aimed at prevention and alleviation of stress from psychosocial problems and the disequilibrium experienced. It utilizes a helping or a therapeutic relationship of varying intensity; fosters access to services through organization and structuring of agency policy, services, and resources for social supports; and intercedes with interlocking environmental systems on the behalf of those who need help. The intervention process thus varies to include the one-to-one relationship oriented to the individual, treatment of family members jointly or as a group, treatment of groups of families or individuals in formed

---

[3] Carol Meyer, *Social Work Practice* (New York: The Free Press, 1970), pp. 153–61.

groups, and the organization and use of agency service structures and manpower to implement the direct work. Indeed, the shift in focus of intervention depends upon the assessed needs and desires of the family or individuals who need or seek help with their difficulties.

Figure 1 illustrates the focal components of casework services oriented to helping individuals, families, and groups. The chart portrays the social casework practitioner at the center of the wheel of service activity which may be consultative or therapeutic and may serve to develop or facilitate the use of other socioenvironmental resources. It may also serve to develop agency policies and patterns of service delivery to reach out and meet needs, or it may extend the professional self through supervisory, administrative, and consultative roles, adding professional knowledge in the use of the non-professional for varied tasks. More broadly, a consultative role may extend the caseworker as consultant and facilitator to school systems, nurseries or day care centers, parent education groups, and family planning and other socioenvironmental systems. Although one casework practitioner may have more interest and acquire more expertise in some focal components of the casework system rather than in others, he has basic knowledge of, and some competence in, all components or foci of activity.

Figure 2 serves to place the foci of casework within the social work practice system. It is important to view the whole of social work as a system and to view casework as a subsystem or cluster of interdependent focal components of the fluid interacting practice system. The organizational relationships of the focal components of the social work system are portrayed in a circular pattern in figure 2. The foci of organization and access, social policy, social planning, and direct services interlock at varying levels in practice, but the focal components of the system tend to cluster in subsystems, depending on whether the processes carried out are interventions addressed to individuals, families, and small groups or to the larger, more complex social systems, such as institutions and communities.

Thus, we can identify the major foci as clusters of the focal components of the social work system, interlocking but differing in major emphasis and elements of underlying knowledge. The components are interdependent, with interventions in one part of the practice system affecting other parts. Group and individual methods are seen as cutting across the totality of the practice system.[4] At points in the transactions of the social work practice system, whether aimed at families or communities, there will be interpenetration and exchange as indicated by the arrows in figure 2. Any strategy for helping poor people through direct casework intervention is also interdependent and interactive with the structure of service networks, social policies, and opportunities that facilitate qualitative changes in the larger environment.

[4] In this formulation *group work* is integrated in the holistic practice system. *Casework* identifies the "case" in services oriented toward clients and is consonant with social work tradition.

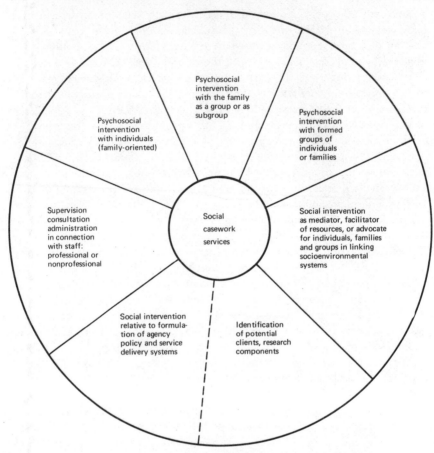

Figure 1. Social Casework Services: Focal Components Directed Toward Individuals, Families, and Groups

The social casework practice subsystem brings into focus the person/family-in-environment with varying needs for counseling, for mediation of environmental problems, for advocacy, for access, and for provision of services. Environmental deprivation cannot be neglected, nor can the suffering within the individual and his maladaptive interpersonal relationships, which are transactional with a noxious environment.

Solutions to poverty that include broad social change or direct help to families at risk, as a major commitment in social work, have been the subject of much controversy. It is contended that provision of direct services to individuals and families should receive less priority. Direct services are described as inadequate to meet the challenge of improved conditions for the poor. The charge among many in social welfare is that social casework does not address itself sufficiently to the structural and institutional arrangements that are the primary sources of human suffering.[5] Holders of this view

---

[5] Bertram Beck, A Reassessment of Casework as a Method, in *Social Work Practice* (New York: Columbia University Press, 1964).

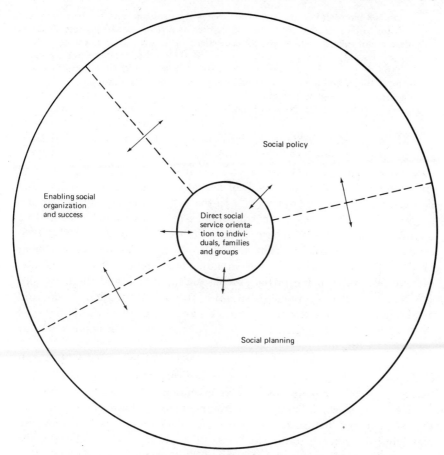

Figure 2. Foci of Social Work Practice System

consider direct help as a Band-Aid approach and emphasize broad-scale solutions. The tendency to polarize these views does not serve the poor or the profession. A systemic view, as outlined here, would move practice toward cooperative and interactive tasks and goals, though major emphases and professional preparation would vary.

In this connection, systems theory as a theoretical framework bears discussion. The theory is consistent with the historical focus of casework on the person-in-situation, and it offers a conceptual framework for identification and assessment of transactional phenomena for casework intervention.

General Systems Theory: A Theoretical Frame

General systems theory provides a frame for viewing the dynamic whole of man in his universe or life space. Social casework has historically viewed the person and his environment as dynamically related. Gordon Hamilton in the early 1930s defined the organismic view and the psychosocial approach of casework, using the concept of person-in-situation. She wrote:

Man is a bio-social Organism—the "case", the problem, and the treatment are always to be regarded by the social worker as a psychosocial process. A social case is not determined by the kind of client (a family, a child, an old person, an adolescent), nor can it be determined by the kind of problem (an economic disability or a behavior problem). A social case is a "living event", within which there are always economic, physical, mental, emotional, and social factors in varying proportions. So when one thinks of a social case one must always consider it in terms of both inner and outer interacting factors.[6]

More recently, William Gordon has referred to the traditional focus on "the person-in-his-life-situation complex" suggesting "the central focus of social work as the interface between or the meeting place of person and environment. The phenomenon of concern at this interface is the transaction between person and environment."[7] In the action intersystem that Gordon conceptualizes, he stresses the transactions of persons coping with their impinging environment. There is less strength, however, for also conceptualizing the holistic qualities of the system with its own unique, emergent properties, which is vital to understanding and treatment of the family. Florence Hollis, referring to the psychosocial approach and the person-in-situation concept in current use, speaks of the person-situation Gestalt and emphasizes both the individual and his situation as factors to be understood in diagnosis and as elements in which change can be brought about by casework treatment.[8]

Using systems theory, this writer evolved a further developed Gestalt concept to emphasize not only the person-in-situation but the family as a primary systemic unit for casework intervention. The concept of systemic configuration of person/family-in-environment more definitively encompasses the transactional nature of the person-family-environmental systems and highlights the integrity and wholeness of a given system, especially the family with its own emergent properties. Thus this formulation suggests a wide-angle lens for viewing the fluid, penetrating, transactional properties of the individual and family, with linking environmental systems as well as emergent properties of the whole.[9] With the refocusing of the lens, a closeup and highly penetrating vision of smaller and smaller parts of any of these systems can be examined for their transactions. The past and current focus of social casework on person-in-situation suggests a holistic, transactional field, although it actually tends to narrow vision. Every client needing help— and most especially poor clients within debilitating environmental con-

---

[6] Gordon Hamilton, *Theory and Practice of Social Casework*, 2nd ed. rev. (New York: Columbia University Press, 1951), pp. 3–4.

[7] William Gordon, Basic Constructs for Integrative and Generative Conception of Social Work, in *The General Systems Approach: Contributions Toward a Holistic Conception of Social Work* (New York: Council on Social Work Education, 1969), pp. 6–7.

[8] Florence Hollis, The Psychosocial Approach to Casework, in *Theories of Social Casework*, ed. Robert Roberts and Robert Nee (Chicago: University of Chicago Press, 1970), p. 58.

[9] Paul Waltzlawick, Janet H. Beavin, and Don D. Jackson, *Pragmatics of Human Communication* (New York: W. W. Norton Co., 1967), pp. 123–25.

ditions—should be viewed as a component of his family system and his environment, unless there is no family in the focal field.

As yet, general systems theory is not sufficiently developed to explain and predict transactional phenomena definitively; it is essentially a framework rather than theory. It has identified universal laws governing organizational entities ranging in complexity and including organisms, personality, physical matter, and sociocultural phenomena. Middle-range concepts that could underlie principles for casework practice are generally lacking. However, systems theory is extremely useful in identifying structural relationships and processes of casework relevant to impoverished people who have disruptive family relationships and multiple environmental problems.

Before going into further detail regarding its particular relevance in application, it is necessary to explain the basic theoretical concepts. Ludwig Von Bertalanffy defines a system as a "complex of components in mutual interaction . . . any 'whole' consisting of interacting components."[10] James Miller further elaborates that the state of each component is constrained by, conditioned by, or dependent on the state of other components, thus predicting organizational relationships among components or parts of a system.[11]

Systems may range from such simple levels of organization as one cell in an organism to such complex social organizations as communities. Properties of systems apply to varying levels of organization, to abstract, physical inanimate matter, and to living organisms. A system may be open or closed. It is the open and living systems we are essentially concerned with in social work. In a closed system there is no exchange of energies or information in any form with the environment. An open system implies the opposite. Human organisms, personalities, and all levels of organization of social groups may be defined as living, open systems, with a dynamic order of parts and processes standing in mutual interaction. The particular substances or properties of the whole of the system result from an organization of lower-level components, which in themselves have varying degrees of organization. Organization of components, with interdependent relationships in the systemic whole, makes it possible to identify an aggregate of characteristics, different from but often lacking in the individual component alone. Thus, the whole of a family system is greater than the sum of its parts (members). The social work practice system is greater than the components embodied in casework, organization, planning, and policy development.

All systems have a hierarchial relationship with larger or smaller systems in the environmental field. The suprasystem is the next higher system in which a given system is a component or a subsystem. The supra-

[10] Ludwig Von Bertalanffy, General System Theory and Psychiatry, in *American Handbook of Psychiatry*, vol. 3, ed. Silvano Arieti (New York: Basic Books, 1966), p. 709.

[11] James Miller, Living Systems: Basic Concepts, in *General System Theory and Psychiatry*, ed. William Gray et al. (Boston: Little, Brown Co., 1969), pp. 68–69.

system of a person is the group he is in at the time. The entire environment of a system includes the suprasystem and all systems at higher levels which contain it.[12] In order to survive, any open system exchanges energy or information with its environment. These exchange processes alter both the system and its environment. For example, for the person—or individual—system, the suprasystem is his family, and his immediate environment is his family minus himself. His entire environment includes his family, his social groups, neighborhood, work, community, and so forth—these are the larger, higher-level systems of which he is a part and with whom he interacts. Every system except the largest has an environment, and every system except the smallest is an environment.[13]

To explicate general systems theory further as a framework for casework focus, using the concept of systemic configuration of person/family-in-environment, requires other central concepts. In this discussion, open and living systems are not being considered in the abstract, like Talcott Parsons's model,[14] which conceptualizes the components of a social system as social roles. System components here imply concrete, living individuals and groups of individuals capable of energy and information exchange in the physical and human interactional environment. They may also take social roles.

The open system is further characterized by permeable boundaries so that inputs of energy and information from the environmental system can be processed and exchanged with output to the environment. The second law of thermodynamics identifies a tendency in physical matter to run a course of entropy, which means "leveling down differences to states of maximum disorder and randomness."[15] The entropic leveling down and disintegration are decreased with negative entropy (or negentropy)—a higher input and exchange of energy and information from the environment, that become a restoring process which repairs the decompensation. This process allows the system to maintain a steady state even though entropic changes may occur over the long run. The open system may achieve an ultimate state independent of the initial conditions, known as equifinality.[16] An open system will therefore appear to have certain characteristics and a will or purpose of its own. If the steady state is disturbed by adding or removing quantities of interactional substances, the system will reestablish itself in a manner determined by the characteristics of the entire system rather than by any of its specific states.[17]

[12] Miller, Living Systems: Basic Concepts, p. 99.

[13] Gordon Hearn, *The General System Approach* (New York: Council on Social Work Education, 1970), p. 65.

[14] Talcott Parsons, Social Systems, in *International Encyclopedia of the Social Sciences*, ed. David L. Sills, vol. 15 (New York: Macmillan Co. and The Free Press, 1968), p. 452.

[15] Von Bertalanffy, General System Theory and Psychiatry, p. 708.

[16] Ibid.

[17] Anatol Rapoport, General System Theory, in *International Encyclopedia of the Social Sciences* (New York: Macmillan Co. and The Free Press, 1968), pp. 452–58.

Systems, although repairing themselves in the negentropic process, may thus maintain themselves at high levels of order and complexity with increasing differentiation. To illustrate in terms of a family system: The impoverished ghetto family alienated from the mainstream is subject to increasing entropic processes from the multiple input of substandard housing, assaults on member self-esteem, deprivation of income and opportunity, physical danger from crime and drugs, and inadequate medical care. These difficulties allow for little energy or informational resources from the environmental systems for restoration, repair, or change. Under the principle of entropic processes, the family system would continue to deteriorate and move toward chaos. In the fluid, interacting processes, a tenuous steady state may occur, although the family is moving toward further deterioration. However, with increased input of good housing, medical care, money income, and opportunities for member self-realization and dignity, the exchange processes with the environment can tend to be restorative (negentropic process), and the family output can become more consistent with the expected role-carrying of the environment, the growth tasks, and higher levels of functioning (differentiation).

In addition, systems have a criterion apparatus or a critical subsystem that controls the entire system and guarantees characteristic or purposeful behavior. This apparatus tends to be embodied in the concept of feedback. The sensory apparatus of the system distinguishes deviations from external or goal-directed states and feeds back mismatch information into the system's behavior-directing centers. Corrections are thus made which reduce the systems deviation (negative feedback) or increase the systems deviation within criterion limits (positive feedback) from its goal or characteristic behavior.[18]

For example, in the person system the perceptual and cognitive apparatus tends to perceive and serve to control deviation from characteristic goals. In the family system, the controls, rules, or seat of power in the organization may vary, but ordinarily are held by a parent. Among poor, disorganized, female-based families as described by Salvador Minuchin, Louise Bandler, and others,[19] the absence of a controller or the transfer of executive control and power to one of the children is observed as disintegrative. It can be postulated that the criterion apparatus of the family system does not function and that chaos will result, without the necessary selective apparatus to judge selectively, from the input of a painful, frustrating environment, the routines that serve purposeful, survival goals. This cursory description of the dynamics of open systems would not be complete without emphasizing that any system has a structure, which is the

[18] Walter Buckley, *Sociology and Modern Systems Theory* (Englewood Cliffs, N.J.: Prentice Hall, 1967), pp. 52–53.

[19] Salvador Minuchin et al. *Families of the Slums* (New York: Basic Books, 1967); Louise S. Bandler, Family Functioning: A Psychological Perspective, and Casework—a Process of Socialization, in *The Drifters*, ed. Eleanor Pavenstadt (Boston: Little, Brown Co., 1967), pp. 226–94.

arrangement of its subsystems and components or the organizational structures underlying the system. The functional units or components in interaction change in time with the input of energy and information; this is known as process. Thus all systems have a structure and process that include the ongoing functioning of the system.

From the foregoing discussion of the central concepts of general systems theory, it is easy to visualize the individual and family systems in a depriving environment and the crucial need to identify the input (nurturing physical and affective resources and information) needed, from a range of linking environmental systems, to stimulate the exchange processes that reduce excessive output of aggression or apathy.

Figure 3 shows the concepts of systemic configuration of person/family-in-environment, using systems theory as a framework for organizing the dynamic and social theory in conceptualizing casework focus. The person is depicted in the chart as a biological-personality system, a component in the family system, and a component in the major systems of the total environment with which he may be linked at a given time. All of these systems are fluid and capable of interpenetrating the boundaries of any system with which they may be linked.

The psyche, or personality system, is identified from its structural organization of id, ego, and superego and not isolated from the biological system variables of energy, cells, organs, and mental apparatus. The person as a psyche and soma is subject to exchange with an environment that may be growth-producing, gratifying, and stimulating of negentropic processes. Conversely, input may be excessive in deprivation of affective and usable information that produces entropic processes and diminution of capacity to survive.

In figure 3 the family is presented as the vital suprasystem for the person, and the transactional whole has its own emergent properties. The figure further identifies the varying socioenvironmental systems within the total environmental space that may be linked with any person/family system. The chart exemplifies the principle that change in the components of a system brings change in the system whole. This concept is applicable at every level of systemic organization. The fluidity and interlocking of systems cue the social caseworker to view the clients' troubles as transactional, along with their historic antecedents and to specify the crucial points of stress and strain among the interlocking systems in charting the directions for intervention.

To illustrate graphically the significance of systems theory as a theoretical framework for casework aimed at helping low-income families, the following case example is presented.[20] It can be seen that problems in any one system, person/family/environment, transact and interpenetrate the permeable boundaries of the interlocking systems.

---

[20] The writer is indebted to Dorothy Yates, field instructor, Columbia University, and Mary Watson, student, for case material.

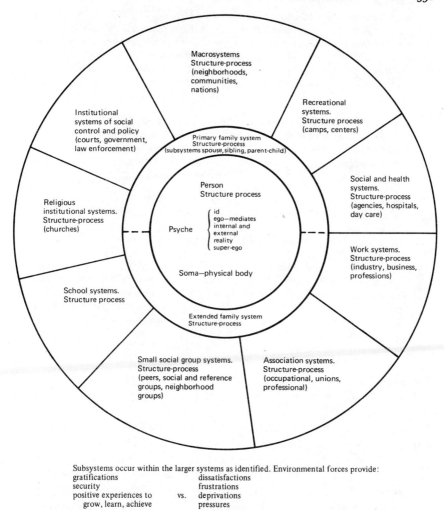

Figure 3. Systemic Configuration of Person/Family-in-Environment
Man is a social being in constant interaction or interplay with his environment

Case Illustration

Mrs. R, a black, forty-two-year-old, obese mother of ten children, was admitted to a state hospital. Prior to admission, Mrs. R, who has an eighth-grade education, resided with her husband and children in a six-room apartment in a deteriorated old building in a ghetto neighborhood. The family received a maximum ADC grant, and Mr. R earned a small income from steady night work. The family managed poorly as their income provided only basic necessities. (They would be currently categorized as the "working poor.")

Mrs. R was diagnosed as a chronic schizophrenic, undifferentiated type. She was hospitalized at the request of the family court when at a court hearing both she and her husband were charged with child neglect. Her bizarre delusional responses led to recommendation of hospitalization. Mrs. R spoke of being unable to take care of her ten children, ranging from two-year-old twins to a fourteen-year-old daughter on whom she relied. Her child care was erratic, and at times she could not feed, change, or train the twins, nor could she touch or acknowledge any of the children. She refused to prepare her husband's meals and refused sexual relationships, fearing pregnancy. She used a contraceptive preparation which had been ineffective. Mr. R had withdrawn from her verbally and emotionally, and generally was away from the home. He had deserted her four years before, but returned when ordered by the court to face a jail sentence or return home.

Mrs. R is essentially nonverbal; her voice has a strained, unnatural sound. She distrusts people and is aloof and withdrawn. She complains of the heavy strain of family responsibility. Mr. R does not see himself as a helpmate and does nothing to maintain the family or marital relationship, nor does he give physical care to the children. Clinic appointments, school appointments, household chores and management, and discipline are left to Mrs. R. She says she resents this and her husband's criticism of her being a poor housekeeper, but she does not speak out about it. She tends to withdraw and appears apathetic.

The six school-age children all have learning difficulties and are in special classes at public school. One child, age ten, is severely retarded and cannot dress herself. All the children in the family are functioning below normal expectations. Little is known of Mrs. R's early life beyond the fact that she was the youngest of nine children and was born on a farm. She moved to the city with her mother during her teens after her father died. She worked in factories, was self-supporting, and lived with her mother until age twenty-six, when she married her present husband. Her mother has subsequently died, and there is no extended family in the city. In the hospital, in addition to appearing isolated, she evidences some delusional ideas.

This case illustration is similar to a magnitude of cases known to hospitals and to voluntary and public agencies that serve people from low-income groups in areas of a central city.

At the outset, one sees a family system in chaos and in transaction with a range of interlocking systems in the environment. The primary focus, as discussed here, would not be simply on Mrs. R as a new paitient in the state hospital with an identified diagnosis of schizophrenia. The focus would be on Mrs. R as a component of her family system and the interlocking social systems, such as the hospital, the family court, Department of Social Services, the ghetto neighborhood, and public schools—and indirectly with the work system, where her husband is a structural part.

The unit of attention may shift with diagnosis and intervention, but primarily the focus is on the family in trouble. There is no attempt to minimize the fact that Mrs. R has a severe emotional illness. Her personality system is disorganized, with an overwhelmed ego that cannot successfully mediate the intrapsychic and environmental forces. Her individual dynamics should be assessed in concert with the dynamics of her family system and the transactions with other linking systems. With this focus, intervention is aimed at family equilibrium, differentiation, and growth in the family system. This practice does not imply that the R family system is seen and treated only as a family group, with help to Mrs. R accruing as residual to shifting the family dynamics in an improved equilibrium of the system.[21] It

[21] The system purists are described by Christian Beels and Andrew Ferber, Family Therapy: A View, *Family Process*, 8: 296 (September 1969).

is important, however, to focus on change of functioning in the family as a dynamic, interactional unit, as well as change in the dynamics of Mrs. R's individual functioning. Intervention is aimed at both the family and individual systems. Treatment may be individual or family group treatment, or both.

The social caseworker who applies systems theory as a frame and focuses on the family unit, with Mrs. R as a component, will intervene in the following directions.

1. Build a trusting relationship with Mrs. R (person system) through regular contact, as a caring, dependable object whose quality of communication and tangible help can stimulate affective contact, a sense of trust, and self-worth. Dealing with her reality, its burdens, and a more realistic appraisal is aimed at improving her reality testing and expansion of ego-functioning.

2. Encourage Mrs. R, in dealing with ward and hospital systems, to participate and enlarge her object relationships and general functioning in her patient role.

3. Intervene in the hospital system to mediate problem situations, including access to knowledge of family planning, and serve as interpreter or advocate for the client in order to reduce stress and support hospital input for nurturance and change.

4. Involve Mr. R (family system) in a greater role of leadership as the sole parent in the home, as is consistent with his capacities and as the family transactions permit.

5. Intervene with the Department of Social Services agency system in the provision of a homemaker (paraprofessional) on a long-term basis and bring routines into the home by which child care can be brought up to standard, without displacing Mr. or Mrs. R but by encouraging their support and accrediting parental strengths.

6. Intervene with housing authorities to provide adequate housing.

7. Intervene with the school system to mediate, interpret, advocate, or plan with school for children to maximize learning. The ten-year-old severely retarded child, who remains in the home, will need special planning depending on her functioning and the extent of care required.

8. Intervene with the family court to mediate and interpret family difficulties and enlist support for the family as a structural unit.

9. Intervene with the family as a group in assessment of family dynamics and with family group treatment as appropriately timed. The aim in

treatment is to improve interpersonal relationships, facilitate appropriate communication and role-carrying, and shift the affective supports within the system to meet individual needs for growth and mastery of developmental tasks.

10. Enroll Mrs. R, as diagnostically indicated, in a formed group aimed at socialization and introduce the other family members who can benefit to community services offering group experience.

The social caseworker's diagnostic assessment of the individual/family and environmental transactions guides the intervention at varying depths in all of the linking systems to achieve reduction of frustration and to increase the supplies of energy and information that will stimulate exchange that is restorative and growth-producing. Systems concepts aid in depicting the fluid, interactional relationship within the person/family systems and those that interlock to form the environment for Mrs. R and the family. The functioning of Mrs. R as a component of her family system is conditioned by and conditions that of other members in the family. The homemaker who enters the family system must also be taken into account in the transactional processes. Serving as a dependable mother surrogate, the homemaker can be responsive to deep and feared dependency needs in Mrs. R's personality system which affect the entire family transaction.

The casework practitioner thus orchestrates a range of services combined with a therapeutic approach not only to strengthen Mrs. R's ego functioning, in individual work, but also to modify the functioning of the family unit. At the hub of the wheel, as illustrated in figure 1, the caseworker must be competent to extend himself as helper in each focal area as specified in the social casework practice system. Families like the R family who are maladaptive, poor, disadvantaged, uneducated, and unaware of services are brought into sharp relief in the areas of social environmental intervention illustrated in the figure. The practitioner has responsibility to contribute from his knowledge of broad client needs to policies and development of a range of services, with delivery patterns that serve to prevent problems and to restore individuals and families, whose maladaptations are associated with substandard living. The aim must be to make available appropriately trained manpower, equipped to render direct helping services in a service network with sufficient resources. Professional knowledge, competence, and skill are basic requirements for the wide responsibilities of social casework practice at the hub of the wheel, especially aimed at poor, dysfunctional families alienated from the mainstream.

Individualizing the Multiproblem Family

Carol H. Meyer

During the last ten years, ever since the publication of the study of social problems undertaken in St. Paul, Minnesota, by Community Research Associates,[1] the professional literature has abounded with material on the multiproblem family. The term "multiproblem family"—literally, "a family with many problems"—has come into general use not as a description but as a pseudodiagnostic classification. It is not derived from an explicated theory, and it does not have the same meaning to everyone who uses it. Yet it has taken on a kind of magical significance as a convenient device by means of which the social worker is presumed to be able to identify a particular group of clients—those families in a low socioeconomic class whose members act out, are umotivated to get help, suffer from character disorders, and fail to function adequately in their social roles. In this article, I shall examine some of the most important characteristics of the families to which we have assigned the label "multiproblem" and suggest the means by which social workers can bring them the help they need.

First, I should like to make a few additional comments about the term "multiproblem." Although it is not a diagnostic term, it is preferable to certain other terms, such as "hard-to-reach," "hard-core," "self-defeating," or "acting-out," which are laden with value judgments or have a pseudo-clinical implication.[2] "Multiproblem" at least does not convey the idea that the family so labeled is judged to be lacking in inner resources, unmotivated, overly dependent, or hopeless. In the absence of a better term, it can be used to identify a group of clients who carry a particularly heavy burden of

[1] Bradley Buell and Associates, *Community Planning for Human Services*, Columbia University Press, New York, 1952.
[2] *Multi-Problem Families and Casework Practice*, New York City Chapter, National Association of Social Workers, New York, 1960 (mimeographed).

Reprinted from *Social Casework*, Vol. 44 (May, 1963), pp. 267–272, by permission of the author and the Family Service Association of Americe.

social problems and to whom the social work profession bears a special responsibility.

Characteristics of Multiproblem Families

Multiproblem families have been the subject of many community studies.[3] From these studies, one is led to conclude that such families exhibit the following characteristics. They are families that have been overwhelmed by the cumulative effects of chronic economic dependency, which are manifested in some of the following difficulties: periodic unemployment, indebtedness, inadequate housing, poor standards of housekeeping, conspicuous marital discord, school failure, delinquency and other major misconduct, chronic illness, alcoholism, narcotics addiction, and prostitution. Also characteristic of these families are the repetition of their difficulties in succeeding generations, their long contact with social agencies, the pervasiveness of their personal and social breakdown, and the fact that they have become troublesome to the communities in which they live. Certain characteristics of the families vary with the particular community, for they are often members of racial minorities, newcomers, or marginal workers. Moreover, the studies emphasize that multiproblem families are resistant to offers of help from social workers and disinclined to ask for service.

This listing of the gross characteristics of multiproblem families offers a composite picture of the client group I am considering here. I would submit, however, that there is only *one* characteristic universal to this group—poverty. The fact that these families are *poor* is the fundamental issue in understanding them and in planning appropriate treatment. No proof has ever been offered that their difficulties are related to particular racial or ethnic backgrounds or to specific psychiatric typologies or to their behavorial patterns. Furthermore, I should like to point out that even the fact of their poverty does not provide an adequate basis for determining what a social worker must do in order to help them. Professional help can be given only if each multiproblem family is individualized in relation to its own unique characteristics and the particular constellation of factors that have created

---

[3] See, for example, L. L. Geismar and Beverly Ayres, *Families in Trouble*, Family Centered Project, Greater St. Paul Community Chest and Councils, St. Paul, Minnesota, 1958; L. L. Geismar and Beverly Ayres, *Patterns of Change in Problem Families*, Family Centered Project, Greater St. Paul Community Chest and Councils, St. Paul, Minnesota, 1959; *Reaching the Unreached Family*, Youth Board Monograph No. 5, New York City Youth Board, New York, 1958; *A Study of Some of the Characteristics of 150 Multiproblem Families*, New York City Youth Board, New York, 1957 (mimeographed); Kenneth Dick and Lydia J. Strnad, "The Multi-problem Family and Problems of Service," *Social Casework*, Vol. XXXIX, June, 1958, pp. 349–55; Elizabeth Wood, *The Small Hard Core*, Citizens' Housing and Planning Council of New York, New York, 1957; Kermit T. Wiltse, "The 'Hopeless' Family," *Social Work*, Vol. III, October, 1958, pp. 12–22.

its special internal and external difficulties. In other words, the treatment of multiproblem families must take place within the frame of reference of social work.

The Pressures of Poverty

From a socioeconomic point of view these are poverty-stricken families who have suffered for generations from unemployment and underemployment. As members of cultural minority groups, they have been the victims of discrimination and of countless forms of exploitation in their jobs as unskilled workers. The lack of steady work inevitably leads to chronic financial insecurity, with all its attendant problems: poor nutrition and lack of regular medical and dental care, hence poor health and often illness; housing that is inadequate in size, comfort, and cleanliness, hence extreme crowding or indifference toward housekeeping and homemaking; children deprived of sufficient clothing, recreational outlets, room and time for homework, and attention from parents preoccupied with making ends meet, hence maladjustment at school, dropout, delinquency, and behavior problems; the exhausting pressures of poverty that lead husband and wife to become disappointed in each other when there seems to be no way out, hence all forms of marital conflict. For many of these families there is the ever-present fact of public assistance and marginal living. In the AFDC program, for example, men have been driven out of their homes through legal statute.[4] Thus the AFDC family has often become a maternal household with a working mother or adolescent and latchkey children who must assume a host of extra responsibilities because the family is fatherless.

Viewed from a socioeconomic standpoint, therefore, "treatment" of the multiproblem family and of the cyclical problems that pervade its life must reside in broad social reform: the promise of full employment throughout the year, legal provisions such as family allowances and health insurance, a higher minimum wage that will at least purchase the necessities of life, more readily available and better co-ordinated neighborhood services, better schools, renovation of slum areas, and more suitable public housing. A better world must be created for the seventy-seven million Americans who now live in poverty and deprivation.[5] The answer to the multiproblem family is to be found, in large part, in eliminating economic insecurity.

Until drastic social and economic reform effects the changes and improvements demanded by the complexities of our largely urban society, we cannot hope to build a social order in which there is no multiproblem family. In the meantime, social workers will have to assume their rightful responsibility for meeting the needs of such families—a responsibility they have traditionally been assigned by society.

[4] Elizabeth G. Meier, "Casework Services to ADC Families," *Public Welfare*, Vol. XIX, January, 1961, pp. 19–22.
[5] *Poverty and Deprivation In the United States: The Plight Of Two-Fifths Of A Nation*, Conference on Economic Progress, Washington, D.C., 1962, p. 2.

Psychosocial Problems

It is not sufficient, however, to consider the multiproblem family only from a socioeconomic point of view. Poverty exacerbates a variety of problems that may have their origin in psychological or emotional malfunctioning. Although behavior disorders in children, parental breakdown, marital conflict, out-of-wedlock pregnancies, school failure, mental illness, neuroses, and character disturbances are not solely problems of the poor, the lack of resources accompanying the state of poverty makes it more difficult for the poor to cope with them. Moreover, each social class expresses its problems in a particular manner. The way in which the lower-class family expresses its problems gives it greater visibility in a society saturated with middle-class values. For example, in a middle-class family, the husband who is in conflict with his wife may take his highball into another room, where he can be alone. But in the lower-class home, where there is no spare room and no chance for solitude, the husband may lose his temper out loud in front of his wife and children, or he may go to the corner bar for solace. Whichever he does, his marital conflict will be apparent to the community.

Another example can be cited. Children in all economic classes are subject to behavior disorders. The poor family trying to cope with such a problem, however, cannot rely on a change of neighborhood, a better school, a camp in the summer, or cultural and recreational outlets that might alleviate the child's difficulty. Neither can the family utilize psychiatric or clinical services that require the payment of a fee. Frequently it cannot even articulate its concerns well enough to communicate with a social agency—if indeed the child's disorder is at all as bothersome to the family as it is to the community.

In summary, working with multiproblem families does not involve dealing with new clinical entities, hereditary problems, or "lower-classisms." It requires dealing with psychosocial problems that have long been familiar to social workers but have been made worse by poverty, lack of resources, and rejection in practically every aspect of life.

As social workers search for means of helping multiproblem families, they must be alert both to their own and to the community's attitudes toward them. Much has been written about "lower-class cultures" and "deviant behavior in lower-class groups," "street-gang culture" and "the maternal family in the lower classes." One may wonder whether a poor person any longer has an individual identity! In my opinion, it is indefensible to write off as "culturally acceptable" to a certain group poverty and its terrible hardships, personality disturbances and their painful results, or the pervasive effect of impaired relationships. How often we have heard that in a particular cultural group it is acceptable for a teen-age girl to have a baby out of wedlock! Whether or not this is a valid generalization is for the sociologist to study. The social worker, on the other hand, must be concerned about the loneliness a teen-age girl feels when she has no husband with whom to share her parenthood, when she cannot return to school, when her friends go out on dates while she stays at home to care for the baby, or when her friends get their first jobs and she must apply for public assistance.

The same kind of generalizations on the cultural acceptability of deviant behavior have been made about adolescent delinquency and about a family's failure to meet socially approved standards in homemaking or in the education of the children. Even if the adolescent who is behaving in a deviant manner—truanting from school, hanging around the streets, participating in delinquent acts or gang warfare, or using narcotics—*is* reflecting what is normal for his primary reference group or his economic class, this generalization cannot form the basis of a plan of treatment. To understand this boy and help him, the social worker must know the nature of his particular family relationships, the kind of upbringing he has had, and how he expresses his personal values and his troubles through behavior that is meaningful to him.

The family that is failing to meet standards may indeed be reflecting the attitudes of its particular cultural or economic group. On the other hand, its lack of interest in household cleanliness and order or in having the children finish high school may be the natural outcome of grinding poverty and discrimination in the midst of a striving and affluent community. The social worker's help, however, must be based on an understanding of why the family is hopeless or hostile. It must be directed toward removing the obstacles that stand in the way of the family's own efforts to meet the expectations of the community.

Treatment of the multiproblem family must be based on an understanding of the manifold sources of its pathology. Walter Miller has stated that this understanding can be facilitated "by clarifying the cultural sources of the pathology and indicating more directly the nature of feasible treatment goals."[6] I agree with this statement, but I should like to add that physiological and psychogenic sources are of equal importance. There is no evidence that a single causative factor produces the multiproblem family. The search for a primary cause is futile; there are many possible sources of pathology—psychological, social, and cultural—which must be analyzed not for multiproblem families as a distinct group in society but for *each* family we attempt to treat.

Amelioration

I should like now to examine some aspects of the problem of ameliorating this client group's serious condition. It is somewhat startling that after almost a century of professional development, social workers are still "discovering"

---

[6] Walter B. Miller, "Implications of Urban Lower-Class Culture for Social Work," *Social Service Review*, Vol. XXXIII, September 1959, p. 234.

multiproblem families; relating themselves to "the poor"; using such so-called new techniques as reaching out, beginning where the client is, making home visits, offering services in terms that the client can understand, accepting cultural differences, raising a cry for community action, and work-ing with indigenous groups. Not one of these techniques is based on a new theoretical formulation; all are as old as social work itself. Yet they are not being employed in precisely the same way as in earlier years. Today our use of these techniques has taken on greater precision and greater depth, because it is based on our expanded knowledge of ego psychology and on the new insights provided by the social sciences.

In the early settlement-house and COS movements, social work practice was based chiefly on the recognition by a few outstanding leaders that an industralized society would inevitably victimize some of its members. What these early-twentieth-century leaders did was to take an aggressively charitable stand in behalf of those who were poor, maladjusted, uprooted, sick, and lonely. A few persons, such as Jane Addams and Lillian Wald, became the embodiment of social work practice. Today, the expression of the humanistic and ethical values of our profession cannot take the same form. We have experienced marked changes in social philosophy, in the organization of social work, and in the availability of knowledge and skills. Although many of our social problems and the goals of social work are similar to those of Jane Addams' day, we have come to recognize that the force for change does not lie in the outstanding abilities of one leader but rather in the capacity of social workers generally to enable clients to participate in bringing about the social changes necessary to productive living.

The content and methods of practice, having become communicable, are shared nowadays by all social workers and are embedded in innumerable community agencies. No longer should social workers rely primarily on exhortation or conviction; because we have a body of accumulated know-ledge and tested skills, we have an obligation to demonstrate the validity of our professional practice and to utilize a scientific method of investigation and treatment. That we have not produced a leader of the stature of Jane Addams in the past fifty years does not show a lack of conviction on the part of the profession; it shows, rather, that the profession is now beyond the need to rely on any one person for its humanitarian spirit.

Even though it no longer suffices to "do good for others" and to romanti-cize our function, the fact remains that we cannot divorce methodology from values. As social workers we cannot operate a social service for the motivated client and deny help to those who, for a multitude of reasons, are uninitiated into our social work system, different from ourselves, over-burdened by problems, difficult to help, and perhaps most in need of the help we can and should give. A set of values must be the basis of all our practice. We have no alternative but to help the multiproblem family as best we can, notwithstanding our own differing attitudes, prejudices, and identifications.

Techniques of Helping

From my earlier discussion, it is obvious that I believe that help to the multiproblem family must be based on the social worker's precise knowledge of the sociocultural and economic forces that shape its way of life, its intimate family relationships, and the behavior and ideals of each family member. The appropriateness of a family's behavior in its daily functioning and the significance of a particular problem to an individual and his family can be understood only if the worker has this knowledge. Understanding of the psychosocial aspects of the multiproblem family's breakdown in functioning or adjustment is now available to the social worker as a result of recent advances in ego psychology. The use of ego psychology in casework practice has been described thus:

> The client who needs help with various problems describes these in terms of everyday behavior and attitudes. Everyday behavior is a complex psychosocial phenomenon. We must analyze it in various ways—as a social role and as family interaction, as an expression of ideals and values, as physical processes, as an expression of psychological processes, such as instinctual drives and defensive operations. Casework practice requires that we use all these frames of reference. [7]

Within this broad scope of concern for the client's external and internal problems, the techniques of working with multiproblem families become self-evident. On the assumption that multiproblem families are living under adverse conditions and are acting in ways alien to the expectations of the community—the same community that has contributed to their problems— social workers can be certain that these families would not willingly come to social agencies for help. Thus, we must reach out to them if we are to demonstrate our concern. It has been aptly stated that "reaching out is neither a physical act nor a technique. It is rather a frame of mind, a psychological readiness, a determination of the social worker to find a way to help the client whether the means is physical, psychological, social, or some combination."[8]

What does reaching out involve for the social agency that wants to help? It may require that the agency locate its office in the same neighborhood as the people it wants to serve; it may mean that the agency maintain an open-door policy for those in need of help, even if the help they need will take a great deal of staff time and will show little immediate result. All the community's resources for prevention and treatment must be mobilized. The agency's staff must be available at night and on week ends, when crises are most likely to occur. Service programs must be of a kind that makes sense to people who do not value talk in a one-to-one interview as a way

[7] Isabel L. Stamm, "Ego Psychology in the Emerging Theoretical Base of Casework," in *Issues in American Social Work*, Alfred J. Kahn (ed.), Columbia University Press, New York, 1959, p. 87.

[8] Walter Haas, "Reaching Out—A Dynamic Concept in Casework," *Social Work*, Vol. IV, July, 1959, p. 44.

of solving their problems. Concrete forms of help are likely to have more significance for the multiproblem family than verbal communication. The programs should include group activities (recreational, educational, or cultural), services within the family's home (homemaker, home economist, or caseworker to help with shopping, meal-planning, housework, child care), and neighborhood services (provisions for day care of preschool and school-age children, interpretation of the family's needs to the schools, work with hospitals toward less waiting on clinic days, help to the managers of housing projects in understanding their tenants).

What does reaching out involve for the caseworker and the group worker? It means that they must discover creative ways of making the help they offer tangible, concrete, and meaningful to clients. As workers *demonstrate* their concern in tangible ways, rather than in words alone, they will have less need to *promise* help. Obviously, however, there are families for whom the traditional interview is a valuable therapeutic technique. No matter what the worker's technique, he must select it on the basis of sound diagnostic understanding of why it is appropriate, not on the basis of whim alone. The technique of reaching out, then, should take its place as one of a range of professional techniques that may improve the effectiveness of social work practice with multiproblem families.

Conclusion

In conclusion, it does not seem inappropriate to quote what Jane Addams said in an article in the *Atlantic Monthly* in 1899:

> We sometimes say that our charity is too scientific, but we should doubtless be much more correct in our estimate if we say that it is not scientific enough. ... A man who would hesitate to pronounce an opinion upon the stones lying by the wayside ... will, without a moment's hesitation, dogmatize about the delicate problems of human conduct, and will assert that one man is a scoundrel and another an honorable gentleman, without in the least considering the ethical epochs to which the two belong. ... In our charitable efforts, we think much more of what a man ought to be than of what he is or of what he may become; and we ruthlessly force our conventions and standards upon him.

About the social worker's role with his clients, Miss Addams said:

> Recently, ... there has come to my mind the suggestion of a principle, that while the painful condition of administering charity is the inevitable discomfort of a transition into a more democratic relation, the perplexing experiences of the actual administration have a genuine value of their own ... The social reformers who avoid the charitable relationship with any of their fellow men take a certain outside attitude toward this movement. They may analyze it and formulate it; they may be most valuable and necessary, but they are not essentially within it. The mass of men seldom move together without an emotional incentive, and the doctrinaire, in his effort to keep his mind free from the emotional quality, inevitably stands aside. He avoids the perplexity, and at the same time loses the vitality.[9]

[9] Jane Addams, "The Subtle Problems of Charity," *Atlantic Monthly*, Vol. LXXXIII, February, 1899, pp. 163–78.

Since 1899 social work has experienced the backing and filling of all professions that have moved from a largely intuitive response to social need to a reliance on scientific thinking. At last we have learned that the development of new content and the refinement of professional methods do not require us to deny the validity of the tested knowledge and skills that have served as the building blocks of present practice. It may be that through our work with multiproblem families and through our continuing recognition of multiple causation and the psychosocial determinants of behavior, we shall achieve the genuine integration of many theories that have significance for social work practice. The social work profession is committed to helping those who need its services. When we discover that our skills are faulty, we must search for new techniques through which our historic values and convictions can be put to work in behalf of our clients. Doing this will not be difficult if we but use the rich scientific and humanistic knowledge now available to us.

Client Value Orientations: Implications for Diagnosis and Treatment

Shirley C. Hellenbrand

The imprint of value orientations is to be found in all aspects of case-work practice. Values are reflected in client, caseworker, and agency. They affect behavior, personality, the nature of client problems, and methods of solving them. This paper will present a theroretical framework within which the cultural determinants of value orientations can be viewed and will examine some of the implications of value orientations for diagnosis and treatment in casework.

The following three propositions are suggested as guideposts for this discussion.

1.   An individual's way of life and his orientation to life problems are determined by a number of factors. His salient environment, as well as his biologic and psychic constitutional endowment, his particular family situation, and other idosyncratic features fashion and color the life experi-ences he will have. A major agent in the individual's approach to these experiences, in his role commitments and role performances, is his culturally conditioned value orientations.

2.   These value orientations and their far-reaching effects on the indi-vidual's functioning need to be part of the data of diagnosis. Treatment concepts and techniques need to be broadened to include a greater variety of approaches that can respond effectively to particular value orientations.

3.   Recognition of differences in cultural value orientations, respect accorded to these differences, and a more intensive attempt to understand them should not constitute a deification of cultural relativism.

Present knowledge about human behavior, incomplete as it is, offers

Reprinted from *Social Casework,* Vol 42 (April, 1961), pp. 163–169, by permission of the author and the Family Service Association of America.

conclusive evidence that answers to many of the problems of clinical diagnosis are intricately linked with the delicate but steely strong threads of cultural patterning. The connections are evident if we look at typical problem "themes," such as a particular type of parent-child relationships, of management or housekeeping practices, of attitudes toward scholastic or vocational achievement and choices, or of reaction toward revealing or discussing intimate problems and anxieties. The diagnostic question is: To what extent are these and other types of behavior reflections of the individual's character structure which evolved from his idiosyncratic responses to his personal life history, and to what extent are they the reflections of his cultural conditioning?

Regardless of origins, the individual's attitudes and behavior may be equally internalized, unconscious, disguised, and defended. Nevertheless, it is of great importance diagnostically to know which set of influences—the personal idiosyncratic or those that are culturally patterned—had priority in fashioning certain attitudes or behavior traits. If problematic attitudes, behavior, and role definitions represent cultural norms, the individual is likely to have less question or conflict about his behavior than if his feelings and his functioning are at variance with his "reference group." A crucial issue in diagnosis and treatment is whether the individual's environment sustains and supports his role interpretations and responds to them in a complementary fashion, or whether the environment implicitly or explicitly questions or condemns them. In order to understand the particular behavior patterns an individual has "chosen," we need to know the nature and variety of the norms of his group and the ranking of these norms on the group's value scale. An understanding of the norms and of their hierarchal order should play a significant part in the caseworker's evaluation of the the possibilities for favorable changes in the client.

As is implied in the preceding statements, treatment should also be closely related to the client's cultural patterning and value orientations. A glance at a few of the key elements in treatment will serve to illustrate the point. For example, motivation is generally considered a major item in treatment prognostication. The nature and degree of motivation, however, depend on a number of factors, one of which is whether or not the client, as a result of his cultural conditioning, believes that personal efforts *can* effect changes in his behavior and in his situation. Another important element in treatment is verbal communication. Ability to communicate verbally is not only related to intelligence and personality but also to the role assigned to language and verbal exchange by a particular culture. The capacity of an individual to use a professional helping relationship, as well as the nature of his ensuing transference reactions, are conditioned not only by his personal life history and character but also by his culturally defined orientations to people. Another element in treatment is the goal of helping the client to achieve greater skill at reality testing and to improve his reality perception. His distortion of reality or his limited perception may not be idiosyncratic but may be colored by cultural definitions and norms.

These examples clearly suggest that the cultural determinants of value orientations have major importance for diagnosis and treatment. The problem of how to use cultural data is complicated by the richness and intricacies of ethnic and class cultures and subcultures in our society. Two questions arise. What kinds of cultural data should we try to obtain and understand? How can we use this knowledge for more effective helping?

Theoretical Schemes

Florence Kluckhohn has proposed a scheme for the "systematic ordering of cultural value orientations within the framework of common–universal problems" which, it seems to me, offers rich possibilities to caseworkers. The basic assumptions of this scheme, which have been described in a number of articles by Kluckhohn[1] and Spiegel,[2] are being used by them in a research project at the Laboratory of Social Relations at Harvard University.

In brief, Kluckhohn's postulates may be recapitulated as follows: (1) There is a limited number of common human problems for which all people at all times must find some solution; (2) there is variability in the solutions to these problems but the variability is neither limitless nor random, it is variability within a range of possible solutions; (3) all variants of all solutions are present in all societies at all times in varying degrees. Kluckhohn also identifies five problems that appear to be crucial to all human groups at all times: (1) human-nature orientation, (2) man-nature orientation, (3) time orientation, (4) activity orientation, (5) relational orientation. For each of these problems she suggests three styles of solution, noting that one will be the "preferred" style and that the others will also be present, ranking lower in the hierarchy of values.

In my opinion, there is an equally crucial question for casework which does not seem to be explicitly formulated in the Kluckhohn scheme: In a particular group, what is the emotional coloring of interpersonal responses? In other words, what is the basic orientation to other people? I can envisage a threefold value classification covering such emotional responses: (1) moving toward, away from, or against others; (2) relating to others trustfully, or with caution, or with suspicion; (3) in terms of affection for others, seeking power over them, or seeking to exploit them. As we know from psychoanalytic theory, responses to people are rarely fortuitous. We also know that certain attitudes are characteristic of certain cultures.[3]

---

[1] Florence Rockwood Kluckholm, "Variations in the Basic Values of Family Systems," *Social Casework*, Vol. XXXIX, Nos. 2–3 (1958), pp. 63–72.

[2] John P. Spiegel, "Some Cultural Aspects of Transference and Counter-Transference," in *Science and Psychoanalysis*, Vol. II, Jules H. Masserman (ed.), Grune & Stratton, New York, 1959.

[3] For example, in *Les Carnets du Major Thompson*, by Pierre Daninos, the Major comments on the typical Frenchman's response, "Je me defends," to the question, "How are things going?" The response is suggestive of the wary attitude of French people toward government, politics, and so on.

Social Class and Value Orientations

For some time, caseworkers and psychiatrists have been increasingly aware that the success or failure of treatment is dependent on more variables than the apparent motivation of the client or patient, the apparent degree of his pathology, and the skill of the therapist. Schaffer and Myers state that "what happens therapeutically to a person who becomes a psychiatric patient is, to a significant degree, a function of his social class position in the community." They continue, "If it is justified to assume the existence of a culture of classes, then one may assume that persons from different classes undergo different kinds of experiences, integrating these experiences in different terms. Thus they have more or less different frames of reference for human relations, or different kinds of orientations for acting with others."[4]

This point is further clarified by Spiegel. He states that these integrations, these frames of reference and orientations, become "behavior without awareness . . . the making of an unconscious discrimination between two or more choices of behavior when the act of discrimination cannot be brought to the status of conscious report because it has never at any time existed in consciousness. Since the value orientations of a culture are outside of awareness to begin with and are learned in childhood only through their indirect impact on conscious behavior, they can be expected to have a powerful effect on the therapeutic relationship."[5]

It seems to me that casework must proceed on the proposition that certain of the "differences" alluded to by Schaffer and Myers stem from *value* orientations that are culturally transmitted, are internalized in the process of development, and are supported in various ways by the milieu and the larger environment. I have already suggested that Kluckhohn's formulation throws significant light on the kind of data needed to deal effectively with problems of diagnosis and treatment. I should like to illustrate the proposition through an analysis, tentative as yet, of several crucial questions of value orientation and their implications for casework with clients from lower-class subcultures. I have chosen this group for two reasons: first, because the members constitute a large proportion of social agencies' clientele and we should, therefore, rightfully be concerned about our effectiveness with them; and, second, because the differences in value orientations are more gross than the subtle differences in the subcultures of the middle class and are, therefore, more visible to our still poorly trained eyes.

At this point, it may be helpful to restate some of the characteristics of lower-class subcultures which seem to have particular pertinence to this.

---

[4] Leslie Schaffer and Jerome K. Myers, "Psychotherapy and Social Stratification," in *Advances in Psychiatry*, Mabel B. Cohen (ed.), W. W. Norton & Co., New York, 1959, p. 87.

[5] John P. Spiegel, *op. cit.*, p. 161.

discussion.[6] The characteristics include: (1) involvement in unskilled or semi-skilled occupations, often seasonal and cyclical and often characterized by long hours of monotonous work; (2) a median of school years per adult much lower than in other classes; (3) housing often inadequate from the point of view of sanitation, privacy, and esthetic appeal; (4) many families of the three- or four-stem type, as a result of frequent separation, desertion, or divorce; (5) a large number of female-based households, frequent serial mating; (6) the peer group's superseding the family as the primary reference group; (7) *carpe diem* as the prevalent philosophy—"Live today, let tomorrow take care of itself"; (8) deep-seated distrust of authority figures transmitted by attitudes, deeds, and words from adults to children; (9) a tendency toward self-centeredness, suspicion of and hostility toward institutional controls, and suspicion among members of the group.

In an analysis of gang delinquency, Miller defines a number of attributes of persons in lower-class subcultures.[7]

Toughness: the emphasis on masculinity is almost compulsive and reaction-formational in nature.

Smartness: to outsmart, to "con," even ingenious aggressive repartee carries status value.

Excitement: alternation between relatively routine activity and danger or risk; "trouble" (any form of illegal activity) is one source of excitement while gambling, use of dope, and sexual activity are others.

Fate: "Everything rides on the dice"; man is a pawn.

Autonomy: the mask of independence and toughness covering strong dependency yearnings; there is a discrepancy between what is overtly expressed and what is covertly desired. Authority and nurturing seem to be connected, and the person often searches for a highly restrictive environment.

It must be emphasized that much careful research is needed to determine the frequency of these attributes and their nature in various subtypes of lower-class culture.

Crucial Questions for Diagnosis and Treatment

Crucial questions for diagnosis and treatment pertain to client conceptions about innate human nature and man's relation to natural or supernatural forces. Although such questions may appear at first glance to be

[6] The characteristics listed are drawn from formulations by: August B. Hollingshead and Frederick C. Redlich, *Social Class and Mental Illness: A Community Study*, John Wiley & Sons, New York, 1958; Henry S. Maas, *et al.*, "Socio-Cultural Factors in Psychiatric Clinic Services for Children," *Smith College Studies in Social Work*, Vol. XXV, No. 2 (1955); Walter B. Miller, "Lower Class Culture as a Generating Milieu of Gang Delinquency," *Journal of Social Issues*, Vol. XIV, No. 3 (1958), also "Implications of Urban Lower-Class Culture for Social Work," *Social Service Review*, Vol. XXXIII, No. 3 (1959).

[7] Walter B. Miller, "Lower Class Culture as a Generating Milieu of Gang Delinquency," *op. cit.*

highly philosophical, almost metaphysical or theological, and to have little relation to the problems of helping people, there is evidence that such conceptions influence attitudes and behavior.

One set of questions may be shown graphically, as follows:

WHAT IS THE CHARACTER OF INNATE HUMAN NATURE?

Evil
Neutral (mixture of good and evil) }Mutable
Good   }Immutable

Spiegel has pointed out that a person's conception of the nature of man has an effect on his personality development, on both his problem formation and his defense formation.[8] The struggle involved in changing a way of behaving and of feeling and reacting is never lightly undertaken. It is necessary to ask if it can be undertaken at all by an individual who believes that man's nature is evil and not likely to be changeable. We might also ask what people in certain segments of lower-class society feel about their essential nature, if we keep in mind Miller's discussion of their characteristics. He points out that in the female-based household the children, from their earliest days, are exposed to the value that men are no good and are not to be relied upon. When the boy first steps outside the home for some affirmation of his masculinity, he is warned, "Don't be like your father," and when he disappoints his mother he is told that he is "just like his father after all." Is it not likely that children in such a culture carry into adulthood a deep-seated feeling about the inevitable and unchanging evil nature of men? They absorb this idea from family "teaching" and it is supported by the larger culture in which they grow up and have their experiences.

Does not treatment need to take into account the imprint of the cultural value system on personality, as well as the more familiar effects of familial jealousies, hostilities, and sexual identifications? A treatment orientation that includes cultural factors might lead to new approaches, perhaps along the lines of re-education and resocialization.

A second crucial question pertains to man's relation to natural and supernatural forces. His orientation may be: (1) subjugation to nature, (2) harmony with nature, or (3) mastery over nature.

The general orientation in America, as is well known, is mastery over nature except, as Spiegel points out, when people are faced with the invincible tragedies of fatal illness and death. Social work, itself, is "all-American" in its adherence to the creed of fight and mastery. It has retained a close philosophical tie to pragmatism, holding to the belief that man can create his own environment and to the principle that the individual has a right to self-determination. These value orientations form the foundation of our treatment approach.

[8] John P. Spiegel, *op. cit.*

In many lower-class subcultures, however, as was noted earlier, man is viewed as a powerless pawn of destiny—"It all rides on the dice." The "family teaching" about powerlessness and inevitability is reaffirmed by the adverse social and economic conditions under which many of these people live. A natural response under such imprisoning circumstances is, "Live today, let tomorrow take care of itself."

It is not possible to suggest treatment techniques for problems of this scope, that is, where outer and inner forces combine to imprison the individual in a destiny which seems so bleak that he can see no purpose in struggling. As a first step to new approaches, we must develop an awareness that the impulse to struggle, to endeavour to intervene actively and purposively in one's destiny, is *not* a dominant trait in all subcultures. We must learn to scrutinize and evaluate clients' value orientations in regard to their relation to nature. If subjugation to nature is the dominant pattern, we may need to intervene energetically by suggesting choices, and by initiating, stimulating, and teaching various forms of social activity. I am not proposing that we return to earlier periods of social work practice and become manipulators. I am merely suggesting that, on the basis of a cultural differential diagnosis, we adapt our treatment "styles" to the needs of the situation. If changes take place in the institutional arrangements in the larger society, which would provide wider choices for individuals and greater chances for achieving goals, the "right to self-determination" would be more realistically based. We might then find fewer clients with the subjugation-to-nature orientation.

Social work orientation is also different from the orientation of certain lower-class subcultures in relation to temporal focus and the modality of human activity. The social work culture is future-oriented while most lower-class subcultures are present-oriented. This time-gulf creates significant differences in the ways the caseworker and the client approach problems of planning, management, and so forth. Similarly, difficulties arise because of differences in their concepts of modalities of activity. The wild alternation between monotonous routines and frequent excursions into excitement, and even danger, by persons in lower-class subcultures is in great contrast to the rational, orderly organization of living that social work holds as a treatment goal. These differences in orientation also have important implications for treatment.

I should like to refer now to the question I raised earlier about the interpersonal or emotional orientation of persons in various cultural groups. The basic emotional orientation of a client to other people will determine to a large extent the nature of his problems as well as the character and fate of the client-worker relationship. In designing a treatment approach, the caseworker must take into account, with certain clients, the status value they place on "toughness," and "conning," their suspicion of authority figures, as well as the discrepancy between their mask of independence and their convert longing for dependence and nurture.

The data we would secure from clients, in response to inquiry about these "crucial questions," should provide us with a rough sketch of the modal personality in a variety of subcultures. Analysis of the typical ways a group operates in relation to life problems would help us become familiar with the variant value orientations of particular groups. At the same time, we need to enlarge our understanding of the multiple ways in which the "salient environment" shapes, reinforces, or weakens cultural value orientations and patterns. Certain kinds of economic and social institutions, such as those that affect occupational opportunities, income distribution, housing, and education are particularly salient. If these institutions circumscribe the human potentialities of certain groups of individuals, the end result can only be an increase in their feelings of defeatism. Study may reveal that certain clinical entities, or at least certain constellations of symptoms and defenses, have a correlation with value orientations of the family and the larger cultural environment. With greater knowledge about the interaction of clinical and cultural variables, we would be in a better position to develop differential treatment methods and procedures and to chart social action programs.

Philosophical and Theoretical Considerations

For obvious reasons, we in this country have a philosophical and intellectual commitment to cultural pluralism. Social workers, in keeping with the ethics of the profession, also have a deep respect for the principle of cultural relativism. The worship of this principle, however, placing it above all others, is naive. There are at least two kinds of conditions that indicate the need for modification of cultural patterns. When these conditions exist, the goal of social work and of the larger society should be directed toward cultural change. One such condition is the existence of a source of danger to the society. For example, a society may have worked out social and economic structures and a set of values that permit its survival at the cost of the well-being of its members. The people may be diseased and physically weak, or continually frightened and anxious. Graham Greene in *Journey into Night,* published about twenty years ago, gives an account of his travels in West Africa, describing villages where the inhabitants are diseased, poorly nourished, apathetic, and in constant terror of the witch doctors who hold top power positions. We need not go so far afield to find cultures in which the physical, emotional, and intellectual development of people is stunted, in which deprivation corrodes their potentialities for growth, and in which such conditions become sources of disease and danger for the whole society. In our country, certain subcultures in lower-class society represent such a danger. It also is possible that some middle- and upper-class subcultures constitute similar, although less visible, sources of pathology and danger. The role of the social worker is not to "respect" such cultures and leave them untouched.

A second condition that calls for modification of cultural patterns is the imbalance between the requirements of a society and the living patterns of its members. A society may change more rapidly than the life patterns and the behavioral characteristics of the people. In general, certain cultural influences and institutional pressures operate to produce personality patterns that are adaptive to the particular society at a particular time. In discussing this concept, Inkeles points out that "integration between personality patterns developed . . . and the requirements of the roles provided and required by the *ongoing* social system may be highly imperfect, and since personality resides in individuals and not in social systems, that personality once developed, becomes a more or less independent entity which is in interaction with the social system."[9]

The current social and economic conditions, and the current demands on members of our society, often make a "poor fit," particularly for persons in some subcultures. Our society doubtless will have need to work out new patterns of living for many people, in order to cope with automation, increase in leisure time, and geographic mobility with its resulting "stranded" nuclear family. The extension of terrestrial boundaries may some day create other new problems. Cultural patterns and value orientations are continually changing and evolving for all groups in our society. Social work should consciously assume responsibility for helping to accelerate the rate of change, either in society or in the living patterns of people, and to give direction to such change.

Operational Problems

I should like to conclude by calling attention to some of the operational problems involved in applying the theory discussed in this paper. One thorny problem is how to secure from clients the data needed to understand the value orientations of different subcultures. How can the differences in frames of reference and the difficulties in communication be sufficiently overcome so that we know what to look for and what and how to understand our interlocutors? A second problem pertains to means of organizing the data. How can these new data be related to existing knowledge about personality development, pathology, and treatment techniques? Social workers sometimes have had a tendency, on the discovery of exciting new concepts, to "redecorate" the house completely, throwing out all the old furniture. For example, there is risk that our present interest in role theory may make us lose sight of psychological theory. We have also tended to add new concepts to old ones, even though they may contradict, rather than complement, each other. The theoretical problem, which has not yet been solved, is how to integrate new and old concepts so that they form a unitary framework of knowledge about personality development and social functioning.

A third problem is how to find a system for classifying various kinds of

---

[9] Alex Inkeles, "Sociological Observations on Culture and Personality Studies," in *Personality in Nature, Society and Culture*, Clyde Kluckhohn, Henry A. Murray and David M. Schneider (eds.), Alfred Knopf, New York, 1953.

problem entities in the person-in-the-situation configuration. Such a classification, it seems to me, must take into account three types of data: (1) personal, idiosyncratic; (2) cultural, value orientation; and (3) the complex role of the salient environment.

A system of classification of problem entities would lay the groundwork for the construction of a network of treatment approaches, each of which might be related in a broad way to a specific problem classification. Any such classification scheme and its correlated treatment techniques, in my opinion, can be only a general guide. I do not believe that the rich variety of human experience can be compressed into neat, tight, diagnostic categories or that a treatment plan, like a blueprint for a house, can be drawn to precise scale. However, there are broad ways of looking at data systematically and of ordering crucial human problems, as is evidenced in Kluckhohn's scheme. I believe caseworkers need to develop a conceptual scheme from their own practice and research which will have usefulness for understanding the person in his total situation and for treatment.

Effect of Value Reevaluation on Current Practice

Francis J. Turner

Over the past two years, the writer has become increasingly aware of a group of clients whose psychosocial stress has originated from two related yet separate phenomena—a personal reevaluation of values and ethics and a recurrence of previously dormant superego concerns. This article examines these two phenomena and offers some knowledge and practice implications of their occurrence. It includes some case illustrations, theoretical comments, implications for learning, and diagnostic and management observations.

It is no surprise that persons in our society are experiencing value and ethical difficulties during a period of rapidly changing value and ethical systems at all levels of society. What is noteworthy is that persons are turning to social work professionals for help in dealing with such problems. This trend is significant in relation to the tradition in which the client's values were considered as a therapeutic no-man's-land and the therapist's values as something to be kept private and rarely shared with the client. Whether social workers adhered to these taboos is, of course, a moot question.

This tradition is now changing. Individuals, groups, and families are turning to us for help with stress in psychosocial functioning directly related to value and ethical conflicts that are sometimes recognized, sometimes not. These clients are diagnostically within the range of normal functioning, yet still in need of skilled help. Such requests require that social work professionals respond in an understanding and helpful way and give this content more consideration.

It should not be surprising that a challenge to one's ethical position or a commitment to change one's value position would have implications for the superego component of personality, especially if the approach to practice is from a developmental base. Each person brings to new situations his whole developmental history, including superego development. These pasts influence how we are affected by or affect our present. But we also know that this is not a one-way influence; new experiences and perceptions can shift, alter, diminish, or increase the extent to which our pasts influence the present and, in turn, alter the way we will function in the future.

It is because these two phenomena—one society-wide and current and the other individual and past-related—can reciprocally influence each other

Reprinted from *Social Casework,* Vol 56 (May, 1975), pp. 285–291, by permission of the Family Service Association of America.

that their simultaneous occurrence becomes of interest and importance therapeutically. Four types of situations that the writer has observed and which are related to this topic are described in the case illustrations below.

Case Illustrations

First, there is the client who initially appears in a mild or moderately severe crisis situation resulting from a shift in life view, the effects of which are only partially recognized and understood.

> Mr. M is an intelligent, successful businessman of forty-five, who experienced a mild crisis reaction that he related to a recent upset in his marriage. This upset had resulted in diminished effective functioning in most life areas, including his business. His sales had dropped off drastically, and he was facing the possibility of losing his position. It was soon evident that his stress was more broadly based than the difficulty with his marriage; he was, in fact, in a process of reevaluating his whole view of life, his commitment to his marriage, and his aspirations.
>
> In brief, he was striving to move from a rigid view of life and duty to a more open one in which self-fulfillment was the goal. This upheaval had reactivated some of his earlier ambivalent feelings toward his father, a man who had high standards and expectations of him that he rarely could meet. These feelings became transferred both to his boss and to the therapist and showed in his wanting to please and to hurt. Only after some of this material was clarified and he began to recognize both his present shifting perceptions and commitments and the strings on him from the past was he able to begin to function in his accustomed self-fulfilling, socially responsible manner and to reexamine his commitment to his marriage.

A second type of client in a value dilemma is the individual who recognizes that he has altered his self-concept along with his perception of desirable behavior and responsibility; the problem that moves him to seek help stems from his inability to follow through on the implications of his value shifts.

> Mrs. J is a twenty-five-year-old woman of above-average intelligence, married to a successful, upwardly mobile man whom she met while both were in the armed forces. She had felt abandoned by her husband and unfulfilled in her role as mother of three. To counter these feelings, she began taking university courses at night and became involved in a women's discussion group. She was significantly influenced by the campus climate and the content of some of her courses and decided to pursue a full university career along with her responsibilities as wife and mother. Although her husband concurred with this plan and encouraged her, the decision evoked a wave of anxiety and marked ambivalence that confused her husband and put severe strains on the marriage. In individual and joint interviews with her and her husband, it quickly became apparent that her decision had evoked both the spectre of her dead father—a controlling, demanding man who viewed women as being second-best—and her feelings about her highly critical, dependent mother, who was still alive. Several stormy interviews took place in which some of the components of the unresolved emancipation from parental demands and expectations were worked through and their influence on her present goals clarified. Following this stage, Mrs. J began to follow through on her decisions and resumed effective functioning as wife and mother.

A third form of value-related problem concerns marital situations where support for the altered life view is not present and where the stress comes from the lack of such support. This problem appears to be the situation in an increasing number of marriages in which there have been several years of a reasonably stable, apparently healthy relationship of essentially mature spouses. Nevertheless, under the influence of recent societal trends, conflict emerges as one or both partners begin to change attitudes toward broad life objectives, role perceptions, or moral stances related to sexual conduct within or outside the marriage. Examples are the man who decides to leave a secure job after several years in order to establish his own business or the woman who wishes for a new career outside the home. In these cases, the conflicts that emerge frequently evoke the same superego immaturities identified earlier.[1]

The fourth cluster of problems in this area is similar to some traditional family problems but with a new dimension. These cases involve value and ethical shifts that have taken place differentially in various family subsystems. Customarily, social workers have seen these from the viewpoint of the parent-system and sibling-system dyad, but currently other kinds of subsystem splits seem to be taking place. Usually social workers have viewed them as normal maturational emancipation struggles and have understood the superego components of the child's struggle. What has not been given sufficient attention is the real value-based struggle. The latter situation is considered here: a situation where there has been a value shift in some component of the family that results in new stress. One example involved a changed perception of the acceptability of parents' arranging an abortion for a fifteen-year-old daughter.

> Mr. and Mrs. N had long been a stable, socially conscious couple with strong church ties. In recent years, Mrs. N had begun to question some of her long-held moral views, and it was concerning the decision on the daughter's abortion that the couple realized how far apart they had grown in their perceptions of acceptable behavior. This differential perception on the part of the parents created additional conflict for the girl who was struggling with her own emerging system of morality. This issue was never resolved for the family, and the daughter eventually left home following the abortion. Mr. and Mrs. N's marriage suffered a serious blow. After several months, they began to make some progress in reestablishing a functioning system with themselves and their other children.

No doubt there are other clusterings of cases.[2] The four categories above identify some situations in which the persons involved have histories of adequate functioning and mastery of many life situations but have met unmanageable difficulties in psychosocial functioning because they, significant others, or significant institutions have altered or questioned earlier-held

---

[1] Elizabeth Bott, Urban Families: The Norms of Conjugal Roles, in *The Psychosocial Interior of the Family*, ed. Gerald Handell (London: George Allen & Unwin, 1968), pp. 141–58.

[2] Eric J. Cleveland and William D. Longaker, Neurotic Patterns in the Family, in *The Psychosocial Interior of the Family*, ed. Handell, pp. 159–85.

positions on values, ethics, or responsibilities. In seeking to resolve these attitudinal changes, they have also found themselves struggling with issues stemming from their own maturational histories. To fully assist these clients, it is necessary to understand both their superego functioning and current social value changes.

Background on the Superego

In the 1923 article "The Ego and the Id," Sigmund Freud redescribed the personality structure in a manner that gave proper emphasis to the superego.[3] Important as this reconceptualization was, professionals have tended to direct more emphasis and interest to the censoring, restricting, inhibiting components of the superego than to some of its more positive components. The fact that the process of superego development affects the person's attitudes to himself, his perceived esteem or lack of it, and his attitudes to authority persons, initially parents and parent-like authorities but ultimately all authorities, has been understressed.

The superego goal for the maturing person is the development of a psychic structure that fosters the establishment of norms, attitudes, and identities in a way that is increasingly autonomous. This stance permits an individual throughout life to set his own life rules and attitudes and to select the societal systems by which he will be influenced, rather than be directed with little autonomy.[4]

It has been generally accepted that by early adulthood a person has developed a functioning and generally stable superego and a self-image reasonably well accommodated to the significant others and systems within which he functions. Apart from some gradual maturing and realignment of life views as identified in the last three of Erik H. Erikson's eight stages, professionals have presumed that there would be little change in a person's ethical stance, although it was understood that other components of self-image and self-attitudes would change.[5]

Values and Ethics

We no longer live in a social system where values are stable in individuals, family systems, ethnic groupings, or larger political or religious systems. Both ethical and value systems are in flux for many individuals and groups. By *ethics* is meant those consciously adhered to, explicit or implicit, codes of behavior that govern the lives of individuals and groups.

---

[3] Sigmund Freud, The Ego and the Id, in *The Standard Edition of the Complete Psychological Works of Sigmund Freud*, ed. James Strachey (London: Hogarth Press, 1961), 9: 19–39.

[4] Eunice F. Allen, Psychoanalytic Theory, in *Social Work Treatment*, ed. Francis J. Turner (New York: The Free Press, 1974), pp. 19–41.

[5] Erik H. Erikson, *Childhood and Society* (New York: W. W. Norton & Co., 1950), pp. 219–34.

Values are those less obvious and less conscious pragmatically oriented preferential choices, almost automatic in operation, that assist individuals to develop patterns of selection from the vast array of daily decisions and choices. The latter are more accurately called value orientations. Although ethics and values or value orientations are separate but related concepts, they do tend to be combined in the general term *values*.

From the ethical aspect, there are many individuals who have drastically altered their long-held convictions about such things as duties to one's country and to one's neighbors, be they old or young, born or unborn. Questions of when one is or is not a human person, when one is or is not alive or dead, are now clearly topics for dispute.

In the area of value orientations, there are interesting and rapid shifts. From a North American society that probably in Florence R. Kluckhohn's scheme had a predominant first-level value orientation to the future, to doing, to individuality, and to man over nature, significant components of society have shifted to a present, being, collateral, man-with-nature orientation.[6] Thus, many persons who had thought their moral and value development had been completed are having to face a new developmental challenge, obviously with differing degrees of success.

Both ethical and value shifts have taken place within the social work profession that must be acknowledged in current practice. Ethically, social workers have had to come to terms with the same questions as society or at least come to terms with their unanswered dilemmas. From a value orientation perspective, there have also been some shifts that are influencing practice styles. The increased interest in present-oriented, here-and-now, short-term therapeutic engagements, the value placed on experiential kinds of therapy, the heavy involvement in groups, and the expanded interest in communities and community action and in environmental and ecological issues all reflect value orientation shifts and reorderings from an individualistic, long-term, future-oriented, insight-based, problem-solving approach.

These comments about value orientations should not be viewed as definitive, but only as indicators of this much-discussed and well-identified social phenomenon. Of more relevance to this article is a brief consideration of what social work has already learned from this development and what implications are emerging for practice.

Implications for Knowledge

One thing we all have learned is that ethical and value systems are not as stable and unchanging as social workers had thought. Whether or not historians or philosophers held this view, practitioners have tended to view moral codes and value systems of themselves and their clients as generally fixed, once professional and personal maturity was achieved. Many social workers have been surprised at the ability of persons to make dramatic

[6] Florence R. Kluckhohn and Fred S. Strodtbeck, *Variations in Value Orientations* (Evanston, Ill.: Row Peterson & Co., 1961).

and fundamental shifts in standards and behavior, a further example of the ongoing learning about one's ability to change and mature. People are highly flexible and adaptable.

Social workers have also learned that the ability to adjust to new norms and values is not as age-related as had been thought. Some of the most flexible persons, in regard to values, observed in recent years have been old, and some of the most restricted and value-constricted have been among the young. It is misleading to overstress the positive results because it is also evident that many personal and social problems arise from these identified changes—problems of both a primary and secondary form. The term *primary* refers to the problems of those individuals for whom value changes produce internal stress and uncertainty that can approach or reach crisis situations. The term *secondary problems* covers those situations that emerge as a result of internal value changes—that is, the effects of the changes on significant others in a person's life, such as parents, spouse, or children.

A further component of value-related problems is their frequent connection to a person's developmental history. Many persons, in the process of working through alterations of formerly held standards, experience a resurgence of developmental gaps and painful experiences. As professionals have learned from crisis work, earlier unsolved issues frequently are reawakened under stress, and such reexperiencing presents to the client and the alert therapist an opportunity to work on them. This opportunity is the so-called second-chance aspect of crisis work.

Because value issues and superego development and functioning are closely related, some unfinished components of superego development can be dealt with in these situations. Because of the high possibility of current-based, value-related contents evoking emotions and material from the past, therapists must be sensitive to the effect of such transferred feelings, especially with negative components.

The above material becomes further complicated in working with adolescents and the family. The struggle for the adolescent to face parental standards and to accept, reject, or modify them in making them his own is sufficiently difficult at any time. It becomes even more crisis prone when the parents are in conflict, transition, or confusion in this area. This kind of situation sets up a reciprocating form of influence which puts further stress and confusion on both the parents and the adolescent, thus exacerbating the superego struggle. If, in addition to this parent-sibling value struggle, a therapist is struggling with his own value conflict or dilemma, the potential for therapeutic confusion is vast.

Superego development is closely related to one's psychosexual development and the formation of attitudes toward acceptable or nonacceptable conduct. However, the sphere of sexual attitudes, beliefs, and practices is one of the areas most influenced currently by societal value shifts. Thus, as persons are influenced by changing societal sexual values, they may reexperience earlier superego conflicts that would complicate the resolution of value issues in this area.

Diagnostic and Management Implications

From the viewpoint of diagnosis, the above information suggests that it is important for social workers to be alert to the possiblity of value dilemmas as a key source of conflict or stress in their clients. At times, these conflicts will be obvious, but this source of stress may not be apparent to the client and can be overlooked or misunderstood by both client and worker. Implied in this description is the necessity to focus more attention than has been common on the value and ethical orientation of clients, particularly when there is a likelihood of these life areas' being in transition, either in the client or in his life space. The worker must also consider the risk of being overenthusiastic about the possibility of value dilemmas and developing a tendency to see them where they do not exist. We do not have sufficient data about the prevalence of this type of situation. However, as a general diagnostic stance, it is better to be aware of the possibility of various presenting situations than to be surprised by their occurrence.

The necessity of anticipating the appearance of revived unfinished developmental material in situations where value shifts are in progress has been described. In such instances, professionals must be interested in developmental history and alert to developmental clues available from current functioning. Indicators of the intensity, consistency, and appropriateness of superego functioning can be derived from such factors as the client's attitudes toward his aggressive and sexual impulses, his attitudes to authority figures, and, most important, his level and profile of self-esteem. When there are concerns of more than a minor nature in these areas accompanying reactions to value matters, the likelihood of intrapsychic, historically based therapeutic complications is high.

From a case management viewpoint, several observations can be suggested. Assuming that both current value stress and earlier-based reactions are present, there are at least three choices open. One would involve focusing only on the present value material, assuming that its resolution would reestablish an adequate level of functioning without having to reexamine earlier material. A second stance would include focusing primarily on developmental material, with the rationale that helping the client resolve unfinished material from the past would free him to deal objectively with the present. The third perspective would involve attempting to find a balance between the two sources of strain and to seek for growth-enabling resolution of both areas. Although the writer's preference is for the latter approach, the decision must be made on the experiences of the individual situation and the theoretical stance of the therapist.

In working with clients in these situations, one of the crucial responsibilities of the therapist is to be aware of his own value dilemmas and value shifts and the extent to which such developments may have reactivated developmental scars that could, in turn, influence his perceptions and reactions to the client-worker relationship. If there is adequate awareness of therapist involvement in the relationship, careful attention must be given to the probable presence of transferred feelings. They will be significant if earlier parent-child conflicts on standards and values are active. Because of the importance of such early experiences, there is the risk of moving too quickly into potentially negative material; the therapist may become the recipient of these negative feelings before the relationship is sufficiently strong to tolerate them. Frequently, discussions of values and moral standards take on a rational, discursive, philosophical format and appear present-oriented, with the result that the affective component and reactions are unperceived or misunderstood.

In situations where the client is struggling to evaluate and to understand, the writer has found it helpful to share personal value concerns and dilemmas. This step seems to help some clients appreciate that the struggle is more widespread than his own and to obtain a more reality-based perception of the worker. It is also useful in helping the client to begin to understand the new demand of current psychosocial functioning—learning to live comfortably with uncertainty and change. Professionals clearly underserve their clients if they convey to them, either overtly or implicitly, certainties in these areas that they do not have or that others do not have. However, when therapists have arrived at value solutions and have found ways of resolving uncertainties, they can be helpful in sharing this success with clients. Clients do expect professionals to share their knowledge and views and the benefits of their experience as a way of answering their own questions. The risks of overusing authority are known, but failure can also result from not sharing knowledge and experience.

When professionals are involved in helping clients explore and struggle with value-related issues, much of the interview content will consist of "reflective thinking," the D material of Florence Hollis's outline.[7] This type of procedure leads the client to reflect upon a range of components of his significant environments and the nature of his responses to them. In these cases, the client should be helped to reflect on both the conceptual and attitudinal component of values and to look at their influence on himself and others. Although the focus will tend to be present-oriented, there will be some reflective consideration of the past and its influence on the present. Support will be needed, especially as the client struggles to risk new ideas or new actions. These are situations in which clients individually and jointly need information, new ideas, and the opportunity to reflect, discuss, and share. Because of this tendency, working with groups of parents, for example, with similar related concerns and value dilemmas can be rewarding to the professionals and helpful to the group members.

Implied in the need for discovery and discourse is the need to look for resources not ordinarily used, such as colleagues from the disciplines of theology and philosophy. Many persons in our society need direct contact with theologians and philosophers in a consultative role to struggle with

---

[7] Florence Hollis, *Casework: A Psychosocial Therapy* (New York: Random House, 1972), pp. 109–24.

moral, personal, and familial value dilemmas. Related to the possible need for information as well as an enabling and corrective experience, the possibility of clients' having mistaken or incorrect views and perceptions of significant others and systems in their lives can not be ignored. Of particular concern are persons who believe they have cut themselves off from significant groups—for example, church or family membership—because of their perceived violation of rules or norms. There has been a dramatic reevaluation of some moral and ethical positions in many societal systems that can accommodate a much wider range of viewpoints and practices than in an earlier day. Tremendous relief and comfort can be available to persons from friends, families, and systems when they find acceptance in lieu of expected rejection.

Another component of work with this kind of client is the question of the length of involvement. There are clients in this category for whom the present emphasis on short-term treatment is both adequate and the treatment of choice. However, factors are emerging to indicate that some identified value-based cases will require a much longer period of treatment, especially in situations where the value issues have revived significant earlier superego material that has to be reassessed. Often, these persons can be helped initially on a short-term basis, especially if a crisis has developed, but they will be underserved if the professionals involved do not offer the opportunity to build on the crisis through some further maturational progress of which they are capable. In this kind of situation, where a form of personal reevaluation and recommitment to the future based on the freedom gained in value shifts is taking place, probably four to six months of contact will be required.

The kinds of situations discussed in this article represent a range of therapeutic opportunities for which several current thought systems offer rich resources. Initially, the developmental and superego concepts are best understood and managed from an ego-psychological framework. Existential thinking is important to fully appreciate the questions of purpose and authenticity that value questions can raise. Crisis theory is necessary to understand the normalcy yet the wide-ranging effects of high-stress situations and their reopening of earlier life episodes. Crisis theory gives some clear indicators of the skills helpful to bring about growth-producing solutions. Finally, role theory is useful both for the therapist and the client to sort out changes in role perceptions and role enactment that result from alterations in ethics and values.

To responsibly understand and aid in such cases, a reexamination and use of social work's traditional knowledge of superego development and functioning, linked to current views on treatment, will provide social work professionals with the necessary knowledge and skill. Some research efforts should be made to clarify the extent and parameters of these cases and to experiment with alternate approaches.

Part 5

Presenting Problems

In this new section of the book a series of articles has been selected each of which deals with a discrete area of social work intervention. They are not presented as a comprehensive overview; rather, they serve as examples of how problem or identified need is an important component of the diagnostic process.

In the first edition some consideration was given to including a section under this heading. The decision not to include it was based on the perception that requests for service, as discussed here, were of a different conceptual order than those qualities of persons which comprise their psychosocial identities as considered in the first four sections.

I have continued to ponder this and have concluded that its absence can be interpreted as implying that the four prior sections are the essential variables in diagnosis, and the request for service secondary. This would in turn imply that variations in modality, method or technique altered only in relation to the former and not the latter. These articles belie this concept. It is evidently not the case any more than the other extreme which would hold that the request for service or the identified problem was the essential independent variable upon which the choice of modality or technique depended.

The concept of problem, as distinct from man's biopsychosocial identity, is an elusive yet essential term for our profession. It is also an elusive term because the focus of our professional attention is directed to several components or subsystems of a client's significant social system rather than on one particular one.

We know that we have resisted identifying the sole object of our professional activity as personality change lest we be seen as attempting to pattern ourselves too closely on the example of other professions. Yet we know that much of our direct work with clients does aim at altering patterns and indeed structures of personality. We have at times attempted to escape this by claiming our unique focus to be the social problems of clients, that vast area of people's interactions with others and with situations. But only by semantic *legerdemain* can we exclude in any concept of social work the altering of personality function. I mention this struggle not in an effort to resolve it but to identify the difficulty that emerges when one attempts to include the concept of problem in a collection such as this.

In attempting to develop a conceptual base that would aid in selecting articles for this section, I struggled with several concepts of "problem" that differentiated situations from the prior four sections where problems were also considered.

After weighing various alternatives, I decided that there are two characteristics present that distinguish these articles from those in other sections. These are (1) normative considerations and (2) fortuitous events. Sometimes only one of the characteristics is present, but more frequently both.

Normative in this sense is used to identify situations that are considered by a significant component of society as being undesirable or as variations from the expected or desired. Thus child abuse, unmarried parenthood, enuresis, school avoidance, anomie and suicide all deal with situations that are variations from society's expectation and that require professional intervention for relief or resolution. In fact, all of the articles but the Grossman article on disaster services in the train wreck have this normative component.

The other variable, the fortuitous event, refers to those chance events of psychosocial living devoid of any concept of responsibility, such as train wrecks, other disasters, housing difficulties, unemployment, relocation, resettlement, economic inequities and other forms of material lacks.

If this conceptual dyad is a valid one for diagnosis and treatment, it is interesting to speculate on the observation that our literature is heavily weighted in favor of the normative articles. Perhaps this is related to the oft-discussed concept that social work still does have a larger component of a social control function than we wish to acknowledge.

Six of the twelve articles in this section relate to some component of child welfare; this phenomenon also appeared in other sections. Several of the articles deal with situations of high current interest, such as abortion and vasectomy; others deal with some of our long-standing social work interests, such as school attendance, unmarried mothers and separation.

An important emphasis in the articles with a normative consideration is the role that values and attitudes play in providing effective service. In abortion situations there are a wide range of personal, societal and ethical issues on the part of both client and therapist that influence the situation. In child abuse cases, our and society's feelings about this phenomenon play an important part in effective intervention. In cases of enuresis, the shame of the child and its parents towards the problem is again an important variable in working effectively with them. The effect of various personal and societal attitudes in situations can be seen in the vasectomy article where the relationship between diminished concern in clients and societal acceptance is discussed.

Of particular interest is the article on stepparenting. This is an important role adjustment increasingly faced by large numbers of persons who have moved in and out of two or more marital situations.

In earlier sections of the book, reference was made to our growing comfort in making use of the range of thought systems which influence current practice. How this diversity enriches the scope of our practice is particularly evident in this section. For example, behavior modification has given us new approaches to the age-old scourge of enuresis. Role theory helps us understand and manage the changing roles faced by the stepparent. Existentialism gives us a basis to both recognize the prevalence of the suffering caused by anomie and a viewpoint with which to confront it. Finally, crisis theory permits us to understand the impersonal kind of disaster, such as a train wreck, and the highly personalized disaster, such as a rape episode.

In the article on school phobia can be seen another component of our multitheory trend. Here the authors identify varying theoretical implications of school phobia but point out that there is growing consensus about the management implications. In the article on the unmarried mother we find Strean encouraging us not to abandon earlier theoretical perceptions but to expand and enrich them in view of further understanding.

Within this section several of the articles are specific in presenting interventive strategies for particular kinds of cases based on the accumulated experience of the setting or authors. This type of suggestion has been long sought and is a welcome one in our field. Too often we have put more time and effort into describing situations rather than presenting precise suggested interventions.

I was interested to note that there were many other kinds of problems and situations traditional to our practice that were not visible in the literature. Rather than focusing on some of the diagnostic and management skills we have developed around traditional problems, we often tend to address problems currently fashionable.

We have been less than dramatic in our literature from the viewpoint of generalizing as a step to theory building. Even though we have a strong tradition of a "problem-solving" approach to practice, the literature still reflects a strong tendency to view problems as discrete entities rather than as contributing to an expansion of problem-solving theory.

It is hoped that within the next few years we can progress in making use of the full range of systems available in current practice to develop a more general understanding of what specific interventive and therapeutic steps are appropriate to different situations. In the meantime it may be necessary to continue to address individual problems separately as demonstrated by these articles, until we build a richer literature on the diagnostic and treatment implications of the presenting problem.

Abortion

Social Work Service to Abortion Patients

Alice Ullmann

On July 1, 1970, abortions were legalized in New York State. In the following fifteen months about 200,000 abortions were performed in New York City. Although this demand on services apparently presented no particular problem to the health care facilities in the city, debates about abortion continue among the health professions, religious groups, and the general public. In the face of much public discussion, it is pertinent to ask how the women who are undergoing abortions are affected. What are the psychological implications of having an abortion? Why do women make that decision? Do they need help in coping with their decision?

Background

Review of the literature about the implications of abortion does not provide a definitive point of view about psychological conflict regarding abortion or psychological sequelae. Psychologically oriented studies are rare and often deal with the psychiatrist's dilemma in recommending therapeutic abortion. Experience with legal abortion in this country is not yet extensive enough to have produced studies; those from other countries are not always pertinent, in view of cultural differences.

Some years ago, Helene Deutsch wrote of the legal and religious influences in the field of abortion over the centuries and pointed out that it is likely that there have been even deeper psychological motivations against abortion. These motivations, she suggested, are connected with the instinct of self-preservation and the urge to motherhood. She also noted that there must be ambivalence, in that the pregnancy is rejected even though becoming pregnant represented a wish fulfillment. Abortion, some women feel, destroys something in themselves. Deutsch further reported that, during menopausal depressions, some women who have had abortions express self-accusation—but more recent thinking indicates that this may represent a vehicle for depression rather than its cause. She also described a change in the relationship between the man and the woman after abortion. Since

Reprinted from *Social Casework,* Vol. 53 (October, 1972), pp. 481–487, by permission of the author and the Family Service Association of America.

Deutsch's work was published in 1945, it may well reflect the mores of that period.[1]

Mary Calderone has also cautioned about the psychological effect of abortions.[2] Most literature, however, does not support these suggestions. In fact the consensus appears to be that "legal abortion can be performed without fear of severe psychic harm to the woman."[3] Liberalization of abortion laws doubtlessly reflects this opinion, and recent polls of physicians and psychiatrists have shown large majorities in favor of legalizing abortion.[4] It is generally agreed that a woman's reaction to abortion is determined by her general psychological state. However, certain psychological symptoms, it is reported, do appear. One of these is guilt, sometimes as a reaction to the clinical procedure, sometimes as a result of the punitive attitude of those caring for the patient. The guilt may be mild or severe. This guilt and the rarity of severe depression are well described by George S. Walter in his review of the literature.[5] The Kinsey group reported that abortion did not effect subsequent sexual behavior of women.[6]

Edward Senay describes women applying for abortion as a population in crisis.[7] In his clinical experience, there were many instances of insomnia, somatic complaints, anxiety, and suicidal ideation, as well as an intense preoccupation with the problem of ending the unwanted pregnancy. This report reflects experience with psychiatric indications for abortion. One might argue that the women who no longer require psychiatric evaluations, and can obtain legal abortions based on the decision between patient and physician, are not under as much psychological stress. A Scandinavian study shows that the majority of women who have undergone legal abortions do not suffer major psychological sequelae.[8] However, it is not known how many women who ask for abortion have preexisting psychological problems which may be exacerbated by the procedure. Senay speaks of this high-risk group and describes a mourning process that almost invariably takes place and can affect a woman in different ways, depending on preexisting psychological status.[9] He reports, also, that specific questioning of the patients will

[1] Helene Deutsch, *The Psychology of Women*, vol. 2: *Motherhood* (New York: Grune and Stratton, 1945).

[2] Mary Calderone, ed., *Abortion in the United States* (New York: Harper & Row, 1968).

[3] George S. Walter, Psychologic and Emotional Consequences of Elective Abortion, *Obstetrics and Gynecology*, 36: 482–91 (September 1970).

[4] Eric Pfeiffer, Psychiatric Indications or Psychiatric Justification of Therapeutic Abortion?, *Archives of General Psychiatry*, 23: 402–07 (November 1970).

[5] Walter, Psychologic Consequences of Abortion.

[6] Paul H. Gebhard et al., *Pregnancy, Birth and Abortion* (New York: Harper & Row, 1958).

[7] Edward C. Senay, Therapeutic Abortion—Clinical Aspects, *Archives of General Psychiatry*, 23: 408–15 (November 1970).

[8] Martin Ekblad, Induced Abortion on Psychiatric Grounds: A Follow-up Study of 479 Women, *Acta Psychiatrica et Neurologica Scandinavica*, suppl. 99 (1955), p. 1.

[9] Senay, Therapeutic Abortion.

elicit reports of guilt, depression, and anxiety. *American Journal of Public Health* of March 1971 contains a number of articles about abortion. In one of these, Henry P. David asks for research in psychosocial factors in abortion.[10] He maintains that more should be known about psychological implications now that more and more states are liberalizing their abortion laws.

Planning a Service

Prior to 1970 the social workers at New York Hospital—a large voluntary, university hospital in New York City—were involved in obtaining psychiatric recommendations for women seeking abortion. These requests originally came at the rate of about one a week, but in the period immediately before July 1970, there were about five a week. Experience with these patients had shown that they reflected the psychological adjustment of almost any patient group. That is, some women were under greater stress than others, some had histories or evidenced symptoms of varying degrees of psychological disorders, some, although under stress, showed general emotional stability. The problems involved in obtaining an abortion on psychiatric grounds caused all of them some stress.

Supporters of legal abortion claim that the procedure is a simple one and often describe it as less traumatic than a tonsillectomy. Experience of the social work staff in interviewing the patients mentioned above, however, showed that the majority of patients had psychological difficulties in making the decision to have the abortion. This group of patients served to make it clear that the women requesting abortion after July 1970 would be under stress of varying degree and that every effort should be made to provide a social work service.[11]

When the new law came into effect, New York Hospital set aside a thirty-bed clinical ward for private and service abortion patients separating them from obstetrical and gynecological patients. The service patients were seen in the clinic first and admitted to the hospital within a few days. Private patients were not seen in the hospital prior to admission.

The social workers turned their attention to the service patients who could be seen prior to admission. Because of the amount of time involved, individual interviews to find problem situations were not feasible. The decision to see patients in groups, therefore, was a logical means of handling the situation. The group session would provide education about the abortion procedure and family-planning methods and had the added benefit of the interest and support of the nursing staff who eventually became coleaders of the groups.

[10] Henry P. David, Abortion: Public Health Concerns and Needed Psychosocial Research, *American Journal of Public Health*, 61: 510–17 (March 1971).

[11] The writer is grateful to the obstetrical and gynecological unit of the Department of Social Work at the New York Hospital for aiding in data collection and providing the patient service, and to Miss Margaret Mushinski for her assistance in preparing the statistical report.

Further rationale for the establishment of the groups was to allow for the expression of conflict regarding the abortion and to help the patient deal with possible adverse family, religious, and social class attitudes. Group censures may cause feelings of isolation as well as guilt and anxiety in the prospective abortion patient who often has to face the procedure alone. Peer groups would offer the patient the opportunity to share her feelings with others in a similar situation. They might support the patient in the decision-making process. The goal of the groups was therefore three-fold: (1) to help the patients share and express feelings of conflict within the group, (2) to help members of the group support each other, and (3) to provide education about abortion and medical procedures and to clear up mistaken ideas about abortion and family planning. It was also hoped that the group process would help to identify those women with significant psychosocial problems or stress so that further help could be offered to those patients.

The Patients

Prospective patients were asked to join the group for a discussion with the social worker, but joining the group was not compulsory. The group meetings took place after every clinic session, and each group met once.

From September 1, 1970, to February 26, 1971, 598 patients were seen in groups, an average of five in each session. This total represented roughly 75 percent of all abortion patients who came to the clinic. Most of those women who did not attend a group session gave as a reason that they wanted to get home. This applied particularly to those coming from out of town. Some who did not wish to join a group explained that they felt they had nothing to discuss, no questions to ask. Each patient coming into a group was asked to complete a small card containing questions on area of residence, age, marital status, race, religion, occupation, source of support, how the patient heard about the service, what birth control methods had been used, and why the patient was seeking an abortion. There were no refusals to fill out the cards although a few patients omitted some items and eighteen patients did not give reasons for seeking the abortion.

As shown in table 1, 60 percent of the patients came from New York City, 5 percent from New York State, and 33 percent from states other than New York. The largest percentage of patients (40 percent) were between the ages of twenty and twenty-four. One-third of the patients were married. Single women comprised 46 percent of the patients, and the remaining 21 percent were divorced, separated, or widowed. The patients were primarily white (68 percent), and the largest percentage of the women were Catholic (47 percent). Almost a third were housewives, a little more than a fifth were employed as clerical or sales personnel, and skilled workers and students were almost equally represented (13 percent and 14 percent, respectively). More than one-half (55 percent) had completed high school, almost a quarter (23 percent) had only an elementary education, and almost a fifth (18 percent) had attended college. The majority of the patients were self-supporting; 21 percent were receiving public assistance.

Table 1.
Percentage Distribution of Respondents'
Characteristics

Characteristics	Percentage of respondents
Age	
Under 19	15
20–24	40
25–29	24
30–34	12
35–39	7
40+	2
Race	
White	68
Black	26
Other	5
Unknown	1
Religion	
Catholic	47
Protestant	34
Jewish	4
Other	10
None	3
Unknown	2
Education	
Elementary	23
High school	55
College	16
College+	2
Unknown	4
Marital status	
Single	46
Married	33
Separated	14
Divorced	6
Widowed	1
Unknown	*a*
Occupation	
Housewife	32
Clerical, sales	21
Student	14
Skilled	13
Professional, managers	10
Unknown	7
Unskilled	3
Area of residence	
New York City	60
New York State	5
Other states	33
Unknown	2
Means of support	
Self	38
Husband	26
Public assistance	21
Parents	11
Other	3
Unknown	1

[a] Less than one percent
N = 598

Table 2.
Methods of Contraception

Methods	Percentage of respondents
None	46
Pill	25
Foam	10
Diaphragm	6
Rhythm	6
Coil	5
Condom	3
Other	2
Jelly	1
Average number of methods per patient[a]	1.1

N = 598
[a] Totals amount to more than 100 percent because there were multiple responses. Percentages were calculated from the number of respondents, not the number of responses.

Table 2 shows that one-quarter of the patients had used the pill for birth control, and 46 percent had used no birth control at all. Table 3 reflects the reasons given for seeking an abortion; the women were given the opportunity to cite more than one reason. Lack of sufficient money was the reason given by the largest percentage of women (43 percent). Being unmarried was cited by 37 percent, even though actually 46 percent were single. This fact is more significant when *single* is considered to include divorced, separated, and widowed, in which case the percentage of unmarried women is actually 67. It is not clear what was meant by the response, *not ready,* but it was included because earlier experience with abortion patients had shown this to be a reason frequently cited. It appears to include a combination of such reasons as lack of money, desire to space children, and general unpreparedness. The work/school category usually represented school for high school students and work for the older women, although there were some women interested in continuing education.

The Groups

When examining the content of the group discussions, the characteristics of the women should be borne in mind. It is possible that women of different ethnic and educational backgrounds would have other concerns about abortion.

Six social workers participated in the program. A nurse clinician acted as coleader to insure that the educational and clinical aspects of abortion could be handled effectively. One of the leaders usually began the meeting with a statement that being admitted for an abortion has caused many women some degree of social and emotional stress and that hospital per-

Table 3.
Reasons for Abortion

Reasons	Percentage of respondents
Money	43
Not married	37
Not ready	31
Work/school	30
Too many children	20
Other	8
Not husband's child	5
Unknown	3
Average number of reasons per patient[a]	1.8

N = 598

[a] Totals amount to more than 100 percent because there were multiple responses. Percentages were calculated from the number of respondents, not the number of responses.

sonnel wanted them to have the opportunity to discuss their questions and concerns. This comment usually brought out requests for information about the abortion procedures, but it appeared that these questions could not be handled through a purely educational approach. Questions about the procedure included who exactly would do the procedure and what the length of anesthesia would be. The questions also reflected fear of the procedure and its aftereffects. For instance, the question of subsequent sterility came up quite often. For many women this would be their first hospitalization, and they wanted to know what it was like to be in a hospital, whether they would be separated from the obstetrical patients, and when they could be visited. They needed education and information, but more than this they were asking for reassurance that the procedure was not harmful.

It was necessary to encourage the group members to express their conflicts on some occasions, but most of the women were very ready to talk about their underlying feelings. The question of guilt came up at every session. It appeared that although abortion had been legalized, it was still felt by many of these patients to be an illegal procedure. Apparently, in this situation, the change in law has come before the change in heart. Religious issues came up very rarely so that the guilt expressed or implied was usually not based on religious conflict. There was discussion about "killing the baby," fear that society would judge them, stress on secrecy, expression of guilt about becoming pregnant and undergoing an unnatural procedure. Often group members tended to appeal to the leaders for alleviation of their guilt. The leaders found that what helped the group most was to receive this reassurance from each other, and they guided the group to talk to each other rather than to the leaders.

It seemed very clear that the majority of women were ambivalent. They described how they suppressed their motherly feelings, which they said they possessed but did not want at this time. They said they did not want to think of the fetus as a baby. There was regret by some that while pregnancy should be a wonderful experience, they could not go through it with now. Many wanted quick admission so that the fetus would not have a chance of becoming "too real."

A frequent topic of discussion was the attitude of the clinic personnel. The women complained they were being talked at, treated like numbers rather than people, and kept waiting too long. They felt the professional staff condemned them. On further discussion it appeared that these reactions had much to do with how the patients felt about themselves; however, the attitude of personnel was a problem at times and certainly bears further exploration. Some patients expressed much anger on such subjects as racism, fathers of the babies, and promiscuous women; again it appeared that some of this feeling was projection of their own anxiety and ambivalence.

Feelings of isolation were also apparent, although the records show that very few patients actually went through planning for the abortion alone. In the groups, however, many patients regretted not being able to discuss their problems with their families. Many out-of-town patients described what it was life to come to New York and to the hospital without family or peer support. Even those who had discussed their plans with families and friends felt that ultimately the decision and experience were personal ones which others could share only to a limited extent.

In some groups, patients talked about their backgrounds and families, their other children, about being or not being married, and about birth control and family-planning. Some blamed birth control device failures, but many admitted to ignorance of birth control methods. This fact is interesting because it was not an educationally deprived group. Knowledge about birth control is apparently not related to education. One might, of course, question the motivation of these women to become pregnant but the group discussions did not deal with this question. The women spoke about their jobs and how to handle job absence. Usually they found someone in the group who had similar experiences and others who had opinions and feelings about these subjects.

Joint leadership was a problem at times. It did provide for nurses and social workers to cooperate in a service to patients and gave them an opportunity to work together. In general, the nurses tended to lean toward more active participation; they taught, guided, and reassured. The social workers tended to encourage the group members to talk to each other and derive help and support from each other. Nurses and social workers met to discuss these differences in approach, but they remained a problem. The nurses were a definite asset in providing information and education about the abortion procedures. However, as the social workers became more familiar with the information, it was not as important to have the nurse handle the educational aspects.

Discussion

No attempt was made at a formal evaluation of the group meetings. A number of patients mentioned during their subsequent hospital stay that they had found the meeting personally helpful and reassuring in relation to staff attitudes. The social work staff felt that the sessions gave patients an opportunity to discuss their questions and concerns with professional staff and with group members having similar experiences. The contact resulted in mutual support and relief of tension. Further evaluation of the group experience would have to be based on study and control groups.

Approximately one patient in every three groups was seen individually subsequent to the group sessions. Some of these patients sought individual service; in other cases the social worker, having identified a disturbed patient during a session, would speak with her afterward, offering help. Service was given most often in relation to ambivalence about the abortion and less frequently in relation to concrete problems such as housing, absence from work, or financial questions. The group sessions were therefore of some help in individual case-finding.

Another area requiring further study and observation is the attitude toward abortion of the professional personnel, who are bound to have some personal conflicts and to be affected both consciously and unconsciously by positive or negative public attitudes. It is quite likely that physicians and nurses—both trained to save lives—find abortion a difficult subject to deal with and have conflict about participating in the procedure. Patients seem to be quickly aware of this feeling. Although social workers are less involved in the actual abortion procedure, they are also likely to have their own conflicts. Another question one might ask is whether men and women have different attitudes about abortion. It would be useful, also, to analyze the contribution of the group leaders and to evaluate the group process in general.

The greatest amount of work, however, needs to be done in the whole area of the nature of emotional conflicts in patients undergoing abortions and the presence or absence of psychological sequelae. For instance, do all women suffer some emotional conflict or ambivalence, and if so, do they all need professional help? Is abortion today a procedure acceptable to most women as a way of limiting family size? Is seeking an abortion symptomatic of other psychological conflict, and does it take place in the presence of other psychological problems? To obtain answers to these questions it would be necessary to conduct personal interviews including follow-up after the abortion.

Summary

This article has examined some of the literature about the psychological aspects of abortion. The 598 patients who came to a large voluntary hospital in New York City and were seen in group-counseling sessions were described, and such subjects as use of birth control and reasons for abortion were considered. The content of the group discussions was examined in an attempt to determine if a need was being met. There was no formal evaluation of the effect of the groups, but it appeared that useful information about abortion was given, that group members expressed their ambivalent feelings, and that they felt that they had derived some benefit from the group experience.

Child Abuse

Working with the Parent in Child-Abuse Cases

Sally A. Holmes, Carol Barnhart, Lucile Cantoni, and Eva Reymer

Child abuse as a concept is relatively new in Western civilization. Historically, children have been accepted as the exclusive property of their parents, who would give them the kind of care they needed and deserved. Parents know best was the rule. An abused child was therefore believed to be a bad child who needed to be punished. Thus, when men like Rousseau, Pestalozzi, and Dewey began to advocate the rights of children, they presented a strange, unwelcome threat to established society. Gradually, however, society has been forced to look at what is happening between some parents and their children, and too often it is not a pretty sight.

One reaction to child abuse takes the form of a bad case of myopia. There is evidence of this reaction in the fact that the writers could find only two articles in SOCIAL CASEWORK in the past twenty years dealing with child abuse. One was by physicians[1] and the other by a social worker not in the family service field.[2] Yet family agencies do work with abusive families. Larry B. Silver, Christina C. Dublin, and Reginald S. Lourie report that of the thirty-four child abuse cases they studied, four of the families were treated by the local family agency.[3] The multiproblem family often includes child abuse as one of its problems. But, in reports, family service caseworkers

Reprinted from *Social Casework*, Vol. 56 (January, 1973), pp. 3–12, by permission of the authors and the Family Service Association of America.

[1] Larry B. Silver, Christina C. Dublin, and Reginald S. Lourie, Agency Action and Interaction in Cases of Child Abuse, *Social Casework*, 52: 164–71 (March 1971).

[2] Maurice J. Boisvert, The Battered-Child Syndrome, *Social Casework*, 53: 475–80 (October 1972).

[3] Silver, Dublin, and Lourie, Agency Action and Interaction, pp. 166–67.

tend to minimize parental attacks on children. In a major article on work with the multiproblem family, Alice Overton refers to abuse in only one sentence: "He acted the tyrant, often beating the children and demanding complete silence in the home."[4] The success of this case is reported in detail, but there is no mention of whether the beating continued, diminished, or stopped.

A second reaction to extreme child abuse is outrage against the parents, which can lead to a child-snatching approach to the problem: Identify the abuse, punish the parents, and remove the child. This view came into focus early in the last century as society came to realize that there was little legal protection for the child. This fact was graphically illustrated in the State of New York in 1871 when a child named Mary Ellen, who was undernourished, beaten, and chained to her bed, was rescued by a group of church workers. The court case was tried under the law against cruelty to animals because there was no law for the protection of children. Shortly thereafter, the Society for the Prevention of Cruelty to Children was founded in New York City.[5]

It is possible, however, to leap too quickly to the solution of removing the child from his home. Many questions may remain unanswered in this process: How much abuse is enough to require removal of the child? If one child is removed, will a sibling be chosen to be abused? Is the emotional damage of losing a parent greater than the danger of abuse? If the child is removed from his parents, to what is he being removed? Who will care for him? Would he be worse off with no parent or with an abusive parent?

There are times when it is clear that a parent is likely to severly injure or kill a child unless the two are separated. Then, action must be taken to remove the child quickly. More often, however, the danger is less obvious. There is room for doubt, and there is a nagging conviction that there must be a better way. A child may be rescued temporarily, only to be returned to the home eventually to more severe abuse than ever. It seems clear that it is necessary to look beyond our outrage in order to give attention to the needs of the abusive parents. It is known that separation from even a severely abusive parent is traumatic for a child. Might it not in many instances be more helpful to the abused child if more determined efforts were made to focus the treatment on his parents?

With this goal in mind, nine staff members of Family Service of Detroit and Wayne County established themselves as a study group in order to develop into more responsive, sensitive, and skillful caseworkers in the treatment of child-abuse cases.[6] Two members were involved with Parents

---

[4] Alice Overton, Serving Families Who "Don't Want Help," *Social Casework*, 34: 304–9 (July 1953).

[5] Ray E. Helfer and C. Henry Kempe, *The Battered Child* (Chicago: University of Chicago Press, 1968).

[6] In addition to the writers, other members of the study group included Armethyst Carswell, Betty Istratoff, Francis M. Moynihan, Francena Tinsley, and Ellen Whitehead.

Anonymous in an agency service to that organization.[7] All members had experience with child abuse in other agencies or in their current caseloads.

For nearly a year, the group met regularly. It began by reading the literature on child abuse, each member reviewing a different aspect. All the members read *The Battered Child, Helping the Battered Child and His Family*, and *The Neglected Battered-Child Syndrome*, which became, in effect, their textbooks.[8]

The group then considered case material and reviewed a total of twenty-three cases. Each case had been handled by a study group member, either in a district office of the agency, through Parents Anonymous, or both through Parents Anonymous and in the agency office.

Definition of Child Abuse

Defining child abuse is not easy. The medical definition emphasizes physical trauma to the child. The legal definition is concerned with the guilt of the parents. Various cultures and subcultures appear to have different standards of what is acceptable treatment for children. The working definition of the study group was developed in relation to the parent's perception of abuse. After inflicting damage to his child, a parent may suffer terrible guilt or he may be so afraid of further harming the child that he is hardly able to touch him at all. The abusive treatment may bear no relation to the child's behavior but relate instead to the parent's negative feelings about himself or his situation. Abuse may be a result of the parent's unrealistic view of the child as the powerful one who fails to meet the parent's needs or is "out to get him."

There is no one kind of abusive parent. Such parents come from all socioeconomic levels and cultural backgrounds, and no one psychiatric diagnosis encompasses the personalities and behavior of all of them. They do, however, share a pattern of parent-child relationships. C. Henry Kempe and Ray E. Helfer describe several conditions under which child abuse is likely to occur:[9]

---

[7] Parents Anonymous is a self-help group for parents who abuse their children and want to stop. It started in California in 1969 and rapidly developed into a national organization. Members join small groups that meet weekly with a professional to discuss individual progress. Members help each other by providing help at the time of crisis and by offering the support of a friendship group. For further information about Parents Anonymous, see Lucile Cantoni, *The First Two Years: Parents Anonymous of Michigan* (Detroit: Parents Anonymous of Michigan, 1974).

[8] Helfer and Kempe, *The Battered Child;* idem, *Helping the Battered Child and his Family* (Philadelphia: J. B. Lippincott Company, 1972); and *The Neglected Battered-Child Syndrome* (New York: Child Welfare League of America, 1963).

[9] Kempe and Helfer, *The Battered Child,* pp. 57–62.

The parent was emotionally or physically abused as a child.

The parents feel isolated, with no one to turn to in time of need.

The spouse is absent, cooperative with the abuse, or fails to provide support for the marital partner.

The parent unrealistically expects the child to gratify his own dependency needs. The child is seen as different from other children.

Some form of crisis, real or imagined, exists that sets the abusive act in motion.

In keeping with its emphasis on treatment of the parent, the study group members found themselves defining child abuse in terms of the abusive parent rather than the abused child. This important difference is particularly significant in handling reactions to child abuse. Although it is almost impossible for caseworkers to deal with their reactions to the pain and cruelty of abusive acts committed against children, they are on more familiar ground if they can see not only the children, but also the parents as hurting, needy people—the kind of people that caseworkers are professionally educated to help.

Resistance to Treating Abusive Parents

Articles in SOCIAL CASEWORK are not the only evidence that caseworkers find it difficult to deal with child abuse. The members of the study group became aware of their own avoidance patterns whenever a group member would relate the more gory aspects of an experience with abuse. It is easy to identify with the child and become angry with the parents. Yet, if the worker happens to have a warm, ongoing relationship with the parent, he wants to deny the abusive act and see only the pleasant side of the parent that is shown, forgetting that, in order to help, he must be able to accept the rage as well as the love in the client.

Abusive parents, however, are likely to be isolated and to suffer from severe deficiencies in interactional skills. The behavior that prevents them from establishing warm relationships with others also makes it difficult for caseworkers to relate to them. Although many abusive parents are charming, likable people, others may be difficult people to like. They may talk too much, they may be critical, they may be withholding and unresponsive. Their insatiable dependency may place heavy demands on the caseworker. The client may go through a series of crises necessitating frequent, tense, and exhausting contacts. Extraordinary outreach is often required, leaving the worker drained and discouraged.

Sometimes it is surprising to realize the subtle ways that client reactions may affect casework. If the client frequently fails to appear, the worker may forget to call back or delay arranging the time for a home visit. If a client speaks of being worried about losing control with the children, the worker may minimize his worry. These difficulties are illustrated by the following case.

> Mrs. A came to the agency expressing feelings of being overwhelmed by her total family situation and by her fear that she could not control her own impulses. The worker focused on Mrs. A's feelings of helplessness with uncontrollable children. Mrs. A failed to keep the next appointment, and two months later the case was closed. Eight months later, Mrs. A called. She was seen once on an emergency basis, put on the waiting list, and seen one month later. In the interview, Mrs. A poured out her feelings about her school-phobic, seven-year-old daughter, her own tension headaches, morning chaos when quarreling children waked her, hiding in bed, problems with nine-year-old Keith, past marital problems, and so forth. The worker selected morning time as the initial focus, but whenever a change in the routine was suggested, Mrs. A would say it would not work. The worker questioned Mrs. A's capacity to change the situation.
>
> The next week, the worker made a home visit. Mrs. A had followed none of the suggestions. Mrs. A later cancelled several appointments.
>
> Three months later, the worker saw Mrs. A once. She was upset about possible mental illness and felt nobody could help her. She did not call back and the case was closed. Five months later, Mrs. A was seeking help at another agency for her child-abuse problem.

In this case, the caseworker did not focus on the client's concern about her lack of impulse control, even though it was expressed in the first interview. The caseworker skirted this difficult area and tried unsuccessfully to help the client without facing this central issue.

Sometimes, even when the parent is being seen for child abuse problems, the caseworker tends to minimize the extent of the abuse, as in the following case.

> Mrs. B was referred to the district office through her Parents Anonymous sponsor. In the first interview, the worker noted ambivalent interaction between the mother and child. Mrs. B continually pushed the child away, placated her with food, then pulled the child to her again. As the sponsor had not seen the mother and child together, she had been unable to pick up the negative interaction and had tended to view the mother as "not a real child abuser." She had wanted to screen out the hurt and minimize for Mrs. B her weakness as a parent

Developing a Treatment Relationship

The initial contact with an abusive parent may be difficult to begin. Often these clients have experienced severe rejection in their lives and have learned to expect rejection. Extensive outreach may be needed. A parent may seek help for some other problem, afraid and ashamed to admit the abuse. From the examination of cases, the study group identified some clues to alert the caseworker to possible child abuse. When several of these clues are found in the same family, workers should become concerned.

The parent expresses fear of being abusive.

The parent expresses fear of losing control.

A referral source (hospital, school, other agency, friend, or relative) expresses suspicion of abuse.

The parent refuses to focus on a child's injury, talking instead about some real or imagined injury of his own, even though the child's injury is clearly traumatic, possibly serious.

A child runs away from home.

Punishment is out of proportion to the behavior, suggesting displacement of the parent's anger.

The parent has unrealistic expectations for the child, particularly if the parent is expecting the child to take a nurturing role toward the parent (role reversal).

Normal child behavior is seen as deliberate abuse of the parent (the child is "out to get me").

The parent asks that the child be placed outside the home.

The home is excessively sloppy or excessively neat.

The child is blamed for family difficulties, such as marital problems.

The parent complains that the child does not even cry when physically punished.

The parent strenuously defends his own parents' bad child-raising techniques.

There is little affection shown between parent and child.

The child, particularly a preschooler, suffers repeated injuries that require medical attention.

There is frequent screaming and demeaning of the child by name-calling—"devil," "bastard," "whore," and so forth.

The client reports that a friend or relative is the abusive parent.

Often, when the caseworker fails to pick up the clues, the client becomes convinced that what he is doing is so terrible that even the caseworker can not talk about it. It is important, therefore, to talk openly about the abuse. At the same time, it is undesirable to have the client's identity revolve around being a child-abuser. There is no point in forcing admissions, nor is it necessary to define and admit to abuse before the problem has been worked on.

Because severely abusive parents are rivalrous with their children, it is important that the caseworker avoid focusing on the child during the early stages of treatment, especially at the time of crisis. In the following example, when the caseworker expressed concern for the child, the child became further endangered.

Mrs. D called late one night to report that she had been beating her ten-year-old John and felt like finishing the job. She was going to run away—take the baby and go to a motel. The caseworker questioned what she had done to John and asked how badly he had been hurt. The caseworker said that if Mrs. D went away, she would need to call another community agency to make sure John was cared for. Mrs. D became very angry and accused the worker of not believing or trusting her. She threatened to kill John to prove that she meant what she said. She put John on the phone and he sobbed that his mother was pointing a gun at him.

Defining Precipitating Factors

Once an abusive parent has been drawn into treatment, how does one offer the help that is needed? The major goal of altering the destructive relationship between parent and child may be facilitated in many ways. One of the first tasks is to find out what is happening. What behavior of the child triggers the irrational response? What are the patterns in the relationship between parent and child? In each of the following examples, the irrational responses of the parents are focused on particular behavior—lessons, eating habits, bed-wetting.

Mrs. E beat her ten-year-old son with a belt. She had unrealistic expectations of him. She expected perfect obedience. She expected him to do household tasks that required more skill than a ten-year-old was likely to have. She also expected him to organize his work in a mature fashion. But what upset her most were his repeated school failures. For weeks after a teacher would complain about him, she would sit him down after school each day to do his lessons. He would not do the work, so she would beat him. This behavior continued all evening until the final lashes in bed just before he went to sleep for the night.

Mrs. F came in to get help with the management of her child. Her chief complaint was that the child did not eat properly. Mrs. F was concerned about both nutrition and manners. In the third interview, Mrs. F sat down and said, "You know, it's not Betty's eating. There is nothing she could do to please me. I feel that she has trapped me by her very existence."

Mrs. G was quite open about her inability to tolerate her six-year-old daughter, Terry. Terry expressed her rebellion through enuresis, which provoked her mother's rejection. Mrs. G threatened "to take off for good." This upset Mr. G who focused his anger against Terry, frequently using physical punishment.

In the next example, the irrational behavior is harder to identify because, instead of attacking the child in anger, the mother withdrew because of her fear of her own violence. In this situation, the irrational response was expressed by keeping an emotional distance between the mother and her child.

Mrs. H came to the agency when her four-year-old was returned to her from foster care. Mrs. H had abused the child, but never seriously enough to warrant court action. Mrs. H had voluntarily placed the child because she was afraid she might abuse her more seriously. When she came to the agency, Mrs. H was catering to her child's every whim, fearing that if she tried to set any limits on the child's behavior, the child might become angry and that she might retaliate with more serious abuse. Mrs. H entertained the child constantly, yet carefully maintained an emotional distance.

The client and caseworker together try to identify the situations—such as the above response—that seem to set off abusive responses. This effort is the first step toward understanding and controlling the parent's irrational perceptions.

Understanding Rage

It is important that clients be aware of the distinction between anger and rage. Anger is the emotional reaction to the present situation in which an individual perceives himself as hurt or mistreated in any way. The person is easily able to identify the reason for his anger and his angry reaction is proportionate to the severity of his perceived injury.

Rage, however, is a well of suppressed anger and fear that has been stored up, often from early childhood, so that its cause can no longer be easily remembered or identified. It simmers beneath the surface of the conscious mind and is a source of terror to the individual who feels the pressure and fears that the dammed-up emotion may burst forth beyond his control. Often, the rage originates from the terror which the individual felt as a child, bearing the brunt of the uncontrolled violence of his own parents. In such a situation, a child is not only frightened but overwhelmed by his own helplessness. He is not allowed to express his anger at being mistreated; he is forced to submit and suppress his anger. As an adult, he re-creates the scene, only this time he is in the powerful position and can act out against his own child the revenge he longed to gain against his parents. An important step in treatment is the client's recognition of the infantile rage and, if possible, some understanding of its source so that he can find new ways to cope with it.

> About two months after starting treatment, Mrs. J was sitting at home very upset. Her child reached over to comfort her. Later Mrs. J described the incident: "That was my mother's hand touching me. I cringed and ran away from it. I wanted to kill her!" Thus, Mrs. J recognized that a major component of her abuse of her child was an acting-out of the rage toward her own mother. In subsequent weeks, Mrs. J remembered many childhood experiences in which her needs were not met, where she was expected to forego her own needs in order to care for her mother, and where she was severely hurt when she failed to care for her mother. As she worked on her current relationship with her mother, Mrs. J found that she no longer had to dedicate her life to the care of her mother. When she could assert herself more effectively with her mother, she could begin to set realistic limits on her child's behavior, without the danger that she would express her pent-up rage against the child.

When an individual is burdened with underlying rage, he becomes fearful of all angry feelings lest they trigger an outburst of the rage over which he feels, at best, only tenuous control. Because he was not allowed to express his anger as a child, he may not know how to express it legitimately as an adult or even understand that anger is an acceptable, normal emotion. The interaction between the caseworker and the client often provides an arena in which the client is able to experiment with new ways of expressing anger. Clients learn that they may express their anger without threat of loss of the relationship or of physical control. Parents Anonymous group meetings are particularly helpful in this regard.

> Mrs. N phoned to say that she had been hurt by Mrs. O's remarks at a previous Parents Anonymous meeting and felt that Mrs. O did not want her in the group. Mrs. N was encouraged to express just how she felt, and it was then suggested that it was important for her to express those same feelings to Mrs. O at the next meeting.
>
> Supported by the caseworker's acceptance of her feelings, Mrs. N was able, with great difficulty, to repeat to the group what she had said. The worker's role in the group meeting was to help each of the women to clarify how she was feeling and to express these feelings to the others. Mrs. O told Mrs. N that she could accept the fact that her own problems were different from Mrs. N's but that she did want her in the group and she did care for her. As they talked out their misunderstanding, the tension subsided. It was a learning experience for the whole group.

Some clients divide people into "good" and "bad." People either "hate" or "love" them. People are either "for" or "against" them. With such unrealistic expectations and no room for human error, it is difficult to sustain long relationships. Again and again, such clients must be reminded that people feel ambivalent emotions toward others, including both love and hate. These clients have been taught from childhood that they can not be angry with people they love. They were forced to deny the hate and fear they felt toward their parents, often building idealized images of the parents to prove their affection. They carry heavy guilt about the hate, having been taught that there must be only love between the parent and child. One of the goals in treatment is to help clients to understand that feelings of hate and anger do exist in every close, loving relationship. Misunderstandings occur and feelings get hurt. Gradually, clients learn to recognize and explore their own negative feelings and to accept them as a legitimate part of any relationship.

Parenting the Parent

Caseworkers are continually faced with the task of meeting parents' dependency needs without infantalizing them. As ways are found to meet their needs, they become better able to perform the role of parent. Because these parents suffer from an overwhelming sense of rejection, it is important always to show them acceptance and concern and to focus on what hurts within the parent. If the caseworker shows concern for the children, the parent is threatened; he immediately feels that the worker can not be concerned for him.

While an extremely dependent client may lean heavily on the caseworker, at the same time he is apt to resent the dependency. The adult part of the client knows the dependent relationship is inappropriate, and negative feelings about past dependent relationships may be projected onto the caseworker. Delicate judgment is required to set limits in a firm but gentle manner, constantly evaluating whether his response is nurturing support or if it goes beyond this to feed the childlike dependency. It is easy to become unduly involved in the client's life, allowing anxiety about the client's behavior to impede his progress toward appropriate independence.

In a group situation, a sibling rivalry may develop, with each member vying for the caseworker's attention and feeling slighted if any member gets extra time. This conflict is a reliving of childhood family experience where parents showed favoritism among siblings. It is important to define limits together.

Educating the Parent

Another task of the caseworker is to fill gaps in the parents' knowledge of normal child development. We must evaluate the parents' understanding of what are realistic expectations for the age level of the child. In the following examples, the parents were ignorant of the developmental needs of their children.

> Mrs. V felt that her own life had been severely restricted by lack of a proper education and was determined that her son would not suffer in this way. Although he was only seven years old, she forced him to sit for hours doing homework, without adequate time for play or exercise. Severe and frequent beatings were used to force the child's compliance.
>
> It was necessary to do a great amount of educating so that Mrs. V could understand the other needs of her child. Because her own needs were so tied up in the child's education, she was encouraged to stay entirely away from any participation in his schooling. As she learned the importance of play and exercise for him, she was able to modify her expectations and greatly reduce both the frequency and the severity of the beatings.
>
> Mrs. W was very angry with her one-year-old child because she kept dropping things from her high chair. When she expressed her frustration about this behavior to her Parents Anonymous group, it was pointed out that this occurrence is common with year-old children. Other group members spoke of similar experiences with their children. When asked the reason for dropping toys, they replied, "The child is out to get you," "They know you don't like it," "They want to show who's boss," and so forth. The caseworker explained that a baby learns about distance this way, by watching things go away from him. He learns about gravity—that they always fall down, never up—and that things which go out of sight don't cease to exist but will come back (like peek-a-boo). A baby learns the fun of interaction with others in this first predictable game. The worker pointed out that if a parent gives a child four items to drop and then picks them up, it is less wearing.
>
> When the mothers understood that the game was a valuable learning experience for the child, they felt that they would be able to play it with a great deal more patience, possibly even with enthusiasm.

Expanding Life Satisfactions

The abusive parent's life is likely to be only minimally satisfying. Such clients usually suffer painfully from low self-esteem and extreme feelings of inadequacy, hopelessness, and despair about their ability to improve their lives. This overwhelming sense of futility and incompetence seriously damages the parent-child relationship. People whose inner resources are so depleted often have few pleasurable activities. They may have internalized the belief that they should not have fun, that their role as parents demands self-sacrifice and martyrdom, and that to set aside any time for themselves is unimportant or even sinful.

Caseworkers need to maintain firmly that the client deserves to have fun and that is is healthier for the child if the parent leads a satisfying life. A pleasurable activity for some clients may be working toward a definite vocational goal. They may have been thwarted in their vocational plans, may be in unsuitable jobs, or may never have thought of themselves as desiring a job. Caseworkers can help to legitimize the clients' desires and reinforce their efforts toward achievement.

Helping Parents Modify Behavior

Many times, clients have adopted behavior which was important to their survival as children but is inappropriate in their role as parents. If parental approval was strongly insisted upon and backed up by physical abuse, for example, approval of others—even his own children—may be overwhelmingly needed by the individual even as an adult. Such a client needs to be helped to recognize the inappropriate seeking of approval as a source of trouble. For example, a child may fail to recognize and approve his mother's efforts to please and may be badly beaten. The mother may be thoroughly confused as to her reason for losing control and may need the caseworker's help to relate her need for approval to the inappropriate expectation of her child.

Housekeeping is often perceived by the mother as an important part of her self-concept. In this symbolic role, the mother's housekeeping behavior often becomes quite inappropriate. Compulsive housecleaning may be a fruitless attempt to build or increase self-esteem. In such a case, any action of the child that disrupts the house will be experienced by the mother as a direct attack against her. At the other extreme is the client who is disorganized and compulsively dirty. This mother feels dirty, worthless, and inadequate, and her housekeeping reflects her self-image. In each case, part of the problem may be the mother's impossibly high expectations of herself. In the first instance, no matter how hard she works, she can not satisfy her own high standards. In the second, she feels like such a failure that she is immobilized before she can begin. The goal is to help the client to set up reasonable standards for herself, to learn why housekeeping has become so overcharged emotionally for her, and to improve her image of herself.

Role reversal is one of the most common categories of inappropriate behavior for the abusive parent. Parenting demands a constant giving of emotional support to the child. The abusive parent not only lacks the ability to give sufficient support, but often demands a parenting type of support from the child instead. The parent's insatiable dependency needs are expressed through the constant demands on the child to assume a parenting role so that the parent can assume the role of the dependent child.

> Mrs. T habitually spent many hours of her day on the telephone. One day she was upset and called the caseworker to complain that Rose, her year-old child, was whiny and crying. Crying could be heard in the background and Mrs. T said the child had been in the playpen in the bedroom by herself for "about forty-five minutes." She pleaded with the child, "Don't cry now or I'll lose control and come in and spank you."
>
> The caseworker talked with Mrs. T about her feelings, and Mrs. T was able partially to understand that the child was upset because she was alone and could sense her mother's rejection. But Mrs. T also felt that Rose was trying to "get" her. She expected adult behavior from her child when she asked her to remain quiet for a long period of isolated play. She asked the child to act the adult part—exert control—so that her mother would not misbehave (come in and spank).
>
> After talking about this and many similar experiences in the group, Mrs. T was gradually able to recognize that she was making unrealistic demands of her child. Slowly, as the group continued to look at what was happening between Mrs. T and her child, the mother began to understand that her child was reacting to demands which were beyond her ability to meet. She was not deliberately out to get her mother.
>
> Mrs. T will probably always feel that her child (and everyone else) should nurture and give to her. She learned, however, that no one can make up for her the nurturing she missed as a child. She must live with that pain and emptiness. She is gradually learning to look elsewhere for the nurturing, to know that she can not expect to receive it from her child. As the mother's demands have become more realistic, the child's behavior has improved, and the relationship has become more tolerable for both parent and child.

Breaking the Barrier of Isolation

Most abusive parents suffer from the fear that they have no one to turn to when they are in need. Whether the isolation is emotional or realistic, there is a defective communication system and a weak support system within the client's environment.

One of the major values of Parents Anonymous is that group members are available to each other in times of crisis. The group process is used to help members recognize their self-defeating patterns of interaction so that they no longer feel alone and isolated. Group members help each other in such practical ways as baby-sitting and alleviating other environmental pressures. Aid in solving these problems helps parents to feel that someone else cares and will nurture and support them.

Caseworkers need to work also with important people in the parents' lives in order to build stronger support systems within the fabric of the client's private life. Sometimes relatives or friends, made aware of the client's isolations and fears, can develop stronger ties with the client and offer needed support.

Helping Parents to Allow for Setbacks

A major problem for many abusive parents is their low self-esteem coupled with their high demands on themselves, a combination that results in a feeling of defeat. A client may have many strengths and be making substantial progress, yet one setback can throw him into despair and self-recrimination. Over and over, such clients must be reminded that progress is erratic and setbacks must be expected. We are all human and we make mistakes. If it is difficult for an abusive parent to allow his children to make mistakes, it is even harder for him to allow them in himself. In the following example, the caseworker actively pointed out the client's strengths.

> Mrs. X called to say she had hit her child. She was very upset at losing control just when she had been doing so well. She felt she had failed the group and could not return. She said she was not really making progress after all. The worker reminded her that progress is slow and erratic, and they reviewed her improvement, remembering how she had been when she began coming to Parents Anonymous and how much she had changed over time. The worker talked about her desire to control herself and her wish to be a responsible parent. When her child had fled to her the day before she had not lost control. She was trying to improve and the group would continue to support her efforts.

Recognizing the Need for Placement

Although the emphasis in treatment is to prevent the separation of the child from the parent, under certain conditions such separation may be necessary and, in fact, the most appropriate treatment plan. Temporary separation of the child from the home may be essential as a way of providing safety for the child when other methods of intervention fail. It may also be a way of assisting the parents to work out their problems without the pressures of caring for the children at the same time. Sometimes, of course, permanent placement is necessary.

The factors the caseworker uses in determining whether placement is necessary involve two major areas: the inner resources of the parent and the external support system. Parents who function adequately most of the time will sometimes undergo periods of physical and emotional stress. If there is no one in the extended family or among friends to care for the children temporarily, a short-term placement facility enables the parents who are under personal stress to get away for short periods of time. This relief allows them to mobilize their resources to face some stressful situations in their lives and possibly prevent a full-blown crisis. When parents feel overburdened with their children and feel there is no escape from them, these feelings often precipitate child abuse.

There are times when parents' inner resources are so minimal and external supports so unavailable that the children must be rescued. It is essential to consider what would be gained by removing the child from the home, and what the alternative care would be. Feelings of rejection, abandonment, and guilt may be expected in both parents and children. These feelings need to be worked out in preparation for the separation so that the child will not go into placement with his original problems compounded by the trauma of separation.

Relationship between Agencies

There are often many agencies involved with an abusive family—school, juvenile court, protective services, guidance clinic, hospital, and so forth. Unfortunately, the multiplicity of agencies involved does not in itself guarantee more effective service to the family. It is important that each agency be clear about its role in the total service.

The authoritative agency is primarily concerned with the protection of the child. Although the caseworker in that agency may recognize that the best way to protect the child is to help the parent, his primary function is to assure the child's safety in whatever way may be necessary. The caseworker in the voluntary agency, on the other hand, can focus on helping the parent deal with the problem of child abuse. Even when his focus is on the parent, however, he must be sensitive to the child's welfare to assure that the child does not become severely damaged while he is treating the parent. The two points of view are complementary. Yet, the manipulative client may distort and play one agency against another in a self-defeating way. It is essential that staff members of the various agencies consult with each other frequently.

A family agency is a voluntary service whose clientele is generally limited to people who recognize that they have problems and are able to work on them without the direct, ongoing pressure of a court or other authoritative agency. For those families who are unable to meet the community's child-care standards without frequent and firm use of the law, the greatest cooperation possible is demanded of all community resources. Not only must social agencies be aware of their needs, but churches, neighbors, schools, the extended family, and formal and informal groups should help in building up the support systems necessary to sustain these dependent parents through the difficult years of child-rearing.

Childhood Enuresis

The Conditioning Treatment of Childhood Enuresis

R. T. T. Morgan and G. C. Young

Enuresis, or bedwetting, is one of the most widespread disorders of childhood, and is a problem frequently encountered by most social workers. It is a source of embarrassment to the sufferer, often invoking ridicule or punishment, and can place an intolerable burden upon intrafamilial relationships—especially in those large families living in overcrowded conditions, where several children may wet the bed. For the majority of enuretics, to be a bedwetter carries adverse emotional consequences, and many exhibit some degree of reactive disturbance. Even where this is not apparently the case, enuresis imposes a limit on the child's choice of activities; few enuretics can happily go camping or to stay with friends. In residential establishments, the daily wash of bed-linen is unpleasant and onerous. Because of its widespread, offensive, embarrassing and potentially disturbing nature, the problem of the management and cure of enuresis should be of concern to any caseworker or residential worker involved with an enuretic child; all too often both natural parents and houseparents are forced into a fatalistic acceptance of, and accommodation to, enuresis as an inevitable correlate of child upbringing. It is the purpose of the present paper to suggest that this need not be so, and to describe a rational and well-validated approach to the cure of enuresis, which deserves careful consideration for the benefit of the child sufferer.

Much confusion and many theories exist regarding the aetiology and treatment of enuresis; the literature is extensive and the folk-lore rich. Confusion is enlarged by the use of enuresis as a paradigmatic battleground between conflicting schools of psychological opinion which present mutually exclusive interpretations of this particular disorder. What is urgently required by the social worker confronted with an enuretic child is a relatively simple and well-substantiated form of treatment which offers a high probability of permanent cure without producing harmful side effects.

Consideration of enuresis in terms of a learning deficiency has led to the development of conditioning techniques as a treatment of enuresis.

Reprinted from *British Journal of Social Work*, Vol. 2 (Winter, 1972), pp. 503–509, by permission of the authors and the Association.

Learning theory postulates that bladder control may be regarded as learned behavior, and enuresis as a failure to acquire or maintain appropriate learned responses. According to the Yerkes–Dodson principle (Eysenck, 1960), the efficiency of learning is affected by drive level, very low or very high levels of drive leading to less effective learning as opposed to some intermediate level which is optimal. This optimal intermediate level of drive varies according to task complexity, and is lower for more complex learning tasks. Application of this principle to the learning of urinary continence suggests three major variables affecting the ability of any particular child to acquire bladder control; (1) the optimal level of drive for a task of a given complexity, (2) the degree of complexity represented to the child by the task of acquiring bladder control, and (3) the level of drive induced by the environment. There are individual differences in the ease with which children acquire control of bladder function, as there are in learning to swim or riding a bicycle, and environmental stresses, whether general or specifically related to toilet training, may affect one child more than another. During the third year of life there seems to exist a 'sensitive period' for the learning of continence, during which the child's sensitivity to appropriate learning situations is most acute. Stresses and anxieties during this period may produce over-optimal levels of drive which act to the detriment of learning and render the child enuretic (Young, 1965b; 1969; MacKeith, 1968; 1972). In the case of the 'secondary' enuretic, who loses bladder control after an appreciable period of normal continence, the learned pattern of control is disrupted by the intrusion of some new anxiety-provoking stimulus, such as disturbances in the family or problems at school. Because appropriate learning is less likely to take place outside the sensitive period, transient stress during the third year of life may produce the lifelong, or 'primary' enuretic, and secondary enuresis may persist even when its provoking stress has disappeared.

Conditioning treatment is based on the assumption that whatever influences may have led to a failure or breakdown of learning, appropriate learning may best be effected by maximizing the impact of the learning situation. The simplification of the learning situation also serves to reduce the decremental effects of whatever over-optimal drive may still be present, by reducing task complexity and thus raising the optimal level of drive according to the Yerkes–Dodson principle.

Treatment itself involves the use at home of a simple commercially produced 'enuresis alarm' (Young, 1965a; Turner, Young and Rachman, 1970).*

The alarm provides a powerful auditory stimulus in the form of a loud buzzer which is activated as urine makes electrical contact between a pair of gauze mats beneath the sleeping child. The alarm, when triggered, is

---

* Such as the 'Eastleigh', manufactured and supplied by N. H. Eastwood & Son, Ltd., 48 Eversley Park Road, London, N.21.

switched off by the child, who then completes urination in the toilet. The alarm thus conditions in the child the two separate responses of awakening and of the inhibition of micturition, both in competition with the response of reflex urination to the stimulus of a full bladder. These responses, repeatedly evoked, eventually supercede that of reflex urination, the learned inhibitory effect of bladder stimulation tending to raise the general tone of the bladder muscle (the detrusor) so that the child not only awakes to urinate, but can eventually sleep for the entire night without either wetting or waking.

It is essential that the alarm is used properly and consistently, and that its use is adequately demonstrated. A high level of interest and involvement on the part of a social worker or houseparent is vital to the success of the treatment. It is necessary to maintain a simple record of wet and dry nights throughout treatment. Some children are punished for wet beds and some parents express the opinion that the child is 'lazy'—it is necessary to counter attitudes likely to increase the child's stress in a situation in which over-optimal drive may already be present. Furthermore, certain management practices such as fluid restriction and 'lifting', which are detrimental to conditioning treatment, should be discouraged. Indeed, it is quite likely that regularly lifting a child may train him to need to urinate at a certain time of night.

The success of conditioning treatment in practice has been well demonstrated. Young (1969) lists 19 clinical studies of such treatment in which the percentage success rate ranged from 63% to 100%. Two carefully conducted studies have found conditioning to be significantly superior to psychotherapy in the treatment of enuresis (Werry and Cohrssen, 1965; De Leon and Mandell, 1966).

The conditioning treatment described above is not new, the first suggestion of such treatment occurring in a paper written by Nye in 1830 (Glicklich, 1951). The therapeutic effects of a signal used to alert nurses to wet beds were accidentally discovered by Pfaundler in 1904, and have been continuously studied ever since. However, the use of conditioning treatment for enuresis has yet to find wide acceptance among social workers and those entrusted with the residential care of children.

Until very recently, it was justifiable to question the efficacy of treating enuresis in the manner described, on the grounds that regardless of patient or treatment variables, approximately one in three children could be expected to relapse to wetting once again following initial cure (Young and Morgan, 1972a). Although not affecting the initial success of conditioning in arresting enuresis, such a relapse rate posed a serious question regarding the long-term usefulness of the treatment. Recently, however, a technique has been developed capable of producing dramatic reduction in relapse by strengthening the pattern of relevant learned responses beyond the level necessary to effect initial arrest of wetting. Known as 'overlearning', the technique requires the child to continue to use an enuresis alarm while drinking up to two pints of fluid in the last hour before retiring, once an initial success criterion of fourteen consecutive dry nights has been achieved (Young and Morgan, 1972b).

Perhaps one of the major reasons for the presently limited acceptance of conditioning treatment by social workers is that, not conversant with such conceptualizations of enuresis, many have permitted certain common and popular assumptions to escape rigorous question. The concept of enuresis as a somatic expression of emotional disturbance is thus traditionally accepted without question. Indeed it is often assumed that the coexistence of enuresis and disturbed behavior in the same child demonstrates a causal relation between the two. Such inference is in contradiction of the research findings of Tapia *et al.* (1960), who found that disturbed children are not especially prone to enuresis, nor enuretics particularly prone to disturbance, and of Baker (1969), who found neither projective personality tests nor assessment of adjustment by psychologists to distinguish enuretics from non-enuretics. The finding that the *persistence* of enuresis relates to familial inadequacies and family disruption, the problem persisting longest where family pathology is most severe (Stein and Susser, 1967), tends to support the view that environmental stresses rather than innate personality disorders are responsible for interference with the normal process of acquisition of bladder control. It is logical to assume that in such circumstances, emotional disturbance and enuresis may coexist, but as quite separate responses to the same external environmental influences. It is thus also logical to give treatment for enuresis as a separate entity, even where it occurs in a context of multiple problems.

A frequent objection to the direct, or 'symptomatic', treatment of enuresis by conditioning techniques is that the elimination of enuresis by these methods may lead to harmful consequences for the child's emotional adjustment. The specific predictions made by opponents of conditioning techniques are that, since a disturbed child is assumed to require an expressive symptom, a substitute symptom will emerge following the removal of enuresis; and that by removing enuresis, disturbance will be increased. Investigation of these predictions has found them to be unsupported. Baker (1969), investigating the 'symptom substitution' prediction, found no supporting evidence in his study of conditioning treatment and its consequences. Most clinicians testify to *improvement* in emotional adjustment following relief from enuresis (Yates, 1970; Young, 1965a). There need, therefore, be little concern that conditioning treatment may do harm to any child.

The above predictions derive from the common assumption that enuresis is a symptomatic expression of deep emotional disturbance, rather than a learning deficit, and that the child thus 'needs' and must not be deprived of his bedwetting. Therapy is directed instead at the inferred disturbance. The behavioral view, however, asserts that enuresis is a useless and troublesome habit from which appropriate training can provide relief. It is unnecessary to assume that because a child cannot control his bladder function, he must 'need' to be unable to do so, and to proceed to 'interpret' the feelings he is presumed to be expressing in somatic form.

Various forms of interpretation of a child's inability to control the act of micturition in the accepted manner have provided a wide variety of possible 'meanings'. One of the most common is the theory of regression, which states that enuresis, being similar to infantile incontinence, represents the attempted return of the older child undergoing stress to the presumed security of infancy. The enuretic may thus be saying, by wetting the bed, 'I will take the privileges of a baby, which you deny me' (Fenichel, 1946). A second range of interpretation is based upon the assertion that urination is equivalent to a sexual act. Fenichel thus regards enuresis as frequently a masturbation-equivalent; although the expected replacement of enuresis by mature forms of sexual gratification at puberty is not found in the age/incidence curves for enuresis (Jones, 1960). As a conversion symptom (i.e. a somatic expression of inner conflict or disorder), enuresis may, writes Fenichel, often be regarded as a 'discharge instrument of the Oedipus impulses'. Such theorists frequently interpret enuresis as an aggressive act—or, where this seems inappropriate, an act of passive submission. Thus enuresis in girls is seen as an active assumption of the male sexual role through fear of males as destructive aggressors—while in boys it is considered to represent assumption of a passive female role through fear of destruction by women consequent upon playing a male sexual role (Gerard, 1937; Fenichel, 1946). Ferenczi (1925) actually produced enuresis in a number of normally continent persons, by suggesting retention of urine to test a professed potency in the inhibition of micturition and thus apparently 'exhausting' the urinary musclature. This procedure was explained as serving to 'unmask a tendency to enuresis with which the patient had been quite unfamiliar and which threw light on important parts of his early infantile history' (Ferenczi, 1925).

It is maintained that when such interpretations of enuresis are rejected as unnecessary elaborations of a learning failure, the removal of enuresis (by conditioning techniques) is superficial; and cannot represent 'real' cure. However, no more elaborate criterion for the cure of enuresis seems necessary, than that bedwetting should be eliminated without harmful side effects; it is difficult to imagine what further 'cure' is required when a formerly wet child is no longer enuretic, and is better adjusted than before. It is questionable to withhold from any child the chance of relief from wet beds, unless conditioning treatment were proven to be either ineffective or harmful. The infant learns bladder control, and learning failure can be countered by the more effective training afforded by an enuresis alarm.

Apart from lack of information and attitudes of reserve, many are deterred from the use of conditioning treatment by the practical problems involved. When an alarm is used in the home situation, parental cooperation is vital, and may well require a high level of supervision by a caseworker. Parents, siblings (and even patients) who sabotage treatment to avoid disturbed nights will not achieve success; cooperation must be secured before treatment is introduced and should be maintained throughout its duration. The presence of overcrowding and multiple occupation present additional problems, and it may be necessary to arrange for a separate bed in cases where an enuretic shares a bed with another member of the family.

It should prove possible in residential establishments to arrange medical screening for possible organic pathology, and the appropriate supervision of treatment could be undertaken by the staff. Older children can assume virtually full responsibility for the conduct of treatment. Young children and those slow to awaken to the alarm will require a staff member to assist, to ensure that the child awakes and to change the wet sheets before resetting the apparatus. Treatment naturally places a burden upon child-care staff, just as it does upon parents, but treatment forms an essential part of caring for an enuretic child.

Conditioning treatment of enuresis, when properly and consistently carried out and followed by a period of overlearning therapy, thus carries great promise of effective and stable cure without harmful side effects. As such it demands careful consideration by all having professional contact with enuretic children.

References

1 BAKER, B. L. (1969) "Symptom Treatment and Symptom Substitution in Enuresis," *J. Abnorm. Psychol., 74,* 42–49.

2 DE LEON, G. and MANDELL, W. (1966) "A Comparison of Conditioning and Psychotherapy in the Treatment of Functional Enuresis," *J. Clin. Psychol., 22,* 326–30.

3 EYSENCK, H. J. (1960) *Handbook of Abnormal Psychology,* Pitman, London.

4 FENICHEL, O. (1946) *The Psychoanalytic Theory of Neurosis,* Routledge & Kegan Paul, London.

5 FERENCZI, S. (1925) "Psycho-analysis of Sexual Habits," *Int. J. Psychoanal., 6,* 372–404.

6 GERARD, M. W. (1937) "Child Analysis as a Technique in the Investigation of Mental Mechanisms: Illustrated by a Study of Enuresis," *Am. J. Psychiat., 94,* 653–68.

7 GLICKLICH, L. B. (1951) "An Historical Account of Enuresis," *Pediatrics, 8,* 859–76.

8 JONES, H. G. (1960) "The Behavioral Treatment of Enuresis Nocturna," in *Behavior Therapy and the Neuroses* (Ed. H. J. Eysenck), pp. 377–403, Pergamon, Oxford.

9 MACKEITH, R. C. (1968) "A Frequent Factor in the Origins of Primary Nocturnal Enuresis: Anxiety in the Third Year of Life," *Develop. Med. Child Neurol., 10,* 465–70.

10 MACKEITH, R. C. (1972) "Is Maturation Delay a Frequent Factor in the Origins of Primary Nocturnal Enuresis?" *Develop. Med. Child Neurol., 14,* 217–23.

11 STEIN, Z. A. and SUSSER, M. (1967) "The Social Dimensions of a Symptom. A Sociomedical Study of Enuresis," *Soc. Sci. & Med. 1,* 183–201.

12 TAPIA, F. JEKEL, J. and DOMKE, H. R. (1960) "Enuresis: An Emotional Symptom?" *J. Nerv. Ment. Dis., 130,* 61–6.

13 TURNER, R. K., YOUNG, G. C. and RACHMAN, S. (1970) "Treatment of Nocturnal Enuresis by Conditioning Techniques," *Behav. Res. & Therapy, 8,* 367–81.

14 WERRY, J. S. and COHRSSEN, J. (1965) "Enuresis—an Etiologic and Therapeutic Study," *J. Pediat. 67,* 423–31.

15 YATES, A. J. (1970) *Behavior Therapy,* John Wiley, New York, Ch. 5.

16 YOUNG, G. C. (1956a) "Condition-

ing Treatment of Enuresis," *Dev. Med. Child Neurol.*, *7*, 557–62.

17 YOUNG, G. C. (1965b) "The Aetiology of Enuresis in Terms of Learning Theory," *Med. Offr.*, *113*, 19–22.

18 YOUNG, G. C. (1969) "The Problem of Enuresis," *Br. J. Hosp. Med.*, *2*, 628–32.

19 YOUNG, G. C. and MORGAN, R. T. T. (1972a) *Analysis of Factors Associated with the Extinction of a Conditioned Response. Behav. Res. & Therapy.* In press.

20 YOUNG, G. C. and MORGAN, R. T. T. (1972b) "Overlearning in the Conditioning Treatment of Enuresis," *Behav. Res. & Therapy*, *10*, 147–51.

Steps in the Return to School of Children with School Phobia

Elisabeth Lassers, Robert Nordan, and Sheila Bladholm

Children with school phobia present a difficult problem that is very upsetting to the child, his family, the community, and the therapist. Suddenly, for little or no apparent reason, the child refuses to go to school. He insists on staying home and may complain of aches and pains. When his parents urge him to go to school, he may cry, perspire, become pale, and show other signs of severe panic that are relieved only when his parents finally allow him to stay home. The longer he stays home, the harder it becomes to send him to school, and he soon develops "school phobia."

A great deal has been written about school phobia, and many views have been expressed about the dynamics and treatment of the problem. The most thorough reviews of the literature with extensive bibliographies are those of Esther Marine (1–3) and Kahn and Nursten (4, 5). In spite of the great divergency of opinion, most authors agree that the child's early return to school is of prime importance, and the focus in this paper is on the appropriate steps before, during, and after returning the child to school (6–18). While most therapists probably use these steps to some extent, we feel that it is relevant to look at them more specifically, to relate them to the casual mention of their use in the literature, and to draw on our own experiences for particular illustrations.

School Phobia

The term "school phobia" needs to be differentiated from truancy and simple school withdrawal. A "truant" is a child who is absent from school without either his parents' or the school's permission. Other children may be kept home for some reason by the parents, and this may be termed "school withdrawal." Both problems are social in nature. The child with school phobia, on the other hand, may *want* to go to school but *cannot* and becomes acutely anxious even at the thought of leaving home. To some

Reprinted from *American Journal of Psychiatry*, Vol. 130 (1973), pp. 265–268. Copyright 1973, the American Psychiatric Association.

extent, "school phobia" is a misleading term, in that it is usually symptomatic of another problem—the tie between parents and child and the resulting conflicts (4).

Most authors suggest that the basic difficulty is a mutual hostile-dependent relationship between mother and child or, much less frequently, between father and child (7–9, 19–25). While the parents overtly urge the child to go to school, they give nonverbal cues interpreted by the child as suggesting that he stay home (6–9, 21, 26–31). When these children are in school, they frequently fear that death or injury will occur to a family member, most likely as a result of their fear that their hostile wishes might come true (8, 9, 13, 15, 16, 23–25, 27, 29, 32–37). The child feels an urgent need to go home, then, to make sure that his "beloved one" is still alive and well. Frequently, there is a precipitating event, such as a death or illness in the family, or the child's own illness (8, 9, 11, 16, 21–23, 38, 39). After this acute precipitating event has passed, the child will then refuse to return to school.

Returning the Child to School

The treatment of school phobia has caused considerable controversy in the literature, with approaches ranging from psychoanalytic therapy (11, 32) and "analytic first aid" (15) to child guidance approaches, conditioning (33), and other rapid treatment methods (10). An early controversy dealt with how quickly to return the child to school; although there are still some authors who feel that an early return to school may interfere with intensive therapy (24, 40), most authors cited in this paper believe that rapid return to school is essential, though they may differ over the method of therapy to be used after the child has been returned to school. Our own experience confirms this belief.

There are several reasons for returning the child quickly. The children who do go back seem to improve rapidly, while those who remain at home become increasingly anxious, so that it becomes more and more difficult to return them to school at a later date. Since a large part of the problem seems to be the mother's difficulty in letting the child go, the successful experience of his being back in school permits both the parent and the child to function in a more usual way; if anxiety continues to be a problem, it can be dealt with in psychotherapy.

How can early return to school be accomplished? In our work, we have found that several steps are necessary which must be initiated as quickly as possible. These steps are set forth below, along with illustrative case reports.

Step I: Physical Examination

Obviously, if the child has a real physical illness that keeps him out of school, lack of attendance cannot be called "school phobia." The first step, then, in dealing with a child who is staying home because of physical complaints is to determine whether there is an organic basis for his condition.

It should be kept in mind, however, that physical symptoms, mostly minor and chronic, such as headaches, gastrointestinal upsets, or mild respiratory symptoms, may be used by the child and his family as an excuse to keep him out of school, thus masking a real school phobia.

Step II: Psychiatric Evaluation

The next step is to rule out an incipient psychosis or other serious pathology, since school avoidance in such cases is usually seen as a secondary symptom rather than as a primary problem. The therapist should conduct an interview with parents and child and then determine the seriousness of the difficulties.

Case 1. Charles was hospitalized at age 13 for "chest pains" but was discharged soon after when examination revealed no organic cause for his complaints. Four months later he was brought to the Child Psychiatry Clinic because he had refused to return to school after his discharge. Charles was spending most of this time in his room, though he slept very little and had frightening nightmares; he was also fearful of members of other races and nationalities and fantasied attacks both upon them and upon members of his family. Charles was anxious, had delusions of grandeur and persecution, and had tenuous reality testing. School avoidance was thus a symptom of psychotic decompensation; immediate hospitalization was recommended.

The second purpose of the diagnostic interview with the child and his parents is to determine the individual and family dynamics involved and the precipitating event that resulted in school phobia. While certain relationships and problems might be expected, they are not always present in every case and, even when found, their expression can vary widely.

Case 2. Randy, a six-and-a-half-year-old black boy, was referred to the clinic after he had been out of school for nearly a year. When he first started kindergarten, he cried and the teacher suggested that he stay home until the following year. The next September, he had a successful first day at school, but on the second day he was hit by a car and suffered a broken leg. After being in the hospital in traction for three weeks and at home in a hip spica cast for seven weeks, he had sufficiently recovered to return to school, but he refused.

Randy came from a severely disorganized ghetto family. He was the eighth of 11 children, and his parents were divorced when he was three and a half years old. His maternal grandmother, to whom his mother was very close, had died when his mother was pregnant with Randy. The mother herself had a history of depression and suicidal attempts. Her tenth child was born two months before Randy was to start first grade, and she was pregnant with her 11th at the time of the interview. Randy's older sister, who had taken a mothering role toward him, had also been pregnant at the time he started kindergarten.

While Randy was not able to verbalize his problems easily, his play fully revealed his concerns. While in the hospital he had been quite lonely, and he was still angry that his mother had not visited him. He knew that his mother was expecting another child and feared that he would again be left alone. Past desertions—by his father, by his mother during other pregnancies, by his sister during hers—all contributed to his anger and his fear of being abandoned once again. The anger could not be expressed, however, since he still needed his mother, and it is likely that he felt that he must stay home to make sure that his mother had not been destroyed by the destructive fantasies he had about her. Randy was still concerned about the injury to his leg, with unresolved castration fears.

Randy's mother was overwhelmed by her own problems and those of her family. Though she was irritated by Randy's demands and clinging behavior, she also worried about him and "loved" him while he was ill and at home. It may be that he was a "special" child to her, since she was pregnant with him when her own mother had died and he had provided comfort to her then; but at the same time, she may have had strong feelings of rejection for him. Whatever the reason, her dependence upon him and her communication of these concerns to him did not promote his easy return to school.

Step III: Finding a Therapeutic Ally

One of the most important steps in returning the phobic child to school is to find one or more persons who can function as a source of strength. This can be someone in the family or someone outside—a teacher, a minister, or even a family friend. This person acts as a kind of aide to the therapist— someone who is more often present and more available to the family on a day-to-day basis, and who can act both as an agent of external control and as a support to parents and child.

Case 3. In the case of Sally, an eight-year-old girl, the family physician provided the extra support that was needed to get her back in school. It was he who had initially referred her to the clinic, since his own examinations and those of several other physicians indicated that there was no physical basis for the child's complaints, and it was his insistence that finally brought the family to the clinic. Sally's complaints of headaches and nightmares began when the family had moved just before school started; this had been the fifth such move in five years, and Sally had recently asked when the family would be moving again. Her mother had been hospitalized four times since Sally was born; the last hospitalization, for a hysterectomy, occurred when Sally was six and precipitated a depression in the mother that she "hid" from the children. Sally had one older sister who was said to be "bad," but who received more of the parents' approval since they prized her independent behavior.

Assessment of the case was made in close collaboration with the referring physician, who then informed Sally's mother of the findings. She put up immediate resistance to accepting Sally's problems as being emotional, indicating that Sally had had a reaction to a penicillin shot, which had kept her home for two weeks, but the doctor assured her that the "reaction" was simply the result of Sally's hyperventilation. He reiterated that he had found no physical problems in his examination and told the mother that she could best help the girl by standing firm and insisting that Sally go to school.

Although the mother agreed to the plan, the doctor felt she was not convinced; but when the social worker checked with the mother a few days later, Sally was in school. The mother admitted that forcing a "sick" child to go to school made her feel guilty, but she was determined to follow her doctor's advice and to keep Sally in class. She asked for help in finding a local agency that would provide therapy for the girl, but later, when she was recontacted, the mother indicated that the family had not followed up on the referral since Sally was still in school and things were going well.

Step IV: The Interpretive Interview

Once the therapist has established that the child is not physically ill or seriously disturbed, has some understanding of the dynamics of the case, and has identified someone who can provide extra support, an interpretive interview is needed to discuss the problems with the family and to set up the expectation that the child can return to school immediately. The therapist should confirm that nothing is physically wrong with the child and indicate that the child is truant unless he goes back to school at once. He should show his willingness to help the family and child find ways to make his return to school easier. If the precipitating cause is obvious, it should be discussed, and fears ("Will I be a bad mother if I make him go to school?") should be dealt with sympathetically. The therapist should be understanding but firm in his resolution that the child return to school, suggesting that the only alternatives are a truancy petition or hospitalization in a psychiatric unit that has classroom facilities. A mild tranquilizer may be prescribed for a few days to alleviate some of the renewed anxiety over the return to school.

Step V: Planning

The therapist, the family, and the school should draw up plans for returning the child to class and set a date in the near future. If at all possible, a face-to-face meeting should be held so that a plan can be worked out among all those involved. In some cases, it may seem advisable to return the child gradually, through a kind of "deconditioning" process, letting him return home after part of the day or permitting him to retire to the principal's office from time to time. In other cases, a complete return may be desirable so that the child has no "outs."

> *Case 4.* The school not only took an active part in planning the return of Jenny, age nine, but was also a source of strength for the family. Just before a minor illness that kept her out of school, Jenny's grades had begun to drop, and later, looking back, the parents realized that the change occurred after her father lost a finger in an accident at work. Jenny began to complain of sore throats and was even hospitalized with tonsillitis; she could not return to school. A crisis was reached two months later when Jenny set two fires within two days.
>
> At the interpretive interview with the parents, it was suggested that Jenny be returned to school immediately, the next day if at all possible. The mother's ambivalent feelings came out at once—she did not want to be a "bad mother" by sending a sick child to school, nor did she want her daughter to miss so much school. With support, she was able to get Jenny off to school the following morning, but Jenny used one of her previous symptoms to foil the plan. She vomited and was sent home. Again the mother, teacher, and principal were contacted, and it was agreed that Jenny would stay in school, even if she did vomit. Jenny tried to find a way home again and was successful: she vomited down the front of her dress. At last, when a final plan of sending extra changes of clothes to school was worked out, Jenny settled down and did not remain out of school any longer.

Step VI: Support

Jenny's case and some of the others discussed show the importance of the therapist's continuing involvement in guiding and supporting the family as it made the critical adjustment of returning the child to school. Phone calls were made, office visits were arranged, and, in some cases, home and school visits were necessary. Sometimes drug therapy was necessary, usually for a limited time. Whatever the need, the therapist should make himself available so that he can provide the help and support that both parents and child need to make the return to school successful.

Step VII: Follow-Up

At the time that the child returns to school (successfully, one hopes) he, his parents, and the school should understand that the therapist will be checking at regular intervals to determine his progress. To the family, this says that the therapist is interested and still available; to the school, it indicates the therapist's willingness to continue to be involved and to provide consultation whenever the teacher or principal needs it. In the cases described here, some contact has been maintained; at last report, all the children except Randy were still in school and coping adequately.

Step VIII: Psychotherapy

Ideally, follow-up would be only one aspect of a total therapeutic plan but, although psychotherapy was offered all the families mentioned above, none accepted. Once the child was back in class and free of overt physical symptoms, the overall anxiety level was apparently reduced enough that further therapy was rejected. Although we have little information concerning the later development and adjustment of the children, neither they nor their siblings have returned to the clinic with the same or other symptoms.

Discussion

School phobia frequently appears as a symptom in response to a subtle, often ambivalent, message from the mother or another family member that life is insecure and the child had better stay at home. Staying at home then leads to a vicious circle of withdrawal from the growth-promoting stimulation of learning and peer relations, further regression and withdrawal, increasing embroilment in a hostile-dependent relationship with parents, more intense anxiety, and more extreme school rejection.

At the same time, in moments of healthier ego functioning, both parents and child know that the child should be in school and, at some point, they reach out for help. If he acts quickly, the therapist can strengthen this functioning through his own authoritative support and the temporary reliance on family members, school personnel, or someone else outside the family in order to work out a plan for the child's immediate return to school. Then, with some of the anxiety of both parents and child relieved, and the message clearly stated that the child must return to school, he can usually go back to class. Once there, the child can use the accomplishment for further growth and the symptoms usually do not reappear (12).

Although the return to school puts an end to the secondary gain of staying at home and induces growth, it does not solve the family's basic problems, for which further therapy may be needed. Unfortunately, in the cases described here, the families were not ready for treatment. It could be argued that they might have been better motivated for further treatment if they had been denied relief of the symptom, but this would be risky since school phobia itself is so crippling and becomes harder to treat the longer the child's return to school is put off.

Conclusions

This paper has focused on the specific steps we have found useful in returning the school-phobic child to school as soon as possible. The first step is to rule out any organic reasons for the symptoms through a physical examination and then to determine the dynamics of the situation through a psychiatric examination. Next the therapist should search for a therapeutic ally, someone who can support the family on a day-to-day basis through the period of crisis. With these steps accomplished, an interpretive interview can be held with the family and the expectation should be set up that the child can return to school immediately. A plan is devised in cooperation with school personnel and, during the critical first days after the child's return, frequent support is given by the therapist. Follow-up contact is made and, if possible, the family is involved in psychotherapy.

References

1 MARINE, E. "School Refusal: Review of the Literature." *Social Service Review* 42:464–478, 1968.

2 MARINE, E. "School Refusal Treatment in Two Agencies: a Follow-up Study of Intervention by a Child Guidance Center and an Attendance and Counseling Division of a School System." Ph.D. dissertation, University of Pittsburgh, 1966.

3 MARINE, E. "School Refusal: Who Should Intervene? (diagnostic and treatment categories)." *J. Sch. Psychol.* 7:63–70, 1969.

4 KAHN, J. H., NURSTEN, J. P. *Unwillingly to School: School Phobia or School Refusal—a Medico-Social Problem,* 2nd ed. New York, Pergamon Press, 1968, pp. 1–19, 227, 271.

5 KAHN, J. H., NURSTEN, J. P. "School Refusal: a Comprehensive View of School Phobia and Other Failures of School Attendance." *Am. J. Orthopsychiatry* 32:707–718, 1962.

6 COHEN, N. J., LEONARD, M. F. "Early Pediatric Management of Acute School Avoidance," in *Modern Perspectives in Child Development.* Edited by Solnit, A., Provence, S., New York, International Universities Press, 1963, pp. 419–441.

7 EISENBERG, L. "School Phobia: a Study in the Communication of Anxiety." *Am. J. Psychiatry* 114:712–718, 1958.

8 ESTES, H. R., HAYLETT, C. H., JOHNSON, A. M. "Separation Anxiety." *Am. J. Psychotherapy* 10:682–695, 1956.

9 FUTTERMAN, E. H., HOFFMAN, I. "Transient School Phobia in a Leukemic Child." *J. Am. Acad. Child Psychiatry* 9:477–494, 1970.

10 KENNEDY, W. "School Phobia: Rapid Treatment of Fifty Cases." *J. Abnorm. Psychol.* 70:285–289, 1965.

11 KLEIN, I. "The Reluctance to Go To School." *Psychoanal. Study Child.* 1:263–279, 1945.

12 LEVENTHAL, T. WEINBERGER, G., STANDER, R. et al. "Therapeutic Strategies with School Phobics." *Am. J. Orthopsychiatry* 37:64–70, 1967.

13 MILLAR, T. P. "The Child Who Refuses to Attend School." *Am. J. Psychiatry* 118:398–404, 1961.

14 REGER, R. "A School Phobia in an Obese Girl." *J. Clin. Psychol.* 18:356–357, 1962.

15 SPERLING, M. "Analytic First Aid in School Phobias." *Psychoanal. Q.* 30:504–518, 1961.

16 SUTTENFIELD, V. "School Phobia: a Study of Five Cases." *Am. J. Orthopsychiatry* 24:368–380, 1954.

17 WARNECKE, R. "School Phobia and its Treatment." *Br. J. Med. Psychol.* 37:71–79, 1964.

18 WARREN, W. "Acute Neurotic Breakdown in Children with Refusal to Go to School." *Arch. Dis. Child.* 23:266–272, 1948.

19 COLM, H. N. "Phobias in Children." *Psychoanal. Psychoanal. Rev.* 40:65–84, 1959.

20 COOLIDGE, J. C., HAHN, P. B., PECK, A. L. "School Phobia: Neurotic Crisis or Way of Life?" *Am. J. Orthopsychiatry* 27:296–309, 1957.

21 DAVIDSON, S. "School Phobia as a Manifestation of Family Disturbance: Its Structure and Treatment." *J. Child Psychol. Psychiatry* 1:270–287, 1961.

22 JARVIS, V. "Countertransference in the Management of School Phobia." *Psychoanal. Q.* 33:411–419, 1964.

23 JOHNSON, A. M., FALSTEIN, E. I., SZUREK, S. A. et al. "School Phobia." *Am. J. Orthopsychiatry* 11:702–711, 1941.

24 WALDFOGEL, S., COOLIDGE, J. C., HAHN, P. B. "The Development, Meaning and Management of School Phobia." *Am. J. Orthopsychiatry* 27:754–780, 1957.

25 WALDFOGEL, S., TESSMAN, E., HAHN, P. B. "Learning Problems: a Program for Early Intervention in School Phobia." *Am. J. Orthopsychiatry* 29:324–332, 1959.

26 EISENBERG, L. "School Phobia: Diagnosis, Genesis and Clinical Management." *Pediatr. Clin. North Am.* 5:645–666, 1958.

27 GLASER, K. "Problems in School Attendance." *Pediatrics* 23:371–383, 1959.

28 MALMQUIST, C. P. "School Phobia: a Problem in Family Neurosis." *J. Am. Acad. Child Psychiatry* 4:293–319, 1965.

29 RADIN, S. S. "Psychodynamic Aspects of School Phobia." *Compr. Psychiatry* 8:119–128, 1967.

30 RODRIGUEZ, A., RODRIGUEZ, M., EISENBERG, L. "The Outcome of School Phobia: a Follow-up Study based on 41 Cases." *Am. J. Psychiatry* 116:540–544, 1959.

31 SPERLING, M. "School Phobias: Classification, Dynamics and Treatment." *Psychoanal. Study Child.* 22:375–401, 1967.

32 BROADWIN, I. T. "A Contribution to the Study of Truancy." *Am. J. Orthopsychiatry* 2:253–259, 1932.

33 GARVEY, W. P., HEGRENES, J. R. "Desensitization Techniques in the Treatment of School Phobia." *Am. J. Orthopsychiatry* 36:147–152, 1966.

34 HERSOV, L. A. "Refusal to Go to School." *J. Child Psychol. Psychiatry* 1:137–145, 1960.

35 MESSNER, A. A. "Family Treatment of a School Phobic Child." *Arch. Gen. Psychiatry* 11:548–555, 1964.

36 PAPPENHEIM, E., SWEENY, M. "Separation Anxiety in Mother and Child." *Psychoanal. Study Child.* 7:95–114, 1952.

37 SPERLING, M. "Mucous Colitis Associated with Phobias." *Psychoanal. Q.* 19:318–326, 1950.

38 COOLIDGE, J. C., TESSMAN, E., WALDFOGEL, S. et al. "Patterns of Aggression in School Phobia." *Psychoanal. Study Child.* 17:319–333, 1962.

39 LEVENTHAL, T., SILLS, M. "Self-image in School Phobia." *Am. J. Orthopsychiatry* 34:685–695, 1964.

40 GREENBAUM, R. S. "Treatment of School Phobias: Theory and Practice." *Am. J. Psychother.* 18:616–634, 1964.

Separation—A Crucial Issue in Foster Care

Jack Adler

Separation of children from their families is a crucial issue in foster care.* Its emotional implications permeate from its beginning through termination. It affects the child who is placed and his family from whom he is separated; caseworkers, child care personnel and foster parents must cope with children's and parents' reactions to separation and its manifestations during placement. This paper examines the nature of separation, its consequences for foster child, his family, and foster care workers, and implications for foster care practice.

During the course of normal child development, separation experiences are inevitable and necessary for maturation and individuation. They take place in the setting of developmental readiness for and pleasure in independent functioning. Although each new step of separate functioning entails anxiety for the very young child, the mother's availability, love and support minimizes this anxiety and makes the process pleasurable. In this respect, separation experiences are viewed as essential and constructive.[1] Precipitous, long term or repeated separations have been found to be destructive.

Significance of Separation to Child

Review of the literature on separation,[2] indicates that is it not a simple delineated event with clearly predictable consequences. The issues involved

---

Reprinted with permission of *Journal of Jewish Communal Services,* Vol. 46 (Summer, 1970), pp. 305–313.

* The term "foster care" refers to all residential settings, including foster homes, group homes, group residences, institutions and residential treatment centers. Since there is no single all inclusive term to describe the adults responsible for the "fostering" of children, the traditional term of foster parents (in foster home care), house parents and child care counselors (in other types of foster care), are used here. All of them become major figures in the child's separation experience.

[1] Margaret Mahler and Kitty La Perriere, "Mother-Child Interaction During Separation-Individuation," *Psychoanalytic Quarterly* (1965), 34: 358–498.

[2] Leon J. Yarrow, "Separation from Parents during Childhood," M. L. and L. W. Hoffman, Eds., *Review of Child Development Research*, Vol. I, Russell Sage, 1964.

J. A. Rose, *A Re-Evaluation of the Concept of Separation for Child Welfare*, Child Welfare League, New York, 1962, pp. 444–58.

are highly complex. The significance to the child of separation from his family depends on many individual and environmental variables. Among these are:

Age at time of separation: Reaction to separation seems to be less severe in very early infancy before the establishment of a significant relationship with the mother figure. If this separation is followed immediately by the provision of an adequate substitute, there should be no serious effects. The most sensitive time may be the period during which the infant is in the process of establishing stable, affectional relationships, approximately between six months and two years. However, each developmental stage may be viewed as critical and has its own sensitivities and vulnerability to separation.

The quality of the relationship with the mother prior to separation: Spitz and Wolf[3] noted that the children showing the most severe reaction to separation were those who had the closest relationship with their mothers prior to separation. Older children who have experienced close relationships with parents may be better equipped to tolerate separation and to establish meaningful relationships with substitute parental figures than the children who have never experienced such intimate relationships.

The character of maternal care subsequent to the initial separation: The nature of the foster care experience is of major significance. Provision of adequate substitute mothering following separation may mitigate the shock and prevent development of serious disturbance. If the child moves into unsatisfactory foster care relationships, the traumatic impact of separation is likely to be strengthened.

The character of the relationship with the parents during separation: If the child is able to maintain a relationship with the parents, the impact of separation is likely to be less severe than if there is abrupt and complete termination of the relationship.

Duration of separation: It may be a single or repeated brief occurrences, as in the case of a child's hospitalization, or a short term placement as a consequence of a mother's hospitalization. A child's reaction to it will be determined by the degree of his emotional maturity, the nature of his relationship with his mother, the process of preparation and the conditions to which he is subjected during placement. Single long term separations, with reunions, are generally associated with factors of stress, resulting from fragmentation of family life. A child subjected to these separations may fear that there will be no family to return to. Here the extent and nature of the child's contact with his natural parents is an important consideration. Repeated long term separations imply continuous family crises. These can be most traumatic and may involve serious emotional deprivation since the original sense of loss and abandonment are reinforced and reactivated by each replacement.

The role of constitutional factors: Developmental studies[4] document the

---

[3] R. A. Spitz and K. Wolf, "Anaclitic Depression," *Psychoanalytic Study of the Child*, 1949, 2: 113–17.

[4] S. Chess, A. Thomas and H. Birch, *Temperament and Behavior Disorders in Children*, N.Y. University Press, N.Y. 1968.

existence of individualized basic sensitivities and response predispositions among infants. The nature of a child's "temperament" may affect his reaction to changes in maternal care, including those resulting from placement.

The scope of the separation problem is extensive. About a quarter of a million children are currently in foster care in the United States and the rate is increasing annually. During the nineteenth century, the principal reasons for placement were death of parents and economic dependency. These factors have for the most part been eliminated as reasons for separating children from their families by advances in medical science, improved medical care, reduction of industrial accidents, and economic assistance through social security and other public and voluntary welfare programs. Family breakdown has become the single most contributing cause for placement of children.[5] An extensive variety of communal social services have been established to prevent disorganization and disruption of family life. Unfortunately, these services are still insufficient, are unevenly distributed geographically, and to a great extent do not reach the socio-economically deprived, underprivileged minority populations in our cities. Lacking such resources, they are apt to suffer a greater incidence of crises, family disorganization and increased need for foster care for their children.

The anxiety and conflict experienced by parents and children as a result of family fragmentation, though immeasurable, represent far-reaching personal and social tragedies. The consequent separation signifies a disruption and loss of emotionally significant relationships, a sense of guilt and failure and exposure to the insecurities of an unknown future. During periods of serious crisis, where life itself may be in danger, children have preferred the security of parental presence to safety away from them. During the period of the London blitz, for example, children seemed less upset about the bombing than by evacuation to the countryside. The war for these children became most meaningful at the moment of separation. The degree of deprivation experienced within their own families, as a result of war conditions, seemed of little significance compared to the experience of being uprooted from their parents.[6] Caseworkers in foster care programs are universally familiar with children's strivings for reunion with their (nuclear) families. They are often puzzled and even upset that children from seriously pathological family environments strive to return to their homes despite the discomforts and frustrations they will face.

Children's reactions to separation vary.[7] In general, most children experience a sense of abandonment. They may feel helpless because they have no control of what is happening to them, and "worthless" because of the

---

[5] H. Maas and R. E. Engler, *Children in Need of Parents*, Columbia University Press, New York, 1959.

[6] Anna Freud and D. Burlingham, *War and the Children*, International University Press, New York, 1943.

[7] N. Littner, *Traumatic Effects of Separation and Placement*, Child Welfare League of America, New York, 1956.

feeling that if they were worthy, their parents would not have placed them. They may blame themselves for imagined offenses which may not have any basis in reality. They may not only consider themselves "bad," but view placement as punishment for it. Their feelings of guilt and anger may be repressed, with resulting anxieties and emergence of neurotic symptoms.

When placed, the child may react with displacement of emotions. He may expect to get from the fostering adults the attitudes and behavior he experienced in his own parents. He may view them as the people who will punish him for imagined or actual sins. Expecting punishment, he may protect himself by "attacking" first or by withdrawing into isolation. If a child is masochistically inclined, he may try to evoke punishment to allay guilt feelings. A child may also hesitate to establish close and significant relationships with the adults because of the fear that if he loves them or is loyal to them his own parents will resent it, or because of a feeling that if he does, he will again be rejected and be subjected to another separation. A similar range of reactions may be expressed in relation to other children in the foster care situation, such as children of the foster parents, other foster children in the home or peers in the group home or cottage.

The older child in placement, especially the adolescent, faces additional difficulties. The general instabilities and vicissitudes which pervade adolescence are aggravated by separation. Intensified feelings of ambivalence toward parents may then be nourished by actual or phantasized feelings of parental rejection. The resolution of the dependence-independence conflict becomes more complex and difficult, negative feelings are more readily displaced or projected, superego deterrents to impulse expression and deep emotional ties which might neutralize tendencies to act out behaviorally within one's natural family may be weakened or absent altogether. As foster (or house) parents are drawn into the vortex of the emotional turmoil that accompanies the strivings for independence on the part of the adolescent foster child, they may become the object of defiance and rebelliousness, rationalized by such expressions as "You can't tell me what to do. *You are not my parents!*"

The child's emotional ties to his family persist during placement. His need to relate to his source or origin continues to be expressed in a variety of ways. The young child will more likely do so through play; the older child may act out unexpressed feelings (interpersonally) or verbalize them in devious ways if he cannot express them directly. It is important to understand and respect this expression and to provide opportunities for the child to work them through in accordance with his readiness and capacities. This may serve to diminish the possibility of repression of these charged feelings and their ultimate expression through neurotic symptoms, neurotic character traits and destructive transference reactions. The tendency to "protect" a child from facing and airing what may be painful feelings about his separation and placement is unrealistic and psychologically unsound. Excluding the infant and the very young, the child should, if at all possible or feasible, be involved actively throughout the intake and placement process. He needs to be aware of what is going on about him so that he can feel assured that there are no realistic alternatives and that at least temporarily his parents cannot care for him. Joint interviews with parents, or in their absence, close relatives, may facilitate the process. Here distortions, misgivings, anger and guilt may be aired, avoiding denial and suppression of feelings. Foster parents (or child care counselors) require preparation for the new arrival who will live with them. The greater their understanding, the better equipped they will be to cope constructively with the child's feelings and transference manifestations. The very young child, especially the infant placed in foster care, needs provision for continuity between the known and the new caretakers. The degree of change in the physical environment can often be decreased by carrying over familiar objects from the old to the new environment. Foster parents or adoptive parents can be helped to avoid, at least in the early stages of placement, drastic changes to which the child may be required to adapt.

The child's emotional investment in his natural family may be intensified after the physical separation occurs because in addition to the psychological distortions about the reality of his family and his experience in it, he may develop a fantasy about it in unrealistic terms. In extreme cases a child may completely replace stark reality with rosy fantasies about his parents in a "family romance" where the disappointing realities are replaced by "ideal" loving parents. It is important to be aware of this if we are to help him accept the realities of his natural family and to bridge the gap between his fantasy and reality in order to facilitate the development of a sense of acceptance, security and identity in his foster care milieu.[8]

Impact of Separation on Parents

We are sensitive to the impact of separation on the children who are placed and efforts are expended to ameliorate the resulting sense of deprivation. The complementary feelings experienced by the parents are generally given insufficient attention in research or practice. Unless this is rectified, we shall continue to be handicapped in coping with its consequences on families and in the placement situation.

Feelings about separation permeate all families and affect all of its members. Fathers and mothers, siblings and relatives, are shaken by the fragmentation of family cohesiveness symbolized by the placement of one or more of its children. Feelings of guilt and anger generated by inner conflicts are intensified by outside pressures. Prevalent community attitudes are generally not sympathetic to parents who place their children. They are not considered as adequate persons or as "good" parents. Consequently their own guilt feelings and sense of failure as parents become intensified. These may be further reinforced by foster parents (or child care personnel) who convey to the children indirectly by implication, or directly by word, deed

[8] H. Riese, "Identity Problems of the Rootless Child," *Journal of the American Medical Women's Association*, Vol. 21, #8 (1966), pp. 652–58.

or derogatory attitudes that they are "rescuing" or "protecting" them from their "irresponsible" parents.[9] This may evoke counter-hostility on the part of parents, who may then react in ways which are destructive to their children's adjustment in the foster care situation.

Some parents may try to alleviate guilt feelings by over-indulging their children during visits; others may disparage the foster parents, child, or the institution. Some may have to maintain the delusion that the child alone or a spouse is responsible for the placement. They may seek out and complain about real or apparent difficulties in the child's adjustment and blame their spouse, the child or foster parents. Parents whose children were placed through the family court because of parental neglect or a child's delinquent behavior may not only be uncooperative but overtly disruptive. The most difficult parents in this group are those with paranoid tendencies who complain to the administrators of the agency, to city and state officials and to the newspapers in order to recover their child from placement. Consideration must be given to the degree of parental disturbance, since this will determine the nature of the reaction. In the process of identifying the degree of parental pathology, the caseworker may find areas of ego strength which can be utilized or developed to increase the parents' capacities to participate constructively in their child's foster care experience.

Parental feelings about separation and placement cannot be ignored; they have to be worked with. They are not always expressed to social workers. Awareness of this is particularly pertinent in work with socially and economically disadvantaged families residing in urban ghetto areas. A caseworker confronted by the overwhelming problems faced by these families may be so preoccupied with efforts to alleviate the stark realities of their existence that he may not be sufficiently attuned to the subtle emotional implications when placement of a child is being considered. There is so much to cope with realistically that he may not pay sufficient attention to the feelings on the part of a mother or father who is about to surrender a child to foster care. If the worker fails to do so, he may inadvertently convey to them the feeling that he is insensitive to their suffering, and they may consequently avoid expressing them. If he is able to help them see that he empathizes with them, perhaps they will feel a greater sense of trust and will more readily work with him around the very complex reality problems facing them.

There are situations where it becomes essential to separate a child from his parents expeditiously. We have in mind conditions within the child's environment which are more harmful to his existence than separation from it. These include cases of chronic neglect and of physical abuse. These children may require long term or permanent placement because their families may never be reintegrated, due to severe parental pathology. In such situations the caseworker, representing the agency, serves as the en-

[9] A. Mandelbaum, "Parent Child Separation: Its Significance to Parents," *Social Work* Vol. 7, #4 (1962), pp. 27–34.

abling agent in developing the type of absorptive home which will provide the child with a sense of security and belonging and enhance the achievement of a positive identity.

Reactions of Foster Parents

Foster parents (as well as child care personnel in residential settings) are also caught in the complex web of emotions generated by separation. Their attitudes and reactions, like those of natural parents, are expressions of their personalities and their life experience. These will affect their capacity to cope with the reality of child–natural parent relationship and to share the child with his parents. Rearing a foster child entails emotional investment. When the child becomes a significant part of the foster family, foster parents and their children may feel threatened by continuing ties between himself and his natural family and the social agency's supervisory activities. The everpresent possibility of losing the child eventually can be a serious threat hanging over all of them like an ominous cloud. When it occurs, reaction will vary with circumstances of the child's departure from the foster home. For example, one highly competent foster father was adamant in his objection to visitation by the natural father of his foster son. Thirty-five years before, as a young child, he had been traumatized by a sudden departure of a foster brother to whom he had become deeply attached. He came home from school one day to find that his foster brother had been removed from his family by his natural parents. When together with his caseworker he was able to work through the trauma of his separation experience, his objections ceased.

Even when the separation is due to joint planning for a foster child's return to his parents, the foster family and the child experience a sense of loss. This is felt more acutely in those situations where a parent insists on his child's return against foster parent and agency advice. Regret about the separation may then be accompanied by hostile feelings toward natural parents and toward the social agency for not preventing the departure. In cases of difficult children who have to be transferred to another foster home or to a residential setting because of their inability to make an adequate or acceptable adjustment, the foster parents and other members of their immediate family are affected. Even though the child's departure may bring a sense of relief, feelings of guilt are experienced and projected anger is expressed.

Attitudes of foster parents, like that of natural parents, are expressions of their personalities and their life experience. These will affect their capacity to cope with the reality of child–natural parent relationship and to share the child with his parents. The maintenance of a harmonious, mutually positive relationship among foster parents, child and natural parents, is not easily achieveable because of the complexity of the conscious and unconscious elements which permeate these relationships.

A study by Gottesfeld[10] sheds light on this issue. He found that foster parents and their children emphasize their roles and de-emphasize the value of natural parents; natural parents do the opposite; foster children are generally neutral in this struggle for their loyalty. These findings suggest that the foster home may become the arena for two rivalrous family groups, each of whom strives to maintain its primacy in the life of the foster child, who in turn does not (outwardly at least) commit himself to either family group. This suggests the possibility that foster children may be inadvertently forced into developing personality structures which inhibit their capacity to commit themselves to anyone or to any important issues in their inter-personal relationships. The consequence of being "neutral" or "playing it safe" may be the development of character constrictions which might hinder the capacities to "feel" as well as to "act." We need to examine whether practices in the child care agencies contribute to this phenomenon. By focusing *separately* on the child, foster and natural parents, caseworkers may inadvertently be encouraging the fragmentation of significant relationships, deterring a sense of unity of purpose and contributing confusion to the child's developing sense of identity.

This fragmentary approach may be considered uneconomical and unrealistic. However, it represents an effort to work with natural parents. What is realistically tragic is the degree of inattention paid to parents following placement. A recent nationwide followup study[11] of children in foster care for ten or more years indicates a significant association between long-term care and agency treatment of parents. A large percentage (73 percent) of the parents of long-term care children had little or no agency treatment; only 15 percent had "adequate or better" contact with the agencies and relationships of significance with them. Related to this is the fact that 16 percent of the long-term care children ultimately returned to their homes.

Natural Foster Families and Child as One Network

The above findings seem to confirm the gap between our society's and our profession's expressed commitment to the fundamental value of pre-serving family ties and the reality of our practice. Higher priorities continue to be given to removal of children from families where adverse conditions exist than to the correction of these disruptive conditions and the reinte-gration of families as soon as possible following placement. Whenever there is a likelihood that a child will eventually return to his family, a continuous relationship between foster and natural parents should be encouraged. Joint concern, planning and activities with and on behalf of the child, might

[10] H. Gottesfeld, "Perceived Role Values in Foster Care," 1966, unpubl., Jewish Child Care Association, New York, 1966.
[11] Henry S. Mass, "Children in Long-Term Foster Care," *Child Welfare*, Vol. 48, #6 (1969), pp. 321–33.

serve to convey to him that his natural and foster families are interested in his welfare. In this respect their importance to him is enhanced and in this sense they will constitute for him an enlarged, significant family group. This might serve to increase his sense of security in relation to his foster and natural family units by providing him with an extended "kinship" family, which is becoming rare in our fragmented, technological society.

There are situations where realistic considerations hinder the realization of joint planning and participation. It may be impossible for severely disturbed or guilt ridden parents to share a child with a foster family. If efforts to overcome the obstacles which hinder a harmonious relationship between natural and foster parents are unsuccessful, the placement situation will have to be reevaluated in order to determine the action necessary to assure the optimum protection for the child. This may entail transfer from a foster home to a group residence, or in extreme cases, court action to deter parental disruptive and destructive acts.

A consistent continuous relationship with a caseworker can serve as a bridge between the natural and foster families. The agency remains a stable factor in the child's life, regardless of changes in workers and foster parents. This needs to be emphasized by word and deed, and if it is done, it may serve to reduce a child's projection that the agency is responsible for his separation. Instead, he may become aware that the agency is a source of his well-being and that its objective is to provide him with the best possible substitute family environment for as long as he requires it.

The complexities and multiplicity of interpersonal relationships in child placement complicate the caseworker's role. Among the numerous functions of providing services to children and their families, the most important and optimum role of the caseworker is, in partnership with the foster and natural families, to keep on creating an environment for the child's healthiest development possible. This requires a high degree of skill, sensitivity, self-awareness, and understanding of the complexity of the emotional inter-relationships. The caseworker, as the representative of the social agency, is in a position to exercise a great deal of power. To avoid its misuse, this power must be exercised with a great deal of care and self-awareness. For example, a caseworker's unresolved conflicts with his own parents may negatively color his attitudes toward natural, foster parents, or child counselors. His over-identification with a child or his caseload may influence him to adopt the role of "rescuer" and "protector," which is not necessarily helpful. In foster care one finds a great deal of devotion and dedication to children on the part of foster parents, child care counselors and caseworkers. This investment is, for the most part, based on genuine and mature concern for the child. When this is the case, the child usually responds favorably to the adult's interest and concern. If it is motivated by neurotic needs on the part of the adult, it may be destructive because it perpetuates dependency, feeds resentment and hinders independent personality growth. In general, children do not want to be "rescued" from their parents, no matter how inadequately the latter may be evaluated in terms of society's standards of parenting and of their individual physical and emotional capacities to exercise it. The emotional ties that bind them to each other continue to generate a hunger for reunion.

Although child welfare practices in general have not kept pace with changing philosophy which strives for conservation and reintegration of families, rather than "rescuing" children from adverse family circumstances, there have been significant achievements in this direction. Greater recognition of the importance of family ties to children and parents and the importance of conserving family cohesiveness, has been reflected historically in the development of supportive child welfare services (financial assistance, family day care, homemaker, etc.), which enable parents to care for their children at home. The increasingly selective use of foster care, greater emphasis on work with parents, use of family treatment techniques, flexibility in agency policies concerning home visits by children and visitation by parents, are indications of the effort among child welfare agencies to reunite children and their parents wherever it is feasible and as soon as it is possible. A large number of agencies are also introducing group techniques in working with foster parents and foster children, particularly with adolescents. In these group sessions, separation and its effects are prevalent topics for discussion. Greater interest and concern with the effects of separation on children and parents are also reflected in current child welfare research.[12] These positive trends need to be extended to encompass the whole field of foster care.

Sensitivity to and cognizance of the significance of the separation experience through increased diagnostic skills, and emphasis on working through its emotional components, can only serve to improve foster care practice. The greatest benefits of so doing will accrue to the children in placement. In the process of helping them master the anxieties of separation we may more effectively help them bridge the physical and emotional gaps between their natural and foster families, heal the psychological wounds inflicted by separation and provide greater consistency in their living and maturing.

---

[12] Shirley Jenkins, "Separation Experiences of Parents Whose Children are in Foster Care." *Child Welfare*, Vol. 48, #6 (1969), pp. 334–40.

The Stepparent Role: Potential for Disturbances in Family Functioning

Irene Fast and Albert C. Cain

If references in the Readers Guide and the Psychological Abstracts are a fair indication, both popular and professional interest in marriage, parenthood and divorce has been at a high level during the past 10 years, but there has been little interest in the problems of families with "step" relationships. Numerically the group concerned is large. In 1948 there were approximately six million stepchildren in the United States, or, about 11 per cent of marriages were remarriages, and in approximately 15 per cent of these the wives had children under the age of 18 by a previous marriage.[1]

The focus of this paper is the unusual social role of the stepparent. The stepparent is selected, not because his problems are likely to be greater than those of his spouse or the stepchild, but because folklore tends to hold him the villain of the piece, and he is therefore perhaps most in need of sympathetic attention. Role theory is chosen as a model in order to highlight the relation of structural factors to interpersonal disturbances frequently found in families with step-relationships. Our aim is to show that organizational disturbance in stepfamilies is inevitable, and that because the social structure of the family normally provides a source of impulse control and regulation of interpersonal relationships, the nature of the disruption causes particular areas of family functioning to be especially vulnerable to dysfunction. Examples of breakdown in interpersonal functioning are selected from a clinical population. These are meant to serve only as clarifying illustrations without implication either that vulnerability inevitably leads to breakdown or that the intensity or mode of disturbances necessarily would be the same in other clinical populations or in a nonclinical one.

The clinical observations are based on approximately 50 case records

Reprinted from *American Journal of Orthopsychiatry*, Vol. 36 (April, 1966), pp. 485–491. Copyright © 1966 the American Orthopsychiatric Association, Inc. Reproduced by permission of the authors and the Association.

[1] We appreciate the cooperation of the Children's Psychiatric Hospital, the Mental Hygiene Clinic, and the Counseling Division of the University of Michigan; Ypsilanti Family Service, the San Fernando Valley Child Guidance Clinic, and therapists in private practice in opening their case files to us and helping in a variety of ways in the preparation of these materials.

from both inpatient and outpatient child guidance settings. There were approximately three times as many families with stepfathers as with stepmothers and a few with both. Approximately half the previous marriages ended in death, and the other half in divorce. The primary patient in the majority of cases was a child. The length of contact varied from diagnostic evaluation to two years of inpatient treatment.

The role definition of stepparent in this society is both poorly articulated and implies contradictory functions as "parent," "stepparent," and "nonparent." Folk tradition describes the stepmother as wicked and cruel. Dictionaries define the term, stepmother, as implying unparent-like behavior[11] or neglect and deprivation of the stepchildren.[2] To enact that role is socially disapproved. Instead, the stepparent is encouraged to assume the role of parent. For this role enactment legal support is also offered, in the explication of the rights and duties entailed by the "in loco parentis" relationship.[4] But the stepparent cannot totally assume the role of father or mother; he is also nonparent. In this society, where some of the most obvious role functions of the father are biological, financial and educational, a stepfather cannot assume responsibility for biological fatherhood, frequently shares financial obligations with the natural father, and almost invariably shares the socialization of the child either contemporaneously as the child divides his time between two homes, or temporally in the course of the two successive marriages.

Attempts at individual resolutions of pressures to be parent, notparent and stepparent were observed in the behavior of almost all stepparents. In a few cases a single role seemed to be expressed with the overemphasis of caricature, e.g., the "real daddy," the tormenting and depriving stepparent, or the nonparent (holding himself severely separate from the child or achieving the closeness of friend or pal rather than parent).

In most, however, the three roles seemed interwoven. A central unsettled question was "how much to be parent." Decisions about some easily identified questions such as the child's place of residence, financial responsibility for him, his use of a surname, could usually be made. But even these relatively public commitments sometimes failed to remain stable. Some were changed by external pressures, others were inappropriately made the child's responsibility. Still others were precariously dependent on the stepparent's mood, or the shifting fortunes of his intrapsychic or interpersonal struggles. More subtle parental relationships, less easily made explicit and less amenable to conscious decision, were even more difficult to stabilize: the maintenance of an appropriate generation barrier; the assumption of the rights and responsibilities of discipline; mutuality with the child in work or play, the offer of the self as an object for identification.

Intrapsychic and interpersonal difficulties often appeared to augment problems based on stepparents' uncertainties about their appropriate roles as parents. Many stepparents were burdened with their wives' or husbands' hypersensitivity to their every act, total nuance, look, omission or suggestion of negative feeling. In the natural parents such overawareness often expressed their own uneasy feelings that their children were only "part of a package deal" and not really wanted, or feelings of guilt toward the children for having "broken" their homes, deprived them of their natural parents, and provided them with stepparents. Stepparents' own feelings that the children were an encumbrance, an unwanted financial burden, a continuous unwelcome reminder of their spouses' previous marriages were sometimes strongly fended off as heinous no matter how strongly balanced by positive feelings. Some stepparents, afraid of being or seeming the traditionally evil stepparent, could not be adequately assertive in discipline. Still others were unable to treat as absurd the stepchild's fantasy-based complaints of overwork, neglect and deprivation.

The stepparent's capacity to assume the role of parent did not depend only on his own willingness and ability. The reciprocal acceptance of himself in that role by spouse and child was essential. In Parson's[7] terms, "the success of ego's action is contingent on alter's re-action." Some children's repudiation of the stepparent as parent was extreme. No gift was accepted. Every punishment was treated as an attack. No identification was made with the stepparent's goals, values or personal characteristics. Every forced accommodation to the stepparent was responded to as though he were an intruder or occupying army. Sibling groups sometimes treated any single child's deviation from total rejection of the stepparent as traitorous to both the displaced parent and to themselves. The natural parent, spouse of the stepparent, usually intensely wished the stepparent to assume the role of parent. But this wish was not unambivalent. Indirect expressions of the wish to maintain exclusive control occurred, for example, in a mother's assumption of more than her share of disciplinary and financial responsibility for the child, or a father's performance of duties more typically the mother's in our society in relation to school and clinic.

The uncertainties about appropriate role behavior, related intrapsychic conflicts and problems due to failures in reciprocal role behavior by other family members found a variety of manifestations. Three seemed particularly prevalent. The first, a denial of any problems, usually occurred early in any clinical contact. It was the statement that the stepparent treated the child as his own, i.e., was completely "parent," an assertion rigidly, even belligerently maintained, usually supported by the spouse during the joint interview and often stated so persuasively that no further clinical inquiry was attempted despite overwhelming evidence of its falsity. A second was the stepparent's development of an acute hypersensitivity to every event as "proof" that he was, or was not, seen as "parent." In addition to the tensions this created for the stepparent himself, a particularly heavy burden was placed on the child whose every act was weighted with such significance that spontaneity and decisive action became difficult. Finally, and perhaps most damaging to the stepchild, was the parents' united focus on the child as the source of all marital dissension and threat to the marriage itself. It is not difficult to see the probable contribution to this outcome of the child's actual wish to separate parent and stepparent, the fact that the difficult step-relationships would not exist at all were it not for the child, and the negative feelings of both marital partners toward the child as reminder of the natural parent's previous spouse.

Whatever the reasons for the stepparent's behavior, his particular pattern of role functioning must affect the role enactment of every other family member. To the extent that the stepparent does not appropriately carry out the role functions of parent, the complementary roles and relationships of the natural parent and of the children will also suffer. As he does function as parent his idiosyncratic enactment of that role also forces modifications in all familial relationships. In either case, then, both the dyadic relationships involving the stepparent and all the other relationships among family members will be modified. As a stepfather behaved as nonparent an intense mother-son bond, not appropriately tempered by a father-son relationship, prevented a boy's adequate individuation. A boy's highly sexualized tie to a sister was used as replacement for an emotionally distant stepmother. A fiercely female mother-daughter competition occurred for a man whose disparate roles as husband to one and father to the other were not adequately defined. When the stepparent did function as parent, subtle role changes also occurred. One adolescent focused on her mother's role changes from woman-about-town to housewife, and more especially, from mother of herself to wife of the intruding stepfather. Sometimes too, a painful but healthy separation between natural parent and child became evident as each developed his appropriately different relationship to the stepparent.

But however strong the stepparent's determination to be parent, however skillful his efforts, he cannot succeed totally. Furthermore, social norms make it inappropriate for him to attempt to completely assume the parent role. They require that he gracefully accede to the parental rights of another, to be nonparent; to share residential, educational, and financial decisions regarding the child with a living parent, or perhaps to accept the moral and religious legacy of a dead one.

Perhaps the most steady reminder that the "stepparent" is also "nonparent" occurs in divorce. The activity of the natural parent, the child's visits with him, the spouse's continued relation with him force awareness and require decisions. But where the natural parent has died, his influence as parent is by no means lost, though sometimes less easily recognized. In some families where the death of one parent terminated the previous marriage, constant unfavorable comparison between stepparent and the overidealized image of the dead parent occurred. One boy's potent identification with his dead parent as worthless and destructive prevented a confidence-giving identification with the stepparent. Other children maintained the relationship with the dead parent in firm beliefs in his continued living existence as a wandering ghost, a benign helper or a vengeful and still powerful punisher.

Whether the natural parent is dead or alive, the child maintains a contemporary relationship to him. The stepparent shares that parental role with the previous parent. He is both "parent" and "nonparent." In some families bitter competition between the stepparent and the previous parent replaced the sharing of rights and responsibilities. Seemingly endless internal ruminations or acrimonious discussion occurred about the child's preference for one over the other; the other parent's spoiling of the child; his relative adequacy in living up to financial obligations; his relative "goodness" as a parent. In some families, particularly those in which embittering divorce proceedings had ended the previous marriage, the couple of the present marriage united in an uncompromising denunciation of the natural parent. In others a withdrawal occurred from any relationship with him. Sometimes the child functioned as go-between, made decisions in relation to the adults for which he was ill equipped, and inevitably was burdened with a frightening degree of power.

Further, because roles and role functions are interlocking networks, rather than simple aggregates of behaviors and relationships,[6] the sharing of any role aspect with another person must affect all other aspects of role functioning. While family members probably could not have formulated this characteristic of role functions in the abstract, they illustrated it very concretely in their behavior. Frequently a stepfather's right to obedience was perceived to increase as he assumed greater financial responsibility. A child's, "You are not my real (biological) mother," denied the stepparent's right to obedience. More subtly, an adolescent felt that repudiation of any identification with her stepfather's values was contingent on her refusing any gifts from him.

The enactment of a special role also has implications for the strength of broader social mores, to the extent that these are sanctions applied to occupants of particular roles. The incest taboo is one of these. In this society sexual relationships between father and daughter are strongly prohibited. Implications for stepparents are less clear: in 1940, 26 states permitted stepfather-daughter marriage; the remainder did not. No clear-cut taboo exists for the situation of "nonparent." As the stepparent is all three of these, the impact of the taboo is weakened. As it loses strength, the roles reciprocally dependent on it are also diffused.

It was our impression that the absence of clear sanctions against sexual relationships between stepparents and children intensified normal difficulties in channeling sexual impulses of family members. In some cases mothers "saw" potential incest in every intimacy between stepfather and child. In others highly sexualized fondling, hugging, and kissing between stepfather and daughter alternated with horrified and embarrassed avoidance of any intimacy. And in a few, overt sexual relationships occurred. The effects were those anticipated[8] though not invariably observed[3,9] by others: pressures toward the breakdown of generation barriers, the abrogation of the primary husband-wife bond, and a blurring of the differential relationships of stepfather as husband and father.

Finally, roles are learned. In the normal course of the establishment of a family, marriage follows courtship, and the birth of children follows a period of marital adjustment. In a marriage in which at least one partner has children from the very beginning, a number of role-learning opportunities ordinarily offered the natural parent are not available. Reciprocal marital role relationships between husband and wife are not worked out prior to the assumption of parental roles. Husband and wife cannot gradually acquire their particular parental role functions beginning early in their relationship with the first casual talk of establishing a family. There is no opportunity to establish a primary husband-wife bond prior to the birth of children. And parents have no time to gradually establish a generation barrier between themselves and their offspring.

It was our impression that the premarital relationship of the stepparent to family members as acquaintance, friend and fiance of the natural parent interfered with his establishing appropriate differential relationships as spouse and parent, and with his function as authority figure. The working out of marital and parental problems simultaneously seemed to encourage the inappropriate involvement of the children in marital dissension. The natural parent's prior relationship to the child, often pathologically intensified during and after the dissolution of the previous marriage made a primary husband-wife bond more difficult to establish, a difficulty often increased by the mother's guilt about taking away from the child the status of "man of the house," and by the child's terror of desertion by his only remaining parent.

Concluding Comments

Some inevitable modifications in the role structure of the family due to the step relationship have been indicated, related areas of vulnerability to interpersonal disturbance noted and illustrations provided of kinds of malfunctioning that were found to occur in a clinical population in cases where the weakening of family role structure did lead to interpersonal disturbances.

The strong tendency in the major professions dealing with interpersonal relationships to use a health-illness model in understanding behavior makes it tempting to see the stepfamily in terms of pathology. Inevitably then, the "cure" for its disturbance will be sought in the best possible approximation of the normative pattern of the nuclear family in this society. We think this is a tactical error. If our analysis is generally correct, attempts to reproduce the nuclear family in the step situation are doomed to failure in any case. More important, an alternative framework is both available and promising of more heuristic formulation of questions. That is, the stepfamily can be conceptualized as a structural variation of importance equal to the Kibbutz pattern in Israel[10]; the working-class family pattern in France[5]; the urban, rural, nuclear extended family structures in this country. From this organizational point of view, then, potentially soluble problems can be formulated concerning, for example, patterns of transition from one marriage to another, processes in the integration of two sibling groups in a single family, or the appropriate allocation of individual and joint functions of the two same-sex parents. Since the stepfamily is likely to be an increasingly common pattern of family organization, the resolution of such problems might well warrant our considerable effort.

Bibliography

1 BARNARD, J. 1956. *Remarriage, a Study of Marriage*. The Dryden Press, New York.

2 *The Concise Oxford Dictionary*, 4th Edition. 1951. Oxford, at the Clarendon Press.

3 KAUFMAN, I., A. L. PECK, and T. CONSUELO. 1954. "The Family Constellation and Overt Incestuous Relations Between Father and Daughter." *Amer. J. Orthopsychiat.* 24:266–77.

4 MERIAM, A. S. 1940. *The Stepfather in the Family*. The University of Chicago Press, Chicago, Ill.

5 MICHEL, A. V. 1960. "Kinship Relations and Relationships of Proximity in French Working-class Households." In *The Family, A Modern Introduction*. N. S. Bell and E. F. Vogel, eds. The Free Press of Glencoe, Ill.

6 NADEL, S. F. 1956. *The Theory of Social Structure*. Cohen and West, Ltd. London.

7 PARSONS, T. 1957. "The Basic Structure of the Interactive Relationship." *Sociological Theory, A Book of Readings*. L. A. Coser and B. Rosenberg, eds. The MacMillan Company, N.Y.

8 SELIGMAN, B. Z. 1931–32. "The Incest Barrier: its Role in Social Organization." *British J. of Psychol.* 22:250–276.

9 SLOANE, P. S., and E. KARPINSKI. 1942. "Effects of Incest Upon the Participants." *Amer. J. Orthopsychiat.* 12:656–74.

10 SPIRO, M. E. 1960. "Is the Family Universal?—the Israeli Case." In *The Family, A Modern Introduction*. N. W. Bell and E. F. Vogel, eds. The Free Press of Glencoe, Ill.

11 *Webster's International Dictionary*. 1960.

Disaster

Train Crash: Social Work and Disaster Services

Leona Grossman

In a fast-moving, technological society it is to be expected that the unpredictabilities in nature as well as human fallibility will continue to result in periodic catastrophes. What science may have accomplished in mastery over the natural environment seems to be balanced out by what its sophisticated technology has confounded.

However horrendous it may seem, the possibility of danger and disaster is indigenous to today's world. Two emerging issues are involved in all such happenings: how to cope and how to prevent. The focus on prevention has received by far the greater emphasis in its concern with such matters of technological safety as prevention of mine casualties, safety devices in factories, railroads, airplanes, and so forth. Investigations into responsibility and the possibility of legal reprisal act as powerful control agents. A fair amount of research has been conducted on natural disasters that have claimed large numbers of lives. It is only recently, however, that serious attention has been given to the human perspective: the intricate processes people use to cope with disasters, which have now been identified as "disaster behavior."

Several case studies and theoretical analyses of disasters have appeared in the literature of disciplines other than social work.[1] In the past ten years, however, the subject has been dealt with only rarely in social work journals.[2]

Reprinted with permission of the National Association of Social Workers, from *Social Work*, Vol. 18, No. 5 (September, 1973), pp. 38–44.

[1] *See*, for example, A. F. C. Wallace, *Tornado in Worcester: An Exploratory Study of Individuals and Community Behavior in an Extreme Situation*, "Disaster Study No. 3" (Washington, D.C.: National Academy of Sciences–National Research Council, 1965); George H. Grosser, Henry Wechsler, and Milton Greenblatt, eds., *The Threat of Impending Disaster: Contributions to the Psychology of Stress* (Cambridge, Mass.: The M.I.T. Press, 1964); R. R. Dynes, *Organized Behavior in Disaster* (Lexington, Mass.: D. C. Heath & Co., 1970); R. I. Leopold and H. Dillon, "Psycho-Anatomy of Disaster: Long-Term Study of Post-Traumatic Neuroses in Survivors of a Marine Explosion," *American Journal of Psychiatry*, 119 (April 1963), pp. 913–921.

[2] Herbert Blaufarb and Jules Levine, "Crisis Intervention in an Earthquake," *Social Work*, 17 (July 1972), pp. 16–19; Richard I. Shader and Alice J. Schwartz, "Management of Reactions to Disaster," *Social Work*, 11 (April 1966), pp. 99–104.

Although written accounts of such incidents usually contain some skew, they still have pragmatic value. Since disasters evoke strong, instantaneous emotional responses, research of the "hard-fact" variety is a bit more difficult.

The Study of Disasters

The literature on behavior in extreme situations can be divided into three general categories: popular and journalistic accounts, official reports, and scientific or professional studies. Popular accounts generally reach a wide audience and convey their message with dramatic impact and strong human appeal, though their scientific usefulness may be limited.[3] Official reports constitute more technical accounts that are frequently found in organizational journals, annual reports, or trade magazines. These are usually pragmatic. Scientific literature is varied and can be subdivided into scholarly studies and professional studies. Thus far, the scholarly studies have been descriptive and usually noninterpretive.[4] Professional studies "employ the concepts, categories of observation, and research techniques of the disciplines they represent," and are usually specific studies dealing with specific variables.[5]

Several scientific studies of behavior in extreme situations are of value in developing generalizations. Those that deal with situations of specific stress offer some possibilities for constructing a "disaster theory."[6]

Behavioral scientists have not been drawn to research on disasters. This may be because they tend to view such extreme events as isolated incidents, without observing the patterns they follow, or because these events do not lend themselves to control by scientific procedures.[7]

Only within the last decade have a few efforts been made to institute systematically controlled studies of disasters. Many of the larger universities have developed research projects with funding from the National Academy of Sciences–National Research Council. These studies have been essentially sociological, initially stimulated, perhaps, by the possibility of nuclear attack.

In 1963 the Disaster Research Center at Ohio State University was instituted and has since conducted field work at approximately seventy-three disaster sites. These studies have concentrated on various aspects of community organization in disaster situations.[8]

---

[3] John R. Hersey, *Hiroshima* (New York: Alfred A. Knopf, 1964).

[4] J. E. Thompson, *The Rise and Fall of the Maya Civilization*, (Norman, Okla.: University of Oklahoma Press, 1954).

[5] Wallace, op. cit.

[6] *See*, for example, Irving L. Janis, *Air War and Emotional Stress* (New York: McGraw Hill Book Co., 1951); A. H. Leighton, "Psychological Factors in Major Disasters," *Medical Projects Reports* (Rochester, N.Y.: University of Rochester, 1951); Bruno Bettelheim, "Individual and Mass Behavior in Extreme Situations," *Journal of Abnormal and Social Psychology*, 38 (October 1943), pp. 417–452; R. A. Lucas, *Men in Crisis* (New York: Basic Books, 1969).

[7] Wallace, op. cit., pp. 14–17.

[8] Dynes, op. cit., pp. 10–14.

Theory

All definitions of disaster include the idea of a destructive force, non-humanly or humanly induced, that strikes without warning and has a widely disruptive impact on normal functioning. Disasters harbor the potential for widespread public upset. In organizing one's thinking about disasters, it is possible to draw upon concepts from several areas of knowledge. There is a large body of material on psychological responses to situations of severe stress.[9] Such studies have revolved around specific situations that attempt to formalize the range of individual responses and evaluate the adaptive and nonadaptive aspects. Related to this are the many and varied analyses of panic behavior that focus on the instinct to flee in critical situations.[10]

Wallace formulated the concept of a "disaster syndrome" that is usually manifested by aimless wandering, stunned or dazed responses, extreme passivity or suggestibility, sleep disturbance, irritability, somatic distresses restlessness, and isolation.[11] Recently this concept has been refined and elaborated into a "post-stress syndrome."[12] In his well-known studies of reactions to the Coconut Grove fire in a Boston nightclub in 1942, Lindemann has connected many of these reactions to the more fundamental processes of bereavement, mourning, and grief.[13]

All these pieces of theory or sets of generalizations fit, at least in part, into reactions to disasters and offer possible explanations for the range of observable behavior. They are drawn from psychological and social psychological theory and are usually based on empirical evidence taken from a number of incidents.

A particularly interesting structural and more sociological framework for understanding the natural history of a disaster has been developed by Powell and Rayner.[14] They divide a disaster into seven sequential phases: warning, threat, impact, inventory, rescue, remedy, and recovery, and attribute specific variables to each phase. All seven of these phases need not occur in each disaster. Some, like the Chicago transit crash to be described, start with impact, omitting the phases of warning and threat.

More important, continued study must be made of treatment following a disaster. The reality of a threat to survival and the urgency of immediate

[9] *See* Grosser et al., op. cit.; Irving L. Janis, *Psychological Stress* (New York: John Wiley & Sons, 1958); Henry Krystal, ed., *Massive Psychic Trauma* (New York: International Universities Press, 1969).

[10] Duane P. Schultz, *Panic Behavior: Discussion and Readings* (New York: Random House, 1964).

[11] Wallace, op. cit.

[12] H. C. Archibald and R. D. Tuddenham, "Persistent Stress Reactions after Combat," *AMA Archives of General Psychiatry*, 12 (May 1965), pp. 475–481.

[13] Erich Lindemann, "Symptomatology and Management of Acute Grief," *American Journal of Psychiatry*, 101 (September 1944), pp. 141–148.

[14] J. W. Powell and J. Rayner, *Progress Notes: Disaster Investigations, July 1, 1951–June 30, 1952.* (Washington, D.C.: Chemical Corps Medical Laboratories, Army Chemical Center, 1952).

rescue have naturally tended to overshadow the covert psychological wounds. These might not immediately express themselves in behavior, but might become embedded in mental functioning and have disturbing residual effects. Some of the recent professional literature on death and mourning has an important relevance.[15] Studies have emphasized the effectiveness of encouraging survivors to talk about their experiences and emotions.[16]

Analysis

The intent of this paper is to discuss and analyze only one part of the total event, that concerning the participation of social workers and their interactions with the victims' friends and relatives. It is not often that one witnesses in such dramatic form the basic application of professional values and skills. Unusual as well is the opportunity to observe collective behavior at this level of emotional intensity and stress.

The article will deal with the participation of a social work staff, some of whom were personally involved while others were more removed and could observe the processes unfold with more perspective. This can be considered a natural history of a disaster, with attempts to analyze selected aspects, speculate on meanings, and hopefully, arrive at a few generalizations. It is particularly valuable, because it offers an unsimulated field experience. Through collective input and corrections by members of the staff and people of other disciplines, the usual pitfalls of bias have been kept to a minimum. The analysis was undertaken immediately following the events in order to reduce the distortion of retrospect.[17]

This undoubtedly would have been a more valid analysis had a team of uninvolved researchers been able to study the situation with complete objectivity. Several disaster rescue centers that are now studying the problems seriously have made this recommendation. Perhaps this is something that the field of social work should consider in relation to its own professional interests and range of experiences.

Train Crash

On October 30, 1972, a crash on a local Chicago railroad claimed the lives of forty-five passengers and left more than three hundred persons injured. The catastrophe occurred at 7:27 A.M. on a Monday, when passengers were on their way to work. These were able-bodied, young to

---

[15] Elisabeth Kubler-Ross, *On Death and Dying* (New York: Macmillan Co., 1970).

[16] S. E. Perry, E. Silber, and D. A. Block, *The Child and His Family in Disaster: A Study of the 1953 Vicksburg Tornado*, "Disaster Study No. 5" (Washington, D.C.: National Academy of Sciences–National Research Council, 1956); Archibald and Tuddenham, op. cit.

[17] The staff met as a group several times immediately following this event. They talked among themselves, checking out their reactions and feelings. After a little while, when they were somewhat removed from the emotional impact of that particular day, they were able to evaluate and conceptualize their experiences.

middle-aged workers, going about their beginning-of-the-week routine. Disaster struck with no warning.

The impact was immediate and critical. Certainly on the part of the victims there was no thought that such an event could conceivably take place. Most of these commuters had been using this transit system for some time. Although the possibility of casualties in daily living exists, the majority of people are not normally preoccupied with such a likelihood. In this era of escalating stress, the only plausible attitude is to maintain a realistic vigilance for the possiblity of crisis. This has some implications for mental health in our present society. It makes added demands on the adaptive capacities of individuals, organizations, and communities.

In this situation, the time of the accident and the fact that it occurred at a train depot situated between two hospitals were among the more fortunate factors in the tragedy. In fact, one of the hospitals, the Michael Reese Hospital and Medical Center, had just completed and rehearsed its disaster plan so that it could immediately mobilize and institute a significant rescue operation. The fire and police departments were also prepared to join the hospital in meeting the immediate challenge. Without these factors the list of deceased might have been significantly longer.

Impact

Although the literature on disasters discusses impact in terms of those who are direct victims of the disaster, the definition needs to be enlarged to include other people also acutely involved. Extreme events such as this one have multiple impact points. One was the impact on family members and friends who, on hearing of the incident, rushed to the scene. This group of people under severe stress remained in communication with the social work staff throughout that eventful day. They came in droves and were directed to the lobby and lounge of the nurses' residence. The initial effect was total chaos.

A second point of impact was on the staff of social workers at Michael Reese Hospital, most of whom did not know of the accident until their arrival that morning. Faced with this challenge, the staff quickly recovered from the initial shock and confusion and, joining the throngs in the nurses' residence, organized themselves into a functioning subsystem.

Morale was high and the staff reacted instantaneously to each task, accepting requests from whoever issued them and attempting to suppress any uncontrollable anxiety. The initial mobilization of forces rapidly assumed a structure in which roles were covertly defined and rational leadership emerged. It was this spirit of cohesiveness that provided the stability required by the fragmented subsystem of relatives and friends. This supports the generalization that "high group morale and cohesiveness will generally minimize the disaster effects of impact."[18] At the termination of

---

[18] Shader and Schwartz, op. cit., p. 101.

the impact phase, the two subsystems (professional and lay) were moving in complementary fashion, each gaining strength from the other. Urgent needs for comfort and help demanded the support and total involvement of the social work staff and in the end neutralized the mechanisms that usually separate professionals from clients.

The staff had to deal with its own set of interpersonal reactions before it could function as an organic whole. Following the initial shock and immediate immersion, there was some recoil, some jockeying for power or status. There was competition for social credits, measured by the number of relatives and friends who looked to them for help. Staff members later reported having been pushed aside by their colleagues and experiencing momentary anger. But such feelings were not reinforced because of the urgency of other needs. The situation itself determined the structure that finally emerged. Each staff member discovered some satisfying level of usefulness, accepted the leadership of others, and developed effective modes of nonverbal communication through symbols and cues. These were important, since time did not always permit speech.

Inventory and Rescue

For the purposes of this analysis these two phases, which Powell and Rayner's model separates, can be combined. One phase flowed into the other. In the inventory phase, survivors began to feel concern for others and to reach out helpfully. At the point of rescue, outside professionals, other hospital staff, nearby service departments, members of the clergy, and volunteer workers moved in to offer further support. As family and relatives engaged in their desperate search for survivors, the professionals were there to inform, guide, and offer hope and comfort.

Great reliance was put on the steady dissemination of information. Lists of the injured and dead were relayed continuously to the social work staff from the hospital's public relations department. Social workers, supported by members of the clergy, acted as the major informers.

The waiting population proved to be admirably controlled. Family members clung together and comforted one another. Strangers sat side by side, locked in their personal thoughts, not speaking but observant of others' reactions. A few people attached themselves to members of the staff, returning periodically for news. They seemed patient when reassured that someone was personally concerned about them. Volunteers stayed with people who seemed lost and confused, or who wanted to talk or cry. Some needed physical comfort such as someone to hold their hand or pat their shoulder. Even staff needed this from each other. The function of touching is frequently underestimated and even frowned upon in a professional relationship, but in this case the taboo was lifted. In essence, the staff responded in a totally human way and the overall effects were appropriate. Food played an important part in the role of comforting. The hospital had supplied generous amounts of coffee and sandwiches for all staff and visitors.

As the day wore on, the tension mounted and families began to search for information with increased anxiety. Their relentless questioning might easily have overtaxed an already fatigued staff who remained, nonetheless, remarkably patient. As it became clear that the remaining groups might have to face the news of a death, the level of staff empathy increased. Relatives and friends were encouraged to express their fears, to cry, and to talk endlessly. Efforts to sustain hope continued; other hospitals were contacted in a further search for more complete information. The increased activity was again used to suppress the mounting anxiety and concern.

A final handful of families had to be directed to the morgue to identify relatives. This tragic episode was handled by one of the priests. Emotional responses were extreme—one Mexican woman experienced an "ataque," others wept or screamed. Families turned to one another in their sorrow; professionals seemed locked out, or chose to remove themselves.

Aftermath

"An experience of extreme danger is not over once the danger is past, even for those who survive it intact. Something has intruded into their emotional life which requires some time to assimilate."[19] This was relevant to all who experienced the Chicago disaster.

Despite the exhaustion of most staff members after this experience there was, nevertheless, a feeling of having accomplished something and of having extended oneself fully to others. But there were also the disquieting feelings of having observed and emphathized with severe loss and grief. In practically each staff member, this aroused repressed memories of past personal loss, and responses ranged from emotional outbursts to attempts at denial. Staff meetings, informal discussions, and group meetings with patients held over a period of several weeks eventually helped to reconcile the arduous events of that day.

A joint decision was made to help those survivors interested in working out their mourning and grief. All those with whom staff members had worked and those who had been treated in the emergency room were notified. Although attendance was small, these follow-up meetings proved meaningful for those who came. Several persons attended a few times, others just once. The groups were composed of survivors, relatives, and staff members.

Analysis of the process in these groups revealed some similarities to ordinary reactions of shock or mourning. To begin with, survivors tended to ruminate over the precise details of the crash in an attempt to work through their own preoccupations. The less verbal members appeared to be listening intently, as if vicariously going through the experience. Most persons seemed to recall minutely what had been happening just before the crash. Many had superstitious reasons for why they survived while others

---

[19] Martha Wolfenstein, *Disaster: A Psychological Essay* (Glencoe, Ill.: Free Press, 1957), p. 135.

were killed. Some wondered about their decision that day not to ride in their usual car, which was subsequently demolished.

Several who came away shaken but not badly injured struggled with reactions of moral censorship in the belief that they should have done more to help others. They were disappointed in themselves, because their immediate response had been to flee from danger rather than turn back to help. One young woman had not even allowed herself to face this truth until well into the meeting. Then, after listening to others, she was able to say what was truly troubling her and evidently had motivated her to attend. Her belief in herself as a helpful person had been shattered by her flight reaction. She prefaced this disclosure by unconsciously citing what appeared to be an irrelevant account of how she had offered shelter and food to a stranger the night before the accident. The comparison between this incident and her behavior at the accident indicated how confused she felt about herself as a "good" person. Some discussion about the range of panic reactions helped to put her feeling of self-worth together again, although she will probably be haunted with this for some time.

The somatic effects of the accident were fairly consistent: headaches, sleep disturbances, startle reactions, and gastric distresses. One survivor experienced immediate amnesia and could not recall how he had escaped without injury from the car that had been demolished and had claimed the highest number of casualties. The method in which he might have escaped worried him and he strained to put together the pieces of his memory. Another survivor had developed a tremor in one hand. Others were grappling with phobias of one kind or another, and practically all the victims were afraid to board the train again.

Survivors discovered that talking to each other had a cathartic effect and as such was a vital part of recovery. They uniformly felt that not even close family members could fully understand and empathize with their experience. Those few relatives who did accompany survivors to the sessions gained a better understanding. In some situations we could almost see the walls that separated relatives and survivors break down and could sense the change of attitude. In one situation the mother of a daughter who had been injured in the crash accompanied the young woman to some of the sessions. She expressed irritation and guilt for not having "been with my daughter in time of need." Through this irrational reaction the staff gained insight into the relationship of overdependency that existed between the two. This experience underscored the importance of working through feelings with close relatives as well as survivors, since guilt reactions are prevalent in both groups. In this case the group discussion helped the participants recognize and accept these emotions while pointing out their irrationality.

In several instances, the emotional reactions to this event were linked to past experiences either real or vicarious. A few of the men had had army experiences and this disaster touched off feelings of horror, fear, shame, disgust, or guilt. Having mutually shared these past experiences, certain of them were able to form bonds and to support each other's feelings. On the other hand, there was the occasional tendency to deprecate and embarrass others for not being "more courageous." These reactions came from persons who used them to hide their own feelings of inadequacy. Depression and sudden outbursts of anger of the "why me" variety were constantly present.

The social work staff were totally involved in these group sessions. Because they themselves had experienced a wide range of emotions they were able to relate with empathy and reflect more openly upon their reactions. This made each group session an existential "experience." Growth in insight, and closer relationships with one another were some of the positive gains from this intense involvement.

Efforts were made to reach out to the families of the deceased. Although each overture seemed to be appreciated, the bereaved families were not interested in talking with each other. They sought the intimacy of family or the comfort of religion, but they seemed to have no immediate wish for contact with strangers.

There remained one more group of survivors—patients who had been seriously enough injured to require hospitalization. This coincided with the traditional role of hospital social work. These patients had the same urgent need to talk of the accident in detail and compare impressions. The feelings of grief and anger felt by those close to them needed attention as well. In one extreme situation there seemed to be a pathological denial of the severity of the survivor's condition, but this was attributed to a preexisting disturbed relationship.

Conclusions

This experience provided verification of some assumptions concerning the behavior of people in stressful situations. Under serious threat, most adults are oriented toward mutual helpfulness rather than toward destructiveness or panic, especially if consolidated leadership is provided to create models for positive action. Even under extreme conditions, behavior can be fundamentally adaptive and orderly. For this to happen, a social structure that permits mutual caring and helpful involvement must exist. In its commitment to the survivors, the social work staff offered such a model. Because of the pressures of daily routine, it is frequently possible to lose sight of these cardinal professional values.

Personal experience, especially of a highly emotional kind, provides significant opportunities for growth through self-reflection and feedback. In this situation members of the staff revealed qualities that had never before surfaced. This produced increased mutual respect. The total experience reconfirmed the effectiveness of the social work role in crisis intervention, in which action as well as a high level of empathy and respect for human dignity are major priorities.

Rape Trauma Syndrome

*Ann Wolbert Burgess and
Lynda Lytle Holmstrom*

Rape affects the lives of thousands of women each year. The Uniform Crime Reports from the Federal Bureau of Investigation indicated a 121-percent increase in reported cases of rape between 1960 and 1970. In 1970, over 37,000 cases were reported in the United States (1). A District of Columbia task force studying the problem in the capital area stated that rape was the fastest growing crime of violence there (2).

The literature on sexual offenses, including rape, is voluminous (3–5), but it has overlooked the victim. There is little information on the physical and psychological effects of rape, the therapeutic management of the victim, and the provisions for protection of the victim from further psychological insult (6–9).

In response to the problem of rape in the greater Boston area, the Victim Counseling Program was designed as a collaborative effort between Boston College School of Nursing and Boston City Hospital to provide 24-hour crisis intervention to rape victims and to study the problems the victim experiences as a result of being sexually assaulted.

The purpose of this paper is to report the immediate and long-term effects of rape as described by the victim.

Method

Study Population

The study population consisted of all persons who entered the emergency ward of Boston City Hospital during the one-year period July 20, 1972, through July 19, 1973, with the complaint of having been raped. The resulting sample was made up of 146 patients: 109 adult women, 34 female children, and 3 male children.

We divided these 146 patients into three main categories: (1) victims of forcible rape (either completed or attempted rape, usually the former);

Reprinted from *American Journal of Psychiatry*, Vol. 131 (1974), pp. 981–986. Copyright 1974, the American Psychiatric Association.

(2) victims in situations to which they were an accessory due to their inability to consent; and (3) victims of sexually stressful situations—sexual encounters to which they had initially consented but that went beyond their expectations and ability to control.

The rape trauma syndrome delineated in this paper was derived from an analysis of the symptoms of the 92 adult women in our sample who were victims of forcible rape. Future reports will analyze the problems of the other victims. Although not directly included in this paper, supplementary data were also gathered from 14 patients referred to the Victim Counseling Program by other agencies and from consultation calls from other clinicians working with rape victims.

A major research advantage in the location of the project at Boston City Hospital was the fact that it provided a heterogeneous sample of victims. Disparate social classes were included in the victim population. Ethnic groups included fairly equal numbers of black and white women, plus a smaller number of Oriental, Indian, and Spanish-speaking women. In regard to work status, the victims were career women, housewives, college students, and women on welfare. The age span was 17 to 73 years; the group included single, married, divorced, separated, and widowed women as well as women living with men by consensual agreement (see table 1). A variety of occupations were represented, such as schoolteacher, business manager, researcher, assembly line worker, secretary, housekeeper, cocktail waitress, and health worker. There were victims with no children, women pregnant up to the eighth month, postpartum mothers, and women with anywhere from 1 to 10 children. The women ranged in physical attractiveness from very pretty to very plain; they were dressed in styles ranging from high fashion to hippie clothes.

Interview Method

The counselors (the coauthors of this paper) were telephoned when a rape victim was admitted to the emergency department of Boston City Hospital; we arrived at the hospital within 30 minutes. We interviewed all the victims admitted during the one-year period regardless of time of day or night. Follow-up was conducted by use of telephone counseling or home visits. This method of study provided an 85-percent rate of direct follow-up. An additional 5 percent of the victims were followed indirectly

Table 1.
Distribution of Marital Status by Age (N = 92)

Marital Status	Age (in Years)				
	17–20	21–29	30–39	40–49	50–73
Single	29	25	0	2	1
Married	2	1	2	2	0
Divorced, separated, or widowed	2	6	7	2	2
Living with a man by consensual agreement	4	5	0	0	0

through their families or reports by the police or other service agencies who knew them. Detailed notes of the interviews, telephone calls, and visits were then analyzed in terms of the symptoms reported as well as changes in thoughts, feelings, and behavior. We accompanied those victims who pressed charges to court and took detailed notes of all court proceedings and recorded the victims' reactions to this process (10, 11). Contact with the families and other members of the victims' social network was part of the assessment and follow-up procedure.

Manifestations of Rape Trauma Syndrome

Rape trauma syndrome is the acute phase and long-term reorganization process that occurs as a result of forcible rape or attempted forcible rape. This syndrome of behavioral, somatic, and psychological reactions is an acute stress reaction to a life-threatening situation.

Forcible rape is defined in this paper as the carnal knowledge of a woman by an assailant by force and against her will. The important point is that rape is not primarily a sexual act. On the contrary, our data and those of researchers studying rapists suggest that rape is primarily an act of violence with sex as the weapon (5). Thus it is not surprising that the victim experiences a syndrome with specific symptomatology as a result of the attack made upon her.

The syndrome is usually a two-phase reaction. The first is the acute phase. This is the period in which there is a great deal of disorganization in the woman's lifestyle as a result of the rape. Physical symptoms are especially noticeable, and one prominent feeling noted is fear. The second phase begins when the woman begins to reorganize her lifestyle. Although the time of onset varies from victim to victim, the second phase often begins about two to three weeks after the attack. Motor activity changes and nightmares and phobias are especially likely during this phase.

The medical regimen for the rape victim involves the prescription of antipregnancy and antivenereal disease medication after the physical and gynecological examination. The procedure usually includes prescribing 25 to 50 mg. of diethylstilbestrol a day for five days to protect against pregnancy and 4.8 million units of aqueous procaine penicillin intramuscularly to protect against venereal disease. Symptoms reported by the patient need to be distinguished as either side effects of the medication or conditions resulting from the sexual assault.

The Acute Phase Disorganization

Impact Reactions

In the immediate hours following the rape, the woman may experience an extremely wide range of emotions. The impact of the rape may be so severe that feelings of shock or disbelief are expressed. When interviewed within a few hours of the rape, the women in this study mainly showed two emotional styles (12): the expressed style, in which feelings of fear, anger, and anxiety were shown through such behavior as crying, sobbing, smiling, restlessness, and tenseness; and the controlled style, in which feelings were masked or hidden and a calm, composed, or subdued affect was seen. A fairly equal number of women showed each style.

Somatic Reactions

During the first several weeks following a rape many of the acute somatic manifestations described below were evident.

1. *Physical trauma.* This included general soreness and bruising from the physical attack in various parts of the body such as the throat, neck, breasts, thighs, legs, and arms. Irritation and trauma to the throat were especially a problem for those women forced to have oral sex.

2. *Skeletal muscle tension.* Tension headaches and fatigue, as well as sleep pattern disturbances, were common symptoms. Women were either not able to sleep or would fall asleep only to wake and not be able to go back to sleep. Women who had been suddenly awakened from sleep by the assailant frequently found that they would wake each night at the time the attack had occurred. The victim might cry or scream out in her sleep. Victims also described experiencing a startle reaction—they become edgy and jumpy over minor incidents.

3. *Gastrointestinal irritability.* Women might complain of stomach pains. The appetite might be affected, and the victim might state that she did not eat, food had no taste, or she felt nauseated from the antipregnancy medication. Victims described feeling nauseated just thinking of the rape.

4. *Genitourinary disturbance.* Gynecological symptoms such as vaginal discharge, itching, a burning sensation on urination, and generalized pain were common. A number of women developed chronic vaginal infections following the rape. Rectal bleeding and pain were reported by women who had been forced to have anal sex.

Emotional Reactions

Victims expressed a wide gamut of feelings as they began to deal with the aftereffects of the rape. These feelings ranged from fear, humiliation, and embarrassment to anger, revenge, and self-blame. Fear of physical violence and death was the primary feeling described. Victims stated that it was not the rape that was so upsetting as much as the feeling that they would be killed as a result of the assault. One woman stated: "I am really mad. My life is disrupted; every part of it upset. And I have to be grateful I wasn't killed. I thought he would murder me."

Self-blame was another reaction women described—partly because of their socialization to the attitude of "blame the victim." For example, one young woman had entered her apartment building one afternoon after shopping. As she stopped to take her keys from her purse, she was assaulted in the hallway by a man who then forced his way into her apartment. She fought against him to the point of taking his knife and using it against him and in the process was quite severely beaten, bruised, and raped. Later she said:

> I keep wondering maybe if I had done something different when I first saw him that it wouldn't have happened—neither he nor I would be in trouble. Maybe it was my fault. See, that's where I get when I think about it. My father always said whatever a man did to a woman, she provoked it.

The Long-Term Process: Reorganization

All victims in our sample experienced disorganization in their lifestyle following the rape; their presence at the emergency ward of the hospital was testimony to that fact. Various factors affected their coping behavior regarding the trauma, i.e., ego strength, social network support, and the way people treated them as victims. This coping and reorganization process began at different times for the individual victims.

Victims did not all experience the same symptoms in the same sequence. What was consistent was that they did experience an acute phase of disorganization; many also experienced mild to moderate symptoms in the reorganization process, as table 2 indicates. Very few victims reported no symptoms. The number of victims over age 30 was small, but the data at least suggest that they might have been more prone to compounded reactions than the younger age groups.

Motor Activity

The long-term effects of the rape generally consisted of an increase in motor activity, especially through changing residence. The move, in order to ensure safety and to facilitate the victim's ability to function in a normal style, was very common. Forty-four of the 92 victims changed residences within a relatively short period of time after the rape. There was also a strong need to get away, and some women took trips to other states or countries.

Changing one's telephone number was a common reaction. It was often changed to an unlisted number. The woman might do this as a precautionary measure or as the result of threatening or obscene telephone calls. The victim was haunted by the fear that the assailant knew where she was and would come back for her.

Another common response was to turn for support to family members not normally seen daily. Forty-eight women made special trips home, which often meant traveling to another city. In most cases, the victim told her parents what had happened, but occasionally the victim contacted her parents for support and did not explain why she was suddenly interested

Table 2.
Severity of Symptoms During Reorganization Process by Age (N = 92)*

	Age (in Years)				
Severity of Symptoms	17–20	21–29	30–39	40–49	50–73
No symptoms: no symptoms reported and symptoms denied when asked about a specific area	7	4	2	0	0
Mild symptoms: minor discomfort with the symptom reported: ability to talk about discomfort and feeling of control over symptom present	12	16	0	2	1
Moderate to severe symptoms: distressing symptoms such as phobic reactions described: ability to function but disturbance in lifestyle present	12	5	1	1	2
Compounded symptoms: symptoms directly related to the rape plus reactivation of symptoms connected with a previously existing condition such as heavy drinking or drug use	7	5	3	3	0
No data available	0	5	4	0	0

* At time of telephone follow-up.

in talking with them or being with them. Twenty-five women turned to close friends for support. Thus 73 of the 92 women had some social network support to which they turned.

Nightmares

Dreams and nightmares could be very upsetting. Twenty-nine of the victims spontaneously described frightening dreams, as illustrated in the following statement.

> I had a terrifying nightmare and shook for two days. I was at work and there was this maniac killer in the store. He killed two of the salesgirls by slitting their throats. I'd gone to set the time clock and when I came back the two girls were dead. I thought I was next. I had to go home. On the way I ran into two girls I knew. We were walking along and we ran into the maniac killer and he was the man who attacked me—he looked like the man. One of the girls held back and said, "No—I'm staying here." I said I knew him and was going to fight him. At this point I woke with the terrible fear of impending doom and fright. I knew the knife part was real because it was the same knife the man held to my throat.

Women reported two types of dreams. One is similar to the above example where the victim wishes to do something but then wakes before acting. As time progressed, the second type occurred: the dream material changed somewhat, and frequently the victim reported mastery in the dream —being able to fight off the assailant. A young woman reported the following dream one month following her rape.

> I had a knife and I was with the guy and I went to stab him and the knife bent. I did it again and he started bleeding and he died. Then I walked away laughing with the knife in my hand.

This dream woke the victim up; she was crying so hard that her mother came in to see what was wrong. The girl stated that in her waking hours she never cries.

Traumatophobia

Sandor Rado coined the term "traumatophobia" to define the phobic reaction to a traumatic situation (13). We saw this phenomenon, which Rado described in war victims, in the rape victim. The phobia develops as a defensive reaction to the circumstances of the rape. The following were the most common phobic reactions among our sample.

Fear of indoors. This occurred in women who had been attacked while sleeping in their beds. As one victim stated, "I feel better outside. I can see what is coming. I feel trapped inside. My fear is being inside, not outside."

Fear of outdoors. This occurred in women who had been attacked outside of their homes. These women felt safe inside but would walk outside only with the protection of another person or only when necessary. As one victim stated, "It is sheer terror for every step I take. I can't wait to get to the safety of my own place."

Fear of being alone. Almost all victims reported fears of being alone after the rape. Often the victim had been attacked while alone, when no one could come to her rescue. One victim said: "I can't stand being alone. I hear every little noise—the windows creaking. I am a bundle of nerves."

Fear of crowds. Many victims were quite apprehensive when they had to be in crowds or ride on public transportation. One 41-year-old victim said:

> I'm still nervous from this, when people come too close—like when I have to go through the trolley station and the crowds are bad. When I am in crowds I get the bad thoughts. I will look over at a guy and if he looks really weird, I will hope something bad will happen to him.

Fear of people behind them. Some victims reported being fearful of people walking behind them. This was often common if the woman had been approached suddenly from behind. One victim said:

> I can't stand to have someone behind me. When I feel someone is behind me, my heart starts pounding. Last week I turned on a guy that was walking in back of me and waited till he walked by. I just couldn't stand it.

Sexual fears. Many women experienced a crisis in their sexual life as a result of the rape. Their normal sexual style had been disrupted. For the women who had had no prior sexual activity, the incident was especially upsetting. For the victims who were sexually active, the fear increased when they were confronted by their husband or boyfriend with resuming sexual relations. One victim said:

> My boyfriend thought it [the rape] might give me a negative feeling to sex and he wanted to be sure it didn't. That night as soon as we were back to the apartment he wanted to make love. I didn't want sex, especially that night. . . . He also admitted he wanted to know if he could make love to me or if he would be repulsed by me and unable to.

This victim and her boyfriend had considerable difficulty resuming many aspects of their relationship besides the sexual part. Many women were unable to resume a normal sexual style during the acute phase and persisted with the difficulty. One victim reported, five months after the assault, "There are times I get hysterical with my boyfriend. I don't want him near me; I get panicked. Sex is OK, but I still feel like screaming."

Clinical Implications

Management of Rape Trauma Syndrome

There are several basic assumptions underlying the model of crisis intervention that we used in counseling the rape victim.

1. The rape represented a crisis in that the woman's style of life was disrupted.

2. The victim was regarded as a "normal" woman who had been functioning adequately prior to the crisis situation.

3. Crisis counseling was the treatment model of choice to return the woman to her previous level of functioning as quickly as possible. The crisis counseling was issue-oriented treatment. Previous problems were not a priority for discussion; in no way was the counseling considered psychotherapy. When other issues of major concern that indicated another treatment model were identified by the victim, referrals were offered if the woman so requested.

4. We took an active role in initiating therapeutic contact as opposed to more traditional methods where the patient is expected to be the initiator. We went to the hospital to see the victim and then contacted her later by telephone.

Management of Compounded Reaction

There were some victims who had either a past or current history of physical, psychiatric, or social difficulties along with the rape trauma syndrome. A minority of the women in our sample were representative of this group. It became quite clear that these women needed more than crisis counseling. For this group, who were known to other therapists, physicians, or agencies, we assumed a secondary position. Support was provided for the rape incident, especially if the woman pressed charges against the assailant, but the counselor worked closely with the other agencies. It was noted that this group developed additional symptoms such as depression, psychotic behavior, psychosomatic disorders, suicidal behavior, and acting-out behavior associated with alcoholism, drug use, and sexual activity.

Management of Silent Rape Reaction

Since a significant proportion of women still do not report a rape, clinicians should be alert to a syndrome that we call the silent reaction to rape. This reaction occurs in the victim who has not told anyone of the rape, who has not settled her feelings and reactions on the issue, and who is carrying a tremendous psychological burden.

Evidence of such a syndrome became apparent to us as a result of life history data. A number of the women in our sample stated that they had been raped or molested at a previous time, often when they were children or adolescents. Often these women had not told anyone of the rape and had just kept the burden within themselves. The current rape reactivated their reaction to the prior experience. It became clear that because they had not talked about the previous rape, the syndrome had continued to develop, and these women had carried unresolved issues with them for years. They would talk as much of the previous rape as they did of the current situation.

A diagnosis of this syndrome should be considered when the clinician observes any of the following symptoms during an evaluation interview.

1. Increasing signs of anxiety as the interview progresses, such as long periods of silence, blocking of associations, minor stuttering, and physical distress.

2. The patient reports sudden marked irritability or actual avoidance of relationships with men or marked change in sexual behavior.

3. History of sudden onset of phobic reactions and fear of being alone, going outside, or being inside alone.

4. Persistent loss of self-confidence and self-esteem, an attitude of self-blame, paranoid feelings, or dreams of violence and/or nightmares.

Clinicians who suspect that the patient was raped in the past should be sure to include questions relevant to the woman's sexual behavior in the evaluation interview and to ask if anyone has ever attempted to assault her. Such questions may release considerable pent-up material relevant to forced sexual activity.

Discussion

The crisis that results when a woman has been sexually assaulted is in the service of self-preservation. The victims in our sample felt that living was better than dying and that was the choice which had to be made. The victims' reactions to the impending threat to their lives is the nucleus around which an adaptive pattern may be noted.

The coping behavior of individuals to life-threatening situations has been documented in the work of such writers as Grinker and Spiegel (14), Lindemann (15), Kübler-Ross (16), and Hamburg (17). Kübler-Ross wrote of the process patients go through to come to terms with the fact of dying. Hamburg wrote of the resourcefulness of patients in facing catastrophic news and discussed a variety of implicit strategies by which patients face threats to life. This broad sequence of the acute phase, group support, and the long-run resolution described by these authors is compatible with the psychological work rape victims must do over time.

The majority of our rape victims were able to reorganize their lifestyle after the acute symptom phase, stay alert to possible threats to their lifestyle, and focus upon protecting themselves from further insult. This latter action was difficult because the world was perceived as a traumatic environment after the assault. As one victim said, "On the exterior I am OK, but inside [I feel] every man is the rapist."

The rape victim was able to maintain a certain equilibrium. In no case did the victim show ego disintegration, bizarre behavior, or self-destructive behavior during the acute phase. As indicated, there were a few victims who did regress to a previous level of impaired functioning four to six weeks following the assault.

With the increasing reports of rape, this is not a private syndrome. It should be a societal concern, and its treatment should be a public charge. Professionals will be called upon increasingly to assist the rape victim in the acute and long-term reorganization processes.

References

1 Federal Bureau of Investigation: *Uniform Crime Reports for the United States*. Washington, DC, U.S. Department of Justice, 1970.

2 *Report of District of Columbia Task Force on Rape*. Washington, DC, District of Columbia City Council, 1973, p 7 (processed).

3 AMIR, M. *Patterns of Forcible Rape*. Chicago, University of Chicago Press, 1971.

4 MACDONALD, J. *Rape: Offenders and Their Victims*. Springfield, Ill., Charles C. Thomas, 1971.

5 COHEN, M., GAROFALO, R., BOUCHER, R. et al. "The Psychology of Rapists." *Seminars in Psychiatry* 3:307–327, 1971.

6 SUTHERLAND, S., SCHERL, D. "Patterns of Response Among Victims of

Rape." *Am. J. Orthopsychiatry* 40:503–511, 1970.

7 HAYMAN, C., LANZA, C. "Sexual Assault on Women and Girls." *Am. J. Obstet. Gynecol.* 109:408–486, 1971.

8 HALLECK, S. "The Physician's Role in Management of Victims of Sex Offenders." *J.A.M.A.* 180:273–278, 1962.

9 FACTOR, M. "A Woman's Psychological Reaction to Attempted Rape." *Psychoanal. Q.* 23:243–244, 1954.

10 HOLMSTROM, L. L., BURGESS, A. W. "Rape: the Victim Goes on Trial." Read at the 68th annual meeting of the American Sociological Association, New York, N.Y., Aug. 27–30, 1973.

11 HOLMSTROM, L. L., BURGESS, A. W. "Rape: the Victim and the Criminal

Justice System." Read at the First International Symposium on Victimology, Jerusalem, Sept. 2–6, 1973.

12 BURGESS, A. W., HOLMSTROM, L. L. "The Rape Victim in the Emergency Ward." *Am. J. Nursing* 73:1741–1745, 1973.

13 RADO, S. "Pathodynamics and Treatment of Traumatic War Neurosis (Traumatophobia)." *Psychosom. Med.* 4:362–368, 1948.

14 GRINKER, R. R., SPIEGEL, J. P. *Men Under Stress.* Philadelphia, Blakiston, 1945.

15 LINDEMANN, E. "Symptomatology and Management of Acute Grief." *Am. J. Psychiatry* 101:141–148, 1944.

16 KÜBLER-ROSS, E. "On Death and Dying." *J.A.M.A.* 221:174–179, 1972.

17 HAMBURG, D. "A Perspective on Coping Behavior." *Arch. Gen. Psychiatry* 17:277–284, 1967.

Vasectomy

Implications of Vasectomy for Social Work Practice

Sarah F. Hafemann and Catherine S. Chilman

It has been estimated that over three million living Americans have had a vasectomy,[1] and the popularity of this procedure as a method of contraception has been growing in recent years. It is important that social workers become well informed on this subject so that they may more effectively carry out their various roles as counselors, educators, and social planners. However, little information has appeared in the professional social work journals about vasectomy and its effects. This article presents an overview of medical, social, and psychological research. Popular attitudes as reflected in the popular press are also surveyed, and some implications for social work practice are suggested.

Medical Aspects of Vasectomy

Vasectomy is a simple, safe surgical procedure performed to sterilize the male. It consists of cutting or blocking the tube (vas or vas deferens) through which sperm pass to the penis. As a method of male sterilization, vasectomy has been widely performed since the 1930s;[2] and today throughout the world it is the most commonly performed operation on the adult male.[3]

Physicians vary widely in the qualifications they demand of patients requesting a vasectomy for sterilization. Some doctors perform the operation with no evaluation of the patient's life situation or personality. Others may require a stable family unit, minimum ages for husband and wife, at least two children including at least one son, a personal interview, the consent of

Reprinted from *Social Casework*, Vol. 55 (June, 1974), pp. 343–351, by permission of the authors and the Family Service Association of America.

[1] Gilbert Kasirsky, *Vasectomy, Manhood and Sex* (New York: Springer, 1972), p. 17.

[2] W. S. Haynes, Vasectomy, *Medical Journal of Australia*, 20: 1045–48 (May 1967).

[3] Stanwood S. Schmidt, Vasectomy: Indications, Technic, and Reversibility, *Fertility and Sterility*, 19: 192–96 (March–April 1968).

both husband and wife, a psychiatric evaluation, and a consultation with another physician.[4]

There may or may not be a physician-required waiting period before the actual operation. Most vasectomies are performed in the doctor's office under local anesthetic. The patient prepares himself at home by bathing and shaving the scrotal area. Then, in the office, the area is cleansed with antiseptic and the doctor manipulates the vas to separate it from other tissues so that it is positioned immediately under the skin. Local anesthetic is then injected into the skin and around the vas. The manipulation and injection are the only parts of the procedure that may be uncomfortable. After the anesthetic has taken effect, an incision of three-quarters to one inch is made on one side of the scrotum and a segment of the vas is lifted out.

Early methods involved cutting the vas and tying it to itself with the two ends pointing in opposite directions.[5] A more recent development includes the use of small tantalum clips to close off the vas.[6] There has been considerable criticism of the earlier method because it seems to lead to a greater chance of the formation of sperm granuloma (small nodules appearing around the cut end of the vas where sperm cells may be escaping) and eventual recanalization (forming of a new channel between the closed ends of the vas).[7] After the vas has been closed off, only a few stitches are required to close the incision in the scrotum. After one side has been completed, the procedure is performed on the other. Some physicians prescribe a sedative or tranquilizer for the patient to take before the operation. Any pain after the anesthetic wears off can usually be managed by aspirin and codeine.

After the operation, the patient should wear a scrotal supporter to prevent strain on the wound. Most men can go back to work the day after the operation, and many vasectomies are scheduled for Friday mornings so the patient will have a weekend in which to recuperate. Intercourse may be resumed one to ten days after the operation.

It is crucial to realize that sterility does not result immediately. Even though no new spermatozoa will be released, there will be mature sperm remaining in the male's reproductive tract. For this reason, sperm counts must be made before other contraceptive measures can be safely abandoned. Samples are obtained either by masturbation or the use of a condom during intercourse. There has been continuing debate whether the samples should be requested after a certain amount of time or after a certain number of ejaculations. Research has shown that approximately 68 percent of any

[4] Harold Lear, Vasectomy—A Note of Concern, *Journal of the American Medical Association*, 219: 1206–07 (February 28, 1972); and D. M. Potts and G. I. M. Swyer, Effectiveness and Risks of Birth-control Methods, *British Medical Bulletin*, 26: 26–32 (January 1970).

[5] Kasirsky, *Vasectomy, Manhood and Sex*, p. 52.

[6] William M. Moss, A Sutureless Technic for Bilateral Partial Vasectomy, *Fertility and Sterility*, 23: 33–37 (January 1972).

[7] Stanwood S. Schmidt, Vasectomy, *Journal of the American Medical Association*, 206: 522 (April 19, 1971); and Donald J. Dodds, Reanastomosis of the Vas Deferens, *Journal of the American Medical Association*, 220: 1498 (June 12, 1972).

remaining sperm is ejaculated at each emission.[8] The suggestion has been made that the first sperm count be made after ten ejaculations instead of waiting twelve to sixteen weeks after the operation.[9]

The operation is considered to be extremely safe in terms of mortality and is also the most effective method of birth control, with a failure rate of .15 pregnancies per year per 100 couples; this rate is slightly lower than that for tubal ligation and considerably lower than for any other contraceptive method.[10]

As far as morbidity rates for vasectomy are concerned, there is great variation depending on interpretation by the patient or the doctor.[11] The most common immediate complications of vasectomy are infection, bruising, and pain. All three can be kept to a minimum by careful surgical technique.[12] Study has shown that these problems are bothersome to only a small proportion of vasectomy patients. At present, the most significant long-range complication appears to be formation of spermatic granulomas which may occur in the epididymus or at the cut end of the vas any time after vasectomy. These may become painful and require surgical removal.

Perhaps the most disconcerting complication of vasectomy is spontaneous recanalization of the vas, with the possibility of a resultant impregnation. The risk of this happening is about one-half to one percent.[13] Some doctors feel that what actually may happen is simple failure to maintain other contraceptive measures until sterility is finally achieved, but others disagree with this viewpoint.[14]

Possible long-term effects of vasectomy on the hormonal balance have also been investigated. Of major importance is the fact that the production of sperm is not affected by vasectomy.[15] Not only do sperm continue to be produced, but also testosterone, the male sex hormone.[16]

There is a sizable body of medical literature available on the subject of reanastomosis (the surgical reversal of sterility due to vasectomy). This operation is extremely difficult to perform and the success rate tends to be low.[17]

[8] Matthew Freund et al., Disappearance Rate of Spermatozoa from the Ejaculate Following Vasectomy, *Fertility and Sterility*, 20: 163–70 (January–February 1969).

[9] Schmidt, Vasectomy, p. 522.

[10] Joseph E. Davis, Vasectomy, *American Journal of Nursing*, 72: 509–13 (March 1972).

[11] Davis, Vasectomy, p. 509.

[12] Stanwood S. Schmidt, Technics and Complications of Elective Vasectomy: The Role of Spermatic Granuloma in Spontaneous Recanalization, *Fertility and Sterility*, 17: 467–81 (July–August 1966).

[13] Davis, Vasectomy, p. 511.

[14] C. D. Muller, Consideration of Sterilization Vasectomy, *Northwest Medicine*, 54: 1,427–30 (December 1955).

[15] R. S. Grewal and M. S. Sachan, Changes in Testicle After Vasectomy: An Experimental Study, *International Surgery*, 49: 460–62 (May 1968).

[16] Raymond G. Bunge, Plasma Testisterone Levels in Man Before and After Vasectomy, *Investigative Urology*, 10: 9 (July 1972).

[17] David Rosenbloom, Reversal of Sterility Due to Vasectomy, *Fertility and Sterility*, 7: 540–45 (November-December 1956).

With restoration of fertility so difficult, it has been proposed that men could protect themselves against the need to have the operation reversed by freezing some of their sperm and placing it in a sperm bank in case another child were wanted at a later date. Although the techniques of sperm banking have been developed, there has been little research on patient demand for this service.

Medical opinion has given greater acceptance to vasectomy in recent years. In 1968, the American Medical Association examined the reasons doctors cited for not performing vasectomies—legal or religious considerations and concern for psychiatric trauma. This editorial concluded that vasectomy for reason of contraception alone should be available to couples who did not display psychiatric contraindications.[18]

Psychological Aspects of Vasectomy

Any couple's experience with vasectomy is complex, with many factors influencing their response to this method of birth control. The research on the psychological aspects of vasectomy reflects the difficulty of studying such subjective phenomena. Much of the work has been colored by the individual bias of the investigator. The relative lack of valid and reliable studies in this area has been a serious omission in the literature of medicine and the behavioral sciences. Work already done can start to answer some of the questions related to vasectomy but a great deal more research is needed.

The medical literature includes several studies reported by doctors who have done vasectomies in their private practices. For the most part, the studies show overwhelming approval of the operation on the part of the patients. These studies, however, have many shortcomings. Usually only surface questions are asked, such as "How would you rate your enjoyment of sexual intercourse since the operation?" and "Would you have the operation if you had it to do all over again?"[19] Characteristically, these studies are conducted over a short period of time, usually six months to a year after the operation. Often the questionnaires do not include open-ended questions but only a checklist for the respondent to complete. It is further reported that many men do not go to their regular family physician for this operation and therefore are not as likely to return to the doctor who performed the actual surgery if difficulties arise.[20]

The studies undertaken by psychiatrists and psychologists specifically to investigate psychosexual results of vasectomy also tend to be unsatisfactory. One of the difficulties is the bias introduced by Freudian theory. Freud's

[18] Voluntary Male Sterility, *Journal of the American Medical Association*, 204: 821–22 (May 27, 1968).

[19] Pauline Jackson et al., A Male Sterilization Clinic, *British Medical Journal*, 4: 295–97 (October 31, 1970).

[20] Elzena Barnes and Glenna B. Johnson, Effects of Vasectomy on Marriage Relationships: A Descriptive Analysis of 26 Cases Seen in Marriage Counseling by Family Service–Travelers Aid, Des Moines, Iowa, 1964 (unpublished).

teachings regarding the Oedipal complex and castration anxiety predispose many researchers to expect pathology to result from vasectomy and thus to direct their investigations toward possible pathological outcomes. Many of these studies are further weakened by the use of very small samples, with the heightened possibility of sampling error. Adequate control groups were not set up in a number of investigations. As with the doctors' studies discussed above, many of these studies have not been conducted over a sufficient length of time.

In addition to the methodological difficulties with much of the published research, a new problem has been introduced in our understanding of this aspect of vasectomy. The rapid increase in the number of men undergoing this surgery and the seeming acceptance of this method of birth control may drastically alter many psychological and social effects of male sterilization. As vasectomy becomes increasingly accepted throughout society, the lessened negative cultural sanctions may make the vasectomized male feel less deviant or defensive. Earlier studies that revealed temporary adverse social-psychological effects for some males might yield fewer negative findings if they were carried out today.

The best-known and most careful research in this area was undertaken by David A. Rodgers and Frederick J. Ziegler. Their first article reports on a group of forty-eight California males who underwent vasectomy. Preoperative tests showed that this sample was "much more representative of the stable, productive, successful group in the culture than either the emotionally disturbed or the economically and socially improvident group" and they appeared to be "motivated primarily by rational considerations and were relatively free of neurotic concerns about the consequences of the operation."[21] A follow-up study of thirty-five of these men between one and two years postoperatively found that although they expressed almost unanimous satisfaction with the operation, the Minnesota Multiphasic Personality Inventory (MMPI) scores indicated evidence of increased psychological disturbance for some of them. The authors suggested that preoperative hypochondriasis or concern over masculinity may be predictive of difficulties following vasectomy.[22]

Rodgers and Ziegler continued their work with a larger study involving forty-two couples who chose vasectomy and thirty-nine couples who chose ovulation suppression pills as their method of birth control. Two subgroups of twenty-two couples each—closely matched in terms of age, early sexual history, education, and income—were also studied. Initial testing and interviews were conducted, and follow-up testing and psychiatric interviews were conducted two years later. When the vasectomy group was compared to the pill group, the first was found to do more poorly, on the

---

[21] David A. Rodgers et al., Sociopsychological Characteristics of Patients Obtaining Vasectomies from Urologists, *Marriage and Family Living*, 25: 335 (August 1963).

[22] David A. Rodgers et al., A Longitudinal Study of the Psycho-Social Effects of Vasectomy, *Journal of Marriage and the Family*, 27: 59–64 (February 1965).

average, in the areas of sexual and psychiatric adjustment and marital satisfaction. Some of the vasectomized men emphasized masculine role behavior which called for modifications in their wife's behavior and in the marriage itself. "We thus infer that the vasectomy husbands are more vulnerable to the threats of the typical husband-wife rivalries than they were preoperatively."[23] In a later discussion of these findings, the authors suggest that the vasectomized men tended to avoid behavior that might call into question either their manliness or the appropriateness of the operation. In so doing they showed an increase in culturally approved masculine behavior, along with a decrease in the kind of behavioral flexibility that would be most conducive to a happy personal life and comfortable marriage.[24]

Despite research evidence of poorer average psychological functioning, the vasectomy group expressed satisfaction with the operation and tended to blame other events for changes in their personal or marital lives. The study further reported that the vasectomy couples felt that the preoperative interview was quite useful in reducing or eliminating confusion about the operation. The postoperative interview was also reported by some to have improved understanding and communication between husband and wife. The authors suggest that such discussion may attenuate the potential traumatic impact of vasectomy.

In attempting to identify the causes of the poorer adjustment of the vasectomy group, a study of prevailing cultural attitudes about vasectomy was undertaken in the mid-1960s. Projective tests were given to a group of seventeen couples of a Protestant church group and 127 undergraduate psychology students to determine their attitudes toward couples using oral contraceptives or vasectomy. The couple using vasectomy was seen in a less favorable light by both groups, but there was no consistent characteristic ascribed to the vasectomy couple. According to the authors, a major problem about this form of contraception for the vasectomized male is the nonspecificity of the negative cultural judgment. Thus, the judgment "could never be completely disconfirmed [sic]."[25]

In a follow-up study, the researchers noted a return to virtual similarity between the oral contraceptive and vasectomy groups over four years' time. Differences in scores on the MMPI and the California Psychological Inventory decreased for both groups of husbands and wives. The investigators expressed some surprise that, in light of some of the earlier studies, they did not find more sizable long-range changes in the psychological functioning of the vasectomy couples. Although the sample was too small to develop predictive capability adequately, it appears that the earlier impression that

[23] Frederick J. Ziegler, David A. Rodgers, and Sali Ann Kriegsman, Effect of Vasectomy on Psychological Functioning, *Psychosomatic Medicine*, 28: 62 (January–February 1966).

[24] David A. Rodgers, Frederick J. Ziegler, and Nissim Levy, Prevailing Cultural Attitudes About Vasectomy: A Possible Explanation of Postoperative Psychological Response, *Psychosomatic Medicine*, 29: 367–75 (July–August 1967).

[25] Ibid., p. 373.

hypochondriacal men or men insecure about their masculinity are unsuited to vasectomy was not validated four years postoperatively. The investigators also stressed that the extensive contact with the study team which provided opportunities to ventilate and discuss areas of concern may have prevented some adverse reactions.[26] It should be recalled, however, that Ziegler and his colleagues studied only a small group of couples, that these people were generally middle-class and economically secure, and that extensive counseling may well have been a factor in mitigating possible negative aftereffects. So far as we now know, the ultimate effects of vasectomy on personal and marital adjustments are not likely to be different from those associated with use of oral contraceptives.

The task of investigating the psychological ramifications of vasectomy is not yet complete, but several old wives' tales may have been disproved. Research findings show that, in all likelihood, vasectomy does not cure sexual problems. Although release from the fear of an unwanted pregnancy may increase a couple's pleasure in lovemaking, a vasectomy apparently does not cure frigidity, impotence, or premature ejaculation. Vasectomy seems not to increase or decrease infidelity, divorce, or separation.[27] It also does not appear that men are pressured to have vasectomies by overbearing wives.

Changing Public Attitudes

It has been suggested that cultural attitudes influence men's adjustment after vasectomy. An examination of the popular press, from 1960 to the present, provides ample evidence of a shift in public opinion about sterilization.

Throughout the early 1960s, vasectomy gained in popularity. In the five-year period of 1959–1964, the incidence of vasectomy doubled. Attitudes changed slowly, however; even in the mid-1960s "to most Americans there [was] something peculiarly disturbing about the words 'abortion' and 'sterilization.' They [were] uncomfortable words, not exactly obscene but not polite either."[28] Advocates of voluntary sterilization did not propagandize so much as they simply attempted to break down prejudices.

The spectacular increase in vasectomy began in 1967 with the first warnings from British doctors of the possibility of blood clots forming as a result of taking birth control pills. The number of vasectomies has doubled every year since then. Several other factors were also responsible: the 1965 Supreme Court ruling in *Griswold* v. *Connecticut* which expanded the right of

---

[26] Frederick J. Ziegler, David A. Rodgers, and Robert J. Prentiss, Psychological Response to Vasectomy, *Archives of General Psychiatry*, 21: 46–54 (July 1969).

[27] D. A. Rodgers and Frederick J. Ziegler, Changes in Sexual Behavior Consequent to Use of Noncoital Procedures of Contraception, *Psychosomatic Medicine*, 30: 495–505 (September–October 1968).

[28] Walter Goodman, Abortion and Sterilization: The Search for Answers, *Redbook*, October 1965, pp. 70–71.

privacy to include birth control; the 1968 decision by Planned Parenthood–World Population to include voluntary sterilization in its program; and the decisions of the United States Department of Health, Education, and Welfare and the Blue Cross–Blue Shield to approve payments for voluntary sterilization. The decline of American puritanism and the growing concern about the problems of overpopulation also influenced the rising popular acceptance of sterilization. A crucial step in the changing of public opinion was the gradual conversion of the medical profession. In 1968, an editorial in the *Journal of the American Medical Association* declared vasectomy to be "safe, quick, effective and legal" and took doctors to task for not performing the operation in the absence of certain contraindications.[29]

The 1970 Senate hearing on the safety of the birth control pill stimulated a further surge of interest in vasectomy. Articles describing vasectomy and discussing its tremendous gain in popularity appeared in numerous popular magazines. The information contained in these articles appeared to be medically accurate; it was stressed that vasectomy is not castration and does not alter sex drive or performance. Husbands who had had vasectomies were portrayed as intelligent, considerate, and assured of their manhood.

The 1970 National Fertility Studies reported:

> By 1970 sterilization was the first choice of contracepting [sic] couples where the wife was 30–44 years old (25 percent, as against 21 percent for the pill); and among couples of all ages intending no more children, sterilization was second only to the pill.[30]

These data reflect practices antedating the Senate hearings on possible adverse side effects of the birth control pill. Statistics obtained today would probably show an even higher use of sterilization.

Female sterilization is more prevelant among blacks than whites and is used by 21 percent of the fertile black couples who desire no more children versus 18 percent for whites. However, vasectomy is nine times more prevalent among whites than blacks. Blacks and low-income people may be reluctant to seek vasectomies because of misinformation about the consequences of the operation. Vasectomy, as opposed to tubal ligation, is most acceptable to low-parity white couples with above-average education and income. Fears of genocide are frequently expressed by some black males. In general, cultural innovations tend to be picked up first by urban people at higher socioeconomic levels.

The pendulum has now begun to swing away from a wholesale endorsement of vasectomy. Concern has been expressed that vasectomy may become a fad. William A. Nolen has urged that couples consider in advance all aspects of vasectomy, including fears regarding the operation, its near-irreversibility, the possibility of divorce or death of spouse or of children,

---

[29] Voluntary Male Sterility, p. 822.

[30] Harriet B. Presser and Larry L. Bumpass, The Acceptability of Contraceptive Sterilization Among U.S. Couples: 1970, *Family Planning Perspectives*, 6: 18–26 (October 1972).

and assumptions that the operation would, of itself, solve marital problems.[31] The issue of formation of sperm antibodies in the vasectomized male has signaled the beginning of a reappraisal of the safety of the operation. Additional medical research addressed to this problem has not yet made its way into the popular press.

At present there are still many couples who have completed their families or have chosen to forego parenthood completely but have not chosen a permanent method of birth control. The incidence of vasectomy is likely to increase as more of these couples learn what vasectomy involves, talk to friends or relatives who have had the operation, and become concerned about the possible deficiences of other birth control methods.

Implications for Social Work Practice

Although not exhaustive, the social and psychological research on vasectomy can provide important leads for social workers. The implications of the available research touch on the areas of prevasectomy screening and postoperative follow-up, marital discord after vasectomy, pregnancy after vasectomy, and the desire for reversal of sterilization.

These implications might well apply to social workers in such activities as program-planning and program development, education, and counseling. They may also apply to social workers in a variety of settings: medical, family service, marriage counseling, family life education, and so on. As literature reviewed in this article suggests, vasectomy involves more than a medical procedure. Social workers, as well as physicians and other human service professionals, have important contributions to make. The social worker involved in such a team approach will require additional training beyond the basic understanding of human sexuality and birth control that all social workers should possess. The training necessary for social workers who frequently work with couples and individuals who may be considering vasectomy should include advanced understanding of vasectomy and alternative contraceptive methods and techniques, including the experience of observing a vasectomy operation; effective counseling and therapy skills; and, finally, a clear and continuing awareness of one's bias and values and those of any sponsoring agency. Implications for counseling and education include consideration of factors related to both prevasectomy decision-making and postoperative adjustments.

Social and psychological prevasectomy screening should probably be conducted in a joint interview with both partners, preferably by a male-female interview team unless special circumstances indicate other approaches. To rule out possible undue influence of one spouse by the other, each should also be interviewed separately. The counselor should explore the reasons both the male and his spouse have for seeking a vasectomy as well as their

---

[31] William A. Nolen, Vasectomy: A Cautionary Note, *McCall's*, June 1972, p. 60.

related attitudes, feelings, and understandings. Before the vasectomy, the couple should be encouraged to consider how their decision might be affected by divorce or death of a spouse or the illness or death of their children, if they have any. Alternatives of adoption and sperm-banking should be explained realistically. (At present, frozen sperm does not seem to last indefinitely, and adoptable children are becoming less available.) Couples should be discouraged from thinking of the surgical reversal of vasectomy as a possibility, since the chance of restoration of fertility is so low. The final decision should be left until the couple have been fully informed, have achieved a clear understanding of the possible complications, and have examined their feelings regarding future changes in their life situation. The social worker should be clear that the couple also have thorough knowledge of alternative birth control measures.

No scale has yet been devised to predict which couples may regret vasectomy or have related social or psychological problems. Contraindications to vasectomy include such factors as impulsiveness, high levels of related anxiety on the part of either partner, hopes that a vasectomy will improve the marital relationship, or a decision based on an overzealous commitment to population control or women's liberation ideology. Social workers should not be too quick, however, to reject couples who manifest some degree of anxiety, insecurity, or difficulty in their relationship, because (1) any surgery is likely to be accompanied by some anxiety; (2) no intimate relationship is completely free of problems; and (3) no individual is completely free of sex-role confusion or insecurity.

In their contributions to the formulation of administrative policy, as well as in their handling of screening interviews, social workers will need to be aware of their own biases about vasectomies for certain couples, for example, very young or childless couples. A possible result of a too-rigid policy regarding acceptance or exclusion is that many couples would seek the operation from physicians who have no screening procedures at all and no provision for follow-up. Policies can be flexible if the couple are provided the opportunity to discuss fully their expectations and anxieties, if the couple have adequate knowledge of vasectomy and of alternative methods of contraception, and if they appear to be comfortable and firm in their decision.

Ideally, every couple who choose vasectomy as a method of birth control should be encouraged to come in for a postoperative interview at the time of the second sperm count. This interview would allow for discussion and clarification of any anxieties or problems that have arisen or may be foreseen. If pre- and postoperative interviews with a knowledgeable and skilled counselor like a social worker become common, it is possible that the rate of postoperative complications might decline.

According to the available research evidence, these postoperative problems involve sexual dysfunction, pregnancy, and a desire for reanastomosis. Sexual dysfunction after vasectomy is usually of psychological origin. For example, if the fear of pregnancy is used by a couple to restrict their sexual activities, a vasectomy eliminates their rationale. With this limit removed, they may find that one or both of them may not wish to engage in more frequent intercourse for a variety of reasons. Skilled marriage counseling may help the couple resolve problems in this area.

According to available evidence, the likelihood of pregnancy following vasectomy is very small. Spontaneous reanastomosis occurs rarely. If the male has received laboratory confirmation of his sterility, the chance of viable sperm remaining in his reproductive tract is also minimal. In the rare case that pregnancy does occur after vasectomy, it may be accompanied by suspicion of the wife's infidelity or the wife's fear that she is suspect. Skilled social workers may be helpful in these cases.

Ill-advised physicians have frequently let the couple work such problems out by themselves; social workers should not ignore such problems and can perform a useful function. A first step is a repeat sperm count to assess the possibility of a reanastomosis. The question of abortion may also be raised. Social pressure on the couple may be great if family and friends have been informed that a vasectomy had been obtained. Some couples may not wish to have a sperm count and will assume that the pregnancy resulted from spontaneous reanastomosis, rather than confront directly the question of infidelity.

Inevitably, some couples will change their minds about vasectomy and will request reanastomosis. The social worker should not hold out bright promise to these people. Vasectomy must be considered as permanent. Because possibility of surgical correction of vasectomy is so slight and because the surgery is so much more complex than the original vasectomy, it may be more fruitful to explore the significance of the reemergent desire for children and the acceptability of substituting other goals or satisfactions. In the case of the death of a child, the desire for another child may be a manifestation of grief and a sense of loss which, with help, can be accepted without the need to restore fertility. In cases of remarriage after divorce or the death of a spouse, the desire to cement the marriage may be expressed by other means than conceiving a child. If a couple's economic or emotional situation has changed and they feel themselves able to care for additional children, adoption or foster care may be suggested.

Most social workers will see problems related to vasectomy in the context of problems within the marriage and family. Ziegler and fellow researchers have suggested that vasectomy may produce changes in the husband's and wife's behavior that may increase marital tension.[32] These changes reflect a polarization of male and female behavior as a result of the male's trying to prove that his masculinity is not impaired. Recent changes in public opinion that give greater social approval to vasectomy may have reduced the likelihood of this possible effect. Social workers should check for increased sex-role rigidity in couples who experience increased marital tension after vasectomy. Techniques useful in marital and family counseling are apt to be appropriate here.

[32] Ziegler, Rodgers, and Kriegsman, Effect of Vasectomy on Psychological Functioning, p. 62.

Within the society as a whole and in their roles as program planners and educators, social workers can contribute to policies that provide freedom of individual decision-making regarding vasectomies and access to high-quality related services for people at all income levels. Recent court cases have affirmed the right of a woman to be sterilized at her own request.[33] There has not been a comparable decision on vasectomy. It is desirable that freedom and rights in this area be scrupulously maintained.

As in many other areas, it is important that social workers not project their own values or bias on their clients. Properly informed, they can join with other professionals in educating the public about vasectomy and in assuring that adequate related services, including counseling, are made available to all persons who desire them.

[33] Vivian Cadden, Very Private Decision, *Good Housekeeping*, May 1972, p. 85.

The Unmarried Mother

Reconsiderations in Casework Treatment of the Unmarried Mother

Herbert S. Strean

An historical overview of social work's philosophy about and orientation to the unmarried mother yields several sequential trends. Until the early 1920's virtually the sole concern of the social agency was the unmarried mother's infant and help to the mother herself was rarely considered. As dynamic psychiatry made its inroads and began to influence social work's thinking and activity, the unmarried mother began to be appreciated in her own right and the purposiveness of her behavior was pondered. With the fairly recent advent of ego psychology and the social sciences, the unmarried mother's complete role network—her relationships to various subsystems, e.g., ethnic group, kinship ties, and so on—has become part of the caseworker's psychosocial diagnosis and enriched his treatment plan for her and her child.[1]

Concomitant with the impact of sociology, anthropology, and social psychology on social work has been the intensification of the profession's sense of social responsibility.[2] The cluster of economic, social, psychological, and health variables that are now seen as impinging on the unmarried mother have pointed to a more pressing need for the provision of community resources.[3] While the social planner and policy-maker have presented valid arguments reiterating that effective casework alone cannot be considered the complete answer to the unmarried mother's plight,[4] as Perlman has pointed out, casework is not dead and individualized services will probably

---

Reprinted with permission of the author and the National Association of Social Workers, from *Social Work*, Vol. 13, No. 4 (October, 1968), pp. 91–100.

[1] *See* Jane K. Goldsmith, "The Unmarried Mother's Search for Standards," *Social Casework*, Vol. 48, No. 2 (February 1957), pp. 69–73; and Vera Shlakman, "Unmarried Parenthood: An Approach to Social Policy," *Social Casework*, Vol. 47, No. 8 (October 1966), pp. 494–502.

[2] Herbert H. Aptekar, "Education for Social Responsibility," *Journal of Education for Social Work*, Vol. 2, No. 2 (Fall 1966), pp. 5–11.

[3] Martin Wright, "Comprehensive Services for Adolescent Unwed Mothers," *Children*, Vol. 13, No. 5 (September–October 1966), pp. 171–176.

[4] *See* Aptekar, *op. cit.*

always be necessary for some people even if optimum provision of resources could be achieved.[5]

It is incumbent on caseworkers not only to locate where they may legitimately offer their expertise in helping the unmarried mother, but constantly to scrutinize their method and avoid the danger to which Kadushin has pointed, namely, the acceptance of traditional practices in lieu of tested theory.[6] It is the purpose of this paper to evaluate some of the conventional diagnostic hypotheses and classical treatment plans that have evolved in casework with the unmarried mother; certain modifications in casework interventions will be proposed that may more accurately meet certain of the unmarried mother's maturational needs and more expediently enhance certain aspects of her psychosocial functioning.

Review of the Literature

Analysis of the past two decades of social work literature reveals that periodicals in the field have been replete with data on the unmarried mother. Most of the articles have aimed at sensitizing social workers to the subtleties and intricacies of the unmarried mother's personality and/or enriching interventions for her. Virtually every paper or book has begun with the axiom that a multitude of factors contribute to a young woman's becoming pregnant out of wedlock.

Until recently, the search for causes has utilized the metapsychological framework of psychoanalysis and the theme pervading most of the literature in the 1940's and '50's was that the unmarried mother had a conflicted relationship with her own mother and was improperly nurtured at early levels of development. In addition to being the recipient of fragmented mothering, she was seen as having often experienced her father as withdrawn and cold.[7] Common to most of these young women has been an alleged narcissistic character structure, i.e., the girls have been described as extremely preoccupied with their own infantile wishes, which they have had to discharge impulsively. The baby she conceived has frequently been considered to be a narcissistic extension of the unmarried mother and her wish to mother the baby seen as similar to psychologically mothering herself.[8]

The level of ego development of most of these girls has been viewed as

---

[5] Helen Harris Perlman, "Casework Is Dead," *Social Casework*, Vol. 48, No. 1 (January 1967), pp. 22–25.

[6] Alfred Kadushin, "The Knowledge Base of Social Work," in Alfred J. Kahn, ed., *Issues in American Social Work* (New York: Columbia University Press, 1959), pp. 39–79.

[7] *See* A. Ferdinand Bonan, "Psychoanalytic Implications in Treating Unmarried Mothers with Narcissistic Character Structures," *Social Casework*, Vol. 44, No. 6 (June 1963), pp. 323–330; and Joseph E. Lifschutz, Theodosia B. Stewart, and Ada M. Harrison, "Psychiatric Consultation in the Public Assistance Agency," *Social Casework*, Vol. 39, No. 1 (January 1958), pp. 3–8.

[8] Bonan, *op. cit.*; Jane G. Judge, "Casework with the Unmarried Mother in a Family Agency," *Social Casework*, Vol. 32, No. 1 (January 1951), pp. 7–14.

"infantile" or "primitive." "They also feel very deprived or depraved."[9] According to most authors, they have not developed mature methods of resolving conflicts and are so self-absorbed that they cannot love others.[10] The young woman has often reported a feeling of being an "ugly duckling" most of her life and conceiving a baby has been in part an attempt to make restitution for her own defects.[11]

The unmarried mother as observed by most psychoanalytically and social work–oriented professionals appears to manifest severe superego lacunae and therefore has been considered delinquent in internalizing societal norms and standards. Not having witnessed in her own home the positive values inherent in a wholesome husband-wife or parent-child relationship, she has been declared incapable of setting standards for her own behavior.[12] Often she has come to the social agency during her fourth or fifth month of pregnancy, seeking specific services; she has tended to withdraw from contact when a plan for the baby has been concluded. Few have taken kindly to the idea of regular casework sessions and if the client has appeared well motivated for continuing treatment, she has been viewed as suspect. The unmarried mother has frequently been described as resistant, defensive, and unresponsive to treatment, usually demanding immediate pragmatic solutions and becoming angry if these are not forthcoming.[13]

The treatment of choice for unmarried mothers has been an ongoing relationship with a female caseworker. Often deserted by the putative father and having experienced emotional abandonment by her own mother, the client allegedly needs "a motherly person who will serve as a refuge during a time of stress."[14] A woman caseworker, it has been concluded, can most appropriately serve as "a healthy object for identification, making it possible [for the client] to accept herself as a woman."[15] Since four out of five unmarried mothers who come to a social agency give the baby up for adoption, it has been alleged that for the mother to give her baby to a woman caseworker is like "making up" with her own mother and thus finalizing a bad experience.[16] (Of the unmarried mothers who do not come to agencies, many do not give their babies up for adoption; of this group, most—especially young Negro women—turn the baby over to their own mothers.[17])

[9] Bonan, op. cit.
[10] Lifschutz, Stewart, and Harrison, op. cit.
[11] Judge, op. cit.
[12] Goldsmith, op. cit.
[13] Rose Bernstein, "The Maternal Role in the Treatment of Unmarried Mothers," Social Work, Vol. 8, No. 1 (January 1963), pp. 58–65; and Bernstein, "Are We Still Stereotyping the Unmarried Mother?" Social Work, Vol. 5, No. 3 (July 1960), pp. 22–28.
[14] Peter Blos, On Adolescence (New York: Free Press, 1961), pp. 27–28.
[15] Lifschutz, Stewart, and Harrison, op. cit., p. 50.
[16] Helen L. Friedman, "The Mother-Daughter Relationship: Its Potential in Treatment of Young Unwed Mothers," Social Casework, Vol. 47, No. 8 (October 1966), pp. 502–507.
[17] Wright, op. cit.

During the last several years the social work field—as reflected in its literature—has slightly altered its focus on the unmarried mother. Instead of concentrating almost exclusively on the client's psychological motives and internal dynamics, the field has been more preoccupied with unmarried motherhood as a social problem, shown more concern for the culture and subculture in which the young woman resides, considered the significant others in her environment, and been quite sensitive to the social values impinging on her.[18] The Negro unmarried mother in particular has received much consideration; she has been reported to be more indifferent and less sensitive to the stigma of illegitimacy because of a greater tolerance of it in her subculture.[19] Although frequently turning over the care of her child to her own mother, the Negro unmarried mother is nonetheless ascribed "an exceptional maternal capacity" and a sexually fertile constitution.[20]

Although the increments to social work's knowledge of the unmarried mother have been substantial and despite valiant attempts on the part of many skilled workers to involve the client in a meaningful casework relationship, as Friedman stated recently, "We are still powerless to alter the script."[21] These clients frequently remain resistant to social work intervention, in many cases seek service but not understanding, usually do not continue treatment after the baby is born, and it has not been uncommon for them to repeat the same experience that brought them to the agency in the first place.[22]

Revised Diagnosis

Re-examination of the literature reported and experimentation in a few selected agencies in the New York and New Jersey area have led to a revised diagnostic picture of the modal unmarried mother. The treatment plan that has evolved in light of this enriched understanding will be presented both theoretically and by case illustrations.

During the year 1966–67 the writer was permitted to read the case records and/or discuss with the caseworker involved procedures utilized in the treatment of fifteen unmarried mothers seen in four different public and private agencies. Seven of these cases were treated either exclusively by a male worker or by a male conjointly with a female caseworker. The remainder were all seen by female workers and served as a control group for this modest pilot study.

Although this study involved a small number of cases and lacked many

---

[18] *Ibid.*; Shlakman, *op. cit.*; and Sidney Furie, "Birth Control and the Lower-Class Unmarried Mother," *Social Work*, Vol. 11, No. 1 (January 1966), pp. 42–49.

[19] Bernstein, "The Maternal Role in the Treatment of Unmarried Mothers," and "Are We Still Stereotyping the Unmarried Mother?"

[20] Bernstein, "The Maternal Role in the Treatment of Unmarried Mothers."

[21] *Op. cit.*

[22] Frances H. Scherz, " 'Taking Sides' in the Unmarried Mother's Conflict," *Social Casework*, Vol. 28, No. 2 (February 1947), pp. 57–60.

of the requirements of a rigorous experimental design, our findings prompted us, nevertheless, to question the traditional view of the unmarried mother, namely, that the answer to the riddle of her behavior resides to a large extent in her relationship to her own mother. Careful review and analysis of many cases illustrated in the literature and of those in treatment at the agencies that the researchers selected at random to visit induced us to hypothesize that the aforementioned conventional view regarding the etiology of the unmarried mother's dynamics provides too narrow a focus and results in a premature closure of her dynamic picture as well as of the casework plan for her.

It appears necessary in light of this study to reconsider seriously the entire family gestalt to which the unmarried mother relates. More often than not, the client is not merely caught in the web of an ambivalent, cold mother-daughter relationship, but frequently has been a pawn in a tempestuous marital relationship. More than occasionally, her birth has stimulated much rivalry between her parents, with the mother clinging to her and the father behaving quite seductively. It is frequently the father's seductiveness that has overstimulated her immature ego and aroused powerful sexual fantasies with which she has found it extremely difficult to cope. As a result, it is not uncommon to find in the histories of unmarried mothers strong prudishness, puritanical attitudes, and other forms of reaction formation defensiveness.[23]

As the power struggle between the girl's parents mounts and she attempts to deal with her divided loyalties, identifying for a time with her mother and then for another period with her father, the potential unmarried mother gradually finds it more and more difficult to fuse and integrate maternal and paternal introjects. She is never quite certain whether she is male or female, and is almost incessantly flirting with each possibility. As adolescence approaches and the need "to prove" herself assumes even more important dimensions, sexual promiscuity becomes one avenue by which to reassure herself of her tenuous femininity.[24]

Quite frequently the girl's parents have separated or become divorced, with the father leaving the home altogether. His absence activates Oedipal and incestuous longings, but because of the girl's recognition of her mother's angry and vitriolic feelings toward her husband, she has to repress and suppress her attachment to her father; she cannot discuss her distress with her mother because of the latter's bias. It is perhaps being left alone with a mother who the young girl feels has deprived her of a father that may account in great measure for what has been referred to as a "pathological and ambivalent mother-daughter relationship." Possibly it is the father's withdrawal that may arouse in the client the self-image of being ugly, "deprived and depraved"—deprived not so much of pregential and pre-Oedipal love from a mother, but of Oedipal contact with a father; depraved

23 Bonan, op. cit.
24 Blos, op. cit.

not so much because of a poor maternal object with whom to identify, but because she has been overwhelmed with sexual fantasies and can no longer cathect them in the direction of her sexually exciting but unavailable father. Schmideberg has pointed out: "Many girls became promiscuous during wartime because their fathers were away."[25]

Unwed Mother's Mother

The author does not wish to negate the tremendous influence of the mother in the unmarried mother's development, but rather to appreciate the mother even more—she is not merely an ambivalent object but a figure who enacts many roles and who is relating to many significant others in the client's environment. All of her interactions and transactions are witnessed by her daughter and affect the latter's self-image and attitude toward the world.

In attempting to comprehend more thoroughly the unmarried mother's own mother, many life histories of the latter were studied. It was found that frequently the mother was recapitulating her own life story with her daughter. Often the victim herself of cold, withdrawn, and punitive fathering, she appeared to arrange to live vicariously through her daughter as the latter subtly but sexually interacted with her father. However, out of jealousy and competition with her daughter, who was achieving what she could not, the mother threw roadblocks into the very dyad that she herself had initiated. This does make her an ambivalent object for identification. However, the ambivalent feelings that the unmarried mother feels toward her own mother are nurtured by her fantasies toward her father, which she cannot share with her mother but must rather keep hidden from her. It is these forbidden and secretive sexual impulses toward the father that are often acted out in a clandestine affair; because they are forbidden, they are expressed in a way that will bring punishment.

What should be emphasized is that the girl's resentment toward her mother arose not so much because the latter failed to nurture her properly at early developmental levels, but because the mother has distorted hetero-sexual attitudes that can only intensify the young girl's conflict. Also of tremendous importance are the client's conflicting feelings toward her father, whom she fantasies as a sexual partner but fears as too engulfing. She is contemptuous of her father because he has not responded maturely as a husband to his wife. If he had been a responsible husband, the girl reasons, then he would have been free enough to relate to his daughter as a growing girl rather than primarily as a sexual object. He has become simultaneously too attractive and too dangerous to his daughter and her developing ego cannot withstand the excruciating dilemma. Therefore, the baby that the

[25] Melitta Schmideberg, "Psychiatric-Social Factors in Young Unmarried Mothers," *Social Casework*, Vol. 32, No. 1 (January 1951), pp. 3–7.

unmarried mother conceives is not only the baby that she wishes to be, but often is the fantasied outcome of incest. Is it any wonder that after the product of incest has been born the client does not want to face her mother figure, the caseworker? Her incestuous guilt is too overwhelming, so that at best she turns the baby over to the mother figure to whom she feels it rightfully belongs, and leaves!

In the majority of cases reviewed it was found that when the father withdrew, the mother-daughter relationship, although desired as a refuge by the daughter, became a battleground with both mother and daughter appearing as two immature girls. The mother was seen by her daughter as unable to provide sexual guidance or advice about men or to cater to her maturing sexual interest and questions. Therefore, it has tentatively been concluded that when the young woman appears infantile, demanding, and hyperdependent in her early casework interviews, this occurs not so much because of a fixation at primitive and infantile levels, but as a regression to earlier modes of satisfaction because present conflicts are too overwhelming and the current environment is not sufficiently supportive.

Most of the mothers studied viewed their teen-age daughters as a potpourri of unintegrated conflicts and impulses with whom a relationship was too burdensome. In several cases the mother herself often turned to sexual affairs as a refuge, frequently looking for "fatherly-type men." As one mother, speaking on her daughter's behalf as well as her own, said: "Neither of us had a good father so we thought we were 'punks' as girls. Getting a guy to 'knock us up' somehow tells us that at least for a while we're O.K." However, because the self-hating impulse has remained active throughout, these women frequently chose men who left them or, if they remained, became insensitive and infantile father figures.

The absence of the father altogether or the presence of a father who deprives his daughter of the satisfactions of being a girl (and not just a sexual object) seems to appear where unmarried motherhood occurs must frequently, namely, among lower socioeconomic Negro families. The girl during the course of her development has usually had some relationships with older men that have frequently been tantalizing, but the consistent unavailability of a mature father figure is ubiquitous. Certainly the host of attendant economic and other social variables inherent in the Negro constellation should not or cannot be minimized; it is, nonetheless, a virtual truism that unmarried motherhood is prevalent in circumstances in which the father is unavailable.[26]

While the importance of the father in a girl's psychosocial development has in general been relatively undefined and the effects of paternal deprivation largely unspecified, we are beginning to become sensitized to the uniquely paternal contributions necessary for a girl's development as she shifts from primary to secondary dependency. As Forrest has pointed out, for a female to be fulfilled as a person and a woman, the father's presence

[26] Wright, *op. cit.*

from infancy through childhood, girlhood, and adolescence aids and abets psychological growth.[27]

How Help is Offered

Because it has been tentatively hypothesized that part of the etiology of the unmarried mother's difficulty is the absence of mature fathering, that the quest for "pre-Oedipal mothering" on her part stems more from a regression to old modes of functioning than from a fixation, and that the client's mother is so flooded with anxiety of her own that renders her incapable of meeting her daughter's maturational needs—especially the need to see her mother function in mature heterosexual relationships—it is proposed that casework intervention must seek to meet these unmet needs.

Is it not possible that the way the unmarried mother experiences casework help as it is presently structured for her may recapitulate the ugly experiences that brought her to the agency in the first place? More than nine times out of ten she is confronted by a female worker who initially wishes to "understand" her rather than immediately give her tangibles, such as advice and information about the baby's delivery and the external factors attending it. What the client usually wants from the caseworker initially, namely, informative advice, is what her mother could not give her. When her initial requests are subjected to study rather than immediately met, she does become "demanding and hostile." If the hostility is not seen as a defensive response to the hurt and anguish the client is feeling because no one cares about her, the kind of power struggle that transpired with her own mother might ensue with the caseworker.

Another feature of the way help is offered to the unmarried mother that repeats past traumas is the absence of a man in the treatment plan. Occasionally the putative father is interviewed if available and sometimes the client's own father is approached, but most social agencies working with unmarried mothers, especially group residences, have a completely female atmosphere. While the less traditional agencies and more modern caseworkers have inaugurated casework plans that include the few men in the girl's life (and with good results), it is the author's finding that this is more the exception than the rule.[28] When a male worker, trained or untrained, becomes part of the treatment plan and if in addition significant men in the girl's environment are sought out, the casework experience for the unmarried mother comes closer to meeting her psychosocial deprivations. Because, according to the writer's data, the most fundamental lacuna in the unmarried mother's ego development has been the lack of men and women working together in her behalf, it is this latter experience, if planfully utilized as part of work with her, that can improve the casework results appreciably.

[27] Tess Forrest, "Paternal Roots of Female Character Development," *Contemporary Psychoanalysis*, Vol. 3, No. 1 (Fall 1966), pp. 21–31.

[28] Francis L. Feldman and Francis H. Scherz, *Family Social Welfare: Helping Troubled Families* (New York: Atherton Press, 1967), p. 386.

Suggested Treatment Model

In several cases by plan and in some cases by accident the following structured approach has been found to be most beneficial in casework treatment of the unmarried mother:

1. Because the unmarried mother comes to an agency in a state of crisis and panic that has been precipitated by her illegitimate pregnancy and frequently exacerbated by her mother's anxiety, her father's withdrawal, and the putative father's emotional and often physical isolation, she will inevitably conduct herself in a regressed, infantile, and demanding manner. The female caseworker, rather than making interpretations about the client's behavior or asking questions in an attempt to clarify her motives, should try to answer her questions immediately. Initially, information should not be provided about agency practice and policy unless the client asks for this; rather, she should be given information that *she wants for herself*. As the client is "given to" in terms of what she wants, the worker is gradually experienced as the nurturing mother who has her psychological daughter's best interests in mind and is genuinely relating to them.

2. With the caseworker's demonstration of concern about matters pertaining to the client's physical care—who the doctor will be, diet, medical prescriptions, appropriate exercises, details of the delivery, and so on—the client usually begins to become more interested in the worker as a person. As a result, she begins to share with the worker the experiences that brought her to the agency, her confusion regarding sexual matters, and her debilitating experiences with her parents. She often comes up with a statement or question that disguises, yet implies, a cry for help as if casework treatment were to begin only now (although contacts have transpired for several weeks). The wish for help is usually couched in statements about her poor self-image and her desire to be rid of it. As the caseworker relates to the client's formulation of her own problems and concerns, the idea of treatment or counseling can be discussed meaningfully and nondefensively by both worker and client.

3. At this stage a male worker should be introduced to the client for counseling. The rationale for this proposal should be explained to the client as follows: "I agree that your relationships with men have caused you a lot of difficulty. I think, therefore, that it would be helpful for you if you had a male caseworker. As you learn to get along with him, I'm quite sure that you'll be able to get along with many other men in the future."

The client initially interprets this proposal to mean that the female caseworker will be "dropping out of the picture." The caseworker should explain: "On the contrary, I'll be around whenever you need me. You are still concerned about doctors, nurses, hospital visits, and the like, and I'm here to help you with these concerns." Invariably, after two or three interviews the client's response is euphoric and ecstatic: "You mean I'll have you both. That's great!"

4. The opportunity to work with a male worker and not lose the female

worker offers the client the opportune situation of which she has been deprived. Given a nonseductive male and a mother figure who is genuinely concerned increases the self-image positively, mobilizes previously intact ego functions, and frequently enables the client to reflect genuinely on herself and her interaction with her environment, present and past.

5. The triadic relationship continues after the birth of the infant and as long as the client needs it. In addition, if the girl's father, mother, or the baby's putative father can be part of the treatment plan, the client feels far from alone but instead enjoys "all the attention I am getting."

6. From time to time, and dictated by the client's needs and requests, both male and female workers see her together. The rationale for this maneuver is explained as follows: "We want you to have the opportunity really to experience a man and a woman working together in your behalf."

Experimentation has been done not only with trained workers but with untrained workers as well. Given appropriate supervision, it has been found that persons with only undergraduate education can adapt to the cited approach, provided it is well structured in advance so that salient client responses can be anticipated and appropriate interventions timed accordingly. The six steps enumerated appear to offer the client an emotionally corrective experience with an unambivalent mother figure and a nonseductive father figure. The treatment is designed to meet the developmental needs of the unmarried mother—to feed her when she needs emotional nourishment, to educate her when she needs information and knowledge, and to offer her fatherly admiration and maternal tenderness when these are required.

Case Illustrations

Miss A, a young Negro woman of 31, had five illegitimate pregnancies. Living in a housing project and on welfare, she was frequently drunk, often depressed, and managed her home and children with extremely limited care and discipline. The management of the project sent a female case aide—an untrained worker—to "see what could be done" before processing an eviction.

The worker found Miss A's house extremely untidy, her children poorly cared for, and Miss A in the third month of her sixth pregnancy. The case aide told Miss A that the management of the project had suggested that she be seen, but before the worker could finish her opening remarks, the client bellowed: "Oh, they want to throw me out because they don't like the way I keep the house!" The worker looked around and said calmly: "I'm sure things are very difficult for you. You must have it very rough." The client spent the next half hour talking about how her children were a burden to her, that meeting their physical needs was impossible, how difficult it was to make ends meet financially, and that the only pleasure she got once in a while was "a little sex and a little drink." The worker remarked that she could understand how sex and drinking could be her only pleasures but wondered if there was anything that she, the worker, could do to bring her some pleasure. Miss A pointed to the children's clothes and her poor furniture, and mentioned that she had limited time for herself. The worker immediately responded: "I'll get in touch with a few places and people and see what can be done."

The worker did get in touch with the department of welfare and other agencies in the community in order to supply Miss A with some of the tangibles she requested. Therefore, with some physical needs met—clothes for the children and mother, mattresses and beds, and a volunteer for some babysitting—the client began, in her second interview, to talk about her current pregnancy and previous ones as well. She said that she knew "damn well that I don't appeal to men" and that all of her sexual affairs turned out to be one-night stands. When the worker took note of the client's feelings of depreciation vis-à-vis men, and said: "You think that the only reason men would have anything to do with you is to go to bed, don't you?" Miss A tearfully reported how she remembered as a little girl wishing that a boy friend of her mother's who intermittently visited the house "could be my father." She then spent some time talking about her wish for a father who "would have really cared about me" but how her mother "just didn't meet up with a good man to live with."

As Miss A continued to talk about her feelings of deprivation in her heterosexual relationships, the worker gradually introduced the subject of a male worker, who was part of the same social service department of the housing project. Miss A did not ask for any explanation of the entrance of the male worker into the situation but seemed to sense the rationale behind the introduction and merely said: "Great!"

In contrast to the manner in which Miss A usually cared for the house, the male worker at his first interview found it to be extremely tidy and the children and Miss A well groomed. This held true at subsequent visits. While Miss A continued to see the female worker about plans for the baby and dealt with the situation quite responsibly, with the male worker she talked about the possibility of working, which he encouraged. Through his efforts, Miss A took a job in the postoffice, did excellent work there (enough to receive part of a maternity leave with pay), and talked with both of her workers about the new "but different" men in her life who "seem to respect me."

While a case situation like Miss A's will remain open for some time and Miss A will see both workers intermittently, at one interview she explained the modifications in her life by saying: "I got a good mommy and daddy— that's all you need to feel good!"

Miss L, a 19-year-old Jewish girl, came to a family agency during her fourth month of pregnancy. Referred by a physician, she blurted out in her first intake interview: "I want to give up my baby for adoption." The female caseworker immediately responded: "Then I think you've come to the right place. That's our business here; maybe we can help you!" The client, a little surprised, said: "Good. I thought you'd want to ask me a bunch of personal questions!" The worker responded: "Oh, I thought *you'd* want to ask *me* a bunch of questions!" The client stated that she did, and asked many pertinent questions about hospital delivery, seeing the baby, nurses, residence, and so on, all of which the worker answered directly, truthfully, and factually. Miss L gladly initiated a second appointment with the same worker, and on leaving said: "Enjoyed it!"

Miss L arrived on time for her second appointment and within a few minutes volunteered without prompting the details of her pregnancy and of previous relationships with young men. She was able to say: "I know I've used sex to make me feel adequate. I guess I've wondered most of my life how much of a female I am!" When the intake worker asked her how she accounted for her "feeling of inadequacy," Miss L described her relationships with her parents. According to her, her mother was extremely concerned with her own appearance and "always squabbled with my father." Her father was described as a "sensitive and passionate man," who "used to tickle me a lot." Further references to Miss L's father led the worker to help her focus on the highly stimulating experiences with him and the longings she felt for him when her parents separated when she was 16. On her own, Miss L dated her sexual acting out with her father's leaving home.

Miss L participated actively in the intake interviews and eventually requested treatment. She was assigned a male worker to whom she eagerly remarked in the first interview: "I need to see a man counselor so that I can get along with men better." Rather quickly she attempted to initiate a mutually seductive relationship with the worker. When he pointed this out to her, she experienced it as a rejection, saying quite pitifully: "No men like me," and recalled relationships with young men in which she felt abandonment and rejection. The worker responded: "Just because it wouldn't be good for treatment for me to have sex with you doesn't mean I want to leave you!" The treatment became quite challenging for Miss L at this point. She found it difficult to believe that a man could like her and yet not go to bed with her. Here the worker was able to say: "If we weren't more interested in seeing you get help it might be fun," thus demonstrating to her that a father figure could have sexual feelings but could control them.

Miss L continued her treatment after the baby was born. The worker was able to involve both of her parents in the delivery and adoption proceedings. Interestingly, Miss L's father asked for treatment himself and was referred for private psychotherapy. The female worker Miss L saw at intake was utilized at strategic times during the process—once when Miss L wanted information about gynecological matters and another time when Miss L was thinking about attending a college that was the worker's alma mater.

Miss L visited both workers after she left the community and went away to college. Eventually she became interested in a career in social work.

Summary and Conclusion

Examination of the social work literature on the unmarried mother and investigation of cases in selected agencies led to the conclusion that the dynamic formulations that have placed the prime etiological factor in the mother-daughter relationship required modification and further elaboration. While the importance of pre-Oedipal nurturing in the mother-daughter relationship should not be discounted in the study, diagnosis, or treatment of the unmarried mother, it was proposed that the client must be viewed within her total family constellation. Important, therefore, is the unmarried mother's perception of her parents' interaction as well as her unique relationship to her father.

De-emphasized in the literature has been the importance of the father's contribution to the unmarried mother's sexual difficulties. His seductiveness and eventual withdrawal were seen as prime factors in the development of the girl's difficulties. The question was raised as to whether the prevalence of unmarried motherhood in certain subcultures may be due, in part, to a high incidence of absence of the father.

A structured treatment plan involving male and female workers who would offer the unmarried mother a corrective emotional experience was presented along with case illustrations.

Existential Psychotherapy and the Problem of Anomie

Donald F. Krill

A characteristic of the present age is the increasing freedom of people from traditional ties and associated systems of mores, folkways, and religious disciplines, coupled with the fact that instead of flowering in their newfound freedom a large share have become muddled, confused, highly anxious, and self-driving, and in general resort to ways of "escaping their freedom."[1] Such modern maladies as alcoholism, increased divorce rates, overuse and experimental use of drugs, and the general entertainment and recreation manias have been linked with this desperate flight or search (which one it is depending, perhaps, on the person).

In 1962 Pollak presented several ideas related to this issue:

> Strangely enough, the clients who represent the greatest challenge to social work and a wider community at the present time do not suffer from the scars of sub-mission to the reality principle. They suffer from the ineffectiveness of having retained the pleasure principle as a guide of living. They lead a life of normless-ness conceptualized by Merton as anomie. . . . With people who are victims of anomie we have no theory of helping and tradition of success. The culture of social work here is faced with the challenge of becoming a rearing and binding, superego demanding profession rather than of being a liberating one. . . . Here social workers will have to come to terms with a phenomena of normlessness which makes liberating or improving efforts miss the mark.[2]

Many respond to this problem by talking all the more vehemently of the need for increased services in education, welfare, and mental health, but while there is truth in this they miss the central point that is being proclaimed by the existentialists: People have lost contact with many basic human realities that they must accept and understand if they are to have a sense of personal direction or meaning in their lives. One need only look at present-

Reprinted with permission of the author and the National Association of Social Workers, from *Social Work,* Vol. 14, No. 2 (April, 1969), pp. 33–49.

[1] Erich Fromm, *Escape from Freedom* (New York: Holt, Rinehart & Winston, 1941).

[2] Otto Pollak, "Social Determinants of Family Behavior." Paper presented at the Mid-Continent Regional Institute, National Association of Social Workers, Kansas City, Mo., April 1962, p. 6.

day common behavior patterns and voiced attitudes to see this. With regard to the concept of human love, closeness, and intimacy, it can be seen that marital disappointments are commonly dealt with by divorce, adultery, alcoholism, increased work (the notion that more money or prestige will change the marriage), and individualized social circles that allow two near-strangers to remain together under the same roof "for the sake of the children." The concept of death is often dealt with by avoidance of it as a fact with implicit meaning for present conduct or weak hopes for some scientific "deep-freeze" solution, and of course by the whole ridiculous ritual of the funeral parlors.

Efforts of the Church

The illusion behind such maneuvers is the widely held belief that one can manipulate and control life in such a way as to bring oneself happiness, security, and freedom from suffering. This idea has been nourished through-out this century by utopian hopes stemming from scientific rationalism. The effort has backfired insofar as men have become increasingly estranged from many realities of the human condition. These attitudes have at the same time considerably weakened the position of the church, which in the past had been the fount for people's sense of direction and meaning and the support for their capacity to endure hardship. Needless to say, the church, especially since the Reformation, has had its part in nurturing the very hopes in scientific rationalism that have weakened its influence. Now the church itself is struggling for a new language and new means with which to express its fundamental ideas, knowing that people have been alienated and disil-lusioned and have come to feel indifferent toward traditional presentations of beliefs and truths.[3]

The church, as mentioned, has always concerned itself with the conflicts, ideas, feelings, and behavior that make up the state of mind called anomie. Presumably, the church should have important contributions to make to the psychiatric and social work professions in their efforts to cope with this problem. An interesting development in society has been furthered by those serious students of or searchers after a religion that refuses to return to Sunday school fantasies, hopes, rituals, and platitudes. The new religious vitality is one that seeks a sense of direction and unity in the intimacy of direct experience with this world of tasks, suffering, and possibilities. The forerunners of this surge were such religious existentialist thinkers as Dostoevsky, Kierkegaard, Berdyaev, Bergson, Jaspers, Marcel, Maritain, Tillich, Niebuhr, Barth, and Buber. This is the true religious revival and has nothing to do with increased church attendance, faith healing, and the renewed interest in Gospel singing. A profound movement toward unity

---

[3] This is the basic conflict in the "Honest to God" debate. *See* John A. T. Robinson, *Honest to God* (Philadelphia: Westminster Press, 1963); and David L. Edwards, *The Honest to God Debate* (Philadelphia: Westminster Press, 1963).

among the world's religions is in progress and this includes a strong effort toward a unity between religion and science as well.

A similar movement has occurred apart from the church, yet seems related to the same precipitating conditions and personal needs. This has expressed itself in the arts and literature and theoretically in the avid interest of many in existential philosophy and Zen Buddhism—two areas of modern thought representing West and East that are remarkably similar in their concern for the discovery of meaning in the direct, immediate experience of life as one lives it.

The existentialist movement in the fields of psychiatry and psychology may well provide a body of knowledge that is highly valuable and useful in our quest for some answers to the problem of anomie. Existentialism is a philosophy derived from man's immediate experience of the world in which he lives—a confrontation with the realities of the human condition and the establishment of a personalized meaning from them. As a philosophy of daily experience it should be capable of speaking meaningfully about ideas that can be grasped by the unsophisticated, much as a novel does.

Pollak's words (". . . becoming a rearing and binding, superego demanding profession") are provocative to the ears of social workers who have identified their goals, along psychoanalytic lines, to be in marked contrast with his suggestion. There is the ring here of paternalism, authoritarianism, and a judgmental attitude. But let us look at what the church has attempted to accomplish over its many centuries of existence and what this may have to say to us through the modern views of existentialism.

The church has always attempted to deal with the sufferings of people by providing them with a sense of meaning that transcends their own self-derived, suffering-based feelings of futility about life. Religious people have found courage to endure through acceptance of what is considered to be divine revelation. The fundamental services of religion to an individual are the provision of guidance in his way of living and the experience of union with an ultimate reality that relates him to others and all that exists through the transcendent power in which he believes. Religious dogmas, orders, sects, rituals, sermons, discussion groups, sacraments, social action, study, prayer, and meditation are some of the varied efforts to accomplish these two basic services. This variety of approaches reflects the church's efforts to serve people of varying capacities and levels of motivation and understanding. The mental health movement faces a similar problem.

Psychiatry cannot be equated with religion, for the sphere of divine revelation and speculation on the mystery of transcendence is beyond the scope and capacity of scientific methods. But the human need for guidance in the management of one's life and the experience of unity through relatedness to others outside oneself are certainly within its realm. It is here that the existentialist movement has attempted to relate a philosophy of life to mankind's problems by focusing, as the church has done, on guidance and relatedness. This is why the existentialist movement is most commonly characterized as stressing meaning in life and authenticity in relationships.

Existentialism Versus Anomie

Elsewhere the writer defined the concern of existentialism as "meaningful living through self-encounter in the situation at hand despite a world of apparent futility."[4] Essentially, this means that one derives or helps another derive an attitude and direction toward life by becoming increasingly aware of life as he lives it and what this living entails. It is for this reason that the problem of anomie—of aimless, futile, normless lives—can be constructively related to by existentialist thought.

The process of growth in existentialism emphasizes the following reality concepts: increasing awareness of self-deceptions that attempt to define the self as fixed and secure; confrontation with the knowledge of personal freedom and its accompanying responsibilities; discovery of meaning in one's sufferings that actually helps establish a direction in life; realization of the necessity of dialogue or intimacy that nurtures change, courage, and self-assertion; and finally a decision for continued commitment that prizes freedom above attachment to childhood strivings and self-deceptions. This commitment is characterized by responsive action in the world of tasks, duties, and possibilities, in contrast to narcissism and self-pity.[5]

Let us contrast this with patterns of thought and behavior implicit in the state of mind labeled anomie. The characteristic of normlessness mentioned by Pollak is a result of several atitudes about oneself and also oneself in relation to others and the world in general. These attitudes are anti-existential in content because of the nature of the implicit beliefs and assumptions about freedom, responsibility, suffering, authenticity, love, and commitment. The sources of these attitudes are many and have been ably described by such social critics as Erich Fromm, Allen Wheelis, Colin Wilson, David Riesman, and William Whyte.

Anomie is derived from a Greek word meaning "lack of law." As a sociological concept it describes the breakdown or failure of those forces (standards, sanctions, norms, rules, values) that ordinarily bind people together in some organized social whole. This social whole it characterized by a sense of duty and obligation of people toward one another that preserves organization. There are different degrees of anomie and it may take several forms, outlined by Cohen as "confrontation by a situation for which there are no relevant rules, vagueness or ambiguity of the relevant rules, or lack of consensus on which rules are relevant and in the interpretation of rules."[6]

---

[4] Donald F. Krill, "Existentialism: A Philosophy for Our Current Revolutions," *Social Service Review*, Vol. 40, No. 3 (September 1966), p. 291.

[5] *Ibid.* This entire article is a development of these ideas.

[6] Albert K. Cohen, "The Study of Social Disorganization and Deviant Behavior," in Robert K. Merton, Leonard Brown, and Leonard S. Cottrell, Jr., eds., *Sociology Today: Problems and Prospects* (New York: Basic Books, 1959), p. 481.

Tiryakian states:

> To liberate the individual from all social constraint, adds Durkheim, is to abandon him to his unlimited wants, to demoralize him and to lead him to despair. What the individual should feel, more acutely than ever before, is the need for moral rules.[7]

He suggests that what is latent in the writings of Durkheim that differentiates the notions of solidarity and anomie are societal analogues of what the existentialist terms an individual's "authentic" and "unauthentic" existence.

Anomic Man

The existentialists have enriched our understanding of "anomic man" in both fictional and philosophical descriptions of the "unauthentic man," the man of "bad faith," and "alienated man." These assessments demonstrate that the anomic state of mind and attitude are not to be limited to delinquent, sociopathic, multiply deprived individuals but apply to an ever increasing number of people at all levels of present-day society. Attitudes typical of anomic man will now be examined.

There is a sense of aimless drifting, or at times being helplessly driven, both of which relate to one's sense of impotence and personal insignificance. One considers oneself as being fixed in place either by tradition, heredity, social position, or psychological and social determinism. One has been formed, or perhaps victimized, by the powers that be or by those that were before.

Paradoxically, along with this sense of missing personal freedom and hence diminished responsibility there is an increased expectation that one's surrounding environment should change in such a way as to bring one increased comfort, protection, and happiness. The experience of suffering is therefore often felt to be unfair, and bitterness as well as envy arises toward others in more fortunate circumstances. Quick and easy solutions are sought to manipulate the environment in order to reduce any personal pain and bring about a state of pleasure or comfort. The variety of efforts is vast and extends from pills and television to infidelity and alcoholism.

A Mexican-American leader recently defended his people, who are accused of filling the jails and reformatories of the Southwest, with this interesting observation:

> When a Mexican kid is brought before the judge he is usually honest in admitting he committed the crime and ready to accept whatever consequences come—leaving his future to God. When an Anglo is in the same situation, he'll do anything possible to avoid a charge of guilty to get out of being punished.[8]

---

[7] Edward A. Tiryakian, *Sociologism and Existentialism* (Englewood Cliffs, N.J.: Prentice-Hall, 1962), p. 31.

[8] Rudolph Gonzales, lecture-discussion given to the Child Psychiatry Department of the University of Colorado Medical Center, Denver, November 1966.

One's sense of self as a feeling, thinking, changing person is replaced by a notion of self as dependent on support from outside. One plays roles or "markets oneself" in such a way as to manipulate others to view one in a specific way that meets one's needs. Relationships are characterized by superficiality, calculation, and "game-playing." Other props used are the identification of self with groups, such as religious, political, or professional, or with slogans and characteristics of models found in society and given acceptance or even acclaim, such as "the good Joe, the hustler, the smart operator, the playboy, the status seeker. . . ."[9] When such supports are challenged or threatened, one is prepared to fight righteously and defend his self-identity to the bitter end.

What is apparent in this entire description is that one hides one's inner self both from others and from one's own sensitive judgement. There is an ongoing effort to gratify needs by actions and manipulations and a fleeing from being alone with oneself. Such exercises as meditation and self-examination become foreign, or if adopted are used with magical, naïve expectations that usually end in disappointment. Intuition and spontaneity tend to be lost or warped.[10] The simple joys to be found in the beauty and mystery of life and responsive participation in the ongoing order of things are rare. One feels alienated from other people, the world, and oneself, yet hides this fundamental panic beneath desperate efforts to grasp, contain, and fortify a sense of identity, false as it is.

Advantages of Existential Psychotherapy

This description of attitudes and behavior is not a presentation of symptoms, but rather a way of life—an anti-existentialist way of living—that has developed to significant proportions in our age. Because anomie can be considered to be an attitude toward life, existential psychotherapy has a unique advantage over many other forms of psychotherapy. The outstanding difference does not lie in techniques or methods, for the existential approach may occur with insight, crisis-oriented, family, group, or supportive therapies. It may be directive, nondirective, or analytical. The uniqueness of existential psychotherapy is that it attempts a philosophical reorientation through the use of therapy content and behavior. There is a process of challenge, re-education, and reconstruction of the patient's basic way of viewing himself, his relation to others, and the world at large.

The mental health professional performing the therapy (hereafter called the therapist) holds to a number of existential philosophical premises based on his perception and understanding of reality. The experiences that are lived through in therapy are utilized to demonstrate and highlight the

[9] A comprehensive elaboration of these "models" is found in Henry Winthrop, "American National Character and the Existentialist Posture," *Journal of Existentialism*, Vol. 6, No. 24 (Summer 1966), pp. 405–419.

[10] This theme is fully developed in Franz E. Winkler, MD, *Man, The Bridge Between Two Worlds* (New York: Harper & Bros., 1960).

philosophical implications of those realities apparent in these experiences. Soon experiences take on new meanings for patients, who are helped to rethink and redevelop their own outlook on life in a fresh manner.

It is true that the patient takes on certain values and philosophical attitudes of the therapist. This occurs in any form of psychotherapy to a certain degree. What is important here is that the therapist knowingly permits this. He has in mind certain existential realities within his philosophical frame of reference that he wants the patient to see, understand, and accept if he is to overcome his problems. The goal in this approach is not insight into early traumas, reassurance, catharsis, or enabling the patient to grow in a nondirective atmosphere. It may include any or all of these, but the goal itself is a philosophical re-education through direct experience.

The relation between anomie and emotional illness must also be understood. Each can exist without the presence of the other; however, in our present society both occur simultaneously and are interrelated in a vast and growing number of cases. The attitudes of anomie actually predispose the person to emotional illness.

The general view among existentialists of the development of emotional disorders stresses the following factors. Two human needs are considered most fundamental: (1) to be loved and to experience a sense of unity with what is other than oneself and (2) to grow through ongoing creative and responsive change. These are interrelated inasmuch as the mature person, at the moment he is authentically creative by responding to the tasks and opportunities of the world about him, is also experiencing a sense of unity by feeling needed or being a vital and unique part of his own specific area of the world (life space).

A child needs the trust and confidence of his parents to develop as a loving and creative person. As he discovers certain creative or loving expressions to be unacceptable to his parents, he experiences the threat of loss of love. With this goes the fear of a disintegration of his sense of self, for one's early identity is dependent on approval and acceptance by one's parents. This fear of parental rejection is equal to the adult fear of death, for the meanings are precisely the same. To live, to preserve some sense of self, a person willingly gives up or hides those aspects of personality that would produce rejection and adapts himself to what he believes his parents want from him, thus making himself acceptable and of worth. This pattern of self-conformity to a necessitated image in childhood continues into adulthood; one relates to others as if it were still necessary to uphold the same image in order to be acceptable and loved.

What is apparent here are the elements of calculated choice of behavior initially and ongoing manipulative efforts to maintain for others a set image of oneself. Trouble results from the fact that manipulative behavior fosters distance rather than love and intimacy in relationships, and also the clinging effort to maintain and express only specific aspects of the self results in frustration of free and creative growth. The two fundamental needs become endangered and the result is symptoms that cry out distress and a need for help. Guilt and anxiety are often seen to be reality based. Anxiety may be experienced when a person realizes that he could act in a spontaneous and creative way that would express his true, responsive self in a situation, yet to do so would endanger the image he feels he must preserve to be acceptable to others and himself. Guilt may occur when he chooses behavior that preserves his own childhood-based image at the expense of a growth possibility. Genuine open communication and sincere efforts of self-examination actually threaten the image that one wishes to maintain and are thus avoided.

Treatment Goals

Anomie encourages a pattern that leads to emotional disturbance insofar as it emphasizes a helpless, weak, predetermined notion of oneself as lacking freedom and responsibility; a manipulative view of human relationships that nourishes superficiality, deceit, and distance; and an avoidance of pain as one tries with various self-deceptions to resist the meaning of guilt and anxiety in order to hide from what is real within oneself. The causes of anomie are sociological and historical, but the existence of anomie is itself an important contribution to mental illness. When anomie is a part of the emotional problem, it should be dealt with and the issue of treatment then becomes partly philosophical in nature.

The specific treatment goals for existential psychotherapy are essentially philosophical achievements in terms of a patient's coming to grips with those aspects of reality that will produce a significant change in his view of life and his relation to it. The five goals that would appear most important are these:

1. Aiding the process of disillusionment.

2. Confronting freedom.

3. Discovering meaning in suffering.

4. Realizing the necessity of dialogue.

5. Accepting the way of commitment.

Therapeutic techniques familiarize the patient with these goals, or realities, both by educational guidance and direct experience, much as the church directed its people toward spiritual growth. The balance of this paper will present methods by which these goals may be achieved. Emphasis will not be on an analytical or long-term insight-oriented psychotherapy from the existential framework, but rather on techniques useful for casework, group work, and reality-oriented psychotherapy.[11]

The description of therapy may seem somewhat disjointed, since the author's intention is to develop an over-all sense of direction for therapy rather than a complete system applicable to all clients. There is, of course, the question of which people would most benefit from this approach.

This same question must now honestly be asked about psychoanalytic psychotherapy. Studies of its results with many clients who seemed appropriate middle-class candidtaes for therapy as well as of persons in low-income groups have clearly indicated its gross ineffectiveness. It has had its successes too, but such studies raise radical questions about whether it is the most useful approach for our age. The entire community psychiatry movement is a vivid response to doubts about traditional methods and efforts toward new, creative approaches.

To what group of clients does Pollak refer when he speaks of "victims of anomie?"[12] Is there a difference between this group and those people who manifest anomic symptoms as a result of depressive conflict? Existential psychotherapy is not being suggested here as a cure-all, nor is it possible to say with assurance exactly what sorts of persons will benefit from it, any more than psychoanalytic practitioners can comfortably state this. May and Frankl have both expressed the view that the existential approach is more attuned to the problems of our age.[13] Fromm, sharing many of the existential concerns about the plight of modern man, has challenged the psychoanalytic approach on this same basis.[14] The reality-oriented psychotherapists (including Glasser, Ellis, Mowrer, and O'Connell) utilize techinques that are closely aligned with the existential treatment goals mentioned, and have worked successfully with neurotics, psychotics, and sociopaths. As early as 1933 Jung made the following relevant comments:

> A psycho-neurosis must be understood as the suffering of a human being who has not discovered what life means to him. . . . Among all my patients in the second half of life—that is to say, over thirty-five—there has not been one whose problem in the last resort was not that of finding a religious outlook on life. . . . This of course has nothing whatever to do with a particular creed or membership of a church. . . . Today this eruption of destructive forces has already taken place, and man suffers from it in spirit. . . . That is why we psychotherapists must occupy ourselves with problems which, strictly speaking, belong to the theologian. But we cannot leave these questions for theology to answer; the urgent, psychic needs of suffering people confront us with them day after day.[15]

---

[11] Two recent books illustrating the existential-analytical view are Avery D. Weisman, MD, *The Existential Core of Psychoanalysis* (Boston: Little, Brown & Co., 1965); and J. F. T. Bugental, *The Search for Authenticity* (New York: Holt, Rinehart & Winston, 1965).

[12] *Op. cit.*

[13] Rollo May, ed., *Existential Psychology* (New York: Random House, 1961), p. 21. Viktor Frankl, *The Doctor and the Soul* (New York: Alfred A. Knopf, 1955), pp. 3–26.

[14] Erich Fromm, D. T. Suzuki, and Richard Demartino, *Zen Buddhism and Psychoanalysis* (New York: Evergreen Publishing Co., 1963), pp. 135–136.

[15] C. G. Jung, *Modern Man in Search of a Soul* (New York: Harcourt, Brace & Co., 1933), pp. 225, 229, and 241.

Aiding the Process of Disillusionment

The major task with this goal is gradually to reveal to the patient the reality that the very way he goes about thinking of himself and relating to other people defeats his purpose. His efforts at self-assurance and manipulation of those to whom he wishes to be close are marked with inconsistencies and self-deceptions that result in alienation and the limited expression of his potentialities. Habit patterns are revealed to him that consistently distort reality in his daily living. This process is anxiety provoking, of course, and requires the accompanying nurture of the therapeutic relationship.

The therapist must be well trained and experienced in the knowledge and operation of self-deception. Perhaps his most direct acquaintance with this is to have undergone psychoanalysis or psychotherapy himself. A corresponding discipline occurs in those religious orders that require intense self-examination by priests, monks, and the like in a search for personal truth. It is perhaps unfortunate that modern Protestant seminaries have for the most part replaced such personal struggle and discipline with rational teaching of history and theory.

A therapist aims initially at understanding the specific, unique patterns his client uses in viewing and relating to his world of tasks and relationships and his sense of self-adequacy. It is often important to develop some historical picture of the client to identify the presence of early patterns that still carry over into his present life adjustment. The existence of these patterns is also identified in the way the patient relates to the therapist. Because of the therapist's ability to maintain himself as a free, authentic person in the therapeutic relationship, he fails to be manipulated by the client's habitual efforts, although his interest and understanding remain solid and intact. As a free person, the therapist has no egotistical investment in curing or failing to cure the client. He offers reality, with himself as a therapeutic agent, but the client must always realize that the choice between change and growth on the one hand and flight toward the security of habitual patterns on the other is his own.

This process of challenging a person's manner of viewing his problem (as well as his general life conduct) can be illustrated in part by the techniques used with an open-ended therapy group for alcoholics conducted by the author. An alcoholic who wishes to join the group is told quite directly at the beginning how his problem will be viewed. This is done in a brief individual orientation session with the therapist. The prospective group member is told that alcoholics usually drink for a specific reason and that reason has to do with feelings that are difficult to bear without the aid of alcohol. Such feelings result from the way he sees himself and also the manner in which he relates to those with whom he wishes to have a close relationship. To benefit from therapy he must abstain from alcohol so that he can experience the feelings behind his drinking and talk about them in the group. By being as open and honest as possible, the group can help him come to an understanding of his problems and change them, so that the suffering caused by inner feelings can be managed better or diminished. It is emphasized that alcoholics can be helped in different ways, but if the client wants group therapy he must accept this notion of the helping process.

In the course of therapy he will usually find opposition to his personal view of his problems. Such ideas as the alcoholic's being born this way, having an incurable disease, or being inherently weak or hopelessly dependent are simply not accepted by the group. What is stressed instead is that the alcoholic never learned appropriate and workable means of expressing and meeting his needs. The manipulative ritual with his spouse is a good example. The cycle of drinking, fighting, threatening separation, confessing failure and appealing for another chance during the hangover period, and the final acceptance by the martyred wife provide several elements of closeness. There is an exchange of feelings, including anger, hurt, despair, contrition, forgiveness, and refound hope. But the closeness is short lived and must be repeated because it fails to deal with the genuine daily relationship struggles between the marital partners.

During therapy it becomes increasingly apparent to the alcoholic that his efforts to control interactions with other group members are related to the specific view he has of himself as a person, which he feels obliged to maintain. Yet this image and his strivings to maintain it are the sources of both his failure at intimacy and his inability to satisfy his needs, as well as an infringement on his ability to think and express himself in new ways.

The following Zen story illustrates how a monk's view of others stemmed from his own self-image. A perceptive friend disillusions his self-complacency.

> Following a heavy rain, two Zen monks were walking together along a muddy road. They came upon a dismayed young maiden in a quandary about how she might cross the road without soiling her low-hanging silk kimono. "Come on, girl," said one monk as he lifted her in his arms and carried her across. The two monks resumed their journey without a word to each other. Finally, at a temple at which they were lodging that evening the second monk could no longer restrain himself: "We monks don't go near females, especially not young and lovely ones. It is dangerous. Why did you do that?" The first monk whimsically replied, "I left the girl there. Are you still carrying her?"[16]

Confronting Freedom

In therapy the process of disillusionment dwells on the negative side of personality wherein values, attitudes, judgments, and behavior are revealed to be colored by childhood assumptions. This view of self is counterbalanced by an increasing awareness of the adult part of oneself, which is characterized by the freedom and responsibility available to a person in his daily functioning. Some basic ideas about the nature of the self and its capacity for freedom are stressed.

The self is never a fixed, closed, totally predetermined form; it is only a person's own fears and self-deceptions that make him think this is the case.

[16] Paul Reps, *Zen Flesh, Zen Bones* (Garden City, N.Y.: Anchor Books, Doubleday & Co., 1961), p. 18.

Everyone is considered to be responsible in accordance with his age. Each is also a completely unique person unlike anyone who ever was or ever will be. His adult self is in a constant process of change and growth. The process of growth requires the ongoing assertion of freedom—the capacity to transcend what one has been before. A person chooses his future direction and utilizes his past knowledge and experiences as he relates to the present, deciding what is to emerge in him. He alone is responsible for his aspirations and whether he strives to fulfill them.

The person comes to see that while he is possessed by childhood strivings that seem to inhibit and interfere with his desired growth, this need not be accepted fatalistically. He chose these patterns as a child because of circumstances that at that time seemed to necessitate them. But as an adult he possesses the same freedom to choose differently and, because he is an adult, the circumstances are no longer the same. It is only his fear that seems to make them so. He can manage new reality-based judgments of situations and how he will respond to them. A certain detachment from identified childhood strivings will be required, and the resulting sense of uncertainty will be painful, yet as a human being he does possess the freedom to accomplish change. His sense of direction will arise entirely from his own unique assessment of the duties, responsibilities, and inner promptings in his daily life. A responsive relatedness to what is going on about him helps him respond to the adult needs and potential within him.

Therapy is partly the teaching of a basic skill: how one may choose a response that is different from the one prompted by identified childhood strivings and their accompanying feelings. It encourages a developing sensitivity to meaning and reality in the confronting therapeutic situation. The client is repeatedly faced with the fact that he does have some choice in the matter at hand, and many of his rationalizations to the contrary are based on his fear and need to maintain old props for security. Therapy, then, does not emphasize the nature of his early bondage that must be relived and changed through the handling of transference manifestations, nor is it viewed as a complete remaking of a person's basic character. Instead, it helps the client to identify actual reality-based choices in the present situation and find satisfaction by asserting himself as a free being.[17] Consistent with the emphasis on the client's capacity to choose freely and decide his own direction from what lies within himself is the therapist's willingness to allow him to accept or reject therapeutic interpretations or suggestions. The therapist is not an authority on the specific manner in which a client is to choose and live his life, although he is an authority on the basic elements of the human condition and what this means with regard to the development of emotional disorders and the way toward growth and change.

A client's direct experience of his freedom to rise above the powerful negative driving forces in his daily life is a crucial therapeutic happening.

[17] A detailed description of this technique is found in Richard L. Sutherland, "Choosing—As Therapeutic Aim, Method and Philosophy," *Journal of Existential Psychiatry*, Vol. 2, No. 8 (Spring 1962), pp. 371–392.

Helping him to recognize choices he had hidden from himself is one way of accomplishing this. There may be many other ways that to date have not been explored and attempted in a sufficiently significant fashion.[18]

The logotherapy of Frankl includes a number of such examples. He sometimes utilizes humor and exaggeration of notions based on a client's neurotic assumptions about his own helpless condition. His aim is always to enable the client to acquire a new perspective on his symptoms and his own nature so that he does not continue to identify his total self with his neurotic symptoms, compulsions, or feelings. He also may suggest that a patient imagine himself to be twenty years older and review his present situation from that vantage point. The patient is able to identify instances in which more desirable choices might have been made by him "back then," and by so doing grasps the importance of the unique opportunity facing him at the present moment.[19]

Kondo, writing on "Zen in Psychotherapy" suggests as an adjunct to therapy the use of sitting meditation, which provides the patient with an experience of "single-mindedness"––an intuitive sense of the unity of body and mind that can enable him to detach himself from old childhood strivings bidding for present control.[20] The exercises of Gestalt psychology are aimed at a similar accomplishment.[21]

Another unique approach is Japan's *Morita* therapy. This is a therapy for hospitalized patients that is related to the philosophy of Zen Buddhism, which itself has many similarities to existentialism. Upon being hospitalized, a patient is placed in solitary confinement for the first several days, with only himself and his thoughts for company. He is asked to maintain a diary from the day of admission. Gradually he is permitted simple work activities and limited contact with a therapist. His range of contacts and tasks is slowly broadened and he begins to experience a sense of satisfaction in performing minor functions and relating to something other than himself. The nature of his problem is interpreted to him by the therapist, who has studied his diary. This interpretation has nothing to do with early trauma or deep insight into childhood relationships. Rather, it is aimed at emphasizing the foolishness and futility of the self-preoccupied existence the patient maintained until his hospitalization. It is further directed at arousing a sense of humility and genuine acceptance of his daily life circumstances as being not only bearable but an intrinsic vehicle for meaning and satisfaction, if he would only perform the tasks required of him instead of brooding over his unhappy lot in life. This treatment approach is continued until the patient is discharged from the hospital in anywhere from one to two months.

What is important in these approaches is the patient's developing

---

[18] One method utilizing casework techniques was described in Gerald K. Rubin, "Helping a Clinic Patient Modify Self-destructive Thinking," *Social Work*, Vol. 7, No. 1 (January 1962), pp. 76–80.

[19] Viktor Frankl, *The Doctor and the Soul* (New York: Alfred A. Knopf, 1957).

[20] Akihisa Kondo, "Zen in Psychotherapy: The Virtue of Sitting," *Chicago Review*, Vol. 12, No. 2 (Summer 1958).

[21] *See* Frederick S. Perls, Ralph F. Hefferline, and Paul Goodman, *Gestalt Therapy* (New York: Julian Press, 1951).

awareness of a different aspect of himself—that part of him is beyond the control of childhood striving and compulsive feelings. This aspect of self can manage a perspective over his total self and situation and thereby direct his choices in new ways. This part of him is also adult, creative, and—most important—real. There are lessons to be learned here from the novelists and film-makers who depict men and women discovering new and critical perspectives of their lives. Dickens' *A Christmas Carol* is a classic example, as is Dostoevsky's *Crime and Punishment*. The same theme occurs in Bergman's film *Wild Strawberries* and Fellini's *8½*. In *La Strada* Fellini presents a delightful vignette in which the feeble-minded heroine of the film is confronted by the clown–high-wire artist in a moment of utter despair. He laughs at her troubled face and tells her how foolish it is to feel her life is completely meaningless. He picks up a pebble and tells her that even this serves some purpose—that if it did not, then there would be no purpose in the entire star-strewn heavens. This statement at this particular time resulted in a profound change in the young woman.

The root of one's hope and sense of dignity lies within the preservation of belief in one's freedom, as well as its assertion over and against the forces that seem determined to defeat one. This is quite apparent in the thinking of many alcoholics involved in the therapy group mentioned earlier. The commitment to abstinence from alcohol emphasized by Alcoholics Anonymous reflects the same idea. One alcoholic who has been "dry" for five years put it this way: "My choice is to drink again and face complete hopelessness or else to refuse alcohol and stand at least a fighting chance for happiness sometime." Here is commitment that accepts suffering and frustration without a guarantee of bliss. What is rewarding is the free and ongoing act of refusing to use alcohol as an escape.

As mentioned, in group therapy the notions about the alcoholic being some predetermined, unchangeable kind of being are challenged. It is important that group members sense the personal belief of the therapist in their capacity for freedom. The therapist must always go beyond the role of a sympathetic nursemaid to the "hopelessly sick and downtrodden."

A technique similar to some of Frankl's ideas was used effectively with this group. It had to do with handling the frustrations of one member as his assertive efforts at communication in the group continually failed. He could state his ideas openly until someone disagreed and requested that he clarify something. Then he experienced a blocking of thought that resulted in his having to back down. Next he would withdraw emotionally from the group and feel increasingly depressed at being overpowered by his own anxiety. It was pointed out that he had identified an important pattern within himself. While it was true that he could not control the rising feelings of anxiety and subsequent blocking, he did have control over how he reacted to this. On the one hand, he could give himself up to the notion that he was impotent and helpless and withdraw from any further efforts. On the other hand, he could strive to maintain attention to the continuing group discussion, so that when his anxiety subsided somewhat he could again assert any ideas he might have on some aspect of the discussion. When he was later able to do this, it was emphasized that he was not allowing the feelings to control him, but could find satisfaction in remaining the assertive kind of person he wanted to be in the group.

Repeated assertion that two parts of an individual can be identified—that which strives for new ways of thought, expression, and action and that which is fearful of this because of certain false assumptions about self and others based on childhood experiences—has been found to be quite meaningful to the group. The question that follows is: "Which of these two parts rules in you?"

Discovering Meaning in Suffering

The central theme in the writings of Dostoevsky and Kazantzakis is that suffering is an inherent part of life and one's growth as a person is dependent on acceptance of and being willing to grapple with this suffering. This same thesis must form a crucial part of psychotherapy. The therapeutic stance is that one can learn from one's suffering, but to do so one must bring it out into the open where it can be faced.

A client will seldom be thrown by the frightening and guilt-ridden aspect of himself if the therapist is not. The therapist must be willing to share the client's sufferings by simply being there, as Rogers emphasizes.[22] His acceptance and deep understanding of this suffering can be conveyed by avoidance of reassurance or easy solutions. He may occasionally reveal examples of his own or another's personal struggles, to emphasize that suffering is a shared human condition.[23] Therapeutic techniques are often used to help a person endure his suffering instead of becoming embittered by it or clinging to weak notions of how it may someday be replaced by pleasure and comfort.

In the group of alcoholics described, an important part of the discussion content is learning to read the underlying meanings in what a person presents. These may be expressions or descriptions of guilt, anxiety, anger, depression, somatic illnesses, or acting-out behavior. Essentially, it is some feeling or behavior that has troubled a person about himself. The group's effort, then, is to examine the factors surrounding the occurrence in order to discover its meaning. Perhaps the person's response was not only natural, but could be considered mature. On the other hand, it may reveal an important aspect of a person's problematic life pattern. Guilt may reveal the inhibition of growth potential in a situation or behavior that is seen as being in conflict with what the person feels he could or should be doing. Anxiety may indicate that he has the potential to behave in a significantly

---

[22] Carl Rogers, "Becoming a Person," in Simon Doniger, ed., *Healing: Human and Divine* (New York: Association Press, 1957), p. 61.

[23] This openness by the therapist is described in Sidney M. Jourard, *The Transparent Self* (Princeton, N.J.: D. Van Nostrand Co., 1964), pp. 39–65. O. Hobart Mowrer also emphasizes such openness in his integrity therapy. A critique of his over-all approach is made by Donald F. Krill in "Psychoanalysis, Mowrer and the Existentialists," *Pastoral Psychology,* Vol. 16 (October 1965), pp. 27–36.

different way but fears the consequences of so doing. Anger is often seen to be a way of blaming others for what are really one's own shortcomings. These concepts of common meanings associated with varying kinds of feelings soon become useful tools for group members to apply to themselves as well as to one another in subsequent meetings.

For example, a relatively new member of the group, 37 years old, commented that he was operating at "low gear" and could see no reason for this other than what he had once been told by a psychiatrist—that he must constantly punish himself because his parents had always been critical of him. Another group member inquired when the depression had become more apparent to him. The onset was pinned down to the previous Saturday night when he had wanted to go to a movie with his wife, who had encouraged him to go alone since she wanted to do her hair that evening. He had accepted this and gone alone. Further questioning by the group led him to see his disappointment and annoyance and his failure to let his wife know what he was feeling. Because he was afraid to show his own needs to her he had avoided any effort either toward changing her decision or attaining a closer understanding with her. The result was loneliness, resentment, and guilt over his own passivity. This incident revealed a pattern in their marital relationship related to his own fear of being hurt if he exposed a dependency need.

Then there is the type of suffering that either must be endured for a long time—perhaps for life—or else evaded by drinking: loneliness and a sense of emptiness, often accompanied by bitterness and envy. The person may have no friends or spouse, or a spouse who resists all efforts at a more intimate relationship. Perhaps the alcoholic, despite his efforts, finds himself unable to be more open and direct even within the therapy group. Here the only creative effort possible may be the continued endurance of suffering. It is natural to envy those whose upbringing, capacities, and circumstances have resulted in a far easier adaptation to life. Yet to endure suffering can still be meaningful. For some it will be a gesture of faith that relates them to a divine force or power. For others it will be a way of remaining true to the human condition—refusing false havens. For still others it will be a means of relating to the fraternity of alcoholics, who often find courage and hope in the continued sobriety of their brothers.

Suffering is a human reality not to be seen as a meaningless, chaotic disruption of a person's life. There is no pleasure principle norm that says to suffer is to be out of kilter with life. The opposite is the case—to live is to accept suffering. Its acceptance depends on some understanding of its hidden meaning—often seeing it as a guide toward potential growth. Suffering gives direction to one's freedom.

Realizing the Necessity of Dialogue

All that has been said with regard to disillusionment, freedom, and suffering would be no more than empty thoughts without the nourishment of dialogue. Creative growth and change are seldom intellectual decisions activated by willpower alone. The supportive sense of intimacy and related-ness involved here does not apply only to the therapeutic relationship. As mentioned, it may be an experience of unity with a deity, with fellow alcoholics, or with the human condition.

What must take place in the dialogue of therapy is revelation by the client of what is unique within himself, to which the therapist responds with interest, concern, acceptance, and validation of the client's feelings about himself. This does not, of course, mean continuing approval, but the willingness of the therapist to grasp and understand what is being revealed, even in the throes of disagreement. Increasing directness and openness of communication are therefore necessary. Also required is the lessening of manipulative efforts to control the relationship. There is a risk in allowing another person to respond to one freely. When a person ceases his efforts to control another's image of him, he often experiences a feeling of extreme panic, for his sense of self seems to be at the mercy of another's unknown response. Yet true dialogue requires this, and one of the most significant accomplishments in therapy is for two persons to be authentic and free in relation to one another. This, of course, requires that the therapist reveal himself as a human being with feelings, thoughts, and spontaneity.[24] The client must come to see himself as co-equal with the therapist by virtue of his humanity, and the therapist, to encourage this, must be adept at avoiding the client's efforts to control him.

The capacities both to trust and verbalize are inseparable from such dialogue. Clients will therefore vary in their ability to relate in the way described, and the therapist must carefully assess the modifiability of the client. For some people an effort to change meaningful relationships will be the goal sought. For others a more open dialogue with the therapist alone will be the only effort to implement this necessary aspect of the human condition.[25]

Group and family therapy are excellent proving grounds for examining methods of communication and the reason for failures of dialogue. In the group of alcoholics again, from time to time the specific ingredients of dialogue are structured. There is the initiator and the listener. Courage is often required to initiate a problem, for the response of others is uncertain. Courage is again needed by the listener in his attempt to develop the picture the initiator has begun through sincere curiosity. Responses such as advice-giving, early intellectual interpretations, and silence are frequently identified as defenses against a closer involvement with the initiator's problem. Genuine interest and an effort to understand more deeply may lead the

---

[24] The concept of therapeutic openness and authenticity is well developed in Helen E. Durkin, *The Group in Depth* (New York: International Universities Press, 1964), sect. 2, pp. 249–276.

[25] A differentiation of therapy goals in accord with categories of client modifiability is described in Donald F. Krill, "A Framework for Determining Client Modifiability," *Social Casework*, Vol. 49, No. 10 (December 1968), pp. 602–611.

listener to disagree with or challenge the initiator, with the accompanying threat of conflict. It may also lead the initiator to expect to receive a satisfactory solution to his problem from the listener, which the listener is fearful he may not be able to produce. On the other hand, the initiator may feel obliged to accept a listener's advice—even though he is doubtful of its applicability—and be silent in an effort to avoid conflict and the risk of displeasing others in their efforts to be of help.

The fears mentioned in efforts at dialogue can often be clarified in such a way that an individual will see and experience the fact that his very maneuvers to preserve a specific self-image negate the possibility of closeness. To become aware of this is also to realize the self-destructive aspects of one's manipulation of others. One may be more secure through feeling one has control of another person, but for genuine love and closeness to occur, the other must be allowed freedom of response. A gesture of love from another whom one feels one has successfully manipulated can be little more than emotional masturbation. One's own growth and knowledge of oneself is also dependent on the free assessment of others whose view is naturally different in some respects from one's own. To resist another's free opinion is to close off an opportunity for personal growth.

Accepting the Way of Commitment

The way of commitment refers to a loyalty to those realities of the human condition one has discovered to be true and meaningful for oneself. The basis for a new philosophy is found in the realization of the nature and pattern of certain childhood strivings and a disillusionment with some previous way of achieving self-security; recognition that there is a part of oneself that is adult, free, and spontaneous; the finding of ongoing direction and a sense of meaning in one's sufferings; and finally through experiencing some possibility of genuine, sincere intimacy with another. As members of the described group of alcoholics stay on in therapy, these reality factors often become part of their lives as is manifested in the framework within which they use therapy sessions and relate to one another's problems. Gradually they have integrated elements of a new life-style.

It is helpful to think in terms of a model of the committed and authentic person as representing the ideal result of an acceptance of the existential realities described in this paper. While such a model would not be an expectation for all patients, it does add clarity and direction to our thinking. The characteristics are the opposite of those describing the state of anomie. One's sense of self is not seen as fixed, determined, or able to be constructed and secured by some set of achievements that prove one adequate because others finally recognize and applaud one. Rather, one's sense of self, as a narcissistic ego, is laughed at for its foolish and self-defeating strivings. Humor—as the capacity to laugh at oneself—is a natural characteristic. The self is seen now as having an ongoing relation to the world, constantly changing as new situations arise, forever being tapped by new possibilities, suspicious of the self-satisfaction that can lead to rigidity. The self as the center of attention and fortification increasingly is lost and replaced by a more avid interest in others, the tasks of one's daily life, and the beauty and wonder of the world about us. As the young English friend of Zorba the Greek said of him, "Zorba sees everything every day as if for the first time."[26] As one disciplines oneself away from self-clinging and delusional attachments to childhood strivings, a creative spontaneity unfolds that is invested in many aspects of one's life—not focused in one isolated area of achievement.

This new state of self is similar to the mindlessness and nothingness in Zen Buddhism, meaning that the mind operates freely without attachment. The inflow of intuitive response with this state of mindlessness is illustrated in a Zen tale of a young man who wanted to learn the art of swordsmanship and apprenticed himself to a master swordsman. He was, however, disappointed when he was refused permission even to hold a sword, but instead had to prepare his master's meals and perform various chores. As the student went about these chores he was periodically assaulted by his master, who would suddenly appear and hit him with a stick. The student was told to defend himself, but every time he prepared for an assault from one direction, it would come from another. Finally, in utter confusion and helplessness, he gave up his hyperalertness. It was only then that he could intuitively sense the direction of the next attack and defend himself adequately. This is a practice of discipline in certain forms of personal combat in Japan even today.

This turnabout way of viewing the self is also the essence of true religious conversion. In religious terms, the self becomes detached from the idols of past devotion and is related now to the will of God, viewing the tasks and relationships of daily life as calling forth a response from oneself that in turn accomplishes a sense of divine unity in the act of free, open, and giving relatedness.

Buber describes this turnabout experience as a change from a reacting "I-it" relation to the world to a responding "I-Thou" relation. Instead of using people in one's environment as objects to support and gratify a self-image, one "enters into relation with the other," whatever form this might take, and such a contact is characterized by awe, respect, care, and creative response.[27] Tillich speaks of this experience as discovering the "courage to be" as a result of experiencing oneself as "being grasped by the power of Being itself." As one feels that one's most ego-gratifying strivings are illusory and false, one also has a sense of being affirmed as worthy and acceptable in spite of the fact that such acceptance has not been earned by the energy expended in these false strivings. The acceptance of this affirmative experience allows one to carry out one's daily tasks with a lessened need for the old security striving. One's "acceptance of being accepted" is seen to be a reunion with the transcendent power of Being that gives meaning to life.[28]

---

[26] Nikos Kazantzakis, *Zorba the Greek* (New York: Simon & Schuster, 1959), p. 51.

[27] The best critique of Buber's thought is found in Maurice S. Friedman, *Martin Buber: The Life of Dialogue* (New York: Harper & Bros. 1959).

[28] Paul Tillich, *The Courage To Be* (New Haven: Yale University Press, 1952).

A nonreligious discussion of this same theme is found in Frankl's logotherapy, which is designed to arouse an awareness of the "task character of life." This concept is developed by using the realities of the patient's everyday life. Considering such factors as family background, the nature of time, awareness of death, ever changing circumstances, and ever changing personality, the therapist emphasizes that every person is singular, is unique. Not only will there never be another like him but even the exact circumstances of a momentary situation will never again be precisely the same, so that each decision possesses uniqueness. He is free to respond to the moment at hand, and when he grasps the tremendous sense of responsibility that goes with his uniqueness (which he bears sole responsibility for shaping), then his daily tasks take on a special meaning never before experienced. When he has truly reached this stage, he loses his self-preoccupation in a new sense of responsible relatedness to daily happenings. This might be labeled a new form of self-concern, but the essential difference is that the direction is outward—giving, doing, creating, and enduring—rather than inwardly striving, securing, protecting, and possessing.

A significant portion of Frankl's logotherapeutic technique is designed to enlighten a patient about the kinds of values or possibilities that seem to await realization or actualization in his concrete life circumstance. Values are seen to be creative, experiential, and attitudinal in nature and vary, of course, with the patient. Creative values may refer to work tasks or even to those that may be artistic or athletic. Experiential values have to do with enjoyment of the world about one and this includes the closeness of an interaction in personal relationships. Attitudinal values are those that can be realized as one accepts and endures suffering that is unavoidable or unchangeable. From this perspective, it is apparent that some values can be identified as real and meaningful for any patient, regardless of the nature of his limits and circumstances.[29]

Mowrer and Glasser state that the key factor in therapy is helping a patient identify for himself clearly how he believes he ought to behave— what values seem important to him personally. He can then identify how his actual decisions and behavior are at odds with the way he wants to be. The necessity of changed behavior is stressed, regardless of the feelings involved, in order to bring about the person's increased acceptance of himself as worthy and hence as acceptable to others. Self-pity and self-preoccupation are replaced by identification of one's value and by commitment.[30]

Conclusion

The problem of anomie should be seen as a way of life in itself that must be countered by philosophical efforts that become meaningful through

[29] Frankl, *op. cit.*
[30] O. Hobart Mowrer, *The Crisis in Psychiatry and Religion* (Princeton, N.J.: D. Van Nostrand Co., 1961); William Glasser, *Reality Therapy: A New Approach to Psychiatry* (New York: Harper & Row, 1965).

the process of psychotherapy. Existentialism is an especially useful philosophical base because it draws its central themes from man's immediate experience of his life. Its emphases on disillusionment, freedom, suffering, authentic relationships, and commitment deal directly with their opposites, which are characteristics of anomie. Existentialism should not be considered a completed philosophical system, but rather a series of emphasized realities that can be adapted to other forms of philosophy and religious belief, depending on the background and thought of the individual therapist.

A danger in the misuse of psychoanalytic thought is the reduction of man to primitive animal drives. Notions of chaos and determinism prevail in this attitude about man's nature, and the resulting pleasure principle goal for people is simply insufficient for those experiencing anomie. The process, common among many psychoanalytically oriented therapists, of classifying and categorizing symptoms and behavioral expressions according to a system based on the primacy of animal drives accentuates this very problem. This process is viewed as "scientific" because it is wholly materialistic, but it is not scientific at all. The belief in the primacy of animal drives is as much a faith as the assumptions espoused in existentialism and other humanistic psychologies.

For the existentialists, man's biological drives are important and must be understood, but they do not fully explain man's nature. As a matter of fact, emphasis on the primacy of instinctual drives is a way of viewing human beings at their minimum level of functioning rather than their maximum level. At this maximum level man has freedom, the power to transcend his egotistical strivings, courage to venture, and a capacity to endure. The spirit is available to men, but they must sometimes seek it out to become aware of its existence. Kazantzakis, in *The Last Temptation of Christ,* expressed the nature of this spirit by proclaiming man as the being who gives wings to matter.

Freud was reported to have said to Binswanger, the existentialist psychoanalyst: "Yes, the spirit is everything. . . . Mankind has always known that it possesses spirit; I had to show it that there are also instincts."[31] Freud's contribution has been immense and he responded honestly and courageously to what he viewed as the problems of his society. But the repression of sexuality, with its resulting neuroses, is not the most common problem in our modern society of *Playboy,* the Hollywood love goddesses, and birth control. To reestablish meaning and direction in people's lives there is a need in the psychotherapeutic method for philosophical guidance and value education. By leaving this up to the church a therapist is being blind to the essential function of therapy for anomic man. This presents an identity problem for many therapists who have long been fond of criticizing and belittling the church, for now, as therapists, they are called on to serve patients in the very way in which for centuries the church has attempted to serve them.

[31] Ludwig Binswanger, *Sigmund Freud: Reminiscences of a Friendship* (New York: Grune & Stratton, 1957), p. 81.

Suicide

Suicide: Answering the Cry for Help

David J. Klugman, Robert E. Litman, and Carl I. Wold

Suicide, which accounts for at least 20,000 deaths per year in the United States, ranks among the first ten causes of adult deaths in this country.[1] In addition to completed suicides, there are numerous suicide attempts and threats. It has been estimated that each year in the United States about half a million people are affected by a range of suicidal crises, making it a major public health problem.[2]

The purpose of this paper is to examine some characteristics of suicidal individuals and to discuss evaluation and treatment approaches and the need for consultation when suicidal crises arise. The professional activity described took place at the Los Angeles Suicide Prevention Center.[3]

Reaction to Crisis

A striking aspect of suicidal people is that they do not form a homogeneous group. They come from a broad spectrum of different life situations and are not seen as similar in personality. Some are stable people with roots in family and community life, while others lead unstable lives, riddled with failure in all their interpersonal dealings. All these people, however, share in common the condition of being in a serious life crisis. They are no longer able to sweep their feelings under the rug of indifference and denial. They

Reprinted with permission of the authors and the National Association of Social Workers. from *Social Work*, Vol. 10, No. 4 (October, 1965), pp. 43–50.

[1] Sam M. Heilig and David J. Klugman, "The Social Worker in a Suicide Prevention Center," *Social Work Practice, 1963* (New York: Columbia University Press, 1963).

[2] Norman L. Farberow and Edwin S. Shneidman, eds., *The Cry For Help* (New York: McGraw-Hill Book Co., 1961). *See also* Louis I. Dublin, *Suicide: A Sociological and Statistical Study* (New York: Ronald Press, 1963).

[3] Robert E. Litman, MD, Edwin S. Shneidman, and Norman L. Farberow, "Los Angeles Suicide Prevention Center," *American Journal of Psychiatry*, Vol. 117, No. 12 (June 1961), pp. 1084–1087. The Suicide Prevention Center has been supported by grants from the National Institute of Mental Health, administered through the University of Southern California School of Medicine.

must face their feelings of hopelessness, helplessness, and dependency. Most commonly their symptoms are those of a severe depressive syndrome—sleep disorder, appetite loss, and psychomotor retardation. Often there are disorganized activity states with exaggerated tension, perturbation, and pan-anxiety.

The crisis may or may not be related to specific life stresses. Such events as a divorce or the death of a loved one, financial loss, or sudden legal involvements may trigger suicidal concerns. In a number of suicidal people, however, there is no discernible precipitating stress. Rather, there seems to have been a slow, steady loss of the ability to function adaptively. With these people there is an erosion process under way such that their roots in life are gradually pulled loose. Relatives, friends, lawyers, helping people, and agencies become alienated and unable to help.

In a suicidal crisis there is a radical change in the person's view of himself and his relationships with others. This often shows itself as an increase in stereotyped perceptions, i.e., it is difficult for people in a suicidal crisis to generate new ideas, feelings, or plans without help from others. A suicidal person is often severely constricted in thinking about his problems. He has so little perspective that the past seems forgotten and the future is unimaginable. His view of the present is rigidly confined to a small number of alternative behaviors of which suicide is one. The following case illustrates this point.

Mr. A, a 38-year-old married man, was referred to the center because of suicidal threats. He had been employed as an aircraft mechanic on the same job for twelve years and had led a quiet, stable life until his wife of ten years had left him in order to be free to see other men. They were not divorced and neither of them wanted to effect a complete separation. Periodically Mrs. A returned to him, contrite about having left, and each time he welcomed her return. However, his disgust with himself and unconscious anger toward her grew as the returns and separations continued. It was noted that he was acutely agitated and depressed, had lost weight, slept very little, and had suffered acute psychological distress. He was about to give up his job, which in the past had provided major satisfactions for him. His conception of his situation was that he could not continue to live with his wife on the present basis but he could not give her up. He loved her and she loved him, but she was now confused and hurting him unintentionally. He hoped that, magically, the situation would prove to be a bizarre mistake, a sort of nightmare. Yet, because of his unbearable anxiety, he could no longer wait for this resolution. He was almost aware of wanting to kill Mrs. A and he was acutely aware of wanting to kill himself.

Mr. A had lost his ability to see himself clearly. The crisis he had entered distorted his view of who he was, where he had been, and what might happen in the future. Nothing satisfied him anymore, nor could he achieve satisfactions. He admitted to feeling helpless and without hope, powerless to change—killing himself seemed the only solution. The center's staff openly disagreed with his conclusion of hopelessness, and he was told that because of his depression his view of himself and his situation was distorted in such a way that realistic alternatives were not available to him. Staff expressed concern about him, pointed up his need for help, and advised him that there was a good chance that with professional aid he could regain healthy perspectives. The offer of help was accepted eagerly and he began working on a plan for his recovery. He was seen briefly each day for a few days, until he entered regular outpatient psychotherapy at another agency.

Ambivalence about Dying

This case raise another important characteristic of suicidal people. They are intensely ambivalent about dying.[4] If someone really intended to die, would he tell others about it who would try to prevent his death? Such communications may cast doubts on the sincerity of the suicidal person. Combined with one's own anxieties about helping a suicidal person, these attitudes impede the helping process. The result is that some suicidal people are not taken seriously, which can tip the balance dangerously toward suicide.

An appreciation of the ambivalent state of the suicidal person helps to make sense of behavior that otherwise appears insincere. During such a crisis, there is an admixture of conflicting feelings. In nearly all cases, regardless of obvious attempts to manipulate other people or dramatic bids for emotional response from others, there are genuine wishes to die and to be rid of tension, pain, or confusion. These death-seeking feelings range from well-thought-out plans to impulsive, erratic outbursts that would be lethal only through a combination of adverse chance factors.

Often the mixed motives include rescue fantasies as well as wishes to die. The suicidal person is looking for a rescuer to serve as an alter ego at a time when his own ego functions are severely impaired. Some of these rescue wishes are realistic, but many are magical in character; both types influence the demands made on the rescue person. Thus Mr. A recognized realistically that he was unable to resolve his dilemma without help, that he was weakened, and that his suicidal feelings served to communicate this to the center's staff. Unrealistically and magically, he hoped the center would make a sudden change in the present relationship between him and his wife. He wished only for his wife to love and care for him by meeting all his needs. He saw the helping person as an all-powerful figure who entered his life to make sweeping changes for the better.

Finally, to appreciate better the ambivalence associated with suicide the rescuer should guard against basing his feelings and actions primarily on the content of the suicidal person's communications. He may hear: "Leave me alone; I don't want your help," from a person crying out loudly for help. Someone who desperately wants to go to a hospital and be taken care of will say: "I'd rather die before going to the hospital." These statements demonstrate vividly the ambivalence about being helped. This ambivalence is especially acute in the case of suicidal men. Approximately twice as many men as women kill themselves. Although a man may feel emotionally incapacitated, he cannot bear to know that others may recognize this.

---

[4] Edwin S. Shneidman and Norman L. Farberow, eds., *Clues to Suicide* (New York: McGraw-Hill Book Co., 1957), chap. 11; and Robert E. Litman, MD, "Emergency Response to Potential Suicide," *Journal of the Michigan State Medical Society*, Vol. 62, No. 1 (January 1963), pp. 68–72.

Helpful Techniques

Just as there are differences in the personality characteristics of suicidal persons, so are there differences in the degree of suicidal risk, which usually falls into one of three broad categories: mild, moderate, or high. An important part of the work at the Los Angeles Suicide Prevention Center has been to evaluate the degree of suicidal risk of patients referred and then to recommend appropriate treatment modalities. Generally, mild-risk patients can be treated optimally at social work or family service agencies, moderate-risk patients at outpatient psychiatric clinics, and high-risk patients in psychiatric hospitals. The purpose of this section is to describe some helpful evaluative and treatment techniques developed at the center.

Telephone contacts

Ninety-five percent of initial patient contacts begin on the telephone; the rest are walk-ins. These calls range from emergencies to situations of little or no suicidal risk; regardless of initial impression, however, every call is treated seriously. As a defensive or testing maneuver the caller will often begin in a joking or hostile way. Unless this is accepted and understood for what it is (a defense against feelings of inadequacy), the caller may not go on to reveal his real suicidal feelings and an important therapeutic opportunity may be lost.

The initial telephone call is regarded as extremely important.[5] Sometimes it is the center's only contact. Great care is therefore accorded to it. Usually from twenty to forty minutes are spent carefully evaluating the situation, trying to form a positive relationship by moving into the situation rather than away from it. Staff want the caller to learn quickly that they are interested, they wish to help him, and improvement is possible regardless of how desperate he feels. Above all, staff try to instill a feeling of hope, pointing out, for example, that the center has helped many people with similar problems or that together some new alternative way of dealing with his problem may be found.

Specifically, the job on the telephone is to get information, to evaluate the situation—especially the suicidal potential—and to recommend a course of action. This is all done concomitantly and questions are woven in whenever possible at appropriate moments. The aim is to give the caller a therapeutic experience; staff avoid asking for information in a formal, routine way. They do ask for identifying information and request the caller to discuss any current stress he is under. Further, they ask if there is any past suicidal behavior and any history of medical or psychiatric treatment. If there is a "significant other" in the patient's life, his name and telephone number, which can be of crucial importance in an emergency, are requested.

[5] Robert E. Litman, MD, Norman L. Farberow, Edwin S. Shneidman, Sam M. Heilig, and Jan A. Kramer, "Suicide-Prevention Telephone Service," *Journal of the American Medical Association*, Vol. 192, No. 1 (April 5, 1965), pp. 21–25.

Staff talk about suicidal feelings and thoughts openly, having learned that this relieves some of the anxiety the patient feels. Evasiveness or secretiveness about suicidal feelings increase his anxiety and the danger of a suicidal act.

Office interviews

In the office staff are able to do a more intensive evaluation of a patient's suicidal potentiality. The following are taken into account: the amount of stress he is under, the symptoms that disturb him, suicidal plan or feelings (in detail), his financial and interpersonal resources, and, finally, his character—that is, whether he had a history of stability or of chronic disorganization and instability. This is usually done in one interview but may be extended to two or more office visits. Staff's attitude throughout is one of interest, encouragement, hope for the patient, and optimism about the eventual outcome. At the conclusion of the interview the patient is asked to complete a shortened form of the Minnesota Multiphasic Personality Inventory, a psychological test consisting of a series of 479 true or false questions, which usually takes about an hour to complete. Selected patients are asked additionally to fill out a social history form or other research materials. An important aspect of the psychological testing and completion of forms is that it forces the patient to think of himself—past, present, and future—which helps to re-establish his identity in his own mind, a valuable therapeutic assist to anyone in a suicidal crisis.

If there is a spouse or a significant other in the patient's life, that person is asked to come in with him. Often this person is the patient's most valuable resource and it is therefore desirable for him to participate in helping the patient to get through the critical period and then to follow up with recommendations made by the center. The following is an example of work in the office with a middle-aged depressed man.

Mr. R, a 50-year-old married man, was referred by his physician because of severe depression and overt threats of suicide. His son, a 27-year-old police officer, had committed suicide two weeks previously by shooting himself in the temple with his service revolver. He left no note and the motives for his death remained a mystery. Mr. R, who had been depressed before this incident, now felt anxious, tense, unable to concentrate, and nearing exhaustion. He thought of death frequently and expressed a desire to follow in his son's footsteps by shooting himself.

Mr. R was employed as an equipment maintenance worker, and had been with the same company for twenty-one years. He was a steady worker but he had no hobbies or social life. He and his wife had been married for thirty years, had raised a family, and Mrs. R was now working in order to help with expenses. She was a thin, tense individual who strove to be a good wife but had become more of a mother to her husband. She was sexually frigid.

Mr. R was the sixth of a family of ten children. His father was an alcoholic who abused the family. Because of the difficult times, Mr. R quit school after the eighth grade. He became a sporadic alcoholic and at such times was ugly and abusive; he was beaten up on several occasions. He continued to drink after his marriage, but stopped thirteen years ago and has not had a drink since. Mrs. R reported that during the years he drank he was able to shout and express his hostility, but after he stopped he apparently had no satisfactory way of expressing his angry feelings and had become more and more depressed.

Mr. R was treated at the center with psychotherapy and antidepressant medication, and his wife was asked to come in for supportive therapy. His depression and suicidal thinking did not abate, and it was concluded that hospitalization would be necessary. When Mr. R was told, he refused to submit to this and threatened to do away with himself first. After careful evaluation of the risk involved, staff decided to continue to see him as an outpatient, but with a focus on the need for hospitalization. After two more weeks of concentrated effort with him, the center enabled Mr. R to accept its recommendation and enter a psychiatric hospital. In the hospital he responded well to a series of electroshock treatments, dropped his suicidal ideation, and was then able to return to work.

Mr. R was rated a high suicide risk based on his age and sex, high stress, depression, and suicidal preoccupation. The center's decision to try to treat him at first as an outpatient was based in part on the stability of his work and married life and the fact that he had never had a previous try at outpatient psychiatric treatment.

Mr. R is representative of many suicidal persons seen at the center. Under the brunt of some overwhelming life stress, they begin to experience distressing physical or mental symptoms that sharply heighten their discomfort. If in addition they happen to be emotionally constricted or immobilized with respect to some potentially constructive relief-bringing action, they may develop a severe depression, fears of becoming mentally ill, or extreme tension and anxiety. Under these conditions of near-intolerable affect, they begin to consider suicide as a relief or escape from their tensions and confusions or as a final resolution of their problems. This is a most critical time for these patients, a time when they are likely to request help. With help available and with someone responding appropriately, the suicidal risk usually subsides within a short period of time.

Suicidal Crisis Consultations

One of the special features of emergency psychotherapy at the Los Angeles Suicide Prevention Center is the emphasis placed by the staff on frequent consultations. These are informal case discussions conducted in a spirit of rapid communication, mutual support, and teamwork, often leading to continuous collaboration by several therapists. The purpose of this section is to describe this type of consultation as a specific therapeutic device for counteracting certain serious technical problems often associated with suicidal crises. Among these are the prevailing sense of urgency and responsibility, the required personal and emotional involvement by the therapist, and the contagious quality of the patient's panic and pessimism.

The stresses may induce problem reactions in the therapist. Among these are overwhelming affects such as anxiety, anger, or hopelessness, constriction of thought, impulsive actions, or complete immobilization. Frequent informal consultations tend to prevent panic and build up the therapist's self-confidence. Fears of overlooking vital points are allayed. Consultations encourage imaginative solutions to problems and help the therapists preserve their feelings of personal identity and sense of humor even though they participate sympathetically in many frustrating interpersonal transactions.

Reasons for consultations

Cases that are unusual, associated with legal complications, bring the clinic into conflict with other community agencies, or involve a high suicide risk should have consultations. In evaluating high suicide danger for the patient, probably the best single indicator is the therapist's awareness of his own anxiety. Therapists feel some anxiety at some point with nearly every case. Failure to experience anxiety while interacting with a suicidal person, whether owing to poor imagination or excessively strong defenses against anxiety, disqualifies a therapist for work in the center. Therapists learn various strategies and techniques for dealing with suicidal persons and, by taking appropriate actions, keep their anxiety at levels suitable for effective work.

The consultation is probably the most usual device for constructively handling anxiety in the therapist, who should be alert enough to recognize when he needs help. For instance, when a therapeutic interaction has such impact on the therapist that his reactions spill over into his private life he needs a consultation quickly.

The therapist's anxiety may be focused in one or more of several possible areas. He may be having difficulty in understanding, evaluating, or diagnosing the personality or reactions of the patient and his relatives. "Do these symptoms mean schizophrenia?" "He says he still enjoys sexual relations. Does this contradict the possibility of suicide?" "Do you think his wife can be trusted to keep an eye on him over the weekend?"

Many problems involve decisions about direct action. "Must he go to the hospital immediately or can hospitalization wait a day or two?" "How can I get her to come to the clinic?" "To which psychiatric agency should this patient be referred?"

Sometimes the therapist feels he is in over his depth. "Whenever I talk to this patient she seems to get worse!" "I'm afraid to let her leave the office because she might hurt her baby!" "Have you ever heard of someone who liked to kill stray cats?" "This man hired a woman to tie him up and choke him into unconsciousness!"

Spirit

The spirit of the consultation, which has been derived historically from the original approach of the center's staff to patients, is probably more important than the content. In the first phase of the center, patients were selected one at a time and studied carefully by a team consisting of a psychiatrist, psychologist, and psychiatric social worker. The patient was nominally the responsibility of the psychiatrist but, in practice, whichever member of the team came to have the longest and most intense relationship with the patient took over the practical responsibility for the therapeutic contact and was referred to as the therapist of record. In later years, as the case load increased, the practice of team collaboration on each case could not be maintained nor was it necessary. Consultations continue the spirit of collaboration. Both the therapist and consultant are members of a team and are responsible for the patient's welfare.

There is a great difference between supervision and consultation. The act of supervising is essentially the direction and critical evaluation of instruction as, for instance, in a school or teaching clinic. To supervise is to inspect with authority. To consult is to confer together, to take counsel, to interact and consider, and to give advice leading to action.

The formal case conference is designed to stimulate the entire staff, to formulate research problems, and to continue the education of all, but often adds extra problems, extra speculations, and extra possibilities for the therapist to consider. By contrast, the informal consultation aims to clarify the problem, reach a decision, and motivate toward action.

The center feels strongly that the consultant must share in the responsibility for the outcome of the case and must feel personally involved in the consultation as the therapist must feel personally involved with the patient. One of the most important functions of the consultant is to point out situations when it is time for the therapist to let the patient go. Sometimes correct tactics require the consultant to take the patient over from the original therapist and become the patient's new therapist.

The consultation should start with a statement by the therapist of the reasons he feels anxious and his idea of the goal of the consultation. For example:

> The problem is that this girl is 17 and a minor, so I don't see how we can keep on seeing her here, without consent from her parents. But she won't tell us her family name or address, and she says she will break off with us and commit suicide if we try to find out.

> I'm afraid this man will not follow our recommendations for more psychotherapy. How can we keep him motivated for treatment now that he has come out of his depression?

> Here is a 50-year-old man, pretty much alone and friendless. The only thing that keeps him going is work, but he is very depressed now and I have to decide whether to insist that he go immediately to the hospital.

The therapist should then give a brief case report. The consultant listens to make sure that nothing vital has been omitted and tries to visualize the circumstances of the problem and imagine possible solutions. Finally, a course of action is determined. In the first example, it was decided that the adolescent patient would be seen for a few more interviews and that her parents would be involved as staff's relationship with her strengthened and she could better accept this necessity. In the second example, it was decided to bring the patient's wife to the clinic, acquaint her with the problem of insufficient motivation in her husband, and try to use her to increase his motivation. In the last example, it was decided to see the patient daily as an outpatient for a while in the hope he would improve. If he did not improve, he would be sent to the hospital.

Emergency consultations are characterized by a lack of formal structure. They may take place in offices, halls, or at lunch. They may involve two or more staff people of the same or different disciplines. For example, the psychiatrist asked a psychiatric social worker where to refer a patient who only spoke Hungarian (the International Institute, a casework agency for the foreign-speaking, was suggested). A clinical psychologist asked a social worker to call a patient's brother to check on additional information about the husband who had left her. In relating the case history, he realized that several important aspects were still unclear to him. A social worker talked for an hour with a discouraged starlet who was going to take an overdose of pills. Next morning he received a letter of gratitude and a nude picture, as well as a promise to come in for an interview. Naturally, he requested some consultation with his colleagues before proceeding with the therapy. The following case was presented by a social worker to the chief psychiatrist for consultation.

> Mr. C, a 32-year-old steel worker, was threatening to commit suicide in reaction to a divorce action by his wife. The referral was initiated by the wife's employer and she joined him on the telephone. No one knew of Mr. C's present whereabouts but he had been trying to reach his wife at her place of work for the past two days, threatening suicide. The wife was afraid of him because of his previous violence and did not want to see him. She and her employer wondered if they could get him to contact the center by some sort of trick. The social worker expressed great concern about Mr. C, who sounded to him like the kind of person who was capable of acting on his impulses and of committing suicide in this context.
>
> The consultant felt the situation was serious and suggested that an appointment be given the wife. Mrs. C was advised that the next time Mr. C called her place of employment he should be told she was going to the center and should be given the center's number to call. Mr. C did call, was referred to the center, and after a long conversation came into the office. The social worker interviewed him and then asked the consultant to talk with him also.
>
> Mr. C was a muscular ex-fighter, former captain of his high school football team, who had always earned a good living as a steel worker but had had bad luck with his two marriages. He was not an alcoholic or chronically unstable, but one received the impression that he was impulsive and had perhaps too many fights—there may have been a trace of brain damage. It was known that he had taken a large overdose of sleeping tablets two weeks before, for which he had been hospitalized, but he had demanded his release from the hospital. He found it hard to put things into words and could not explain exactly why he felt compelled to commit suicide. He felt that he would have to do something if he did not get to see his wife; that something would be to kill himself.
>
> Two things were picked up by the social worker and the consultant: (1) The patient felt warmly toward his mother and father in another city and was concerned about the effect of his suicide on them. (2) His suicide threat represented a need for some sort of action. The possibility of substitute action was emphasized with him. After consultation and discussion, it was decided that Mr. C would return to his home town. A long-distance telephone call was made to his parents and his father took a plane to come and meet him.

It can be seen from this case that at each point where doubt existed the consultation helped resolve the indecision so that the participants could move toward further action and resolution of the problem.

Summary

In order to facilitate recognition of suicidal persons the following common characteristics are noted: (1) an objective and/or subjective breakdown in coping abilities accompanied by feelings of collapse and helplessness, (2) severely constricted perceptions of themselves and their difficulties, (3) acute ambivalence about dying and living and receiving help. Various techniques have been developed at the Los Angeles Suicide Prevention Center for evaluating suicide risk and recommending appropriate action. These techniques have the effect of interrupting death thoughts and suggesting action directed toward continued living. Therapists work under special stress owing to the prevailing sense of urgency and great responsibility, the required personal involvement, and the contagious quality of the patient's panic and pessimism. Frequent informal consultations are mandatory as a technical device to maintain the therapists' morale and keep anxiety at an optimal level. These informal case discussions are conducted in a spirit of rapid communication, mutual support, and collaborative teamwork.